Freedom in the World
2014

The findings of *Freedom in the World 2014* include events
from January 1, 2013, through December 31, 2013.

Freedom in the World 2014
The Annual Survey of Political Rights and Civil Liberties

Arch Puddington
General Editor

Aili Piano
Managing Editor

Jennifer Dunham, Bret Nelson, Tyler Roylance
Associate Editors

Freedom House • New York, NY and Washington, DC
Rowman & Littlefield • Lanham, Boulder,
New York, Toronto, London

ROWMAN & LITTLEFIELD

Published in the United States of America
by Rowman & Littlefield
A wholly owned subsidiary of The Rowman & Littlefield Publishing Group, Inc.
4501 Forbes Boulevard, Suite 200, Lanham, Maryland 20706
www.rowman.com

Unit A, Whitacre Mews, 26-34 Stannary Street, London SE11 4AB

Copyright © 2015 by Rowman & Littlefield

All rights reserved. No part of this book may be reproduced in any form or by any electronic or mechanical means, including information storage and retrieval systems, without written permission from the publisher, except by a reviewer who may quote passages in a review.

British Library Cataloguing in Publication Information Available

Library of Congress Cataloging-in-Publication Data Available

ISBN: 978-1-4422-4706-2 (cloth : alk. paper)
ISBN: 978-1-4422-4707-9 (electronic)
ISSN: 0732-6610

∞™ The paper used in this publication meets the minimum requirements of American National Standard for Information Sciences—Permanence of Paper for Printed Library Materials, ANSI/NISO Z39.48-1992.

Printed in the United States of America

Contents

Acknowledgments — 1

Freedom in the World 2014: The Democratic Leadership Gap — 3
Arch Puddington

Introduction — 20

Country Reports — 21

Related and Disputed Territory Reports — 781

Survey Methodology — 833

Tables and Ratings — 847
    Table of Independent Countries — 847
    Table of Related and Disputed Territories — 853
    Combined Average Ratings: Independent Countries — 854
    Combined Average Ratings: Related and Disputed Territories — 855
    Table of Electoral Democracies — 856

The Survey Team — 858

Selected Sources — 870

Freedom House Board of Trustees — 877

About Freedom House — 878

Acknowledgments

Freedom in the World 2014 could not have been completed without the contributions of numerous Freedom House staff members and consultants. The section titled "The Survey Team" contains a detailed list of the writers and advisors without whose efforts this project would not have been possible.

Aili Piano served as the project director for this year's survey. Jennifer Dunham, Bret Nelson, and Tyler Roylance provided extensive research, analytical, editorial, and administrative assistance, and Michael Johnson and Haley Klausmeyer provided additional research and administrative support. Ronald Eniclerico, Anne Kosseff-Jones, Shannon O'Toole, Sarah Repucci, and Eliza Young served as additional country report editors. Overall guidance for the project was provided by David J. Kramer, president of Freedom House, Arch Puddington, vice president for research, and Vanessa Tucker, vice president for analysis. A number of Freedom House staff offered valuable additional input on the country reports and/or ratings process

Freedom House would like to acknowledge the generous financial support for *Freedom in the World* by the Smith Richardson Foundation, the Lilly Endowment, and the Schloss Family.

Freedom in the World 2014:
The Democratic Leadership Gap

by Arch Puddington, Vice President for Research

As the year 2013 neared its end, the world stepped back from ordinary affairs of state to signal its deep respect for a true giant of the freedom struggle, Nelson Mandela. Praise for Mandela's qualities as dissident, statesman, and humanitarian came from every part of the globe and from people of all stations in life. Former U.S. president Bill Clinton tellingly described Mandela as "a man of uncommon grace and compassion, for whom abandoning bitterness and embracing adversaries was not just a political strategy but a way of life."

But the praise bestowed on the father of post-apartheid South Africa was often delivered with more than a note of wistfulness. For it was apparent to many that the defining convictions of Mandela's career—commitment to the rule of law and democratic choice, rejection of score settling and vengeance seeking, recognition that regarding politics as a zero-sum game was an invitation to authoritarianism and civil strife—are in decidedly short supply among today's roster of political leaders.

Indeed, the final year of Mandela's life was marked by a disturbing series of setbacks to freedom. For the eighth consecutive year, *Freedom in the World*, the report on the condition of global political rights and civil liberties issued annually by Freedom House, showed a decline in freedom around the world.

While the overall level of regression was not severe—54 countries registered declines, as opposed to 40 where gains took place—the countries experiencing setbacks included a worrying number of strategically or economically significant states whose political trajectories influence developments well beyond their borders: Egypt, Turkey, Russia, Ukraine, Azerbaijan, Kazakhstan, Indonesia, Thailand, Venezuela. The year was also notable for the growing list of countries beset by murderous civil wars or relentless terrorist campaigns: Central African Republic, South Sudan, Afghanistan, Somalia, Iraq, Yemen, Syria.

In short, this was not a year distinguished by political leaders who showed much inclination toward "abandoning bitterness and embracing adversaries." To make matters worse, some of those who bear responsibility for serious atrocities and acts of repression were not only spared the world's opprobrium, but in some cases drew admiring comments for their "strong leadership" and "statesmanship."

Perhaps the most troubling developments took place in Egypt, whose first competitively elected president, Mohamed Morsi, was removed from office in an old-fashioned military coup, albeit backed by the acclamation of many citizens. While Morsi and his political movement, the Muslim Brotherhood, had exhibited authoritarian tendencies during their short period of leadership, the military and allied forces arrayed around General Abdul Fattah al-Sisi have moved ruthlessly to both eliminate the Brotherhood from political life and marginalize the liberal secular opposition and other elements of society that are critical of the interim government. Since the July takeover, the authorities have killed well over a thousand demonstrators, arrested practically the entire Brotherhood leadership, coopted or intimidated the media, persecuted civil society organizations, and undermined the rule of law. The government also failed to quell a rise in Islamist militancy, including attacks on security forces and sectarian violence in the form of arson and lynchings aimed at the Coptic Christian community.

In just six months, Egypt's post-coup leadership systematically reversed a democratic transition that had made halting progress since 2011. The interim authorities are coming to resemble, and in some areas exceed, the regime of deposed strongman Hosni Mubarak. Meanwhile, the U.S. government has refused to label the seizure of power a coup, issued little more than pro forma objections to the authorities' killings and arrests, and on occasion praised the conduct and supposed democratic aspirations of the military leadership. Other countries have moved to solidify relations with al-Sisi.

In Syria, the regime of Bashar al-Assad managed to deflect criticism of its criminal brutality by agreeing to the removal of chemical weapons whose existence it had long denied, even as its ruthless drive to wipe out the opposition intensified. Chemical arms were never central to Assad's military strategy, and their abandonment has had no effect on aerial bombing and artillery barrages, often directed at urban civilian targets, or the use of blockades on food and humanitarian aid as a war tactic. These and other abuses have combined to produce over 115,000 deaths, two million refugees, and five million internally displaced persons. Syria now earns the lowest scores in the entire *Freedom in the World* report.

Assad is not the only leader to distract the world from domestic repression through superficial, self-serving gestures of reasonableness. A series of opportunistic maneuvers by Vladimir Putin—brokering the Syrian chemical weapons agreement, granting political asylum to former American intelligence contractor Edward Snowden, and approving pardons for several high-profile political prisoners—were enough to change the subject from the Russian leader's persecution of vulnerable populations at home and campaign of intimidation against neighboring countries just months before the opening of the Winter Olympics in Sochi.

In fact, the authoritarian regime created by Putin, now in his 15th year as the country's paramount leader, committed a string of fresh outrages during 2013. The authorities brought spurious criminal charges against protesters and opposition leaders, convicted a dead man—corruption whistleblower Sergey Magnitsky—of tax evasion in an absurd bid to discredit him, and adopted a measure that outlawed "propaganda of nontraditional sexual relations," triggering violence, job dismissals, and venomous verbal attacks against LGBT people by parliamentarians and other public figures.

MODERN AUTHORITARIANISM IN ACTION

While freedom suffered from coups and civil wars during the year, an equally significant phenomenon was the reliance on more subtle, but ultimately more effective, techniques by those who practice what is known as modern authoritarianism. Such leaders devote full-time attention to the challenge of crippling the opposition without annihilating it, and flouting the rule of law while maintaining a plausible veneer of order, legitimacy, and prosperity.

Central to the modern authoritarian strategy is the capture of institutions that undergird political pluralism. The goal is to dominate not only the executive and legislative branches, but also the media, the judiciary, civil society, the economy, and the security forces. While authoritarians still consider it imperative to ensure favorable electoral outcomes through a certain amount of fraud, gerrymandering, handpicking of election commissions, and other such rigging techniques, they give equal or even more importance to control of the information landscape, the marginalization of civil society critics, and effective command of the judiciary. Hence the seemingly contradictory trends in *Freedom in the World* scores over the past five years: Globally, political rights scores have actually improved slightly, while civil liberties scores have notably declined, with the most serious regression in the categories of freedom of expression and belief, rule of law, and associational rights.

A result of this approach is that elections are more likely to be peaceful and at least superficially competitive, even as authoritarian (or aspiring authoritarian) incumbents use multiple tools to manipulate the electoral environment as needed. In Zimbabwe, for example, the elections of 2013 were less objectionable than in past years, if only due to the absence of widespread violence perpetrated by security forces loyal to President Robert Mugabe. Although observers judged that procedures on election day were relatively fair, the outcome was strongly influenced by policies and abuses meant to tilt the playing field months before the balloting took place.

The past year was notable for an intensification of efforts to control political messages through domination of the media and the use of legal sanctions to punish vocal critics.

In Venezuela, the leading independent television station, Globovision, was neutralized as a critical voice after it was sold under government pressure to business interests that changed its political coverage. In Ecuador, President Rafael Correa, having pushed through legislation in 2012 that threatened to cripple media coverage of elections, ensured that the law was implemented during the balloting in 2013. In Russia, the Putin regime, having gained dominance over the national television sector, folded a respected state-run news agency, RIA Novosti, into a consolidated media entity, Russia Today, that is likely to be more aggressively propagandistic. Among other alarming remarks, designated Russia Today chief Dmitriy Kiselyov has said that gay people "should be banned from donating blood, sperm. And their hearts, in case of the automobile accident, should be buried in the ground or burned as unsuitable for the continuation of life." In Ukraine, associates of President Viktor Yanukovych and his family have gained control of key media outlets and censored coverage of major political issues. In China, the authorities pressured foreign news organizations by delaying or withholding visas for correspondents who had exposed human rights abuses or whose outlets published investigative reports about the business dealings of political leaders and their families. And in Turkey, a range of tactics have been employed to minimize criticism of Prime Minister Recep Tayyip Erdoğan. They include jailing reporters (Turkey leads the world in the number of imprisoned journalists), pressuring independent publishers to sell their holdings to government cronies, and threatening media owners with reprisals if critical journalists are not silenced.

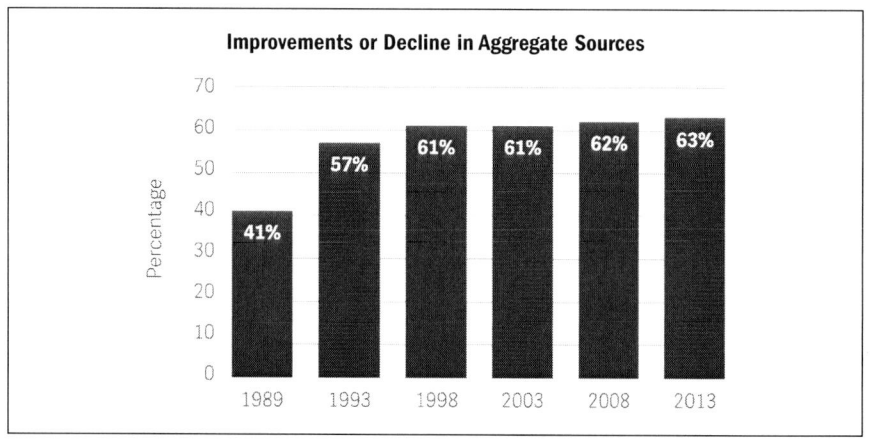

FREEDOM'S TRAJECTORY IN 2013

As in the seven preceding years, the number of countries exhibiting gains for 2013, 40, lagged behind the number with declines, 54. Several of the countries experiencing gains were in Africa, including Mali, Côte d'Ivoire, Senegal, Madagascar, Rwanda, Togo, and Zimbabwe. However, some of these improvements represented fragile recoveries from devastating crises or slight increases from quite low baselines. There were also important declines on the continent, including in Central African Republic, Sierra Leone, Uganda, South Sudan, the Gambia, Tanzania, and Zambia. In the Middle East, in addition to Egypt and Syria, deterioration was recorded for Bahrain, Lebanon, and the territory of Gaza.

An assessment of the *Freedom in the World* political rights indicators over the past five years shows the most pronounced declines in sub-Saharan Africa and the greatest gains in the Asia-Pacific and Middle East and North Africa (MENA) regions, though there has been significant rollback of the improvements associated with the Arab Spring. Eurasia registered the lowest scores for political rights, while MENA had the worst scores for civil liberties categories. Latin America saw declines on most indicators, especially in the civil liberties categories, such as freedom of expression and freedom of association.

MAJOR DEVELOPMENTS AND TRENDS IN 2013 INCLUDED:

- **Anti-LGBT Measures in Russia, Africa:** There were some positive developments for the rights of LGBT people, especially in the United States, where state-level legislative action and court decisions significantly expanded marriage rights, and in several European and Latin American countries. But these gains were overshadowed by hostile measures adopted or more vigorously enforced in other countries, most notably Russia and parts of Africa. In Cameroon, the penal code forbids "sexual relations with a person of the same sex," but people are prosecuted on the mere suspicion of being gay. During the year the executive director of the Cameroonian Foundation for AIDS was found murdered in Yaoundé, his neck broken, feet smashed, and face burned with an iron. In Zambia, same-sex relations are punishable by prison sentences of up to 15 years, and members of the LGBT community have faced increased persecution, including arrests and trials. In Uganda, an anti-LGBT bill passed by the parliament (though not signed by President Yoweri Museveni at year's end) allows penalties of up to life in prison for banned sexual activity. It would also punish individuals for the "promotion" of homosexuality and for not reporting violations within 24 hours, a provision likely to affect health workers and advocates for LGBT rights.

- **Volatility in South Asia:** At year's end, events in Bangladesh seemed ready to spin out of control, with demonstrations, strikes, an election boycott, and repressive measures against the political opposition. Yet developments elsewhere in South Asia suggested some reason for hope in a subregion that has experienced years of violence and political instability. Pakistan held elections that were deemed competitive and reasonably honest, allowing the first successful transfer of power between two elected, civilian governments. Bhutan benefited from a peaceful rotation of power after the opposition won parliamentary elections for the first time. The Maldives held a largely free and fair presidential election despite several delays and repeated interference by the Supreme Court, and there were also successful elections amid many obstacles in Nepal. On a less positive note, Sri Lanka experienced a decline due to violence directed at religious minorities by hard-line Buddhist groups, often with official sanction.

- **Rebounding from Conflict in West Africa:** Both Mali and Côte d'Ivoire registered impressive improvements after suffering through periods of lethal internal conflict. In 2012, Mali's designation had plummeted from Free to Not Free after Islamist militants gained control of the country's northern regions and a military coup overthrew the elected government in the south. But French-led forces succeeded in driving back the militants, and civilian government was restored through presidential and parliamentary elections. These developments enabled Mali to achieve a Partly Free designation for 2013. Côte d'Ivoire's years of political and ethnic strife were punctuated by a 2011 conflict that erupted after President Laurent Gbagbo refused to accept the election victory of his rival, Alassane Ouattara. Since Gbagbo's surrender and arrest, the country has made steady progress toward the consolidation of democratic institutions, especially during 2013, with major improvements in the civil liberties environment.

- **Xenophobia in Central Europe:** While attention has focused on the rise of anti-immigration and Euroskeptic parties in Britain, France, the Netherlands, Austria, and other Western European countries, more virulently xenophobic groups have been at work to the east. Like Golden Dawn in Greece, Bulgaria's Ataka party has gained strength at the expense of the political mainstream as the country's economy has suffered, and the current protest-battered government relies on it for a legislative majority. Ataka and smaller ultranationalist parties regularly used racist rhetoric in their electoral campaigns in 2013, and they have recently targeted refugees from Syria and Muslim citizens. In Hungary, Jobbik focuses its attacks on Jews and Roma, and although its popularity has softened over the past several years, it still holds 11 percent of the seats in parliament. The Slovak National Party (SNS) currently has no seats in that country's legislature, but its slurs against Roma, Hungarians, and LGBT people continue to poison the political atmosphere.

GLOBAL FINDINGS

The number of countries designated by *Freedom in the World* as Free in 2013 stood at 88, representing 45 percent of the world's 195 polities and slightly more than 2.8 billion people—or 40 percent of the global population. The number of Free countries decreased by two from the previous year's report.

The number of countries qualifying as Partly Free stood at 59, or 30 percent of all countries assessed, and they were home to just over 1.8 billion people, or 25 percent of the world's total. The number of Partly Free countries increased by one from the previous year.

A total of 48 countries were deemed Not Free, representing 25 percent of the world's polities. The number of people living under Not Free conditions stood at nearly 2.5 billion people, or 35 percent of the global population, though it is important to note that more than half of this number lives in just one country: China. The number of Not Free countries increased by one from 2012.

The number of electoral democracies stood at 122, four more than in 2012. The four countries that achieved electoral democracy status were Honduras, Kenya, Nepal, and Pakistan.

One country rose from Not Free to Partly Free: Mali. Sierra Leone and Indonesia dropped from Free to Partly Free, while the Central African Republic and Egypt fell from Partly Free to Not Free.

EURASIA: FEW GLIMMERS IN A DARK YEAR

Developments in Eurasia during 2013 proved the adage that in global affairs there is one standard for countries with energy wealth and another, more rigorous standard for everyone else. Three states in the subregion that suffered declines for the year—Russia, Azerbaijan, and Kazakhstan—are locked in a downward spiral that has been ongoing for over a decade, but they are rich in natural gas and oil, and thus have largely escaped the condemnation of democratic governments. Russia, in fact, is looking forward to hosting the Winter Olympics next month, while Kazakhstan and Azerbaijan have played host to various other international competitions, cultural festivals, and diplomatic gatherings.

The year-by-year assault on democratic freedoms through much of Eurasia has brought it to the point where its scores on political rights indicators are lower than those of any other region, now slightly worse than the aggregate scores for Middle Eastern countries. Three Eurasian states, Belarus, Turkmenistan, and Uzbekistan, are included in Freedom House's list of the world's most repressive countries.

A signal development during 2013 was Russia's use of bullying tactics—especially punitive trade restrictions—to discourage neighboring countries from initialing Association Agreements with the European Union. Threats, table thumping, and the promise of tenuous rewards were enough to persuade Armenia to scuttle its plans for closer EU integration and join a Russian-led customs union instead. In dealing with Ukraine, Russia first employed threats of economic retaliation and then offered a major loan and energy-price deal to convince President Viktor Yanukovych to abandon the EU agreement. Yanukovych's actions came after months of pledges to sign the pact, and the betrayal triggered ongoing, mammoth street protests in Kyiv by Ukrainians demanding a European and democratic orientation for their country.

Georgia and Moldova, which boast Eurasia's best rankings on the *Freedom in the World* scale, did initial their EU agreements despite concerted Russian pressure. In Georgia, a presidential election that was widely regarded as fair and honest marked a further step toward the consolidation of democracy.

Notable Gains or Declines:

- **Azerbaijan**'s civil liberties rating declined from 5 to 6 due to ongoing, blatant property rights violations by the government in a year in which the state also cracked down on the opposition and civil society in advance of presidential elections.

- **Kazakhstan** received a downward trend arrow due to broad extralegal enforcement of its already strict 2011 law on religious activity, with raids by antiterrorism police on gatherings in private homes.

- **Russia** received a downward trend arrow due to increased repression of two vulnerable minority groups in 2013: the LGBT community, through a law prohibiting "propaganda of nontraditional sexual relations," and migrant laborers, through arbitrary detentions targeting those from the Caucasus, Central Asia, and East Asia. Both efforts have fed public hostility against these groups.

- **Ukraine** received a downward trend arrow due to violence against journalists and media manipulation associated with the controversy over President Viktor Yanukovych's decision to forego a European Union agreement and accept a financial assistance package from Russia—a decision made without public consultation and against the wishes of a large portion of the Ukrainian people.

MIDDLE EAST AND NORTH AFRICA: TUNISIA PERSEVERES ON THE MARCH TO DEMOCRACY

After two high-profile assassinations of secularist leaders and months of deadlock between the ruling Islamist-led coalition and the largely secularist opposition, Tunisia once again found a way forward in 2013 through compromise and moderation on both sides. The Islamist government agreed to step down in favor of a neutral caretaker government that will rule until elections are held under a new constitution in 2014. The agreement was a significant breakthrough for the country that began the Arab Spring of 2011 and remains the best hope for genuine, stable democracy in the Arab world.

Developments were less positive among the Gulf monarchies, whose bitter resistance to democratic reform included fresh restrictions on the opposition in Bahrain.

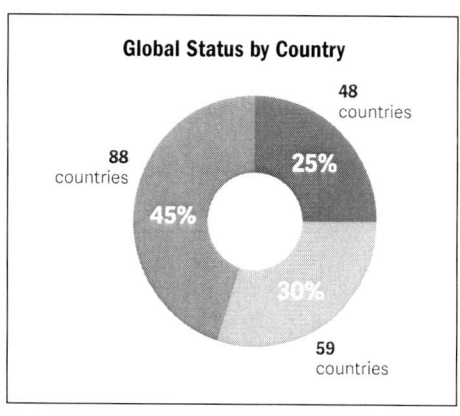

Global Status by Country

48 countries — 25%
59 countries — 30%
88 countries — 45%

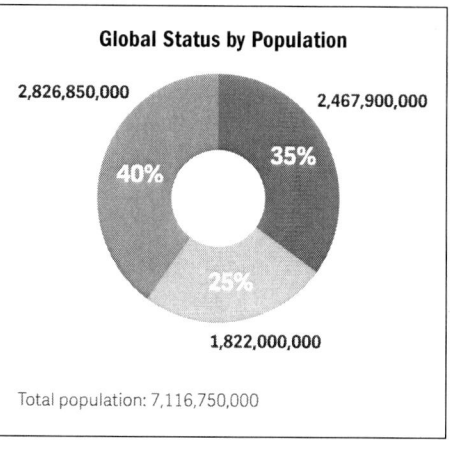

Global Status by Population

2,826,850,000 — 40%
2,467,900,000 — 35%
1,822,000,000 — 25%

Total population: 7,116,750,000

Notable Gains or Declines:

- **Egypt**'s political rights rating declined from 5 to 6 and its status declined from Partly Free to Not Free due to the overthrow of elected president Mohamed Morsi in July, violent crackdowns on Islamist political groups and civil society, and the increased role of the military in the political process.

- **Tunisia**'s civil liberties rating improved from 4 to 3 due to gains in academic freedom, the establishment of new labor unions, and the lifting of travel restrictions.

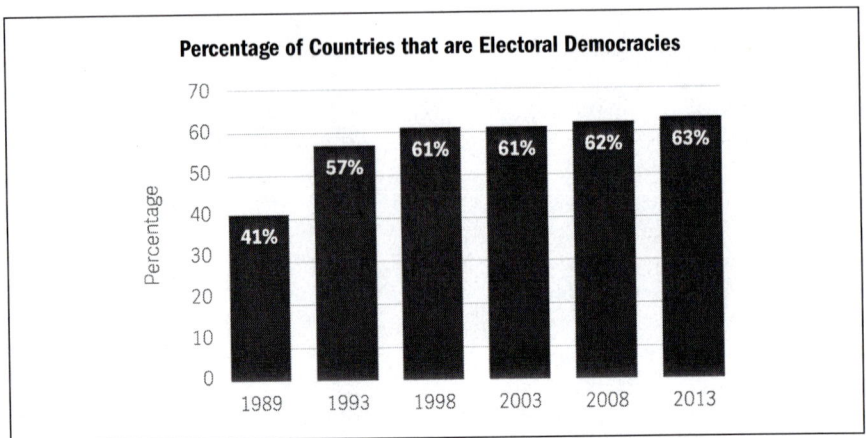

- **Iraq**'s political rights rating improved from 6 to 5 due to an increase in political organizing and activity by opposition parties during provincial elections held in April and June.

- The **Gaza Strip**'s political rights rating declined from 6 to 7 due to the continued failure to hold new elections since the term of the 2006 Palestinian legislature expired in 2010.

- **Bahrain** received a downward trend arrow due to a new ban on unapproved contact between political societies and foreign officials or organizations as well as a government move to dissolve the Islamic Scholars' Council.

- **Lebanon** received a downward trend arrow due to political paralysis stemming from the Syrian conflict that prevented the passage of a new electoral law and led to the postponement of national elections until late 2014.

- **Syria** received a downward trend arrow due to the worsening conditions for civilians in the past year, the increased targeting of churches for destruction and kidnapping of clergy, the implementation of harsh Sharia-inspired restrictions in some areas, and unchecked violence against women, including the use of rape as a weapon of war.

LATIN AMERICA AND CARIBBEAN: VENEZUELA ON THE BRINK

The death of Venezuelan president Hugo Chávez in March triggered hopes that his successors might moderate his authoritarian course and seek common ground with the political opposition. Instead, the new president, Nicolás Maduro, moved in the opposite direction. He took measures to reduce the opposition's ability to serve as a check on government policy, blamed opposition leaders (and the United States) for power outages and other symptoms of government ineptitude, further weakened the independent media, made threats against civil society organizations, and dispatched security forces to retail outlets to enforce price controls on consumer goods prior to municipal and regional elections. Many analysts warned at year's end that Venezuela would require a major shift in policy if it is to avoid an economic and social crisis.

A positive note was a national election in Honduras that observers deemed generally fair and competitive. While the vote was an indication of progress toward political normalcy after the 2009 coup that removed President Manuel Zelaya from office (Zelaya's wife was the runner-up in the 2013 presidential race), Honduras still confronts high rates of poverty and spiraling crime statistics.

Both Chile and Uruguay burnished their images as leading South American democracies. Uruguay adopted several important reform measures, including the legalization of same-sex marriage, while Chile conducted successful elections that returned former president Michelle Bachelet to office for a second term.

Cuba also registered a small step forward due to the easing of visa restrictions and the growth of the private economic sector, though the island remains among the world's most repressive countries as measured by *Freedom in the World*.

Notable Gains or Declines:

- **Nicaragua**'s political rights rating improved from 5 to 4 and its civil liberties rating improved from 4 to 3 due to the positive impact of consultations on proposed constitutional reforms, advances in the corruption and transparency environment, and gradual progress in women's rights and efforts to combat human trafficking.

- The **Dominican Republic**'s civil liberties rating declined from 2 to 3 due to a decision by the Constitutional Court to retroactively strip the citizenship of tens of thousands of Dominicans of Haitian descent.

- **Panama**'s political rights rating declined from 1 to 2 due to concerns that authorities were not investigating allegations of corruption against President Ricardo Martinelli and other officials, as well as verbal attacks against, and the withholding of information from, journalists who write about government corruption.

- **Cuba** received an upward trend arrow due to a modest decline in state surveillance, a broadening of political discussion in private and on the internet, and increased access to foreign travel and self-employment.

- **Belize** received a downward trend arrow due to reports of corruption across several government ministries related to the sale of passports and other documents, as well as an inadequate response by law enforcement agencies.

- **Saint Kitts and Nevis** received a downward trend arrow due to the government's improper efforts to block consideration of a no-confidence motion that had been submitted by opposition legislators in December 2012.

- **Venezuela** received a downward trend arrow due to an increase in the selective enforcement of laws and regulations against the opposition in order to minimize its role as a check on government power.

ASIA-PACIFIC: NEW LEADERSHIP, LITTLE CHANGE IN CHINA

Despite official rhetoric about fighting corruption, improving the rule of law, and inviting input from society, the new Chinese Communist Party leadership under President Xi

Jinping has proven even more intolerant of dissent than its predecessors. After intellectuals and other members of civil society called in early 2013 for the party to adhere to China's constitution and reduce censorship, the authorities responded with campaigns to intensify ideological controls. New judicial guidelines expanded the criminalization of online speech, confessions and "self-criticisms" reminiscent of the Mao era reappeared on television screens, and police arrested dozens of activists affiliated with the New Citizens Movement who had advocated reforms including asset disclosures by public officials.

Even potentially positive changes fell short. Although authorities began to close the country's infamous "reeducation through labor" camps, they increasingly turned to criminal charges with potentially longer sentences and various alternative forms of administrative or extralegal detention to punish human rights defenders, anticorruption activists, petitioners, and religious believers. And despite announced reforms that will increase the number of families permitted to have two children, the intrusive regulations and harsh practices used to enforce the country's long-standing birth quotas remained in place.

A bright spot was the determination of high-profile dissidents as well as large numbers of ordinary citizens to assert their rights and challenge injustice in the face of heavy obstacles. Public protests, online campaigns, journalistic exposés, and activist networks scored several victories during the year, including the release of individuals from wrongful detention. Nevertheless, the ability of Chinese citizens to share breaking news, uncover corruption, or engage in public debate about political and social issues was hampered by increased internet controls and crackdowns on prominent social-media commentators and grassroots antigraft activists.

Notable Gains or Declines:

- **Indonesia**'s civil liberties rating declined from 3 to 4 and its status declined from Free to Partly Free due to the adoption of a law that restricts the activities of nongovernmental organizations, increases bureaucratic oversight of such groups, and requires them to support the national ideology of Pancasila—including its explicitly monotheist component.

- **Bhutan**'s political rights rating improved from 4 to 3 due to an increase in government transparency and a peaceful transfer of power after the opposition won parliamentary elections for the first time, and its civil liberties rating improved from 5 to 4 due to an increase in open and critical political speech, the political opposition's greater ability to hold demonstrations, and the growing independence of the judiciary.

- **Japan**'s civil liberties rating improved from 2 to 1 due to a steady rise in the activity of civil society organizations and an absence of legal restrictions on religious freedom.

- The **Maldives**' political rights rating improved from 5 to 4 due to the largely free and fair presidential election held in November 2013, despite several delays and repeated interference by the Supreme Court.

- **Papua New Guinea**'s political rights rating improved from 4 to 3 due to efforts by Prime Minister Peter O'Neill and his government to address widespread official abuse and corruption, enabling successful prosecutions of several former and current high-ranking officials.

- **Tonga**'s political rights rating improved from 3 to 2 due to the orderly implementation of constitutional procedures in response to the prime minister's incapacitation by illness, and the opposition's increasing ability to hold politically dominant nobles accountable to the electorate.

- **South Korea**'s political rights rating declined from 1 to 2 due to high-profile scandals involving corruption and abuse of authority, including alleged meddling in political affairs by the National Intelligence Service.

- **Pakistan** received an upward trend arrow due to the successful transfer of power between two elected, civilian governments following voting that was widely deemed free and fair.

- **Afghanistan** received a downward trend arrow due to the deteriorating security environment linked to the drawdown of NATO troops, which resulted in an increase in violence against aid workers and women in public office.

- **Bangladesh** received a downward trend arrow due to increased legal harassment and attacks on bloggers, the passage of restrictive amendments to the Information and Communication Technology Act, and the deaths of dozens of protesters during demonstrations over verdicts by the country's war crimes tribunal.

- **Malaysia** received a downward trend arrow due to rampant electoral fraud and structural obstacles designed to block the opposition from winning power, a decision by the highest court to forbid non-Muslims from using the term "Allah" to refer to God, and worsening hostility and prejudice faced by the LGBT community.

- **Sri Lanka** received a downward trend arrow due to intensified attacks by hard-line Buddhist groups against the Christian and Muslim minorities, including their properties and places of worship, often with official sanction.

SUB-SAHARAN AFRICA: A PATTERN OF GAINS AND REVERSALS

For the past decade or so, Africa has been the most volatile region, suffering from a disproportionate share of the world's coups and insurgencies. But its recent history also includes a number of instances in which regimes installed by force have given way to elected civilian rule. In 2013, gains were noted in Mali, Madagascar, and Côte d'Ivoire, all of which were recovering from coups and civil conflicts. The past year also featured modest improvements for countries with authoritarian records, including Rwanda, Togo, and Zimbabwe. At the same time, there were declines for Zambia and Sierra Leone, which had been credited with promising reforms or openings in recent years.

Notable Gains or Declines:

- **Mali**'s political rights rating improved from 7 to 5, its civil liberties rating improved from 5 to 4, and its status improved from Not Free to Partly Free due to the defeat of Islamist rebels, an improved security situation in the north, and successful presidential and legislative elections that significantly reduced the role of the military in politics.

- The **Central African Republic**'s political rights rating declined from 5 to 7, its civil liberties rating declined from 5 to 7, and its status declined from Partly Free to Not Free due to the Séléka rebel group's ouster of the incumbent president and legislature, the suspension of the constitution, and a general proliferation of violence by criminal bands and militias, spurring clashes between Muslim and Christian communities.

- **Sierra Leone**'s political rights rating declined from 2 to 3 and its status declined from Free to Partly Free due to high-profile corruption allegations against bankers, police officers, and government officials as well as long-standing accounting irregularities that led to the country's suspension from the Extractive Industries Transparency Initiative.

- **Côte d'Ivoire**'s civil liberties rating improved from 5 to 4 due to further openings in the environment for freedoms of expression, assembly, and association, as well as for minority groups, as the security situation stabilized under the new government.

- **Madagascar**'s political rights rating improved from 6 to 5 due to the holding of competitive and peaceful presidential and parliamentary elections that were deemed free and fair by international and regional observers.

- **Rwanda**'s civil liberties rating improved from 6 to 5 due to increasing critical commentary on social media, as illustrated by the unhindered online debates regarding Paul Kagame's presidential tenure.

- **Senegal**'s civil liberties rating improved from 3 to 2 due to improvements in the media environment and for freedom of assembly since President Macky Sall took office in 2012.

- **Togo**'s political rights rating improved from 5 to 4 due to successful elections for the national legislature, which suffered from alleged irregularities but were generally deemed fair by international observers and did not feature serious violence.

- **Zimbabwe**'s political rights rating improved from 6 to 5 due to a decline in harassment and violence against political parties and opposition supporters during the 2013 elections.

- **South Sudan**'s civil liberties rating declined from 5 to 6 due to increased armed conflict and mass killings along ethnic lines, triggered by intolerance for dissent within the ruling party and politically motivated arrests in December.

- **Uganda**'s political rights rating declined from 5 to 6 due to the continued, repeated harassment and arrest of prominent opposition leaders, the passage of the Public Order Management Bill to further restrict opposition and civil society activity, and new evidence of the limited space for alternative voices within the ruling National Resistance Movement.

- **Benin** received a downward trend arrow due to increasing efforts by the executive to consolidate power, as demonstrated by the continued detention of alleged coup plotters despite a judge's dismissal of their charges, the placement of the judge under house arrest, and politicized bans on a number of planned demonstrations and protests throughout the year.

- **The Gambia** received a downward trend arrow due to worsening restrictions on civil liberties, including amendments to the Information and Communication Act and the Criminal Code Act that further limited open and free private discussion, and a ban on the use of Skype and other voice communication programs in internet cafés.

- **Tanzania** received a downward trend arrow due to an increase in acts of extrajudicial violence by security forces, mob and vigilante violence, and violence against vulnerable groups including women, albinos, members of the LGBT community, and those at high risk of contracting HIV.

- **Zambia** received a downward trend arrow due to the ruling party's ongoing repression and harassment of the political opposition, including the increased use of the Public Order Act, hindering its ability to operate in general and to campaign in by-elections.

EUROPE AND NORTH AMERICA: DYSFUNCTION IN THE UNITED STATES, AN UNCERTAIN FUTURE FOR TURKEY

The United States in 2013 endured a level of government gridlock not seen in over a century. The long-running standoff between the administration of President Barack Obama and his Republican Party opponents in Congress culminated in a two-week partial shutdown of the federal government. Ultimately, the Republicans backed down and a budget agreement was adopted. But little progress was made on a broad set of important issues. For example, Republican resistance played a major role in thwarting Obama's proposed overhaul of the country's immigration laws, which would include a path toward citizenship for some undocumented immigrants.

The U.S. government pledged to redouble its efforts to close down the military prison facility at Guantanamo Bay, Cuba, where scores of terrorism suspects have been held without trial since 2001. However, only a handful of detainees were released and placed in other countries during 2013; at year's end there were over 150 detainees at the facility.

The administration also found itself under criticism from civil libertarians at home and a number of foreign governments for the eavesdropping and data-collection tactics of the National Security Agency (NSA). The intelligence agency's sprawling activities, including its collection of communications metadata on American citizens and its intrusive monitoring of close foreign allies, was made public through a series of leaks by Edward Snowden, a contractor who had worked for the NSA. Fearing arrest, Snowden fled to Hong Kong and then to Russia, where he was granted asylum.

A special presidential commission set up to review the NSA's practices after the leaks did not find violations of Americans' constitutional rights, but it did recommend a series of changes in intelligence policy and procedures. The administration separately came under fire during the year after prosecutors gained access to the telephone records of journalists who worked for the Associated Press as part of an internal investigation into leaked national security information.

Among the most important developments in Europe during 2013 was the escalating crisis surrounding the Erdoğan government in Turkey. In his early years in power, Erdoğan was widely praised—and credited in this report—for introducing overdue democratic reforms. Then came a period in which reform efforts seemed to stall. More recently, key democratic institutions have faced intense pressure, and basic civil liberties have experienced setbacks.

A series of "deep state" trials, in which hundreds of prominent Turks have been charged with alleged conspiracies to overthrow the government, have raised serious questions about the rule of law and selective justice. These concerns have only been compounded by the government's ongoing purge of law enforcement officials and prosecutors in response to corruption cases recently brought against Erdoğan's allies. Just as troubling is the prime minister's campaign against critical voices in the media. A government that several years ago was in serious negotiations on EU membership is notorious today as a major adversary of press freedom.

Erdoğan's increasingly authoritarian tendencies were on display in his imperious reaction to the year's protests over a development plan that would eliminate a cherished Istanbul park. Reprisals by the authorities extended to protesters, businesses accused of sheltering them, and social-media users who commented on the events, among others. With increasing frequency, the prime minister and his allies blamed their troubles on supposed plots by international cabals.

Notable Gains or Declines:

- **Italy**'s political rights rating improved from 2 to 1 due to parliamentary elections that were generally considered to be free and fair as well as progress in the adoption and implementation of anticorruption measures.

- **Turkey** received a downward trend arrow due to the harsh government crackdown on protesters in Istanbul and other cities and increased political pressure on private companies to conform with the ruling party's agenda.

CONCLUSION: FREEDOM IN THE WORLD AT 41

This year marks the 41st edition of *Freedom in the World*. From the beginning, the survey used scholarly research to inform the policy debate. It was conceived as an instrument that would employ rigorous methods to measure the state of global freedom, after which the findings would be publicized in order to alert policymakers and the press to democracy's gains and setbacks, as well as the major threats to free societies.

At the time the report was launched, there was reason for concern, if not alarm, about the condition of world freedom. For the first time since the early years of the Cold War, democracy seemed to be in retreat, and the world's democratic powers were mired in doubt and confusion. By contrast, the two communist giants, China and the Soviet Union, appeared firmly in control of their societies. The most recent effort at reform in the communist world, the Prague Spring of 1968, had been crushed by military invasion, and the rest of Eastern Europe had digested the message that liberalization was not on the agenda. Asia, Africa, Latin America, and the Middle East were dominated by strongmen, white-minority regimes, military juntas, and absolute monarchs. Even Western Europe, where democracy was generally well entrenched, had its dictatorships—in Greece, Spain, and Portugal.

The state of freedom reached its nadir in 1975, when 40 countries, just 25 percent of the world's independent states, were ranked as Free, compared with 65 countries, or 41 percent, ranked as Not Free. At that point in history, the democratic universe was restricted to Western Europe, North America, and a few other scattered locales, and recent trends gave little cause for optimism about the future.

But for the next quarter-century, the state of freedom experienced a period of progress unprecedented in human history. After the embrace of democracy by the European dictatorships, military governments gave way to civilian rule in Latin America, followed by the beginning of political change in South Korea, Taiwan, and other Asian states. Then came the unraveling of the communist world, first in the East European satellites and then in the Soviet Union itself. The collapse of Soviet communism—and the effective demise of Marxism as a political system—had additional ripple effects, as elites in Africa, Latin America, and Asia could no longer claim that right-wing dictatorships were necessary to forestall the spread of communist totalitarianism.

Thus by 2000, the number of countries designated as Free had surged to 86, or 45 percent of the total, while the number of Not Free states had declined to 48, or 25 percent. With the end of the 1990s Balkan wars and a modest surge of democratic governance in Africa, the Middle East remained the only major part of the world that had been relatively untouched by what Samuel Huntington labeled the third wave of democracy.

Since then, the state of freedom has been situated somewhere between stagnation and decline. On the one hand, few of the countries that moved toward democracy in the previous decades sank back into authoritarian rule. Europe's postcommunist countries have maintained a high standard of rights and liberties, in part due to the EU's imposition of democracy criteria for new member states. There have been problems in Latin America—most prominently in Venezuela—but on balance the region has experienced the longest period of stable democracy in its history.

On the other hand, the march of democracy has met with a wall of resistance in three major settings: China, Eurasia, and the Middle East.

THE AUTHORITARIAN RESISTANCE

During the 1990s, when the foundations for its economic miracle were being set, many predicted that China would rather quickly evolve toward a more liberal and perhaps democratic system. If the immediate results were not democracy as understood in Washington and Brussels, it would at least be a system that was less repressive, more tolerant of criticism, and more subject to the rule of law. Instead, the Chinese Communist Party leadership has developed a complicated apparatus of controls and punishments designed to maintain rigid one-party rule and prevent the expression of dissent, while at the same time enabling China to become a global economic powerhouse.

In the immediate aftermath of the Soviet unraveling, there were also expectations that a number of the new independent states, including Russia, would opt for democracy and reject the authoritarian institutions of communist times. But with a few peripheral exceptions, the bulk of the Eurasian states have remained in or returned to various forms of despotism. Across the region, the political opposition has been jailed, forced into exile, or made irrelevant; the media have been coopted or censored; and public wealth has been plundered by ruling elites and their cronies in the business community.

The Middle East seemed especially impervious to liberalization until the Arab Spring. Yet the sudden emergence of protest movements in Tunisia, Egypt, and Bahrain, and the armed conflicts arising from similar efforts to overthrow dictatorships in Libya and Syria, were greeted by democratic governments more with apprehension than enthusiasm. Their authoritarian counterparts had no such misgivings, displaying unalloyed hostility toward the prospect of democratic change in the Arab heartland. The region's surviving dictatorships and monarchies have worked actively to undermine local democrats and give encouragement to the forces of repression, counterrevolution, or extremism.

While the official ideologies of today's authoritarian powers vary considerably, their leaders clearly form alliances in order to advance common goals. They have studied how other dictatorships were destroyed and are bent on preventing a similar fate for themselves. At one level, a loose-knit club of authoritarians works to protect mutual interests at the United Nations and other international forums, subverting global human rights standards and blocking precedent-setting actions against fellow despots. More disturbingly, they collaborate to prop up some of the world's most reprehensible regimes. This is most visible at present in Syria, where Russia, China, Iran, and Venezuela have offered diplomatic support, loans, fuel, or direct military aid to the Assad regime.

THE DEMOCRACIES' CRISIS OF CONFIDENCE

In an earlier period, it was the United States and its allies that were the guarantors of political change in the world. Self-assured and optimistic, they provided the material resources and diplomatic muscle that tipped the balance in favor of freedom movements and struggling new democracies. In this undertaking, a range of private actors also played a critical role. Trade unions from North America and Europe made it possible for Poland's Solidarity movement to survive under duress; a transnational alliance of intellectuals mobilized behind Václav Havel during Czechoslovakia's Velvet Revolution; activists worldwide joined together to press for an end to South African apartheid.

If Poland and South Africa were once the causes that inspired freedom's allies, today the animating cause is—or should be—the Middle East. Egypt's coup and Assad's apparent resurgence notwithstanding, the forces of change have been unleashed, and for the first time popular demands for self-government, freedom of thought, and an end to oppression have been placed squarely on the table.

Unfortunately, the American government has failed to recognize the historic moment that presents itself in the region. It is true that there have been setbacks, that democratic forces have made mistakes, and that rigid geostrategic priorities sometimes conflict with the goals of democratic change. But there is a real danger that policymakers will become locked into a defeatist loop, seeing validation for their inaction in the very problems it produces. The Arab world is clearly in flux, and the question is whether those committed to free societies will prevail or whether the Middle East will fall prey to new forms of repressive rule. Observers who might prefer to turn back the clock should remember that decades of authoritarian misrule, not demands for democracy, led to the institutional weaknesses and extremist elements now in plain view.

The cause is far from lost. While today's authoritarians impress many with their self-assurance and determination, a closer examination suggests that modern despots devote much of their time to holding actions against popular demands for change. Recently, the leaderships in Russia and China have attempted to develop overarching ideas that would justify their ruling policies. The predictable answers—"traditional" Russian values and a kind of neo-Maoist nationalism—smack more of incoherence than confidence in the future.

It is noteworthy that those who, at considerable personal risk, have joined the struggle for change in Egypt, Tunisia, and Bahrain are not chanting in praise of the "China Dream" or issuing appeals to Vladimir Putin. The United States may not be the most popular country in the Middle East, but desire for the democratic benefits it enjoys—free elections, freedom of expression, and guarantees against police-state predation—lies at the heart of the ongoing uprising in the Arab world. Similar demands can be heard on the streets or are uttered more furtively in virtually every authoritarian state, Russia and China included.

The democratic world was experiencing a period of self-absorption much like today's when Freedom House launched *Freedom in the World* during the 1970s. Once it had overcome its crisis of confidence, America helped propel a historic surge of democratization in parts of the world where self-government was almost unknown. A similar era of change could be in the offing, and some democracies—including a number in Europe—have done their best to play a constructive role. But if there is no reassertion of American leadership, we could well find ourselves at some future time deploring lost opportunities rather than celebrating a major breakthrough for freedom.

Jennifer Dunham, Bret Nelson, Aili Piano, Tyler Roylance, and Vanessa Tucker contributed to the preparation of this report.

Introduction

The *Freedom in the World 2014* survey contains reports on 195 countries and 14 related and disputed territories. Each country report begins with a section containing the following information: **population, capital, political rights rating** (numerical rating), **civil liberties rating** (numerical rating), **freedom rating** (the average of the political rights and civil liberties ratings), **freedom status** (Free, Partly Free, or Not Free), **"electoral democracy" designation**, and a **10-year ratings timeline**. Each territory report begins with a section containing the same information, except for the capital and the electoral democracy designation. The population figures are drawn primarily from the *2013 World Population Data Sheet* of the Population Reference Bureau.

The **political rights** and **civil liberties** ratings range from 1 to 7, with 1 representing the most free and 7 the least free. The **status** designation of Free, Partly Free, or Not Free, which is determined by the average of the political rights and civil liberties ratings, indicates the general state of freedom in a country or territory. Any improvements or declines in the ratings since the previous survey are noted next to the relevant number in each report. Positive or negative trends that were not sufficient to trigger a ratings change may be highlighted by upward or downward **trend arrows**, which are located next to the name of the country or territory. A brief explanation of ratings changes or trend arrows is provided for each country or territory as required. For a full description of the methods used to determine the survey's ratings, please see the chapter on the survey's methodology.

The **10-year ratings timeline** lists the political rights and civil liberties ratings and status for each of the last 10 years. Each year that is included in the timeline refers to the year under review, *not* the edition of the survey. Thus, the ratings and status from the *Freedom in the World 2014* edition are listed under "2013" (the year that was under review for the 2014 survey edition).

Following the section described above, each country and territory report is divided into two parts: an **introduction** and an analysis of **political rights and civil liberties**. The introduction provides a brief review of major events during the survey year. The political rights and civil liberties section summarizes each country or territory's degree of respect for the rights and liberties that Freedom House uses to evaluate freedom in the world. This section is composed of seven parts that correspond to the seven main subcategories in the methodology. The scores for each subcategory, and any changes from the previous year, are noted next to the relevant subheading.

↓ Afghanistan

Political Rights Rating: 6
Civil Liberties Rating: 6
Freedom Rating: 6.0
Freedom Status: Not Free
Electoral Democracy: No

Population: 30,552,000
Capital: Kabul

Trend Arrow: Afghanistan received a downward trend arrow due to the deteriorating security environment linked to the drawdown of NATO troops, which resulted in an increase in violence against aid workers and women in public office.

Ten-Year Ratings Timeline For Year Under Review (Political Rights, Civil Liberties, Status)

Year Under Review	2004	2005	2006	2007	2008	2009	2010	2011	2012	2013
Rating	5,6,NF	5,5,PF	5,5,PF	5,5,PF	5,6,NF	6,6,NF	6,6,NF	6,6,NF	6,6,NF	6,6,NF

INTRODUCTION

Events in Afghanistan during 2013 were shaped in large part by the ongoing drawdown of North Atlantic Treaty Organization (NATO) forces and preparations for the April 2014 presidential election.

In June, NATO-led coalition forces transferred full responsibility for the country's security to the Afghan military and police, which continued to be plagued by illiteracy, corruption, involvement in drug trafficking, and high rates of desertion. Afghan forces also suffered an increase in combat deaths, suggesting the need for considerably more training and support before they could handle combat operations on their own. In November, President Hamid Karzai's refusal to sign the final draft of the new U.S.-Afghan Bilateral Security Agreement (BSA), which had received the approval of a national assembly of Afghan elders that was convened for that purpose, caused additional uncertainty, as international donors were awaiting the pact's conclusion before committing to financial pledges beyond 2014. The U.S. government declared in mid-December that it was not willing to make any further changes to the BSA, which had been negotiated in good faith. The potential loss of the U.S. troop presence was already having a negative effect on the Afghan economy, which relied heavily on foreign aid.

In preparation for the 2014 presidential and provincial elections, the Independent Election Commission (IEC) approved 11 candidates to run for president. Among the nominees was a brother of the current president as well as former warlords accused of perpetrating serious human rights abuses. Though voter registration resulted in the addition of over 3 million new voters by mid-November when its third phase came to an end, the process was reportedly tainted by irregularities, with registration cards allegedly being sold or handed to individuals without verifying identity documents. More than 20 million registration cards have been issued in the country since the first post-Taliban elections, despite the estimated number of voters being only 12 million.

The year featured a threefold increase in deadly attacks against aid workers, making Afghanistan the most dangerous place for relief work in the world. Female public officials and employees were also targeted with abductions and killings. Concerns about a regressive trend on women's rights were exacerbated by a Ministry of Justice proposal to reinstate public stoning as a punishment for convicted adulterers in a draft penal code.

POLITICAL RIGHTS: 11 / 40
A. Electoral Process: 3 / 12

Afghanistan's president is directly elected for up to two five-year terms and has the power to appoint ministers, subject to parliamentary approval. In the directly elected lower house of the National Assembly, the 249-seat Wolesi Jirga (House of the People), members stand for five-year terms. In the 102-seat Meshrano Jirga (House of Elders), the upper house, two-thirds of members are indirectly elected by the provincial councils for three- or four-year terms, and one-third are appointed by the president for five-year terms. Ten of the Wolesi Jirga seats are reserved for the nomadic Kuchi community, including at least three women, and another 65 seats are reserved for women. Provisions for women's representation have also been implemented for the Meshrano Jirga and provincial councils.

Karzai, the incumbent, initially emerged as the outright winner of the 2009 presidential election with more than 50 percent of the vote, but the confirmation of large-scale fraud significantly reduced his total, necessitating a November runoff against his main opponent, former foreign minister Abdullah Abdullah. However, Abdullah withdrew before the vote, arguing that the flaws in the electoral system had not been adequately addressed, and Karzai was declared the winner.

The September 2010 parliamentary elections also proved to be deeply flawed, with low voter turnout and widespread fraud. Karzai did not inaugurate the new parliament until January 2011, ruling by decree in the interim, and it was not until August 2011 that disagreements over 62 candidates for the 249-seat lower house were resolved, with the IEC agreeing to replace only nine of the seated lawmakers. Afghanistan's district council elections, which were scheduled to take place in 2010, were canceled.

In September 2013, Karzai appointed the five members of the Independent Election Complaints Commission for the upcoming April 2014 presidential and provincial elections, prompting opposition members to accuse him of installing cronies on the panel. Meanwhile, of the 27 presidential candidates who filed their nominations with the IEC by a deadline in early October, 11 were deemed qualified to run. An additional 2,360 individuals submitted their nominations for provincial elections. Soon after all nominations were submitted, Human Rights Watch demanded that Karzai repeal recent laws that constrained the IEC from disqualifying candidates who have violated human rights.

Due to overall security concerns, registration centers for the 2014 elections had opened in only 387 of 399 districts as of August 2013. Over a third of the approximately three million new voters registered by mid-November were women. Meanwhile, the Free and Fair Election Foundation of Afghanistan reported thousands of instances in which voter cards were issued to individuals without valid identification documents. There were also allegations that voter cards were on sale for $5, bought by campaign managers aiming to boost their candidates' performance.

NATO generals expressed confidence that Afghan security forces would be able to provide security for roughly 95 percent of the polling centers during the 2014 elections. However, there was a shortage of policewomen to be posted at women's polling centers, with only 2,000 available out of the 13,000 deemed necessary.

B. Political Pluralism and Participation: 6 / 16

Violence and insecurity continue to restrict political activity nationwide, particularly outside urban areas, with regular attacks against government officials at all levels. Afghanistan uses the single non-transferable vote (SNTV) electoral system, under which most candidates for elected office run as independents and participate in fluid alliances. Parties lack a formal role within the legislature, weakening their ability to contribute to stable political, policymaking, and legislative processes.

Women accounted for about 16 percent of the candidates in the 2010 parliamentary elections, where roughly 41 percent of registered voters were women; 69 female candidates were elected. There were two women among the 41 candidates for the 2009 presidential election. While there are no women candidates in the upcoming 2014 presidential election, 273 women are running for provincial seats.

On the whole, female electoral participation has been limited by threats, harassment, and social restrictions on traveling alone and appearing in public. There have also been attacks against women parliamentarians. In one notable incident in August 2013, a militant attack in Ghazni Province injured Rooh Gul, a female member of the upper house from Farah Province, and killed her daughter and a security guard. Also that week, Taliban insurgents kidnapped Fariba Ahmadi Kakar, a lower house member who was traveling in Ghazni with her children. She was freed the following month after the government agreed to release Taliban prisoners.

C. Functioning of Government: 2 / 12

In November 2013, the Afghan government convened a four-day assembly of thousands of Afghan elders to approve a new BSA with the United States, intended to determine the scope and terms of the U.S. military presence in Afghanistan after 2014. The United States and its allies planned to end direct combat operations that year but are considering continuing smaller training and counterterrorism missions through 2024. Though the draft agreement was backed by the elders, Karzai rejected their recommendation, suggesting that the matter be deferred to his successor after the April 2014 election. The United States made it clear that this would not be possible, threatening to resort to a "zero option" whereby it would leave no forces in Afghanistan. This impasse, which remained unresolved at year's end, jeopardized billions of dollars in aid money, with international donors awaiting an agreement before deciding on their post-2014 financial commitments to Afghanistan.

Corruption, nepotism, and cronyism remain rampant at all levels of government, and woefully inadequate salaries encourage corrupt behavior by public employees. Afghanistan was ranked 175 of 177 countries and territories surveyed in Transparency International's 2013 Corruption Perceptions Index. Findings released in July by the 2013 Global Corruption Barometer found that roughly half of the Afghans surveyed reported paying a bribe in the past year. In terms of institutions, Afghans see the judiciary and civil service as the most corrupt, with religious bodies and the media as least corrupt.

The international community, concerned that government corruption is crippling all efforts toward security and development, has pressed the Karzai administration to make the issue its top priority. There were 21 convictions in March 2013 linked to the massive Kabul Bank fraud scandal that emerged in 2010 and undermined confidence in Afghan financial institutions. Among those convicted were the bank's founder and its former chief executive, who received five-year prison sentences and were ordered to pay hundreds of millions of dollars in restitution. The sentences were considerably more lenient than those sought by prosecutors, and they did not come with confiscation orders, leaving it unclear whether or how the money could be recovered. In a July meeting to assess progress on the benchmarks set by the previous year's Tokyo donor conference, at which Afghanistan had pledged to tackle corruption, it was determined that only 3 of the 17 benchmarks had been achieved, raising concerns about the disbursement of roughly $4 billion pledged in aid.

CIVIL LIBERTIES: 15 / 60 (-1)
D. Freedom of Expression and Belief: 6 / 16

Afghan media continue to expand and diversify, but they face major challenges including physical attacks and intimidation. Despite a 2007 media law intended to clarify press freedoms and limit government interference, a growing number of journalists have been arrested, threatened, or harassed by politicians, security services, and others in positions of power as a result of their coverage. Afghanistan remains a dangerous place for journalists, with 24 confirmed killed since 1992, according to the Committee to Protect Journalists, though none were reported killed in 2013.

Media diversity and freedom are markedly higher in Kabul than elsewhere in the country, but some local leaders and warlords display a limited tolerance for independent media in their areas. Dozens of private radio stations and several private television channels currently operate, conveying a range of viewpoints and often carrying criticism of the government. Some independent outlets and publications have been denounced or fined for content that "opposes Islam and national values," and in April 2013 Karzai supported a request by conservative clerics to ban television programs that are considered "counter to social morality." Rapidly expanding use of the internet and mobile telephones has broadened the flow of information, particularly for urban residents, but Taliban attacks on mobile-phone infrastructure has worked against this trend.

Religious freedom has improved since the fall of the Taliban government in late 2001, but it is still hampered by violence and harassment aimed at religious minorities and reformist Muslims. The constitution establishes Islam as the official religion. Blasphemy and apostasy by Muslims are considered capital crimes. While faiths other than Islam are permitted, non-Muslim proselytizing is strongly discouraged. Hindus, Sikhs, and Shiite Muslims—particularly those from the Hazara ethnic group—face official obstacles and discrimination by the Sunni Muslim majority. Militant groups have targeted mosques and clerics as part of the larger civil conflict. In September 2013, agents of Afghanistan's National Directorate of Security (NDS) killed two gunmen who had shot and injured at least three worshippers at a Shiite mosque in Kabul.

Aside from constitutional provisions regarding the role of Islam in education, academic freedom is not officially restricted, but insurgents have attacked or destroyed schools associated with the government or foreign donors, particularly girls' schools. An assailant in Faryab Province in May 2013 reportedly used a toxic agent to sicken 75 middle-school girls. More than 74 schoolgirls had taken ill the previous month in Takhar Province, and a similar chemical attack was suspected. In mid-November, the police defused a bomb near a girls' high school in Ghazni Province. The quality of school instruction and resources remains poor. Higher education is subject to bribery and prohibitively expensive for most Afghans.

E. Associational and Organizational Rights: 4 / 12 (-1)

The constitution guarantees the rights to assembly and association, subject to some restrictions, but they are upheld erratically from region to region. Police and other security personnel have occasionally used excessive force when confronted with demonstrations or protests.

The work of hundreds of international and Afghan nongovernmental organizations (NGOs)—numbering 287 and 1,911 respectively in 2013—as well as over 4,000 other associations is not typically constrained by the authorities in a formal sense, but these groups' ability to operate freely and effectively is impeded by the security situation. There was a threefold increase in deadly attacks against NGO staff members in 2013, with at least 36 people killed, compared with 11 in 2012. The number of kidnappings or abductions also rose dramatically. Among other incidents during the year, five Afghan aid workers with the International Rescue Committee were kidnapped and killed along with a local official in Herat Province in August. Six Afghans working for a French charity were shot and killed in Faryab Province in November, a day after three local development workers were killed by a bomb in Uruzgan Province. Civil society activists, particularly those who focus on human rights or accountability issues, continue to face threats and harassment.

Despite broad constitutional protections for workers, labor rights are not well defined, and there are currently no effective enforcement or dispute-resolution mechanisms. Child labor is reportedly common.

F. Rule of Law: 2 / 16

The judicial system operates haphazardly, and justice in many places is administered on the basis of a mixture of legal codes by inadequately trained judges. The Supreme Court, composed of religious scholars who have little knowledge of civil jurisprudence, is particularly in need of reform. Corruption in the judiciary is extensive, and judges and lawyers are often subject to threats from local leaders or armed groups. Traditional or mob justice is the main recourse for the population, especially in rural areas. In two widely publicized incidents of vigilantism during 2013, a group of local residents attacked a male doctor and female patient in Sar-i-Pul Province in June because he was treating her in a room without a chaperone, and an individual suspected of planting a bomb that killed 18 people in Ghazni Province was beaten and stoned to death in October.

Prison conditions are extremely poor, with many detainees held illegally. The NDS as well as some warlords and political leaders maintain their own prisons and do not allow access to detainees. A UN report released in January 2013 found an increase in incidents of torture in Afghan incarceration facilities.

In October 2013, UN representatives in Afghanistan stated that there was a 16 percent increase in Afghan civilian casualties in the first eight months of 2013 compared with the same period a year earlier, including a 54 percent increase in four eastern provinces. There was also an increase in the deaths of women and children. Nearly three-quarters of the civilian deaths were caused by Taliban attacks, mostly bombings. The second-largest cause was increased fighting between militants and Afghan security forces.

In a prevailing climate of impunity, government officials, as well as warlords in some provinces, sanction widespread abuses by the police, military, local militias, and intelligence forces under their command, including arbitrary arrest and detention, torture, extortion, and extrajudicial killings. The Afghanistan Independent Human Rights Commission (AIHRC) receives hundreds of complaints of rights violations each year. In addition to abuses by security forces, the reported violations have involved land theft, displacement, child trafficking, domestic violence, and forced marriage. There was an increase in kidnappings for ransom during 2013, raising concerns that the foreign troop withdrawal would empower not just the Taliban but also criminal gangs.

G. Personal Autonomy and Individual Rights: 3 / 16

Over 474,000 civilians were displaced within the country as of mid-2013, according to the Office of the UN High Commissioner for Refugees (UNHCR). Humanitarian agencies and Afghan authorities are ill-equipped to deal with the displaced. Factors like the poor security situation and widespread land grabbing have prevented refugees from returning to their homes, and many congregate instead around major urban centers. In the absence of a properly functioning legal system, the state remains unable to protect property rights.

Private business activity is heavily influenced by criminal groups, particularly in connection with the vast narcotics trade. In 2013 there was a 49 percent increase in opium production, part of a three-year trend that is expected to continue after the 2014 withdrawal of coalition combat forces, whose presence is associated with a third of legal investment and employment in Afghanistan. The country is not just the world's largest opium producer, but also one of the largest per capita consumers, with over a million opiate addicts in a population of some 30 million.

Though women have formal rights to education and employment, and some are participating in public life, societal discrimination and domestic violence remain pervasive, with the latter often going unreported because of social acceptance of the practice. Women's choices regarding marriage and divorce remain circumscribed by custom and discriminatory laws, and the forced marriage of young girls to older men or widows to their husbands' male relations is a problem, with the UN Children's Fund (UNICEF) reporting that nearly 40 percent of Afghan girls are married before the legal age of 16.

As reported in March 2013, more than two-thirds of the women incarcerated in Afghanistan's main women's prison, Badam Bagh, are jailed for "moral crimes," such as leaving their husbands or refusing an arranged marriage. Meanwhile, according to an unpublished UN study described in the media in September, close to 70 percent of female Afghan police officers have confronted sexual violence or harassment in the workplace. There were also deadly attacks on high-ranking women in law enforcement, with two senior policewomen murdered within a three-month period in Helmand Province.

Many observers have expressed fears that gains made in women's rights over the past 12 years could be lost after coalition forces withdraw. In May 2013, women's rights activists suggested and then retracted revisions to Afghanistan's Elimination of Violence against Women Act, after it appeared that any requests for amendment would result in the outright annulment of the law by conservative legislators. In November, the Justice Ministry proposed the reinstatement of public stoning as a punishment for convicted adulterers and flogging for sex between unmarried people in a draft revision of the country's penal code, drawing condemnation from Human Rights Watch and other groups. Under existing law, various forms of extramarital sex, including sex between adult men, can be punished with imprisonment. Women who report rapes are sometimes jailed for having extramarital sex. In December, a UN Assistance Mission in Afghanistan report criticized the government for not enforcing the 2009 Elimination of Violence against Women Law, which criminalizes child marriage, forced marriage, forced self-immolation, rape, and other acts of violence against women.

In October, the AIHRC began a campaign against the sexual exploitation of young boys and men by powerful individuals. The commission linked the illegal trade to the practice of trafficking in dancing boys (*bacha bazi*).

Albania

Political Rights Rating: 3
Civil Liberties Rating: 3
Freedom Rating: 3.0
Freedom Status: Partly Free
Electoral Democracy: Yes

Population: 2,774,500
Capital: Tirana

Ten-Year Ratings Timeline For Year Under Review (Political Rights, Civil Liberties, Status)

Year Under Review	2004	2005	2006	2007	2008	2009	2010	2011	2012	2013
Rating	3,3,PF	3,3,PF	3,3,PF	3,3,PF	3,3,PF	3,3,PF	3,3,PF	3,3,PF	3,3,PF	3,3,PF

INTRODUCTION

A coalition led by the opposition Socialist Party (PS) won a decisive victory in June 2013 parliamentary elections, ousting a bloc headed by two-term prime minister Sali Berisha and his Democratic Party (PD). The PS-led coalition was bolstered by the Socialist

Movement for Integration (LSI), which had withdrawn from the government in April. Berisha conceded defeat after the vote and resigned as party chairman. PS chairman Edi Rama took office as prime minister, pledging to tackle persistent corruption and other obstacles to European Union (EU) membership, and his cabinet was approved by the parliament in September.

The Central Election Commission (CEC) was crippled by partisan infighting, and a range of electoral irregularities were reported, but international monitors praised the competitive and relatively peaceful campaign as well as the voting and counting processes on and after election day. The fairly positive assessment and the smooth transfer of power played a role in the European Commission's October recommendation that Albania be granted EU candidate status, four years after the country first applied. However, the European Council decided against the move in December, putting it off for another year.

POLITICAL RIGHTS: 27 / 40 (+3)
A. Electoral Process: 8 / 12

The unicameral, 140-member Kuvendi (Assembly) is elected through proportional representation in 12 regional districts of varying size. All members serve four-year terms. The prime minister is designated by the majority party or coalition, and the president—who does not hold executive powers but heads the military and plays an important role in selecting senior judges—is chosen by the parliament for a maximum of two five-year terms.

Preparations for the June 2013 parliamentary elections were seriously disrupted by political deadlock in the CEC. After the LSI left the PD-led government in April, the parliamentary majority dismissed the CEC member nominated by the LSI and appointed a replacement nominated by the Republican Party, a member of the governing coalition. The three remaining opposition-backed members of the seven-seat commission resigned in protest, and the opposition refused to name replacements. As a result, the CEC operated with just four members throughout the election period, preventing it from making crucial decisions that require a five-vote majority. Earlier, the CEC failed to decide on seat distribution for the country's electoral districts, leading the parliamentary majority to intervene and set the allotments using outdated 2009 population figures.

Other problems reported by monitors from the Organization for Security and Cooperation in Europe (OSCE) included the partisan use of administrative resources, pressure on public employees and students to attend campaign events, alleged vote buying, some cases of family or proxy voting, and various missed deadlines. However, the observer mission found that the overall campaign was vibrant, competitive, and largely peaceful, despite an election-day shooting incident in which an LSI supporter was killed and two other people, including a PD candidate, were injured.

According to the final results, the PS captured 65 seats, the LSI took 16, and two smaller PS-allied parties—the Human Rights and Unity Party (PBDNJ), which represents ethnic Greeks, and the Christian Democratic Party—each garnered 1 seat. Meanwhile, the PD won 50 seats and its junior partners—the nationalist Justice, Integration, and Unity Party and the Republican Party—took 4 and 3 seats, respectively. Voter turnout was reported at 53.5 percent.

B. Political Pluralism and Participation: 13 / 16 (+3)

The two main political parties, the PD and the PS, are sharply polarized and given to personality-driven rivalry, though in 2012 they cooperated on electoral reforms in a process that was criticized by smaller parties. Berisha and the PD had worked to consolidate partisan control over state institutions, particularly after violent antigovernment protests in early 2011, and the PS lost the crucial Tirana mayoralty in flawed 2012 municipal voting.

However, the Socialists' clear victory in 2013 restored confidence in the ability of opposition forces to secure a rotation of power through elections.

Ethnic minorities were able to campaign freely in their own languages in 2013, and voters had access to ballot materials in minority languages. The PBDNJ represents ethnic Greek interests in politics and government. The Romany minority and other marginalized groups are reportedly vulnerable to political exploitation and vote-buying schemes.

C. Functioning of Government: 6 / 12

Corruption is pervasive, and the EU has repeatedly called for rigorous implementation of antigraft measures. The electoral framework lacks robust transparency provisions on campaign financing, requiring no disclosures before election day. Convictions of high-ranking officials and judges for corruption and abuse of power remain rare. In July 2013, the Supreme Court declined to review a February appellate ruling that sharply reduced the prison sentences of businessmen and former defense officials who had been convicted in connection with a 2008 arms depot explosion that killed 26 people. Fatmir Mediu, the defense minister at the time, had escaped punishment through parliamentary immunity and a general amnesty at the end of 2012. A number of other senior officials, including new parliament speaker Ilir Meta and new PD leader Lulzim Basha, have been cleared of corruption charges in controversial court rulings in recent years.

In December, several court officials were arrested after video recordings published in the media allegedly showed them collecting bribes on behalf of judges. Also that month, former defense minister Arben Imami was charged with corruption regarding tenders for Defense Ministry television advertisements. Albania was ranked 116 out of 177 countries and territories surveyed in Transparency International's 2013 Corruption Perceptions Index.

CIVIL LIBERTIES: 40 / 60 (+1)

D. Freedom of Expression and Belief: 13 / 16

While the constitution guarantees freedom of expression, the intermingling of powerful business, political, and media interests inhibits the development of independent news outlets; most are seen as biased toward either the PS or the PD. Reporters have little job security and remain subject to lawsuits, intimidation, and in some cases physical attacks by those facing media scrutiny. Berisha's government sometimes placed financial pressure on critical outlets, and government-friendly media have reportedly been favored in state advertising purchases. Most election-related media regulations were weakly enforced in 2013. A June CEC ruling required broadcasters to air recordings prepared by political parties during their newscasts, raising concerns about editorial independence. The government does not limit internet access.

The constitution provides for freedom of religion, and it is generally upheld in practice. The government typically does not limit academic freedom, though students and teachers have faced political pressure ahead of elections.

E. Associational and Organizational Rights: 9 / 12 (+1)

Freedoms of association and assembly are generally respected. In September 2013, an appeals court convicted two Republican Guard commanders of manslaughter for the shooting deaths of three antigovernment protesters in January 2011, rejecting the murder convictions and stiff sentences sought by prosecutors. The ruling meant that the men would serve no further prison time, as their pretrial detention exceeded the sentences handed down to them. Demonstrations since 2011 have been relatively peaceful.

Nongovernmental organizations function without restrictions but have limited funding and policy influence. In what was hailed as a major victory for civil society, nationwide protests led by students and environmental activists prompted Prime Minister Rama to announce in November 2013 that Albania would reject a U.S. request to host the destruction of Syrian chemical weapons.

The constitution guarantees workers the rights to organize and bargain collectively, and most have the right to strike. However, effective collective bargaining remains limited, and union members have little protection against discrimination by employers. Child labor is a problem, and informal child workers sometimes face hazardous conditions.

F. Rule of Law: 9 / 16

The constitution provides for an independent judiciary, but the underfunded courts are subject to political influence. In July 2013, the High Council of Justice, which is led by President Bujar Nishani, appointed seven candidates seen as PD allies to the powerful Tirana appeals court. Meanwhile, Nishani blocked former prosecutor general Ina Rama's request to be reinstated as an appeals court judge, which is her right under the law, and the Tirana appeals court reopened a closed abuse-of-power investigation into Rama related to a prosecutor's 2009 firing. Rama had finished her tenure as prosecutor general in late 2012, having clashed repeatedly with the PD government. She had also complained that court officials effectively protected one another when accused of wrongdoing. In September 2013, a former judge in Durres was acquitted of criminal charges related to his deliberate stalling of an appeal in a murder case, which had allowed the release of an organized crime figure who was then arrested for a new murder. The justice minister retains the power to open or close judicial disciplinary procedures. Judges sometimes face threats and physical violence. In January, a judge in Vlora was injured when an unidentified attacker threw acid at her face.

Police reportedly engage in abuse of suspects during arrest and interrogation. Prison inmates suffer from poor living conditions and lack of adequate medical treatment, often relying on family to provide food and other supplies. A November 2013 jailbreak raised concerns about corruption in the prison system and led to a series of firings and arrests of prison officials.

In an effort to combat rising crime rates, the new government in October 2013 restructured the police force, replacing commanders and disbanding several units, including the traffic police. Two high-ranking officers were murdered in separate incidents during the year. Albania is known as a transshipment point for heroin smugglers and a key site for cannabis production. Traditional tribal law and revenge killings remain a problem in parts of the north.

Roma face significant discrimination in education, health care, employment, and housing. A 2010 law bars discrimination based on race and several other categories, including sexual orientation and gender identity, and a May 2013 reform of the criminal code introduced protections against hate crimes and hate speech based on sexual orientation and gender identity. However, bias against gay and transgender people remains strong in practice.

G. Personal Autonomy and Individual Rights: 9 / 16

A raft of property-restitution cases related to confiscations during the communist era remains unresolved, and illegal construction is a major problem. The World Bank's 2014 Doing Business rankings listed Albania as one of the world's four worst countries for obtaining construction permits.

Women are underrepresented in politics and business, and the three largest political parties were fined in September 2013 for the failure of their candidate lists to meet a 30 percent quota for women. Just 25 of the 140 members elected to parliament in June 2013 were women. However, the new cabinet included a record six women, including the first female defense minister. Domestic violence is believed to be widespread, though the parliament has adopted some measures to combat the problem in recent years. A criminal code amendment passed in May 2013 made sexual violence within marriage a specific offense. Albania is a source country for trafficking in women and children.

Algeria

Political Rights Rating: 6
Civil Liberties Rating: 5
Freedom Rating: 5.5
Freedom Status: Not Free
Electoral Democracy: No

Population: 38,289,500
Capital: Algiers

Ten-Year Ratings Timeline For Year Under Review (Political Rights, Civil Liberties, Status)

Year Under Review	2004	2005	2006	2007	2008	2009	2010	2011	2012	2013
Rating	6,5,NF	6,5,NF	6,5,NF	6,5,NF	6,5,NF	6,5,NF	6,5,NF	6,5,NF	6,5,NF	6,5,NF

INTRODUCTION

Two years after Algeria lifted its 19-year state of emergency and promised constitutional and electoral reforms, protests against stagnant economic and political conditions continued. Laws relating to political and civil liberties were criticized for failing to protect basic rights, and harassment of the political opposition and civil society was ongoing.

A January 2013 attack by Islamist militants at a gas plant at In Amenas, a southeastern town near the Tunisian border, killed 40 oil workers, including 39 foreigners. Unprecedented in its scale in Algeria, the attacks raised concerns about regional security in the wake of the overthrow of longtime Libyan ruler Mu'ammar al-Qadhafi in 2011, which led to the widespread dispersion of Qadhafi-era weapons.

Algeria expects to hold presidential elections in 2014, prompting speculation about whether ailing president Abdelaziz Bouteflika, 76, will run and the circumstances likely to surround his succession.

POLITICAL RIGHTS: 12 / 40

A. Electoral Process: 4 / 12

Algeria's upper house of Parliament, the National Council, has 144 members serving six-year terms; 96 members are chosen by local assemblies, and the president appoints the remaining 48. The size of the People's National Assembly, the lower house of Parliament, was increased from 389 to 462 members directly elected for five-year terms in advance of the May 2012 elections. The president is directly elected for five-year terms, and constitutional amendments passed in 2008 abolished the two-term limit, allowing Bouteflika to run for a third term in 2009. The amendments also increased the president's powers relative to the premiership and other entities. Bouteflika, who took office in 1999, won a third term in April 2009, taking about 90 percent of the vote amid widespread accusations of fraud.

In parliamentary elections held in May 2012, the National Liberation Front (FLN) won 221 seats, the military backed National Democratic Rally (RND), 70, and the Green Algeria Alliance—comprised of multiple Islamist parties—47. The government estimated participation in the elections at approximately 42 percent. Foreign observers from the European

Union, United Nations, Arab League, and other institutions declared the elections largely free and fair. Opposition candidates and some human rights groups, however, asserted that the results were manipulated by the Ministry of the Interior, and that participation rates were much lower than the government stated. Fifteen parties that won a combined 29 seats announced that they would boycott the new Parliament. The election commission set up by the Algerian government itself condemned the elections as "not credible," although FLN and RND members on the commission refused to sign the final report. In September 2012, Bouteflika appointed former water resources minister Abdelmalek Sellal the new prime minister. Sellal presented a reform plan to the Parliament in October that stressed the need to continue with political reforms, enhance security, boost the economy, and fight corruption.

B. Political Pluralism and Participation: 4 / 16

The Ministry of the Interior must approve political parties before they can operate legally. The 2012 elections were also supervised by a judicial body, the National Election Observation Commission. A January 2012 law liberalized the party registration process, and 23 new political parties were allowed to register for the first time since 1999. The FLN, RND, Green Algeria Alliance (comprised of the Movement for the Society of Peace [MSP], Ennahda, and Islah parties), the Front of Socialist Forces, the Workers Party, and a number of smaller parties sit in the current Parliament.

The military and intelligence services play an important role in politics despite their ongoing rivalries. In recent years, a power struggle developed between the ailing Bouteflika, who reportedly suffered a stroke in April 2013, and General Mohamed "Toufik" Mediène, the powerful head of the Department of Intelligence and Security (DRS), over rumors that Bouteflika's younger brother would succeed him. Shake-ups in the cabinet and the DRS in September and October 2013, respectively, suggested Bouteflika's desire to assert more control over the government and limit the power of the DRS.

Although parties cannot form explicitly along ethnic or religious lines, minorities, particularly the country's indigenous Amazigh groups, are able to participate actively in the political process.

C. Functioning of Government: 3 / 12

High levels of corruption plague Algeria's business and public sectors, especially the energy sector. In 2012, Algerian courts sentenced Mohamed Boukhari, the former executive officer of state-owned Algeria Telecom, to 18 years in prison for accepting bribes from two Chinese firms over a period of three years. Despite the existence of anticorruption laws, low levels of judicial independence, bloated bureaucracies, and a lack of government transparency contributed to problems of corruption. Algeria was ranked 94 out of 177 countries and territories surveyed in Transparency International's 2013 Corruption Perceptions Index.

CIVIL LIBERTIES: 23 / 60 (-1)
D. Freedom of Expression and Belief: 6 / 16 (-1)

There is an array of restrictions on press freedom, but the situation has improved since the peak of Algeria's civil war in the mid-1990s. Privately owned newspapers have been published for nearly two decades, and journalists have been aggressive in their coverage of government affairs. However, most newspapers rely on the central government for printing, and the state-owned advertising agency favors progovernment newspapers, encouraging self-censorship. A new press law adopted in December 2011 was criticized by journalists and human rights activists for containing vague language that reinforces the government's ability to block reporting on certain sensitive topics, including those deemed to undermine the country's security or economic interests. In 2013, there was widespread secrecy surrounding the health of Bouteflika, as well as a near-complete media blackout surrounding the In Amenas terrorist attack. Both government officials and private entities use criminal defamation laws to pressure independent newspapers. In September, blogger Abdelghani Aloui was arrested for posting allegedly defamatory cartoons of Bouteflika on his Facebook page and charged with "glorification of terrorism" and "insulting state institutions"; he remained imprisoned at year's end.

A July 2009 cybercrime law gives authorities the right to block websites "contrary to the public order or decency," and a centralized system monitors internet traffic. In February 2011, amid protests against the government, activists in Algiers and the northwestern city of Annaba accused the government of shutting down the internet and disrupting social-networking activities.

Algeria's population is overwhelmingly Sunni Muslim; small non-Muslim communities do not face harassment. However, non-Muslims may gather to worship only at state-approved locations, proselytizing by non-Muslims is illegal, and the government in 2008 began enforcing an ordinance that tightened restrictions on minority faiths. In 2013, some Christians faced harassment at their places of worship. Security services monitor mosques for radical Islamist activity, but Muslims are also sometimes harassed for a perceived lack of piety. Academic freedom is largely respected, though debate is somewhat circumscribed.

The climate produced by the Arab Spring has led to increased fears of government surveillance among citizens and a reluctance to express opinions on sensitive subjects such as slow or absent political reforms and high levels of political corruption, especially through social media.

E. Associational and Organizational Rights: 5 / 12

Despite the lifting of the state of emergency in 2011, the government has nevertheless continued to forcibly disrupt and discourage public gatherings and protests. International human rights groups criticized the suppression of demonstrations in advance of the May 2012 elections. In 2013, activists protesting government policies also faced arrest, often on vague charges, and others were apprehended when they protested the detention of their colleagues. In February, three activists—Taher Bela'bas, Khaled Dawi, and Ali Ghabshi—were fined and handed jail terms ranging from one to two months for participating in a January protest against rising unemployment in the eastern province of Ouargla. In April, the leader of the banned Islamist Salvation Front, Ali Belhadj, was detained during a protest in Tizi Ouzou.

A January 2012 law on associations was criticized for continuing to restrict the formation, funding, and operations of civil society. Permits are required to establish nongovernmental organizations (NGOs), and those with Islamist leanings are regarded with suspicion by the government. Reports of NGOs facing barriers to registration continued in 2013. Algerian authorities reportedly prevented 96 Algerian civil society activists from travelling to Tunisia for the World Social Forum in 2013.

Workers can establish independent trade unions, but the main labor federation, the General Union of Algerian Workers, has been criticized for being too close to the government and failing to advocate aggressively for workers' interests. Algerian authorities have increasingly clamped down on efforts to form independent unions and to organize, including using administrative measures to prevent independent unions from operating. Authorities have blocked peaceful demonstrations and strikes, arbitrarily arrested trade unionists, and prosecuted some of them on criminal charges that appear to have little basis in fact or are based on the peaceful exercise of their union activities. In one incident in September 2013, a peaceful demonstration by the Contractual Workers Union in front of the government compound in Algiers was violently broken up by the authorizes, and 20 people were arrested; they were released later that day.

F. Rule of Law: 5 / 16

The judiciary is susceptible to government pressure. International human rights activists have accused the security forces of practicing torture, and have also highlighted lengthy delays in bringing cases to trial. Prison conditions in Algeria generally do not meet international standards due to overcrowding and poor nutrition and hygiene. In 2013, Algeria's bid to a fill vacant seat on the UN Human Rights Council was denied because of an unfulfilled request for human rights experts to visit Algeria.

In 2005, a referendum approved the Charter for Peace and National Reconciliation, which offered amnesty to most militants and government agents for crimes committed during Algeria's 1991–2002 civil war. Human rights organizations criticized the charter for not addressing the issue of the roughly 7,000 people who disappeared during the war, and for allowing perpetrators of human rights violations from both sides to escape justice. The 2005 charter provided for compensation to the families of the war's victims and the disappeared, but the broad amnesty program prevents discussion of the period.

Attacks on Algerian police officers and political officials by Al-Qaeda in the Islamic Maghreb (AQIM) continued throughout 2013. In January, militants led by former AQIM leader Mokhtar Belmokhtar attacked the Tigentourine gas plant gas plant at In Amenas, a southeastern town near the Tunisian border, jointly operated by British Petroleum, Norway's Statoil, and Algerian state energy company Sonatrach. After a four-day siege, the plant was stormed by Algerian forces; a total of 40 oil workers, including 39 foreigners, died in the incident. At least one arrest has been made in connection to the attacks; the militants reportedly had inside knowledge of the facility.

Algeria's ethnic composition is a mixture of Arabs and Berbers, with Arabs traditionally forming the country's elite. In recent years, following outbreaks of antigovernment violence in the Berber community, officials have made more of an effort to recognize Berber cultural demands. Tamazight, the Berber language, is now a national language. The Berber-dominated Rally for Culture and Democracy (RCD) party was one of the few parties to boycott the May 2012 elections entirely.

Same-sex sexual relations are illegal and punishable with two months to two years in prison. Although no one was prosecuted under that law in 2013, at least two individuals were detained for immoral behavior.

G. Personal Autonomy and Individual Rights: 7 / 16

While most citizens are free to move throughout the country and travel abroad, the authorities closely monitor and limit the movement of suspected terrorists. Access to visas for non-Algerians is carefully controlled. Men of military draft age are not allowed to leave the country without government consent.

Women continue to face discrimination at both the legal and societal levels, but 2013 saw their access to elected office expand. A November 2011 law required that female candidates comprise one-third of any candidate list for legislative elections. As a result, women occupy 146 seats—about a third—in the recently elected People's National Assembly, a higher percentage than in any other Arab country. Women's rights groups praised the outcome, but some questioned whether the female lawmakers would be able to have an impact on the overall political system. Under the family code, which is based on Islamic law, women do not enjoy equal rights in marriage, divorce, and inheritance. Algeria is one of the few countries in the region to allow women to transfer their nationality to their children, regardless of the father's nationality. A law adopted in January 2009 criminalized all forms of trafficking in persons, but the government has made little effort to enforce it, according to the U.S. State Department's 2013 Trafficking in Persons Report.

Andorra

Political Rights Rating: 1
Civil Liberties Rating: 1
Freedom Rating: 1.0
Freedom Status: Free
Electoral Democracy: Yes

Population: 73,526
Capital: Andorra la Vella

Ten-Year Ratings Timeline For Year Under Review (Political Rights, Civil Liberties, Status)

Year Under Review	2004	2005	2006	2007	2008	2009	2010	2011	2012	2013
Rating	1,1,F	1,1,F	1,1,F	1,1,F	1,1,F	1,1,F	1,1,F	1,1,F	1,1,F	1,1,F

INTRODUCTION

The Andorran government has worked in recent years to address the country's reputation as a tax haven and bring its financial laws into compliance with the standards of the Organization for Economic Cooperation and Development (OECD), including a value-added tax of 4.5 percent that went into effect in January 2013. In June, Andorra announced that it would collect its first income tax starting in 2016. A number of laws enacted in February also aimed to align Andorra with international standards, addressing issues including organizational requirements and operations in the financial sector. In November, the government signed the OECD Multilateral Convention on Mutual Administrative Assistance in Tax Matters.

Also during the year, the Supreme Court of Justice ruled in January in favor of a man who claimed discrimination because Andorra denied him survivor benefits after his husband's death. The couple had married in Spain, and Andorra does not allow same-sex marriage.

POLITICAL RIGHTS: 39 / 40

A. Electoral Process: 12 / 12

Andorra is governed under a parliamentary system. Two "co-princes," the French president and the bishop of La Seu d'Urgell, Spain, serve jointly as ceremonial heads of state. Popular elections are held every four years for the 28-member Consell General, which selects the executive council president—the head of government. Half of the members are chosen in two-seat constituencies known as parishes, and the other half are chosen through a national system of proportional representation.

The last elections were held in April 2011, after two years of government deadlock. The Democrats for Andorra (DA) won 20 seats, followed by the Social Democratic Party (PS) with 6 and the Lauredian Union with 2. Antoni Martí became the new head of government.

B. Political Pluralism and Participation: 15 / 16

The people have the right to establish and join different political parties, and the 2011 elections marked a change of power from the PS to the DA. However, more than 50 percent of the population consists of noncitizens who do not have the right to vote. Under Andorra's restrictive naturalization criteria, one must marry a resident Andorran or live in the country for more than 20 years to qualify for citizenship. Prospective citizens are also required to learn Catalan, the national language.

C. Functioning of Government: 12 / 12

In June 2011, the Council of Europe's Group of States against Corruption (GRECO) released a report finding "shortcomings" in Andorra's bribery laws and calling for tougher penalties for bribery and influence peddling. GRECO also highlighted inadequate campaign finance laws. A GRECO compliance report published in November 2013 concluded that Andorra had satisfactorily implemented only 3 of the 20 recommendations from the 2011 report.

CIVIL LIBERTIES: 57 / 60
D. Freedom of Expression and Belief: 16 / 16

Freedom of speech is respected across the country. There are two independent daily newspapers, *Diari d'Andorra* and *El Periòdic d'Andorra*, and two free weekday papers, *Diari Bondia* and *Diari Més*. There is only one Andorran television station, operated by the public broadcaster Ràdio i Televisió d'Andorra. Residents also have access to broadcasts from neighboring France and Spain. Internet access is unrestricted.

Although the constitution recognizes the state's special relationship with the Roman Catholic Church, the government no longer subsidizes it. Religious minorities like Mormons and Jehovah's Witnesses are free to seek converts. Despite years of negotiations between the Muslim community and the government, there is no proper mosque for the country's roughly 1,000 Muslims. While requests to convert public buildings or former churches for this purpose have been denied, the government does provide the Muslim community with public facilities for various religious functions. Academic freedom is respected.

E. Associational and Organizational Rights: 11 / 12

Freedoms of assembly and association are generally respected, and domestic and international human rights organizations operate freely. While the government recognizes that both workers and employers have the right to defend their interests, the right to strike is not legally guaranteed. There are also no laws in place to penalize antiunion discrimination or regulate collective bargaining, although a 2009 law guarantees unions the right to operate. In March 2012, a survey by the Union of Workers of Andorra la Vella collected widespread complaints about workplace corruption, as well as physical and psychological abuse of workers. Although the government expressed concern over the report, no specific steps have been taken to investigate the issues in question. In October and November 2012, police unions organized a strike to protest unfulfilled promises, especially in the area of pension reform.

F. Rule of Law: 15 / 16

The government generally respects the independence of the judiciary. Defendants enjoy the presumption of innocence and the right to a fair trial. Police can detain suspects for up to 48 hours without charge. In November 2013, the UN Committee against Torture evaluated Andorra's prison conditions and reported that although they meet international standards, there were three reports of torture under investigation.

Although they do not have the right to vote, noncitizen residents receive most of the social and economic benefits of citizenship under Andorran law. In 2012, Andorra introduced a new law on residency, which applies to all those seeking nonwork residency permits.

Applications are assessed under three categories: passive residency for individuals who can show they are financially self-sufficient, business residency for individuals who own foreign companies, and cultural residency for renowned artists and other public figures.

Immigrant workers, primarily from North Africa, complain that they lack the rights of citizens. Nearly 7,000 such immigrants have legal status, but many hold only "temporary work authorizations." Temporary workers are in a precarious position, as they must leave the country when their job contract expires, leaving them vulnerable to potential abuse by employers.

G. Personal Autonomy and Individual Rights: 15 / 16

Citizens enjoy freedom of movement and have the right to own property. Legislation passed in 2012 fully opened the economy to foreign investors as well, allowing noncitizens to own up to 100 percent of any commercial entity.

Women enjoy the same legal rights as men. Half of the seats in the legislature are held by women. However, there are no specific laws addressing the problem of violence against women, nor are there any government departments for women's issues or government-run shelters for battered women. Abortion is illegal, except to save the life of the mother.

Andorra does not allow same-sex marriage or unions. However, the Supreme Court of Justice ruled in January 2013 in favor of a man's right to claim his late husband's social security survivor benefits, citing a nondiscrimination clause in Andorra's constitution. The couple had wed in Spain, which recognizes same-sex marriage.

Angola

Political Rights Rating: 6
Civil Liberties Rating: 5
Freedom Rating: 5.5
Freedom Status: Not Free
Electoral Democracy: No

Population: 21,635,000
Capital: Luanda

Ten-Year Ratings Timeline For Year Under Review (Political Rights, Civil Liberties, Status)

Year Under Review	2004	2005	2006	2007	2008	2009	2010	2011	2012	2013
Rating	6,5,NF	6,5,NF	6,5,NF	6,5,NF	6,5,NF	6,5,NF	6,5,NF	6,5,NF	6,5,NF	6,5,NF

INTRODUCTION

The long-ruling Popular Movement for the Liberation of Angola (MPLA) tightened its grip on power after winning the 2012 elections. The mostly urban-based antigovernment protests that began in 2011 expanded in 2013. Demonstrators faced violent dispersal and intimidation—hundreds were arrested, and several were killed. In late November 2013, a group of opposition parties led by the National Union for the Total Independence of Angola (UNITA) urged the government to end the political violence.

Meanwhile, the government continued to subject the independent media to legal and physical harassment, and corruption remained rampant. Poor management of public debt, combined with a devastating drought and a weak global economy, resulted in a moderate slowing of Angola's gross domestic product (GDP) growth in 2013.

POLITICAL RIGHTS: 11 / 40
A. Electoral Process: 4 / 12

In 2010, the MPLA-dominated parliament approved a new constitution that abolished direct presidential elections, stipulating instead that the leader of the largest party in the parliament would become the president. The 220-seat unicameral National Assembly, whose members serve four-year terms, has little power, and 90 percent of legislation originates from the executive branch. The constitution also mandates that, as of 2012, the president may serve a maximum of two five-year terms, and directly appoints the vice president, cabinet, and provincial governors. President Jose Eduardo dos Santos has been in power for 34 years, making him one of the longest-serving heads of state in Africa.

After a number of delays, parliamentary elections were held in August 2012. While the African Union deemed the elections "free, fair, transparent and credible," the polls were deeply flawed. The MPLA's 72 percent of the vote marked a notable decline from its 82 percent showing in 2008, though the party still maintained its overwhelming dominance in the National Assembly, garnering 175 of 220 seats. UNITA is the largest opposition party, holding 32 seats; the Broad Convergence for Angola's Salvation-Electoral Coalition (CASA-CE) holds 8 seats, the Social Renewal Party (PRS) holds 3, and the National Front for Angolan Liberation (FNLA) holds 2. The MPLA-dominated National Assembly easily reelected dos Santos in September 2012.

B. Political Pluralism and Participation: 6 / 16

While five political parties are represented in the National Assembly, the ruling MPLA dominates Angola's party system. In a rare show of coordination, the four opposition parties abandoned the National Assembly on November 28, protesting the MPLA's "intransigence" and demanding a discussion on "violence and political persecution" in Angola. The opposition parties have since returned to the assembly, but declared they would be willing to leave it indefinitely. MPLA representatives have stated that the National Assembly functioned during Angola's three-decade civil war without opposition and could do so again if the opposition parties chose to depart.

Adding to the nation's political instability, dos Santos has been largely absent from the country since June 2013, reportedly due to serious health concerns. The president missed the Angolan Independence Day celebrations on November 11 and former South African president Nelson Mandela's funeral on December 10.

C. Functioning of Government: 1 / 12

Corruption and patronage are endemic and bribery often underpins business activity. A 2011 International Monetary Fund report stated that $32 billion in government funds, believed to be linked to the national oil company Sonangol, could not be accounted for.

Corruption in Angola has led to increased scrutiny on dos Santos, his family, and his allies, who are among the richest people in the world. In 2013, Forbes named Isabel dos Santos, the president's oldest daughter, the wealthiest woman in Africa, with an estimated net worth of $3 billion. Angola was ranked 153 out of 177 countries and territories surveyed in Transparency International's 2013 Corruption Perceptions Index.

CIVIL LIBERTIES: 18 / 60
D. Freedom of Expression and Belief: 7 / 16 (-1)

Despite constitutional guarantees of freedom of expression, the state owns the only daily newspaper and national radio station, as well as the main television stations. These outlets, along with private media owned by senior officials and members of the dos Santos family, act as mouthpieces for MPLA; censorship and self-censorship are common.

Angolan authorities have consistently prevented independent journalists from reporting the news, denying them access to official information and events, preventing them from broadcasting, and threatening them with detention and prosecution. Security forces have also targeted journalists, particularly those covering antigovernment protests and reporting on corruption. In September 2013, for instance, the rapid intervention police arrested three journalists—Rafael Marques de Morais, who runs the anticorruption website Maka Angola; Alexandre Neto, the head of the Media Institute of Southern Africa (MISA) in Angola; and Coque Mukuta, a correspondent for Voice of America—while they were interviewing antigovernment protesters. The journalists were threatened, beaten, and eventually released without charge.

Religious freedom is respected, though a high membership threshold to acquire legal status has kept many groups from registering. Since 1991, over 1,000 applications by religious groups have been denied. The government has yet to grant legal status to any Muslim groups, and there have been reports that it intervenes selectively to close Muslim schools, community centers and mosques. In November 2013, the Minister of Foreign Affairs Georges Chikoti denied accusations that Muslims were being persecuted.

Approximately 15 percent of Angolans are evangelical, according to the Angolan government. After accusing evangelical churches of "false advertisement" and of "exploiting the Angolan people" the government decided in February 2013 to close the Universal Church and other Brazilian evangelical churches such as the Pentecostal Evangelical Church New Jerusalem. On March 31, the government lifted the ban only for the Universal Church, which was then the only evangelical church recognized by the Angolan state.

There are no government restrictions on academic freedom though in interviews with members of Angola's most prestigious universities, there are certain topics that professors avoid for fear of repercussions.

E. Associational and Organizational Rights: 4 / 12

The constitution guarantees freedoms of assembly and association, though in recent years, police and security forces have violently dispersed peaceful demonstrations and intimidated and arrested protesters. In 2013, security forces banned or dispersed at least six demonstrations and made over 400 arrests. The protests—in Luanda and other cities and towns—sought to express concerns over social justice, corruption, forced evictions, police violence against street vendors, and the unexplained disappearance in May 2012 of two activists, Isaías Cassule and António Alves Kamulingue. Most of the detainees were quickly released, although the authorities reportedly abused many of the demonstrators while in custody. One protester, Emilio Catumbela—who was detained in May during a peaceful demonstration calling for information about Cassule and Kamulingue—was charged with attempted murder and kept in prison with little or no access to legal counsel, until his release on June 24, 2013.

In November, internal government communications were leaked to Angolan media outlets revealing that Cassule and Kamulingue had been abducted, tortured, and killed by the State Intelligence and Security Services (SINSE). Dos Santos dismissed SINSE's director following the revelations; UNITA called for a massive protest to demand the president's resignation. On November 22, the Interior Ministry banned the protest a day before it was scheduled to begin, citing security concerns. The following day, police arrested 292 activists in several provincial towns and in Luanda, alleging that they were distributing subversive propaganda. UNITA's offices were broken into and ransacked by the police, and Manuel de

Carvalho, a CASA-CE legislator, was killed by dos Santos's presidential guard. At Carvalho's funeral, the persecution of opposition members continued, with security forces using tear gas against hundreds of mourners.

Meanwhile, the government allowed a pro-government demonstration on November 23 in Luanda, organized by "Friends of the Good and Peace," a group with strong government ties.

Several hundred nongovernmental organizations (NGOs) operate in Angola, many of them advocating for transparency, human rights protections, and political reform. The most active organizations are often subject to government inspections, bogged down with excessive bureaucracy, and sometimes threatened with closure.

The constitution includes the right to strike and form unions, but the MPLA dominates the labor movement, and only a few weak independent unions exist.

F. Rule of Law: 4 / 16

The courts in general are hampered by a lack of training and infrastructure, a large backlog of cases, corruption, and extensive political influence, particularly from the executive. The president appoints Supreme Court judges to life terms without legislative input.

In mid-2013, 11 unsubstantiated charges were brought against journalist Marques by 7 Angolan generals, a civilian, two mining companies, and a private security company. He was held for several hours for questioning and released only amid significant international pressure.

In October 2013, an international arrest warrant was issued for General Bento dos Santos Kanganba, President dos Santos' nephew; Brazilian police alleged that he had been running a human trafficking and money laundering operation in Austria, Brazil, Portugal, and South Africa, as well as Angola. The Angolan judiciary has yet to execute the warrant.

There is no efficient protection against unjustified imprisonment, pretrial detention, extortion or torture. Both government and private security personnel have committed murders and other abuses in connection with the diamond-mining industry in the Lunda Norte and Lunda Sul provinces of Angola.

According to Amnesty International, Angolan jails are overcrowded, do not provide basic sustenance, and are plagued by sexual abuse. They also contain a number of political prisoners, advocates of the Cabindan autonomy movement, and members of peaceful activist groups. One prisoner, 17-year-old Nito Alves, was arrested in September 2013, one week after helping to organize a protest, and placed in solitary confinement for weeks without access to medical care, lawyers, or family. Alves was freed in November, but still faces charges for violating a state security law for printing shirts calling for the resignation of dos Santos.

In mid-2013, on the occasion of its own 50th anniversary, the secessionist movement FLEC renewed its call for talks on independence for the oil-rich region of Cabinda. There was no public response from the Angolan government; FLEC supporters continue to be randomly arrested in Cabinda.

The law criminalizes same-sex sexual activity, although there were no reported cases of this law being enforced. Still there are reports in some communities of persecution of members of the LGBT community.

G. Personal Autonomy and Individual Rights: 3 / 16

The problem of landmines remains serious. In the last five years alone, the Halo Trust found and destroyed an average 690 landmines a month. International funding for demining is declining, however, and the Angolan government has not stepped in. As a result, demining rates are decreasing, restricting Angolans' freedom of movement, particularly in the rural areas.

Securing entry and exit visits from Angola remains difficult and mired in corruption. Nevertheless, the inflows of migrants from neighboring countries, as well as from Brazil, China, and Portugal, have increased. In May 2013, the Director of the National Service of Migration and Foreigners, José Paulino da Cunha, declared that over 1 million illegal immigrants were living in Angola thanks to corrupt government officials, companies that hire illegal workers, and some religious sects. The director added that the government was spending US$1 million per month to expatriate illegal migrants and planned to invest more in border control.

The Angolan police have forcefully evicted an estimated 80,000 people from informal settlements in and around Luanda. In February 2013, 5,000 people were told to leave their homes in the Maiombe neighborhood in Cacuaco without adequate notice, resettlement provisions or compensation. Dozens of those evicted were arbitrarily arrested, charged with illegal land occupation, convicted, and given prison sentences or large fines after summary trials.

Extortion and unlawful violence during government roundups of street vendors in Luanda and its suburbs is frequent, led by armed police, tax office representatives, and agents without proper credentials.

Access to quality education is limited to Angola's elite and the expat community. The rest of Angola's population has access only to a barely functioning educational system thanks to underpaid and often absent and corrupt teachers and a severely damaged infrastructure.

Women enjoy legal protections, and occupy cabinet positions and multiple seats in the National Assembly. However, de facto discrimination and violence against women is on the rise, even after a new law on domestic violence took effect in 2011. Child labor is a major problem, and there are frequent reports of trafficking in women and children for prostitution or forced labor.

Angola's GDP grew an average 11 percent between 2004 and 2013. Still, some 70 percent of the nation's citizens live on less than $2 a day, and as much as 10 percent of the population is struggling for food as the result of a recent drought that has affected about 1.8 million people.

Antigua and Barbuda

Political Rights Rating: 2
Civil Liberties Rating: 2
Freedom Rating: 2
Freedom Status: Free
Electoral Democracy: Yes

Population: 100,000
Capital: St. John's

Ten-Year Ratings Timeline For Year Under Review (Political Rights, Civil Liberties, Status)

Year Under Review	2004	2005	2006	2007	2008	2009	2010	2011	2012	2013
Rating	2,2,PF	2,2,F	2,2,F	2,2,F	2,2,F	3,2,F	3,2,F	3,2,F	2,2,F	2,2,F

INTRODUCTION

Tensions between the ruling United Progressive Party (UPP) and the opposition Antigua Labour Party (ALP) continued to build throughout 2013 as Antigua and Barbuda prepared for general elections scheduled for March 2014. The ALP accused the UPP of engaging in unlawful acts to influence the elections, and challenged the constitutionality of numerous government initiatives before the High Court, including the alleged gerrymandering of boundaries, de-registration of voters, and unconstitutional amendments to the law governing the Electoral Commission.

On January 28, 2013, the World Trade Organization granted Antigua authorization to circumvent U.S. intellectual property laws in order to recoup lost revenue by selling up to US$21 million in online music, movies, games, and software without having to pay copyright fees as the result of a long-standing trade dispute with the United States over Antigua's online gambling sites. The remote gaming industry had been Antigua's second largest employer until the United States prohibited its citizens from accessing Antigua's gambling sites.

POLITICAL RIGHTS: 31 / 40

A. Electoral Process: 11 / 12

The 1981 constitution establishes a parliamentary system, with a governor general representing the British monarch as ceremonial head of state. The bicameral Parliament is composed of the 17-seat House of Representatives (16 seats for Antigua, 1 for Barbuda), to which members are elected for five-year terms, and an appointed 17-seat Senate. Antigua and Barbuda's prime minister is typically the leader of the majority party or coalition that emerges from the legislative elections.

In the 2004 elections, the opposition United Progressive Party (UPP), led by Baldwin Spencer, defeated Prime Minister Lester Bird and the ruling Antigua Labour Party (ALP). The 2009 parliamentary elections returned Spencer and the UPP to power with 9 seats in the 17-seat lower house; the ALP took 7 seats, while the Barbuda People's Movement (BPM) retained the single seat representing Barbuda. While the elections were deemed fair and competitive by the Organization of American States, a March 2010 High Court ruling invalidated the election of Spencer and others due to electoral irregularities. The Eastern Caribbean Court of Appeals, however, overturned the verdict in October 2010.

In May 2013, the Eastern Caribbean Court declared null and void amendments made by Prime Minister Spencer in December 2011 to the Representation of the People Act; the amendments had altered the procedures and composition of the Antigua and Barbuda Electoral Commission (ABEC) and removed power from the Supervisor of Elections. The ALP had challenged the amendments as unconstitutional in 2012. In August, the UPP-led government passed new legislation to reinstate the changes, though a November decision by the High Court declared the amendments unconstitutional.

In December 2013, the High Court ruled that proposed changes to 15 electoral boundaries in advance of the 2014 elections were constitutional and permissible. The changes had been challenged by the ALP, which denounced them as gerrymandering and an attempt to engineer an electoral victory for the UPP.

The ALP also challenged the constitutionality of 2010 amendments to the nation's electoral laws that would have required voters to re-register for the 2014 elections. Re-registration began in September, and was fraught with obstacles, including power outages, long lines, and computer failures, and needed to be extended for a fifth week.

B. Political Pluralism and Participation: 13 / 16

Political parties can organize freely and there is a significant opposition vote and representation in the government. The victory of Baldwin Spencer and the UPP in 2004 marked the end of a political dynasty led by the Bird family that lasted over half a century. In November 2012 party elections, Lester Bird lost his position as ALP leader to Gaston Browne, representing the first time in 66 years that the party will not be led by a member of the Bird family.

C. Functioning of Government: 7 / 12

On February 13, 2013, four government-appointed senators voted with the opposition to defeat the Spencer administration's plan to implement its Citizenship by Investment Program. Two of the senators were dismissed for not supporting the policies of their own party, a move Spencer defended as being in accordance with the Westminster system of parliamentary governance. The other two senators offered to resign, though Spencer ultimately allowed them to retain their positions. The Citizenship by Investment Program, which allows investors to directly acquire citizenship and passports by donating money to a charity or by purchasing real estate, became law on April 11.

Antigua continued throughout 2013 to refuse to comply with the United States' request for the extradition of American investor R. Allen Stanford, who was convicted of fraud by a U.S. court in 2012. Stanford had been sentenced to 110 years in prison for running a $7 billion Ponzi scheme in which clients were encouraged to invest in certificates of deposit from the Stanford International Bank of Antigua with false promises of security and high returns. In February 2013, a group of defrauded investors sued the government of Antigua and Barbuda, claiming that top officials were aware of Stanford's scheme and benefited from it. While the government has since taken steps to reform the country's financial regulatory environment, no Antiguan officials connected to the Stanford case have been brought to trial. Leroy King, former chief executive of Antigua's Financial Services Regulatory Commission (FSRC), faces multiple charges in the United States of fraud, conspiracy, and money laundering related to his alleged involvement in Stanford's scheme.

CIVIL LIBERTIES: 49 / 60
D. Freedom of Expression and Belief: 14 / 16

Antigua and Barbuda generally respects freedom of the press. However, defamation remains a criminal offense punishable by up to three years in prison, and politicians often file libel suits against opposing party members. Prime Minister Spencer committed to repealing defamation and libel laws in April 2013, and the attorney general announced in November that a bill to decriminalize the practices might be introduced in early 2014.

On March 3, 2013, a journalist for the online news website Caribarena was reportedly shot at after covering a West Indies cricket match. The website's management reported receiving verbal threats several days earlier, allegedly by an unidentified ALP official, related to the website's ongoing investigation of a government agreement with a Japanese debt settlement company. A series of alleged cyberattacks shut down the website in July, and the editors fled the country following harassment of their families and the vandalization of their homes. Media outlets are concentrated among a small number of firms affiliated with either the current government or its predecessor. There are no restrictions on access to the internet.

The government generally respects religious and academic freedoms.

E. Associational and Organizational Rights: 9 / 12

Freedom of association and assembly are guaranteed under the Constitution, and the government generally respects these rights in practice. Nongovernmental organizations are active but inadequately funded and often influenced by the government. Demonstrators are occasionally subject to police harassment. Labor unions can organize freely and bargain collectively. The Industrial Court mediates labor disputes.

F. Rule of Law: 13 / 16

The country's legal system is based on English common law. In recent years, the Antiguan courts have increasingly asserted independence through controversial decisions against the government.

Crime continues to be a problem. The government has responded with increased community policing, the reintroduction of roadblocks, and stiffer fines for firearms violations. An increase in gun-related crimes and the shooting death of a woman at her workplace in February 2013 prompted the Minister of National Security to announce government plans to begin to actively enforce the death penalty for the first time since 1991. The country's prison is at 247 percent occupancy, and conditions are very poor. The abuse of inmates has been reported, though visits by independent human rights groups are permitted. The government issued a call for proposals for the design and construction of a new prison in May 2013, and was reviewing proposals at year's end.

Personal Autonomy and Individual Rights: 13 / 16

The 2005 Equal Opportunity Act bars discrimination on the basis of race, gender, class, political affinity, or place of origin. However, societal discrimination and violence against women remain problems. Women hold only 10 percent of the elected seats of the House of Representatives. Same-sex sexual activity remains criminalized under a 1995 law, and there have been cases of excessive force and discrimination of people based on sexual orientation at the hands of the police. Antigua and Barbuda serves as both a destination and transit country for the trafficking of men, women, and children for the purposes of forced labor and prostitution.

Argentina

Political Rights Rating: 2
Civil Liberties Rating: 2
Freedom Rating: 2.0
Freedom Status: Free
Electoral Democracy: Yes

Population: 41,267,000
Capital: Buenos Aires

Ten-Year Ratings Timeline For Year Under Review (Political Rights, Civil Liberties, Status)

Year Under Review	2004	2005	2006	2007	2008	2009	2010	2011	2012	2013
Rating	2,2,F	2,2,F	2,2,F	2,2,F	2,2,F	2,2,F	2,2,F	2,2,F	2,2,F	2,2,F

INTRODUCTION

Popular support for President Cristina Fernández de Kirchner fell in 2013 due to the Argentine economy's estimated 25 percent annual inflation rate, an effective ban on foreign currency exchange, and the increasing centralization of the executive branch. Declining public services and public safety, as well as the government's judicial reform proposal prompted demonstrations in April 2013 in which an estimated one million Argentines participated. The government's popularity was also hit by its slow response to massive floods that scourged La Plata and Buenos Aires in April, killing more than 50 people and destroying thousands of homes.

The Argentine government continued to pressure opposition media in 2013 through the discriminatory allocation of official advertising. After years of delays due to injunctions, in October the Supreme Court upheld the controversial 2009 Media Law. Hailed as a victory for freedom of speech by supporters by limiting the power of large media conglomerates, opponents alleged that the government could use it to silence critical outlets.

In July 2013 the government announced a joint venture between YPF—an oil company formerly owned by a Spanish corporation that the Argentine government had nationalized the previous year—and Chevron. The move followed a disappointing production year, and aims to exploit Argentina's massive shale gas reserves, the second largest in the world.

Fernandez underwent unexpected brain surgery in early October to remove a build-up of blood near her brain, causing her to cease campaigning for allies in midterm elections held on October 27. The elections reduced the president's majority in Congress, giving new momentum to the opposition.

POLITICAL RIGHTS: 31 / 40
A. Electoral Process: 11 / 12

As amended in 1994, the constitution provides for a president elected for four years, with the option of reelection for one additional term. Presidential candidates must win 45 percent of the vote to avoid a runoff. The National Congress consists of the 257-member Chamber of Deputies, whose members are directly elected for four-year terms, with half of the seats up for election every two years; and the 72-member Senate, whose members are directly elected for six-year terms, with one-third of the seats up for election every two years.

Fernández—originally elected in 2007 after her husband, Néstor Kirchner, finished his term—won reelection in October 2011, garnering 54 percent of the vote, the largest margin of victory in the first round of an Argentine presidential election since the return of democracy in 1983. Fernández continued to centralize power around the executive even after Néstor Kirchner's sudden death in October 2010.

In the October 2013 midterm elections, 127 of the 257 seats in the Chamber of Deputies and 24 of the 72 seats in the Senate were at stake, as were provincial deputies, senators, and a governorship. Fernández's Front for Victory (FPV) coalition won 33 percent of the vote nationwide, allowing the president to maintain a slim majority in both houses of the National Congress. However, it lost 12 of 23 provinces, and placed third in the city of Buenos Aires. Observers said the strong showing by moderate opposition figures in effect marked the end of an era of "Kirchnerismo," the political movement of Fernández and her late husband. The prospect of changing the constitution, which requires a two-thirds congressional majority, to allow Fernandez to run for a third term became close to impossible.

B. Political Pluralism and Participation: 14 / 16

The right to organize political parties is generally respected. Major parties include the Justicialist Party (also known as the Peronist Party), which holds two opposing factions: the center-left FPV faction, and the center-right Federal Peronism faction. Other parties include the centrist Radical Civic Union, the center-right Republican Proposal, and the socialist Broad Progressive Front. In recent years, the Renewal Front, a breakaway faction within Fernández's party, has gained prominence. The Peronists have been a dominant force in politics since 1946, although in Argentina's multiparty political system, opposition parties do have a realistic ability to compete.

C. Functioning of Government: 6 / 12

Corruption plagues Argentine society and scandals are common. Former president and current senator Carlos Menem was convicted in June 2013 of trafficking arms while in office in the 1990s, but remains free because of parliamentary immunity. Former secretary of transportation Ricardo Jaime was indicted twice in 2010 on separate charges of embezzlement that reportedly occurred during his tenure from 2003 to 2009; while his trial had not begun by the end of 2013, he was found guilty in a separate trial in September 2013 of removing evidence during a raid on his house. Vice President Amado Boudou was also accused of embezzlement and influence peddling in 2012; his criminal investigation continued through the end of 2013. Finally, a scandal broke out in April 2013 concerning money laundering and official corruption involving Lazaro Baez, a construction tycoon and close business associate of the late Nestor Kirchner. Baez faces allegations of embezzlement, facilitated by an illegal relationship with the Argentine government. A criminal investigation continued at year's end. Argentina was ranked 106 out of 177 countries and territories surveyed in Transparency International's 2013 Corruption Perceptions Index.

Meanwhile, the government's manipulation of INDEC, the national statistics agency, in recent years has resulted in distorted economic figures, as well as the agency's loss of domestic and international credibility. In February 2013, Argentina became the first country to be censured by the IMF for not providing accurate economic data. A new consumer price index, more in line with IMF recommendations, was in the works at year's end and was expected to be released in early 2014.

CIVIL LIBERTIES: 49 / 60
D. Freedom of Expression and Belief: 14 / 16

Freedom of expression is guaranteed by law, and Congress decriminalized libel and slander in 2009. However, the Fernández government has increasingly pressured opposition media through verbal attacks, the selective distribution of official advertising to progovernment outlets, and directives prohibiting private companies from advertising in opposition outlets. The government also proposed a bill in May 2013 to expand the government's stake in Papel Prensa, the country's sole newsprint manufacturer. The main target of the government's actions has been Grupo Clarín, Argentina's largest media conglomerate and a vocal critic of the Fernández government. After a years-long battle, Fernández's government won a significant victory in October 2013 when the Supreme Court upheld the controversial 2009 Media Law, which aimed to diversify ownership in the heavily concentrated broadcast sector. Under the new provisions, Grupo Clarín will be forced to surrender all but 24 of its current holding of 158 broadcast licenses.

While the Senate passed a freedom of information bill in 2010 that would apply to all branches of the government, the time limit for action by the Chamber of Deputies lapsed in 2013, requiring the legislative process to begin anew. Several Argentine provinces have passed their own freedom of information laws, though enforcement and funding problems have undermined their impact.

The constitution guarantees freedom of religion, and anti-Semitism is reportedly on the decline. In June 2010, Fernández appointed the first Jewish foreign minister in Argentine history. Nevertheless, the country's Jewish community, the largest in Latin America, remains a target of discrimination and vandalism. The 1994 bombing of a Jewish cultural center continues to play a role in Argentine politics; in 2006, Argentine prosecutors formally accused top Iranian officials with orchestrating the bombing, though no convictions have been made. In 2013, the governments of Iran and Argentina set up a truth commission to investigate the bombing, prompting concerns that the Fernandez administration was interested in deepening Argentina's economic ties with Iran at the expense of pursuing justice. Academic freedom is a cherished Argentine tradition and is largely observed in practice.

E. Associational and Organizational Rights: 11 / 12

The rights of freedom of assembly and association are generally respected. For example, an estimated one million protestors marched peacefully across Argentina in April, criticizing Fernandez's management of the economy, crime and unemployment, and a combative political environment. Civic organizations are robust and play a major role in society, although some fall victim to Argentina's pervasive corruption. Labor is dominated by Peronist unions, though union influence has diminished dramatically in recent years due to internal divisions.

F. Rule of Law: 11 / 16

The justice system remains plagued by scores of incompetent and corrupt judges who retain their positions through tenure. The lower courts are highly politicized, and the relatively independent Supreme Court received heightened pressure from the government in the fall of 2013, specifically surrounding the Grupo Clarín case. In June 2013, Argentina's Supreme Court struck down part of a judicial reform, pushed through Congress by Fernández, that called for direct elections of members of the Council of Magistrates, the body that nominates and disciplines judges. Critics said the reform endangered the independence of the judiciary.

Police misconduct, including torture and brutality of suspects in custody, is endemic. Arbitrary arrests and abuse by police are rarely punished in the courts, owing to intimidation of witnesses and judges, particularly in Buenos Aires province. Prisons are overcrowded, and conditions remain substandard throughout the country.

In 2005, the Supreme Court ruled that laws passed in the 1980s to protect the military from prosecution were unconstitutional. The decision laid the foundation for the prosecution of past military crimes, leading previous president Néstor Kirchner to initiate prosecution proceedings against former officials involved in Argentina's dirty war, a period between 1955 and 1983 that saw the use of brutal tactics by a series of right-wing military regimes to silence dissent. Prosecutions of perpetrators of human rights violations committed during that era have continued under the Fernández administration. Twelve military and police officers, including Ricardo Cavallo and Alfredo Astiz, were convicted of torture, murder, and forced disappearance in October 2011 and sentenced to life in prison. Jorge Videla, a former military dictator and principal architect of the dirty war, died in prison in May 2013 after receiving a life sentence in 2010 for crimes against humanity.

Argentina's indigenous peoples, who represent between 1.5 and 3.5 percent of the population, are largely neglected by the government. Approximately 70 percent of the country's rural indigenous communities lack title to their lands. While the Kirchner administration has returned lands to several communities, most disputes remain unresolved. Forced evictions of indigenous communities still occur, despite laws prohibiting the practice. In July 2013, the Supreme Court ordered the local government of La Primavera and the National Institution of Indigenous Rights to submit a plan of action for mapping territory claimed by the Qom community. The mandate specified that the Qom community must participate in the process. The ruling came amidst a period of political pressure and police violence against the Qom community in the province of Formosa. Particularly since 2010, the Qom have suffered from abusive authority, specifically violent evictions, in their quest to regain ancestral territory.

G. Personal Autonomy and Individual Rights: 13 / 16

Women actively participate in politics in Argentina. In addition to the 2011 reelection of Fernández as president, women comprised nearly 35 percent of the seats in the Chamber of Deputies after the October 2013 elections. Decrees mandate that one-third of National Congress members be women. Argentina's Supreme Court ruled in March 2012 that women who have an abortion after being raped can no longer be prosecuted; an estimated 500,000 illegal abortions are performed in Argentina each year. Domestic abuse remains a serious problem, and women face economic discrimination and gender wage gaps.

In 2002, Buenos Aires became the first South American city to pass a domestic partnership law, and Argentina became the second country in the Americas—after

Canada—to legalize same-sex marriage nationwide in July 2010. Sex-trafficking remains a problem in Argentina, and in December 2012, three judges unexpectedly acquitted 13 defendants accused of kidnapping a woman and forcing her into prostitution. The verdict led to accusations that members of the judiciary were complicit in the sex-trafficking trade.

Armenia

Political Rights Rating: 5
Civil Liberties Rating: 4
Freedom Rating: 4.5
Freedom Status: Partly Free
Electoral Democracy: No

Population: 3,048,000
Capital: Yerevan

Note: The numerical ratings and status listed above do not reflect conditions in Nagorno-Karabakh, which is examined in a separate report.

Ten-Year Ratings Timeline For Year Under Review (Political Rights, Civil Liberties, Status)

Year Under Review	2004	2005	2006	2007	2008	2009	2010	2011	2012	2013
Rating	5,4,PF	5,4,PF	5,4,PF	5,4,PF	6,4,PF	6,4,PF	6,4,PF	6,4,PF	5,4,PF	5,4,PF

INTRODUCTION

Armenia held presidential elections in February. International observers noted that the vote was well-administered and that authorities had demonstrated a general respect for freedom of assembly and expression. There were no debates between the candidates, but the media provided campaign coverage of all candidates as required by law. However, pressure on voters, abuse of administrative resources, and interference in the voting process remained concerns. As in previous elections, observers noted procedural violations and irregularities in the tabulation of votes. Grave violations were observed on election day, particularly regarding the interference of proxies from the ruling party.

The incumbent, President Serzh Sarkisian of the governing Republican Party of Armenia (HHK), won a second five-year term with 59 percent of the vote. His closest challenger, Raffi Hovannisian of the Heritage party, received a remarkably high 36.7 percent. Hovannisian's popularity was largely a result of his active campaigning, characterized by direct American-style voter outreach considered unusual in Armenian politics. Despite his unexpectedly strong showing on election day, Hovannisian rejected the results, triggering a six-week standoff during which he made various inconsistent political demands and organized several protests calling for the election's annulment. Authorities responded with restraint and upheld the public's right to peacefully assemble. While Sarkisian assumed his post, his administration offered to engage in negotiations that could allow the opposition to play a greater role in the political process. Hovannisian rejected the offer. Hovannisian's inconsistent demands and unwillingness to engage in negotiations cost him public support, as demonstrated by his poor performance in mayoral elections held in Yerevan in May.

Over the last two years, Armenia had been in negotiations with the European Union (EU) on forging an association agreement. However, Sarkisian indicated in September that Armenia would instead join a Russian-led customs union. Following the decision, which was unpopular with the public, Russia reduced planned increases in gas prices to Armenia.

In November, Turkey announced that it would consider opening its land border with Armenia as an incentive to move forward with peace negotiations over Nagorno-Karabakh, an ethnic Armenian enclave within Azerbaijan's borders that split from Azerbaijan amid a war following the collapse of the Soviet Union. After three years of deadlock, Armenian and Azerbaijani leaders agreed to renew peace talks that month. Although no substantial progress was made to resolving the territorial dispute by year's end, both sides vowed to continue the dialogue in 2014. The Nagorno-Karabakh border remains heavily militarized.

POLITICAL RIGHTS: 14 / 40 (+1)

A. Electoral Process: 5 / 12

Armenia is not an electoral democracy. The unicameral National Assembly is elected for five-year terms, with 90 seats chosen by proportional representation and 41 through races in single-member districts. The president is elected by popular vote for up to two five-year terms. Elections since the 1990s have been marred by irregularities. International monitors reported issues with the 2013 presidential election and it was assessed as falling short of democratic standards.

In the 2012 parliamentary elections, the ruling HHK secured a majority with 69 seats. The HHK's former coalition partner, the Prosperous Armenia party (Bargavaj Hayastan Kusaktsutyun, or BHK), secured 37 seats, and the Armenian Revolutionary Federation (HHD) and Rule of Law party each took 6 seats. Historic representation was also granted to the Armenian National Congress (HAK), the formerly anti-institution opposition coalition led by former president Levon Ter-Petrosian, which won 7 seats. Many ministers retained their posts following the elections, including Prime Minister Tigran Sarkisyan of the HHK, though members of BHK in the outgoing cabinet were replaced by appointees from HHK.

The HAK, BHK, and HHD all declined to propose a candidate to challenge Sarkisian in the February 2013 presidential election. Hovannisian, the most serious challenger, vehemently rejected Sarkisian's victory. Hovannisian and his proxies filed a large number of complaints with the Central Elections Commission (CEC), requesting the invalidation of dozens of polling station results and a number of recounts, as well as the disqualification of the incumbent's candidacy based on allegations of campaign-spending violations. The CEC rejected all complaints challenging the legitimacy of Sarkisian's victory and declared him the official winner on February 25. The elections commission has a track record of unduly rejecting complaints based on formalities and court decisions on complaints cannot be appealed. According to the Organization for Security and Cooperation in Europe (OSCE), redress for electoral complaints is inadequate, failing to meet standards described in paragraph 5.10 of the 1990 OSCE Copenhagen Document. President Sarkisian was sworn in to his second five-year term in April.

B. Political Pluralism and Participation: 6 / 16 (+1)

People have the right to organize in different political parties in Armenia, but the ruling party's access to and abuse of administrative resources prevents the existence of a level political playing field. However, there was increased space for parties to campaign during the 2013 presidential election; contenders were allowed to operate fairly openly and candidates were more active in their voter outreach than in the past. Voters lack access to the information necessary to make informed choices and fear retribution for voting against the ruling party. There were no reports of physical attacks on candidates during the 2013 presidential election campaign. One minor challenger was shot and injured in late January, but no links between the shooting and the campaign were reported.

C. Functioning of Government: 3 / 12

Corruption is pervasive, and bribery and nepotism are reportedly common among government officials, who are rarely prosecuted or removed for abuse of office. Corruption is also believed to be a serious problem in law enforcement. A five-year initiative to combat graft, announced in 2008, has not made meaningful headway against the country's entrenched culture of corruption. In 2013, Armenia took steps to develop a strategy to improve control over public internal finances and improve competition in the public procurement of medicines. However, anticorruption measures remain largely ineffective due to a lack of successful implementation and enforcement.

Despite a 2003 law on freedom of information, government agencies have remained reluctant to disclose public information. In 2011, Armenia joined the Open Government Partnership initiative, a project dedicated to promoting government accountability that has several dozen nations as members. However, nongovernmental organizations (NGOs) monitoring progress on implementation claim that government bodies still do not adequately disclose public information as required by the project.

CIVIL LIBERTIES: 29 / 60
D. Freedom of Expression and Belief: 8 / 16

There are limits on press freedom. The authorities use informal pressure to maintain control over broadcast outlets, the chief source of news for most Armenians. There are two public television networks, and dozens of private channels with varying degrees of national reach; the owners of most private channels have close ties to the government. A 2010 digital broadcasting law mandated a reduction in the maximum number of television stations in the capital and in nine other regions; the new law also obliged a number of stations to focus on content other than domestic news and political affairs. In 2011, the law led to the denial of a digital license to GALA TV, the sole remaining television station that regularly criticized the government; the station is almost certain to be forced from the airwaves when the country completes the switchover from analog to digital broadcasting in 2015. In 2013, the government continued to deny a license to the independent television station A1+ despite a 2008 ruling in the network's favor by the European Court of Human Rights. The station returned to the airwaves in 2012 with the help of the privately owned ArmNews TV, which granted A1+ a contract to broadcast a news bulletin over its frequency.

Although libel was decriminalized in 2010, journalists face high fines under the civil code for defamation and insult. In February 2013, a coalition of NGOs issued a statement emphasizing that civil suits against the media with high fines remain a serious problem; the NGOs also expressed concern that courts tend to grant motions aimed at preventing media outlets in such cases from accessing their property and assets. Violence against journalists remains a problem, particularly during election periods. The Committee to Protect Freedom of Expression, an Armenian NGO, reported an uptick in violence against and pressure on journalists in 2013. Eleven of the 56 incidents of pressure on journalists that it documented in 2013 were in connection with the Yerevan mayoral elections on May 5. In one such incident a journalist was verbally and physically assaulted when he refused to stop filming the incumbent mayor during his arrival at a lavish campaign event. The authorities do not interfere with internet access.

Freedom of religion is generally respected, though the dominant Armenian Apostolic Church enjoys certain exclusive privileges, and members of minority faiths sometimes face societal discrimination. In May 2013, the law governing obligatory military service was amended to conform to European standards, allowing civil service as an alternative for conscientious objectors. Since the adoption of the new law, Jehovah's Witnesses have not faced prosecution for refusing military service, which had previously been a problem in Armenia. By November, all of the members of the Armenian Jehovah's Witnesses community who had been imprisoned for their conscientious objection to military service were released. Armenia's Jehovah's Witnesses, however, complain that the government has failed to respond to applications by 41 conscientious objectors to the new civil service program, leading to criminal cases against 12 such applicants.

The government generally does not restrict academic freedom. Public schools are required to display portraits of the president and the head of the Armenian Apostolic Church and teach the church's history.

E. Associational and Organizational Rights: 6 / 12

In the aftermath of the 2008 post-election violence, the government imposed restrictions on freedom of assembly. Major opposition rallies in 2011—combined with criticism from the Council of Europe—led the government to allow demonstrations in the capital's Freedom Square, the traditional venue for political gatherings since the late 1980s. However, authorities have been known to create artificial obstacles, such as setting up unexplained roadblocks, for people attempting to travel from the provinces to participate in such rallies. On several occasions, law enforcement and state-run media called the rallies following the February presidential election unauthorized and illegal, even though Hovannisian informed police of the demonstrations on a daily basis in accordance with the Law on Peaceful Assembly of the Republic of Armenia. Police reportedly blocked some protest routes without providing adequate explanation. Police did not interfere with most of the large antigovernment demonstrations that took place immediately after the election, but scuffles between protesters and law enforcement officers occurred in April when Sarkisian was inaugurated. Clashes between demonstrators and police took place on several other occasions during the year. A number of protesters were arrested at a rally in August against increases in public transportation costs; demonstrators were also arrested at a separate protest against Armenia's decision to join the customs union with Russia in September. A minor opposition figure attempted to stage an antigovernment revolution in November, but police and special forces officers responded with force, breaking up crowds and arresting scores of demonstrators.

Registration requirements for NGOs are cumbersome and time-consuming. More than 3,500 NGOs are registered with the Ministry of Justice, though many of these are not operational because of a lack of funding or capacity. The government provides financial assistance to certain organizations, but research conducted by the Yerevan Center for Freedom of Information, an NGO, suggests that some state-financed NGOs are completely inactive, raising the possibility that those groups' primary purpose is to launder money. While the constitution provides for the right to form and join trade unions, labor organizations are weak and relatively inactive in practice.

F. Rule of Law: 6 / 16

The judiciary is subject to political pressure from the executive branch and suffers from considerable corruption. Under a project implemented by the World Bank, the country in 2013 increased the speed of processing cases at first instance courts and made some improvements to judicial infrastructure, including the renovation of courthouses, new buildings for the Forensic Center and the Academy of Justice, and new information communications technologies. However, these changes did not improve public perceptions of the judiciary, which 75 percent of polled Armenians believe to be an extremely corrupt institution. Police make arbitrary arrests without warrants, beat detainees during arrest and interrogation, and use torture to extract confessions. Prison conditions in Armenia are poor, and threats to prisoner health are significant. In September, President Sarkisian issued an amnesty releasing several hundred prisoners, including HAK activist Tigran Arakelian, who was widely regarded as

Armenia's "last political prisoner." In 2012, the government launched a four-year prison reform plan that will include the adoption of a new criminal code, inmate rehabilitation, and the practice of suspended sentences.

Although members of the country's tiny ethnic minority population rarely report cases of overt discrimination, they have complained about difficulties in receiving education in their native languages. Members of the Yezidi community have sometimes reported discrimination by police and local authorities.

Homosexuality was decriminalized in 2003, but the LGBT community still faces violence and persecution. In August 2013, law enforcement supported a bill that would ban all "nontraditional sexual relationships." The bill was withdrawn after human rights groups criticized the proposal, likening it to anti-LGBT laws that were recently passed in Russia. In May, PINK Armenia and Women's Resource Centre organized a diversity march in support of LGBT rights, which was met by four times as many counterdemonstrators. While police prevented the violence from escalating to a large scale, counterdemonstrators were permitted to get close to the LGBT rights marchers, attacking some of them.

G. Personal Autonomy and Individual Rights: 9 / 16

Citizens have the right to own private property and establish businesses, but an inefficient and often corrupt court system and unfair business competition hinder such activities. Key industries remain in the hands of so-called oligarchs and influential cliques who received preferential treatment in the early stages of privatization following the fall of the Soviet Union. Illegal expropriation of private property by the state remains problematic. Thousands of residents and business owners in central Yerevan were forced off their property, on the grounds of "prevailing public interest" during the wave of construction projects that begin sweeping the capital about a decade ago, including the mostly vacant luxury apartments and shops on Northern Avenue.

According to the electoral code, women must occupy every sixth position—or 20 percent—on a party's candidate list for the parliament's proportional-representation seats. There were no female candidates in the presidential election in 2013. Fourteen out of the 131 seats in parliament are held by women. Domestic violence and trafficking in women and girls for the purpose of prostitution are believed to be serious problems.

Australia

Political Rights Rating: 1
Civil Liberties Rating: 1
Freedom Rating: 1.0
Freedom Status: Free
Electoral Democracy: Yes

Population: 23,100,000
Capital: Canberra

Ten-Year Ratings Timeline For Year Under Review (Political Rights, Civil Liberties, Status)

Year Under Review	2004	2005	2006	2007	2008	2009	2010	2011	2012	2013
Rating	1,1,F	1,1,F	1,1,F	1,1,F	1,1,F	1,1,F	1,1,F	1,1,F	1,1,F	1,1F

INTRODUCTION

With the ruling center-left Labor Party polling poorly as national elections approached, Prime Minister Julia Gillard was ousted in a June party leadership vote and replaced as party leader and prime minister by the more popular Kevin Rudd, her predecessor, whom she ousted in 2010 in a similar fashion. Distaste for the political infighting and the passage under Gillard of a controversial carbon tax contributed to a big victory for the conservative Liberal Party/National Party coalition over Labor in the September 2013 general elections. Economic and fiscal concerns also contributed to the coalition's electoral edge. The economy, which has benefited from the export of commodities to China and has been insulated from the economic recession experienced in the United States and Europe, nevertheless slowed in 2013, in part due to weak commodity prices and a strong currency.

Asylum seekers coming to Australia by boat remained one of the country's most divisive political issues, and Rudd soon after taking office announced that no one arriving by sea to Australia without a visa would be resettled there; refugees would instead be resettled in Papua New Guinea or Nauru. Rudd's government also announced a bounty of $180,000 for information leading to the arrest of human smugglers and launched a $27 million media campaign in Australia to advertise this policy change. Abbott's government took an even harder line, announcing that boats arriving from Indonesia would be turned back. In his first term as prime minister, Rudd had rejected his Liberal Party predecessor's "Pacific Solution" of putting asylum seekers in detention centers in Nauru and Papua New Guinea for processing, but rising numbers of people risking the perilous sea journey had led Rudd to open a new detention center on Christmas Island in 2008. Escalating violence, suicides, hunger strikes, and arson by detainees at the facility pressing their demand for resettlement in Australia led the Gillard government to readopt the Pacific Solution in 2012, in a move strongly criticized by human rights groups. However, the number of arrivals did not drop; in the first half of 2013, some 13,000 asylum seekers arrived by boat, many died at sea, and incidents of violence and self-harm among asylum seekers also persisted, and political pressure for a new approach intensified.

Australia officially ended its combat mission in Afghanistan. At year's end, only about 400 service members remained in Afghanistan to provide training and support to Afghan forces. Public support for the mission had fallen significantly in recent years. As of October 2013, according to the Australian Defense Department, there was a total of 40 operational deaths and 261 seriously wounded from Australia's 12 years in Afghanistan. Australia had contributed the largest non-NATO contingent in Afghanistan, and the largest number of special forces personnel after the United States and the United Kingdom.

POLITICAL RIGHTS: 39 / 40

A. Electoral Process: 12 / 12

A governor general, appointed on the recommendation of the prime minister, represents the British monarch as head of state. The prime minister is the leader of the majority party or coalition in Parliament.

Voting is compulsory, and citizens participate in free and fair multiparty elections to choose representatives for the bicameral Parliament. The Senate, the upper house, has 76 seats, with 12 senators from each of the six states and two from each of the two mainland territories. Half of the state members, who serve six-year terms, are up for election every three years; all territory members are elected every three years. All 150 members of the House of Representatives, the lower house, are elected by popular preferential voting to serve three-year terms, and no state can have fewer than five representatives.

Kevin Rudd replaced Julia Gillard as prime minister on July 1, 2013. Her government fell after Rudd bested her with a 55 to 45 vote in March to secure leadership of the Labor Party. Rudd tried to shore up Labor's poor image and flagging popularity, even shifting to a hardline position on asylum seekers. However, voters were disenchanted with Labor and

Rudd. In the 150-seat House of Representative, Labor won 55 seats versus 90 for Tony Abbott's Liberal Party and its coalition. In the 76-seat Senate, Labor won 31 seats versus 33 for the Liberal coalition. This was one of the worst showings for Labor in a federal election.

B. Political Pluralism and Participation: 15 / 16

Since World War II, political power has alternated between the Labor Party and the Liberal Party/National Party coalition. The left-leaning Green Party and independent legislators joined Labor in a coalition after it failed to win a majority of House seats in 2010 elections.

In the September 2013 federal elections, Abbott and his Liberal/National coalition scored a decisive 90-seat majority in the 150-seat lower house. (Labor took 55 seats; the rest went to smaller parties and independents.) Newly elected senators would not take office until mid-2014, but the results of the Senate elections would leave the Liberal coalition with 34 seats, Labor with 31, the Green Party with 9, and one each going to the Democratic Labor Party and an Independent. Since the Green Party generally opposes the Liberal/National coalition, Abbott will need support from several of the senators from small parties to pass controversial measures, including his campaign pledge to repeal the carbon tax.

Native aboriginal peoples continue to fight for a bigger voice in politics. In the September 2013 elections, the first indigenous woman was elected to the federal parliament. Other minorities are also slowly but steadily finding success in local and national politics. A Pakistan-born female environmental engineer chosen by the Greens in 2012 to fill an upper house seat in the New South Wales legislature would be the first Muslim lawmaker in Australia, and Malaysia-born Chinese-Australian Penny Wong became the first openly gay cabinet member in the Gillard government in 2010.

C. Functioning of Government: 12 / 12

Australia is regarded as one of the least corrupt societies in the world, ranking 9 out of 177 countries and territories surveyed in Transparency International's 2013 Corruption Perceptions Index. A high degree of transparency and accountability prevails in the functioning of government. Government policies and actions are openly discussed, examined, and criticized in parliament, the media, and research.

CIVIL LIBERTIES: 58 / 60

D. Freedom of Expression and Belief: 16 / 16

While the constitution does not protect freedoms of speech and the press, citizens and the media can freely criticize the government without reprisal. Some laws restrict publication and dissemination of material that promotes or incites terrorist acts. Ownership of private print media is highly concentrated. There are numerous public and private television and radio broadcasters.

Religious and academic freedoms are respected. Antiterrorism laws bar mosques and Islamic schools from spreading anti-Australian messages.

E. Associational and Organizational Rights: 12 / 12

Freedoms of assembly and association are not codified in law, but the government respects these rights in practice. Workers can organize and bargain collectively.

F. Rule of Law: 15 / 16

The judiciary is independent, and prison conditions generally meet international standards. Antiterrorism laws have tightened since 2001, among them legislation enacted in 2005, with a 10-year sunset clause, that includes police powers to detain suspects without charge, "shoot to kill" provisions, the criminalization of violence against the public and Australian troops overseas, and authorization for the limited use of soldiers to meet terrorist threats on domestic soil. After more than a decade of antiterrorism laws and more than 40 arrests, legal scholars and opponents of antiterrorism laws continue to question whether these measures are needed and effective. Australian immigration has expanded use of electronic biometric captures of fingerprints and facial images for visitors since 2011, with emphasis on those from countries deemed a high risk for Islamic extremism, such as Yemen and Somalia.

In 2011, the military was embroiled in a series of scandals involving rape, homophobia, and sexual predation. In 2012, the government officially apologized to victims after a government-commissioned study found more than 1,000 claims of abuse dating back to the 1950s. In March 2013, Gillard issued the first national government apology for Australia's decades-long forced-adoption policy, which had ended in the 1970s. The state had strong-armed unmarried mothers into placing their babies for adoption and had handed the babies over to married couples that had no children; thousands or tens of thousands of such forced adoptions were believed to have taken place.

Rudd in July declared that no asylum seekers arriving by sea would be allowed to resettle in Australia. Instead, he announced a deal with Papua New Guinea by which asylum seekers trying to enter Australia would be sent to Papua New Guinea for assessment and would be resettled there if they were determined to be refugees; a similar deal was later struck with Nauru. Opponents say the new policy violates Australia's obligations to asylum seekers under the United Nations Convention on Refugees, and criticize the living conditions at the detention centers. According to Rudd's government, the policy had an almost immediate impact, with 1,585 people arriving by boat in August, compared to 4,236 the previous month. There were also reports of Iranian detainees asking for repatriation to their home country rather than resettlement in Papua New Guinea. Abbott, who had made a campaign promise to "stop the boats," retained Rudd's new approach and took an even harder line, ordering the military to develop a border protection plan and to turn boats back to Indonesia, where many asylum seekers paid human smugglers to take them by boat into Australia.

Racial tensions involving South Asian and other immigrant groups have grown in recent years, especially in Melbourne, where the bulk of interracial violence has occurred. Foreign university student enrollment has suffered. With tuition from foreign students an important source of income for universities, the government in 2012 reduced the cost of applying for a student visa; it has also made verbal assurances of safety for foreign students.

G. Personal Autonomy and Individual Rights: 15 / 16

An open and free market economy, Australia ranks high in individual economic freedom and is regarded overall a good place to do business.

Aborigines comprise about 2 percent of the population. Underrepresented at all levels of government and lagging considerably behind other groups in key social and economic indicators, including life expectancy and employment, they also suffer higher rates of incarceration, are more frequently involved in violent crimes, and are reportedly routinely mistreated by police and prison officials. Women enjoy equal rights and are gaining greater parity in pay and promotion in public and private sector jobs. Since 2012, they can also serve in military combat positions. However, violence against women remains a serious problem, particularly within the Aboriginal population.

Gay men and lesbians can serve in the military, and federal law grants legal residence to foreign same-sex partners of Australian citizens. However, a 2004 amendment to the Federal Marriage Act defines marriage as a union between a man and a woman. In 2012, lawmakers voted to reject a bill to legalize gay marriage. In October 2013, the legislature of the

Australian Capital Territory (ACT) voted to legalize same-sex marriage; however, the federal government challenged the territorial law, and in December, the Australian High Court ruled that the territory did not have the authority to legalize same-sex marriage. Same-sex civil partnerships are recognized in the ACT and four Australian states.

Austria

Political Rights Rating: 1
Civil Liberties Rating: 1
Freedom Rating: 1.0
Freedom Status: Free
Electoral Democracy: Yes

Population: 8,511,000
Capital: Vienna

Ten-Year Ratings Timeline For Year Under Review (Political Rights, Civil Liberties, Status)

Year Under Review	2004	2005	2006	2007	2008	2009	2010	2011	2012	2013
Rating	1,1,F	1,1,F	1,1,F	1,1,F	1,1,F	1,1,F	1,1,F	1,1,F	1,1,F	1,1,F

INTRODUCTION

In a September 29, 2013, general election, the two largest Austrian political parties—Chancellor Werner Faymann's center-left Social Democratic Party of Austria (SPÖ) and the center-right People's Party of Austria (ÖVP)—narrowly won a combined majority in the lower house of parliament. That allowed them to continue governing in a grand coalition, as they had done since 2008, and for most years since 1986. However, their vote shares slipped after both parties were implicated in a rash of corruption scandals. The Freedom Party of Austria (FPÖ), a far-right nationalist party, won more than 20 percent of the vote, up significantly from the previous election in 2008.

POLITICAL RIGHTS: 38 / 40

A. Electoral Process: 12 / 12

The lower house of the Federal Assembly, the Nationalrat (National Council), has 183 members chosen through proportional representation at the district, state, and federal levels. Members serve five-year terms, extended from four in 2008. The president, who is elected for a six-year term, appoints the chancellor, who needs the support of the legislature to govern. The 62 members of the upper house, the Bundesrat (Federal Council), are chosen by state legislatures for five- or six-year terms.

In the September election the SPÖ won 52 seats in the Nationalrat, and the ÖVP took 47. Their combined vote share of 50.9 percent, down from 78.8 percent in 2002, was their worst since World War II, and their combined number of seats fell from 108. Both parties were weakened by corruption scandals and by their pro-European Union (EU) policies; Austria, which has the lowest unemployment rate in the EU, is nevertheless experiencing rising public discontent with bailouts for other members of the Eurozone.

The FPÖ took 40 seats, up 6 from the previous election. Team Stronach for Austria, a new euroskeptic, pro-business party founded in 2012 by Austrian-born Canadian car-parts magnate Frank Stronach, performed worse than expected, garnering 5.7 percent of the vote, for 11 seats. After briefly exploring the possibility of a conservative coalition with the FPÖ and Team Stronach, the ÖVP backed away from that option. (In 2000, the EU briefly suspended ties with Austria, imposing diplomatic sanctions in response to the inclusion of the far-right, xenophobic FPÖ in an ÖVP-led coalition government.) In December, SPÖ and the ÖVP reached an agreement to continue governing as a grand coalition. The Austrian Green Party won 12.3 percent of the vote, for 24 seats. The far-right Alliance for the Future of Austria (BZÖ), which had split from the FPÖ in 2005 and was considered less extreme, failed to win any seats, falling short of the 4 percent threshold necessary for inclusion in the Nationalrat. Another new party, the centrist, pro-business New Austria (NEOS), won nine seats. Voter turnout was about 75 percent.

B. Political Pluralism and Participation: 15 / 16

Though Austria has competitive political parties and free and fair elections, the traditional practice of grand coalitions has fostered disillusionment with the political process. The participation of Slovene, Hungarian, and Roma minorities in local government remains limited despite governmental efforts to provide bilingual education, media, and access to federal funds. There is little minority representation in the Federal Assembly. After the 2013 elections the Nationalrat included one Muslim man and three Turkish-born Muslim women.

C. Functioning of Government: 11 / 12

Recent corruption scandals have damaged the reputation of Austria's political class. In January 2013, former interior minister Ernst Strasser was sentenced to four years in prison for bribery. Strasser had resigned his seat in the European Parliament in 2011 after accepting a bribe offered by British reporters posing as lobbyists. Also in January, the Green Party released a report on a parliamentary corruption investigation, estimating that corruption reduced the nation's economic output by about 5 percent, or €17 billion ($22 billion), in 2012. In June, Wolfgang Duchatczek, deputy governor of the Austrian central bank, was one of a group of nine people charged in connection with bribes allegedly paid to win contracts to supply banknotes to Azerbaijan and Syria. Rudolf Fischer, a former deputy chief executive of Telekom Austria—which had been linked to a number of corruption scandals—in August was convicted of diverting funds to the FPÖ, and received a three-year prison sentence, all but six months of which was suspended.

In June 2012, ongoing corruption scandals led the parliament to pass an ethics reform bill that tightened disclosure rules for political contributions and gifts. Later that year, Gabriela Moser, the head of a parliamentary committee investigating alleged corruption involving Faymann, resigned, asserting that opposition from the SPÖ and the ÖVP was limiting her effectiveness. Austria was ranked 26 out of 177 countries and territories surveyed in Transparency International's 2013 Corruption Perceptions Index.

CIVIL LIBERTIES: 58 / 60

D. Freedom of Expression and Belief: 16 / 16

The federal constitution and the Media Law of 1981 provide the basis for free media in Austria, and the government generally respects these provisions in practice. However, libel and slander laws protect politicians and government officials, and a large number of defamation cases have been brought by public officials, particularly from the FPÖ, in recent years. Despite a 2003 law to promote media diversity, media ownership remains highly concentrated. There are no restrictions on internet access.

While there is no official censorship, Austrian law prohibits any form of neo-Nazism or anti-Semitism, as well as the public denial, approval, or justification of Nazi crimes, including the Holocaust. However, the FPÖ has been accused of anti-Semitic rhetoric in recent years. In January 2013, a court sentenced a prominent neo-Nazi figure, Gottfried Kuessel, to nine years in prison for helping start a website to disseminate Nazi views. Two other defendants in the case also received prison sentences. The website had been shut down by authorities in 2011.

Additionally, the FPÖ has been criticized for fueling anti-Muslim feelings in Austria through controversial ad campaigns. A number of recent high-profile court cases have centered on the balance between freedom of speech and the prohibition of hate speech, including the February 2011 conviction of lecturer Elisabeth Sabaditsch-Wolff for denigrating Islamic teachings during an FPÖ-sanctioned seminar.

Religious freedom is constitutionally guaranteed. Austrian law divides religious organizations into three legal categories: officially recognized religious societies, religious confessional communities, and associations. Many religious minority groups have complained that the law impedes their legitimate claims for recognition and demotes them to second- or third-class status. There are no government restrictions on academic freedom.

E. Associational and Organizational Rights: 12 / 12

Freedoms of assembly and association are protected in the constitution and in practice. Nongovernmental organizations operate without restrictions. Trade unions are free to organize and to strike, and they are considered an essential partner in national policymaking. Some 40,000 civil servants demonstrated in Vienna in December 2013 against the government's handling of pay negotiations.

F. Rule of Law: 15 / 16

The judiciary is independent, and the Constitutional Court examines the compatibility of legislation with the constitution. The quality of prisons generally meets high European standards.

Residents are usually afforded equal protection under the law. However, immigration has fueled some resentment toward minorities and foreigners. Austria has one of the world's highest numbers of asylum seekers per capita, and the Office of the UN High Commissioner for Refugees has criticized Austria's strict asylum law. Some asylum seekers can be deported while appeals are pending, and new arrivals are asked for full statements within 72 hours. In addition, the number of people who have been naturalized has fallen dramatically since the establishment of a more restrictive national integration policy in 2009. In January 2013, the government rejected demands for easing its asylum rules by about 40 mostly Pakistani and Afghan refugees who had been holding a hunger strike in a Vienna church.

G. Personal Autonomy and Individual Rights: 15 / 16

Roma and other ethnic minorities face discrimination in the labor and housing markets. The labor ministry has sought to promote integration of younger immigrants by providing German-language and job training.

A 1979 law guarantees women's freedom from discrimination in various areas, including the workplace. However, the income gap between men and women remains significant. The 2009 Second Protection Against Violence Act increased penalties for perpetrators of domestic violence and authorized further measures against chronic offenders. Women made up 33 percent of the Nationalrat after the 2013 elections.

A 2009 law permits civil partnerships for same-sex couples, giving them equal rights to pension benefits and alimony. However, it does not provide same-sex couples with the same adoption rights as heterosexual couples or equal access to assisted reproductive technologies. In February 2013, the European Court of Human Rights ruled that Austrian law discriminated against unmarried same-sex couples by not allowing the biological children of one of the partners to be adopted by the other partner. In July, the Austrian parliament approved an amendment to the civil code to allow such adoptions. But it rejected a bill that would grant gay couples unrestricted adoption rights.

Azerbaijan

Political Rights Rating: 6
Civil Liberties Rating: 6 ↓
Freedom Rating: 6.0
Freedom Status: Not Free
Electoral Democracy: No

Population: 9,418,000
Capital: Baku

Ratings Change: Azerbaijan's civil liberties rating declined from 5 to 6 due to ongoing, blatant property rights violations by the government in a year in which the state also cracked down on the opposition and civil society in advance of presidential elections.

Note: The numerical ratings and status listed above do not reflect conditions in Nagorno-Karabakh, which is examined in a separate report.

Ten-Year Ratings Timeline For Year Under Review (Political Rights, Civil Liberties, Status)

Year Under Review	2004	2005	2006	2007	2008	2009	2010	2011	2012	2013
Rating	6,5,NF	6,5,NF	6,5,NF	6,5,NF	6,5,NF	6,5,NF	6,5,NF	6,5,NF	6,5,NF	6,6,NF

INTRODUCTION

On October 9, 2013, President Ilham Aliyev won a third term in a predictable landslide victory amid significant evidence of massive electoral fraud. As in previous election cycles, the government stepped up the use of intimidation and other tactics to suppress dissent and ensure an unchallenged victory at the polls. During the year, the authorities employed excessive force to break up antigovernment protests, introduced restrictive laws to limit freedoms of expression and association, and jailed journalists and government critics.

A wave of protests swept the country early in the year in response to the perceived corruption of local elites and the deadly abuse of military conscripts. In January, new laws introducing increased fines for participating in or organizing unsanctioned protests came into force, and authorities quickly put them to use. Dozens of protesters were arrested in the first few months of 2013, and some remained in detention at year's end.

Other restrictive measures adopted in 2013 limited the financing and activities of civil society organizations. The nation's strict criminal defamation laws were expanded to include online content, and government critics who were active on social media were fined, detained, and suffered harassment from authorities.

POLITICAL RIGHTS: 6 / 40
A. Electoral Process: 1 / 12

Azerbaijan's constitution provides for a strong presidency, and the 125-member Milli Majlis (National Assembly) exercises little or no independence from the executive branch. The president and members of parliament serve five-year terms; a 2009 referendum eliminated presidential term limits.

Elections since the early 1990s have been considered neither free nor fair by international observers. In the October 2013 presidential election, Aliyev won with 84.6 percent of the vote. Jamil Hasanli, who was nominated as a backup candidate by the opposition

National Council of Democratic Forces, placed a distant second with 5.5 percent. The council, an umbrella organization formed in May to unite opposition factions and push for reform, had originally nominated well-known filmmaker Rustam Ibragimbekov, but his registration was rejected on the grounds that he had dual Russian-Azerbaijani citizenship.

The Organization for Security and Cooperation in Europe (OSCE) strongly criticized the government's limitations on freedom of expression and assembly surrounding the presidential election, pressure placed on voters and candidates, and widespread fraud at every stage of the voting process. Nevertheless, a delegation from the European Parliament (EP) initially called the elections "free, fair and transparent." Some critics speculated that the positive assessment was the result of successful lobbying efforts on the part of the Azerbaijani government and European business interests in the country. The EP ultimately backed away from its own findings and supported the conclusions of the OSCE, calling on Baku to implement the OSCE's recommended reforms as a precondition for moving forward on a strategic partnership deal between Azerbaijan and the European Union.

The most recent parliamentary elections, held in November 2010, followed the established trend of increasing manipulation, and the ruling New Azerbaijan Party (YAP) emerged with 71 seats, up from 61 in the 2005 polls. The remainder went to 41 independents and 10 minor parties, none of which garnered more than three seats.

B. Political Pluralism and Participation: 3 / 16

The political environment in Azerbaijan lacks pluralism. President Aliyev's YAP has dominated the political playing field in all electoral contests since its founding in 1995. Amendments to the electoral code in 2009 removed candidates' access to public campaign funding and reduced the official campaign period to 22 days, significantly limiting the ability of the opposition to connect with voters; the amendments also shortened the period for processing complaints. Changes made to laws governing freedom of assembly and nongovernmental organizations (NGOs) in 2012 and 2013 further restricted the opposition's capacity to campaign by raising fines for participation in unauthorized rallies and limiting sources of funding for public initiative groups.

Opposition groups are also marginalized by the state-controlled media, which grant them almost no coverage outside of the official campaigning period. Leaders of opposition groups are subject to arbitrary arrests on dubious charges as well as physical violence and other forms of intimidation. International observers determined that in the months prior to the 2013 election, authorities arrested 14 opposition politicians, journalists, and human rights activists, who were still in custody as of the end of the year.

Among those arrested in 2013 were Tofiq Yaqublu, leader of the Musavat party, and Ilqar Mammadov, chairman of the Republican Alternative (REAL) movement, who were detained on February 4 and remained on trial for "organizing social disorder" and "resisting authorities" at year's end. In the spring, several members of the opposition youth movement Nida (Exclamation) were arrested in connection with use of social media to promote antigovernment protests in March. Dashqin Malikov, an active member of the opposition People's Front Party, was arrested on trumped-up drug charges in March and sentenced to two and a half years in prison in July. Also in March, the leader of the Nakhchivan branch of the Musavat party was beaten by unidentified attackers and hospitalized with serious head injuries.

Parties representing minority groups do not play a significant role in politics in Azerbaijan.

C. Functioning of Government: 2 / 12

Corruption is widespread, and wealth from the country's massive oil and gas exports creates ever greater opportunities for graft. Because critical institutions, including the media and judiciary, are largely subservient to the president and ruling party, government officials are rarely held accountable for corruption. Several investigative reports published by foreign media in early 2012 revealed evidence that President Aliyev and his immediate family controlled prodigious private assets, including monopolies in the economy's most lucrative sectors. In response, the president in July 2012 signed a series of legal amendments that allowed companies' organizational structures and ownership to remain secret, significantly limiting journalists' ability to uncover corruption.

The consolidation of power within the president's immediate family continued in 2013, with First Lady Mehriban Aliyeva winning an election for deputy chief of the YAP in June. Some observers speculated that Aliyev could be planning to eventually transfer the presidency to his wife. He was named to the same position in 2001, two years before he succeeded his father, Heydar Aliyev, as president.

In 2013, the government created a web portal to provide information about its agencies. However, due to the site's unnecessarily complex login procedure, it was unclear whether it amounted to an improvement in the accessibility of public information.

CIVIL LIBERTIES: 16 / 60 (-1)
D. Freedom of Expression and Belief: 4 / 16

While the constitution guarantees freedom of the press, the authorities severely restrict the media in practice. Broadcast media generally reflect progovernment views. Most television stations are controlled by the government, which also controls approval of broadcast licenses. Although there is more pluralism in the print media, some 80 percent of newspapers are owned by the state, and circulation and readership are relatively small. Independent and opposition papers struggle financially and have faced heavy fines and imprisonment of their staff. State-owned companies rarely if ever advertise in such papers. Those who supply information to opposition newspapers have at times been subjected to threats and arrest. In early 2012, the state demolished kiosks owned by the private companies Qasid and Qaya, which distributed the independent newspapers *Yeni Musavat* and *Azadliq*. Local radio broadcasts of key international news services, including the British Broadcasting Corporation (BBC), Radio Free Europe/Radio Liberty (RFE/RL), and Voice of America, were banned in 2009.

Defamation remains a criminal offense punishable by exorbitant fines and imprisonment. Journalists are threatened and assaulted with impunity, and several have been jailed on fabricated charges of drug trafficking, ethnic hatred, high treason, and hooliganism, among other offenses. Many are convicted and face long jail sentences. In March 2013, Vugar Gonagov and Zaur Guliyev, the executive director and editor in chief of Khayal TV, were each given three-year suspended sentences and released after being tried on charges of inciting mass disorder and abuse of office for uploading a video to YouTube that depicted the governor of Quba District insulting local residents.

Also in March, newspaper editor Avaz Zeynalli was convicted of extortion and tax evasion and sentenced to nine years in prison. He had been in detention since October 2011, when parliamentarian Gular Ahmadova claimed he tried to blackmail her. Zeynalli had been reporting on allegations of corruption against Ahmadova, who was ultimately convicted in December 2013 and sentenced to three years in prison.

Website editor Nijat Aliyev, who was arrested on drug charges in May 2012 for his activism during antigovernment protests surrounding that year's Eurovision song contest, faced new charges in January 2013 of illegally distributing religious materials, provoking mass disorder, and inciting racial hatred. He was convicted in December and sentenced to 10 years in prison. Youth activist Anar Aliyev, who was also arrested during the Eurovision protests, was convicted in April and sentenced to eight years in prison on multiple charges ranging from disrupting public order to insulting the flag. Separately, blogger Rashad Ramazanov was sentenced in November to nine years in prison for drug possession after regularly criticizing official corruption and human rights abuses online.

Internet-based reporting and social networking have increased significantly in recent years as methods of sidestepping government censorship and mobilizing protesters. The government has repeatedly blocked some websites that feature opposition views and intimidated the online community through harsh treatment of critical bloggers. Defamation legislation was amended in June 2013 to specifically include online content and commentary, even on social media.

The government restricts the practice of "nontraditional" minority religions—those other than Islam, Orthodox Christianity, and Judaism—through burdensome registration requirements and interference with the importation and distribution of printed religious materials. A 2009 law required religious groups to reregister with the authorities and religious figures to be recertified. It also barred foreign citizens from leading prayers. A 2011 amendment to the law significantly increased fines for distribution of unapproved religious material and prescribed multiyear prison sentences for leaders of unsanctioned religious services. Well-known Islamic theologian Taleh Bagirzade was arrested in April 2013 after he criticized the government in a sermon. He was sentenced in November to two years in prison for drug possession.

The authorities have linked academic freedom to political activity in recent years. Some professors and teachers have reported being dismissed for links to opposition groups, and students have faced expulsion and other punishments for similar reasons.

E. Associational and Organizational Rights: 2 / 12

The government restricts freedom of assembly, especially for opposition parties. In early 2013, a wave of protests broke out in Ismayilli and Baku over perceived corruption among local elites and the abuse of military conscripts. New legal amendments increasing fines for organizing and participating in unauthorized protests came into effect in January 2013. Dozens of people were arrested and more than 20 fined in connection with the local protests under the new rules. In May, further legal restrictions on freedom of assembly were adopted, extending the maximum periods of administrative detention for certain offenses.

Legislation that took effect in February requires NGOs to register all grants and donations with the Ministry of Justice. In addition, under legal amendments introduced in March, NGOs are obliged to inform authorities of all donations over $250, and those that fail to acquire proper registration are prohibited from opening or maintaining bank accounts. The rules have been used to put pressure on both local and foreign organizations. NGOs reported during the year that the authorities had increased restrictions on their activities, requiring permission to hold even simple trainings and other events.

Although the law permits the formation of trade unions and the right to strike, the majority of trade unions remain closely affiliated with the government, and most major industries are dominated by state-owned enterprises.

F. Rule of Law: 4 / 16

The judiciary is corrupt, inefficient, and subservient to the executive branch. Arbitrary arrests and detention are common, particularly for members of the political opposition. Detainees are often held for long periods before trial, and their access to lawyers is restricted. Police abuse of suspects during arrest and interrogation reportedly remains common; torture is sometimes used to extract confessions. Prison conditions are severe, with many inmates suffering from overcrowding and inadequate medical care. Protesters detained during 2013 reported ill-treatment in custody. Most were arrested arbitrarily and denied legal counsel in closed pretrial hearings.

Some members of ethnic minority groups, including the small ethnic Armenian population, have complained of discrimination in areas including education, employment, and housing. Although homosexuality was decriminalized in 2001, antidiscrimination laws do not specifically protect LGBT people, who reportedly face police harassment and other forms of bias or abuse.

G. Personal Autonomy and Individual Rights: 6 / 16 (-1)

Hundreds of thousands of ethnic Azeris who were displaced by the war in Nagorno-Karabakh in the early 1990s remain subject to restrictions on their place of residence and often live in dreadful conditions.

As part of a citywide redevelopment project, the government evicted many Baku residents in 2011 and 2012 in preparation for the Eurovision Song Contest in 2012, forcibly removing and illegally demolishing the homes of those who refused to be resettled. In general, respect for property rights has plummeted in recent years as the state appears able to seize any property it wishes and options for recourse are extremely limited for ordinary citizens. Significant parts of the economy are controlled by corrupt elite, which severely limits equality of opportunity. Supporters of the political opposition face job discrimination, demotion, and dismissal.

Traditional societal norms and poor economic conditions restrict women's professional roles, and they remain underrepresented in government. Women hold 19 seats in the parliament. Domestic violence is a problem, and the country is believed to be a source, transit point, and destination for the trafficking of women for prostitution. A 2005 law criminalized human trafficking, but the U.S. State Department's 2013 *Trafficking in Persons Report* placed Azerbaijan on its Tier 2 Watch List for the sixth consecutive year.

Bahamas

Political Rights Rating: 1
Civil Liberties Rating: 1
Freedom Rating: 1.0
Freedom Status: Free
Electoral Democracy: Yes

Population: 349,589
Capital: Nassau

Ten-Year Ratings Timeline For Year Under Review (Political Rights, Civil Liberties, Status)

Year Under Review	2004	2005	2006	2007	2008	2009	2010	2011	2012	2013
Rating	1,1,F	1,1,F	1,1,F	1,1,F	1,1,F	1,1,F	1,1,F	1,1,F	1,1,F	1,1,F

INTRODUCTION

The Bahamian tourism industry continues to suffer from the global economic crisis that struck in late 2008. In 2013, the International Monetary Fund downgraded the economic growth projections for the Bahamas due to the slow global economy. Marijuana cultivation and trafficking by foreign nationals residing in the country have led the United States to keep the Bahamas on the list of major drug-producing and drug-transit countries.

In 2013, criminal activity targeting tourists in the Bahamas contributed to negative international press. This image problem was further compounded by reports of beatings by Bahamas security forces of refugees from Cuba.

POLITICAL RIGHTS: 38 / 40

A. Electoral Process: 12 / 12

The Bahamas is governed under a parliamentary system, and the governor general is appointed by the British monarch as head of state. The lower house of the bicameral Parliament, the 38-member House of Assembly, is directly elected for five-year terms. The 16 members of the upper house, the Senate, are appointed for five-year terms by the governor general based on recommendations made by the prime minister and the opposition leader. The head of the majority party or coalition in Parliament typically serves as prime minister.

The Progressive Liberal Party (PLP) regained power in general elections held in May 2012, winning 29 seats, while the Free National Movement (FNM) took 9 seats. Following the elections, Perry Christie, who had been prime minister in the 2000s, resumed the post.

B. Political Pluralism and Participation: 16 / 16

Political parties can organize freely, although the PLP and FNM dominate politics in a two-party system. Power rotates regularly between these two parties.

C. Functioning of Government: 10 / 12

Corruption remains a problem at all levels of government. Top officials frequently face allegations of administrative graft, domestically and from abroad. Parliament passed a freedom of information bill in February 2012; while the government has pledged to enforce the law, it has not specified when it would come into effect. The Bahamas was ranked 22 out of 177 countries and territories surveyed in Transparency International's 2013 Corruption Perceptions Index.

CIVIL LIBERTIES: 58 / 60

D. Freedom of Expression and Belief: 16 / 16

The Bahamas has a well-developed tradition of respecting press freedom. The privately owned daily and weekly newspapers express a variety of views, as do the government-run radio station and four privately owned radio broadcasters. Strict and antiquated libel laws dating to British legal codes are seldom invoked. Access to the internet is unrestricted, and religious and academic freedoms are respected.

E. Associational and Organizational Rights: 12 / 12

Freedoms of assembly and association are generally protected. Constitutional guarantees of the right to form nongovernmental organizations (NGOs) are generally respected, and human rights organizations have broad access to institutions and individuals. A proposed law, the Civil Society Organization Encouragement Act, will for the first time register civil society organizations separately instead of under the Companies Act. Labor, business, and professional organizations are generally free from government interference. Unions have the right to strike, and collective bargaining is prevalent.

F. Rule of Law: 15 / 16

The independent judicial system is headed by the Supreme Court and a court of appeals, with the additional right of appeal to the Privy Council in London under certain circumstances. The death penalty was last carried out in 2000, and it was ruled unconstitutional in 2006. However, in light of the rising crime rate, government representatives have issued calls for resuming capital punishment.

After a dramatic rise in the rates of murder, rape, and robbery in 2011, the government amended existing laws and introduced new legislation related to the functioning of the criminal justice system, including amendments to the Penal Code, the Dangerous Drugs Act, the Firearms Act, the Bail Act, the Sexual Offences Bill, and the Court of Appeal Act. Crime rates continued to fall somewhat in 2013, indicating that anticrime measures have achieved some success. However, some high-profile cases against tourists attracted the attention of the cruise ship industry and led to negative domestic and international press, damaging the country's reputation. In 2013, the murder rate increased by 7 percent, from 111 cases in 2012 to 119 in 2013. There was a small decrease in armed robberies in 2013 to 1,022 cases, down from 1,106 in 2012.

NGOs have occasionally documented cases of prisoner abuse and arbitrary arrest. Overcrowding in the country's prison remains a major problem, and juveniles are often housed with adults, increasing the risk of abuse. The correctional training institute established in 2005 has worked to segregate violent and nonviolent offenders. However, the institute continues to face problems of limited capacity, including inadequate space to segregate offenders and insufficient numbers of trained personnel.

The Bahamas remains a major transit point for migrants coming from other Caribbean islands, especially Cuba and Haiti, who are trying to reach the United States. Discrimination against Haitian immigrants persists, and at least 30,000 undocumented Haitians reside in the Bahamas. Strict citizenship requirements and a stringent work-permit system leave Haitians with few rights. Reports also emerged in 2013 of mistreatment of Cuban refugees by guards in a notorious detention center, which led to protests in Miami.

G. Personal Autonomy and Individual Rights: 15 / 16

Although the law does not protect against gender discrimination, criminal "quid pro quo" sexual harassment is prohibited. Violence against women, including domestic violence, is a serious problem. Despite laws against domestic violence, police are often reportedly reluctant to intervene in domestic disputes. Women hold only 12 percent of the seats in Parliament. Discrimination against same-sex relationships is not prohibited by the constitution, and efforts have been promoted to weave anti-LGBT clauses into existing marriage acts. Basic rights such as foreign travel, internal movement, emigration, and repatriation are constitutionally protected and respected in practice.

⬇ Bahrain

Political Rights Rating: 6
Civil Liberties Rating: 6
Freedom Rating: 6.0
Freedom Status: Not Free
Electoral Democracy: No

Population: 1,336,000
Capital: Manama

Trend Arrow: Bahrain received a downward trend arrow due to a new ban on unapproved contact between political societies and foreign officials or organizations as well as a government move to dissolve the Islamic Scholars' Council.

Ten-Year Ratings Timeline For Year Under Review (Political Rights, Civil Liberties, Status)

Year Under Review	2004	2005	2006	2007	2008	2009	2010	2011	2012	2013
Rating	5,5,PF	5,5,PF	5,5,PF	5,5,PF	5,5,PF	6,5,PF	6,5,NF	6,6,NF	6,6,NF	6,6,NF

INTRODUCTION

In an effort to break through the political crisis that has plagued Bahrain since antigovernment protests erupted in February 2011, the government held its first talks with the opposition in more than 18 months in February 2013. This National Dialogue made little progress, as the regime continued to crackdown on protesters and harass the country's majority Shiite population, leading the opposition to boycott the dialogue repeatedly throughout the year.

Large numbers of demonstrators continued to stage public protests critical of the regime. Most of these remained peaceful, although some opposition forces became increasingly violent and confrontational over the course of the year. In a response to repeated police brutality, attacks against security forces increased considerably during the year. For its part, the regime continued to use strong-arm tactics by detaining hundreds over the course of the year, sentencing dozens of activists to long prison terms, and torturing those detained. Several protesters were killed by police during the year. As they had in 2012, Bahraini authorities systematically targeted human rights defenders in 2013, including arresting prominent activists Naji Fateel of the Bahrain Youth Society for Human Rights and Sayed Muhafedha of the Bahrain Center for Human Rights.

Security forces also continued to target journalists and sought to further restrict freedom of speech. In July, with the support of both chambers of the parliament, King Hamad issued a new "anti-terrorism" decree which stated that protesters who demonstrate in spite of a state ban or without government permission can be stripped of their citizenship and fined. In September, the Justice Minister ordered Bahraini nongovernmental organizations (NGOs) and political societies to seek government permission before meeting with or communicating with international organizations.

POLITICAL RIGHTS: 6 / 40
A. Electoral Process: 3 / 12

Bahrainis approved a National Charter in 2001, and the country was proclaimed a constitutional kingdom the following year. However, leading Shiite groups and leftists boycotted local and parliamentary elections in 2002 to protest campaigning restrictions and gerrymandering aimed at diminishing the power of the Shiite majority. The 2002 constitution gives the king power over the executive, legislative, and judicial authorities. He appoints cabinet ministers and members of the 40-seat Consultative Council, the upper house of the National Assembly. The lower house, or Council of Representatives, consists of 40 elected members serving four-year terms. The National Assembly may propose legislation, but the cabinet must draft the laws. Bahrain's main Shiite opposition grouping, Al-Wefaq, withdrew its 18 members from the Council of Representatives in February 2011 to protest the government's crackdown. The opposition then boycotted interim elections held that September to fill the seats, and as a result, all 40 seats are now held by government supporters.

B. Political Pluralism and Participation: 2 / 16

While formal political parties are illegal, the government has generally allowed political societies or groupings to operate. A 2005 law makes it illegal to form political associations based on class, profession, or religion, and requires all political associations to register with the Ministry of Justice. In February 2011, Bahraini activists, mostly from economically depressed Shiite communities, organized small demonstrations to call for political reform and an end to sectarian discrimination. A brutal police response galvanized support for the protest movement, and tens of thousands of demonstrators converged on central Manama. In March 2011, the government declared martial law and summoned troops from regional allies including Saudi Arabia to backstop a prolonged crackdown. While the government claimed that political societies remained free to operate, it has imprisoned key opposition leaders, including Hassan Mushaima (Haq), Ibrahim Sharif (Democratic Action Society), Abd al-Jalil Singace (Haq), Matar Ibrahim Matar (Al-Wefaq), and Jawad Fairuz (Al-Wefaq). Mushaima, Sharif, and Singace were sentenced to life in prison for their activism. After a lengthy appeal process, Bahrain's courts upheld their sentences in January 2013. In December the president of al-Wefaq, Ali Salman, was arrested, charged with inciting unrest, and banned from traveling.

The government re-launched the National Dialogue in February 2013 in an attempt to re-engage the opposition in the political process. For their part, opposition representatives participated haltingly and cautiously throughout the year, staging several boycotts due to the ongoing crackdown against protesters, continued arrests of opposition leaders, and rising levels of police brutality. Senior members of Al-Wefaq continued to be detained in 2013, including Khalil al-Marzooq, who was arrested for his criticisms of the government during a rally in September. Al-Wefaq's president, Ali Salman, was charged with inciting hatred and spreading false news after giving a speech criticizing the government in December.

The government has maintained a heavy security presence in primarily Shiite villages since 2011. Security forces restricted the movements of Shiite citizens, periodically destroyed property, and continued to arrest regime critics and activists.

C. Functioning of Government: 3 / 12

Bahrain has some anticorruption laws, but enforcement is weak, and high-ranking officials suspected of corruption are rarely punished. A source of frustration for many citizens is the perception that Khalifa bin Salman al-Khalifa, the king's uncle and Bahrain's prime minister since 1971, is both corrupt and a key opponent of reform. A British investigation into illicit payments allegedly made by a British-Canadian citizen to Aluminum Bahrain in 2013 was dropped, although it is widely believed that the payments occurred and that the Bahraini Prime Minister was either aware of them or involved. Bahrain was ranked 57 out of 177 countries and territories surveyed in Transparency International's 2013 Corruption Perceptions Index.

C. Discretionary Political Rights Question B: -2 / 0

Shiites are underrepresented in government and face various forms of discrimination. Fears of Shiite power and suspicions about their loyalties have limited employment opportunities for young Shiite men and fueled government attempts to erode the Shiite majority, mostly by granting citizenship to foreign-born Sunnis. In 2013 the regime continued its systematic sectarian discrimination and continued to recruit foreign Sunnis to serve in the country's security services and to take up Bahraini citizenship.

CIVIL LIBERTIES: 10 / 60 (-2)

D. Freedom of Expression and Belief: 2 / 16 (-1)

Restrictions on freedom of expression continued in 2013. The government owns all broadcast media outlets, and the private owners of the three main newspapers have close ties to the state. The government and its supporters have used the press to smear human rights and opposition activists repeatedly since 2011, most notably in separate campaigns against the former opposition newspaper *Al-Wasat* and its editor, Mansur al-Jamri. Self-censorship is encouraged by the vaguely worded 2002 Press Law, which allows the state to imprison journalists for criticizing the king or Islam, or for threatening "national security." Human rights activist Nabeel Rajab, who was arrested in 2012 for criticizing the government on the Twitter microblogging service, remained in prison during 2013. Zainab al-Khawaja, another prominent rights activist and daughter of high-profile imprisoned activist Abd al-Hadi al-Khawaja, also remained in prison during 2013 for criticizing the government.

The prominent blogger Ali Abdulemam, a regular contributor to the popular opposition web forum Bahrain Online, was sentenced in absentia to 15 years in prison by a military court in 2011. After spending two years in hiding, he was escaped Bahrain to Great Britain in April. In July, prominent blogger and journalist Muhammad Hassan Sadef and photographer Hussain Hubail were arrested in anticipation of opposition protests planned for August 14. Sadef was released in October while Hubail remained in custody at year's end. In May, six Bahrainis were sentenced to a year in jail for criticizing the king on Twitter. The government continued to block a number of opposition websites during the year, including those that broadcast live events, such as protests. In October police raided and shut down a public exhibition dedicated to the Arab Uprisings.

Islam is the state religion. However, non-Muslim minorities are generally free to practice their faiths. All religious groups must obtain a permit from the Ministry of Justice and Islamic Affairs to operate legally, though the government has not punished groups that operate without a permit. In 2010, the government stripped Ayatollah Hussein Mirza Najati, one of the country's top Shiite clerics, of his Bahraini nationality. Police and military forces destroyed over 40 Shiite places of worship during the spring 2011 crackdown. The government has promised to rebuild at least 12 of the mosques, but had not begun widespread efforts to do so in 2012. The government intensified its crackdown on prominent Shiite religious figures in 2013. Police raided the home of the country's top religious scholar Issa Qassim in May, a move that promoted large protests and Al-Wefaq to boycott the National Dialogue for two weeks. In September, the Justice, Islamic Affairs and Endowments Ministry labeled the Islamic Scholars Council—the largest organization of Shiite clerics in Bahrain—an illegal organization and moved to have it dissolved.

Academic freedom is not formally restricted, but scholars who criticize the government are subject to dismissal. In 2011, a number of faculty and administrators were fired for supporting the call for democracy, and hundreds of students and some faculty were expelled. Those who remained were forced to sign loyalty pledges.

E. Associational and Organizational Rights: 1 / 12 (-1)

Citizens must obtain a license to hold demonstrations, which are banned from sunrise to sunset in any public arena. Police regularly use violence to break up political protests, most of which occur in Shiite villages. In July 2013, King Hamad decreed additions to Bahrain's antiterrorism law that imposed heavy penalties on those convicted of demonstrating unlawfully, including large fines and the stripping of citizenship. The decree was the result of ongoing protests throughout the year and rising levels of violence. Several Bahraini protesters were killed by police in 2013, including an 8-year old boy who the opposition claimed was killed by tear gas in January. Hussain al-Jazeri was shot and killed by police in February while protesting. His brother Mahmud was also killed that same month. Several protesters were arrested and received prison sentences.

The 1989 Societies Law prohibits any NGO from operating without a permit. In 2010, the government dissolved the board of directors of the Bahrain Human Rights Society, an independent NGO, and assigned a government-appointed director to run the organization. The authorities blocked visits by foreign NGOs during 2012. Among others, Richard Sollom of Physicians for Human Rights was denied entry in 2012, as were delegations from the International Trade Union Confederation and the International Labour Organization. In April 2013 the government cancelled a visit by torture expert Juan Mendez, the UN special rapporteur on torture. In September, the Ministry of Justice ordered all groups to get government permission before meeting with non-Bahraini diplomats and officials in an effort to limit the amount of contact opposition and human rights networks have with potentially supportive foreign governments and international organizations. The order also required a government official to be present at any interaction.

Bahraini human rights defenders continued to be targeted in 2013. Sayed Muhafadha, a leading member of the outlawed Bahrain Center for Human Rights, was briefly detained in January. Naji Fateel of the Bahrain Youth Society for Human Rights was arrested, tortured, and sentenced to 15 years in prison in September.

Bahrainis have the right to establish independent labor unions, but workers must give two weeks' notice before a strike, and strikes are banned in a variety of economic sectors. Private-sector employees cannot be dismissed for union activities, but harassment of unionist workers occurs in practice. Foreign workers lack the right to organize and seek help from Bahraini unions. A 2009 decision that shifted responsibility for sponsoring foreign workers from private employers to the Labor Market Regulatory Authority did not apply to household servants, who remain particularly vulnerable to exploitation. Among the several thousand people known to have been fired in 2011 for allegedly supporting the prodemocracy protests were key officials in the General Federation of Bahraini Trade Unions. In 2012, the government prevented a delegation from the International Trade Union Confederation and the International Labour Organization from entering the country to participate in the annual congress of the General Federation of Bahrain Trade Unions.

F. Rule of Law: 1 / 16

The king appoints all judges, and courts have been subject to government pressure. Members of the royal family hold all senior security-related offices. Bahrain's antiterrorism law prescribes the death penalty for members of terrorist groups and prison terms for those who use religion to spread extremism. Critics have argued that the law's definition of terrorist crimes is too broad and that it has encouraged the use of torture and arbitrary detention.

Bahrain's criminal courts and those responsible for personal status laws are largely beholden to political interests. The country's judicial system is seen as corrupt and tilted in favor of the ruling family and its backers. Although Bahrain has criminalized torture and claims it does not hold political prisoners, its prisons are full of human rights and prodemocracy activists. Prison conditions are mixed. Prisoners report frequent rough treatment. While some detainees are periodically denied access to family and lawyers, others enjoy limited opportunities for phone calls and other amenities. In August, prisoners at the Dry Dock prison on the island of Muharraq rioted over poor conditions and for being denied family visits. Over 40 prisoners were injured.

In November 2011, the Bahrain Independent Commission of Inquiry (BICI) concluded that security personnel had used excessive force during the crackdown earlier that year. The BICI found no evidence that Iran or other foreign elements were behind the uprising, contradicting a key government claim. The regime implemented one BICI recommendation in July 2013, when it created a police ombudsman to investigate allegations of brutality and the excessive use of force by security forces. While several police were sentenced to prison terms during the year, including one unnamed officer who was sentenced to seven years in jail in February for killing a protester in 2011, sentences for those convicted of killing protesters have been light compared to political activists. In March, two others were sentenced to 10 years in prison for the death of Ali Issa Ibrahim Saqer while he was detained in 2011, but their prison sentences were reduced to five years by the High Criminal Court of Appeals in September. In December, two police officers, including a member of the royal family, were acquitted on charges that they had tortured doctors during the spring 2011.

Throughout the year, protesters were accused of detonating a series of car bombs targeting police; at least two police officers were killed and several others were injured in the bombings. Courts sentenced dozens of protesters to long prison terms for illegally protesting or on suspicion of complicity in bomb attacks. In September, nine boys under the age of 18 were abducted by security forces, allegedly tortured, and detained on charges that they were behind recent fire-bomb attacks. Hundreds children were arrested and detained during 2013, some being sentenced to jail, for allegedly participating in protests.

G. Personal Autonomy and Individual Rights: 6 / 16

The government continued to obstruct foreign travel by key opposition figures and activists in 2013. After having visited Bahrain earlier in the year, British Airways authorities denied Maryam al-Khawaja entry on a flight to Manama in August. Authorities also restricted movement inside the country, particularly for residents of largely Shiite villages outside Manama. A tight security cordon blocked easy access to the capital.

Although women have the right to vote and participate in elections, they are underrepresented politically. Women are generally not afforded equal protection under the law. The government drafted a personal status law in 2008 but withdrew it in 2009 under pressure from Shiite clergy; the Sunni portion was later passed by the parliament. Personal status and family law issues for Shiite Bahrainis are consequently still governed by Sharia (Islamic law) court rulings based on the interpretations of predominantly male religious scholars, rather than by any formal statute.

⬇ Bangladesh

Political Rights Rating: 3
Civil Liberties Rating: 4
Freedom Rating: 3.5
Freedom Status: Partly Free
Electoral Democracy: Yes

Population: 156,595,000
Capital: Dhaka

Trend Arrow: Bangladesh received a downward trend arrow due to increased legal harassment and attacks on bloggers, the passage of restrictive amendments to the Information and Communication Technology Act, and the deaths of dozens of protesters during demonstrations over verdicts by the country's war crimes tribunal.

Ten-Year Ratings Timeline For Year Under Review (Political Rights, Civil Liberties, Status)

Year Under Review	2004	2005	2006	2007	2008	2009	2010	2011	2012	2013
Rating	4,4,PF	4,4,PF	4,4,PF	5,4,PF	4,4,PF	3,4,PF	3,4,PF	3,4,PF	3,4,PF	3,4,PF

INTRODUCTION

Bangladesh was racked by ongoing political and social unrest in 2013, fueled by tensions between the ruling Awami League (AL) government and opposition parties in the run-up to national elections scheduled for January 2014, and between Islamist groups and secularist protesters. In addition to violence and killings surrounding street protests that took place throughout the year, restrictions were placed on both traditional and online media. Meanwhile, the collapse of a factory building in April, in which more than 1,100 workers died, highlighted unsafe working conditions in the garment industry.

The International Crimes Tribunal (ICT)—established by the AL government in 2010 to prosecute those suspected of committing war crimes or other atrocities against civilians during the 1971 war of independence—started handing down verdicts in early 2013. In February, the tribunal sentenced Abdul Quader Mollah, leader of the Islamist Jamaat-e-Islami (JI) political party, to life imprisonment. The sentencing triggered increased tensions between JI supporters and a coalition of nationalist and secularist forces, who led a series of large-scale peaceful protests termed the "Shahbagh movement" in the capital of Dhaka. The protesters demanded that convicted war criminals receive the death penalty. Violent clashes between the two factions erupted when the tribunal handed down a death sentence to JI vice president Delwar Hossain Sayedee in late February, leading to the death of dozens of protesters, mostly at the hands of security forces. In September, Mollah's original life sentence was changed by the Supreme Court to the death penalty, prompting further protests by JI supporters; he was executed in December.

POLITICAL RIGHTS: 24 / 40 (-1)

A. Electoral Process: 9 / 12

Terms for both the unicameral National Parliament and the largely ceremonial presidency are five years. Under provisions contained in the 15th amendment to the constitution, Parliament is composed of 350 members, of whom 300 are directly elected, and 50 are women nominated by political parties—based on their share of the elected seats—and then voted on by their fellow lawmakers. The president is elected by Parliament.

In national elections held in December 2008, an electoral alliance led by the AL won an overwhelming 263 seats, with the AL taking 230. The Bangladesh Nationalist Party (BNP) took 30 seats, and its ally, JI, took 2. Independents and minor parties captured the remainder. While the 2008 elections were deemed free and fair by European Union observers and other monitoring groups, more recent local government polls have been marred by more extensive violence and intimidation, as well as suspected rigging.

The BNP boycotted participation in subnational elections in 2013 to demand the reinstatement of the Caretaker Government (CG) system, which had been eliminated in 2011. Under the CG system, a theoretically nonpartisan government would take power temporarily to oversee parliamentary voting.

B. Political Pluralism and Participation: 10 / 16 (-1)

Bangladesh has a strong two-party system in which power alternates regularly between political coalitions led by the AL and BNP. The BNP-led opposition continued in 2013 to intermittently boycott Parliament and rigidly oppose the AL government's initiatives, making regular use of hartals (strikes) and mass protests.

The level of political violence in Bangladesh remains relatively high, and increased in the lead-up to national elections planned for January 2014; the human rights group Odhikar registered more than 500 deaths and more than 24,000 people injured as a result of inter- or intraparty clashes during 2013, a substantial uptick from the previous year.

Harassment of the opposition was widespread in 2013, ranging from charges filed against senior BNP members to limitations placed on political activities, particularly rallies and processions. In March 2013, following a BNP rally that turned violent, nearly 200 opposition activists were arrested, including BNP acting secretary general Mirza Fakhrul Islam Alamgir. Of those detained, 154 faced charges, including several top leaders.

Members of the JI also faced pressure in 2013; police raided the party's headquarters in Dhaka following violent protests it organized countrywide in response to the Shahbagh protests calling for the death penalty for war criminals. A February 2010 Supreme Court decision effectively reinstated a ban on religious political parties. In August 2013, a high court ruled that the JI would be required to amend its charter to conform to the constitution and reregister in order to contest the 2014 national elections.

The military does not generally play a dominant role in politics.

C. Functioning of Government: 5 / 12

Endemic corruption and criminality, weak rule of law, limited bureaucratic transparency, and political polarization have long undermined government accountability. Moreover, regular opposition boycotts of Parliament have significantly hampered the legislature's role in providing thorough scrutiny of government policies, budgets, and proposed legislation. The 2009 Right to Information Act mandates public access to all information held by public bodies and overrides secrecy legislation, but has been unevenly implemented.

Bangladesh was ranked 144 out of 177 countries and territories surveyed by Transparency International in its 2013 Corruption Perceptions Index. Under the present government, anticorruption efforts have been weakened by patchy or biased enforcement and subversion of the judicial process. In particular, the Anticorruption Commission (ACC) has become ineffective and subject to overt political interference. Its powers were weakened further in November 2013, when the ACC law was amended to withdraw its authority to bring cases against officials without permission from the government. Meanwhile, dozens of pre-2009 cases against Prime Minister Sheikh Hasina Wajed and other AL politicians were dropped after the AL assumed power, while those against BNP politicians, including party leader Khaleda Zia and her family, have remained open, and additional charges have been filed by the AL government.

CIVIL LIBERTIES: 29 / 60 (-2)
D. Freedom of Expression and Belief: 8 / 16 (-1)

Bangladesh's media environment remained relatively unfettered in 2013, though the legal and regulatory framework allows for some restrictions, and the government showed signs of intolerance during the year. In April, Mahmudur Rahman, the editor of the opposition-oriented *Amar Desh* newspaper, was arrested and charged with sedition. Print media are generally given more leeway than broadcasters when covering sensitive topics. In May 2013, several television stations were shuttered by authorities as they attempted to cover unfolding protests in Dhaka.

Journalists continue to be threatened and attacked with impunity by organized crime groups, party activists, and Islamist factions, which sometimes leads to self-censorship on sensitive topics. One journalist—a blogger associated with the Shahbagh movement—was killed in 2013, according to the Committee to Protect Journalists. On a number of occasions during the year, journalists were harassed or attacked while trying to cover the protests engulfing the country. Some journalists received threatening telephone calls from intelligence agencies seeking to prevent negative coverage.

Attempts to censor internet-based content increased in 2013. The video-sharing site YouTube remained blocked until June following a global uproar over a 2012 anti-Islam video produced in the United States. Facebook and some individual blogs were also blocked for shorter periods during the year, allegedly due to carrying antireligious content. In March 2013, an official committee was formed to monitor blogs and social media and to identify individuals who produced or posted anti-Islamic content. Bloggers faced increased physical attacks and legal charges in 2013, with many accused of blasphemy; several were arrested in April. Amendments to the Information and Communication Technology Act that passed in October would expand police powers and increase the penalties for violations; activists criticized the broad provisions and vowed to challenge the law's constitutionality. Various forms of artistic expression, including books and films, are occasionally banned or censored.

A 2011 amendment to the constitution confirmed Islam as the official religion, but also reaffirmed the secular nature of the state. Muslims form an overwhelming majority; about 10 percent of the population is Hindu, and there are smaller numbers of Buddhists and Christians. Although religious minorities have the right to worship freely, they face societal discrimination as well as harassment and legal repercussions for proselytizing, and physical attacks occasionally target minority groups and their houses of worship.

Religious minorities remain underrepresented in politics and state employment, but the secularist AL government has appointed several members of such groups to leadership positions. It has also initiated curriculum reform in Islamic schools. The government rejected demands by Islamist parties during the year to implement a new blasphemy law.

In early 2013, attacks against Hindus and Buddhists took place across Bangladesh as part of the violent protests organized by Islamists against the war crimes verdicts, affecting hundreds of homes, businesses, and temples. Members of the Ahmadiyya sect are considered heretical by some Muslims, and despite increased state protection since 2009, they have encountered physical attacks, boycotts, and demands that the state declare them non-Muslims. They are also occasionally denied permission to hold religious events.

While authorities largely respect academic freedom, research on sensitive political and religious topics is reportedly discouraged. Political polarization at many universities, including occasional clashes involving the armed student wings of the three main parties, inhibits education and access to services.

E. Associational and Organizational Rights: 6 / 12 (-1)

The rights of assembly and association are provided for in the constitution, but the government is empowered to ban gatherings of more than four people, and it regularly exercised this provision in 2013. Nevertheless, many demonstrations took place during the year, including strikes and rallies called by the BNP, as well as protests both in favor of and opposing the war crimes trials. Authorities sometimes try to prevent rallies by arresting party activists, and protesters are frequently injured and occasionally killed during clashes in which police use excessive force. Dozens of pro-JI protesters were killed early in the year, while in May, several dozen activists belonging to the Hefazat-i-Islami religious group were killed by security forces in Dhaka following a day-long protest rally.

Numerous nongovernmental organizations (NGOs) operate in Bangladesh. While most are able to function without onerous restrictions, they must obtain clearance from the NGO Affairs Bureau (NAB)—which reports to the prime minister's office—to use foreign funds. The bureau is also empowered to approve or reject individual projects after a review period of 45 days. Groups such as Odhikar that are seen as overly critical of the government, particularly on human rights issues, have been subject to harassment and surveillance of staff and are regularly denied permission for proposed projects. In August 2013, Odhikar secretary Adilur Rahman Khan was arrested for allegedly spreading false information after he criticized extrajudicial killings by the security forces; he spent two months in detention before being released on bail. The government announced plans in 2013 to bring the Grameen Bank, a key nonprofit and one of the country's largest and most influential microfinance institutions, under the direct control of the central bank.

Labor union formation is hampered by a 30 percent employee-approval requirement, restrictions on organizing by unregistered unions, and rules against unionization by certain categories of civil servants. Organizations and individuals that advocate for labor rights have faced increased harassment over the past several years. The Bangladesh Center for Workers'

Solidarity (BCWS) was stripped of its legal status by the NAB in 2010 for allegedly inciting labor unrest; although criminal charges were dropped against its leaders in 2013, little substantive progress was made on investigating the April 2012 murder of BCWS organizer Aminul Islam, despite evidence that security forces were complicit in his death.

F. Rule of Law: 6 / 16

Politicization of the judiciary remains an issue, despite a 1999 Supreme Court directive ordering the separation of the judiciary from the executive. Political authorities have continued to make appointments to the higher judiciary, in some cases demonstrating an overt political bias, leading to protests from the Supreme Court Bar Association. Harassment of witnesses and the dismissal of cases following political pressure are also growing issues of concern.

The court system is prone to corruption and severely backlogged with an estimated two million pending cases. Pretrial detention is often lengthy, and many defendants lack counsel. The indigent have little access to justice through the courts. Prison conditions are extremely poor, severe overcrowding is common, and juveniles are often incarcerated with adults. Suspects are routinely subject to arbitrary arrest and detention, demands for bribes, and physical abuse by police. Torture is often used to extract confessions and intimidate political detainees. Criminal cases against ruling party activists are regularly withdrawn on the grounds of "political consideration," which has undermined the judicial process and entrenched a culture of impunity.

Security forces including the Rapid Action Battalion, a paramilitary unit composed of military and police personnel, have been criticized for extrajudicial executions. According to Odhikar, there were 329 extrajudicial killings by law enforcement agencies in 2013, a dramatic increase from the previous year; most were committed by the police. The Directorate General–Forces Intelligence, a military intelligence unit, has been responsible for a number of cases of abuse during interrogations. Although the AL government initially promised a "zero-tolerance" approach on torture and extrajudicial executions, high-level officials routinely excuse or deny the practices, and the rate of custodial deaths has increased since the AL took office. Abductions and enforced disappearances are also a growing concern, according to the International Crisis Group and other organizations, with several dozen cases recorded in 2013. In a positive step, a law criminalizing custodial torture or death—with mandated minimum fines for perpetrators—was passed by Parliament in October 2013.

Law enforcement abuses are facilitated by legislation such as the 1974 Special Powers Act, which permits arbitrary detention without charge, and Section 54 of the criminal procedure code, which allows detention without a warrant. A 2009 counterterrorism law includes an overly broad definition of terrorism and generally does not meet international standards; a June 2013 amendment to the law allowed the use of materials posted on social media as evidence in cases. The National Human Rights Commission, reestablished in 2010, is empowered to investigate and rule on complaints against the armed forces and security services, and it can request reports from the government at its own discretion.

Revisions in 2009 and 2011 to the International War Crimes Tribunal Act of 1973 and the current tribunal's procedural rules were intended to help meet international standards on issues such as victim and witness protection, the presumption of innocence, defendant access to counsel, and the right to bail. However, the trials conducted thus far have fallen short of these standards, with concerns raised regarding political interference, due process shortcomings, and inadequate protection given to witnesses and defense lawyers. During the year, the ICT handed down a number of sentences, with most defendants receiving the death penalty. Abdul Quader Mollah was executed in December, prompting fears of increased instability.

Following the Shahbagh protests, the law governing the tribunal was amended in February 2013 to allow prosecutors as well as the defense to appeal sentences.

Violence by nonstate actors remains a concern. Protests by Islamist political parties and other pressure groups—some of which involved violence—were a key feature of 2013, though terrorist attacks by Islamist militant groups have been negligible since a 2006 crackdown, and the AL government has been aggressive in arresting cadres and closely monitoring their activities. Separately, casualties from clashes involving Maoist militants have declined dramatically in recent years; according to the South Asia Terrorism Portal, just 18 people were killed in 2013.

Members of ethnic and religious minority groups, women, and LGBT (lesbian, gay, bisexual, and transgender) individuals face some discrimination under law, as well as harassment and violations of their rights in practice. Indigenous people in the Chittagong Hill Tracts (CHT) remain subject to physical attacks and property destruction by Bengali settlers, as well as occasional abuses by security forces. Roughly 230,000 ethnic Rohingyas who fled forced labor, discrimination, and other abuses in Burma in the early 1990s remain in Bangladesh and are subject to some harassment. In June 2012, authorities began turning away Rohingya and other refugees seeking to escape new outbreaks of ethnic and sectarian violence in Burma, and in August officials suspended the activities of international aid organizations providing humanitarian assistance to the refugees, claiming that such aid was encouraging further influxes. However, refugees continued to cross over the Burma-Bangladesh border in 2013.

A criminal ban on homosexual acts is rarely enforced, but societal discrimination remains the norm, and dozens of attacks on LGBT individuals are reported every year. Transgender people face persecution, though government-supported projects have recently attempted to integrate this group into mainstream society. In November 2013, the government announced that it would officially consider transgender people to be a separate, third gender.

G. Personal Autonomy and Individual Rights: 9 / 16

The ability to move within the country is relatively free, as is foreign travel, with the exception of travel to Israel, which is not permitted.

Land rights for the Hindu minority remain tenuous. The 2011 Vested Properties Return Act allows Hindus to reclaim land that was seized from them by the government or other individuals. However, human rights groups have critiqued the government for its slow implementation of the law. Tribal minorities have little control over land decisions affecting them, and Bengali-speaking settlers continue to illegally encroach on tribal lands in the CHT. In 2009 the AL government announced plans to set up a commission that would allocate land to indigenous tribes, but the panel's activities have suffered from delays and interruptions, and it has not addressed land disputes effectively.

Property rights are unevenly enforced, and the ability to engage freely in private economic activity is somewhat constrained. Business activities throughout the country are hindered by corruption and bribery, inadequate infrastructure, and official bureaucracy and regulatory hurdles, according to the Global Competitiveness Report. State involvement and interference in the economy is considerable.

Child labor is widespread. Worker grievances fuel unrest at factories, particularly in the rapidly expanding and lucrative garment industry, where strikes and protests against low wages and unsafe working conditions are common. In April 2013, more than 1,100 workers were killed when a factory building collapsed on the outskirts of Dhaka, prompting some foreign companies to cease sourcing production in the country and others to push for improved working conditions. However, reforms of the system are hampered by the fact that a growing number of factory owners are also members of Parliament or owners of influential media outlets.

Under the personal status laws affecting all religious communities, women have fewer marriage, divorce, and inheritance rights than men, which increases their socioeconomic insecurity, according to a September 2012 Human Rights Watch report. However, Parliament that month passed the Hindu Marriage Bill, which aims to grant legal and social protection to members of the Hindu community, particularly women. In rural areas, religious leaders sometimes impose flogging and other extrajudicial punishments on women accused of violating strict moral codes, despite Supreme Court orders calling on the government to stop such practices. Women also face discrimination in health care, education, and employment. In 2013, Islamic clergy and women's groups remained at loggerheads over implementation of the National Women Development Policy, which holds that women and men should have equal political, social, and economic rights.

Rape, dowry-related assaults, acid throwing, and other forms of violence against women occur regularly. A law requiring rape victims to file police reports and obtain medical certificates within 24 hours of the crime in order to press charges prevents most cases from reaching the courts. Police also accept bribes to quash rape cases and rarely enforce existing laws protecting women. The Acid Survivors Foundation (ASF), a local NGO, recorded 69 acid attacks during 2013; they affected 85 victims, most of them women. While attacks have declined since the passage of the Acid Crime Prevention Act in 2002, investigations remain inadequate. A 2010 law offers greater protection to women and children from domestic violence, including both physical and mental abuse. Giving or receiving dowry is a criminal offense, but coercive requests remain a problem, as does the country's high rate of early marriage. Odhikar noted a decrease in dowry-related violence against women in 2013, with around 150 murders recorded during the year.

Women and children are trafficked both overseas and within the country for the purposes of domestic servitude or sexual exploitation, while men are trafficked primarily for labor abroad. The government has taken steps to raise awareness and prosecute sex traffickers somewhat more vigorously, with dozens convicted each year and some sentenced to life in prison. A comprehensive antitrafficking law, passed by Parliament in 2012 and finally approved by the cabinet in August 2013, would provide further protection to male as well as female victims, and increased penalties for traffickers.

Barbados

Political Rights Rating: 1
Civil Liberties Rating: 1
Freedom Rating: 1.0
Freedom Status: Free
Electoral Democracy: Yes

Population: 253,269
Capital: Bridgetown

Ten-Year Ratings Timeline For Year Under Review (Political Rights, Civil Liberties, Status)

Year Under Review	2004	2005	2006	2007	2008	2009	2010	2011	2012	2013
Rating	1,1,F	1,1,F	1,1,F	1,1,F	1,1,F	1,1,F	1,1,F	1,1,F	1,1,F	1,1,F

INTRODUCTION

In February 2013, elections confirmed Freundel Stuart of the ruling Democratic Labour Party (DLP) as prime minister, albeit with a very narrow majority. Stuart had assumed the post in 2010 following the death of then prime minister David Thompson.

Barbados continued to grapple with the impact of the global recession, with a sluggish economy and high crime rate. The tourist arrival rate dropped by 6.3 percent in 2013. Central government debt rose to 94 percent of GDP in September 2013, thus putting enormous strain on the economy. The island nation currently uses more than 13 percent of government revenues to service its debt.

POLITICAL RIGHTS: 40 / 40
A. Electoral Process: 12 / 12

Members of the 30-member House of Assembly, the lower house of the bicameral Parliament, are directly elected for five-year terms. The governor general, who represents the British monarch as head of state, appoints the 21 members of the Senate: 12 on the advice of the prime minister, 2 on the advice of the leader of the opposition, and the remaining 7 at his own discretion. The prime minister is appointed by the governor general and is usually the leader of the political party with a majority in the House.

Elections were held on February 21, 2013. In a narrow win, the ruling DLP won 16 of 30 seats in the House of Assembly. The Barbados Labour Party (BLP), under former prime minister Owen Arthur, took the remaining 14 seats.

B. Political Pluralism and Participation: 16 / 16

Political parties are free to organize. Historically, power has alternated between two centrist parties, the DLP and the BLP. Other political organizations without representation in Parliament include the People's Empowerment Party, an opposition force favoring trade union rights and greater state intervention in the economy.

C. Functioning of Government: 12 / 12

Barbados is largely free from governmental corruption. The country was ranked 15 out of 177 countries and territories surveyed in Transparency International's 2013 Corruption Perceptions Index.

CIVIL LIBERTIES: 59 / 60
D. Freedom of Expression and Belief: 16 / 16

Freedom of expression is respected. Public opinion expressed through the news media, which are free from censorship and government control, has a powerful influence on policy. Newspapers, including the two major dailies, are privately owned. Four private and two government-run radio stations operate. The single broadcast television station, operated by the government-owned Caribbean Broadcasting Corporation, presents a wide range of political viewpoints. The DLP has so far failed to make good on its promise to introduce a new Freedom of Information Act. Access to the internet is not restricted.

The constitution guarantees freedom of religion, which is widely respected for mainstream religious groups. However, members of Barbados's small Rastafarian community have protested prison regulations that require inmates to have their long dreadlocks cut off while in detention, and have also reported discrimination in the areas of education and employment. Academic freedom is fully respected.

E. Associational and Organizational Rights: 12 / 12

Barbados's legal framework provides important guarantees for freedom of assembly, which are upheld in practice. The right to form civic organizations and labor unions is respected. Two major labor unions, as well as various smaller ones, are active.

F. Rule of Law: 16 / 16

The judicial system is independent, and the Supreme Court includes a high court and a court of appeals. Barbados has ratified the Caribbean Court of Justice as its highest appellate court. There are occasional reports and complaints of the use of excessive force by the Royal Barbados Police Force to extract confessions, along with reports that police do not always seek warrants before searching homes.

Barbados has been more successful than other Caribbean countries in combating violent crime, though the crime rate in 2013 remained at high levels. The drug trade continues to be an important problem for Barbados, as the island has become a transshipment point for cocaine originating from Venezuela.

The government has taken some positive steps to address overcrowding in the prison system and to discharge prison personnel accused of beating inmates, but there has not been substantial progress in their prosecution. Although the death penalty remains mandatory for certain capital crimes, it has not been implemented since 1984. In October 2011, the government announced plans to update the Corporal Punishment Act, the Juvenile Offenders Act, and the Prevention of Cruelty Act, in response to rulings by the Inter-American Court of Human Rights that found Barbados in violation of the American Convention on Human Rights; however, no steps had been taken by the end of 2013.

Barbadian authorities have been criticized for excessively restrictive migration policies, including the treatment of foreign nationals at airports. In several separate cases, visitors from Jamaica claim to have been sexually abused and even raped by Barbadian immigration officers. In October 2013, the Caribbean Court of Justice ruled in favor of Jamaican Shanique Myrie, deciding that Barbados had violated her rights of entry as stipulated in the Treaty of Chaguaramas (which established the Caribbean Community). Myrie was subjected to a body cavity search upon arrival in Barbados and then deported. Barbados was ordered to pay approximately 77,000 Barbadian dollars (US$39,000) in damages.

G. Personal Autonomy and Individual Rights: 15 / 16

Women comprise roughly half of the country's workforce, although the World Economic Forum reported that in 2013 women earned 25 percent less than men for comparable work. Women are underrepresented in the political sphere, comprising only 17 percent of the elected House. Violence against and abuse of women continues to be widespread despite domestic violence laws, and police responsiveness is often slow and inadequate. The United States has kept Barbados on its Tier 2 Watch List for human trafficking because the island nation does not fully comply with minimum standards, a claim which the Barbadian government has disputed.

Human rights groups have criticized Barbados for some of the harshest laws against same-sex sexual activity in the Western Hemisphere, which effectively put the country in violation of its obligations under the American Convention on Human Rights. Although Barbados has not repealed these laws since the United Nations' 2008 Universal Periodic Review (UPR) recommended it do so, the 2013 UPR did not mention the laws.

Belarus

Political Rights Rating: 7
Civil Liberties Rating: 6
Freedom Rating: 6.5
Freedom Status: Not Free
Electoral Democracy: No

Population: 9,463,000
Capital: Minsk

Ten-Year Ratings Timeline For Year Under Review (Political Rights, Civil Liberties, Status)

Year Under Review	2004	2005	2006	2007	2008	2009	2010	2011	2012	2013
Rating	7,6,NF	7,6,NF	7,6,NF	7,6,NF	7,6,NF	7,6,NF	7,6,NF	7,6,NF	7,6,NF	7,6,NF

INTRODUCTION

President Alyaksandr Lukashenka, in power since 1994, continued to preside over an authoritarian system that crushes political dissent while offering citizens a basic, if increasingly unstable, standard of living. The country faced a precarious economic situation in 2013, with ongoing European Union sanctions against key regime figures, Russian pressure on Belarusian state-owned firms like Belaruskali, and a reduction in Russian oil and gas subsidies late in the year. Belarus depends heavily on Russian economic support; the oil and gas subsidies comprised 15.9 percent of its gross domestic product as of 2012. Russia had already acquired, in 2011, full control of the Belarusian pipelines carrying Russian energy exports to Europe. Chinese investors have also attempted to use Belarus as a foothold for access to European markets, and are building a new industrial complex outside of Minsk. Meanwhile, Belarus has sought to develop a gambling industry, as Russia and other countries in the region have curtailed their own gaming sectors.

POLITICAL RIGHTS: 4 / 40

A. Electoral Process: 0 / 12

The president is elected for five-year terms, and there are no term limits. The 110 members of the Chamber of Representatives, the lower house of the rubber-stamp National Assembly, are popularly elected for four years from single-mandate constituencies. The upper house, the Council of the Republic, consists of 64 members serving four-year terms; 56 are elected by regional councils and 8 are appointed by the president.

Serious and widespread irregularities have marred all recent elections. In December 2010, Lukashenka won a fourth term in a deeply flawed presidential vote, though some opposition candidates were allowed to run. When approximately 15,000 protesters turned out to question the legitimacy of the balloting, the authorities arrested more than 700 people, including seven of the nine opposition presidential candidates, and many of them remained in jail for long periods. Three of the former candidates were later sentenced to prison terms ranging from five to six years.

During the 2012 parliamentary elections, the authorities blocked key opposition figures from running for office, harassed critics of the regime, denied the opposition access to the media, failed to administer the elections fairly, and prevented observers from independently verifying the vote count. Further, the regime pressured workers at state-owned enterprises to participate in the process. No opposition candidates won seats.

The legal framework for the elections does not meet democratic standards. Most members of the election commissions support Lukashenka.

B. Political Pluralism and Participation: 3 / 16

There is no official progovernment political party. Opposition parties have no representation in the National Assembly, and most lawmakers are unaffiliated with any party. Lukashenka systematically destroys any potential alternative to his rule—a poll in September 2013 found that 81.5 percent of respondents could not name a candidate who could compete successfully with him in presidential elections. Most people have no idea who actually sits in the parliament.

At the end of 2013, the authorities continued to hold 10 political prisoners, including Ales Byalyatski, leader of the Viasna human rights group; former opposition presidential candidate Mikalay Statkevich; Eduard Lobau, of the unregistered Young Front political movement; and entrepreneur Mikalay Autukhovich. During the year, three political prisoners completed their terms: Tell the Truth campaign activist Vasil Parfyankou, Young Front leader Zmitser Dashkevich, and Belarus Christian Democracy Party cochair Pavel Sevyarynets. However, even after their release they faced multiple legal restrictions on their personal freedoms. In July, a Minsk court rescinded the two-year suspended sentence of Iryna Khalip, a prominent journalist and the wife of former Belarusian presidential candidate Andrey Sannikau, for her alleged participation in protests following the December 2010 election.

The authorities harass dissidents on a daily basis, forcing some, such as physician Ihar Pasnou, into psychiatric hospitals. Under this intense pressure, the opposition remains deeply divided on the best tactics for opposing the regime and currently has little support among the public.

C. Functioning of Government: 1 / 12

The constitution vests most power in the president, giving him control over the government, courts, and even the legislative process by stating that presidential decrees have a higher legal force than ordinary legislation.

The state controls 70 percent of the Belarusian economy, feeding widespread corruption. Graft is also encouraged by an overall lack of transparency and accountability in government. Under presidential decrees, information on the work of about 60 government ministries and state-controlled companies, including the Ministry of Information, the Minsk city executive committee, and the state broadcaster, is classified. Belarus was ranked 123 out of 177 countries surveyed in Transparency International's 2013 Corruption Perceptions Index.

CIVIL LIBERTIES: 10 / 60
D. Freedom of Expression and Belief: 3 / 16

The government systematically curtails press freedom. Libel is both a civil and a criminal offense, and a 2008 media law gives the state a monopoly over information about political, social, and economic affairs. Belarusian national television is completely under the control of the state and does not present alternative or opposition views. The state-run press distribution monopoly limits the availability of private newspapers. The authorities routinely harass and censor the remaining independent media outlets, including by using physical force, confiscating equipment, and revoking journalists' credentials. Freelancing and working for a foreign, unaccredited news outlet can be punished as criminal offenses. The authorities do allow the publication of two independent newspapers: *Nasha Niva* and *Narodnaya Volya*. During a June 2013 visit to Belarus, Dunja Mijatović, the media freedom representative of the Organization for Security and Cooperation in Europe, called on the authorities to cease detaining journalists and social media activists. She noted the chilling effect these detentions have on other journalists.

More than half of the population uses the internet daily or several times a week. Every day, more than 400,000 Belarusians—equivalent to the audience size for state television—visit news websites. The government has sought greater control over the internet through both legal and technical means. The 2008 media law subjects internet outlets to the same restrictions as traditional media, and the government owns the country's sole internet service provider. A 2010 presidential decree requires internet café owners to identify users and track their activities, and a 2012 law codified the provisions of the decree. The authorities have repeatedly blocked access to social-networking sites, such as the Russian VKontakte and U.S.-based Facebook and Twitter, while the state security service harasses online opposition activists. In April 2013, the independent news platforms Belarusian Partisan and Charter97.org, and the websites of Viasna and the Belarusian Association of Journalists, experienced the largest in a series of denial-of-service attacks. Following threats and arrests, many online editors now work from Poland and Lithuania.

Despite constitutional guarantees of religious equality, government decrees and registration requirements have increasingly restricted religious activity. Legal amendments in 2002 provided for government censorship of religious publications and barred foreigners from leading religious groups. The amendments also placed strict limitations on religious groups that have been active in Belarus for fewer than 20 years. The government in 2003 signed a concordat with the Belarusian Orthodox Church, which enjoys a privileged position. The authorities have discriminated against Protestant clergy and ignored anti-Semitic attacks.

Academic freedom is subject to intense state ideological pressures, and institutions that use a liberal curriculum or are suspected of disloyalty face harassment and liquidation. Regulations stipulate immediate dismissal and revocation of degrees for students and professors who join opposition protests. Mandatory assignment of university graduates to state-sanctioned, low-paid jobs for two years after graduation is another factor that forces many young people to pursue higher education in European universities.

Wiretapping by state security agencies limits the right to free private discussion.

E. Associational and Organizational Rights: 1 / 12

The government restricts freedom of assembly for critical independent groups. Protests and rallies require authorization from local authorities, who can arbitrarily deny permission. When public demonstrations do occur, police frequently break them up and arrest participants.

Freedom of association is severely restricted. More than a hundred of the most active nongovernmental organizations (NGOs) were forced to close down between 2003 and 2005, and participation in an unregistered or liquidated political party or organization was criminalized in 2005. Registration of groups remains selective. As a result, most human rights activists operating in the country face potential jail terms ranging from six months to two years. In the eight years since 2005, at least 18 individuals were convicted, including five who were sentenced to prison terms. Regulations introduced in 2005 ban foreign assistance to NGOs, parties, and individuals deemed to have promoted "meddling in the internal affairs" of Belarus from abroad.

Independent trade unions face harassment, and their leaders are frequently fired and prosecuted for engaging in peaceful protests. No independent trade unions have been registered since 1999. Over 90 percent of workers have fixed-term contracts; these workers can be dismissed when their contracts expire. Mandatory unpaid national work days, postgraduate employment allocation, the use of compulsory labor by addicts confined to state rehabilitation facilities, and restrictions on leaving employment in specific industries have led labor activists to conclude that all Belarusian citizens experience forced labor at some stage of their life.

F. Rule of Law: 1 / 16

Although the constitution calls for judicial independence, courts are subject to significant executive influence. The right to a fair trial is often not respected in cases with political overtones. Human rights groups continue to document instances of beatings, torture, and psychological pressure during detention in cases involving leaders of the democratic opposition. Ihar Ptsichkin, a man who had been serving a three-month jail sentence for driving without a license, died in prison in August 2013; his body reportedly showed signs of having been beaten. Several lawyers for the political opposition have been disbarred. The power to extend pretrial detention lies with a prosecutor rather than a judge, in violation of international norms.

Belarusian authorities arrested Russian businessman Vladislav Baumgertner, chief executive of the Uralkali potash company, for alleged "abuse of office" as he was returning to Russia after meeting with the prime minister in August 2013. He was imprisoned and then placed under house arrest in late September in an apartment rented for him in Minsk. Baumgertner had withdrawn Uralkali from a joint venture with Belarus's state-run potash company Belaruskali, depriving Belarus of considerable revenue. Belaruskali, the country's most profitable enterprise, had been accused of making side deals in violation of the two firms' export pricing agreement. Baumgertner was eventually allowed to return to Russia in November, after Uralkali agreed to sell a minority stake to a Belarusian businessman.

Ethnic Poles and Roma often face discrimination. Belarusian identity is under threat as well, as Russian language is taking over, especially in urban areas. In August 2013, police destroyed seven Romany homes, apparently built without permits, in the city of Zhlobin before a visit by Lukashenka. No compensation was provided. LGBT (lesbian, gay, bisexual, and transgender) people also face discrimination and regular police harassment. In February 2013, the Justice Ministry refused to register a gay rights NGO, meaning it cannot operate legally in the country.

G. Personal Autonomy and Individual Rights: 5 / 16

An internal passport system limits freedom of movement and choice of residence. In September 2013, Lukashenka proposed a $100 exit fee for shoppers who cross the border to buy better-made foreign goods, but he renounced the idea by the end of the month due to its unpopularity. Some opposition activists have been turned back at the border or detained for lengthy searches. Belarus's command economy severely limits economic freedom.

There are significant discrepancies in income between men and women, and women are poorly represented in leading government positions. Domestic and sexual violence against women were considered to be persistent and underreported, and there are no specific clauses addressing domestic violence or sexual harassment in the criminal code. As a result of extreme poverty, many women have become victims of the international sex trade.

Belgium

Political Rights Rating: 1
Civil Liberties Rating: 1
Freedom Rating: 1.0
Freedom Status: Free
Electoral Democracy: Yes

Population: 11,164,000
Capital: Brussels

Ten-Year Ratings Timeline For Year Under Review (Political Rights, Civil Liberties, Status)

Year Under Review	2004	2005	2006	2007	2008	2009	2010	2011	2012	2013
Rating	1,1,F	1,1,F	1,1,F	1,1,F	1,1,F	1,1,F	1,1,F	1,1,F	1,1,F	1,1,F

INTRODUCTION

King Albert II abdicated on July 21, 2013, at the age of 79, and his son, Crown Prince Philippe, 53, became king. The monarchy is largely ceremonial, although the king retained constitutional authority to mediate between parties during the process of forming a government—a role played by Albert during a 541-day political stalemate that followed 2010 parliamentary elections.

In July, Prime Minister Elio Di Rupo oversaw the completion of a state reform package that would grant more autonomy to regional and local governments in areas including welfare, labor, and health care policy. The reform was to take effect in July 2014.

Ethnic and linguistic conflicts had prompted a series of constitutional amendments in 1970, 1971, and 1993 that devolved considerable power from the central government to the three regions in the Belgian federation: French-speaking Wallonia in the south; Flemish-speaking Flanders in the north; and Brussels, the capital, where French and Flemish share the same official status. Cultural and economic differences between the regions have contributed to political rifts between Flemish and Francophone parties across the ideological spectrum, with the wealthier Flemish north seeking increased self-rule and reduced taxpayer support for the less prosperous Wallonia. Voting takes place along strict linguistic lines; with the exception of the bilingual district encompassing Brussels, parties are only permitted to run in their respective linguistic regions.

After 2010 parliamentary elections, coalition negotiations stalled over issues linked to the balance of power between Flanders and Wallonia. A deal was finally reached in November 2011, after Flemish and Francophone parties reached a compromise on the separation of the contentious Brussels-area electoral district. Di Rupo, of the Francophone Socialist Party, became the first French-speaking prime minister in more than 30 years. The next federal and regional elections were set to take place in 2014.

POLITICAL RIGHTS: 40 / 40
A. Electoral Process: 12 / 12

Belgium's Parliament consists of two houses: the House of Representatives and the Senate. The 150 members of the House are elected directly by proportional representation. There are 71 seats in the Senate, with 40 filled by direct popular vote and 31 by indirect vote. Members serve four-year terms in both houses. The prime minister, who is the leader of the majority party or coalition, is appointed by the monarch and approved by Parliament. The party system is highly fragmented, with separate Flemish and Walloon parties representing all traditional parties of the left and right.

B. Political Pluralism and Participation: 16 / 16

The separatist New Flemish Alliance (N-VA) had won 27 seats in the House of Representatives in the 2010 parliamentary elections, the most of any party, but was excluded from Di Rupo's government. Di Rupo's Francophone Socialist Party had 26 seats. The Francophone Movement for Reform held 18 seats. The Christian Democratic and Flemish (CD&V) party had 17 seats.

The xenophobic Vlaams Blok party was banned in 2004 for violating the country's antiracism laws. It changed its name to Vlaams Belang (Flemish Interest) and removed some of the more overtly racist elements from its platform. However, the party maintains its opposition to immigration and its commitment to an independent Flanders. It held 12 seats.

C. Functioning of Government: 12 / 12

Corruption is relatively rare in Belgium, which was ranked 15 out of 177 countries and territories surveyed in Transparency International's 2013 Corruption Perceptions Index. In March 2013, Finance Minister Steven Vanackere resigned over a scandal involving a January deal by a state-owned bank to buy back shares at favorable terms from two Christian labor organizations linked to Vanackere's CD&V; Vanackere admitted no wrongdoing.

CIVIL LIBERTIES: 57 / 60
D. Freedom of Expression and Belief: 15 / 16

Freedoms of speech and the press are guaranteed by the constitution and generally respected by the government. Belgians have access to numerous private media outlets. However, concentration of newspaper ownership has increased in recent decades, leaving most of the country's papers in the hands of a few corporations. Internet access is unrestricted.

Freedom of religion is protected. About half of the country's population identifies itself as Roman Catholic. However, members of a number of minority religions have complained of discrimination by the government, which has been criticized for its characterization of some non-Catholic groups as "sects." In March 2013, Foreign Minister Didier Reynders called for closer scrutiny of the preaching of Muslim clerics in Belgium, warning that some imams were preaching radical Islamist views.

In April 2010, the Chamber of Deputies approved a ban on the partial or total covering of the face in public locations; although it did not specifically mention the veils worn by some Muslim women, these were widely seen as the target. The ban took effect in July 2011. Offenders face a fine of up to €137.50 ($180) or a week in jail. In June 2013, a Belgian court sentenced a French Islamist, Brahim Bahrir, to 17 years in prison for "attempted murder for terrorist motives." He had stabbed two police officers in Brussels in June 2012, after riots earlier in June that followed the arrest of a woman who refused to remove her veil.

The government does not restrict academic freedom.

E. Associational and Organizational Rights: 12 / 12

Freedom of assembly is respected. Freedom of association is guaranteed by law, except for groups that practice discrimination "overtly and repeatedly." Employers found guilty of firing workers because of union activities are required to reinstate the workers or pay an indemnity. In February 2013, as many as 40,000 people joined a demonstration in Brussels organized by unions to protest government austerity measures, including wage and welfare benefit freezes.

F. Rule of Law: 15 / 16

The judiciary is independent, and the rule of law generally prevails in civil and criminal matters. Although conditions in prisons and detention centers meet most international standards, many continue to suffer from overcrowding.

Specific antiracism laws penalize the incitement of discrimination, acts of hatred, and violence based on race, ethnicity, or nationality. While a 2009 government decision regularized 25,000 illegal immigrants, there have been complaints about the treatment of rejected asylum seekers and illegal immigrants awaiting deportation, who can sometimes be held in unsanitary conditions in the Brussels airport for several months.

In March 2013, the federal minister for asylum and migration policy, Maggie De Block, rejected a call from Flanders integration minister Geert Bourgeois to require Roma immigrants to Flanders to undergo an integration course.

In April 2013, police raided over 45 homes across the country and arrested six men suspected of recruiting Islamist militants to join the ongoing antigovernment insurgency in Syria. The police operation targeted a group called Sharia4Belgium, which had agitated for Islamic law in Belgium until announcing that it was disbanding in October 2012.

In October 2013, Belgium extradited to the United States Nizar Trabelsi, a Tunisian man who had been held in Belgian custody since 2001. He was convicted in 2003 by a Belgian court of plotting to carry out a suicide bombing at a Belgian air base where U.S. soldiers were stationed. In September, the Council of State, Belgium's highest administrative court, had rejected Trabelsi's appeal of his extradition, in which he claimed that he would be subject to "inhumane" treatment by the United States. The Belgian government said it had received assurances from U.S. officials that Trabelsi would be tried in a civilian court rather than a military tribunal, and would not face the death penalty.

G. Personal Autonomy and Individual Rights: 15 / 16

The law provides for the free movement of citizens at home and abroad, and the government does not interfere with these rights. However, individual communities may expel Roma from city limits at the discretion of the local government. The European Court of Justice in April 2013 ruled that a Flemish law infringed on workers' freedom of movement within the European Union by requiring employers based in the region to write contracts in Dutch, even for non-Dutch-speaking employees from abroad; the law stipulated that noncompliance could result in cancellation of a contract.

The government actively promotes equality for women. The state Institute for the Equality of Men and Women is empowered to initiate sex-discrimination lawsuits. In the 2010 elections, women won about 40 percent of the seats in the Chamber of Deputies, and 37 percent of the seats in the Senate. Belgium legalized same-sex marriage in 2003, and in 2006 it gave gay and lesbian couples the right to adopt children. In 2011, Di Rupo became the country's first openly gay prime minister. Belgium is a source, destination, and transit point for trafficked persons. However, according to the U.S. State Department's 2013 Trafficking in Persons Report, the country complies fully with the minimum standards for eliminating trafficking.

In December, the Senate passed a bill that would make the country the first in the world to legalize euthanasia for terminally ill children, despite opposition from religious groups. The measure still required the approval of the House of Representatives to become law. Belgium legalized euthanasia for terminally ill adults in 2002.

⬇ Belize

Political Rights Rating: 1
Civil Liberties Rating: 2
Freedom Rating: 1.5
Freedom Status: Free
Electoral Democracy: Yes

Capital: Belmopan
Population: 333,887

Trend Arrow: Belize received a downward trend arrow due to reports of corruption across several government ministries related to the sale of passports and other documents, as well as an inadequate response by law enforcement agencies.

Ten-Year Ratings Timeline For Year Under Review (Political Rights, Civil Liberties, Status)

Year Under Review	2004	2005	2006	2007	2008	2009	2010	2011	2012	2013
Rating	1,2,F	1,2,F	1,2,F	1,2,F	1,2,F	1,2,F	1,2,F	1,2,F	1,2,F	1,2,F

INTRODUCTION

Like other Central American countries, Belize struggled with the negative effects of organized crime, gang violence, drug trafficking, and corruption in 2013. Criminal trafficking networks involved in the sale of illegal narcotics, counterfeit merchandise, timber, exotic animals, humans, and weapons were uncovered last year. Several corruption cases were uncovered, including one involving the illegal sale and distribution of Belizean nationality documents and passports to people from Asia, Africa, and the Middle East, and another involving alleged extortion from a government contractor.

POLITICAL RIGHTS: 36 / 40 (-1)
A. Electoral Process: 12 / 12

Belize achieved independence from Britain in 1981 but has remained a member of the British Commonwealth. The head of state is the British monarch, who is represented by a governor general. Members of the 31-seat House of Representatives, the lower house of the bicameral National Assembly, are directly elected for five-year terms. The 12 members of the Senate are currently appointed to five-year terms, though Belizeans voted in a 2008 referendum to change to an elected Senate following the 2012 general elections.

Control of the government has alternated between the center-right United Democratic Party (UDP) and the center-left People's United Party (PUP). The UDP swept the 2008 national elections, amid public dissatisfaction with corruption, increased taxation, and rising crime rates under a PUP government; the UDP's Dean Barrow became prime minister. The UDP narrowly held on to power in 2012 when it captured 50.4 percent of the national vote and 17 seats in the House of Representatives to the PUP's 47.5 percent and 14 seats; turnout was 73.2 percent. The PUP alleged that the elections were not free and fair, claiming that there were credible, documented reports of abuse and illegality in the electoral process. The Organization of American States' first ever Electoral Observation Mission (EOM) to Belize noted similar problems, including complaints of voter-list irregularities and concerns that party activists were electioneering outside of polling centers. Although the EOM still characterized the elections as free and fair, it did call on the government to pass campaign finance legislation, noting that political financing is unregulated in Belize.

B. Political Pluralism and Participation: 14 / 16

There are no restrictions on the right to organize political parties and the UDP and PUP participate in a competitive two-party system. The interests of Mestizo, Creole, Mayan, and Garifuna ethnic groups are generally represented in the National Assembly. One female candidate won office in the March 2012 elections; Belize had previously been the only country in the Americas where no woman served in its elected lower house of government.

C. Functioning of Government: 10 / 12 (-1)

Given the recent increase in corruption, gang violence, organized crime, and drug trafficking, there has been an inadequate response by law enforcement agencies. Government corruption is a serious and growing problem. Belize is the only country in Central America that is not a party to the UN Convention against Corruption. Since 2009, Transparency International has not had enough access to data that would allow Belize to be included on the organization's annual Corruption Perceptions Index. After running on an anti-corruption platform and winning the 2008 election, Dean Barrow's popularity suffered as the result of several corruption scandals involving members of his administration. Corruption scandals have continued in Barrow's second term. A UDP member from the Corozal District allegedly stole $50,000 from the Karl Heusner Memorial Hospital. Allegations pertaining to the misallocation of funds committed to the repair of San Estevan Road continue. The Minister of State in the Immigration Ministry, Elvin Penner, was fired from the cabinet in September after he was found to have been involved in the illegal issuance of a Belizean passport to a South Korean man who had never been to Belize and who was incarcerated in a Taiwanese jail at the time of the passport's issuance. Three immigration officers were also suspended and investigations into former deputy mayor of Belize City Eric Chang, an alleged accomplice of Penner's, are ongoing. The media has also reported on allegations that more than 150 nationality applications were also signed by Penner. In October and November, a whistleblower accused Minister of State Edmund Castro of having been involved in visa irregularities as well. The Ministry of Natural Resources was hit with allegations of questionable payments to UDP-connected individuals. In September, four employees of the Social Investment Fund (SIF) were fired and its executive director resigned amid an extortion scandal involving a contractor hired to renovate the Dangriga market.

CIVIL LIBERTIES: 51 / 60
D. Freedom of Expression and Belief: 15 / 16

Belize has a generally open media environment. The constitution guarantees freedom of the press, but there are exceptions in the interest of national security, public order, and morality. Journalists or others who question the financial disclosures of government officials may face up to three years in prison or up to US$2,500 in fines, but this law has not been applied in recent years. The Belize Broadcasting Authority has the right to prior restraint of all broadcasts for national security or emergency reasons, though this too is rarely invoked. Despite the availability of diverse sources of media, including privately owned weekly newspapers, radio and television stations, concerns over government control of the broadcast industry remain after the attempted nationalization of Belize Telemedia Limited, the country's largest telecommunications company. While the government does not restrict internet access or use, internet penetration is low due to lack of infrastructure and high costs.

Residents of Belize enjoy full freedom of religion, and academic freedom is respected.

E. Associational and Organizational Rights: 11 / 12

Freedoms of assembly and association are generally upheld, and demonstrations are usually peaceful. A large number of nongovernmental organizations are active, and labor unions remain politically influential despite their shrinking ranks. Official boards of inquiry adjudicate labor disputes, and businesses are penalized for labor-code violations. However, the government has done little to combat antiunion discrimination, and workers who are fired for organizing rarely receive compensation.

F. Rule of Law: 12 / 16

The judiciary is independent, and the rule of law is generally respected. However, concerns remain that the judicial system is vulnerable to political interference. A 2011 report by the American Bar Association scored Belize poorly on 16 out of 28 factors in evaluating its prosecutorial and criminal justice system, and it found that only one in ten murders leads to a conviction. Defendants can remain free on bail or in pretrial detention for years amid a heavy case backlog; about one-fifth of the country's detainees are awaiting trial.

Although overall crime decreased in 2013, violent crime, money laundering, gang violence, and drug trafficking remain serious concerns. Extrajudicial killings and the use of excessive force by police remain concerns, and Belizeans lack confidence in a police force they perceive as highly corrupt. Belize has been on the U.S. list of "major" drug-producing and transit countries since 2011 because of large numbers of drugs and weapons traveling across its border with Mexico and weak anticorruption measures. The government established a committee to investigate decriminalizing marijuana in 2012. Belize agreed in 2013 to share tax information with international officials. According to the International Center for Prison Studies, Belize has the world's 9th-highest prisoner-to-public ratio, with about 476 inmates per 100,000 inhabitants. Its prisons do not meet minimum international standards, although prison conditions are generally better than its neighbors.

While the government actively discourages ethnic discrimination, some Spanish-speaking immigrants in the country lack legal status and face discrimination.

G. Personal Autonomy and Individual Rights: 13 /16

The Barrow government faced criticism for its 2009 takeover of Belize Telemedia. Although the Supreme Court upheld the nationalization in 2010, the Belizean Court of Appeals ruled in June 2011 that the move was unconstitutional. The Belizean government nationalized Telemedia a second time in July 2011, believing that it had addressed the issues that the court had found to be illegal; in June 2012, however, the Court of Appeals once again found the nationalization unconstitutional. The government has appealed the Court's decision and litigation remains pending as of September 2013.

In June 2013, the government took control of the International Business Companies Registry and the International Merchant Marine Registry of Belize, both of which were being managed by a private company. The company, Belize International Services Limited, launched legal action, saying it had an agreement with the government to manage the registries until 2020; the government claimed that the agreement was invalid and resisted the characterization of the take-over as nationalization.

In a long-awaited decision on government appeals to 2007 and 2010 Supreme Court rulings, the Belizean Court of Appeals ruled in July that more than 30 Mayan communities in southern Belize have rights to their ancestral lands, but that the government is not responsible to provide documentation of that ownership or to prevent third parties from using the land. Indigenous communities continue to criticize the government's concessions that permit foreign corporations to exploit their lands.

Violence against women and children remains a serious concern, as does the prevalence of child labor in agriculture. Gender disparities are profound; Belize ranks 107 out of 136 countries on the World Economic Forum's 2013 Global Gender Gap Report.

Belize is a source, transit, and destination country for women and children trafficked for prostitution and forced labor and there is concern that Belize is emerging as a sex tourism destination.

There have been reports of discrimination against people living with HIV/AIDS, despite the government's efforts to educate the public about the illness. LGBT (lesbian, gay, bisexual, and transgender) persons face legal and societal discrimination. The Belizean government revised its gender policy in May 2013 to include sexual orientation. While female same-sex sexual activity is legal, male same-sex sexual activity is illegal and can result in 10 years' imprisonment. The Supreme Court is still considering the constitutionality of this provision. Gay and lesbian foreigners are legally prohibited from entering Belize.

⬇ Benin

Political Rights Rating: 2
Civil Liberties Rating: 2
Freedom Rating: 2.0
Freedom Status: Free
Electoral Democracy: Yes

Population: 9,645,000
Capital: Porto-Novo

Trend Arrow: Benin received a downward trend arrow due to increasing efforts by the executive to consolidate power, as demonstrated by the continued detention of alleged coup plotters despite a judge's dismissal of their charges, the placement of the judge under house arrest, and politicized bans on a number of planned demonstrations and protests throughout the year.

Ten-Year Ratings Timeline For Year Under Review (Political Rights, Civil Liberties, Status)

Year Under Review	2004	2005	2006	2007	2008	2009	2010	2011	2012	2013
Rating	2,2,F	2,2,F	2,2,F	2,2,F	2,2,F	2,2,F	2,2,F	2,2,F	2,2,F	2,2,F

INTRODUCTION

While Benin continues to be among the most stable democratic countries in West Africa, 2013 saw some deterioration in the political climate amid a scandal involving a second alleged coup attempt in two years, controversy surrounding proposed constitutional reform, and an unexpected dissolution of the government. Tensions have been increasing between President Thomas Boni Yayi and the opposition after they accused him and the Autonomous National Electoral Commission of irregularities in the 2011 presidential poll when he won his second term in office.

In March 2013, authorities claimed that they had foiled a coup attempt; they arrested the former head of Cotonou's gendarmerie company and an accountant for alleged involvement. This followed an alleged 2012 attempt to poison Yayi for which Yayi's niece, his doctor, and a former commerce minister remain in prison. Patrice Talon, a wealthy businessman and former political ally and supporter of Yayi, is accused by the administration of having coordinated both attempts. In 2012, Talon fled to France, which has so far refused administration requests to extradite him. In May, Judge Angelo Houssou dismissed the government's case against the alleged poisoners and alleged 2013 coup plotters; when Houssou later attempted to travel to Nigeria, police stopped him and seized his passport. Houssou fled to the United States in December and was seeking asylum there, saying his life had been threatened in Benin.

Controversy and robust public debate surrounded Yayi's efforts to pass constitutional amendments through the National Assembly in 2013. The president denied accusations that he would use the changes to secure another term for himself by extending the presidential term limit. Instead, his administration argued that the amendments would modernize the government and allow them to better combat corruption. Despite Benin's tradition of public consultation during periods of serious political reform, harking back to the 1990 national conference at which the current constitution was agreed upon, the attempted constitutional reform was criticized for undue haste and lack of engagement with civil society. In June, the president did not renew the mandate of Robert Dossou, the president of the Constitutional Court and an individual well known for opposing changes to the constitution. In September, the law commission of the National Assembly rejected the proposed amendments, with a number of Yayi's former allies opposing the reform.

In August 2013, Yayi made a surprise move to dismiss his cabinet, ultimately replacing about half of the ministers and eliminating the recently recreated position of prime minister, reportedly amid disagreements between the prime minister and the president. Many of the new appointments had little prior experience in the position for which they had been chosen and some of those dismissed reportedly opposed revising the constitution. The administration claimed the restructuring was in order to "breathe a new dynamic" into the government ahead of planned antipoverty reforms. In October, Yayi again restructured his cabinet, this time saying it was for technical reasons, creating one new position and drawing accusations of disorganization.

POLITICAL RIGHTS: 32 / 40
A. Electoral Process: 8 / 12

The president is elected by popular vote for up to two five-year terms and serves as both the chief of state and head of government. Delegates to the 83-member, unicameral National Assembly and the prime minister all serve four-year terms. In April 2013, a revised Electoral Code was unanimously passed in the National Assembly; its revisions included making the Electoral Commission (the CENA) a permanent body and requiring presidential candidates to prove nationality and residency of Benin. The controversial requirement in the draft code prohibiting presidential candidates from having dual nationality was removed before the final draft after heated debate in the National Assembly. However, Benin continued a long pattern of municipal elections characterized by disorganization and delay; elections scheduled for April 2013 were initially postponed to allow time for the new Electoral Code to come into effect, but had not been held by year's end.

Despite delays, serious problems with the new electronic voting system, and doubts about the performance of the Autonomous National Electoral Commission, international observers deemed the 2011 presidential and legislative polls largely free and fair. Five major opposition parties of the south united for the first time since independence to form the Build the Nation Union (UN), which fielded former prime minister Adrien Houngbédji as its candidate for president. In March 2011, Yayi was reelected with 53 percent of the vote. Houngbédji, who received 36 percent, refused to accept the results and appealed to the Constitutional Court. The court confirmed Yayi's victory, leading to mass opposition demonstrations that were dispersed with tear gas and other police violence.

Houngbédji's refusal to accept the results undermined the opposition's campaign for the April legislative polls. Yayi's coalition gained a majority, winning 49 of 83 National Assembly seats, with 41 going to his core party, the Cowrie Forces for an Emerging Benin (FCBE). This majority is enough to push through legislation but not constitutional reform, assuaging concerns that Yayi would seek to amend the constitution to allow for a third term. At the end of 2011, the position of prime minister, abolished since 1998, was reinstated.

B. Political Pluralism and Participation: 16 / 16

Historically, Benin has been divided between northern and southern ethnic groups. Yayi's support comes primarily from the north, while the main opposition parties, including Adrien Houngbedji's Democratic Renewal Party (PRD), hail primarily from the south. There are dozens of different small political parties, and they are typically allowed to operate openly regardless of ethnic or regional affiliation.

While Yayi's coalition has typically held a clear majority in the National Assembly, the links between the many disparate parties that it comprises have long been tenuous. This year's controversy over the proposed constitutional revision led a number of ministers to defect and form a new parliamentary group, weakening Yayi's hold over the legislature.

C. Functioning of Government: 8 / 12

Yayi came to power in 2006 on an anticorruption platform and subsequently enacted a number of measures to combat graft, including an internationally praised audit of 60 state-run companies. In August 2011, the National Assembly voted unanimously to pass an antigraft law, initially proposed by Yayi in 2006, which requires government employees to declare their assets when they enter and leave office, and in 2013 a National Anti-Corruption Authority (ANLC) was created. Despite these moves, Yayi has generally not lived up to his promises on corruption, and his antigraft measures have gradually deteriorated over the last few years as his tolerance for opposition appears to wane. Despite the creation of the ANLC, for example, the president directly appoints its members, posing a potential conflict of interest, and by the end of 2013 they had not yet been given the resources to carry out their mandate, despite having received a number of cases.

Yayi's unsuccessful push to revise the constitution in 2013 was criticized for a lack of transparency, particularly for his perceived attempt to accelerate the process; civil society representatives complained that there had been no public consultation process.

CIVIL LIBERTIES: 48 / 60 (-2)
Freedom of Expression and Belief: 15 / 16

Constitutional guarantees of freedom of expression are largely respected in practice, though they were more at risk around the 2011 elections as the High Authority of Broadcasting (HAAC) handed out sanctions and suspensions with particular ease. Domestic respect for the HAAC has declined since 2011, when the president appointed a new chairman whom many considered to be a Yayi partisan. In a continuation of problems for the private television station Canal 3, which in 2012 had been suspended for "undermining national unity," the director of the station was in January 2013 fined and sentenced to three months in prison for airing a press conference in which the president's former spokesman accused administration members of corruption. The spokesman was sentenced to six months in prison; however, by the end of the month, Yayi had issued a pardon for both individuals.

Libel and defamation remain criminalized in Benin, though they are rarely prosecuted. A pluralistic press publishes articles that are highly critical of both government and opposition leaders, though most media outlets receive direct financial support from politicians and few are considered genuinely independent.

The government actively seeks to ensure religious and academic freedoms. While the majority of Beninese identify themselves as either Muslim or Christian, many also practice some form of voodoo. Confrontations between religious groups are rare. Benin reportedly has the world's fastest-growing Roman Catholic population. Yayi is frequently criticized by the opposition for favoring the country's evangelical Christian population, though these criticisms are generally thought to be unfounded.

E. Associational and Organizational Rights: 11 / 12 (-1)

Freedom of assembly is respected, and requirements for permits and registration have often been ignored. Nonetheless, demonstrators encountered more problems than usual surrounding the 2011 elections, as widespread opposition demonstrations were at times violently suppressed by the police and some protesters were arrested. In 2013, a number of peaceful protests were allowed to proceed unhindered, including those organized by an opposition protest movement known as Red Wednesday. At the same time, the organizers of some planned protests said their demonstrations had been banned, including one led by opposition politicians opposing the planned constitutional amendments and another by trade unions protesting alleged fraud related to employment examinations for the Ministry of Finance.

Nongovernmental organizations and human rights groups operated freely in 2013. The right to organize and join labor unions is constitutionally guaranteed, even for government employees and civil servants. The right to strike, however, is more limited; in 2011 a new law extended a ban on the right to strike for military personnel and police officers to include customs officers and water and forestry workers. Unions played a central role in the country's democratization and were a vocal force supporting Yayi's opponent, Houngbédji, in the 2011 presidential election.

F. Rule of Law: 12 / 16 (-1)

The judiciary's independence is generally respected by the executive branch, but the courts are highly inefficient and susceptible to corruption, largely due to their serious and persistent lack of funding. Nevertheless, the Constitutional Court demonstrated remarkable independence in 2010, when it ruled on a number of complex issues regarding electoral reform, and in 2011, during a controversy that erupted when Houngbédji refused to accept the presidential election result. However in 2013, Yayi chose not to renew Dossou's mandate as president of the Constitutional Court, a decision critics claimed was connected to his opposition to constitutional changes. In June, the nation's judges went on strike for 72 hours to protest the treatment of Houssou, the judge who dismissed the government's cases against the alleged poisoners and coup plotters, and to draw attention to what they called Yayi's "provocative" appointment of a number of new judges. In November 2013, lawyers for the government filed a complaint against Houssou at the Supreme Court, accusing him of illegally attempting to leave the country. By the end of the year Houssou had applied for and been granted asylum in the United States.

Prisons are harsh and overcrowded, and criminal cases are rarely processed in a timely manner. In 2012, Benin ratified an international treaty indicating its commitment to abolish the death penalty. A new Code of Criminal Procedure was passed by the National Assembly in March 2012, but in August the Constitutional Court concluded that provisions for the death penalty that it contained were unconstitutional. The National Assembly amended the code, which was finally promulgated by Yayi in March 2013. There have been no executions in Benin for 26 years. The new code also bans torture as a sentence for a crime, though it may still be permissible as a disciplinary measure in jails.

Relations among Benin's ethnic groups are generally amicable, although regional divisions occasionally flare up, particularly between the north and south. Minority ethnic groups are well represented in government agencies, the civil service, and the armed forces. Constitutional restrictions prohibiting discrimination based on race, gender, and disability are in place, but these are not extended to sexual orientation. Nonetheless, the only law directly restricting homosexuality is the Penal Code of 1996 that imposes a higher age restriction on the age of consent for same-sex sexual activity (21) than for heterosexual activity (13).

G. Personal Autonomy and Individual Rights: 10 / 16

Due to the high level of poverty economic activity continues to be restricted. But gradual improvements have been seen since 2010 in the bureaucracy around starting a business. In 2013 for example, the government reduced some of the fees associated with the process, streamlining commercial registry into one place, and reducing the confusion and costs associated with the starting a company.

Although the constitution provides for gender equality and a national gender promotion policy aims to achieve gender equality by 2025, women enjoy fewer educational and employment opportunities than men, particularly in rural areas. A family code promulgated in 2004 improved women's inheritance, property, and marriage rights, and prohibited forced marriage and female genital mutilation, but these laws have not been well enforced. Women hold only 8 of the total 83 seats in the National Assembly, down from 11 in the previous Assembly.

Human trafficking is widespread in Benin; the vast majority of victims are girls trafficked inside the country from rural to urban areas. A law formally outlawing the trafficking of children was passed in 2006, but there is no legislation specifically addressing the trafficking of adults. In the Walk Free Foundation's 2013 Global Slavery Index, Benin was ranked as having the world's seventh-highest prevalence of enslaved people per capita.

Bhutan

Political Rights Rating: 3
Civil Liberties Rating: 4
Freedom Rating: 3.5
Freedom Status: Partly Free
Electoral Democracy: Yes

Population: 733,000
Capital: Thimphu

Ratings Change: Bhutan's political rights rating improved from 4 to 3 due to an increase in government transparency and a peaceful transfer of power after the opposition won parliamentary elections for the first time, and its civil liberties rating improved from 5 to 4 due to an increase in open and critical political speech, the political opposition's greater ability to hold demonstrations, and the growing independence of the judiciary.

Ten-Year Ratings Timeline For Year Under Review (Political Rights, Civil Liberties, Status)

Year Under Review	2004	2005	2006	2007	2008	2009	2010	2011	2012	2013
Rating	6,5,NF	6,5,NF	6,5,NF	6,5,NF	6,5,NF	4,5,PF	4,5,PF	4,5,PF	4,5,PF	3,4,PF

INTRODUCTION

The opposition party won national parliamentary elections in 2013, and the first transfer of parliamentary power to an opposition party in Bhutan's history followed. In the run-up to the elections, Bhutanese voters apparently had been angered by the country's economic dependence on India, and by the ruling party's focus on promoting the concept of "gross national happiness" in international forums rather than attending to the economic needs of the country's residents.

As Bhutan's democracy has become more consolidated following a recent transition to a constitutional monarchy, other aspects of its political culture have become freer as well. The media environment has become increasingly liberalized, adding to a climate of free expression. In 2013, the country drafted a freedom of information law that would force government officials and ministries to operate more transparently, putting the onus on ministries to publish information about their decisions. It had yet to pass at year's end.

The freer media climate and more competitive politics have also resulted in greater condemnation of corruption. In 2013, the home minister and speaker of parliament were convicted of corruption charges in a landmark case.

POLITICAL RIGHTS: 28 / 40 (+6)

A. Electoral Process: 10 / 12 (+2)

The constitution provides for a bicameral Parliament, with a 25-seat upper house, the nonpartisan National Council, and a 47-seat lower house, the National Assembly. Members of both bodies serve five-year terms. The current king, Jigme Khesar Namgyel Wangchuck, formally succeeded his father as king in November 2008, though he had been in power since the outgoing king's abdication in 2006. The monarchy remains highly popular with the public. The king appoints 5 members of the National Council, and the remaining 20 are elected; the lower house is entirely elected, and the head of the majority party is nominated by the king to serve as prime minister.

The logistics of voting and vote counting remain heavily dependent on expertise and technology from India. In the 2013 parliamentary elections, held over two rounds in May and July, the opposition People's Democratic Party won 32 of 47 seats. The Druk Peace and Prosperity Party had dominated the first national elections in 2008, winning 45 seats in Parliament, but in 2013 it won only 15 seats. International monitors deemed the 2013 national elections free and fair, and had also deemed the 2012 local elections free and fair. Although the 2013 national elections created uncertainty, the free vote and peaceful transfer of power were seen as signs of a healthy democratic system.

B. Political Pluralism and Participation: 10 / 16 (+2)

Political parties, previously illegal, were allowed to begin registering in 2007, and Bhutan now has two major parties and at least two smaller ones. Although the law officially bars clergy from voting, monks and other religious leaders voted in previous elections. While international monitors have deemed recent elections free and fair, they have also noted that Nepali speakers have been turned away from voting. No party exists to represent Nepali speakers. Bhutan's electoral rules stipulate that political parties must not be limited to members of any regional or demographic group.

Participation was relatively low for local elections held in 2011 and 2012, due partly to voter apathy and distrust that the polls would result in concrete change. Low turnout had also been attributed to the remoteness of parts of Bhutan, where officials and voters had to walk for miles to reach polling stations. However, turnout for the 2013 national elections was high—it was estimated at about 80 percent of eligible voters, roughly the same as for the 2008 parliamentary polls.

C. Functioning of Government: 9 / 12 (+2)

Bhutan has in recent years made a rapid transition from a system in which the monarch and his advisers had enormous influence over the elected Parliament to one in which the elected Parliament determines its own policies. Although the king still has some influence over ministerial positions, in general the party in control of Parliament now selects its own cabinet, and staffs it with its own choices for ministerial posts. The cabinet has increasingly taken on the role of governing, not deferring to the monarch for guidance on most issues, though Bhutan still relies on India for defense and many foreign policy issues. The king remains the head of state and retains the right to appoint some members of the Supreme Court and the heads of national commissions.

Although corruption exists in Bhutan, the country has in recent years made significant strides in addressing graft by senior government officials. Courts have pursued and won cases against some of the most powerful political elites in the country, setting examples for lower-ranking officials; these types of prosecutions would not have occurred even five years ago. In March 2013, a district court convicted Home Minister Minjur Dorji and National Assembly speaker Jigme Tshultim of corruption charges related to the improper distribution of land; they were sentenced to one year and two and a half years in prison, respectively. The court also ordered that the plots they had illegally distributed be returned to the government.

In the fall of 2013, Bhutan published a draft right to information law that would guarantee greater government transparency and put the onus on government officials and agencies to release information about every major decision to the public. It had not yet been passed at year's end. The 2006 Anti-Corruption Act established whistleblower protections, and the Anti-Corruption Commission (ACC) is tasked with investigating and preventing graft. In 2011, the National Assembly passed an anticorruption law that strengthened and expanded the ACC's mandate. Bhutan was ranked 31 out of 177 countries and territories surveyed in Transparency International's 2013 Corruption Perceptions Index.

Discretionary Political Rights Question B: -1 / 0

The Bhutanese government has for decades attempted to diminish and repress the rights of ethnic Nepalis, and to force many of them to leave the country, changing the makeup of the population of the country.

The government expelled a large percentage of Nepali speakers in the early 1990s, after previously stripping them of their citizenship. Many fled to Nepal as refugees. The government maintains that many Nepali speakers left Bhutan voluntarily or had been illegal immigrants. At the high point, over 108,000 such refugees lived in extremely poor conditions in Nepal and were denied reentry to Bhutan. A resettlement effort aimed at transferring the refugees to third countries began in 2007. According to the Office of the UN High Commissioner for Refugees (UNHCR), by the end of 2013 roughly 80,000 of the refugees had been resettled in third countries, with the majority resettled in the United States. About 38,100 refugees from Bhutan remain in Nepal's camps.

CIVIL LIBERTIES: 27 / 60 (+3)

D. Freedom of Expression and Belief: 9 / 16 (+1)

The law protects freedom of speech and of the press. However, defamation can carry criminal penalties, and a 1992 law prohibits criticism of the king and has strict provisions on "words either spoken or written that undermine or attempt to undermine the security and sovereignty of Bhutan by creating or attempting to create hatred and disaffection among the people." Journalists sometimes practice self-censorship, although not as much as in the past, and have had difficulty obtaining information from government bodies.

State media dominated press coverage prior to the start of reforms under which Bhutan shifted to a constitutional monarchy. A 2006 media law led to the establishment of two independent radio stations. Since then, the government has liberalized the issuing of media licenses, allowing more outlets to emerge. The state-owned *Kuensel* and two independent weeklies, the *Bhutan Times* and the *Bhutan Observer*, generally publish progovernment articles; they are allegedly favored with advertising revenue by the government and government-linked companies. Independent media outlets in general depend heavily on revenue from government advertising. Many newspapers struggle to make enough money to operate, with financial problems recently exacerbated by a decrease in readership following the elections. The internet is accessed by about 30 percent of Bhutan's population, a figure that is growing significantly every year.

The constitution protects freedom of religion. While Bhutanese of all faiths can worship relatively freely, the Drukpa Kagyupa school of Mahayana Buddhism is the official religion and reportedly receives various state subsidies. The Christian minority has allegedly been subject to harassment by the authorities in the past, and permits for the construction of Hindu temples are apparently difficult to obtain. Few restrictions on academic freedom have been reported, though nongovernmental organizations (NGOs) claim that the teaching of Nepali and Sanskrit is banned.

E. Associational and Organizational Rights: 4 / 12 (+1)

The constitution guarantees freedom of assembly, but the government must approve the purpose of any protests, and often does not, essentially restricting demonstrations. Citizens must get government approval to form political parties and hold political rallies, and this approval process seriously restricts party organization. However, small antigovernment gatherings appeared in urban areas in the run-up to the 2013 elections. In recent years, security forces have arrested Bhutanese refugees based in Nepal who entered Bhutan to demonstrate for the right to return home.

NGOs that work on issues related to ethnic Nepalis are not allowed to operate, but other local and international NGOs increasingly have worked freely. Under the 2007 Civil Society Organization Act, all new NGOs must register with the government. The constitution protects the right of workers to form associations, but not for the purpose of conducting strikes. Most of the country's workforce is engaged in subsistence agriculture.

F. Rule of Law: 6 / 16 (+1)

Since 2007, Bhutan has moved decisively away from a traditional monarchy and toward a constitutional and judicial-based rule of law and a constitutional monarchy. An independent Judicial Service Council created in 2007 controls judicial appointments and promotions. Until a new Supreme Court was finally seated in early 2010, the king served as the final arbiter of appeals, but the Supreme Court now does so. The judiciary is generally considered independent.

The civilian police force generally operates within the law. Prisons in Bhutan for the most part meet international standards. There are dozens of political prisoners being held in the country, according to NGOs. This is a decrease from the hundreds of prisoners kept behind bars in the past; most were jailed for being part of banned political groups from the past, such as the local communist party or parties that advocated for rights for ethnic Nepalis.

The Nepalese minority population, as well as people with disabilities, face significant discrimination. LGBT (lesbian, gay, bisexual, and transgender) individuals also face discrimination, though one Bhutanese NGO represents LGBT people.

G. Personal Autonomy and Individual Rights: 8 / 16

The government requires that Bhutanese wear traditional dress on certain occasions and at certain times. Women participate freely in social and economic life but continue to be underrepresented in government and politics. Domestic violence is problematic, and rapes are underreported. In 2013, the legislature approved the Domestic Violence Prevention Act, which allows the National Commission for Women and Children (NCWC) more freedom to create programs that address the problem.

Bolivia

Political Rights Rating: 3
Civil Liberties Rating: 3
Freedom Rating: 3.0
Freedom Status: Partly Free
Electoral Democracy: Yes

Population: 11,000,000
Capital: La Paz (administrative), Sucre (judicial)

Ten-Year Ratings Timeline For Year Under Review (Political Rights, Civil Liberties, Status)

Year Under Review	2004	2005	2006	2007	2008	2009	2010	2011	2012	2013
Rating	3,3,PF	3,3,PF	3,3,PF	3,3,PF	3,3,PF	3,3,PF	3,3,PF	3,3,PF	3,3,PF	3,3,PF

INTRODUCTION

A favorable court ruling in April 2013 cleared the way for President Evo Morales to seek a third term in office in the 2014 general elections, drawing objections from opposition leaders who said such a move would be unconstitutional. Also during the year, independent media outlets continued to face threats and government pressure in response to their critical reporting, and new legislation restricted union organizing within worker cooperatives. In May, Morales announced that he was expelling the U.S. Agency for International Development (USAID) from the country, accusing it of conspiring against his government.

POLITICAL RIGHTS: 29 / 40

A. Electoral Process: 11 / 12

Bolivia is a presidential republic. The president is directly elected, and presidential and legislative terms are both five years. The Plurinational Legislative Assembly consists of a 130-member Chamber of Deputies and a 36-member Senate, in which all senators and 53 deputies are elected by proportional representation, and 70 deputies are elected in individual districts. Seven seats in the Chamber of Deputies are reserved for indigenous representatives. The 2009 constitution includes a presidential runoff provision to replace the previous system, in which the legislature had decided elections when no candidate won an outright majority.

In the 2009 presidential election, Morales was reelected with 64 percent of the vote amid a record 95 percent turnout. Monitors from the European Union characterized the election as generally free and fair, but reported some misuse of state resources, a complaint echoed by opposition leaders. Some opposition members also claimed they were targeted with criminal investigations, causing them to flee the country.

Morales's Movement for Socialism (MAS) party also dominated the 2009 legislative elections, taking 88 seats in the lower house and 26 seats in the Senate. The right-leaning Plan Progress for Bolivia–National Convergence (PPB-CN) placed second with 37 deputies and 10 senators, followed by the National Unity Front with three deputies and the Social Alliance with two. Meanwhile, the remainder of Bolivia's nine departments approved regional autonomy statutes, joining four that had already done so in 2006. In April 2010 regional elections, MAS candidates won governorships in six of the nine departments, but opposition candidates from the left and right became mayors in 7 of the 10 principal cities.

In a controversial April 2013 ruling, the Plurinational Constitutional Tribunal determined that Morales's first term in office did not count toward the constitutionally mandated two-term limit, since it had begun before the current constitution was adopted. The ruling allows Morales to run for a third term in office in the 2014 election.

B. Political Pluralism and Participation: 11 / 16

Citizens have the right to organize political parties. The MAS draws support from a diverse range of social movements, unions, and civil society actors. Since the election of Morales in 2005, the country's traditional political parties have all but collapsed, giving way to a series of new formations and short-lived opposition coalitions. Following the 2010 local and regional elections, the Movement Without Fear party—a group previously allied with the MAS and led by former La Paz mayor Juan del Granado—emerged as a centrist alternative to the ruling party. As of December 2013, the Supreme Electoral Tribunal reported that 14 political parties, one political alliance, and two citizen political organizations were legally recognized.

There are some allegations that prosecutions against members of the opposition are politically motivated. In a high-profile case, opposition senator Roger Pinto Molina sought and was granted political asylum by the Brazilian government in 2012. He faced corruption and other criminal charges after he denounced corruption in the government. Pinto spent 15 months in the Brazilian embassy in La Paz because the Morales administration refused safe passage across the Bolivian border, but he escaped to Brazil in August 2013.

C. Functioning of Government: 7 / 12

Corruption remains a problem in Bolivia, affecting a range of government entities and economic sectors, including extractive industries. Anticorruption legislation enacted in 2010 has been criticized for permitting retroactive enforcement. The government has established an Anti-Corruption Ministry, outlined policies to combat corruption, and opened investigations into official corruption cases. In 2011, legislators voted to prosecute former presidents Gonzalo Sánchez de Lozada and Jorge Quiroga for approving hydrocarbon contracts that are alleged to have contravened national interests. Three former ministers were also included in the indictment. In September 2012, the U.S. government announced that it would not extradite Sánchez de Lozada. In October 2013, the prosecutor filed corruption charges and requested house arrest for Quiroga. Separately, corruption of law enforcement bodies in connection with the illegal drug trade has been a long-standing problem. Bolivia was ranked 106 out of 177 countries and territories surveyed in Transparency International's 2013 Corruption Perceptions Index.

CIVIL LIBERTIES: 38 / 60 (-2)
D. Freedom of Expression and Belief: 14 / 16

Although the constitution guarantees freedom of expression, the media are subject to some limitations in practice. Press associations have complained that the language of a 2010 antiracism law is vague and contributes to a climate of self-censorship. In particularly serious cases, the law allows publication of racist or discriminatory ideas to be punished with fines, the loss of broadcast licenses, and prison sentences of up to five years. In many instances a public apology can result in the waiver of such sanctions. In February 2011, the government created a Ministry of Communications, raising hopes that the "right to communication" established in the new constitution would be enforced. Since the ministry's establishment, however, two successive ministers have failed to promote the passage of a law to that end, leaving in question the constitution's guarantee of freedom of expression.

Most media outlets are privately owned, and radio is the leading source of information. The print sector has undergone a wave of consolidation and the closing of some newspapers. Online media are growing in importance as a source of news. Many private newspapers and television stations feature opposition rather than progovernment opinion pieces; the opposite holds true in state media. The 2011 telecommunications law aims to allocate 33 percent of all broadcast licenses to state-run media, another 33 percent to commercial broadcasters, and 17 percent each to local communities and indigenous groups.

Journalists and independent media operate in a somewhat hostile environment, and attacks continued to be reported in 2013. In May, amid clashes between supporters and detractors of the mayor of Caranavi, protesters broke into the offices of community radio station La Voz de la Mayoría, threatened a reporter, and destroyed equipment. In October, Marianela Montenegro, a journalist and owner of Canal 33 in Cochabamba, presented a complaint to the Inter-American Commission on Human Rights alleging that she had received threats and been harassed by the government in response to criticism aired on her station. Also during the year, some government officials accused the newspaper *Página Siete*, which reports aggressively on official corruption, of serving Chilean interests in Bolivia's territorial dispute with that country; in 2012, the paper was the subject of a government lawsuit for allegedly inciting racism through its reporting on a speech by Morales.

In 2012, the Constitutional Tribunal struck down Article 162 of the penal code, which made it a crime to criticize a government official in the exercise of his or her office. The decision brought Bolivia into accordance on this issue with three international conventions ratified by the government: the Universal Declaration of Human Rights, the American Convention on Human Rights, and the International Covenant on Civil and Political Rights.

Freedom of religion is guaranteed by the constitution. The 2009 constitution ended the Roman Catholic Church's official status and created a secular state. The government does not restrict academic freedom.

E. Associational and Organizational Rights: 9 / 12 (-1)

Bolivian law provides for the rights of peaceful assembly and freedom of association, though protests sometimes turn violent. The Morales government has been highly critical of nongovernmental organizations, especially those that supported 2011 indigenous protests that resulted in a police crackdown.

The right to form labor unions is guaranteed by the constitution. Labor and peasant unions are an active force in society and have significant political influence. In April 2013, Bolivia ratified the International Labour Organization's 2011 Domestic Workers Convention. Also that month, a new law established regulations for workers' cooperatives—nonprofit organizations created on a voluntary basis by autonomous workers who simultaneously own the organizations. Among other provisions, the measure prevents members of cooperatives dedicated to production, services, and public services from joining a union in that cooperative. Critics have pointed out that this rule violates the right to association.

F. Rule of Law: 6 / 16 (-1)

The judicial system has faced ongoing systemic challenges in recent years. Judicial elections were held in 2011 to remedy a crisis in the judicial branch, which had been rocked by resignations, charges of corruption, and a backlog of cases. The elections were marred by procedural problems and voter discontent. Candidates for the Supreme Court, the Constitutional Tribunal, and other entities were nominated through a two-thirds vote in the legislature, which allowed the MAS to dominate the selection process. Election officials ruled that candidates were not permitted to campaign openly, and that information about the candidates would be disseminated through official channels. In results that were interpreted as a defeat for the government, voters cast null ballots in numbers that exceeded the overall valid vote. Nevertheless, 56 new high court judges took office in January 2012, and Bolivia became the first country in Latin America to swear in elected judges to its highest tribunals. The Constitutional Tribunal's contentious 2013 decision to allow Morales to seek a third presidential term was interpreted as a sign of political bias among the new justices.

The country's courts continue to face a daunting caseload. Prosecutorial independence is viewed as weak, and enforcement at times focuses on opposition members and sympathizers, with former presidents and many opposition politicians facing charges ranging from graft to treason.

Bolivian prisons are overcrowded, and conditions for prisoners are extremely poor. In October 2013, the minister of justice reported to the UN Human Rights Committee that about 20 percent of inmates had been sentenced, while the remaining 80 percent were in pretrial detention. Trial dates are frequently postponed. A 1988 law passed at the urging of the United States that substantially lengthened prison sentences for drug-related crimes has contributed to prison overcrowding, as has an increase in urban crime rates. In response to overcrowding, the government approved a pardon in 2012, but found that the results were not satisfactory. A new pardon issued in September 2013, set to last for a year, authorized a number of categories of prisoners, including women with children, to apply for release.

While the 2009 constitution and jurisdictional law recognize indigenous customary law regarding conflict resolution, reform efforts have not fully resolved questions pertaining to the jurisdiction and proper application of indigenous customary law. This lack of clarity has allowed some perpetrators of vigilante crimes, including lynching, to misrepresent their actions as a form of indigenous justice. A February 2012 report by the UN Office of the High Commissioner for Human Rights stated that lynchings had substantially decreased over the previous two years, though violent extrajudicial punishment remains a problem in many parts of Bolivia.

Bolivia is the world's third-largest producer of the coca leaf, after Colombia and Peru. By law, 12,000 hectares of land are designated for the legal cultivation of the crop, although a study on local coca consumption released in November 2013 and partially financed by the European Union suggests that the limit of legal cultivation should be 14,705 hectares. In an August report, the UN Office on Drugs and Crime (UNDOC) estimated that another 25,300 hectares were used for unregulated coca production destined for the illegal cocaine trade during 2012, representing a 7 percent decrease from the previous year. UNDOC attributed the decrease to the Morales government's policies of control and eradication.

The 2009 constitution recognizes 36 indigenous nationalities, declares Bolivia a "plurinational" state—changing the official name of the country from the Republic of Bolivia to the Plurinational State of Bolivia—and formalizes local political and judicial control within indigenous territories. In general, racism is rife in the country, especially against indigenous groups. Indigenous people from the country's Andean west who move to Santa Cruz de la Sierra and some other areas in the eastern lowlands for economic reasons are subject to considerable discrimination and occasional violence, some of which involves organized armed gangs. The 2010 antiracism law contains measures to combat discrimination and imposes criminal penalties for discriminatory acts. In 2011, police violently dispersed a protest by indigenous groups opposed to a planned highway through their territory; a criminal investigation into police abuses was ongoing at the end of 2013. The government announced in April that it would postpone the highway project until the end of 2015 and focus on eliminating extreme poverty in the affected region, known as the Isiboro-Sécure Indigenous Territory and National Park (TIPNIS).

G. Personal Autonomy and Individual Rights: 9 / 16

While the law protects freedom of movement, protesters often block highways and city streets, disrupting internal travel.

The constitution prohibits discrimination based on gender and sexual orientation, but it reserves marriage only for opposite-sex couples, and there is no provision for same-sex civil unions. Women enjoy the same formal rights to property ownership as men, but discrimination is pervasive, leading to disparities in property ownership and access to resources. Women's political representation has increased in recent years. Ballot-alternation requirements resulted in women winning 44 percent of the seats in the Senate in 2009, but only 28 percent of the seats in the Chamber of Deputies. Gender-parity election rules were also applied to the 2011 judicial elections, resulting in gender parity in elected judges. Violence against women is pervasive, and the justice system is ineffective at safeguarding women's broader legal rights. A law adopted in March 2013 increased the penalties for rape and domestic abuse, among other provisions targeting violence against women. More than half of Bolivian women are believed to suffer domestic violence at some point during their lives.

Child labor and forced labor are ongoing problems. Child labor in cooperatively run mines and in agriculture is common, and a 2012 study by the United Nations reported instances of forced child labor in mining, agriculture, and the drug trade. Forced labor has also been reported on agricultural estates in the Chaco region. In 2012, authorities achieved their first forced-labor conviction. Human trafficking continues to be a problem in Bolivia. The government enacted an antitrafficking law in 2012, but the U.S. State Department's 2013 *Trafficking in Persons Report* found that implementation was lacking, placing the country on its Tier 2 Watch List.

Bosnia and Herzegovina

Political Rights Rating: 3
Civil Liberties Rating: 3
Freedom Rating: 3
Freedom Status: Partly Free
Electoral Democracy: Yes

Population: 3,800,000
Capital: Sarajevo

Ten-Year Ratings Timeline For Year Under Review (Political Rights, Civil Liberties, Status)

Year Under Review	2004	2005	2006	2007	2008	2009	2010	2011	2012	2013
Rating	4,3,PF	4,3,PF	3,3,PF	4,3,PF	4,3,PF	4,3,PF	4,3,PF	4,3,PF	3,3,PF	3,3,PF

INTRODUCTION

In the summer of 2013, the European Union (EU) suspended two aid programs to Bosnia and Herzegovina (BiH), citing the inability of the country's two entities—Bosniak-Croat Federation of Bosnia and Herzegovina (the Federation) and the Republika Srpska—to work together on preparations for receiving the assistance. The programs were worth a combined total of €9.5 million ($13.2 million). In September, the EU canceled an agriculture program due to a similar lack of progress. The following month, it canceled an additional €47 million ($65.4 million) in aid, citing leaders' failure to agree on reforms to address a 2009 European Court of Human Rights (ECHR) ruling, which had found the constitution discriminatory for allowing only members of BiH's three major ethnic groups—Bosnian Muslims (Bosniaks), Bosnian Croats, and Bosnian Serbs—to run for the state-level presidency or serve in the upper house of parliament. While several former Yugoslav constituent republics have already joined the EU or have made significant progress toward accession, BiH's political stagnation continues to impede its path toward EU membership in 2013.

BiH made some progress in anticorruption efforts during the year. Authorities broke up fraud schemes run by police and customs officers and opened investigations into alleged corruption by senior officials in the Federation, including the president.

The country's first postwar census took place in October. The results, expected in early 2014, will effectively serve as formal recognition of the ethnic cleansing that took place during the 1992–1995 civil war, which ended following the U.S.-backed Dayton Accords. Given that many political posts are awarded under a population-based ethnic quota system, Bosniak, Croat, and Serb political and religious leaders urged members of their respective ethnic groups to identify themselves as such on the census form. Citizens have the option to reject ethnic labels on the form, but doing so excludes them from holding some government positions.

POLITICAL RIGHTS: 24 / 40 (-1)
A. Electoral Process: 8 / 12

The Dayton Accords created a loosely knit nation composed of two states, or entities—the Federation, whose citizens are mainly Bosniak and Croat, and the largely Serb Republika Srpska—that operate under a weak central government. The role of head of state is performed by a three-member presidency comprising one Bosniak, one Serb, and one Croat; each is elected to a four-year term, which the three presidents serve concurrently.

The Parliamentary Assembly, a state-level body, has two chambers. The 15-seat upper house, the House of Peoples, consists of five members from each of the three main ethnic groups, elected by the Federation and Republika Srpska legislatures for four-year terms. The lower house, the House of Representatives, has 42 popularly elected members serving four-year terms, with 28 seats assigned to representatives from the Federation and 14 to representatives from the Republika Srpska. The House of Representatives elects the prime minister, who leads the state-level government. The Federation and the Republika Srpska have their own presidents, parliaments, and other governing bodies, which are responsible for policymaking on the entity level.

The most recent elections held in 2010 were deemed generally free and fair. In that year's tripartite presidential election, incumbent Željko Komšić of the Social Democratic Party (SDP) was reelected as the Croat member of the presidency, Bakir Izetbegović of the Party of Democratic Action (SDA) won the Bosniak seat, and Alliance of Independent Social Democrats (SNSD) incumbent Nebojša Radmanović was reelected as the Serb member. Hardline Bosnian Serb nationalist Milorad Dodik of the SNSD was elected president of Republika Srpska, and Živko Budimir of the Croatian Party of Rights of BiH (HSP BiH) was elected president of the Federation.

In the 2010 parliamentary elections, the SNSD remained the dominant party in the Republika Srpska's legislature, while the more moderate and largely Bosniak SDP secured a plurality of seats in the Federation's legislature. The Croat Democratic Union of BiH (HDZ BiH) remained the most popular party among Bosnian Croats.

In the 2012 local elections, the long-established nationalist parties—the SDA, the HDZ BiH, and the Serb Democratic Party (SDS)—prevailed.

B. Political Pluralism and Participation: 10 / 16 (-1)

Political parties typically organize and operate freely, though the political arena in the Federation is generally limited to Bosniaks and Croats, while Serbs dominate politics in the Republika Srpska. Recent opinion polls show deep frustration among Bosnia's residents with the country's politicians, but no viable alternatives have emerged to challenge the established parties. Coalitions at all levels of government shift frequently.

The Federation government has been in a state of crisis since in May 2012, when an alliance between the SDP and the SDA collapsed. The SDP subsequently won support from five other parties to form a parliamentary majority, but was unable to eject a number of entity-level cabinet ministers belonging to the SDA and two other parties not represented in the new parliamentary alliance. In February 2013, after several unsuccessful attempts to dismiss these ministers, the SDP-led coalition in the Federation's lower house passed a no-confidence measure against the entity-level government. The SDA blocked the motion in the upper house by invoking a constitutional mechanism that allowed them to claim that Bosniak national interests were at risk. The no-confidence measure was then referred to the Federation's Constitutional Court, which was unable to rule due to open seats on its bench. In March, the SDA blocked the appointment of a Bosniak judge to the court, again claiming the move would harm Bosniak national interests. Federation President Budimir defused some tension in July by agreeing to appoint judicial candidates acceptable to the SDA, but the court apparently had yet to rule on the no-confidence measure at year's end.

In the Republika Srpska, President Dodik ordered a government reshuffle in February, citing the entity government's failure to address poor economic conditions. Prime Minister Aleksandar Džombić was replaced by Željka Cvijanović, one of Dodik's close allies. Cvijanović took power in March, becoming Republika Srpska's first female prime minister. She emphasized a commitment to maintaining the entity's autonomy, but also stressed the importance of EU membership for both the Republika Srpska and the whole of BiH. Her position stood in contrast to Dodik's continued agitation for the Republika Srpska's independence, a notion BiH's international patrons have rejected. Many argue that Dodik's separatist rhetoric is intended to distract from the Republika Srpska's economic struggles.

In September, the SDS announced that it would withdraw from Dodik's SNSD-led, state-level coalition, citing the SNSD's announcement that it would seek the removal of a state-level SDS cabinet member.

The Office of the High Representative (OHR), which was created by the Dayton Accords, operates under the auspices of the United Nations and has the authority to remove elected officials if they are deemed to be obstructing the peace process. In recent years, the OHR has been reluctant to intervene in the country's politics.

Under the Dayton Accords, representatives from each of the three major ethnic groups, at both state and entity levels, may exercise a veto on legislation deemed harmful to their interests. As a result, Bosniaks, Serbs, and Croats must agree on major legislation before it can advance. Such consensus is rarely reached.

BiH's leaders have not enacted reforms in response to a 2009 ruling by the ECHR that the country's constitution is discriminatory for allowing only Bosniaks, Bosnian Croats, and Bosnian Serbs to run for the presidency or serve in the upper house of parliament. The provisions exclude candidates from the Jewish, Romany, and other smaller minorities, as well as those who identify simply as Bosnian. In October 2013, EU authorities moved to cut funding for the rest of 2013 by 54 percent, the equivalent of €47 million ($65.4 million), due to the government's inability to resolve to the constitution issue and after the country's leaders failed to establish a single, state-level EU liaison. EU deputy director general for enlargement Joost Korte said in December that the money had been redirected to fund projects in Kosovo, as well as regional housing initiatives.

C. Functioning of Government: 6 / 12

Corruption remains a serious problem. Enforcement of legislation designed to combat corruption has historically been weak due to the lack of strong and independent anticorruption agencies and a dearth of political will to address the issue; the country's complex institutional framework also provides many avenues for corrupt behavior among politicians. However, the country made some progress on anticorruption efforts in 2013. Budimir was arrested in April, along with several other officials, and charged with granting pardons to convicts in exchange for bribes. He was released in May after the BiH Constitutional Court ordered a revision of the earlier decision to jail him, but in November, Budimir was again indicted in connection with the scandal, this time alongside several other suspects including Justice Minister Zoran Mikulić. In June, authorities broke up a livestock smuggling scheme in Republika Srpska that involved a number of police officers. In September, a number of senior customs officials were detained on suspicion of involvement in tax evasion, customs evasion, and money laundering schemes worth millions of euros. BiH was ranked 72 of 177 countries surveyed in Transparency International's 2013 Corruption Perceptions Index.

CIVIL LIBERTIES: 37 / 60
D. Freedom of Expression and Belief: 10 / 16

The constitution and the human rights annex to the Dayton Accords provide for freedom of the press, but this right is not always respected in practice. While a large number of independent broadcast and print outlets operate, they tend to appeal to narrow ethnic audiences, and most neglect substantive or investigative reporting. The public broadcaster, BiH Radio Television (BHRT), which is designed to cater to multiethnic audiences, has faced growing political pressure in recent years. Attacks on journalists take place occasionally, and reporters have faced pressure from government officials. In September 2013, a fire was set on the office doorstep of the Sarajevo-based weekly newspaper *Slobodna Bosna*, which is known for its investigative work. That same day, graffiti threatening journalist Nermin Bise, who has covered sensitive political topics, was discovered in Mostar.

Citizens enjoy freedom of religion, but only in areas where their particular ethnic group represents a majority. In August 2013, three young Serb men in the Republika Srpska city of Zvornik attacked four Muslims, including a 73-year-old, while they were traveling to mosque on the religious holiday of Eid al-Fitr. One person was arrested in connection with the attack. Acts of vandalism against holy sites of all three major faiths continue to occur.

While the authorities do not restrict academic freedom at institutions of higher education, academic appointments are heavily politicized, with ethnic favoritism playing a significant role. Primary and secondary school curriculums are also politicized. Depending on their ethnicity, children use textbooks printed in Croatia, Serbia, or Sarajevo. In areas of the Herzegovina region, students are often divided by ethnicity, with separate classrooms, entrances, textbooks, and class times.

E. Associational and Organizational Rights: 7 / 12

The constitution provides for freedoms of assembly and association, and the various levels of government generally respect these rights in practice. Nonetheless, nongovernmental organizations—particularly those that are critical of the authorities—have faced intimidation in the past.

Although there are no legal restrictions on the right of workers to form and join labor unions, discrimination against union members persists. Unemployment in BiH is among the highest in Europe, and many workers have reportedly declined to file anti-union-related complaints with labor inspectors for fear of losing their jobs. However, courts in both the Federation and Republika Srpska frequently rule in favor of workers when faced with such cases.

F. Rule of Law: 10 / 16

The judiciary remains susceptible to influence by nationalist political parties, and faces pressure from the executive branch. The lack of a single, supreme judicial body and the existence of four separate court systems—for the central state, Republika Srpska, the Federation, and the self-governing Brčko district—contributes to overall inefficiency. The country has made some efforts to reduce its case backlog, but the number of pending in the court system cases remains high. The police do not always fully inform people of their rights upon arrest; prisons are overcrowded and prisoners sometimes face abuse. Witness protection programs are also not always available to those who need them.

The state court—which handles organized crime, war crimes, corruption, and terrorism cases—has made progress on adjudicating cases in the areas of organized crime and war crimes. However, in July 2013, the ECHR decided that a state-level court had ruled improperly when it retroactively applied the 2003 criminal code against two men convicted of war crimes in 2006 and 2007; the ECHR ruled that their crimes had been committed before 2003, and thus the 1976 criminal code—under which the men would have received lighter penalties—should have been applied. The ECHR ruled that BiH pay each man €10,000 ($13,600) in damages. In October, Bosnia's war crimes court ordered retrials for the two men, as well as another man who had also been convicted of war crimes in 2007; the ECHR ruling could result in the overturning of dozens of rulings in war crimes cases in which the 2003 criminal code was applied.

Members of the LGBT (lesbian, gay, bisexual, and transgender) community face discrimination and occasional physical attacks, as well as harassment in the country's media. Entity-level laws do not protect LGBT people from discrimination. While state-level laws do offer such protection, such measures are often disregarded.

G. Personal Autonomy and Individual Rights: 10 / 16

In a rare display of ethnic unity, thousands of people demonstrated in June in Sarajevo against the central government's failure to pass a law on citizen identification numbers; due to government inaction, children born after February 2013 were not issued identification numbers, leaving them without passports or the documentation required to receive medical care. A baby girl died in June because her parents lacked the necessary paperwork to travel abroad for treatment, sparking the protests. After months of infighting, the government in November passed a law that divided identification registration districts along the territorial lines established after the country's 1992–1995 civil war.

Individuals face discrimination in employment, housing, and social services in regions that are not dominated by their own ethnic group. Women are legally entitled to full equality with men, but are underrepresented in politics and government and face discrimination in the workplace. Sexual harassment remains problematic, and improper behavior frequently goes unpunished. Police are also largely unresponsive to violent domestic disputes, particularly in rural areas. According to the U.S. State Department, BiH is a source, destination, and transit country for men, women, and children trafficked for the purpose of prostitution and forced labor. The government does not full comply with the minimum standards for the elimination of trafficking, but has made significant efforts to do so, including improving national funding for anti-trafficking activities. However, sub-national laws on trafficking are inconsistent with national and international law. In May 2013, the Brčko district adopted amendments to its criminal code relating to human trafficking that brought the district in line with international norms.

Botswana

Political Rights Rating: 3
Civil Liberties Rating: 2
Freedom Rating: 2.5
Freedom Status: Free
Electoral Democracy: Yes

Population: 1,866,000
Capital: Gaborone

Ten-Year Ratings Timeline For Year Under Review (Political Rights, Civil Liberties, Status)

Year Under Review	2004	2005	2006	2007	2008	2009	2010	2011	2012	2013
Rating	2,2,F	2,2,F	2,2,F	2,2,F	2,2,F	3,2,F	3,2,F	3,2,F	3,2,F	3,2,F

INTRODUCTION

Elected governments, all led by the Botswana Democratic Party (BDP), have ruled the country since it gained independence from Britain in 1966, and the BDP—led by President Seretse Khama Ian Khama—continued to dominate the political scene in 2013.

In June 2013, the High Court ruled that the government could not forcibly relocate the residents of Ranyane, a small settlement of the traditionally marginalized San people. In another significant ruling in September, the Botswana Court of Appeal rejected gender-biased customary laws.

In December, gunmen allegedly from the police or Botswanan security forces shot and seriously injured Costa Kalafatis, reviving concerns about the rule of law under Khama and the government's targeting of the Kalafatis family. Kalafatis's older brother, John Kalafatis, an alleged organized crime suspect, had been murdered in 2009; three members of the Botswana Defence Force had been convicted of the killing, which occurred amid a spate of extrajudicial killings by security forces, and had reportedly been ordered by the president's Directorate of Intelligence and Security (DIS). In 2012, Khama issued a "conditional" pardon to the three convicted men. Additionally, the father of both Costa and John Kalafatis had died in early 2013 as a result of injuries he had sustained the previous year in an attack by unknown assailants.

POLITICAL RIGHTS: 28 / 40

A. Electoral Process: 10 / 12

In 2008, then president Festus Mogae retired before the end of his term, leaving 10-year vice president Khama to assume the presidency; Khama is the son of Seretse Khama, an independence leader and Botswana's first president. Mogae was the second successive president to resign before the end of his term, leading critics to accuse the BDP of subverting democratic institutions through an "automatic succession" process whereby the president prematurely steps aside to allow the vice-president to assume the presidency without a formal vote. Despite being elected indirectly, the president holds significant power. While the president can prolong or dismiss the legislature, the legislature is not empowered to impeach the president.

Members of the 63-seat National Assembly are elected for five years, and choose the president to serve a five-year term. Of the National Assembly's 63 members, 57 are directly elected, 4 are nominated by the president and approved by the assembly, and 2—the president and the attorney general—are ex-officio members.

Under Khama, the BDP won 45 of the 57 directly elected National Assembly seats in the 2009 elections with 53.3 percent of the vote. The Botswana National Front (BNF) won

6 seats, while the Botswana Congress Party (BCP) took 4. Parliament confirmed Khama for a full presidential term following the elections, which observers declared free and fair.

B. Political Pluralism and Participation: 10 / 16

The BDP is the dominant party, but has suffered splits in recent years, including with the 2010 formation of a new opposition party, the Botswana Movement for Democracy (BMD), by leaders of the so-called Barata-Pathi faction. However, shuffling of legislators between the BMD and BDP has subsequently diminished the former's representation in parliament and sapped it of key leaders. The BDP and Khama look set to secure another commanding electoral victory in elections set for 2014.

Democracy advocates have alleged that power has become increasingly centralized around Khama, with many top jobs going to military officers and family members. The 2007 Intelligence and Security Services Act created the DIS within the Ministry of Justice, Defense, and Security with substantial powers (for example, the director can authorize arrests without warrants) and without strong parliamentary oversight mechanisms. Director Issac Kgosi is a close confidant of Khama from the military, though relations between the two have soured recently.

The House of Chiefs, a national body that serves primarily in an advisory role, represents the country's eight major Setswana-speaking tribes and some smaller ones. Groups other than the eight major tribes tend to be left out of the political process; under the Territories Act, land in ethnic territory is distributed under the jurisdiction of majority groups. Due in part to their lack of representation in the House of Chiefs, minority groups are subject to patriarchal Tswana customary law despite having their own traditional rules for inheritance, marriage, and succession.

C. Functioning of Government: 8 / 12

Botswana's anticorruption body has special powers of investigation, arrest, and search and seizure, and the body generally boasts a high conviction rate. Nevertheless, there are almost no restrictions on the private business activities of public servants (including the president, who is a large stakeholder in the tourism sector), and political ties often play a role in awarding government jobs and tenders. A number of high-profile officials have been cleared of corruption charges in recent years. Most notably, in 2011, the minister of justice, defense and security (and cousin of Khama), Ramadeluka Seretse—who had been charged with corruption in 2010 for failing to disclose his position as a shareholder in a company, owned by his wife, that won a massive defense contract in 2009—was acquitted of all charges. In 2012, the Directorate of Public Prosecution's appeal of the acquittal was dismissed by the Court of Appeals. Botswana was ranked 30 out of 177 countries and territories surveyed in Transparency International's 2013 Corruption Perceptions Index.

Botswana does not have a freedom of information law, and critics accuse the government of excessive secrecy. Khama had yet to hold a domestic press conference by the end of 2013.

CIVIL LIBERTIES: 46 / 60

D. Freedom of Expression and Belief: 13 / 16

Botswana has a free and vigorous press, with several independent newspapers and magazines. The private Gaborone Broadcasting Corporation television system and two private radio stations have limited reach, though Botswana easily receives broadcasts from neighboring South Africa. State-owned outlets dominate the local broadcast media, which reach far more residents than the print media, yet provide inadequate access to the opposition and government critics. The country's only broadsheet printing company, Printing and Publishing Company Botswana, is reportedly commercially tied to senior BDP officials and has been accused of pre-publication censorship. In addition, the government sometimes censors or otherwise restricts news sources or stories that it finds undesirable. The 2008 Media Practitioners Act, which had not yet been implemented due to legal challenges by opponents, established a media regulatory body and mandated the registration of all media workers and outlets. The government does not restrict internet access, though such access is rare outside cities.

Freedom of religion is guaranteed, but all religious organizations must register with the government. There are over 1,000 church groups in Botswana. Academic freedom is generally respected.

E. Associational and Organizational Rights: 10 / 12

The government generally respects the constitutional rights of assembly and association. Nongovernmental organizations (NGOs), including human rights groups, operate openly without harassment. However, the government has barred organizations supporting the rights of the San (an indigenous tribal population) from entering the Central Kgalagadi Game Reserve (CKGR), the subject of a long-running land dispute, and demonstrations at the reserve have been forcibly dispersed. In March 2013, representatives of the NGO Lesbians, Gays and Bisexuals of Botswana (LEGABIBO) filed a case with the High Court of Botswana, seeking review of a decision by the Director of Civil and National Registration and the Minister of Labour and Home Affairs to refuse to register the group. The case was pending at year's end.

While independent labor unions are permitted, workers' rights to strike and bargain collectively are sometimes restricted. In 2011, almost 100,000 public sector workers—including "essential" workers in the health sector—staged an eight-week strike, leading to the closure of all public schools, while many clinics and hospitals were forced to close or partially shut down. Unions demanded a 16 percent wage increase but eventually settled for only 3 percent. The government fired nearly 2,600 striking health workers and demanded that they re-apply for their jobs following the settlement. In 2012, unions in the country appealed to the International Labour Organization (ILO) concerning restrictions in the country, including the 2009 deregistration of the Botswana Federation of Public Sector Unions (BOFEPUSU) umbrella group. The complaint was still pending at the end of 2013.

F. Rule of Law: 12 / 16

The courts are generally considered to be fair and free of direct political interference (with the prominent exception of high-profile corruption charges), although the legal system is affected by staffing shortages and a large backlog of cases. Trials are usually public, and those accused of the most serious violent crimes are provided with attorneys. Civil cases, however, are sometimes tried in customary courts, where defendants have no legal counsel. The 2007 Intelligence and Security Services Act created the DIS in the office of the president. Critics charged that it vested too much power in the agency's director—including allowing him to authorize arrests without warrants—and lacked parliamentary oversight mechanisms. Security forces have also been accused of politically motivated extrajudicial killings in the past, and the shooting of Costa Kalafatis in December 2013 revived concerns about violence by security personnel.

Occasional police abuse to obtain evidence or confessions has been reported, and Botswana has been criticized by rights groups for continuing to use corporal and capital punishment. Prisoners suffer from poor health conditions, though the government has responded by building new facilities and providing free HIV treatment to inmates. However, the government required prisoners who were not citizens to pay for such treatment, a policy that was currently being challenged in the courts.

Since 1985, authorities have relocated about 5,000 San, who tend to be marginalized in education and employment opportunities, to settlements outside the CKGR. Almost all of the remaining San fled in 2002 when the government cut off water, food, health, and social services in the area. In 2006, a three-judge panel of the Lobatse High Court ordered the government to allow the San to return to the CKGR. Several hundred San have since gone back, though disagreement remains as to how many will be allowed to live in the reserve; relatives of those involved in the case are not allowed to enter the area without a permit. By court order, the issue is being mediated by the Botswana Centre for Human Rights. In 2010, those San who had returned to CKGR lost a court battle with the government to reopen a water hole on the reserve. In 2011, an appeals court overturned the decision, ruling that the San have rights to subsurface water, which led to the reopening of the Mothomelo borehole and the return of many San to the area. The government insists that the San have been relocated to give them access to modern education and health facilities and have been adequately compensated, and it rejects claims that it simply wanted unrestricted access to diamond reserves in the region. In 2012, the government began establishing police camps in the CKGR to combat poaching. The rights group Survival International claimed the camps were also intended to intimidate local San.

Separately, in the June 2013 High Court ruling, the court ordered the government to stop forcibly relocating the San residents of Ranyane. San activists alleged that the government was carrying out the relocations because Ranyane was situated in a corridor used by commercial farmers to move their livestock from one area to another. Despite the ruling, there were reports that the government continued to pressure the residents to relocate.

Undocumented immigrants from Zimbabwe face increasing xenophobia and are subject to exploitation in the labor market. In 2010, the government announced a set of new immigration policies to halt the flow of undocumented immigrants into the country, mostly from Zimbabwe. The new policies introduced an online passport system, mandated electronic permits for visitors and immigrants, and increased the number of official workplace inspections. There were regular deportations. Botswana has built a fence along its border with Zimbabwe, ostensibly to control foot-and-mouth disease among livestock, but the barrier is popularly supported as a means of halting illegal immigration.

While same-sex sexual activity is not explicitly criminalized, "unnatural offences" are punishable by up to seven years in prison. However, there were no reported cases during the year.

G. Personal Autonomy and Individual Rights: 11 / 16

With the exception of the restrictions imposed on the San, citizens of Botswana generally enjoy freedom of travel and internal movement. Botswana is viewed as one of the least corrupt countries in Africa, and the regulatory framework is considered conducive to establishing and operating private businesses.

Women are underrepresented in the government, comprising less than 8 percent of the National Assembly seats following the 2009 elections. Women enjoy the same rights as men under the constitution, though customary laws limit their property rights, and women married under traditional laws have the same legal status as minors. The 2004 Abolition of Marital Powers Act established equal control of marriage estates and equal custody of children, removed restrictive domicile rules, and set the minimum marriage age at 18. However, enforcement of the act is not uniform and generally requires the cooperation of traditional authorities, which is not always forthcoming. In September 2013, the Botswana Court of Appeal upheld a 2012 High Court ruling that struck down as unconstitutional a customary law favoring a youngest-born son over older sisters in awarding inheritance, setting a precedent for the supremacy of civil over customary law in Botswana. The court unanimously upheld the High Court's ruling in the case of *Ramantele v. Mmusi and Others*, finding that Edith Mmusi and her three sisters were entitled to inherit their family home.

Domestic violence and trafficking for the purposes of prostitution and labor remain significant problems. Same-sex sexual relations are illegal and can carry a prison sentence of up to seven years. A 2010 amendment to the Employment Act outlaws workplace dismissal based on an individual's sexual orientation or HIV status.

Brazil

Political Rights Rating: 2
Civil Liberties Rating: 2
Freedom Rating: 2.0
Freedom Status: Free
Electoral Democracy: Yes

Population: 195,527,000
Capital: Brasília

Ten-Year Ratings Timeline For Year Under Review (Political Rights, Civil Liberties, Status)

Year Under Review	2004	2005	2006	2007	2008	2009	2010	2011	2012	2013
Rating	2,3,F	2,2,F	2,2,F	2,2,F	2,2,F	2,2,F	2,2,F	2,2,F	2,2,F	2,2,F

INTRODUCTION

More than a million Brazilians took to the streets nationwide in June 2013 to protest poor public services, high taxes and living costs, and political corruption. An increase in bus fares at a time when billions were being spent—often inefficiently—on facilities for the 2016 Olympic Games served as the catalyst for the protests, which were the largest in decades. In response, the government proposed a package of reforms, including an investment of $23 billion in city transportation and additional spending on health care and education. On June 25, Congress voted to reject a constitutional amendment that would have limited the ability of prosecutors to investigate politicians, which had been a major source of the protesters' anger. Congress also passed a law, previously rejected, that devoted all royalties from new oilfields to education and health care. Despite these measures, President Dilma Rousseff was unable to recover lost public confidence in her presidency, and her approval rating fell from 63 percent to 42 percent in the aftermath of the protests.

Police brutality continued to be a problem in 2013, drawing increased calls for independent civilian oversight over security forces. Although the year's large demonstrations were generally peaceful, police violence increased as smaller and more disruptive protests continued into the fall. Influenced by anarchist groups, these protests featured arson and looting, and the police response included stun grenades and tear gas.

Revelations that the U.S. National Security Agency had been spying on the Brazilian government and Brazil's national oil company, Petrobras, led to a souring of the country's relations with the United States, as well as a renewed push by the Brazilian Congress to pass legislation that would force foreign-based internet companies to store locally gathered information in Brazil.

POLITICAL RIGHTS: 33 / 40

A. Electoral Process: 11 / 12

Brazil is governed under a presidential system, and elections are generally free and fair. The president is directly elected for up to two four-year terms. Rousseff, the candidate of the Workers' Party (PT) and the chosen successor of outgoing president Luiz Inácio Lula da Silva, won the 2010 presidential election with 56 percent of the vote, defeating José Serra of the Brazilian Social Democracy Party (PSDB).

In Brazil's bicameral National Congress, the Senate's 81 members serve eight-year terms, with a portion coming up for election every four years, and the 513-member Chamber of Deputies is elected for four-year terms. After the 2010 congressional elections, the PT became the largest party in the lower house, with 87 seats, and in combination with allied parties it controlled well over 300 seats. In the Senate, where two-thirds of the seats were up for renewal, the PT emerged with a total of 14, while its broader coalition secured at least 50. Aside from the PT, the three largest parties are the centrist, PT-allied Brazilian Democratic Movement Party (PMDB), with 78 seats in the lower house and 21 in the Senate; the centrist opposition PSDB, with 54 and 10; and the conservative opposition Democrats (DEM), with 43 and 6. Seventeen other parties are also represented in Congress.

B. Political Pluralism and Participation: 14 / 16

Brazil has an unfettered multiparty system marked by vigorous competition between rival parties. The electoral framework encourages the proliferation of parties, a number of which are based in a single state. The summer 2013 protests provided a political opening for the rise of additional independent parties.

While the PT has been in power for 12 years, no single force has been able to dominate both the executive and legislative branches in recent years. A 2007 Supreme Court decision outlawed party switching after elections, though lawmakers have continued to switch parties on occasion for financial and other inducements. Accordingly, some parties display little ideological consistency; the sheer number of parties means that the executive branch must piece together diverse coalitions to pass legislation.

C. Functioning of Government: 8 / 12

In spite of the Rousseff administration's public intolerance of corruption, official graft remains an endemic problem in Brazil. In September 2013, the Supreme Court narrowly ruled to reopen the trial of 25 prominent PT members who were found guilty in 2012 of corruption in a vote-buying scandal, angering those who expected the landmark verdicts and prison sentences to be upheld.

Rousseff maintained her strong stance against corruption in 2013, signing an anti-corruption "Clean Company" law in August. She also promoted legislation that would ban secret voting in Congress—a key demand of the June protesters. That bill was unanimously passed by the Chamber of Deputies in September; a watered-down version passed the Senate in November which bans the secret ballot only in cases of presidential vetoes or stripping a congressperson of his/her seat. Brazil was ranked 72 out of 177 countries and territories surveyed in Transparency International's 2013 Corruption Perceptions Index.

A long-awaited freedom of information act, which covers all branches of government at all levels, went into effect in May 2012, though numerous states and cities had not yet implemented the law by the end of 2013.

CIVIL LIBERTIES: 48 / 60

D. Freedom of Expression and Belief: 15 / 16

The constitution guarantees freedom of expression, and both libel and slander were decriminalized in 2009. A bill stipulating educational degree requirements for journalists passed the lower house in 2012 and was expected to pass the Senate in 2014. While deemed a threat to freedom of speech by some critics, the legislation was supported by Brazil's principal journalist association.

The press is privately owned, and there are dozens of daily newspapers and a variety of television and radio stations across the country. The print media have played a central role in exposing official corruption. However, journalists—especially those who focus on organized crime, corruption, or human rights violations committed under the military governments that ruled Brazil prior to 1985—are frequently the targets of violence. At least 25 journalists were attacked by police during the first two weeks of the protests in June 2013, and there were also instances of brutality during Pope Francis's visit to Brazil in July.

The judicial branch, particularly judges outside large urban centers, remained active in preventing media outlets from covering numerous stories during 2013, often those involving politicians. In a positive development, the gunman behind the 2010 murder of a radio journalist was convicted in August and sentenced to 27 years in prison.

The government does not impose restrictions on access to the internet. A stalled "internet bill of rights," which would guarantee basic rights for internet users and intermediaries, was revived after the summer 2013 protests, and Congress was reviewing the proposed law at year's end.

The constitution guarantees freedom of religion, and the government generally respects this right in practice. Academic freedom is not restricted.

E. Associational and Organizational Rights: 10 / 12

Freedoms of association and assembly are generally respected, as is the right to strike. The nationwide protests of 2013 were largely peaceful, but they featured several instances of police brutality. Industrial labor unions are well organized, and although they are politically connected, Brazilian unions tend to be freer from political party control than their counterparts in most other Latin American countries. Labor issues are adjudicated in a system of special labor courts. Tens of thousands of workers representing the education, medical, and transportation sectors initiated a one-day national strike and day of protest across Brazil in July. The generally peaceful protesters, called to action by Brazil's trade union federations, demanded a 40-hour work week and improved working conditions.

F. Rule of Law: 10 / 16

Brazil's largely independent judiciary is overburdened and plagued by corruption. The judiciary is often subject to intimidation and other external influences, especially in rural areas, and public complaints over its inefficiency are frequent. Access to justice also varies greatly due to Brazil's income inequality. However, Brazil's progressive 1988 constitution that mandates civic rights such as access to health care has translated into an active judiciary, often ruling in favor of citizens against the state.

During the last 10 years, Brazil has maintained an average annual homicide rate of 26 per 100,000 residents, compared with a global average of approximately 7 per 100,000. Impunity and corruption perpetuates a culture of violence in Brazil; violent crime is also related to the illegal drug trade. Highly organized and well-armed drug gangs frequently clash with the military police or with private militias comprising off-duty police officers, prison guards, and firefighters. The long-term presence of special Pacifying Police Units

(UPP) has successfully pacified several of the city's dangerous *favelas*, or slums, though the sustainability of this peace remains in question, as does the government's ability to successfully expand the program to other impoverished areas. Moreover, allegations of increased violence by the UPP in 2013 raised concerns about their tactics. In October, a group of 10 officers were charged with killing a suspect who lived in Rio de Janeiro's Rocinho favela, then hiding his body. The suspect was epileptic and allegedly died during an interrogation session in which he was tortured.

Corruption and violence remain entrenched in Brazil's police forces. According to UN figures, more than 2,000 people are killed by the police each year. Torture is used systematically to extract confessions from suspects, and extrajudicial killings are portrayed as shootouts with dangerous criminals. Police officers are rarely prosecuted for abuses, and those charged are almost never convicted. In August 2013, President Rousseff signed a law creating the National Mechanism to Prevent and Combat Torture. The watchdog body will consist of 11 experts with the unprecedented power to visit any civilian or military facility where torture or ill-treatment are documented and ask authorities to initiate investigations in cases of alleged torture. The body will also make policy recommendations aimed at reducing the prevalence of torture. Separately, in a blow against impunity, a court convicted 23 police officers in April for their part in the bloody suppression of a 1992 São Paulo prison riot in which 111 inmates died. The officers were each sentenced to 156 years in prison.

The prison system is anarchic, overcrowded, and largely unfit for human habitation. Brazil's prisons held 550,000 inmates in 2013, representing the world's fourth-largest prison population, and three-quarters more than the system's intended capacity. Overcrowding sometimes results in men and women being held in the same facilities.

Racial discrimination, long officially denied as a problem in Brazil, began to receive both recognition and remediation after former president Lula took office in 2003. Afro-Brazilians earn less than 50 percent of the average earnings of other citizens, and they suffer from the highest homicide, poverty, and illiteracy rates. The 2010 Statute of Racial Equality recognized the right of *quilombos*—communities of descendants of escaped slaves—to receive title to their land. It also called for the establishment of nonquota affirmative action policies in education and employment, as well as programs to improve Afro-Brazilians' access to health care. In 2013, the first beneficiaries of a 2012 affirmative action law on education began classes. The law requires public universities to reserve half of their admission spots to the mostly poor students attending public schools, as well as to increase the number of students of African descent in accordance with the racial composition of each state.

Brazil's indigenous peoples account for less than 1 percent of the total population. Half of the indigenous population lives in poverty, and most indigenous communities lack adequate sanitation and education services. Unresolved and often violent land disputes between indigenous communities and rural farmers continued in 2013, as landowners often refused to leave their land demarcated for indigenous use under Brazil's constitution. In October 2013, several indigenous groups waged a week-long campaign to demand the demarcation of their territory; approximately 600 demarcation plans were pending at the end of 2013.

While discrimination based on sexual orientation is prohibited by law, violence against members of the LGBT (lesbian, gay, bisexual, and transgender) community remains a problem. Brazil's Supreme Court ruled in May 2011 that gays and lesbians have the right to form civil unions, and that couples in civil unions have the same rights as married couples with regard to alimony, health, and retirement benefits, as well as adoption rights.

G. Personal Autonomy and Individual Rights: 13 / 16

Brazilians generally enjoy freedom of movement and choice of residence, but the owners of large estates control nearly 60 percent of the country's arable land, while the poorest 30 percent of the population hold less than 2 percent. Land invasions are organized by the grassroots Landless Workers' Movement, which claims that the seized land is unused or illegally held. Progress on land reform has been slow, due in part to a strong farm caucus and the economic importance of large-scale agriculture. In May and June 2013, land disputes became particularly violent in the agricultural state of Mato Grosso do Sul. Several Terena Indians were injured, and one was killed, in confrontations with police and farmers over land occupation and forced evictions.

A 2003 legal code made women equal to men under the law for the first time in the country's history. Upon entering office, President Rousseff vowed to push women's rights onto the national and international agenda, and women make up almost a third of her cabinet. The head of Petrobras is the only female head of a major oil company worldwide. Women make up 27 percent of the senior managers of Brazil's leading companies, compared with a global average of 21 percent. In March 2013, the Senate gave final approval to a constitutional amendment that extended to household workers, many of whom are women, the same rights and duties of all regulated Brazilian workers.

Brazil's law on violence against women is exemplary in the region. Nevertheless, violence against women and children is commonplace, and protective laws are rarely enforced. According to the UN Entity for Gender Equality and the Empowerment of Women (UN Women), a woman is assaulted every 15 seconds in the city of São Paulo. In the first three months of 2013, 1,822 rapes were reported in the state of Rio de Janeiro, and only 70 men were arrested. In August, Rousseff signed a law that allows public health centers to administer emergency-contraception drugs in cases of rape. Abortion is illegal in Brazil, with rare exceptions; approximately one in four women that have illegal abortions each year end up in the hospital due to complications.

Although Brazil abolished slavery in 1888, thousands of rural laborers still work under slavery-like conditions. Landowners who enslave workers face two to eight years in prison, in addition to fines. Measures to fight the impunity of employers, including mobile inspection units and a public "black list" of offending companies and landowners, have proven effective in reducing slave labor in rural Brazil. In May 2012, the Congress passed a constitutional amendment that allows the government to confiscate all property of landholders found to be using slave labor, among other penalties.

Approximately 3.7 million minors work in Brazil, according to a 2011 national survey. The government has sought to address the problem by cooperating with various nongovernmental organizations, increasing inspections, and offering cash incentives to keep children in school. Human trafficking continues from and within Brazil for the purpose of forced labor and commercial sexual exploitation.

Brunei

Political Rights Rating: 6
Civil Liberties Rating: 5
Freedom Rating: 5.5
Freedom Status: Not Free
Electoral Democracy: No

Population: 400,000
Capital: Bandar Seri Begawan

Ten-Year Ratings Timeline For Year Under Review (Political Rights, Civil Liberties, Status)

Year Under Review	2004	2005	2006	2007	2008	2009	2010	2011	2012	2013
Rating	6,5,NF	6,5,NF	6,5,NF	6,5,NF	6,5,NF	6,5,NF	6,5,NF	6,5,NF	6,5,NF	6,5,NF

INTRODUCTION

In 2013, Sultan Hassanal Bolkiah Mu'izzaddin Waddaulah announced new provisions to Brunei's Penal Code based on Sharia (Islamic law). The new rules, which will come into effect in 2014, include harsher penalties for a variety of crimes, including stoning for adultery, limb amputation for theft, flogging for abortion, and others.

Energy wealth has long allowed the government to stave off demands for political reform by employing much of the population, providing citizens with extensive benefits, and sparing them an income tax. Despite a declining gross domestic product growth rate, Brunei remains the fourth-largest oil producer in Southeast Asia and the ninth-largest exporter of liquefied natural gas in the world. In December 2010, Brunei and Malaysia moved forward with a "milestone" offshore oil exploration deal in which both countries agreed to a 50-50 sharing partnership for a period of 40 years.

POLITICAL RIGHTS: 7 / 40

A. Electoral Process: 0 / 12

Brunei is a constitutional sultanate. Its constitution was drafted in 1959. Brunei achieved political independence from the United Kingdom in 1984, though in practice the country has been self-governed since 1959. The sultan is the head of state and prime minister, and continues to wield broad powers under a long-standing state of emergency imposed in 1984. No direct legislative elections have been held since 1962, when elective provisions of the constitution were suspended after the leftist and antimonarchist Brunei People's Party (BPP) won all 10 elected seats in the 21-member council. While the most recent constitutional amendment in 2004 expanded the size of the Legislative Council and included 15 elected seats, there is no timetable for any Council elections, and in practice the size and composition of the Legislative Council has differed from constitutional provisions with members appointed by the Sultan.

The Sultan is technically advised by the Council of Cabinet Ministers, Legislative Council, Privy Council and Religious Council. Citizens convey concerns to their leaders through government-vetted councils of elected village chiefs.

B. Political Pluralism and Participation: 3 / 16

The reform efforts of Sultan Hassanal have been largely superficial and are designed to attract foreign investment. The unicameral 33-member Legislative Council, which was reinstated in 2004 after being suspended since 1984, has no political standing independent of the sultan. While the 2004 constitutional amendment expanded the body to 45 seats, 15 of which would be elected, in 2005 Hassan appointed most members of a new, 29-member Council, which included five indirectly elected members representing village councils. Most of the other members of this body were either relatives or loyalists. Following the completion of its first five-year term, the Legislative Council was disbanded in March 2011 and replaced with a newly appointed and expanded 33-member council in June 2011. The council's mounting oversight activity and queries aimed at the government reflect a growing demand for accountability and responsible spending; in January 2013, members of the Council met with village council leaders, where issues such as pensions and healthcare were raised. These tentative reforms were considered preparations for an eventual succession and the expected depletion of the country's oil and gas reserves, which account for about 90 percent of state revenues.

Hassanal instituted a significant reshuffle of the Cabinet of Ministers in May 2010. While many ministers retained their positions, and the sultan continued to hold the posts of prime minister, minister of defense, and minister of finance, the changes that were instituted signified a small step toward improving governance. The new cabinet included the country's first woman cabinet member as deputy minister for culture, youth, and sports.

Genuine political activity by opposition groups remains extremely limited. In 2007, the Registrar of Societies disbanded the People's Awareness Party and forced the president of the Brunei National Solidarity Party (PPKB) to resign. The PPKB was then deregistered without explanation in 2008, leaving the National Development Party as Brunei's sole remaining legal political party. Headed by a former political prisoner, exile, and insurgent leader, the NDP was permitted to register in 2005 after pledging to work as a partner with the government and swearing loyalty to the sultan.

C. Functioning of Government: 3 / 12

The government claims to have a zero-tolerance policy on corruption, and its Anti-Corruption Bureau has successfully prosecuted a number of lower-level officials in recent years. The sultan's brother and former finance minister, Prince Jefri Bolkiah, has faced a number of legal challenges, including a 2008 arrest warrant, over accusations that he misappropriated state funds, and he was ordered to return significant personal assets to the state after a drawn out court case that went as high as the Privy Council in London. Brunei was ranked 38 out of 176 countries surveyed in Transparency International's 2013 Corruption Perceptions Index, an increase from 2012.

Discretionary Political Rights Question A: 1 / 0

Citizens have the opportunity to convey concerns to their leaders through government-vetted councils of elected village chiefs.

CIVIL LIBERTIES: 23 / 60
D. Freedom of Expression and Belief: 6 / 16

Journalists in Brunei face considerable restrictions. Officials may close newspapers without cause and fine and imprison journalists for up to three years for reporting deemed "false and malicious." The national sedition law was amended in 2005 to strengthen prohibitions on criticizing the sultan and the national "Malay Muslim Monarchy" ideology. The country's main English-language daily newspaper, the *Borneo Bulletin*, is controlled by the sultan's family and often practices self-censorship. A second English-language daily, the *Brunei Times*, was launched by prominent businessmen in 2006 to attract foreign investors. A smaller, Malay-language newspaper and several Chinese-language papers are also published. Brunei's only television station is state run, but residents can receive Malaysian broadcasts and satellite channels. The country's internet practice code stipulates that content must not be subversive or encourage illegitimate reform efforts.

Approximately 67 percent of the population is Muslim, 13 percent is Buddhist, and 10 percent is Christian (approximately half of whom are Catholic). The constitution allows for the practice of religions other than the official Shafeite school of Sunni Islam, but proselytizing by non-Muslims is prohibited. Non-Shafeite forms of Islam are actively discouraged, in part due to concerns about security and foreign investment. Christianity is the most common target of censorship, and the Baha'i faith is banned. Marriage between Muslims and non-Muslims is not allowed. Muslims require permission from the Ministry of Religious Affairs to convert to other faiths, though official and societal pressures make conversion nearly impossible. In July 2013, the government enacted regulations banning non-Muslims from eating in Muslim-owned restaurants and eateries during Ramadan.

Islamic courts oversee family-related matters and handle approximately 27 criminal offenses. In October 2013, the government announced that stricter Sharia-based laws would be included in the Penal Code in 2014. The new rules would apply only to Muslims and these would increase the number of criminal offenses handled by Sharia courts to more than 95. While Brunei already implements many Sharia-based laws, the amendment is expected to include harsher punishments for a number of crimes, including stoning for adultery, limb amputation for theft, and flogging for abortion; other punishable offenses include failure to preform Friday prayer and cross-dressing.

The study of Islam, Malay Muslim Monarchy ideology, and the Jawi (Arabic script used for writing the Malay language) is mandatory in all schools, public or private. The teaching of all other religions is prohibited.

Academic freedom is generally respected, though in January a Myanmar professor at Universiti Brunei Darussalam (UBD) resigned his position, citing academic censorship.

E. Associational and Organizational Rights: 3 / 12

Emergency laws continue to restrict freedoms of assembly and association. Most nongovernmental organizations are professional or business groups. All groups must register and name their members, and registration can be refused for any reason. No more than 10 people can assemble for any purpose without a permit. Brunei only has three, largely inactive, trade unions, all of which are in the oil sector and represent only about 5 percent of the industry's labor force. Strikes are illegal, and collective bargaining is not recognized. Civil servants may not join a political party.

The law guarantees the right to form and join a union, though there is no provision for collective bargaining. Only a single union exists, that of the Brunei Shell Petroleum workers. Strikes are prohibited.

F. Rule of Law: 6 / 16

The constitution does not provide for an independent judiciary. Although the courts generally appear to act independently, they have yet to be tested in political cases. Final recourse for civil cases is managed by the Privy Council in the United Kingdom. Sharia takes precedence in areas including divorce, inheritance, and some sex crimes, though it does not apply to non-Muslims. Amendments to the Penal Code are expected to be enforced in 2014, which will increase the number of offenses covered by Sharia courts. A backlog of capital cases results in lengthy pretrial detention for those accused of serious crimes. Caning is mandatory for 42 criminal offenses, including immigration violations, and is commonly carried out, though an attending doctor can interrupt the punishment for medical reasons.

Religious enforcement officers raid homes to arrest people for *khalwat*, the mingling of unrelated Muslim men and women. However, most first offenders are fined or released due to a lack of evidence. The authorities also detain suspected antigovernment activists under the

Internal Security Act, which permits detention without trial for renewable two-year periods. Prison conditions generally meet international standards.

G. Personal Autonomy and Individual Rights: 8 / 16

Freedom of movement is respected in the country, though all government employees—domestic and foreign—must apply for permission to travel abroad. The government utilizes an informant system to monitor suspected dissidents, and emails, chat-rooms and cellphone messages are monitored for subversive content; however, social media is not censored and foreign press widely available.

Same-sex relations are illegal, and in practice, individuals do not disclose sexual orientations, which has likely led to the low occurrence of societal and official discrimination in employment, ownership, access to services, etc.

Brunei's many "stateless" people, mostly longtime ethnic Chinese residents, are denied the full rights and benefits of citizens, while migrant workers, who comprise approximately one quarter of the workforce, are largely unprotected by labor laws and vulnerable to exploitation. Workers who overstay visas are regularly imprisoned and, in some cases, caned or whipped.

Islamic law generally places women at a disadvantage in cases of divorce and inheritance. All women in government-run institutions and schools are required or pressured to wear traditional Muslim head coverings. An increasing number of women have entered the workforce in recent years, comprising 50.4 percent of the civil service in 2010. Brunei appointed its first female attorney general, Hayati Salleh, in 2009; she was formerly the first female High Court judge. Women have access to family planning and free healthcare. In 2014, Brunei maintained its position at 88th place, down from 75th place in 2012, in the World Economic Forum's Global Gender Gap report, particular in the areas of economic participation and educational attainment. Brunei serves as a destination, transit, and source country for the trafficking of men and women for forced labor and prostitution.

Bulgaria

Political Rights Rating: 2
Civil Liberties Rating: 2
Freedom Rating: 2.0
Freedom Status: Free
Electoral Democracy: Yes

Population: 7,300,000
Capital: Sofia

Ten-Year Ratings Timeline For Year Under Review (Political Rights, Civil Liberties, Status)

Year Under Review	2004	2005	2006	2007	2008	2009	2010	2011	2012	2013
Rating	1,2,F	1,2,F	1,2,F	1,2,F	2,2,F	2,2,F	2,2,F	2,2,F	2,2,F	2,2,F

INTRODUCTION

The center-right government of Prime Minister Boyko Borisov and his Citizens for the European Development of Bulgaria (GERB) party resigned in February 2013 amid a wave of protests that included several fatal self-immolations. The protests were triggered by a sharp rise in electricity prices, but demonstrators aired broader grievances related to persistent poverty, official corruption, and an entrenched nexus of political, business, and organized crime interests in the country.

President Rosen Plevneliev appointed a technocratic caretaker government that served until parliamentary elections were held in May, two months ahead of schedule. GERB emerged with a plurality, but it was unable to form a majority coalition. The opposition Bulgarian Socialist Party (BSP) consequently formed a government with the Movement for Rights and Freedoms (DPS), a mainly ethnic Turkish party, that controlled exactly 50 percent of the legislature and relied on support from the ultranationalist Ataka party to produce a quorum and pass legislation.

The government's June appointment of a controversial 32-year-old media tycoon as head of the State Agency for National Security (DANS) ignited fresh protests, and although the decision was quickly reversed, large demonstrations continued through the end of the year. The mostly peaceful protesters sought deeper democracy and rule of law, and expressed frustration with the entire political class. They demanded the government's resignation and proposed electoral reforms that would open the door to new parties or even nonpartisan candidates. Meanwhile, Plevneliev expressed support for the protesters and defied the government with a rare budget veto in early August, though it was soon overturned. European Union (EU) justice commissioner Viviane Reding also voiced sympathy with the demonstrators, saying their anticorruption demands matched those of the European Commission.

POLITICAL RIGHTS: 31 / 40 (-3)

A. Electoral Process: 10 / 12 (-1)

The unicameral National Assembly, composed of 240 members, is elected every four years in 31 multimember constituencies. The president, elected for up to two five-year terms, is the head of state, but has limited powers. The legislature chooses the prime minister, who serves as head of government.

Observers from the Organization for Security and Cooperation in Europe (OSCE) generally praised the conduct of the May 2013 parliamentary elections, but noted an election-eve incident in which prosecutors seized hundreds of thousands of extra ballots from a printer owned by a GERB municipal official. The printer maintained that the ballots were set aside due to production defects, but prosecutors disputed that claim, and opposition parties held press conferences on the day before the election, alleging a possible fraud plot. GERB complained that the accusations violated a mandatory 24-hour period of media silence before election day. Observers noted widespread allegations of vote buying and other irregularities, with prosecutors opening dozens of criminal investigations. According to Transparency International Bulgaria, the number of registered complaints about alleged violations was significantly higher than in 2011 and 2009.

Amid low turnout of 51.3 percent, four factions won seats, down from six in the previous elections. GERB led the voting with 97 seats, followed by a BSP-led electoral bloc with 84, the DPS with 36, and Ataka with 23. The BSP formed a coalition government with the DPS, relying on support from Ataka to achieve a simple majority. Plamen Oresharski, a former finance minister who was elected on the BSP list but is not a party member, became prime minister, and some cabinet posts were assigned to nonpartisan technocrats.

Delyan Peevski, the DPS lawmaker and media mogul whose June appointment as DANS director set off renewed protests, was required to give up his parliamentary seat in order to take the new post. However, a court ruled in October that he was still a member of parliament because the chamber had not formally voted on his departure as a lawmaker before the DANS appointment was reversed. The ruling triggered clashes between police and protesters.

B. Political Pluralism and Participation: 14 / 16 (-1)

The BSP has long represented the center-left, while GERB, which was founded in 2006 and took power in 2009, is the latest in a series of center-right parties to rise and fall in

Bulgaria's multiparty system. In a sign of disaffection with the major parties, about a quarter of voters in the May 2013 elections chose small parties that failed to cross the 4 percent threshold to win seats.

Electoral campaigns must be conducted in the Bulgarian language. While the ethnic Turkish minority is represented by the DPS, the Romany minority is more marginalized. Small Romany parties are active, and many Roma reportedly vote for the DPS, but the parliament elected in 2013 was reportedly the first since 1991 to include no Romany members, down from one member in the previous parliament. Moreover, Ataka and smaller nationalist parties regularly used anti-Roma rhetoric in their campaigns, and police efforts to combat vote buying in Romany areas may have had an intimidating effect, according to international observers. Nationalist parties also repeatedly used hate speech aimed at ethnic Turks, Muslims, and Syrian refugees, among other groups.

C. Functioning of Government: 7 / 12 (-1)

Corruption is a serious concern in Bulgaria. The Peevski affair touched off major protests because it was seen as a symbol of broader corrupt collusion among the political and economic elite. Peevski's New Bulgarian Media Group (NBMG), owned on paper by his mother, consistently supports whatever party is in power, and its rapid expansion has been backed by the Corporate Commercial Bank (KTB), owned by Tsvetan Vassilev. The bank in turn receives much business from state-owned enterprises, creating a triangular relationship. Peevski's appointment as DANS director was made with no public debate. Protesters denounced a number of other government nominees and officials for their alleged links to powerful businessmen and, in at least one case, to organized crime. A recording leaked in April featured Borisov improperly discussing a corruption case against a former agriculture minister with the Sofia city prosecutor and the accused. Bulgaria was ranked 77 out of 177 countries and territories surveyed in Transparency International's 2013 Corruption Perceptions Index.

Although the leadership's lack of transparency and accountability were core grievances behind six months of daily protests that had broad support in Bulgarian society, the BSP-led government failed to respond to the demonstrators' demands for reform, reinforcing their sense of exclusion and causing an indefinite impasse.

CIVIL LIBERTIES: 47 / 60
D. Freedom of Expression and Belief: 14 / 16

Bulgarian media have become more vulnerable to political and economic pressures as some foreign media firms withdraw from the struggling market and domestic ownership becomes more concentrated. NBMG controls about 40 percent of the print sector, the distributor for about 80 percent of newspapers, and the fourth-largest television broadcaster, among other assets. Although the state-owned media generally provide balanced coverage, ineffective legislation leaves them exposed to political influence. Journalists continued to face the threat of violence during 2013. Ataka leader Volen Siderov and his supporters were involved in at least two incidents, forcing their way into the public television station in June and assaulting a television crew from SKAT TV in July. A talk-show host was beaten by an unidentified attacker in June, and the vehicle of another host was set on fire in front of her home in September. Journalists covering a protest were reportedly attacked by police in one instance in July. The government does not place restrictions on internet access.

Religious freedom is generally upheld, but Muslims and members of other minority faiths have reported instances of harassment and discrimination, and some local authorities have blocked proselytizing or the construction of minority religious buildings. The government does not restrict academic freedom, though students occupied many of the country's universities beginning in October 2013, shutting down classes in solidarity with the broader antigovernment protests.

E. Associational and Organizational Rights: 11 / 12

The authorities generally respect freedoms of assembly and association. The large and frequent protests during 2013 were generally peaceful and did not prompt widespread police abuses, although police beatings of demonstrators in February triggered Borisov's resignation. Another incident occurred during an attempt by protesters in July to blockade the parliament building; police ultimately dispersed the blockade using excessive and indiscriminate force, according to human rights groups. Police clashed with protesters outside the parliament again in November. A gay pride parade in Sofia proceeded without incident in September, having been postponed from June for security reasons.

Nongovernmental organizations operate freely, and the surge in activism and public engagement during 2013 was welcomed as a major awakening for Bulgarian civil society. Workers have the right to join trade unions, but public employees cannot strike or bargain collectively, and private employers often discriminate against union members without facing serious repercussions. A large union federation announced in July 2013 that it would join the antigovernment protests.

F. Rule of Law: 11 / 16

Bulgaria's judiciary has benefited from legal and institutional reforms associated with EU accession, but practical gains in efficiency and accountability have been lacking. The EU has noted ongoing flaws in the judicial appointment and disciplinary processes.

Organized crime is a serious problem, and scores of suspected contract killings over the past decade have gone unsolved. In March 2013, Interior Ministry officials were implicated in a scandal involving the illegal wiretapping of a wide range of political and business figures. Incidents of mistreatment by police have been reported, and prison conditions remain inadequate in many places.

Ethnic minorities, particularly Roma, continue to face discrimination in employment, health care, education, and housing. Discrimination based on sexual orientation is illegal, but societal bias reportedly persists. Thousands of Syrian refugees entered the country during 2013, overwhelming government preparations and drawing hostility from ultranationalist groups. Anti-immigrant rallies were held in multiple cities in November, and some speakers were subsequently prosecuted for hate speech. A series of assaults targeting minorities, immigrants, and refugees were reported during the year.

G. Personal Autonomy and Individual Rights: 11 / 16

The informal, untaxed "shadow economy" accounts for a large share of the country's gross domestic product, and organized crime is believed to play an influential role in private business activity.

Women remain underrepresented in political life, accounting for just a quarter of the National Assembly seats after the 2013 elections, though the OSCE reported a high level of participation by women in the administration of the May elections. Domestic violence is an ongoing concern. The country is a source of human-trafficking victims, of whom Roma make up a disproportionately large share.

Burkina Faso

Political Rights Rating: 5
Civil Liberties Rating: 3
Freedom Rating: 4.0
Freedom Status: Partly Free
Electoral Democracy: No

Population: 18,015,000
Capital: Ouagadougou

Ten-Year Ratings Timeline For Year Under Review (Political Rights, Civil Liberties, Status)

Year Under Review	2004	2005	2006	2007	2008	2009	2010	2011	2012	2013
Rating	5,4,PF	5,3,PF	5,3,PF	5,3,PF	5,3,PF	5,3,PF	5,3,PF	5,3,PF	5,3,PF	5,3,PF

INTRODUCTION

Despite being surrounded by neighbors experiencing political crises, Burkina Faso has been spared similar upheaval thanks to its relative internal stability and robust security apparatus. Nevertheless, the country has experienced a series of protests over the last three years, including large demonstrations in June and July 2013 that opposed alterations to the constitution and the creation of a new Senate; the protests successfully stalled the proposed body's creation.

In September, Romuald Tuina, an ex-presidential guard who had been wanted for bank robbery, shot a gun at the entrance of the presidential palace in what was taken as an attempt to assassinate President Blaise Compaoré. Tuina was then shot dead at the scene. He was believed to have acted alone, and the attempt was not judged to be politically motivated.

The turmoil in neighboring Mali resulted in continued tension along its border with Burkina Faso, including a steady influx of refugees.

POLITICAL RIGHTS: 17 / 40

A. Electoral Process: 5 / 12

Compaoré, a former army captain, has held power since ousting populist president Thomas Sankara as an army captain in 1987. With his Congress for Democracy and Progress (CDP) party, Compaoré went on to win Burkina Faso's first democratic elections in 1991. In 2000, two-term presidential limits were reintroduced, but the law was not retroactive, allowing Compaoré, who had already served two seven-year terms, to run for reelection again. Compaoré won presidential elections in 2005 and 2010, the last for which he was eligible under the current term-limit rules.

The CDP won a comfortable majority in concurrent parliamentary and municipal elections held in December 2012. The CDP took 70 seats in the 127-seat, unicameral National Assembly. The next two largest parties—the Alliance for Democracy and Federation-African Democratic Rally (ADF-RDA) and the new Union for Progress and Change (UPC)—won 19 seats each; smaller parties hold the remaining seats. In total, pro-Compaoré parties control 97 seats. Members of the National Assembly serve five-year terms.

International monitors have judged recent elections in Burkina Faso to be generally free but not entirely fair, due to the ruling CDP's privileged access to state resources and the media. Some reported problems with the 2010 presidential election included traditional leaders mobilizing voters for the incumbent, inadequate numbers of voting cards and ballots at the polls, incorrect electoral lists, and the use of state resources for Compaoré's campaign.

The 2012 parliamentary and municipal elections were run more efficiently and were generally considered free by domestic and international observers, though the opposition claimed that the ruling party still possessed privileged access to state resources.

Compaoré has not attempted to change the constitution to give himself another term in office—an issue that concerns the opposition—and under Article 37 of the current constitution he would have to leave office in 2015. In May 2013, Compaoré announced the creation of a new Senate with 89 members, 29 of whom would be appointed directly by the president, with the rest appointed by local officials. The opposition expressed fears that the new Senate could be more amenable to altering Article 37 in addition to further concentrating power in the hands of the president.

Electoral reforms in 2009 extended the right to vote in presidential elections and referendums to Burkinabé living abroad, but not until the 2015 presidential election. A 2010 law requires that all voters show picture identification when arriving at the polls.

B. Political Pluralism and Participation: 8 / 16

The constitution guarantees the right to form political parties, and 13 parties are currently represented in the legislature. The 2009 reforms also included an injunction against the practice of switching parties after elections. UPC is the main opposition party and one of the three largest in the country; other parties that genuinely oppose the government are small. The ruling CDP controls much of the resources and limits the playing field for opposition parties, many of which it has coopted. ADF-RDA, while formally the largest opposition party, supported Compaoré or his party in both the 2005 and 2010 elections.

Corruption among military elites and in recruiting practices bred resentment among the ranks in 2011, leading to large protests and vandalism by mutineers. Hundreds of soldiers were arrested and prosecuted in 2012, at which time Compaoré assumed the role of minister of defense and initiated reforms that are ongoing. One reform involved partial disarmament in order to prevent protests within the military.

Minority rights are generally respected in politics, although a small, educated elite, the military, and labor unions dominate the scene.

C. Functioning of Government: 4 / 12

Corruption remains widespread, despite a number of public and private anticorruption initiatives. The courts have been unwilling or unable to adequately prosecute many senior officials charged with corruption. The government stepped up anticorruption efforts in 2012, firing the head of the country's notoriously corrupt customs office in January; no firings or high-profile arrests were made in 2013. Burkina Faso was ranked 83 out of 177 countries and territories surveyed in Transparency International's 2013 Corruption Perceptions Index.

In 2012, parliament voted to give all presidents since Burkina Faso's 1960 independence immunity from prosecution, despite an opposition boycott of the vote.

CIVIL LIBERTIES: 36 / 60

D. Freedom of Expression and Belief: 13 / 16

Although freedom of expression is constitutionally guaranteed and generally respected, many media outlets practice self-censorship. Journalists occasionally face criminal libel prosecutions, death threats, and other forms of harassment and intimidation. In October 2012, two journalists at the private weekly *L'Ouragan* were sentenced to 12 months in prison for defamation, and their paper was suspended for six months for publishing allegations of corruption against the state prosecutor's office. In July 2013, state media employees, dissatisfied with working conditions and censorship, participated in protests organized by the

Autonomous Syndicate of Information and Culture Workers. The journalists staged a sit-in in front of the Ministry of Communications building in Ouagadougou. Minister of Communications Alain Edouard Traoré responded by insisting that the government does not issue directives to journalists, only attempts to offer guidance. Along with the state-owned outlets, there are over 50 private radio stations, three private television stations, and several independent newspapers. The government does not restrict internet access.

Burkina Faso is a secular state, and freedom of religion is respected. Academic freedom is also unrestricted.

E. Associational and Organizational Rights: 8 / 12

The constitution provides for the right to assemble, though demonstrations are sometimes suppressed or banned. While many nongovernmental organizations operate openly and freely, human rights groups have reported abuses by security forces. Violent protests broke out in February 2011 throughout the country in reaction to the death of a student, Justin Zongo, in police custody. While initially composed mainly of students, the protests later swelled to include soldiers, police, and teachers. The government imposed some reforms after the protests and took steps to increase the wages of civil servants and to reduce corruption. New protests erupted in the capital and second largest city, Bobo Dioulasso, in June and July 2013 against perceived plans to alter Article 37 of the constitution, as well as the rising cost of staples such as sugar and rice. The protests were dispersed with tear gas.

The constitution guarantees the right to strike, and unions are able to engage freely in strikes and collective bargaining, although only a minority of the workforce is unionized.

F. Rule of Law: 7 / 16

The judicial system is formally independent, but it is subject to executive influence and corruption. The courts are further weakened by a lack of resources and citizens' poor knowledge of their rights.

Human rights advocates in Burkina Faso have repeatedly criticized the military and police for committing abuses with impunity. Police often use excessive force and disregard pretrial detention limits. The sentencing in August 2011 of three police officers charged with the torture and death of Zongo was seen as a positive step.

Discrimination against various ethnic minorities occurs but is not widespread. However, gay men and lesbians, as well as those infected with HIV, routinely experience discrimination. In an effort to address discrimination against the disabled, Burkina Faso ratified the Convention on the Rights of Persons with Disabilities in 2009 and adopted a new law on the protection and promotion of the rights of the disabled in April 2010. Civil society actors also noted increased government efforts since 2010 to provide access to health care and a decrease in costs for maternal health services.

The crisis in neighboring Mali that began in 2012 has resulted in more than 40,000 refugees fleeing to Burkina Faso over the last two years, including many into the country's already drought-ridden Sahel region. Clashes between ethnic groups along the Mali-Burkina Faso border left 25 people dead in May 2012, and the situation remained tense throughout 2013 as local farmers vied for land with Malian refugees.

G. Personal Autonomy and Individual Rights: 8 / 16

The constitution provides for freedom of movement within the country, although security checks on travelers are common. Equality of opportunity is hampered in part by the advantages conferred on CDP members, who receive preferential treatment in securing public contracts.

While illegal, gender discrimination remains common in employment, education, property, and family rights, particularly in rural areas. There are 20 women in the 127-seat National Assembly. Reforms in 2009 established a 30-percent quota for women on all party candidate lists in municipal and legislative elections, but the law is vague regarding implementation. In the north, early marriage contributes to lower female school enrollment and a heightened incidence of obstetric fistula. Human rights groups have recorded a significant drop in the prevalence of female genital mutilation since its criminalization in 1996.

Burkina Faso is a source, transit, and destination country for trafficking in women and children, who are subject to forced labor and sexual exploitation. According to the U.S. State Department's 2013 Trafficking in Persons Report, Burkina Faso does not comply with the minimum standards for eliminating human trafficking; it is placed in Tier 2 of the report. However, the report noted the government's reform efforts as evidenced by a larger number of children—1,427—intercepted from traffickers in 2012.

Burma (Myanmar)

Political Rights Rating: 6
Civil Liberties Rating: 5
Freedom Rating: 5.5
Freedom Status: Not Free
Electoral Democracy: No

Population: 53,300,000
Capital: Nay Pyi Taw

Ten-Year Ratings Timeline For Year Under Review (Political Rights, Civil Liberties, Status)

Year Under Review	2004	2005	2006	2007	2008	2009	2010	2011	2012	2013
Rating	7,7,NF	7,7,NF	7,7,NF	7,7,NF	7,7,NF	7,7,NF	7,7,NF	7,6,NF	6,5,NF	6,5,NF

INTRODUCTION

Burma's nominally civilian government made progress in peace negotiations with ethnic armed groups and continued its relaxation of controls over the media and civil society in 2013. However, the year was marked by weak government enforcement of the rule of law, increasing arrests of political activists for "unlawful public demonstrations," a gradual resurgence of political confrontation between the government and the opposition regarding proposed reforms of the 2008 constitution, and intensifying rivalry within the parliament, as well as between the government and parliament, that led to the suspension of a constitutionally mandated bill.

The country was also shaken by anti-Muslim riots, especially after March 2013. At least 77 people were killed, thousands of residents were displaced, and hundreds of properties, including religious sites, were destroyed. The government's failure to protect victims and punish perpetrators was well documented in the media. Beginning in July, a series of bomb explosions hit several major cities, killing at least three people and injuring 10 others, including an American tourist. Separately, contentious disputes over land grabbing and socially irresponsible business projects continued during the year.

POLITICAL RIGHTS: 9 / 40

A. Electoral Process: 3 / 12

The military, which had long controlled all executive, legislative, and judicial functions, handed power to the current government in March 2011 following the 2010 national elections, which were neither free nor fair. The process of drafting the 2008 constitution, which the elections put into effect, was closely controlled by the military and excluded key stakeholders such as the National League for Democracy (NLD). Although the charter establishes a parliament and a civilian president, it also entrenches military dominance and allows the military to dissolve the civilian government if it determines that the "disintegration of the Union or national solidarity" is at stake. The charter's rights guarantees are limited by existing laws and may be suspended in a state of emergency. The military retains the right to administer its own affairs, and members of the outgoing military government received blanket immunity for all official acts. The military budget is still not publicly available, although some parliamentary scrutiny of military affairs has recently become possible.

The bicameral legislature consists of the 440-seat People's Assembly, or lower house, and the 224-seat Nationalities Assembly, or upper house. A quarter of the seats in both houses are reserved for the military and filled through appointment by the commander in chief, an officer who has broad powers and is selected by the military-dominated National Defense and Security Council (NDSC). The legislature elects the president, though the military members have the right to nominate one of the three candidates, with the other two nominated by the elected members of each chamber.

Ahead of the 2010 elections, the military leadership handpicked the election commission and wrote election laws designed to favor military-backed parties, leading the opposition NLD to boycott the polls. There were many allegations of rigged "advanced voting" and other irregularities. Ultimately, the military-supported Union Solidarity and Development Party (USDP) captured 129 of the 168 elected seats in the upper house and 259 of 330 elected seats in the lower house. The USDP also secured 75 percent of the seats in the 14 state and regional assemblies. The Rakhine Nationalities Development Party (RNDP) and the Shan National Democracy Party (SNDP) earned the second-highest percentage of seats in the Nationalities Assembly and People's Assembly, respectively. However, the vote for ethnic minority parties would likely have been higher had balloting not been canceled in several minority-dominated areas. The National Democratic Force (NDF), a breakaway faction of the NLD that decided to contest the elections, won just four seats in the upper house and eight in the lower.

Outgoing prime minister Thein Sein, who had retired from the military to register as a civilian candidate, was chosen as president by the new parliament. Military ruler Than Shwe officially retired, but he reportedly retained influence through his allies in the new government.

In April 2012, the NLD participated in by-elections for both chambers of the parliament. The party won all 37 seats at stake in the lower house, with one seat going to party leader and longtime political prisoner Aung San Suu Kyi. In the upper house, the NLD captured four of the six seats that were contested, with the other two going to the USDP and the SNDP. However, voting was postponed in three constituencies in war-torn Kachin State.

B. Political Pluralism and Participation: 6 / 16

The 2010 Political Party Registration Law gave new political parties only 60 days to register, mandated that existing parties reregister, and required parties to expel members currently serving prison terms. However, during the 2012 by-elections, there were fewer restrictions on party organization and mobilization, with only sporadic reports of mild interference. Many parties, including the NLD, convened meetings and rallies throughout the country.

Tu Ja, a former leader of ethnic Kachin rebels, was denied permission to form a political party and contest the 2010 and 2012 elections. In October 2013 he was granted approval to establish the Kachin State Democracy Party, which he would lead as chairman. However, minority groups continued to face restrictions on their political rights and electoral opportunities. In September 2013, the upper house of parliament took up a draft bill that would amend the Political Parties Registration Law to prohibit residents without full citizenship from forming political parties and contesting elections. The bill was introduced by the RNDP to curb political participation by the ethnic Rohingya minority, who were rendered stateless by a 1982 law and lack full citizenship documents.

C. Functioning of Government: 3 / 12

Since 2011 the government has allowed members of the parliament to speak about democratic rights. While the legislators' time to speak has often been severely limited, many of their speeches receive coverage in the domestic media, and they are not harassed for their remarks. Nevertheless, most of the parliament lacks electoral legitimacy, and the military remains a powerful force in politics and policymaking.

In July 2013, in the context of his personal and to some extent institutional rivalry with the president, the speaker of the parliament challenged the government's approach to peace talks with ethnic rebel groups, demanding direct involvement by the parliament and the military-dominated NDSC.

In August, the parliament decided to postpone discussion of a bill proposed by the Union Election Commission that would allow just 1 percent of constituents to initiate a recall process for elected lawmakers. The measure was supported by military members of parliament and opposed by elected members.

Although Aung San Suu Kyi has gained influence since joining the parliament in early 2012, she has been accused of failing to strongly challenge incumbent interests or alter state policy. Since August 2012 she has headed the parliamentary Committee for Rule of Law and Stability, which is tasked with supervising the compliance of four entities—the legislature, the judiciary, the civil service, and the media—with the rule of law. After a year of studying public complaints, investigating courts in many parts of the country, and meeting clients and officials, the committee submitted a seven-page report to the parliament. The report called for judicial independence and advised the authorities to work for peace. However, critics argued that the report lacked substantive detail and that communal violence, hate speech, corruption, and human rights violations in ethnic minority regions have continued unabated under the watch of the committee.

In December 2012, the government appointed Aung San Suu Kyi to head a commission charged with investigating a November crackdown on local residents protesting the Letpadaung Mining Project, which is operated under a contract between the military-owned Union of Myanmar Economic Holdings Company (UMEHL) and China's Wanbao Mining. The commission's report, published in March 2013, urged the Chinese company to increase compensation payments to local farmers whose land was lost to the project. The commission did not recommend that the project's expansion be halted. Local communities, protesters, and international human rights groups strongly criticized the report.

In a system that still lacks transparency and accountability, corruption and economic mismanagement are rampant at both the national and local levels. Burma was ranked 157 out of 177 countries surveyed in Transparency International's 2013 Corruption Perceptions Index. The government's economic reforms continue to be marred by widespread allegations that they primarily benefit family members and associates of senior government officials. Tax evasion by top companies, including large construction firms, has drawn public attention. While the space for public debate of sensitive economic issues is still limited, there is a growing consensus that the country's future development will require more transparency.

Discretionary Political Rights Question B: -3 / 0

The government has long used violence, displacement, and other tactics to alter the demographics of states featuring ethnic unrest or insurgencies. In May 2013, authorities in Rakhine State reaffirmed a 2005 regulation barring Rohingya Muslims in two townships from having more than two children per couple. Another local order requires Rohingya couples to obtain official permission to marry. Rohingya Muslims who violate the order by cohabiting or having sex out of wedlock can face up to 10 years' imprisonment. According to the Arakan Project, there were 535 Rohingya men serving sentences for unauthorized marriages in mid-2013. Children born to unrecognized couples or beyond the two-child limit are denied legal status and services. Also during 2013, the authorities pressured internally displaced Rohingyas to register as "Bengalis," which would suggest that they are migrants from Bangladesh. Those who refused to identify as Bengalis were beaten and arrested.

CIVIL LIBERTIES: 17 / 60
D. Freedom of Expression and Belief: 7 / 16

The government has allowed a more open media environment in recent years. An official censorship board was dissolved in 2012, and private daily newspapers were authorized in December 2012 for the first time since the 1960s. In November 2013, the lower house of parliament passed a Printing and Publishing Enterprise Bill after a consultative process that included input from its own committees, the Ministry of Information, the Interim Press Council, and media practitioners. The final bill, which had yet to be signed into law at year's end, was widely viewed as a step forward for press reform, as it would abolish prison sentences and reduce financial penalties for those found to be printing or publishing without registration. Two other media reform bills made progress toward adoption during the year. Despite such gains, a number of restrictions and abuses remain. The year's worst violation of press freedom took place in December, when a reporter in Shan State was sentenced to three months' imprisonment for investigating and documenting judicial corruption. She was the first journalist to be jailed under the current government. Separately, an edition of *Time* magazine was banned in June due to its cover story on Buddhist religious violence against Muslims. The government justified the ban as a measure "to prevent further conflict."

Previous constraints on internet access have largely unraveled, and the primary limitations on the medium's growth are now bandwidth and the cost of connections. Internet activity is still subject to criminal punishment under broadly worded legal provisions. Legislation enacted in 2013 amended the Electronic Transactions Law, which has routinely been used to criminalize political activism. Under the amended Section 33, internet users would face fines or prison terms of 3 to 7 years, down from 7 to 15 years, for "any act detrimental to" state security, law and order, community peace and tranquility, national solidarity, the national economy, or national culture—including "receiving or sending" related information. Separately, journalists and others have faced organized cyberattacks and attempts to infiltrate their e-mail accounts.

The 2008 constitution provides for freedom of religion. It distinguishes Buddhism as the majority religion, but also recognizes Christianity, Islam, Hinduism, and animism. At times the government interferes with religious assemblies and attempts to control the Buddhist clergy. Buddhist temples and monasteries were kept under close surveillance after monk-led protests and a subsequent crackdown in 2007, and more recently in connection with some clergy's anti-Muslim activities. The authorities have also discriminated against minority religious groups, refusing to grant them permission to hold gatherings and restricting educational activities, proselytizing, and construction of houses of worship.

Anti-Muslim riots affected major cities during 2013, and there was an outpouring of hate speech against the Muslim minority. Social media played an undisputed role in amplifying racial and religious tensions, though they were also stoked by some state institutions and mainstream news websites. The 969 Movement, a loosely organized Buddhist group that agitates for the protection of Buddhist privileges, urged boycotts against Muslim-run businesses and disseminated anti-Muslim propaganda. It has also been accused of instigating violence. Some Buddhist monks have aggressively promoted a draft law that would restrict interfaith marriages.

Although the former military junta imposed severe restrictions on academic freedom, there have been signs of more open academic discussion since 2011, as well as eased restrictions on private education. There are growing efforts to reform the University of Rangoon, with significant support from foreign partners. Political indoctrination, however, remains a problem, especially in history texts. Academics, like journalists, have been subject to cyberattacks and alleged surveillance.

People continue to impose some restrictions on their private discussions to avoid harassment by both state and nonstate actors, particularly in the context of religious violence. In February 2013, lawmakers established a special committee to identify a pseudonymous blogger who had criticized the parliament.

E. Associational and Organizational Rights: 4 / 12

Section 18 of the Peaceful Assembly and Peaceful Procession Law, which was adopted in July 2012, requires those who plan to stage a peaceful demonstration to obtain permission from the government. Proceeding without permission is punishable by one year in prison and a fine of 10,000 to 30,000 kyats ($12 to $35). According to a report released by Assistance Association for Political Prisoners (Burma) in October 2013, at least 29 people have been sentenced under Section 18, and 15 remained incarcerated. A bill under consideration in the parliament would repeal the section.

In November 2013 the parliament unveiled a draft Association Registration Law featuring simple, voluntary registration procedures for local and international nongovernmental organizations (NGOs) and no restrictions or criminal punishments. It had yet to be enacted at year's end. Although conditions have improved in recent years, both local and foreign NGOs continue to face regular restrictions on their activities, especially in ethnic minority regions.

The government violates workers' rights and represses union activity. Independent trade unions, collective bargaining, and strikes are illegal. However, garment workers have held strikes in Rangoon in recent years, with fewer repercussions than in the past. Various commercial and other interests continue to use forced labor despite a formal ban on the practice in 2000.

F. Rule of Law: 1 / 16

The judiciary is not independent. Judges are appointed or approved by the government and adjudicate cases according to its decrees. Administrative detention laws allow individuals to be held without charge, trial, or access to legal counsel for up to five years if the government concludes that they have threatened the state's security or sovereignty.

In keeping with President Thein Sein's pledge to release all political prisoners in Burma by the end of 2013, the government set up the Committee for Scrutinizing Remaining Political Prisoners in February 2013—with some civil society representation—to define the category of political prisoners, identify those still behind bars, report to the president, and coordinate a framework for their release. With a series of presidential pardons, the government subsequently released almost all of the political prisoners, including 57 in December

2013 alone. The government insists that all political prisoners have been freed, but according to civil society members of the committee, there are at least 33 prisoners of conscience still behind bars. Critics also note that releases of political prisoners have often coincided with high-profile diplomatic events, and freed inmates are warned that they must complete their old sentences if they commit new offenses.

In 2013 the government met with 16 ethnic armed groups and reached an agreement that there should be a nationwide cease-fire accord and a political solution to the civil conflicts. Both government and parliamentary leaders publicly said Burma should adopt a form of federal union. However, multiple negotiations continued throughout the year, and fighting persisted in some areas. Some of the country's worst human rights abuses still take place in ethnic minority regions, mostly committed by government troops. The Kachin, Chin, Karen, and Rohingya minorities are frequent victims. In 2012, renewed fighting in Kachin areas resulted in over 100,000 people being displaced from their homes. Tens of thousands of ethnic minorities in Shan, Karenni, Karen, and Mon States still live in squalid relocation centers as a legacy of previous military campaigns.

The practices of Chinese companies in various extractive industries in Burma, in addition to the migration of hundreds of thousands of Chinese workers and businesspeople, have led to rising anti-Chinese sentiment in recent years.

LGBT (lesbian, gay, bisexual, and transgender) people face societal discrimination and harassment by police. The penal code assigns up to 10 years in prison for sex "against the order of nature," and although the law is rarely enforced, it is sometimes used by police for harassment or extortion. However, LGBT rights showed some progress in 2013, including the holding of public or semipublic pride events in Rangoon and Mandalay.

G. Personal Autonomy and Individual Rights: 5 / 16

When a household receives any guest staying overnight, the host family is required to register the guests at a neighborhood administrative office, submitting the guests' proof of citizenship and paying a "small donation" to the neighborhood fund. A joint team of township and neighborhood authorities occasionally visit houses to check for unregistered guests. In the aftermath of bomb blasts occurring in some major cities in October 2013, for instance, the authorities conducted checks in almost all city neighborhoods. Guests and households who fail to register them face prison sentences or fines.

Burmese women of some classes have traditionally enjoyed high social and economic status, but women remain underrepresented in the government and civil service. Notwithstanding the prominence of Aung San Suu Kyi, few women have achieved public recognition during the current political opening. There is a dearth of laws to protect women from violence and exploitation. Domestic violence and human trafficking are concerns, and women and girls in displacement or refugee camps are at an increased risk of sexual violence and exploitation by traffickers. In the past, the Women's League of Burma has accused the military of systematically using rape and forced marriage as weapons against ethnic minorities during counterinsurgency campaigns. There are complaints that both the government and ethnic armed groups do not allow women's participation in peace negotiations.

Burundi

Political Rights Rating: 5
Civil Liberties Rating: 5
Freedom Rating: 5.0
Freedom Status: Partly Free
Electoral Democracy: No

Population: 10,900,000
Capital: Bujumbura

Ten-Year Ratings Timeline For Year Under Review (Political Rights, Civil Liberties, Status)

Year Under Review	2004	2005	2006	2007	2008	2009	2010	2011	2012	2013
Rating	5,5,PF	3,5,PF	4,5,PF	4,5,PF	4,5,PF	4,5,PF	5,5,PF	5,5,PF	5,5,PF	5,5,PF

INTRODUCTION

Political violence and extrajudicial killings were less prevalent in Burundi in 2013 compared with their 2010–2011 peak. Nevertheless, there were reports of violence and intimidation against civil society and opposition members perpetrated by Imbonerakure, the youth wing of the ruling National Council for the Defense of Democracy (CNDD). Tensions between rival political parties also began to rise as the country prepared for the 2015 general elections.

In January 2013, Burundi underwent its Universal Periodic Review (UPR) by the United Nations Human Rights Council (UNHRC), which provided 174 recommendations. More than 25 recommendations related specifically to concerns about freedoms of expression, association, and assembly. Restrictions on press freedom increased in 2013, including through a widely criticized media law that was signed in June. Just weeks after the new law went into effect, a journalist was arrested for allegedly breaching state security and was held in a secret prison by intelligence services.

POLITICAL RIGHTS: 12 / 40

A. Electoral Process: 4 / 12

A new constitution was adopted in 2005 after a series of agreements ended Burundi's 12-year civil war, which began with the 1993 assassination of a newly elected Hutu president and ultimately killed more than 300,000 people. Under the charter, the president, who is elected to a five-year term, appoints two vice presidents, one Tutsi and one Hutu, and they must be approved separately by a two-thirds majority in both the lower and upper houses of Parliament. While the lower house—the 100-seat National Assembly—is directly elected for a five-year term by proportional representation, locally elected officials choose members of the Senate, also for five-year terms. Each of Burundi's 17 provinces chooses two senators—one Tutsi and one Hutu. Carefully crafted constitutional arrangements require the National Assembly to be no more than 60 percent Hutu and no less than 40 percent Tutsi, with three additional deputies from the Twa ethnic minority, which is also allocated three senators. In both houses, a minimum of 30 percent of the legislators must be women.

Local elections in May 2010 were beset with electoral irregularities and repression, including serious government restrictions on freedom of movement for opposition leaders, the arrest of dozens of opposition activists, and a ban on all opposition party meetings. In response, most opposition parties boycotted the presidential and parliamentary polls that June and July. As a result, the ruling CNDD—a largely Hutu party associated with a former rebel group—captured 81 percent of the vote for the lower house, followed by the opposition Unity for National Progress (UPRONA) with almost 12 percent and the CNDD-allied Front for Democracy in Burundi (FRODEBU) with nearly 6 percent. In the Senate, the

CNDD took 32 seats, leaving UPRONA with 2. Incumbent president Pierre Nkurunziza of the CNDD was reelected with some 92 percent of the vote.

According to opposition parties and human rights organizations, the ostensibly independent election commission failed to adequately investigate allegations of preelectoral violence and release some individual polling-place results. Political rifts and violence in 2010 were mainly between rival Hutu groups, rather than between Hutu and Tutsi as in the past. Political polarization increased, and several leading opposition figures—including Agathon Rwasa, leader of the political party and former rebel group National Liberation Forces (FNL)—fled the country, fearing for their safety.

In preparation for the 2015 elections, the National Assembly and Senate approved a new electoral commission in December 2012, but an alliance of 10 opposition parties rejected the panel due to the reappointment of the commission's chairman and communications head. In March 2013, the ruling party and opposition met during a UN-backed electoral workshop and agreed on a roadmap for the 2015 polls as well as the adoption of an electoral code by December, though the code was still pending at year's end. Nevertheless, Nkurunziza indicated that he might run for president, defying the two-term limit set by the constitution. The CNDD argued that Nkurunziza's first term did not count toward the two-term limit, since in 2005 he had been chosen unopposed by a newly elected Parliament as part of the peace accords, rather than directly elected as in 2010.

B. Political Pluralism and Participation: 6 / 16

There are more than two dozen active political parties in Burundi, ranging from those that champion radical Tutsi positions to those that hold extremist Hutu views. Most are small in terms of membership, and many Tutsi have now joined formerly Hutu-dominated parties. The current government, appointed in September 2010, consists of members from the three political parties represented in Parliament: the largely Hutu CNDD, the country's largest party; the mainly Tutsi-led UPRONA; and FRODEBU. Many political parties include youth groups that intimidate and attack opponents.

A few opposition leaders who fled Burundi after the polarizing 2010 elections returned from exile or announced plans to return in 2013, reportedly to prepare for the 2015 elections. Nevertheless, repression against opposition voices persisted. Rwasa, who returned to Burundi in August 2013, was subsequently prevented from addressing his supporters at a public rally, and in September the public prosecutor launched an investigation against him for his alleged role in the massacre of some 160 Congolese refugees in 2004. Opposition parties regard these events as politically motivated attempts to undermine Rwasa's presidential ambitions.

There were fewer incidents of political violence between the ruling and opposition parties in 2013 than during the peak of violence in 2010–2011, though clashes between supporters of rival parties increased during the year as tensions began to rise ahead of the 2015 elections. There were also reports of increasing violence and intimidation against civil society and opposition members by Imboncrakure. Impunity has been the norm for the majority of political violence and extrajudicial killings in recent years.

C. Functioning of Government: 2 / 12

Corruption remains a significant problem. Burundi was ranked 157 out of 177 countries and territories surveyed in Transparency International's 2013 Corruption Perceptions Index. In July 2012, prominent antigraft activist Faustin Ndikumana was convicted under an anticorruption law and sentenced to five years in prison for making "false declarations" in his reporting on bribes that judges were allegedly forced to pay for their appointments. In

May 2012, 14 people were convicted for the April 2009 assassination of the deputy head of Burundi's largest anticorruption organization, the Anticorruption and Economic Malpractice Observatory, despite concerns that the investigation had targeted the wrong suspects and exonerated police and military officers who were known to have been involved. The jail sentences ranged from 10 years to life imprisonment.

CIVIL LIBERTIES: 22 / 60

D. Freedom of Expression and Belief: 8 / 16

Freedom of speech is legally guaranteed, but press laws restrict journalists through broad, vaguely written provisions. In June 2013, the president signed a new media law that was widely criticized for violating the constitutional right to free expression. The law limits the protection of journalistic sources, requires journalists to meet certain educational and professional standards, and bans the publication of stories related to national defense, security, public safety, and the state currency. The law also provides the media regulatory body with the power to issue or withdraw press cards in defamation cases. The legislation removed the penalty of imprisonment for offenses like defamation, but replaced it with crippling fines of between $2,000 and $6,000. The sums are more than the annual salaries of many Burundian journalists.

Radio is the primary source of information for the majority of the population. The media are dominated by the government, which owns the public television and radio stations; it also runs *Le Renouveau*, the only daily newspaper. There are several private broadcast media outlets, though most have a limited range. The British Broadcasting Corporation, Radio France Internationale, and Voice of America are available via FM transmissions in the capital. Print runs of most newspapers remain small, and readership is limited by low literacy levels. Access to the internet remains largely confined to urban areas.

Despite the recent emergence of a more pluralistic press, journalists have been arbitrarily arrested, harassed, or threatened on numerous occasions. Hassan Ruvakuki, a reporter for Radio France Internationale who had been sentenced to life in prison in 2012 on dubious charges of involvement in a 2011 rebel attack, was granted a conditional release in 2013 after he agreed to withdraw an appeal of his conviction. In June 2013, shortly after the promulgation of the new media law, intelligence services arrested Lucien Rukevya, a journalist and producer for the state-run National Radio and Television of Burundi, for his alleged involvement with M23 rebels in the Democratic Republic of the Congo. Accused of breaching state security, he was held in a secret prison for the first 24 hours of his detention and eventually released after 10 days. Two other journalists from a private radio station were subsequently summoned by the police for questioning.

While journalists have been increasingly willing to convey criticism of the government, they continue to engage in self-censorship and are sometimes censored by authorities. In May 2013, the media regulator ordered the Iwacu press group to suspend the posting of comments on its web forum for 30 days for failing to moderate comments that allegedly disturbed national unity and incited ethnic hatred.

Freedom of religion is generally observed, though in March 2013 police launched a brutal assault on a large crowd of adherents of a local spiritual movement who were making a monthly pilgrimage to Businde. The officers killed nine people and beat numerous others. Members of the same movement have been arbitrarily arrested and denied due process on other occasions since late 2012.

For many years, civil strife and Tutsi social and institutional dominance had impeded academic freedom by limiting educational opportunities for the Hutu, but this situation has improved since 2005.

E. Associational and Organizational Rights: 4 / 12

The constitution provides for freedoms of assembly and association, though onerous and costly registration requirements prevent many local nongovernmental organizations (NGOs) from receiving official legal recognition. Registration must be completed in person at the Ministry of Interior in Bujumbura, which is difficult for many in remote areas to reach, and extensive documentation is required.

Constitutional protections for organized labor are in place, and the right to strike is guaranteed by the labor code. The Confederation of Burundi Trade Unions has been independent since its establishment in 1995. Most union members are civil servants and have bargained collectively with the government.

There is modest but important civil society activity with a focus on human rights. In June 2011, members of the newly created National Independent Human Rights Commission were sworn in, and a 2012 assessment by Human Rights Watch found that the commission had so far been able to investigate politically sensitive cases and operate independently. In 2013, the commission led a consultation process that assessed threats against Burundian human rights defenders (HRDs), with the aim of drafting a law to support the protection of HRDs. Members of human rights groups that criticize the authorities are often subject to intimidation, threats, or surveillance, and bans on opposition organizations have been common during periods leading up to national elections. In 2013, opposition groups were prevented from holding public meetings, and some peaceful demonstrations were violently dispersed, such as a February rally held in support of Ruvakuki, the imprisoned journalist.

F. Rule of Law: 4 / 16

Burundi's judiciary is hindered by corruption, a lack of resources and training, and executive interference in legal matters. The current judicial system struggles to function effectively or independently and cannot handle the large number of pending cases, many of which are politically sensitive. In December 2012, a new draft law for the creation of a truth and reconciliation commission (TRC) to provide accountability for past abuses was submitted to Parliament, though an independent analysis of the draft found that the presidentially appointed body would lack independence. The pending TRC would also allow amnesty to be granted for crimes under international law, and there are concerns that the body could be used as a political tool to selectively punish the opposition, especially in the lead-up to the 2015 elections. The law had yet to be adopted at the end of 2013.

Crimes, especially those related to political violence, often go unreported or uninvestigated. An unusually large number of extrajudicial executions have been reported in recent years, though there were fewer in 2013 than in 2010–2012. According to Transparency International's 2013 Global Corruption Barometer, 82 percent of Burundians surveyed feel that the police are either corrupt or extremely corrupt. Prisons are overcrowded, unhygienic, and at times life-threatening.

Impunity for police brutality remains widespread. In March 2013, a police officer shot journalist Patrick Niyonkuru without warning for seeking information about a police roadblock in Bujumbura. In a rare occurrence, the government reacted to the shooting swiftly, bringing the officer to trial; he was sentenced to 15 years in prison.

Albinos face a particular threat from discrimination and violence. An albino girl was kidnapped and killed in May 2012; several suspects were arrested, and a verdict in their trial was pending at the end of 2013.

134   Freedom in the World 2014

G. Personal Autonomy and Individual Rights: 6 / 16

The constitution provides for freedom of movement, though citizens are restricted from traveling outside their communities without a special permit on Saturday mornings as part of a government effort to encourage participation in local service projects.

Women have limited opportunities for advancement in the economic and political spheres, especially in rural areas. Sexual and domestic violence are serious problems but are rarely reported to law enforcement agencies. The 2009 penal code criminalizes gay and lesbian sexual activity, and punishments include up to two years in prison.

Cambodia

Political Rights Rating: 6
Civil Liberties Rating: 5
Freedom Rating: 5.5
Freedom Status: Not Free
Electoral Democracy: No

Population: 14,400,000
Capital: Phnom Penh

Ten-Year Ratings Timeline For Year Under Review (Political Rights, Civil Liberties, Status)

Year Under Review	2004	2005	2006	2007	2008	2009	2010	2011	2012	2013
Rating	6,5,NF	6,5,NF	6,5,NF	6,5,NF	6,5,NF	6,5,NF	6,5,NF	6,5,NF	6,5,NF	6,5,NF

INTRODUCTION

Prime Minister Hun Sen and his Cambodia Peoples Party (CPP) won the July 2013 national elections amid widespread reports of voter list irregularities and fraud. The opposition Cambodian National Rescue Party (CNRP) rejected the results and led an unsuccessful call for the creation of an independent committee to investigate the irregularities. All 55 elected CNRP officials subsequently boycotted parliament, resulting in a single-party legislature forming a government without the CNRP. Sam Rainsy, long-time opposition leader and head of the CNRP, returned from exile in June, while hundreds of thousands of Cambodians participated in CNRP protests throughout the second half of the year calling for independent investigations of the election results.

Crackdowns on activists continued throughout the year. Police injured five protestors in March and some two dozen in May who were demonstrating against the government's forced eviction of several hundred residents from Boeung Kak Lake for land development. More than 30 garment factory workers were injured by police in May while protesting low pay and dangerous working conditions.

The trials of former top Khmer Rouge leaders in the Extraordinary Chambers in the Courts of Cambodia (ECCC) concluded in October, with a verdict expected in 2014.

Relations with China continued to improve in 2013, with Beijing funding several massive infrastructure projects throughout Cambodia. Natural resource extraction initiatives and infrastructure projects by China, Vietnamese and European firms, and multinational organizations continue to negatively impact residents' livelihoods and the environment due to endemic corruption and a lack of legal protections.

POLITICAL RIGHTS: 10 / 40 (+1)

A. Electoral Process: 3 / 12

The current Cambodian constitution was promulgated in 1993 by former King Norodom Sihanouk, who died in October 2012. The monarchy remains highly revered as a symbol of national unity, but has little political power. King Norodom Sihamoni currently sits on the throne, having succeeded his ailing father in 2004.

The prime minister and cabinet must be approved by a majority vote in the 123-seat National Assembly, whose members are elected by party-list voting to serve five-year terms. The upper house of the bicameral parliament, the Senate, has 61 members, of whom two are appointed by the king, two are elected by the National Assembly, and 57 are chosen by local legislators. Senators serve six-year terms.

Elections in Cambodia are marred by vote buying and fraudulent ballots, and the opposition is hampered by serious legal and sometimes physical harassment. Voting is tied to a citizen's permanent resident status in a village, township, or urban district, and this status cannot be changed easily.

In the July 2013 national elections, the CPP captured 68 of 123 seats, marking its worst showing since 1998. The elections were marred by reports of duplicate voter names, vote buying, and large groups of voters casting ballots in communes where they were not registered; the NEC identified over 250,000 duplicate names and 290,000 missing names from voter rolls. The CNRP rejected the official results, charging that it had won 63 seats, and—despite the NEC's findings—unsuccessfully petitioned for the creation of an independent authority to investigate its claims. As a result, 55 CNRP parliamentarians boycotted the results by refusing to take their seats in parliament at the assembly's September 23 opening session. The CPP nominated Hun Sen for his fifth term as prime minister, and the single-party legislature formed a government without the CNRP. By year's end, the legislature continued to be run solely by the CPP.

B. Political Pluralism and Participation: 4 / 16 (+1)

The constitution outlines the right of Cambodians to participate in multiparty democracy, but in practice space for the opposition is restricted. Harassment or threats against opposition supporters is not uncommon, and the CPP delivers vital jobs and financial rewards to supporters. Opposition leaders face legal suits for criticizing the ruling party.

In June 2013, longtime opposition leader Sam Rainsy returned to Cambodia; Rainsy had been living in exile since 2010 following charges related to allegations he made that the government had ceded territory along the border to Vietnam. In 2012, Rainsy fused his Sam Rainsy Party with opposition leader Kem Sokha's Human Rights Party to form the CNRP, creating the strongest opposition against the CPP in recent years. In May 2013, progovernment media carried remarks of an audio recording of Sokha allegedly expressing doubts about the existence of a Khmer Rouge-era prison; Sokha charged that the comments had been taken out of context in order to weaken the political opposition before the July elections. In June, the CPP-run National Assembly pushed through a law criminalizing genocide denial—a move widely viewed as a measure to increase anti-Sokha public sentiment—after having stripped 27 opposition lawmakers of their parliamentary status. The CPP used the lawmakers' membership in multiple parties as a pretext for this action, as many CNRP parliamentarians were members of the now-defunct SRP and HRP. The group Article 19 condemned the genocide denial law for having been adopted in a deeply flawed manner, violating freedom of expression, and imposing harsh penalties on violators.

C. Functioning of Government: 3 / 12

Corruption is a serious problem that hinders economic development and social stability. A 2010 law established the Anti-Corruption Unit (ACU), though its implementation has been slow. The ACU investigated corruption allegations against state-owned Telecom Cambodia director-general Lao Saroeun in May. Many in the ruling elite abuse their positions for private gain. While increased investment in mining, forestry, agriculture, textile manufacturing, tourism, hydropower, and real estate has brought notable economic growth in recent years, these enterprises frequently involve land grabs by powerful politicians, bureaucrats, and military officers.

Nepotism and patronage undermine the functioning of a proper, transparent bureaucratic system. Following unexpectedly poor showings in the 2013 elections, the CPP forced several party members to resign so that the sons of high-ranking party leaders, including Prime Minister Hun Sen and Interior Minister Sar Kheng, could take seats in parliament.

CIVIL LIBERTIES: 20 / 60

D. Freedom of Expression and Belief: 9 / 16

The government does not fully respect freedom of speech. The 2010 penal code continues to criminalize defamation and bars written criticism of public officials or institutions. The government has used lawsuits, criminal prosecution, and occasionally violent attacks as means of intimidation. Criticism of government policy is not well tolerated, and authorities are especially sensitive to media coverage of land grabs and extralegal resource extraction. The Ratanakkiri Provincial Court in August 2013 dropped charges against a military policeman and his wife who were accused of the September 2012 slaying of journalist Hang Serei Odom while he was investigating military involvement in timber smuggling. The death of Chut Wutty, an environmentalist killed in 2012 while assisting investigations into illegal logging, also remains unsolved. Independent radio owner Mam Sonando was arrested in 2012 on secession charges for coverage of a heavy-handed government crackdown on land protesters in Kratie, though international pressure prompted his release in May 2013.

Print journalists are somewhat freer to criticize the government, but the print media reaches only about 10 percent of the population. There are roughly 20 privately owned print and broadcast outlets, including several owned and operated by the CPP and opposition parties, though several have closed in recent years due to financial difficulties. Broadcast licensing processes remain opaque. There are no restrictions on access to foreign broadcasts via satellite.

The majority of Cambodians are Theravada Buddhists and can generally practice their faith freely, but societal discrimination against religious and ethnic minorities remains a problem. Terrorist attacks by Islamist militants elsewhere in Southeast Asia in recent years have raised new suspicions about the 2.4 percent of the population who are Cham Muslims.

Teachers and students practice self-censorship regarding discussions about Cambodian politics and history. Criticism of the prime minister and his family is often punished.

E. Associational and Organizational Rights: 3 / 12

The government's tolerance for freedoms of association and assembly has declined over the past few years. Crackdowns are unpredictable and often harsh. Hundreds of thousands of Cambodians from across the country participated in major protests in the second half of 2013 calling for independent investigations into the results of the July elections. Police shot and killed a bystander at a checkpoint and wounded several others at a CNRP rally in September, though the CNRP massive demonstrations in late October and at the end of December calling for an independent investigation into the election results were tolerated.

Violence against activists continued in 2013, especially regarding issues surrounding forced evictions and workers' rights. On November 22, the Supreme Court released on bail Yorm Bopha, a Boeung Kak activist imprisoned since September 2012 on ostensibly manufactured charges of assault. Her case was sent back to the Court of Appeals, which had upheld her conviction earlier in the year. Protests surrounding the controversial Boeung Kak

Lake, a community from which the government has forcibly evicted several hundred residents for land development, are especially vulnerable to retaliation; police injured 5 protesters in March and another 20 in May.

Civil society groups work on a broad spectrum of issues and offer social services, frequently with funding from overseas. Those that work on social or health issues, as opposed to justice and human rights, generally face less harassment from the state.

Cambodia has a small number of independent unions and workers have the right to strike, though many face retribution. Tensions between garment workers and law enforcement officials grew in 2013 as workers protested low wages and poor or dangerous working conditions. Police arrested eight demonstrators at a Nike factory in Kampong Speu province on June 3, and the factory later fired nearly 300 of the demonstrators. The government raised the minimum wage several times throughout the year from $61 a month to $100 in response to protests, but challenges to labor rights remain. A lack of resources and experience limit union success in collective bargaining, and union leaders report harassment and physical threats.

F. Rule of Law: 2 / 16

The judiciary is marred by inefficiency, corruption, and a lack of independence. There is a severe shortage of lawyers, and the system's poorly trained judges are subject to political pressure from the CPP, which has also undermined the Khmer Rouge tribunal. Abuse by law enforcement officers, including illegal detention and the torture of suspects and prisoners, is common. Impunity of elites and sham trials are common. In June 2013, former Bavet governor Chhouk Bandith was convicted for the 2011 shooting of three protesters; he was sentenced to only one and a half years in prison. On February 8, 2013, Minister of Information Khieu Kanharith released guidelines prohibiting lawyers from providing interviews to media outlets without approval of the CPP-associated Bar Association. Jails are severely overcrowded, and inmates often lack sufficient food, water, and health care.

On September 25, the Supreme Court ordered the release of Born Samnang and Sok Sam Oeun, who had been convicted of killing union leader Chea Vichea in 2004 and had served five years in prison. Domestic and international rights groups had long said the defendants were scapegoats in an effort to deflect a legitimate investigation into the death of the labor activist.

Government interference and lack of capacity continues to beset the ECCC, which was established to try the leaders of the genocidal Khmer Rouge regime. The trials faced repeated setbacks during 2013, including a $7 billion budget shortfall, two strikes of unpaid court workers, and the March 14 death of former Khmer Rouge foreign minister and defendant Ieng Sary while on trial. The ECCC has found only one major regime official guilty, former chief of the Tuol Sleng prison, Kang Kck "Duch" Ieu; he was sentenced in 2010 to 35 years in prison, a term later reduced to 19 years. The trial against defendants Nuon Chea, 86, and Khieu Samphan, 81, concluded in October, with a verdict expected in 2014. The remaining leader, Ieng Thirith, was declared mentally unfit to stand trial and released in 2012.

Minorities, especially those of ethnic Vietnamese descent, often face discrimination. The government has cracked down harshly on minority protests, notably the ethnically Vietnamese Khmer Krom community, though no specific incidents have been reported in recent years.

G. Personal Autonomy and Individual Rights: 6 / 16

The constitution guarantees the right to freedom of travel and movement, and the government generally respects this right in practice. However, reports surfaced in September

2013 that police prevented protesters in Svay Rieng province from traveling to Phnom Penh to participate in opposition demonstrations.

Land and property rights are regularly abused for the sake of private development projects. Some groups estimate the state has seized around 22 percent of Cambodia's land in concessions to private developers. Over the past several years, hundreds of thousands of people have been forcibly removed from their homes in both rural and urban areas—with little or no compensation or relocation assistance—to make room for commercial plantations, mine operations, factories, and high-end office and residential developments. Senior officials and their family members are frequently involved in these ventures, alongside international investors.

Women suffer widespread economic and social discrimination, lagging behind men in secondary and higher education. Rape and violence against women, including acid attacks, is common. The state convicted an acid attack perpetrator in January 2013, the first since the passage of a 2011 law outlawing the practice. However, advocates maintain that attacks are still frequent due to ease of access to such chemicals. Men, women, and children are frequently trafficked to and from Cambodia for prostitution and forced labor, and the government has done little to address the issue or provide assistance to victims.

Cameroon

Political Rights Rating: 6
Civil Liberties Rating: 6
Freedom Rating: 6.0
Freedom Status: Not Free
Electoral Democracy: No

Population: 21,500,000
Capital: Yaoundé

Ten-Year Ratings Timeline For Year Under Review (Political Rights, Civil Liberties, Status)

Year Under Review	2004	2005	2006	2007	2008	2009	2010	2011	2012	2013
Rating	6,6 NF	6,6 NF	6,6 NF	6,6 NF	6,6 NF	6,6 NF	6,6 NF	6,6 NF	6,6 NF	6,6 NF

INTRODUCTION

In April 2013, Cameroon elected its first Senate—a body that had been established under a series of constitutional reforms in 1996, but had not yet been realized. The body, however, has little authority; it is unable to reject presidential appointments or conduct investigations of the executive branch. Elections for municipal councilors and members of the National Assembly were held on September 30, resulting in landslide wins for President Paul Biya's Cameroon People's Democratic Movement (CPDM).

Biya turned 80 in 2013, and also began his fourth decade in office. His grip on power remains undiminished, and, despite rumors of ill health, he has suggested that he plans to run for the presidency again in 2018. Biya has not groomed a successor, and fears persist that his death in office would create a power vacuum. However, the election in June of a Senate president, 79-year-old Marcel Niat Njifenji, provided for a constitutional successor who would serve as a placeholder until elections could be held.

The persecution of those suspected of homosexual activity continued unabated in 2013. A prominent gay rights activist was murdered in Yaoundé in July.

POLITICAL RIGHTS: 8 / 40 (+1)
A. Electoral Process: 3 / 12 (+1)

Biya determines Cameroon's electoral calendar. On April 14, 2013, the country held long-delayed elections for its first Senate, which has 100 members. Seventy senators were indirectly elected by 10,636 members of the country's 360 municipal councils, while 30 senators were appointed by Biya, three from each of the country's 10 regions. The CPDM won 56 of the elected seats, while the main opposition party, the Anglophone-led Social Democratic Front (SDF), won the remaining 14. The SDF leader, John Fru Ndi, lost his Senate bid in the party's northwestern stronghold, an embarrassing defeat that pointed to a possible generational shift in party leadership. Fru Ndi accused CPDM leaders of vote buying.

Direct elections for municipal councilors and the 180-seat National Assembly were held on September 30 after three postponements and a year of delay. Twenty-nine political parties took part in the legislative elections and 35 in the municipal elections. Results released in October showed that the CPDM took 148 of the 180 assembly seats; the SDF took 18, and smaller parties took the remainder. The CPDM won 305 of the 360 contested municipal council seats. Both the April and the September elections were generally described by observers as free and fair.

Presidential elections in 2011, in which Biya claimed 78 percent of the vote, were widely viewed as tainted, as had been previous presidential, legislative, and municipal elections. The country's electoral commission, Elections Cameroon (ELECAM), had been formed in 2006 to address concerns about the fair management of previous elections. The commission's board remains dominated by appointees with close ties to the ruling party, despite the 2011 appointment of six additional board members with ties to civil society and the clergy. ELECAM introduced biometric voter registration for the September 30 National Assembly elections, which was credited with raising both voter registration and participation to new levels. Some 70 percent of the country's 5.4 million registered voters reportedly went to the polls.

B. Political Pluralism and Participation: 3 / 16

Despite having almost 300 political parties, Cameroon remains essentially a one-party state controlled by Biya. The country's numerous opposition parties remain highly fragmented, preventing any one from becoming a credible threat to the CPDM; efforts to form loose coalitions of rival parties have failed. The SDF is the largest opposition party and has a national base, but other opposition groups suffer from ethnic and regional biases that sharply limit their membership.

State patronage and Biya's control of high-level appointments help his CPDM retain its hold on power, as does de facto state control over the timing of the release of mandated public funding for campaigning political parties and the government's payment of village chiefs' salaries; voting recommendations by village chiefs are often still followed absolutely.

Several political rivals of Biya have been imprisoned on corruption charges. Critics raised questions about the timing of the release after three years' imprisonment of Haman Adama, the former minister of basic education; charges against her were dropped September 19 after she paid back to the government the money it said she had taken. Just days after her release and days prior to the municipal and National Assembly elections, Adama joined CPDM campaign activities in her home town, the country's northern city of Garoua, where she was popular and where support for the CPDM was weak.

The Baka people, who face discrimination in Cameroon, are not represented in either house of parliament or in the top levels of government.

C. Functioning of Government: 2 / 12

Corruption remains systemic. Generous fuel subsidies placate the car-owning middle and upper-middle classes. Biya initiated an anticorruption campaign called Opération Épervier, or "Operation Sparrowhawk," in 2006, but critics have accused him of using it to remove potential political opponents. In September 2012, Marafa Hamidou Yaya, a former minister and presidential hopeful whom Biya had fired in 2011, was sentenced to 25 years in prison for embezzlement. In October 2013, a court sentenced former prime minister Inoni Ephraim and former minister of state Atangana Mebara to 20 years in prison for corruption. The two had been charged with embezzling millions of dollars from state-run companies while in office.

Cameroon ranked 47 out of 58 countries worldwide and 14 out of 17 African countries included in the 2013 Resource Governance Index of revenue transparency and accountability in the oil, gas, and mining sectors. Cameroon was ranked 144 out of 177 countries and territories surveyed in Transparency International's 2013 Corruption Perceptions Index.

CIVIL LIBERTIES: 16 / 60
D. Freedom of Expression and Belief: 7 / 16

The constitution guarantees free speech, but genuine freedom of expression remains elusive. Although the 1996 constitution ended prepublication censorship, the charter's Article 17 gives officials the power to ban newspapers based on a claimed threat to public order. Defamation remains a criminal offense; in June, a reporter was fined and briefly jailed after being convicted of criminal defamation for reporting in 2011 that the wife of a musician had been arrested; the editor of the weekly *Paroles* magazine served two months in prison following criminal defamation charges for reporting on allegations of mismanagement at a Douala bus company. In September, the National Communications Council banned 11 media outlets for what it described as ethics violations; the move followed a similar announcement from the council in April, when it had banned two television programs and three radio programs, and suspended seven journalists. There are no restrictions on internet use, but internet penetration is very low, at just over 6 percent in 2013.

While there is general religious freedom, the government in 2013 shut down dozens of Pentecostal churches, calling them a security threat. There are no legal restrictions on academic freedom, but state security informants operate on university campuses. Public criticism of the government and membership in opposition political parties can have a negative impact on professional opportunities and advancement.

E. Associational and Organizational Rights: 3 / 12

Freedoms of assembly and association, while legally protected, are subject to significant restrictions, including a requirement that organizers notify the government before assemblies take place. In practice, this policy led to frequent suppression of the right to free assembly. In July, about 80 members of the Southern Cameroons National Council (SCNC), a banned organization that advocates for the partition of Cameroon's English-speaking south from the rest of the country, were arrested while attending a meeting in a private home. Civil society is growing, but organizations can face stiff government opposition if they become too critical. Trade unions, strikes, and collective bargaining are permitted, but subject to numerous restrictions.

F. Rule of Law: 2 / 16

The judiciary is subordinate to the Ministry of Justice, and courts are weakened by political influence and corruption. Lengthy pretrial detentions are commonplace.

The security forces act with impunity for human rights violations that include excessive use of force, torture and other abuse, and extrajudicial executions. Prisons are overcrowded and conditions are sometimes life threatening, and torture and abuse of detainees is widespread.

In February, a French family was kidnapped and held for two months by members of the Nigerian Islamist group Boko Haram in the Waza National Park in Cameroon's far north. A Nigerian government report indicated that the abductors had received a $3 million ransom, but did not indicate the money's source.

Discrimination against the LGBT (lesbian, gay, bisexual, and transgender) community is rife. Article 347 of the penal code forbids "sexual relations with a person of the same sex," but in practice, most people are prosecuted with no evidence of actual sexual activity, but rather on suspicion of being gay. There are persistent reports of forced anal exams as well as other forms of abuse. On July 15, Eric Ohena Lembembe, the executive director of the Cameroonian Foundation for AIDS, was found murdered in Yaoundé, his neck broken, feet smashed, and face burned with an iron. Two prominent Cameroonian lawyers who regularly defend people accused of homosexuality, Alice Nkom and Michel Togué, have received threats, including against the safety of their children, and Togué's office was burglarized in June. There was a suspicious fire at an HIV-prevention center in Douala.

G. Personal Autonomy and Individual Rights: 4 / 16

Travel is largely unrestricted, although Nigerian militant activity in Cameroon's far north has increased insecurity in the region. Bribery is commonplace and operates in all sectors, from gaining school admissions to fixing traffic infractions. There were reports that Cameroonians seeking to resettle abroad could base fraudulent asylum claims on bogus police reports and medical records they had purchased, and even on news articles alleging persecution that were written in exchange for bribes.

In recent years, Cameroon has bolstered its commercial legal system in a bid to make contracts easier to enforce. Yet Cameroon still ranked 175 out of 189 countries included in the World Bank's 2014 rankings on the ease of enforcing contracts, and 168 in the World Bank's 2014 rankings on the ease of doing business. Agribusinesses operate with little or no consultation with local inhabitants, and a lack of transparency means people are usually unaware of potential environmental hazards. Concerns have been raised about the government's failure to recognize indigenous forest peoples' right to prior consent when logging concessions are granted.

The constitution guarantees equal rights to men and women, but traditional legal values often take precedence, and do not always provide women full rights. Although the penal code criminalizes rape against women, perpetrators are declared innocent if the victim has reached puberty and freely consents to marriage. Female genital mutilation is still practiced, particularly in isolated areas of the extreme north, east and southwest regions. Women won 56 National Assembly seats in the September elections, a significant increase, and 20 Senate seats.

Despite an anti–human trafficking law passed in 2011, Cameroon remains a source, transit and destination country for forced labor and sex trafficking of children, as well as a source country for women who have been subject to forced labor and forced prostitution in Europe.

Canada

Political Rights Rating: 1
Civil Liberties Rating: 1
Freedom Rating: 1.0
Freedom Status: Free
Electoral Democracy: Yes

Population: 35,250,000
Capital: Ottawa

Ten-Year Ratings Timeline For Year Under Review (Political Rights, Civil Liberties, Status)

Year Under Review	2004	2005	2006	2007	2008	2009	2010	2011	2012	2013
Rating	1,1,F	1,1,F	1,1,F	1,1,F	1,1F	1,1,F	1,1,F	1,1,F	1,1,F	1,1,F

INTRODUCTION

In May, the Canadian Federal Court ruled that electoral fraud had been committed in several districts during the 2011 federal elections, but determined that the fraud was not severe enough to overturn the results. In an effort to increase representation in provinces with the fastest growing populations, a bill was passed in December that adds 30 seats to the House of Commons.

Numerous corruption investigations that took place during the year resulted in the resignation of a senator and the chief of staff, as well as the suspension of three additional senators. An ongoing inquiry into corruption within Québec's construction industry revealed that the largest labor federation was under the control of organized crime. Toronto mayor Rob Ford was also embroiled in scandal during the year after he admitted in November to having smoked crack cocaine. After he refused to resign, the Toronto Council voted to remove most of his authority by late November.

The proposed Charter of Québec Values, intended to restrict religious expression by public sector employees, was heavily debated throughout the year amongst political parties and the public.

POLITICAL RIGHTS: 39 / 40 (-1)

A. Electoral Process: 12 / 12

Canada is governed by a prime minister, a cabinet, and Parliament, which consists of an elected 308-member House of Commons and an appointed 105-member Senate. Senators may serve until age 75. Lower-house elections are held every four years, with early elections called only if the government loses a parliamentary no-confidence vote. The British monarch is head of state, represented by a ceremonial governor-general who is appointed on the advice of the prime minister.

In early elections held in 2011, the Conservative Party triumphed, securing 166 seats to form a majority government. Placing second with 103 seats was the social democratic New Democratic Party (NDP), which became the leading opposition party for the first time. The center-left Liberal Party won 34 seats, while the Bloc Québécois, which favors Québec separatism, suffered a devastating defeat, with just 4 members elected to Parliament. The Green Party captured 1 seat.

On May 23, 2013, the Canadian Federal Court ruled that electoral fraud had been committed in several electoral districts during the 2011 election, but that the fraud was not severe enough to overturn the voting results. The fraudulent activity involved voter suppression tactics used by someone who accessed the Conservative Party's database to make misleading phone calls, or robocalls, to non-Conservative voters to misinform them that their polling stations had been relocated. The chief electoral officer released a report in March recommending that political parties be held liable for the misuse or loss of voter information; a second report to be released before the 2015 federal election will detail sanctions and penalties for such violations.

Prime Minister Stephen Harper made significant changes to his cabinet in July, including the promotion of four female ministers from the backbenches. In December, the Fair Representation Act received royal assent to add 30 new seats to the House of Commons in an effort to increase effective representation of provinces with growing populations. The new seats will be distributed among Alberta, British Columbia, Ontario, and Québec, and will be in effect for the 2015 elections.

B. Political Pluralism and Participation: 16 / 16

Canadians are free to organize in different political parties, and the political system is open to the rise and fall of competing parties. Both Conservative and Liberal governments have been elected to the House of Commons since the 1980s. A total of 18 political parties competed in the 2011 elections, as well as 61 independent candidates.

C. Functioning of Government: 11 / 12 (-1)

Canada has a reputation for clean government and a record of vigorous prosecution of corruption cases. However, the country has been criticized for failing to effectively combat bribery of foreign public officials in international business transactions. In January 2013, a Calgary-based oil company was fined US$10.35 million, the largest penalty to date, for bribing a government official from Chad. The government strengthened the Corruption of Foreign Public Officials Act in June with amendments that will allow the government to more easily prosecute Canadian individuals and companies that bribe foreign officials.

Efforts to address corruption in Québec continued during the year along with the ongoing inquiry led by France Charbonneau, a Québec Superior Court justice. The Charbonneau Commission, which has focused on corruption in the construction industry, led to the resignation of Montréal mayor Gérald Tremblay and neighboring Laval mayor Gilles Vaillancourt in 2012. Vaillancourt was arrested in May 2013, along with 36 others, on charges of gangsterism, fraud, corruption, and money laundering; no charges were brought against Tremblay. Michael Applebaum, who became interim mayor of Montréal following Tremblay's resignation, was arrested on corruption charges in June. The commission's public hearings and investigations throughout 2013 revealed that the construction branch of Québec's largest labor federation was under the control of organized crime. The Charbonneau Commission is expected to release an interim report in January 2014 and a final report in 2015.

The Canadian Senate was also rocked by scandal in 2013, stemming from improper expense reports prepared by four senators. The controversy emerged over the manipulation of rules allowing senators to claim living expenses when working in the capital if they live more than 100 kilometers away. In May, the Senate and external auditors released a report that revealed the improperly claimed living allowances of senators Patrick Brazeau, Mike Duffy and Mac Harb. News then surfaced that while Senator Duffy had voluntarily repaid US$90,000 of improperly claimed expenses, the Prime Minister's chief of staff, Nigel Wright, had written Duffy a personal check to reimburse him. Wright resigned in May and Senator Harb resigned in August. In September it was announced that Senator Pamela Wallin had also submitted false claims. The Senate voted in November to suspend Senators Duffy, Brazeau and Wallin; however, no criminal charges were filed.

Canada was ranked 9 out of 177 countries and territories surveyed in Transparency International's 2013 Corruption Perceptions Index.

CIVIL LIBERTIES: 59 / 60 (+1)

D. Freedom of Expression and Belief: 16 / 16

Canada's media is generally free; journalists are mostly protected from violence and harassment in their work and are able to express diverse views. However, defamation remains a criminal offense, punishable by up to five years in prison. No statutory laws protect confidential sources, and the courts often decide whether or not to respect source confidentiality on a case-by-case basis. A gag law was passed in Alberta in December, making it illegal to advocate for a strike by public employees. A 2012 bill designed to increase accountability by amending the Access to Information Act and the Privacy Act continued to raise concerns as it moved through the House of Commons. Press freedom advocates claimed that the bill would undermine the journalistic and programming integrity of Canadian Broadcasting Corporation, the country's public broadcaster; however, the bill had yet to become law at year's end. Despite the existence of Canada's Access to Information Act, there are many challenges to obtaining information, including lengthy delays and excessive costs. Media ownership continues to become more concentrated.

While the Harper government vowed at the end of 2012 to permanently shelve proposed legislation that would have allowed them to monitor the digital activity of internet users via their service providers without a warrant, a similar bill was introduced in November with the intention of combatting cyberbullying. Press freedom critics have argued that the language that defines this crime is too vague, and like the previous proposed legislation, this bill allows Internet service providers and telecommunications companies to provide customer information to the government without a warrant. The bill would also allow police to remotely access personal computers and cellphones. The bill had yet to become law at year's end.

Religious freedom is protected by the constitution and other legislation. However, there have been cases of societal discrimination based on religious affiliation, including numerous acts of violence and vandalism against Canada's Jewish and Muslim communities. There has also been controversy over the legality of wearing religious clothing and face coverings in public. In November 2013, the Charter of Québec Values bill was introduced in the province's legislature, with the aim of restricting "overt" and "conspicuous" religious symbols, including headgear and the wearing of large crosses by public sector employees. The proposed charter caused significant debate, with public hearings on the bill scheduled for January 2014. Academic freedom is respected. However, a policy prohibiting federally funded scientists from speaking to the media about their research, even after it has been published, continued to be enforced in 2013.

E. Associational and Organizational Rights: 12 / 12 (+1)

Freedoms of association and assembly are generally respected. However, police conduct during the protests surrounding the 2010 meeting of the Group of 20 (G20) in Toronto included the use of excessive force and illegal imprisonment. During 2013, 31 police officers faced disciplinary charges related to their response to the G20 protest. One officer was convicted in September on criminal charges of assault with a weapon for striking a protester with a baton while he was held down by other officers.

The police response to the 2012 demonstrations in Québec staged by students and the general public occasionally turned violent; authorities arrested some 2,500 people, used tear gas against demonstrators, and resorted to the tactic of kettling. A Quebec government-appointed commission initiated an investigation into the police conduct around the demonstrations in June, and public hearings began in September; the commission's report had yet to be released at year's end. In October, at least 40 people were arrested in New Brunswick when a protest against shale gas extraction (fracking) near land belonging to the Elsipogtog Mi'kmaq Nation turned violent.

Trade unions and business associations enjoy high levels of membership and are well organized. However, the Conservative government has adopted a tough line with unions representing public workers and has interfered with the rights of workers to organize, strike, and bargain collectively.

F. Rule of Law: 15 / 16

The judiciary is independent. Canada's criminal law is based on legislation enacted by Parliament; its tort and contract law is based on English common law, with the exception of Québec, where it is based on the French civil code. A 2012 anticrime law increased mandatory minimum sentences, provided for harsher sentences for young offenders, and eliminated conditional sentences such as house arrest or community service for some crimes. Critics argued that the new law would increase both the number of people in prison and detention costs, and inflict unconstitutional punishments on people. According to the Annual Report of the Office of the Correctional Investigator (2012–2013), the country's prison population was the highest ever. The number of visible minorities in prison has risen by 75 percent in the last decade; while the aboriginal population comprises about 4 percent of Canada's population, they represent close to a quarter of all inmates.

According to human rights groups, a 2012 immigration law, which took effect in 2013, creates an unfair system by increasing detention time for refugees and granting sole discretion to the minister of citizenship and immigration to designate certain countries of origin as "safe." The new law also imposes a waiting period of five years before refugees can apply for permanent residence. Significant cuts in funding for refugee health care also came into effect this year.

While authorities have taken important steps to protect the rights of the country's indigenous population, they remain subject to multiple forms of discrimination and have unequal access to education, health care, and employment. There are frequent controversies over control of land in various provinces, including the building of gas and oil wells on traditional territories.

G. Personal Autonomy and Individual Rights: 16 / 16

Women's rights are protected in law and in practice. Women hold approximately 25 percent of the seats in the lower house of Parliament, some 37 percent in the Senate, and about 31 percent in the cabinet. Women have made major economic gains and are well represented in the labor force, though they still earned 28 percent less than men for the same work in Ontario in 2012. Indigenous women and girls face racial and economic discrimination, as well as high rates of gender-based violence. In 2012, Canada enacted a National Action Plan to Combat Human Trafficking. Canada legalized same-sex marriage in 2005; however, despite advances in legal equality, lesbian, gay, bisexual, and transgender (LGBT) Canadians continue to occasionally face discrimination and be the targets of hate crimes.

Cape Verde

Political Rights Rating: 1
Civil Liberties Rating: 1
Freedom Rating: 1.0
Freedom Status: Free
Electoral Democracy: Yes

Population: 514,600
Capital: Praia

Ten-Year Ratings Timeline For Year Under Review (Political Rights, Civil Liberties, Status)

Year Under Review	2004	2005	2006	2007	2008	2009	2010	2011	2012	2013
Rating	1,1,F	1,1,F	1,1,F	1,1,F	1,1,F	1,1,F	1,1,F	1,1,F	1,1,F	1,1,F

INTRODUCTION

The year 2013 was marked by slowing economic growth (estimated at 4.1 percent) and dangerously expanding public debt. President Jorge Carlos Fonseca and Prime Minister José Maria Neves and their two political parties worked together toward Cape Verde's stability.

The cooperation did not impede institutionalized checks and balances. For example, the opposition Movement for Democracy (MPD) contested the validity of the law establishing the Council of Communities, which addresses migration and the diaspora, because it was passed without a two-thirds majority. Although Fonseca also questioned it, he approved the law after a Supreme Court review.

POLITICAL RIGHTS: 37 / 40

A. Electoral Process: 12 / 12

Cape Verde's president (head of state) and members of the 72-seat National Assembly are elected by universal suffrage for five-year terms. The prime minister is nominated by the National Assembly and appointed by the president.

In the February 2011 legislative elections, the African Party for Independence of Cape Verde (PAICV) secured 38 seats, while the MPD garnered 32 seats and the Democratic and Independent Cape Verdean Union (UCID) took 2. In the August 2011 presidential election, former MPD foreign minister Jorge Carlos Fonseca claimed 54 percent of the vote in a second-round runoff. International observers declared the elections to be free and fair.

B. Political Pluralism and Participation: 15 / 16

Cape Verde had only one political party, the socialist PAICV, until a multiparty system was introduced in 1991. Since then, the PAICV and the center-right MPD have dominated politics. The leader of the UCID has stated that the party's main goal for 2016 is to prevent the PAICV and the MPD from achieving an absolute majority.

C. Functioning of Government: 10 / 12

In January, the secretary of state for public administration admitted that there were "serious ethical problems and strong indication of corruption" in Cape Verde's civil service. To combat this, he declared that the government was preparing an Ethics Code for the Civil Service. In April, six workers from the Ministry of Finance and one unemployed youth were arrested under suspicion of embezzlement of the government coffers and money laundering.

Cape Verde's infrastructural development has generated multiple allegations of corruption at the municipal and national levels. In January, the leader of the MPD accused the government of lack of transparency and mismanagement of Cape Verde's public works. Following confirmation in March of cost overruns and tender mismanagement in the construction of the island of Fogo's ring road, the MPD accused the government of using the money originally allocated to build homes for supporters and buy Jeeps for the prime minister.

Partly as a result of these accusations, Cape Verde dropped from second to third in the 2013 Ibrahim Index of African Governance. Cape Verde was ranked 41 out of 177 countries and territories in Transparency International's 2013 Corruption Perceptions Index.

In early 2013 the government announced a series of reforms that would transfer a larger share of central government funds to the municipalities in 2014. Later in the year, the president of the Commission on Parliamentary Reform introduced a draft proposal to promote transparency and ethical behavior in the National Assembly. The proposal would be implemented in 2014.

CIVIL LIBERTIES: 53 / 60

D. Freedom of Expression and Belief: 15 / 16

While government authorization is needed to publish newspapers and other periodicals, freedom of the press is guaranteed in law and generally respected in practice. The independent press is small but vigorous, and there are several private and community-run radio stations. State-run media include radio and television stations. The government does not impede or monitor internet access. In May the president argued for the introduction of new legal procedures that ensure that the media has easier access to information from public institutions.

According to the 2012 U.S. Department of State's International Religious Freedom Report, there were no societal or governmental incidents of religious intolerance, and the constitution requires the separation of church and state. However, 77 percent of Cape Verdeans belong to the Roman Catholic Church, which enjoys a somewhat privileged status. Academic freedom is respected, and higher education has expanded rapidly.

E. Associational and Organizational Rights: 11 / 12

Freedoms of assembly and association are legally guaranteed and observed in practice. Nongovernmental organizations operate freely. The constitution also protects the right to unionize, and workers may form and join unions without restriction. Strikes are uncommon. A 72-hour prison guard strike took place in October 2013 to force the government to respect the terms of the agreement that was reached with the union and the workers' association in May 2013.

F. Rule of Law: 14 / 16

Cape Verde's judiciary is independent. However, the capacity and efficiency of the courts are limited, and lengthy pretrial detention remains a problem. The occasional use of the military as a domestic police force is generating some concern. In August, an MPD legislator accused the military corps deployed to protect turtles in Boa Vista of using excessive force against the local population.

Following a spike in crime in 2012, the Cape Verdean government implemented the Strategic Plan for Homeland Security (PESI), which contributed to a marked decrease in crime nationwide.

Ethnic divisions are not a salient problem in Cape Verde. Still, the government and Cape Verdean society struggle to deal with a fast-growing number of immigrants, particularly from Guinea-Bissau, Senegal, Nigeria, and China.

G. Personal Autonomy and Individual Rights: 13 / 16

While discrimination based on gender is legally prohibited, problems such as violence against women, wage discrimination, and unequal access to education persist. To address these issues, the government adopted a series of legislative reforms, including a 2010 law criminalizing gender violence and a National Action Plan to fight gender violence (2009–2011). Same-sex sexual acts are legal as of the 2004 Penal Code. The first Gay Pride March took place in 2013.

Central African Republic

Political Rights Rating: 7 ↓
Civil Liberties Rating: 7 ↓
Freedom Rating: 7 ↓
Freedom Status: Not Free
Electoral Democracy: No

Population: 4,676,000
Capital: Bangui

Status Change: The Central African Republic's political rights rating declined from 5 to 7, its civil liberties rating declined from 5 to 7, and its status declined from Partly Free to Not Free due to the Séléka rebel group's ouster of the incumbent president and legislature, the suspension of the constitution, and a general proliferation of violence by criminal bands and militias, spurring clashes between Muslim and Christian communities.

Ten-Year Ratings Timeline For Year Under Review (Political Rights, Civil Liberties, Status)

Year Under Review	2004	2005	2006	2007	2008	2009	2010	2011	2012	2013
Rating	6,5,NF	5,4,PF	5,4,PF	5,5,PF	5,5,PF	5,5,PF	5,5,PF	5,5,PF	5,5,PF	7,7,NF

INTRODUCTION

A rebellion against the government of President François Bozizé that began in December 2012 culminated in a coup in March 2013, leading the situation in the Central African Republic (CAR) to deteriorate significantly throughout 2013. The rebel group responsible for the coup was known as Séléka; it was created in August 2012 from three older rebel groups: a faction of the Union of Democratic Forces for Unity (UDFR); an offshoot of the Convention of Patriots for Justice and Peace (CPJP) known as the Fundamental CPJP; and a lesser-known group, the Convention of Patriots for Salvation and Kodro. Séléka's original demands were for the proper implementation of earlier peace accords between the government and rebel groups, including payments for demobilized rebels fighters and release of prisoners. The group was led by Michel Djotodia, who came from the CAR's predominantly Muslim northeast. Most of Seleka's soldiers come from the same region, although Chadian and Sudanese mercenaries have also played an important role in the group's actions.

As the rebels advanced and the central government quickly lost control over large areas of the country, the Economic Community of Central African States (ECCAS) decided in late December 2012 to send a multinational force to the CAR and the Chadian government pledged a force of 2,000 soldiers. January 2013 meetings in Libreville, the capital of Gabon, between Séléka representatives and Bozizé produced a power-sharing agreement that seemed to have the potential to deescalate the situation by creating a unity government; Djotodia would become vice prime minister and Bozizé would retain the presidency until his term ended in 2016. However, Séléka did not halt its military campaign, taking control of towns in northern and southeastern CAR, and finally seizing Bangui on March 24 in an attack that killed 13 South African soldiers and wounded 27. Bozizé immediately fled the county, and Djotodia suspended the constitution, dissolved the parliament, and declared himself president. Soon after, he created a transitional government and promised elections within

18 months of the swearing in of a transitional president. In August, Djotodia was sworn in to that position and a transitional charter went into effect.

The coup left the CAR internationally isolated, with the African Union (AU) suspending the country and foreign governments refusing to recognize Djotodia as its leader. In September, Djotodia ordered Séléka to disband, but the order had little practical effect.

The CAR was already plagued by various armed groups, including combatants from the Lord's Resistance Army in the southeast of the country and poachers and traffickers from neighboring countries in the Vakaga region. The coup and subsequent instability led to a proliferation of armed groups and an increase in weapons in the country. Infighting within Séléka itself has further heightened tensions.

In early October, at the request of France, the UN Security Council resolution asked for the creation of MISCA (The International Support Mission to CAR), led by the African Union, which already had troops on the ground. On December 5, the Security Council authorized MISCA with a one year mandate that allows the use of force to protect civilians. By the end of December, MISCA was comprised of 4,000 soldiers with 2,000 more to be added by the beginning of 2014. During this time, France increased its troops to 1,600 soldiers.

This troop increase was in response to the worsening of violence during the end of November and particularly December. By early November, and in response to Seleka targeting of Christian civilians, a new Christian militia—the anti-Balaka—that includes ex-army soldiers and supporters of ex-president Bozize, started fighting both Seleka and attacking Muslim communities throughout the country. As a result of a Seleka attack in Bangui, by the end of December over 1,000 civilians were killed while nearly half the population of the city fled. Similarly, hundreds of Muslims have been killed by anti-Balaka militias and entire villages burned. Both groups have recruited child soldiers and by the end of the year, the UN estimates that up to 6,000 children are fighting for one of the rebel factions.

POLITICAL RIGHTS: 0 / 40 (-16)

A. Electoral Process: 0 / 12 (-7)

Bozizé came to power through a coup in 2003, but his government transitioned to civilian rule and voters approved a new constitution in 2004. According to the constitution, members of the unicameral, 105-seat National Assembly were elected by popular vote for five-year terms. The president, who was elected for a five-year term and eligible for a second term, appointed the cabinet and dominated the legislative and judicial branches.

Presidential and legislative elections were held in January 2011 after being delayed twice the previous year. Bozizé, with the backing of the National Convergence Kwa Na Kwa (KNK) coalition, won the presidential poll, defeating four candidates with 66 percent of the vote, later revised downward to 64 percent by the Constitutional Court. The KNK won 63 out of the 105 seats in concurrent National Assembly elections. The polls were considered free, and security officers did not intimidate voters as they had in previous elections. However, the opposition criticized both elections as unfair.

In the March 2013 coup, the self-appointed president, Djotodia, suspended both the constitution and parliament. He also appointed the members of the weak transitional government. The transitional charter was put in place in August, but there were no specific plans to write a new constitution.

B. Political Pluralism and Participation: 1 / 16 (-6)

Prior to the coup, the KNK coalition was the country's leading political force, and other parties operated freely. In 2012, the government sometimes withheld approval for meetings of opposition groups.

The coup and the precarious security situation around the country have effectively blocked political participation throughout 2013. Although there are no laws prohibiting new parties, the coup and the security situation make competitive political groupings impossible, and the lack of explicit plans to hold elections makes it impossible for opposition parties to organize through elections in the immediate future. Séléka and anti-Balaka rebels have terrorized the population, other armed groups have proliferated, and sectarian tensions and violence have skyrocketed, rendering free political choice meaningless. Due to the sectarian and religious nature of these tensions, political pluralism and participation have been heavily curtailed.

C. Functioning of Government: 0 / 12 (-2)

The coup removed all elected office holders from power and imposed a nontransparent, unelected regime. The deteriorating security situation means the new government cannot provide basic protection and services.

Until the March 2013 coup, corruption remained pervasive in all branches of government, despite some steps toward reform in recent years. Diamonds accounted for about half of the country's export earnings, but a large percentage circumvented official channels. Since the coup, Séléka has taken control of the diamond industry. Without a functioning government, the CAR cannot protect or regulate the extraction of natural resources, and the Kimberley Process, a multi-government scheme to stop the trade of "conflict diamonds," suspended exports of the country's diamonds in May.

Discretionary Political Rights Question B: -1 / 0 (-1)

The deliberate targeting of Christians by Séléka sparked unprecedented clashes between the country's Muslim and Christian populations, and the creation of the Christian anti-Balaka militias as a response has further exacerbated these clashes.

CIVIL LIBERTIES: 6 / 60 (-13)

D. Freedom of Expression and Belief: 4 / 16 (-4)

Until Bozizé's ouster in March, the government generally respected the right to free speech, but many journalists practiced self-censorship. It was illegal to broadcast information that was "false" or that could incite ethnic or religious tension. The state dominated the broadcast media, but private radio stations existed. Several private newspapers offered competing views, though they had limited influence due to low literacy levels and high poverty rates. There were no government restrictions on the internet, but the vast majority of the population is unable to access it. The progressive decline of the security situation as a result of the rebel advance and coup severely restricted the movement of journalists and their ability to report. Although freedom of speech and the press are protected under the transitional charter, there were reports of threats and violence against journalists at the hands of Seleka and of the transitional government. Both radio stations and newspapers stopped operating for a few days in early and late December, as a result of the increase in violence during this period.

Before the coup, the constitution guaranteed religious freedom, but the Bozizé government prohibited activities that it considered subversive or fundamentalist, and the constitution banned the formation of religious-based parties. However, since the Séléka takeover, sectarian violence between Muslims, mostly aligned with the rebels, and the country's Christian population has increased severely. In early October 2013, over 70 people were killed in separate incidents between Muslims and Christians in Bangassou and Gaga, while anti-Balaka revenge killings in early December led to the bloodiest Seleka attack, with over 1,000 civilians killed in the capital, Bangui.

Academic freedom was generally respected under Bozizé, but in 2013 universities have had difficulty functioning due to the security situation. By early 2013, as many as half of the schools where closed and taken over by militia groups, with universities shutting down as well. The coup also had a chilling effect on private political discussion.

E. Associational and Organizational Rights: 1 / 12 (-3)

Until the March 2013 coup, freedoms of assembly and association were constitutionally protected and generally upheld in practice. However, permission was required to hold public meetings and demonstrations, and authorities sometimes denied such requests. The rights to unionize and strike were constitutionally protected and generally respected, though only a small percentage of workers were unionized.

Since the coup, however, freedom of assembly is effectively curtailed as a result of the security situation, which has also made it impossible for organizations to operate effectively. Members of humanitarian organizations were harassed and attacked, both by Séléka members and forces loyal to Bozizé, and the offices of international aid organizations were looted. The security situation also made it difficult for unions to function properly.

F. Rule of Law: 0 / 16 (-3)

Prior to the coup, corruption, political interference, and lack of training had undermined the judiciary. The president appointed judges, and proceedings were prone to executive influence. Limitations on police searches and detention were often ignored. While the penal code prohibited torture, police brutality remained a serious problem. The military and members of the presidential guard continued to commit human rights abuses, including extrajudicial killings, with impunity. Prison conditions remained poor.

The rule of law was severely compromised by the coup, after which the judiciary operated under the threat of the rebel government. There were widespread reports of atrocities, including torture and extrajudicial killings, committed by Séléka and by anti-Balaka groups. The violence greatly exacerbated existing insecurity in the CAR, where several armed groups—including the Ugandan rebel group the Lord's Resistance Army—already operated. Djotodia was unsuccessful in his attempt to disband Seleka, and reports indicated that fighting between various factions of Séléka was contributing to the overall violence.

The humanitarian situation was dire: in late December, the United Nations estimated that over 710,000 people had been displaced within the CAR; about 100,000 people were sheltering at Bangui's airport at the end of the year. According to the United Nations, about 71,500 additional people had fled to nearby countries. Food security was a major concern. Additionally, Muslim civilians were deliberately targeted by Seleka rebels, while anti-Balaka militias targeted Christian civilians in return, sending thousands from each group in hiding.

G. Personal Autonomy and Individual Rights: 1 / 16 (-3)

In 2013, increased insecurity restricted the movement of citizens and greatly undermined the protection of private property. Private businesses were looted and destroyed regularly by both of the major rebel groups and Séléka mined diamond-producing areas for its own benefit.

Even before the coup, constitutional guarantees for women's rights were not enforced, especially in rural areas. There was no specific law criminalizing domestic abuse, which is widespread, and there was a high incidence of sexual violence against women by state and nonstate actors.

Chad

Political Rights Rating: 7
Civil Liberties Rating: 6
Freedom Rating: 6.5
Freedom Status: Not Free
Electoral Democracy: No

Population: 12,200,000
Capital: N'Djamena

Ten-Year Ratings Timeline For Year Under Review (Political Rights, Civil Liberties, Status)

Year Under Review	2004	2005	2006	2007	2008	2009	2010	2011	2012	2013
Rating	6,5,NF	6,5,NF	6,6,NF	7,6,NF	7,6,NF	7,6,NF	7,6,NF	7,6,NF	7,6,NF	7,6,NF

INTRODUCTION

The government of longtime president Idriss Déby appointed a new prime minister—Joseph Djimrangar Dadnadji—in January. However, on November 21, the prime minister tendered his resignation ahead of a planned motion of censure against his government. Dadnadji had ordered five cabinet reshuffles in 10 months, and his government was criticized for demanding arbitrary arrest of deputies and failing to control the high cost of living and chronic instability. The same day, President Déby appointed Kalzeubet Pahimi Deubet, an economist, to lead the new government.

Security forces in Chad claimed to have foiled a coup against the president following two separate clashes on May 1 at a military barracks and in a residential neighborhood in the capital in which several people were killed. In the aftermath of the fighting, two generals and two members of parliament were among those arrested on suspicion of conspiracy. Many observers have stated that these arrests were politically motivated in order to crack down on government critics; some have also questioned whether the coup may have been staged for this purpose. Chad's borders with Libya and Sudan saw an increase in rebel activity throughout the year, contributing to instability even as Chad's military deployments to conflicts elsewhere in the region allowed it to maintain a central role in regional politics. In March, the Union of Forces of Resistance (UFR), a rebel coalition that had ended its armed rebellion against the government in 2010, warned that it could again take up arms, accusing Déby of not following through with his agreement to hold talks with the group. In April, Déby accused the Libyan government of hosting a training camp for Chadian mercenaries and UFR rebels who sought to destabilize the country, a charge that Libya denied.

Early in the year, Chad sent 2,000 troops to Mali to help drive out Islamist fighters as part of an intervention spearheaded by France, Déby's long-term ally. In April, however, Déby announced that he would pull the country's troops out of Mali, saying they had accomplished their mission; the withdrawal began in May. Chad has contributed substantially to the African Union peacekeeping force in the Central African Republic, but it has also been accused of supporting and training the Séléka rebels who are fighting the government there.

According to the UN High Commissioner for Refugees, 434,479 refugees reside in Chad—mainly from Sudan, the Central African Republic, and Nigeria—and almost 20,000 internally displaced persons (IDPs).

POLITICAL RIGHTS: 5 / 40

A. Electoral Process: 3 / 12

Chad has never experienced a free and fair transfer of power through elections. Déby, a former military commander, ousted dictator Hissène Habré in 1990, and has won four presidential elections, in 1996, 2001, 2006, and 2011. The president is elected for five-year terms, and a 2005 constitutional amendment abolished term limits. The executive branch dominates the judicial and legislative branches, and the president appoints the prime minister. The unicameral National Assembly consists of 188 members elected for four-year terms.

Legislative elections originally due in 2006 were repeatedly postponed due to insufficient equipment and staffing, as well as delays in voter registration, but finally took place in February 2011. In the National Assembly, Déby's Patriotic Salvation Movement (MPS) party won 117 seats and 14 more went to Déby's allies, securing an absolute majority for the president. The most successful opposition party won only 10 seats.

The European Union praised the peaceful and fair conduct of the elections, despite some logistical problems. However, the opposition claimed that irregularities occurred both before the vote—due to the government's media dominance and the use of state resources to benefit the ruling party—and during the elections, including issues with electoral rolls and voter registration cards. They also pointed to the Independent Electoral Commission's official results page, which showed irregularities. A request by opposition parties to reprint voter registration cards was rejected.

Citing irregularities before and during the parliamentary elections, the three main opposition candidates boycotted the presidential poll in April 2011, which Déby won with 89 percent of the vote.

B. Political Pluralism and Participation: 1 / 16

More than 70 political parties operate in Chad, although a number of them were created by the government to divide the opposition. Only the ruling MPS has significant influence. Despite rivalries within Déby's northeastern Zaghawa ethnic group, members of that and other northern ethnic groups continue to control Chad's political and economic systems, causing resentment among the country's more than 200 other ethnic groups. Despite comprising 45 percent of the population, Christians in the south of the country have been excluded from political power in Chad for more than 20 years. Déby's strong hold on power and political instabilities in the border regions of the country further exacerbate the obstacles to their political participation.

In May, following the government's claim to have foiled a coup attempt, two members of parliament—opposition member Gali Gata Ngoté and MPS member Routouang Yoma Golom—were arrested and charged with conspiracy; they were provisionally released later in the month. The arrests appeared to violate the immunity legally guaranteed to the country's parliamentarians; only the National Assembly can remove a member's immunity, and it had not done so in these cases.

C. Functioning of Government: 1 / 12

Corruption is rampant within Déby's inner circle. Despite becoming an oil producer in 2003, Chad remains one of the world's poorest nations; according to the UN Development Programme, Chad currently occupies position 184 out of a total of 187 states on the 2013 Human Development Index. Weaknesses in revenue management and oversight facilitate the diversion of oil revenues from national development projects to private interests and growing military expenditures. However, fighting corruption has not been a government priority and criticizing the government for corruption can be dangerous. An anticorruption blogger and writer was arrested on March 22 on defamation charges. Chad was ranked 163 out of 177 countries and territories surveyed in Transparency International's 2013 Corruption Perceptions Index.

CIVIL LIBERTIES: 16 / 60
D. Freedom of Expression and Belief: 7 / 16

The constitution provides for freedom of the press and expression. However, both are severely restricted, and self-censorship is common. Broadcast media are controlled by the state. The High Council of Communication (HCC) exerts control over most content on the radio—the most important means of mass communication—and while there are roughly a dozen private stations, they face high licensing fees and the threat of closure for critical coverage. In 2008, the HCC banned reporting on the activities of rebels or any other information that could harm national unity. A small number of private newspapers circulate in the capital, and internet access is not restricted, but the reach of both is limited by poverty, illiteracy, and inadequate infrastructure.

A 2010 media bill eliminated imprisonment as a punishment for libel, slander, or insulting the president, but introduced heavy fines or prison time for inciting racial and ethnic hatred and "condoning violence." In 2013, several journalists faced prosecution related to their work in cases that drew condemnation from international rights organizations, and dozens of government critics were arrested. On August 19, Eric Topona, the secretary general of the Union of Chadian Journalists (UJT), was convicted of defamation and given a three-year suspended prison sentence. Topona had been arrested in May on the charge of "endangering constitutional order." The same day, blogger and writer Jean Laokolé—who covered issues such as corruption for the popular *Blog de Makaila* and had been arrested in March—was convicted of "defamation" and "abortive conspiracy against public order," with a three-year suspended sentence. Later in August, Moussaye Avenir de la Tchiré, managing editor of the news publication *Abba Garde* and the UJT treasurer, was given a two-year suspended sentence and fined after being convicted of "incitement to hatred and a popular uprising." De la Tchiré had also been arrested in May, a month that saw a string of arrests of government critics following the government's claim to have foiled a coup attempt. In October, newspaper editor Samory Ngaradoumbé was arrested for spreading malicious rumors based on an article he published on Chadian peacekeepers defecting in Mali.

Although Chad is a secular state, religion is a divisive force. Muslims, who make up slightly more than half of the population, hold a disproportionately large number of senior government posts, and some policies favor Islam in practice. At the same time, the authorities have banned Muslim groups that are seen as promoting violence. The government does not restrict academic freedom, but funds meant for the education system have reportedly been lost to corruption.

E. Associational and Organizational Rights: 4 / 12

Despite the constitutional guarantee of free assembly, the authorities ban demonstrations by groups thought to be critical of the government. The arrest of government critics in 2013 made demonstrations even more dangerous. Insecurity has severely hindered the activities of humanitarian organizations in recent years. Although the country has been relatively stable since 2011, recurrent bandit attacks on humanitarian workers make access to the population difficult.

The constitution guarantees the rights to strike and unionize, but a 2007 law imposed new limits on public sector workers' right to strike. Nevertheless, public sector workers did strike for three weeks in the fall of 2011 and in July 2012, demanding promised wage increases. Both protests ended with deals with the government, which also signed an agreement on salaries with union leaders in March.

F. Rule of Law: 2 / 16

The rule of law and the judicial system remain weak, and the political leadership heavily influences the courts. According to Amnesty International, judicial harassment of political opponents had been frequent throughout 2012 and was exacerbated with the arrest of two parliamentarians in May. Civilian leaders do not maintain control of the security forces, which routinely ignore constitutional protections regarding search, seizure, and detention. Human rights groups credibly accuse the security forces and rebel groups of killing and torturing with impunity. Prison conditions are inhumane, and many inmates are held for years without charge.

In January, the ruling MPS government proposed changes to two articles of the constitution, generating concern among the opposition. Article 71 of the constitution requires that the president be completely divorced from all professional or business activities not connected to his presidential duties, including the activities of his own party. The MPS contended that the president should be allowed to participate in party events. The second change—and the one that reportedly generated the most opposition—would remove permanent tenure for Supreme Court judges. While the ruling party claims that judicial independence is guaranteed by other constitutional provisions, the opposition argues that eliminating secure tenure would expose judges to political pressure.

In July 2012, the Senegalese government agreed to establish a special court to try former Chadian president Hissène Habré—who has been living in exile in Senegal—for political killings and torture committed during his rule. Senegal's long-awaited decision came after an International Court of Justice ruling earlier that month that it either try Habré or extradite him to Belgium. On February 8, a special tribunal called the Extraordinary Chambers was inaugurated in Dakar, Senegal, to oversee the first crimes-against-humanity trial by one country of a former leader of another. Habré was arrested in Dakar on June 30 and charged July 2 with crimes against humanity, war crimes, and torture. In November, the Court of Justice of the Economic Community of West African States (ECOWAS) rejected Habré's request to suspend the proceedings, clearing the way for the trial to go forward.

Clashes are common between Christian farmers of the various southern ethnic groups and Muslim Arab groups living largely in the north. Turmoil linked to ethnic and religious differences is exacerbated by clan rivalries and external interference along the insecure borders. Communal tensions in eastern Chad have worsened due to the proliferation of small arms and ongoing disputes over the use of land and water resources.

While same-sex sexual activity has never been criminalized in Chad, cultural and legal restrictions mean that same-sex and transgender activities remain secretive. No nongovernmental organizations related to LGBT (lesbian, gay, bisexual, and transgender) rights function in Chad.

G. Personal Autonomy and Individual Rights: 3 / 16

Although guaranteed in the constitution, the government restricts the movement of citizens within the country and controls the movement of both IDPs and refugees. Government control of the economy, repression of minority rights, and lack of security in certain areas of the country also exacerbate freedom of movement, employment, and education.

Chadian women face widespread discrimination and violence. In the 2011 elections, 24 female members were elected to the National Assembly, or about 13 percent. Female genital mutilation is illegal, but routinely practiced by several ethnic groups. Chad is a source, transit, and destination country for child trafficking, and the government has not made significant efforts to eliminate the problem. The U.S. State Department again placed Chad on the Tier 2 Watch List in its 2013 Trafficking in Persons Report.

Chile

Political Rights Rating: 1
Civil Liberties Rating: 1
Freedom Rating: 1.0
Freedom Status: Free
Electoral Democracy: Yes

Population: 17,600,000
Capital: Santiago

Ten-Year Ratings Timeline For Year Under Review (Political Rights, Civil Liberties, Status)

Year Under Review	2004	2005	2006	2007	2008	2009	2010	2011	2012	2013
Rating	1,1,F	1,1,F	1,1,F	1,1,F	1,1,F	1,1,F	1,1,F	1,1,F	1,1,F	1,1,F

INTRODUCTION

Former president Michelle Bachelet was returned to office in a December runoff election, defeating Evelyn Matthei, a conservative former labor minister. During the campaign, the center-left Bachelet endorsed free education for all Chileans following two years of student protests for more equitable and affordable schooling.

Tension between Chile's Mapuche Indians and the government escalated in 2013 as the Mapuche demanded the return of approximately 1 million acres of territory. Early in the year, violence in the Mapuche heartland of Araucanía resulted in multiple deaths, including that of a Mapuche activist. In one arson attack, a prominent farmer and his wife were burned alive, a tactic commonly used by the Mapuche. No one had been arrested by year's end.

The year marked the 40th anniversary of the 1973 military coup that toppled Socialist president Salvador Allende. The nation remains divided over the coup, and only a minority of those responsible for the estimated 3,000 Chileans killed or disappeared during the ensuing rule of General Augusto Pinochet have been tried. Although 260 people were convicted in 2013 as reported by Amnesty International, only 60 have been sent to jail, due in part to a 1978 amnesty law.

POLITICAL RIGHTS: 39 / 40

A. Electoral Process: 12 / 12

The president of Chile is elected for a four-year term, and consecutive terms are not permitted. The Senate's 38 members serve eight-year terms, with half up for election every four years, and the 120-member Chamber of Deputies is elected for four years.

General elections held in November 2013 were considered free and fair. The center-left New Majority coalition—formerly known as Concertación—won 67 seats in the Chamber of Deputies and 12 in the Senate. Parties affiliated with the conservative Alliance coalition won 49 seats in the lower house and 7 in the Senate.

Bachelet, who previously served as president from 2006 to 2010, garnered the most votes in November's presidential election, but failed to reach the 50 percent threshold required to secure victory. In a runoff held on December 16, Bachelet defeated the conservative Matthei, receiving 62 percent of the vote.

B. Political Pluralism and Participation: 15 / 16

Chile has a multiparty political system with two dominant coalitions. The center-left New Majority coalition is composed of the Christian Democratic Party, the Socialist Party, the Party for Democracy, and the Communist Party. The center-right Alliance coalition consists of the Independent Democratic Union and the National Renewal party.

In 2005, the Senate passed reforms that repealed some of the last vestiges of military rule, ending authoritarian curbs on the legislative branch and restoring the president's right to remove top military commanders.

C. Functioning of Government: 12 / 12

Levels of official corruption are low by regional standards. Congress passed significant transparency and campaign-finance laws in 2003 that contributed to Chile's reputation for good governance. A 2007 law further improved transparency by offering protections for public employees who expose corruption. A freedom of information law was enacted in 2008, and in practice the government grants the public access to all unclassified information. Chile was ranked 22 out of 177 countries and territories surveyed in Transparency International's 2013 Corruption Perceptions Index.

CIVIL LIBERTIES: 56 / 60 (-1)
D. Freedom of Expression and Belief: 16 / 16

Guarantees of free speech are generally respected, though some laws barring defamation of state institutions remain on the books. Topics such as human rights violations committed during the dictatorship remain extremely sensitive, and journalists investigating such issues were threatened, harassed, and robbed in 2013. Approximately 95 percent of newspaper titles are owned by two private companies, and 60 percent of radio stations are owned by a Spanish media group. There are no government restrictions on the internet.

The constitution provides for freedom of religion, and the government generally upholds this right in practice. The government does not restrict academic freedom.

E. Associational and Organizational Rights: 11 / 12

The rights to form nongovernmental organizations and to assemble peacefully are largely respected. Although the government regularly granted permits for large student demonstrations during 2011 and 2012, police often used excessive force against protesters. An estimated 15,000 people joined a protest organized by the Mapuche in October 2013 to demand the return of ancestral lands. The protests became violent as demonstrators threw rocks and police used water cannons to disperse the protesters. Despite laws protecting worker and union rights, antiunion practices by private employers are reportedly common.

F. Rule of Law: 14 / 16 (-1)

The constitution provides for an independent judiciary, and the courts are generally free from political interference. The right to legal counsel is constitutionally guaranteed, but indigent defendants have not always received effective representation.

The government has developed effective mechanisms to investigate and punish police abuse and corruption. However, excessive force and human rights abuses committed by the Carabineros—a national police element of the armed forces—still occur. An official body created two years ago to monitor human rights released a report in December 2012 highlighting ongoing police violence. While acknowledging progress toward a culture of respect for human rights in the Carabineros, the report condemned the "irregular and disproportionate use of anti-riot shotguns" and highlighted complaints about sexual aggression against female demonstrators. The Carabineros continued to use excessive force against members of the Mapuche indigenous community in 2013. Chile's prisons are overcrowded and violent. Inmates suffer from physical abuse as well as substandard medical and food services.

In August 2013, the lower chamber approved a watered-down version of the Hinzpeter Law, a public security bill introduced by the administration of outgoing conservative president Sebastián Piñera. Its most contentious aspects—those giving the Carabineros greater powers during public demonstrations and increased sanctions for protesters—were removed. The Senate rejected the legislation in October, sending it back to the lower house; by year's end, disagreement between the two houses, coupled with the center-right's electoral defeat, resulted in the bill's demise.

Approximately 1 million Chileans identify themselves with indigenous ethnic groups. While they still experience societal discrimination, their poverty levels are declining, aided by government scholarships, land transfers, and social spending. A 1993 law paved the way for the return of their ancestral land, but rather than appeasing the Mapuche, it prompted additional land claims, land seizures, and violence. The Pinochet-era antiterrorism law, which allowed for secret witnesses, pretrial detention, and the use of military courts, was historically used against the Mapuche. As amended in 2010, the law presumes innocence and carries a reduced sentence for arson—one of the principal tactics of the Mapuche. However, in violation of the 2010 accord, the old law continues to be used by prosecutors in a way that discriminates against the Mapuche. A UN special rapporteur criticized the ongoing use of the legislation in 2013, as well as the failure of Piñera to make good on his promise to constitutionally recognize the Mapuche people, a pledge he made early in 2013. The "Plan Araucanía"—a development plan for the southern Araucanía area, one of Chile's poorest regions and the homeland of the Mapuche—was implemented in summer 2012 and continued into 2013. The plan financed construction of new schools and hospitals, funded the building of new roads, and provided financial support to victims of violence.

LGBT (lesbian, gay, bisexual, and transgender) people continue to face societal bias, despite a 2012 antidiscrimination law that covers sexual orientation and gender identity. Violent attacks are reported each year, and authorities have allegedly failed to pursue the cases energetically. Chilean law does not permit transgender people to change gender indicators on identity documents, a restriction that led the country's first transgender congressional candidate to end her campaign in May 2013.

G. Personal Autonomy and Individual Rights: 15 / 16

President Bachelet made great strides to reduce gender discrimination during her first term, including by appointing women to half of the positions in her cabinet. She also enacted new laws to increase women's labor rights and to eliminate the gender pay gap. However, violence against women and children remains a problem. In June 2013, the European Union and UN Women signed an agreement establishing a joint fund to support gender equality in Chile, focusing on eliminating violence against women, women's economic empowerment, and women's political participation and leadership. As the former head of UN Women, Bachelet is expected to continue to promote gender equality in her second administration. The 2012 antidiscrimination law, which addresses gender bias, allows individuals to file antidiscrimination lawsuits and includes augmented hate-crime sentences for violent crimes.

While all forms of compulsory labor are illegal, forced labor, particularly among foreign citizens, continues to occur in the agriculture, mining, and domestic service sectors.

China

Political Rights Rating: 7
Civil Liberties Rating: 6
Freedom Rating: 6.5
Freedom Status: Not Free
Electoral Democracy: No

Population: 1,357,400,000
Capital: Beijing

Note: The numerical ratings and status listed above do not reflect conditions in Hong Kong or Tibet, which are examined in separate reports.

Ten-Year Ratings Timeline For Year Under Review (Political Rights, Civil Liberties, Status)

Year Under Review	2004	2005	2006	2007	2008	2009	2010	2011	2012	2013
Rating	7,6,NF	7,6,NF	7,6,NF	7,6,NF	7,6,NF	7,6,NF	7,6,NF	7,6,NF	7,6,NF	7,6,NF

INTRODUCTION

Chinese Communist Party (CCP) general secretary Xi Jinping, who had assumed his post as part of a broader leadership rotation at the November 2012 party congress, was named state president by the country's largely symbolic parliament in March 2013. Throughout the year, Xi attempted to consolidate his power amid ongoing infighting within the CCP. The 2012 purge of former Chongqing party secretary Bo Xilai was completed in September, when he was sentenced to life in prison on corruption charges. Former domestic security chief Zhou Yongkang, who had been viewed as Bo's most powerful patron, was rumored to be under investigation for corruption at year's end.

Xi initially raised hopes among reform-minded intellectuals that the CCP under his leadership might be more tolerant of dissent and loosen political controls. However, despite a reinvigorated anticorruption drive, official rhetoric about improving the rule of law, and invitations for input from society, such optimism faded as the year progressed. After intellectuals and members of civil society urged the party to adhere to China's constitution and a rare strike by journalists at a major newspaper sparked broader calls to reduce censorship, the authorities responded with campaigns to intensify ideological controls. The state-led anticorruption drive proved opaque and selective, and the latter half of 2013 was marked by crackdowns on grassroots anticorruption activists, new judicial guidelines expanding the criminalization of online speech, and the detention of both prominent social-media commentators and ordinary users.

In November, the CCP Central Committee chosen at the party congress a year earlier convened for its crucial third plenum, announcing a series of modest reforms in the economic, social, and legal spheres. They included a decision to close the country's infamous "reeducation through labor" camps, where individuals can be detained without trial, but the authorities continued to use various alternative forms of administrative or extralegal detention—as well as formal criminal charges with potentially longer sentences—to punish human rights defenders, anticorruption activists, petitioners, and religious believers. Another reform expanded the categories of families permitted to have two children, though the intrusive regulations and harsh practices used to enforce the country's long-standing birth quotas remained in place.

Despite CCP hostility toward organized dissent, both high-profile dissidents and ordinary citizens continued to assert their rights and challenge injustice during 2013. Public protests, online campaigns, journalistic exposés, and activist networks scored several victories, including the release of individuals from wrongful detention. Nevertheless, the ability of Chinese citizens to share breaking news, uncover corruption, or engage in public debate about political and social issues was hampered by the increased internet controls and crackdowns.

POLITICAL RIGHTS: 2 / 40

A. Electoral Process: 0 / 12

The CCP has a monopoly on political power, and its Politburo Standing Committee (PSC) sets government and party policy. At the 18th Party Congress in November 2012, a new PSC was announced following an opaque, internal selection process. The committee shrank from nine to seven members, only two of whom—new CCP general secretary Xi Jinping and his deputy, Li Keqiang—had served on the previous panel. Party members—who number some 80 million nationwide, or about 6 percent of the population—hold almost all top posts in the government, military, and internal security services, as well as in many economic entities and social organizations.

The country's legislature, the 3,000-member National People's Congress (NPC), is elected for five-year terms by subnational congresses, formally elects the state president for up to two five-year terms, and confirms the premier after he is nominated by the president. However, the NPC is a largely symbolic body. Only its standing committee meets regularly, while the full congress convenes for just two weeks a year to approve proposed legislation. In March 2013, Xi was appointed president and Li was named premier, solidifying Xi's role as the top leader in the party and the government. He also heads the military as chairman of the party and state military commissions.

The country's only competitive elections are for village committees and urban residency councils, which hold limited authority and are generally subordinate to the local CCP committees. The nomination of candidates remains tightly controlled, and many of the elections have been marred by fraud, corruption, and attacks on independent candidates.

B. Political Pluralism and Participation: 1 / 16

The CCP does not tolerate any form of organized opposition or independent political parties. Citizens who attempt to form opposition parties or advocate for democratic reforms have been sentenced to long prison terms in recent years. Democracy advocate and 2010 Nobel Peace Prize winner Liu Xiaobo remained behind bars in 2013, having been sentenced in 2009 to 11 years in prison for his role in organizing the prodemocracy manifesto Charter 08. His wife, Liu Xia, has been under strict house arrest since 2010; her brother was sentenced in June 2013 to 11 years in prison on what were widely perceived as trumped-up fraud charges in retaliation for Liu Xia's brief contact with activists and foreign journalists.

Over the course of the year, more than 65 political reform activists across the country were detained, many for their connection to the New Citizens' Movement, a loosely organized network of individuals seeking to promote the rule of law, transparency, and human rights. One of the movement's leaders, Beijing lawyer Xu Zhiyong, was detained in July and indicted in December on charges of "gathering a crowd to disturb public order," having organized small protests to urge officials to disclose their assets and circulated photographs of the demonstrations online; he faces a prison term of up to five years if convicted.

In addition to advocates of democracy and political reform, tens of thousands of grassroots activists, petitioners, Falun Gong practitioners, Christians, Tibetans, and Uighurs are believed to be in prison or extrajudicial forms of detention for their political or religious views, although complete figures are unavailable. In October 2013, the U.S. Congressional-Executive Commission on China published a partial list of over 1,300 current political prisoners.

C. Functioning of Government: 2 / 12

Corruption remains endemic despite increased government antigraft campaigns. Top party leaders acknowledged growing public resentment over the issue in 2013. In January, Xi Jinping vowed to crack down on corruption by both senior leaders and low-level bureaucrats, while party bodies issued directives instructing officials to curb ostentatious displays of wealth. However, the leadership rejected more fundamental reforms, such as requiring officials to publicly disclose their assets, creating genuinely independent oversight bodies, or lifting political constraints on journalists and law enforcement agencies.

Thousands of officials are investigated and punished each year by government or CCP entities, but prosecution is selective and decision-making highly opaque, with informal personal networks and internal CCP power struggles influencing both the choice of targets and the outcomes. The highest-level target in 2013 was former Chongqing party chief and Politburo member Bo Xilai, who was sentenced to life in prison in September on charges of bribery and abuse of power. Although the authorities tightly controlled information and public discussion about Bo's August trial, the unprecedented release of select excerpts and updates on the proceedings via an official microblog, including Bo's relative defiance in contesting the prosecution's case, surprised many observers and drew considerable public attention.

Many lower- and mid-level officials were also disciplined, demoted, dismissed, or prosecuted during the year, often after bloggers or journalists exposed evidence of their corruption online. Authorities encouraged the public to submit corruption complaints through official channels rather than airing them publicly or anonymously on the internet, and launched state-run whistleblower websites. They also cracked down on independent anticorruption initiatives and harassed those who exposed earlier cases. Foreign media outlets faced reprisals including website blocking and visa delays after publishing stories on apparent influence peddling by top officials and their families.

CCP officials increasingly seek input from academics and civic groups regarding certain policy areas, though without relinquishing control over the decision-making process. Since open-government regulations took effect in 2008, many agencies have become more forthcoming in publishing official documents. However, implementation has been incomplete. Government bodies retain great discretion to classify or withhold information, including on vital public matters such as food safety, home demolitions, and environmental disasters. Courts have largely hesitated to enforce information requests. The poor quality of official responses has dampened citizens' initial enthusiasm to lodge complaints. China was ranked 80 out of 177 countries surveyed in Transparency International's 2013 Corruption Perceptions Index, but was excluded from the organization's public opinion–based Global Corruption Barometer because Chinese survey companies were reportedly reluctant to participate.

Discretionary Political Rights Question B: -1 / 0

The government continues to pursue policies, including large-scale resettlement and work-transfer programs, that are designed in part to alter the demography of ethnic minority regions, especially Tibet and the Xinjiang Uighur Autonomous Region. [Note: Tibet is examined in a separate report.]

CIVIL LIBERTIES: 15 / 60
D. Freedom of Expression and Belief: 4 / 16

Despite relative freedom in private discussion and citizen efforts to push the limits of permissible public speech, China's media environment remains extremely restrictive. All Chinese television, radio, and print outlets are owned by the CCP or the state. Moreover, all media outlets are required to follow regularly issued CCP directives to avoid certain topics or publish content from party mouthpieces. Routinely censored topics include calls for greater autonomy in Tibet and Xinjiang, independence for Taiwan, the 1989 Tiananmen Square crackdown, the persecuted Falun Gong spiritual group, the writings of prominent activists, and critical commentary regarding CCP leaders. Other directives issued in 2013 barred or "guided" reporting on antigovernment protests, torture, certain cases of official corruption, and fatal industrial accidents. Outlets that disobey official guidance risk closure, and journalists face dismissal and sometimes imprisonment. Pressure on investigative journalism remained intense during the year, as several respected periodicals and journalists faced suspension, dismissals, or tighter supervision. Meanwhile, regulators introduced various restrictions, including prior censorship for television documentaries, tightened controls on outlets' use of foreign sources or microblogs, and plans to require Chinese journalists to pass a new ideological exam in order to receive their press cards.

According to the New York–based Committee to Protect Journalists, at least 32 journalists were behind bars in China as of December 2013, including a number of Uighurs and Tibetans; the total number of Chinese citizens jailed for freedom of expression violations, especially on the internet, was much higher. Several journalists faced questionable charges of bribery, defamation, or "spreading false rumors" in 2013, but no convictions were reported as of year's end. In January, despite the risk of punishment, journalists at the Guangzhou-based *Southern Weekly* pushed back against official interference by going on strike after propaganda officials altered a New Year's editorial urging greater adherence to China's constitution. The journalists' protest sparked a wider outcry against censorship, both online and in street demonstrations, by segments of Chinese society ranging from students and intellectuals to popular entertainment figures. Some analysts suggested that officials' alarm at the incident contributed to the intensified media and internet controls later in the year.

Harassment of foreign reporters, including occasional physical attacks, and intimidation of their Chinese sources and staff continued during the year. The authorities used the threat of visa denials to retaliate against foreign journalists and news organizations they deemed objectionable. One correspondent—veteran journalist Paul Mooney, who is known for his human rights reporting—was unable to take up a position with Reuters after the government refused to issue him a visa in November. Over two dozen other foreign journalists, most of them from Bloomberg and the *New York Times*, faced de facto expulsion after authorities refused to issue visas and press cards in apparent retribution for articles about the wealth and business connections of top party leaders and their families. Following international pressure, most of the reporters received their documents by year's end. The websites of Bloomberg and the *Times* have been blocked since 2012, and other foreign news outlets experienced temporary blocking during 2013. Some international radio and television broadcasts, including the U.S. government–funded Radio Free Asia, remain jammed.

China's population of internet users surpassed 600 million in 2013, remaining the world's largest. According to official figures, mobile-telephone users exceeded one billion, with over 460 million people accessing the internet via their mobile devices. The government maintains an elaborate apparatus for censoring and monitoring internet and mobile-phone communications. The authorities block websites or force the deletion of content they deem politically threatening, and sometimes detain those who post such information. The U.S.-based social-media platforms Twitter and Facebook remain blocked, and Chinese internet companies are obliged to adhere to official censorship directives. Nevertheless, domestic microblogging services—with over 300 million users in 2013—have grown rapidly in influence since 2010 as a source of news, an outlet for public opinion, and a tool for mobilization. Over the last few years, users were frequently able to outpace censors to expose government malfeasance, publicize breaking stories, or comment critically on sensitive topics.

However, in 2013 the authorities launched a sweeping crackdown aimed at reasserting control over online discussion. In August, Xi Jinping reportedly gave a speech to party cadres in which he urged them to "wage a war to win over public opinion" and "seize the ground of new media." Four days later, Chinese-American businessman Charles Xue, whose web commentaries on social and political issues were shared with 12 million followers on the Sina Weibo microblogging platform, was detained for allegedly soliciting prostitutes. He was later shown handcuffed on state television, criticizing the way he had used his microblog to influence public opinion, reinforcing suspicions of a politically motivated prosecution. Other public figures with large microblog followings also faced growing pressure in the form of deletions, locked accounts, and selective arrests and interrogations.

In September, the country's highest judicial authorities issued a legal interpretation that expanded the scope and severity of criminal offenses covering online speech and allowed prosecutors to initiate criminal defamation cases in defense of public order or state interests. Under the guidelines, a user could receive up to three years in prison for content deemed false or defamatory if the circumstances are deemed "serious," meaning the post was viewed more than 5,000 times or reposted more than 500 times. Chinese and international legal experts criticized the threshold as extremely low for such a severe punishment. Throughout August and September, in addition to the high-profile bloggers, police detained and interrogated hundreds of social-media users, with most subject to brief periods of detention rather than full criminal prosecution. The harsh judicial interpretation and growing number of arrests had an immediate and palpable chilling effect on online discourse, more so than previous government attempts to increase control over social media. Data from social-media analysis firms pointed to a decline in traffic and political discussion on Sina Weibo, especially among users with large followings. A growing number of Weibo users also shifted to Tencent's WeChat, a social-media application organized around closed communities and therefore less conducive to viral dissemination of news and nationwide public debate.

Religious freedom is sharply curtailed by the formally atheist Communist Party. All religious groups must register with the government, which regulates their activities, oversees clergy, and guides theology. Some groups, including certain Buddhist and Christian sects, are forbidden, and their members face harassment, imprisonment, and torture. The largest among them is the Falun Gong spiritual group. In 2013, the party launched a new three-year initiative to coerce its adherents to renounce their beliefs. While some Falun Gong practitioners were released from detention as part of the closure of labor camps, authorities seized hundreds of others in home raids, sending them to extralegal detention centers for forced conversion or sentencing them to long prison terms. In October 2013, Wang Hongxia, a former English teacher from Sichuan Province, was sentenced to 12 years in prison for helping fellow Falun Gong adherents to hire defense lawyers. Other unregistered groups, including unofficial Protestant and Roman Catholic congregations, operate in a legal gray zone. Some are able to meet quietly with the tacit approval of local authorities, but "house church" gatherings were raided or harassed in several provinces in 2013, with congregants facing detention and beatings.

Authorities intensified curbs on Islam among the Uighur population of Xinjiang in 2013, conducting pervasive house searches, making hundreds of arrests, monitoring religious leaders, and destroying thousands of publications. Several clashes between Uighur residents and police—some sparked by restrictions on religious practice—led to dozens of deaths. In March, 20 Uighurs were sentenced to prison terms of up to 15 years on charges of "inciting splittism" or engaging in "terrorist" communications, but overseas Uighur groups maintained that the individuals had merely listened to overseas radio broadcasts and discussed religious and cultural topics online. Official restrictions on journalists' access to the region made it difficult to independently verify the details of such cases. The authorities continued to enforce policies marginalizing use of the Uighur language in education and restricting religious attire.

Academic freedom remains restricted with respect to politically sensitive issues. The CCP controls the appointment of top university officials, and many scholars practice self-censorship to protect their careers. Two professors known for their outspoken criticism of one-party rule were dismissed from their positions at prominent universities in Beijing and Shanghai in 2013. Political indoctrination is a required component of the curriculum at all levels of education.

E. Associational and Organizational Rights: 3 / 12

Freedoms of assembly and association are severely restricted. Citizens risk criminal punishment for organizing demonstrations without prior government approval, which is rarely granted. Nevertheless, workers, farmers, and urban residents held tens of thousands of protests during 2013, reflecting growing discontent over wrongdoing by officials, especially land confiscation, widespread corruption, pollution, and fatal police beatings. The government has struggled to suppress protests without exacerbating public frustration, as some aggrieved protesters resort to violence against officials and symbols of authority. The authorities use force in some cases, while employing softer strategies to deter or disperse large gatherings in others. In March, the authorities responded to an 18-day uprising over land grabs by villagers in Guangdong Province with about 3,000 security officers who cut electricity and phone services, beat protesters, and fired tear gas and stun grenades into the crowds, arresting at least nine people and injuring dozens. Officials in Yunnan Province, by contrast, thwarted a protest movement in Kunming over the construction of a petrochemical plant by summoning local activists for questioning, prohibiting workers to take leave on the day of a scheduled protest, and threatening to fire executives at public institutions if employees were allowed to attend the protest.

The central government ranks provincial and city officials based on the number of petitioners who travel from their jurisdictions to Beijing to report injustices, affecting their chances of promotion. As a result, local officials routinely intercept and harass petitioners, at times detaining them in illegal "black jails" and labor camps to stop them from visiting Beijing. Detained petitioners are reportedly subject to beatings, psychological abuse, and sexual violence. In November 2013, state media reported that the authorities planned to abolish the ranking system to encourage disputes to be settled locally, and have implemented pilot programs in Zhejiang and Jiangsu Provinces. However, some experts warned that without the pressure to reduce numbers of petitioners, local officials would have even fewer incentives to address grievances.

Nongovernmental organizations (NGOs) are required to register, obtain a government sponsor, and follow strict regulations, including vague prohibitions on advocating non-CCP rule, "damaging national unity," or "upsetting ethnic harmony." Nevertheless, the number of civil society groups, especially those whose work is not politically sensitive or is focused on service provision, continued to expand during the year, while informal activist networks scored minor victories on more difficult issues. Official statistics showed that more than half a million civil society organizations were formally registered in 2013. Millions of other groups are thought to operate without registration or as commercial entities. In December, the Ministry of Civil Affairs announced plans to abolish the requirement to obtain a government sponsor for certain types of civil society organizations. Meanwhile, the authorities continue to deny registration to groups promoting issues disfavored by the CCP. In November, Hunan Province authorities denied a gay rights activist's attempt to set up an NGO, declaring that it would violate Chinese morality, though no law bans same-sex activity. Despite restrictions on obtaining foreign donations, experts observed that domestic charitable giving is on the rise and civil society groups are increasingly taking a rights-based approach in advocacy.

The only legal labor union is the government-controlled All-China Federation of Trade Unions (ACFTU), which has long been criticized for failing to properly defend workers' rights. Nevertheless, workers have asserted themselves informally via strikes, collective petitioning, and selection of negotiating representatives. They have also used social media to bolster solidarity. Arbitration mechanisms established under 2008 labor laws have proven disappointing to workers, who complain of biased mediators, lengthy procedures, and employers' failure to comply with rulings. Collective bargaining is legal but rarely leads to success if not accompanied by strikes and social-media campaigns. The hiring of subcontractors has enabled employers to bypass contract protections in the 2008 legal reforms. Amendments to the law that took effect in July are designed to limit the use of subcontractors, but implementation was uncertain. Workers are routinely denied social insurance and other legal benefits, while dangerous workplace conditions continue to claim many tens of thousands of lives each year. The use of juveniles in government-sanctioned "work-study" programs remains a serious problem.

F. Rule of Law: 2 / 16

The CCP controls the judiciary. Party political-legal committees supervise the operations of courts at all levels, and allow party officials to influence verdicts and sentences. Most judges are CCP members. Their appointment, salaries, and promotions are largely determined by party and government officials at the same bureaucratic level. CCP influence is especially evident in politically sensitive cases, such as the prosecution of activists or officials like Bo Xilai who have fallen out of favor.

Adjudication of minor civil and administrative disputes is fairer than in politically sensitive or criminal cases. However, even in commercial litigation and civil suits involving private individuals, previous limited progress toward the rule of law has stalled or been reversed. Judges have increasingly been pressured to resolve civil disputes through mediation, sometimes forced, rather than actual adjudication. In March 2013, a new chief justice possessing a law degree was appointed, replacing a CCP veteran with no formal legal training. Following official statements surrounding the CCP Central Committee's third plenum that acknowledged the need for greater transparency and judicial autonomy from local authorities, some experts speculated about a possible reduction of political control over parts of the judiciary in the coming years.

The country's growing contingent of civil rights lawyers continued to face restrictions and physical attacks in 2013. Lawyers were prevented from seeing their clients, disbarred, beaten, and in some cases detained. Prominent lawyer Gao Zhisheng remained imprisoned and at risk of torture at year's end. In May, plainclothes police beat and detained 11 lawyers as they were attempting to investigate abuses at an extralegal detention center in Sichuan Province.

Criminal trials, which often amount to mere sentencing announcements, are frequently closed to the public, and the conviction rate is estimated at 98 percent. In January 2013, amendments to the Criminal Procedure Law took effect. They include improvements for ordinary criminal proceedings, including exclusion of evidence obtained through torture, access for lawyers to their clients, and the possibility of witnesses being cross-examined. However, legal experts raised concerns that the revised law includes exceptions for cases of "endangering state security," "terrorism," and "major bribery"—categories often employed to punish nonviolent activism and political expression. The amendments allow such suspects to be detained in an unspecified location for up to six months, and notification of families is not strictly required, essentially legalizing the practice of enforced disappearances.

Torture remains widespread, either for the purpose of extracting confessions or forcing political and religious dissidents to recant their beliefs. Security agents routinely flout legal protections, and impunity is the norm for police brutality and suspicious deaths in custody. Overall, detention facilities are estimated to hold three to five million people. Conditions are generally harsh, with reports of inadequate food, regular beatings, and deprivation of medical care; the government generally does not permit visits by independent monitoring groups. A lengthy magazine exposé and independent documentary published in mid-2013 described systematic torture at the Masanjia "reeducation through labor" camp in northeast China, including electric shocks and the use of specialized torture devices, contributing to public pressure to abolish the camps.

Following years of such pressure, the authorities in January had issued a preliminary announcement that the decades-old network of "reeducation through labor" camps, which permit individuals to be held for up to four years without a judicial hearing, would be abolished by year's end. The camps were believed to hold several hundred thousand citizens, including a substantial contingent of political and religious prisoners, alongside petty criminals, prostitutes, and drug offenders. Throughout the year, the media and human rights groups reported the closure of camps and the release of prisoners, including prisoners of conscience. In late December, the Standing Committee of the NPC formally approved the camps' abolition and the release of remaining detainees, though it affirmed the legitimacy of existing sentences to prevent victims from suing for redress.

However, according to media reports and a detailed report published by Amnesty International in December, alternative nonjudicial detention systems were used during the year to hold the same categories of detainees previously subject to reeducation through labor, though often for shorter terms. Some camps were transformed into coercive drug-rehabilitation centers, and prostitutes were sent to "custody and education centers," both of which typically involve forced labor. Some petitioners and Falun Gong detainees who had failed to "reform" were sent directly to other types of extralegal facilities for indefinite detention. More broadly, a growing number of activists, petitioners, microbloggers, and Falun Gong practitioners have been confined in extralegal "black jails," "legal education centers," or psychiatric facilities. Others faced formal prosecution, with some receiving harsher sentences than those possible via the labor camp system.

Fifty-five crimes, including nonviolent offenses, carry the death penalty, though the CCP's November 2013 reform plans included a gradual reduction in the applicability of capital punishment. The number of executions each year is a state secret. An estimate by the San Francisco–based Duihua Foundation put the number at 3,000 for 2012. While still more than the combined total for the rest of the world, this represents a sharp decline from an estimated 12,000 annual executions a decade earlier. Executed prisoners remain the primary source of organs for transplant operations, though the government reiterated plans in August 2013 to phase out the practice in the coming years. Some experts continued to raise concerns that those imprisoned for their religious beliefs or ethnic identity have also been used as sources for organs.

The CCP controls and directs the security forces at all levels. During 2013, the party continued to expand investment in its apparatus for "stability maintenance," a term that encompasses maintaining law and order, suppressing peaceful dissent, and closely monitoring the populace. Key components include state intelligence agencies, such as the Public Security Bureau; paramilitary forces like the People's Armed Police; and extralegal CCP-based entities like the 610 Office, stability-maintenance units, and administrative enforcers called *chengguan*.

In 2013, the government reportedly allocated 769 billion yuan ($125 billion) for internal security, an increase of more than 8 percent from 2012. The total surpassed the military budget for the third consecutive year. The spending has fueled a lucrative market for surveillance and police equipment. Analysts reported that some party chiefs were attempting to curb the growing power of the internal security apparatus, noting that the CCP portfolio overseeing the legal system was downgraded in rank during the November 2012 party congress.

Chinese laws formally prohibit discrimination based on nationality, ethnicity, race, gender, religion, or health condition, but they do not guarantee equal treatment for all segments of society in practice. Ethnic and religious minorities, the disabled, and people with HIV/AIDS face widespread de facto discrimination, in some cases with official encouragement. This includes discrimination in access to employment and education. Separately, despite international legal protections for asylum seekers and refugees, Chinese law enforcement agencies continue to seek out and repatriate North Korean defectors, who face imprisonment or execution upon return.

G. Personal Autonomy and Individual Rights: 6 / 16

The *hukou* (household registration) system remains in place, limiting the ability of China's 800 million rural residents and migrant workers to fully access urban social services, such as education for their children. Since *hukou* status is hereditary, subject to change only for those who meet strict income or educational requirements, China faces a growing underclass of low-wage migrant workers, many now living in cities for decades but denied the same benefits as their neighbors holding urban *hukou*. In late 2013, senior leaders vowed to carry out an overhaul of the *hukou* system by gradually lifting registration restrictions, first in smaller cities and then in the larger ones. Several ministries submitted reform proposals, but no regulatory changes had been made by year's end.

According to the U.S. Congressional-Executive Commission on China, an estimated 14 million people were affected by restrictions on foreign travel and acquiring passports, many of them Uighurs and Tibetans. Political and religious dissidents, human rights defenders, and certain scholars were also prevented from traveling abroad or to Hong Kong, and some were placed under house arrest during politically sensitive times.

Property rights protection remains weak in practice. Urban land is owned by the state, even if the buildings that sit on it are privately owned. Rural land is collectively owned by villages. Farmers enjoy long-term lease rights to the land they farm, but are barred from selling or developing it. Low compensation standards and weak legal protections have facilitated land seizures by local officials, who often evict the residents and transfer the land rights to developers. Corruption is endemic in such projects, and local governments rely on land development as a key source of operating revenue, funds for debt repayment, and economic growth statistics that are critical to officials' careers. According to the State Bureau of Letters and Visits, an estimated four million disputes resulting from land grabs and property demolition occur each year. Residents who resist eviction, seek legal redress, or organize protests often face violence at the hands of local police or hired thugs.

Since the 1980s, the space for private business has expanded dramatically. Since the early 2000s, however, the resurgence of state-owned enterprises—which dominate key industries such as utilities, energy, banking, and transportation—and limits on private access to lending from state banks has impeded the growth of the private sector. Chinese citizens are legally permitted to establish and operate private businesses. However, those without official protection can find themselves at a disadvantage vis-à-vis competitors, in legal disputes, or in dealings with regulators. Foreign companies can similarly face arbitrary regulatory obstacles, demands for bribes and other inducements, or negative media campaigns.

China's population controls mandate that couples must obtain government permission before giving birth. Most urban couples are limited to one child and rural residents to two. Compliance is enforced by intrusive government directives—such as required implantation of long-term contraception devices—and the inability of unregistered children to obtain *hukou* status, except upon payment of substantial fines. Birth and sterilization quotas remain crucial to the career advancement of local officials. Consequently, compulsory abortion and sterilization still occur, though less frequently than in the past. According to the U.S. Congressional-Executive Commission on China, regulations in 22 of 31 provincial-level administrative units explicitly endorse abortions as an enforcement tool, an increase from the previous year. Relatives of unsterilized women or couples with unapproved births are subject to high fines, job dismissal, reduced government benefits, and occasionally detention. These controls, combined with commercial ultrasound technology and societal pressures favoring boys, have led to sex-selective abortion and a general shortage of females, exacerbating the problem of human trafficking.

At the end of 2013, the NPC Standing Committee announced a limited relaxation of China's population-control policies, specifying that couples in which both of the spouses are only children would be allowed to have two children. Demographers estimate that the change could lead to one or two million additional births per year, on top of the current 15 million per year. Party leaders said local authorities would gradually implement the reforms over the coming months.

Domestic violence affects one-quarter of Chinese women, according to official figures. The problem is addressed in scattered provincial-level laws; national-level provisions are not comprehensive. Many claims are not recognized by courts, leaving victims unprotected. A draft Anti-Domestic Violence Law has stalled but remained on the NPC's legislative agenda in 2013. Several laws bar gender discrimination in the workplace, and gender equality has reportedly improved over the past decade, but bias remains widespread, including in job recruitment and college admissions. Women remain severely underrepresented in important CCP and government positions.

Colombia

Political Rights Rating: 3
Civil Liberties Rating: 4
Freedom Rating: 3.5
Freedom Status: Partly Free
Electoral Democracy: Yes

Population: 48,028,235
Capital: Bogotá

Ten-Year Ratings Timeline For Year Under Review (Political Rights, Civil Liberties, Status)

Year Under Review	2004	2005	2006	2007	2008	2009	2010	2011	2012	2013
Rating	4,4,PF	3,3,PF	3,3,PF	3,3,PF	3,4,PF	3,4,PF	3,4,PF	3,4,PF	3,4,PF	3,4,PF

INTRODUCTION

The Colombian government and the Revolutionary Armed Forces of Colombia (FARC) rebel group continued to engage in a formal peace process throughout 2013, making some progress toward ending the country's long-running internal conflict. Negotiators reached an agreement in May on rural development, and in November the teams announced an accord on political rights for demobilized guerrillas. At year's end the two sides were working toward an accord on drug trafficking, the third of the six issues on the agenda, along with victims' rights, rebel disarmament, and implementation of a prospective agreement. Opinion polls showed that Colombians continued to back the process, though skepticism regarding its chances for success remained high. The primary opposition to the talks came from President Juan Manuel Santos's predecessor, Álvaro Uribe, and his supporters, who considered the process a negotiation with terrorists.

Public approval of the Santos administration declined sharply following a series of popular protests that peaked in August and early September. The demonstrations began in late June, driven by grievances regarding economic policies in rural areas, with roadblocks erected by farmers, miners, and truckers. Over the next two months the protests spread to Bogotá and other cities. A harsh police response led to several deaths and many injuries, as well as government concessions on prices and tariffs.

Progress remained uneven on implementation of the landmark 2011 Victims and Land Law, which recognized the legitimacy of claims by victims of conflict-related abuses, including those committed by government forces. While over 150,000 affected citizens had received compensation by midyear, resettlement of displaced people who lost their land during the conflict continued at a slow pace, and a backlog of land claims grew throughout 2013. Moreover, according to Human Rights Watch, as of September the legal process for land restitution had resulted in the successful return of land to just three families, although several hundred others had received favorable judgments.

Santos formally announced in November that he would seek reelection in 2014. Uribe, meanwhile, declared his candidacy for the Senate at the head of a conservative list of candidates. In December, the elected mayor of Bogotá, Gustavo Petro, was removed from office under an order by the inspector general, who cited mismanagement of a new garbage collection plan, prompting outrage and protests by the mayor and his supporters.

POLITICAL RIGHTS: 28 / 40 (+1)
A. Electoral Process: 10 / 12

The directly elected president is eligible for two consecutive four-year terms. Congress is composed of the Senate and the Chamber of Representatives, with all seats up for election every four years. Of the Senate's 102 members, two are chosen by indigenous communities and 100 by the nation at large using a closed-list system. The Chamber of Representatives consists of 166 members elected by closed-list proportional representation in multimember districts.

The 2010 legislative elections, while less violent than previous campaigns, were marred by vote buying, murky campaign-finance practices, and intimidation in some areas, particularly former strongholds of right-wing paramilitary groups. Uribe's allies won a substantial majority in both chambers, with the two largest parties in his coalition, the Social Party of National Unity (Partido de la U) and the Conservative Party, taking 47 and 38 seats in the lower house and 28 and 22 seats in the Senate, respectively. Two other Uribe-allied factions, the National Integration Party and Radical Change, took 12 and 15 seats in the lower house and 9 and 8 seats in the Senate. The largest opposition party, the Liberal Party, won 37 seats in the lower house and 17 seats in the Senate. Several smaller parties and indigenous representatives divided the remainder.

The 2010 presidential election was relatively peaceful. Santos, the former defense minister, benefited from his association with the Uribe administration's security achievements. He overcame an ideologically diverse array of opponents in the first round and ultimately defeated Green Party member and former Bogotá mayor Antanas Mockus in a June runoff with 69 percent of the vote.

In regional and local elections held in 2011, Santos's Partido de la U, the Liberal Party, and independents won the greatest share of governorships and mayoralties. Although the elections were generally viewed as an improvement over those of 2007, 41 candidates were killed, and interference by armed actors, particularly paramilitary successor groups, skewed the results in many rural municipalities.

The Electoral Observation Mission, a monitoring group, has stated that it regards the power of local barons and potential vote fraud as the biggest risks for the 2014 elections, rather than violence by nonstate actors.

B. Political Pluralism and Participation: 11 / 16 (+1)

The traditional Liberal-Conservative partisan duopoly in Congress has in recent years been supplanted by a rough division between urban, modernizing forces and more conservative, often rural factions aligned with former president Uribe. Factional divides within both right- and left-wing parties in 2013 exacerbated the ongoing problem of party fragmentation, although the hawkish right coalesced around Uribe, who declared his candidacy for a Senate seat in 2014 at the head of a list of conservative politicians. In a decision that could facilitate the future political aspirations of left-wing guerrillas, in July 2013 the Council of State determined that candidates could legally run under the banner of the Patriotic Union, a political offshoot of the FARC founded in the 1980s and subsequently subjected to a massive campaign of violence. Meanwhile, Santos's National Unity coalition continued to enjoy the loose support of a significant majority of legislators in both chambers in 2013.

While general progress remains slow, the government has undertaken a series of steps to incorporate indigenous and Afro-Colombian voices into national political debates in recent years, including training programs to increase Afro-Colombian communities' governance capacity and awareness of their broader political rights.

C. Functioning of Government: 7 / 12

The "parapolitics" scandal, which linked scores of politicians to illegal paramilitary groups, resulted in the investigation, arrest, or conviction of over 90 legislators by the close of the 2006–2010 Congress, with investigations and trials continuing in 2013. Separately, in October a judge ordered the reopening of an investigation into links between former president Uribe and paramilitary groups.

Corruption occurs at multiple levels of public administration. Graft scandals have emerged in recent years within an array of federal government agencies. In addition, contracting abuses in Bogotá led to the 2011 removal of Mayor Samuel Moreno from office and the arrests of both him and his brother, Senator Iván Moreno. Their cases proceeded throughout 2013, as further revelations about the extent of corruption in the Bogotá government continued to emerge. Colombia was ranked 94 out of 177 countries surveyed in Transparency International's 2013 Corruption Perceptions Index. Part of the responsibility for combatting corruption rests with the inspector general, who is charged with monitoring the actions of elected officials. However, the aggressiveness of current inspector general Alejandro Ordóñez, who has removed multiple mayors and bureaucratic officials from office or suspended their right to stand for election, induced a backlash following Gustavo Petro's removal as Bogotá mayor in December 2013. In arguing for a revision of the inspector's powers, critics pointed to the lack of due process, the essentially political nature of many of the alleged offenses, and the conservative Ordóñez's apparent focus on officials whose ideologies differ from his own.

CIVIL LIBERTIES: 34 / 60

D. Freedom of Expression and Belief: 12 / 16

The constitution guarantees freedom of expression, and opposition views are commonly expressed in the media. However, dozens of journalists have been murdered since the mid-1990s, many for reporting on drug trafficking and corruption. Most of the cases remain unsolved, and although violence has declined in recent years, a local press watchdog recorded at least 123 threats and other abuses against the press in 2013. Two journalists were murdered, including Édison Alberto Molina, a reporter in Antioquia who was killed in September and had frequently discussed local government corruption. Self-censorship is common, and slander and defamation remain criminal offenses. The government does not restrict access to the internet or censor websites, and Twitter and other social-media platforms have become important arenas of political discourse.

The constitution provides for freedom of religion, and the government generally respects this right in practice. The authorities also uphold academic freedom, and university debates are often vigorous, though armed groups maintain a presence on many campuses to generate political support and intimidate opponents.

E. Associational and Organizational Rights: 5 / 12

Constitutional rights regarding freedoms of assembly and association are restricted in practice by violence. Although the government provides extensive protection to hundreds of threatened human rights workers, trust in the program varies widely, and scores of activists have been murdered in recent years, mostly by paramilitary groups and the criminal organizations that succeeded them following a government-backed demobilization process in 2005. Although the Santos administration has reiterated respect for nongovernmental organizations (NGOs), violations against activists have risen since Santos took office. Victims' and land rights campaigners are especially threatened by former paramilitaries seeking to smother criticism of their ill-gotten assets. The nongovernmental organization We Are Defenders stated that 78 human rights defenders were murdered in 2013, with paramilitary successor groups the most frequent victimizers.

The wave of protests that occurred in 2013 started in Catatumbo, a volatile region in Norte de Santander Department, and four people were killed during demonstrations there in June. The protesters demanded increased attention to rural issues. By August, what organizers labeled an "agrarian strike" had inspired further protests in various departments and cities, including Bogotá. Following violence and serious economic disruption, Santos was forced to acknowledge the protesters' demands and agree to several new agricultural assistance policies.

More than 2,600 labor union activists and leaders have been killed over the last two decades, with attacks coming from all of Colombia's illegal armed groups. Killings have declined substantially from their early-2000s peak, but the National Labor School reported 26 murders in 2013. Although a special prosecutorial unit has substantially increased prosecutions for such assassinations since 2007, most have avoided those who ordered the killings. A Labor Action Plan linked to a 2011 free trade agreement with the United States called for enhanced investigations of rights violations and stepped-up enforcement regarding abusive labor practices, but it has resulted in only minor improvements to date.

F. Rule of Law: 7 / 16

The justice system remains compromised by corruption and extortion. Although the Constitutional Court and Supreme Court have demonstrated independence from the executive in recent years, revelations of questionable behavior involving justices on both courts in 2013 resulted in diminished support for the judiciary in opinion polls. In November a member of the Superior Judicial Council, the judicial branch's main oversight body, was forced to resign following allegations that he had taken a bribe from an army officer facing trial for human rights abuses. A long-debated justice reform bill that failed to pass in 2012, with significant political fallout, remained dormant in 2013.

Many soldiers work under limited civilian oversight, though the government has in recent years increased human rights training and investigated a greater number of military personnel for violations. Collaboration between security forces and illegal armed groups declined following the 2005 paramilitary demobilization, but rights groups report official toleration of paramilitary successor groups in some regions. Primary responsibility for combating them rests with the police, who lack the resources of the military, are frequently accused of colluding with criminal groups, and are largely absent from many rural areas where the groups are active. However, many of the paramilitary groups' key leaders have been killed or arrested in recent years, as have several of Colombia's most wanted drug traffickers.

The systematic killing of civilians to fraudulently inflate guerrilla death tolls has declined substantially since a 2008 scandal over the practice led to the firing of dozens of senior army officers. More than 2,000 people may have been killed in this fashion, and thousands of security personnel remained under investigation at the end of 2013. Dozens of defendants were convicted in cases that were transferred to civilian courts—including, for the first time, two colonels, who were convicted in July and September 2013. Other cases proceeded slowly due to a shortage of prosecutors and delaying tactics by defense lawyers.

Jurisdiction over human rights violations is a sensitive issue. Convictions of high-ranking officers for forced disappearances added to tensions between military and civilian justice institutions and prompted the December 2012 passage of a government-sponsored constitutional amendment that expanded the jurisdiction of the military justice system. Domestic and international outcry over the amendment continued in 2013, especially following the June passage of implementing regulations that, according to rights groups, could have allowed extrajudicial execution cases to be transferred to military courts. However, in October the Constitutional Court struck down the amendment on the basis of procedural errors, without ruling on its substance.

While violence has subsided since the early 2000s and homicides declined by 8 percent in 2013, some areas, particularly resource-rich zones and drug-trafficking corridors, remain highly insecure. Following a series of military blows against the FARC leadership between 2008 and 2011, the rebel group reorganized and focused on new tactics, including multiple attacks carried out by small units. The Peace and Reconciliation Foundation, an authoritative nongovernmental monitor, registered about 2,000 attacks in 2013, roughly matching the figures from each of the previous three years. FARC guerrillas and paramilitary successor groups regularly extort payments from businesspeople and engage in forced recruitment, including of minors. The use of landmines in the internal conflict has added to casualties among both civilians and the military.

Impunity for crime in general is rampant. Debate continued in 2013 on legal and policy questions related to the Legal Framework for Peace, a constitutional reform enacted in 2012. Rights groups cautioned that it could allow broad impunity for all armed actors accused of atrocities during the conflict between rebel guerrillas and paramilitary groups. The Constitutional Court confirmed the law's constitutionality in August 2013, though the decision emphasized the legal necessity of prosecuting and punishing all alleged crimes against humanity.

G. Personal Autonomy and Individual Rights: 10 / 16

Freedom of movement, choice of residence, and property rights are restricted by violence, particularly for vulnerable minority groups. Colombia's more than 1.7 million indigenous inhabitants live on over 34 million hectares granted to them by the government, often in resource-rich, strategic regions that are increasingly contested by the various armed groups. Indigenous people are frequently targeted by all sides. The Office of the UN High Commissioner for Refugees and the Constitutional Court have warned in recent years that many groups face extinction, often after being displaced by the conflict.

Afro-Colombians, who account for as much as 25 percent of the population, make up the largest segment of Colombia's over 4 million displaced people, and 80 percent of Afro-Colombians fall below the poverty line. Consultation with Afro-Colombians is constitutionally mandated on issues affecting their communities, but activists expressed dismay over shortcomings in the government's consultation process for the Victims and Land Restitution Law in 2011.

Child labor is a serious problem in Colombia, as are child recruitment into illegal armed groups and related sexual abuse. Sexual harassment, violence against women, and the trafficking of women for sexual exploitation remain major concerns. Thousands of rapes have occurred as part of the conflict, generally with impunity. The country's abortion-rights movement has challenged restrictive laws, and a 2006 Constitutional Court ruling allowed abortion in cases of rape or incest, or to protect the woman's life. Same-sex marriage has become a controversial issue, with a series of judicial and administrative decisions in 2013 allowing and then annulling same-sex marriages as the country awaited a clear ruling on the matter from the Constitutional Court.

Comoros

Political Rights Rating: 3
Civil Liberties Rating: 4
Freedom Rating: 3.5
Freedom Status: Partly Free
Electoral Democracy: Yes

Population: 791,761
Capital: Moroni

Ten-Year Ratings Timeline For Year Under Review (Political Rights, Civil Liberties, Status)

Year Under Review	2004	2005	2006	2007	2008	2009	2010	2011	2012	2013
Rating	4,4,PF	4,4,PF	3,4,PF	4,4,PF	3,4,PF	3,4,PF	3,4,PF	3,4,PF	3,4,PF	3,4,PF

INTRODUCTION

In April, the government reported that it had foiled an attempted coup perpetrated by both Comoran nationals and foreigners. A former minister and the son of former president Ahmed Abdallah Abderemane were arrested in connection with the coup attempt. Corruption remained a serious problem, and a case against former president Ahmed Abdallah Sambi was pending at year's end.

In 2013, President Ikililou Dhoinine continued to push aggressive fiscal management and governance reforms in response to stagnant economic growth, rampant corruption, and high unemployment. The unemployment rate hovers around 15 percent, and unemployment among young adults is around 45 percent. In late 2012, the International Monetary Fund and the World Bank's International Development Association announced $176 million in debt relief for Comoros, representing a 59 percent reduction of its future external debt service over a period of 40 years. In June 2013, the Islamic Development Bank rescheduled Comoran debt and pledged $55 million for development projects. The European Development Fund allocated $18 million toward education and road infrastructure.

Large numbers of Comorans illegally emigrate to the French-administered island of Mayotte to settle or to seek entry into metropolitan France, and the economy depends heavily on remittances and foreign aid. In September, Dhoinine criticized restrictions on movement between Comoros and Mayotte, which the government claims as part of its territory.

POLITICAL RIGHTS: 25 / 40
A. Electoral Process: 9 / 12

Since 1996, Comorans have voted freely in several parliamentary and presidential elections. The unicameral Assembly of the Union consists of 33 members, with 9 selected by the assemblies of the three islands and 24 by direct popular vote; all members serve five-year terms. Each of the three islands is semi-autonomous, with directly elected assemblies and governors. A 2009 referendum approved constitutional reforms increasing the powers of the federal government at the expense of the individual island governments. The reforms instituted a rotation of the federal presidency among the islands every five years.

Dhoinine won the presidential elections in 2010 with the support of then president Sambi, becoming the first president from the island of Mohéli. The constitutional court upheld the election results despite irregularities reported on the island of Anjouan. In the December 2009 legislative elections, the president's supporters won 19 of the 24 directly elected seats. In September 2013, the constitutional court ruled that the end of the mandate for the president and governors must be respected.

B. Political Pluralism and Participation: 11/ 16

Political parties operate freely. They are mainly defined by their positions regarding the division of power between the federal and local governments, and are generally formed in support of particular leaders. The current main political groups are the Convention for the Renewal of the Comoros (CRC) and the Camp of the Autonomous Islands.

A major cabinet reshuffle in July 2013 was widely regarded as a purge of politicians loyal to Sambi.

C. Functioning of Government: 5 / 12

Corruption remains a major problem. There are reports of corruption at all levels of the government, judiciary, and civil service, as well as among the police and security forces. In 2011, the opposition CRC, led by former president Azali Assoumani, filed a complaint in a Moroni court against Sambi for alleged misuse of public funds while in office. The allegations concern the sale of Comoros nationality to citizens of Gulf countries, which supposedly generated $200 million that was never accounted for during financial reconciliations. The case was still pending at the end of 2013. Comoros was ranked 127 out of 177 countries and territories surveyed in Transparency International's 2013 Corruption Perceptions Index.

CIVIL LIBERTIES: 30 / 60
D. Freedom of Expression and Belief: 10 / 16

The constitution and laws provide for freedoms of speech and the press, though self-censorship is reportedly widespread. In November 2013, two journalists from the newspaper

L'Observateur des Comores were arrested for contempt of court after publishing a speech by a public prosecutor denouncing evidence of judicial corruption. That same month, radio personality Abdallah Agwa of La Baraka FM was arrested for inciting hatred after approaching the corruption issue on air. The internet is available and unrestricted by the government.

Islam is the state religion, and 98 percent of the population is Sunni Muslim. Tensions have occasionally arisen between Sunni and Shiite Muslims, and non-Sunni Muslims are reportedly subject to restrictions, detentions, and harassment. In March 2013, 19 Shiites were arrested for practicing and propagating Shia doctrine. Conversion from Islam and non-Muslim proselytizing are illegal. Academic freedom is generally respected.

E. Associational and Organizational Rights: 6 / 12

The government typically upholds freedoms of assembly and association. A few human rights and other nongovernmental organizations (NGOs) operate in the country. In May 2013, the human rights NGO Lawyers Without Borders established a branch in Moroni. Workers have the right to bargain collectively and to strike, but collective bargaining is rare.

F. Rule of Law: 8 / 16

The judicial system is based on both Sharia (Islamic law) and the French legal code, and is subject to influence by the executive branch and other elites. Minor disputes are often settled informally by village elders. Harsh prison conditions include severe overcrowding and inadequate sanitation, medical care, and nutrition.

In April, the government arrested 15 alleged coup plotters, including Mahamoud Ahmed Abdallah, the son of former president Ahmed Abdallah. Seven of those arrested were foreigners. The plotters were awaiting trial at year's end.

Same-sex sexual activity is punishable by imprisonment and fines.

G. Personal Autonomy and Individual Rights: 6 / 16

The law prohibits discrimination based on gender, and the government has taken steps to improve the political participation of women. However, in practice, women are still underrepresented at the political level; only one parliamentarian is female. Economic equality also remains a key challenge, as women have far fewer opportunities for education and salaried employment than men, especially in rural areas. In accordance with modern law and some matriarchal customary laws, women have equal rights with regard to inheritance; in some cases they are the beneficiaries of all inheritable property. However, this is complicated by the concurrent application of Islamic law limiting gender equality. In addition, a poor system of land registration and women's difficulty securing bank loans often negate the benefits of land ownership in practice. Sexual violence is believed to be widespread, but is rarely reported to authorities. In 2012, the National Assembly passed a new labor code criminalizing the trafficking of children, but Comoran children are often victims of forced labor within the country.

Congo, Republic of (Brazzaville)

Political Rights Rating: 6
Civil Liberties Rating: 5
Freedom Rating: 5.5
Freedom Status: Not Free
Electoral Democracy: No

Population: 4,355,000
Capital: Brazzaville

Ten-Year Ratings Timeline For Year Under Review (Political Rights, Civil Liberties, Status)

Year Under Review	2004	2005	2006	2007	2008	2009	2010	2011	2012	2013
Rating	5,4,PF	5,5,PF	6,5,NF	6,5,NF	6,5,NF	6,5,NF	6,5,NF	6,5,NF	6,5,NF	6,5,PF

INTRODUCTION

The repression of opposition parties and independent media outlets in the Republic of Congo continued in 2013; in June, the government suspended three newspapers for printing articles linking President Denis Sassou-Nguesso to an assassination decades earlier.

Six soldiers were convicted in September 2013 for their role in an arms depot explosion in Brazzaville the previous March; 26 others were acquitted. A French investigation into crimes against humanity allegedly committed by General Norbert Dabira began in August 2013, though he was released pending his trial.

Congo is one of sub-Saharan Africa's major oil producers, but corruption and decades of instability have contributed to poor humanitarian conditions and extreme poverty for much of the population. Congo was ranked 142 out of 186 countries on the 2013 UN Human Development Index. In March 2013, Brazil announced the cancellation of US$352 million in debt for the Congo. A French investigation into Sassou-Nguesso and his family for alleged embezzlement of public funds to acquire assets in France has been ongoing since 2010.

POLITICAL RIGHTS: 7 / 40

A. Electoral Process: 1 / 12

The 2002 constitution limits the president to two seven-year terms, although Sassou-Nguesso has held office since seizing power in 1997 after a brief civil war; he had previously been president from 1979 until 1992. In 2009, Sassou-Nguesso eliminated the post of prime minister, becoming both head of state and head of government. The Senate consists of 72 members, with councilors from each department electing six senators for five-year terms. Half of them come up for election every three years. Members of the 139-seat National Assembly are directly elected for five-year terms. Irregularities, opposition boycotts and disqualifications, and the absence of an independent electoral commission consistently tarnish elections in Congo.

Sassou-Nguesso was reelected in 2009 with 78 percent of the popular vote in a peaceful election that was criticized by both opposition parties and nongovernmental organizations (NGOs) for irregularities. The next presidential election is scheduled for 2016.

Sassou-Nguesso's Congolese Labor Party (PCT) took 89 of the 139 available seats in the July 2012 National Assembly elections amid concerns that he was considering constitutional amendments to remove presidential term limits. The PCT and its allies now control 117 of the body's seats. The elections were marred by accusations of fraud, low voter turnout, and postelection violence. The next Senate election is set for July 2014, and the next National Assembly election is planned for 2018.

B. Political Pluralism and Participation: 3 / 16

Most of the more than 100 registered political parties in Congo are personality-driven and ethnically based. Members of Sassou-Nguesso's northern Mbochi ethnic group dominate key government posts, while the opposition remains weak and fragmented. The PCT and its allies control 95 percent of Congo's legislative seats, and hold most senior positions in the government. Voters elected seven opposition candidates in 2012, all of whom belong to the Pan-African Union for Social Democracy (UPADS), though the courts overturned the elections of four of these candidates.

The government regularly restricts opposition parties' rights, especially during the most recent presidential and legislative elections. Indigenous populations are often excluded from the political process, in part due to stigmatization by majority ethnic groups, cultural barriers, and geographical isolation.

C. Functioning of Government: 3 / 12

Corruption, especially in the extractive industries, remains pervasive in Congo, though reform measures were undertaken in 2013 that included a public anticorruption campaign and efforts to draft an anticorruption law. In 2004, the country was barred from the Kimberley Process because it could not account for the origins of its diamonds, and in 2006 the International Monetary Fund (IMF) delayed debt relief due to the high level of corruption in the country. Both the World Bank and the IMF proceeded with a debt relief program for the country in 2010. Congo became fully compliant with the Extractive Industries Transparency Initiative (EITI) in February 2013. Compliance with these standards comes as a result of increased accuracy in reporting revenue from oil exploitation in the country, and requires the government to have procedures in place to disclose annual government income from extractive industry activities. The Congo also cooperates with the African Peer Mechanism Review, and a national Anti-Corruption Commission was created in 2009. The state oil company is directly under the control of the president's family and advisers.

In July, the chairman of the Anti-Corruption Oversight Committee and four members of the Committee were arrested for alleged misappropriation of funds. The National Commission for Fighting Corruption and Fraud released a report in November that described systemic corruption among the "majority of civil servants."

French authorities have been investigating Sassou-Nguesso and his family for the alleged embezzlement of public funds to acquire assets in France, including real estate and bank accounts, since 2010. Domestic prosecutions for corruption have been limited and are often politically motivated when they do occur. Congo was ranked 154 out of 177 countries and territories surveyed in Transparency International's 2013 Corruption Perceptions Index.

CIVIL LIBERTIES: 23 / 16 (+1)

D. Freedom of Expression and Belief: 8 / 16

While the constitution provides for freedom of speech and of the press, the government's respect for press freedom is limited. Speech that is perceived as inciting ethnic hatred, violence, or civil war is illegal, and the government can impose fines for defamation and incitement to violence. During the election campaign period in 2012, opposition parties reported a lack of access to state media. The High Council for Freedom of Communication (CSLC) suspended three independent newspapers in June 2013 for alleged defamation and incitement of violence. The papers had reprinted a 1977 article linking the president to the assassination of then military ruler Marien Ngouabi. A fourth paper that had not published the article was nonetheless suspended for two months for failing to comply with the CSLC.

With no nationwide radio or television stations, most citizens get their news from local broadcast sources, and the state publishes the only daily newspaper. The government systematically censors journalists, and uses government-owned media to counter critical reports in the independent media. Self-censorship among journalists is common. Most of the newspapers published in Brazzaville are privately owned, and some print articles and editorials critical of the government. There are no government restrictions on internet access, though sites that "radically criticize" the government are only permitted to operate outside of the country.

Religious and academic freedoms are generally guaranteed and respected.

E. Associational and Organizational Rights: 6 / 12

Freedoms of assembly and association are provided for in the constitution, though security forces have shown little tolerance for political demonstrations. Groups must receive official authorization to hold public assemblies. Nongovernmental organizations generally operate without interference, so long as they do not challenge the ruling elite. Workers' rights to join trade unions and to strike are protected, and collective bargaining is practiced freely, though rarely. Most workers in the formal business sector, including the oil industry, belong to unions, which have also made efforts to organize informal sectors, such as agriculture and retail trade. Members of the security forces and other essential services are not allowed to form unions.

Police detained two leaders of the national teachers' union without charge in April during a 10-week-long national teachers' strike; they were only released once they had apologized for their participation and called for the end of the strike. Hundreds of students were tear gassed by police in April when they attempted to protest the government response to the teachers' strike. In August, police briefly arrested several trade union representatives from the bank workers' union, and allegedly forced one unionist to sign a memorandum of understanding on the collective agreement.

F. Rule of Law: 2 / 16

Congo's underfunded judiciary is subject to corruption and political influence, and crippled by institutional weakness and a lack of technical capability. However, for the most part the authorities respect court orders, though they are rarely issued.

Traditional courts are the dominant judicial system in rural Congo, presiding over local property, inheritance, and domestic cases. The Human Rights Commission (HRC), charged with addressing complaints about abuses committed by security forces, is largely ineffectual and does not enjoy the trust of the people, as most of its members are presidential appointees. The president of the HRC was placed under de facto house arrest for much of the year, and the Commission did not meet regularly in 2013.

The government generally maintains control over security forces, though there are instances in which members of the security forces act with impunity. There have been reports of arbitrary arrests and suspects being tortured and dying during apprehension or in custody. Prison conditions are life threatening. The death penalty is still on the books, though executions are not carried out.

In September 2013, six soldiers were convicted of involvement in an explosion in a Brazzaville arms depot in March 2012 that killed at least 240 people, seriously injured 2,300, and displaced 17,000 families. The accused leader of the group was sentenced to 15 years' hard labor for deliberately setting fire to the depot, and the former deputy secretary general to the National Security Council was sentenced to 5 years' labor for his role in the explosion. Twenty-six others others were acquitted of wrongdoing linked to the blast.

In August, General Norbert Dabira was briefly arrested in France, where he owns a home, for crimes against humanity for his role in the 1999 disappearance of returning refugees from the neighboring Democratic Republic of Congo. He was released pending his trial, which was not scheduled by the end of 2013.

Indigenous groups are often concentrated in isolated rural areas, are not registered to vote, and are actively discriminated against, leaving them politically marginalized. In particular, native Mbendjele Yaka suffer discrimination, with many held in lifetime servitude. Ethnic discrimination is common in hiring practices, and urban neighborhoods tend to be segregated. The National Action Plan on the Improvement of Quality of Life of Indigenous Peoples, introduced in 2009 and set to end in 2013, established benchmarks for measures to improve the lives of the Congolese indigenous population. This plan set the stage for the adoption of Africa's first law on indigenous rights in February 2011.The Promotion and Protection of Indigenous Populations Act contains provisions on cultural rights, education, and land rights, explicitly prohibiting forced assimilation and discrimination; the law has widely known nationally and accelerated the process of improving access to basic services for indigenous populations.

While there is no law that specifically prohibits same-sex sexual relations, people found to have committed a "public outrage against decency" face punishments of up to two years in prison; however, this is rarely enforced.

G. Personal Autonomy and Individual Rights: 7 / 16 (+1)

Harassment by military personnel and militia groups inhibits travel, though such practices have declined. The judicial system offers few protections for business and property rights.

Despite constitutional safeguards, legal and societal discrimination against women persists. Equal access to education and employment is limited, and civil codes regarding marriage formalize women's inferior status. Most women work in the informal sector, and do not receive employment benefits or protection from abusive employers. Violence against women is reportedly widespread. Rape, including marital rape, is illegal, but this common crime is rarely reported or prosecuted. Abortion is prohibited in all cases except to save the life of the mother. There are no restrictions on access to contraceptives. Women are underrepresented in government and decision-making positions, holding just 13 seats in the National Assembly, 10 Senate seats, and 4 positions in a cabinet comprised of 37 individuals.

The government has made a significant effort to improve maternal morbidity and mortality, including providing free Caesarean sections since 2011. Congo has seen a 50 percent decrease in the number of women dying during childbirth over the previous 10 years, with the most significant rate of decrease occurring over the past 2 years. Congo's continued progress puts it on track to be 1 of only 12 countries to meet the 2015 Millennium Development Goal for maternal mortality.

Congo is a destination for and source of human trafficking, and substantial improvements to the prevention and prosecution of the practice have not occurred.

Congo, Democratic Republic of (Kinshasa)

Political Rights Rating: 6
Civil Liberties Rating: 6
Freedom Rating: 6.0
Freedom Status: Not Free
Electoral Democracy: No

Population: 71,128,000
Capital: Kinshasa

Ten-Year Ratings Timeline For Year Under Review (Political Rights, Civil Liberties, Status)

Year Under Review	2004	2005	2006	2007	2008	2009	2010	2011	2012	2013
Rating	6,6,NF	6,6,NF	5,6,NF	5,6,NF	6,6,NF	6,6,NF	6,6,NF	6,6,NF	6,6,NF	6,6,NF

INTRODUCTION

Violence and insecurity in the context of endemic official corruption and impunity persisted in the Democratic Republic of Congo (DRC) in 2013, though military and diplomatic advances were made against the M23 rebel movement in the country's eastern provinces. The M23 declared an end to its rebellion in November, and M23 leader Bosco Ntaganda surrendered to the International Criminal Court (ICC), signaling a victory for the international justice body. However, the ongoing presence of numerous other rebel groups in the DRC's eastern provinces continues to have a major destabilizing effect on the region. The national military continued to be implicated in human rights violations during the year, with little effective civilian control over its activities. Rule of law, especially regarding rampant sexual violence perpetrated by government and rebel forces, was almost entirely absent.

Massive corruption in the government, security forces, and extractive industries persists, paralyzing the proper functioning of the government and sustainable development efforts intended to raise the standard of living for the country's citizens. The DRC's membership in the Extractive Industries Transparency Initiative (EITI) was suspended in April. A new mineral certification program was implemented in July, although its effects remained to be seen as of the end of the year.

Journalists and human rights advocates continued to face threats, unlawful detention, and beatings by both state security forces and rebel groups around the country. Opposition lawmakers were arrested and imprisoned for speaking out against the government.

In February, 11 Great Lakes regional states signed a new peace deal in Addis Ababa aimed at bringing stability to the DRC and the region at large. Signatories agreed to a policy of non-interference in Congolese affairs and to avoid supporting armed groups, while the DRC committed to strengthening its security sector, consolidating state authority, and promoting economic development. The agreement provided for the establishment of a regional oversight mechanism as well as a national mechanism by which to oversee the implementation of the deal.

In September, a national dialogue opened between the government, members of civil society, and opposition parties to address endemic problems of poverty and corruption, in keeping with the February agreement. The September conference was hampered, however, by a boycott by some opposition members, who cited grievances related to the disputed 2011 presidential election and claimed that President Joseph Kabila would use the platform to push a constitutional change and extend his mandate beyond two terms.

POLITICAL RIGHTS: 9 / 40

A. Electoral Process: 3 / 12

The president of the DRC is elected for up to two five-year terms. The president nominates a prime minister from the leading party or coalition in the 500-seat National Assembly, whose members are popularly elected to serve five-year terms. Provincial assemblies elect the 108-seat Senate, as well as provincial governors, for five-year terms.

The DRC's November 2011 presidential and National Assembly elections were marked by a lack of preparation, changes in the structure and function of the electoral commission, and limited international logistical support. A number of changes to the country's electoral law were enacted prior to the elections despite opposition protests, including eliminating the requirement for a run-off if no presidential candidate won more than 50 percent of the vote in the first round. The amendment was seen by opposition parties as an intentional manipulation to secure Kabila's reelection. Kabila was declared the winner despite widespread criticism of the election by international observers, defeating longtime opposition figure Étienne Tshisekedi, 49 percent to 32 percent, according to the Independent National Electoral Commission (CENI).

The National Assembly elections suffered similar problems. Kabila's People's Party for Reconstruction and Democracy (PPRD) won 61 seats, down from the 111 seats it held prior to November 2011, while Tshisekedi's Union for Democracy and Social Progress (UDPS) took 41. Kabila's coalition, the Alliance of the Presidential Majority (AMP), won 260 of the 500 seats. Tshisekedi supporters protested the results, and numerous civil society groups called for new elections.

The legitimacy of CENI is questionable, as four of its seven members are appointed by the presidential coalition, and it does not include members of civil society. CENI was restructured and reestablished in June 2013, prompting hope that the electoral process might be revitalized.

B. Political Pluralism and Participation: 4 / 16

According to CENI, there are about 445 political parties in the DRC. Political parties are often divided along ethnic, communal, or regional lines, and usually lack national reach. The AMP requires members to have national representation, ensuring that the PPRD remains in the majority within the coalition. Other major parties include the UDPS and Movement for the Liberation of Congo (MLC). Nearly 100 different parties and many independents are represented in the parliament. Opposition politicians and their supporters faced violence and harassment by police in the run-up to the 2011 polls.

There were cases of politically motivated arrests of opposition leaders in 2013. Eugène Diomi Ndongala, the president of the Christian Democrats opposition party and a Tshisekedi supporter, was detained in April on charges supporters say were politically motivated, and was still in custody at year's end as his trial continued. In August, lawmaker Muhindo Nzangi of the Social Movement for Renewal (MSR) was sentenced to three years in jail on the charge of threatening national security after making comments on the radio critical of the government. As a result, the MSR suspended its participation in the ruling coalition and boycotted September's national unity conference.

The majority of the DRC's indigenous population does not take part in the political process because of ethnic discrimination and lack of access to institutions in rural areas. The government does not effectively protect their political rights.

C. Functioning of Government: 2 / 9

Corruption and impunity continue to be serious problems. The clandestine trade in mineral resources by rebels and elements of the Armed Forces of the Democratic Republic of Congo (FARDC) help finance violence and deplete government revenues from the sector. Massive corruption in the government, security forces, and mineral extraction industries continues to paralyze the proper functioning of the government and sustainable development efforts intended to raise the standard of living for its citizens.

Recruitment for government posts is often determined by nepotism, and political interference is rampant. The complicated system of taxation and regulation has made bribery and corruption a regular aspect of business dealings. Hundreds of millions of dollars are embezzled every year. Beginning in 2012, civil servants and members of the military were paid electronically, with the aim of curbing corruption and ensuring regular, accurate payments.

Despite incremental improvements in revenue reporting, there is little transparency in the state's financial affairs. As a result, the EITI in April suspended the DRC's membership for one year. The law does not provide for public access to government information. The DRC was ranked 154 out of 177 countries and territories surveyed in Transparency International's 2013 Corruption Perceptions Index.

CIVIL LIBERTIES: 11 / 60

D. Freedom of Expression and Belief: 7 / 16

Although guaranteed by the constitution, freedoms of speech and the press are limited. Radio is the dominant medium in the country, and newspapers are found mainly in large cities. The content of private television and radio stations is occasionally restricted, but lively political debate is growing in urban areas. The government does not monitor online communications or restrict access to the internet, but use is limited by lack of infrastructure.

Freedom of the press is significantly restrained through criminal defamation and libel laws as well as threats, detentions, and attacks against journalists; nevertheless, Kabila and his government are often criticized in the media. Journalists in the conflict-ridden east are frequently subject to threats, censorship, and violence. Government soldiers raided the Radio Tujenge Kabambare community station in January, confiscating equipment and detaining and beating two staff members; the station had previously aired reports critical of the military. In May, radio presenter Guillain Chanjabo was found murdered near the northeastern city of Bunia after having been missing for 12 days; local journalists staged peaceful protests and some media outlets suspended broadcasts to pressure the government to investigate his disappearance. In July, radio station manager Simplexe Musangu was detained and held for more than 100 days after rebel gunmen forced him to broadcast a message calling for the independence of southeastern Katanga province. The government ordered the radio station suspended for 30 days following the incident, though the suspension lasted for 37 days. In August, a radio journalist spent two days in solitary confinement for being late in reading an official government press release on the radio in Shabunda, in eastern South Kivu province.

In September, the DRC's state broadcasting regulator, the High Council for Broadcasting and Communication (CSAC), was ordered by a court to pay the owner of a private television station $40,000 for damage done to his business interests by prolonged and repeated suspensions of his station's programs.

Freedom of religion is guaranteed by the constitution and generally respected in practice. Although religious groups must register with the government in order to be recognized, unregistered groups operate unhindered. There are no formal government restrictions on academic freedom.

E. Associational and Organizational Rights: 3 / 12

The constitution guarantees freedoms of assembly and association, though these are limited in practice. Groups holding public events must register with local authorities in advance, and security forces occasionally act against unregistered demonstrations and marches. In April 2013, 12 people were sentenced to 20 years in jail each for planning to hold a demonstration protesting mismanagement by local authorities. The charges were eventually reduced to between 5 and 12 months, and the judge who issued the original verdict was suspended for failing to justify his ruling.

Authorities often target human rights activists and opposition political party members who are critical of the government. In August, a peaceful sit-in by supporters of Muhindo Nzangi—a member of the National Assembly who had been sentenced to three years in prison for publicly criticizing the government's management of the conflict in the east of the country—was violently interrupted by police, who arrested five demonstrators.

There are about 5,000 registered nongovernmental organizations (NGOs) in the DRC, though they often have narrow scopes devoted to ethnic and local concerns. NGOs are generally able to operate, though domestic human rights advocates are subject to harassment, arbitrary arrest, and detention. In June, the National Assembly approved a law establishing a forum for civil society to express their views on government policies and actions.

Congolese who fulfill a residency requirement of 20 years can form and join trade unions, though government employees and members of state security forces are not permitted to unionize. It is against the law for employers to retaliate against strikers. Unions organize strikes regularly. Some labor leaders and activists face harassment.

F. Rule of Law: 0 / 16

Kabila appoints members of the judiciary, which remains subject to corruption and political manipulation. The courts are concentrated in urban areas, leaving the majority of the country reliant on customary courts. Military courts are often used, even in civilian cases, and are subject to interference by high-ranking military personnel. The judiciary is susceptible to bias against opposition party members and civil society. Prison conditions are life-threatening, and long periods of pretrial detention are common.

Civilian authorities do not maintain effective control of the security forces. The FARDC are largely undisciplined, and soldiers and police regularly commit serious human rights abuses, including rape and torture. Low pay and inadequate provisions commonly lead soldiers to seize goods from civilians. Most government and government-allied forces enjoy apparent impunity for even the most heinous crimes. In May 2013, 12 senior FARDC officers were suspended and 11 were arrested for their alleged involvement in a mass rape in November 2012. Between February and June, at least four soldiers were found guilty of acts of torture.

The ICC continues to pursue cases in the DRC, including the trials of rebel leader Germain Katanga and Jean-Pierre Bemba, a former DRC vice president and the leader of the MLC. Both trials continued through the end of 2013.

In February, the M23 split into factions, with Sultani Makenga taking over the larger group and Ntaganda taking the smaller. In March, Bertrand Bisimwa was announced as the M23's new president by Makenga's faction. The same month, Ntaganda, along with several hundred combatants, fled to Rwanda, where he turned himself in to stand trial before the ICC on charges of war crimes and crimes against humanity, leaving Makenga's group as the sole M23 faction.

According to a 2012 UN Security Council report, Rwanda and Uganda have been actively involved in providing material and command support to the M23 rebels. In August 2013, Rwanda, with a temporary seat on the UN Security Council, blocked a proposal to impose sanctions on two M23 commanders accused of human rights violations in eastern Congo, arguing that doing so would compromise regional peacemaking efforts. Rwanda was reportedly providing supplies to M23 fighters as late as September 2013.

In January, the UN Security Council approved the use of unmanned drone aircraft to provide better military reconnaissance for its peacekeeping force, the UN Organization

Stabilization Mission in the Democratic Republic of the Congo (MONUSCO). The drones were to be deployed in August, but procurement difficulties delayed this until December. In March, the United Nations created a new intervention brigade comprised of 3,000 troops from three African countries and charged with confronting and disarming armed groups in the DRC's eastern region, including the M23. The brigade has the strongest mandate ever given for such a force, and brings the total number of uniformed personnel in MONUSCO to about 22,000.

In August, M23 launched an assault on the eastern city of Goma. The UN brigade and the Congolese army took action against the group on August 21, responding to rebel aggression with artillery fire, arrests, and the recovery of firearms in the surrounding security zone. During the fighting, one UN peacekeeper was killed and several others wounded. Three days later, however, demonstrators in Goma demanded that UN troops take a more aggressive stance against M23 rebels. The protests turned violent and led to the deaths of several civilians, though reports differed as to whether UN forces or the FARDC were responsible for the deaths.

The combined operations of the UN brigade and government troops represented the most significant military victory since the beginning of the rebellion, and forced the M23 to announce a unilateral ceasefire and resume negotiations in September. The government rejected an amnesty for senior rebels allegedly responsible for human rights violations. The M23 declared an end to its rebellion in November, though prospects for long-term peace in the eastern region are hampered by the presence of several other rebel groups. These included two Ugandan groups—the Lord's Resistance Army (LRA) and the Islamist Allied Democratic Forces (ADF)—as well as the Democratic Forces for the Liberation of Rwanda (FDLR) and the Mai Mai Bakata Katanga. Most armed group activity occurred in North and South Kivu, Katanga, and Orientale Provinces.

The impact of years of fighting on civilians has been catastrophic, with over five million conflict-related deaths since 1998. The DRC was ranked 186 out of 187 countries in the UN Development Programme's 2013 Human Development Index.

Ethnic discrimination, including against indigenous populations, is a major problem. There are reports of indigenous people being kidnapped and forced into slavery. Rwandophone minorities in the Kivu provinces have been the victims of violence and hate speech for decades.

The constitution prohibits discrimination against people with disabilities, but they often find it difficult to find employment, attend school, or access government services. There are no laws specifically prohibiting same-sex sexual relations, but individuals can still be prosecuted for these acts under public decency laws.

G. Personal Autonomy and Individual Rights: 1 / 16

Although the law provides for freedom of movement, security forces seeking bribes or travel permits restrict this right in practice. In conflict zones, various armed groups and soldiers have seized private property and destroyed homes. As of mid-2013, 2.6 million Congolese had been internally displaced due to violence in the east.

The Congolese economy, reliant on the extraction of natural resources, has grown an average of 6 percent over the past decade, and expanded by 8.5 percent in 2013, though only 4 percent of Congolese are employed in the formal economy. A new mineral certification program aimed at stopping armed groups from benefiting financially from the lucrative mineral trade took effect in July. Property rights are recognized in the constitution, but the expropriation of private property is common. The majority of land in the DRC is held through customary tenure, and this lack of legal title to the land leads to regular confiscation of property.

Despite constitutional guarantees, women face discrimination in nearly every aspect of their lives, especially in rural areas. There is no equality for women either in practice or in law. Violence against women and girls, including sexual and gender-based violence, has soared since fighting began in 1994, though sex crimes often affect men and boys as well. The M23 rebels and FARDC soldiers have been implicated in kidnappings, killings, and rape. Mass rapes continued in 2013, and convictions remain rare. Abortion is prohibited, and women's access to contraception is extremely low. Women are also greatly underrepresented in government, making up only 9 percent of the National Assembly and 6 percent of the Senate. Women must have their husband's permission to seek employment, engage in legal transactions, and often for access to family planning services.

The law prohibits all forced or compulsory labor, though this still occurs commonly around the country, including forced child labor in mining, street vending, and agriculture. The forced recruitment of young men and boys by M23 forces, as well as by Rwandan military officials on behalf of the M23, has been documented. The M23 has also reportedly forced civilians to work for them, at times imposing tolls on vehicles passing through its territory. The recruitment and use of child soldiers by other rebel groups is also widespread.

In 2012, the government entered a UN-backed plan to end the use of child soldiers in the FARDC, and has made progress toward doing so. Several hundred child soldiers forcibly recruited to rebel forces were freed in 2013 with the help of UN peacekeepers. The DRC is both a source and destination country for the trafficking of men, women, and children for the purposes of labor and sexual exploitation.

Costa Rica

Political Rights Rating: 1
Civil Liberties Rating: 1
Freedom Rating: 1.0
Freedom Status: Free
Electoral Democracy: Yes

Population: 4,700,000
Capital: San José

Ten-Year Ratings Timeline For Year Under Review (Political Rights, Civil Liberties, Status)

Year Under Review	2004	2005	2006	2007	2008	2009	2010	2011	2012	2013
Rating	1,1,F	1,1,F	1,1,F	1,1,F	1,1,F	1,1,F	1,1,F	1,1,F	1,1,F	1,1,F

INTRODUCTION

Public confidence in President Laura Chinchilla's administration continued to decline in 2013 as resignations and corruption scandals plagued her government. Crime and drug-related violence remained a significant threat as Mexican drug cartels increased their activity in Costa Rica. Corruption, insecurity, and unemployment were the chief concerns of Costa Ricans as the country prepared for national elections in February 2014.

While the quality of life in Costa Rica is relatively high for the region, economic growth is hampered by the national debt, inflation, and cost-of-living increases. Though foreign direct investment reached record levels in 2011, and the economy grew in 2012 and 2013, poverty rates and unemployment also increased. Difficulties in passing reforms to deal with the growing public debt led the Moody's rating agency to downgrade the outlook for Costa Rica's bond rating from stable to negative in September 2013.

POLITICAL RIGHTS: 37 / 40 (-1)

A. Electoral Process: 12 / 12

The president of Costa Rica and members of the 57-seat, unicameral Legislative Assembly are elected for single four-year terms and can seek a nonconsecutive second term. A special chamber of the Supreme Court chooses an independent national election commission. Ahead of the 2010 elections, Costa Rica approved reforms to its electoral law, including revised regulations on political party and campaign financing, and new quotas for women's participation in political parties. The main political parties are the National Liberation Party (PLN), the Citizens' Action Party (PAC), the Libertarian Movement Party (PML), and the Social Christian Unity Party (PUSC).

In February 2010, Laura Chinchilla of the PLN became Costa Rica's first female president. She captured nearly 47 percent of the vote, defeating Ottón Solís of the PAC and Otto Guevara of the PML. In concurrent legislative elections, the PLN captured 24 seats, the PAC won 11, the PML took 9, the PUSC won 6, and the Accessibility without Exclusion Party (PASE) captured 4, with the remaining 3 seats going to other smaller parties. In April 2011, the PAC's Juan Carlos Mendoza was elected president of the Assembly; Mendoza's election marked the first time in 46 years that the president of the Assembly was not a member of the ruling party.

B. Political Pluralism and Participation: 15 / 16

Since 1949, power in Costa Rica has alternated between the PLN and the PUSC. Dissatisfaction with party politics and political scandals resulted in defections from the PLN in the early 2000s. The newly formed PAC then became a rising force in Costa Rican politics as the PUSC collapsed under the weight of scandal.

C. Functioning of Government: 10 / 12 (-1)

Every president since 1990 has been accused of corruption after leaving office, with the exception of Óscar Arias, who served from 2006 to 2010. In December 2012, an appeals court overturned the corruption conviction of former president Miguel Ángel Rodríguez. Rodríguez was convicted in 2011 on corruption charges related to a business deal between the Costa Rican Electricity Institute and Alcatel, a French telecommunications company. He returned to court in October 2013 to face embezzlement charges. Costa Rica was ranked 49 out of 177 countries and territories surveyed in Transparency International's 2013 Corruption Perceptions Index.

As with her predecessors, President Chinchilla's government has been plagued by corruption revelations. Scandals and routine cabinet changes reinforced the lack of confidence in her administration; 13 cabinet ministers resigned for various reasons during her first two years in office.

In March 2012, Finance Minister Fernando Herrero; his wife, presidential consultant Floriasbel Rodriguez; and Tax Administrator Francisco Villalobos were accused of evading taxes by undervaluing their property. Herrero and Rodriguez had also benefited from irregular bidding on a state-owned oil refinery project, which led to an investigation of Vice President Luis Lieberman and Minister of Education Leonardo Garnier for influence peddling. Chinchilla's refusal to dismiss them resulted in a standoff with the Legislative Assembly. Minister of Public Works Francisco Jimenez resigned in May 2012 amid allegations of corruption surrounding a road project along the San Juan River.

In May 2013, a jet used by Chinchilla to travel to Peru and Venezuela was reportedly linked to drug traffickers. The scandal forced the resignation of three administration officials, including Presidency Vice Minister Mauricio Boraschi, who was also head of the Office of Intelligence and Security and the antidrug commissioner.

The lack of confidence in the Chinchilla administration has had a dramatic impact on citizen attitudes toward democracy, as support for the political system have declined during her presidency. A September 2012 opinion poll indicated that Chinchilla had the lowest approval rating in the hemisphere. In October 2013 her approval rating dropped to 9 percent.

CIVIL LIBERTIES: 53 / 60
D. Freedom of Expression and Belief: 16 / 16

The Costa Rican media are generally free from state interference. A February 2010 Supreme Court ruling removed prison terms for defamation. There are six privately owned dailies, and both public and commercial broadcast outlets are available, including at least four private television stations and more than 100 private radio stations. There have been reports of abuse of government advertising and direct pressure from senior officials to influence media content. Internet access is unrestricted.

In April 2013, lawmakers removed a controversial provision from a 2012 law that threatened prison terms for those who published secret political information. Journalists had challenged the original measure at the Supreme Court. The revised law excludes prison sentences when the information's release is in the public interest.

The government upholds freedom of religion. Academic freedom is respected.

E. Associational and Organizational Rights: 11 / 12

The constitution provides for freedoms of assembly and association, and numerous non-governmental organizations (NGOs) are active. Although labor unions organize and mount frequent protests with minimal governmental interference, employers often ignore minimum wage and social security laws, and the resulting fines are insignificant.

F. Rule of Law: 13 / 16

The judicial branch is independent, with members elected by the legislature. However, there are often substantial delays in the judicial process, resulting in lengthy pretrial detention. There have been complaints of police brutality, and organized criminal networks are suspected of having infiltrated law enforcement institutions. An attempted prison break at a maximum-security facility in May 2011 led to an investigation of prison conditions, which revealed corruption, overcrowding, guard shortages, and guard-initiated abuse. Deadly prison riots in January and October 2012 underscored the severity of overcrowding in prisons, which has more than quintupled since 2009.

The country's Pacific coast serves as a major drug transshipment route. Analysts have noted the presence of several Mexican drug cartels operating within the country.

During her first year in office, President Chinchilla created a national antidrug commission, hired 1,000 new police officers, earmarked additional funds for the country's judicial investigation agency, and made plans to expand prison capacity. In February 2011, she introduced a 10-year crime reduction plan, which aimed to promote interagency coordination to combat growing public insecurity, crime, and narcotics trafficking. The country's homicide rate fell to an estimated 10 murders for every 100,000 people in 2012, the first drop since 2004. In 2013, it was reported that more than 80 percent of the arrests in the country were related to drug trafficking. There have been concerns that crime is overwhelming local courts and other state institutions in some areas in the south of the country.

A 2006 law permits security forces to raid any home, business, or vehicle where they suspect undocumented immigrants, who can then be detained indefinitely. Abuse and extortion of migrants by the Border Guard have also been reported. Legislation governing migration issues imposes fines for employers who hire undocumented immigrants and controls on marriages between Costa Ricans and foreigners.

Indigenous rights are not a government priority, and NGOs estimate that about 73 percent of the country's 70,000 indigenous people have little access to health and education services, electricity, or potable water. Costa Ricans of African descent have also faced racial and economic discrimination.

G. Personal Autonomy and Individual Rights: 13 / 16

Women face discrimination in the economic realm. Female household workers are subject to exploitation and lack legal protections. Despite the existence of domestic violence legislation, violence against women and children is a major problem.

Costa Rica remains a transit and destination country for trafficked persons. In 2013, Costa Rica was a Tier 2 country in the U.S. State Department's *Trafficking in Persons Report*. A new law against human trafficking went into effect in February 2013. In addition to establishing penalties for human trafficking and organ trafficking, the law established a fund for victims and prevention efforts, to be financed by a $1 dollar increase in the exit tax paid by visitors upon departure.

Chinchilla faced criticism from civil society organizations and LGBT (lesbian, gay, bisexual, and transgender) rights advocates in 2010 when she supported a referendum put forth by conservative groups against same-sex unions. However, the Constitutional Court ruled that year that holding a referendum on this issue was unconstitutional. In October 2011, the Supreme Court ruled against sexual orientation as grounds for discrimination by overturning a regulation that had prohibited same-sex conjugal visits for prisoners. In May 2012, PLN legislator Justo Orozco, known for his antigay views, was elected president of the Legislative Assembly's Human Rights Committee. His election was criticized by the LGBT community, which called on Chinchilla to speak out in support of LGBT rights. In July 2013 the legislature passed the Law of Young People, which some believed created a loophole for the legalization of gay marriage. However, the Family Court ruled in September that the language in the bill applied only to unions between a man and a woman.

Côte d'Ivoire

Political Rights Rating: 5
Civil Liberties Rating: 4
Freedom Rating: 4.5
Freedom Status: Partly Free
Electoral Democracy: No

Population: 21,141,693
Capital: Yamoussoukro (official), Abidjan (de facto)

Ratings Change: Côte d'Ivoire's civil liberties rating improved from 5 to 4 due to further openings in the environment for freedoms of expression, assembly, and association, as well as for minority groups, as the security situation stabilized under the new government.

Ten-Year Ratings Timeline For Year Under Review (Political Rights, Civil Liberties, Status)

Year Under Review	2004	2005	2006	2007	2008	2009	2010	2011	2012	2013
Rating	6,6,NF	6,6,NF	7,6,NF	7,5,NF	6,5,NF	6,5,NF	7,6,NF	6,6,NF	5,5,PF	5,4,PF

INTRODUCTION

Throughout 2013, Côte d'Ivoire continued to grapple with the aftermath of a 2010–2011 civil conflict sparked by a disputed presidential election; the crisis left some 3,000 people dead and an estimated one million others displaced. Local and regional elections were held in April 2013, marking the first such voting in over a decade. While violence was limited, several opposition parties boycotted the polls, and postelection protests were dispersed with tear gas. President Alassane Ouattara's Rally of the Republicans (RDR) party continued to dominate both local and national politics, while former president Laurent Gbagbo's Ivoirian Popular Front (FPI) party remained in disarray. Dialogue between the two parties has stalled, and progress toward reconciliation has been fitful and slow.

Investigations into massacres committed during and after the 2010–2011 postelection crisis have been stymied by repeated delays and an apparent lack of political will. There were some new arrests of pro-Gbagbo figures in 2013, but few if any targeting members of the pro-Ouattara camp. In August, judicial authorities ordered the release pending trial of 14 allies of the Gbagbo regime, including Gbagbo's son and the former head of the FPI, in a tentative but important step toward accommodation with the opposition.

Separately in August, the legislature passed two laws that eased restrictions on nationality and citizenship, which have proven perennial sources of conflict in the country. Lawmakers also enacted land-tenure legislation that extended the implementation period of a 1998 law designed to codify land transactions.

Conditions for the press continued to improve, with violence and legal harassment against journalists declining compared with previous years. However, among other ongoing problems, the government continued to selectively suppress unfavorable coverage in the media. In July, the authorities temporarily suspended an opposition newspaper for publicizing the names of alleged political prisoners being held by the regime.

POLITICAL RIGHTS: 17 / 40 (+4)
A. Electoral Process: 6 / 12 (+1)

The constitution provides for the popular election of a president and a unicameral National Assembly—currently comprised of 255 members—for five-year terms. The last presidential election, held in two rounds in October and November 2010 after years of delays, triggered an internal conflict when Gbagbo, the incumbent, refused to concede the internationally recognized victory of Ouattara, who secured 54 percent of the vote in the November runoff. Gbagbo was ultimately arrested with the assistance of French and UN troops, and Ouattara was able to assume office by April 2011. Ouattara ally and former rebel leader Guillaume Soro became prime minister. Soro and other former rebel commanders, to whom Ouattara is greatly indebted, continue to exert significant influence over policy decisions.

The first largely peaceful and fair parliamentary elections in over a decade were held in December 2011. Ouattara's RDR party won 127 seats in the unicameral National Assembly, while the Democratic Party of Côte d'Ivoire–African Democratic Rally (PDCI-RDA) placed second with 77 seats. Thirty-five independents and four smaller parties divided the remainder. Gbagbo's party, the FPI, boycotted the vote, accusing the electoral commission of bias and the security forces of intimidation. After the elections, Soro was chosen as speaker of parliament, and Jeannot Ahoussou-Kouadio of the PDCI-RDA became prime minister. Daniel Kablan Duncan, also of the PDCI-RDA, replaced him in November 2012.

The RDR won a majority of contests in the April 2013 local and regional elections, followed by the PDCI-RDA; independent candidates won 72 municipalities, though many rejoined their respective political parties (especially the RDR) after polling was complete. The elections were largely free of violence, but supporters of losing candidates protested in the streets, in some cases setting up roadblocks and burning tires. Security forces responded with tear gas. Several opposition parties boycotted the elections, demanding changes to the composition of the Independent Election Commission, and the FPI suspended 15 of its members for registering as independent candidates.

B. Political Pluralism and Participation: 7 / 16 (+3)

The conduct of the long-delayed 2013 local and regional elections represented further progress in the country's gradual return to normal multiparty political activity, without major interference from armed groups or the outright exclusion of major regions. However, the RDR and PDCI-RDA remain the most powerful parties. Gbagbo's FPI is weak and disorganized, and did not received state funding due to its boycott of the parliamentary and local elections. In June 2013, the FPI set a number of conditions for a resumption of dialogue with the RDR, including the release of political prisoners and the establishment of a committee to monitor negotiations between the two parties. In December, representatives of the FPI held direct talks with the RDR—the first in a decade. Nevertheless, Gbagbo's supporters continued to reject the UN-mediated reconciliation framework, on the grounds that Ouattara is seeking victor's justice through both the political and judicial processes.

The two-year mandate of the national Dialogue, Truth and Reconciliation Commission (CDVR) concluded in September 2013, with many observers complaining that it had failed to complete its mission. While the body was designed to be impartial, it was headed by a prominent politician and Ouattara ally, Charles Konan Banny. The CDVR never held promised public hearings at which victims would confront perpetrators of violence during the 2011 postelection crisis. The commission argued that its work was stymied by a lack of resources and the continuing persecution of Gbagbo's supporters. In July, criminal charges—including vague offenses like "destabilization activities"—were confirmed against another 84 Gbagbo allies, lending credence to the CDVR's complaints and further eroding trust between the FPI and the RDR. The release of 14 of the detainees on bail in August was seen as a positive step, though they still faced trial. At year's end the president was considering a request to extend the CDVR's mandate so that it could accomplish its goals.

The parliament passed two laws in August that were aimed at easing restrictions on nationality and citizenship. The first allows both male and female foreigners who marry Ivoirian nationals to acquire citizenship, removing restrictions on foreign men; the second extends citizenship to foreign-born residents who have lived in the country since before independence, along with their descendants, as well as to foreign nationals born in Côte d'Ivoire in 1961–1973 and their descendants. Citizenship has been a perennial source of conflict since Ivoirian nationalists adopted former president Henri Bédié's concept of "Ivoirité" to exclude perceived foreigners (including Ouattara) from the political process. While the effects of the two laws remain to be seen, they constitute an important advance toward inclusion across ethnic and regional divides.

C. Functioning of Government: 4 / 12

Corruption is a serious problem, and perpetrators rarely face prosecution or public exposure. Ouattara instructed his ministers to sign a code of ethics in 2011, and in September his administration passed two ordinances designed to strengthen the legal framework for curbing corruption and to establish a High Authority for Good Governance. Critics initially worried that these efforts would leave too many loopholes for officials to escape punishment; their effectiveness remains to be seen. In August, the president of the National Public Procurement Regulating Authority announced that it would audit a series of no-bid procurement contracts awarded over the last several years. Estimates suggested that approximately 40 percent of all contracts were sole source in 2012 alone. Côte d'Ivoire was ranked 136 out of 177 countries and territories surveyed in Transparency International's 2013 Corruption Perceptions Index.

The National Assembly adopted legislation in April that authorized the president to govern by decree until the end of the year, including on matters of economic and social policy. The FPI condemned the move as illegal, while Ouattara and his supporters deemed it necessary to ensure efficiency while the government continues to reckon with the aftermath of the 2011 crisis.

CIVIL LIBERTIES: 28 / 40 (+7)

D. Freedom of Expression and Belief: 10 / 16 (+2)

Freedom of speech and of the press is protected by the constitution and by the country's laws, although there are prohibitions on speech that incites violence, hatred, or rebellion. Conditions for the press have eased considerably since the end of the internal conflict. Violence, legal harassment, and other obstacles to reporting have declined, and a number of private news outlets have opened or resumed operations. However, many such problems persist. The Ouattara government has continued to use legal and regulatory mechanisms to suppress critical coverage in some cases. In January 2013, two bloggers were arrested for "interfering with disaster relief" after they started a blog to help victims of a New Year's Eve stampede in Abidjan that killed more than 60 people; they were released after four days. In July, the opposition newspaper *Le Quotidien d'Abidjan* was suspended for seven days for publishing a list of political prisoners held by the Ouattara regime; the country's state-controlled press council claimed that publication of the list could incite rebellion. In November, the editor in chief of *Tomorrow Magazine* was killed in what may have been a botched robbery attempt, and a journalist working for *Le Nouveau Réveil* was abducted and later released.

In December 2013, the National Assembly passed an Access to Information law; the law's provisions included the appointment of an information commissioner. The impact of the law had yet to be evaluated.

Legal guarantees of religious freedom are typically upheld, though the political divide between north and south often overlaps with a religious divide between Muslims and Christians. Religious and traditional organizations have been instrumental in leading the postconflict reconciliation process at the local level.

Academic freedom suffered severely during the civil conflict. Public universities throughout the country were closed in 2011, occupied by armed forces from both sides, and used as military bases and training grounds. They were reopened to students only in September 2012. A university police force was created and, after the minister of higher education was attacked by students at Félix Houphouët-Boigny University in May 2013, student unions are required to sign a "charter for nonviolence in university settings"—a measure that has been credited with curbing violence on campus.

E. Associational and Organizational Rights: 7 / 12 (+2)

The constitution protects the right to free assembly, but it is often denied in practice. In February, security forces fired tear gas at pro-Gbagbo protesters in Abidjan, and in May, police again used tear gas to disperse a peaceful protest by students demanding improved conditions at the country's largest university. Nevertheless, conditions continued to improve compared with previous years. Former FPI president Pascal Affi N'Guessan was reportedly able to hold public meetings in different parts of the country, largely without incident, following his release on bail in August.

Freedom of association also continued to improve in 2013. Both domestic and international nongovernmental organizations generally operated freely.

The right to organize and join labor unions is constitutionally guaranteed, and workers have the right to bargain collectively. Unions suffered greatly during the 2011 crisis, becoming disorganized and largely ineffectual. However, there were signs of increasing union activity in 2013. Public-sector workers launched a 72-hour strike in January, demanding wage increases and the release of long-delayed arrears allowances. In April, primary and secondary school teachers in Abidjan mounted a strike to demand the repayment of levies deducted from their salaries and the return of previously confiscated union dues.

F. Rule of Law: 5 / 16 (+1)

The judiciary is not independent, and judges are highly susceptible to external interference and bribes. A number of high-profile cases from the postelection crisis and its aftermath remain unresolved, including the killing of seven peacekeepers in June 2012 and the massacre of at least 14 individuals at an internally displaced persons camp in Nahibly in July 2012. Even as these investigations languished in 2013, new probes were launched. In May, a pro-Ouattara warlord was arrested for illegally squatting in a protected forest; human rights groups have accused him of several massacres in western Côte d'Ivoire both during and after the postelection crisis. Also in May, 57 mass graves were exhumed in and around Abidjan, at least 36 of which contained the bodies of individuals killed during the crisis.

The government has contested jurisdiction with the International Criminal Court (ICC) in some cases involving Gbagbo allies. Upon his release on bail in August 2013, Gbagbo's son Michel began lobbying for the release of other FPI detainees, including his mother, currently under indictment by the ICC for alleged crimes against humanity. In September, the government announced that it would try the former first lady in a domestic court, rather than transferring her to the ICC. Also in September, the ICC unsealed an additional arrest warrant for a former Gbagbo aide, Charles Blé Goudé, who was accused of committing crimes against humanity as a youth militia commander during the 2011 crisis. The warrant raised the prospect of another conflict over jurisdiction, as the government has announced its intention to try the former commander at home.

The Special Investigation Cell, created in June 2011 to investigate crimes committed during and after the postelection crisis, remains understaffed and susceptible to political meddling. The justice minister has on several occasions replaced or removed the cell's investigative judges, and the number of judicial police officers has been reduced from 20 to 4. Prosecutors complain that the government has prevented them from initiating investigations against pro-Ouattara forces; to date, not a single member of the pro-Ouattara Republican Forces of Côte d'Ivoire (FRCI) has been arrested for human rights abuses committed during the crisis. The government has renewed the cell's mandate, but its effectiveness remains in doubt.

The security situation improved slowly but steadily in 2013, with an increase in cooperation between the governments of Côte d'Ivoire, Liberia, and Ghana to curb violence and mercenary activities in the countries' porous border regions. Cross-border attacks in March resulted in the temporary displacement of approximately 8,000 Ivoirians. Despite such instability along the border, thousands of Ivoirian refugees have now returned to their homes, and violence continues to abate. In July, the mandate of the UN Operation in Côte d'Ivoire (UNOCI) was extended through June 2014 with a reduced strength of approximately 7,000 military personnel, down from the existing 10,000.

Members of the LGBT (lesbian, gay, bisexual, and transgender) community reportedly face societal prejudice as well as physical violence and harassment by security forces in Côte d'Ivoire.

G. Personal Autonomy and Individual Rights: 6 / 16 (+2)

Freedom of movement within the country continued to improve along with the security situation in 2013, although illegal roadblocks and extortion by security forces remained problems, particularly in the west. In August the parliament extended by 10 years the "grace period" for landholders to prove their legal claims to their properties. This may facilitate a transition to secure land ownership for some of the thousands of Ivoirians whose claims are caught between customary inheritance and a 1998 law designed to codify and formalize property rights in the country.

Despite constitutional protections, women suffer significant legal and economic discrimination. In a country dominated by subsistence agriculture, 75 percent of rural woman live below the poverty line, and women typically need permission from their families to cultivate food crops, according to a June 2013 World Bank report. However, a 2012 law on marriage equality stipulated that both husband and wife should manage household affairs; the previous law designated the man as head of the household. The law allows a woman to perform actions such as opening a bank account, obtaining a job, or starting a business without her husband's permission; its effectiveness in practice remains to be seen. Rape was common during the 2011 crisis and remains widespread. The law does not include provisions that specifically penalize spousal rape and mandates onerously high standards of evidence to prosecute domestic violence cases. Rape is routinely reclassified as indecent assault, and perpetrators are often released if victims fail to provide costly medical certificates. The government is working on a national strategy to combat sexual violence, but no legislation has yet been proposed.

Croatia

Political Rights Rating: 1
Civil Liberties Rating: 2
Freedom Rating: 1.5
Freedom Status: Free
Electoral Democracy: Yes

Population: 4,253,000
Capital: Zagreb

Ten-Year Ratings Timeline For Year Under Review (Political Rights, Civil Liberties, Status)

Year Under Review	2004	2005	2006	2007	2008	2009	2010	2011	2012	2013
Rating	2,2,F	2,2,F	2,2,F	2,2,F	2,2,F	1,2,F	1,2,F	1,2,F	1,2,F	1,2,F

INTRODUCTION

Croatia formally became the 28th member of the European Union (EU) in July 2013 after its EU bid had stalled in recent years over concerns about insufficient cooperation with the International Criminal Tribunal for the former Yugoslavia (ICTY), among other issues.

More than two decades following the outbreak of the conflicts accompanying Yugoslavia's collapse, this political milestone followed a key agreement with Slovenia, which had previously refused to ratify Croatia's EU accession treaty. Croatia and Slovenia had been engaged in a 20-year dispute over a Slovenian bank, Ljubljanska Banka, which had received savings from Yugoslav citizens in the 1970s. When another Slovenian bank acquired its assets in 1994, thousands of non-Slovene customers lost their deposits, prompting several government-supported lawsuits in Croatia. After years of requests from Slovenia, Croatia suspended the suits in March, and the countries agreed to seek a final ruling on the issue from the Bank for International Settlements. In April, Slovenia ratified Croatia's EU accession treaty.

Three days before joining the EU, Croatia adopted a law exempting crimes committed before 2002 from the purview of European arrest warrants—evidently to prevent the extradition of a Yugoslav-era Croatian secret police chief wanted in Germany for questioning in a murder case. Under the threat of EU sanctions, Croatia amended the law in December 2013 to repeal the exemption. Also in December, Croatian voters overwhelmingly supported a referendum to effectively ban gay marriage through a constitutional amendment.

Throughout the year, Croatia struggled with recession and a high budget deficit. In response, the government pursued belt-tightening measures to shore up the economy, including unpopular public-sector wage cuts.

POLITICAL RIGHTS: 36 / 40
A. Electoral Process: 12 / 12

The president, who serves as head of state, is elected by popular vote for a maximum of two five-year terms. Members of the 151-member unicameral parliament (Sabor) are elected to four-year terms. The prime minister is appointed by the president and requires parliamentary approval.

Ivo Josipović of the Social Democratic Party (SDP) was elected president in January 2010. In the December 2011 parliamentary elections, the center-left opposition Kukuriku coalition, comprising the SDP and three other parties, placed first with 80 seats. The Croatian Democratic Union (HDZ) and its coalition partners, the Croatian Civic Party and the Democratic Centre, followed with 47 seats. The SDP's Zoran Milanović succeeded Jadranka Kosor of the HDZ as prime minister that month.

B. Political Pluralism and Participation: 15 / 16

Following Croatia's first multiparty elections in 1990, the center-right HDZ ruled until 1999. Power has since alternated between the HDZ and the center-left SDP, including at the presidential level. Several smaller parties have also won representation in the parliament.

The Sabor comprises 140 members from 10 districts; in addition, 8 seats are set aside for ethnic minorities, including 3 for ethnic Serbs. Another three seats are reserved for representatives for Croatians living abroad. Roma are generally underrepresented in government.

C. Functioning of Government: 9 / 12

In a March 2013 report on Croatia's accession preparations, the European Commission (EC) noted progress on Croatia's anticorruption efforts, including the introduction of a new Criminal Code—effective January 1—which enforces stiffer penalties for various forms of corruption. Also in early 2013, a long overdue commission was appointed to monitor conflicts of interest among public officials. The EC praised law enforcement for continuing its proactive approach to high-profile corruption cases. However, the EC also noted that sentences in corruption cases are relatively weak, and more effort is needed to clean up corruption within public procurement processes.

In 2013, the trial continued in the so-called Fimi media case, which includes indictments against former HDZ officials, including Ivo Sanader, who served as prime minister from 2003 to 2009. Individual former members of the HDZ and the HDZ itself stand accused of funneling money from public companies to a slush fund from 2003 to 2009. Sanader has been indicted for corruption six times since 2010. Most recently, in September 2013, Sanader was indicted for allegedly forcing the utility company HEP to sell electricity to two aluminum companies at below-market rates while serving as prime minister. Separately, following a lengthy investigation, Croatian officials in August arrested 16 suspects, including nine police officers, on bribery charges related to the illegal smuggling of immigrants. In November, authorities arrested Nadan Vidošević, a prominent businessman and politician who led the Croatian Chamber of Commerce for 18 years, for allegedly embezzling 32 million kuna ($5.7 million) from the chamber through a fake-invoicing scheme.Croatia was ranked 57 out of 177 countries and territories surveyed in Transparency International's 2013 Corruption Perceptions Index.

CIVIL LIBERTIES: 50 / 60

D. Freedom of Expression and Belief: 14 / 16

The constitution guarantees freedoms of expression and the press, and these rights are generally respected. However, journalists face political pressure, intimidation, and attack. In January, a leading Balkan press watchdog criticized the arrest of Jasna Babić, an investigative reporter sued for libel by a businessman. In an unprecedented move by the authorities, a court ordered Babić jailed for two days after she repeatedly missed hearings in the case. Babić was released January 24. Four days later, she apologized in court to the businessman, who dropped the suit. Internet access is unrestricted.

The constitution guarantees freedom of religion. A group needs at least 500 members and five years of registered operation to be recognized as a religious organization. Members of the Serbian Orthodox Church continue to report cases of intimidation and vandalism, although such incidents are declining. Little progress has been made in restoring property nationalized by the communists to non-Roman Catholic groups.

Academic freedom is guaranteed by law, though subjects such as sexual health remain taboo in the socially conservative country. For example, in January 2013 the government introduced a health education program in primary and secondary schools that proved controversial for including curriculum on sexual health and homosexuality. Allied with conservative lawmakers, the Croatian Catholic Church launched a PR war against the program, including a leafleting campaign asserting that the sexual education curriculum would undermine traditional values while promoting the "disease" of homosexuality. In May, the Constitutional Court suspended the program, arguing that the government failed to consult with parents on the curriculum.

E. Associational and Organizational Rights: 12 / 12

The constitution provides for freedoms of association and assembly. In June 2013, Zagreb held its largest-ever gay pride parade, and multiple interest groups held protests throughout the year. In September, 46,000 doctors and nurses went on strike over benefit cuts imposed by the government in response to the economic crisis. A variety of nongovernmental organizations operate in Croatia without interference or harassment. The constitution allows workers to form and join trade unions, though unlawful dismissals of union members have been reported.

F. Rule of Law: 11 / 16

In 2013, Croatia continued implementing reforms to improve judicial independence and efficiency. The State Judicial and Prosecutorial Councils functioned independently, working to develop a track record of merit-based appointments and taking a more proactive approach to cases of misconduct by judicial officials. Under a new judicial appointments system that came into effect in January, all candidates must complete the State School for Judicial Officials, representing an effort to increase professionalism. Despite some progress on improving efficiency, the case backlog remains above the EU average. Prison conditions do not meet international standards due to overcrowding and poor medical care.

The legacy of the 1991–1995 war in Croatia remains a sensitive issue. In 2013, veterans protested a government plan to introduce bilingual public signs—in Croatian (in the Latin alphabet) and in Serbian (in Cyrillic script)—to serve the Serb minority, which comprises 4.4 percent of the population nationwide and over 30 percent in some municipalities. Nevertheless, the government continued implementing the project.

Throughout the year, Croatia continued to cooperate with the ICTY, which in May convicted six former Bosnian Croat leaders of war crimes during the 1992–1995 conflict; crimes included murdering and deporting Bosnian Muslims in an effort to create a Croat mini-state in Bosnia-Herzegovina, and the 1993 destruction of the iconic, 16th century Ottoman bridge in the Bosnian city of Mostar. In a landmark domestic verdict, a Croatian court in January held the state responsible for the killing of two Serb civilians in an attack after the 1995 Operation Storm campaign against the separatist Serb Krajina region. The court ordered the government to pay damages to the families of two of the nine elderly civilians killed by assailants wearing Croatian military uniforms in a majority-Serb village two months after Operation Storm. However, more effort is reportedly needed to tackle impunity in war crimes cases, initiate and quickly process investigations, and improve witness protection.

Respect for minority rights has improved over the past decade. Incidents of harassment against returning Serbs have declined in recent years, and Croatia has been implementing both an antidiscrimination act and hate-crime legislation. Roma face widespread discrimination, including poor access to primary and secondary education.

G. Personal Autonomy and Individual Rights: 13 / 16

The 2011 Housing Care Program, established to aid returning refugees, continues to be implemented, but slowly. The constitution prohibits gender discrimination, but women have a higher unemployment rate and earn less than men for comparable work. Women hold 26 percent of the seats in parliament, well below the 40 percent target under law. Domestic violence against women is believed to be widespread and underreported, though law enforcement is strengthening its capacity to combat such crimes. Croatia remains a transit country for women trafficked to Western Europe for prostitution.

In 2013, a coalition of religious and conservative civic groups called "In the Name of the Family" spearheaded a campaign to effectively ban gay marriage through a referendum to amend Croatia's constitution to define marriage as between a man and a woman. After a successful signature-gathering campaign by the group, parliament voted in November to hold the referendum on December 1. The measure passed with nearly 66 percent voter approval, and the government confirmed that the constitution would be amended.

⬆ Cuba

Political Rights Rating: 7
Civil Liberties Rating: 6
Freedom Rating: 6.5
Freedom Status: Not Free
Electoral Democracy: No

Population: 11,258,000
Capital: Havana

Trend Arrow: Cuba received an upward trend arrow due to a modest decline in state surveillance, a broadening of political discussion in private and on the internet, and increased access to foreign travel and self-employment.

Ten-Year Ratings Timeline For Year Under Review (Political Rights, Civil Liberties, Status)

Year Under Review	2004	2005	2006	2007	2008	2009	2010	2011	2012	2013
Rating	7,7,NF	7,7,NF	7,7,NF	7,7,NF	7,6,NF	7,6,NF	7,6,NF	7,6,NF	7,6,NF	7,6,NF

INTRODUCTION

During 2013, the Cuban government continued its systematic use of short-term "preventative" detentions—along with harassment, beatings, and "acts of repudiation"—to intimidate the political opposition, isolate dissidents from the rest of the population, and maintain political hegemony through the control of all public spaces. The strategy aimed to neutralize the opposition without leaving any legal trace of repression that could be denounced by human rights organizations and hamper international trade and investment. Such repressive actions intensified during politically sensitive periods, especially surrounding the visits of foreign dignitaries and on the December 10 anniversary of the signing of the Universal Declaration of Human Rights.

Political repression was combined with continued—if somewhat halting and unevenly executed—economic and civic reforms, including the further growth of self-employment, the launch of nonagricultural cooperatives, and a migration reform that included the elimination of the exit visa requirement for foreign travel for the first time in January. While the travel reforms were implemented in a fairly broad and consistent manner, with most leading dissidents taking full advantage, those who dared to criticize the government or organize their supporters while abroad were routinely harassed upon returning. On the positive side, the allowance for Cuban citizens to remain abroad without losing their residency was expanded to 24 months, from 11 months, and former émigrés were now able to apply to regain their lost right to reside on the island.

The year also featured a coming together of various dissident and human rights groups, such as the Cuban Patriotic Union (UNPACU), the Damas de Blanco (Ladies in White), the Cuban Commission for Human Rights and National Reconciliation (CCDHRN), and Estado de Sats (State of Sats), to collaborate on common goals. The leaders of these groups gained a higher international profile through foreign travel. This was especially true for the blogger and free speech activist Yoani Sánchez, who went on an 80-day journey to more than a dozen countries between March and May, and Guillermo "Coco" Fariñas and Berta Soler, who met with U.S. president Barack Obama in Miami late in the year.

The summer rollout of the first nonagricultural cooperatives was seen by some observers as the government's way of guarding against the emergence of a private small and medium-sized enterprise sector with its own economic interests and political influence. The island's first public cybercafés opened in June, with very high prices. Self-employment expanded to 444,000 licensees by the end of the year, and the number of licensable occupations rose to 201, from 178 in 2010. Still, enforcement of self-employment regulations increased significantly in the autumn, reining in private 3D cinemas, arcades, door-to-door resellers of household goods, and resellers of imported clothing. A similar pattern of opening and restriction was apparent in the December announcement of "free" automobile sales, followed by the unveiling of exorbitant prices ranging from $40,000 to $250,000.

POLITICAL RIGHTS: 1 / 40
A. Electoral Process: 0 / 12

Longtime president Fidel Castro and his brother, current president Raúl Castro, have long dominated the one-party political system, in which the Communist Party of Cuba (PCC) controls all government and most civil institutions. The 1976 constitution provides for a National Assembly, which designates the Council of State. This body in turn appoints the Council of Ministers in consultation with its president, who serves as chief of state and head of government.

Raúl Castro replaced his brother as president of the Council of Ministers and the Council of State in 2008. In April 2011, the PCC held its Sixth Congress. In addition to electing Raúl Castro as head of the party, delegates appointed a greater number of high-level military officials to the PCC Politburo and Central Committee. In the February 2013 National Assembly elections, as in previous elections, voters were asked to either support or reject a single PCC-approved candidate for each of the 612 seats, and all 612 candidates were elected. Two-thirds of them were entering the legislature for the first time. The new National Assembly reelected

Raúl Castro for a second five-year term as president, which will be his last as stipulated for all senior officials by a new law. The 2013 elections were also notable in that a large number of women, young people, and Afro-Cubans were elected to office.

In the last few years, the "revolutionary generation" has begun to gradually pass power to a trusted younger "successor generation." For example, a PCC national conference in January 2012 imposed a limit of two five-year terms on elected officials, and the 53-year-old Miguel Díaz-Canel Bermúdez was appointed first vice president of the Council of State after the February 2013 elections. Raúl Castro publicly announced that his new term, ending in 2018, would be his last.

B. Political Pluralism and Participation: 0 / 16

All political organizing outside the PCC is illegal. Political dissent, whether spoken or written, is a punishable offense, and dissidents are systematically harassed, detained, physically assaulted, and frequently sentenced to years of imprisonment for seemingly minor infractions. The regime has called on its neighborhood-watch groups, known as Committees for the Defense of the Revolution, to strengthen vigilance against "antisocial behavior," a euphemism for opposition activity. This has led to the use of "acts of repudiation," or supposedly spontaneous mob attacks, to intimidate and silence political dissidents. In recent years, dissident leaders have reported an increase in intimidation and harassment by state-sponsored groups as well as short-term detentions by state security forces. According to the CCDHRN, after rising sharply from 2,074 in 2010 to 6,602 in 2012, the number of politically motivated short-term detentions declined slightly to 6,424 in 2013, though the rate increased late in the year.

C. Functioning of Government: 1 / 12

Corruption remains a serious problem, with a culture of illegality permeating the mixture of limited private enterprise and a vast state-controlled economy. The Raúl Castro government has made the fight against corruption a central priority, with long sentences for both high-placed Cuban nationals and foreign businessmen who are convicted of economic crimes. However, the steady revelation of new cases of high-level corruption indicates that the problem is chronic and not easily resolved. Cuba was ranked 63 out of 177 countries surveyed in Transparency International's 2013 Corruption Perceptions Index.

CIVIL LIBERTIES: 11 / 60 (+1)

D. Freedom of Expression and Belief: 3 / 16 (+1)

The Cuban news media are owned and controlled by the state. The independent press is considered illegal and their publications "enemy propaganda." Government agents routinely infiltrate the ranks of independent journalists and report on their activities, often accusing them of being mercenaries working at the behest of foreign powers. Independent journalists, particularly those associated with the island's dozen small independent news agencies or human rights groups, are subject to harassment. Nevertheless, some state media have begun to cover previously taboo topics, such as corruption in the health and education sectors. The national newspaper *Granma* has begun to publish letters to the editor complaining about economic issues, and state television, while generally a mouthpiece of the PCC, has recently inaugurated a new program, *Cuba Dice* (Cuba Says), that features "man-on-the-street" interviews. A number of publications associated with the Roman Catholic Church have emerged as key players in debates over the country's future, including *Espacio Laical*, *Palabra Nueva*, and *Convivencia*. Low-circulation academic journals such as *Temas* are similarly able to adopt a relatively open and critical posture, given their limited mass appeal.

Access to the internet remains tightly controlled and prohibitively expensive. The estimated effective internet penetration rate is 5 percent, one of the lowest in the world, while nearly 30 percent of the population has occasional access to e-mail and a circumscribed, domestic "intranet." In June 2013, the government announced the opening of 118 "Nauta" internet cafés across the island, increasing public access. However, one hour of computer time at these cafés costs the equivalent of a week's average salary, and users are required to show identification and sign a pledge not to engage in "subversive" activities online. Household access to the internet is not currently available to the public, with only a select few permitted to legally connect at home. There are plans to begin enabling access via smartphones, but prices are expected to be prohibitive for the vast majority of the population.

To the extent possible given these severe restrictions, online activity has flourished on the island, including many semi-independent online news portals, rigorous debates on Twitter and Facebook, "revolutionary" blogs that are also occasionally critical of government policies, and the use of thumb drives to share information among those without regular internet access. Twitter has become an important tool for human rights activists to disseminate photographs, films, and written reports on abuses, with a small community of around 150 users employing their mobile phones to reach a global audience.

There are an estimated 100 independent, journalistic bloggers working on the island. Although some have kept their distance from the political opposition and restricted their activities to the internet, others have faced harassment and detention for supporting dissidents and human rights activists. A growing group of cyberactivists led by pioneering blogger Yoani Sánchez have recently begun to hold public gatherings and link up with other independent civil society groups. While traveling abroad in 2013, after being repeatedly prevented from doing so, Sánchez announced her intention to launch an independent online newspaper in 2014.

A recent example of important online discussion focused on the musician Robertico Carcassés, who dared to call for greater civil liberties and political freedoms—including direct presidential elections, an end to the "self-embargo," greater access to information, an end to political demonization, and the liberalization of auto sales—during a nationally televised concert in support of Cuban intelligence agents jailed in the United States.

The Roman Catholic Church has been playing an increasingly important role in civil society, enabling discussion of topics of public concern and offering material assistance to the population. Nevertheless, there remain official obstacles to complete religious freedom. Churches are not allowed to conduct ordinary educational activities and many church-based publications are subject to censorship and self-censorship.

The government restricts academic freedom. Teaching materials for many subjects must contain ideological content. Affiliation with PCC structures is generally needed to gain access to educational institutions, and students' report cards carry information regarding their ideological commitment. There have been numerous instances of the expulsion of university students who are considered dissidents, such as San Miguel Molina Cobas, who was expelled from medical school in 2013 for belonging to UNPACU. Despite the elimination of the exit permit, university faculty must still obtain permission from superiors to travel to academic conferences abroad if the travel is undertaken as part of their work responsibilities.

E. Associational and Organizational Rights: 0 / 12

According to the constitution, citizens' limited rights of assembly and association may not be "exercised against the existence and objectives of the Socialist State." Nearly all of the politically motivated short-term detentions carried out in recent years have targeted members of independent associations, parties, or unions. During 2013, there were 179 cases of physical assault, 153 "acts of repudiation," and 153 cases of vandalism to activists' homes. Such incidents became especially common in the last three months of the year. The 1,123 detentions recorded in December were the most in any single month for a decade, with the exception of the 1,158 that took place in March 2012 surrounding a papal visit.

The December increase reflected a crackdown on human rights activists as they sought to celebrate the United Nations' International Day of Human Rights on December 10. One particularly prominent target of harassment and detention on this day was Antonio Rodiles, the founder of Estado de Sats, who was the victim of an "act of repudiation," caught on film, that included undercover state security agents mixed in with parading school children.

Recent initiatives by emergent nongovernmental organizations, such as the independent Cuban Legal Association (CubaLex) and its consulting services, have been forcefully rebuffed by the state. Workers do not have the right to strike or bargain collectively, and independent labor unions are illegal.

F. Rule of Law: 2 / 16

The Council of State controls the courts and the judicial process as a whole. From 1991 to 2007, the United Nations voted annually to assign a special investigator on human rights to Cuba, which consistently denied the appointee a visa. The investigator position was terminated in 2007. Cuban government representatives signed two UN human rights treaties in 2008, but neither has been ratified or implemented on the island. Cuba does not grant international humanitarian organizations access to its prisons but did recently allow a group of foreign correspondents access to some prisons. The CCDHRN estimates that there are currently 102 political prisoners, with 87 behind bars and another 15 on parole, under constant surveillance and periodically detained. In September 2013, the government announced that it would accept the majority of 292 recommendations issued by the UN Human Rights Council as part of the Universal Periodic Review process, but that it rejected "guaranteeing freedom of speech and peaceful assembly, as well as the free activity of human rights defenders, independent journalists, and those in opposition to the government" because it considered such recommendations "politically biased, constructed on false bases, and incompatible with constitutional principles and the internal juridical order."

While racial discrimination has long been outlawed as state policy, Afro-Cubans have reported widespread discrimination and profiling by law enforcement officials (many of them Afro-Cuban themselves). Many Afro-Cubans have only limited access to the dollar-earning sectors of the economy. Autonomous racial advocacy or civil rights organizations are illegal. Berta Soler, the current leader of the dissident group Ladies in White, is Afro-Cuban, as is Guillermo "Coco" Fariñas, a longtime human rights activist and member of UNPACU.

Cuba has made important strides in redressing discrimination against the LGBT (lesbian, gay, bisexual, and transgender) community, thanks in part to the advocacy work of Mariela Castro Espín, director of the National Center for Sexual Education (CENESEX) and Raúl Castro's daughter. In 2010, Fidel Castro issued an apology for the regime's past persecution of LGBT individuals. Nonetheless, a bill proposing the legalization of same-sex marriage has been stalled in the National Assembly since 2008. Moreover, the authorities do not recognize the work of independent, grassroots LGBT rights groups, and their efforts have often been attacked by CENESEX.

G. Personal Autonomy and Individual Rights: 6 / 16

Freedom of movement and the right to choose one's residence and place of employment are restricted. Cubans working abroad or for foreign companies on the island are not paid directly, but rather through the Cuban state, in violation of International Labour Organization statutes. In January 2013, the government implemented a new migration law that rescinded the exit visa and letter of invitation that were previously required to travel abroad. It also created a legal process for émigrés to regain their residency, lengthened Cuban travelers' ability to remain abroad from 11 months to 24 months without forfeiting residency rights, and rescinded the automatic state seizure of all assets and real estate of émigrés. Despite legal language that leaves much arbitrary discretion in state hands, the law's relatively broad implementation represented a dramatic step forward in restoring fundamental rights. Still, while many of the island's leading dissidents have traveled abroad and returned, several former political prisoners from a 2003 crackdown are unable to travel abroad, since they are technically still on parole. Moreover, many Cuban exiles are prevented from returning to the island to visit or live.

Only state enterprises can enter into economic agreements with foreigners as minority partners; ordinary citizens cannot participate. There are very few fully private foreign businesses in Cuba. The number of self-employment licenses has rapidly expanded in recent years, growing from 157,000 in October 2010 to 444,000 by the end of 2013. The number of legal occupations for self-employment increased from 178 to 201 over the same period. Despite the quantitative increase, the quality of the vast majority of these occupations remains limited, with almost no professional jobs included in the expanded list of legal occupations. A new income-tax law and new cooperative regulations were issued in late 2012, but it is unclear whether these will help jumpstart the economic modernization process, which seemed to stall during the latter half of 2013 as officials cracked down on entrepreneurs such as the resellers of imported clothing and operators of private cinemas and arcades. Private credit and wholesale access to inputs remain largely nonexistent, severely curtailing any expansion of the private sector beyond survival-oriented microenterprises.

The Cuban constitution establishes the full equality of women, and nearly 49 percent of the National Assembly seats are held by women. About 40 percent of all women work in the official labor force, and they are well represented in most professions. However, the ongoing economic reforms have begun to widen the gender gap in the labor force.

Cyprus

Political Rights Rating: 1
Civil Liberties Rating: 1
Freedom Rating: 1.0
Freedom Status: Free
Electoral Democracy: Yes

Population: 1,135,000
Capital: Nicosia

Note: The numerical ratings and status listed here do not reflect conditions in Northern Cyprus, which is examined in a separate report.

Ten-Year Ratings Timeline For Year Under Review (Political Rights, Civil Liberties, Status)

Year Under Review	2004	2005	2006	2007	2008	2009	2010	2011	2012	2013
Rating	1,1,F	1,1,F	1,1,F	1,1,F	1,1,F	1,1,F	1,1,F	1,1,F	1,1,F	1,1,F

INTRODUCTION

Presidential elections in February resulted in the triumph of the Democratic Rally (DISY). Nicos Anastasiades replaced Demetris Christofias of the Progressive Party of the Working People (AKEL), who opted not to run for reelection.

Cyprus's recession continued to intensify in 2013 as the banking crisis worsened, necessitating a European Union (EU)-funded bailout. The country entered into intense negotiations with the EU and the International Monetary Fund (IMF) in March, shortly after Anastasiades took office. In return for €10 billion ($13 billion) in emergency loans, Cyprus agreed to close its second largest bank, the Cyprus Popular Bank, and use uninsured deposits—those over €100,000—to pay for poorly performing investments. It is estimated that larger depositors, many of whom are Russian, may lose 47.5 percent of their holdings. The terms of the loan also required Cyprus to implement austerity measures, including tax increases, pension reductions, and a cut in welfare benefits. This provoked mass protests that, while peaceful, led to concerns of extreme nationalism, xenophobia, and racism taking hold on the island. In face of its economic troubles, the government of Cyprus continued the development of natural gas reserves in its territorial waters, further increasing tensions with Turkey and Northern Cyprus.

POLITICAL RIGHTS: 37 / 40 (-1)
A. Electoral Process: 11 / 12

Cyprus's president is elected by popular vote to a five-year term. The unicameral House of Representatives has 80 seats filled through proportional representation for five-year terms. The Turkish Cypriot community has 24 reserved seats, which have not been occupied since Turkish Cypriot representatives withdrew from the chamber in 1964.

Presidential elections were held in February 2013. Anastasiades of the conservative DISY party emerged as the victor, winning 57.5 percent of the vote in the run-off phase. Running on a platform of efficient negotiations with the EU and the IMF over the bailout agreement, Anastasiades defeated AKEL's Stavros Malas, whose platform opposed austerity.

In the most recent legislative elections, which were held in May 2011, DISY took 20 seats, AKEL won 19 seats, and the Democratic Party (DIKO) took 9 seats; 3 small parties captured the remaining 8 seats. AKEL and DIKO originally formed a coalition government, but DIKO withdrew in August 2011 following a massive explosion on a naval base that killed 13, called into question the competence of AKEL leadership, and brought to a head differences between DIKO and AKEL over reunification talks with Northern Cyprus.

B. Political Pluralism and Participation: 16 / 16

Democratic governance in Cyprus remains healthy. Elections feature a diversity of parties, and the system is open to their rise and fall—as demonstrated by the 2013 elections, which saw the presidency change hands from AKEL to DISY.

Minority groups participate fully in the political process in Cyprus. Following a 2004 ruling against Cyprus by the European Court of Human Rights (ECHR), a law was passed allowing Turkish Cypriots living in the south to vote and run for office in Greek Cypriot elections. Turkish Cypriots cannot run for president, as the constitution states that a Greek Cypriot should hold that post and a Turkish Cypriot should be vice president (the vice presidency remains vacant). The Maronites (Levantine Catholics), Armenians, and Latins (Roman Catholics) elect special nonvoting representatives.

C. Functioning of Government: 10 / 12 (-1)

The banking and sovereign debt crisis has limited the ability of Cyprus's president and legislature to determine the country's policies. External powers—the EU and the IMF—increasingly influence the legislative process and restrict the ability of the governing party to act autonomously.

The influence of the EU and IMF over democratic decision making was particularly evident in the March 2013 negotiations surrounding the €10-billion loan package. The EU and IMF were able to use the loan to insist that depositors bear the major brunt of the bank bailout and to force the government to pass austerity measures. The Anastasiades government struggled to find solutions that balanced the demands of external creditors with the desires of its populace.

Corruption is not a major problem in Cyprus, but there is evidence that its banking system has served as a tax haven and has permitted the laundering of illegally obtained money from Russia and other countries. Parliamentary hearings on freedom of information in May 2009 indicated that many legal requests for information are not fulfilled, mostly due to lack of resources. Research by the Open Cyprus Project in 2010 suggests that this problem continues: 72 percent of their requests for information were met with complete administrative silence and only 7 percent resulted in full disclosure. Cyprus was ranked 31 out of 177 countries and territories surveyed in Transparency International's 2013 Corruption Perceptions Index.

CIVIL LIBERTIES: 55 / 60

D. Freedom of Expression and Belief: 15 / 16

Freedom of speech is constitutionally guaranteed and generally respected. A vibrant independent press frequently criticizes the authorities, and several private television and radio stations compete effectively with public stations. Although Turkish Cypriot journalists can enter the south, Turkish journalists based in the north have reported difficulties crossing the border. Access to the internet is unrestricted.

Freedom of religion is guaranteed by the constitution and protected in practice. Nearly all inhabitants of the south are Orthodox Christians, and some discrimination against other religions has been alleged. State schools use textbooks containing negative language about Turkish Cypriots and Turkey.

E. Associational and Organizational Rights: 11 / 12

Freedoms of association and assembly are generally respected. Doros Polycarpou, director of the local human rights group KISA, was tried but acquitted for rioting and illegal assembly after organizing a multicultural unity festival in December 2010 at which violent clashes took place. Cyprus's frequent austerity protests have been almost uniformly peaceful. Nongovernmental organizations generally operate without government interference. Workers have the right to strike and to form trade unions without employer authorization.

F: Rule of Law: 15 / 16

Cyprus's independent judiciary operates according to the British tradition, upholding due process rights. However, the ECHR ruled against Cyprus in 2009 for failure to provide a timely trial in a case that lasted nearly six years. The problem of indefinite detentions of asylum seekers has improved somewhat since the country's ombudsperson filed complaints on the matter in 2008, but long-term detention of migrants continues. The Council of Europe and other groups have noted cases of police brutality, including targeted beatings of minorities. Prison overcrowding has decreased but remains a problem.

The economic crisis has bolstered the fortunes of far-right, anti-immigration elements in Cypriot politics, including the National Popular Front (ELAM) party. Attacks on immigrants have become more frequent, including the firebombing of a building in which farmworkers from Egypt were sleeping. There have also been allegations that ELAM uses summer camps to indoctrinate young people and conduct military training activities. In response, the justice minister has announced that the police are investigating the organization.

A 1975 agreement between the two sides of the island governs treatment of minorities. Asylum seekers face regular discrimination, especially in employment, and KISA has warned of racially motivated attacks.

G. Personal Autonomy and Individual Rights: 14 / 16

Since 2004, all citizens have been able to move freely throughout the island using a growing number of border crossings. While the Greek Cypriots have thwarted attempts to lift international trade and travel bans on the north, trade has increased between the two sides.

The status of property abandoned by those moving across the Green Line dividing the two sides of the island after the 1974 invasion is a point of contention in reunification talks. A 1991 law states that property left by Turkish Cypriots belongs to the state. Under the law in the north, Greek Cypriots can appeal to the Immovable Property Commission, which in 2010 was recognized by the ECHR as an adequate local authority for the resolution of property disputes. As of the end of 2013, a total of 5,704 applications have been lodged with the commission and 594 had been settled; approximately $235 million has been dispersed.

Gender discrimination in the workplace, sexual harassment, and violence against women are problems in Cyprus. Women are underrepresented in government, with only one women in the cabinet and seven in the legislature. While the government has made genuine progress in preventing human trafficking and launched a new antitrafficking plan in 2010, Cyprus remains a transit and destination country, and prosecution is weak. Though the LGBT community in Cyprus is protected by a variety of antidiscrimination measures, they are not protected from rhetorical violence. Same sex couples also do not have the right to enter into either marriages or civil unions, and transgender individuals are not allowed to officially change their sex.

Czech Republic

Political Rights Rating: 1
Civil Liberties Rating: 1
Freedom Rating: 1
Freedom Status: Free
Electoral Democracy: Yes

Population: 10,500,000
Capital: Prague

Ten-Year Ratings Timeline For Year Under Review (Political Rights, Civil Liberties, Status)

Year Under Review	2004	2005	2006	2007	2008	2009	2010	2011	2012	2013
Rating	1,1,F	1,1,F	1,1,F	1,1,F	1,1,F	1,1,F	1,1,F	1,1,F	1,1,F	1,1,F

INTRODUCTION

Miloš Zeman of the center-left Party of Civic Rights–Zemanovci (SPOZ) won the Czech Republic's first direct presidential elections in January 2013.

In June, Prime Minister Petr Nečas of the Civic Democratic Party (ODS) resigned amid a spying and corruption scandal. Rather than appointing a replacement from the ruling government, President Zeman instead selected a long-time ally, Jiří Rusnok, as caretaker in a move that critics denounced as a power grab. Rusnok's interim government lost a no-confidence vote in August, leading to his resignation and prompting early legislative elections in October. However, no single party won enough seats to form a government without entering into a coalition, and a new prime minister had yet to be appointed at year's end.

After numerous failed attempts at recovery, the Czech Republic moved out of its longest-ever recession in September; the economy had been contracting since the third quarter of 2011.

POLITICAL RIGHTS: 37 / 40 (-1)
A. Electoral Process: 12 / 12

The Czech Republic is an electoral democracy. The 200 members of the Chamber of Deputies, the lower house of Parliament, are elected to four-year terms by proportional representation. The Senate has 81 members elected for six-year terms, with one-third up for election every two years.

The president is directly elected under a 2012 constitutional amendment. The president can veto legislation and appoints judges, central bank officials, the prime minister, and other cabinet members, but the post holds few other formal powers. The country held its first direct presidential elections in January 2013, though no candidate received an absolute majority. A run-off vote was held later that same month between Minister of Foreign Affairs Karel Schwarzenberg of the center-right Tradition Responsibility Prosperity 09 (TOP 09) party and former prime minister Miloš Zeman of the SPOZ. Zeman—who had criticized austerity measures implemented by the government in previous years and took a strong stance against corruption—won with almost 55 percent of the vote amid a turnout of 59 percent.

Early legislative elections were held in October in response to the resignation of Prime Minister Nečas following a spying and corruption scandal. The center-left Czech Social Democratic Party (ČSSD) finished first in the October vote, capturing 50 seats, followed closely by ANO 2011—a new protest party—with 47 seats. The Communist Party of Bohemia and Moravia (KSČM) placed third with 33 seats, while TOP 09, the center-right Civic Democratic Party (ODS), the populist the Úsvit (Dawn of Direct Democracy) Party, and the Christian Democratic Union-Czech People's party (KDU–ČSL) all crossed the parliamentary threshold of 5 percent. A ruling coalition and new prime minister had not yet been negotiated by year's end.

B. Political Pluralism and Participation: 15 / 16

Historically, the two main political parties were the ČSSD and the center-right ODS. However, the resignation of the Nečas government in 2013 proved detrimental to the popularity of ODS, which received just 16 seats in the snap elections in October, down from 53 seats in the 2010 elections.

The other two right-leaning parties in the Nečas government, TOP 09 and the Public Affairs (VV) party, also suffered significant losses of popularity. VV splintered in 2012, following the conviction of one of its leaders, Vít Bárta, on bribery charges; the party announced in September that it would not run in the October elections. Some former VV members, including Bárta, joined the newly established Úsvit Party, which was formed by the businessman Tomio Okamura.

Several other new parties were founded in 2013; the most popular among them ANO 2011, started by the billionaire Andrej Babiš. The Roma Democratic Party (RDS)—which was established in 2013 to represent the country's Romany minority—did not reach the 5 percent parliamentary threshold.

C. Functioning of Government: 10 / 12 (-1)

The country was shaken by several high-profile corruption scandals in 2013. In January, outgoing President Václav Klaus caused national outrage by granting a broad amnesty that resulted in the release of more than 6,000 low-level and elderly inmates; Klaus's amnesty also halted several high-profile graft investigations, triggering widespread public anger. The Senate impeached the president in March, just days before his term ended; he was charged with high treason for allegedly violating the constitution with the amnesty, though the Constitutional Court cleared him several weeks later.

An intricate spying and corruption scandal emerged during the summer of 2013, involving one of Prime Minister Nečas's close aides, Jana Nagyová, who allegedly ordered intelligence agencies to spy on Nečas's wife. In June, Czech anticorruption forces raided the government's offices and arrested several politicians and advisors, including Nagyová, who was charged with abuse of power and bribery; charges of corruption against three other members of Parliament were dropped after the Supreme Court ruled that they were protected by immunity. Nečas divorced his wife in August and married Nagyová in September, which observers believed was an effort to avoid testifying against her in court. The Czech Republic was ranked 57 of 177 countries in Transparency International's 2013 Corruption Perceptions Index.

After Nečas's resignation, President Zeman refused to appoint a candidate chosen by the out-going center-right coalition, and instead selected an ally, his former minister of finance, Jiří Rusnok. Opponents criticized the move as a power grab; Rusnok's caretaker government lost a no-confidence vote in the Chamber of Deputies in August, leading to the dissolution of the Parliament and early elections in October.

CIVIL LIBERTIES: 57 / 60

D. Freedom of Expression and Belief: 16 / 16

Freedom of expression is respected, though the constitution-based Charter of Fundamental Rights and Freedoms limits this right in cases of threats against individual rights, state and public security, public health, and morality.

Most media outlets are owned by private foreign companies and do not appear to be influenced by the state. However, the acquisition of several outlets by wealthy businessmen in recent years has raised concerns regarding their independence and influence. In June 2013, Andrej Babiš, the country's second-richest man and leader of ANO 2011, purchased one of the largest publishing houses, MAFRA.

Public television and radio have a reputation of producing highly analytical and in-depth reports. In the second half of 2013, personnel changes at the Czech Television (CT) and allegations of censorship, however, prompted fears of politicization at the channel. In November, 23 editors criticized CT's management in an open letter. The government generally upholds freedom of religion. Tax benefits and financial support are provided to registered religious groups. Promoting denial of the Holocaust or past communist crimes is illegal, as is inciting religious hatred. In 2012, the lower house approved legislation under which the state would return some of the church land confiscated under the 1948–1989 communist regime and pay compensation for the rest. The Supreme Court upheld the law in June 2013 after left-wing opposition groups filed a challenge.

Academic freedom is respected and generally free from political intrusion. Ceremonial presidential approval is required for academic positions. In what was considered an unparalleled interference in academic freedom, President Zeman refused to approve the appointment of Martin Putna for a professorship at Prague's Charles University in May 2013. Zeman's decision caused a public uproar, as Putna was openly gay and often critical of the president. The president subsequently agreed to endorse Putna after meeting with the minister of education.

E. Associational and Organizational Rights: 12 / 12

Czechs may assemble peacefully, form associations, and petition the government. The Prague Pride Parade—the annual event of the LGBT (lesbian, gay, bisexual, and transgender) community—took place without any major incidents in 2013.

In 2012, there were approximately 80,000 registered nongovernmental organizations (NGOs) in the country, most of which struggled with poor funding. The 2012 Civil Code scheduled to come into force in January 2014 is expected to give rise to large-scale changes in the nonprofit sector, including amendments to NGOs' legal status and tax exemptions.

Trade unions and professional associations function freely but are weak in practice. The largest trade union, the Czech-Moravian Confederation of Trade Unions (ČMKOS), incorporates more than 30 member unions and has around 400,000 members. The 2007 Labor Code was amended in 2012, lowering workers' severance pay, among other changes. Workers have the right to strike, though this right is limited for public employees in jobs deemed essential, such as hospital workers and air traffic controllers.

F. Rule of Law: 14 / 16

The judiciary is largely independent, though its complexity and multilayered composition has led to a slow delivery of judgments. A 2010 report produced by the country's counterintelligence agency found that corruption within the Czech Republic's judicial system was "very sophisticated," making detection difficult.

The rule of law generally prevails in civil and criminal matters, though corruption also remains a problem within law enforcement agencies. The arrest of the CSSD's David Ráth in 2012 on corruption charges and the 2013 investigation into the ODS government were praised by many as proof of an increasingly independent police force and prosecution. However, the unsuccessful prosecution of three members of Parliament in the Nagyová scandal due to immunity, as well as the unwillingness of the Czech Bar Association to turn over important files related to the case demonstrated ongoing problems in prosecuting high-level crime.

Prisons suffer from overcrowding and poor sanitation. In July 2013, the European Court of Human Rights (ECHR) ruled that the Czech Republic had violated its prohibition of inhuman or degrading treatment by allegedly abusing a detainee, Vladimir Kummer, while in custody. In August, the police promised better treatment of detainees.

The 2009 Antidiscrimination Act covers a wide range of areas and provides for equal treatment regardless of sex, race, age, disability, belief, or sexual orientation. However, members of the Roma community sometimes face threats and violence from right-wing groups, and Romany children continue to face discrimination in the country's public school system. Despite a landmark ECHR decision in 2007 that found the placement of Roma pupils in "special schools" discriminatory and the government's repeated efforts to address the issue, Romany children continue to face segregation in the education system. Roma also face discrimination in the job market and suffer from significantly poorer housing conditions.

Several anti-Roma protests occurred during the summer of 2013, some of which turned into violent clashes with police. Police arrested at least 75 people in August during violent rallies in České Budějovice and Ostrava.

A new immigration bill tabled in May received harsh criticism from NGOs and migrants' rights advocates. The draft, among other things, requires a work permit for EU citizens staying longer than three months, discriminates against spouses who are not EU-citizens, and allows immigration police to detain minors.

Asylum seekers are routinely detained in the Czech Republic. In 2012, only 49 of 753 applicants were granted asylum. Conditions in detention centers are generally poor. The remote location of detention and reception centers also limits the ability of NGOs to visit them.

G. Personal Autonomy and Individual Rights: 15 / 16

Gender discrimination is legally prohibited. However, sexual harassment in the workplace appears to be fairly common, and women are underrepresented at the highest levels of government and business—their parliamentary presence decreased from 44 to 39 seats in

2013 in the 200-member Chamber of Deputies. Three of the nine candidates in the January 2013 presidential elections were women. Trafficking of women and girls for the purpose of prostitution remains a problem.

Denmark

Political Rights Rating: 1
Civil Liberties Rating: 1
Freedom Rating: 1.0
Freedom Status: Free
Electoral Democracy: Yes

Population: 5,600,000
Capital: Copenhagen

Ten-Year Ratings Timeline For Year Under Review (Political Rights, Civil Liberties, Status)

Year Under Review	2004	2005	2006	2007	2008	2009	2010	2011	2012	2013
Rating	1,1,F	1,1,F	1,1,F	1,1,F	1,1,F	1,1,F	1,1,F	1,1,F	1,1,F	1,1,F

INTRODUCTION

In municipal elections held in November 2013, the ruling Social Democrat Party maintained its leadership positions in Copenhagen, Aarhus, Odense, and Aalborg, but lost several other mayorships. Social Democrats won 29.5 percent of votes overall, while the opposition Liberal Party won 26.6 percent.

The year also saw the continuation of the so-called Taxgate scandal, which concerned the 2011 leaking of a tax audit of Prime Minister Helle Thorning-Schmidt when she was opposition leader. Meanwhile, in February, well-known media personality Lars Hedegaard survived an assassination attempt in his home due to his support of anti-Muslim cartoons published by the newspaper *Jyllands-Posten* in 2005.

POLITICAL RIGHTS: 40 / 40

A. Electoral Process: 12 / 12

Denmark has been a monarchy since the Middle Ages, though the monarch's role became largely ceremonial after the promulgation of the first democratic constitution in 1849. The country was occupied by Nazi Germany during World War II despite its attempts to maintain neutrality, and in 1949, it joined NATO.

Denmark has had a conflicted relationship with the European Union (EU), securing opt-outs from the bloc's 1992 Maastricht Treaty on justice, foreign, and monetary policy, and opting not to adopt the euro in 2000.

The current constitution, adopted in 1953, established a single-chamber parliament (the Folketing) and retained a monarch, currently Queen Margrethe II, with mostly ceremonial duties. The parliament's 179 representatives are elected at least once every four years through a system of modified proportional representation. The leader of the majority party or government coalition is usually chosen to be prime minister by the monarch. Danish governments most often control a minority of seats in the parliament, ruling with the aid of one or more supporting parties. Since 1909, no single party has held a majority of seats, helping to create a tradition of compromise.

The territories of Greenland and the Faroe Islands each have two representatives in the Folketing. They also have their own elected institutions, which have power over almost all areas of governance, except foreign and financial policy. In 2009, Greenland passed the

Self-Government Act, which gave it greater control over government functions, including its security apparatus and judicial system.

Prime Minister Anders Fogh Rasmussen of the Liberal Party resigned in April 2009 after being named NATO secretary general; he was replaced by finance minister Lars Løkke Rasmussen (no relation).

Parliamentary elections in September 2011 led to a change of government, with Helle Thorning-Schmidt leading the Social Democratic Party to power after forming a coalition with the Social Liberal Party, the Socialist People's Party, and the Red-Green Party. Although Thorning-Schmidt's coalition was able to narrowly defeat Rasmussen's center-right coalition, the Social Democratic Party itself suffered its worst electoral result since 1903 and won fewer seats in Parliament than Rasmussen's Liberal Party. As a result of the election, Thorning-Schmidt became Denmark's first female prime minister.

B. Political Pluralism and Participation: 16 / 16

Postwar Danish politics were dominated by the Social Democratic Party. However, in the 2001 elections, a right-wing coalition led by Anders Fogh Rasmussen's Liberal Party won control by pledging to reduce immigration and lower taxes. The coalition, which served for two terms, also included the Conservative People's Party and was supported by the anti-immigrant and Euroskeptic Danish People's Party.

The Social Democrats have historically been firmly anchored in the working class, but as their traditional voters were hollowed out due to structural changes in the Danish economy during the post-war period, they lost their once-dominant position in Danish politics. Many of their core positions on social services and an expansive public sector were adopted by parties across the spectrum during the post-war period. The Liberal Party has experienced a similar dynamic, with their positions on the importance of economic competitiveness spreading for example to the Social Democrats and other parties. The differences between the two major parties are thus differences of degree and emphasis, rather than deeply held ideological differences.

C. Functioning of Government: 12 / 12

Levels of corruption are generally very low in Denmark, which was ranked 1 out of 177 countries surveyed in Transparency International's 2013 Corruption Perceptions Index. However, the so-called Taxgate scandal, in which information regarding a 2010 tax audit of then-opposition leader Helle Thorning-Schmidt was leaked to the press, continued to unfold throughout 2013. The leak occurred just one week before the 2011 general election and had allegedly been carried out by Thorning-Schmidt's political opponents. Throughout 2013, an independent commission investigated whether Troels Lund Poulsen, at the time tax minister of the then-ruling Venstre party, was involved in leaking the information to the press. Poulsen and other Venstre party members had also been accused of interfering in the audit itself; Thorning-Schmidt was found not to have violated any tax laws. The commission faced some criticism for spending large amounts of money while yielding few results.

CIVIL LIBERTIES: 58 / 60
D. Freedom of Expression and Belief: 16 / 16

The constitution guarantees freedom of expression. The media reflect a wide variety of political opinions and are frequently critical of the government. The state finances radio and television broadcasting, but state-owned television companies have independent editorial boards. Independent radio stations are permitted but tightly regulated.

Since the September 2005 publication of the controversial cartoons by the Danish newspaper *Jyllands-Posten* depicting the Prophet Muhammad, Denmark has been hit with a string of attempted terrorist attacks. In February 2013, controversial public intellectual and journalist Lars Hedegaard—an outspoken supporter of the publication of the cartoons and critic of Muslim immigration and integration—survived an assassination attempt in his home when an assailant rang his doorbell and shot at him at close range, but missed. At year's end no organization or individual had claimed responsibility for the attack, and the police were without leads. The cartoonist Kurt Westergaard, who had drawn the most contentious of the cartoons, was attacked in his home in January 2010 by a Somali assailant with ties to the Al-Shahab. Westergaard escaped unharmed, and the intruder, Mohamed Geele, was apprehended by police and sentenced to 9 years in 2011.

After complaints from the Turkish ambassador to Denmark in March 2010, the Danish attorney general charged the Danish-based, Kurdish-language satellite television station Roj-TV with promoting the Kurdistan Workers' Party, which the EU and the United States consider a terrorist organization. In August 2013, the station declared bankruptcy, citing fines imposed by the Copenhagen City Court in 2012 of 5.2 million kroner ($885,000), which were doubled by the Eastern High Court in July. The station was the first Danish media organization to face prosecution for promoting terrorism, and the trial has been criticized across the political spectrum for harming freedom of speech and being unduly influenced by Turkish political pressure on the Danish government.

Access to the internet is not restricted, and Denmark's internet penetration rate is among the highest in the world.

Freedom of worship is legally protected. However, the Evangelical Lutheran Church is subsidized by the government as the official state religion. The faith is taught in public schools, though students may withdraw from religious classes with parental consent. At present, about half of all schoolchildren are exempted from the catechism taught in public schools. In 2009, religious and political symbols were banned from judicial attire. Denmark denies religious worker visas, thereby restricting access to missionaries entering the country from abroad.

E. Associational and Organizational Rights: 12 / 12

The constitution provides for freedoms of assembly and association. Demonstrations during 2013 were peaceful. Civil society is vibrant, and workers are free to organize. The labor market is mainly regulated by agreements between employers' and employees' organizations.

In April 2013, there was a four-week lockout of 50,000 elementary and middle-school teachers affecting more than 500,000 students. The dispute between the teachers' union (DFL) and the Local Authorities Association (KL) centered on a new reform that would end the national collective bargaining mechanism for deciding the ratio of hours teaching and preparing for class, instead leaving it to individual schools to negotiate. The government ended the lockout in May 2013 by passing legislation in Parliament defining teaches' working conditions that effectively sided with the Local Authorities Associations.

F. Rule of Law: 15 / 16

The judiciary is independent, and citizens enjoy full due-process rights. The court system consists of 100 local courts, two high courts, and the 15-member Supreme Court, with judges appointed by the monarch on the government's recommendation. Prisons generally meet international standards.

Discrimination is prohibited under the law. Asylum seekers and immigration remained divisive issues in 2013. Strict immigration laws introduced in 2002 were tightened further in 2010 and 2011. However, Helle Thorning-Schmidt's socialist government did honor one of its campaign pledges when new, less restrictive, immigration laws regarding family reunification cases and permanent residency came into effect in 2012. The reforms included the elimination of a fee to apply for family reunification and the replacement of an immigration test with a Danish language exam. Denmark continues to have some of the harshest immigration laws in Europe.

The European Court of Human Rights in 2010 called on Denmark to stop deporting asylum seekers to Greece, their point of entry to the EU; a binding decision from the Strasbourg court was pronounced in January 2011, compelling Denmark to stop the practice.

G. Personal Autonomy and Individual Rights: 15 / 16

Women enjoy equal rights in Denmark and represent half of the workforce. However, disparities have been reported in the Faroe Islands and Greenland. Denmark was the first country in the world to adopt same-sex civil unions in 1989 and in 2012 parliament overwhelmingly passed same-sex marriage legislation enabling same-sex couples to wed in the Lutheran state church of their choosing. Priests are not obligated to officiate, but must find a colleague who will.

Denmark is a destination and transit point for women and children trafficked for the purpose of sexual exploitation. Following the 2003 adoption of legislation that defined and criminalized such trafficking, the government began working regularly with nongovernmental organizations in their trafficking-prevention campaigns.

Djibouti

Political Rights Rating: 6
Civil Liberties Rating: 5
Freedom Rating: 5.5
Freedom Status: Not Free
Electoral Democracy: No

Population: 939,000
Capital: Djibouti

Ten-Year Ratings Timeline For Year Under Review (Political Rights, Civil Liberties, Status)

Year Under Review	2004	2005	2006	2007	2008	2009	2010	2011	2012	2013
Rating	6,5,NF	6,5,NF	6,6,NF	7,6,NF	7,6,NF	7,6,NF	7,6,NF	7,6,NF	7,6,NF	7,6,NF

INTRODUCTION

President Ismail Omar Guelleh's administration continued to stifle political rights and civil liberties in 2013. A tense political climate following February 2013 legislative elections was characterized by opposition protests, the use of excessive force by police against demonstrators, the ongoing detention of independent journalists, and the pursuit of opposition figures.

In July, the European Parliament passed a resolution expressing strong concerns about the situation in Djibouti, citing various violations of freedom of expression and attempts to suppress opposition members and demonstrators. The resolution also placed pressure on the Djiboutian regime to begin negotiations with opposition groups over the contested elections. Though these negotiations initially appeared promising, talks stalled in October. The Union for National Salvation (USN) sent a request to the African Union to mediate, but the African Union has not publicly acknowledged or responded to the request. The USN released a statement at the end of the year citing increasing government repression including the arrest of more than a dozen party members in December alone.

POLITICAL RIGHTS: 9 / 40
A. Electoral Process: 3 / 12

Djibouti's ruling Union for a Presidential Majority (UMP) coalition party has effectively usurped the state. A constitutional amendment passed by the National Assembly in 2010 removed the two-term limit for presidents, reduced presidential terms from six years to five, and specified that candidates must be between the ages of 40 and 75. The changes allowed Guelleh to stand for a third term in 2011. The decision sparked a series of antigovernment protests in which at least two were killed and hundreds arrested, including the leaders of three opposition parties. The 2011 presidential campaign was marred by the harassment of opposition leaders and a clampdown on public gatherings. Guelleh ultimately faced only one challenger and won with 81 percent of the vote.

The 65 members of the unicameral legislature, the National Assembly, are directly elected for five-year terms. The 2010 constitutional changes provided for the formation of a bicameral parliament comprising the existing National Assembly and a newly created senate, though steps to establish one have yet to be taken.

On February 22, 2013, the electorate voted in the first legislative polls contested by the opposition since 2003. In the weeks prior to the election, the Union for National Salvation (USN) opposition coalition accused the government of censorship after its websites could not be accessed domestically. Sixty observers from the African Union, the Arab League, the United Nations, and the European Union, among other organizations, oversaw the legislative elections. Although the observers declared the elections free and fair, the opposition alleged foul play and refuted the ruling party's official total of 55 seats, to 10 for the USN. Opposition protests in the days following the election were met with a heavy-handed police response, including the use of tear gas, as well as the arrest of 500 protesters and the death of 6. The opposition filed a formal complaint to the constitutional committee, citing allegations of double voting and ballot-stuffing, and questioning the speed with which preliminary results were released. The claim was rejected on a legal technicality—that it was not filed within 10 days of the release of election results—and was subsequently dismissed.

In March, Prime Minister Dileita Mohamed Dileita resigned after 12 years in the post, citing pressure from Guelleh. He was replaced by Defense Minister Abdoulkader Kamil Mohamed. Changes were also made in the departments of interior, defense, and justice, among others.

B. Political Pluralism and Participation: 3 / 16

The Djiboutian constitution provides full political rights, but these rights are often ignored in practice. While Djibouti technically has a multiparty political system, the ruling UMP party has seized all state power. Political parties are required to register with the government. Six political parties joined to form the USN coalition in the run-up to the February 2013 legislative elections. USN spokesman Daher Ahmed Farah was arrested and jailed over a dozen times since his return from exile in January. In April, Minister of Interior Hassan Omar Mohamed alleged that USN was an electoral coalition, not a legitimate party, and that the demonstrations undertaken after the election were therefore illegal. In May, the government threatened to dissolve the USN due to such activities, and in June, police arrested 13 USN officials, including the group's president, Ahmed Youssouf.

Opposition parties have traditionally been disadvantaged by Djibouti's first-past-the-post electoral system, as well as the government's abuse of the administrative apparatus. In November 2012, the electoral law was amended to award 20 percent of seats proportionally, a distinction from the previous system under which the party that received the majority in a district won the entirety of that district's seats. Under the previous system, the UMP won 62 percent of the vote but captured all 55 seats in the National Assembly in the 2003 elections. In 2013, the UMP won more than 80 percent of the vote and captured 55 of the 65 seats in the National Assembly. The 10 seats won by the opposition constituted the first time the ruling party had conceded any seats in the National Assembly.

C. Functioning of Government: 3 / 12

Djibouti is not an electoral democracy. President Guelleh won a third term in 2011 following an opposition boycott of the election. The UMP has assumed full control of the state and policy formation. Efforts to curb corruption have met with little success. Government corruption is a serious problem and public officials are not required to disclose their assets. In April 2013, the Guelleh administration launched the "Djibouti Fights Corruption" initiative, which included an internet-based platform that documents government anticorruption efforts. Djibouti ranked 94 out of 177 countries and territories surveyed in Transparency International's 2013 Corruption Perceptions Index. Though there are no laws granting citizens access to government information, the government has made legislation publicly available and created mechanisms for citizens to request access to information.

CIVIL LIBERTIES: 20 / 40

D. Freedom of Expression and Belief: 7 / 16

Despite constitutional protections, freedom of speech is not upheld in practice. There are no privately owned or independent media operated domestically, though political parties are allowed to publish a journal or newspaper. The government owns the principal newspaper, *La Nation*, as well as *Radio-Television Djibouti*, which operates the national radio and television stations. Strict libel laws lead journalists to practice self-censorship. Former journalist and opposition spokesperson Daher Ahmed Farah has been a regular target of the administration, and has been in and out of prison since February. Also arrested during the February protests, schoolteacher Mohamed Elmi Rayaleh died in police custody in August. Local human rights groups alleged that the government secretly cremated Rayaleh, whose family was not allowed at his burial.

While the government typically places few restrictions on internet access, opposition parties claimed their websites were censored during the 2013 legislative elections. Additionally, opposition internet radio station La Voix de Djibouti, run by Djiboutian exiles in Europe, has been regularly blocked. The website's technician, Maydaneh Abdallah Okieh, has been detained in Djibouti's Gabode prison since May 2013 on charges of defaming the police and insulting a police officer after he posted Facebook photos of police breaking up an opposition protest. Though sentenced to 45 days in prison, Okieh remained in Gabode until October and was denied medical care throughout his detention.

Four La Voix journalists—Farah Abadid Hildid, Houssein Ahmed Farah, Moustapha Abdourahman Houssein, and Mohamed Ibrahim Waïss—who had been released on bail in June 2011 were summoned back to court in July 2013 because the initial charges against them were changed to the more serious charge of "inciting a disturbance of public order," which carries strict penalties. Three of the men were again arrested, each in separate incidents, in December. Waïss was jailed for seven days after covering a women's demonstration in Buldhuqo, a working-class neighborhood that the government had recently demolished. The women were protesting the government's unfulfilled promise to provide them land in another neighborhood.

Islam is the state religion, and 99 percent of the population is Sunni Muslim. Freedom of worship is respected both legally and in practice. Academic freedom is generally upheld.

E. Associational and Organizational Rights: 3 / 12

Freedoms of assembly and association are nominally protected under the constitution, but are not respected in practice. More than 500 opposition figures were arrested for participating in protests following the 2013 elections. The protests turned violent, with some demonstrators throwing petrol bombs and security forces firing tear gas and rubber bullets. Opposition protests continued for several months before negotiations with between President Guellah and the USN began. Demonstrations resumed after the talks broke down. USN representatives alleged that dozens of members, including top party leaders, were arrested during a September protest.

Local human rights groups who cover politically sensitive matters do not operate freely and are often the target of government harassment and intimidation. The Djiboutian Observatory for the Promotion of Democracy and Human Rights, a group created in the memory of human rights activist Jean Paul Noel Abdi, who died in 2012, is still awaiting government approval for its NGO status. Women's rights groups are the exception to these government restrictions; the government generally supports their educational efforts and trainings. It remains uncertain how active a role the government's National Human Rights Commission plays in upholding domestic human rights.

Though workers may legally join unions and strike, the government has been known to intimidate union leadership and obstruct union activities. The government discourages truly independent unions and has been accused of meddling in their internal elections and harassing union representatives. The general secretary of the Union of Djibouti Workers, is reportedly under constant police surveillance, and his family moved to Ethiopia after receiving repeated threats. Approval for union status is seemingly arbitrary and follows a long and complex registration process. Taxi drivers were prevented from establishing a union in 2013. The Djiboutian government has also frozen union bank accounts and kept unions from receiving external funds, presumably to limit support from diasporans and international unions' rights organizations.

F. Rule of Law: 4 / 16

The judicial system is based on the French civil code, though Sharia (Islamic law) prevails in family matters. The courts are not independent of the government. A lack of resources often delays legal proceedings. Security forces frequently make arrests without a proper decree from a judicial magistrate, in violation of constitutional requirements. Constitutional amendments made in 2010 abolished the death penalty. Prison conditions are harsh, but have improved in recent years.

Allegations of politically motivated prosecutions are common. In 2010, Djiboutian businessman Abdourahman Boreh was convicted in absentia on charges of terrorism. Boreh, an opposition leader who planned to stand against Guelleh in the 2011 presidential elections, received a 15-year prison sentence. Boreh fled to the United Kingdom in 2008 and is currently based in the United Arab Emirates. In 2013, the Djiboutian government brought two suits in London and Emirati commercial courts seeking to freeze Boreh's assets on the grounds that he abused his position as chairman of the Djibouti Port and Free Zone Authority from 2003 to 2008 for private gain. The British court initially struck down the charges against Boreh in June, only to issue a worldwide freeze of $111.5 million in Boreh's assets in September. An appeal is scheduled for 2015. In October, the Dubai International Financial Centre (DIFC) courts froze $5 million of Boreh's assets upon the request of the Djiboutian government.

Representatives from minority groups including the Afar, Yemeni Arabs, and non-Issa Somalis, are represented in all major Djiboutian governance institutions (cabinet, legislature, lower-level bureaucracy, etc.). However, the majority Issa do hold more prominent positions in both government and the private sector. Minority ethnic groups and clans suffer discrimination and social and economic marginalization.

Homosexual conduct is criminal under Djiboutian law and there are no laws in place to prevent discrimination against the lesbian, gay, bisexual, and transgender (LGBT) community. Generally, matters of sexual preference or orientation are not discussed publicly.

G. Personal Autonomy and Individual Rights: 6 / 16

There are few employment prospects in the formal sector. Higher educational opportunities are also generally limited. In September 2013, the government destroyed hundreds of shops, restaurants, and stalls that were operating in Djibouti City without license as part of its Djibouti Clean City campaign. Though the government claimed it warned owners of the maneuver in advance and would help them relocate, no such assistance has yet been offered. Shop owners complained of the loss of their livelihoods amid the city's rising rent costs.

Though the law provides equal treatment for all Djiboutian citizens, women have fewer employment opportunities and are paid less than men for the same work. Women face discrimination under customary practices related to inheritance and other property matters, divorce, and the right to travel. The law prohibits female genital mutilation, but more than 90 percent of women are believed to have undergone the procedure. An estimated 50 percent of girls are now receiving primary education following efforts to increase female enrollment. While the law requires at least 20 percent of upper-level public service positions to be held by women, women still hold only about 10 percent of legislative seats.

Dominica

Political Rights Rating: 1
Civil Liberties Rating: 1
Freedom Rating: 1.0
Freedom Status: Free
Electoral Democracy: Yes

Population: 70,625
Capital: Roseau

Ten-Year Ratings Timeline For Year Under Review (Political Rights, Civil Liberties, Status)

Year Under Review	2004	2005	2006	2007	2008	2009	2010	2011	2012	2013
Rating	1,1,F	1,1,F	1,1,F	1,1,F	1,1,F	1,1,F	1,1,F	1,1,F	1,1,F	1,1,F

INTRODUCTION

The Eastern Caribbean Supreme Court (ECSC) ruled on March 11 that the opposition Dominica United Workers Party (UWP) failed to make the case in their appeal that the parliamentary membership of Prime Minister Roosevelt Skerrit and Education Minister Petter Saint-Jean should be disqualified as a result of their dual citizenship at the time of the 2009 elections. The UWP boycotted the election of President Charles Savarin, who took office on October 2, claiming that the prime minister had failed to consult the opposition leader, Hector John, on Savarin's nomination.

Former radio journalist Lennox Linton was elected to lead the UWP in September. A long-time critic of the majority Dominica Labour Party (DLP) government, Linton continued in 2013 to accuse Prime Minister Skerrit of violating the Integrity in Public Office Act.

POLITICAL RIGHTS: 38 / 40

A. Electoral Process: 12 / 12

Dominica's unicameral House of Assembly consists of 30 members who serve five-year terms; 21 members are directly elected, 5 senators are appointed by the prime minister, and 4 by the opposition leader. The president, who is the ceremonial head of state, is elected by the House of Assembly for a five-year term, and the prime minister is appointed by the president.

In December 2009 legislative elections, the DLP captured 18 seats, and the UWP took only 3. Although the elections were deemed generally fair by regional observer teams, opposition members accused the DLP of misconduct during the campaign. They also said Prime Minister Skerrit and Minister of Education and Human Resource Development Saint-Jean were ineligible to hold office because they held dual citizenship at the time of the elections. The courts rejected all complaints in 2010 except the dual citizenship case. In January 2012, a High Court judge ruled that the 2009 elections of Skerrit and St. Jean had been constitutional and that they should retain their posts; however, the UWP filed an appeal. In March 2013, the ECSC dismissed the appeal on the grounds that the UWP had failed to prove its case.

Following the resignation of President Nicholas Liverpool for health reasons, in September 2012 parliament elected DLP candidate Eliud Williams to finish Liverpool's term. The UWP boycotted the election, arguing that the process leading to Williams's nomination was unconstitutional. The case went to the ECSC, which had yet to issue a decision by year's end. Meanwhile, in September 2013 the government elected former minister of security Charles Savarin as president. The UWP contested Savarin's as well as two prior nominations, and again boycotted the election.

The Elections Commission took steps in 2013 to initiate the process of issuing multipurpose identification cards that will be used for voting.

B. Political Pluralism and Participation: 16 / 16

The dominant political parties are the ruling social-democratic DLP and the opposition centrist UWP. The right-wing Dominica Freedom Party has not been represented in parliament since 2005. Although opposition members complained of unequal access to state media during the campaign period of the 2009 elections, political parties are relatively free to organize.

C. Functioning of Government: 10 / 12

The government generally implements anticorruption laws effectively. As an offshore financial center, Dominica passed a series of laws in November 2011 to combat money laundering and the financing of terrorism. In February 2013, the Integrity in Public Office Commission (IPO) was scheduled to consider a 2012 complaint against Prime Minister Skerrit. Lennox Linton, a radio journalist at the time, accused Skerrit of using his influence as chairman of cabinet to secure concessions for luxury villas for which he allegedly holds ownership claims. The hearing had been repeatedly postponed, with Skerrit's attorney, Tony Astaphan, questioning the commission's objectivity. Astaphan then claimed that commission members had leaked confidential information to Linton; Linton later said that Astaphan had himself provided the information to Linton's source. Just days before the scheduled hearing, a high court judge granted Skerrit's legal team leave to apply for judicial review of the IPO's actions, and the IPO subsequently postponed the hearing indefinitely. Dominica was ranked 41 out of 177 countries in the 2013 Corruption Perceptions Index.

CIVIL LIBERTIES: 57 / 60

D. Freedom of Expression and Belief: 15 / 16

Freedom of expression is constitutionally guaranteed, and the press is generally free in practice. Four private weekly newspapers are published without interference, and there are both public and private radio stations. Citizens have unimpeded access to cable television and the internet. However, the country lacks access to information legislation, and defamation remains a criminal offense punishable by imprisonment or fines. Libel lawsuits and threats are commonly used by the Skerrit government against members of the media, resulting in self-censorship. In March, the ECSC overruled a lower court decision against Linton for defamation, ordering the accountant to whom Linton had paid damages to cover Linton's court costs. In November, the ECSC granted leave to appeal the matter to the Privy Council. Police searched Linton's home and car on January 16 as part of an investigation of leaked IPO information.

Freedom of religion is protected under the constitution and other laws. While the majority of the population is Roman Catholic, Protestants and others practice freely, Academic freedom is respected.

E. Associational and Organizational Rights: 12 / 12

The authorities uphold freedoms of assembly and association, and advocacy groups operate without interference. Workers have the right to organize, strike, and bargain collectively, and laws prohibit anti-union discrimination by employers. Nevertheless, less than 30 percent of the private sector is unionized.

F. Rule of Law: 15 / 16

The judiciary is independent, and the rule of law is enhanced by the courts' subordination to the inter-island ECSC. In 2013 the government informed the British government of its intention to establish the Caribbean Court of Justice as its final court of appeal, replacing the Privy Council in London. The government awaited a response at year's end. The judicial system generally operates efficiently, though staffing shortfalls remain a problem.

The Dominica police force, which assumed responsibility for security after the military was disbanded in 1981, operates professionally and with few human rights complaints.

Dominica's small indigenous population, the Carib-Kalingo, faces a variety of challenges, including a higher poverty rate than the rest of the country, encroachment on its territory by farmers, and difficulties in obtaining loans from banks. Rastafarians also report discrimination and profiling by the police.

G. Personal Autonomy and Individual Rights: 15 / 16

Women are underrepresented in government and hold just four seats in the House of Assembly. No laws mandate equal pay for equal work in private sector jobs, or criminalize domestic abuse, which is a significant problem. Same-sex relations are criminalized with punishments of imprisonment, and the prime minister announced in May that the government has no intention of overturning these laws.

Dominican Republic

Political Rights Rating: 2
Civil Liberties Rating: 3 ↓
Freedom Rating: 2.5
Freedom Status: Free
Electoral Democracy: Yes

Population: 10,260,000
Capital: Santo Domingo

Ratings Change: The Dominican Republic's civil liberties rating declined from 2 to 3 due to a decision by the Constitutional Court to retroactively strip the citizenship of tens of thousands of Dominicans of Haitian descent.

Ten-Year Ratings Timeline For Year Under Review (Political Rights, Civil Liberties, Status)

Year Under Review	2004	2005	2006	2007	2008	2009	2010	2011	2012	2013
Rating	2,2,F	2,2,F	2,2,F	2,2,F	2,2,F	2,2,F	2,2,F	2,2,F	2,2,F	2,3,F

INTRODUCTION

An October 2013 ruling by the Constitutional Court of the Dominican Republic threatened to retroactively strip thousands of Dominicans of Haitian descent of their citizenship; the move generated a substantial amount of international criticism and charges of xenophobia.

Although the Dominican Republic has experienced stronger economic growth than most Latin American countries, its growth decelerated in early 2013 to just about 1.6 percent. In July 2011, demonstrations against fiscal and economic measures, including tax increases and electricity tariffs, paralyzed transportation and trade.

POLITICAL RIGHTS: 30 / 40 (-1)

A. Electoral Process: 10 / 12

The Dominican Republic's bicameral National Congress consists of the 32-member Senate and the 183-member Chamber of Deputies, with members of both chambers elected to four-year terms.

Leonel Fernández of the Dominican Liberation Party (PLD) was elected president in 1996 and reelected in 2004. Capitalizing on the Dominican Republic's economic growth during Fernández's presidency, the PLD captured 31 of 32 Senate seats in the May 2010 legislative elections, while the Social Christian Reformist Party (PRSC) took the remaining seat. In the Chamber of Deputies, the PLD secured 105 seats, the Dominican Revolutionary Party (PRD) won 75, and the PRSC took 3. The PLD also won a majority of the municipal elections. The opposition subsequently presented allegations of electoral fraud to the Organization of American States (OAS), and international observers noted that campaigning resources were not equally distributed between government and opposition candidates. The OAS also noted certain irregularities, including vote buying, though it certified the results.

The PLD's Danilo Medina was victorious in the presidential election held on May 20, 2012, winning 51 percent of the vote and defeating PRD candidate Hipólito Mejia; Fernández was barred by the constitution from seeking another consecutive term. Medina took office in August, pledging to reduce poverty, improve the country's educational system, and expand infrastructure projects.

The country's 38th constitution, which was promulgated in January 2010, removed restrictions on non-consecutive presidential reelection, which would allow Fernández to run for president again in 2016.

B. Political Pluralism and Participation: 11 / 16 (-1)

Since the mid-1990s, Dominican politics have been defined by competition between the PLD, the opposition PRD, and the smaller PRSC.

Haitians face persistent systematic discrimination in political and social life, and do not have full political rights. Thus, Dominicans of Haitian descent have been denied full participation in national life such as attending university, obtain legal employment or a marriage license.

C. Functioning of Government: 9 / 12

Official corruption remains a serious problem. In December 2012, protestors in Santo Domingo demanded an end to government corruption and insisted on imprisonment for most of the officials in the Fernández administration. In October 2013, Dominican prosecutors froze the assets of former Public Works minister Víctor Díaz Rúa as part of an investigation into charges of fraud, money laundering and embezzlement. Rúa had generally been regarded as one of the Dominican Republic's "untouchables."

The Dominican Republic was ranked 123 out of 177 countries and territories surveyed in Transparency International's 2013 Corruption Perceptions Index.

CIVIL LIBERTIES: 43 / 60 (-1)
Freedom of Expression and Belief: 15 / 16

The law provides for freedoms of speech and the press, and the government generally respects these rights. There are five national daily newspapers and a large number of local publications. The state-owned Radio Television Dominicana operates radio and television services. Private owners operate more than 300 radio stations and over 40 television stations, most of which are small, regional broadcasters. Journalists reporting on possible collusion between drug traffickers and state officials have faced intimidation, and some have been killed. Internet access is unrestricted but not widely available outside of large urban areas.

Constitutional guarantees regarding religious and academic freedom are generally observed.

E. Associational and Organizational Rights: 10 / 12

Freedom of assembly is generally respected. Freedom of association is constitutionally guaranteed, but is limited for public servants. The government upholds the right to form civic groups, and civil society organizations in the Dominican Republic are some of the best organized and most effective in Latin America. Labor unions are similarly well organized. Although legally permitted to strike, they are often subject to government crackdowns. In November 2012, police used tear gas and fired guns on union-led demonstrators protesting tax reforms deemed to be unfavorable to the working class; several protestors were wounded.

F. Rule of Law: 8 / 16

The judiciary is politicized and riddled with corruption, and the legal system offers little recourse to those without money or influence. However, reforms implemented in recent years have included measures aimed at promoting greater efficiency and due process. The 2010 constitution sought to further modernize the judiciary, creating a Constitutional Court and Judiciary Branch Council, as well as mandating retirement for Supreme Court magistrates over the age of 75 years.

Extrajudicial killings by police remain a problem, and low salaries encourage endemic corruption in law enforcement institutions. According to the country's National Human Rights Commission, at least 290 people were killed by police in 2012. In November 2012,

Amnesty International called for a reform to the nation's police services following the shooting by police of a university student during a demonstration against tax increases in Santo Domingo. Prisons suffer from severe overcrowding, poor sanitation, and routine violence.

The Dominican Republic is a major transit hub for South American drugs, mostly cocaine, en route to the United States. Local, Puerto Rican, and Colombian drug smugglers use the country as both a command-and-control center and a transshipment point. Involvement by elements in the Dominican Republic's police and army in drug smuggling remains a major concern. In 2013, Dominican police operations on the outskirts of Santo Domingo discovered for the first time in the Caribbean a cocaine-processing laboratory.

G. Personal Autonomy and Individual Rights: 10 / 16 (-1)

The mistreatment of Haitian migrants continues to mar the Dominican Republic's international reputation, but no strategy has been adopted to handle this growing problem. The 2010 constitution removed the possibility of Dominican citizenship for children born of illegal Haitian migrants. Despite important advances in relations with Haiti, especially after the January 2010 earthquake, Dominican authorities continued to illegally deprive Dominicans of Haitian descent of their nationality, leaving them without access to health care, education, employment, or the right to vote. This virtual statelessness increases their chance of being subjected to arbitrary detentions and mass expulsion, without judicial review, and in violation of bilateral agreements with Haiti. In October 2013, the Constitutional Court ruled that a 2010 law limiting Dominican citizenship to children born to legal immigrants could be retroactively applied; the decision could strip four generations of Dominicans of Haitian descent—about 250,000 Dominicans—of their citizenship.

Recent proposals to reduce the recommended prison time for some acts of domestic violence and sexual abuse, such as sexual abuse of a minor, has led to an outpouring of protest from human rights and women's groups. The trafficking in women and girls, child prostitution, and child abuse are major concerns. The 2010 constitution includes one of the most restrictive abortion laws in the world, making the practice illegal even in cases of rape, incest, or to protect the life of the mother. The new constitution also defines marriage as solely between a man and a woman, making the country one of the few in the world to ban same-sex marriage at the constitutional level.

East Timor

Political Rights Rating: 3
Civil Liberties Rating: 4
Freedom Rating: 3.5
Freedom Status: Partly Free
Electoral Democracy: Yes

Population: 1,108,000
Capital: Dili

Ten-Year Ratings Timeline For Year Under Review (Political Rights, Civil Liberties, Status)

Year Under Review	2004	2005	2006	2007	2008	2009	2010	2011	2012	2013
Rating	3,3,PF	3,3,PF	3,4,PF	3,4,PF	3,4,PF	3,4,PF	3,4,PF	3,4,PF	3,4,PF	3,4,PF

INTRODUCTION

East Timor began operating without direct international support for the first time in 2013. The UN Integrated Mission in Timor-Leste (UNMIT) departed in late 2012, and the last personnel from the Australian-led International Stabilization Force (ISF) withdrew in March, leaving local authorities with sole responsibility for security.

The country's stability rested in part on continuity in Timorese leadership, dominated by figures from the independence struggle such as Prime Minister Kay Rala Xanana Gusmão and President Taur Matan Ruak, and also on heavy government spending on infrastructure and other development projects. A May 2013 report by the International Crisis Group warned of government leaders' overreliance on their personal authority rather than institutional arrangements to solve problems, as well as the need for reforms before current independence leaders retire from public service and revenue from oil and gas reserves is depleted.

Economic growth was a critical concern in the government's 2014 budget and its 2011 strategic development plan. East Timor remains one of the poorest countries in Southeast Asia, and the state budget draws heavily on revenue from its well-regarded and ably managed Petroleum Fund. The fund reached over $14.9 billion in 2013, though at current rates and with no additional planned projects it was expected to be exhausted by 2025.

High-level corruption accusations have continued into Gusmão's second term, though the judiciary has had some success in delivering convictions. The conviction of former justice minister Lúcia Lobato was upheld by the Supreme Court in January 2013.

Allegations emerged in 2013 that Australia had spied on East Timor's government in 2004 during discussions over a gas deal; East Timor claimed that the spying put it at a disadvantage in negotiations over potential oil and gas royalties and opened a case with the International Court of Justice at The Hague.

POLITICAL RIGHTS: 29 / 40
A. Electoral Process: 11 / 12

The directly elected president is a largely symbolic figure, with formal powers limited to the right to veto legislation and make certain appointments. The leader of the majority party or coalition in the 65-seat, unicameral Parliament becomes prime minister. The president and members of Parliament serve five-year terms, with the president eligible for a maximum of two terms.

East Timor successfully completed presidential and parliamentary elections in 2012, and despite some minor technical problems, the voting was deemed largely free and fair by observers. The first round of the presidential contest in March was led by Francisco Guterres, known as Lú-Olo, the party chairman of the Revolutionary Front for an Independent East Timor (Fretilin), and José Maria Vasconcelos, better known as Taur Matan Ruak, the former head of the National Defense Force (F-FDTL). Ruak, who ran as an independent but received last-minute support from Gusmão's National Congress for Timorese Reconstruction (CNRT) party, won in the second round in April with 61 percent of the vote.

Due to the 3 percent electoral threshold to enter Parliament, only 4 out of 21 competing parties garnered seats in the July legislative elections. Gusmão secured a second term as prime minister after the CNRT captured 30 seats, just short of the number needed to form a government alone. The CNRT entered into a coalition with the Democratic Party, which won 8 seats, and the new National Reconstruction Front of East Timor–Change (Frenti-Mudança), which had broken from Fretilin in 2011 and took 2 seats in the elections. The new government took office in August. Fretilin, which had led the first elected government from 2001 to 2007, secured 25 seats and remained in opposition.

B. Political Pluralism and Participation: 12 / 16

The main players in Timorese politics are the governing coalition controlled by Gusmão's CNRT and Fretilin, led by former prime minister Mari Alkatiri, who does not have a seat in Parliament. Independence heroes and their rivalries dating back to the anti-Indonesian resistance movement continue to dominate national politics, at times causing governmental paralysis and even violence. A 2006 political and security crisis resulted in widespread rioting, armed clashes with the police, numerous deaths, and the displacement of over 150,000 people.

There is a significant opposition vote, but Parliament has shown little initiative in its government oversight functions or the development of draft legislation; draft bills introduced by the government are rarely debated. Nevertheless, there were some signs of progress in 2013. Despite not serving in Parliament, Alkatiri led an ad hoc committee that succeeded in slightly reducing the government's proposed budget, demonstrating the first signs of a credible policy alternative. Gusmão responded positively to the budget debates by proposing that ministers report to Parliament every three months.

Cultural, ethnic, and religious minorities have full political rights and electoral opportunities in East Timor. Women hold 25 of the 65 seats in Parliament. Amendments to the election laws in 2011 required one-third of candidates on party lists for parliamentary elections to be women.

C. Functioning of Government: 6 / 12

Despite a relatively large cabinet of 55 members, power is concentrated in the 15-member Council of Ministers and the person of Gusmão, who also holds the portfolio of the Ministry of Defense and Security. The government has been criticized for not spending down its budget and delaying obligatory payments, due in part to mismanagement, limited human resources, and political impasse.

Voter frustration with corruption and nepotism has plagued both Fretilin- and CNRT-led governments. An anticorruption commission was created in 2009 with a broad mandate, except for powers of prosecution. In 2012, former justice minister Lobato was found guilty of corruption on a government procurement project and sentenced to five years in prison; her appeal was rejected in December 2012, and a subsequent extraordinary appeal to the Supreme Court was rejected in January 2013. In March, Secretary of State for Institutional Strengthening Françisco da Costa Soares Borlaco was charged with abuse of power during his tenure as director general of the Ministry of Finance; in May Parliament suspended him from his current position; in June, he was acquitted. In November, three high-level officials from the Ministry of the Environment—a former secretary of state, a former chief of staff, and a former treasurer—were sentenced to between one and five years in prison for crimes ranging from active corruption to falsification of documents. A contract with a Chinese company to supply school furniture came under fire during the year; the same company had won a contract in 2008 to build power plants and a national electricity grid, but failed to complete the project, forcing the government to turn to other companies and incur a significant loss and delay.

East Timor was ranked 119 out of 177 countries and territories surveyed in Transparency International's 2013 Corruption Perceptions Index.

CIVIL LIBERTIES: 34 / 60
D. Freedom of Expression and Belief: 12 / 16

Journalists are often treated with suspicion, particularly by government officials, and in many cases practice self-censorship; authorities regularly deny access to government information. The 2009 penal code decriminalized defamation but retained provisions against "slanderous denunciation," and defamation remains part of the civil code. Two journalists from different newspapers were indicted in 2012 for allegedly writing false accounts of a prosecutor's handling of a fatal 2011 traffic accident. In March 2013, neither were found guilty of a criminal act, but they were ordered to pay small fines as civil compensation. A National Code of Ethics, drafted by several media organizations, was adopted by journalists in November at the National Congress of Journalists.

The free flow of information remains hampered primarily by poor infrastructure and scarce resources. Radio is the medium with the greatest reach. The country has four major daily newspapers, some of which are loosely aligned with the ruling or opposition parties. Printing costs and illiteracy rates generally prevent the expansion of print media. In 2013, only about 1 percent of the population had access to the internet.

Freedom of religion is protected in the constitution, and East Timor is a secular state, though approximately 97 percent of the population is Roman Catholic. Protestant groups have reported some cases of discrimination and harassment. Academic freedom is generally respected. While religious education is included in the school curriculum, parents may remove their children from the classes.

E. Associational and Organizational Rights: 7 / 12

Freedoms of association and assembly are constitutionally guaranteed. However, a 2004 law regulates political gatherings and prohibits demonstrations aimed at "questioning constitutional order" or disparaging the reputations of the head of state and other government officials. The law requires that demonstrations and public protests be authorized in advance. Nongovernmental groups can generally operate without interference, though the government extended its ban on *pencak silat* martial-arts clubs in July 2013 after rivalry among the clubs led to several violent incidents during the first half of the year.

Workers, other than police and military personnel, are permitted to form and join labor organizations, bargain collectively, and strike; in practice, however, labor organizations are slow to form. In 2011, the government approved a law governing the right of workers to strike, which reduced the time required for written notification prior to a strike from 10 days to 5 days. A new labor law implemented in 2012 established a minimum wage of $115 per month, among other provisions. Unionization rates are low due to high levels of unemployment and informal economic activity.

F. Rule of Law: 6 / 16

The country suffers from weak rule of law and a prevailing culture of impunity. There is a considerable backlog in the understaffed court system; mobile courts were introduced in 2008 to improve access to justice outside of the capital. Due process rights are often restricted or denied, owing largely to a dearth of resources and personnel. Alternative methods of dispute resolution and customary law are widely used, though they lack enforcement mechanisms and have other significant shortcomings, including unequal treatment of women. According to a 2013 Asia Foundation report, while those who have knowledge of the formal court system have confidence in it, most Timorese have greater confidence in local justice mechanisms.

Internal security continued to improve in 2013. Gang violence—sometimes directed by rival elites or fueled by land disputes—continued sporadically, including clashes among *pencak silat* groups, though these are now banned. A dissident group, the Committee for the Popular Defense of the Democratic Republic of East Timor (CPD-RDTL), which rejects the current political system and government and advocates a return to the 1975 constitution and declaration of independence by Fretilin, raised its profile in 2013 when its members, mostly former anti-Indonesian guerrilla fighters, wore military fatigues and occupied land. They were forcibly evicted by the government, but concern about CPD-RDTL's plans persisted through the end of the year.

The military (F-FDTL) and police (PNTL) are constitutionally subject to oversight by a civilian secretary of state; Prime Minister Gusmão currently holds the relevant ministry's portfolio. Tension between the police and the military contributed to the 2006 political and security crisis, but it has since diminished significantly. Disputes regarding promotions are particularly acute in the PNTL, though the government made progress in 2013 on resolving the matter. While police officers and F-FDTL soldiers are regularly accused of excessive force and abuse of power, the courts have had some success in prosecuting them.

The status and reintegration of the thousands of Timorese refugees living in the Indonesian province of West Timor—having fled a 1999 Indonesian crackdown in East Timor following that year's referendum on independence—remained unresolved in 2013. The Timorese government has long encouraged the return of the refugees, but concerns over access to property and other rights, as well as the status of former militia members, continues to hinder their return.

The law bans discrimination based on sexual orientation, and hate crimes based on sexual orientation are considered an aggravating circumstance in the penal code. Issues like sexual orientation and gender identity reportedly receive little public attention, but a small number of LGBT (lesbian, gay, bisexual, and transgender) advocacy organizations have been established.

G. Personal Autonomy and Individual Rights: 9 / 16

Citizens enjoy freedom of unrestricted travel, but travel by land to the enclave of Oecusse is hampered by visa requirements and Indonesian and Timorese checkpoints. The country's citizens also enjoy free choice of residence and employment, though unemployment rates are high, and an estimated 80 percent of the population still works in subsistence farming.

While Timorese have the right to establish businesses, property rights are complicated by the legacies of the Portuguese and Indonesian administrations. Community property comprises approximately 90 percent of the land in East Timor, and land reform remains an unresolved and contentious issue. In February 2012, the outgoing Parliament passed three land laws that facilitated grant titles for plots with uncontested ownership, created a legal category for communal land, and established a system to resolve land disputes outside of the court system. However, then president José Ramos-Horta vetoed the laws, citing a lack of societal consensus, among other reasons. A new draft land law was amended and presented to Parliament in 2013, and was pending at year's end.

Equal rights for women are constitutionally guaranteed, but discrimination and gender inequality persist in practice and in customary law. Despite a 2010 law against domestic violence, gender-based and domestic violence remain widespread. A 2013 report by the UN Development Programme noted that many victims of domestic violence are deterred from seeking justice by factors including the desire to preserve family networks, the economic dependence of victims on perpetrators, community pressure, and perceived consequences of working within the formal justice system—such as abandonment or divorce. East Timor is a source and destination country for human trafficking into forced labor and prostitution.

Ecuador

Political Rights Rating: 3
Civil Liberties Rating: 3
Freedom Rating: 3.0
Freedom Status: Partly Free
Electoral Democracy: Yes

Population: 15,789,000
Capital: Quito

Ten-Year Ratings Timeline For Year Under Review (Political Rights, Civil Liberties, Status)

Year Under Review	2004	2005	2006	2007	2008	2009	2010	2011	2012	2013
Rating	3,3,PF	3,3,PF	3,3,PF	3,3,PF	3,3,PF	3,3,PF	3,3,PF	3,3,PF	3,3,PF	3,3,PF

INTRODUCTION

President Rafael Correa easily won a new term in February 2013 general elections, while an alliance led by his Movement for a Proud and Sovereign Homeland (PAIS) party captured an overwhelming majority in the legislature. Although the voting itself was deemed generally free and fair, preelection factors—including changes to the seat-allocation rules in 2012—were believed to have favored the incumbents.

Also during the year, the National Assembly passed a Communications Law that could lead to new restrictions on the media, and cases of harassment or attacks aimed at journalists continued to be reported. Civil society groups faced tighter regulation under a presidential decree issued in June, while individual activists faced prosecution under sabotage and terrorism laws for their role in organizing protests.

POLITICAL RIGHTS: 24 / 40

A. Electoral Process: 7 / 12

The 2008 constitution provides for a directly elected president who may serve up to two four-year terms. The unicameral, 137-seat National Assembly is elected for four-year terms, with 116 members elected in 24 provinces (each province elects at least 2 representatives and then one additional representative for every 200,000 inhabitants), 15 through nationwide proportional representation, and 6 in multimember constituencies representing Ecuadorians living abroad. The president has the authority to dissolve the legislature once in his term, which triggers new elections for both the assembly and the presidency. The assembly can likewise dismiss the president, though under more stringent rules. The president enjoys line-item veto power over legislation.

In the February 2013 presidential election, Correa was reelected with over 57 percent of the vote in the first round, followed by Guillermo Lasso Mendoza of the Creating Opportunities Movement (CREO) with 22 percent. In concurrent legislative elections, Correa's Alianza PAIS took 100 of the 137 seats, followed by Lasso's CREO with 11, the Social Christian Party with 6, Patriotic Society and Avanza with 5 each, and five smaller factions with one seat each.

International observers found that the elections were generally free and fair. The Organization of American States (OAS) reported that voters cast their votes freely and without obstacles. According to the OAS, new electoral legislation banning public institutions from advertising during the campaign, establishing predetermined spaces for the candidates to campaign, and prohibiting private individuals from contracting and disseminating electoral propaganda created a more equal environment for political competition among candidates in comparison with previous elections.

However, the OAS also observed that because those rules were effective only during the official six-week campaign period, competition that occurred between candidates in the precampaign period was unregulated. Separately, the local nongovernmental organization (NGO) Citizen Participation reported that the eight presidential candidates received equal government funds to campaign as stated by the law, but media coverage of the elections tended to favor Correa.

Other factors may have influenced the outcome of the voting long before election day. Changes to the parliament's seat-allocation formula enacted by Correa in January 2012 favored larger parties, prompting critics to warn that they would benefit PAIS. A government-sponsored revision of the electoral law had removed language that would have forced Correa to take a leave of absence during the presidential race, though he ultimately requested voluntary leave in late December in order to campaign full time. The National Electoral Council that supervised the 2013 elections was appointed in 2011, and the Council of Popular Participation was criticized for a lack of transparency in its selection of the body's members.

B. Political Pluralism and Participation: 11 / 16

For decades, Ecuador's political parties have been largely personality-based, clientelist, and fragile. Correa's PAIS party remains by far the largest in the legislature. The opposition includes the newly created CREO, the Social Christian Party, and the Patriotic Society Party. Pachakutik is loosely affiliated with the Confederation of Indigenous Nationalities (CONAIE), the leading national organization representing indigenous groups.

The 2008 constitution mandated the reregistration of political organizations as a requirement for eligibility to participate in the 2013 general elections. The process drew controversy as it unfolded during 2012, with reports that voters were signed up to support parties without their knowledge, among other irregularities. A total of 42 political organizations were legally recognized—11 at the national level and 31 at the provincial level.

C. Functioning of Government: 6 / 12

Ecuador has long been racked by corruption. The weak judiciary and lack of investigative capacity in government oversight agencies contribute to an atmosphere of impunity. Corruption investigations fall under the jurisdiction of the Transparency and Social Control (FTCS) branch of government, created by the 2008 constitution. As of November 2013, the FTCS had 64 corruption cases under investigation, ranging from irregularities in public contracting to disputed fees at educational institutions. In May, the agency launched a national anticorruption plan aimed at eradicating the problem by 2017. In an assessment of the current situation, the FTCS found that clientelist practices, impunity, excessive discretion, fragmented anticorruption policies, lack of correspondence between offenses and sanctions, and collusion were among the factors that have favored the persistence of corruption in the country. Ecuador was ranked 102 out of 177 countries surveyed in Transparency International's 2013 Corruption Perceptions Index.

CIVIL LIBERTIES: 36 / 60

D. Freedom of Expression and Belief: 13 / 16

The environment for freedom of expression did not improve in 2013. As of mid-December, the press watchdog Fundamedios reported 174 cases of verbal, physical, or legal harassment against journalists during the year. Correa continued his use of national broadcasts to castigate opposition and indigenous leaders, and his 2012 reforms of the electoral law barred the media from influencing the electoral campaign. In addition to Correa's regular verbal attacks on the press, the government uses its unlimited access to public-service airtime to interrupt news programming on privately owned stations and discredit journalists.

The courts ruled on a number of disputes involving freedom of expression during the year. In April, opposition assembly member Clever Jimenez and journalist Fernando Villavicencio were sentenced to 18 months in prison, along with a fine and an obligatory public apology to Correa, after being convicted of defamation. Activist Carlos Figueroa was sentenced to six months in prison. The three had sued Correa over his response to a police revolt in September 2010, and the president had filed a defamation case in retaliation after their lawsuit was dismissed. Separately, in September 2013, a judge censored a book on unsolved killings among noncontacted indigenous peoples.

International press freedom groups and human rights commissions criticized the new Communications Law approved by the National Assembly in June. Among other provisions, the legislation would create powerful regulatory bodies with questionable independence, place excessive controls on content, and impose onerous obligations on journalists and media outlets. The law employs vague language that could be used to censor critical reporting. For example, it introduces the offense of "character assassination," prohibiting the dissemination of information that may undermine the prestige of an individual or institution or reduce its public credibility. Opposition politicians and civil society members challenged the legislation before the Constitutional Court.

In December, the National Assembly approved a new criminal code containing elements that may affect freedom of expression. Fundamedios highlighted provisions penalizing the propagation of any distinction that may erode equality, the dissemination of unauthorized personal information, the publication of false news that may hinder the economy, and the defense of someone sentenced for a crime. The new criminal code also retained existing libel and terrorism clauses.

Freedom of religion is constitutionally guaranteed and generally respected in practice. Academic freedom is not restricted.

E. Associational and Organizational Rights: 7 / 12

Numerous protests occur peacefully. However, national security legislation that predates the Correa administration provides a broad definition of sabotage and terrorism, which includes acts against persons and property by unarmed individuals. The use of such charges, along with other criminal and civil laws, against protesters has increased under Correa. Indigenous organizations in particular complain that the government is criminalizing protest by targeting leaders for legal harassment and using more aggressive police tactics against demonstrators. The Ecumenical Commission for Human Rights reported that 15 people were charged with sabotage and 10 others were accused of terrorism during 2012. In July 2013, opposition assembly member and indigenous leader Pepe Acacho was sentenced to 12 years in prison for his participation in a 2009 protest over a government-sponsored water bill that resulted in a civilian's death. In June, a former leader of the teacher's union, Mery Zamora, received an eight-year prison sentence for sabotage, having encouraged students to protest against the government during the 2010 police revolt. Both defendants appealed their sentences.

The right to organize political parties, civic groups, and unions is unabridged in law. However, domestic and international NGOs have come under increasing government scrutiny and regulation. Presidential decree 16, published in June 2013, has created great concern among civic activists. Among other contentious provisions, it introduced onerous requirements for forming an NGO, granted officials broad authority to dissolve them, and obliged organizations to register all of their members. NGOs were given one year to comply with the new rules. Critics contended that the regulations violated international standards, and activists challenged the constitutionality of the decree in Ecuadorian courts. NGO representatives also testified on the matter before the Inter-American Commission on Human Rights in October. A July 2011 presidential decree had already outlined broadly worded regulations for foreign-sponsored NGOs, forbidding activities that are "incompatible with public security and peace." Correa has accused many NGOs of forming part of a right-wing conspiracy to bring down his government. On December 4, the NGO Pachamama was dissolved under this new regulation after the government accused some of its members of having initiated a violent protest.

The country's labor unions have the right to strike, though the labor code limits public-sector strikes. There are more labor unions in the public than in the private sector, and it is estimated that only a small portion of the workforce is unionized, partly because many people work in the informal sector. The criminal code that was approved in December 2013 prescribes one to three years in prison for public servants who agree on something that may "impede, suspend, or obstruct the execution of a law or regulation."

F. Rule of Law: 6 / 16

The highest judicial bodies established under a 2011 judicial reform are the nine-member Constitutional Court and the 21-member National Court of Justice, whose judges were appointed in 2012. Opposition members and a panel of foreign experts cited problems in the appointment process for the National Court of Justice, including a lack of transparency. The primary criticism regarding the selection of justices for the Constitutional Court was that the members of the selection committee were too closely aligned with the government. A new attorney general was appointed in April 2011, and the system used by the Council of Popular Participation to vet candidates was similarly criticized for a lack of transparency.

Judicial processes remain slow, and many inmates reach the time limit for pretrial detention while their cases are still under investigation. Prisons are seriously overcrowded, and torture and ill-treatment of detainees and prisoners are widespread. Various projects to reform the penal and criminal procedure codes in order to improve efficiency and fairness were undertaken in 2009 and 2010, but rising crime—partly blamed on prisoners who were released to relieve overcrowding—pushed the focus of debate away from comprehensive reform. In the 2011 referendum that adopted the government's judicial reforms, voters endorsed more restrictive rules on pretrial detention. These and other changes were included in the new criminal code that was approved in December 2013. The new code introduces specific crimes such as hired killings and femicide, and imposes tougher sentences for existing offenses.

Indigenous people continue to suffer discrimination at many levels of society. In the Amazon region, indigenous groups have attempted to win a share of oil revenues and a voice in decisions on natural resources and development. The government has maintained that it will not hand indigenous groups a veto on core matters of national interest.

With over 55,000 refugee visas granted since 1999, Ecuador is the largest recipient of refugees in Latin America. The government provides refugees with access to health facilities, schools, and small-business loans. However, the implementation of presidential decree 1182, initially adopted in May 2012, has raised concerns among defenders of refugee rights. The UN refugee agency reported that the decree introduced restrictive admissibility procedures and adopted a narrower refugee definition than that established in the 1984 Cartagena Declaration on Refugees. Human Rights Watch pointed out that the Cartagena Declaration includes those who have fled their country due to generalized violence, which is the case with most Colombians who seek refuge in Ecuador.

G. Personal Autonomy and Individual Rights: 10 / 16

Women took 53 of 137 assembly seats in the 2013 elections, and the 2008 constitution calls for a significant female presence in public office. The election law requires that women account for 50 percent of the party lists in national legislative elections. Violence against women is common, as is employment discrimination. The 2008 constitution does not provide for same-sex marriage, but civil unions are recognized. Trafficking in persons, generally women and children, remains a problem.

Egypt

Political Rights Rating: 6
Civil Liberties Rating: 5
Freedom Rating: 5.5
Freedom Status: Not Free
Electoral Democracy: No

Population: 84,700,000
Capital: Cairo

Status Change: Egypt's political rights rating declined from 5 to 6 and its status declined from Partly Free to Not Free due to the overthrow of elected president Mohamed Morsi in July, violent crackdowns on Islamist political groups and civil society, and the increased role of the military in the political process.

Ten-Year Ratings Timeline For Year Under Review (Political Rights, Civil Liberties, Status)

Year Under Review	2004	2005	2006	2007	2008	2009	2010	2011	2012	2013
Rating	6,5,NF	6,5,NF	6,5,NF	6,5,NF	6,5,NF	6,5,NF	6,5,NF	6,5,NF	5,5,PF	6,5,NF

INTRODUCTION

Political support for President Mohamed Morsi waned during the first half of 2013, with critics alleging that he was more focused on consolidating power for himself and his Muslim Brotherhood–affiliated Freedom and Justice Party (FJP) than working to resolve Egypt's severe economic and governance problems. Morsi's June 2012 election had ended a period of military rule after the ouster of longtime authoritarian president Hosni Mubarak amid popular protests in February 2011. However, he had alienated many Egyptians in November 2012, when he claimed extensive executive powers in a decree that he defended as necessary to ensure the adoption of a new constitution in a chaotic political environment. Opponents denounced the decree as a blatant power grab and later criticized the resulting constitution as a highly problematic document written by an unrepresentative, overwhelmingly Islamist constituent assembly.

In the spring of 2013, a small group of activists calling themselves Tamarrod (Rebellion) began organizing a petition campaign, gathering signatures to demand the withdrawal of confidence from the Morsi government and early elections. The campaign climaxed in millions-strong demonstrations across the country on June 30, the anniversary of Morsi's inauguration.

The military intervened shortly after those protests began, first declaring a 48-hour window for Morsi to respond to popular demands. Military officers then detained him on July 3, suspending the constitution and installing an interim government led by Adli Mansour, chairman of the Supreme Constitutional Court. Under a plan outlined by Mansour, a new constitution was drafted by a small panel of jurists and revised by a 50-member committee that was far from demographically or politically representative, with only five women, four Copts, and one Islamist member. The panel undermined its transparency by conducting secret votes on a number of occasions. The draft was finalized and released to the public in early December, and was expected to be put up for a popular referendum in January 2014. The final document gave enhanced powers to the military, the judiciary, and the police, among other antidemocratic features.

Morsi supporters demonstrated continually against the interim government, and were met with harsh crackdowns by security forces that resulted in more than 1,000 deaths. The authorities methodically arrested and prosecuted Muslim Brotherhood leaders, and the courts ultimately outlawed the organization. Attacks on the Coptic Christian minority, a longstanding problem, increased dramatically after both the coup and related attacks on Islamist protesters, as many Islamists believed that the Coptic community was complicit in Morsi's overthrow and the repression of the Islamist community. Islamist militants also increasingly mounted attacks on police and military targets.

The military-backed government enjoyed high levels of popular support, though discontent among activists and revolutionary groups soon swelled, particularly after Mansour issued a law in November that gave police free rein to ban and disperse protests. By year's end the authorities had declared the Muslim Brotherhood a terrorist organization and were arresting both Morsi supporters and non-Islamist democracy activists who objected to the restoration of a Mubarak-style regime.

POLITICAL RIGHTS: 9 / 40 (-7)

A. Electoral Process: 1 / 12 (-2)

Mubarak and his National Democratic Party (NDP) dominated the Egyptian political system from October 1981 until February 2011, when the president was deposed in a popular uprising. The Supreme Council of the Armed Forces (SCAF), a group of senior army officers, then took control, dissolving the NDP-controlled legislature and promising an orderly transition to civilian rule. The SCAF exercised executive powers until Morsi was elected president in June 2012. Observers of the election, the first genuinely competitive presidential contest in Egypt's history, reported that election-day conduct was generally consistent with international standards, but criticized a number of factors in the electoral process, including restrictions on election observers, violations of ballot secrecy, and the disqualification of several well-known candidates. Morsi led the first round on May 23–24, taking over 24 percent of the vote. Mubarak-era prime minister Ahmed Shafik placed second with roughly 23 percent. In the June 16–17 runoff, Morsi won the presidency with 51.7 percent of the vote.

Morsi exercised executive powers until his forcible removal on July 3, 2013. The military appointed an interim government, with Mansour as president and Hazem al-Beblawi as prime minister. Though the government claimed to be civilian in nature, Mansour cited the July 3 declaration of the head of the armed forces, Abdel Fattah al-Sisi, as the source of his authority. In August the government appointed 19 generals to serve as provincial governors, and the military remained heavily involved in the political system throughout the year.

There was no legislative body in place in the second half of the year. The last elections for the People's Assembly, Egypt's lower house of parliament, were completed in January 2012, with nearly 70 percent of the new chamber held by Islamist parties that were illegal before Mubarak's ouster. The Democratic Alliance, led by the Muslim Brotherhood's FJP, won 235 of the 498 elected seats, and a bloc led by the Salafist party Al-Nour won 123 seats. A coalition of liberal parties, the Egyptian Bloc, won 34 seats, and the center-right Wafd party won 38. Several smaller groups took the remainder. Including the 10 members nominated by the SCAF in its role as de facto executive, there were just 10 women and 13

Coptic Christians in the new assembly. However, the chamber was dismissed in mid-June 2012, after the courts ruled various electoral laws unconstitutional.

The upper house, the Consultative Council, traditionally functioned solely in an advisory capacity. The president appointed 90 of its members, and 180 were directly elected. Elections for the council in early 2012 were marred by problems including low turnout, with less than 15 percent of eligible voters participating. The FJP's Democratic Alliance won about 60 percent of the elected seats, with a total of 105 seats. Al-Nour's bloc placed second with 45 seats, or 25.5 percent of elected spots, followed by Wafd with 14, the Egyptian Bloc with 8, and small parties and independents with the remainder. Morsi chose the chamber's appointed members in December of that year. In the absence of the People's Assembly, the upper chamber exercised legislative functions until it was dissolved following the July 2013 coup.

Under a plan laid out by the interim government, parliamentary and presidential elections would be held in 2014 after a referendum on the new constitution. However, the draft finalized in December would allow a six-month gap between the two elections, which could be held in either order, meaning a new president could serve without the check of a legislature for much of the year. The Supreme Electoral Commission was created in September 2013, and political parties began to organize and identify candidates in October. However, the ongoing political violence and repression, and the increasing likelihood that al-Sisi would run for president, left virtually no space for constructive political debate or other normal preelection activities, dimming the prospects for free and fair balloting.

B. Political Pluralism and Participation: 6 / 16 (-4)

The legal and electoral framework of the Mubarak era ensured the almost complete dominance of the NDP, and although a court ruling following Mubarak's ouster dissolved the party, many of its leading figures remained active in politics. The 2012 electoral victories of long-banned Islamist groups and the formation of several new parties across the political spectrum seemed to represent a dramatic shift toward political pluralism, but this trend was reversed in 2013.

Following Morsi's ouster, the Muslim Brotherhood was once again banned—affecting both its political party, the FJP, and its larger structure as a nongovernmental organization—and its assets were seized. Members and supporters of the Brotherhood, including nearly all of its leadership and Morsi himself, were arrested en masse and later charged with a variety of offenses, including incitement of violence, violation of public order, the use of FJP headquarters as a weapons warehouse, and the use of live ammunition and violence against the public. At the end of December, the Muslim Brotherhood was declared a terrorist organization, effectively allowing the government to charge anyone participating in a Muslim Brotherhood demonstration with terrorism offenses. Morsi was held incommunicado for months before finally appearing at a trial hearing in November, at which he lambasted the new government and insisted that he was Egypt's legitimate president. Although his supporters continued to organize rallies and protests long after the coup, they repeatedly faced arrest and deadly police violence, including a single day of crackdowns on August 14 that killed an estimated 700 people at protest encampments. The draft constitution finalized in December 2013 banned parties based on religion, making it very unlikely that Islamists would be able to participate freely in the political system, with the possible exception of Al-Nour, which supported the military overthrow of Morsi and cooperated with the interim government.

The military has played an assertive role in the political process since ousting Morsi, using massive demonstrations by its supporters to bolster the legitimacy of its actions. Shortly before the August crackdown on pro-Morsi protesters, al-Sisi appealed directly to the Egyptian people for their backing in the military's battle against "violence and terrorism."

Separately, video released in October showed senior members of the military discussing strategies to shape media coverage of their leadership.

C. Functioning of Government: 2 / 12 (-1)

Morsi's ouster and the dissolution of the Consultative Council in July 2013 left no elected officials in the executive or legislative branches. All subsequent legislation was enacted in the form of decrees by the military-backed interim government. Under the interim regime, as with the Mubarak, SCAF, and Morsi governments before it, there was very little transparency in government operations and budget making, and the military is notoriously opaque regarding its own extensive interests throughout the Egyptian economy. There was a civil society consultation process for the new draft constitution, though civic and opposition groups did not have a significant impact on the final document.

Corruption is pervasive at all levels of government. Egypt was ranked 114 out of 177 countries surveyed in Transparency International's 2013 Corruption Perceptions Index. Given the urgency of ongoing events and the general level of political crisis, many of the major corruption revelations and prosecutions of past years have faded from public attention, and there remain very weak mechanisms for investigating and punishing corrupt behavior.

CIVIL LIBERTIES: 22 / 60 (-3)

D. Freedom of Expression and Belief: 6 / 16 (-2)

Freedom of expression at first appeared to improve after Morsi took power, for example when he banned the pretrial detention of journalists in August 2012, but it soon became clear that Morsi was as hostile to critical media coverage as his predecessors. Physical attacks on journalists grew during Morsi's tenure, and a number were arrested on charges including "insulting the president." Among the best-known cases was that of Bassem Youssef, a television comedian who was arrested in March 2013 and charged with insulting Morsi and Islam. Those charges were eventually dropped. Youssef's show returned briefly in October 2013, but he soon faced a new investigation for criticizing the military leadership. The show's broadcaster, CBC, pulled it from the air on November 1.

While the media were already highly polarized before the coup, making unbiased information difficult to obtain, the authorities shut down three major Islamist television channels following Morsi's ouster and raided the Egyptian offices of Qatar's Al-Jazeera network, which was widely criticized for displaying a pro-Morsi slant. Similar repressive actions continued through the end of 2013. In September, the government took a number of television channels off the air; although some of them broadcast pro-Morsi views, at least one stridently opposed Morsi and supported the military. Police also raided the Cairo office of the Turkish broadcaster TRT, which the government accused of siding with Morsi, and the offices of the Muslim Brotherhood's party newspaper. Scores of journalists were arbitrarily detained by the interim government, including Ahmed Abu Deraa, a reporter for an Egyptian daily who was arrested in Sinai in early September. He was given a six-month suspended sentence by a military tribunal in October for "intentionally spreading false news about the military," having reported on the army's troubled campaign against Islamist militants in the region.

State media and most remaining private television stations reflect largely promilitary views, especially in their coverage of protests and related violence. Most private outlets embraced the government crackdown on Morsi supporters, including by adopting almost verbatim the government's defense of its actions. At least four journalists were killed during or after the August 14 raids on pro-Morsi sit-ins. Reporters and photographers, particularly those from foreign news outlets, were targeted during the operations.

On December 29, police arrested four journalists from Al-Jazeera English on charges that they aired false news, were broadcasting illegally, and met with a terrorist group—the Muslim Brotherhood.

Censorship, both official and self-imposed, is widespread. A video leaked in October showed senior army leaders discussing the need for a reassertion of "red lines" on media criticism of the military, which they worried had been lost since the 2011 uprising. The officers complained that scrutiny of the government was not "normal," and encouraged al-Sisi to pressure media owners to self-censor their coverage of military affairs.

Islam is the state religion, and most Egyptians are Sunni Muslims. Coptic Christians form a substantial minority, and there are very small numbers of Jews, Shiite Muslims, and Baha'is. As in the 2012 constitution, the draft constitution completed in December 2013 would endow Christians with a right to their own personal status law.

Sectarian bloodshed has increased in recent years, with Christians typically bearing the brunt of the violence, and religious divisions became increasingly politicized following Morsi's fall from power. Many Morsi supporters believed that the Coptic community was in some way responsible for his overthrow, and attacked Copts and their property in retaliation. After the bloody August 14 dispersal of pro-Morsi sit-ins, Islamist mobs assaulted Christians and damaged or destroyed dozens of churches and businesses. Security forces reportedly failed to intervene.

Also in the period after the coup, many Muslims were caught up in the government's crackdown on the Brotherhood and its perceived supporters. Anyone whose appearance or dress suggested adherence to a conservative form of Islam was reportedly at risk of arrest or harassment. The government in September banned approximately 55,000 unlicensed imams from delivering sermons and required license applicants to receive training from Al-Azhar University or certification by another state-supervised institution. The move was designed to silence preachers whom the government considered extremist.

Academic freedom improved somewhat after the fall of Mubarak. University leaders were no longer appointed by the government, and a series of Mubarak-era education officials resigned. Universities were a center of pro-Morsi and antigovernment demonstrations following the July 2013 coup. A ban on political activity at universities did not dampen the considerable pro-Morsi demonstrations that sprouted up after the beginning of the new academic year. Confrontations, many of them violent, between students and security forces continued throughout the term. The authorities used excessive force in trying to disperse these protests, including in the shooting death of student Khaled al-Haddad at Al-Azhar University.

Freedom of private discussion has generally been quite high in recent years, including under the interim government. However, there is a danger that the escalating political polarization and the growing tendency of rival groups to engage in vigilante justice will increase the risks of this kind of speech.

E. Associational and Organizational Rights: 4 / 12 (-1)

Freedoms of assembly and association are restricted, but protests have been a key forum for political expression since the 2011 uprising. Protests frequently turn violent, and police are quick to crack down on demonstrators, often using excessive force.

Millions protested against the Morsi administration in the days prior to the July 2013 coup, and there were near-constant protests and sit-ins following Morsi's removal. Human rights groups have documented authorities' use of live ammunition to disperse such demonstrations, including a July 27 attack that killed at least 80 people, the August 14 crackdown that killed some 700 protesters, and an assault in early October that left 53 dead. Supporters of the interim government accused the Islamists of carrying weapons to ostensibly peaceful rallies and instigating violence against their opponents. More than 105 police officers were killed in the August crackdown on Islamist protest camps.

A state of emergency and a related curfew that lasted from August to November gave police broad discretion to break up demonstrations and detain participants without regard to due process. In late November, the interim president signed a new law that permanently gives police great leeway to ban and forcibly disperse gatherings of 10 or more people. The law also prohibits all protests at places of worship and requires protest organizers to inform police at least three days in advance. Protests against the law were violently suppressed, with police assaulting, sexually abusing, and arresting dozens of non-Islamist liberal activists. Prominent activists such as Alaa Abdel-Fattah were rounded up over the subsequent week. Also that month, a group of 21 female Islamist protesters, including several juveniles, received long prison sentences on charges related to an October pro-Morsi demonstration. Following significant public outcry, an appeals court in December reduced the penalties to suspended sentences or probation.

Nongovernmental organizations (NGOs) are barred from receiving foreign grants without the approval of the Social Affairs Ministry, and the ministry is allowed to dissolve NGOs without a judicial order. The Mubarak regime watched NGOs closely, and government officials continued to harass them after Mubarak's fall. In December 2011, security forces raided the offices of 17 domestic and international civil society groups, confiscating equipment and temporarily detaining some staff. In January 2012, 43 NGO workers were indicted on charges of operating an organization and receiving funds from a foreign government without a license. All 43 were convicted in absentia in June 2013, receiving sentences ranging from suspended terms to five years in prison.

The labor movement made important advances during and after the 2011 uprising, as strikes played a significant role in increasing pressure on Mubarak to step down. Workers were granted the right to establish independent trade unions and formed an independent union federation, ending the long-standing monopoly of the state-allied federation. Labor activists criticized Morsi's November 2012 adoption of Decree No. 97, an amendment to the 1976 labor law that increased government control over unions. Such control was most evident in a provision setting a maximum age of 60 for board members of the historically state-dominated Egyptian Trade Union Federation (ETUF), which would lead to the dismissal of more than 160 of 524 members and allow the Morsi government to fill any vacancy for which there was no runner-up in the most recent election.

The labor movement continued to have difficult relations with the government after Morsi's ouster. In September 2013, the minister of manpower, Kamal Abu Eita, removed the leader and a number of Muslim Brotherhood–affiliated members of the ETUF board, claiming that they did not support a new labor law the ministry had drafted. Abu Eita did not push back against two government crackdowns on strikes at the Suez Steel Company and the Scimitar Petroleum Company in August.

F. Rule of Law: 4 / 16

The Supreme Judicial Council, a supervisory body of senior judges, nominates and assigns most members of the judiciary. However, the Justice Ministry controls promotions and compensation, giving it undue influence over the courts. The judiciary was at the center of the political process following the removal of Morsi from power in July 2013. Supreme Constitutional Court chairman Adli Mansour served as interim president, and judges played a leading role in the drafting of the new constitution. The final draft released to the public in December enhanced the judiciary's autonomy, including by allowing it to receive its budget in a lump sum and permitting the Supreme Constitutional Court to appoint its own chief justice.

Military tribunals lack independence. Verdicts are based on little more than the testimony of security officers and informers, and are reviewed only by a body of military judges and the president. Charges brought in military courts are often vague and trumped up, according to human rights organizations. Activists have continually demanded an end to military trials of civilians, but these continued in 2013. Following the coup, a number of activists were tried in military courts. Like the 2012 constitution before it, the 2013 draft constitution left the matter of military trials of civilians to be regulated by legislation, and used such broad language to delineate the jurisdiction of military courts that they could take on virtually any case.

Police brutality and the near-complete impunity enjoyed by security forces were key catalysts for the 2011 protests that overthrew Mubarak, but there has been no effort at comprehensive security-sector reform in the years since, regardless of the regime in power. General prison conditions are very poor; inmates are subject to torture and other abuse, overcrowding, and a lack of sanitation and medical care. In a widely publicized incident in August 2013, a group of 36 people detained in the crackdown on Muslim Brotherhood protest camps died while in police custody.

Egypt was under a state of emergency from 1981 until May 31, 2012. Under the Emergency Law, "security" cases were usually referred to executive-controlled exceptional courts that denied defendants many constitutional protections. The Emergency Law empowered the government to tap telephones, intercept mail, conduct warrantless searches, and indefinitely detain suspects without charge if they were deemed a threat to national security. The military-backed government that unseated Morsi reinstated the state of emergency on August 14 as it violently broke up the camps of pro-Morsi demonstrators. The state of emergency was extended multiple times until November 12, when an administrative court ended it and lifted a related curfew.

G. Personal Autonomy and Individual Rights: 8 / 16

Egypt's past constitutions have typically limited women's rights to those compatible with Islamic law. The 2013 draft constitution represents a modest improvement, as it clearly affirms the equality of the sexes. The extent to which this results in practical improvements for women is not yet clear, as implementation will depend on future laws and court rulings.

Some existing laws and many traditional practices discriminate against women. Job discrimination is evident in the civil service. Muslim women are placed at a disadvantage by laws on divorce and other personal status issues. However, Christians are not subject to such provisions of Islamic law. Domestic violence is common, and sexual harassment on the street has drawn increased attention in recent years. Spousal rape is not illegal, and the penal code allows for leniency in so-called honor killings. Other problems include forced marriages, increases in human trafficking, and high rates of female genital cutting.

Violence against women has surfaced in new ways since Mubarak's ouster, particularly as women have participated in more demonstrations and faced increased levels of sexual violence in public. In the four days of protests leading up to the July 2013 coup, human rights groups documented at least 91 cases of sexual assault against women in Cairo's Tahrir Square. Security forces have also engaged in sexual abuse of female protesters and activists, including in November 2013 as they arrested those demonstrating against the new protest law.

There are few rights for the LGBT (lesbian, gay, bisexual, and transgender) community. Gay men especially have been jailed under laws against "moral depravity" and "violating the teachings of religion." In October 2013, 14 men were arrested at a medical center and accused of engaging in "indecent acts." Some familiar with the center said it was a common venue for men to solicit male prostitutes.

El Salvador

Political Rights Rating: 2
Civil Liberties Rating: 3
Freedom Rating: 2.5
Freedom Status: Free
Electoral Democracy: Yes

Population: 6,300,000
Capital: San Salvador

Ten-Year Ratings Timeline For Year Under Review (Political Rights, Civil Liberties, Status)

Year Under Review	2004	2005	2006	2007	2008	2009	2010	2011	2012	2013
Rating	2,3,F	2,3,F	2,3,F	2,3,F	2,3,F	2,3,F	2,3,F	2,3,F	2,3,F	2,3,F

INTRODUCTION

The Salvadoran government continued to work in 2013 to transform the gang truce between the Mara Salvatrucha (MS-13) and the 18th Street gangs of the previous year into a sustainable peace. While the truce has reduced the country's murder rate by over half, its long-term success is in doubt given the lack of resources available domestically and internationally and the lack of transparency with which the government has facilitated and supported the truce. It has also become a political issue in advance of the February 2014 presidential election.

The independence of the Salvadoran government to make decisions concerning its people was challenged in 2013 following public and private pressure applied by U.S. officials, programs associated with the Bolivarian Alliance for the Peoples of Our Americas (ALBA), litigation by multinational corporations, and infiltration by transnational criminal organizations.

The United States' support for initiatives such as the Public-Private Partnership (P3) law in May, debate on a second Millennium Corporation Compact for El Salvador in September, and investment in a number of programs related to the Partnership for Growth have caused friction between El Salvadorian president Mauricio Funes, his party, the Farabundo Martí National Liberation Front (FMLN), and the business sector and civil society.

POLITICAL RIGHTS: 35 / 40

A. Electoral Process: 12 / 12

El Salvador's president is elected for a five-year term, and the 84-member, unicameral Legislative Assembly is elected for three years. Residential voting and absentee voting from Salvadorans living in the US will be available in 2014.

El Salvador held legislative and local elections in March 2012, with a turnout of 51 percent of registered voters. The Nationalist Republican Alliance (ARENA) captured 33 seats and the FMLN 31; they were followed by Grand Alliance for National Unity (GANA) with 11, the National Conciliation (CN) with 7, and the Party of Hope (PES) and the Democratic Change Party (PDC) with 1 seat each. In municipal elections, ARENA captured 116 and the FMLN 95 mayorships; the CN, PES, and GANA shared the remaining 51. An electoral observer mission from the Organization of American States (OAS) made a number of recommendations to improve the legitimacy of El Salvador's electoral process, including the passage of campaign finance and accountability laws, as well as measures to increase female representation in the national and municipal-level governments.

B. Political Pluralism and Participation: 14 / 16

A 1979–1992 civil war pitted El Salvador's Christian Democratic Party (PDC) government, the right-wing oligarchy, and the military, with support from the United States, against the leftist FMLN. In 1989, the conservative ARENA captured the presidency, and the civil war ended in 1992 with the signing of a peace treaty. ARENA held the presidency for two decades until the FMLN emerged victorious in 2009 with the more-centrist Mauricio Funes as its presidential candidate. While the FMLN has supported Funes on several issues since taking office, important disagreements have, at times, caused a rift between the president and his party. The FMLN and ARENA are the country's two largest political parties, although there is growing support for former president Antonio Saca's GANA party.

Following the loss of several ARENA congressmen, the FMLN surpassed ARENA as the largest legislative bloc in November 2012. Increasing frustration with the abandonment of the party on whose ticket they had won office led ARENA deputies to propose reforms to the constitution that would impose one-to-three-year prison sentences on members of congress who abandoned their party for another or to become independent.

There is increasing concern that foreign governments and multinational corporations are exerting ever greater influence over decisions made by local and national government officials. In September 2013, U.S. senator Patrick Leahy argued that El Salvador should have to demonstrate greater progress toward fighting corruption and making its judiciary more independent before the U.S. Congress would authorize $277 million in aid to the country. Canadian gold mining company Pacific Rim is suing El Salvador for $315 million because it claims that the government failed to issue permits for the company to remove gold from the ground. There is also concern with the amount of power that Venezuela has over domestic policy given its $800 million worth of assets in El Salvador through a joint initiative with FMLN mayors, Alba Petróleos.

After the former inspector general of the National Civil Police (PNC) resigned in January 2012, claiming that the military had gained too much influence over the nation's security institutions, several officers who had been under investigation for ties to drug trafficking and organized crime were promoted or appointed to key positions.

C. Functioning of Government: 9 / 12

Corruption remains a serious problem in El Salvador, and few high level public officials have ever been charged or convicted. In June 2013, however, President Funes announced the creation of a new anti-extortion unit. In July, the Constitutional Chamber agreed to support an investigation into former president Francisco Flores and several prominent businessmen for illicit enrichment. Funes announced in September that his government would establish a Financial Crimes Division of the National Police in order to tackle money laundering by drug-trafficking organizations. That month, the attorney general's office raided a number of homes and served arrest warrants that alleged fraud, embezzlement, the falsification of identity and of documents, and corruption in the Public Works Ministry during the administration of president Tony Saca (2004–2009). In October, President Funes ordered his ministers to cooperate with the attorney general in his investigation of an unnamed ex-president for money laundering and tax evasion. El Salvador was ranked 83 out of 177 countries surveyed in Transparency International's 2013 Corruption Perceptions Index.

While President Funes maintains very high approval ratings, questions surrounding his administration's lack of transparency regarding the government's facilitation of a March 2012 truce between the MS-13 and the 18th Street gangs linger. After initially denying involvement with the truce, the government eventually acknowledged it and held several meetings with representatives of civil society, political parties, the business community, and the OAS in order to devise a long-term plan to sustain the peace. However, the president has not clarified the government's involvement in facilitating the agreement and continues to be vague about the ongoing negotiations. Mayors across the political spectrum have continued to support the truce, creating so-called sanctuary cities (also known as "peace zones" and "violence-free municipalities") where gang members surrender their weapons and cease to engage in all criminal activities. In June, Attorney General Luis Martinez accused former minister of justice and public security David Munguía Payés of obstructing police anti-gang operations. Meanwhile, in October, critics accused Minister of Justice and Public Security Ricardo Perdomo of politicizing the debate over the truce in advance of the 2014 elections. International security analysts have accused President Funes of downplaying the severity of organized crime, money laundering and drug trafficking in El Salvador.

CIVIL LIBERTIES: 42 / 60
D. Freedom of Expression and Belief: 15 / 16

The constitution provides for freedom of the press, and this right is generally respected in practice. The staff of the newspaper *El Faro* have received threats and reported being followed after reporting in May 2011 about connections between gang leaders, politicians, and businessmen, as well as the March 2012 gang truce. In July 2013, President Funes vetoed a bill that would have established fines of up to $25,000 against individuals who defame presidential candidates. The congress also passed a Special Law for the Right to Rectification or Response in July that required media outlets to print any letter written by anyone offended by the outlet's reporting. Failure to do so could result in a fine or a prison sentence. The media are privately owned, but ownership is confined to a small group of powerful businesspeople who often impose controls on journalists to protect their political or economic interests. ARENA-aligned Telecorporación Salvadoreña owns three of the five private television networks and dominates the market. There is unrestricted access to the internet and the government and private organizations have worked to extend internet access to the poor.

The government does not encroach on religious freedom, and academic freedom is respected.

E. Associational and Organizational Rights: 8 /12

Freedoms of assembly and association are generally upheld. Public protests during recent constitutional conflicts have not been obstructed. The Legislative Assembly passed a controversial law in 2010 criminalizing gang membership, which critics feared would threaten freedom of association and would not succeed in addressing gang-related crime. While there was hope that the Salvadoran government might repeal the law as part of its new approach to public security, there has been no movement to do so. El Salvador's nongovernmental organizations (NGOs) generally operate freely, but some have reported registration difficulties. In an act of intimidation in November, armed men broke into and burned the records of Pro-Búsqueda, a Salvadoran non-profit that works to locate children missing from the war. Labor unions have long faced obstacles in a legal environment that has traditionally favored business interests.

F. Rule of Law: 9 / 16

Although El Salvador's judicial system remains weak and judges and others continue to speak out against the corruption and obstructionism that still permeates the entire judiciary, the Constitutional Chamber of the Supreme Court continues to demonstrate its independence. In December 2012, the Constitutional Chamber ruled that elements of the regulations issued by the Funes administration to implement the Access to Information Law were unconstitutional. In March 2013, the Chamber ruled against the Legislative Assembly's appointment of four out of five magistrates on the Court of Accounts. In May, the Chamber ruled that President Funes' appointments of two former military officials to the positions of minister of justice and public security and PNC, respectively, violated the constitutional requirement that those positions be staffed by civilian authorities. In July, the Chamber blocked the introduction of a new vehicle tax. In October, it declared unconstitutional the Legislative Assembly's selection of Salomón Padilla as president of the Supreme Court on the grounds that his previous political ties to the FMLN should have disqualified his selection.

Justice system officials continue to be criticized for brutality, corruption, arbitrary arrest, and lengthy pretrial detention. The country's prison system continues to operate at over 300 percent of its capacity, and nearly 30 percent of inmates have not been convicted of a crime. In September 2013, President Funes announced plans to reduce prison overcrowding by building a new prison, increasing space at an existing prison in Izalco, and expanding work farms and the use of electronic ankle bracelets.

The U.S. Treasury Department named MS-13 a transnational criminal organization in October 2012 and imposed sanctions on six Salvadoran leaders in June 2013 by adding them to its Specially Designated Nationals List. El Salvador remained one of the most violent countries in the hemisphere in 2013, though crime rates were down from their high in 2011. El Salvador has remained on the U.S. list of "major" drug producing and transit countries since 2011, and the country has been criticized for not attacking organized crime. In August, authorities arrested Roberto Herrerra of the Texis Cartel, and on September 17 additional cartel members, including a former legislator, a police inspector, and a public defender, were arrested.

Salvadoran law, including a 1993 general amnesty, bars prosecution of crimes and human rights violations committed during the civil war, but the authorities have faced criticism from NGOs and the Inter-American Court of Human Rights (IACHR) for failing to adequately investigate such crimes. The Constitutional Chamber of the Supreme Court announced in September that it would consider repeal or nullification of the law. The Attorney General's office also announced its intention to investigate several civil war era massacres including those at El Mozote and the Sumpul River. The Legislative Assembly elects a human rights ombudsman for a three-year term. David Morales was elected to the position in August.

G. Personal Autonomy and Individual Rights: 10 / 16

Discrimination on the basis of sexual orientation is widespread in El Salvador even though it is prohibited by law. Human rights NGO Comcavis Trans reported that four transgender women and one gay man had been killed as of September.

There are no national laws regarding indigenous rights. Access to land and credit remain a problem for indigenous people, along with poverty, unemployment, and labor discrimination. Businesses and private citizens are subject to regular extortion by organized criminal groups. While women are granted equal rights under the constitution, they are often discriminated against in practice, including in employment. Abortion is illegal, even when the life of the mother is at risk, and can be punishable by prison time. In May 2013, the Constitutional Chamber of the Supreme Court ruled to affirm this law, stating that the "rights of the mother cannot be privileged over the fetus." In July, a young woman was sentenced to 30 years in prison on charges of aggravated homicide for having an abortion. Violence against women, including domestic violence, is a serious problem. Several police officers were arrested in separate incidents in 2013 for abusing their wives or girlfriends, and an aide in the Legislative Assembly was convicted of assault against his girlfriend and sentenced to six years in prison in May. Despite governmental efforts, El Salvador remains a source, transit, and destination country for the trafficking of women and children for the purposes of prostitution and forced labor.

Equatorial Guinea

Political Rights Rating: 7
Civil Liberties Rating: 7
Freedom Rating: 7.0
Freedom Status: Not Free
Electoral Democracy: No

Population: 760,800
Capital: Malabo

Ten-Year Ratings Timeline For Year Under Review (Political Rights, Civil Liberties, Status)

Year Under Review	2004	2005	2006	2007	2008	2009	2010	2011	2012	2013
Rating	7,6,NF	7,6,NF	7,6,NF	7,6,NF	7,7,NF	7,7,NF	7,7,NF	7,7,NF	7,7,NF	7,7,NF

INTRODUCTION

In May 2013, Equatorial Guinea held elections for its lower house, the Chamber of Deputies, and its newly established Senate; it also held municipal elections. The results were a predictable landslide for the ruling Democratic Party of Equatorial Guinea (PDGE), with one member of the country's main opposition party, the Convergence for Social Democracy (CPDS), winning a seat in each chamber. Numerous opposition figures were summarily detained ahead of the elections and many other basic rights were curtailed.

The country's president, Teodoro Obiang Nguema Mbasogo, 71, is Africa's longest-serving head of state, having taken power in 1979 after deposing and executing his uncle, Equatorial Guinea's first president. His hold on power is considered absolute, and he is expected to run in the next presidential election, to be held in 2015 or 2016. In May 2012, Obiang appointed his eldest son, Teodoro Nguema Obiang Mangue, known as Teodorín, to the newly created post of second vice president, putting him second in line for the presidency and, according to the government, providing him with diplomatic immunity from international corruption charges. Teodorín faces money-laundering investigations by France and the United States. Another of Obiang's sons, Gabriel Mbega Obiang Lima, is minister of mines, industry, and energy, and is also viewed as a potential successor but with more moderate tendencies. Mbega's mother, who is Obiang's second wife, is from São Tomé and is not Fang, unlike the rest of the Obiang clan, which could prove an insurmountable obstacle to becoming president.

Equatorial Guinea is sub-Saharan Africa's third-largest oil producer, and hydrocarbons account for some three-quarters of its gross domestic product (GDP). The country has the continent's highest GDP per capita, yet it ranks 136 out of the 187 countries and territories in the 2013 UN Development Programme (UNDP) Human Development Index. According to the UNDP, per capita income in Equatorial Guinea increased more than 9-fold between 1985 and 2012, but the expected years of schooling for residents decreased to 7.9, from 8.7. The government has spent lavishly on selected infrastructure projects over the past five years, including work on a new capital, Oyala, located just west of Mongomo, the home city of Obiang and most of the rest of the political elite, near Equatorial Guinea's border with Gabon.

POLITICAL RIGHTS: 1 / 40
A. Electoral Process: 0 / 12

Under constitutional reforms approved in a November 2011 referendum, Equatorial Guinea replaced its unicameral system with a bicameral parliament consisting of a 70-seat Senate alongside a 100-seat Chamber of Deputies. Parliamentary and municipal elections were held on May 26, 2013, and Obiang's PDGE won 54 of the 55 contested Senate seats (Obiang appointed the remaining 15 members), and 99 of the 100 seats in the lower house. The CPDS, one of two opposition parties that independently contested the election, took the two seats that were not won by the PDGE, as well as the five local councilor slots did not go to the ruling party, of more than 300 nationwide.

Voting was held amid widespread reports of irregularities and intimidation of opposition members, and independent monitoring was very limited. Equatorial Guinea does not have an independent electoral body; the PDGE oversaw the National Election Commission, which was led by the country's interior minister, a prominent PDGE figure.

Obiang had swept the most recent presidential elections, in 2009, winning 95.4 percent of the vote. The election reportedly featured intimidation and harassment of the opposition by security forces and was widely regarded as rigged.

B. Political Pluralism and Participation: 1 / 16

Political opposition is limited and kept under strict control by the regime. The CPDS, the primary opposition party, is routinely denied access to the media and its access to campaign funds mandated by the constitution is routinely delayed.

The regime's control of the media, judiciary, police, and military make it difficult for new opposition groups to take hold within the country. Opposition figures are routinely detained for indefinite periods without arrest warrants. Membership in the PDGE is generally a prerequisite for government and many private-sector jobs, and the country's tiny middle class is kept mollified with generous fuel subsidies.

C. Functioning of Government: 0 / 12

Despite public praise of democracy and good governance by Obiang, progress toward these goals at home has been almost nonexistent, and graft is rampant. The constitutional changes approved in 2011 created a Court of Auditors to investigate corruption. Teodorín is under investigation by France and the United States for laundering tens of millions of dollars allegedly received through corruption in Equatorial Guinea, and using the proceeds to buy property and luxury goods.

Other members of Obiang's extended family have been placed in key government positions. According to the country's official website, there are nearly 90 ministers, vice ministers, and secretaries of state in a country with a population of just under 800,000, creating a ready source for patronage appointments.

The budget process is opaque, with even the most basic information difficult to find; the Open Budget Survey for 2012 gave the country a score of zero, the lowest possible result. The government generally negotiates directly with companies for oil concessions rather than awarding them on a competitive basis. Equatorial Guinea was delisted from the Extractive Industries Transparency Initiative in 2010, and has not reapplied.

CIVIL LIBERTIES: 7 / 60
D. Freedom of Expression and Belief: 4 / 16

Press freedom is severely limited in Equatorial Guinea, despite constitutional protections. Journalists who criticize the president, his family, or the security forces face reprisals and usually exercise self-censorship. Government press censorship is authorized by a 1992 law. Opposition party and exile group websites, along with Facebook, were blocked, presumably by the government, in the lead-up to the 2013 elections. Libel remains a criminal offense. There are only a handful of private newspapers or magazines, but they face intense financial and political pressure and are unable to publish regularly. The only private radio and television network belongs to the president's son, Teodorín. The government on occasion has imposed news blackouts about subjects such as the Arab Spring uprisings.

The constitution protects religious freedom, though in practice it is sometimes affected by the country's broader political repression. Official preference is given to the Roman Catholic Church and the Reform Church of Equatorial Guinea. Academic freedom is also politically constrained, and self-censorship among faculty is common. University professors and teachers have reportedly lost their positions due to their political affiliations; one such professor was Enrique Nsolo Nzo, who was fired from his post at the National University of Equatorial Guinea after being beaten, detained, and released without charge on May 8 while preparing a banner for a political demonstration. The government reportedly uses informants and electronic surveillance to monitor members of the opposition, nongovernmental organizations, and journalists, including the few members of the foreign press in the country.

E. Associational and Organizational Rights: 0 / 12

Freedom of association and assembly are severely restricted, making it difficult for civil society groups and trade unions to operate. Associations and political parties were required to register with the government through a difficult process. Requests for peaceful protests against the government ahead of the May 26 elections were denied and several organizers were detained. These included Clara Nsegue Eyí (also known as Lola Mba Ndong), a founder of the Democratic Party for Social Justice, which the government has refused to register. She was arrested on May 13 and sent back to the town where she was born, Mongomo, in the mainland section of the country. She was released two weeks later, but re-arrested in late June after she defied an order to remain in Mongomo and returned to the capital, Malabo, where she lived. She was held until October 9. During that time, she was never charged with an offense or brought before a court.

In June, a request by the CPDS to stage a protest rally in Malabo against the election results was turned down by the interior minister, who cited "substantial grounds for danger." Nevertheless, between 50 and 100 CPDS members demonstrated for half an hour outside their party headquarters in Malabo on June 25 before being dispersed by security forces. Several CPDS party members living in the country's mainland were prohibited by security forces for several days from flying to Malabo ahead of the planned demonstration.

The constitution provides for the right to organize unions, but there are many legal barriers to collective bargaining. While it has ratified key International Labour Organization conventions, the government has refused to register a number of trade unions. The country's only legal labor union is the Unionized Organization of Small Farmers.

F. Rule of Law: 0 / 16

The judiciary is not independent, and judges in sensitive cases often consult with the office of the president before issuing a ruling. The government continued its policy of arbitrary arrests and detentions without trial in 2013, often holding prisoners incommunicado. The government often uses charges of "destabilization" of the country to justify arrests of political opponents. Agustín Esono Nsogo, a teacher and relative of a cofounder of the opposition Popular Union party, was arrested in October 2012, and accused of such activities; he continues to be held without charge or trial.

Torture and excessive force by the police occur routinely, and graft is endemic in the security forces. Military justice still operates under a system dating back to General Francisco Franco's rule in Spain (Equatorial Guinea's colonial ruler until 1968), and civilians can face trial in military courts for certain offenses. Prisons—several of which are located on military bases—are overcrowded and conditions harsh. The central prison in Malabo, known as Black Beach, is located inside a former military compound. The death penalty is legal, although no executions have been reported since 2010.

While discrimination and stigma against LGBT (lesbian, gay, bisexual, and transgender) individuals exists, homosexuality is not illegal, and according to reports, discussions of sexual orientation are not completely off-limits.

G. Personal Autonomy and Individual Rights: 3 / 16

Freedom to travel within the country was impeded by the government. Equatorial Guinea has one of the most difficult business environments in the world. According to the World Bank's *Doing Business* report for 2014, the country required 18 steps and 135 days to start a business, ranking it 185 among 189 countries.

Constitutional and legal guarantees of equality for women are largely ignored. Women won 22 percent of the seats in the Chamber of Deputies in the 2013 elections. Violence against women is reportedly widespread.

The U.S. State Department's 2013 Trafficking in Persons report ranks Equatorial Guinea as a Tier 3 source and destination country for women and children trafficked for the purposes of forced labor and prostitution, particularly in Malabo and in Bata, the largest city on the mainland, and says the government does not fully comply with minimum standards to combat trafficking.

Eritrea

Political Rights Rating: 7
Civil Liberties Rating: 7
Freedom Rating: 7.0
Freedom Status: Not Free
Electoral Democracy: No

Population: 5,765,000
Capital: Asmara

Ten-Year Ratings Timeline For Year Under Review (Political Rights, Civil Liberties, Status)

Year Under Review	2004	2005	2006	2007	2008	2009	2010	2011	2012	2013
Rating	7,6,NF	7,6,NF	7,6,NF	7,6,NF	7,6,NF	7,7,NF	7,7,NF	7,7,NF	7,7,NF	7,7,NF

INTRODUCTION

President Isaias Afwerki's personal authority was publicly challenged in 2013 for the first time in more than a decade when, on January 21, more than 100 soldiers occupied the Ministry of Information, took over the state-run television channel, Eri-TV, and demanded democratic reforms, including the implementation of Eritrea's constitution and the release of thousands of political prisoners. The revolt was quelled within hours, as the government reportedly negotiated with the soldiers. Their message was pulled off the air mid-broadcast, and calm was restored following negotiations in which the soldiers agreed to return to their barracks. Reports suggest there were between 60 and 200 arrests in the days following the incident, though details are vague due to the intense secrecy surrounding the Eritrean regime.

Several other incidents in 2013 suggested that, for some, discontent with the regime was reaching a breaking point. A number of high-profile defections were confirmed, including Eritrea's former information minister, two senior Air Force pilots, and the national football team, all of whom left the country in late 2012. In October, more than 250 Eritreans and Somalis tragically drowned as they tried to reach the Italian island of Lampedusa in an overcrowded boat. Another 200 people were missing, and presumed dead. The incident illustrated to many the plight of ordinary Eritreans.

POLITICAL RIGHTS: 1 / 40

A. Electoral Process: 0 / 12

Following Eritrea's formal independence from Ethiopia in 1993, Isaias Afwerki was chosen by a Transitional National Assembly to serve as president until elections could be held. He has remained in charge ever since. His rule has become harshly authoritarian, particularly since the end of a bloody border war with Ethiopia in 2000.

A new constitution, ratified in 1997, called for "conditional" political pluralism and an elected 150-seat National Assembly, which would choose the president from among its members by a majority vote. This system has never been implemented, and national elections planned for 2001 have been postponed indefinitely. The Transitional National Assembly is comprised of 75 members of the ruling party—the People's Front for Democracy and Justice (PFDJ)—and 75 elected members. In 2004, regional assembly elections were conducted, but they were carefully orchestrated by the PFDJ and offered no real choice to voters.

B. Political Pluralism and Participation: 0 / 16

Created in 1994, the PFDJ is the only legal political party. The PFDJ and the military are in practice the only institutions of political significance in Eritrea, and both entities are strictly subordinate to the president.

C. Functioning of Government: 1 / 12

Corruption is a major problem. The government's control over foreign exchange effectively gives it sole authority over imports, and those in favor with the regime are allowed to profit from the smuggling and sale of scarce goods such as building materials, food, and alcohol. According to the International Crisis Group, senior military officials are the chief culprits in this trade. The UN Eritrea and Somalia Monitoring Group has accused senior officers of running a lucrative criminal network smuggling people and arms out of the country.

The government operates without public scrutiny and few outside a small clique around the president have any insight into how policy and budget decisions are made and implemented.

CIVIL LIBERTIES: 2 / 60

D. Freedom of Expression and Belief: 0 / 16

The law does not allow independent media to operate in Eritrea, and the government controls all broadcasting outlets. A group of 10 journalists arrested in 2001 remains imprisoned without charge, and the government refuses to provide any information on their status. According to the Committee to Protect Journalists, at least 28 journalists were in prison in Eritrea at the end of 2012. In September 2013, a dissident group drawing inspiration from January's army mutiny said it had begun circulating an underground newspaper in Asmara written by a team based inside and outside the country.

The government controls the internet infrastructure and is thought to monitor online communications. Foreign media are available to those few who can afford a satellite dish.

The government places strict limits on the exercise of religion. Since 2002 it has officially recognized only four faiths: Islam, Orthodox Christianity, Roman Catholicism, and Lutheranism as practiced by the Evangelical Church of Eritrea. Members of Evangelical and Pentecostal churches face persecution, but the most severe treatment is reserved for Jehovah's Witnesses, who are barred from government jobs and refused business permits or identity cards. According to Amnesty International, members of other churches have been jailed and tortured or otherwise ill-treated to make them abandon their faith. As many as 3,000 people from unregistered religious groups are currently in prison because of their beliefs. Abune Antonios, patriarch of the Eritrean Orthodox Church, has been under house arrest since speaking out against state interference in religion in 2006.

Academic freedom is constrained. Students in their last year of secondary school are subject to obligatory military service. Academics practice self-censorship and the government interferes with their course content and limits their ability to conduct research abroad. Eritrea's university system has been effectively closed, replaced by regional colleges whose main purposes are military training and political indoctrination. Freedom of expression in private discussions is limited. People are guarded in voicing their opinions for fear of being overheard by government informants.

E. Associational and Organizational Rights: 0 / 12

Freedoms of assembly and association are not recognized. The government maintains a hostile attitude toward civil society, and independent nongovernmental organizations (NGOs) are not tolerated. A 2005 law requires NGOs to pay taxes on imported materials, submit project reports every three months, renew their licenses annually, and meet government-established target levels of financial resources. The six remaining international NGOs that had been working in Eritrea were forced to leave in 2011. The government placed strict controls on UN operations in the country, preventing staff from leaving the capital.

The government controls all union activity. The National Confederation of Eritrean Workers is the country's main union body and has affiliated unions for women, teachers, young people, and general workers.

F. Rule of Law: 0 / 16

The judiciary, which was formed by decree in 1993, is understaffed, unprofessional, and has never issued rulings at odds with government positions. Most criminal cases are heard by the Special Court, composed of PFDJ loyalists chosen by the president himself. The International Crisis Group has described Eritrea as a "prison state" for its flagrant disregard of the rule of law and its willingness to detain anyone suspected of opposing the regime, usually without charge, for indefinite periods. In 2013, the UN High Commissioner for Human Rights reported that there were between 5,000 and 10,000 political prisoners in Eritrea. They include surviving members of a group of ruling party-members who publicly criticized Afwerki in May 2001. Eleven of them were arrested for treason, along with a number of journalists, but were never charged. Many of the jailed dissidents and journalists were subsequently reported to have died in custody, but the government refuses to divulge information about them.

Torture, arbitrary detentions, and political arrests are common. Prison conditions are harsh, and outside monitors such as the International Committee of the Red Cross are denied access to detainees. Juvenile prisoners are often incarcerated alongside adults. In some facilities, inmates are held in metal shipping containers or underground cells in extreme temperatures. Prisoners are often denied medical treatment. The government maintains a network of secret detention facilities.

The Kunama people, one of Eritrea's nine ethnic groups, face severe discrimination. LGBT (lesbian, gay, bisexual, and transgender) individuals face legal and social discrimination due to the criminalization of same-sex sexual relations.

G. Personal Autonomy and Individual Rights: 2 / 16

Freedom of movement, both inside and outside the country, is tightly controlled. Eritreans under the age of 50 are rarely given permission to go abroad, and those who try to travel without the correct documents face imprisonment. The authorities adopt a shoot-on-sight policy toward people found in locations deemed off-limits, such as mining facilities and areas close to the border. Eritrean refugees and asylum seekers who are repatriated from other countries are also detained. These strict penalties fail to deter tens of thousands of people from risking their lives to escape the country each year.

Government policy is officially supportive of free enterprise, and citizens are in theory able to choose their employment, establish private businesses, and operate them without harassment. In reality, a conscription system ties most able-bodied men and women to obligatory military service and can also entail compulsory labor for enterprises controlled by the political elite. The official 18-month service period is frequently open-ended in practice, and conscientious-objector status is not recognized. The government conducted raids in several cities in October 2013, detaining young men of fighting age and sending them to military training camps. Reports suggest as many as 1,500 men were seized in Asmara alone. The government imposes collective punishment on the families of deserters, forcing them to pay heavy fines or putting them in prison. The enforced contraction of the labor pool, combined with a lack of investment and rigid state control of private enterprise, has crippled the national economy. The government levies a compulsory 2 percent tax on income earned by citizens living overseas, and those who do not pay place their relatives back home at risk of arrest.

Women hold some senior government positions, including four ministerial posts. The government has made attempts to promote women's rights, with laws mandating equal educational opportunity, equal pay for equal work, and penalties for domestic violence. However, traditional societal discrimination against women persists in the countryside. While female genital mutilation was banned by the government in 2007, the practice remains widespread in rural areas.

The U.S. State Department's 2013 Trafficking in Persons Report ranks Eritrea at Tier 3, describing it as a source country for individuals subjected to forced labor and sexual exploitation.

Estonia

Political Rights Rating: 1
Civil Liberties Rating: 1
Freedom Rating: 1.0
Freedom Status: Free
Electoral Democracy: Yes

Population: 1,283,000
Capital: Tallinn

Ten-Year Ratings Timeline For Year Under Review (Political Rights, Civil Liberties, Status)

Year Under Review	2004	2005	2006	2007	2008	2009	2010	2011	2012	2013
Rating	1,1,F	1,1,F	1,1,F	1,1,F	1,1,F	1,1,F	1,1,F	1,1,F	1,1,F	1,1,F

INTRODUCTION

Diminishing support for Prime Minister Andrus Ansip's pro-business Reform Party was reflected in local elections held in October, which the left-leaning Center Party won, taking roughly 32 percent of the vote nationwide and maintaining control of the city council in Tallinn. Reform won only 14 percent, and its coalition partner, Pro Patria and Res Publica won about 17 percent. The Social Democrats finished fourth, with 12 percent of the vote.

There were a number of allegations during the run-up to the elections that the Center Party had used public funds to pay for parts of its election campaign. Just prior to the elections, a former member of the Center Party alleged that the party's current deputy chair had been involved in a money-laundering scheme. Meanwhile, the vast majority of lawmakers in the Riigikogu, or parliament, registered to stand in the municipal elections. Known in Estonia as "decoy ducks," these high-profile politicians sign up for local polls in order to boost voter turnout for their respective parties, and have no intention of actually accepting municipal posts. The practice has drawn criticism by some for confusing voters and potentially distorting the political process in Estonia's municipalities.

The Reform Party struggled with corruption allegations in 2013. Senior party members have been implicated in a business corruption scandal involving a now-defunct company owned by the environment minister's father. In December, Culture Minister Rein Lang resigned amid allegations that he had improperly installed one of his allies as the editor in chief of an independent newspaper.

POLITICAL RIGHTS: 39 / 40
A. Electoral Process: 12 / 12

The 1992 constitution established a 101-seat, unicameral Riigikogu, whose members are elected for four-year terms. A prime minister serves as head of government, and is chosen by the president and confirmed by the parliament. The president is elected by parliamentary ballot to a five-year term, filling the largely ceremonial role of head of state. Observers have deemed recent elections free and fair.

In parliamentary elections held in March 2011, the Reform Party won 33 seats, with its coalition partner, the Union of Pro Patria and Res Publica (IRL), capturing 23 seats. The opposition Center Party took 26 seats, and the Social Democratic Party (SDE) won 19 seats. In August 2011, the parliament reelected President Toomas Hendrik Ilves to a second five-year term. The parliament in April rejected legislation, backed by the Center Party, which would have amended the constitution to allow for direct presidential elections.

The Reform Party performed poorly in the 2013 municipal elections, while the Center Party posted strong results. Igor Gräzin, a Reform Party MP, suggested in a November interview that voters had become disenchanted with the governing party due to slow economic growth in Estonia and because the party had failed to effectively articulate a clear vision for the country.

B. Political Pluralism and Participation: 15 / 16

Estonia's political parties organize and operate freely, though only citizens may be members. The conservative, pro-business Reform Party has dominated the government since 2007. However, support for the Reform Party declined markedly in 2013 in the wake of corruption scandals, including a high-profile 2012 financing scandal, and due to Prime Minister Andrus Ansip's continued support for European Union (EU) bailout packages for heavily indebted EU member nations; Estonia has contributed some €2 billion to back such efforts. The left-leaning Center Party draws much of its support from Estonia's Russian-speaking population. The Center Party and the SDE, respectively, were the first- and second-most popular parties in the country in 2013, according to opinion polls.

Only citizens may participate in national elections; as a result, ethnic Russian residents of Estonia whose citizenship remains undetermined cannot vote in national polls. Resident noncitizens are permitted to vote in local elections, but may not run as candidates.

C. Functioning of Government: 12 / 12

There are occasional problems with government corruption in Estonia. Over the past two years, there have been heavily publicized allegations of money laundering within both the Reform Party and the Center Party, but no criminal convictions have followed. In March, the daily *Postimees* reported that Center Party head and Tallinn mayor Edgar Savisaar had requested the resignations of four Tallinn officials because they had not returned 5 percent of their gross wages to the Center Party, which all Tallinn city officials who belonged to the party were apparently obliged to do under a 2005 agreement. The revelations prompted allegations of influence-peddling, but prosecutors declined to pursue a criminal case. In October, just ahead of municipal elections, former Center Party member Tarmo Lausing alleged that he during the 2000s had aided in the funneling of some €20,000 (US$27,200) of unclear origin to the Center Party at the request of Kadri Simson, a member of parliament and the Center Party's current deputy chair. Prosecutors declined to pursue the allegations, saying the statute of limitations had expired. A similar scandal within the Reform Party had erupted in 2012 and led to the resignation of Justice Minister Kristen Michal, but an investigation into that controversy was abandoned due to a lack of evidence. In October, the Riigikogu began debating a slate of campaign-finance reforms that included a provision requiring parties to release financial reports more frequently; the proposed reforms were in part the result of a public-input program Ilves had initiated following 2012 financial scandals.

Separately, top members of the Reform Party including Environment Minister Keit Pentus-Rosimannus have been implicated in the so-called Autorollo case, a corruption case involving a defunct trucking company that had been owned by Pentus-Rosimannus's father. However, senior government officials only rarely face corruption trials. There were a number of successful corruption prosecutions against local officials in 2013. Estonia was ranked 28 out of 177 countries and territories surveyed in Transparency International's 2013 Corruption Perceptions Index.

CIVIL LIBERTIES: 56 / 60

D. Freedom of Expression and Belief: 16 / 16

The government generally respects freedom of the press. However, in December, culture minister Rein Lang of the Reform Party resigned amid allegations that he had pressured the independent newspaper *Sirp* to install one of his allies as its new editor. Lang denied that he was stepping down in connection with those claims. Public and private television and radio stations operate in Estonia, and there are a number of independent newspapers, including at least one in Russian. In November 2010, lawmakers passed a measure authorizing fines for outlets that disseminated news deemed libelous, as well as for journalists who refused to reveal sources under certain circumstances. It is illegal in Estonia to insult court officials or police officers in connection with their official responsibilities, but in July legislation decriminalizing such speech was introduced. The Tartu County Court, in separate rulings in February and March, issued suspended jail sentences and lengthy probation terms against individuals who had posted to the internet insults against a prominent judge. In October a judge banned investigative journalist Katariina Krjutškova of the business daily *Äripäev* from sitting in on court proceedings for the Autorollo case over claims that Krjutškova had disrespected the court in a recent article. In May, the Tallinn city government said it would pursue a civil defamation suit against *Äripäev*, days after the newspaper had published details of a bribery case that had concluded with the 2012 convictions of two Tallinn city officials. The *Äripäev* reports suggested that senior members of the city hierarchy were behind the bribery scheme, and Tallinn officials argued that the newspaper had damaged the city, its government, and its residents. However, the Harju County Court threw out the case in October and ordered the Tallinn government to pay *Äripäev*'s legal fees.

In October, the European Court of Human Rights (ECHR) ruled that the Estonian news website Delfi SA was responsible under Estonian defamation laws for the content of anonymous comments left on its stories, in part because Delfi had a commercial interest in maintaining a robust comment section. A spokeswoman for the ECHR indicated that the decision applied only to details of Estonian law and did not create a precedent applicable in other countries. International anticensorship activists nevertheless expressed concern over the ruling.

In May, the European Commission referred Estonia to the European Court of Justice, saying that the Ministry of Economic Affairs, which regulates Estonia's telecommunication sector, could not also own the largest television and radio broadcast network operator in the country, Levira. The ministry had indicated earlier in the year that it would sell Levira but has yet to do so.

Religious freedom is respected in law and in practice.

A public school teacher in Narva who planned to run in local elections as an SDE candidate resigned in September, claiming that his job had been threatened for political reasons by the school's principal, a member of the Center Party. A 2011 law mandated that public, Russian-language high schools must teach 60 percent of their curriculum in the Estonian language. In July, the government rejected a petition from Tallinn's city council to allow four public secondary schools in the city to waive that requirement.

E. Associational and Organizational Rights: 12 / 12

The constitution guarantees freedoms of assembly and association, and the government upholds those rights in practice. Civil society is vibrant, and the government involves nongovernmental organizations and ordinary citizens in the drafting of legislation. Workers may organize freely, strike, and bargain collectively, although public servants at the municipal and state levels may not strike. The Confederation of Estonian Trade Unions has reported private-sector violations of union rights, including workers being threatened with dismissal or pay cuts if they formed unions.

F. Rule of Law: 14 / 16

The judiciary is independent and generally free from government interference. Laws prohibiting arbitrary arrest and detention and ensuring the right to a fair trial are largely observed. The Justice Ministry reported in May that legal procedures for criminal and misdemeanor cases accelerated significantly in 2012 following various reforms; the average length of pretrial detention also reportedly decreased in 2012. The country's prison system continues to suffer from overcrowding and prisoners have poor access to health care.

In March, the ECHR ruled that Estonia must pay a combined total of about €50,000 to four men who claimed that Estonian authorities had abused them when they were detained following a 2007 riot that accompanied the relocation of a Soviet-era World War II memorial in Tallinn. The ECHR found that Estonian authorities had violated one plaintiff's right to protection against ill-treatment, and had failed to adequately investigate his and three other plaintiffs' allegations of ill-treatment at the hands of authorities.

Though women enjoy the same legal rights as men, Estonia has the largest gender pay gap in the EU, with women earning about 28 percent less than men per hour.

G. Personal Autonomy and Individual Rights: 14 / 16

Estonia's constitution allows citizens and noncitizens holding government-issued identity documents to travel inside Estonia and abroad. Though corruption in the business sector is problematic, Estonian residents enjoy a high level of economic freedom.

Violence against women, including domestic violence, remains a problem. Estonia is a source, transit point, and destination for women trafficked for the purpose of prostitution. Estonia criminalized human trafficking in 2012, becoming the last EU country to do so.

In August 2012, the Justice Ministry released a draft of a new law that would allow same-sex couples to register their cohabitation, allowing same-sex couples some protections that married opposite-sex couples receive. Despite support from the Reform Party and the SDE it has not advanced, and faces opposition from the IRL and some religious groups.

Ethiopia

Political Rights Rating: 6
Civil Liberties Rating: 6
Freedom Rating: 6.0
Freedom Status: Not Free
Electoral Democracy: No

Population: 89,200,000
Capital: Addis Ababa

Ten-Year Ratings Timeline For Year Under Review (Political Rights, Civil Liberties, Status)

Year Under Review	2004	2005	2006	2007	2008	2009	2010	2011	2012	2013
Rating	5,5,PF	5,5,PF	5,5,PF	5,5,PF	5,5,PF	5,5,PF	6,6,NF	6,6,NF	6,6,NF	6,6,NF

INTRODUCTION

Despite a relatively smooth political transition following the 2012 death of Prime Minister Meles Zenawi, the Ethiopian government in 2013 continued harassing and imprisoning political opponents, journalists, and the country's Muslim population under Meles's successor, Hailemariam Desalegn of the ruling Ethiopian People's Revolutionary Democratic Front (EPRDF).

Tensions with Eritrea showed signs of easing in 2013, after Ethiopia announced a willingness to hold peace talks. Though no formal dialogues were held, domestic and regional developments suggested a possible movement toward normalization of relations. Ethiopian troops had carried out a series of incursions into Eritrea in 2012—the first since the end of the war in 2000—reportedly in pursuit of rebels responsible for kidnapping a group of foreign tourists in Ethiopia's Afar region.

Violence resumed in Ethiopia's Ogaden region in 2013 after talks failed between the government and the Ogaden National Liberation Front (ONLF), a separatist group that has fought for independence since 1991. Talks between the government and the ONLF had been convened in Kenya but broke down in 2012 without agreement. In October 2013, the ONLF conducted a series of attacks against Ethiopian military posts that resulted in the deaths of 24 Ethiopian soldiers.

Ethiopia ranked 33 out of 52 countries surveyed in the Mo Ibrahim Index of African Governance, below average on the continent and among the bottom in the East Africa region. The country's modest gains in the index are largely due to its improvement in human development indicators; its lowest score was in the category of Participation and Human Rights.

POLITICAL RIGHTS: 7 / 40

A. Electoral Process: 1 / 12

Ethiopia's Parliament is made up of a 108-seat upper house, the House of Federation, and a 547-seat lower house, the House of People's Representatives. The lower house is filled through popular elections, while the upper chamber is selected by the state legislatures; members of both houses serve five-year terms. The lower house selects the prime minister, who holds most executive power, and the president, a largely ceremonial figure who serves up to two six-year terms. In October 2013, Mulatu Teshome, Ethiopia's ambassador to Turkey, was selected as Ethiopia's new president.

The 2010 parliamentary and regional elections were tightly controlled by the EPRDF. Voters were threatened with losing their jobs, homes, or government services if they did not turn out for the ruling party. Opposition meetings were broken up, and candidates were threatened and detained. Opposition-aligned parties saw their 160-seat presence in Parliament virtually disappear, with the EPRDF and its allies taking all but two of the 547 seats in the lower house. Hailemariam will remain prime minister until elections in 2015.

B. Political Pluralism and Participation: 2 / 16

Shorn of their representation in Parliament and under pressure by the authorities, opponents of the EPRDF find it difficult to operate. Opposition parties held peaceful demonstrations in June 2013, the first to be allowed by the government since 2005. Later in the year, however, opposition parties—including the Blue Party and the Unity for Democracy and Justice Party—accused the government of arresting large groups of their members and holding them without charge.

Political parties are often ethnically based. The EPRDF coalition is comprised of four political parties representing several ethnic groups. The government tends to favor Tigrayan ethnic interests in economic and political matters, and the EPRDF is dominated by the Tigrayan People's Liberation Front. While the 1995 constitution grants the right of secession to ethnically based states, the government acquired powers in 2003 to intervene in states' affairs on issues of public security.

C. Functioning of Government: 4 / 12

All of Ethiopia's governance institutions are dominated by the EPRDF, which tightly controlled the succession process following the death of Meles in 2012.

Corruption remains a significant problem in Ethiopia. EPRDF officials reportedly receive preferential access to credit, land leases, and jobs. Petty corruption extends to lower level officials, who allegedly solicit bribes in return for processing documents. In 2013, the

Ethiopian government attempted to demonstrate its commitment to fighting corruption after the release of a World Bank study the previous year that detailed corruption in the country. As part of the effort, the Federal Ethics & Anti-Corruption Commission (FEACC) made a string of high-profile arrests of prominent government officials and businessmen throughout the year. In October, Hailemariam opened the conference of the National Anti-Corruption Coalition, outlining a national anticorruption strategy and urging other officials to support the initiative. Ethiopia ranked 111 out of 177 countries and territories surveyed in Transparency International's 2013 Corruption Perceptions Index.

CIVIL LIBERTIES: 11 / 40

D. Freedom of Expression and Belief: 3 / 16

The media is dominated by state-owned broadcasters and government-oriented newspapers. One of the few independent papers in the capital, *Addis Neger*, closed in 2009, claiming harassment by the authorities. Privately owned papers tend to steer clear of political issues and have low circulations. In 2013, three news outlets were either banned or shut down indefinitely. A 2008 media law criminalizes defamation and allows prosecutors to seize material before publication in the name of national security. According to the Committee to Protect Journalists (CPJ), Ethiopia had the second-highest number of jailed journalists in Africa after Eritrea as of December 2013. Restrictions on journalists perceived to be sympathetic to widespread protests by the Muslim community are particularly tight. In August 2013, Darsema Sori and Khalid Mohammed of Radio Bilal, which has covered the demonstrations, were arrested and held without charge.

Journalists reporting on opposition activities face serious harassment and the threat of prosecution under Ethiopia's sweeping 2009 Antiterrorism Proclamation. An estimated 11 journalists have been convicted under the law since 2011, three of whom remained in prison in 2013. Two additional journalists remain on trial under the law. In September 2013, Reeyot Alemu, a *Feteh* newspaper columnist serving a five-year sentence on terrorism charges at Kaliti prison, undertook a four-day hunger strike to protest visitation restrictions and threats of solitary confinement. Reeyot's health is said to have deteriorated significantly in prison. In July 2012, six journalists were convicted of terrorism. While five were convicted in absentia, the sixth, Eskinder Nega, received 18 years in prison. The judge said that he had consorted with the political group Ginbot 7, a designated terrorist entity in Ethiopia. The United States, the European Union, and the UN High Commissioner for Human Rights expressed dismay at the verdicts. The UN Working Group on Arbitrary Detention characterized Eskinder's detention as a violation of international law and recommended his "immediate release." He continued to publish from prison in 2013, appearing in both the *New York Times* and the *Guardian*. Both Eskinder and Reeyot's cases are being appealed to the African Commission on Human and Peoples' Rights under the African Union.

Due to the risks of operating inside the country, many Ethiopian journalists work in exile. CPJ says Ethiopia has driven 49 journalists into exile in the past 5 years. Authorities use high-tech jamming equipment to filter and block news websites seen as pro-opposition. Legislation adopted in May 2012 criminalizes the use of telecommunications devices to transmit any "terrorizing message." Critics said the vaguely worded law also effectively banned the use of Skype and other voice-over-internet protocol services that cannot be closely monitored by the government. According to Human Rights Watch (HRW), since 2010 the Ethiopian government has developed a robust and sophisticated internet and mobile framework to monitor journalists and opposition groups, block access to unwanted websites, and collect evidence for prosecutions in terrorism and other trials.

The constitution guarantees religious freedom, but the government has increasingly harassed the Muslim community, which has grown to rival the Ethiopian Orthodox Church as the country's largest religious group. Muslim groups accuse the government of trying to impose the beliefs of an obscure Islamic sect, Al-Ahbash, at the expense of the dominant Sufi-influenced strain of Islam. Before his death, Meles accused the Muslim community of being a source of extremism, claiming it had links to Al-Qaeda.

Academic freedom is often restricted in Ethiopia. The government has accused universities of being pro-opposition and prohibits political activities on campuses. There have been reports of students being pressured into joining the EPRDF in order to secure places at universities. The Ministry of Education closely monitors and regulates official curricula, and the research, speech, and assembly of both professors and students is frequently restricted. In March 2013, authorities arrested Addis Ababa University student Manyazewal Eshetu for posting "unconfirmed information" after he wrote about government corruption on his Facebook page. Manyazewal was later released without charge.

The presence of the EPRDF at all levels of society inhibits free private discussion. Many people are wary of speaking against the government for fear of being overheard by party officials. The EPRDF maintains a network of paid informants, and opposition politicians have accused the government of tapping their telephones.

E. Associational and Organizational Rights: 0 / 12

Freedoms of assembly and association are guaranteed by the constitution but limited in practice. Organizers of large public meetings must request permission from the authorities 48 hours in advance. Applications by opposition groups are routinely denied. Ongoing peaceful demonstrations have been held by members of the Muslim community since December 2011 with violent responses from security forces. The protesters allege government interference in religious affairs and politically motivated selection of members of the Ethiopian Islamic Affairs Supreme Council. Tens of thousands participated in demonstrations following Eid holiday prayers in August; the protesters were met with a heavy-handed police response that resulted in hundreds of arrests and an unconfirmed number of deaths. Twenty-nine demonstration leaders have been charged under the antiterrorism law with conspiracy and attempting to establish an Islamic state; their trial remains ongoing. Trial proceedings have been closed to the public, media, and the individuals' families. According to HRW, some defendants claimed that they have been restricted access to legal counsel. Though momentum has slowed, protests remain ongoing.

The 2009 Charities and Societies Proclamation restricts the activities of foreign nongovernmental organizations (NGOs) by prohibiting work on political and human rights issues. Foreign NGOs are defined as groups receiving more than 10 percent of their funding from abroad, a classification that includes most domestic organizations as well. NGOs have struggled to maintain operations as a result of the law, which also requires them to reregister with the authorities. According to Justice Ministry figures, there were 3,522 registered NGOs before the law was passed. Estimates of the number of NGOs since the passage of the law ranged from 1,500 to 1,700 as of the end of 2013. In 2010, the Human Rights Council (HRCO) and the Ethiopian Women Lawyers' Association (EWLA) had their bank accounts frozen for violating the rules on receiving foreign funds. An appeal against the ruling by the HRCO was rejected by the Supreme Court in October 2012. Both organizations have dramatically reduced their operations. As of 2013, HRCO shut down three-quarters of its offices and shed 85 percent of its staff, while the EWLA scaled down its staff by 70 percent.

Trade union rights are tightly restricted. Neither civil servants nor teachers have collective bargaining rights. All unions must be registered, and the government retains the authority to cancel registration. Two-thirds of union members belong to organizations affiliated with the Confederation of Ethiopian Trade Unions, which is under government influence. Independent unions face harassment, and trade union leaders are regularly imprisoned. There has not been a legal strike since 1993.

F. Rule of Law: 3 / 16

The judiciary is officially independent, but its judgments rarely deviate from government policy. The 2009 antiterrorism law gives great discretion to the security forces, allowing the detention of suspects for up to four months without charge. It was used in 2011 to detain more than 100 members of opposition parties; terrorist suspects were denied legal assistance while they awaited trial. In April 2013, nearly 30 individuals suspected of having links to Al-Qaeda and the Somali Islamist group Al-Shabaab were charged under the antiterrorism law. Conditions in Ethiopia's prisons are harsh, and detainees frequently report abuse. A HRW report released in October 2013 documented human rights violations in Addis Ababa's Maekelawi police station, including verbal and physical abuse, denial of basic needs, and torture.

Domestic NGOs estimated that there were up to 400 political prisoners by the end of 2012, though estimates vary significantly. In August 2013, Tesfahun Chemeda, an engineer who had been sentenced to life in prison in 2010 for holding political views that dissented from the EPRDF, died in Kaliti prison. He had reportedly been tortured repeatedly, and human rights groups have called for an investigation into his death.

Repression of the Oromo and ethnic Somalis, and government attempts to co-opt their parties into subsidiaries of the EPRDF, have fueled nationalism in both the Oromia and Ogaden regions. Persistent claims that war crimes have been committed by government troops in the Ogaden area are difficult to verify, as independent media are barred from the region.

G. Personal Autonomy and Individual Rights: 5 / 16

Private business opportunities are limited by rigid state control of economic life and the prevalence of state-owned enterprises. All land must be leased from the state. The government has evicted indigenous groups from various areas to make way for projects such as hydroelectric dams. It has also leased large tracts of land to foreign governments and investors for agricultural development in opaque deals. Up to 70,000 people have been forced to move from the western Gambella region, although the government denies the resettlement plans are connected to land investments. Journalists and international organizations have persistently alleged that the government has withheld development assistance from villages perceived as being unfriendly to the ruling party.

Women are relatively well represented in Parliament, holding 28 percent of seats and three ministerial posts. Legislation protects women's rights, but they are routinely violated in practice. Enforcement of the law against rape and domestic abuse is patchy, with cases routinely stalling in the courts. In December 2012, the government made progress against forced child labor, passing a National Action Plan to Eliminate the Worst Forms of Child Labor and updating its list of problematic occupations for children. Same-sex sexual activity is prohibited by law and punishable with imprisonment.

Fiji

Political Rights Rating: 6
Civil Liberties Rating: 4
Freedom Rating: 5
Freedom Status: Partly Free
Electoral Democracy: No

Population: 860,000
Capital: Suva

Ten-Year Ratings Timeline For Year Under Review (Political Rights, Civil Liberties, Status)

Year Under Review	2004	2005	2006	2007	2008	2009	2010	2011	2012	2013
Rating	4,3,PF	4,3,PF	6,4,PF	6,4,PF	6,4,PF	6,4,PF	6,4,PF	6,4,PF	6,4,PF	6,4PF

INTRODUCTION

In September 2013, interim president Ratu Epeli Nailatikau signed a new Fijian constitution into law. The document was submitted in March by Prime Minister Frank Bainimarama to replace a draft developed by an independent committee the previous year. The new constitution will create a parliament with a single chamber, elected through proportional representation, and is expected to pave the way for parliamentary elections.

Opposition groups criticized some aspects of the new constitution, particularly a provision to grant amnesty to all involved in Fiji's 2006 coup, which Bainimarama led. Opponents also say it does not provide sufficient protections for civil rights and liberties, and that the government did not provide a long enough period of public comment.

Fiji's ties with Australia and New Zealand—traditional trade partners and major aid donors—improved as the country moved closer to holding elections. Formal ties with both countries were restored in July 2012. In 2013, Australia pledged to increase bilateral aid by 18 percent to $57 million for fiscal year 2013–2014, while New Zealand lifted travel restrictions and restored academic aid for Fijian students.

POLITICAL RIGHTS: 7 / 12

A. Electoral Process: 0 / 12

The interim government has essentially ruled by decree since the military overthrew the civilian government of Laisenia Qarasa in December 2006.

The new constitution, signed into law in September 2013, provides for a single 50-member chamber of parliament with a national constituency that is selected through a proportional representation system. This replaces the old two-tier system. No ethnic group has any reserved seats or receives preferential treatment. The party with the greatest number of seats will select one of its own members as prime minister to head a government. The president is elected from parliament between two candidates—one each named by the prime minister and leader of the opposition. As head of state, the president holds largely a ceremonial role to represent the government in an annual speech to the parliament on its programs and policies, for example. The president can hold two three-year terms and can only be removed for inability or misbehavior by a tribunal appointed by the Chief Justice at the Prime Minister's request. The parliament has a four-year term. The voting age was lowered to 18 years. Citizens overseas can vote, but only those residing in Fiji can run in elections.

Parliamentary elections are expected in September 2014. A Canadian firm was hired to create a new voter roll. Registration has been taking place at hundreds of sites throughout Fiji since June 2012, and embassies have been registering voters overseas since September 2012. A new election office website began operation in February 2013 to provide updates on the registration process and to allow voters to verify their registration for accuracy. By year end, more than 540,000 voters had registered to vote including 588 Fijians in New Zealand, and permanent registration centers had opened in major locations across Fiji. The interim government has said it will establish a full-time professional elections office to conduct elections and educate voters.

B. Political Pluralism and Participation: 5 / 16

Political affiliations tend to be associated with ethnicity: Indo-Fijians mostly support the Labour Party while indigenous Fijians back the United Fiji Party (UFP). All political parties are also required to have English names to appeal to all ethnic groups; in January 2013, Soqosoqo Duavata ni Lewenivanua changed its name to the Social Democratic Liberal Party (SDL).

On January 14, 2013, the interim government passed the Political Parties (Registration) Conduct Funding and Disclosure Decree to require all political parties to register by February 18, 2013, in order to participate in the 2014 elections. Critics say the registration period is too short and that the new requirement is to block them from running in the 2014 elections. In late May, four parties—Labour, the National Federation, SDL, and the People's Democratic Party—were approved, while leaders of the United People's Party and the National Alliance Party had to dissolve the two groups because they could not meet registration requirements. In June 2013, three of the four parties almost lost their approved status after initial failure to pay *Fiji Sun* to publish their party asset declarations. The interim government designated *Fiji Sun* as the only place to publish these financial reports. The three political parties argued that they should be free to publish their financial statements in other newspapers or there should have been an open, competitive bid among vendors for this contract. Bainimarama has said he will form a political party and contest in the 2014 elections.

C. Functioning of Government: 2 / 12

Official abuse and corruption are serious problems. Numerous officials have been removed from office for abuse and corruption charges by the interim government, though opponents have criticized the government for not living up to its own standards regarding transparency and accountability. Bainimarama, for example, has refused to disclose his income and assets, and has blocked the publication of military budgets and government finances since he took power in 2006.

CIVIL LIBERTIES: 30 / 60
D. Freedom of Expression and Belief: 11 / 16

The interim government has improved Fiji's communications infrastructure, expanded electronic access to government services, and expanded public access to the Internet by reducing costs and opening public Internet centers across the country, even winning a special recognition from the International Telecommunication Union in February 2013. Nevertheless, it has maintained its hard-line approach to controlling the media. In February 2013, the *Fiji Times* and its editor-in-chief were fined, respectively, $169,000 and $5,600 for contempt of court for republishing a November 2011 article from a New Zealand newspaper that questioned the independence and integrity of the Fijian judiciary. The editor-in-chief was also sentenced to six months in prison. One month later, the *Fiji Times* and its six directors were charged with breach of the Media Industry Development Decree of 2010, which requires Fijian citizenship and permanent residence for all directors. One director did not reside in Fiji during his tenure, and the newspaper was fined $2,700 in May 2013.

In August 2013, the Citizens' Constitutional Forum and the editor of its newsletter were found in contempt of court for criticizing the judiciary in an article published the previous year. The high court imposed a $20,000 fine and sentenced the editor to a three-month prison sentence.

Freedom of religion is generally respected, though the interim government has restricted the activities of religious organizations that have spoken out against it. In 2010 and 2011, permits for the Methodist Church—the largest in Fiji—to hold its annual conference were withheld and church officials were banned from traveling overseas to attend church meetings and conferences. The permits were granted in 2012 and 2013 and the travel restrictions lifted; in September 2013, the church announced it would no longer allow its ministers to voice political views.

Most indigenous Fijians are Christians; Indo-Fijians are generally Hindus. Ethnic tensions have made Hindu temples targets of violence, though there were no reports of attacks in 2013.

While academic freedom is generally respected, the education system suffers from a lack of resources. The interim government has been dismantling the old system, which gave preferential treatment to indigenous Fijians in college admission, scholarships, and other areas.

E. Associational and Organizational Rights: 3 / 12

The interim government has severely restricted freedom of assembly and association. The lifting of public emergency regulations in June 2012, however, allowed meetings to be held without a permit as long as they were not held in public spaces. Relations between the interim government and labor unions and other groups critical of the government have been tense. The Essential National Industries Decree of 2011 limited trade union and collective bargaining rights for those employed in industries that are considered essential to Fiji's economy, including the sugar industry, the airline industry, utility companies, banks, and telecommunication firms. The decree banned strikes in these industries under a penalty of $50,000 or five years in jail, and required that all union officials be employees of the company whose workers they represented.

F. Rule of Law: 6 / 16

Dismissal of judges following the 2009 suspension of the constitution and their replacement by appointees of the interim government have raised questions about judicial independence. The dismissals also exacerbated an already serious backlog of cases. A new tax court was launched in March 2013 to fast-track cases, though resources were insufficient.

Police misconduct is a problem. Prisons are overcrowded and have poor sanitary and living conditions. A new detention center opened in the capital in July 2013, and has provided some relief.

The new constitution has been criticized for granting the government too much leeway to carry out pretrial detentions, as well as for providing immunity to government officials for torture and other human rights violations. Those involved in the 2006 coup, too, would be granted amnesty.

Indigenous Fijians receive preferential treatment in many areas. A 2011 study reported that an estimated 250,000 Fijians—many of them educated and skilled Indo-Fijians—had left the country in the last 25 years because of discrimination, economic hardship, and political instability. Nevertheless, the interim government recognizes indigenous land rights and amended the Land Act in February 2013 to bar further conversion of native lands to freehold status.

G. Personal Autonomy and Individual Rights: 10 / 16

Fiji was the first Pacific Island nation to decriminalize homosexuality in 2010 when the interim government abolished anti-sodomy laws. The new 2013 constitution also bans discrimination based on sexual orientation and gender identity. However, conservative social mores and absence of explicit anti-discrimination protections mean the LGBT community continues to suffer from discrimination and violence.

Discrimination and violence against women are also widespread. A study by the Fiji Women's Crisis Center released in December 2013 reported widespread violence against women in Fiji, including more than 60 percent of all Fijian women have been victims of violence in domestic relationships. The interim government has pledged greater equality and protection for women. It also said it would increase the number of female police officers by 15 percent and place more women in front line and leadership positions; the first female police division chief was appointed in January 2013. The interim government has also pledged to provide greater medical services for battered women and children, and to train health workers to coordinate medical management, referrals, counseling, and treatment to victims of abuse and violence.

Fiji is a source country for the trafficking of children for sexual exploitation and a destination for the trafficking of men and women for forced labor and prostitution. The first human trafficking for prostitution case was heard in February 2013, and the International Labor Organization is assisting investigation of 121 case of child labor. A new crime unit was launched in May 2013 to monitor the movement of Chinese migrants in Fiji, who have been repeatedly linked to human trafficking, money laundering, prostitution, and other illegal activities. The Chinese community has assailed the policy as discriminatory.

Finland

Political Rights Rating: 1
Civil Liberties Rating: 1
Freedom Rating: 1.0
Freedom Status: Free
Electoral Democracy: Yes

Population: 5,440,000
Capital: Helsinki

Ten-Year Ratings Timeline For Year Under Review (Political Rights, Civil Liberties, Status)

Year Under Review	2004	2005	2006	2007	2008	2009	2010	2011	2012	2013
Rating	1,1,F	1,1,F	1,1,F	1,1,F	1,1,F	1,1,F	1,1,F	1,1,F	1,1,F	1,1,F

INTRODUCTION

The year 2013 saw no notably dramatic political developments in Finland. An employer-union agreement on wages was reached in 2013 that affected almost all Finnish workers, and the left-leaning parties in the government coalition suffered from defending unpopular austerity measures and not supporting the trade unions. The controversial right-wing, euroskeptic opposition Finns Party (formerly "The True Finns Party") consolidated their political gains in 2013, including with a high-profile but unsuccessful vote of no-confidence against Prime Minister Jyrki Katainen over his role in commissioning a €700,000 ($955,000) report without a competitive bidding process. True Finns remained the third most popular party according to opinion polls at the end of the year, having risen to second place for some of the year.

The debate—both public and within the government—about the European Union's economic bailouts for heavily indebted eurozone members continued in 2013. The solvent Finns, seeing themselves as fiscally prudent, expressed frustration at sending funds to southern European countries perceived as less financially responsible. Finland is the only country in the EU that has reserved the right to put any bailout to a parliamentary vote. A bill approving the Spanish bailout package passed Parliament in July 2012, with a comfortable majority and was widely considered a confidence vote on Katainen's government. The government survived a confidence vote raised by the Finn's Party brought on by the Cyprus bailout package, although less comfortably.

POLITICAL RIGHTS: 40 / 40
A. Electoral Process: 12 / 12

The president, whose role is mainly ceremonial, is directly elected for a six-year term. The president appoints the prime minister and deputy prime minister from the majority party or coalition after elections; the selection must be approved by Parliament. Representatives in the 200-seat unicameral Parliament, or Eduskunta, are elected to four-year terms. Finland joined the European Union (EU) in 1995 and is the only Nordic country to have adopted the euro as its currency.

The so-called rainbow coalition currently in government is led by Prime Minister Jyrki Katainen of the moderate conservative National Coalition Party (KOK); the coalition comprises the KOK, the Social Democratic Party (SDP), the Left Alliance, the Green League, the Swedish People's Party, and the Christian Democrats. Pro-EU and pro-euro former finance minister Sauli Niinistö of the KOK handily won the presidency in February 2012, defeating the Green League candidate, Pekka Haavisto, with 63 percent to 37 percent of the vote. Elections are considered free and fair.

B. Political Pluralism and Participation: 16 / 16

Finland boasts a robustly free political environment with a strong opposition free to organize on every political level. The Åland Islands—an autonomous region located off the southwestern coast whose inhabitants speak Swedish—have their own 30-seat Parliament, as well as a seat in the national legislature. The indigenous Sami of northern Finland also have their own legislature, but are not represented in the Eduskunta.

C. Functioning of Government: 12 / 12

Corruption is not a significant problem in Finland, which was ranked 3 out of 177 countries surveyed in Transparency International's 2013 Corruption Perceptions Index. However, the Chancellor of Justice in September 2013 found that there had been a lack of transparency and good governance practices in the government's commissioning of a report, without launching a competitive bidding process, for which it paid €700,000 ($955,000). A parliamentary inquiry into the issue in June had absolved Katainen of any legal wrongdoing. A court in April 2012 had found Parliament member and former foreign minister Ikka Kanerva guilty of accepting bribes and neglecting his official duties as chairman of the Regional Council of Southwest Finland's managing board, and handed down a 15-month suspended jail sentence. Three codefendants received harsher sentences. A 2010 law requires candidates and parties to report campaign donations of more than €800 ($1,030) in local elections or €1,500 ($1,930) in parliamentary elections.

CIVIL LIBERTIES: 60 / 60
D. Freedom of Expression and Belief: 16 / 16

Finnish law provides for freedom of speech, which is respected in practice. Finland has a large variety of newspapers and magazines and protects the right to reply to public criticism. Newspapers are privately owned but publicly subsidized, although at a lower level than in neighboring Scandinavian countries. Many are controlled by or support a particular political party. In 2012 and 2013, a new value added tax on subscriptions to newspapers and magazines contributed to financial difficulties for this sector. In March 2010, the Finnish police launched an internet tip-off system in an effort to simplify the process of reporting threats of violence and racist slander.

Finns enjoy freedom of religion. The Evangelical Lutheran Church and the Orthodox Church are both state churches and receive public money from the income taxes of members; citizens may exempt themselves from contributing to those funds, but must renounce their membership. Religious communities other than the state churches may also receive state funds. Religious education is part of the curriculum in all secondary public schools, but students may opt out in favor of more general instruction in ethics. Academic freedom is respected.

E. Associational and Organizational Rights: 12 / 12

Freedoms of association and assembly are upheld in law and in practice. Workers have the right to organize and bargain collectively, though public sector workers who provide services deemed essential may not strike. Approximately 70 percent of workers belong to trade unions. In October 2013, a 2-year deal covering 93 percent of all Finnish workers was finalized between the three biggest Trade Union Confederations, the Central Organisation of Finnish Trade Unions (SAK), the Confederation of Unions for Professional and Mangerial Staff (AKAVA), the Finnish Confederation of Salaried Employees (STTK), and the Confederation of Finnish Industries (EK), providing very minor wage increases. Exempt from the agreement by choice are Finnair and the cabin crew union SLSY, which were intermittently continuing their own negotiations and on strike at year's end.

F. Rule of Law: 16 / 16

The constitution provides for an independent judiciary. The president appoints Supreme Court judges, who in turn appoint lower-court judges. Finland has been criticized by the European Court of Human Rights for slow trial procedures. The Ministry of the Interior controls police and Frontier Guard forces. Ethnic minorities and asylum seekers report occasional police discrimination. The criminal code covers ethnic agitation and penalizes anyone who threatens a racial, national, ethnic, or religious group. In October 2013, retail magnate Juha Kärkkäinen was sentenced to 90 income-based day fines for anti-Semitic writings that appeared in his free newspaper *Magneetti Media*. A 2012 ruling by the country's Supreme Administrative Court led to a new interpretation of Finland's immigration law that might allow several hundred rejected asylum seekers to stay in Finland and receive residency permits if their home countries refuse to receive forcible deportations. A little over half of all the asylum applications ruled on in 2013 were rejected.

Immigration issues remained divisive in 2013, in part fueled by the rapid political ascent of the True Finns starting in 2011. The political identity of the True Finns on the subject of immigration remains a controversial subject, both within and outside the party. While leader Timo Soini has sought to maintain a more moderate stance on immigration, several high-profile party members who serve in Parliament also belong to the nationalist group Suomen Sisu. True Finns MP Olli Immonen became the group's chair in March 2013. This faction has expressed fierce disagreement with the party leadership on the immigration issue. Controversial MP James Hirvisaari was expelled from the True Finns in October 2013 for posting pictures online of a friend performing a Nazi salute in Parliament; his expulsion was interpreted by some as an effort to shift the party's image toward the political mainstream.

However, the True Finns' main political emphasis in 2012 and 2013 was on opposition to EU bailouts rather than immigration.

The constitution guarantees the Sami people cultural autonomy and the right to pursue their traditional livelihoods, which include fishing and reindeer herding. Their language and culture are also protected through public financial support. However, representatives of the community have complained that they cannot exercise their rights in practice and that they do not have the right to self-determination with respect to land use. While Roma also make up a very small percentage of the population, they are more significantly disadvantaged and marginalized.

G. Personal Autonomy and Individual Rights: 16 / 16

Property rights, intellectual as well as physical, are upheld in Finland. Finland has one of the most expansive legal definitions of "Freedom to Roam" in the world. Provided the privacy of a private residence is not violated and no environmental damage is incurred, anybody is free to use any land, public and private, for outdoor recreation purposes, without having to seek permission beforehand. There are no major obstacles to establish business, which boasts a well-regulated, transparent and open economy.

Women enjoy equal rights in Finland. Women hold approximately 43 percent of the seats in Parliament, and 9 of 19 cabinet ministers are women. Despite a law stipulating equal pay for equal work, women earn only about 85 percent as much as men with the same qualifications. Domestic violence is an ongoing concern. Legislation to legalize same-sex marriage in Finland was voted down in a parliamentary committee in February 2013. A citizens' initiative was then drafted and signed by over 167,000 Finns, leading to the presentation of a same-sex marriage bill to Parliament in December. An amendment to the constitution in 2012 allowed for citizens' initiatives, which required Parliament to consider petitions that attracted more than 50,000 signatures. Finland is the only Nordic country not to have legalized same-sex marriage. Finland remains a destination and a transit country for trafficked men, women, and children. Amendments to the Alien Act in 2006 allow trafficked victims to stay in the country and qualify for employment rights.

France

Political Rights Rating: 1
Civil Liberties Rating: 1
Freedom Rating: 1.0
Freedom Status: Free
Electoral Democracy: Yes

Population: 63,851,000
Capital: Paris

Ten-Year Ratings Timeline For Year Under Review (Political Rights, Civil Liberties, Status)

Year Under Review	2004	2005	2006	2007	2008	2009	2010	2011	2012	2013
Rating	1,1,F	1,1,F	1,1,F	1,1,F	1,1,F	1,1,F	1,1,F	1,1,F	1,1,F	1,1,F

INTRODUCTION

President François Hollande of the center-left Socialist Party (PS) continued to struggle with a weak economy in 2013, a year after he won the presidency by defeating incumbent Nicolas Sarkozy of the center-right Union for a Popular Movement (UMP). In May,

Parliament approved labor reform legislation backed by Hollande that allowed businesses more leeway to fire employees or reduce pay and hours during economic downturns, in exchange for better benefits for workers on short-term contracts, which had become the most common means of hiring new workers. However, Hollande faced criticism for not taking stronger measures to revive the economy and reduce unemployment, which remained over 10 percent through the end of 2013.

The issue of the integration of immigrants and Muslims into French society—a priority since youth riots swept the nation's cities in 2005—remained prominent throughout 2013, as a ban on Islamic head scarves in public spaces led to a number of violent incidents. The government deported nearly 20,000 Roma immigrants in 2013, double the previous year's total.

In April, the National Assembly passed legislation to legalize gay marriage. Hollande signed the law in May despite months of mass protests by opponents of the measure.

POLITICAL RIGHTS: 38 / 40
A. Electoral Process: 12 / 12

The French president and members of the lower house of Parliament, the 577-seat National Assembly, are elected to five-year terms. The upper house, the 348-seat Senate, is an indirectly elected body whose members serve six-year terms. The prime minister is appointed by the president. In April 2012, Hollande won the first round of the presidential election with 28.6 percent of the vote, ahead of Sarkozy, who took 27.2 percent. Marine Le Pen, the daughter of Jean-Marie Le Pen and his successor as head of the far-right National Front, placed third, with 17.9 percent. Hollande won the election in a runoff against Sarkozy in May, with 51.6 percent of the vote to Sarkozy's 48.4 percent, becoming France's first Socialist president since François Mitterrand left office in 1995.

In June 2012, the PS and its allies won an absolute majority of 314 seats in the National Assembly, while the UMP and its allies took 229 seats. In 2011, the PS had taken control of the Senate for the first time in the history of France's Fifth Republic.

B. Political Pluralism and Participation: 15 / 16

Parties organize and compete on a free and fair basis. The center-left PS and the center-right UMP are the largest parties, though the far-right, anti-immigration National Front party receives significant support. National Front leader Marine Le Pen won nearly 18 percent of the vote in the first round of the 2012 presidential election, placing third behind Hollande and Sarkozy. Since taking over the FN in 2011, Le Pen has sought to give it a new image as a mainstream party.

The 2012 parliamentary elections yielded a record eight new members from immigrant backgrounds. However, they comprised just 2 percent of the new National Assembly, prompting renewed calls from minority rights groups for a law ensuring ethnic diversity in politics.

C. Functioning of Government: 11 / 12

In 2010, Labor Minister Éric Woerth was accused of corruption for allegedly accepting illegal donations from L'Oréal heiress Liliane Bettencourt on behalf of Nicolas Sarkozy's 2007 presidential campaign. In March 2013, Sarkozy was placed under formal investigation on a charge of "exploiting the frailty" of Bettencourt by soliciting donations from her after she was declared to be suffering from dementia. The case against Sarkozy was dropped in October, though 10 others, including Woerth, still face trial in the case. Sarkozy's campaign organization was still under criminal investigation for allegedly accepting money from then Libyan leader Muammar al-Qaddafi in 2007.

International Monetary Fund managing director Christine Lagarde, who served as finance minister in Sarkozy's cabinet, was questioned by French judges in May 2013 over her decision to send a case involving businessman Bernard Tapie, a Sarkozy backer, to arbitration in 2007. Tapie had won a judgment of 285 million euros ($366 million) after suing the government for fraud over a 1993 deal in which he sold his stake in sporting goods maker Adidas to Credit Lyonnais, a bank that was state-owned at the time. Tapie was arrested in June 2013 and placed under formal investigation for fraud.

Budget Minister Jérôme Cahuzac, who had led the Hollande government's crackdown in tax evasion, resigned in March 2013 after being placed under investigation for tax fraud and money laundering. Cahuzac admitted on April 2 that he had lied to Hollande and Parliament by denying reports that he held secret bank accounts in Switzerland and Singapore. Later that month, at Hollande's order, all 38 members of his cabinet publicly declared their assets. France was ranked 22 out of 177 countries and territories surveyed in Transparency International's 2013 Corruption Perceptions Index.

CIVIL LIBERTIES: 57 / 60
D. Freedom of Expression and Belief: 15 / 16

The media operate freely and represent a wide range of political opinions. Though an 1881 law forbids "offending" various personages, including the president and foreign heads of state, the press remains lively and critical. Reporters covering criminal cases or publishing material from confidential court documents have occasionally come under pressure by the courts to reveal their sources.

While internet access is generally unrestricted, a domestic security law, which came into effect in March 2011, allows the filtering of online content. A separate March 2011 decree requires internet companies to provide user data, including passwords, to authorities if requested. In July 2013, Twitter said it gave Paris prosecutors data that could identify users who posted anti-Semitic comments in 2012. Several activist groups, including the French Union of Jewish Students and SOS Racisme, had sued Twitter to force it to identify those who had posted the messages under pseudonyms.

Freedom of religion is protected by the constitution, and strong antidefamation laws prohibit religiously motivated attacks. Denial of the Nazi Holocaust is illegal. France maintains the policy of *laïcité,* whereby religion and government affairs are strictly separated. A 2004 law bans "ostentatious" religious symbols in schools.

In October 2010, the Senate nearly unanimously passed a bill banning clothing that covers the face, including the burqa and niqab, in public spaces. The ban went into effect in April 2011. Violators of the ban can be fined up to €150 (US$215) or ordered to take citizenship lessons, and a man who forces a woman to wear a niqab can be fined €30,000 (US$43,000). In March 2013, the Court of Cassation, France's highest appeals court, ruled that a Muslim woman had been illegally dismissed in 2007 for wearing a head scarf to work at a private child care center in a Paris suburb. In June 2013, two men attacked a pregnant Muslim woman wearing a head scarf in the Paris suburb of Argenteuil, shouting anti-Islamic slurs and cutting off her hair; she suffered a miscarriage. Rioting broke out in the immigrant neighborhood Trappes in the Paris suburbs on July 18, 2013, after police stopped a woman for wearing a veil covering her face. A 16-year-old girl in Trappes filed charges accusing two skinheads of attacking her on August 13 for wearing a head scarf. In August, *Le Monde* reported that the official High Council for Integration had proposed a new ban on wearing religious symbols, including head scarves, at universities, citing "growing tensions" over religious differences on campuses.

On July 2, 2013, a committee of the European Parliament voted to remove the legal immunity of National Front leader Marine Le Pen, a member of the legislature, in order to allow prosecutors to pursue charges brought against her in 2011 for incitement of hatred and discrimination. The case concerned a 2010 speech in which she compared Muslims praying in the streets to the German occupation of France in World War II. A controversial September 2011 directive banned street prayer.

Academic freedom is respected by French authorities.

E. Associational and Organizational Rights: 12 / 12

Freedoms of assembly and association are respected. In June 2013, authorities in Toulouse barred a rally by a far-right youth group, following the death of a leftist student who had been beaten in a clash between far-left and far-right youths in Paris.

Nongovernmental organizations can operate freely. Trade union organizations are strong despite fractionalization, declining density and a lack of legal protections relative to more corporatist European countries.

F. Rule of Law: 15 / 16

France has an independent judiciary, and the rule of law is firmly established. Prisons are overcrowded, and suicides are common. The country's antiterrorism campaign has included surveillance of mosques, and terrorism suspects can be detained for up to four days without charge.

In July 2013, *Le Monde* reported that the French foreign intelligence service, the General Directorate for External Security (DGSE), was collecting data on nearly all communications, including telephone calls, e-mails, and social media posts, sent in and out of France. The report came days after Hollande rebuked the United States for using similar data collection methods to spy on allies including France, a practice revealed by documents leaked by former U.S. National Security Agency contractor Edward Snowden. In October, the government again made official protests after *Le Monde* reported that the NSA had intercepted some 70 million telephone communications in France in one 30-day period from December 2012 to January 2013.

French law forbids the categorization of people according to ethnic origin. No official statistics are collected on ethnicity, but minorities are underrepresented in leadership positions in both the private and public sectors. In May 2013, the National Assembly approved legislation to ban the word "race" from the penal code, fulfilling a campaign pledge by Hollande. In March 2013, the independent French Consultative Commission on Human Rights reported that the number of racist acts reported to police rose by more than 23 percent in 2012, and cited growing intolerance toward immigrants.

In 2013, France reportedly deported a record 19,380 Roma, up from about 9,400 in 2012 and 6,400 in 2011, increasing sharply under Hollande despite his previous criticism of Sarkozy for such expulsions. After Valls said in September that most Roma were incapable of integrating into French society and should be deported, the European Commission warned France that it could face sanctions if it did not respect the rights of Roma as European Union citizens. In October, police took a 15-year-old Roma girl, high school student Leonarda Dibrani, off a school bus to be deported with her family to Kosovo. Responding to criticism of her treatment, Hollande said she would be allowed to return to France to continue her education if she wished—but without her family.

Corsica continues to host a sometimes-violent separatist movement. In 2001, the government devolved some legislative powers to the island and allowed teaching in the Corsican language in public schools. As of 2013, Corsica had the highest murder rate in Europe.

G. Personal Autonomy and Individual Rights: 15 / 16

Gender equality is protected in France, and constitutional reforms in 2008 institutionalized economic and social equality. However, in the 2013 Global Gender Gap report, France ranked the lowest (tied with Mauritania) among countries that responded to a question on wage equality. Some electoral lists require the alternation of candidates by gender. After the 2012 elections, women held a record 27 percent of seats in the National Assembly. Women hold 22 percent of Senate seats, and have served in key cabinet posts, as well as serving as prime minister.

Discrimination based on sexual orientation is prohibited by law. In April 2013, the National Assembly approved legislation to legalize same-sex marriage, despite mass protests by conservative opponents, including a Paris demonstration that drew at least 340,000 people (according to police) in January. Hollande signed the bill into law on May 18, a day after the Constitutional Council rejected a legal challenge by the UMP. France became the 14th nation in the world to make gay marriage legal, and the ninth in Europe.

Right groups and academic studies have reported evidence of labor market discrimination against French Muslims, reflected in hiring patterns and income differentials.

Gabon

Political Rights Rating: 6
Civil Liberties Rating: 5
Freedom Rating: 5.5
Freedom Status: Not Free
Electoral Democracy: No

Population: 1,601,495
Capital: Libreville

Ten-Year Ratings Timeline For Year Under Review (Political Rights, Civil Liberties, Status)

Year Under Review	2004	2005	2006	2007	2008	2009	2010	2011	2012	2013
Rating	5,4,PF	6,4,PF	6,4,PF	6,4,PF	6,4,PF	6,5,NF	6,5,NF	6,5,NF	6,5,NF	6,5,NF

INTRODUCTION

Local and regional elections took place on December 14, with the president's dominant Gabonese Democratic Party (PDG) retaining an overwhelming majority of seats. Biometric identification was used for the first time, and election observers say more than 50 percent of eligible voters went to the polls, up sharply from the last municipal elections in 2008.

The discovery in March of a young girl's mutilated body on a beach in Libreville reignited public anger about ritual killings, and in May first lady Sylvia Bongo Ondimba led a march of several thousand people against the practice. The government banned a concurrent demonstration organized by nongovernmental organizations (NGOs) with close ties to the opposition who said the government was not doing enough to prevent the practice. Several leaders of the banned march were arrested. In June, a senator was arrested and accused of ordering the ritual murder of a 12-year-old girl.

Gabon's president, Ali Bongo Ondimba, has spent a great deal of effort trying to prove that he is different than his father, whom he succeeded after four decades in office, reducing the size of the presidential cabinet and eliminating ghost workers from the public payroll. But the government is still mired in corruption, and the country's oil revenue wealth still ends up disproportionately benefiting a wealthy elite. Despite ambitious growth plans and one of the highest per capita incomes in sub-Saharan Africa, Gabon's human development indicators remain well below average for a middle-income county. Public impatience is growing at the country's poor infrastructure—especially outside of Libreville—water shortages, and frequent power cuts.

POLITICAL RIGHTS: 9 / 40
A. Electoral Process: 2 / 12

The 120 members of the National Assembly are elected by popular vote for five-year terms, while members of the 91-seat Senate are indirectly elected by regional and municipal officials for six-year terms. Presidential term limits were abolished in 2003, and the president, who is elected by popular vote for seven years, can dissolve the National Assembly. President Omar Bongo died in June 2009 after 41 years in power. In snap presidential elections the following August, his son Ali was elected with 42 percent of the vote against several senior PDG figures, who ran as independents. Although the opposition challenged the official results amid violent protests, the Constitutional Court upheld Bongo's victory following a recount the next month.

National Assembly elections in 2011 were boycotted by some opposition parties over the government's failure to implement biometric technology for voter registration, and the ruling PDG won all but seven seats. Five of the remaining seven seats went to parties allied with the PDG, while opposition parties Union for the New Republic (UPNR) and the Social Democratic Party (PSD) took one seat each. Small parties hold the remaining seats.

Regional and municipal elections were held on December 14, and the results were a predictable landslide for the ruling PDG, which claimed 1,517 of the 2,404 council seats nationwide. Although the PDG was the only party to have a candidate in each of the country's 122 constituencies, it failed to win a majority everywhere, including the northern Fang stronghold of Oyem and in the economic capital Port-Gentil, where it won 36 out of the 73 councilor seats. For the first time, voters used biometric registration.

B. Political Pluralism and Participation: 4 / 16

The government is dominated by the PDG, which has held power since it was formed in 1968. Political opposition is fragmented and weak, and many opposition parties are effectively under the umbrella of the ruling PDG. The principal opposition party, the National Union, was dissolved in January 2011 after it claimed victory in the 2009 presidential election and established a parallel government. Though banned, the party maintains its headquarters, but it is not allowed to organize public meetings. It has been in disarray since the death of its president in October 2011.

Some 20 opposition parties formed a loose coalition, the Union of Forces of Change (UFC) in September, 2012, but within months that group splintered amid accusations that some of the opposition parties were too conciliatory. A new group of about a dozen parties, the Union of Forces for an Alternative (UFA), was formed. Several leading opposition figures at one time were part of the government of Omar Bongo and are believed to have personally profited from his rule.

C. Functioning of Government: 3 / 12

President Bongo has taken several measures to lessen corruption, including contracting the American construction giant Bechtel to run the National Infrastructure Agency in an effort to lessen the possibility of kickbacks and bribes from domestic ministries. In September, the government announced that a corruption investigation had uncovered some 3,000 fake civil servants out of the 70,000-person civil service.

While the country's anticorruption commissioner says he has scores of open cases, the requisite special tribunal to try anticorruption cases has not been established. Graft is widespread. Investigations in other countries, especially France and the United States, have revealed extensive patronage under Omar Bongo's regime.

In February, after five years of trying to obtain approval, Gabon was delisted as a candidate from the Extractive Industries Transparency Initiative (EITI) because it failed to submit a validation report. It is no longer recognized as an EITI implementing country. Gabon was ranked 106 out of 177 countries and territories surveyed in Transparency International's 2013 Corruption Perceptions Index.

CIVIL LIBERTIES: 25 / 60

D. Freedom of Expression and Belief: 10 / 16

Press freedom is guaranteed by law. The only two daily newspapers are both government owned, although there are some two dozen private weeklies and monthlies and half a dozen private radio and television stations. While criticism of the government is usually permitted, most journalists practice self-censorship, and the National Communications Council (NCC), the government's main regulatory body, rarely permits criticism of the president.

In May, the NCC suspended two newspapers for six months each for lack of respect: the private weekly *Ezombolo* because of an April 22 column that criticized Bongo's record in office, and the satirical supplement *Le Gri-Gri de la Griffe* for indecency. It also suspended newspaper *La Calotte* for two months after it published articles critical of a minister and a deputy minister.

In March, environmental activist Marc Ona Essangui was sentenced to a six-month suspended sentence for defamation. During a November 2012 television debate, Ona accused Bongo's chief of staff, Liban Souleymane, of having a controlling interest in Olam Gabon, a joint-venture between a Singaporean agricultural company and Gabon that is believed to be worth more than $200 million. Olam has been accused of land grabbing and environmental damage in Gabon. The contract is not public. Internet access is not restricted by the government.

Religious freedom is enshrined in the constitution and largely upheld by the authorities. The government does not directly restrict academic freedom.

E. Associational and Organizational Rights: 4 / 12

The rights of assembly and association are legally guaranteed, and NGOs are an important counterweight to the lack of an effective opposition. Generally, NGOs are free to investigate and report on civil liberties abuses. But their numbers are small. In addition, public protests must be approved by the government and harsh tactics have been used by security forces to keep order. There are several Facebook forums in which opposition to the government by Gabonese inside the country is expressed.

Unions are relatively strong, and the private industrial sector is almost entirely unionized. However, union members are occasionally blacklisted and there have been threats to workers who have supported labor unions. The country's powerful oil union, the National Organization of Oil Employees (ONEP), staged a one-week strike in March to protest the country's high numbers of undocumented oil workers.

F. Rule of Law: 6 / 16

The judiciary is not independent, and is subject to political influences. Prison conditions are harsh and there is severe overcrowding in the country's nine prisons. Pre-trial detention is often lengthy.

Legal prohibitions against arbitrary arrest and detention are not always observed. In October, a student at Omar Bongo University who was a leader in campus protest movements, Firmin Ollo Obiang, was arrested by the General Directorate of Investigations (DGR), the country's internal security force, and held for just under a week. An anonymous complaint accused him of disrupting public order.

The country's large population of African immigrants is subject to harassment and extortion, especially during roundups by security forces. Most of Gabon's several thousand members of the indigineous Baka ethnic group live in extreme poverty in remote forest communities and are often exploited as cheap labor.

Bias against lesbian, gay, bisexual, and transgender (LGBT) persons remained an issue, and most members of the LGBT community chose to keep their identities a secret to avoid housing and employment discrimination. But there were no reports of violence directed at any LGBT members.

G. Personal Autonomy and Individual Rights: 5 / 16

International attention in 2013 focused on an upsurge in ritual killings, which often peak before elections because certain body parts, including genitals, are believed to enhance strength. Senator Gabriel Eyeghe Ekomie was stripped of his parliamentary immunity in December 2012 after a man convicted of killing a young girl told the court he had done so on the senator's orders. Eyeghe Ekomie was arrested in June after failing to appear in court, the first time a senior politician in Gabon has been detained in such a case.

Gabon's relatively stable economy makes it far easier than elsewhere for traffickers to lure young women under 18 to the country. Teenagers from Mali, Benin, and Togo are trafficked into Gabon and forced to do manual labor, while girls are sent to households or brothels without their consent and made to work without pay. The Walk Free Foundation describes this as "modern slavery"; in its 2013 Global Slavery Index it ranked Gabon tenth in the world in the prevalence of slavery, with an estimated 13,000 to 14,000 people enslaved. There are a relatively large number of women in senior government and private sector positions. However, there is no law against sexual harassment, rape is rarely prosecuted, and there is no specific mention of spousal rape in the law.

⬇ Gambia

Political Rights Rating: 6
Civil Liberties Rating: 6
Freedom Rating: 6.0
Freedom Status: Not Free
Electoral Democracy: No

Population: 1,884,155
Capital: Banjul

Trend Arrow: The Gambia received a downward trend arrow due to worsening restrictions on civil liberties, including amendments to the Information and Communications Act and the Criminal Code Act that further limited open and free private discussion, and a ban on the use of Skype and other voice communication programs in internet cafés.

Ten-Year Ratings Timeline For Year Under Review (Political Rights, Civil Liberties, Status)

Year Under Review	2004	2005	2006	2007	2008	2009	2010	2011	2012	2013
Rating	4,4,PF	5,4,PF	5,4,PF	5,4,PF	5,4,PF	5,5,PF	5,5,PF	5,6,NF	6,6,NF	6,6,NF

INTRODUCTION

The government's repression of opposition leaders and journalists continued in 2013. Two legal reforms—an amendment to the media code restricting internet freedom and an amendment to the criminal code increasing fines for providing "false information" to public servants—further narrowed the space for journalists and civil society to operate.

Baba Leigh, an imam who criticized President Yahya Jammeh's decision to execute nine death row inmates in 2012, was released in April 2013 after five months of detention without charge. Jammeh continues to denounce sexual minorities in the name of Islam. Changes to the criminal code have made sexual minorities' personal freedoms more precarious.

POLITICAL RIGHTS: 7 / 40

A. Electoral Process: 2 / 12

The president is elected by popular vote for unlimited five-year terms. Of the 53 members of the unicameral National Assembly, 48 are elected by popular vote, with the remainder appointed by the president; members serve five-year terms. Elections are violent and rigged. In the run-up to the November 2011 presidential poll, the government-controlled Independent Electoral Commission (IEC) installed a new biometric voter registration system, though it stated that 1,897 voters had nonetheless registered at least twice. The IEC failed to share the electoral register with opposition parties, significantly shortened the campaign period, and hampered the ability of opposition parties to campaign. Clashes between opposition supporters and the ruling Alliance for Patriotic Reorientation and Construction (APRC) during the campaign resulted in three deaths. Jammeh secured his fourth term as president with 72 percent of the vote; opposition parties rejected the results as fraudulent. The Economic Community of West African States (ECOWAS) refused to send election observers, while the Commonwealth Observer Group said the elections were fundamentally flawed.

After the denial of an opposition request to postpone the March 29, 2012, legislative elections to ensure a level playing field, six of the seven opposition parties boycotted this vote. Facing no opposition for over half of the available seats, the ARPC won 43 seats, the National Reconciliation Party captured 1 seat, and independent candidates took the remaining 4 seats. Observers from the African Union noted irregularities, including a "gross imbalance" between the resources of the ARPC and other parties and the presence of security personnel and traditional chiefs in polling stations. ECOWAS again refused to send observers.

B. Political Pluralism and Participation: 5 / 16

Jammeh's government continues to repress opposition. Visiting opposition websites has been outlawed since April 2012. Ousainou Darboe of the opposition United Democratic Party (UDP) has claimed that public servants may be fired for being sympathetic to the opposition. In August, Dodou Kassa Jatta—who had run as an independent in the 2012 legislative elections—fled the country. Sources reported that he believed that security forces would murder him in a ritual sacrifice. UDP activist Momodou Lamin Shyngle Nyassi was told by the minister of presidential affairs that he would be arrested if he returned to The Gambia from the United States, where he was on tour with Darboe. Malang Fatty, a political opponent seeking asylum abroad, was arrested in September along with those assisting him: Amadou Sanneh, national treasurer of the UDP; Fatty's brother, who asked Sanneh to write a letter promoting Fatty's case for asylum; and the commissioner of oaths who authorized the letter. The government allegedly tortured the detainees and televised their forced confessions to political offenses.

C. Functioning of Government: 0 / 12

Official corruption remains a serious problem. In 2012, Jammeh's focus on economic development led to increased anticorruption efforts, including the establishment of an

Anti-Corruption Commission and the sentencing of several high-ranking security officials on drug and corruption charges. However, several sentenced officials eventually re-joined the government after paying fines, and government officials allegedly participated in the trafficking of drugs through the country. The Gambia was ranked 127 out of 177 countries and territories surveyed in Transparency International's 2013 Corruption Perceptions Index.

CIVIL LIBERTIES: 14 / 60 (-2)
D. Freedom of Expression and Belief: 4 / 16 (-1)

The government does not respect freedom of the press. Laws on sedition give the authorities discretion in silencing dissent, and independent media outlets and journalists are subject to harassment, arrest, and violence. Three UDP leaders were convicted of sedition in July 2013 after one leader had attempted to seek asylum abroad after alleging that he had been subject to death threats by the Gambian government. In July, the National Assembly amended the Information and Communications Act to impose harsher penalties—up to 15 years in jail and up to three million delasis ($82,000) in fines—on people who use the internet to criticize or publish political cartoons about government officials. The minister of presidential affairs is quoted as saying, "If you cannot say anything good about the country, then you should keep quiet." In April, the National Assembly also passed the Criminal Code Amendment Bill, which increased the punishments for anyone convicted of providing "false information" to a public servant. The definition of public servant was also expanded to include elected officials that are not defined as such in the constitution. In addition, in April the government banned internet telecommunications services such as Skype.

Ownership of private television outlets is prohibited, and media outlets Teranga FM, the *Standard,* and the *Daily News* continue to be banned. Journalists are often jailed without charge, or detained more than the 72 hours allowed by law, while their whereabouts are withheld. Fatou Camara, a talk show host who had previously been Jammeh's press secretary, fled the country in October after being released from jail; she faced charges of sedition.

Religious freedom is formally protected. Although there are no formal government restrictions on academic freedom, it appears to be limited at the University of The Gambia, with the presence of security forces on campus, the discouragement of political speech and activities, and the departure of prominent scholars from the university in recent years. Open and free private discussion is limited by fears of government surveillance and retaliation.

E. Associational and Organizational Rights: 3 / 12 (-1)

Freedoms of assembly and association are legally protected but constrained by state intimidation in practice. Associational rights are limited in effect by the regime's use of judicial measures and arbitrary detention to intimidate opponents. The 2013 amendment to the Information and Communications Act further threatens associational freedoms of opponents by formalizing punishments for people "inciting dissatisfaction." Nongovernmental organizations (NGOs) operate in the country but, like journalists, human rights advocates are constantly under threat of judicial reprisals and detentions. Because freedom of association is limited, few NGOs aggressively tackle political issues. Workers, except for civil servants and members of the security forces, have the right to form unions, strike, and bargain for wages, though a climate of fear generated by the state dissuades workers from taking action.

F. Rule of Law: 1 / 16

Although the constitution provides for an independent judiciary, Jammeh selects and dismisses judges. The judicial system recognizes customary law and Sharia (Islamic law), primarily with regard to personal status and family matters. Impunity for the country's security forces is a problem. A 1995 decree allows the National Intelligence Agency (NIA) to search, arrest, or seize any person or property without a warrant in the name of state security. Prisons are overcrowded and unsanitary. Torture of prisoners has been reported as routine. In 2013, the Gambian judiciary established a Judicial Complaints Committee to receive complaints, arbitrated by certain members of the judiciary.

In August 2012, Jammeh ordered the execution of 9 of the 47 inmates on death row, depriving them access to a fair trial, an attorney, or their families. Baba Leigh, an imam who criticized this decision, was released in April 2013 after five months' detention without charge.

The Gambia's ethnic groups coexist in relative harmony, though critics have accused Jammeh of giving preferential treatment to his Jola ethnic group. In 2013, Jammeh called the country's majority Mandinka ethnic group "treasonous."

Consensual same-sex sexual relationships between men are a criminal offense, with punishments of between 5 and 14 years in prison. The LGBT (lesbian, gay, bisexual, and transgender) community was targeted alongside drug traffickers and murderers in the anti-crime operation called "Operation Bulldozer" in 2012. In his speech at the UN General Assembly in September 2013, Jammeh declared homosexuality as "one of the biggest threats to human existence." Amnesty International has reported that the passage of the Criminal Code Amendment Act heightened threats to sexual minorities.

G. Personal Autonomy and Individual Rights: 6 / 16

Women enjoy fewer opportunities for higher education and employment than men. Sharia provisions regarding family law and inheritance restrict women's rights. Rape and domestic violence are common, despite laws prohibiting violence against women. Female genital mutilation (FGM) remains legal and widely practiced. The two-year trial of Isatou Touray, the chief executive of the Gambia Committee on Traditional Practices (GAMCOTRAP)—a local group working to combat FGM that is often harassed by the government—ended in acquittal in November 2012. Critics said the trial was politically motivated.

The Gambia is a source, destination, and transit country for the trafficking of women and children. There are legal penalties for trafficking and the government investigated some operations, including one that revealed 79 potential victims in January 2013, but there has been no formal declaration that they were trafficked. In December 2013, the National Assembly passed a domestic violence bill, supported by the UN Development Programme, intended to reduce sexual violence and empower women to bring perpetrators of sexual offenses and domestic violence to justice.

Georgia

Political Rights Rating: 3
Civil Liberties Rating: 3
Freedom Rating: 3.0
Freedom Status: Partly Free
Electoral Democracy: Yes

Population: 4,500,000
Capital: Tbilisi

Note: The numerical ratings and status listed above do not reflect conditions in South Ossetia or Abkhazia, which are examined in separate reports.

Ten-Year Ratings Timeline For Year Under Review (Political Rights, Civil Liberties, Status)

Year Under Review	2004	2005	2006	2007	2008	2009	2010	2011	2012	2013
Rating	3,4,PF	3,3,PF	3,3,PF	4,4,PF	4,4,PF	4,4,PF	4,3,PF	4,3,PF	3,3,PF	3,3,PF

INTRODUCTION

The heated personality conflict between President Mikheil Saakashvili and Prime Minister Bidzina Ivanishvili that fuelled partisan politics before and after the 2012 parliamentary elections gradually subsided in early 2013. Ivanishvili's new government demonstrated political will to ensure a transparent and democratic process for the presidential vote held in October, which was judged by domestic and international observers as transparent and fair.

Giorgi Margvelashvili of the Georgian Dream Movement (GDM) won 62 percent of votes in the first round of October's presidential election, surpassing the 50 percent threshold needed for an outright win. His primary challengers—David Bakradze of Saakashvili's United National Movement (UNM) and Nino Burjanadze of the Democratic Movement-United Georgia party—received 22 and 10 percent of the vote, respectively.

Constitutional changes introduced by Saakashvili in 2010 to transform the country's political structure from a presidential to a parliamentary system came into force following Margvelashvili's inauguration in November. In June, Ivanishvili, who had expressed a desire to exit politics on numerous occasions since being sworn in as prime minister in October 2012, announced his intention to leave his post after the presidential election. In November, Ivanishvili nominated his long-term protégé, 31-year-old interior minister Irakli Garibashvili, as his replacement as prime minister. Parliament voted to confirm Garibashvili as the new prime minister in November.

The media environment in Georgia became less polarized and more transparent in 2013. Key 2011 legislation that required media outlets to disclose their ownership structures was successfully implemented, and a permanent "must carry, must offer" rule was introduced in July, increasing voters' access to information.

POLITICAL RIGHTS: 25 / 40 (+1)

A. Electoral Process: 8 / 12 (+1)

Georgia is an electoral democracy. International observers generally considered the October 2012 parliamentary elections as free and fair, noting increased competitiveness and a range of largely peaceful political activities, including mass demonstrations by the opposition. GDM captured 85 seats in the 2012 elections, leaving the UNM in the minority with 65 seats. In Georgia's first peaceful transfer of power through elections since independence in 1991, Saakashvili conceded defeat and pledged to fully cooperate with the new government.

Presidential elections in October 2013 were widely regarded as free and fair. The campaign environment was remarkably less polarized than in previous years. While observers reported some violations, they also noted virtually no cases of abuse of administrative resources or pressure on voters, which have been serious issues in past elections. Another notable improvement was reduced numbers of so-called special voting stations set up for public servants in penitentiaries, police stations, medicinal facilities, and military bases; employees of these institutions were encouraged to vote as civilians in their local communities. Election observers welcomed this development as positive step in reducing opportunities for influencing the vote of government employees. The Central Election Commission was also praised for its professionalism during the election.

B. Political Pluralism and Participation: 10 / 16

The unicameral Parliament has 150 seats, with 77 chosen by party list and 73 in single-member districts. According to the constitution, the president appoints the cabinet and can serve up to two five-year terms. Under a package of constitutional amendments adopted in 2010, the bulk of executive authority shifted from the president to the prime minister in 2013, and new rules surrounding votes of no confidence will make it difficult for Parliament to remove the prime minister.

Saakashvili's UNM dominated Georgian politics from 2004 to 2012, when growing dissatisfaction with the ruling party's perceived consolidation of power helped fuel support for the GDM. This new party, founded by Ivanishvili in 2012, merged older opposition factions and benefited from Ivanishvili's extensive personal wealth. Though Ivanishvili left the political scene in November 2013, it remained to be seen how much influence he will continue to wield, given his close relationship with his successor. While polling has indicated that around 70 percent of the population disapproves of Ivanishvili's departure, many Georgians have also expressed frustration with his administration's failure to deliver on campaign promises, particularly pledges to improve the country's sagging economy, and its lack of a clear vision.

C. Functioning of the Government: 7 / 12

Major electoral irregularities were absent from the presidential elections in October and the duly elected candidate entered into office without incident. The political environment with regard to adopting and implementing legislation was also relatively calm.

Since the parliamentary elections and changeover of government in 2012, civil society participation in lawmaking has strengthened, with parliament considering the opinions of civil society coalitions on important legislative decisions in 2013, such as amendments to the law on broadcasting, and the labor code. Civil society has played a more active role in policymaking in certain areas of government, particularly the judicial sector. However, on other issues, such as the controversial construction of hydropower plants, which were initiated by the previous government and continued by its successor, lawmakers neglected to properly include civil society consultation. In December, Transparency International Georgia released a report highlighting persistent corruption risks in the practice of noncompetitive government contracts. While the amount of direct contracts dropped drastically immediately following the parliamentary elections in 2012, they began to rise again towards the end of 2013 indicating that corruption in this area continues to be a problem. The study shows that in recent years several companies, who are owned or partially owned by current and former members of parliament, substantially profited from this practice, receiving hundreds of direct, noncompetitive contracts totaling more than 100 million GEL.

While notable progress has been made with respect to lower- and mid-level corruption, particularly in comparison with the country's neighbors, Georgia continues to suffer from corruption at the highest levels of government. Little was accomplished in 2013 to address these issues. Georgia was ranked 55 out of 177 countries and territories surveyed in Transparency International's 2013 Corruption Perceptions Index.

After the GDM took power in late 2012, authorities arrested and interrogated numerous former officials from the Saakashvili administration on charges of abuse of power and bribery, among others. A number of the allegations related to illegal surveillance of the GDM, prompting the UNM to accuse the new government of pursuing a political vendetta. The international community urged the new leadership to maintain respect for due process, warning that using prosecutions to seek political retribution could jeopardize Georgia's bid for NATO membership. GDM officials denied that the cases were politically motivated and invited NATO to monitor the investigations. Transparency International Georgia monitored the ensuing legal proceedings and found that both the defense and prosecution had enjoyed equal opportunities to present their cases. In the first major conviction related to these trials, the former head of prisons, Bachana Akhalaia, was found guilty in October 2013 of abuse of power in connection to the death of seven prisoners during authorities' crackdown on a prison riot in 2006. Akhalaia was sentenced to three years and nine months in prison. In November, outgoing president Saakashvili pardoned Akhalaia, who nonetheless remains in detention on abuse of power charges related to a separate case. There was some speculation that Saakashvili himself may be investigated for abuse of power in connection to several cases, including illegal media raids, privatizing scandals and reducing sentences of politically connected convicts, after leaving office.

CIVIL LIBERTIES: 38 / 60 (+2)
D. Freedom of Expression and Belief: 12 / 16

The constitution provides guarantees for press freedom, and the print media offer a range of political views. The state television and radio outlets were converted into public-service broadcasters in 2005, but critics maintain that the stations show a pro-UNM bias that continued even after the 2012 elections. The major private television stations received heavy subsidies from the UNM government and displayed a pro-government slant. In the weeks following the 2012 parliamentary elections that brought the GDM to power, ownership changes reduced the dominance of pro-UNM stations, leading to a steady reduction in media polarization in 2013. Legal amendments banning offshore ownership of broadcasters and requiring stations to reveal their ownership structures were successfully implemented in 2013. In August, Ivanishvili decided to close TV9, the pro-GDM station he had founded prior to parliamentary elections to compete with pro-UNM coverage on Imedi TV and Rustavi 2. Prior to his decision, media watchdogs had warned Ivanishvili that his proximity to the station was inappropriate.

In July 2013, "must carry, must offer" legislation, which was originally implemented during the campaign period before the parliamentary elections, became a permanent fixture in Georgian media legislation. The law grants national broadcast reach to all television stations with an audience of at least 20 percent of the population. Media monitoring during the campaign period revealed far less polarization among outlets. The authorities do not restrict access to the internet.

E. Associational and Organizational Rights: 8 / 12 (+1)

Freedom of religion is respected for the country's large Georgian Orthodox Christian majority and some traditional minority groups, including Muslims and Jews. However, members of newer groups—including Baptists, Pentecostals, and Jehovah's Witnesses—have faced harassment and intimidation by law enforcement officials and Georgian Orthodox extremists. Since political changes began in Egypt in 2011, there has been an influx of Coptic Christian immigrants. Some reports indicate that Orthodox authorities have denied Coptic Christians permission to worship in Orthodox churches.

The government does not generally restrict academic freedom, though there have been reports of politically motivated academic dismissals and appointments.

Freedoms of association and assembly were generally upheld in 2013, including in the run-up to the presidential election; ahead of the poll, authorities advocated for restraint from violence, and law enforcement successfully minimized clashes with police during political rallies. However, a small LGBT rights rally held in May in Central Tbilisi to mark the international day against homophobia was disrupted when counter-demonstrators broke through a police cordon and attempted to attack the participants; police were reportedly forced to bus the activists out of the city in avoid further attacks.

Nongovernmental organizations (NGOs) are able to register and operate without arbitrary restrictions. NGOs were active in monitoring the preelection environment in 2013. NGOs have generally reported that Ivanishvili's government has been more accessible and has engaged more actively in dialogue with civil society than the previous administration. Obtaining funding for NGOs is a challenge; local business support for charities tends not to be directed toward organizations that work on government policy and reform issues. A 2011 law allows the government to provide financial support for projects administered by NGOs and universities.

The constitution and the Law on Trade Unions allow workers to organize and prohibit antiunion discrimination. The Amalgamated Trade Unions of Georgia, the successor to the Soviet-era union federation, is the principal trade union bloc. It is not affiliated with the government and receives no state funding. Union influence remains marginal in practice. Civil society groups raised concerns in 2012 that the labor code did not protect employees from being fired on political grounds. In June 2013, amendments were passed to the labor code, which among other improvements requires employers to provide written and reasonable argumentation for the cause of the dismissal.

F. Rule of Law: 8 / 16 (+1)

The judiciary has traditionally suffered from significant corruption and pressure from the executive branch. The need for comprehensive reform of the justice system came to the fore in September 2012, when leaked videos showing the apparent abuse and rape of inmates at a prison outside of Tbilisi were broadcast on television. The images sparked public outrage, leading Saakashvili to appoint the country's ombudsman as the new minister for prisons and call for an overhaul of correctional institutions.

After coming to power in October 2012, the GDM initiated a series of penitentiary reforms that have more than halved the prison population, improved access to health care for inmates, and reduced prison deaths. The reduction of the prison population stemmed in part from an amnesty granted to more than 8,000 inmates in January. The move was received somewhat uneasily by the public, who feared a resulting rise in crime.

The new GDM administration has also demonstrated an effort to increase transparency and fairness within the judicial system. In May 2013, the government adopted amendments to the Law on Common Courts that made several improvements to the administration of court procedures, including allowing media coverage of court proceedings, which was forbidden under the former law. There has also been an increase in the number of defense cases since the change in government and a decrease in the number of prosecution cases, indicating a less heavy reliance on the plea bargain. State-appointed attorneys are more frequently presenting defense cases in court, which demonstrates a greater confidence in objective justice. In the first half of 2013, the number of successful requests from the prosecutor for imprisonment decreased by 25 percent compared to the same period in 2012.

Despite these improvements, several areas in the judicial system remained unreformed. Since the 2012 prison abuse scandal, the government has failed to create a formal mechanism for the regular public monitoring of detention facilities. Since 2007, only the ombudsman has had oversight of Georgia's penitentiaries.

The government generally respects the rights of ethnic minorities. Antidiscrimination regulations cover bias based on sexual orientation, but societal discrimination against LGBT people remains strong.

G. Personal Autonomy and Individual Rights: 10 / 16

Freedom of residence and freedom to travel to and from the country are observed. Populist fears of too many foreigners buying land in Georgia led to the passing of a new law in June 2013, which temporarily prohibits the sale of land to non-Georgians or foreign entities until the end of 2014.

Georgia has gradually established legislation to address the problem of domestic violence, including a 2012 law that upgraded domestic violence from an administrative to a criminal offense. However, the ombudsman and NGOs have reported that police fail to pursue rape and domestic violence cases adequately, and these crimes are believed to be underreported.

Georgia is a source, transit, and destination country for trafficking in persons according to the U.S. State Department's 2013 Trafficking in Persons Report. While the government does not fully comply with the minimum standards for the elimination of trafficking, it has made significant efforts to do so. The new government finalized an anti-trafficking action plan for 2013–2014, which President Saakashvili signed in March 2013.

Germany

Political Rights: 1
Civil Liberties: 1
Freedom Rating: 1
Freedom Status: Free
Electoral Democracy: Yes

Population: 80,572,000
Capital: Berlin

Ten-Year Ratings Timeline For Year Under Review (Political Rights, Civil Liberties, Status)

Year Under Review	2004	2005	2006	2007	2008	2009	2010	2011	2012	2013
Rating	1,1,F	1,1,F	1,1,F	1,1,F	1,1,F	1,1,F	1,1,F	1,1,F	1,1,F	1,1,F

INTRODUCTION

Chancellor Angela Merkel's Christian Democratic Union (CDU) and its Bavarian sister party, the Christian Social Union (CSU), won a solid plurality in September 2013 parliamentary elections, clearing the way for Merkel's third term as chancellor. The Christian Democrats' victory was seen as a public endorsement of Merkel's leadership through the European debt crisis of the past several years, during which Germany had maintained a strong economy with low unemployment, while insisting that weaker members of the Eurozone submit to austerity measures in return for bailout loans. However, despite Merkel's triumph, the CDU's junior coalition partner in the outgoing government, the Free Democratic Party (FDP), failed to reach the five percent threshold to qualify for seats in the Bundestag, the lower house, for the first time since 1949, losing all 93 of its seats. The CDU in late November reached an agreement with its center-left rival, the Social Democratic Party (SPD), to form a so-called grand coalition government, as they did during Merkel's first term

(2005–2009). Among other pledges, the agreement called for legislation to set a national minimum wage for the first time.

POLITICAL RIGHTS: 39 / 40
A. Electoral Process: 12 / 12

The German constitution provides for a lower house of parliament, the 622-seat Bundestag (Federal Assembly), elected at least every four years through a 50-50 mixture of proportional representation and single-member districts; as well as an upper house, the Bundesrat (Federal Council), which represents the country's 16 states. The country's head of state is a largely ceremonial president, chosen jointly by the Bundestag and a group of state representatives to serve up to two five-year terms. In Germany's federal system, state governments have considerable authority over matters such as education, policing, taxation, and spending. The chancellor, the head of government, is elected by the Bundestag and usually serves for the duration of a four-year legislative session, which can be cut short only if the Bundestag chooses a replacement in a so-called constructive vote of no confidence.

In the September 22, 2013, federal elections, Merkel led the CDU/CSU to a combined 41.5 percent of the vote, according to preliminary results, up 7.7 points from the 2009 elections. They won a total of 311 seats in the 630-seat Bundestag—the best showing for the Christian Democrats since 1990, when Germany reunified and Chancellor Helmut Kohl won a third term—but they fell five seats short of an absolute majority. Their current coalition partner, the pro-free market FDP, fell to 4.8 percent, down from 14.6 percent in 2009, and failed to meet the 5 percent threshold to qualify for seats. The SPD, led by former finance minister Peer Steinbrück, took 25.7 percent, up from their historic low of 23 percent in 2009, for 193 seats. The environmentalist Greens dropped to 8.4 percent, from 11.9 percent, for 63 seats. The radical Left party fell to 8.6 percent, from 11.9 percent, taking 64 seats. A new party, Alternative for Germany, which called for exiting the Eurozone and curbing immigration, took 4.7 percent, narrowly failing to qualify for seats.

While the SPD, the Greens and the Left together won enough seats to make up a majority for a left-wing coalition, the SPD had previously ruled out governing with the Left.

B. Political Pluralism and Participation: 15 / 16

For historical reasons, political pluralism is somewhat constrained. Under electoral laws intended to restrict the far left and far right, a party must receive either 5 percent of the national vote or win at least three directly elected seats to be represented in parliament. The Constitutional Court, Germany's highest court, outlawed the Socialist Reich Party (a successor to the Nazi Party) in 1952 and the Communist Party of Germany in 1956 on the grounds that their goals disregarded the principles of the constitution. However, the former ruling party of communist East Germany—the Socialist Unity Party, renamed the Party of Democratic Socialism—participated in state governments after reunification. It then merged with Labor and Social Justice–The Electorate Alternative, a party of former left-wing SPD members, to form the new Left party ahead of the 2005 elections. The main extreme right party, the National Democratic Party of Germany (NPD), is hostile to immigration and the EU, and has been accused of glorifying Adolf Hitler and the Third Reich. In December 2012, the opposition-controlled Bundesrat voted to petition the Constitutional Court to ban the NPD, but the government did not back the move.

The September 2013 federal elections resulted in the first black members of the Bundestag, with one each from the CDU and the SPD. The CDU also saw its first Muslim deputy elected to the Bundestag. Overall, the number of Bundestag members from immigrant backgrounds rose from 21 to 34.

C. Functioning of Government: 12 / 12

Germany is free of pervasive corruption. The government is held accountable for its performance through open parliamentary debates, which are covered widely in the media. In April 2013, prosecutors brought corruption charges against former president Christoph Wulff, who resigned in 2012 amid allegations that he had accepted favors from wealthy friends while serving as governor of Lower Saxony state. In August, a court in Hanover said Wulff would stand trial only on less serious charges of receiving and granting favors. The trial opened in November; Wulff became the nation's first former head of state to stand trial. Germany was ranked 12 out of 177 countries and territories surveyed in Transparency International's 2013 Corruption Perceptions Index.

CIVIL LIBERTIES: 57 / 60
D. Freedom of Expression and Belief: 15 / 16

Freedom of expression is enshrined in the constitution, and the media are largely free and independent. However, hate speech is punishable if publicly pronounced against specific segments of the population and in a manner that incites hatred, such as racist agitation and anti-Semitism. It is also illegal to advocate Nazism, deny the Holocaust, or glorify the ideology of Hitler. Internet access is generally unrestricted. In July 2013, *Der Spiegel* magazine reported that documents leaked by former U.S. National Security Agency (NSA) contractor Edward Snowden showed that the NSA, collaborating with German intelligence agencies, had secretly collected extensive data on communications in Germany. In October, reports that the NSA had monitored Merkel's official cellphone prompted her to call U.S. President Barack Obama to demand assurances that she was not under surveillance, which she said would be an unacceptable breach of trust between allies.

Freedom of belief is legally protected. However, Germany has taken a strong stance against the Church of Scientology, which it deems an organization pursuing commercial interests rather than a religion. A number of federal states have also denied the Jehovah's Witnesses the official "public law corporation" status, which has been granted to 180 other religious groups in the country. Eight states have passed laws prohibiting female Muslim schoolteachers from wearing the headscarf, while Berlin and the state of Hesse have adopted legislation banning headscarves for all civil servants. Academic freedom is generally respected. In February 2013, Education Minister Annette Schavan resigned after her doctorate was revoked over alleged plagiarism. A similar plagiarism scandal had felled Defense Minister Karl-Theodor zu Guttenberg in 2011.

E. Associational and Organizational Rights: 12 / 12

The right of peaceful assembly is not infringed upon, except in the case of outlawed groups, such as those advocating Nazism or opposing the democratic order. Civic groups and nongovernmental organizations operate without hindrance. Trade unions, farmers' groups, and business confederations are free to organize. In March 2013, the Interior Ministry banned three Salafist Islamic extremist associations, which it said sought to replace democracy with Sharia (Islamic law). Police the same day arrested four men linked to the Salafist movement for allegedly plotting to kill Markus Beisicht, leader of the far-right Pro-NRW party. In 2012, Pro-NRW had displayed caricatures of the Prophet Muhammad in front of an Islamic school in Bonn, setting off violent clashes between Muslim protesters and police. In December, all 16 German states petitioned the Federal Constitutional Court to ban the National Democratic Party (NPD), calling it a neo-Nazi antidemocratic group. Previous attempts to outlaw the party had failed, most recently in 2003. The party held seats in two eastern state parliaments, in Saxony and

Mecklenberg-Western Pomerania, and reportedly had received some 20 million euros in state funding since 2003.

F. Rule of Law: 15 / 16

The judiciary is independent, and the rule of law prevails. Prison conditions are adequate, though the Council of Europe has criticized elements of the practice of preventive detention. In May 2013, Beate Zschaepe, 38, was tried in Munich for murder for being part of an anti-immigrant neo-Nazi terrorist cell that killed 10 people—nine small business owners mostly of Turkish origin and one policewoman—between 2000 and 2007. The cell had also allegedly carried out two bombings. Four men accused of providing support to the cell or acting as accessories to its crimes were also defendants in the trial. The trial continued through the end of 2013. In August 2013, a special parliamentary committee in August 2013 issued a report calling for more effective surveillance of neo-Nazi groups, criticizing "major failures" in the investigation of the cell's serial killings. Among other recommendations, the committee urged police to recruit more minorities, blaming deeply ingrained biases for causing investigators to mistakenly blame the killings on Turkish gangsters, and to discount the threat posed by racist and xenophobic extremism. The three-member cell was tracked down in November 2011, when two men committed suicide and Zschaepe was arrested. The head of the domestic intelligence agency had resigned in July 2012 after it emerged that the agency had destroyed files on the case and made other mistakes that allowed the cell to evade capture for years.

In 2013, Germany received nearly 127,000 asylum applicants, the most since 1999 and by far the most in the EU for the year (France was second, with 65,000 applicants). In August, far-right extremists led by the NPD protested the opening of a new shelter for asylum seekers in eastern Berlin.

G. Personal Autonomy and Individual Rights: 15 / 16

Women's rights are well protected under antidiscrimination laws. However, gender wage gaps persisted in 2013, with women's wages and salaries approximately 22 percent less than men's wages for the same work. Women held 6 of the 16 federal cabinet positions in the new government and 36 percent of the seats in parliament after the September 2013 elections. However, women held just 12 percent of seats on corporate boards in 2013, and several female executives at prominent companies either resigned or were fired in 2013. In April, Merkel agreed to back the introduction of legally binding quotas for female representation on corporate boards starting in 2020, requiring that they be at least 30 percent women. The November coalition agreement between the CDU and the SPD included a pledge to introduce legislation setting that requirement earlier, as of 2016.

Limited same-sex partnership rights are respected. In February 2013, the Constitutional Court ruled in favor of a challenge to the existing ban on adoption by same-sex couples of one of the partners' adopted children. Currently, a person in a same-sex partnership could adopt only the biological children of his or her partner. The court ordered the government to draft new legislation making the change by June 2014. In June 2013, the same court ruled that the unequal tax benefits for marriage and civil unions were unconstitutional, and ordered that civil partners be granted the same treatment, retroactive to the introduction of civil unions in 2001.

The November coalition agreement included a pledge to grant dual citizenship to German-born children of immigrants for the first time. The change would most prominently affect the descendants of Turks who came to Germany as "guest workers" in the 1960s and 1970s. The Turkish population in Germany was about three million.

# Ghana

Political Rights Rating: 1
Civil Liberties Rating: 2
Freedom Rating: 1.5
Freedom Status: Free
Electoral Democracy: Yes

Population: 26,088,000
Capital: Accra

Ten-Year Ratings Timeline For Year Under Review (Political Rights, Civil Liberties, Status)

Year Under Review	2004	2005	2006	2007	2008	2009	2010	2011	2012	2013
Rating	2,2,F	1,2,F	1,2,F	1,2,F	1,2,F	1,2,F	1,2,F	1,2,F	1,2,F	1,2,F

INTRODUCTION

On August 29, 2013, the Supreme Court dismissed an election petition filed by the National Patriotic Party (NPP) challenging the results of the December 2012 presidential election, and reaffirmed John Mahama of the National Democratic Congress (NDC) as the duly elected president. The Supreme Court hearings on the case, which began in April and continued for nearly 50 days of sittings, were broadcast live on television and radio, enhancing the transparency of the process. While the final judgment highlighted several instances of electoral irregularities, the court ruled that these were not sufficient to have affected the overall result of the presidential election. NPP presidential candidate Nana Akufo-Addo promptly accepted the Supreme Court verdict, and other members of the NPP honored Akufo-Addo's request not to launch an appeal. Ghanaians, including NPP supporters, reacted peacefully to the announcement of the verdict.

Ghana's economy continues to experience high rates of economic growth, due mainly to revenues from oil and gas production at the Jubilee offshore oilfield, which was discovered in 2007. However, many international and domestic stakeholders expressed concerns about the government's ability to manage the economy effectively and transparently. During 2013, Ghana missed its fiscal deficit targets and experienced double-digit inflation rates, while the government struggled to reduce corruption.

Ghana's strong economic and diplomatic ties to China, the country's largest provider of aid and second largest trading partner, remain relatively robust, despite the arrest of 169 Chinese citizens in a crackdown on illegal gold-mining operations during May and June and Ghana's subsequent deportation of approximately 4,600 undocumented Chinese immigrants.

POLITICAL RIGHTS: 37 / 40

A. Electoral Process: 12 / 12

Since 1992, Ghana has experienced an uninterrupted period of competitive multiparty elections. The president and vice president are directly elected on the same ticket for up to two four-year terms. Members of the unicameral, 275-seat Parliament are also elected for four-year terms.

On December 7, 2012, Mahama was elected with just 50.7 percent of the vote, while Akufo-Addo took 47.7 percent. In concurrent parliamentary elections, the NDC captured 148 seats and the NPP took 123. Limited technical problems, including the breakdown of some new biometric voter machines used to register and identify voters, led to the extension of voting by a day at many polling places. Although international and domestic observers praised the elections as free, fair, and peaceful, the opposition disputed the results and questioned the neutrality of the Electoral Commission (EC). On December 28, 2012, the NPP filed a legal" suit before the Supreme Court contesting the presidential election results. The NPP's suit claimed that violations of the electoral law and widespread irregularities should invalidate some 4.6 million votes from over 11,000 polling stations.

The Supreme Court began hearing the case in April 2013 and rendered its final judgment on August 29. The nine-member panel of justices dismissed the NPP's petition, and ruled that Mahama had been fairly elected. For many domestic and international observers, the peaceful resolution of the legal challenge underscored the consolidation of democracy and respect for rule of law in Ghana.

Some problems that arose in the administration of the 2012 elections have led to calls from civil society groups for electoral reforms—such as a more inclusive process of appointing EC commissioners and the adoption of statutory guidelines to govern election timetables—as steps to help avoid another disputed election.

B. Political Pluralism and Participation: 15 / 16

Two rival parties, the NPP and the NDC, dominate the political system. Ghana's multiparty system provides ample opportunity for the meaningful participation of opposition parties in the political process. The country has experienced two peaceful, democratic transfers of power between presidents from the opposing NPP and NDC, in 2000 and in 2008. Moreover, the legal framework provides for equal participation in political life for the country's various cultural, religious, and ethnic minorities.

C. Functioning of Government: 10 / 12

Political corruption continues to be a problem, despite the existence of robust legal and institutional frameworks to combat it. During 2013, the media, nongovernmental organizations (NGOs), and opposition parties criticized the NDC administration for its inability to reduce corruption and prosecute officials suspected of malfeasance. In April, a ministerial committee was established to investigate government officials affiliated with the Ghana Youth Employment and Entrepreneurial Development Agency (GYEEDA) who allegedly granted interest-free loans worth $100 million to several private companies without parliamentary approval. In November, Mahama announced a raft of initiatives to address the GYEEDA controversy including the suspension of exiting GYEEDA contracts, the recovery of misappropriated funds, and the development of legislation to enhance GYEEDA transparency and accountability. By the end of the year, the Economic and Organized Crime Office (EOCO) interrogated over 30 government officials, including current and past government ministers implicated in the scandal, while three companies made commitments to refund approximately 55 million Cedis to the government. The "GYEEDA Scandal" follows on the heels of another major corruption scandal, known as the "Woyome Scandal," involving NDC financier Alfred Woyome, who was arrested and charged with fraud in 2012. The case continued through the end of the year.

During 2013, the government took some positive steps in addressing the problem of corruption. The Commission on Human Rights and Administrative Justice (CHRAJ) in June proposed a budget of $33 million over the next 10 years for the implementation of the National Anti-Corruption Action Plan (NACAP). However, parliament was unable to pass the NACAP by year's end. Ghana ranked 63 out of 177 countries surveyed in the 2013 Corruption Perceptions Index published by Transparency International (TI). Meanwhile, the 2013 Global Corruption Barometer, another TI report, found that the sectors where Ghanaians perceived the highest levels of corruption were the police, political parties, and the judiciary. According to the 2013 Global Corruption Barometer, 38 percent of Ghanaians who interacted with the educational system reported paying bribes, while 79 percent of those who interacted with the police reported making illegal payments.

NGOs demanded greater government accountability and transparency. In the run-up to the 2012 elections, government spending spiked significantly due to increases in civil service wages, causing many donors to question the administration's ability to meet its fiscal targets in 2013. Although the government received international praise for introducing revenue-management legislation within the oil and gas industry in 2012, NGOs have voiced concerns about government compliance with the legislation. Furthermore, a Right to Information Bill aimed at increasing government transparency has not yet been passed by Parliament, though it was approved by the cabinet.

CIVIL LIBERTIES: 47 / 60

D. Freedom of Expression and Belief: 14 / 16

Freedom of expression is constitutionally guaranteed and generally respected in practice. Ghana has a diverse and vibrant media landscape that includes state and privately owned television and radio stations, and several independent newspapers and magazines. However, the government occasionally restricts press freedom through harassment and arrests of journalists reporting on politically sensitive issues. In March, two photojournalists from state-owned newspapers were brutally beaten by security officials while they were taking photos of Mahama during Ghana's Independence Day celebrations. The Ghana Journalist Association (GJA) and the Media Foundation for West Africa condemned the attack and demanded an immediate probe. The Ghana Armed Forces conducted an investigation of the incident and in April exonerated the military personnel involved of any misconduct. However, public uproar over the exoneration led the country's chief of defense staff in May to apologize to the photojournalists and say they would be compensated.

Despite the repeal of criminal libel and sedition laws in 2001, another law prohibiting "publishing false news with intent to cause fear or harm to the public or to disturb the public peace" has at times been loosely applied. On July 2, the Supreme Court found Ken Kuranchie, editor in chief of the *Daily Searchlight* newspaper, guilty of criminal contempt and sentenced him to 10 days in jail over two editorials that criticized the Supreme Court's handling of part of the case challenging the 2012 presidential election. The president of the GJA condemned the ruling as a violation of Kuranchie's freedom of speech and a challenge to media freedom in Ghana.

Religious freedom is constitutionally and legally protected and largely respected in practice by the government. During 2013, there were no major reports of government or societal abuses of religious freedom. Academic freedom is legally guaranteed and upheld in practice.

E. Associational and Organizational Rights: 11 / 12

The rights to peaceful assembly and association are constitutionally guaranteed and generally respected. Permits are not required for meetings or demonstrations. NGOs are generally able to operate freely and play an important role in ensuring government accountability and transparency. Under the constitution and 2003 labor laws, workers have the right to form and join trade unions. However, the government forbids action in a number of essential industries, including fuel distribution, public transportation, and the prison system.

F. Rule of Law: 12 / 16

Judicial independence in Ghana is constitutionally and legally enshrined. While the judiciary has demonstrated greater levels of impartiality in recent years, corruption remains an important challenge as courts lack necessary resources and judges are poorly paid. Generally, the government and private interests comply with judicial decisions. The NPP's acceptance of the Supreme Court's August 29 ruling on the election challenge underscores the legitimacy of the judiciary. Initiatives to improve the judicial process have reaped positive results. The Accra Fast Track High Court and automated commercial courts have enhanced the speed and efficiency of the judicial process, while a judicial complaints unit has actively investigated cases of judicial impropriety. Many prisoners experience lengthy pretrial detention.

There were numerous reports of police brutality, negligence, and corruption in 2013. In May, police personnel from the Accra Regional Command were allegedly caught on video brutally assaulting land guards, prompting the inspector general of police, Mohammed Ahmed Alhassan, to order an immediate investigation. The Police Intelligence and Professional Standards Unit (PIPS) has attempted to improve the image of the police by investigating cases of police misconduct. Alhassan in July 2013 said that between 2010 and June 2013, 108 police officers were fired for involvement in criminal activities and that 371 had received sanctions or demotions during that period.

Ghana's prisons are overcrowded and conditions are often life-threatening. In June, the CHRAJ encouraged Ghana's ratification of the UN Optional Protocol to the Convention against Torture as a mechanism to ensure more humane treatment of inmates. The government continues to cooperate with the UN Refugee Agency to protect the rights of the almost 20,000 refugees and asylum seekers in Ghana. However, a report launched in June by the Human Rights Advocacy Center (HRAC) found inadequate health and sanitation conditions at the Ampain Refugee Camp, which houses Ivorian refugees.

Although communal and ethnic violence occasionally flares in Ghana, there were no reports of such incidents during the year. Moreover, violent crime rates have declined, and there were no major acts of political terror.

Ghanain law prohibits "sexual intercourse with a person in an unnatural manner." However, it is unclear if this law applies to same-sex sexual acitvity between consenting adults, and there were no reports of adults being prosecuted for same-sex sexual activity. Ghana's LGBT community continued to face societal discrimination. In January, a nominee to President Mahama's cabinet, Nana Oye, faced stiff opposition and condemnation from religious and other societal groups for her support of human rights for the LGBT community.

G. Personal Autonomy and Individual Rights: 10 / 16

Economic freedom in Ghana continues to improve. According to the 2014 Economic Freedom Index Ghana ranked 66th in the world and 5th in sub-Saharan Africa. More specifically, the country recorded a marginal increase in its economic freedom score due to improvements in business freedom, control of government spending and corruption. Nonetheless, weak rule of law, corruption, and an underregulated property rights system remain important impediments to economic freedom and business confidence.

Bribery is common practice for those trying to gain access to the nation's public services. These span interactions with traffic police, gaining admittance to educational institutions, starting a business, and registering property.

Despite equal rights under the law, women suffer societal discrimination, especially in rural areas where opportunities for education and wage employment are limited. However, women's enrollment in universities is increasing, and there are a number of high-ranking women in the current government: 6 members of the current cabinet are women, while women won 30 of the 275 seats in the December 2012 parliamentary elections.

Women continue to be affected by domestic violence and rape, and the practice of female genital mutilation continues in northern Ghana. In 2013, HRAC reported a high incidence of violence against girls in schools, while a 2012 HRAC study found that on average, two spousal murders where reported every month. According to a March 2013 statement by Minister of Gender, Children, and Social Protection Nana Oye Lithur, the government has worked to combat gender-based violence by expanding the police's domestic violence and victim support unit to 97 locations, creating gender-based violence courts in Accra and Kumasi, establishing domestic violence shelters, and providing training for police and service providers likely to encounter domestic violence situations.

Ghana serves as a source, transit point, and destination for the trafficking of women and children for labor and sexual exploitation. The police's Anti-Human Trafficking Unit (AHTU) maintains nine regional units, but they are underfunded and have limited capacity. In 2012, the AHTU received 117 reported cases of suspected trafficking.

Greece

Political Rights: 2
Civil Liberties: 2
Freedom Rating: 2
Freedom Status: Free
Electoral Democracy: Yes

Population: 11,100,000
Capital: Athens

Ten-Year Ratings Timeline For Year Under Review (Political Rights, Civil Liberties, Status)

Year Under Review	2004	2005	2006	2007	2008	2009	2010	2011	2012	2013
Rating	1,2,F	1,2,F	1,2,F	1,2,F	1,2,F	1,2,F	1,2,F	2,2,F	2,2,F	2,2,F

INTRODUCTION

The sovereign debt crisis, which emerged in Greece in late 2009, continues to shape the country's economic and political landscapes. Greece entered its sixth consecutive year of economic contraction in 2013. Although there are projections for modest growth in 2014, poor economic performance poses an ongoing challenge to political rights and civil liberties.

In May 2010, the European Union (EU) and the International Monetary Fund (IMF) stepped in to provide a €110 billion ($135 billion) rescue plan in order to help prevent a Greek debt default. In return for this funding, the government was required to implement a number of austerity and modernization measures to make Greece's economy more competitive. These steps were met with a series of national strikes and protests. Greece's debt levels continued to grow as the economy contracted and tax revenues shrank.

Additional austerity measures were passed in July 2011 as a condition for the release of bailout funds, resulting in further protests and strikes. After a failed attempt to hold a referendum on the bailout package, Prime Minister George Papandreou of the Panhellenic Socialist Movement (PASOK) stepped down on November 11. Lucas Papademos, the former head of the Bank of Greece, was appointed to lead a new coalition government. In February 2012, his government passed additional austerity measures, thereby securing a second, €130 billion ($170 billion) bailout that included a voluntary 53.5 percent write-off on privately held Greek debt.

Papademos resigned in April 2012, having shepherded through a series of politically unpalatable austerity measures, and May elections resulted in a hung Parliament. Following a second round of elections in June, the New Democracy party, which received 29.7 percent of the vote and 129 seats, was able to form a coalition government with PASOK, which captured 12.3 percent and 33 seats, and the Democratic Left (DIMAR), which took 6.3 percent and 17 seats. Antonis Samaras of New Democracy was named the new prime minister. This coalition passed yet another round of austerity measures in October in order to assure the release of funds from the EU and IMF.

On June 11, 2013, as the government was negotiating yet another round of austerity measures and facing increased demands that it begin firing public employees, the Samaras administration decided to abruptly close the doors of National Hellenic Broadcasting (ERT), the principle responsibilities of which were three public television stations, four national public radio stations, a satellite television channel, and a major state orchestra. That evening, ERT's broadcast signals went blank, and some 2,600 employees were laid off. A Greek government spokesperson, Simos Kedikoglou, assured citizens that a smaller, more efficient, and more independent broadcaster would emerge in September and that ERT's employees would be eligible to be hired by this organization. The closure, which was accomplished by a ministerial decree and without the full participation of the coalition government's two junior partners, PASOK and DIMAR, sparked a political crisis. Unions organized strikes and many members of the public rallied to the support of ERT employees, dozens of whom occupied the broadcaster's headquarters, producing pirate web broadcasts, until police forcibly removed them in November. On June 21, DIMAR pulled out of the coalition government in protest of the ERT closure. New Democracy and PASOK were able to reorganize their coalition, but their majority is now razor-thin. In August 2013, a transitional broadcasting entity, Public Television (DT), announced the hiring of 577 employees with short-term contracts and began regular broadcasts. The creation of a new broadcasting corporation is planned for 2014.

In its new formulation, the government passed an additional series of austerity measures on July 18. The continuous push for austerity has led to growing poverty and homelessness, with unemployment reaching 27.9 percent in June and youth unemployment reaching 62.9 percent in May.

The right-wing extremist party Golden Dawn, which entered Parliament in the June 2012 elections, capturing 6.9 percent of the vote and 19 seats, has sought to capitalize on the social unrest. Emboldened by increasing levels of public support, the party embarked on a campaign of violence aimed at immigrants, the political left, and members of the LGBT (lesbian, gay, bisexual, and transgender) community. Those targeted by Golden Dawn supporters have reportedly experienced inadequate police protection, and there has even been some evidence of police complicity in the violence. Following the September 18, 2013, murder of Greek rapper and anti-fascist activist Pavlos Fyssas, to which Golden Dawn supporter Giorgos Roupakias confessed, the government launched a crackdown on the party. Six parliamentarians, including the party's president, Nikolaos Mihaloliakos, were arrested on charges of belonging to or founding a criminal organization. Arrest warrants were issued for dozens more party members. Mihaloliakos and two other members of the party's parliamentary contingent are being held in jail pending trial; the three other parliamentarians have been released, but are not allowed to leave the country. The legislators deny the charges against them and say that they are the victims of political persecution. The crackdown has also resulted in a shake-up of Greece's police forces, as the government has sought to root out officers affiliated with Golden Dawn.

POLITICAL RIGHTS: 35 / 40
A. Electoral Process: 12 / 12

All 300 members of the unicameral Parliament are elected by proportional representation for four-year terms. The largely ceremonial president is elected by a supermajority of Parliament for a five-year term. The prime minister is chosen by the president and is usually the leader of the majority party in Parliament. The installation of an unelected technocrat, Lucas Papademos, as prime minister of an interim government of national unity in 2011 was condemned by many in the media as undemocratic.

The country has generally fair electoral laws, equal campaigning opportunities, and a system of compulsory voting that is weakly enforced. Since 2010, documented immigrants are allowed to vote in municipal elections.

In October, Parliament voted to strip the six arrested Golden Dawn lawmakers of their parliamentary immunity so that their prosecution could proceed. Although immunity was intended as a protection against politically motivated prosecution, its removal in the case was viewed as part of a larger effort to neutralize a significant antidemocratic force.

B. Political Pluralism and Participation: 15 / 16

Greece's multiparty system features vigorous competition between rival parties. The political landscape since 1980 has been dominated by two parties, PASOK and New Democracy. PASOK's electoral fortunes have tumbled since the beginning of the sovereign debt crisis. It was surpassed in 2012 elections by the Coalition of the Radical Left (SYRIZA), which is presently the main opposition party; the governing coalition unites traditional rivals PASOK and New Democracy.

Greece's largest minority population, the Muslim minority of the province of Thrace, is allowed full political rights and currently has three representatives in Parliament.

C. Functioning of Government: 8 / 12

Corruption remains a problem in Greece. In October 2013, former PASOK minister of defense Akis Tsochatzopoulos was sentenced to 20 years in prison in connection with the laundering of up to €50 million ($67.8 million) in bribes from European armaments manufacturers. Sixteen of his associates were also found guilty. It remains to be seen if this groundbreaking trial will affect the level of political corruption in Greece. Greece was ranked 80 out of 177 countries surveyed in Transparency International's 2013 Corruption Perceptions Index, the worst ranking of any country in Western Europe.

Although there have been more prosecutions for tax evasion over the past year, Greek officials have largely avoided clamping down on tax evaders. The unwillingness of the Greek government to fully pursue tax evasion is demonstrated by the controversy surrounding the October 2012 publication, by journalist Kostas Vaxevanis, of a list of 2059 Greek citizens who transferred funds to the Swiss bank HSBC. The publication of the list—supposedly lost after being given to Finance Minister Giorgos Papakonstantinou in 2010—ignited a firestorm of criticism directed towards Greece's political class. After being acquitted in November 2012 of violating Greece's data privacy laws, Vaxevanis was re-indicted two weeks later. He was retried and again declared innocent in November 2013.

CIVIL LIBERTIES: 48 / 60

D. Freedom of Expression and Belief: 14 / 16

The constitution includes provisions for freedoms of speech and the press. The closure of ERT in June diminished the diversity of voices in the public sphere and deprived the country of its only non-Athenian nationally distributed channel, the Thessaloniki-based ET3. Still, citizens enjoy access to a broad array of privately owned print and broadcast outlets, and internet access is unrestricted. There are, however, some limits on speech that incites fear, violence, and public disharmony, as well as on publications that offend religious beliefs, are obscene, or advocate the violent overthrow of the political system. Also, political interests occasionally attempt to squelch free speech; in additional to the prosecution of Vaxevanis, some journalists have been physically assaulted by police while covering anti-austerity protests over the past three years.

Freedom of religion is guaranteed by the constitution, though the Orthodox Church receives government subsidies and is considered the "prevailing" faith of the country. Members of some minority religions face discrimination and legal barriers, such as permit requirements to open houses of worship and restrictions on inheriting property. The constitution prohibits proselytizing, but this law is almost never enforced. Opposition to the construction of an official mosque in Athens remains substantial; Muslim inhabitants are forced to worship in improvised mosques.

Academic freedom is respected in Greece, and the educational system is free of political indoctrination. Private conversation is open and free.

E. Associational and Organizational Rights: 11 / 12

Freedoms of assembly and association are guaranteed by the constitution, and the government generally protects these rights in practice, though there are some limits on groups representing ethnic minorities.

Nongovernmental organizations generally operate without interference from the authorities, and workers have the right to form and join unions. Major anti-austerity protests and strikes have occurred frequently in recent years, including large-scale demonstrations during 2013. The vast majority of participants are peaceful, but the protests often turn violent as anarchist elements and the police confront each other.

The right of immigrants and immigrant advocacy groups to assemble is more problematic. Golden Dawn has attempted to intimidate and break up such assemblies. In some cases, the police have not adequately defended the rights of immigrants to assemble.

F. Rule of Law: 10 / 16

The judiciary is independent, and the constitution provides for public trials. Prisons suffer from overcrowding, as do immigrant detention centers. The end of 2012 and the beginning of 2013 saw a major crackdown on illegal immigration that was criticized by human rights organizations for being too indiscriminate, for inhumane conditions in the detention centers, and for the state's failure to implement an adequate system for processing asylum applications. Immigrants are disproportionately affected by institutional problems in the judicial system. Bureaucratic delays force many into a semi-legal status whereby they cannot renew their documents, putting them in jeopardy of deportation.

Acts of political violence continue to constitute a problem. During 2012, 154 acts of racially motivated violence were recorded in Greece, according to an April 2013 report by the Racist Violence Recording Network, with many of them focused in Athens and Patra, two of the epicenters of Golden Dawn activity. There is significant evidence of police complicity, with multiple reports of officers refusing to intervene. Golden Dawn also targets leftists and members of the LGBT community.

G. Personal Autonomy and Individual Rights: 13 / 16

The country's Romany community continues to face considerable governmental and societal discrimination. A 2006 law designed to address domestic violence has been criticized for not giving the state the power to protect the rights of women. Women continue to face discrimination in the workplace and hold only 21 percent of the seats in Parliament, a 4 percent increase over the 2009 election, but lower than Greece's Eurozone counterparts. The country serves as a transit and destination country for the trafficking of men, women, and children for the purposes of sexual exploitation and forced labor.

Grenada

Political Rights Rating: 1
Civil Liberties Rating: 2
Freedom Rating: 1.5
Freedom Status: Free
Electoral Democracy: Yes

Population: 111,582
Capital: St. George's

Ten-Year Ratings Timeline For Year Under Review (Political Rights, Civil Liberties, Status)

Year Under Review	2004	2005	2006	2007	2008	2009	2010	2011	2012	2013
Rating	1,2,F	1,2,F	1,2,F	1,2,F	1,2,F	1,2,F	1,2,F	1,2,F	1,2,F	1,2,F

INTRODUCTION

In January, Prime Minister Tillman Thomas requested the governor-general to dissolve Parliament to prepare for early elections. The country's struggling economy and a 30 percent unemployment rate were the main issues in the ensuing election campaign. Grenada faces unsustainable debt levels and has yet to fully rebuild after devastation by Hurricane Ivan in 2004, which damaged 90 percent of the island's buildings and destroyed the country's main export crop, nutmeg.

In elections on February 19, Prime Minister Thomas and his National Democratic Congress (NDC) lost their 11 seats in the House of Representatives; the New National Party (NNP) captured all 15 seats. Organization of American States (OAS) electoral monitors deemed the elections fair, but recommended that the government review its electoral law and introduce campaign finance regulations.

POLITICAL RIGHTS: 38 / 40

A. Electoral Process: 12 / 12

Grenada is governed under a parliamentary system. The bicameral Parliament consists of the directly elected, 15-seat House of Representatives, whose members serve five-year terms, and the 13-seat Senate, to which the prime minister appoints 10 members and typically the opposition leader appoints 3. The prime minister is generally the leader of the majority party in the House of Representatives and is appointed by the governor-general, who represents the British monarch as head of state.

Prime Minister Thomas's government and his NDC party were plagued by infighting and dissent. While elections were not constitutionally due until October, in January Thomas requested the governor-general to dissolve Parliament. The election took place February 19, a little over a month later. In addition to the NDC and the NNP, the newly formed National United Front (NUF), representing a breakaway faction of the NDC, competed in the elections. Voter turnout was 87 percent. The elections gave a landslide victory to the NNP, which captured all 15 seats in the House of Representatives with 59 percent of the vote; the NDC received 41 percent of the vote and the NUF received less than 1 percent. Keith Mitchell, who had served as prime minister from 1995 to 2008, was sworn in as prime minister the following day.

The OAS Electoral Observer Team commended the government on implementation of a new voter registration system. However, it expressed concerns over the lack of campaign financing regulations, and recommended a comprehensive review of the Representation of the Peoples Act, which governs the conduct of elections.

Due to the lack of parliamentary opposition after the elections, the governor-general appointed three former NDC ministers to the Senate. In April, Prime Minister Mitchell announced the appointment of Grenada's first female governor-general, Dr. Cécile La Grenade. In September, La Grenade acted in her role as head of state to dismiss the supervisor of elections, Judy Benoit. Benoit had failed to comply with a cabinet-mandated decision to integrate the Electronic Government for Regional Integration Project (EGRIP) into the electoral computer system, which Benoit claimed would infringe on the independent mandate of the Office of the Supervisor of Elections and violate the Office's integrity. Benoit requested a judicial review of her dismissal; however, a date had yet to be set by year's end for the hearing.

B. Political Pluralism and Participation: 16 / 16

Grenada's main political parties are the center-left NDC and the conservative NNP, which regularly rotate in power. A number of smaller parties exist and competed in the last elections, including Grenada United Labour Party, the People's Labour Movement, and the newly formed NUF. Parties are free to form and operate.

C. Functioning of Government: 10 / 12

Corruption remains a contentious political issue in Grenada. The Prevention of Corruption Act and the Integrity in Public Life Act were passed in 2007. While the Integrity Commission was operationalized in 2010, it has yet to commence its work. However, the new NNP government announced its intention to implement the Integrity in Public Life Act, and allocated funds for the Integrity Commission in its 2013 budget statement.

CIVIL LIBERTIES: 51 / 60
D. Freedom of Expression and Belief: 15 / 16

The right to free expression is guaranteed in the constitution and is generally respected in practice. In July 2012, Grenada became the first Caribbean country to decriminalize defamation. However, seditious libel remains a criminal offence with a possible two-year prison sentence. The government also passed the retrogressive Electronic Crimes Act on September 9, which includes sanctions for "offensive" electronic communications, with a prison sentence of up to one year. The government subsequently responded to international pressure, announcing on September 23 that it would make necessary changes so the law does not restrict free speech; however, no changes to the law had been made by year's end. While Grenada has no daily newspapers, there are several privately owned weeklies. The government owns a minority stake in a private corporation that operates the principal radio and television stations, and there are several independent stations.

Citizens of Grenada generally practice their religious beliefs freely, and there are no official restrictions on academic freedom.

E. Associational and Organizational Rights: 11 / 12

Constitutional guarantees regarding freedoms of assembly and association are respected. Independent non-governmental organizations are free to operate. Workers have the right to strike and to organize and bargain collectively, though employers are not legally bound to recognize a union if the majority of the workers do not join.

F. Rule of Law: 12 / 16

The constitution provides for an independent judiciary, which is generally respected by the government. Grenada is a member of the Organization of Eastern Caribbean States court system and is a charter member of the Caribbean Court of Justice (CCJ), but still relies on the Privy Council in London as its final court of appeal. Detainees and defendants are guaranteed a range of legal rights, which are mostly respected in practice. However, Grenada's prisons are significantly overcrowded. In December 2011, five police officers allegedly beat to death Oscar Bartholomew, a Grenadian-Canadian man on holiday. In March 2013 manslaughter charges were dropped and the officers returned to work pending a coroner's inquest into the death, which was delayed again in September and had yet to take place at year's end.

G. Personal Autonomy and Individual Rights: 13 / 16

The constitution prohibits gender discrimination, and Grenada's Employment Act (1999) and Education Act (2002) prohibit discrimination based on sex. However, in practice cultural norms and traditional practices perpetuate discrimination. New domestic violence legislation came into effect in 2011, but enforcement has been limited. While women's political representation increased to a record one-third of the lower house following the 2013 elections, women were appointed to just 2 of the 13 Senate seats. Grenada's Criminal Code criminalizes same-sex sexual conduct with prison sentences of up to 10 years, and gay men and lesbians face significant social discrimination.

Guatemala

Political Rights Rating: 3
Civil Liberties Rating: 4
Freedom Rating: 3.5
Freedom Status: Partly Free
Electoral Democracy: Yes

Population: 15,400,000
Capital: Guatemala City

Ten-Year Ratings Timeline For Year Under Review (Political Rights, Civil Liberties, Status)

Year Under Review Rating	2004	2005	2006	2007	2008	2009	2010	2011	2012	2013
	4,4,PF	4,4,PF	3,4,PF	3,4,PF	3,4,PF	4,4,PF	4,4,PF	3,4,PF	3,4,PF	3,4,PF

INTRODUCTION

The Guatemalan criminal justice system continued to demonstrate progress in 2013, with investigations, prosecutions, and guilty verdicts in a number of high-profile cases related to government corruption, murder, extortion, and organized crime. According to the attorney general's office, the number of convictions nearly doubled between 2009 and 2012. In May, former dictator Efraín Ríos Montt was convicted on charges of genocide and crimes against humanity and sentenced to 80 years in prison. Only 10 days later, however, Guatemala's Constitutional Court (CC) overturned the ruling, citing procedural irregularities and returning the case to the lower court.

Attorney General Claudia Paz y Paz and her office continued to receive crucial international support in 2013, while the UN-backed International Commission Against Impunity in Guatemala (CICIG)—a team of police and prosecutors tasked with investigating corruption, violence, and organized crime within Guatemalan public institutions, political parties, and civil society—showed modest improvements in reforming the country's justice system during the year. Colombian Ivan Velasquez Gomez replaced Francisco Dall'Anese as head of CICIG in September.

POLITICAL RIGHTS: 24 / 40

A. Electoral Process: 9 / 12

The Republic of Guatemala, which was established in 1839, has endured a history of dictatorship, foreign intervention, military coups, and guerrilla insurgencies. Civilian rule followed the 1985 elections, and a 36-year civil war—which claimed the lives of more than 200,000 people—ended with a 1996 peace agreement. The Guatemalan National Revolutionary Unit guerrilla movement became a political party, and two truth commissions began receiving complaints of human rights violations committed during the conflict.

The constitution stipulates a four-year presidential term and prohibits reelection. Members of the 158-seat, unicameral Congress of the Republic are elected to four-year terms.

Elections take place within a highly fragmented and fluid multiparty system. In 2011, Guatemalans voted to elect a president, all 158 members of the parliament, mayors for each of the 333 municipalities, and 20 members of the Central American Parliament. The Patriotic Party (PP) and National Unity for Hope (UNE) captured two-thirds of the seats in parliamentary elections; nine other parties took the remaining 54 seats. After no candidate won a majority of votes in the first round of the presidential election, the PP's Otto Peréz Molina defeated Manuel Baldizón of the Renewed Democratic Liberty (LIDER) in a November runoff with 54 percent of the vote. The elections were generally considered free and fair despite accompanying violence, and electoral observers reported irregularities including intimidation, vote buying, and the burning of ballots and electoral boxes. The electoral authority, the Supreme Electoral Tribunal, was criticized for its slow transmission of election results.

B. Political Pluralism and Participation: 10 / 16

At least 36 candidates, party activists, and their relatives were killed in campaign-related violence surrounding the 2011 elections. Both the LIDER and the PP violated campaign spending laws, and five municipal elections had to be repeated due to irregularities.

The government uses the military to maintain internal security, despite restrictions on this practice imposed by the 1996 peace accord. Only 12 percent of the seats in the Congress of the Republic are held by members of the indigenous community, who make up 44 percent of the population. The indigenous population had a more significant representation at the local government level.

C. Functioning of Government: 5 / 12

Despite efforts to combat corruption, serious problems remain. Peréz ordered the closing of the National Fund for Peace (Fonapaz), a governmental organization created by the 1996 peace accords in order to support municipal development projects, in January 2013 because the institution had become so corrupt that it was beyond saving. However, the Social Development Fund, which replaced it, is reportedly similarly plagued by corruption. On October 15, Pérez announced that the military would intervene in the Tax Administration Superintendence, the agency that collects taxes and customs duties for the central government, due to problems in five customs houses that collected less tax than expected.

Vice President Roxana Baldetti Elias has been linked to several high-profile scandals and has purchased luxury items, including several multimillion dollar homes, with unexplained wealth.

In May 2013, former president Alfonso Portillo was extradited to the United States, where he was indicted in 2010 for allegedly embezzling state funds while in office (2000–2004) and laundering the money through Guatemalan, European, and U.S. banks. His case was ongoing at year's end.

In October 2013, five people with close ties to Antigua mayor Vivar Marroquin were sentenced to between two and three years in prison for extortion and fraud. Marroquin himself and several associates await trial on charges of fraud, money laundering, and abuse of authority.

Guatemala's Human Rights Ombudsman reported that it had received 140 denouncements against state institutions for denying or making difficult access to information during the first half of 2013. The office received 275 complaints in 2012. Guatemala was ranked 123 out of 177 countries and territories surveyed in Transparency International's 2013 Corruption Perceptions Index.

CIVIL LIBERTIES: 32 / 60 (-1)
D. Freedom of Expression and Belief: 12 / 16

While freedom of speech is protected by the constitution, journalists often face threats and practice self-censorship when covering drug trafficking, corruption, organized crime, and human rights violations. Threats come from public officials, drug traffickers, individuals aligned with companies operating in indigenous communities, and local security forces. As of mid-October 2013, there had been more than 80 attacks or threats against journalist, including murders in Guatemala City, Zacapa, and Jutiapa. The website of *El Periodico* newspaper has been targeted by several cyber-attacks, and its editor and reporters were threatened following investigations into government corruption. In November, Pérez filed a complaint against José Rubén Zamora Marroquín, the editor of *El Periodico*, accusing him of coercion, blackmail, extortion, violating the constitution, and insulting the president. A judge ordered him not to leave the country and set a hearing for February 2014. In December, a judge issued a restraining order against Zamora that prohibits him from criticizing or physically approaching Baldetti and her family. In November, César Pérez Méndez, the director of the daily newspaper *El Quetzalteco*, reported receiving several deaths threats believed to be related to his paper's coverage of local corruption in Quetzaltenango. Also in November, members of the National Civil Police pepper sprayed 28 journalists in two separate incidents while they were trying to cover a high-profile crime story.

On May 6, Pérez signed a law that created the Program to Protect Journalists, and several mining company employees and government officials were sentenced to jail time in 2013 for threatening journalists. Nevertheless, threats and attacks against journalists increased in 2013, many of which were linked to the Ríos Montt trial. The Central American Institute for Social Democracy Studies and the private office of the UN special rapporteur on freedom of Opinion and expression, Frank La Rue, were burglarized on July 31, during which documents and computers were stolen.

The press and most broadcast outlets are privately owned. Mexican businessman Remigio Ángel González owns a monopoly of broadcast television networks and has significant holdings in radio. Newspaper ownership is concentrated in the hands of business elites, and most papers have centrist or conservative editorial views.

The constitution guarantees religious freedom. However, indigenous communities have faced discrimination for openly practicing the Mayan religion. The government does not interfere with academic freedom, but scholars have received death threats for questioning past human rights abuses or continuing injustices. On January 17, the offices of the Association for the Advancement of Social Sciences were burglarized shortly before the organization was scheduled to publish a report related to its work on the history of the police.

E. Associational and Organizational Rights: 6 / 12 (-1)

The constitution guarantees freedom of assembly, though police frequently threaten force and have at times used force against protesters. The constitution guarantees freedom of association, and a variety of nongovernmental organizations (NGOs) operate in Guatemala, although they do confront significant obstacles. According to the Human Rights Defenders Protection Unit in Guatemala, attacks against human rights defenders rose from 305 in 2012 to 568 during the first eight months of 2013 alone. According to the Guatemalan Human Rights Defenders Protection Unit, a domestic NGO, 18 human rights defenders were killed through November 2013; a total of 13 had been killed in all of 2012. The safety of members of international NGOs worsened during the Rios Montt trial and continued through the end of the year. In October, Interior Minister Mauricio López Bonilla threatened to deport foreigners "meddling in Guatemala's internal affairs."

Guatemala is home to a vigorous labor movement, but workers are frequently denied the right to organize and face mass firings and blacklisting, especially in export-processing zones. Trade union members are also subject to intimidation, violence, and murder, particularly in rural areas during land disputes. According to the International Trade Union Confederation, Guatemala is the most dangerous country in the world for trade unionists. In June, the Committee on Freedom of Association drew international attention to the murder of trade union members and other labor issues in Guatemala. In 2010, the United States filed a formal complaint against Guatemala under the Dominican Republic-Central America Free Trade Agreement, alleging government failure to protect workers' rights. In August 2011, the United States further requested a dispute settlement panel to address its complaint. Representatives from Guatemala and the United States signed an 18-point Enforcement Plan in April, but the United States reiterated that "significant work" was needed on the part of Guatemala as late as October.

F. Rule of Law: 6 / 16

The judiciary is troubled by corruption, inefficiency, capacity shortages, and the intimidation of judges and prosecutors. Witnesses and judicial-sector workers continue to be threatened and, in some cases, murdered. In December 2012, a federal prosecutor and six others were murdered in Huehuetenango. A November 2012 CICIG report accused 18 judges of "creating spaces of impunity" for organized crime and corrupt officials, including shielding suspected criminals from prosecution and making questionable rulings in their favor. According to the CICIG's 2013 report, impunity levels have decreased from 93 percent to 70 percent since the commission's inception.

Police continue to be accused of torture, extortion, kidnapping, extrajudicial killings, and drug-related crimes, although there were several notable prosecutions in 2013. In September, Baltazar Gomez, former director of the National Civil Police, was convicted and sentenced to 16 years in prison for stealing at least 350 kilograms of cocaine in 2009. As of November 2013, authorities had registered more than 1,500 complaints against police; over 300 current and former police officers were arrested for various crimes, including murder and kidnapping. Prison conditions are harsh, and facilities are overcrowded and rife with gang- and drug-related violence and corruption. Prisoners, including Byron Lima Oliva, who is serving time for his involvement in the murder of Bishop Juan Gerardi, have been known to come and go from prison without authorization.

Even after four years of declining homicide rates, Guatemala remains one of the most violent countries in Latin America. Over 5,200 people were murdered in 2013. Violence related to the shipment of drugs from South America to the United States has spilled over the border from Mexico, with rival Mexican and Guatemalan drug gangs battling for territory. These groups have operated with impunity in the northern jungles, which serve as a storage and transit hub for cocaine en route to the United States. The local drug problem has also worsened, as traffickers have paid Guatemalan associates in cocaine rather than cash. The Pérez administration reacted to this situation by expanding the military's role in fighting crime, including creating special task forces to investigate kidnappings, robberies, extortion, and homicides, and building five military bases along well-known drug trafficking routes. Human rights activists are concerned that the bases will be built in areas that have experienced serious conflicts over land, natural resources, and indigenous rights, and in areas that bore the brunt of military repression during the armed conflict.

In May 2013, a 30-day state of siege was declared in four municipalities around the El Escobal mining project: San Rafael Las Flores and Casillas in Santa Rosa, and Jalapa and Mataquescuintla in Jalapa. In July, eight police officers were murdered in their police station in Salcaja, Quetzaltenango, allegedly the result of one of the officers' theft of drugs. Authorities appear to have arrested most, if not all, of those involved in the killing. In September, 29 people were shot and 11 killed in San Jose Nacahuil, outside Guatemala City. Authorities believe the attack was caused by a store owner's refusal to pay protection money, and they arrested eight members of the 18th Street gang in October in connection with the violence.

Citizens continue to take the law into their own hands. According to the Mutual Support Group, there were 39 percent more lynchings during the first 10 months of 2013 compared to the same period in 2012.

Prosecutions of perpetrators of past human rights atrocities continued in 2013. The trial of Ríos Montt—whose May conviction was overturned by the Constitutional Court 10 days later—is scheduled to resume in 2015, a delay that has prompted international criticism from human rights groups. Former guerrilla Fermin Felipe Solano Barillas was arrested in May 2013 for his involvement in the 1988 murders of 22 civilians, and was scheduled to go on trial in February 2014. On September 20, former chief of police Hector Bol de la Cruz was sentenced to 40 years in prison for his participation in the 1984 disappearance of union leader Fernando García. Two former police officers had been sentenced in October 2011 to 40 years in prison for García's kidnapping and disappearance.

Indigenous communities suffer from especially high rates of poverty, illiteracy, and infant mortality. Indigenous women are particularly marginalized. Discrimination against the Mayan community continues to be a major concern. The government in recent years has approved the eviction of indigenous groups to make way for mining, hydroelectric, and other development projects. Several large indigenous communities have reportedly been forcibly evicted in the Polochic Valley with killings, beatings, and the burning of houses and crops. In August 2013, Pérez announced the creation of a cabinet position dedicated to indigenous people.

Clashes between government forces and indigenous people led to the deaths of seven demonstrators at Cuatro Caminos in May 2012. A colonel and eight soldiers were awaiting trial for the killings as of the end of 2013.

Members of the LGBT (lesbian, gay, bisexual, and transgender) community continue to be targets of violent attacks.

G. Personal Autonomy and Individual Rights: 8 / 16

Private businesses continue to experience high rates of extortion by gangs and organized crime. They also suffer from high rates of contraband smuggling.

The constitution prohibits discrimination based on gender, though gender inequalities persist in practice. Sexual harassment in the workplace is not penalized. Young women who migrate to the capital for work are especially vulnerable to harassment and inhumane labor conditions. Physical and sexual violence against women and children, including domestic violence, remain widespread, with perpetrators rarely prosecuted. While Guatemala now has its first female attorney general and vice president, women remain underrepresented in politics and hold just 13 percent of the seats in the Congress of the Republic.

Guatemala has one of the highest rates of child labor in the Americas. According to the U.S. State Department, the government does not fully comply with the minimum standards for eliminating trafficking but is making efforts to do so, including launching a program to provide specialized services for trafficking victims. Guatemala created an investigative body to combat trafficking in July 2012. The kidnapping of children for illegal adoption remains a concern, as does the trafficking of women and children for labor and sexual slavery. In October 2013, authorities claimed to have dismantled five criminal networks dedicated to international trafficking for either labor exploitation, sexual exploitation, or the trafficking of organs.

Guinea

Political Rights Rating: 5
Civil Liberties Rating: 5
Freedom Rating: 5.0
Freedom Status: Partly Free
Electoral Democracy: No

Population: 11,800,000
Capital: Conakry

Ten-Year Ratings Timeline For Year Under Review (Political Rights, Civil Liberties, Status)

Year Under Review	2004	2005	2006	2007	2008	2009	2010	2011	2012	2013
Rating	6,5,NF	6,5,NF	6,5,NF	6,5,NF	7,5,NF	7,6,NF	5,5,PF	5,5,PF	5,5,PF	5,5,PF

INTRODUCTION

In September, Guinea held its first parliamentary elections since a 2008 coup and the violent suppression of opposition protests that followed. The months preceding the elections were marred by violence, leaving dozens of people dead and hundreds injured, and the election results were criticized as unfair by a coalition of opposition parties.

Also during the year, Guinea continued to be plagued by corruption scandals, one of which involved an inquiry by the U.S. Federal Bureau of Investigation (FBI), and there was little progress on the adjudication of atrocities committed by security forces during the 2009 antigovernment protests.

Despite its rich natural resources—Guinea is the world's largest exporter of bauxite, an aluminum ore—the majority of the population lives in poverty. Investment in the country's lucrative mining sector continues to lag as a result of ongoing political instability. Guinea's economic growth underperformed forecasts by a full percentage point in 2012, and the Ministry of Finance warned that investor wariness linked to political uncertainty threatened growth targets for 2013 as well.

POLITICAL RIGHTS: 17 / 40 (+2)
A. Electoral Process: 6 / 12 (+1)

The president is elected by popular vote for up to two five-year terms. The legislature was dissolved in 2008 amid a coup precipitated by the death of incumbent president Lansana Conté. The leader of the coup, Captain Moussa Dadis Camara, was shot and seriously injured in late 2009 by a member of his own guard following the violent repression of an opposition rally, in which security forces killed more than 150 people and raped and beat hundreds of others. A political accord then facilitated a return to civilian rule in 2010, establishing a power-sharing government and an interim legislature, the 155-member National Transitional Council (CNT).

In a presidential election held later in 2010, longtime opposition leader Alpha Condé of the Rally of the Guinean People (RPG) defeated former prime minister Cellou Dalein Diallo of the Union of Democratic Forces of Guinea (UFDG) in a runoff vote, 52.5 percent to 47.5

percent. Most domestic and international observers validated the election, and Diallo eventually accepted the results.

The first parliamentary elections since the 2008 coup were held in September 2013 after repeated delays. The months preceding the elections were marred by violence, ethnic and religious tensions, and disputes over the rules governing the polls, which opposition parties alleged were designed to favor the RPG. Recurrent protests resulted in over 50 deaths between January and September; in the week before the elections, opposition protesters shot and killed a police officer in training, provoking clashes that left 70 people wounded.

The election results were released three weeks after ballots were cast. The RPG won a total of 53 seats in the National Assembly, which serves five-year terms. Of the assembly's 114 seats, 38 are awarded through single-member constituency races, and 76 are filled through nationwide proportional representation. The opposition UFDG won 37 seats, the Union of Republican Forces (UFR) won 10, and a dozen smaller parties divided the remainder. In October, a coalition of opposition parties declined to participate in further vote counting and called for the results of the elections to be annulled. The National Electoral Commission (CENI) admitted to irregularities, but nevertheless defended the validity of the results.

The new constitution that was adopted as part of the political transition in 2010 established a number of independent entities to secure democratic rights, including the CENI, a national human rights body, and a constitutional court.

B. Political Pluralism and Participation: 8 / 16

The main political parties are the RPG and the UFDG. There are more than 130 registered parties, most of which have clear ethnic or regional bases. In October 2012, 44 political parties merged with the RPG to form the RPG-Rainbow coalition. Many of these parties signed a joint declaration in April 2013 that disavowed violence and fraud in the months leading up to the parliamentary elections, though the declaration did little to prevent abuses before or during the polls. During the elections, some 1,700 candidates vied for the 114 parliamentary seats.

UN-backed reforms continue to bring the country's notoriously undisciplined armed forces under civilian oversight and to prevent military meddling in politics. In February, President Condé appointed a close ally as head of the armed forces when a plane crash killed his predecessor and five other top army officials.

C. Functioning of Government: 3 / 12 (+1)

Corruption is a serious problem, and many government activities are shrouded in secrecy. A scandal erupted in 2013 over former president Conté's decision to award a mining license worth billions of dollars to BSG Resources, a company owned by Israeli diamond magnate Beny Steinmetz. The FBI launched an investigation into the deal in January due to its possible violation of the United States's Foreign Corrupt Practices Act. Investigators accused Conté's wife, Mamadie Touré, of receiving kickbacks from BSG, and the Conté regime of destroying evidence that it received millions of dollars in bribes in return for its cooperation in the deal. President Alpha Condé has cooperated with the investigation in the expectation that the mining concession would ultimately be returned to state control. In the wake of the scandal, the government created a commission to reevaluate all 18 mining contracts in effect in Guinea. However, critics contend that the commission is powerless and that reform will depend on companies' willingness to voluntarily renegotiate the terms of their contracts.

Guinea was ranked 150 out of 177 countries and territories surveyed in Transparency International's 2013 Corruption Perceptions Index.

CIVIL LIBERTIES: 24 / 40

D. Freedom of Expression and Belief: 9 / 16

The 2010 constitution guarantees media freedom. In June 2010, the CNT passed two new media laws: one decriminalized press offenses and more clearly defined defamation provisions, while the other created a new media regulatory body. Nevertheless, attacks on the press persist. In August 2013, soldiers in the president's personal security detail assaulted and closed a privately owned radio station for its coverage of local protests against a presidential visit, then beat several journalists associated with the station over the next several days. The press also came under increased scrutiny in the months preceding the September parliamentary polls, and some reporters were accused of intentionally inciting ethnic and partisan tensions.

There are more than 200 newspapers in Guinea, though most have small circulations. While the state controls the national radio station and the only television broadcaster, there are more than 30 radio stations. Due to the high illiteracy rate, most of the population accesses information through radio; internet access remains limited to urban areas.

Religious rights are respected in practice, although there have been rare cases of discrimination against non-Muslims in government employment, as well as restrictions on Muslims' freedom to convert to other religions. Academic freedom has been hampered to some degree by government influence over hiring and curriculum content. Free private discussion, limited under previous authoritarian governments, continued to improve in 2013.

E. Associational and Organizational Rights: 6 / 12

Freedom of assembly is enshrined in the constitution but repressed in practice. Clashes between protesters and state security forces were routine in the months prior to the 2013 parliamentary elections, resulting in dozens of deaths and hundreds of injuries. Freedom of association is generally respected, and there were no reports of government harassment of human rights activists in 2013.

Although workers are allowed to form trade unions, strike, and bargain collectively, they must provide 10 days' notice before striking, and strikes are banned in broadly defined essential services. Members of Guinea's labor unions were active in calling for the annulment of mining licenses awarded under dubious circumstances during Conté's presidency.

F. Rule of Law: 4 / 16

The judicial system has demonstrated some degree of independence since 2010, and the government made modest efforts in 2013 to prosecute human rights violations committed over the last several years. In particular, these efforts have focused on identifying and charging the perpetrators of the massacre of opposition protesters at Conakry stadium in 2009. A panel of magistrates was empowered to investigate the massacre, and Lieutenant Colonel Moussa Tiégboro Camara and Colonel Abdoulaye Chérif Diaby were indicted in 2012 for their involvement. Another high-profile suspect, Lieutenant Colonel Claude Pivi—Guinea's minister for presidential security—was charged in June 2013. However, a lack of political and financial support has stymied progress in the investigations. Pivi remained at his post at year's end, a request to interview former military ruler Camara was still pending, and some suspects have languished in pretrial detention for longer than the two years permitted under Guinean law.

The courts are severely understaffed and underfunded, and security forces continue to engage in arbitrary arrests, torture of detainees, and extrajudicial executions with impunity. Prison conditions remain harsh and are sometimes life threatening.

While the law prohibits discrimination based on race or ethnicity, discrimination by the country's three major ethnic groups—the Peul, Malinké, and Soussou—in employment and place of residence is common. Tensions among these groups are common as well, and multiple incidents of violence before the parliamentary elections in September pitted progovernment Malinké tribesmen against the largely opposition-oriented Peul.

Antidiscrimination laws do not protect LGBT (lesbian, gay, bisexual, and transgender) people. Gay and lesbian sexual activity is a criminal offense that can be punished with up to three years in prison, and although this law is rarely enforced, LGBT people have been arrested on lesser charges.

G. Personal Autonomy and Individual Rights: 5 / 16

Freedom of movement is hindered by rampant crime and bribe-seeking soldiers at security checkpoints, and private business activity is hampered by corruption and political instability, among other factors. A new centralized Agency for the Promotion of Private Investments was established in December 2011 to improve the country's business environment by making the registration process faster and less expensive.

Societal discrimination against women is pervasive. While women have legal access to land, credit, and business, they are disadvantaged by inheritance laws and the traditional justice system. Guinean law allows husbands to forbid their wives from working. Rape and sexual harassment are prevalent but underreported due to fears of stigmatization. Security personnel openly raped more than 100 women during 2007 and 2009 crackdowns on protesters. Advocacy groups are working to eradicate the illegal but nearly ubiquitous practice of female genital mutilation, which according to some estimates affects up to 96 percent of all girls and women in Guinea.

Guinea-Bissau

Political Rights Rating: 6
Civil Liberties Rating: 5
Freedom Rating: 5.5
Freedom Status: Not Free
Electoral Democracy: No

Population: 1,677,047
Capital: Bissau

Ten-Year Ratings Timeline For Year Under Review (Political Rights, Civil Liberties, Status)

Year Under Review	2004	2005	2006	2007	2008	2009	2010	2011	2012	2013
Rating	4,4,PF	3,4,PF	4,4,PF	4,4,PF	4,4,PF	4,4,PF	4,4,PF	4,4,PF	6,5,NF	6,5,NF

INTRODUCTION

Elections have yet to be held for a new president or legislature in the aftermath of the 2012 military coup, which occurred between the two rounds of presidential elections. After the coup, the Economic Community of West African States (ECOWAS) brokered a transition pact and political agreement signed by the military command and many political parties. The third-place candidate in the first-round presidential election, Manuel Serifo Nhamadjo, was named acting president.

On January 17, 2013, the main opposition party, the African Party for the Independence of Guinea-Bissau and Cabo Verde (PAIGC), and four other parties joined the political transition pact and the political agreement. The signing of these documents facilitated parliamentary review of both, as well as the drafting of a new transition roadmap and the formation of a new government of national unity. The international community considered the latter as a condition for the resumption of aid to Guinea-Bissau.

On April 30, a new "Regime Pact" and an "Agreement of Principles for the Return to Normalcy" were presented. To enhance inclusiveness, the parliamentary committee in charge of the review invited religious leaders, nongovernmental organizations (NGOs), and party leaders to participate. The documents that emerged envisioned general elections in November 2013 and the end of the political transition by December 31, 2013; the appointment of an inclusive transitional government; and the election by the National People's Assembly of the president of the National Electoral Commission on a proposal from the Supreme Council of Magistrates.

On June 6, the interim president appointed a broad-based, inclusive transitional government with PAIGC participation and led by Duarte Barros, who was retained as interim prime minister. On June 12, the National People's Assembly elected the new National Electoral Commission leadership, presided over by Supreme Court judge Augusto Mendes.

Nevertheless, instability continued in Guinea-Bissau throughout 2013. The transition was deferred from December 31 to the spring of 2014, and elections initially set for November 24 were postponed to March 2014 due to financial and planning difficulties. Moreover, corruption continued to plague the country, bolstered by Guinea-Bissau's prominent role in international narcotrafficking.

POLITICAL RIGHTS: 9 / 40 (+2)

A. Electoral Process: 3 / 12 (+1)

Under the constitution, members of the National People's Assembly are elected by popular vote for a four-year term. In the 2008 legislative elections—the last to take place—the PAIGC took 67 seats in the 100-seat National People's Assembly, the Party of Social Renewal (PRS) won 28 seats, and the Republican Party for Independence and Development captured 3 seats. In accordance with a transition pact brokered by the Economic Community of West African States (ECOWAS) in May 2012, the People's National Assembly was reinstated in 2013 and Mr. Manuel Serifo Nhamadjo (PAIGC) became Acting President of the Republic. The parliamentary term, which was due to end in November 2012, was extended until the new parliamentary and presidential elections scheduled for April 2014. Before the coup, the president was elected for a five-year term, with no term limits; the president appointed the prime minister.

On June 28, the interim president, Manuel Serifo Nhamadjo, issued a decree announcing that presidential and legislative elections would be held on November 24. On November 15, Nhamadjo issued another decree rescheduling the elections for March 16, 2014. The delay was justified by the fact that the funding needed to cover the costs of the election had only been secured a few weeks prior to the November election date. Additionally, the national voter registration had not been completed.

Shortly thereafter it was announced that voter registration would take place between December 1 and 22, 2013. The process generated controversy even before starting, since the Guinea-Bissau Office for the Technical Support to the Electoral Process (GTAPE) and the United Nations Development Program (UNDP) both wanted to manage the funds donated to cover the election costs.

B. Political Pluralism and Participation: 5 / 16

In 2013 there were over 30 parties in Guinea-Bissau. The top two political parties in Guinea-Bissau—PAIGC, PRS—and their much smaller counterparts such as the Party for

Democratic Convergence (PCD) are competitive but unpredictable and institutionally weak. They routinely suffer from military interference and shifting personal cliques.

In 40 years since independence Guinea-Bissau has never seen a president finish his mandate, due to their untimely death or military coups.

C. Functioning of Government: 1 / 12 (+1)

Corruption is pervasive, driven in large part by the illicit drug trade. With weak institutions and porous borders, Guinea-Bissau has become a major transit point for Latin American drug traffickers moving cocaine to Europe. Powerful segments of the military, police, and government are reportedly complicit in the trade, and the judiciary—either through lack of resources or collusion in the crimes—does not investigate or prosecute corruption cases.

Since the 2012 coup, drug trafficking and illegal exploitation of timber and fish have been on the rise. During an extraordinary session on June 13, the National People's Assembly requested the government to urgently address the rapid depletion of the few remaining forests in the country and related ecosystems.

Guinea-Bissau was ranked 46 out of 52 countries surveyed in the 2013 Ibrahim Index of African Governance, and 163 out of 177 countries and territories surveyed in Transparency International's 2013 Corruption Perceptions Index.

CIVIL LIBERTIES: 23 / 60
D. Freedom of Expression and Belief: 10 / 16

Although the constitution provides for freedoms of speech and the press, these freedoms are currently challenged. Journalists regularly face harassment and intimidation, especially regarding the military's alleged involvement in drug trafficking and its role in the coup. According to the president of the journalists' union, insecurity, poor salaries, difficult work conditions, and limited access to information and technology condition journalists' work. There are no reports that the government restricts access to the internet but the lack of infrastructure and low levels of education greatly limit its use by Guineans.

Religious freedom is legally protected and usually respected in practice. Academic freedom is similarly guaranteed and upheld.

E. Associational and Organizational Rights: 5 / 12

The government generally does not interfere with freedom of assembly as long as protesters secure the necessary authorizations (that are generally reasonable). NGOs were subject to harassment following the 2012 coup, but many have become more vocal in their opposition to the transitional government, human rights abuses, and increased economic and social insecurity. Workers are allowed to form and join independent trade unions, but few work in the wage-earning formal sector. The right to strike is protected, and government workers frequently exercise this right. Teachers have repeatedly gone on strike over salary delays, undermining already low education standards. Health workers also went on a seven-day strike in June.

F. Rule of Law: 3 / 16

Scant resources and endemic corruption severely challenge judicial independence. Judges and magistrates are poorly trained, irregularly paid, and highly susceptible to corruption and political pressure. There are essentially no resources to conduct criminal investigations, and few formal detention facilities. The limited capacity of the security and justice sectors results in the lack of effective civilian oversight over the defense and security forces, which threatens the political process and the functioning of state institutions. Furthermore, this weak capacity contributes to a persistent culture of impunity, lack of accountability, and insecurity. In 2013, a number of cases of human rights violations and abuses were reported, several of which were tied to the military. Soldiers were at the same time perpetrators and victims. On October 8, one Nigerian military official was lynched and killed after being accused of kidnapping a boy. In November, the third Guinean military personnel was beaten to death at the Cumere Military Training Center in just two months. On November 5 Orlando Viegas, Guinea-Bissau's minister of state for transport telecommunications and one of the PRS's vice presidents, was seriously beaten and forced to seek refuge at the UN offices in Bissau.

On a positive note, the arrest by U.S. agents of former navy chief Bubo Na Tchuto in April, as well as drug- and weapons-trafficking charges announced by a U.S. court against armed forces chief of staff Antonio Indjai, did mark a turning point in the fight against drug trafficking in Guinea-Bissau. Apparently without the knowledge or support of the Guinea-Bissau government, Na Tchuto was arrested in a U.S. undercover sting operation due to his role as a kingpin of the international drug trade.

Old rivalries between ethnic groups were revived in the aftermath of the coup and often expressed in disputes over cattle, land and water.

Same-sex sexual activity is legal. There are no reports of violence against the LGBT community but social taboos limit public expression.

G. Personal Autonomy and Individual Rights: 5 / 16

Women face significant traditional and societal discrimination, despite some legal protections. They generally do not receive equal pay for equal work and have fewer opportunities in education and employment. Women of certain ethnic groups cannot own or manage land or inherit property. A 2011 law bans female genital mutilation (FGM) and establishes penalties of up to five years in prison for violators. In response to persistent high levels of domestic violence, in August 2013 the national assembly approved a new law that criminalizes domestic violence, establishing prison sentences of up to 12 years for aggressors and establishing support centers for women. Forced marriages still occur but following NGO pressure some of these young women are freed. Trafficking in persons, especially children, is a serious problem, despite efforts by NGOs to raise awareness, improve law enforcement, and repatriate victims. In one of several instances, the police stopped the illegal trafficking of 60 boys from Kassala to Gambia in November 2013.

Guyana

Political Rights: 2
Civil Liberties: 3
Freedom Rating: 2.5
Freedom Status: Free
Electoral Democracy: Yes

Population: 800,000
Capital: Georgetown

Ten-Year Ratings Timeline For Year Under Review (Political Rights, Civil Liberties, Status)

Year Under Review	2004	2005	2006	2007	2008	2009	2010	2011	2012	2013
Rating	2,2,F	3,3,PF	2,3,F	2,3,F	2,3,F	2,3,F	2,3,F	2,3,F	2,3,F	2,3,F

INTRODUCTION

The government's unwillingness to implement or enforce anti-corruption laws has resulted in the withdrawal of international banks from Guyana. The country is the second-poorest in the Caribbean behind Haiti, though some observers believe its pervasive corruption could cause its standard of living to drop even further.

POLITICAL RIGHTS: 31 / 40

A. Electoral Process: 11 / 12

Guyana's 1980 constitution provides for a strong president and a 65-seat National Assembly, with members elected every five years. The president appoints two additional, nonvoting members. The leader of the party with a plurality of parliamentary seats becomes president for a five-year term and appoints the prime minister and cabinet.

Guyana gained independence from Britain in 1966 and was ruled by the autocratic, predominantly Afro-Guyanese People's National Congress (PNC) for the next 26 years. In 1992, Cheddi Jagan of the largely Indo-Guyanese People's Progressive Party (PPP) won the presidency in Guyana's first free and fair elections. He died in 1997, and the office passed to his wife, Janet, who resigned in 1999 for health reasons. She was succeeded by Finance Minister Bharrat Jagdeo of the PPP-C, an alliance of the PPP and the Civic Party. Jagdeo was elected in his own right in 2001.

In November 2011 elections, the PPP-C captured 32 seats, while the newly established Partnership For National Unity took 26 seats, and the Alliance For Change (AFC) won 7 seats. PPP-C leader, 61-year-old economist Donald Ramotar, became president in December. Denis Marshall, the chairperson of a Commonwealth Observer Group for the 2011 national and regional elections in Guyana, noted that, despite some minor issues, the elections represented progress in strengthening Guyana's democratic processes.

Some observers contend that the parliamentary opposition's one-vote majority has resulted in a stalemate in the National Assembly, with little legislative progress being made, and that President Ramotar's role has as a result been limited to a largely ceremonial one.

B. Political Pluralism and Participation: 13 / 16

Guyanese politics are dominated by a tense split between descendants of indentured workers from India, known as Indo-Guyanese, who generally back the PPP-C, and Afro-Guyanese, who largely support the PNC-Reform (PNC-R) party. In 2004, the political climate showed brief signs of improving when the PPP-C and PNC-R announced that they had reached agreement on a wide variety of issues. However, the emerging harmony was disrupted when a police informant revealed the existence of death squads that enjoyed official sanction and had killed some 64 people. An investigation exposed apparent links to the home affairs minister, Ronald Gajraj, but he was largely exonerated by an official inquiry in 2005.

The 2006 elections strengthened the hand of the ruling PPP-C, but also demonstrated that some Guyanese are beginning to vote across racial lines, as symbolized by the establishment of the multiracial AFC. In the 2011 elections, the PPP-C won for the fifth straight time, although the multiracial AFC gained more weight. The main opposition to the PPP-C minority government is the Partnership for National Unity (People's National Congress–Reform/ Guyana Action Party/National Front Alliance/Working People's Alliance). Together with the AFC, both parties have a one-vote majority over the ruling party.

C. Functioning of Government: 7 / 12

Guyana is rife with corruption. The country is a transshipment point for South American cocaine destined for North America and Europe, and counternarcotics efforts are undermined by corruption that reaches high levels of the government. The informal economy is driven primarily by drug proceeds and may be equal to between 40 and 60 percent of formal economic activity.

Opposition leaders have called for an anti-corruption commission for years, though little progress has been made. Guyana was ranked 136 out of 177 countries and territories surveyed in Transparency International's 2013 Corruption Perceptions Index. A 2013 visit to Guyana by a committee of experts of the Inter-American Convention against Corruption (MESICIC) of the Organization of American States (OAS) issued several recommendations to ameliorate corruption in Guyana. Thus, the committee advised the establishment of an articulated anti-corruption strategy, better coordination between police and the Office of Public Prosecutions, and more financial and human resource investments in several government oversight bodies (e.g., the Audit Office, Public Service Appellate Tribunal, or the Judicial Service Commission).

CIVIL LIBERTIES: 41 / 60 (+1)
D. Freedom of Expression and Belief: 15 / 16

Although freedom of the press is generally respected, an uneasy tension between the state and the media persists. Several independent newspapers operate freely, including the daily *Stabroek News* and *Kaieteur News*. However, opposition party leaders complain that they lack access to state media. The state owns and operates the country's sole radio station, which broadcasts on three frequencies. In 2009, the Guyana Press Association denounced a government initiative to license media professionals as an attempt to impose control over the profession. Government officials occasionally use libel lawsuits to suppress criticism. The government also closed an internationally funded media-monitoring unit, established in 2006 to monitor media ahead of national elections. There have recently been indications the government is considering reintroducing a media-monitoring unit, though opposition leaders have suggested that such a department could be used to suppress dissenting views.

Guyanese generally enjoy freedom of religion, and the government does not restrict academic freedom.

E. Associational and Organizational Rights: 10 / 12 (+1)

The government largely respects freedoms of assembly and association. However, in June 2012, police reportedly shot and killed three men who were part of a political protest against rising electricity prices in the town of Linden. An additional 20 people were injured as a result of the police firing live ammunition and teargas into the crowd of protesters. The subsequent Linden Commission of Inquiry appointed to clarify responsibility for lives lost appeared initially to be bogged down by partisan disputes. Its final report blamed the police for the fatalities, but exonerated the Minister of Home Affairs of responsibility.

There were no notable crackdowns of political protests in 2013.

The right to form labor unions is also generally upheld, and unions are well organized. However, employers are not required to recognize unions in former state enterprises.

F. Rule of Law: 7 / 16

The judicial system is independent, but due process is undermined by shortages of staff and funds. In 2005, Guyana cut all ties to the Privy Council in London, the court of last resort for other former British colonies in the region, and adopted the Trinidad-based Caribbean Court of Justice as its highest appellate court. Prisons are overcrowded, and conditions are poor.

The Guyana Defence Force and the national Guyana Police Force are under civilian control. Racial polarization has seriously eroded law enforcement, with many Indo-Guyanese complaining that they are victimized by Afro-Guyanese criminals and ignored by the predominantly Afro-Guyanese police. Meanwhile, many Afro-Guyanese claim that the police are manipulated by the government for its own purposes. Official inquiries have repeatedly called for improved investigative techniques, more funding, community-oriented policing, better disciplinary procedures, greater accountability, and a better ethnic balance in the police force, but the government has taken few concrete steps to implement the proposed reforms. Police officers have also been accused of soliciting bribes.

While racial clashes have diminished in the last decade, long-standing animosity between Afro- and Indo-Guyanese remains a serious concern. A 2002 Racial Hostility Bill increased penalties for race-based crimes.

G. Personal Autonomy and Individual Rights: 9 / 16

Guyana is home to nine indigenous groups with a total population of about 80,000. Human rights violations against them, particularly with respect to land and resource use, are widespread and pervasive. Indigenous peoples' attempts to seek redress through the courts have been met with unwarranted delays by the judiciary.

Violence against women, including domestic abuse, is widespread. Rape often goes unreported and is rarely prosecuted. The Guyana Human Rights Association has charged that the legal system's treatment of victims of sexual violence is intentionally humiliating. The 2010 Sexual Offenses Act makes rape gender-neutral and expands its definition to include spousal rape and coercion and child abuse; the new law also provides for offenses committed against the mentally disabled.

"Sodomy" is punishable with a maximum sentence of life in prison, and cross-dressing is criminalized for both men and women. In September 2013, the Constitutional Court ruled that cross-dressing in public is illegal only if done for an "improper purpose." Police routinely intimidate gay men.

Along with Cuba and Uruguay, Guyana is one of only three nations in Latin America that permits elective abortion.

Haiti

Political Rights: 4
Civil Liberties: 5
Freedom Rating: 4.5
Freedom Status: Partly Free
Electoral Democracy: No

Population: 10,400,000
Capital: Port-au-Prince

Ten-Year Ratings Timeline For Year Under Review (Political Rights, Civil Liberties, Status)

Year Under Review	2004	2005	2006	2007	2008	2009	2010	2011	2012	2013
Rating	7,6,NF	7,6,NF	4,5,PF	4,5,PF	4,5,PF	4,5,PF	4,5,PF	4,5,PF	4,5,PF	4,5,PF

INTRODUCTION

Political tensions continued to escalate in 2013 as legislative and municipal elections initially scheduled for November 2011 were delayed for another year, causing Haiti to descend toward political crisis. The government made some moves to strengthen the regulatory framework on corruption and improve its capacity to respond to rights violations, and the establishment of an interministerial commission on human rights was considered a promising development toward compliance with international human rights treaties. In practice, however, enjoyment of civil liberties did not markedly improve; detainees and internally displaced people continued to face harrowing conditions and abuse and members of the lesbian, gay, bisexual and transgender (LGBT) community faced attacks. Threats to and harassment and illegal arrests of human rights defenders also continued in 2013, and opposition groups and human rights observers responded to the unlawful arrest of attorney André Michel with outrage. In a positive step for rule of law, a court heard an appeal to a 2012 dismissal of human rights charges against Haiti's former dictator Jean-Claude Duvalier, and summoned both Duvalier and his alleged victims to testify.

POLITICAL RIGHTS: 18 / 40 (-1)
A. Electoral Process: 4 / 12 (-1)

Haiti's constitution provides for a president directly elected for a five-year term, a bicameral parliament composed of a 30-member Senate and a 99-member Chamber of Deputies, and a prime minister appointed by the president. Senators are elected for six-year terms, with one-third coming up for election every two years, and deputies for four-year terms.

Presidential and parliamentary elections held in November 2010 were marred by widespread reports of fraud, voter intimidation, violations of electoral laws, illegal exclusion of political parties and candidates, and problems with the composition of the Provisional Electoral Council. Following a dispute over first-round results, musician Michel Martelly won the presidential election in a March 2011 second round that saw low voter turnout. Meanwhile, after parliamentary runoff elections, the Inité coalition of Martelly's predecessor, René Préval, held 46 seats in the lower house and 6 of the 11 Senate seats at stake. Smaller parties divided the remainder.

Midterm parliamentary and municipal elections due to take place in November 2011 had yet to take place by the end of 2013, posing a grave threat to the democratic functioning of the government. The resulting vacancies have crippled the Senate and the President has replaced some 130 elected mayors with political appointees, offsetting the balance of power provided for in the constitution. According to the constitution, elections are to be organized by a Permanent Electoral Council (CEP) that has never been fully realized in practice. Constitutional amendments adopted in 2011 after a fraught process reformed the CEP appointment process by centralizing appointment powers in the three branches of government. Discrepancies between the constitutional amendments as published and those that had been ratified as well as subsequent irregularities in appointments to the new CEP resulted in political impasse and yet again paralyzed the CEP's proper formation.

In December 2012, the executive and legislative branches agreed to establish an extraconstitutional Transitional College of the Permanent Electoral Council (CTCEP) to plan the overdue 2011 elections. The CTCEP began operations in April 2013, including the drafting of a new electoral law to replace the Electoral Law of 2008 that governed the previous round of elections. Amidst growing tensions and accusations of intentional delays, the CTCEP transmitted the proposed law to a presidential commission in July, which in turn passed on the law to the Chamber of Deputies only days before its last session of the year. The Chamber reportedly held a vote on the law on the eve of their recess, though some parliamentarians contested that an affirming vote actually took place. The Senate passed a modified version of the law in October, which was ultimately approved by the Chamber during an emergency session. The final law was published in December 2013. While this moved Haiti closer toward holding the long overdue elections, the process continues to be undermined by the highly contested legitimacy of the CTCEP and other irregularities in the process.

B. Political Pluralism and Participation: 9 / 16

There are significant concerns about the ability of opposition parties to compete freely in elections. In the November 2010 election, the Provisional Electoral Council excluded 15 presidential candidates from participation in the elections without providing legal justification or explanation. Sixteen political parties—including Fanmi Lavalas, Haiti's most popular—were also excluded. Historically, special interests dominated by a French-speaking, mostly light-skinned minority have captured state agencies and limited Haiti's largely black, Creole-speaking, poor majority from influencing politics and lawmaking. The capture has resulted in policies skewed toward the interests of the elite mercantile class and the politically powerful.

Haiti is highly dependent on foreign aid and insufficient investments in state capacity have continued to hinder the state from effectively asserting a central role in development, resulting in donor countries and international organizations wielding significant influence over policy-making. The United Nations Stabilization Mission in Haiti (MINUSTAH) has maintained a presence in Haiti since 2004 and the UN Security Council voted to renew the mission for an additional year in October 2013. MINUSTAH faces growing opposition from the Haitian people, who lack agency in setting the terms of the presence and increasingly perceive it as an occupying force, especially in light of the mission's role in introducing a cholera epidemic that has killed over 8,300 people since 2010 and its repeated embroilment in sexual abuse. In May, the Senate unanimously passed a resolution calling on MINUSTAH to withdraw by May 2014, but the non-binding resolution is unlikely to be realized.

C. Functioning of Government: 5 / 12

Delayed elections, corruption allegations, and diversions from rule of law have resulted in staggering political strife between the executive and legislative branches and have impaired effective governance. The Martelly administration has made targeting corruption a priority, and took some steps to improve the regulatory framework in 2013, including increasing the budget and geographic reach of the national anti-corruption unit (ULCC). The ULCC reported an increase in compliance with the legal requirement that government officials declare their assets. The Senate finally passed a new anti-corruption law first introduced almost a decade prior, though the law had not passed the chamber of deputies by the end of 2013. But corruption allegations persisted, including against top administration officials. Two of several administration officials who resigned in late 2012 and 2013 cited corruption and lack of political will to introduce transparency measures as their reasons for resignation. Prime Minister Laurent Lamothe has been accused of mismanagement of emergency disaster-relief funds. In July 2013, Judge Jean Serge Joseph, who was presiding over a corruption case against members of Martelly's family and government, died under suspicious circumstances. Moreover, the terms of the commissioners on the Supreme Court of Auditors, which was responsible for auditing government accounts, expired in 2013, and Martelly declined to install the new members appointed by the Senate, proposing instead the formation of a vetting commission, raising concerns about illegal executive-branch interference. Haiti was ranked 163 out of 177 countries surveyed in Transparency International's 2013 Corruption Perceptions Index.

CIVIL LIBERTIES: 25/ 60 (+1)
D. Freedom of Expression & Belief: 10 / 16

The country hosts two major daily newspapers and a number of less frequent publications, though circulation is fairly limited and the vast majority is in French, making it difficult for Creole-speaking Haitians to access written news. Radio is the main form of media in Haiti. There are several hundred radio stations across Haiti, though most lack national reach.

Television stations are far less common, and the total television audience in Haiti is below 10 percent due to lack of electricity and resources. Internet access is similarly hampered. The constitution guarantees freedom of expression, but press freedom is constrained by the feeble judiciary and law enforcement's inability to afford adequate protection to journalists facing threats and violence. Media and observers have expressed concern regarding executive branch interference with freedom of the press.

The government generally respects religious and academic freedoms. However, the absence of an effective police force has led to poor protection for those who are persecuted for their views.

E. Associational and Organizational Rights: 5 / 12

The 1987 constitution guarantees freedoms of assembly and association, but these rights are often not respected in practice. Popular demonstrations against the government continued in 2013, as people protested the election delay, alleged corruption, and persecution of government dissidents. These demonstrations were sometimes met by violent police responses. While Haiti has rich civil society traditions at the local level, many of its formally organized civil society groups have been co-opted by political and economic elites. Persecution of human rights defenders and political dissidents, in the form of harassment, threats, and illegal arrests, continued to escalate in 2013. Human rights attorney Patrice Florvilus received death threats and faced police harassment before being summoned to court on baseless criminal charges after providing legal representation to victims of police brutality, prompting an outcry from the human rights community and grassroots groups. In October, André Michel, an attorney pursuing the corruption claims against Martelly's wife and son, was detained and unlawfully arrested following repeated harassment and death threats. The incident spurred national outrage and demonstrators physically removed Michel from the prosecutor's office where he was awaiting a hearing to the Port-au-Prince Bar Association, spurring prosecutor Francisco René to label him a fugitive of justice. Lawyers and judges of the Port-au-Prince bar entered in a strike to call for the resignation of René and the judge pursuing Michel's case. The government's actions drew severe criticism from Haitian and international human rights groups. In November, the Ministry of Justice recalled René from his post, ending the month-long strike.

While the ability to unionize is protected under the law, unions and workers frequently face harassment and other repercussions for organizing. New labor regulations passed in 2009 that introduced minimum health and safety standards and a stratified minimum wage system for the commercial and industrial sectors took effect in October 2012. The minimum wage increases apply only to a small segment of the population, however, and are underenforced. A study of five of Haiti's 24 export garment factories released in October 2013 by the U.S.-based Worker Rights Consortium found that employers withheld over 30 percent of the wages their employees were entitled to under the law.

F. Rule of Law: 4 / 16

The judicial system is underresourced, inefficient, and frail, and is burdened by a large backlog of cases, outdated legal codes, and poor facilities. Official court business is conducted in French rather than Creole, rendering large portions of proceedings only marginally comprehensible to those involved. Police are regularly accused of abusing suspects and detainees, and impunity continues to be a problem. The ponderous legal system guarantees lengthy pretrial detentions in inhumane prison conditions. The Office of Citizen Protection (OPC), Haiti's ombudsman office, estimated that more than 7,000 people, or 70 percent of Haiti's total prison population, were being held without conviction of a crime in 2013.

Severe overcrowding results in prisoners having far less space per person than international standards, even for emergency settings; a June 2013 UN report estimated that each detainee had only about .61 square meters of personal space, an amount the report said was equivalent to one-third of a single-bed mattress. The cramped conditions contribute to rapid spread of disease. In October, the government reinstituted a bureau for the control of prolonged preventative detention (BUCODEP) with a goal of reducing pretrial detention by 50 percent, and announced plans to construct several new prisons. But the grave situation of persons in detention did not notably improve during 2013.

Investments in strengthening the judiciary were welcomed. OPC is improving its reach but is constrained by underfunding. In May, Martelly issued a decree establishing an interministerial commission on human rights, hailed by the UN as an important development that could help Haiti move toward improved compliance with international human rights treaties. The newly appointed CSPJ, an administrative and disciplinary organ tasked with promoting independence of the judiciary, was still in its nascent stages in 2013, and politically motivated judicial appointments and interference in judicial proceedings persisted. In a potentially major development for rule of law, an appellate court heard arguments on the reinstating of human rights charges against former dictator Jean-Claude Duvalier that had been dismissed in 2012. The court summoned Duvalier to court and heard testimony from his alleged victims. The hearing, held in February, was lauded by human rights groups as a step toward ending impunity, but the fact that a decision was still pending at year's end caused some to fear political intervention in the final outcome.

G. Personal Autonomy and Individual Rights: 6 / 16 (+1)

Spotty record keeping at the national level and corruption in the enforcement process have long resulted in severe inconsistencies in property rights enforcement, and in turn, those with political and economic means frequently rely on extra-judicial means of enforcing actual or purported rights. In 2013, Haiti undertook measures to spur investment, though often at the expense of other rights enforcement. The investment climate continues to be undermined by a fragmented regulatory framework, lack of law enforcement and endemic corruption.

Widespread violence against women and children has received increasing attention since a 2010 earthquake that killed more than 200,000 people and caused 1.5 million to lose their homes, leading to massive displacement. While impunity is still pervasive, efforts of the Ministry of Women, grassroots women's groups, and legal organizations have helped improve the response to sexual violence, including more effective prosecutions and the introduction of new laws that empower victims. Trafficking of children out of the country, especially to the Dominican Republic, also reportedly increased sharply after the earthquake. A new adoption law that went into effect in November included provisions to increase the protection of children and to make trafficking a criminal offense. An estimated 300,000 children serve as *restavek*, or child domestic servants. LGBT individuals face discrimination and violence; in July, religious leaders marched against LGBT rights, setting off a wave of violent attacks against individuals. However, the LGBT rights movement appears to be gaining momentum.

A combination of relocations, forced evictions and reclassifications has resulted in a significant decline in the official internally displaced population living in camps after the earthquake. Forced evictions were often carried out without prior notice and with police or other government participation. Several eviction attempts were violent, involving burning of tents, beatings and shootings. In April, following an altercation surrounding a violent eviction attempt from Camp Acra Adoken, two residents were taken into police custody and severely beaten. One of the residents died in police custody.

Honduras

Political Rights Rating: 4
Civil Liberties Rating: 4
Freedom Rating: 4.0
Freedom Status: Partly Free
Electoral Democracy: Yes

Population: 8,600,000
Capital: Tegucigalpa

Ten-Year Ratings Timeline For Year Under Review (Political Rights, Civil Liberties, Status)

Year Under Review	2004	2005	2006	2007	2008	2009	2010	2011	2012	2013
Rating	3,3,PF	3,3,PF	3,3,PF	3,3,PF	3,3,PF	4,4,PF	4,4,PF	4,4,PF	4,4,PF	4,4,PF

INTRODUCTION

Honduras faced serious institutional crises in 2013. Congress expanded its authority early in the year, further weakening the judiciary after a constitutional crisis in December 2012. With a new, compliant court in place, the legislature passed several controversial laws, including one that empowered it to remove any elected official.

The Honduran government also faced a major fiscal crisis, unable to pay for various expenditures, including the salaries of public-sector employees, due to mounting debt. Rising poverty, inequality, and unemployment further undermined confidence in the government. Honduras retained the highest murder rate in the world in 2013 as drug traffickers, organized criminals, and street gangs preyed upon society, often in collusion with the authorities.

In November 2013, National Party (PN) candidate and head of Congress Juan Orlando Hernández was elected president with a plurality in a disputed vote. His closest challenger, Xiomara Castro, was the wife of former president José Manuel Zelaya, who was deposed in a 2009 coup. Despite allegations of fraud, irregularities, and campaign violence, the elections marked the emergence of several new political parties.

POLITICAL RIGHTS: 20 / 40 (+2)

A. Electoral Process: 7 / 12 (+1)

The president is elected by popular vote for a single four-year term. The leading candidate must only win a plurality, and there is no runoff system. Members of the 128-seat, unicameral National Congress are also elected for four-year terms using proportional representation by department.

General elections held in November 2013 were the first since the controversial 2009 elections, which were overseen by an interim government following the coup that removed Zelaya from office. Hernández of the PN won 36.8 percent of the vote in a field of eight candidates. Castro of the Liberation and Refoundation Party (Libre) won 28.8 percent, followed by Liberal Party (PL) candidate Mauricio Villeda with 20 percent and Salvador Nasralla of the Anti-Corruption Party (PAC) with 14 percent. The remaining four candidates each won less than 1 percent of the vote. In the legislative elections, the PN won 47 seats, Libre won 39, the PL won 26, the PAC won 13, and the Innovation and Unity Party (PINU), Democratic Unification Party (PUD), and Christian Democrats won one seat each.

While the European Union Electoral Observation Mission's preliminary report stated that the elections were transparent, other observers noted a number of anomalies and irregularities, including the harassment of international observers by immigration officials, vote buying, problems with voter rolls, and potential fraud in the transmission of tally sheets to the country's electoral body, the Supreme Electoral Tribunal (TSE). In addition, more than a dozen Libre activists and candidates were murdered during the campaign season, four of them immediately before and after the elections. Castro and the Libre party contested the results and demanded a recount, which the TSE partially conducted; in the end, nearly all complaints were rejected and the TSE certified Hernández's victory. Libre proceeded to challenge the results in the constitutional chamber of the Supreme Court, which had not yet ruled at year's end.

B. Political Pluralism and Participation: 9 / 16 (+1)

Honduras endured decades of military rule and intermittent elected governments, with the last military regime giving way to civilian authorities in 1982. However, the military remained powerful in subsequent decades; no president exercised his constitutional authority to veto the military and choose its leaders until 1999.

Under civilian rule, power alternated between the PL and the PN. In the 2005 presidential election, Zelaya of the PL defeated the PN's Porfirio Lobo. Political polarization increased under Zelaya's administration amid poor policy performance and faltering public institutions. Zelaya was removed from power and forcibly deported in a coup on June 28, 2009, with the participation of the Supreme Court and the military.

Lobo was elected president in late 2009 despite condemnation from the international community, much of which continued to recognize Zelaya as president. In May 2011, President Lobo signed an agreement that permitted Zelaya to return to Honduras without having to face any criminal charges. The agreement also paved the way for Zelaya's organization, the National Front for Popular Resistance (FNRP), to register as a political party. In February 2012 the FNRP created Libre.

In 2013, Libre, the PAC, and the Patriotic Alliance Party (ALIANZA) all participated in elections for the first time. The elections were notable for the disruption of the dominance of the PL and the PN, which had ruled Honduras for more than three decades.

C. Functioning of Government: 4 / 12

Corruption remains a serious problem. Army officers have been found guilty of involvement in drug trafficking and other crimes. The police force is highly corrupt, and officers are known to engage in criminal activities ranging from drug trafficking and extortion to extrajudicial killings. In August 2013, four police officers were convicted in the extrajudicial killing of two men. A purge of the police initiated in 2012 had resulted in many suspensions, but few firings or arrests, by the end of 2013.

A 2006 transparency law was marred by claims that it contained amendments designed to protect corrupt politicians. However, the Institute for Access to Public Information has made some efforts to enforce transparency rules and punish entities that fail to respond properly to information requests. Legislation that transparency advocates warned would grant numerous government officials increased power to categorize information as classified was under debate at the end of 2013. In June Attorney General Luís Alberto Rubi and his assistant resigned following allegations of financial misdeeds in his office. Honduras was ranked 140 out of 177 countries and territories surveyed in Transparency International's 2013 Corruption Perceptions Index.

CIVIL LIBERTIES: 31 / 60 (-2)

D. Freedom of Expression and Belief: 11 / 16

Since the 2009 coup, authorities have systematically violated the constitution's press freedom guarantees. Numerous radio and television stations reported continued harassment in 2013, including police surveillance, assaults, threats, blocked transmissions, and power outages. Lobo continued his verbal attacks against journalists in 2013. Honduras is considered one of the most dangerous countries in the world for journalists, with 29 killed since the 2009 coup, including several known Zelaya supporters.

Three journalists were murdered in 2013. Globo TV reporter Aníbal Barrow was kidnapped and killed in June, followed by cameraman Manuel Murillo in October and reporter Juan Carlos Argeñal Medina in December. Media ownership is concentrated in the hands of a few powerful business interests, and many journalists practice self-censorship, particularly since the coup. Internet use is generally unrestricted, but access was impaired following the coup by multiple politically motivated power outages and cuts in telephone service.

Freedom of religion is generally respected. Academic freedom is also usually honored, but scholars have faced pressure to support the privatization of the national university.

E. Associational and Organizational Rights: 6 / 12

Constitutional guarantees of freedoms of assembly and association have not been consistently upheld. In addition to the violent suppression of peaceful demonstrations in 2009, police were accused of using excessive force during confrontations with striking and demonstrating teachers in August 2010 and March 2011. The 2006 Citizen Participation Law protects the role of civil society groups and individuals in the democratic process. However, human rights defenders and political activists continued to face significant threats following the 2009 coup, including harassment, surveillance, and detentions, as well as the murder of a number of coup opponents.

Labor unions are well organized and can strike, but labor actions often result in clashes with security forces. In March 2012, the American Federation of Labor–Congress of Industrial Organizations filed a complaint with the U.S. Department of Labor, charging that Honduras had violated provisions of the Central American Free Trade Agreement by competing unfairly and violating workers' rights.

F. Rule of Law: 5 / 16 (-2)

Congress and business elites exert excessive influence over the Supreme Court and its decisions. In December 2012, Congress violated the constitution by voting to remove four of the five justices in the Supreme Court's constitutional chamber after it ruled several laws unconstitutional, one regarding so-called "model" cities and another related to procedures in the ongoing attempt to purge the National Police. An appeal by the fired magistrates was denied in February 2013, and in January 2013 Congress passed the laws that had been struck down, as well as legislation aimed to assert Congress's supremacy by allowing it to remove any elected official. It also passed laws restricting the ability of judges in the Supreme Court's constitutional chamber to participate in deliberations of the full court should they fail to reach a unanimous decision, and removed the right of citizens to challenge the constitutionality of laws.

Approximately 80 percent of crimes committed in Honduras are never reported, according to the government, and only 3.8 percent of reported crimes are investigated by police. The vast majority of inmates are awaiting trial. Prison conditions are harsh, the facilities are notoriously overcrowded, and the state routinely permits prisoners to be in charge of disciplining other prisoners. In February 2012, a prison fire in Comayagua killed an estimated 360 inmates, nearly 60 percent of whom had not been charged or convicted of any crime. There is an official human rights ombudsman, but critics claim that the office's work is politicized. The ombudsman not only supported and justified the 2009 coup, but also publicly declared his opposition to the Truth and Reconciliation Commission set up to examine the coup and rights abuses in its aftermath. As many as 74 lawyers have been murdered since the coup. In

September 2012, Manuel Eduardo Diaz Mazariegos, human rights prosecutor in Choluteca, was murdered near his office.

Honduras had the highest murder rate in the world in 2013. At the close of the year, the National University reported a homicide rate of 83 per 100,000 inhabitants. Most murders are attributed to organized crime, including transnational youth gangs and Mexican drug-trafficking syndicates. The government has made membership in a gang punishable by up to 12 years in prison, and uses the military to help maintain order. However, police officers and vigilantes have committed extrajudicial killings, arbitrary arrests, and illegal searches. Hundreds of juveniles have reportedly been killed in "social cleansing" campaigns. Police corruption has been a major impediment to fighting crime and maintaining citizen security.

In May 2012, President Lobo appointed Juan Carlos Bonilla, who was alleged to have participated in death-squad activities, as police chief; he was dismissed in December 2013 in advance of the change of presidential administrations. The government increasingly relied on the military to fight crime in 2013, creating two new military police units. In June, Congress authorized merging the position of Minister of Defense with Secretary of Security.

The LGBT (lesbian, gay, bisexual, and transgender) community faces discrimination, harassment, and physical threats. At least 89 LGBT activists and individuals have been murdered since the 2009 coup. In February 2011, a special unit was established in the attorney general's office to investigate crimes against the LGBT community. The police force also established a new Sexual Diversity Unit. However, a prominent LGBT activist was beaten by police and arrested in a bar raid in January 2013. In September the offices of the nongovernmental group LGBT Rainbow Association were robbed.

G. Personal Autonomy and Individual Rights: 9 / 16

The conflict over fertile land in the Bajo Aguán region in northern Honduras persisted in 2013 as peasants, landowners' private security forces, and state forces clashed. More than 50 people, most of them landless peasants, have died in the conflict since 2009. In September 2012, prominent human rights attorney Antonio Trejo Cabrera was murdered shortly before he was to testify before the Inter-American Commission on Human Rights in Washington, D.C., regarding abuses committed by the landowners in the region. A report released in February 2013 implicated military death squads in some of the killings.

Indigenous and Afro-Honduran residents have faced various abuses by property developers and their allies in recent years, including corrupt titling processes and acts of violence. In 2013 the government transferred approximately 1.6 million acres of land on the Caribbean coast and Nicaraguan border to Miskito communities to help protect forests from ranchers and developers, though some questioned the timing of the government's transfer. The clearing of land for clandestine airstrips used in the drug trade has accelerated deforestation and increased pressure on indigenous groups in remote areas of the country.

Violence against women is a serious problem, and the murder rate for female victims has risen dramatically in recent years. These murders, like most homicides in Honduras, go unpunished. Women remain vulnerable to exploitation by employers, particularly in the low-wage *maquiladora* (assembly plant) export sector. Child labor is a problem in rural areas and in the informal economy, and school dropout rates are high. Honduras is both a source and transit country for human trafficking. Women and children are particularly vulnerable to sex trafficking. A May 2012 antitrafficking law established new penalties for forced labor and prostitution of adults. Honduras was placed on the Tier 2 Watch List in the U.S. Department of State's 2013 *Trafficking in Persons Report*, which found that it had not increased its efforts to battle human trafficking since the previous report.

Hungary

Political Rights Rating: 1
Civil Liberties Rating: 2
Freedom Rating: 1.5
Freedom Status: Free
Electoral Democracy: Yes

Population: 9,900,000
Capital: Budapest

Ten-Year Ratings Timeline For Year Under Review (Political Rights, Civil Liberties, Status)

Year Under Review	2004	2005	2006	2007	2008	2009	2010	2011	2012	2013
Rating	1,1,F	1,1,F	1,1,F	1,1,F	1,1,F	1,1,F	1,1,F	1,2,F	1,2,F	1,2,F

INTRODUCTION

Since its landslide electoral victory in 2010, a coalition led by the Alliance of Young Democrats–Hungarian Civic Union (Fidesz) party of Prime Minister Viktor Orbán has used its two-thirds parliamentary majority to push through some 600 new laws, reforming or restructuring the media, the judiciary, pensions, and the health care and education systems. This process continued in 2013 with several new laws, as well as two new amendments to the constitution, which had been drafted by Fidesz in 2011. Ombudsman Mate Szabo sought to annul a controversial constitutional amendment adopted in March, but the appeal was rejected by the Constitutional Court in May. Another constitutional amendment, adopted in September, included modifications to recent laws that have elicited criticism from the European Union (EU) and various international watchdogs.

Hungary continued to face economic challenges in 2013, though the government has said that the budget deficit for 2013 and 2014 will fall below the EU-mandated ceiling of 3 percent of gross domestic product. On March 1, Orbán announced the appointment of his close ally, György Matolcsy—who had spearheaded unorthodox financial policies as economy minister—to head the central bank. In April, one of the bank's deputy heads resigned to protest the appointment.

POLITICAL RIGHTS: 36 / 40

A. Electoral Process: 12 / 12

Voters elect representatives every four years to a 386-seat, unicameral National Assembly under a mixed system of proportional and direct representation. (As of 2014, the number of seats in the legislature will be reduced to 199.) The National Assembly elects both the president and the prime minister. The president's duties are mainly ceremonial, but he can influence appointments and return legislation for further consideration before signing it into law.

In April 2010 parliamentary elections, a conservative opposition bloc consisting of Fidesz and the much smaller Christian Democratic People's Party (KDNP) captured 263 seats, giving it a two-thirds majority and the ability to amend the constitution. The incumbent Hungarian Socialist Party (MSzP) won just 59 seats. The far-right Movement for a Better Hungary (Jobbik) entered the parliament for the first time with 47 seats, and the liberal Politics Can Be Different (LMP) party, also new to the legislature, captured 16 seats. An independent took the remaining seat. Orbán, who had served as prime minister from 1998 to 2002, reclaimed the post in May. The current president, founding Fidesz member János Áder, was elected in 2012 after the head of state elected in 2010 resigned amid a plagiarism scandal.

A December 2011 electoral law redrew parliamentary districts and changed the seat-allocation formula. The redistricting was ostensibly designed to reduce the overall number of lawmakers and mitigate wide variation in the size of constituencies. The reforms also gave ethnic Hungarians living abroad easier access to citizenship and the right to vote. According to the government, some 480,000 such people—the approximate equivalent of 6 percent of Hungary's in-country electorate—have applied for citizenship since the law was passed, and thousands have registered to vote.

Another package of electoral legislation was passed by the parliament in November 2012, though its legal validity was undermined in late December 2012 when the Constitutional Court found that it and several other laws had been improperly adopted as "temporary" additions to the constitution. In January 2013, the court struck down several elements of the election law on substantive—rather than procedural—grounds; the rejected provisions included a ban on campaign advertising in private media and the introduction of mandatory voter registration at least 15 days before an election, a change that had been expected to reduce turnout among uncommitted voters. Some elements of the voided law later reappeared as part of the controversial and wide-ranging omnibus constitutional amendment passed in March. The law limiting campaign ads to public media was one of those modified by the constitutional amendment passed in September in an apparent effort to quell sharp criticism from the EU and international watchdog organizations.

B. Political Pluralism and Participation: 15 / 16

Relations between Hungary's main political parties, the center-left MSzP and the conservative Fidesz, have deteriorated in the last several years amid growing polarization.

Hungary's next parliamentary elections will take place in 2014. According to an October 2013 poll by Ipsos, Fidesz was leading, with the support of 49 percent of voters who stated an established party preference and an intention to vote. Only 28 percent of that group said they would cast ballots for the MSzP, while around 40 percent of potential voters were still undecided. In October 2012, former MSzP prime minister Gordon Bajnai launched the centrist umbrella organization Together 2014 (E14), which in October 2013 finalized an electoral alliance with MSzP; the two parties have agreed to field single candidates in the first round of district voting. However, the opposition remains fragmented.

Hungary's constitution guarantees the right of ethnic minorities to form self-governing bodies, and all 13 recognized minorities have done so. Despite their large population, Roma hold just four seats in the current National Assembly. The 2011 constitution restricts voting rights for people considered to have "limited mental ability," raising concerns that citizens could be improperly prohibited from participating in politics.

C. Functioning of Government: 9 / 12

Corruption remains a notable problem in Hungary, which ranked 47 out of 177 countries and territories surveyed in the 2013 Corruption Perceptions Index by Transparency International (TI). A study published by TI in 2012 reported rampant collusion between the public sector and privileged private businesses as well as nontransparent campaign spending by both major parties.

In September 2012, the parliament passed a law creating a state monopoly on the sale of tobacco, ostensibly with the aim of reducing teen smoking; the bidding process was criticized for its secrecy, and the list of license recipients, published in April 2013, included many people and businesses with close ties to Fidesz.

Shortly following the uproar over the licenses, the parliament passed an amendment to reduce the scope of publicly available information under the country's Freedom of

Information Act. In May, President Áder vetoed the original version of the bill, which gave only two government bodies total access to public data. Áder signed a new draft of the bill into law in July over the objections of advocacy groups, which said it could allow arbitrary denial of information requests.

In June, lawmakers amended the country's public procurement law. In a July 10 post to its website, TI Hungary characterized the amendment as a missed opportunity to enhance transparency and rein in corruption.

In September 2013, an audio recording surfaced that apparently featured an illegal negotiation over public procurement between the deputy mayor of Budapest's Zugló district and a construction contractor.

In 2012, several senior police officials were arrested on suspicion of accepting regular bribes to advance the business interests of restaurant and nightclub tycoon László Vizoviczki. The case was ongoing at year's end.

Hungary's independent Fiscal Council, which was responsible for overseeing budgetary policy, was dissolved at the end of 2010 after criticizing tax measures enacted by Orbán's government. A new council, installed in January 2011, consists of the head of the Central Bank, the head of the State Audit Office, and a third member nominated by the president.

CIVIL LIBERTIES: 52 / 60
D. Freedom of Expression and Belief: 15 / 16

Under media legislation that took effect in 2011, outlets must register with the new National Media and Infocommunications Authority (NMHH), which can revoke licenses for infractions. A new Media Council under the NMHH can close outlets or impose fines of up to $950,000 for failing to register or airing content that incites hatred. Fidesz, with its parliamentary supermajority, controls appointments to the Media Council, whose members serve nine-year terms. The head of the NMHH is directly appointed by the president, based on the recommendation of the prime minister. He or she automatically becomes a candidate to the presidency of the Media Council, but must be confirmed by a two-thirds parliamentary majority. The council president nominates the heads of all public media outlets for approval by a Fidesz-dominated board of trustees. Annamaria Szalai, the first head of the NMHH and Media Council, died in April 2013; Monika Karas was named in August to replace Szalai.

Despite amendments to media legislation in 2011, 2012, and 2013, international press freedom organizations insist that the laws do not adequately protect media independence. In April 2013, Klubradio, a radio station critical of the Fidesz government, finally regained control of its main frequency after a two-year legal battle against the Media Council, which had prevented it from renewing its broadcasting license for five frequencies after the license expired in early 2011. A few weeks earlier, the NMHH began an investigation into whether a January opinion piece in the daily *Magyar Hirlap* had violated the country's media law by inciting hatred toward the Roma. In May, the newspaper was fined 250,000 forints ($1,100).

While foreign ownership of Hungarian media is extensive, domestic ownership is largely concentrated in the hands of Fidesz allies. The government is the country's largest advertiser and has withdrawn most advertising from independent media since the 2010 elections. There is anecdotal evidence that private companies withhold advertising from independent media to avoid losing government contracts. In 2011, Dániel Papp, cofounder of Jobbik, was named as editor in chief of the news office at the MTVA media fund, which is responsible for the management of all public media. Extensive layoffs followed. In December 2013, German media group ProSiebenSat1 sold TV2, Hungary's largest broadcaster, to its chief executive and financial director amid speculation about the new owners' links to Fidesz-affiliated conservative media conglomerates.

Under an amendment to the country's penal code adopted by the parliament in November 2013, anyone who knowingly creates or distributes false or defamatory video or audio recordings may face a prison sentence of one to three years. The impetus for the widely criticized amendment was a fabricated video published by the news website HVG.hu in October. The video shows locals apparently being bribed to vote for Fidesz ahead of by-elections in the southern city of Baja. The communications director for MSzP resigned after admitting that he had submitted the recording to HVG, though he insisted that he had not known the video was staged. Separate revisions to the criminal code that took effect in July require ISPs to block content deemed illegal by a court order. Websites hosting illegal content are placed on a nonpublic "blacklist" operated by the NMHH. The government may take action if ISPs fail to heed the blocking orders.

The constitution guarantees religious freedom and provides for the separation of church and state. Adherents of all religions are generally free to worship. However, hundreds of religious organizations lost their registered status and budgetary allocations for social and charitable services in 2012 in connection with a law that shifted the power to recognize religious denominations from the courts to the parliament. Deregistered groups were stripped of legal standing and told to apply for recognition as associations. The law was originally adopted in 2011, but voided on procedural grounds before going into effect. A new version was passed in early 2012, then nullified on substantive grounds in early 2013. After the Constitutional Court's second decision, the substance of the voided law reappeared within the constitutional amendment adopted in March 2013, causing widespread concern that the document was being used to circumvent the court's authority. Some adjustments to the rules concerning religious registration were included in the constitutional amendment adopted in September. Religious communities now have the same legal standing as recognized churches, and courts, rather than the parliament, are tasked with assessing their status. However, a two-thirds parliamentary majority must still approve the right of any religious community or church to receive tax and other benefits reserved for "accepted churches."

Anti-Semitism remains a problem in Hungary, particularly among far-right groups. People within the government have honored fascist historical figures, though the ruling party generally distances itself from the strongly xenophobic statements and actions of groups like Jobbik. In July 2013, a member of the European Parliament for Jobbik, Csanád Szegedi, was asked by the party to resign following the disclosure of his Jewish ancestry. Jobbik claimed he was being penalized not for being Jewish, but for attempting to suppress the disclosure through bribery.

The state generally does not restrict academic freedom.

E. Associational and Organizational Rights: 12 / 12

The constitution provides for freedoms of assembly and association, and the government generally respects these rights in practice. Nongovernmental organizations operate without restrictions.

In October 2013, Jobbik proposed that civic groups receiving more than 1 million forints ($4,400) annually from foreign sources should be required to register as "agent organizations," but the proposal was voted down in the parliament. In December, the parliament adopted a new law that required nongovernmental organizations (NGOs) benefitting from the 1 percent tax scheme—under which taxpayers can assign 1 percent of their income tax to an NGO of their choice—to register. The National Tax and Customs Administration (NAV) was empowered to administer the process.

The government recognizes workers' rights to form associations, strike, and petition public authorities. Trade unions represent less than 30 percent of the workforce.

F. Rule of Law: 11 / 16

The independence of the judiciary came under scrutiny in 2011 and 2012 following the adoption of a reform package granting extensive administrative powers to the National Judicial Office (OBH), a body whose leader is elected by a two-thirds parliamentary majority for a nine-year term. A legal provision reducing the mandatory retirement age of judges, prosecutors, and notaries from 70 to 62—seen by critics as a way for the government to purge the judiciary and stack it with supporters—was annulled in 2012 after being struck down by the Constitutional Court.

The court has struck down a number of key laws passed since 2010. However, some of the "temporary [constitutional] provisions" invalidated by the court in December 2012 were nevertheless voted into the constitution via a two-thirds majority in 2013. Moreover, the March 2013 amendment prohibits the Constitutional Court from examining the substantive constitutionality of future proposed constitutional amendments and strips the court of the right to refer in its rulings to legal decisions made prior to January 2012, when the current constitution came into effect. In defiance of the latter restriction, the court's judges began citing their past rulings as early as June 2013.

Prisons are generally approaching Western European standards, though overcrowding, inadequate medical care, and poor sanitation remain problems. Inmates do not have access to independent medical staff to assess abuse allegations. The 2011 constitution introduced the possibility of life sentences without parole, prompting human rights groups to argue that such sentences would conflict with the International Covenant on Civil and Political Rights.

Hungary has taken a number of steps to improve monitoring of Romany legal rights and treatment, but Roma, who form Hungary's largest ethnic minority, still face widespread discrimination and poverty. Romany students continue to be segregated and improperly placed in schools for children with mental disabilities. In August 2013, a court handed down sentences ranging from 13 years to life in prison without parole to four members of a neo-Nazi gang for a series of murders and attacks on Romany families in 2008 and 2009. The ruling party is not always vocal in its condemnation of anti-Roma behavior.

In 2012, the Constitutional Court struck down a 2011 law that prescribed fines for homeless people living in public areas. The substance of this law reappeared in the constitutional amendment of March 2013, and the parliament in September passed a law empowering local governments to ban homeless people from certain areas.

G. Personal Autonomy and Individual Rights: 14 / 16

Women possess the same legal rights as men, but they face employment discrimination and tend to be underrepresented in high-level business and government positions. Women hold only 35 of 386 seats in the National Assembly. The right to life from conception is protected under the 2011 constitution, but access to abortions remained largely unrestricted in 2013.

In November, Human Rights Watch released a report documenting domestic violence in Hungary and claiming that insufficient legal protections as well as problems in the implementation of existing laws further endanger female survivors of domestic violence. The issue of violence against women took center stage earlier in the year, when politician Jozsef Balogh was accused of brutally beating his partner. Months later, Balogh confessed to the assault and was expelled from Fidesz, but refused to resign from the parliament or from his position as mayor of the village of Fulophaza. Acting in response to a civil initiative, the parliament added a law on domestic violence to the criminal code in October 2012; the law came into effect in July 2013. Hungary is a transit point, source, and destination for trafficked persons, including women trafficked for prostitution.

Same-sex couples can legally register their domestic partnerships. However, the 2011 constitution enshrines the concept of marriage as a union between man and woman and fails to directly prohibit discrimination based on sexual orientation. In December 2012, the Constitutional Court annulled provisions of the 2011 family protection law that defined family as the marriage and offspring, biological or adopted, of one man and one woman. The same day, the parliament amended the country's civil code, removing references to domestic partnerships (whether same-sex or opposite-sex) except in the context of division of property and the right to demand spousal support after the dissolution of the partnership. A separate law on same-sex partnerships remained in effect at the end of 2013.

Iceland

Political Rights Rating: 1
Civil Liberties Rating: 1
Freedom Rating: 1
Freedom Status: Free
Electoral Democracy: Yes

Population: 323,000
Capital: Reykjavik

Ten-Year Ratings Timeline For Year Under Review (Political Rights, Civil Liberties, Status)

Year Under Review	2004	2005	2006	2007	2008	2009	2010	2011	2012	2013
Rating	1,1,F	1,1,F	1,1,F	1,1,F	1,1,F	1,1,F	1,1,F	1,1,F	1,1,F	1,1,F

INTRODUCTION

Parliamentary elections in April 2013 saw the decisive ousting of the ruling center-left Social Democratic Alliance (SDA)/Left-Green Movement government, led by Prime Minister Jóhanna Sigurðardóttir of the SDA, and its replacement with a center-right alliance of the Progressive Party and the Independence Party. Sigmundur Davíð Gunnlaugsson, the leader of the Progressive Party, became Iceland's new prime minister. The new center-right government put a halt to the country's negotiations for EU membership, until the question could be put to referendum. The date of the referendum had not been set at year's end.

In March, parliament declined to pass a constitutional draft that had been crafted through an experimental crowd-sourcing process set in motion by Sigurðardóttir's government; the major principles of the draft had been endorsed by voters in a nonbinding referendum in October 2012. The new center-right government elected in April does not support the draft constitution, and since the current constitution mandates that two separate parliaments must pass constitutional changes, Iceland's experimental approach to constitutional reform will not bear fruit for at least two parliamentary election cycles.

Iceland continues to deal with the fallout of its 2008 financial crash—in which a major credit crisis forced the government to nationalize three large banks—both domestically and internationally. In 2013, a number of bankers were charged with various financial crimes pertaining to the crash by the country's special prosecutor for economic crimes. A ruling by the court of the European Free Trade Association in January 2013 on the repayment terms to compensate Dutch and British depositors at Icesave—an online savings account brand owned and operated by the private Landsbanki, which collapsed in 2008—sided with Iceland against the Netherlands and the United Kingdom. The ruling found that while the UK and the Netherlands had chosen to bail out their national depositors with outstanding assets in the bankrupt Icelandic banks, the state of Iceland could not be sued to repay the Dutch and

UK depositors, not for the principal nor for the interest accrued. The ruling stabilized the Icelandic economy and was seen as a boon to the then-opposition. In April 2011, voters had defeated a referendum on repayment plan for British and Dutch depositors at Icesave. Landsbanki announced in 2012 that a sale of its assets should fully cover repayment to all British and Dutch depositors, over a series of years. However the bank applied for a loan extension in 2013, saying it wanted to prevent destabilizing the recovering Icelandic economy and feared that rapidly buying large amounts of foreign currency to service the debt could do so. A decision was pending by year's end.

POLITICAL RIGHTS: 40 / 40
A. Electoral Process: 12 / 12

The Icelandic constitution, adopted in 1944, vests power in a president, a prime minister, the 63-seat unicameral legislature (the Althingi), and a judiciary. The Althingi is arguably the world's oldest parliament, established in approximately 930 AD. The largely ceremonial president is directly elected for a four-year term. Ólafur Ragnar Grímsson won the presidential election and his fifth term in July 2012, defeating independent journalist Thóra Arnórsdóttir.

The legislature is also elected for four years, but can be dissolved for early elections in certain circumstances. The prime minister is appointed by the president. In the April 2013 parliamentary elections, the center-left coalition of SDA and the Left-Green Movement lost half the seats it held in the Althingi, in the biggest loss of seats any governing coalition in Iceland has experienced since the country's independence in 1944. Opposition to unpopular austerity measures, to taxation levels, and to EU ascension negotiations, as well as high levels of personal debt, were seen as major voter concerns during the election campaign. The Althingi now comprises the Progressive Party and the Independence Party, with 19 seats each, as well as the SDA with 9 seats, the Left-Green Movement with 7, and two new parties—Bright Future and the Pirate Party—with 6 and 3 seats, respectively.

B. Political Pluralism and Participation: 16 / 16

Three major political parties and three smaller parties are represented in the Althingi. The center-right Independence Party has historically dominated Icelandic politics until 2009, when Sigurðardóttir's center-left SDA/Left-Green coalition took power and elections left leftist parties in the majority for the first time in Iceland. The severe banking crisis of 2008 spawned several new political parties and movements in Iceland and the 2013 parliamentary elections were contested by 15 political parties, as opposed to 7 in the 2009 elections. The most viable of these new parties has proven to be the Best Party, led by comedian Jón Gnaar, who won the mayoralty of Reykjavik in 2010. Initially a satirical joke party, Best Party, as well as its sister party in the Althingi, Bright Future, have developed coherent, left-leaning agendas. In October 2013, Gnaar announced that he would not run for reelection in Reykjavik's 2014 municipal elections and that the Best Party would dissolve and join forces with Bright Future.

Foreigners can vote in municipal elections if they have been residents for at least five years, or three years for citizens of Scandinavian countries.

C. Functioning of Government: 12 / 12

While corruption is not a serious problem in Iceland, the country has experienced politically tinged business-fraud scandals in recent years, in particular in connection with 2008's banking crash. A special prosecutor to investigate the financial collapse was appointed by parliament in 2009 in response to mounting public anger and to ensure accountability for the financial crisis; his mandate was expanded to economic crimes more generally in 2011.

In September 2013, about 140 cases were under investigation, approximately half of which were related to the crisis. Cases have been brought against all major banks involved in the crash, and more cases are expected to come under investigation in the coming years. In December 2013, 15 top managers of both Kaupthing and Landsbanki, Iceland's two biggest banks at the time of the crash, were sentenced to between 3 and 5 years in prison, for charges of market manipulation. Former prime minister Geir Haarde, who faced charges of negligence was found guilty of one count in April 2012 but not sentenced to any punishment and Baldur Guðlaugsson, former undersecretary of the Ministry of Finance, was convicted of insider trading and sentenced to two years in prison in February 2012.

Iceland was ranked 12 out of 177 countries surveyed in Transparency International's 2013 Corruption Perceptions Index.

CIVIL LIBERTIES: 60 / 60
D. Freedom of Expression and Belief: 16 / 16

The constitution guarantees freedoms of speech and the press. In June 2010, parliament unanimously passed the Icelandic Modern Media Initiative, which mandates the establishment of stringent free speech and press freedom laws and focuses on the protection of investigative journalists and media outlets. Iceland's wide range of print publications includes both independent and party-affiliated newspapers. The autonomous Icelandic National Broadcasting Service competes with private radio and television stations. Private media ownership is concentrated, with the Norðurljós (Northern Lights) Corporation controlling most of the private television and radio outlets and two of the three national newspapers. Internet access is unrestricted.

The constitution provides for freedom of religion. About three-quarters of Icelanders belong to the Evangelical Lutheran Church. The state supports the church through a special tax, which citizens can choose to direct to the University of Iceland instead. A 2008 law requires the teaching of theology in grades 1 through 10. Academic freedom is respected, and the education system is free of excessive political involvement.

E. Associational and Organizational Rights: 12 / 12

Freedoms of association and peaceful assembly are generally upheld. Peaceful protests occurred in September and October 2011 against IMF austerity measures and the government's failure to protect Icelanders from housing foreclosures. Many nongovernmental organizations operate freely and enjoy extensive government cooperation. The labor movement is robust, with more than 80 percent of all eligible workers belonging to unions. All unions have the right to strike. There were no significant strikes in 2013.

F. Rule of Law: 16 / 16

The judiciary is independent. The law does not provide for trial by jury, but many trials and appeals use panels of several judges. The constitution states that all people shall be treated equally before the law, regardless of sex, religion, ethnic origin, race, or other status. Prison conditions generally meet international standards.

The Act on Foreigners was amended in 2004 to allow home searches without warrants in cases of suspected immigration fraud, among other changes.

G. Personal Autonomy and Individual Rights: 16 / 16

Women enjoy equal rights, and more than 80 percent of women participate in the workforce. However, a pay gap exists between men and women despite laws designed to prevent disparities. Iceland topped the World Economic Forum's 2013 ratings on gender equality.

Following the 2013 elections, women hold 40 percent of seats in the Althingi. In 2009, Sigurðardóttir became Iceland's first female prime minister and the world's first openly lesbian head of government. Parliament unanimously passed a law legalizing same-sex marriage in 2010, full equal rights to same-sex couples on adoption and assisted pregnancy were enshrined in a 2006 law passed by Parliament. A comprehensive law on transgender issues was adopted in 2012, to simplify legal issues pertaining to gender reassignment surgery and ensure full and equal rights to transgender Icelanders as well as guaranteed relevant health care. A committee was appointed in 2008 to develop new strategies to combat human trafficking in Iceland, and parliament passed a law criminalizing human trafficking in 2009.

India

Political Rights Rating: 2
Civil Liberties Rating: 3
Freedom Rating: 2.5
Freedom Status: Free
Electoral Democracy: Yes

Population: 1,276,508,000
Capital: New Delhi

Note: The numerical ratings and status listed above do not reflect conditions in Indian-controlled Kashmir, which is examined in a separate report.

Ten-Year Ratings Timeline For Year Under Review (Political Rights, Civil Liberties, Status)

Year Under Review	2004	2005	2006	2007	2008	2009	2010	2011	2012	2013
Rating	2,3,F	2,3,F	2,3,F	2,3,F	2,3,F	2,3,F	2,3,F	2,3,F	2,3,F	2,3,F

INTRODUCTION

In September 2013, the Hindu nationalist Bharatiya Janata Party (BJP) nominated Narendra Modi, the chief minister of Gujarat, as its candidate for prime minister in the 2014 general elections, in which it hoped to unseat the ruling coalition led by the secular Indian National Congress party. Although Modi had a reputation for good economic management in his state, he has also been accused of failing to stop 2002 sectarian riots in which some 1,000 Gujarati Muslims were killed. The issue of communal violence, though in decline over the long term, remained acutely relevant during the year, as the country recovered from 2012 ethnic and religious clashes in which half a million people were displaced from northeastern states. New violence erupted in September 2013, when confrontations between Hindus and Muslims killed 40 people and displaced roughly 40,000 Muslims near the Uttar Pradesh town of Muzaffarnagar. Separately, a terrorist attack, possibly orchestrated by the Islamic extremist group Indian Mujahideen, killed 16 people in the southern city of Hyderabad in February.

Despite the concerns about Modi's past, analysts argued that his probusiness stance gave the BJP an advantage over the Congress-led United Progressive Alliance (UPA) government, which has struggled to rally support in the wake of high-profile corruption scandals and an economic slowdown in recent years. Malfeasance in the awarding of telecommunications licenses and coal-mining contracts was alleged to have caused large public losses, and former telecommunications minister Andimuthu Raja, first charged in 2011, remained on trial at the end of 2013 for bribery, forgery, and abusing his position. The scandals had fueled the growth of an anticorruption protest movement in 2011, and the formation of a new antigraft political faction, the Aam Aadmi (Common Man) Party, in 2012. The government's popularity was battered further that year, when it undertook a set of controversial economic reforms, including reducing subsidies for diesel and cooking gas, in an effort to decrease fiscal deficits and stave off a potential downgrade from credit rating agencies. The cuts led to protests across India and the withdrawal of one partner from the governing coalition.

The ruling coalition announced in 2013 that it would support the creation of a 29th state, Telangana, carved out of southern Andhra Pradesh, before the 2014 polls. Both houses of Parliament and the state assembly would have to approve a bill to establish the new state. The decision was widely viewed as politically opportunistic. Groups in Andhra Pradesh's inland districts have lobbied for the creation of Telangana for decades, saying the state government disproportionately favors the coastal Seemandhra region when allocating resources. Their opponents fear the loss of the present capital, Hyderabad, a commercial hub that would become part of the new state. Protests against the split crippled Andhra Pradesh in October, as striking power plant workers left an estimated 21 million people without electricity. Nationally, other regions with movements seeking statehood saw increased strikes and demonstrations.

POLITICAL RIGHTS: 34 / 40

A. Electoral Process: 11 / 12

Under the supervision of the Election Commission of India, elections have generally been free and fair. Members of the lower house of Parliament, the 545-seat Lok Sabha (House of the People), are directly elected for five-year terms (except for two appointed members representing Indians of European descent). The current, 15th Lok Sabha will complete its term on May 31, 2014. The Lok Sabha determines the leadership and composition of the government. Most members of the less powerful 250-seat upper house, the Rajya Sabha (Council of States), are elected by state legislatures using a proportional-representation system to serve staggered six-year terms; up to 12 members are appointed. Executive power is vested in a prime minister and cabinet. The president, who plays a largely symbolic role but possesses some important powers, is chosen for a five-year term by state and national lawmakers. In July 2012, former finance minister and senior Congress Party leader Pranab Mukherjee was elected as the 13th president of India. Manmohan Singh has been prime minister since 2004.

In the last parliamentary elections in 2009, the UPA decisively defeated the BJP-led National Democratic Alliance, its closest rival. The polls were mostly peaceful, though Maoist militant attacks in parts of the country led to 17 deaths during the first phase of voting. Electronic voting machines, also used in the 2004 elections, helped reduce election-day irregularities. Congress itself won 206 of 543 lower house seats, and the UPA won 260 seats overall. The UPA also made alliances with independent parties that gave it a significant majority, leading to a more stable government.

At the state level, Karnataka, Delhi, Tripura, Rajasthan, Nagaland, Mizoram, Meghalaya, Madhya Pradesh, and Chhattisgarh each held assembly elections during 2013. In Delhi, after Congress lost control of the assembly and the BJP failed to win the majority, the untried Aam Aadmi Party formed a minority government.

B. Political Pluralism and Participation: 14 / 16

India hosts a dynamic multiparty system. The Congress Party ruled at the federal level for nearly all of the first 50 years of independence, but the BJP became a major factor in Parliament in the 1990s and led a governing coalition from 1998 to 2004. Also during the 1990s, a pattern of single-party governments gave way to ruling coalitions involving large numbers of parties. The change stemmed in part from the rise of new parties that held power and legislative seats in a single state or region

Political participation is affected to a certain degree by insurgent violence in some areas, powerful economic interests, and ongoing practical disadvantages for some marginalized segments of the population. Nevertheless, women and religious and ethnic minorities vote in large numbers and are represented in government. As of 2013, the vice president was a Muslim, the prime minister was a Sikh, and the speaker of the Lok Sabha was a Dalit woman. A number of states were headed by female chief ministers.

C. Functioning of Government: 9 / 12

Political corruption has a negative effect on government efficiency and economic performance. India was ranked 94 out of 177 countries and territories surveyed in Transparency International's 2013 Corruption Perceptions Index. Though politicians and civil servants are regularly caught accepting bribes or engaging in other corrupt behavior, a great deal of corruption goes unnoticed and unpunished.

Domestic and international pressure has led to legislation and activism to counter this trend. Federal initiatives include the 2005 Right to Information Act, which is widely used to improve transparency and expose corrupt activities. While this legislation has had clear positive effects, over a dozen right-to-information activists have reportedly been killed since late 2009.

CIVIL LIBERTIES: 43 / 60 (+1)
D. Freedom of Expression and Belief: 13 / 16

The private media are vigorous and diverse. Investigations and scrutiny of politicians make the news media one of the most important components of India's democracy. Nevertheless, revelations of close relationships between politicians, business executives, lobbyists, and some leading media personalities have dented public confidence in the press in recent years. While radio remains dominated by the state and private radio stations are not allowed to air news content, the television and print sectors have expanded considerably over the past decade, with many of the new outlets targeting specific regional or linguistic audiences.

Despite this vibrant media landscape, journalists continue to face a number of constraints. The government has used security laws, criminal defamation legislation, hate-speech laws, and contempt-of-court charges to curb critical voices on social media as well as traditional media platforms. According to the Committee to Protect Journalists, at least three journalists were killed because of their work in 2013, more than in any of the previous four years.

Internet access is largely unrestricted, though officials periodically implement overbroad blocks on supposedly offensive content to prevent unrest. Under Indian internet crime law, the burden is on website operators to remove content if requested to do so, and they face possible criminal penalties. Potentially inflammatory books and films are also occasionally banned or censored. A nationwide Central Monitoring System, launched in April 2013 and reportedly active in at least some states, will allow authorities to intercept any digital communication in real time. The surveillance does not require judicial oversight, and India does not have a privacy law to protect citizens in case of abuse.

Freedom of religion is constitutionally guaranteed in India and is generally respected. However, legislation in several states criminalizes religious conversions that take place as a result of "force" or "allurement." Hindus make up over 80 percent of the population, but the state is secular. An array of Hindu nationalist organizations and some local media outlets promote antiminority views.

Academic freedom is generally robust, though intimidation of professors and institutions over political and religious issues sometimes occurs. Scholars and activists accused of sympathizing with Maoist insurgents have faced pressure from authorities and alleged torture by police.

E. Associational and Organizational Rights: 11 / 12

There are some restrictions on freedoms of assembly and association. Section 144 of the criminal procedure code empowers the authorities to restrict free assembly and impose curfews whenever "immediate prevention or speedy remedy" is required. State laws based on this standard are often abused to limit the holding of meetings and assemblies. Nevertheless, protest events take place regularly in practice. Peaceful demonstrations associated with anticorruption activist Anna Hazare drew tens of thousands of people into the streets in 2011 and 2012, and similar activity to protest violence against women occurred in 2013.

Human rights organizations operate freely, but continue to face threats, legal harassment, excessive police force, and occasionally lethal violence. While India is home to a strong civil society sector and academic community, foreign monitors and journalists are occasionally denied visas to conduct research trips in the country on human rights and other topics. Under certain circumstances, the Foreign Contributions (Regulation) Act permits the federal government to deny nongovernmental organizations access to foreign funding. The government has been accused of abusing this power to target political opponents.

While workers in the formal economy regularly exercise their rights to bargain collectively and strike, the Essential Services Maintenance Act has enabled the government to ban certain strikes.

F. Rule of Law: 9 / 16 (+1)

The judiciary is independent of the executive branch. Judges have displayed considerable activism in response to public-interest litigation matters. However, in recent years some judges have initiated contempt-of-court cases against activists and journalists who expose judicial corruption or question verdicts. Contempt-of-court laws were reformed in 2006 to make truth a defense with respect to allegations against judges, provided the information is in the public and national interest. The lower levels of the judiciary in particular have been rife with corruption, and most citizens have great difficulty securing justice through the courts. The system is severely backlogged and understaffed, with an estimated 32 million cases pending in lower courts and 66,000 at the Supreme Court. This leads to lengthy pretrial detention for a large number of suspects, many of whom remain in jail beyond the duration of any sentence they might receive if convicted. According to the International Centre for Prison Studies, 66 percent of the country's approximately 385,000 prisoners were on or awaiting trial at the end of 2012. The creation of various fast-track courts to clear the backlog has prompted charges that due process is being denied in some instances.

The criminal justice system fails to provide equal protection to marginalized groups. Muslims, who make up some 13 percent of the population, are underrepresented in the security forces as well as in the foreign and intelligence services. Particularly in rural India, informal councils often issue edicts concerning social customs. While these bodies play a role in relieving the overburdened official courts, their decisions sometimes result in violence or persecution aimed at those perceived to have transgressed social norms, especially women and members of the lower castes.

Police torture, abuse, and corruption are entrenched in the law enforcement system. The police also suffer from understaffing in relation to the size of the population. Citizens frequently face substantial obstacles, including demands for bribes, in getting the police to file a First Information Report, which is necessary to trigger an investigation of an alleged crime. Custodial rape of female detainees continues to be a problem, as does routine abuse of ordinary prisoners, particularly minorities and members of the lower castes. According to the Working Group on Human Rights in India and the United Nations, 14,231 people died in police custody between 2001 and 2010, and approximately 1.8 million people are victims of police torture every year. This is likely an underestimate, since it only includes cases registered with the National Human Rights Commission (NHRC).

The NHRC is headed by a retired Supreme Court judge and handles roughly 8,000 complaints each year. While it monitors abuses, initiates investigations, makes independent assessments, and conducts training sessions for the police and others, its recommendations are often not implemented and it has few enforcement powers. The commission also lacks jurisdiction over the armed forces, one of the principal agents of abuse in several parts of the country, further hampering its effectiveness. The NHRC nevertheless makes a substantial contribution to accountability by submitting reports to international bodies such as the UN Human Rights Council, often contradicting the government's account of its performance.

Security forces operating in the context of regional insurgencies continue to be implicated in extrajudicial killings, rape, torture, arbitrary detention, kidnappings, and destruction of homes. The criminal procedure code requires the government to approve the prosecution of security force members, but approval is rarely granted, leading to impunity. The Armed Forces Special Powers Act (AFSPA) grants security forces broad authority to arrest, detain, and use force against suspects in restive areas; civil society organizations and multiple UN human rights bodies have called for the act to be repealed. In northeastern Manipur, much of which is designated a "disturbed area" for the purposes of the act, activist Irom Sharmila Chanu has been on a hunger strike since November 2000 to demand the revocation of the AFSPA, but has faced continual arrests and forced feeding by the authorities. A number of other security laws allow detention without charge or based on vaguely worded offenses.

The Maoist insurgency in several parts of India is of serious concern to the government. Deaths related to this left-wing extremism peaked in 2010 with 1,180 across India, according to the South Asia Terrorism Portal (SATP). The group documented 421 related fatalities—including 159 civilians—in 2013. Twenty-seven people were killed when Maoist militants ambushed a convoy of state-level Congress party representatives returning from a political rally in Chhattisgarh in May. Among other abuses, the rebels have allegedly imposed illegal taxes, seized food and shelter, and engaged in abduction and forced recruitment of children and adults. Local civilians and journalists who are perceived to be progovernment have been targeted by the Maoists. Security forces responding to the threat, including paramilitary troops and police, have also been accused of serious human rights abuses. Tens of thousands of civilians have been displaced by the violence and live in government-run camps.

Separately, in India's seven northeastern states, more than 40 insurgent factions—seeking either greater autonomy or complete independence for their ethnic or tribal groups—attack security forces and engage in intertribal violence. Such fighters have been implicated in numerous bombings, killings, abductions, and rapes of civilians, and they operate extensive extortion networks. The number of deaths related to the northeastern insurgencies declined from 316 in 2012 to 252 in 2013, according to the SATP. These levels represent a substantial reduction compared with the 852 killed in 2009 and the more than 1,000 killed in each of the two years prior to that.

The constitution bars discrimination based on caste, and laws set aside quotas in education and government jobs for historically underprivileged scheduled tribes, scheduled castes (Dalits), and groups categorized by the government as "other backward classes." However, members of the lower castes and minorities continue to face routine discrimination and violence. Dalits are often denied access to land and other public amenities, abused by landlords and police, and forced to work in miserable conditions. Indian Muslims are more likely than the general population to be poor and illiterate, with less access to government employment, medical care, and loans.

G. Personal Autonomy and Individual Rights: 10 / 16

Freedom of movement is hampered in some parts of the country by insurgent violence or communal tensions. Property rights are somewhat tenuous for tribal groups and other marginalized communities, and members of these groups are often denied adequate resettlement opportunities and compensation when their lands are seized for development projects. While many states have laws to prevent transfers of tribal land to nontribal groups, the practice is reportedly widespread. In 2013, the Land Acquisition, Rehabilitation, and Resettlement Bill was passed into law, providing increased rights to people threatened with displacement for industrial and infrastructure projects. It takes effect January 1, 2014.

Rape, harassment, and other transgressions against women are serious problems, and lower-caste and tribal women are particularly vulnerable. The fatal gang rape of a woman on a Delhi bus in December 2012 caused mass demonstrations and drew international attention. The government responded by enacting significant legal reforms, and a special court sentenced four men to death for the crime less than nine months later. However, less publicized rape investigations and trials are still lagging nationwide. Despite the criminalization of dowry demands and hundreds of convictions each year, the practice continues. According to India's most recent National Family Health Survey report, released in 2009 and covering the years 2005 and 2006, 37 percent of married women between ages 15 and 49 have experienced physical or sexual violence at the hands of their husbands. A 2006 law banned dowry-related harassment, widened the definition of domestic violence to include emotional or verbal abuse, and criminalized spousal rape. However, reports indicate that enforcement is poor.

Muslim personal laws and traditional Hindu practices discriminate against women in terms of inheritance, adoption, and property rights. The malign neglect of female children after birth remains a concern, as does the banned but growing use of prenatal sex-determination tests to selectively abort female fetuses.

A landmark 2009 decision by the Delhi High Court struck down Section 377 of the Indian penal code, which criminalized homosexual behavior. However, a panel of the Supreme Court reversed that ruling in December 2013, finding that an act of Parliament would be required to change the code. An appeal was pending at the end of 2013. Widespread discrimination against LGBT (lesbian, gay, bisexual, and transgender) people continues in practice, including violence and harassment in some cases, though transgender people receive varying degrees of official recognition across the country.

Article 23 of the constitution bans human trafficking, and bonded labor is illegal, but the practice is fairly common. Estimates of the number of affected workers range from 20 to 50 million. Children are also banned from working in potentially hazardous industries, though in practice the law is routinely flouted.

Indonesia

Political Rights Rating: 2
Civil Liberties Rating: 4
Freedom Rating: 3.0
Freedom Status: Partly Free
Electoral Democracy: Yes

Population: 248,527,000
Capital: Jakarta

Status Change: Indonesia's civil liberties rating declined from 3 to 4 and its status declined from Free to Partly Free due to the adoption of a law that restricts the activities of nongovernmental organizations, increases bureaucratic oversight of such groups, and requires them to support the national ideology of Pancasila—including its explicitly monotheist component.

Ten-Year Ratings Timeline For Year Under Review (Political Rights, Civil Liberties, Status)

Year Under Review	2004	2005	2006	2007	2008	2009	2010	2011	2012	2013
Rating	3,4,PF	2,3,F	2,3,F	2,3,F	2,3,F	2,3,F	2,3,F	2,3,F	2,3,F	2,4,PF

INTRODUCTION

A much-criticized revision of Indonesia's mass organization law was passed by the parliament in July 2013. The measure imposes new restrictions and additional state supervision on the operations of nongovernmental organizations (NGOs), and obliges them to adhere to the national ideology of Pancasila, whose five core principles notably include monotheism.

The legislation came amid a multiyear pattern of discrimination and violence against religious minorities, which continued unabated in 2013. Major incidents during the year included the forced sealing of multiple Ahmadiyya mosques in West Java, several mob attacks against other houses of worship in East and West Java, attacks against Sufi Muslim boarding school property in southern Aceh, and the demolition of a Protestant church in West Java. The only individual to stand trial for a deadly mob attack against a Shiite Muslim community in 2012 was acquitted in April.

Despite such mob violence, Indonesia continued to make progress in combating terrorism during the year. In June, a key bomb maker received a 10-year sentence for recruiting and training militants, and a terrorist cell member was sentenced to seven years in prison for his role in a plot to bomb police targets in Jakarta. However, Muslim-Buddhist strife centered on the plight of the Muslim Rohingya minority in Burma, which spilled into Indonesia when a bomb was set off at a Buddhist temple in Jakarta in August, injuring several people. The perpetrators were allegedly linked to those behind a foiled bomb plot against the Burmese embassy in Jakarta in May. Both criminal cases were ongoing at year's end.

In the eastern provinces of Papua and West Papua, where the central government's exploitation of natural resources has stirred resentment and separatist action, members of the security forces continued to enjoy relative impunity for abuses against civilians. Freedom of expression was routinely restricted, and gatherings were forcibly dispersed. Information regarding Papua incidents is limited due to restrictions on journalists. In April, two protesters were killed and 20 arrested during a pro-independence demonstration. A local journalist was severely beaten by three police officers in August, and in September police opened fire on civilians during a security sweep, leading to at least one death. Also in September, the prime minister of Vanuatu urged the United Nations to appoint a special representative to review the human rights situation in Papua.

POLITICAL RIGHTS: 30 / 40

A. Electoral Process: 11 / 12

Elections in Indonesia are considered to be free and fair by independent monitoring groups. The House of Representatives (DPR), with 560 seats, is the main parliamentary chamber. The 132-member House of Regional Representatives (DPD) is responsible for monitoring laws related to regional autonomy. In March 2013, the Constitutional Court ruled that the DPD can propose bills on regional autonomy and the relationship between central and local governments; previously, the chamber could only review legislation and make recommendations. Presidents and vice presidents can serve up to two five-year terms, and all legislators also serve five-year terms.

Voters for the DPR can select either a party list or an individual candidate, but candidates are seated based on the number of direct votes they receive. The April 2009 elections yielded a significant turnover in the DPR's membership, with approximately 75 percent of the chamber consisting of new lawmakers. The Democratic Party of President Susilo Bambang Yudhoyono (SBY) won the contest, raising its share of seats to 148, from 55 in 2004. The Golkar party garnered 106 seats, and the Indonesian Democratic Party–Struggle (PDI-P) took 94. Religious parties generally fared poorly, though the Prosperous Justice Party (PKS), with its strong anticorruption platform, captured 57 seats. Five smaller parties divided the remainder. In the presidential election that July, SBY easily secured a second five-year term with 61 percent of the vote in the first round, defeating former president Megawati Sukarnoputri of PDI-P and Jusuf Kalla of Golkar, the outgoing vice president. SBY's new running mate, former central bank governor Boediono, became vice president.

In April 2012, the DPR passed an amended election law that increased the vote threshold for parties to enter the parliament from 2.5 percent to 3.5 percent, making it more difficult for small parties to win seats in the upcoming 2014 elections. In 2013, discrepancies between the eligible voter list of the General Election Commission (KPU) and identity numbers provided by the Home Affairs Ministry led to delays in the finalization of the 2014 voter list, with the eligibility of as many as 65 million voters in jeopardy. Inaccuracies in the voter list have affected past elections.

Direct elections for provincial and district leaders, including provincial and district parliaments, began in 2005. Combined with the decentralization of political and fiscal power to the district and subdistrict levels in 1999, these direct elections have often led to tensions between the central government and local authorities, with the latter at times ignoring court or central government rulings, and are often marred by violence and contested results. Between 2008 and 2011, approximately 90 percent of district election results were contested at the Constitutional Court. In October, Constitutional Court chief justice Akil Mochtar, together with a member of parliament and an incumbent district head, were arrested for their alleged role in fixing rulings on contested district elections. Local direct elections have also proven to be extremely costly and have led to electoral fatigue and increased local conflict. The central government has in recent years considered ending direct elections for mayors and district heads, while maintaining them for provincial governors.

Under a law passed in August 2012, the hereditary sultan of Yogyakarta will be that region's unelected governor. The position will become nonpartisan, and the sultan will be subject to a verification process with minimum requirements—such as education—every five years beginning in 2016. The prince of Paku Alaman will similarly be deputy governor of the region.

B. Political Pluralism and Participation: 13 / 16

The right to organize political parties is respected in Indonesia, though in recent years the election laws have been amended to reduce the number of parties in parliament and the number of parties eligible to field a presidential candidate. In 1999, 48 parties competed; in 2013, only 12 parties passed verification processes for the 2014 elections. Parties must have chapters in all provinces, three quarters of the districts in those provinces, and at least half of the subdistricts in each district. Parties or coalitions must attain 25 percent of the popular vote or 20 percent of the seats in the DPR to nominate candidates for president. Proposed amendments to reduce the threshold for fielding a presidential candidate were rejected in October 2013. All political parties must satisfy national-level requirements to compete in district and provincial elections, except for those in the autonomous province of Aceh, where local-level parties are permitted under a 2005 peace agreement that ended a long-running insurgency.

Despite the relatively high bar for eligibility, one new national party, Partai NasDem, passed verification in 2013 and will compete in the 2014 elections, while two parties that competed for the first time in 2009, Partai Gerakan Indonesia Raya (Gerindra) and Partai Hati Nurani Rakyat (Hanura), will participate again in 2014. It is estimated that 90 percent of the candidates for the 2014 elections are incumbents.

Some local governments have discriminated against minorities by restricting access to national identification cards, birth certificates, marriage licenses, and other bureaucratic necessities, limiting their political rights and electoral opportunities.

C. Functioning of Government: 6 / 12

Elected officials and legislative representatives determine the policies of the government, but corruption remains endemic, including in the parliament and other key institutions such as the police. Indonesia was ranked 114 out of 177 countries surveyed in Transparency International's 2013 Corruption Perceptions Index.

Among other high-profile cases during the year, Democratic Party lawmaker Angelina Sondakh was sentenced in January to four and half years in prison and another eight years in November after a Supreme Court appeal by the Corruption Eradication Commission. She was sentenced for receiving bribes related to construction contracts for the Youth and Sports Ministry, part of a larger corruption scandal that ensnared former Democratic Party treasurer Muhammad Nazaruddin in 2012 and has harmed SBY's reformist credentials. Nazaruddin's wife, Neneng Sri Wahyuni, was sentenced to six years in prison in March for her role in rigging a procurement tender for a solar energy project. In August, Rudi Rubiandini, the head of a special government task force to manage Indonesia's upstream oil and gas activities, was arrested for allegedly receiving a bribe related to energy contracts. In September, former police inspector general Djoko Susilo was sentenced to 10 years in prison for corruption and money laundering, which was increased to 18 years at the Jakarta High Court in December after an appeal by the defendant. That case received widespread attention due to a long-running conflict between the Corruption Eradication Commission (KPK) and the national police. Also in September, former senior Health Ministry official Ratna Dewi Umar was sentenced to five years in prison for graft related to the procurement of medical equipment. In December, former PKS president and lawmaker Luthfi Hasan Ishaaq was sentenced to 16 years in prison for taking bribes to arrange a beef import quota increase for a private company.

A 2009 anticorruption law diluted the authority and independence of both the KPK and the Anticorruption Court (Tipikor), allowing the creation of regional corruption courts. Tipikor had been established partly to counteract the acquittals commonly issued in regular, regional courts. Even those who are convicted in such courts often receive light sentences or benefit from mass pardons. Regional anticorruption court judge Asmadinata was dismissed by an ethics panel in July 2013 and formally named as a bribery suspect by the KPK in September. Two other ad hoc regional anticorruption court judges—Heru Kisbandono and

Kartini Marpaung—had been jailed in March and April in the same case, which involved procurement violations by a former provincial parliament speaker.

Civil society groups are able to comment on and influence pending policies or legislation to a certain extent. For example, a judicial review that led to the 2012 dissolution of the energy regulator BPMigas was launched at the request of 42 organizations. However, government transparency is limited by obstacles including a 2011 law that criminalized the leaking of state secrets to the public. Critics warned that the law—which also gave the State Intelligence Agency (BIN) greater authority to gather information on those suspected of terrorism, espionage, or threatening national security—could lead to abuse of power given the broad definitions of secret information.

CIVIL LIBERTIES: 34 / 60 (-1)
D. Freedom of Expression and Belief: 12 / 16

Indonesia hosts a vibrant and diverse media environment, though press freedom is hampered by a number of legal and regulatory restrictions. Strict but unevenly enforced licensing rules mean that thousands of television and radio stations operate illegally. Foreign journalists are not authorized to travel to the restive provinces of Papua and West Papua without special permission. Reporters often practice self-censorship to avoid running afoul of civil and criminal libel laws.

In addition to legal obstacles, reporters sometimes face violence and intimidation, which in many cases goes unpunished. The Alliance of Independent Journalists (AJI) recorded slightly fewer cases of violence against journalists in 2013, a total of 40 reduced from 56, in addition to 20 separate incidents against journalists in Papua, the latter an increase from the prior year. An AJI report accused the military of responsibility for 8 out of 30 violent assaults against journalists from January 2012 to August 2013.

Some progress was made in 2013 to hold officials accountable. In July, a local Religious Affairs Agency chief was sentenced to five months in jail for sending a death threat to a journalist who was reporting on salary cuts at the agency. In September, an air force officer was sentenced to three months in jail for his assault on a journalist who was covering a military plane crash in 2012, and in April three marines were sentenced to 11 months each for assaulting four journalists who were reporting on demolitions of unauthorized buildings.

Freedom of expression is generally upheld, though censorship and self-censorship of books and films for allegedly obscene or blasphemous content is fairly common. A 2012 documentary film about mass killings of suspected communists in 1965 is banned. Since 2011, authorities in Aceh have cracked down on "punks" for supposedly insulting Islam. Those rounded up by police are subjected to "reeducation," which includes the forcible shaving of their punk-rock hairstyles and a traditional cleansing ceremony. In 2013, despite the agreement of the hosts to remove the swimsuit portion of the competition, protests led by the hard-line Islamic Defenders Front (FPI) forced the Miss World competition finale to be moved from Jakarta to Bali.

The 2008 Law on Electronic Information and Transactions (ITE) extended libel and other restrictions to the internet and online media, criminalizing the distribution or accessibility of information or documents that are "contrary to the moral norms of Indonesia" or related to gambling, blackmail, or defamation.

Indonesia officially recognizes Islam, Protestantism, Roman Catholicism, Hinduism, Buddhism, and Confucianism. Since 2006, individuals have had the option of leaving the religion section of their national identity cards blank, but those who do not identify with a recognized religion face discrimination in practice. Atheism is not accepted, and the criminal code contains provisions against blasphemy, penalizing those who "distort" or "misrepresent" official faiths. The central government has often failed to respond to religious intolerance in recent years, and societal discrimination has increased. A 2006 joint ministerial decree requires religious groups seeking to build houses of worship to obtain the written approval of 60 immediate neighbors and a recommendation from the local Interreligious Harmony Forum (FKUB), composed of representatives from recognized religious groups according to the demographic breakdown of each district. Protestant congregations have struggled to secure local permission to build churches in parts of Java, even when authorized by the Supreme Court.

Violence and intimidation against Ahmadiyya, a heterodox Islamic sect with approximately 400,000 Indonesian followers, continued in 2013. Hostile acts against the group have increased since 2008, when the Religious Affairs Ministry recommended that it be banned nationwide, and the government, seeking a compromise, instead barred Ahmadis from proselytizing. The central government in 2013 affirmed its refusal to ban Ahmadiyya, but it continues to tolerate discrimination by local governments. In April and May in West Java, four Ahmadi mosques were sealed by local authorities and an Ahmadi community was attacked by a mob, with damage to 29 buildings. Also in May, a mob attacked and damaged a mosque in East Java. Another Ahmadi mosque was allegedly closed by the FPI in West Java in October.

The Shiite Muslim minority has also suffered violence and intimidation in recent years. In April 2013, a suspect in a 2012 mob attack on a Shiite community in Sampang, East Java, that left two people dead and many buildings damaged was acquitted of all charges. In September, Sampang residents independently initiated and signed a peace agreement between Shiite and Sunni Muslims. The agreement, among other provisions, allows for the return of the Shiites to their villages on the condition that they not proselytize or file any lawsuits against the other residents. However, the majority of Sampang residents still had not returned at year's end. Forced conversion of Shiites has been an increasing concern, primarily due to public statements by Religious Affairs Minister Suryadharma Ali. In 2013, Suryadharma said the government would not require conversion, but would still require the displaced Sampang Shiites to undergo an official "enlightenment" program.

In February 2013, a Human Rights Watch report on Indonesian religious rights noted the repeated failure of the national and local governments to protect religious minorities, citing problems including local governments that bow to hard-line groups, failure to investigate violence, and bias on the part of prosecutors.

Academic freedom in Indonesia is generally respected.

E. Associational and Organizational Rights: 8 / 12 (-1)

Freedom of assembly is usually upheld, and peaceful protests are common in the capital. However, authorities have restricted the right to assembly in conflict areas. Flag-raising ceremonies and independence rallies in Papua are routinely disbanded, often violently, and participants have been prosecuted. In April 2013, police opened fire on a group of protesters in the province, causing two deaths; the protest was held to mark the 50th anniversary of the transfer of Papua to Indonesian authority.

Indonesia hosts a strong and active array of civil society organizations, with an estimated 28,000 officially registered, though some human rights groups are subject to monitoring and interference by the government. Moreover, independence activists in Papua and the Maluku Islands, and labor and political activists in Java and Sulawesi, remain targets for human rights abuses. No high-level official has been convicted for any serious human rights violation since the fall of Suharto. The new law on mass organizations passed in July 2013, replacing a 1985 law, covers all civic and religious NGOs, including media. It received widespread criticism for provisions that undermine freedoms of association, expression, and religion. Under the new law, the government can dissolve organizations that do not espouse the principles of Pancasila. Organizations cannot commit blasphemy or advocate non-Pancasila ideologies, including Marxism-Leninism, atheism, and communism. The law also narrows the types of activities associations can undertake, increases bureaucratic controls by requiring all organizations to register with the government and submit to regular reviews of their activities, allows the government to dissolve noncompliant organizations, and includes other vague requirements that leave considerable discretion to local governments and courts. In addition, foreign groups are forbidden from activities that disrupt the stability and integrity of the country or its diplomatic relations.

Workers can join independent unions, bargain collectively, and with the exception of civil servants, stage strikes. The labor movement is generally fragmented, and enforcement of minimum-wage and other labor standards is weak. However, the labor laws include generous severance pay and strike provisions. Some unions have resorted to violence in their negotiations with employers, and labor-related demonstrations are widespread. Approximately 10 percent of workers in the formal economy—which accounts for one-sixth of the total economy—belong to unions. Household workers are currently excluded from labor law protections.

F. Rule of Law: 5 / 16

The judiciary, particularly the Constitutional Court, has demonstrated its independence in some cases, but the court system remains plagued by corruption and other weaknesses. The arrest of the Constitutional Court chief justice on graft charges in 2013 was a blow to public confidence in legal institutions. Low salaries for judicial officials and impunity for illegal activity perpetuate the problems of bribery, forced confessions, and interference in court proceedings by military personnel and government officials at all levels.

Effective police work has proven critical to Indonesia's recent successes in fighting terrorism, but the security forces in general remain rife with corruption and other abuses, and personnel regularly go unpunished or receive light sentences for human rights violations. In recent years the police have been faulted for failing to prevent or mitigate mob attacks on religious minority communities. In 2010 the national police issued a regulation allowing officers to use live ammunition to quell situations of "anarchic violence." In 2012, the International Crisis Group released a report highlighting the increasing rate of attacks on police by angry crowds. The report attributed the hostility to the cumulative effects of police brutality, bribery, and lack of accountability. In March 2013, three police officers were given lenient sentences of between two and five years in prison for torturing and killing a man in their custody in 2011.

Information garnered through torture is permissible in Indonesian courts, and torture carried out by law enforcement officers is not a criminal offense. The Indonesian Legal Aid Institute found in 2010 that up to 80 percent of detainees suffered from acts of violence in police custody. Student activists are the most prone to arbitrary arrest, followed by farmers and journalists. Poor prison governance is compounded by endemic overcrowding. Prisons are estimated to be overcrowded by an average of 45 percent, with some up to 400 percent over capacity. Prison riots and protests over lack of services have led to numerous jailbreaks. Prisoners are able to bribe guards for additional services and luxuries, and illegal activity is common. The International Crisis Group has reported on terrorist recruitment in prisons. In 2012, the DPR passed a Juvenile Court Law that raised the minimum age of incarceration to 14 years, ordered the creation of juvenile detention centers within five years, and prohibited the publication of court details about minors. Minors are often incarcerated with adults; prior to the new law, minors aged 8 and above were held criminally responsible for their acts and subject to incarceration.

The military (TNI) has in the past enjoyed relative impunity for criminal activities and human rights abuses, though internal reform efforts and public pressure has led to some improvements. Cases against TNI members for military crimes are tried in military courts; while cases for nonmilitary crimes are supposed to be tried in civilian courts, in practice they are not. In March 2013, three members of the Kopassus special forces unit raided a prison in Yogyakarta and killed four detainees who were awaiting trial for the killing of a soldier. They were tried in military courts and received between 3 and 11 years in prison in September. Five other soldiers were tried as accessories and sentenced to 21 months in prison.

Since the 1950s, separatists have waged a low-grade insurgency in the provinces of Papua and West Papua, where there is a large military presence. In February 2013, the Free Papua Movement (OPM) allegedly killed eight soldiers in a pair of attacks, marking the most deadly incident of its kind in recent years. Conflict between security forces and protesters is common, as are extrajudicial killings, tribal conflict, and conflict related to labor disputes at foreign-operated mines. Government and military officials often accuse human rights activists of being part of the separatist movement, and visits by foreigners, particularly foreign journalists, are highly restricted, perpetuating the lack of access to independent information and increasing impunity. In October, in a sign of potential improvement, the governor of West Papua announced that reporters would be allowed into the region and their safety guaranteed. According to the organization Papuans Behind Bars, as of December there were 70 political prisoners jailed in West Papua. In March, the government announced that it would increase the military presence in the region to facilitate construction of 14 new highways in Papua and West Papua. Corruption has undermined the central government's efforts to improve economic conditions in Papua. Special autonomy status was introduced in 2001 to undercut separatist agitation, but it provided for increased economic rather than political autonomy.

A 2000 law on human rights provides for the establishment of ad hoc human rights courts to hear cases related to gross violations committed before 2000. To date, no court has been set up to deal with violations during the Suharto era (1967–1998), including in Aceh. In August 2013, the human rights organization Komnas HAM published a report detailing gross human rights violations perpetrated by security forces in Aceh during the nearly 30-year insurgency that ended in 2005.

Since 2006, a number of districts have issued local ordinances based on Sharia (Islamic law). Many are unconstitutional, contradict Indonesia's international human rights commitments, or are unclear, leading to enforcement problems. The central government and various parties have failed to take decisive action, apparently for political reasons. Many of the ordinances seek to impose an Islamic dress code, Koranic literacy requirements, and bans on prostitution. Other measures are more extreme. In 2009, the Aceh regional parliament passed legislation that, among other provisions, allows stoning for adultery and public lashing for same-sex sexual acts. A draft revision under consideration in 2013 would remove the stoning penalty. Separately, a local administration in Aceh passed a bylaw that bans women from riding astride motorcycles, and another administration passed one banning dancing. Local regulations unrelated to Sharia have also been criticized for violating constitutional protections.

In recent years, hard-line Islamist groups such as the FPI have engaged in raids and extrajudicial enforcement of Sharia bylaws, and pressured local governments to close churches and non-Sunni mosques. Their violent activities are not supported by large Islamic organizations such as the Nahdlatul Ulama, but the groups exert outsized influence and often have the support of high-ranking government officials. Security forces have been criticized for tacitly aiding them by ignoring their abuses.

Ethnic Chinese, who make up less than 3 percent of the population but are resented by some for reputedly holding much of the country's wealth, continue to face harassment. LGBT (lesbian, gay, bisexual, and transgender) people also suffer discrimination, and gay-themed events have encountered resistance from local officials and open hostility from hard-line Islamist groups. Many local bylaws criminalize homosexuality, and a 2008 anti-pornography law labels same-sex sexual acts as "deviant."

G. Personal Autonomy and Individual Rights: 9 / 16

Freedom of travel and choice of residence, employment, and higher education are generally respected in Indonesia. However, the ability to obtain private business licenses and public employment is often limited by the need for bribes or other inducements. Corruption also affects businesses' daily operations and routine interactions with the state bureaucracy.

Property rights are threatened by mining and logging activity on communal land and state appropriation of land claimed by indigenous groups, particularly in Kalimantan. In May 2013, the Constitutional Court reviewed a 1999 law and ruled that indigenous people have the right to manage "customary forest" lands they inhabit. Before the ruling, such lands were under state control, allowing the government to grant concessions to extractive industries.

Discrimination against women persists, particularly in the workplace. A 2008 law states that 30 percent of a political party's candidates and board members must be women. While only 101 women were elected to the 560-seat DPR in 2009, this was an increase over the 63 in the previous term. Trafficking of women and children for prostitution and forced labor continues, despite the passage of new laws and stricter penalties. Abortion is illegal, except to save a woman's life. National legislation deems rape a criminal offense, but adults over 15 years of age must have corroboration and witnesses for rape charges; while spousal rape is not specified in the criminal code, it is covered under domestic violence legislation. A September 2013 UN study found that 19.5 percent of rural male respondents, 26.2 percent of urban male respondents, and 48.6 percent of Papuan male respondents reported having raped a partner or nonpartner. Sharia-based ordinances in a number of districts infringe on women's constitutional rights. A draft Gender Equality Bill stalled in parliament in 2012 due to objections that it contradicted Sharia on issues such as inheritance and allowed interreligious marriage. Several local governments have in recent years called for virginity tests for female high school students and drafted related local bylaws. A draft national criminal code under consideration in 2013 would ban adultery and cohabitation by unmarried couples.

The 2008 antipornography law applies not just to published images but to speech and gestures that "incite sexual desire," drawing concerns that it could be used to persecute women. Significantly, the law invites the "public" to participate in the discouragement of pornographic acts, leading to extrajudicial enforcement. A Constitutional Court ruling in 2010 upheld the law.

Iran

Political Rights Rating: 6
Civil Liberties Rating: 6
Freedom Rating: 6.0
Freedom Status: Not Free
Electoral Democracy: No

Population: 76,500,000
Capital: Tehran

Ten-Year Ratings Timeline For Year Under Review (Political Rights, Civil Liberties, Status)

Year Under Review	2004	2005	2006	2007	2008	2009	2010	2011	2012	2013
Rating	6,6,NF	6,6,NF	6,6,NF	6,6,NF	6,6,NF	6,6,NF	6,6,NF	6,6,NF	6,6,NF	6,6,NF

INTRODUCTION

In the first presidential election since the disputed 2009 vote in which hard-liner Mahmoud Ahmedinejad won a second term, centrist cleric Hassan Rouhani secured a first-round victory on June 14, 2013. The result underscored the Iranian electorate's support for Rouhani's program of moderation in domestic and foreign policy. However, his ability to deliver on his campaign promises was complicated by the need to negotiate with rival conservative factions that continued to control key institutions, such as the parliament, judiciary, and security forces.

In the months after Rouhani's inauguration in August, some early signs of social and political opening were observed. The new administration adopted a more conciliatory approach and tone with the outside world. At home, Rouhani called for lifting curbs on social-media access and eased restrictions on the press. Nearly a dozen well-known political prisoners were released, including Iran's most prominent human rights activist, Nasrin Sotoudeh, though key opposition leaders remained under house arrest. The new administration also took practical steps to guarantee academic freedom.

POLITICAL RIGHTS: 7 / 40 (+1)
A. Electoral Process: 3 / 12 (+1)

None of the elections held since the 1979 Islamic revolution have been regarded as free or fair. The most powerful figure in the government is the supreme leader, currently Ayatollah Ali Khamenei. He is chosen by the Assembly of Experts, a body of 86 clerics who are elected to eight-year terms by popular vote, from a list of candidates vetted by the Guardian Council. The supreme leader, who has no fixed term, is the commander in chief of the armed forces and appoints the leaders of the judiciary, the heads of state broadcast media, and the Expediency Council. The president is elected by popular vote for up to two four-year terms. All candidates for the presidency and the 290-seat, unicameral parliament are vetted by the Guardian Council, which consists of six Islamic theologians appointed by the supreme leader and six jurists nominated by the head of the judiciary and confirmed by the parliament, all for six-year terms.

Ahead of the March 2012 parliamentary elections, the Guardian Council disqualified one-third of the registered candidates, including incumbent members of parliament, opposition reformists, and supporters of Ahmadinejad, who had increasingly clashed with Khamenei and rival conservative factions. Members of two leading reformist political groupings, the Islamic Participation Front and the Islamic Revolution Mujahedin Organization, as well as the Freedom Movement, were barred from taking part in the legislative elections. Though there were no claims of systematic fraud, several sitting lawmakers accused the Islamic Revolutionary Guard Corps (IRGC) of rigging activities. The official results were seen as favoring the conservative supporters of the supreme leader.

In preparation for the 2013 presidential election, the parliament passed amendments to the election law in January. The changes were largely viewed as politically motivated and designed to diminish the role of Ahmadinejad's executive branch in conducting elections. Under the law, a new executive board composed of representatives aligned with the supreme leader was charged with overseeing the Interior Ministry's administration of the balloting. In May, the Guardian Council approved just eight of the 680 candidates who had registered for the presidential poll. Several leading contenders, including former president Akbar Hashemi Rafsanjani, were disqualified on what many considered to be political grounds, leaving a much narrower field of candidates, most of whom had close ties to Khamenei. Despite crackdowns on journalists and restrictions on the internet in the run-up to the vote, no major election irregularities were reported, and Rouhani's victory—with nearly 51 percent of the vote amid 72 percent turnout—appeared to reflect the choice of the voters.

Local council elections, slated for the winter of 2011 but postponed due to security concerns, were held in conjunction with the presidential election. A number of electoral problems were reported, including the disqualification of prominent political, cultural, and civic figures and the intimidation of reformist candidates.

B. Political Pluralism and Participation: 2 / 16

The constitution permits the establishment of political parties, professional syndicates, and other civic organizations, provided that they do not violate the principles of "freedom, sovereignty, and national unity" or question the Islamic basis of the republic. All political parties, associations, and nongovernmental organizations (NGOs) must register with the Ministry of Interior and are subject to arbitrary restrictions. Opposition politicians and party groupings have suffered especially harsh repression since the disputed 2009 presidential election, with many leaders—including former lawmakers and cabinet ministers—facing arrest, prison sentences, and lengthy bans on political activity. Since February 2011, the former presidential candidates and prominent opposition leaders Mir Hussein Mousavi and Mehdi Karroubi, and Mousavi's wife Zahra Rahnavard, have been kept under strict house arrest without trial, incommunicado, and with only limited access to family members. At least two leading reformist parties, the Islamic Participation Front and the Islamic Revolution Mujahedin Organization, have had their licenses revoked by a court and are prevented from functioning freely.

Though non-Muslim minorities cannot hold senior government or military positions, the constitution grants five parliamentary seats to recognized religious minorities (Armenian Christians, Chaldean Christians, Zoroastrians, and Jews). The political participation and representation of religious and ethnic minorities remains weak at the national and local levels. A Zoroastrian candidate from the city of Yazd won a seat in the 2013 local council elections, reportedly marking the first victory of its kind since the 1979 revolution.

C. Functioning of Government: 2 / 12

In addition to the restrictions imposed on the elected presidency by the supreme leader and other unelected institutions, the powers of the parliament are limited by the Guardian Council. Article 94 of the constitution vests the council with the authority to review all legislation passed in the parliament, and to approve or reject bills on the basis of their adherence to Islamic precepts and constitutional law. The Guardian Council regularly invokes its supervisory powers to block legislation passed in parliament. It has acted as the single most important obstacle to the parliament's legislative jurisdiction since the 1979 revolution.

Corruption is pervasive at all levels of the bureaucracy, and oversight mechanisms to ensure transparency are weak. The hard-line clerical establishment and the IRGC, to which it has many ties, have grown immensely wealthy through their control of tax-exempt foundations that dominate many sectors of the economy. The Ahmadinejad administration gravely damaged fiscal transparency and accountability through the abolition of independent financial watchdogs and the murky transfer of profitable state companies to the IRGC and other semigovernmental conglomerates. Iran was ranked 144 out of 177 countries surveyed in Transparency International's 2013 Corruption Perceptions Index.

CIVIL LIBERTIES: 10 / 60
D. Freedom of Expression and Belief: 2 / 16

Freedom of expression is severely limited. The government directly controls all television and radio broadcasting. Satellite dishes are popular, despite being illegal. Censorship, both official and self-imposed, is widespread, and cooperation with Persian-language satellite news channels based abroad is banned. In January 2013, over a dozen journalists working for mainly reformist newspapers were arrested for allegedly cooperating with "antirevolutionary" news outlets based outside Iran. Many were released without being formally charged. The security apparatus's harassment of the family members of Iranian journalists working abroad, including the employees of Radio Free Europe/Radio Liberty, persisted in 2013.

The Press Supervisory Board has extensive power to prosecute journalists for such vaguely worded offenses as "mutiny against Islam," "insulting legal or real persons who are lawfully respected," and "propaganda against the regime." Warnings and threats of prosecution are often used to induce self-censorship. In the run-up to the 2013 election, authorities clamped down on news and information by issuing warnings to at least six publications and blocking several pro-Ahmadinejad websites. In October 2013, the Press Supervisory Board banned the reformist newspaper *Bahar* for publishing an article that questioned the authority of the first Shiite imam, Ali, as a political rather than a religious leader. Authorities arrested the managing editor of the newspaper and the author of the article, and both were later released on bail.

Freedom of the press has slightly improved since Rouhani's election. Honoring a campaign promise, the new president withdrew 50 government motions filed against Iranian journalists and media outlets by his predecessor. The government also lifted some restrictions on previously banned topics, such as the economic impact of international sanctions, the fate of opposition leaders, criticism of the country's nuclear policy, and the future of U.S.-Iranian relations. Iran still ranks second in the world for the number of jailed journalists, with 35 behind bars as of December 2013, according to the New York–based Committee to Protect Journalists. In October, authorities released two high-profile journalists, Isa Saharkhiz and Bahman Ahmadi Amouyi, who had been imprisoned since 2009.

Internet penetration has skyrocketed in recent years, and many Iranians used mobile-telephone cameras and social-networking sites to provide some of the only independent coverage of the 2009 postelection crackdown. The authorities have consequently established draconian laws and practices to restrict access to communication tools, persecute dissidents for their online activity, and strengthen the government's vast censorship apparatus. Key international social-media sites like Facebook, Twitter, and YouTube were blocked after the 2009 election, hampering the opposition's ability to communicate and organize. The 2010 Computer Crimes Law is freighted with vaguely defined offenses that effectively criminalize legitimate online expression; the law also legalizes government surveillance of the internet. The first phase of a national intranet, aimed at disconnecting the population from the global internet, was launched in September 2012.

Iranian filmmakers are subject to tight restrictions, and many have been arrested or harassed since the 2009 election. In September 2013, the House of Cinema, an independent professional association that supported some 5,000 Iranian filmmakers and artists, reopened after the government forced its closure in January 2012.

Religious freedom is limited in Iran, whose population is largely Shiite Muslim but includes Sunni Muslim, Baha'i, Christian, Jewish, and Zoroastrian minorities. The Special Court for the Clergy investigates religious figures for alleged crimes and has generally been used to persecute clerics who stray from the official interpretation of Islam or criticize the supreme leader. Sunnis enjoy equal rights under the law but face discrimination in practice; there is no Sunni mosque in Tehran, and few Sunnis hold senior government posts. Sufi Muslims have also faced persecution by the authorities. Since the leader of the Sufi order Nematollahi Gonabadi was arrested in 2009 and sentenced to four years in prison, security forces have repeatedly clashed with members of the order in Gonabad and Kavar.

The constitution recognizes Zoroastrians, Jews, and Christians as religious minorities, and they are generally allowed to worship without interference, so long as they do not proselytize. Conversion by Muslims to a non-Muslim religion is punishable by death. Pressure on Christian converts and churches persisted in 2013. In May, plainclothes security forces arrested three Christian converts during a worship session in Isfahan. Also that month, the authorities shut down Iran's oldest Persian-language Protestant church in Tehran and arrested one of its pastors. In August, a court upheld the eight-year prison sentence of Iranian-American Christian convert Saeed Abedini.

Iranian Baha'is, thought to number between 300,000 and 350,000, are not recognized as a religious minority in the constitution, enjoy virtually no rights under the law, and are banned from practicing their faith. Under Ahmadinejad, concerted efforts to intimidate, imprison, and physically attack Baha'is were carried out with impunity by security forces, paramilitary groups, and vigilantes. Baha'i students are barred from attending university and prevented from obtaining their educational records. Seven Baha'i leaders who were arrested in 2008 remain imprisoned for their religious beliefs and the management of their community's administrative affairs.

Academic freedom is limited. Since 2009, between 50 and 150 university faculty members have been forced to retire or dismissed based on their personal and political opinions. A 2010 government directive barred Iranian scholars and citizens from contact with over 60 European and U.S.-based foundations, think tanks, and educational institutions. Since the 2009 presidential election, the IRGC-led Basij militia has increased its presence on campuses, and vocal critics of the regime are more likely to face persecution and prosecution. According to Iran's largest student organization, between 2009 and 2012, 396 students were banned from pursuing their studies because of their political activities. During the same period, 634 were arrested, with 30 of them sentenced to long prison terms, for exercising their rights to assembly, association, and free expression.

However, in September 2013, Iran's Ministry of Research, Science, and Technology (MSRT) announced that it would no longer target and expel students for their political and personal beliefs. Moreover, it announced that students banned from education in 2011, 2012, and 2013 would be allowed to reenroll. Those barred from pursuing their studies prior to 2011 would be required to retake the nationwide university exam. In another sign of positive change, the MSRT set up an internal committee to review the cases of university faculty members who were dismissed or forced into retirement by the previous government. Moreover, several hard-line heads of universities were dismissed from their positions, including Sadreddin Shariati of Allameh Tabatabai University, the country's top institution for the humanities, who was instrumental in implementing gender segregation on campus and eliminating 13 branches of the social sciences from the university's curriculum.

E. Associational and Organizational Rights: 1 / 12

The constitution guarantees the right to assembly, but it prohibits public demonstrations that "are detrimental to the fundamental principles of Islam," a vague provision that is frequently invoked to deny permit requests. Vigilante and paramilitary organizations that are officially or tacitly sanctioned by the government—most notably the Basij and Ansar-i Hezbollah—regularly play a major role in breaking up demonstrations. Even peaceful, nonpolitical demonstrations have been met with brutal violence.

Human rights discourse and grassroots activism are integral parts of Iranian society. However, the security services routinely arrest and harass secular activists as part of a wider effort to control NGOs. In early 2013, authorities summoned and arrested dozens of ethnic Arab civil society activists in Khuzestan to preempt unrest ahead of the anniversary of violent 2005 protests in the province. However, since the June 2013 elections, signs of greater tolerance for civic activism, especially on less politically charged issues, have been observed. During the summer, security forces permitted several grassroots campaigns focused on environmental topics to operate freely, without harassment or arrests.

Iranian law does not allow independent labor unions, though workers' councils are represented in the Workers' House, the only legal labor federation. Workers' public protests and May Day gatherings are regularly suppressed by security forces. In 2013, the authorities denied workers the right to hold a May Day rally, aside from officially organized ceremonies, for the sixth consecutive year.

F. Rule of Law: 3 / 16

The judicial system is not independent, as the supreme leader directly appoints the head of the judiciary, who in turn appoints senior judges. Suspects are frequently tried in closed sessions without access to legal counsel. Judges commonly accept coerced confessions and disregard torture or abuse during detention. Political and other sensitive cases are tried before revolutionary courts, where due process protections are routinely disregarded and trials are often summary. In September 2013, authorities released 11 prominent political prisoners, including human rights lawyer Nasrin Sotoudeh. This marked the largest release of high-profile prisoners in one day since the 2009 postelection protests.

The government practice of pressuring lawyers to abandon the cases of political and social detainees is widespread in Iran. Lawyers who resist such pressure can face harassment, interrogation, and incarceration. Since 2009, at least 42 attorneys have been arrested, given long prison sentences, and barred from practicing law. In recent years, the government has progressively intervened in the affairs of the Iranian Bar Association, an independent body responsible for issuing licenses to lawyers, overseeing their performance, and legally protecting them.

The country's penal code is based on Sharia (Islamic law) and provides for flogging, amputation, and execution by stoning or hanging for a range of social and political offenses; these punishments are carried out in practice. Iran routinely ranks second only to China in number of executions, with hundreds carried out each year. While many inmates are executed for drug-related offenses, a number of political prisoners convicted of *moharebeh* (enmity against God) have also received death sentences. Iran's overall execution rate increased significantly under Ahmadinejad. In 2013 the authorities announced 334 executions, but human rights organizations estimate that as many as 290 individuals were executed without official acknowledgment.

Although the constitution prohibits arbitrary arrest and detention, such abuses are frequently employed, and family members of detainees are often not notified for days or weeks. Suspected dissidents have been held in unofficial, illegal detention centers. Prison conditions in general are notoriously poor, and there are regular allegations of abuse, rape, torture, and death in custody.

The constitution and laws call for equal rights for all ethnic groups, but in practice these rights are restricted by the regime. Minority languages are prohibited in schools and government offices. Minority rights activists are consistently threatened and arrested. Ethnic Kurds, Arabs, Balochis, and Azeris complain of discrimination. Kurdish opposition groups suspected of separatist aspirations, such as the Democratic Party of Iranian Kurdistan (KDPI), are brutally suppressed. Non-Muslim minorities also face some discrimination in employment and education opportunities.

Sexual orientation is a subject of government scrutiny. The penal code criminalizes all sexual relations outside of traditional marriage, and Iran is among the few countries where individuals can be put to death for consensual same-sex conduct.

G. Personal Autonomy and Individual Rights: 4 / 16

The constitution guarantees the freedom of movement for all Iranians. However, among other restrictions, the government has prevented many political activists and journalists from leaving the country. Property rights and economic freedoms are affected by state controls, international sanctions, and the dominant role of clerical and military entities in the economy. Non-Muslims, particularly members of the Baha'i community, face economic discrimination. Authorities regularly deny Baha'is business licenses and often pressure their private employers to fire them.

A woman cannot obtain a passport without the permission of her husband or a male relative. Women are widely educated; a majority of university students are female. They are nevertheless excluded from most leadership roles. Women currently hold just 3 percent of the seats in the parliament, and they are routinely barred from running for higher office. Female judges may not issue final verdicts. Women do not enjoy equal rights under Sharia-based statutes governing divorce, inheritance, and child custody, though some of these inequalities are accompanied by greater familial and financial obligations for men. A woman's testimony in court is given only half the weight of a man's, and the monetary compensation awarded to a female victim's family upon her death is half that owed to the family of a male victim. Women must conform to strict dress codes and are segregated from men in some public places.

Iraq

Political Rights Rating: 5
Civil Liberties Rating: 6
Freedom Rating: 5.5
Freedom Status: Not Free
Electoral Democracy: No

Population: 35,100,000
Capital: Baghdad

Ratings Change: Iraq's political rights rating improved from 6 to 5 due to an increase in political organizing and activity by opposition parties during provincial elections held in April and June.

Ten-Year Ratings Timeline For Year Under Review (Political Rights, Civil Liberties, Status)

Year Under Review	2004	2005	2006	2007	2008	2009	2010	2011	2012	2013
Rating	7,5,NF	6,5,NF	6,6,NF	6,6,PF	6,6,NF	5,6,NF	5,6,NF	5,6,NF	6,6,NF	5,6,NF

INTRODUCTION

Political violence in Iraq increased sharply during 2013. Suicide attacks and car bombings at mosques and in neighborhoods left mass casualties while politicians, members of the

Iraqi Security Forces, journalists, and others who dared to enter the public arena were also targeted in bombings and shootings. These attacks were not only more numerous than in the past, they were also better coordinated and more dispersed, even reaching into the normally calm Kurdish city of Erbil. The vast majority of attacks were attributed to the Islamic State in Iraq (formerly Al Qaeda in Iraq), which in July announced a merger with jihadist groups in Syria and rebranded itself the Islamic State in Iraq and Greater Syria (ISIS). But as the year progressed Shi'a militias in the south and even in Baghdad began to be active again, threatening Sunnis.

The first six months of 2013 saw mass demonstrations against the government by Sunnis. These began in Anbar and spread to Nineveh, Salaheddin, Diyala, Baghdad, and Kirkuk. Protestor demands ultimately focused on repealing Iraq's anti-terrorism and de-Ba'athification laws, both of which Sunnis feel target them, and the release of detainees. Other demonstrations against specific government policies also took place in 2013, such as a Baghdad protest against the high pensions of former parliamentarians. Although protest in 2013 was generally non-violent, it was often repressed by the state, sometimes violently. In April, the Iraqi Security Forces (ISF) attacked a protest camp in Hawija, a district in the disputed Kirkuk governorate, provoking clashes between Sunnis and the ISF there. This prompted the Kurdish government to deploy its own troops in the disputed area, a move viewed as a provocation in Baghdad.

POLITICAL RIGHTS: 12 / 40 (+1)
A. Electoral Process: 7 / 12

Although it conducts meaningful elections, the operation of democracy in Iraq remains seriously impaired by sectarian and insurgent violence, widespread corruption, and the state's limited administrative capacity. Under the constitution, the president and two vice presidents are elected by the parliament and appoint the prime minister, who is nominated by the largest parliamentary bloc. Elections are held every four years. The prime minister is tasked with forming a cabinet and running the executive functions of the state. The parliament consists of a 325-seat lower house, the Council of Representatives, and a still-unformed upper house, the Federal Council, which would represent provincial interests. Members of the Council of Representatives serve four-year terms and are elected through multi-member open lists for each province. Eight seats are reserved for minorities, and these are distributed across provinces with significant minority populations. At least one-fourth of the seats must go to women. Seven members of the current Council of Representatives received compensatory seats distributed to parties that reached a high threshold nationally. Amendments passed to Iraq's Provincial Powers Law in June significantly furthered decentralization, which most Iraqi political groups now see as a way to prevent the state's break up, avoid conflict, and improve governance. However, outside the Kurdish region, in practice most power remains at the center.

The Maliki government was formed in 2010 after nearly nine months of intense negotiations. Ayad Allawi's Iraqiyyah coalition had received two more seats than Maliki's State of Law coalition in the elections. However, Maliki was able to attract enough allies to form the largest parliamentary bloc after the elections and thus form the government, a move approved by Iraq's Federal Supreme Court (FSC) but one that many Iraqis viewed as illegitimate.

On April 20, Iraq held elections for its provincial councils, its first since the departure of U.S. forces. Elections were not held in the Kurdistan Regional Government, in Kirkuk, or in the two majority Sunni provinces, Nineveh and Anbar. These latter provinces were forced to postpone their elections until June due to security problems. Maliki's State of Law coalition lost ground among Shi'a to both the Sadrists and the Islamic Supreme Council of Iraq but remained dominant. The Sunni vote was fragmented. While the election was considered fair, it was marred by sectarianism and violence. The major coalition lists and most political parties were generally either predominantly Sunni or Shi'a. Notably, Prime Minister Maliki's State of Law list, although expanded to include many more parties than it had in the provincial elections of 2009, was overwhelmingly Shi'a. A suicide bomber attacked a ballot counting center in Ramadi, killing three and mortar rounds and small bombs disrupted some polling. At least 15 candidates were also assassinated in the run-up to elections. Security concerns and disenchantment with the performance of government resulted in a turnout of only around 50 percent nationally, with Baghdad's turnout a mere 33 percent.

Home to one-fifth of the country's population, the autonomous Kurdish region constitutes a distinct polity within Iraq, with its own flag, military, and language. The Kurds held parliamentary elections for the 111-seat regional legislature in September and the Gorran opposition unseated the powerful Patriotic Union of Kurdistan (PUK) as the second largest party, after the Kurdistan Democratic Party (KDP), in the legislature. Provincial elections scheduled for November were delayed by the Kurdistan Regional Government because of problems with voter rolls and candidate lists. The Kurds also elect their own president, but in June the Kurdish parliament extended Massoud Barzani's term for two additional years without any legal basis. Eleven seats in the legislature are reserved for minorities and at least 30 percent of the seats must go to women. Elections for the Kurdistan Parliament are based on a closed party-list proportional representation system in which all three Kurdish provinces form one district. The Kurdish region's political leaders profess their commitment to remaining part of Iraq, but Kurdish security forces maintain a de facto border for the region, Iraqi Arabs are often treated as foreigners, and the regional government frequently acts in its own interest over Baghdad's objections.

Suffrage is universal for those over 18 in Iraq. Parliamentary seats are apportioned to provinces according to population estimates. As these lines are the boundaries of historic divisions there is no gerrymandering, but Iraq has not held a census since 1987 and population figures are in dispute. Elections are held regularly and are conducted by secret ballot. Voter lists are sometimes flawed, but this is generally acknowledged and investigated by the Independent High Electoral Commission (IHEC). IHEC oversees and manages the electoral process with technical assistance from international organizations. However, the Council of Representatives nominates, confirms, and oversees the nine members of IHEC's Board of Commissioners, leaving open the possibility for political pressure. Maliki has also increased his control over the IHEC. Iraqi electoral law allows for election monitoring. The 2013 provincial elections were monitored by the media, Iraqi political party representatives, Iraqi NGOs, and international observers. The Kurdish parliamentary elections were monitored by 2,800 international observers. The large parties that have dominated Iraqi government suffered a setback with a change in the parliamentary and provincial electoral laws made this year. Now surplus seats will be allotted not on the largest-remainder formula of the past law, in which surplus seats only went to those parties and coalitions that had already won seats, but on a more proportional formula giving all groups on the list a chance at winning surplus seats. This legal change comes three years after Iraq's FSC struck down the previous election law as insufficiently proportional and therefore undemocratic. This ruling, unpopular with the Prime Minister, supports arguments that the FSC is, in fact, independent or growing more so.

B. Political Pluralism and Participation: 5 / 16 (+1)

Article 39 of Iraq's constitution guarantees the freedom to form and join associations and political parties. However, law regulates that this exclude the Ba'ath party. Iraqis do form political parties of their choice and compete in elections, usually in large numbers. Over 250 political entities (individuals and parties, but mostly parties) and 50 coalitions competed for the 378 seats in the April provincial council elections. Many of these parties are personal vehicles, but some are programmatic.

Iraq's Justice and Accountability Commission (formerly the De-Ba'athification Commission) is still operating, limiting some individuals' ability to participate in politics. In 2013, the Justice and Accountability Commission removed nearly 150 candidates from the lists for the provincial elections. These candidates were overwhelmingly either Sunni or secular.

Iraq's ballot is secret, and Iraqis are free to make their own political choices.

C. Functioning of Government: 1 / 12

The Council of Representatives has been increasingly sidelined by the prime minister. Increasing violence has also encouraged Maliki's dominance, especially on issues related to security. The role of Iran in Iraq's policymaking is debated, with many believing that Iranian state preferences constrain Iraqi policymakers, especially under the current government.

Corruption is pervasive in Iraq. Transparency International's Corruption Perceptions Index ranks Iraq near the bottom of its scale, at 171 out of 177. A survey of 31,000 civil servants by Iraq's Integrity Commission found that more than 50 percent of them felt corruption was increasing. Members of the group reported paying, on average, four bribes a year. The Integrity Commission is one of several government efforts to combat corruption. In addition to conducting studies it also investigates corruption charges, and the organization was very active in 2013, issuing an arrest warrant for the governor of Diyala province and promising to publish files on high officials. While the number of corruption cases prosecuted in Iraq is increasing, most corruption goes unpunished. This is due to the pervasive environment of fear in the country, the interference of politicians in the legal system, and the sheer number of cases to be investigated.

Discretionary Political Rights Question B: -1 / 0

Although there has been a relative decline in targeted killings, the millions of IDPs generally remained so due to the threat of sectarian violence.

CIVIL LIBERTIES: 13 / 60
D. Freedom of Expression and Belief: 5 / 16

Article 38 of the Iraqi Constitution guarantees freedom of expression and of the media, although it makes both conditional on respect for public order and morality. News publications in Iraq are numerous, though many of these are owned by political parties. Freedom of the media is limited in practice by the threat of violence. Several journalists were killed in 2013, and many more received threats. As a result, self-censorship is widespread. Government officials frequently bring criminal libel charges against journalists. Media freedom has also been eroded by the state's ability to justify silencing dissenting views in the media. For example, after the provincial elections in April, Iraq's Media and Communications Commission revoked the licenses of ten satellite stations, including Al Jazeera, for inciting violence and sectarianism. Individual journalists were also detained for minor crimes or for insulting public figures, the latter especially in the three Kurdish provinces. However, in July, the Council of Representatives decided not to take up a controversial Information Technology Crimes bill, which had been criticized by journalists and others for specifying life imprisonment and large fines for vaguely defined crimes such as using computers to undermine the country's economic, political, military, or security interests. Journalists critical of those in power continued to face arrest, threats and attacks in Kurdistan, evidenced by the December killing of journalist Kawa Garmyane, who had made allegations of corruption against leaders of the Patriotic Union of Kurdistan (PUK).

The Iraqi constitution guarantees freedom of belief. But during 2013, religious minorities suffered both from the general climate of violence and from being specifically targeted. In June, a gunman opened fire on an Assyrian church in Baghdad, and two stores owned by Christians in the same neighborhood were bombed. In October, an attack on an ethnic minority Shabak village killed 15. Yezidis, Manicheans, and Sabian Mandaeans were also attacked in 2013. Baha'is and other unrecognized religious minorities also face serious persecution while converts from Islam to other religions face specific threats. Since 2003 many Christians have fled Iraq, and scores of churches have been destroyed. Religious and ethnic minorities in northern Iraq—including Turkmens, Arabs, Christians, and Shabaks—have reported instances of discrimination and harassment by Kurdish authorities, though a number have fled to the Kurdish-controlled region due to its relative security.

The Academic Freedom Monitor lists five deaths, injuries, or disappearances of scholars in Iraq in 2013. Professors and teachers in Iraq may be threatened with violence if they do not give students certain grades or certificates, and they carefully censor themselves for fear of reprisals from both the government and non-state actors.

E. Associational and Organizational Rights: 4 / 12

Iraqis have a constitutional right to freedom of assembly and peaceful demonstration. However, the state limited the exercise of this right in 2013. Demonstrators must seek approval seven days prior to holding a demonstration. Permits are sometimes denied without explanation.

Sunni protests have been largely peaceful, but there have been several exceptions, especially in Hawija, Fallujah, Mosul, and Ramadi. The state's response to protests, however, has often been excessively violent, especially in the attack on the Hawija protest camp in April, which killed at least 50 civilians. In July, a journalist and three others standing in Tahrir Square holding banners expressing criticism of the government were arrested for protesting without a permit, and many other protestors were also detained for this reason in 2013. The government's rationales for disbanding the peaceful August protests against ministerial pensions cited problems with permits, but also a need to protect protestors from terrorism and to prevent them from inciting hatred or violence.

Although they are required to register with the government, there are many Non-Governmental Organizations (NGOs) operating in Iraq, and both the Council of Representatives and the Kurdistan Regional Government have passed laws supportive of their role in policy-making and implementation. NGOs in Iraq suffer less from direct state repression than from the fear of reprisals from non-state actors. NGO leaders complained in 2013 that the state became less willing to protect them.

Iraq's legislation governing trade unions dates from 1987 and prohibits the unionization of public sector workers, strikes by essential service workers, and any non-state sanctioned union. The only state-sanctioned union is the General Federation of Iraqi Workers, and this was effectively taken over by the executive branch in April. The Council of Representatives has indicated that it will soon pass a new labor law that was drafted in 2010 with input from the International Labor Organization.

F. Rule of Law: 0 / 16

Iraq's judiciary is subject to political manipulation, especially by the executive branch and in high-profile cases. In lower-profile cases tribal and religious forces also influence rulings, as does corruption. These same factors also affect judicial appointments and dismissals. The executive selectively implements judicial rulings and Iraq's judges live under the constant threat of violence.

The treatment of Iraqi detainees became a focus of the Sunni protest movement and other critics of the Iraqi government and received a great deal of attention in 2013. Iraq's controversial Counterterrorism Law has permitted the ISF to round up large numbers of people at once, typically Sunnis. Female relatives of male suspects have also been detained to encourage suspects to turn themselves in. Not only does Iraq detain individuals with almost no justification, those detained are often held without trial for long periods of time without contact with their families. Some detainees disappear, and mistreatment—probably even torture to elicit false confessions that are then accepted by the courts—is routine. Iraq executed at least 169 prisoners in 2013. There are over a thousand prisoners now being held on death row, drawing concerns from the international community over Iraq's ability to provide them with fair trials.

Statistics on the number of deaths and attacks in Iraq have varied from organization to organization since they began to be compiled after the U.S. invasion. But by every measure violence and death in Iraq accelerated rapidly this year. For 2012, Iraq Body Count recorded 4,574 civilian deaths from violence and the Government of Iraq recorded 1,317. For 2013, Iraq Body Count's preliminary data puts the number 9,571, and the Iraqi government's number is 7,154, including security forces and militants.

Shi'a were especially targeted by suicide and vehicle bombs in their places of worship and daily lives. In October, a truck bomb exploded outside a school, killing 15, including 14 children in Tal Afar, a Turkmen Shi'a town. Baghdad continued to suffer the bulk of the violence, but there were many more attacks than in the past outside the capital, or even in multiple cities at once. In July, the Al-Qaeda affiliate Islamic State in Iraq attacked prisons in Abu Ghraib and Taji, freeing approximately 500 prisoners.

G. Personal Autonomy and Individual Rights: 4 / 16

An estimated 1.2 million Iraqis remain internally displaced, down from the 2.7 million recorded in 2008. The humanitarian assistance that many of them rely on has been stretched to meet the needs of the Syrian refugees entering Iraq's Kurdish areas and Iraqi refugees returning to Iraq to escape Syria's civil war.

Iraq has a quota system that guarantees women a quarter of the seats in the Council of Representatives, and this percentage was recently extended formally to the provincial councils. Thirty-six of the 111 members of the Kurdish legislature are women. Yet female parliamentarians feel marginalized in the Council of Representatives. Iraq has only one female minister, the Minister of Women's Affairs. Also, religious and tribal leaders now manage issues such as marriage, divorce, inheritance, and custody that used to be dealt with by Iraq's pre-2003, more egalitarian Family Statutes Law. In December the Council of Ministers put off consideration of a Shi'a personal status law that would have permitted marriage for girls as young as nine. In 2013 one-quarter of Iraqi women in their early twenties reported having married before the age of 18. So-called "honor killings," human trafficking, and domestic violence are all anecdotally reported to be on the rise. Outside of the Kurdistan Regional Government the legal system allows honor killings to be dealt with more leniently than other types of murders.

Ireland

Political Rights Rating: 1
Civil Liberties Rating: 1
Freedom Rating: 1
Freedom Status: Free
Electoral Democracy: Yes

Population: 4,600,000
Capital: Dublin

Ten-Year Ratings Timeline For Year Under Review (Political Rights, Civil Liberties, Status)

Year Under Review	2004	2005	2006	2007	2008	2009	2010	2011	2012	2013
Rating	1,1,F	1,1,F	1,1,F	1,1,F	1,1,F	1,1,F	1,1,F	1,1,F	1,1,F	1,1,F

INTRODUCTION

Ireland was rocked by a banking scandal in 2013 after leaked tapes exposed irresponsible and disrespectful behavior by bankers during the 2008 bailout of the Anglo Irish Bank. The revelations added to many citizens' frustration with recent austerity measures and belief that those who caused the turmoil were bailed out, while the rest of the country suffered. After a sluggish first half of the year, however, in September, the country managed to emerge from its second recession in five years. The unemployment rate also dropped to a three-and-a-half-year low.

The Convention on the Constitution, which was established in December 2012, held several public sessions throughout 2013, discussing changes to the electoral system, same-sex marriage, and the role of women, among other topics. The proposals of the 100-member institution—composed of a chairman, 29 members of the Parliament, 4 party representatives, and 66 randomly selected citizens—are nonbinding, but the government has committed to responding to each of them.

Ireland's European Union (EU) presidency in the first half of 2013 was regarded as a success, with its biggest achievement being a deal reached on the EU's 2014–2020 budget.

In July, Irish law was modified to allow for abortions in limited circumstances.

POLITICAL RIGHTS: 39 / 40
A. Electoral Process: 12 / 12

The Irish Parliament (Oireachtas) consists of a lower house (the Dáil), whose 166 members are elected by proportional representation for five-year terms, and an upper house (the Seanad, or Senate) with 60 members, 11 appointed and 49 elected by various interest groups. The Senate is mainly a consultative body, in which members serve five-year terms. The prime minister, or taoiseach, is chosen by Parliament. The president, whose functions are largely ceremonial, is directly elected for a seven-year term.

In the 2011 parliamentary elections, the Fine Gael party won 76 seats in the lower house, but lacked a majority and was forced to enter into a coalition with the Labour Party, which took 37 seats. The Fianna Fáil party captured only 20 seats. The Green Party failed to enter Parliament, while Sinn Féin won 14 seats; independents and two smaller parties took the remaining seats. Enda Kenny of Fine Gael was elected prime minister.

Kenny has argued in favor of abolishing the Senate, contending it is too expensive to maintain and has no real powers. In an unexpected political defeat for the government, a referendum held in October 2013 on abolishing the body narrowly failed.

Throughout 2013, the Constitutional Convention discussed several changes to the current electoral system of proportional representation. Among other issues, the Convention suggested keeping the current system, but changing the size of constituencies, and lowering the voting age to 16 years.

B. Political Pluralism and Participation: 16 / 16

Ireland's two largest parties—Fianna Fáil and Fine Gael—do not differ widely in ideology but represent opposing sides of the nation's 1922–1923 civil war. Smaller parties include the Labour Party, Sinn Féin, and the Green Party. Fianna Fáil dominated politics after Ireland became independent, holding power for 61 out of 79 years before its 2011 ouster due to corruption scandals and the mismanagement of the 2008 economic crisis. Holding two-thirds of the seats, Enda Kenny's Fine Gael–Labour coalition currently holds the largest parliamentary majority in Ireland's history. In 2013, opinion polls indicated that popularity was shifting between Fianna Fáil and Fine Gael throughout the year.

C. Functioning of Government: 11 / 12

Corruption—including cronyism, political patronage, and illegal donations—is a recurring problem. After 15 years of hearings, the Mahon Tribunal released its final report in March 2012, finding that corruption had affected "every level of Irish political life." The tribunal also found that former prime minister Patrick "Bertie" Ahern had not been forthright about money he received while finance minister, leading to his resignation from Fianna Fáil in March 2012.

Tapes leaked in the summer of 2013 about the 2008 bailout of the Anglo Irish Bank caused national outrage. The recordings suggested that the bank's executives had been aware of the institution's dire financial problems but did not reveal the gravity of the situation until after the government had committed to saving the bank. Ireland was ranked 21 out of 177 countries and territories surveyed in Transparency International's 2013 Corruption Perceptions Index.

CIVIL LIBERTIES: 58 / 60
D. Freedom of Expression and Belief: 16 / 16

The media are free and independent, and internet access is unrestricted. The print media present a variety of viewpoints. Over the past few years, advertising revenues have been falling, and at least a dozen outlets have closed down. The state may censor material deemed indecent or obscene. Reforms to Ireland's defamation legislation made in 2009 introduced the offense of blasphemous libel, with penalties of up to €25,000 (US$33,500). In January 2013, controversy erupted when the National Newspapers of Ireland trade association began suing websites for linking to articles published by its newspapers, claiming that such links represented copyright infringement.

After the suicide of Minister for State Shane McEntee in late 2012, the parliamentary Committee on Transport and Communications launched an investigation into cyber-bullying. A barrage of negative coverage on social media had reportedly factored into McEntee's suicide. The committee's report, published in July 2013, recommended that a new body be established to regulate social media, but that had not occurred by year's end.

Freedom of religion is constitutionally guaranteed. Although the country is overwhelmingly Roman Catholic, there is no state religion, and adherents of other faiths face few impediments to religious expression. According to the 2012 WIN-Gallup International "Religiosity and Atheism Index," Ireland suffered one of the biggest declines in religiosity between 2005 and 2012, with the percentage of those considering themselves religious dropping from 69 percent to 47 percent. This decline was partly due to the discovery of numerous sex abuse scandals within the clergy in recent years. While the Catholic Church operates approximately 90 percent of Ireland's schools—most of which provide religious education—parents may exempt their children from religious instruction; the constitution also requires equal funding for students requesting instruction in other faiths. Academic freedom is respected.

E. Associational and Organizational Rights: 12 / 12

The right of public assembly and demonstration is respected. There were several protests in 2013 against austerity cuts, the bank debt burden, and a property tax introduced in 2012. In February, protests organized by the Irish Congress of Trade Unions drew more than 110,000 people nationwide.

Freedom of association is upheld, and nongovernmental organizations can operate freely. Labor unions operate without hindrance, and collective bargaining is legal and unrestricted.

F. Rule of Law: 15 / 16

The legal system is based on common law, and the judiciary is independent. In early 2013, the government moved forward with public sector salary and pension cuts; judges alleged that the reductions undermined their independence. Prison conditions have been highlighted as dangerous, unsanitary, and overcrowded, among other issues.

The Irish Travellers, a traditionally nomadic group of about 25,000 people, are not recognized as an ethnic minority and face discrimination in housing and hiring.

The Provisional Irish Republican Army (IRA)—which disarmed in 2005 after fighting for unification with Northern Ireland for 36 years—is outlawed. Several splinter groups, which have emerged over the past decades, occasionally engage in violent acts, though the threat has been more moderate in recent years. In July 2013, Irish police raided a meeting of the New IRA splinter group and arrested eight of its members, charging them with being part of an illegal group.

G. Personal Autonomy and Individual Rights: 15 / 16

While employment discrimination on the basis of gender or sexual orientation is prohibited, gender inequality in wages persists, and women continue to be underrepresented in the political sphere; women comprise only 15 percent of the members of the lower house of Parliament. A 2012 law reduces state funding for parties if fewer than 30 percent of their candidates are women in the next general election. A groundbreaking law was passed in July 2013, allowing for limited abortion rights in cases where the woman's life is under threat, including the risk of suicide. Civil liberties groups welcomed the new law but argued its limited scope and the cumbersome application process still infringe on women's rights. Around 4,000 women travel to the United Kingdom each year for legal and safe abortion services.

The 2010 Civil Partnership and Certain Rights and Obligations of Cohabitants Act legally recognized same-sex couples, though it denies them some rights awarded to heterosexual married couples, such as adoption. The government has promised to hold a referendum on the issue of same-sex marriage before the next general election, scheduled for 2016.

Reports released by the Commission to Inquire into Child Abuse in 2009 documented decades of widespread physical and emotional abuse against children in state institutions and by Catholic priests, as well as collusion to hide the abuse. The 2011 Cloyne report revealed similar abuse and subsequent cover-ups in the diocese of Cloyne. The government has taken steps to address the abuse, which has declined in recent decades. The government has also moved to end the Catholic Church's monopoly on Ireland's primary education system, as 3,000 schools currently remain under the church's control.

Israel

Political Rights Rating: 1
Population: 8,054,000
[*Note:* There are an estimated 340,000 Israeli settlers in the West Bank, about 20,000 in the Golan Heights, and over 200,000 in East Jerusalem.]
Civil Liberties Rating: 2 **Capital:** Jerusalem
Freedom Rating: 1.5
Freedom Status: Free
Electoral Democracy: Yes
Note: The numerical ratings and status above reflect conditions within Israel itself. Separate reports examine the West Bank and the Gaza Strip.

Ten-Year Ratings Timeline For Year Under Review (Political Rights, Civil Liberties, Status)

Year Under Review	2004	2005	2006	2007	2008	2009	2010	2011	2012	2013
Rating	1,3,F	1,2,F	1,2,F	1,2,F	1,2,F	1,2,F	1,2,F	1,2,F	1,2,F	1,2,F

INTRODUCTION

With the border between Israel and the Gaza Strip quieter than in late 2012 when Israeli forces carried out an eight-day campaign against Gaza-based militants, the country turned to domestic policy issues involving African asylum seekers, gender equality in prayer practices at the Western Wall, moves toward civil marriage, and resettlement of Bedouin villages in the Negev. Although minority rights and discrimination remained in the political spotlight, Israeli-Palestinian peace negotiations—largely insulated from the press—were ongoing at the end of 2013.

Political Rights: 36 / 40
A. Electoral Process: 12 / 12

A largely ceremonial president is elected by the 120-seat parliament, the Knesset, for seven-year terms. The prime minister is usually the leader of the largest party in the Knesset, members of which are elected by party-list proportional representation for four-year terms. At just 2 percent, the threshold for a party to win parliamentary representation favors niche parties and leads to unstable coalitions. A new bill—being considered by year's end—proposes raising the threshold to 3.25 percent.

Israeli elections are free and fair. In the January 2013 Knesset elections, incumbent prime minister Benjamin Netanyahu's right-leaning Likud–Yisrael Beitenu coalition led with 31 seats, followed by the newly formed centrist party Yesh Atid (There Is a Future) with 19, the Labour Party with 15, the right-wing Habayit Hayehudi (Jewish Home) with 12, the ultra-Orthodox parties Shas and United Torah Judaism with 11 and 7, respectively, and six smaller parties with 2 to 6 seats each. Netanyahu formed a governing coalition including Yesh Atid and Habayit Hayehudi, while excluding the two ultra-Orthodox parties.

B. Political Pluralism and Participation: 14 / 16

Israel hosts a diverse and competitive multiparty system. However, parties or candidates that deny Israel's Jewish character, oppose the democratic system, or incite racism are prohibited. In 2010, a Knesset plenum voted to strip Haneen Zoabi, a member of the Arab party Balad, of some parliamentary privileges following her participation in an attempt by activists to break Israel's maritime blockade of Gaza. In December 2012, a special nine-judge panel of the High Court voted unanimously to overturn the ruling. In the 2013 elections, Zoabi secured one of Balad's three seats; another Arab party, United Arab List (Ta'al), won four seats.

Palestinian citizens of Israel enjoy equal political rights under the law but face some discrimination in practice. Palestinian citizens of Israel currently hold 12 seats in the 120-seat Knesset—though they constitute some 20 percent of the population—and no Arab party has ever been formally included in a governing coalition. Arabs generally do not serve in senior positions in government. Although Israeli identity cards have not classified residents by ethnicity since 2005, Jewish Israelis can often be identified by the inclusion of their Hebrew birth date. Calls to impose a loyalty oath have marginalized Arab Israelis, though such proposals have been rejected.

After Israel annexed East Jerusalem in 1967, Arab residents were issued Israeli identity cards and given the option of obtaining Israeli citizenship, though most declined for political reasons. These noncitizens can vote in municipal as well as Palestinian Authority elections, and remain eligible to apply for Israeli citizenship. However, Israeli law strips noncitizens of their Jerusalem residency if they leave the city for more than three months.

A 2003 law denies citizenship and residency status to Palestinian residents of the West Bank or Gaza who are married to Israeli citizens; it was most recently renewed in April 2013. While the measure was criticized as blatantly discriminatory, supporters cited evidence that 14 percent of suicide bombers acquired Israeli identity cards via family reunification. A 2011 law allows the courts to revoke the citizenship of any Israeli convicted of spying, treason, or aiding the enemy.

Under the 1948 Law of Return, Jewish immigrants and their immediate families are granted Israeli citizenship and residence rights; other immigrants must apply for these rights.

C. Functioning of Government: 10 / 12

Corruption scandals in recent years have implicated several senior officials. Ehud Olmert resigned as prime minister in 2008 amid graft allegations, and was indicted in 2009. In July 2012, he was found not guilty in two major corruption cases, though he was convicted of breach of trust. Another corruption case against Olmert was pending at the end of 2013. Separately, Yisrael Beitenu leader Avigdor Lieberman was indicted for fraud and breach of trust in December 2012, prompting his resignation as foreign minister. He was acquitted in November 2013, however, allowing him to return to his cabinet post. Israel was ranked 36 out of 177 countries and territories surveyed in Transparency International's 2013 Corruption Perceptions Index. The relative frequency of high-level corruption investigations is coupled with a strong societal intolerance for graft. Transparency International's 2013 Global Corruption Barometer survey showed that nearly all Israelis are willing to combat corruption and report violations.

CIVIL LIBERTIES: 45 / 60

D. Freedom of Expression and Belief: 12 / 16

The Israeli media are vibrant and independent, and freely criticize government policy. All Israeli newspapers are privately owned, though ownership is concentrated among a small number of companies, some of which display a clear partisan bias. Internet access is widespread and unrestricted. The Israel Broadcasting Authority operates public radio and television services, and commercial broadcasts are widely available. Most Israelis subscribe to cable or satellite television. The diversity and editorial independence of both print and broadcast media have been threatened over the past several years by financial difficulties in the industry. Print articles on security matters are subject to a military censor, and while the scope of permissible reporting is generally broad, press freedom advocates have warned of more aggressive censorship in recent years. The Government Press Office has occasionally withheld press cards from journalists, especially Palestinians, to restrict them from entering Israel, citing security considerations. A series of "Prisoner X" incidents—state-enforced media blackouts regarding secret prisoners held in isolation—were challenged by ACRI during 2013.

Legislation passed in March 2011 requires the state to fine or withdraw funds from local authorities and other state-funded groups that hold events commemorating the 1948 displacement of Palestinians—known as Al-Nakba (The Catastrophe)—on Israeli independence day; that support armed resistance or "racism" against Israel; or that desecrate national symbols. In July 2011, the Knesset passed the Boycott Law, which exposes Israeli individuals and groups to civil lawsuits if they advocate an economic, cultural, or academic boycott of the State of Israel or West Bank settlements, even without clear proof of financial damage. Challenges to this law by civil rights groups were ongoing in 2013.

While Israel's founding documents define it as a "Jewish and democratic state," freedom of religion is respected. Christian, Muslim, and Baha'i communities have jurisdiction over their own members in matters of marriage, divorce, and burial. The Orthodox establishment generally governs these personal status matters among Jews, drawing objections from many non-Orthodox and secular Israelis, though as of 2012, one non-Orthodox rabbi won the right to receive state funding. In another milestone case in 2011, an Israeli Jew won the right to an identity card that excluded his Hebrew birth date. Nevertheless, in October 2013 the Supreme Court ruled against an appeal that would have allowed several individuals to have state-issued identity cards declare their "nationality" to be "Israeli" rather than "Jewish."

Ultra-Orthodox Jews were exempt from compulsory military service under the 2002 Tal Law, which expired in July 2012 after the High Court of Justice ruled it unconstitutional. By the end of 2013, a bill that would subject Haredi youth to military conscription or civilian national service—with a four-year transition period—had passed its first reading in the Knesset.

Muslim and Christian religious authorities are occasionally discriminated against in resource allocation and upkeep of religious sites, though the state budget officially assigns funds according to need. Citing security concerns, Israel occasionally restricts Muslim worshippers' access to the Temple Mount, or Haram al-Sharif, in Jerusalem.

Repeatedly during 2012 and into 2013, Jewish women were arrested at the Western Wall for donning prayer shawls traditionally worn by men, in violation of rules set for the location by ultra-Orthodox religious officials. In December 2012, the government formed a commission to evaluate the status of public prayer at the site in light of these ongoing gender concerns. By the end of 2013, a government-appointed committee was discussing a compromise proposal known as the Sharansky-Mandelblit plan.

Primary and secondary education is universal, with instruction for the Arab minority based on the common curriculum used by the Jewish majority, but conducted in Arabic. In 2010, the government mandated the teaching of Arabic in all state schools. School quality is generally worse in mostly Arab municipalities, and Arab children have reportedly had difficulty registering at mostly Jewish schools. Israel's universities are open to all students based on merit, and have long been centers for dissent. In late 2012, the Council of Higher Education attempted to shut down the Department of Politics and Government at Ben Gurion University, ostensibly for political reasons. In February 2013, the council reversed the decision. Also in late 2012, the government granted Ariel College in the West Bank university status, leading the Council of Presidents of Israeli Universities to file a motion at the High Court of Justice opposing the designation. In December 2013 the court rejected the petition. Periodic road closures and other security measures restrict access to Israeli universities for West Bank and Gaza residents.

E. Associational and Organizational Rights: 11 / 12

Israel has an active civil society, and demonstrations are widely permitted, though groups committed to the destruction of Israel are banned from demonstrating. Thousands of Israelis participated in social protests in 2012, following massive 2011 demonstrations over the cost of living. In 2013, ACRI submitted a letter to the Knesset's internal affairs committee that alleged undue police violence, arrests and detention and "warning conversations" with activists. A law that took effect in 2012 requires nongovernmental organizations (NGOs) to submit financial reports four times a year on support received from foreign government sources. In July 2013, two MKs proposed a bill to curtail foreign governmental funding to Israeli NGOs that advocate a boycott of Israel or armed struggle against Israel, demand that Israeli soldiers be tried in international courts, incite racism, or deny Israel's existence as a Jewish and democratic state. In December, the bill crossed the first hurdle, passing a vote in the Ministerial Committee for Legislation.

Workers may join unions of their choice and have the right to strike and bargain collectively. Three-quarters of the workforce either belong to Histadrut, the national labor federation, or are covered by its social programs and bargaining agreements. Both sector-specific and general strikes are common, but they typically last less than 24 hours.

F. Rule of Law: 11 / 16

The judiciary is independent and regularly rules against the government. The Supreme Court hears direct petitions from citizens and Palestinian residents of the West Bank and Gaza Strip, and the state generally adheres to court rulings. In April 2012, the Knesset debated a bill that would have allowed it to override Supreme Court decisions, though no such measure had been enacted by the end of 2013.

The Emergency Powers (Detention) Law of 1979 provides for indefinite administrative detention without trial. According to B'Tselem, at year's end there were 4,768 Palestinians in Israeli jails, including 150 administrative detainees. A temporary order in effect since 2006 permits the detention of suspects accused of security offenses for 96 hours without judicial oversight, compared with 24 hours for other detainees. Israel outlawed the use of torture in 2000, but milder forms of coercion, including binding, kicking, slapping and threatening violence against relatives, are permissible to extract security information. Hunger strikes by Palestinian detainees have become increasingly common.

According to Defence for Children International (DCI) Palestine, there were 195 Palestinian children being held in Israeli jails by year's end, including 14 youths aged 12 to 15. Although Israeli military law prohibits children younger than 12 from being detained, some still were. DCI-Palestine also reported that the military declined to open an investigation into any of the seven complaints the group lodged regarding treatment of Palestinian minors. Most are serving sentences of several weeks or months—handed down by a special court for minors created in 2009—for throwing stones or other projectiles at Israeli troops in the West Bank; acquittals on such charges are very rare. Palestinian youths typically do not spend more than a year in jail for stone throwing. East Jerusalem Palestinian minors are tried in Israeli civil juvenile courts.

Arab citizens of Israel tend to receive inferior education, housing, and social services. The state's Israeli Lands Administration owns 93 percent of the land; 13 percent of that is owned by the Jewish National Fund (JNF-KKL). In 2005, the Supreme Court and attorney general ruled against the JNF-KKL's marketing property only to Jews. The Knesset made several unsuccessful attempts to override those rulings. Still, in practice, the JNF-KKL continues its Jewish-only land-leasing policy, partly as a result of a land-swap arrangement put in place in 2005 with the Israel Lands Authority.

Palestinian citizens of Israel (other than the Druze) are not drafted, though they may volunteer. Those who do not serve are ineligible for the associated benefits, including scholarships and housing loans. In June 2013 the Knesset discussed a proposed national service law that would provide preferential access to housing, jobs, and other services for those who have completed military or other national service.

In July 2013, the Israel Airports Authority announced new luggage-screening techniques that would make the process more egalitarian. At the end of 2013 the courts were reviewing the constitutionality of 2011 legislation that would allow Jewish communities of up to 400 residents in the Negev and Galilee to exclude prospective residents based on "social suitability." In September 2013, ACRI submitted a petition to the High Court against the Israel Lands Authority to challenge the use of such screening processes by the Negev community of Carmit, which is larger than 400 families.

There are about 110,000 Bedouin in the Negev region, most of whom live in dozens of towns and villages not recognized by the state. Those in unrecognized villages cannot claim social services and have no official land rights, and the government routinely demolishes their unlicensed structures. In June 2013, a Bedouin settlement bill, known as the Prawer-Begin Plan, passed its first reading in the Knesset. Critics asserted that the plan would entail the eviction and displacement of tens of thousands of Bedouins. In December 2013, the plan was halted.

In January 2012, the Knesset passed legislation allowing migrants and asylum seekers (mostly from Eritrea and Sudan) who entered Israel irregularly and have been involved in criminal proceedings to be administratively detained, without trial, for up to three years, or indefinitely if they come from countries designated as hostile. With the number of asylum seekers now 53,000, this Anti-Infiltration Law was overturned in September 2013, though only a small fraction of the prisoners had been released six weeks later. In December, the Knesset passed an amendment requiring new arrivals to be detained for a year in an "open facility" where head counts are required three times daily; some may be detained indefinitely. A June 2013 law caps the amount of money an undocumented migrant may send out of the country, unless a relative is in "grave danger."

G. Personal Autonomy and Individual Rights: 11 / 16

Security measures can lead to entrance delays at some public places, though military checkpoints are restricted to the West Bank. By law, all citizens must carry national identification cards. The West Bank separation barrier restricts the movement of some East Jerusalem residents. Formal and informal local rules that prevent driving on Jewish holidays can also hamper freedom of movement.

Women have achieved substantial parity at almost all levels of Israeli society. However, Arab women and religious Jewish women face some discrimination. Many ultra-Orthodox Jewish communities enforce gender separation. In January 2012, the Supreme Court ruled against gender-segregated buses, though many women still sit at the rear of buses on certain bus lines, and there are occasionally violent Haredi attacks on buses where the practice is not observed, along with attacks against women and girls deemed to be dressed immodestly. Marriages between Jews and non-Jews are not recognized by the state unless conducted abroad. A law passed in 2010 permits nonreligious civil unions, but they are restricted to cases where the individuals have no religion, and they are seldom used. A more comprehensive bill on civil unions was introduced by the Yesh Atid party in October 2013. It is opposed by the Jewish Home party, and by year's end the legislation had not advanced.

Since 2006, Israel has recognized same-sex marriages conducted abroad, and a Tel Aviv family court granted the first same-sex divorce in December 2012. Nonbiological parents in same-sex partnerships are eligible for guardianship rights, and openly gay Israelis are permitted to serve in the military. As of July 2013, the Israel prison service permits same-sex conjugal visits.

Both the UN and the U.S. State Department have identified Israel as a top destination for trafficked women in recent years. The government has opened shelters for trafficking victims, and a 2006 law mandates prison terms of up to 20 years for perpetrators.

About 100,000 legal foreign workers enjoy wage protections, medical insurance, and guarantees against employer exploitation, as long as they don't leave their original employers. A 2011 amendment to the Israel Entry Law restricts the number of times foreign workers can change employers and may limit them to working in a specific geographical area or field.

Italy

Political Rights Rating: 1
Civil Liberties Rating: 1
Freedom Rating: 1.0
Freedom Status: Free
Electoral Democracy: Yes

Population: 59,831,000
Capital: Rome

Ratings Change: Italy's political rights rating improved from 2 to 1 due to parliamentary elections that were generally considered to be free and fair as well as progress in the adoption and implementation of anticorruption measures.

Ten-Year Ratings Timeline For Year Under Review (Political Rights, Civil Liberties, Status)

Year Under Review	2004	2005	2006	2007	2008	2009	2010	2011	2012	2013
Rating	1,1,F	1,1,F	1,1,F	1,1,F	1,2,F	1,2,F	1,2,F	1,1,F	2,1,F	1,1,F

INTRODUCTION

Italy held parliamentary elections February 2013. Early elections were called after former prime minister Silvio Berlusconi's coalition, People of Freedom (PDL), withdrew its support from the government in December 2012, leading Mario Monti to resign as prime minister and President Giorgio Napolitano to dissolve Parliament.

The elections ended in a hung parliament: a center-left coalition obtained 55 percent of the seats in the lower house, the Chamber of Deputies, but in the upper house, the Senate, three factions—a center-left coalition led by the Democratic Party (PD), PDL, and the new Five Star Movement (M5S) led by comedian Beppe Grillo—received similar shares of the vote, and no group emerged with a majority of seats. As the leading parties struggled to form a coalition, Napolitano was unable to dissolve the Parliament and call for new elections since he was nearing the end of his term and the constitution forbids the president from dissolving parliament during his last six months in office.

Political party leaders failed to agree on a successor to Napolitano. After five failed attempts to select a president, Napolitano was persuaded to abandon his retirement and accept a second term. Napolitano immediately pushed to forge a consensus for a coalition government. On April 28, Enrico Letta of the PD was sworn in as prime minister of a grand coalition government comprising the PD, the PDL, and Monti's Civic Choice party.

Serious economic problems faced the new government; in 2013, Italy's public debt rose above 130 percent of its gross domestic product (GPD), and the unemployment rate rose to 12.5 percent in December, with youth unemployment hitting record highs of just over 40 percent. In its 2014 budget, the government tried to balance pro-growth initiatives with austerity measures.

POLITICAL RIGHTS: 37 / 40 (+2)

A. Electoral Process: 12 / 12 (+1)

The president, whose role is largely ceremonial but sometimes politically influential, is elected for a seven-year term by Parliament and regional representatives. The bicameral Parliament consists of the 630-member Chamber of Deputies and the 315-member Senate; most members of both houses are popularly elected to five-year terms. The president may appoint up to five senators for life. The president also appoints the prime minister, who is often, but not always, the leader of the largest party in the Chamber of Deputies. The prime minister proposes a Council of Ministers that needs to be confirmed by the Parliament.

In general elections, most members of both houses are elected through closed party-list proportional systems, with a system of thresholds that encourages political groups to form coalitions. A so-called majority bonus guarantees that whatever grouping emerges with the most votes at the national level will get at least 340 of the seats in the lower house; in the upper house, victory in a given region ensures the winning party or coalition a 55 percent majority of that region's allotment of seats. In December, two controversial aspects of the electoral law—the majority bonus and the closed party-lists—were ruled unconstitutional by the Constitutional Court. Although there was widespread agreement that the electoral law needed to be changed, politicians were unable to agree on what should replace it.

Parliamentary elections took place on February 24 and 25. The pre-election environment was positively assessed by the Organization for Security and Cooperation in Europe (OSCE), and the actual competition was considered free and fair. In elections for the Chamber of Deputies, the center-left "Italy Common Good" coalition led by the PD's Pier Luigi Bersani earned the most votes and claimed 345 seats, including the majority bonus. A center-right bloc, led by Berlusconi and composed of the PDL and Northern League (LN), garnered 125 seats. The M5S, running on a populist, anti-establishment platform, gained 109 seats, while Monti's centrist Civic Choice coalition, claimed 47 seats. In the upper house, the outcome reflected a similar alignment among the four groups: the center-left took 121 seats; the center-right won 117 seats; M5S, 54 seats; and Civil Choice, 189 seats. Voter turnout was just over 75 percent, well below the past 20-year average of 83.28 percent.

Still with no government formed, the presidential election process began on April 18. However, the first five rounds produced inconclusive results due to the pervasive disagreement among—and in some cases within—Italian political parties. In consideration of the severe situation, Napolitano, who was 87, accepted the entreaties of most of the major political parties to stand for a second term. On April 20, Napolitano garnered 738 votes, easily surpassing the 504 needed, and he became the first Italian president to be re-elected to a second term.

Napolitano's first act was to break the political impasse through encouraging the creation of a grand coalition government. Following Napolitano's repeated calls on Parliament to display unity and a sense of responsibility, Letta was sworn in as prime minister of a coalition government after sealing an alliance with Berlusconi and Monti. At the end of September, a new political crisis was triggered when Berlusconi ordered PDL ministers to resign, but Letta refused to accept the resignations and called a vote of confidence. On October 2, Letta's government won the vote by a significant margin after many PDL members said they would not support Berlusconi in his effort to bring down the government down.

B. Political Pluralism and Participation: 15 / 16

The Italian party system is characterized by a high level of pluralism and political competition. However, its structure is very unstable since political coalitions easily change their compositions, and new political parties are often created. In February, two new political groupings contested the elections: Civic Choice and M5S. The M5S relied heavily on the internet as a participation tool, using its blog to select its candidate for the presidential election and to vote on the expulsion from the party of a senator who did not conform to the movement's rules.

In order to protect linguistic minorities, the electoral law stipulates that parties representing such groups can participate in the allocation of seats in the lower house if they obtain at least 20 percent of the vote in the constituency in which they are applying. As result of the 2013 elections, the German-speaking Südtiroler Volkspartei (SVP) gained five representatives in the Chamber of Deputies and four in the Senate.

C. Functioning of Government: 10 / 12 (+1)

Since the end of 2012, Italy has adopted several initiatives to strengthen its anticorruption policy. In November 2012, Italian authorities passed the Anticorruption Law, which set out a framework to improve public administration accountability, regulated conflicts of interest, built up whistleblower protection, and codified new types of corruption-related offenses. The law established a National Anticorruption Authority, which would have the power to investigate and adopt guidelines for public officials. Since 2011, Italy has been an active member of the Open Government Partnership that is a multilateral initiative of 64 countries dedicated to the implementation of open government reforms through government and civil society collaboration. In this context, in March 2013 the government adopted a legislative decree that established greater transparency of information within public administration. In June, Italy ratified the Criminal Law Convention on Corruption and the Civil Law Convention on Corruption. Italian efforts to prevent and reduce corruption were positively evaluated by the 2013 Compliance Report of the Council of Europe's Group of States against Corruption (GRECO).

In a landmark case that saw the first definitive conviction of Berlusconi in at least 24 cases involving him over the course of his political career, the former prime minister's conviction on tax-fraud charges and sentence of four years' imprisonment were upheld by the Supreme Court in August. (Berlusconi, 76, was not expected to serve time in prison, as convicts over 70 rarely do in the country.) At the end of November the Senate imposed a temporary ban on holding public office that had been part of Berlusconi's sentence and that had stemmed from the new Anticorruption Law. Currently, Berlusconi is also appealing a conviction and seven-year sentence imposed by a Milan court for abuse of office and paying for sex with an underage prostitute.

CIVIL LIBERTIES: 53 / 60
D. Freedom of Expression and Belief: 15 / 16

Freedom of expression and the press are constitutionally guaranteed and they are exercised by a large variety of media. There are more than 100 daily newspapers, most of them locally or regionally based, as well as political party papers, free papers, and weekly publications. Political party newspapers are the only category supported by public funds; the others are financed by advertising and sales. Despite the rapid growth of the online news industry, traditional media still play a large role in news consumption. Media concentration remains a major concern; however, it has improved somewhat since Berlusconi left office. When Berlusconi was prime minister, he controlled up to 90 percent of the country's broadcast media through state-owned outlets and his own private media holdings; although he has left office, he is still the main shareholder in television conglomerate Mediaset, and other media companies. Internet access is generally unrestricted.

In October 2013, the lower house passed a bill to abolish jail time as a punishment for defamation; the bill had yet to be considered by the Senate at year's end. The law was considered by press freedom groups to be a step in the right direction, particularly as several journalists had recently been handed jail sentences for defamation; however, the groups criticized the law's retention of criminal liability for defamation.

Religious freedom is constitutionally guaranteed and respected in practice. Although Roman Catholicism is the dominant faith, and the state grants some privileges to the Catholic Church, there is no official religion. Agreements between the government and a number of religious groups have been signed, but an omnibus religious freedom law has yet to be passed.

E. Associational and Organizational Rights: 12 / 12

Italian citizens are free to assemble, establish social and political associations, and organize demonstrations. The constitution recognizes the right to strike, but places restrictions on strikes by those employed in essential services such as transport, sanitation, and health, as well as a number of self-employed professions, such as lawyers, doctors, and truck drivers.

F. Rule of Law: 12 / 16

The judicial system is undermined by long trial delays and the influence of organized crime. A March 2013 report by the European Commission showed Italy having high numbers of pending civil cases in proportion to its population, in comparison with other EU countries, and the lowest number of judges per capita after Malta. Italian prisons are overcrowded, with more than 64,000 detainees held in 206 jails built for about 47,668, according to an October 2013 report by the Ministry of Justice. Despite legal prohibitions against torture, there have been reports of excessive use of force by police, particularly against illegal immigrants. The country continued to make some gains against organized crime in 2013. According to a report released by the Ministry of Interior in August 2013, during the previous 12 months police forces arrested 1,697 mafia members and seized €4,9 billion (about US$6.6 billion) in mafia assets.

Italy is a major entry point for undocumented immigrants trying to reach Europe, and the government has been criticized for holding illegal immigrants in overcrowded and unhygienic conditions and denying them access to lawyers. After more than 350 African migrants died in October while attempting to reach the Italian island of Lampedusa, a commission in the Italian Senate voted in favor of decriminalizing clandestine immigration. This crime was introduced in 2009 as part of the Security Law that imposes fines on illegal immigrants and grants authorities the power to detain them for up to six months without charges. According to a UNHCR advocacy paper, several issues undermine the integration of refugees and the reception of asylum seekers, and a general reform is needed to align Italian policies and practices with international standards. As result, in September the government announced an increase from 3,000 to 16,000 spaces in specialized reception centers for asylum seekers and refugees.

G. Personal Autonomy and Individual Rights: 14 / 16

Italian citizens enjoy a high level of personal autonomy as well as freedom of residence, movement and work both in Italy and abroad. The right to education is guaranteed by the constitution. Pertaining to the education of immigrant children, Italy provides the right to instruction in the same manner as it does for Italian citizens, regardless of their legal status.

Gender-based discrimination is prohibited by law. Women benefit from generous maternity-leave provisions, and considerable education opportunities. Following the February elections, female political representation increased in both the Chamber of Deputies (now 28 percent) and in the Senate (now 27 percent), but it is still far from equal. According to the 2013 Global Gender Gap report, Italian women face severe obstacles in both labor force participation and wage equality. Violence against women continues to be a serious problem. In October, Italy adopted the so-called Femicide Law, which increased penalties for domestic abuse, sexual violence, and stalking.

Although Italian law specifically bans discrimination on the basis of sexual orientation, members of the LGBT (lesbian, gay, bisexual, transgender) community do not have the same legal rights as other Italian citizens. There is no legal recognition of same-sex relationships, and same-sex couples may not adopt children together. In the past decades, a number of bills on civil unions have been presented into the Parliament, but they were regularly rejected by conservative members. In September, the lower house passed a bill targeting anti-LGBT discrimination; however, it was unclear whether the Senate would approve it. LGBT organizations say that the effectiveness of the bill has been undermined by the adoption of broad free-speech exemptions for political and religious organizations. According to a 2013 Amnesty International report, the Italian nongovernmental organization Gay Helpline received information about 750 verbal and physical anti-LGBTI (lesbian, gay, bisexual, transgender, and intersex) attacks in 2011. The same report said that according to the group Transgender Europe, 20 transgender individuals had been murdered in the country between 2008 and March 2013.

Despite some recent improvements, the Heritage Foundation still rates Italy as a moderately free economy due to the perpetuation of structural problems that seriously undermine the access to economic opportunities and resources. Such problems include an excessive fiscal burden; pandemic tax evasion; a large and inefficient public sector that discourages private investments, both domestic and foreign; and a regulatory framework that is hostile to business and encourages corruption. As a result, Italy is currently one of the slowest growing countries in the EU.

Jamaica

Political Rights: 2
Civil Liberties: 3
Freedom Ratings: 2.5
Freedom Status: Free
Electoral Democracy: Yes

Population: 2,712,000
Capital: Kingston

Ten-Year Ratings Timeline For Year Under Review (Political Rights, Civil Liberties, Status)

Year Under Review	2004	2005	2006	2007	2008	2009	2010	2011	2012	2013
Rating	2,3,F	2,3,F	2,3,F	2,3,F	2,3,F	2,3,F	2,3,F	2,3,F	2,3,F	2,3,F

INTRODUCTION

Jamaica continued to struggle in 2013 with high levels of crime, sluggish economic growth, and a public sector in need of major reform. In April, the official unemployment rate was 16.3 percent, the highest in the last decade. That month, Prime Minister Portia

Simpson-Miller approved an agreement to receive a loan of about $958 million from the International Monetary Fund (IMF). Some Jamaicans criticized the loan, claiming it would exacerbate the country's already-deep debt.

POLITICAL RIGHTS: 34 / 40 (+1)

A. Electoral Process: 12 / 12

Jamaica's bicameral Parliament consists of the 60-member House of Representatives, elected for five years, and the 21-member Senate, with 13 senators appointed on the advice of the prime minister and 8 on the advice of the opposition leader. The leader of the party or coalition holding a majority in the House of Representatives is appointed as prime minister by the governor general. The British monarch is represented as head of state by a governor general, who is nominated by the prime minister and approved by the monarch.

In September 2007, the conservative Jamaica Labour Party (JLP) won a majority of seats in the House of Representatives, ending 18 years in power for the People's National Party (PNP).

In September 2011, JLP leader and prime minister Bruce Golding abruptly announced his resignation, a move widely interpreted to have stemmed from his involvement with alleged drug trafficker Christopher "Dudus" Coke, which had caused Golding to lose support within his own party and among the electorate. In October 2011, the JLP elected Minister of Education Andrew Holness to become Golding's successor as party leader and prime minister. Holness called for early general elections at the end of the year. On December 29, 2011, the PNP captured 41 seats in Parliament, while the JLP took only 22. Simpson-Miller became prime minister in January 2012 as a result of the elections; she had previously held the position in 2006 and 2007.

B. Political Pluralism and Participation: 13 / 16

Jamaica achieved independence from Britain in 1962. Since then, power has alternated between the social democratic PNP and the more conservative JLP.

Powerful criminal gangs in some urban neighborhoods maintain influence over voter turnout in return for political favors, which has called into question the legitimacy of election results in those areas.

C. Functioning of Government: 9 / 12 (+1)

Corruption remains a serious problem in Jamaica. Long-standing relationships between elected representatives and organized crime, in which criminal gangs guaranteed votes in certain neighborhoods in exchange for protection has been highlighted in recent years as the U.S. government pressed for the extradition of Coke. The gang Coke reputedly led, the Shower Posse, was based in Tivoli Gardens, an area of Kingston that Prime Minister Golding represented in Parliament. In May 2010, a public outcry over ties between the JLP and Coke prompted Golding to order Jamaican security forces into Tivoli Gardens to arrest Coke, leading to days of violence in which 73 civilians and several police officers were killed. Coke was finally apprehended in late June, reportedly while on his way to surrender at the U.S. embassy. In August 2011, after being extradited to the United States, he pled guilty to drug trafficking and assault charges under a plea bargain; he was sentenced to 23 years in prison in June 2012.

Government whistleblowers who object to official acts of waste, fraud, or abuse of power are not well protected by Jamaican law, as is required under the Inter-American Convention against Corruption. Implementation of the 2002 Corruption Prevention Act has been problematic. Opposition leaders have accused the government of having connections to scams originating in Jamaica in which victims are told they have won the lottery, only to have their personal information stolen. The government has addressed the matter by amending a handful of laws, including the Evidence Act in November 2012. Jamaica was ranked 83 out of 177 countries and territories surveyed in Transparency International's 2013 Corruption Perceptions Index.

CIVIL LIBERTIES: 40 / 60
D. Freedom of Expression and Belief: 15 / 16

The constitutional right to free expression is generally respected. While newspapers are independent and free of government control, circulation is generally low. Broadcast media are largely state owned but are open to pluralistic points of view. Journalists occasionally face intimidation in the run-up to elections. The country enacted an access to information law in 2002.

Freedom of religion is constitutionally protected and generally respected in practice. While laws banning Obeah—an Afro-Caribbean shamanistic religion—remain on the books, they are not actively enforced. The government does not hinder academic freedom.

E. Associational and Organizational Rights: 9 / 12

Freedoms of association and assembly are generally respected. Jamaica has a small but robust civil society and active community groups. Approximately 20 percent of the workforce is unionized. Labor unions are politically influential and have the right to strike.

F. Rule of Law: 6 / 16

The judicial system is headed by the Supreme Court and includes a court of appeals and several magistrates' courts. The Trinidad-based Caribbean Court of Justice is the highest appellate court. A growing backlog of cases and a shortage of court staff at all levels continue to undermine the justice system.

Extrajudicial killings by police remain a major problem in Jamaica, accounting for 12 percent of murders each year, according to Amnesty International. Between 2006 and 2012, the government paid an estimated J$365 million (US$3.8 million) to victims of such violence, and it reportedly owes an additional J$400 million (US$4.4 million).

In May 2013, Amnesty International criticized Jamaican authorities for failing to appoint a commission of inquiry into security forces' conduct during the violence in Tivoli Garden in 2010 that led to the killing of dozens of civilians.

Ill-treatment by prison guards has been reported, and conditions in detention centers and prisons are abysmal. Vigilante violence remains a common occurrence in Jamaica.

According to recent reports, children from abusive homes are routinely placed into police custody together with common criminals for periods of up to two weeks. With the assistance of a European Union grant, several new human rights projects have been initiated. The projects focus on the rehabilitation of prison inmates, reducing impunity among the country's security forces, and providing legal assistance to people who were not accorded their rights.

Kingston's insular "garrison" communities remain the epicenter of most violence and serve as safe havens for gangs. Jamaica is a transit point for cocaine shipped from Colombia to U.S. markets, and much of the island's violence is the result of warfare between drug gangs known as posses. Contributing factors include the deportation of Jamaican-born criminals from the United States and an illegal weapons trade.

According to Jamaican police, murders in the country rose from 839 during the first nine months of 2012 to 884 for the same period in 2013. The police stated that 693 of the killings were related to gang violence.

G. Personal Autonomy and Individual Rights: 10 / 16

Harassment and violence against members of the LGBT (lesbian, gay, bisexual, and transgender) community remains a major concern and is frequently ignored by the police. Sodomy is punishable by 10 years in prison with hard labor. Although Simpson-Miller stated that she would hire a gay man or lesbian to serve in her cabinet, her administration has made no attempts to repeal the country's anti-LGBT laws. In October 2012, two gay Jamaicans initiated a legal challenge to these laws with the Inter-American Commission on Human Rights. According to the Jamaican Forum of Lesbians, All-Sexuals and Gays, nine gay men were killed in 2012 and at least two were killed in 2013.

A court case against Jamaica's anti-sodomy laws was ongoing at year's end. Protests against Jamaica's very restrictive social and legal climate for gays and lesbians erupted in front of the United Nations building in New York in September 2013.

Legal protections for women are poorly enforced, and violence and discrimination remain widespread. A number of highly publicized rape cases of young girls have led to public protests and a renewed debate about prevention and punishment of the crime. Women are underrepresented in government, holding just seven seats in the House of Representatives.

Japan

Political Rights Rating: 1
Civil Liberties Rating: 1
Freedom Rating: 1.0
Freedom Status: Free
Electoral Democracy: Yes

Population: 127,301,000
Capital: Tokyo

Ratings Change: Japan's civil liberties rating improved from 2 to 1 due to a steady rise in the activity of civil society organizations and an absence of legal restrictions on religious freedom.

Ten-Year Ratings Timeline For Year Under Review (Political Rights, Civil Liberties, Status)

Year Under Review	2004	2005	2006	2007	2008	2009	2010	2011	2012	2013
Rating	1,2,F	1,2,F	1,2,F	1,2F	1,2,F	1,2,F	1,2,F	1,2,F	1,2,F	1,1,F

INTRODUCTION

The governing Liberal Democratic Party (LDP), which had recaptured the lower house of parliament in late 2012 after three years in opposition, secured a majority in the upper house as well in July 2013. The victory gave Prime Minister Shinzo Abe a greater degree of legislative control than many of his recent predecessors as he presided over a tentative economic revival. Abe's government faces a dilemma in squaring a push for economic reform with a simultaneous assertion of a more nationalist foreign policy that has exacerbated tensions with China and South Korea in particular.

Also during the year, Japan and particularly its northeastern regions continued to suffer from the financial, human, and environmental repercussions of the 2011 "triple disaster," in which a powerful earthquake, subsequent tsunami, and nuclear meltdown devastated the coastal region north of Tokyo.

POLITICAL RIGHTS: 37 / 40
A. Electoral Process: 12 / 12

Japan is a parliamentary democracy with a purely symbolic monarchy. It has a bicameral parliament, the National Diet, in which the lower house, the House of Representatives, plays the dominant role, particularly through its control over the budget. Of the lower house's 480 members, 300 are elected in single-member plurality districts. The remaining 180 members are elected on the basis of proportional representation in 11 multimember constituencies. All members serve four-year terms. The upper house, the House of Councillors, has 242 members elected through a combination of multimember constituencies and nationwide proportional representation voting. All members serve six-year terms, with half of the seats up for election every three years. The prime minister must have the support of a majority in the lower house.

Elections in Japan are free and fair. In December 2012, the opposition LDP recaptured the lower house with a surprisingly clear election victory, taking 294 of the 480 seats. The then governing Democratic Party of Japan (DPJ) was sharply reduced to 57 seats, followed by the newly formed Japan Restoration Party with 54 and the LDP-allied New Komeito with 31. Six smaller parties and five independents divided the remainder.

The LDP consolidated its parliamentary control in the July 2013 upper house elections, capturing 65 of the 121 seats at stake for a new total of 135. Its coalition partner, New Komeito, won 11 for a total of 20. The DPJ, meanwhile, took only 17 seats, leaving it with 59. Five smaller parties and two independents also won seats.

In November, the Supreme Court faulted the 2012 elections for perpetuating disparities in population between the largest and smallest single-member districts, but it declined to annul the results in affected districts. Disparities remain wide even after a small reduction in seats (from 480 to 475) to take effect in the next Lower House election.

B. Political Pluralism and Participation: 15 / 16

Japanese political parties compete vigorously for voters' attention and support. Most parties can be classified as centrist, with the governing LDP falling right of center, and the opposition DPJ falling squarely in the center. The main exception to this tendency has been the Japan Communist Party, which has long been represented in the Diet and retains a membership of over 300,000. Not all parties clearly fit along an ideological left-right spectrum. New Komeito, which is part of the governing coalition, has its roots in the Buddhist lay organization Soka Gakkai, though its support extends beyond the membership of this organization today. It espouses pacifist policies but aligns with the LDP on many other matters. The array of parties has changed rapidly over the past decade as factions split from and then rejoin the LDP or DPJ.

Party membership rates remain high in Japan, with the two largest parties counting more than a million citizens as members. Voter turnout for the upper house elections in July 2013 was recorded at 52.6 percent. Lower house elections generally feature a slightly higher turnout; a reported 59.3 percent of eligible voters cast ballots in December 2012.

While all citizens have equal political rights under the law, women remain underrepresented in political office in practice. Just 39 of 480 lower house members are women. However, the 2013 upper house elections gave women just over 16 percent of the chamber's seats, a fairly large share by historical standards.

C. Functioning of Government: 10 / 12

For a significant part of the postwar era, national bureaucracies have had more policymaking power in Japan than in other developed democracies. Under the so-called "developmental state" model, Japanese politicians have contented themselves with setting overall guidelines for national goals and aspirations. Frequent changes of political personnel in the cabinet further contributed to this relative lack of control by elected officials.

The close collaboration between national ministries, the political leadership, and corporate groups has been cited to explain the decades-long dominance of the LDP. Retired bureaucrats often join corporations or political parties where they continue to benefit from and act through close association with their successors. In some areas, such as construction, this has led to corruption. Japan was ranked 18 out of 177 countries assessed in Transparency International's 2013 Corruption Perceptions Index.

CIVIL LIBERTIES: 53 / 60 (+2)
D. Freedom of Expression and Belief: 14 / 16 (+1)

Japan's news media are overwhelmingly private and independent. Competition is vigorous between television, radio, and print outlets. National and regional newspapers continue to log some of the highest subscription rates in the world. Online media are slowly establishing themselves as well. However, the country's press clubs, or *kisha kurabu*, lead to some homogeneity of news coverage by fostering close relationships between the major media and bureaucrats and politicians. There are few media outlets whose editorial stance diverges from a centrist commitment to the status quo. NHK, the national broadcaster, is charged with political neutrality, but controversy has erupted over Abe's appointments to the NHK board hinting at a politicization of NHK reporting.

Japanese of all faiths can worship freely. Religious groups are permitted to remain unlicensed, but registering with government authorities as a "religious corporation" brings tax benefits and other advantages. While the terrorism perpetrated by the Aum Shinrikyo cult in 1995 led to its designation as a terrorist organization, there are no lingering legal restrictions on religious activities by nonviolent groups. Remaining ties between the state and Shinto organizations have led to vigorous protests and civil rights litigation in the past.

There are no restrictions on academic freedom. While many institutions of higher education are public, their direct ties with the Ministry of Education have been loosened in recent years, most noticeably through the limited privatization of national universities in the *hojinka* process of 2006.

E. Associational and Organizational Rights: 11 / 12 (+1)

The constitution guarantees freedoms of assembly and association. Massive peaceful protests against the restarting of two nuclear reactors in the wake of the 2011 Fukushima meltdown took place in 2012, and similar antinuclear protests continued on a smaller scale throughout 2013. Protests against the U.S. military presence remain frequent in Okinawa.

Nongovernmental organizations (NGOs) have become more active in Japan over the past decade, and bureaucratic hurdles to their formation have largely been eliminated. Common areas of NGO activity include human rights, social welfare, and environmental protection.

Union mobilization is widespread, though it typically takes the form of enterprise-level unions rather than industrial-sector or general unions. Attempts to unionize part-time workers have been freely allowed, though they have not generated a large-scale response.

F. Rule of Law: 15 / 16

Japan's judiciary is independent. There are several levels of courts, and suspects generally receive fair public trials by an impartial tribunal within three months of being detained. For serious criminal cases, a judicial panel composed of professional judges and *saiban-in* (lay-judges), selected from the general public, rule on defendants. While arbitrary arrest and imprisonment is not practiced, the police may detain suspects for up to 23 days without charge in order to extract confessions. Prison conditions comply with international standards, though prison officials sometimes use physical and psychological intimidation to enforce discipline or elicit confessions.

Organized crime is regarded as fairly prominent, particularly in the construction and nightlife industries. Reports of organized crime groups' ability to extort public corporations have flared up occasionally in the past, but are declining.

The constitution prohibits discrimination based on race, creed, sex, or social status. However, entrenched societal discrimination prevents Japan's estimated three million *burakumin*—descendants of feudal-era outcasts—and the indigenous Ainu minority from gaining equal access to housing and employment, though such forms of discrimination are slowly waning as the Japanese population freely moves within the country, weakening traditional social distinctions. Japan-born descendants of colonial subjects (particularly Korean and Chinese) continue to suffer similar disadvantages.

Antidiscrimination laws do not cover sexual orientation or gender identity, and laws on rape and prostitution do not address same-sex activity. LGBT (lesbian, gay, bisexual, and transgender) people reportedly face social stigma and some cases of harassment.

G. Personal Autonomy and Individual Rights: 13 / 16

Japanese citizens enjoy broad personal autonomy in their choices of residence, profession, and education.

Although women enjoy legal equality, discrimination in employment and sexual harassment on the job are common. Violence against women often goes unreported due to concerns about family reputation and other social mores. Japan is a destination, source, and transit country for people trafficked for forced labor and sexual exploitation.

Jordan

Political Rights: 6
Civil Liberties: 5
Freedom Rating: 5.5
Freedom Status: Not Free
Electoral Democracy: No

Population: 7,300,000
Capital: Amman

Ten-Year Ratings Timeline For Year Under Review (Political Rights, Civil Liberties, Status)

Year Under Review Rating	2004	2005	2006	2007	2008	2009	2010	2011	2012	2013
	5,4,PF	5,4,PF	5,4,PF	5,4,PF	5,5,PF	6,5,PF	6,5,NF	6,5,NF	6,5,NF	6,5,NF

INTRODUCTION

Jordan has largely avoided the massive popular upheavals seen in much of the Middle East; however, demonstrations have become prominent in the country. Calls to maintain economic subsidies and reduce unemployment have garnered strong support from a coalition of leftists, Islamists, the youth, and some tribal elites. Demands for the king to step down have been rare. In February 2011, the king was quick to calm growing dissent by sacking the prime minister and later passing a new constitution. Parliament was dissolved in October

2012 and fresh elections were held in January 2013 under a new electoral framework. Abdullah Ensour, a veteran politician and economist, was reappointed prime minister in March. He is the fifth prime minister to serve since early 2011.

Parliamentary elections in January preserved the status quo. Gerrymandering and the preponderance of the single non-transferable vote system have maintained the political dominance of powerful East Bank tribes and independent businessmen loyal to the regime. Jordan's Muslim Brotherhood has boycotted the past two elections citing the unfair electoral laws that give less weight to the large urban centers from which much of their support derives. The influx of over 500,000 refugees from the conflict in Syria has added to social and economic pressures.

POLITICAL RIGHTS: 11 / 40 (+1)

A. Electoral Process: 2 / 12

King Abdullah II holds broad executive powers, appoints and dismisses the prime minister and cabinet, and may dissolve the bicameral National Assembly at his discretion. However, in a break from previous practices, Prime Minister Abdullah Ensour and his 19-member cabinet were first nominated by the parliament before their appointment. Legislative representatives in the Chamber of Deputies, or lower house, are elected through universal adult suffrage. The Senate is appointed by the king and constitutes the upper house of the bicameral National Assembly. Regional governors are appointed by the central government and fall under the purview of the Ministry of Interior.

Parliamentary elections in January 2013 were the first under the newly adopted Election Law in which voters cast two ballots. One vote is cast for a party list where candidates are selected through proportional representation in a single nationwide constituency. Another candidate is selected through the old single non-transferable vote (SNTV) system based on local electoral districts. The Chamber of Deputies was expanded from 120 to 150 seats, of which 27 deputies are selected through closed party lists. The Senate was also enlarged to 75 seats.

The recently established Independent Electoral Commission administered the elections. International observers noted instances of vote buying and criticized the unfair electoral laws. Political campaigning was seen as noncompetitive and relatively absent in wide areas of the country due to the overall influence of tribal affiliations, a lack of financing, and boycotting by opposition groups. The elections were carried by East Bank tribal elites and independent businessmen loyal to the regime. Turnout was recorded at 56.5 percent of registered voters. Parliamentarians were inaugurated in February and held their first ordinary session in November. Municipal elections were also held in August with regime loyalists taking most seats. Violence and other irregularities were reported by local observers. Turnout was 37.3 percent and as low as 10.5 percent in Amman.

B. Political Pluralism and Participation: 6 / 16 (+1)

Jordanians are free to join political parties, although in practice, votes are cast along non-partisan and tribal lines. Changes to the Political Party Law in 2012 reduced many bureaucratic obstacles while increasing demographic and geographic requirements meant to ensure that new political parties enjoy nationwide support. In a change from previous practice, the new law resulted in the election of 27 out of 150 deputies from nationwide party lists. However, flaws within the electoral law, gerrymandering, and the small role of the nationwide constituency are not conducive to genuine political competition. Urban areas account for over two thirds of the population but less than one third of seats in the Chamber of Deputies. The Chamber of Deputies is heavily imbalanced in favor of rural districts, whose residents are generally of Transjordanian (East Bank) origin. Christian and Circassian minorities are guaranteed nine and three seats, respectively. Palestinian-Jordanians and supporters of the Muslim Brotherhood are heavily concentrated in larger cities. The Brotherhood's Islamic Action Front (IAF), seen as the country's strongest party, has boycotted the 2010 and 2013 parliamentary elections to protest inherent disadvantages in the system.

In a speech that reached headlines in November, King Abdullah promised to further devolve executive powers to elected officials and push the consolidation of the country's 23 political parties into two opposition coalitions. Progress on this matter has yet to be enacted.

C. Functioning of Government: 3 / 12

Key powers and decision-making abilities are ultimately vested in the king. The Chamber of Deputies may approve, reject, or amend legislation proposed by the cabinet, but it cannot enact laws without the assent of the royally appointed Senate. King Abdullah is empowered to dismiss parliament, as well as the prime minister and cabinet. The king can delay parliamentary elections for up to two years and may rule by royal decree during periods in which parliament is not in session. Civil society groups have complained over a lack of inclusion in policymaking, particularly in deliberations over the amendments to the Press and Publications Law. Disputes between parliamentarians have resulted in scuffles and in October a deputy was arrested for firing an assault rifle outside the chamber.

The government has recently undertaken several efforts to combat widespread corruption. The National Integrity Commission was formed in December 2012 to investigate allegations, while the Privatization Review Committee, formed in January 2013, will review the practice of privatizing state-run enterprises that has led to scandals in the past. Prime Minister Ensour also launched a five year anti-corruption strategy in June. While investigations and arrests rarely lead to serious punishment, recently there have been some high-profile cases. The former head of the Jordan Phosphates Mining Company, who is also the husband of the king's aunt, was sentenced in absentia to 37.5 years in prison and a fine of JOD 284.4 million (US$401 million) for abuse of office. A former intelligence director was sentenced to a heavy fine and 13 years jail time in November 2012. Jordan ranked 66 out of 177 countries in the Corruption Perceptions Index, last compiled by Transparency International in 2013.

CIVIL LIBERTIES: 24 / 60
D. Freedom of Expression and Belief: 7 / 16

Freedom of expression is restricted by numerous laws that criminalize defamation, the denigration of government, and the incitement of sectarian strife. In practice, this has resulted in the arrest of traditional and online journalists for criticizing the king, exposing corruption, and violating a vague requirement in the Press and Publications Law (PPL) mandating media objectivity. The government exerts political pressure on editors to control the media. Self-censorship is pervasive, particularly when discussing the royal family, foreign leaders, and certain societal taboos.

Most broadcast news outlets remain under state control, but satellite dishes and the internet give residents access to foreign media. While there are dozens of private newspapers and magazines, the government has broad powers to close them and often engages in pre-censorship of news stories. In June, journalists protested the blocking of nearly 300 news websites by the government over their failure to meet burdensome registration requirements introduced in September 2012. The majority of these remained inaccessible at year's end.

Islam is the state religion. Christians are recognized as religious minorities and can worship freely. Baha'is and Druze are allowed to practice their faiths, although a lack of state recognition has resulted in de facto discrimination. The government monitors sermons at mosques, and preachers cannot practice without written government permission. Only state-appointed councils may issue religious edicts, and it is illegal to criticize these rulings.

Academic freedom is generally respected, and Jordanians openly discuss political developments within established red lines. However, there have been reports of a heavy intelligence presence on some university campuses, as well as some violent incidents. In March, five students were attacked by a mob after rumors circulated they had desecrated a Koran on campus. Police also intervened during violent clashes between tribes at a university in April.

E. Associational and Organizational Rights: 3 / 12

Restrictions on freedom of assembly remain in place. Under the recent changes to the Public Gatherings Law, prior permission is not required to stage a demonstration. Nonetheless, this year dozens of protestors in cities such as Amman, Tafilah, and Karak were detained on charges of "subverting the regime," "insulting the king," "vandalizing property," or "holding unlawful gatherings with the purpose of committing crime." After post-election protests turned deadly in January where one protester was killed in Mafraq and another in Ma'an, tear gas was used to disperse rioters in several cities.

Freedom of association is limited. The Ministry of Social Development has the authority to reject registration and foreign funding requests for nongovernmental organizations (NGOs) and can disband organizations it finds objectionable. In June 2012, the government denied US$350,000 in foreign funds to the migrant workers and legal assistance group Tamkeen with no explanation. NGOs supporting associations with political purposes are prohibited and all board members must be vetted by state security.

Workers have collective bargaining rights but must receive government permission to strike. More than 30 percent of the workforce is organized into 17 unions. According to a 2013 study by the Phenix Centre for Economic and Informatics Studies, a total of 601 labor-related demonstrations took place in the first half of 2013, mainly in urban centers and on the initiative of individual workers.

F. Rule of Law: 6 / 16

The judiciary is subject to executive influence through the Justice Ministry and the Higher Judiciary Council, most of whose members are appointed by the king. Provincial governors can order administrative detention for up to one year under a 1954 Crime Prevention Law that leaves little room for appeal. Prison conditions are poor, and inmates reportedly experience severe beatings and other abuse by guards. In May, a man detained on drug charges died in Juweida prison in Amman; subsequent medical examinations revealed instances of torture. A public prosecutor charged six police officers under Article 208 of the penal code, which bans torture, but the case was referred to a special police court that lacks transparency and independence. Torture allegations are rarely prosecuted or result in little more than minor disciplinary penalties.

While most trials in civilian courts are open and procedurally sound, the quasi-military State Security Court (SSC) may close its proceedings to the public. Dozens of protestors, particularly those affiliated with *Al-Hirak*, a youth protest movement, as well as journalists, faced trials under the SSC this year for undermining the regime, damaging relations with a foreign state, or insulting the king. In September, King Abdullah instructed the government to make revisions to the SSC Law to ensure its use is limited to high crimes including espionage, drugs, terrorism, treason, and money counterfeiting.

Poor living conditions and restrictions on freedom of movement have resulted in repeated riots at the Zaatari camp in northern Jordan, home to over 100,000 Syrian refugees. The camp is the fifth-largest population center in Jordan. The camp has been subject to riots in 2013 over poor living conditions. In October, the government announced plans to deport thousands of Syrians who had failed to obtain work permits. While the majority of Syrian refugees live and work in cities, they are only legally permitted to work inside the camps. There have been reported incidents of border authorities rejecting single Syrian men of military age or with refugees with Palestinian origins, against international norms on non-refoulement.

G. Personal Autonomy and Individual Rights: 8 / 16

Women enjoy equal political rights but face legal discrimination in matters involving inheritance, divorce, and child custody, which fall under the jurisdiction of Sharia (Islamic law) courts. In the recent elections, women constituted 52 percent of the electorate but represented 13 percent of all candidates. Ten percent of seats in the lower house of parliament are reserved for women and the upper house contains eight female senators. Christian and Circassian minorities are guaranteed nine and three seats, respectively, in the Chamber of Deputies. Jordanians of Palestinian origin are marginalized from jobs in the public sector and security forces, which are dominated by East Bank tribes. Jordan was ranked 119 out of 189 economies in the 2014 World Bank Ease of Doing Business study due to obstacles in obtaining credit, protecting investors, enforcing contracts, and resolving insolvency.

Under the new passport law passed in August, women are no longer required to obtain their husbands' permission when applying for a passport. Nonetheless, they are still unable to pass down citizenship to children from non-Jordanian fathers. Women that suffer domestic abuse are often detained in administrative detention and can only be released once a male member of her family gives his assurance that she will not be harmed. Men who commit "honor crimes" against women often receive lenient sentences. Women's rights activists have staged campaigns on these issues and more, including against an article in the penal code that allows alleged rapists to avoid prosecution by marrying their victims and to punish more severely those convicted of honor crimes.

There has been a recent rise in early and forced marriages of Syrian refugees as young as 12. Child marriages accounted for 25 percent of all marriages among Syrian refugees, up from 12 percent in 2011. Although the legal age of marriage is 18, girls can be married younger if a court deems it is in her best interest. Many parents take the decision to marry off their daughters, often to older men, due to financial difficulties or out of fear of sexual violence in the camps. Syrian refugees have also been turned away from public schools due to overcrowding despite their right to free education. Labor rights organizations have raised concerns about poor working conditions, forced labor, and sexual abuse in Qualifying Industrial Zones, where mostly female and foreign factory workers process goods for export. Jordan is a destination and transit country for human trafficking for forced labor and, to a lesser extent, prostitution.

⬇ Kazakhstan

Political Rights Rating: 6
Civil Liberties Rating: 5
Freedom Rating: 5.5
Status: Not Free
Electoral Democracy: No

Population: 17,031,000
Capital: Astana

Trend Arrow: Kazakhstan received a downward trend arrow due to broad extralegal enforcement of its already strict 2011 law on religious activity, with raids by antiterrorism police on gatherings in private homes.

Ten-Year Ratings Timeline For Year Under Review (Political Rights, Civil Liberties, Status)

Year Under Review	2004	2005	2006	2007	2008	2009	2010	2011	2012	2013
Rating	6,5,NF	6,5,NF	6,5,NF	6,5,NF	6,5,NF	6,5,NF	6,5,NF	6,5,NF	6,5,NF	6,5,NF

INTRODUCTION

Authorities in Kazakhstan continued to harass and detain independent journalists in Kazakhstan throughout 2013, repeatedly blocking attempts by employees of publications that had been shut down to open new outlets. The government continued to strictly enforce a 2011 law on religion that criminalized about one third of previously legal organizations, as well as believers who continued to meet without registration; authorities frequently prosecuted beyond the boundaries of the law, sentencing religious adherents to forced psychiatric treatment, fining them for saying prayers or reading scripture, and restricting their foreign travel. In October, Kazakhstan announced that it would end military conscription by 2016.

POLITICAL RIGHTS: 6 / 40

A. Electoral Process: 2 / 12

The Kazakhstani constitution grants the president considerable control over the legislature, the judiciary, and local governments. Under the current constitutional rules, President Nursultan Nazarbayev may serve an indefinite number of five-year terms.

The upper house of the bicameral Parliament is the 47-member Senate, with 32 members chosen by directly elected regional councils and 15 appointed by the president. The senators serve six-year terms, with half of the 32 elected members up for election every three years. The lower house (Mazhilis) has 107 deputies, with 98 elected by proportional representation on party slates and nine appointed by the Assembly of Peoples of Kazakhstan, which represents the country's various ethnic groups. Members serve five-year terms.

The ruling party, Nur Otan, is headed by the president and dominates the legislature. Parties must clear a 7 percent vote threshold to enter the Mazhilis, and once elected, deputies must vote with their party. Parties are barred from forming electoral blocs. A 2009 electoral law amendment guarantees the second-ranked party at least two seats in the Mazhilis if only one party passes the 7 percent threshold. Aside from Nur Otan, two parties—Ak Zhol and the Communist People's Party—won representation in the 2012 Mazhilis elections, with each earning just over 7 percent of the vote. However, neither is considered an opposition party.

Kazakh Communist Party leader Nursultan Nazarbayev won an uncontested presidential election in December 1991, two weeks before Kazakhstan gained its independence from the Soviet Union, and has never left office. Constitutional changes removed term limits for Nazarbayev and have consistently consolidated power for the president and his ruling party. Changes in 2007 also eliminated individual district races for the lower house of Parliament, leaving only party-slate seats filled by nationwide proportional representation. Elections under the new rules that August produced a one-party legislature, with the pro-presidential Nur Otan party taking 88 percent of the vote and no opposition parties clearing the 7 percent threshold for representation. Although Nazarbayev rejected a proposal to hand him the presidency for life in 2009, a constitutional amendment in 2010 gave him immunity from prosecution and made his family's property effectively inviolable. Nazarbayev was most recently elected in a snap presidential election in April 2011 with 96 percent of the vote. His three little-known competitors all publicly expressed support for him. Nur Otan won all 16 Senate seats at stake in indirect upper house elections in 2011. In the 2012 election for the current lower house, Nur Otan took 83 of the 107 seats, Ak Zhol won 8, and the Communist People's Party secured 7. Monitors from the Organization for Security and Co-operation in Europe (OSCE) noted that the elections did not meet democratic norms.

B. Political Pluralism and Participation: 3 / 16

A 2002 law raised the number of members that a party must have to register from 3,000 to 50,000; modest amendments in 2009 lowered the number to 40,000. In December 2012, a court invoked laws against "extremism" to ban the unregistered opposition Algha Party, as well as the People's Front opposition movement. It also found Algha leader Vladimir Kozlov guilty of heading an illegal group, inciting social hatred, and calling for the violent overthrow of the constitutional order. He was sentenced to seven and a half years in prison.

In May 2013, the wife and daughter of billionaire opposition leader Mukhtar Ablyazov were arrested in Italy and hastily deported to Kazakhstan. The move was widely viewed as an attempt to pressure Ablyazov to return to Kazakhstan, where he faces embezzlement charges believed by many opposition activists to be politically motivated. Senior officials in Italy later overturned the decision and acknowledged that their documents were valid and they could return. In July 2013, French authorities arrested Ablyazov and held him without bail on a warrant issued by Ukraine on behalf of Kazakhstan – which has no extradition treaty with France. Also in July, authorities continued to pressure the few remaining opposition groups, disrupting a meeting in Almaty of the Azat (Freedom) party and arresting two of its leaders. Its chairman, prominent businessman Bolot Abilov, announced in September his decision to abandon politics.

Political parties based on ethnic origin, religion, or gender are prohibited.

C. Functioning of Government: 1 / 12

Corruption is widespread at all levels of government. In January 2013, Commander General Aleksandr Sorokin of Kazakhstan's Air Defense Forces was arrested for taking bribes to overlook faulty mechanical tests on a plane that crashed in December 2012, killing 27 people. In July, Sorokin was sentenced to eleven years in prison. Kazakhstan's ranking fell to 140 out of 177 countries surveyed in Transparency International's 2013 Corruption Perceptions Index.

CIVIL LIBERTIES: 19 / 60

D. Freedom of Expression and Belief: 4 / 16

While the constitution provides for freedom of the press, the government has repeatedly harassed or shut down independent media outlets. Most of the country's outlets, including publishing houses, are controlled or influenced by members of the president's family and other powerful groups. Libel is a criminal offense, and the criminal code prohibits insulting the president; self-censorship is common.

Independent media frequently suffer attacks, arrests, and pressure from authorities. Police used emergency powers to arrest or detain journalists attempting to cover unrest in Zhanaozen and neighboring cities in late 2011. After Zhanaozen, raids on independent media outlets and the harassment and detention of journalists sharply increased. New regulations in 2012 gave the Ministry of Culture and Information expanded powers to combat "unofficial or negative information" about any crisis, and courts shut down dozens of independent newspapers, television channels, and news websites on charges of "extremism."

Most of the few remaining independent media faced continued pressure throughout 2013, and authorities consistently blocked attempts to open new publications to replace those that had been banned. In February, for example, Tatyana Trubacheva, the former editor of *Golos Respubliki*, was fined for starting a new periodical, even though its print run of less than 100 issues legally allowed it to avoid registration.

The government has a record of blocking websites that are critical of the regime. The list of banned websites expanded significantly since 2012, with hundreds of new sites added. The authorities also intensified measures to restrict circumvention tools like Tor and virtual private networks, which enable secure and uncensored internet access and are popular with opposition journalists and activists.

The constitution guarantees freedom of worship, and some religious communities practice without state interference. However, laws passed in 2005 banned all activities by unregistered religious groups and gave the government great discretion in outlawing organizations it designated as "extremist." Local officials have harassed groups defined as "nontraditional," such as Protestant Christians, Jehovah's Witnesses, and Muslims. A 2011 law required reregistration of all religious groups, gave the government unprecedented authority to regulate religious communities, and forbade religious expression in government institutions. The process of reregistration was used to cull around one-third of the country's religious organizations, exposing unregistered believers to arrest and prosecution.

These new rules continued to be enforced strictly in 2013, and in many cases local authorities and courts prosecuted believers beyond the authority of the law. In two cases—of Aleksandr Kharlamov, an atheist journalist, and Bakhytzhan Kashkumbayev, a Pentecostal pastor—courts sentenced defendants to forced psychiatric care for their religious beliefs, though no such provision exists in the legislation. Religious communities were raided and fined across the country, often by police divisions dedicated to counter-terrorism operations, resulting in charges of reading scripture or saying prayers without special licenses which also are not stipulated in legislation. In April 2013, according to religious freedom group Forum 18, police in Stepnogorsk attempted to entrap leaders of a protestant church by sending young women to proposition them in a sauna, with plainclothes and regular police following in hopes of arresting them.

The government reportedly permits academic freedom, except regarding criticism of the president and his family. Corruption in the education system is widespread, and students frequently bribe professors for passing grades.

E. Associational and Organizational Rights: 3 / 12

Despite constitutional guarantees, the government imposes restrictions on freedom of association and assembly. Unsanctioned opposition gatherings are frequently broken up by police. Nongovernmental organizations (NGOs) continue to operate despite government harassment surrounding politically sensitive issues. In March 2013, Vadim Kuramshin, a rights activist who lobbied on behalf of abused prison inmates, was transferred to the Petropavlovsk maximum security labor camp, a prison he had often criticized. Kuramshin had originally been sentenced to one year in prison, but was re-sentenced to 12 years in

December 2012 after violating travel restrictions imposed on him a few months before in order to attend an OSCE conference, where he delivered a critical presentation.

Workers can form and join trade unions and participate in collective bargaining, although co-opted unions and close links between the authorities and big business make for an uneven playing field. Migrant workers from neighboring countries often face poor working conditions and a lack of legal protections. Child labor in agriculture has been reported. In 2012, dozens of people were convicted for participating in the 2011 Zhanaozen protests by striking oil workers and their supporters, described by prosecutors as "mass disorder."

F. Rule of Law: 4 / 16

The constitution makes the judiciary subservient to the executive branch. Judges are subject to political bias, and corruption is evident throughout the judicial system. Conditions in pretrial facilities and prisons are harsh. Police at times abuse detainees and threaten their families, often to obtain confessions, and arbitrary arrest and detention remain problems.

Members of the sizable Russian-speaking minority have complained of discrimination in employment and education. The Russian and Kazakh languages officially have equal status, but in 2011, newly rigorous Kazakh-language testing for candidacy in the presidential election eliminated many opposition candidates.

Kazakhstan decriminalized homosexual activity in 1998, but the LGBT (lesbian, gay, bisexual, and transgender) community continues to face societal discrimination.

G. Personal Autonomy and Individual Rights: 8 / 16

While the rights of entrepreneurship and private property are formally protected, equality of opportunity is limited by bureaucratic hurdles and the control of large segments of the economy by clannish elites and government officials. Astana residents whose homes have been demolished to make way for large construction projects have said they were denied legally guaranteed compensation.

Traditional cultural practices and the country's economic imbalances limit professional opportunities for women. Domestic violence often goes unpunished, as police are reluctant to intervene in what are regarded as internal family matters. Despite legal prohibitions, the trafficking of women for the purpose of prostitution remains a serious problem.

Kenya

Political Rights Rating: 4
Civil Liberties Rating: 4
Freedom Rating: 4.0
Freedom Status: Partly Free
Electoral Democracy: Yes

Population: 44,200,000
Capital: Nairobi

Ten-Year Ratings Timeline For Year Under Review (Political Rights, Civil Liberties, Status)

Year Under Review	2004	2005	2006	2007	2008	2009	2010	2011	2012	2013
Rating	3,3,PF	3,3,PF	3,3,PF	4,3,PF	4,3,PF	4,4,PF	4,3,PF	4,3,PF	4,4,PF	4,4,PF

INTRODUCTION

Kenya experienced a turbulent year in 2013. The March presidential and parliamentary elections—the first since a disputed 2007 presidential vote led to deadly ethnic conflict—were relatively peaceful and well-organized. Prior to the campaign period, all parties pledged to work to avoid violence, and this was aided by a stepped-up security presence. However, the elections suffered from serious problems with voter registration, vote tabulation, and confusion over the number and definition of rejected ballots. Uhuru Kenyatta, son of Kenya's first president, Jomo Kenyatta, was ultimately declared the winner following a controversial Supreme Court ruling.

Throughout 2013, the impending International Criminal Court (ICC) trials of Kenyatta and his deputy president, William Ruto, for crimes against humanity in connection with the 2007–2008 postelection violence loomed large. Witnesses against them disappeared or withdrew amid threats, and civil society organizations and media outlets that focused on the trials faced intimidation. In December, the government passed a highly repressive media law, in a further example of threats to civil society activities and free expression in Kenya.

In September, a terrorist attack by the Somali Islamist group Al-Shabaab on the Westgate shopping complex in Nairobi resulted in the deaths of nearly 70 civilians and security personnel. The attack and its aftermath served as a reminder both of the continuing weakness of rule of law in Kenya and the ongoing mistreatment of the country's ethnic Somali population by the security services.

POLITICAL RIGHTS: 22 / 40 (+1)
A. Electoral Process: 7 / 12 (+1)

The 2010 constitution included wide-ranging reforms, such as limiting previously expansive executive powers and shifting some authority from the central government to local officials. Under the new charter, the president and deputy president, who can serve up to two five-year terms, are directly elected by majority vote; they are also required to win 25 percent of the votes in at least half of Kenya's newly created 47 counties. The National Assembly consists of 349 elected members (290 directly elected, 47 special women representatives, and 12 nominated by each party according to their share of the assembly vote), plus 1 ex-officio member elected as speaker. The newly created Senate consists of 67 elected members (47 directly elected, 16 special women representatives, 2 representing youth, and 2 representing people with disabilities), plus 1 ex-officio member elected as speaker.

The March 4, 2013, presidential, parliamentary, and county elections were Kenya's first held under the new constitution and legal framework. There were 8 presidential candidates and over 20 parties competing for legislative seats, aligned into four main groupings—the Jubilee Coalition, the Coalition for Reforms and Democracy (CORD), the Amani Coalition, and the EAGLE Alliance. As in the past, political alliances were formed primarily along ethnic lines, rather than ideology. During the campaign, Jubilee candidates Kenyatta and Ruto used their upcoming ICC trials to drum up support, framing the indictments as part of an alleged attempt by the West to impose its agenda on Africa.

Election observers—including the U.S.-based Carter Center, the European Union, and the Commonwealth, as well as regional and domestic bodies—noted important improvements compared with 2007, but also serious shortcomings. With all sides, including the political parties and the media, agreeing prior to the campaign to promote calm and refrain from using potentially inflammatory language, the election period was mostly peaceful. However, some observers pointed to a harsher security environment and a large degree of self-censorship.

Voting itself was more organized and streamlined than in 2007, especially considering the high turnout at most polling stations; nationwide, turnout was reported at about 86 percent. However, there were serious questions surrounding the tabulation of results: the electronic transmission system implemented by the Independent Electoral Boundaries

Commission (IEBC) failed, and the manual delivery of ballots was delayed and not transparent. Moreover, there was significant confusion initially over the total number of rejected, or invalid, ballots, as well as controversy over whether to include the rejected ballots in the total number of votes cast in the presidential vote.

On March 9, the IEBC declared Kenyatta the winner of the presidential election with 50.07 percent of the vote, with his closest challenger, CORD candidate and former prime minister Raila Odinga, winning 43.7 percent. Kenyatta's vote share—which was calculated without including the rejected ballots—allowed him to claim victory in the first round by a very narrow margin. Odinga, citing widespread irregularities, filed a challenge to the result with the Supreme Court on March 16. Despite high tensions, observers noted that all sides made efforts to preserve calm and not resort to violence, although police used tear gas to disperse Odinga supporters who gathered in front of the Supreme Court building the day their candidate filed his appeal. On March 30, the court upheld the result despite acknowledging several errors in the electoral process, asserting that they did not alter the outcome. While recent judicial reforms had increased the legitimacy of the Supreme Court as an arbiter, the decision nevertheless had questionable legal merit, since it used the number of valid votes cast rather than all votes cast—which would have included the rejected ballots—in its calculations. However, Odinga announced that he would accept the decision and called on his followers to do the same, and there were only sporadic incidents of violence and protest following the court ruling.

Meanwhile, the Jubilee Coalition claimed 167 of the National Assembly seats, 30 of the Senate seats, and 18 of the gubernatorial races. CORD won 141 of the National Assembly seats, 28 of the Senate seats, and 23 of the gubernatorial races. These elections were not free of controversy, and there were more than 180 petitions to either the High or Magistrate Courts. However, this was far less than expected, and the vast majority of these petitions were ultimately rejected.

The framework for the 2013 elections was guided by the requirements set forth in the new constitution, but some aspects, such as campaign finance reform, were not implemented. The IEBC's central members were appointed through a credible process with legislative oversight, yet their effectiveness was hampered by the problems with vote tabulation. In addition, the IEBC's capacity was hindered by ambiguity regarding its mandate and interference from the legislature. For instance, voter registration was delayed by the legislature in order to implement a biometric system, giving the IEBC only 30 days to register voters. Last-minute amendments to the Election Act extended the deadline for nominating candidates to 45 days before the election, leaving the IEBC little time to oversee disputes.

B. Political Pluralism and Participation: 10 / 16

People have the right to organize into political parties that represent a range of ideological, regional, and ethnic interests, and there are no significant impediments to party formation. Opposition party leaders and members are not routinely harassed by the state, but in 2013 there were sporadic outbursts of violence committed by party activists and affiliated ethnic gangs. Kenyan political parties are notoriously weak, often amalgamated into coalitions designed only to contest elections.

In the 2013 elections, there were impediments to political choice posed by domestic economic interests. There was pervasive use of unverified sums of money during campaigns due to the absence of an adequate campaign finance law and evidence of direct vote buying by candidates of both parties.

The new constitution was intended to reduce the role of ethnicity in elections. Although the Political Parties Act requires each party to have at least 1,000 members in 24 of the 47 counties as a mechanism for ensuring diversity, ethnicity remains an entrenched political factor, as the major coalitions reflected distinctive—though rarely exclusive—ethnic groupings. The stipulation that all voters must possess a National Identity Card impeded historically marginalized groups from greater access to the political process, in particular nearly seven million pastoralists from the upper Rift Valley and North Eastern Provinces. Finally, ongoing extrajudicial harassment by the security forces on the substantial Somali population diminished their electoral opportunities.

C. Functioning of Government: 5 / 12

Corruption is a serious problem in Kenya. While the new constitution includes measures for increased accountability and transparency, official prosecutions of corruption have yielded meager results, and no top officials have been successfully prosecuted. In 2013, the new head of the Ethics and Anti-Corruption Commission, Mumo Matemu, was charged with corruption during his time at the Agricultural Finance Corporation. Transparency International's 2013 Corruption Perceptions Index ranked Kenya 136 out of 177 countries surveyed.

Weak institutional capacity has undermined attempts at increased transparency regarding the budget-making process and other actions of the government. There is little input from civil society, and uncertainty exists regarding the allocation of public contracts. For instance, requests made in 2013 by the International Monetary Fund to publicize agreements between the government and mining corporations were denied. In June, reporters were evicted from the parliamentary media center. Ambiguities surrounding the devolution of power to Kenya's counties have led to conflicts between governors and the central government.

CIVIL LIBERTIES: 31 / 60 (-3)

D. Freedom of Expression and Belief: 11 / 16 (-2)

The new constitution strengthened protections for freedoms of speech and of the press, and there is a large, independent, and active media in Kenya. In practice, however, several laws restrict these rights, and the government and security forces harass members of the press, leading to self-censorship in some cases. Media outlets deliberately avoided reporting on the shortcomings of the IEBC, government corruption, or the ICC proceedings, often under threat of reprisals. In April, Bernard Wesonga, a reporter for the *Star* newspaper, was murdered in Mombasa, apparently for reporting on illegal sales of expired fertilizer. Later that month, two journalists for the private KTN network were threatened for reporting on possible foul play in connection with the 2012 death of former interior minister George Saitoti. In the aftermath of the Westgate attack, authorities threatened and summoned several reporters who documented looting of the mall by the police and military.

In early December, parliament passed the Kenya Information and Communication (Amendment) Bill and the Media Council Bill, which provided for wide-ranging government control of the media sector. Among the bills' provisions, a new government-controlled board would have the authority to regulate all forms of journalism, including the power to impose potentially crippling fines on media houses and individual journalists for alleged violations of a code of conduct, which will be drafted by legislators.

The authorities generally uphold freedom of religion on civil matters. The Islamic (*Kadhi*) court system is subordinate to the superior courts of Kenya. The Kadhi courts adjudicate cases related to personal status, marriage, divorce, or inheritance for people who profess the Muslim religion and who voluntarily submit to the courts' jurisdiction. Religious groups are required to register with the government, which permits them to apply for tax-exempt status. Religious tension has risen in recent years due to terrorist attacks carried out in Kenya by Al-Shabaab, the Kenyan government's decision in late 2011 to send troops to

Somalia to fight the group, and extrajudicial attacks and harassment by the security forces against the mainly Muslim ethnic Somali population.

Academic freedom is the norm in Kenya, though the education system suffers from structural and funding problems.

Increasing intimidation from the security forces and ethnically affiliated gangs such as the Mungiki has inhibited open and free private discussion. In addition, since September 2012 the government has increased its ability to monitor text and internet communications for hate speech, potentially limiting free discussion, including surrounding the March elections.

E. Associational and Organizational Rights: 7 / 12 (-1)

The constitution guarantees freedom of assembly. Local police must be notified in advance of any public meetings, and may prohibit such meetings. In May, security forces dispersed a protest outside parliament against a proposed increase in legislators' salaries. In August, police dispersed a protest of mine workers over an alleged breach of contract in Kwale. In November, the government attempted to block a peaceful demonstration in Nairobi against the media bills and proposals to limit foreign funding of nongovernmental organizations (NGOs).

There is freedom for Kenya's active NGO sector, but in 2013 there was a reduction in the leeway given to such groups. Nearly 200 NGOs were deregistered for alleged financial impropriety. In particular, human rights NGOs and those supportive of the ICC proceedings have been targeted. In August, security officers killed human rights activist Hassan Guyo in the northern town of Moyale, and in September unidentified gunman killed human rights lawyer Peter Wanyonyi Wanyama in the western town of Bungoma. The Law Society of Kenya also reported increased threats against its members. In October, supporters of Kenyatta in the National Assembly proposed amendments to the Public Benefit Organization Bill that would have capped foreign funding of NGOs at 15 percent, among other provisions. While these were blocked in December—amid pressure from international and domestic organizations—they nevertheless had a chilling effect.

Trade unions are active in Kenya, with approximately 40 unions representing over 1 million workers. Most of the unions are affiliated with the sole approved national federation, the Central Organization of Trade Unions. The 2007 Labor Relations Act establishes broad criteria for union registration, leaving authorities with limited grounds for suspending or refusing to register a union. However, there are restrictions on the right to strike, and the relevant government bodies have been accused of failing to adequately enforce labor laws and protections. In July 2013, a teachers' strike lasted for nearly a month. However, in September a proposed strike by the Nairobi county government over collective bargaining rights was banned.

F. Rule of Law: 6 / 16

The new constitution enhanced the independence of the judiciary. Chief Justice Willy Mutunga has built the judiciary's image as a trusted institution, and has overseen the creation of a new Supreme Court, Court of Appeal, and High Court. The new Judicial Services Commission handles the vetting and appointment of judges, and has been cited as an early success. In 2013, the judiciary received an increased budget, including the use of an aircraft to reach rural areas. However, instances of corruption at lower levels of the court have increased.

Rule of law does not prevail in many civil and criminal matters. According to a 2013 survey conducted by Transparency International Kenya, the police were considered the most corrupt institution in Kenya. The 2010 constitution created the position of police inspector general and the National Police Service Commission, meant to oversee police reform.

However, little progress has been made in this process, and in August 2013 the newly appointed police commissioner, Johnston Kavuludi, received a serious death threat.

In December 2013, the ICC prosecutor requested an adjournment in Kenyatta's case, citing the withdrawal of witnesses and a lack of cooperation from the government. During the year, several witnesses were murdered, disappeared, or subjected to violent intimidation. Despite these events, the trial of Ruto, along with his codefendant, former radio journalist Joshua arap Sang, began in September.

Kenya's Truth, Justice, and Reconciliation Commission (TJRC), formed in the aftermath of the 2007–2008 violence, released its report in May 2013. However, in December parliament passed a bill giving the National Assembly the power to amend parts of the TJRC report. That included potentially removing the names of prominent Kenyans from the report, including Kenyatta, and manipulating its findings.

There is little protection from political terror or unjustified imprisonment, especially for certain segments of the population. Arbitrary arrests, beatings, and extrajudicial killings remained prevalent in 2013. On March 30, police opened fire on a protest against the Supreme Court's election verdict in Kisumu, killing 5 people and injuring more than 20. There was evidence that the police tried to cover up this incident, which occurred in an Odinga stronghold. Prison conditions are dangerous and often life-threatening due to problems such as severe overcrowding and poor hygiene.

There were also continued tensions between security forces and Muslim populations throughout 2013. These tensions were exacerbated in the aftermath of the brutal terrorist attack launched on September 21 by Al-Shabaab at Nairobi's Westgate shopping complex in Nairobi, in which an undetermined number of heavily armed militants entered and laid siege to the mall. The security services did not regain complete control of the complex for three days. In October, the National Intelligence Service killed Sheik Ibrahim Ismail and three others in Mombasa over their alleged ties to Al-Shabaab, sparking clashes between Muslim youths and the security forces in the city. A ban on the Mombasa Republican Council—a group that advocated the secession of mainly Muslim Coast Province (which under the new constitution is now six separate districts)—continued in 2013, and the trial of seven of its leaders remained unresolved. Authorities continued to target suspected members and supporters of the group.

Significant groups and communities are not given equal treatment under the law. Kenyan security forces deliberately target ethnic Somalis—both Kenyan citizens and refugees from the war in neighboring Somalia—subjecting them to systematic arrest, torture, and rape. In recent years, there has been increased pressure to expel the nearly 500,000 Somali refugees residing in Kenya, many whom live in the massive Dadaab refugee camp. Additionally, friction between Kenya's numerous ethnic groups often leads to discrimination and violence. In late 2012 and early 2013, dozens of people were killed and thousands displaced in clashes between the Pokomo and Orma communities in the Tana River valley. Between March and June, there was a string of violent clashes between the Degodia and Gare in Wajir, in the northeast. In August, clan violence in the northern district of Moyale left approximately 20 people dead.

An estimated 200,000 people internally displaced by the 2007–2008 postelection violence still have not returned to their homes. There is evidence of discrimination during the process of resettlement and allocation of land in favor of the Kikuyu group—to which Kenyatta belongs—over the Kalenjin.

Consensual same-sex sexual activity is criminalized, with a maximum of 21 years in prison for sex between men. Members of the LGBT (lesbian, gay, bisexual, and transgender) community faced discrimination, abuse, and violent attacks in 2013.

G. Personal Autonomy and Individual Rights: 7 / 16

Citizens generally enjoy freedom of travel, residence, employment, and education. However, the prevalence of petty corruption inhibits these freedoms. There is also continued discrimination based on gender and ethnicity, as well as banditry in rural areas, that hinders these rights.

Kenyans have the right to establish private businesses, but often are required to pay petty bribes during the process. There is discrimination based on gender and ethnicity that limits access to property and economic opportunity. Criminal networks and ethnic gangs such as the Mungiki frequently impede economic activity through extortion and threats.

Rape and domestic violence are reportedly common but rarely prosecuted, and spousal rape is not criminalized. Customary law often trumps statutory law, leaving women with little legal recourse. Underage marriage is illegal but still occurs. The brutal rape of a 16-year-old girl in October, and the lenient punishment given to her attackers, sparked protest and renewed concern over gender-based violence. Female genital mutilation has declined among some ethnic groups but continues to be widely practiced among others, including the Somali and Kisii populations. Women remain underrepresented in parliament. A constitutional provision requiring that at least one-third of the members of elective bodies be women was not implemented for the 2013 elections, and there was evidence that the creation of special women's seats allowed political parties to sideline women during the primaries. Only 16 women were directly elected to the National Assembly, and none were directly elected to the Senate or to a governorship.

Kiribati

Political Rights Rating: 1
Civil Liberties Rating: 1
Freedom Rating: 1.0
Freedom Status: Free
Electoral Democracy: Yes

Population: 106,000
Capital: Tarawa

Ten-Year Ratings Timeline For Year Under Review (Political Rights, Civil Liberties, Status)

Year Under Review	2004	2005	2006	2007	2008	2009	2010	2011	2012	2013
Rating	1,1,F	1,1,F	1,1,F	1,1,F	1,1,F	1,1,F	1,1,F	1,1,F	1,1,F	1,1,F

INTRODUCTION

In June 2013, the government of Kiribati purchased 6,000 acres of land in Fiji to help prepare for damage caused by climate change; the land is intended to be used for farming in the event that rising sea levels damage Kiribati's farmland. Kiribati, which consists of 33 atolls scattered across 811 square kilometers, faces an existential threat from climate change.

Kiribati's size, remote location, and lack of resources seriously limit economic development options. The economy largely depends on interest from a trust fund built on royalties from phosphate mining, remittances from workers overseas, and foreign assistance. In September 2013, Kiribati and the United States signed a maritime boundary treaty to formalize jurisdiction over ocean resources. The treaty must be ratified by both countries before it comes into effect.

POLITICAL RIGHTS: 36 / 40
A. Electoral Process: 12 / 12

The president of Kiribati is popularly elected in a two-step process whereby the unicameral House of Parliament nominates candidates from its own ranks and voters then choose one to be president. Forty-four representatives are popularly elected to the House of Parliament for four-year terms. The attorney general holds a seat ex officio, and the Rabi Island Council nominates one additional member. (Although Rabi Island is part of Fiji, many residents were originally from Banaba Island; British authorities forced their relocation when phosphate mining made Banaba uninhabitable.) The president, vested with executive authority by the constitution, is limited to three four-year terms.

Parliamentary elections took place over two rounds in 2011. The ruling Pillars of Truth party won 15 seats, and the opposition Karikirakean Tei-Kiribati and Maurin Kiribati parties took 10 seats and 3 seats, respectively. Tong, who took office in 2003, was elected for another term in the January 2012 presidential elections.

B. Political Pluralism and Participation: 16 / 16

Citizens enjoy a high degree of political freedom. Political parties are loosely organized and generally lack fixed ideologies or formal platforms. Geography, tribal ties, and personal loyalties influence political affiliations.

C. Functioning of Government: 8 / 12

Official corruption and abuse are serious problems. International donors have demanded improvements in governance and transparency. In March 2013, Tong addressed a scandal in which Kiribati passports were allegedly sold to a firm that was reportedly a front for illegal arms shipping; Tong insisted that illegal passport sales had ended in 2004.

In August 2013, two-thirds of parliament members passed a bill to remove their parliamentary protection against civil and criminal liability for actions done or statements made in the course of their legislative duties. In September, nine lawmakers called on the president to dismiss two cabinet members for misconduct. They alleged that Teberannang Timcon, the minister for communication, transport and tourism, had received a sitting allowance of $924, which is much higher than normal, and that Kirabuke Teiaua, Minister for Energy, endorsed it. In October, both Timeon and Teiaua resigned after nine legislators called for their resignation in September. Within days, replacements were appointed and Tangariki Reete jointed the cabinet as the new Minister of Women, Youth, and Social Affairs.

CIVIL LIBERTIES: 55 / 60
D. Freedom of Expression and Belief: 15 / 16

Freedom of speech is generally respected. Several newspapers are published once or twice a week in print or online, including the *Te Ukera* (state-owned), *Te Mauri* (church-owned), and *Kiribati Star* (privately owned). The privately owned *Kiribati Independent* publishes once every two weeks, and resumed publication in January 2013 at the advice of its attorney. The government had ordered its closure in June 2012, alleging improper registration. No charges were ever filed and the government had not reported progress on its investigation. In March, poor management and financial problems forced the closure of the state-owned television station Kiribati TV, meaning there is no domestic television service. Kiribati has one state-owned and one private radio station.

There have been no reports of religious oppression or restrictions on academic freedom. Access to and the quality of education at all levels, however, is seriously restricted by a lack of resources, and secondary education is not available on all islands.

E. Associational and Organizational Rights: 12 / 12

Freedoms of assembly and association are generally respected. Many nongovernmental organizations are involved in development assistance, education, health, and advocacy for women and children. Workers have the right to organize unions, strike, and bargain collectively, though only about 10 percent of the workforce is unionized. The largest union, the Kiribati Trade Union Congress, has approximately 2,500 members. The government is the largest employer.

F. Rule of Law: 15 / 16

The judicial system is modeled on English common law and provides adequate due process rights. There is a High Court, a Court of Appeal, and magistrates' courts; final appeals go to the Privy Council in London. The president makes all judicial appointments. Traditional customs permit corporal punishment. Councils on some outer islands are used to adjudicate petty theft and other minor offenses. A 260-person police force performs law enforcement and paramilitary functions. Kiribati has no military; Australia and New Zealand provide defense assistance under bilateral agreements.

G. Personal Autonomy and Individual Rights: 13 / 16

Citizens enjoy freedom of movement, though village councils have used exile as a punishment. Discrimination against women is common in the traditional, male-dominated culture. Sexual harassment is illegal and not reported to be widespread. Spousal abuse and other forms of violence against women and children are often associated with alcohol abuse. Despite domestic and international calls for greater female participation in politics, Tong has resisted efforts to reserve a set amount of seats in parliament for female lawmakers. Tong's proposal for a ministry for women and youths in 2012 failed to receive adequate support in parliament. Kiribati is a source for sex trafficking, with girls reportedly prostituted for crew aboard foreign fishing vessels in the country's territorial waters.

Homosexuality is punishable by law and there are no protections against discrimination or hate crimes.

Kosovo

Political Rights Rating: 5
Civil Liberties Rating: 4
Freedom Rating: 4.5
Freedom Status: Partly Free
Electoral Democracy: No

Population: 1,824,000
Capital: Priština

Ten-Year Ratings Timeline For Year Under Review (Political Rights, Civil Liberties, Status)

Year Under Review	2004	2005	2006	2007	2008	2009	2010	2011	2012	2013
Rating	6,5,NF	6,5,NF	6,5,NF	6,5,NF	6,5,NF	5,4,PF	5,4,PF	5,4,PF	5,4,PF	5,4,PF

INTRODUCTION

Kosovo celebrated its fifth anniversary of independence in 2013, a year after the International Steering Group officially ended its supervisory mandate in Kosovo. At the end of 2013, 105 countries had recognized Kosovo's statehood.

During the year, Kosovo and Serbia continued to pursue a "dialogue" led by the European Union (EU). Originally launched in March 2011, the dialogue is aimed at improving bilateral relations between the two countries and putting both on the path to EU membership. In February, President Atifete Jahjaga of Kosovo met with her Serbian counterpart, Tomislav Nikolić, in Brussels, marking the first presidential meeting between the countries since Kosovo's 2008 unilateral declaration of independence from Serbia, which Belgrade continues not to recognize.

After many setbacks, the EU-led talks yielded what some called a landmark agreement in April between Prime Minister Hashim Thaçi of Kosovo and Serbia's prime minister, Ivica Dačić. Under the nuanced deal reached in Brussels, Kosovo effectively granted its Serb minority, which comprises about 9 percent of the population, increased autonomy in exchange for Belgrade's recognition of Priština's authority in majority-Serb areas, where Serbia has long funded shadow government structures. The parties also agreed not block each other's EU bids. The dialogue continued throughout 2013, as Kosovo and Serbian leaders worked to implement the April agreement.

In September, a member of the EU's rule of law mission to Kosovo, known as EULEX, was fatally shot in northern Kosovo, representing EULEX's first fatality since deploying in 2008. Also in September, an EU-led court in Kosovo acquitted Fatmir Limaj, a politician and former Kosovo Liberation Army (KLA) commander, of war crimes in the high-profile "Klecka" case. Limaj has now been acquitted of war crimes three times.

In late October, the EU and Kosovo began negotiating a Stabilization and Association Agreement, a key pre-accession instrument, with a goal of signing it in mid-2014. The negotiations marked a milestone in Kosovo's European integration efforts.

POLITICAL RIGHTS: 17 / 40 (+1)

A. Electoral Process: 6 / 12

Members of the unicameral, 120-seat Assembly are elected to four-year terms. The Assembly elects the president, who serves a five-year term. The prime minister is nominated by the president and requires Assembly approval.

Kosovo held early elections in December 2010 following the collapse of Prime Minister Thaçi's government. Significant fraud in parts of Kosovo, including vote buying, necessitated reruns in several municipalities in January 2011. Later that month, the election commission announced that Thaçi's Democratic Party of Kosovo (PDK) had won 34 seats in the Assembly, while the Democratic League of Kosovo (LDK) took 27 seats. The Vetëvendosje (Self-Determination) opposition movement finished strong in third with 14 seats.

In February 2011, parliament elected Thaçi to his second term as prime minister despite a 2010 report by Council of Europe rapporteur, Dick Marty, which linked him and other high-level Kosovo officials to an organized crime network that had been active during and after the 1998–1999 conflict with Serbia. Most controversially, the report alleged that the group harvested organs from prisoners held by the KLA.

In February 2011, parliament also elected businessman Behgjet Pacolli of the New Alliance for Kosovo (AKR) as president, but the Constitutional Court overturned Pacolli's election the following month, saying the vote had not been conducted properly. Jahjaga, then deputy director of the Kosovo police, succeeded Pacolli that April.

B. Political Pluralism and Participation: 9 / 16 (+1)

The ruling coalition—led by the PDK and a handful of smaller parties, including the AKR—has a slim parliamentary majority of 65 seats. There is little substantive difference in policy between the mainstream political parties, many of which are led by former KLA members who try to use this affiliation to attract support. The notable exception is Self-Determination, which has matured from a grassroots youth opposition movement into a legitimate, though still fringe, political party focused on affirming and defending Kosovo's national sovereignty.

In the Assembly, 10 seats are reserved for ethnic Serbs and another 10 for other ethnic minorities. While several political parties represent the Serb minority, the population itself is not fully integrated into the electoral process or Kosovo's institutions. Most Serbs in northern Kosovo boycotted the 2010 parliamentary elections, though 40 percent of the roughly 55,000 Serbs in the southern enclaves below the Ibar reportedly participated.

Belgrade has continued to fund "parallel" public health, education, and other services in majority-Serb enclaves. While these structures have weakened in southern Kosovo in recent years, the EU-led agreement made in April 2013 aimed to diminish them in the north as well. However, northern Kosovo Serb authorities do not recognize Priština's legitimacy, rejected the EU-backed deal reached in April, and created their own legislature. Northern Kosovo also saw a strong boycott movement in the November 3 local elections, and turnout was low. While voting was taking place in November in Mitrovica, a northern Kosovo town divided by the Ibar into ethnic Serb and Albanian sections, masked men entered a polling station in the northern, majority-Serb area of the city and released tear gas canisters and smashed ballot boxes. The attack prompted monitors from the Organization for Security and Cooperation in Europe (OSCE) to leave that site and two others nearby. Polls in the area were rerun later in November, with both domestic and international forces providing security. While voter turnout improved for the Mitrovica rerun compared to the first vote, overall turnout for the November polls in northern Kosovo was low.

In September 2012, the International Steering Group, a body representing 25 countries, ended its oversight of Kosovo. While considered a political "milestone," the move was largely symbolic, as North Atlantic Treaty Organization (NATO) peacekeepers, EULEX, and a scaled-back team from the UN Interim Administration Mission in Kosovo (UNMIK) continue to monitor conditions on the ground. The end of the supervisory mandate reflected progress in state-building following Kosovo's period of supervised independence. South of the Ibar, Priština has made significant advancements in the decentralization process of granting self-rule to Serb enclaves, which has helped to weaken "parallel" structures in those areas. The International Civilian Office, which oversaw legislation and decisions by the government, closed in 2012.

C. Functioning of Government: 3 / 12

Corruption remains a serious problem. A legislative framework to combat corruption is in place, including a new four-year anti-corruption strategy and action plan adopted in February 2013, but implementation is mixed. Graft and misconduct remain widespread in key areas such as law enforcement. In May 2013, the former head of Kosovo's anticorruption task force was sentenced to five years in prison for extorting money from suspects he had investigated. In June, three government officials were convicted on corruption-related charges in a high-profile case pursued by EULEX, though former deputy prime minister Bujar Bukoshi was acquitted of abuse of office and other charges. The EULEX-backed anticorruption department of the Kosovo police launched at least six investigations into abuse of office, bribery, fraud, and other crimes in 2013. Kosovo was ranked 111 out of 177 countries and territories surveyed in Transparency International's 2013 Corruption Perceptions Index.

Discretionary Political Rights Question B: -1 / 0

Despite significant improvements in conditions and government assistance over the past five years, ethnic Serbs continue to live in isolated enclaves within Kosovo, and interethnic hostility has persisted. Many displaced minorities—including the estimated 97,000 who remain in Serbia after fleeing Kosovo—have struggled to reclaim lost property and address other grievances.

CIVIL LIBERTIES: 26 / 60

D. Freedom of Expression and Belief: 8 / 16

The constitution protects freedoms of expression and the press, with exceptions for speech that provokes ethnic hostility. A wide variety of print and television outlets operate, but journalists are subject to political pressure, including from their editors; outside the newsroom, journalists report frequent harassment and intimidation, and attacks are occasionally reported. On December 1, a television news crew reported being attacked by a security guard at a municipal building in eastern Kosovo while covering a story related to November's elections. Also on December 1, unknown assailants torched the car of Fatmir Šeholi, a correspondent for the Serbian news agency Tanjug, in Gračanica, a majority-Serb municipality near the capital. In its October 2013 progress report, the European Commission (EC) urged authorities to step up efforts to investigate and prosecute attacks on journalists. In 2012, after months of outcry from local media, legislators removed provisions in the criminal code criminalizing defamation and potentially forcing journalists to reveal their sources. International officials in Kosovo have been accused of occasionally restricting media independence. Internet access is unrestricted.

The constitution guarantees religious freedom. The predominantly Muslim ethnic Albanians enjoy this right in practice, as does the Serb minority. Nevertheless, the Muslim community increasingly complains of discrimination. In 2013, Kosovo began implementing a 2012 agreement with Serbia within the EU-led dialogue to create a special multiethnic police force to better protect religious and cultural sites. Attacks on Serbian Orthodox religious sites have declined over the last decade, though several Serbian Orthodox cemeteries were desecrated in February 2013.

Academic freedom is not formally restricted, but appointments at the University of Priština are politicized. Kosovo's education system is largely segregated along ethnic lines.

E. Associational and Organizational Rights: 6 / 12

The government, EULEX, and NATO peacekeepers generally respect legislative guarantees on freedom of assembly, though demonstrations have occasionally been restricted for security reasons, and the constitution includes safeguards for public order and national security. In May 2013, thousands of people protested in Priština against the arrest of seven former KLA members on charges of war crimes. In June, police used force, including pepper spray, on protestors demonstrating against the parliament's approval of the April deal with Serbia. Nongovernmental organizations generally function freely. The courts can ban groups that infringe on the constitutional order or encourage ethnic hatred. The constitution protects the right to establish and join trade unions. However, workers face intimidation, and private sector unions are nearly nonexistent.

F. Rule of Law: 5 / 16

In 2013, authorities continued to implement reforms contained in 2010 laws on the Judicial and Prosecutorial Councils. As part of this process, a new court system was introduced in January 2013, whereby seven basic courts and one appellate court replaced the former network of municipal and district courts. The appellate court handles cases in majority-Serb municipalities, including in the north, which has lacked a fully functional judiciary capable of processing civil and criminal cases. Also in January, a new criminal code came into force, overhauling Kosovo's judicial and criminal justice systems. The new code contains provisions on corruption, organized crime, human trafficking, and other key issues. However, case backlogs remain high, and the EC has suggested that the judiciary must establish a track record of implementing the new reforms to improve independence, efficiency, and impartiality.

Ethnic Albanian officials rarely prosecute cases involving Albanian attacks on non-Albanians. In August 2013, Amnesty International (AI) slammed UNMIK, responsible for overseeing post-conflict Kosovo's security and civilian administration, for failing to investigate the abduction and murder of Kosovo Serbs after the 1998–1999 war, which allegedly contributed to a climate of impunity. EULEX has also been criticized for failing to prioritize war crimes investigations, particularly those allegedly committed by former KLA members. However, 2013 saw some progress on these issues. In November, EULEX indicted 15 former KLA members, including government officials with close ties to the ruling PDK, for allegedly abusing civilian prisoners in 1998 at a KLA detention center. The trial began in December. In an ongoing high-profile case, former KLA commander Limaj and nine other defendants stood accused in 2013 of killing and torturing ethnic Serb prisoners at a KLA detention center in the village of Klecka in 1999. While an EU-led court in September found that prisoners were "unlawfully killed" at the camp, it said the prosecution had failed to prove that Limaj and the other defendants were linked to the crimes. Prison conditions generally meet international standards despite issues such as poor medical care.

Kosovo authorities are cooperating with EULEX's investigation into the allegations in Dick Marty's 2010 report. In April 2013, a Kosovo court convicted five men from a clinic mentioned in Marty's report of participating in a 2008 organ trafficking scheme.

Kosovo's Roma, Ashkali, Gorani, and other minority populations face discrimination and difficult socioeconomic conditions.

G. Personal Autonomy and Individual Rights: 7 / 16

Freedom of movement for ethnic minorities is a significant problem; returnees to Kosovo still face hostility and bleak economic prospects, and property reclamation by displaced persons remains problematic. In September 2013, President Jahjaga signed into law an amnesty for Kosovo Serbs who had agitated against Priština's authority after 2008 in an effort to help integrate the northern Kosovo Serbs.

Kosovo's unemployment rate is 31 percent, and even higher among young people. The gray economy accounts for a considerable share of overall economic production.

Kosovo is a principal transit point along the heroin-trafficking route between Central Asia and Western Europe. Organized crime is endemic, especially in northern Kosovo.

Patriarchal attitudes often limit women's ability to gain an education or secure employment. Women are underrepresented in politics despite rules that they must occupy every third spot on each party's candidate list. Women in rural areas remain effectively disenfranchised through family voting—in which the male head of a household casts ballots for the entire family—though attitudes toward women's rights continue to liberalize in urban areas. Domestic violence is a serious problem, as is discrimination against sexual minorities. LGBT persons face societal pressure to hide their sexual orientation or gender identity. Kosovo is a source, transit point, and destination for human trafficking.

Kuwait

Political Rights Rating: 5
Civil Liberties Rating: 5
Freedom Ratings: 5.0
Freedom Status: Partly Free
Electoral Democracy: No

Population: 3,500,000
Capital: Kuwait City

Ten-Year Ratings Timeline For Year Under Review (Political Rights, Civil Liberties, Status)

Year Under Review	2004	2005	2006	2007	2008	2009	2010	2011	2012	2013
Rating	4,5,PF	4,5,PF	4,4,PF	4,4,PF	4,4,PF	4,4,PF	4,5,PF	4,5,PF	5,5,PF	5,5,PF

INTRODUCTION

Kuwait's political tensions and suppression of critical speech continued in 2013 as a result of the country's ongoing parliamentary crisis. In June the country's Constitutional Court threw out the December 2012 elections and in July voters took to the polls for the sixth time in six years. Islamist and liberal candidates won a majority of seats. The country's outspoken opposition boycotted the vote and remains mostly unrepresented in government.

The government continued to deal with criticism harshly throughout the year. Although the number of protests declined in 2013, security forces still forcefully suppressed public gatherings. Authorities also systematically sought to crush any expression of criticism, most notably by continuing to crackdown on dissent on social media platforms like Twitter and Facebook. Dozens of activists were sentenced to lengthy prison terms during the year on charges of criticizing Kuwait's emir, Sheik Sabah al-Ahmed al-Sabah. Included among those charged or imprisoned for criticizing the country's rulers were the journalists Zayed al-Zaid and Ayyad al-Harbi as well as Mussallam al-Barak, a former MP. During Ramadan, the emir issued a blanket pardon for those convicted of criticizing him, although prosecutions of critical speech began again in October.

POLITICAL RIGHTS: 16 / 40 (-1)

A. Electoral Process: 2 / 12

The emir appoints the prime minister and cabinet and shares legislative power with the 50-member National Assembly, which is elected to four-year terms by popular vote. The emir has the authority to dissolve the National Assembly at will but must call elections within 60 days. The parliament can overturn decrees issued by the emir while it is not in session. It can also veto the appointment of the country's prime minister, but it then must choose from among three alternates put forward by the emir. The parliament also has the power to remove government ministers with a majority vote. The electorate consists of men and women over 21 years of age who have been citizens for at least 20 years; members of most security forces are barred from voting.

Controversy over Kuwait's parliamentary elections sparked widespread protest and unrest in 2012. In the February 2012 parliamentary elections, opposition candidates gained a majority of seats. The emir suspended parliament after Kuwaiti MPs, concerned about government corruption, challenged the authority of the al-Sabah family, and sought to investigate allegations of graft among the emir's cabinet members. In June 2012, Kuwait's Constitutional Court tossed out the results of the February elections ruling the emir's December 2011 dissolution of the government was unconstitutional. Tens of thousands of Kuwaitis responded by holding regular protests, with hundreds being injured by a harsh security response. The opposition boycotted the second 2012 elections, leading progovernment candidates to capture the majority of seats.

The parliamentary crisis spilled over into 2013. In June the Constitutional Court once again ordered the dissolution of the parliament after opposition challenges to new electoral laws were dismissed. Although the country's opposition leaders continued to boycott and criticize the government, the protest movement from the previous fall had largely run out of steam by mid-year. The country held its third round of parliamentary elections in 16 months in July. Over 400 candidates ran for office. Turnout was around 50 percent for the July elections. Only two women were elected. Shiites lost more than half their seats from December, winning only 8 seats. The emir reappointed Jaber Mubarak al Hamad al-Sabah as prime minister and the cabinet was sworn in in August.

B. Political Pluralism and Participation: 9 / 16 (-1)

Formal political parties are banned. While political groupings, such as parliamentary blocs, have been allowed to emerge, the government has impeded their activities through harassment and arrests. In October 2012, the emir issued a royal decree reducing the number of candidates each voter could vote for from four to one, a move the opposition claims was designed to limit their power. While the opposition has the right to run for office, the country's long-standing political crisis and the opposition's year-long boycott has left them under-represented in parliament.

C. Functioning of Government: 5 / 12

Charges of government corruption were at the heart of the 2012 crisis, and the opposition continues to pressure the government to address this problem. In August 2011, allegations emerged that up to 18 members of parliament received large cash deposits into their personal bank accounts. The transactions have widely been interpreted as evidence of government bribery and fueled protests in the fall of 2011 that spilled over into 2012. Parliamentary efforts to investigate corruption have been obstructed by the government. In May 2012, a commission established by the government concluded its investigation into the August case after claiming it found no evidence of fraud. In October 2012, the public prosecutor formally ended the state's inquiry, also citing lack of evidence. Kuwait ranks 69 out of 177 in Transparency International's 2013 Corruption Perceptions Index.

CIVIL LIBERTIES: 23 / 60 (-1)
D. Freedom of Expression and Belief: 6 / 16 (-1)

Kuwaiti authorities continue to limit press freedom. Kuwaiti law punishes the publication of material that insults Islam, criticizes the emir or the government, discloses secret or private information, or calls for the regime's overthrow. In April the government proposed a new law that called for a $1 million fine for criticizing the emir. The law remained pending at the end of the year. Several journalists and citizens were prosecuted in 2013 for criticizing the emir, either on Twitter, in the press, or in public speeches. Among the most prominent, the journalist Ayyad al-Harbi from the website Sabr, was sentenced to two years in prison in January for criticizing the emir. Others sent to prison for using Twitter to criticize the government included Rashed al-Enezi, who received a two-year sentence in January and Muhammad Eid al-Ajmi, who was sentenced to five years. In June, school teacher Huda al-Ajmi was sentenced to 11 years for her criticism of the government on Twitter. Zayed al-Zaid who works for the website Alaan was jailed in February for a month for alleging government corruption. Former MP Musallam al-Barrak, who was arrested in 2012 on charges of having "undermined the status of the emir" was sentenced to five years in April for criticizing the emir, although that charge was overturned in May on appeal. He continued to face other charges and possible imprisonment for leading the 2012 protest movement. Three former MPs, Falah al-Sawagh, Badir al-Dahoom, and Khalid al-Tahoos who were sentenced to three years in jail in February for criticizing the emir at a public rally, had their jail terms thrown out on appeal in July. In late July, during the last week of Ramadan, the emir pardoned all of those convicted of insulting him earlier in the year.

In April 2012, parliament passed a new law criminalizing blasphemy, making insulting the prophet Muhammad a capital offense, though the law was rejected by the emir.

Kuwait has more than 10 daily and weekly Arabic newspapers and two English-language dailies and all are privately owned. The state owns four television stations and nine radio stations, but there are also a number of private outlets, including the satellite television station Al-Rai. Foreign media outlets have generally operated relatively freely in Kuwait. Kuwaitis enjoy access to the internet, though the government has instructed internet service providers to block certain sites for political or moral reasons.

Islam is the state religion, but religious minorities are generally permitted to practice their faiths in private. Shiite Muslims, who make up around a third of the population, enjoy full political rights but have experienced a rise in harassment in the aftermath of the Iraq war and the uprising in Bahrain. Kuwaiti Salafis and Sunni Islamists have criticized the country's Shiites for alleged links to Iran. In September, authorities banned the popular Sunni cleric Shafi al-Ajmi from appearing on television after he criticized Shiites and expressed support for al-Qaeda affiliated groups operating in Syria. Five other clerics were suspended in September for supporting the toppled Muslim Brotherhood in Egypt and for supporting the Islamist rebels in Syria during their Friday sermons. Academic freedom is generally respected. Kuwait allows relatively open and free private discussion, often conducted in traditional gatherings (*diwaniyat*) that typically only include men.

E. Associational and Organizational Rights: 4 / 12

Freedoms of assembly and association are guaranteed by law, though the government constrains these rights in practice. Kuwaitis must notify authorities of a public meeting or protest, but the authorities allowed some peaceful protests to take place without a permit. Peaceful demonstrations were held throughout 2012, mostly in response to charges of government corruption and the parliamentary crisis. In October 2012, the government declared that public assemblies of more than 20 people were illegal. Tens of thousands of demonstrators routinely defied the new restrictions, prompting police to respond with tear gas and violence to disperse crowds; hundreds were injured. Small protests continued into the early part of 2013, although they decreased over the spring and summer. Police continued to forcefully break up public gatherings in 2013. In December Kuwaiti courts acquitted 70 citizens, including ex-MP Musallem Barak, of criminal charges after they stormed the parliament in 2011.

Members of Kuwait's more than 100,000 stateless residents, known as *bidoon*, have also staged regular protests over the last two years calling for greater rights. They are considered illegal residents, do not have full citizenship rights, and often live in wretched conditions. In January 2012, the government announced that it would deport bidoon who participated in protests, throw out their citizenship applications, and dismiss those serving in the army if they or their family members were determined to have participated in demonstrations. In March 2013, parliament passed a bill that would begin granting citizenship to 4,000 of the country's stateless residents.

The government routinely restricts the registration and licensing of nongovernmental organizations (NGOs), forcing dozens of groups to operate without legal standing or state assistance. Representatives of licensed NGOs must obtain government permission to attend foreign conferences. Non-public sector workers have the right to join labor unions and bargain collectively, but Kuwait's labor law mandates that there be only one union per occupational trade. Migrant workers enjoy limited legal protections against mistreatment or abuse by employers.

F. Rule of Law: 7 / 16

Kuwait lacks an independent judiciary. The emir appoints all judges, and the executive branch approves judicial promotions. Authorities may detain suspects for four days without charge. Detainees, especially bidoon, have been subjected to torture. In 2011, police arrested a Kuwaiti citizen, Mohammed al-Mutairi, for alcohol possession, which is illegal in Kuwait. A parliamentary investigation revealed that authorities tortured al-Mutairi for six days before killing him and then engaged in a cover-up. Controversy surrounding the case forced the resignation of Minister of the Interior Sheikh Jaber al-Khaled al-Sabah in February 2011, and 16 police officers were brought up on charges. In January 2012, two of the officers were sentenced to life in prison but in June 2013, their sentences were increased to the death penalty by Kuwait's highest court. Four others received sentences of 15 to 16 years. Three other officers received smaller sentences ranging from two years in prison to fines, while the remaining officers were acquitted. The government permits visits by human rights activists to prisons, where overcrowding remains a problem.

G. Personal Autonomy and Individual Rights: 6 / 16

The 1962 constitution provides men and women with equal rights. Kuwaiti women have the right to vote and run as candidates in parliamentary and local elections. For the first time in Kuwait's history, four women won seats in the 2009 parliamentary elections. Three Kuwaiti women were victorious in the December 2012 vote. In the July 2013 elections only two won seats. Women also comprise more than 60 percent of the student body at several leading Kuwaiti universities. Nevertheless, women face discrimination in several areas of law and society and remain underrepresented in the workforce. Women are offered some legal protections from abuse and discrimination, but they are only permitted to seek a divorce in cases where they have been deserted or subjected to domestic violence. Women must have a male guardian in order to marry and are eligible for only one half of their brother's inheritance. As of 2009, married women have the right to obtain passports and to travel without their husband's permission. Domestic abuse and sexual harassment are not specifically prohibited by law, and foreign domestic servants remain particularly vulnerable to abuse and sexual assault.

Same-sex sexual activity is illegal in Kuwait and is punishable by up to ten years in prison. In October officials from the Health Ministry called for clinical tests to be held at Kuwait's port's of entry in an attempt to identify and bar LGBT people from entering Kuwait or any of the other Gulf Cooperation Council countries. Transgender women reportedly face abuse from officials and are subject to prosecution under a 2007 law that criminalizes "imitating the opposite sex."

Kyrgyzstan

Political Rights Rating: 5
Civil Liberties Rating: 5
Freedom Score: 5.0
Freedom Status: Partly Free
Electoral Democracy: No

Population: 5,665,000
Capital: Bishkek

Ten-Year Ratings Timeline For Year Under Review (Political Rights, Civil Liberties, Status)

Year Under Review	2004	2005	2006	2007	2008	2009	2010	2011	2012	2013
Rating	6,5,NF	5,4,PF	5,4,PF	5,4,PF	5,4,PF	6,5,NF	5,5,PF	5,5,PF	5,5,PF	5,5,PF

INTRODUCTION

In 2013, the administration of President Almazbek Atambayev continued to use questionable legal maneuvers to persecute political opponents, while corruption remained a serious issue. Kyrgyzstan remained sharply divided along ethnic lines, and ongoing nationalist protests threatened foreign investment, nearly crippled the country's important tourism sector, and pushed the state into a risky renegotiation with its largest investor.

Azimjon Askarov, an ethnic Uzbek independent journalist and human rights defender, remained in prison in 2013, serving a life sentence on charges of inciting ethnic hatred and complicity in the murder of an ethnic Kyrgyz police officer during the June 2010 violence. It is widely believed that he was prosecuted in retribution for his reporting on issues such as police corruption.

POLITICAL RIGHTS: 14 / 40
Electoral Process: 6 / 12

Constitutional changes adopted in 2010 expanded the unicameral parliament from 90 to 120 deputies, with no party allowed to hold more than 65 seats. Parliamentary elections are to be held every five years. The president, who shares executive power with the prime minister, serves a single six-year term with no possibility of reelection and has the power to veto legislation.

The changes were adopted amid political and ethnic upheaval in the country. In April 2010, then president Kurmanbek Bakiyev fled the country amid antigovernment protests in Bishkek, leading to the formation of an interim government. In June 2010, ethnic rioting swept the southern cities of Osh and Jalalabad, leaving at least 470 people dead. Ethnic Uzbeks suffered the brunt of the violence, and local security forces were accused of abetting attacks on Uzbek communities. Later the same month, a referendum that international observers deemed generally fair confirmed longtime opposition figure Roza Otunbayeva as interim president through December 2011 and approved the constitutional reforms.

Parliamentary elections held in October 2010 were deemed a significant improvement over a deeply flawed 2007 vote by Organization for Security and Cooperation in Europe (OSCE) observers. The nationalist Ata-Jurt party led with 28 of 120 seats, followed by Otunbayeva's Social Democratic Party of Kyrgyzstan (SDPK) with 26, Ar-Namys with 25, Respublika with 23, and Ata-Meken with 18. Ata-Jurt, the SDPK, and Respublika formed a coalition government in December, leaving Ar-Namys and Ata-Meken in opposition. Atambayev, of the SDPK, became prime minister. The coalition remained stable but failed to coordinate on a legislative agenda before the October 2011 presidential election.

The presidential poll was seen by the OSCE observers as free and competitive, though marred widespread problems with voter lists and numerous faults in the tabulation process. Atambayev defeated 15 other candidates and took 63 percent of the vote. In December, a new coalition composed of the SDPK, Respublika, Ata-Meken, and Ar-Namys was formed, with Omurbek Babanov of Respublika as prime minister. The coalition lasted eight months, collapsing in August 2012 after Babanov and Atambayev publicly clashed over their respective roles under the new constitution, revealing unsettled legal issues with the semi-presidential/parliamentary system that have yet to be resolved. In September, the SDPK took the lead in a new coalition with Ata-Meken and Ar-Namys, and Jantoro Satybaldiyev, a close ally of the president, became prime minister.

Local elections were held in August 2013; violence broke out between opposing parties in Kara-Su over accusations of ballot stuffing, leaving one person stabbed and another shot.

B. Political Pluralism and Participation: 6 / 16

Kyrgyzstani citizens have the freedom to organize their own political parties and groupings, especially at the local level, but thresholds for electoral support in every region prevent locally organized groups from participating in national politics. For example, the Uluttar Birimdigi party, which won 2012 city council elections in Osh (amid widespread reports of voter intimidation) and is represented by Osh mayor Melis Myrzakmatov, has no national representation and is unlikely to achieve it due to the regionally divided political landscape. Political parties remain primarily the extension of a single strong personality, rather than ideological organizations with political platforms they seek to implement.

The aim of the 2010 constitutional reforms was to ensure political pluralism and prevent the reemergence of an authoritarian, superpresidential system. Since 2012, however, observers have noted signs that Atambayev was beginning to reclaim powers given to the prime minister's office under the new constitutional rules and to use the executive branch to target political enemies. Atambaev's SDPK party has been accused by opposition members and outside observers alike of using centralized resources to determine electoral and judicial outcomes, and opposition parties often react with protests that sometimes turn violent. Although the presidential administration has used party mechanisms to control government appointments, the parliament itself does function separately from the executive and the propresidential party does not have a majority. In March 2013, three leading lawmakers from the opposition Ata-Jurt party—Kamchybek Tashiev, Sadyr Japarov, and Talant Mamytov—were convicted on questionable charges of attempting to violently overthrow the government and sentenced to 12 to 18 months in prison. They had been arrested in 2012 after holding a nonviolent protest in Bishkek to demand the nationalization of a gold mine run by a Canadian company. In a June 2013 appeal hearing, protesters supporting the lawmakers stormed the courtroom and attacked the judges, who subsequently overthrew the conviction. In August, the Supreme Court restored their convictions and the Central Election Commission stripped them of their seats in the parliament. In October, Atambaev personally fired the two judges who had granted the opposition appeal, which opposition members claimed as evidence for their argument that the prosecution was politicized from the beginning.

C. Functioning of Government: 4 / 12

Corruption is pervasive in Kyrgyz society, and despite many rounds of constitutional and statutory changes, Kyrgyzstan has been trapped in a cycle of predatory political elites who rotate from opposition to power and use government resources to reward clients and punish opponents. The nepotistic practices of Bakiyev, whose sons and brothers were prominent in business and government, were a significant source of popular dissatisfaction prior to his ouster in 2010. The interim government charged some members of the Bakiyev regime with corruption, but the results in the largely unreformed courts have been inconclusive.

A new anticorruption office within the State Committee of National Security (GKNB) was formed in 2012. Although the office was initially used to target the administration's political enemies in Parliament or city government, in March 2013, it arrested Rakhmatillo Amiraev, head of the Kyrgyz Interior Ministry Academy, and his deputy for accepting bribes. The corruption service continues to target only high-profile cases inside the government, without making meaningful efforts to combat institutional corruption at all levels. Alleged corruption among traffic police has led to public safety hazards and chaos on Kyrgyzstan's roads.

In April 2013, convicted criminal Aziz Batukaev was released from prison, where he was serving a 16-year sentence for multiple murders, on what was later proved to be a fraudulent medical leave to treat leukemia. He subsequently fled to Chechnya; investigations later revealed that he had lived a life of privilege in prison. Deputy Prime Minister Shamil Atakhanov resigned in the wake of the revelations. Kyrgyzstan was ranked 150 out of 177 countries and territories surveyed in Transparency International's 2013 Corruption Perceptions Index.

Discretionary Political Rights Question B: -2 / 0

Southern Kyrgyzstan has yet to fully recover from the ethnic upheaval of June 2010, which included numerous, documented instances of government involvement or connivance in ethnically motivated violence against ethnic Uzbeks in the region with the aim of tipping the political and economic balance in favor of the Kyrgyz elite. The some initial steps have been made to restore Uzbek-language media, the political economy of the South remains deeply altered.

CIVIL LIBERTIES: 25 / 60
D. Freedom of Expression and Belief: 9 / 16

The media landscape remained bifurcated along ethnic lines in 2013, with improved conditions for Kyrgyz-language media since 2010 and continuing challenges for both Uzbek-language outlets and critical Russian-language media. Independent Uzbek-language media virtually ceased to exist in southern Kyrgyzstan after the June 2010 ethnic violence, as several Uzbek television and radio outlets were closed down. A small number of outlets have opened, but Uzbek media representation remains a small fraction of what it was before the conflict and staff for remaining publications continued to be persecuted. Prosecutions for inciting hatred have focused exclusively on minority writers despite the prevalence of openly racist and anti-Semitic articles in Kyrgyz-language media. In March 2013, police raided the Russian-language opposition paper *Tribuna* on an "anonymous tip" and claimed to find grenades stored in its offices. Later that month, the editor of one of the only remaining Uzbek language newspapers was arrested on charges related to the disappearance of an ethnic Kyrgyz resident during the ethnic violence of 2010. The government removed a block, however, on the Russia-based Central Asian news website Ferghananews.com.

The government has generally permitted a broad range of religious practices, but all religious organizations must register with the authorities, a process that is often cumbersome and arbitrary. Proselytizing, private religious education, and the wearing of headscarves in schools were banned in 2009. The government monitors and restricts Islamist groups that it regards as a threat to national security, particularly Hizb ut-Tahrir, an ostensibly nonviolent international movement calling for the creation of a caliphate.

The government does not formally restrict academic freedom. In May, Aleksander Knyazev, a former professor at Bishkek's Kyrgyz-Slavic University and outspoken ethnic Russian critic of the government, was denied reentry to the country.

E. Associational and Organizational Rights: 5 / 12

Tight official restrictions on freedom of assembly have not been altered since the Bakiyev era, but enforcement has been eased considerably in practice. Small protests and civil disobedience demonstrations, such as road blocking, continue to be held regularly.

Nongovernmental organizations (NGOs) participate actively in civic and political life, and public advisory councils were established in the parliament and most ministries in 2011, permitting improved monitoring and advocacy by NGOs. However, rising nationalism continues to affect both ethnic Kyrgyz and ethnic Uzbek NGO activists. Human rights workers who support Uzbek abuse victims continue to face threats, harassment, and physical attacks. In October, parliament considered legislation against "foreign agent" NGOs similar to what was enacted in Russia in June but ultimately declined to enact it after criticism from NGOs, the press and foreign governments. Azimjon Askarov, an ethnic Uzbek independent journalist and human rights defender, remained in prison in 2013, serving a life sentence on charges of inciting ethnic hatred and complicity in the murder of an ethnic Kyrgyz police officer during the June 2010 violence. It is widely believed that he was prosecuted in retribution for his reporting on issues such as police corruption.

The law provides for the formation of trade unions, and unions are generally able to operate without obstruction. However, strikes are prohibited in many sectors. Legal enforcement of union rights is weak, and collective bargaining agreements are not always respected by employers.

F. Rule of Law: 4 / 16

The judiciary is not independent and remains dominated by the executive branch. Corruption among judges, who are underpaid, is widespread. Defendants' rights, including the presumption of innocence, are not always respected, and there are credible reports of torture during arrest and interrogation.

The ongoing trials of the Bakiyev family and their accomplices, including a case against 28 former government officials and special forces members for the alleged killing of 86 demonstrators in April 2010, have been marred by numerous procedural violations and threats against lawyers in the courtroom. Additionally, Human Rights Watch has documented systematic rights violations at trials of ethnic Uzbeks in 2010 and 2011, with defendants attacked in courtrooms, tortured in detention, and convicted on flimsy or fabricated evidence. The legal proceedings in these cases have been marked by protests against prosecutors, witness intimidation, and multiple venue changes. In April 2013 the lawyers for an ethnic Uzbek from Jalalabad were attacked inside the Supreme Court, where their client's January acquittal of 2010 murder charges was being appealed by prosecutors.

The widespread and extensively documented violence against the Uzbek community in southern Kyrgyzstan in 2010 cast a harsh light on the plight of ethnic minorities. Uzbeks, who make up nearly half of the population in Osh, had long demanded more political and cultural rights, including greater representation in government, more Uzbek-language schools, and official status for the Uzbek language. Osh mayor Melis Myrzakmatov was dismissed in December 2013 without protests and threats of riots that occurred when the Provisional Government attempted to remove him in 2010; he is blamed by many for facilitating the 2010 violence, anti-Uzbek sentiment and obstructing justice for Uzbeks after the violence.

Same-sex sexual activity is not illegal, but the LGBT (lesbian, gay, bisexual, and transgender) community reportedly faces severe discrimination and the risk of abuse, including by police.

G. Personal Autonomy and Individual Rights: 7 / 16

The government generally respects the right of unrestricted travel to and from Kyrgyzstan. However, barriers to internal migration include a requirement that citizens obtain permits to work and settle in particular areas of the country.

Personal connections, corruption, organized crime, and widespread poverty limit business competition and equality of opportunity. Companies that had belonged to the Bakiyev family were nationalized in 2010 pending a new process of privatization. That year's ethnic violence affected property rights in the south, as many businesses, mainly owned by ethnic Uzbeks, were destroyed or seized. In 2013, nationalist politicians and multiple protests supporting them called for the state to seize assets held by foreign companies, especially in the mining sector. Massive protests and clashes with police in the Issyk Kul region led the government to temporarily declare a state of emergency in late May. In October, the provincial governor of Issyl Kul was briefly held hostage in a gasoline-soaked car and threatened with immolation unless the state nationalized its largest mine, Kumtor. Nationalist thugs frequently attack foreign mining operations, often with no interference from local authorities, and in August video evidence emerged of local strongmen who claimed to be backed by national politicians attempting to extort $3 million from Canadian mining company Centerra to prevent further protests or even a "revolution."

Despite achieving notable leadership positions, women remain underrepresented in high levels of government. Cultural traditions and apathy among law enforcement officials discourage victims of domestic violence and rape from contacting the authorities. An international inquiry criticized the government response to rape cases from the 2010 ethnic violence as "inadequate if not obstructive," and female victims of sexual violence were not eligible for compensation given by the state to others who suffered physical or economic harm in the turmoil.

The trafficking of women and girls into forced prostitution abroad is a serious problem, and some victims report that the authorities are involved in trafficking. The practice of bride abduction persists despite being illegal, and few perpetrators are prosecuted. In January 2013, Atambaev signed a law to increase the maximum penalty for the crime from 3 years in prison to 10, and legally obligated prosecutors to investigate it regardless of whether the victim presses charges. Interviews with human rights activists in 2013 indicated the law was slow to change patterns of prosecution or social attitudes.

Laos

Political Rights Rating: 7
Civil Liberties Rating: 6
Freedom Rating: 6.5
Freedom Status: Not Free
Electoral Democracy: No

Population: 6,700,000
Capital: Vientiane

Ten-Year Ratings Timeline For Year Under Review (Political Rights, Civil Liberties, Status)

Year Under Review Rating	2004	2005	2006	2007	2008	2009	2010	2011	2012	2013
	7,6,NF	7,6,NF	7,6,NF	7,6,NF	7,6,NF	7,6,NF	7,6,NF	7,6,NF	7,6,NF	7,6,NF

INTRODUCTION

The Lao government in 2013 continued to pursue economic opening while maintaining tight control over political space. The government drew international criticism throughout the year for failing to investigate the December 2012 disappearance of international antipoverty activist Sombath Somphone, who remained missing at year's end.

Having won 128 of 132 seats in 2011 elections, the Lao People's Revolutionary Party (LPRP), the only party allowed under the constitution, maintained its control over the National Assembly. Though the Assembly is largely a rubber-stamp legislature, it has undertaken a more active and ambitious legislative agenda in recent years. The LPRP's economic aspirations for the country have fostered tangible improvements in Laos' legal framework in recent years.

Laos was formally approved for entry to the World Trade Organization (WTO) in October 2012 and joined the organization in February 2013. In order to accede to the WTO, the government adopted dozens of legal reforms to meet international standards in areas ranging from intellectual property rights to environmental protection. Such reforms are not expected to foster significant political opening, but may lay a foundation for increasing rule of law and good governance in the coming years.

Preparations for the controversial Xayaburi and Don Sahong dams on the Mekong River continue despite major concerns over their impact on the livelihoods of thousands of Lao and on the environment. The Lao government in 2013 also furthered controversial Chinese-backed infrastructure projects amid continued strong bilateral relations with China. The Lao government's decision in 2013 to construct a $7.2-billion rail line through a loan from China, whose costs some estimates showed totaling more than 80 percent of the country's GDP, drew criticism as a fiscally irresponsible venture that demonstrated authorities' lack of attention to the country's needs.

POLITICAL RIGHTS: 1 / 40 (+1)

A. Electoral Process: 0 / 12

The 1991 constitution makes the LPRP the sole legal political party and grants it a leading role at all levels of government. The party's 61-member Central Committee and 11-member Politburo make all major decisions. Legislative elections are held every five years but elections are not considered free and fair. The LPRP vets all candidates for election to the National Assembly, whose members elect the president. In 2011 the legislature increased in size from 115 members to 132. International observers have not been permitted to monitor elections.

B. Political Pluralism and Participation: 0 / 16

The constitution prohibits political parties other than the LPRP. National Assembly candidates are not required to be members of the LPRP, but all candidates have to be approved by Assembly-appointed committees and in practice almost all are members of the party.

Ethnic minorities and women are represented in the Politburo, Central Committee, and National Assembly. However, village-level leadership is responsible for many of the decisions affecting daily life and fewer than 3 percent of village chiefs are women.

C. Functioning of Government: 1 / 12 (+1)

The National Assembly has grown more robust and responsive in recent years. It had reportedly produced 90 pieces of updated or new legislation in recent years in order to meet international legal standards required for WTO accession. In 2012, the Assembly passed the Law on Making Legislation, which increases legislative transparency by requiring proposed bills at the central and provincial levels to be published for comment for 60 days and, once passed, to be posted for 15 days before coming into force. The government is increasingly using laws, rather than decrees, to govern, though there is still little room for the public to influence policy.

Corruption by government officials is widespread. Laws aimed at curbing graft are rarely enforced, and government regulation of virtually every facet of life provides many opportunities for bribery. Displacement of villagers for dams and other government projects without proper compensation is common, though some in the government have begun to talk seriously about a strategy to address the country's land issues. Senior officials in government and the military are sometimes involved in commercial logging, mining, and other extractive enterprises. Laos was ranked 140 out of 177 countries surveyed in Transparency International's 2013 Corruption Perceptions Index.

CIVIL LIBERTIES: 11 / 40

D. Freedom of Expression and Belief: 4 / 16

Self-censorship is extremely high, and authorities use legal and intimidation tactics against critics of the state. The state owns nearly all media, though some non-government outlets, primarily Chinese entertainment magazines, have cropped up in recent years. A few independent local-interest radio shows have emerged. Journalists who criticize the government or discuss controversial issues risk punishment under the criminal code. Some Lao can access Radio Free Asia and other foreign broadcasts from Thailand. The Ministry of Information, Communication, and Technology in January 2012 ordered off the air the country's first call-in radio show, "Wao Kao," for discussing land grabs and other sensitive issues. While few Lao have access to the internet, online content is not heavily censored owing to a lack of government capacity to monitor and block access.

Religious freedom is constrained. The religious practice of the majority Buddhist population is somewhat restricted through the LPRP's control of clergy training and supervision of temples. Discrimination against animists and other non-Buddhists does occur. Christians enjoy somewhat more freedom to worship, though the government has arrested practitioners for proselytizing.

Academic freedom is not respected. University professors cannot teach or write about politically sensitive topics, though Laos has invited select foreign academics to teach courses in the country, and some young people go overseas for university education. Government surveillance of the population has been scaled back in recent years, but searches without warrants still occur.

E. Associational and Organizational Rights: 0 / 12

The government severely restricts freedom of assembly, prohibiting participation in organizations that engage in demonstrations or public protests, or that in any other way cause "turmoil or social instability." Protests are rare and violators can receive sentences of up to five years in prison. Two activists arrested in 1999 for participating in a peaceful protest remain behind bars on charges of treason. After signing the International Covenant on Civil and Political Rights in 2009, Laos created a legal framework for nongovernmental organizations (NGOs), allowing such groups to be licensed. This law has affected primarily foreign NGOs, which have proliferated in the country in recent years. There are some domestic nongovernmental welfare and professional groups, but they are prohibited from pursuing political agendas and are subject to strict state control. Reports of the government prohibiting NGOs to meet with villagers relocated to make way for a power plant surfaced in 2013. Despite significant international pressure, the disappearance of development activist Sombath Somphone, last seen taken by police in December 2012, remains unsolved.

All unions must belong to the official Lao Federation of Trade Unions. Strikes are not expressly prohibited, but workers rarely stage walkouts, and they do not have the right to bargain collectively.

F. Rule of Law: 2 / 16

The courts are corrupt and controlled by the LPRP. The U.S. Embassy in March accused the Lao government of blocking a U.S. investigation into the whereabouts of three missing Lao-Americans. Long procedural delays are common, particularly for cases dealing with public grievances. Security forces often illegally detain suspects. Torture of prisoners is occasionally reported and prisoners must bribe officials to obtain better food, medicine, family visits, and more humane treatment.

Discrimination against members of ethnic minority tribes is common. The Hmong, who fielded a guerrilla army allied with U.S. forces during the Vietnam War, are particularly distrusted by the government and face harsh treatment. Although some Hmong who are loyal to the LPRP have been elected to the national legislature, poorer and more rural Hmong have been forced off their land to make way for extractive industries. The government restricts the activity of over 4,000 Hmong who were forcibly repatriated from Thailand in 2009 and living in camps in Borikhamxay province.

Refugees who arrive in Laos are often mistreated and deported. Despite international opposition, authorities in May deported nine young North Korean defectors for repatriation.

G. Personal Autonomy and Individual Rights: 5 / 16

All land is owned by the state, though citizens have rights to use it. On some occasions, the government has awarded land to citizens with government connections, money, or links to foreign companies. Traditional land rights still exist in some areas, adding to confusion and conflict over access. With no fair or robust system to protect land rights or ensure compensation for displacement, development projects often spur public resentment. The Xayaburi dam, a $3.5-billion venture that would be used primarily to sell electricity to Thailand, has displaced over 900 people and activists say it will negatively affect the livelihoods of 200,000 more. Plans for another major dam downstream, the Don Sahong dam, are underway.

Marriage to foreign citizens requires approval by the government.

Although laws guarantee women many of the same rights as men, gender-based discrimination and abuse are widespread. Tradition and religious practices have contributed to women's inferior access to education, employment opportunities, and worker benefits. Trafficking in persons, especially to Thailand, is high. The Lao government adopted in 2012 a national action plan to combat trafficking, though little substantive action has followed and, according to the U.S. Trafficking in Persons Report 2013, rates of prosecution and conviction of accused traffickers declined in 2012.

Latvia

Political Rights Rating: 2
Civil Liberties Rating: 2
Freedom Rating: 2.0
Freedom Status: Free
Electoral Democracy: Yes

Population: 2,000,000
Capital: Riga

Ten-Year Ratings Timeline For Year Under Review (Political Rights, Civil Liberties, Status)

Year Under Review	2004	2005	2006	2007	2008	2009	2010	2011	2012	2013
Rating	1,2,F	1,1,F	1,1,F	2,1,F	2,1,F	2,1,F	2,2,F	2,2,F	2,2,F	2,2,F

INTRODUCTION

In January 2013, Latvia's parliament (Saeima) passed legislation aimed at adopting the euro currency, and President Andris Bērziņš signed the law the following month. In July, European Union (EU) officials gave final approval for Latvia to adopt the euro, which it was expected to do at the start of 2014. However, Latvian residents remained wary of the ongoing sovereign-debt crisis within the eurozone, and there was little public enthusiasm for joining the bloc. Harmony Center—a leftist party that draws significant support from Latvia's Russian-speaking population and opposed the country's adoption of the euro—performed strongly in municipal elections held in June. The party has campaigned against austerity programs enacted since the global economic downturn began in 2008.

The parliament passed legislation in June banning the display of Soviet and Nazi symbols at public events, but President Bērziņš had not signed the law by year's end. In October, amendments to Latvia's citizenship law, approved by the parliament in May, took effect. The amendments allow many Latvians living abroad to become dual citizens, and provide newborns, regardless of where they were born, with citizenship if at least one parent is a Latvian citizen. The law also grants children of noncitizens born after August 1991 Latvian citizenship if they are already permanent residents and if their parents pledge to help them learn the Latvian language, a provision previously criticized by the Organization for Security and Cooperation in Europe (OSCE) as restrictive.

In November, Prime Minister Valdis Dombrovskis resigned over a deadly accident at a Riga supermarket in which 54 people were killed when the roof caved in, saying he took "political responsibility" for the disaster. His resignation was unexpected, as he had not faced notable criticism over the accident. Snap elections were not expected, as parliamentary polls were already set for October 2014. However, a permanent government had yet to be formed by the end of the year.

POLITICAL RIGHTS: 33 / 40

A. Electoral Process: 12 / 12

The Latvian constitution provides for a unicameral, 100-seat parliament, whose members are elected to four-year terms. The parliament elects the president, who serves up to two four-year terms; recent elections have generally been considered free and fair. The prime minister is nominated by the president and approved by the parliament.

Bērziņš, a multimillionaire former banker and a member of the Union of Greens and Farmers (ZZS), was elected president in 2011. In snap parliamentary elections held that year, Harmony Center captured the majority of the votes for the first time, winning 31 seats, and the Zatlers Reform Party (ZRP), formed by former president Valdis Zatlers, finished second with 22 seats. The center-right Unity coalition secured 20 seats, followed by the conservative

National Alliance with 14 and the ZZS with 13. Despite its first-place finish, Harmony Center was shut out of the new government, and the ZRP, Unity, and the National Alliance formed a 56-seat governing coalition, with Valdis Dombrovskis of Unity returning as prime minister; Dombrovskis stepped down in November in the wake of the supermarket disaster.

Harmony Center's position as the dominant party in Riga's city government was reaffirmed in local elections held in June 2013; Harmony Center also posted a strong performance in several other major cities. The For Latvia and Ventspils party—led by the mayor of Ventspils, Aivars Lembergs, who faced a number of corruption charges in recent years—won a landslide victory in Ventspils local elections.

B. Political Pluralism and Participation: 14 / 16

Latvia's political parties organize and compete freely. Latvian political candidates cannot run as independents, and those who belonged to communist or pro-Soviet organizations after 1991 may not hold public office. Residents who do not hold Latvian citizenship may not vote, hold public office, or work in government offices. Noncitizens may join political parties, as long as the party does not count more noncitizens than citizens as members. Approximately 14 percent of Latvia's residents are noncitizens; most are ethnic Russians, but Latvia's noncitizen population also includes many Poles, Ukrainians, and Belarusians. Elections to the Latvian Noncitizens' Congress took place in June 2013, but the organization has no official political powers. All residents of Latvia are eligible to vote for representatives to the Latvian Noncitizens' Congress.

C. Functioning of Government: 7 / 12

Corruption is a serious problem and exists at every level of government. Many citizens have little faith that politicians will act in voters' best interests, according to 2013 research by anticorruption watchdog Transparency International, which also reported that some 25 percent of respondents said they had paid bribes to government officials. Several corruption cases were opened against government officials in the city of Riga in 2013. In one case, former Riga transportation official, Leonards Tenis, was charged in February with accepting bribes from a number of vehicle manufacturers, including Germany's Daimler AG. Criminal corruption proceedings against Mayor Lembergs of Ventspils involving allegations of bribery, money laundering, and tax evasion were also ongoing at the year's end. Latvia was ranked 49 out of 177 countries and territories surveyed in Transparency International's 2013 Corruption Perceptions Index.

CIVIL LIBERTIES: 51 / 60

D. Freedom of Expression and Belief: 15 / 16

The government generally respects freedom of the press, but investigative journalists and whistleblowers sometimes face criminal charges as a result of their reporting. Libel is a criminal offense. Newspapers publish a wide range of political viewpoints, but there has been evidence of increasing business and political influence on the media. Private television and radio stations broadcast programs in both Latvian and Russian. By law, 65 percent of both national and regional broadcasts must be in Latvian or subtitled or dubbed in Latvian. The government does not place restrictions on the internet.

In July 2013, the European Court of Human Rights (ECHR) awarded €20,000 ($28,000) to journalist Ilze Nagla, ruling that a Latvian judge had inappropriately authorized a search of her home in 2010 after she reported on the salaries of senior officials at state-owned companies. The ECHR found that the judge who approved the search of Nagla's home had not adequately established that the police's interest in obtaining evidence trumped Nagla's right to protect her sources. Nagla had received the information from a researcher at the University of Latvia, who had accessed various companies' income-tax files by exploiting a security vulnerability on the Latvian tax authority's website.

A Russian-speaking reporter, Andrey Khramtsov, was charged in May 2013 with inciting public disorder after questioning people in Riga as to whether they would violate a proposed measure banning the public display of Nazi or Soviet symbols. In December 2012, Leonīds Jākobsons—owner of the online Russian-language news outlet *Kompromat*, which covers organized crime and government corruption, was arrested and charged with illegally obtaining electronic communication data. The case was brought in relation to Jākobsons's attempt in 2011 to publish e-mails sent by Riga mayor Nils Ušakovs of Harmony Center that appeared to show that he had engaged in corrupt activities. In early 2013, Jākobsons accused Latvian authorities of forcing him to spend a month in a mental institution in 2012; police claimed he went to the facility voluntarily, having agreed to spend time there for observation in connection with the allegations against him. Meanwhile, the 2010 murder of Grigorijs Ņemcovs—the publisher of *Million*, a Russian-language newspaper focusing on political corruption—remains unsolved, as does a 2012 attack against Jākobsons that resulted in his hospitalization.

Freedom of religion is generally respected; however, religious groups that have been registered with the government for more than 10 years have certain privileges that newer groups do not, including various tax benefits, the right to own property, and permission to worship in public places. Academic freedom is generally respected.

E. Associational and Organizational Rights: 12 / 12

Freedoms of assembly and association are protected by law, and the government generally respects these rights in practice. However, organizers of public demonstrations must obtain permission to hold events 10 days in advance. In June 2013, the parliament passed legislation banning the display of Soviet and Nazi symbols at public events, but Bērziņš had not signed the law by year's end. The legislation was introduced in response to highly controversial demonstrations in Riga organized each year by Latvia's ethnic Russians to commemorate the Soviet victory over Nazi Germany, as well as an annual Waffen SS veterans' parade. Both events took place without major incident in 2013.

The government does not restrict the activities of nongovernmental organizations. Workers may establish trade unions, strike, and engage in collective bargaining.

F. Rule of Law: 12 / 16

While judicial independence is generally respected, inefficiency, politicization, and corruption continue to be problems, and citizens distrust both the police and the courts, according to recent polling by Transparency International. Lengthy pretrial detention remains a concern, and law enforcement officials have allegedly abused prisoners. Prisons continue to suffer from overcrowding, and many detainees have poor access to health care.

In January 2013, the ECHR ruled in favor of a disabled man who claimed that he had been held against his will at a state social-care institution for more than 10 years without the possibility of challenging his confinement in court; he was awarded €15,000 ($21,000). Also in January, the ECHR awarded €5,000 ($7,000) to a man who alleged that a Latvian court had failed to consider his claim that an undercover police officer had incited him to engage in narcotics transactions that had resulted in his conviction on drug-trafficking charges.

G. Personal Autonomy and Individual Rights: 12 / 16

Citizens and noncitizens may travel freely within the country and internationally. Latvia in recent years has implemented some reforms to improve the environment for businesses and workers, though corruption represents a major impediment to many business activities.

Same-sex marriage was banned in 2005, and members of the LGBT (lesbian, gay, bisexual, and transgender) community face discrimination. A 2012 report by the Council of Europe's European Commission against Racism and Intolerance found that Latvia had made some improvements in combatting hate crimes, implementing nondiscrimination training for police, providing education for children of ethnic minorities, and increasing the participation of minorities in political life. However, it also noted that few racially motivated crimes are investigated or prosecuted and ethnic Roma face particularly severe discrimination.

Women enjoy the same legal rights as men, but they often face employment and wage discrimination. Domestic violence is not frequently reported, and police do not always take meaningful action when it is. Latvia is both a source and destination country for women and girls trafficked for the purpose of forced prostitution.

Income inequality in Latvia is high, and the country has the third-lowest minimum wage in the EU. The welfare system is inadequate; a May 2013 European Commission report indicated that 40 percent of Latvia's population was at risk of social exclusion or poverty. Poor economic conditions and high unemployment have prompted many young, highly educated people to leave Latvia. The country's 2011 census showed that Latvia lost some 13 percent of its population between 2000 and 2011.

⬇ Lebanon

Political Rights Rating: 5
Civil Liberties Rating: 4
Freedom Rating: 4.5
Freedom Status: Partly Free
Electoral Democracy: No

Population: 4,822,000
Capital: Beirut

Trend Arrow: Lebanon received a downward trend arrow due to political paralysis stemming from the Syrian conflict that prevented the passage of a new electoral law and led to the postponement of national elections until late 2014.

Ten-Year Ratings Timeline For Year Under Review (Political Rights, Civil Liberties, Status)

Year Under Review	2004	2005	2006	2007	2008	2009	2010	2011	2012	2013
Rating	6,5,NF	5,4,PF	5,4,PF	5,4,PF	5,4,PF	5,3,PF	5,3,PF	5,4,PF	5,4,PF	5,4,PF

INTRODUCTION

The Syrian conflict continued to spill over into Lebanon in 2013, as sectarian elements associated with both of the main Lebanese political coalitions, March 8 and March 14, became involved in the fighting in Syria. Faced with political deadlock and concerns about increased violence, the country's leaders failed to form a new government after the incumbent prime minister resigned in March, postponed parliamentary elections until late 2014, and adopted similar stopgap measures regarding key security and judicial appointments.

The number of Syrian refugees in Lebanon passed the one million mark in September 2013, according to the office of the UN High Commissioner for Refugees (UNHCR). The influx of largely Sunni Muslim refugees added friction to the country's confessional divisions, with verbal and physical attacks persisting amid occasionally xenophobic and racist rhetoric by some politicians. The Syrians' arrival also placed an additional fiscal burden on the government and strained the country's already overextended infrastructure and basic services.

Militant activity linked to the war in Syria included a series of cross-border kidnappings and shootings between supporters and opponents of the Syrian government, which caused dozens of deaths. A low-intensity conflict in the city of Tripoli, ongoing since at least June 2011, continued during 2013, killing roughly 50 people. The fighting centered on a longstanding rivalry between an Alawite community in the Jabal Mohsen neighborhood, seen as being aligned with the Alawite-led government of Syria, and a Sunni community in the Bab al-Tebbaneh neighborhood, which is sympathetic to the Syrian rebel movement.

Two bombings in July and August 2013 struck the southern suburbs of Beirut in what was widely seen as retaliation for the Lebanese Shiite militant group Hezbollah's open involvement in the Syrian war on the government's side. The first attack injured 53 people, and the second attack killed 27 and injured 338. A previously unknown Sunni militant group claimed responsibility for the second bombing. Two other bombs were simultaneously triggered on a Friday after the noon prayer in front of two mosques in Tripoli in August. A total of 47 people were killed and several hundred wounded in those attacks, which were attributed to the Syrian government. Two Sunni sheikhs from the city—said to be close to the Syrian regime—were arrested and charged, in addition to a Syrian army officer who was charged in absentia. A double suicide bombing aimed at the Iranian embassy killed at least 22 people in November, and in December a senior Hezbollah commander and a Sunni politician were assassinated in separate attacks in Beirut.

Also during 2013, radical Sunni preacher Ahmad al-Assir in April called on his followers to join the fighting in Syria, and clashes broke out for two days in the southern city of Sidon in June between his supporters and the Lebanese army. Al-Assir fled and went into hiding. More than 40 people were killed in the fighting. One of the men killed in these clashes, Nader Bayoumi, allegedly died under torture in custody of the Lebanese army and intelligence.

POLITICAL RIGHTS: 16 / 40 (-1)

A. Electoral Process: 4 / 12 (-1)

The president is selected every six years by the 128-member National Assembly, which in turn is elected for four-year terms. The president and parliament nominate the prime minister, who, along with the president, chooses the cabinet, subject to parliamentary approval. The unwritten National Pact of 1943 stipulates that the president must be a Maronite Christian, the prime minister a Sunni Muslim, and the speaker of the National Assembly a Shiite Muslim. Parliamentary seats are divided among major sects under a constitutional formula that does not reflect their current demographic weight. Shiites comprise at least a third of the population, but they are allotted only 21 percent of parliamentary seats, for example. The sectarian political balance has been periodically reaffirmed and occasionally modified by foreign-brokered agreements like the 1989 Taif Accords and the 2008 Doha Agreement.

The last parliamentary elections were held in June 2009. Although they were conducted peacefully and judged to be free and fair in some respects, vote buying was reported to be rampant, and the electoral framework retained a number of fundamental structural flaws linked to the country's sectarian political system. The March 14 and March 8 coalitions won 71 and 57 seats, respectively, and Saad Hariri—the son of former prime minister Rafiq Hariri, who was assassinated in 2005—was named prime minister. The government collapsed in 2011 when Hezbollah-allied ministers resigned in protest of Hariri's cooperation with a special UN tribunal investigating the 2005 assassination, and a new cabinet headed by Hezbollah-backed prime minister Najib Miqati took office.

Miqati resigned in March 2013 after the pro-Hezbollah camp refused to extend the term of Ashraf Rifi as director general of the Internal Security Forces beyond April 1. The disagreement reflected rising political tensions linked to the Syrian civil war. President Michel Suleiman nominated Tammam Salam as a consensus candidate for prime minister, but he was unable to form a government for the remainder of the year, leaving Miqati in office in a caretaker capacity.

Parliamentary elections were due in June 2013, but disagreement between the different factions over the electoral law led the parliament to extend its own term, delaying elections until November 2014 in a move that some civil society activists protested as unconstitutional. Suleiman and others brought the matter before the Constitutional Council, but members boycotted its sessions, thwarting a quorum four times. The term extension consequently became legal by default.

Suleiman's presidential term was set to expire in May 2014, feeding discussion on the need to extend his term in office as well, to prevent a void in the executive branch. If such a measure were implemented, Suleiman would be the third consecutive president whose term had to be extended since the end of the civil war in 1989. Many politicians were reportedly concerned about the dangers of moving forward with either legislative or presidential elections as long as the Syrian conflict continued.

B. Political Pluralism and Participation: 9 / 16

Two major factions have dominated Lebanese politics since 2005: the March 8 coalition, of which Shiite Hezbollah is the most powerful member and which is seen as aligned with the Syrian regime; and the March 14 bloc, which is headed by Sunni Muslims, generally supportive of the Syrian opposition, and associated with Saudi Arabia, Europe, and the United States. Christian factions are divided between the two blocs.

These divisions blurred during the 2013 debate over the electoral law, with most major Christian parties endorsing a proposal that would replace the existing system of 26 multimember constituencies—in which seats are allotted by sect but candidates seek votes from all residents of the district—with a single nationwide constituency in which members of a given sect could vote only for representatives from that sect, and seats would be distributed by party-list proportional representation. Critics said the measure would entrench the sectarian political system more deeply and give a large majority to Hezbollah and its allies. The president, Miqati, Druze political leader Walid Jumblatt, and core members of the March 14 coalition expressed their strong opposition. Parliament speaker Nabih Berri of the largely Shiite Amal Movement floated a hybrid bill that mixed the current electoral law and the controversial new proposal, but he withdrew it in May after strong opposition from Hariri's Future Movement. No new electoral legislation had been passed by year's end.

C. Functioning of Government: 3 / 16

Sectarian and political divisions, exacerbated by foreign interference and more recently the Syrian civil war, have frequently prevented Lebanese governments from forming and operating effectively and independently after elections. The authority of the government is also limited in practice by the power of autonomous militant groups, such as Hezbollah. For much of 2013, the government ruled in a caretaker capacity, and the parliament exceeded its electoral mandate. Moreover, the Internal Security Forces director was replaced by a deputy on a temporary basis after he reached retirement age in April, and the term of military chief Jean Qahwaji, who would reach retirement age in September, was extended by two years in July.

The sectarian political system and the powerful role of foreign patrons effectively limit the accountability of elected officials to the public at large. Political and bureaucratic corruption is widespread, businesses routinely pay bribes and cultivate ties with politicians to win contracts, and anticorruption laws are loosely enforced. More than 60 percent of respondents said corruption in Lebanon had "increased a lot" in the past two years, according to Transparency International's 2013 Global Corruption Barometer. Lebanon was ranked 127 out of 177 countries and territories assessed in the organization's 2013 Corruption Perceptions Index.

CIVIL LIBERTIES: 32 / 60
D. Freedom of Expression and Belief: 11 / 16

Freedom of expression and freedom of the press are guaranteed by law, and the media are considered more open than in many other countries in the region. However, nearly all media outlets have ties to sectarian leaders or groups, and consequently practice self-censorship and maintain a specific, often partisan, editorial line.

In addition, the law stipulates that the president and religious leaders cannot be insulted. A supporter of Christian politician Michel Aoun's Free Patriotic Movement was arrested in June 2013 for insulting the president on the Twitter microblogging service, but was later freed on bail. The case was ongoing at year's end.

Censorship of artistic work is still prevalent, especially when the work involves politics, religion, sex, or Israel. Authorities banned the screening of a French film depicting homosexuality and a local short film about temporary marriage among Shiites at the October 2013 Beirut International Film Festival. However, authorities have in general become more cautious about arbitrary censorship, especially after activists in 2012 launched the Virtual Censorship Museum, an online database of censorship actions in Lebanon since the 1940s.

Freedom of religion is guaranteed in the constitution and protected in practice. However, informal religious discrimination is common. In a widely publicized case in July 2013, a Sunni man who eloped with a young Druze woman was later castrated by her family. Citizens' religious affiliation is automatically included in their official documents, unless they request its removal. Every religious group manages its own family and personal status laws, and has its own religious courts to adjudicate such matters. Proselytizing, while not punishable by law, is strongly discouraged by religious leaders and communities, sometimes with the threat of violence. Blasphemy is a criminal offense that carries up to one year in prison. Strife between religious groups has persisted to some extent since the 1975–1990 civil war, and such differences—particularly between Sunnis and Shiites—have again been exacerbated by the civil war in neighboring Syria.

Academic freedom is generally unimpaired.

E. Associational and Organizational Rights: 7 / 16

The constitution guarantees freedoms of assembly and association, and the government generally respects these rights, though police have cracked down in the past on demonstrations against the government or the Syrian regime.

Civil society organizations have long operated openly in Lebanon, with some constraints. All nongovernmental organizations (NGOs) must be registered with the Lebanese Interior Ministry. The ministry may force the NGO to undergo an approval process and investigate its founders, and representatives of the ministry must be invited to observe voting on bylaws and boards of directors.

Trade unions are often tightly linked to political organizations, and in recent years they have been subordinate to their political partners. The Palestinian population of Lebanon, estimated at about 400,000, is not permitted to participate in trade unions. In February and March, public-sector workers and teachers held large demonstrations calling on the government to pass legislation that would raise salaries. The protest actions temporarily paralyzed government bodies and public schools.

F. Rule of Law: 5 / 16

Political forces hold sway over an officially independent judiciary. The Supreme Judicial Council is composed of ten judges, eight of whom are nominated by the president and the cabinet. Other judges are nominated by the Judicial Council, approved by the Justice Ministry, and vetted by opposition and government parties. The delay in forming a new government during 2013 prevented the appointment of 46 new judges who had finished their internships at the Institute of Judiciary Studies.

While the regular judiciary generally follows international standards of criminal procedure, these standards are not followed in the military courts, which have been tasked with cases against Islamist militants, human rights activists, and alleged Israeli spies. In 2013, military judges issued warrants related to the crackdown on Ahmad al-Assir in Sidon and handled charges against a former city council member from Baalbek who was accused of spying for Israel. The use of torture remains widespread among Lebanese security forces despite a formal ban, and human rights groups continue to report arbitrary arrests and poor prison conditions.

The roughly 400,000 Palestinian refugees living in Lebanon are denied citizenship rights and face employment and property restrictions. A 2010 law allowed them access to social security benefits, end-of-service compensation, and the right to bring complaints before labor courts, but closed off access to skilled professions and did not remove restrictions on property ownership.

Iraqi and Sudanese refugees in Lebanon do not enjoy official refugee status and thus face arbitrary detention, deportation, harassment, and abuse. In 2012, security forces detained a number of Syrian refugees and threatened to return them to Syria, and a number of kidnappings stemming from the Syrian conflict went uninvestigated.

Lebanon grants Syrian refugees who enter the country legally a free six-month residency permit with a possible six-month extension, and provides subsidized and sometimes free access to public education and healthcare. Female refugees have reported being sexually harassed by employers and landlords.

LGBT (lesbian, gay, bisexual, and transgender) people face both official and societal discrimination and harassment. NGOs work to uphold their human rights, however, and social acceptance of the LGBT community is more common in urban and cosmopolitan areas, particularly in Beirut.

G. Personal Autonomy and Individual Rights: 9 / 16

Women are granted equal rights in the constitution, but they are disadvantaged under the sectarian personal status laws on issues such as divorce, inheritance, and child custody. NGOs have been lobbying for a change in some of these laws; in October 2013, women demonstrated in front of the main Shiite religious authority and called for revisions of its child custody law.

Under a 1925 law, women cannot pass their nationality to non-Lebanese husbands and children, and a draft law proposed by reformers was rejected in January 2013. Women's NGOs protested in September when they learned that over 100 people had been granted citizenship under a decree that was not made public in the official gazette. The naturalized citizens included clerics, Jordanian royals, and the relatives of politicians, leading to a public outcry and accusations of discrimination and favoritism.

In the aftermath of a high-profile case in which a woman was allegedly beaten to death by her husband, and a media campaign by the NGO KAFA, the parliament advanced a long-stalled bill to address domestic violence in July 2013. However, the measure was modified with input from some religious authorities, and among other flaws it failed to identify spousal rape as a crime. The bill had yet to win final passage at year's end.

Lesotho

Political Rights Rating: 2
Civil Liberties Rating: 3
Freedom Rating: 2.5
Freedom Status: Free
Electoral Democracy: Yes

Population: 2,241,768
Capital: Maseru

Ten-Year Ratings Timeline For Year Under Review (Political Rights, Civil Liberties, Status)

Year Under Review	2004	2005	2006	2007	2008	2009	2010	2011	2012	2013
Rating	2,3,F	2,3,F	2,3,F	2,3,F	2,3,F	3,3,F	3,3,PF	3,3,PF	2,3,PF	2,3,F

INTRODUCTION

Drought has plagued Lesotho for over a decade, leading to food shortages for as many as 725,000 people, although conditions improved somewhat in 2013. Lesotho suffers an adult HIV/AIDS prevalence rate of approximately 23 percent, one of the world's highest. The government offers free HIV testing to all citizens, but only about 25 percent of the country's infected citizens receive antiretroviral treatment.

In 2013, two senior politicians were indicted on corruption charges. Water Minister Timothy Thahane became the first cabinet minister to be dismissed due to corruption.

POLITICAL RIGHTS: 31 / 40
A. Electoral Process: 10 / 12

King Letsie III serves as ceremonial head of state. The lower house of Parliament, the National Assembly, is comprised of 120 seats; 80 are filled through first-past-the-post constituency votes and 40 through proportional representation. Members serve five-year terms, and the leader of the majority party becomes the prime minister. The Senate—the upper house of Parliament—consists of Lesotho's 22 traditional principal chiefs, who wield considerable authority in rural areas, and 11 other members appointed on the advice of the prime minister.

Despite pre-election violence and a deeply divided result, the May 2012 parliamentary elections were free and fair. Prime Minister Pakalitha Mosisili's newly formed Democratic Congress (DC) won the most votes and 48 seats in the National Assembly but was unable to form a government. A few days later, All Basotho Convention (ABC) leader Tom Thabane—whose party won 30 seats—announced a 65-seat coalition with the Lesotho Congress for Democracy (LCD), which had captured 26 seats, and the Basotho National Party, which claimed 5. Despite fears that the results would be contested and that Mosisili and his supporters would refuse to hand over power, Thabane peacefully took over as prime minister in June.

B. Political Pluralism and Participation: 13 / 16

Lesotho was dominated by the LCD until the 2012 election, when an ABC-led coalition took power for the first time. The DC, which won the most seats, was formed after 45 members of Parliament broke off from the LCD before the 2012 election. More than 15 parties and several independent candidates contested the 2012 elections, and 12 gained representation.

C. Functioning of Government: 8 / 12

While the government has aggressively prosecuted cases of graft, political corruption remains a problem. According to the African Peer Review Mechanism, corruption is rife in all sectors of government and public services, and cronyism is prevalent in state bidding procedures. Since 2012, all government officials must declare their financial interests as a condition of office, though implementation was spotty in 2013. The anticorruption watchdog, the Directorate on Corruption and Economic Offenses (DCEO)—which became autonomous in 2012—indicted two senior politicians on corruption charges in 2013. In February, DC deputy leader and former minister of natural resources Monyane Moleleki was charged with fraud and corruption over the alleged diversion of $1.6 million in state resources to electrify villages in his constituency. In October, Thahane, the minister of energy, meteorology, and water affairs, became the first cabinet minister to be sacked for corruption after the DCEO indicted him for illegally benefiting from loans intended for farmers while he was finance minister in 2010. Lesotho was ranked 55 out of 177 countries and territories surveyed in Transparency International's 2013 Corruption Perceptions Index.

CIVIL LIBERTIES: 41 / 60

D. Freedom of Expression and Belief: 14 / 16

Freedoms of speech and the press are generally respected, and independent newspapers and radio stations routinely criticize the government. However, state-owned print and broadcast media tend to reflect the views of the ruling party, and the state controls Lesotho's largest radio station and its only television station. Critical media outlets and journalists face severe libel and defamation penalties, and reporters are occasionally harassed, threatened, and attacked. While media coverage of the May 2012 election was more professional and expansive than during previous elections, the state-run Lesotho Broadcasting Service allocated more radio and television airtime to the DC party; private broadcast coverage favored opposition parties. The government does not restrict internet access, though access is restricted by socio-economic constraints.

Lesotho is a predominantly Christian country, and freedom of religion is widely observed. The government does not restrict academic freedom.

E. Associational and Organizational Rights: 7 / 12

Freedoms of assembly and association are generally respected, though demonstrations are sometimes broken up violently. Local and international nongovernmental organizations (NGOs) generally operate without restrictions. While labor rights are constitutionally guaranteed, the union movement is weak and fragmented. Many employers in the textile sector—Lesotho's largest formal employer—do not allow union activity.

F. Rule of Law: 11 / 16

Courts are nominally independent, but higher courts are subject to outside influence. The large backlog of cases often leads to trial delays and lengthy pretrial detention. Mistreatment of civilians by security forces reportedly continues. Prisons are dilapidated, severely overcrowded, and lack essential health services; instances of torture and use of excessive force have been reported. The police were accused of committing several extrajudicial killings in 2013, and 3 suspects died in custody, including one under investigation at year's end. An independent ombudsman's office is tasked with protecting citizens' rights, but its enforcement powers are weak. In 2013, the Lesotho Mounted Police Service launched a course on management skills to prevent human rights violations.

Tensions between the Basotho and the community of Chinese migrant traders have grown in recent years as Chinese-owned small businesses have become more successful.

G. Personal Autonomy and Individual Rights: 9 / 16

The constitution bars gender-based discrimination, but customary practice and law still restrict women's rights in the areas of property and inheritance. While their husbands are alive, women married under customary law have the status of minors in civil courts and may not enter into binding contracts. Nonetheless, women are prevalent in senior political and economic positions in Lesotho, including in government and senior management. Domestic violence is reportedly widespread. "Sodomy" is illegal but reportedly the law is not enforced. Still, lesbian, gay, bisexual, and transgender individuals face societal discrimination. Lesotho saw its first-ever gay pride march in May, organized by a local gay rights advocacy organization that first registered in 2010.

Liberia

Political Rights Rating: 3
Civil Liberties Rating: 4
Freedom Rating: 3.5
Freedom Status: Partly Free
Electoral Democracy: Yes

Population: 4,400,000
Capital: Monrovia

Ten-Year Ratings Timeline For Year Under Review (Political Rights, Civil Liberties, Status)

Year Under Review	2004	2005	2006	2007	2008	2009	2010	2011	2012	2013
Rating	5,4,PF	4,4,PF	3,4,PF	3,4,PF	3,4,PF	3,4,PF	3,4,PF	3,4,PF	3,4,PF	3,4,PF

INTRODUCTION

In 2013, Liberia celebrated a decade of relative peace and stability after 14 years of civil war. However, the country still faced endemic problems of corruption, nepotism, procedural injustice, and ineffective oversight of the natural-resources and land-management sectors. Institutions devoted to fighting corruption typically lack the resources and mandate to function effectively, and President Ellen Johnson-Sirleaf—now in her second term—is regularly accused of nepotism in filling key positions. In September, one of her sons, Robert Sirleaf, resigned his post as chairman of the National Oil Company of Liberia (NOCAL); the president had previously suspended a second son from his post as deputy governor of the central bank, and a third son remained head of the National Security Agency. Corruption is especially pervasive in the natural-resources sector, as well as the justice and security sectors, where poorly trained and underpaid judges and police officers solicit bribes and extortion payments from citizens.

Media freedom is threatened by onerous libel laws. In August, the editor of the prominent newspaper *FrontPage Africa* was jailed for failing to pay US$1.5 million in libel damages to a former agriculture minister, and a publication ban was imposed on the paper. Although the ban was lifted and the editor was released in November, the case provoked outrage from international rights groups and underscored the need for legal reforms.

Academic freedom remained fairly strong in 2013, but dilapidated, underfunded schools impeded access to education in practice. In August, administrators at the University of Liberia revealed that all of the 25,000 students who took the university's entrance exam that year had failed.

POLITICAL RIGHTS: 26 / 40

A. Electoral Process: 9 / 12

The bicameral legislature consists of a 30-member Senate and a 73-member House of Representatives; senators are elected to nine-year terms, and representatives to six-year terms. In 2005, as part of a peace agreement, half of the senators were elected to six-year terms only, allowing staggered senatorial elections to be introduced in 2011. The president can serve up to two six-year terms.

In the October 2011 parliamentary elections, incumbent president Johnson-Sirleaf's Unity Party (UP) secured a plurality of 24 seats in the House and 4 of the 15 seats at stake in the Senate. The opposition Congress for Democratic Change (CDC) placed second with 11 House seats and 2 in the Senate. Several smaller parties and independents divided the remainder. In the concurrent presidential race, Johnson-Sirleaf captured 43.9 percent of the vote, while the CDC's Winston Tubman took 32.7 percent, and Prince Johnson of the National Union for Democratic Progress (NUDP) secured 11.6 percent. Johnson-Sirleaf was reelected after winning 90.7 percent of the vote in a November runoff, leaving Tubman with only 9.3 percent.

Although opposition members alleged fraud and corruption, international and local observers found that the elections had been comparatively free, fair, and peaceful, with isolated incidents of violence before and after the voting. A day prior to the vote, police clashed with pro-CDC demonstrators, resulting in at least two deaths and numerous injuries. The government briefly shut down radio and television stations with perceived pro-CDC biases.

B. Political Pluralism and Participation: 11 / 16

The organizational and policymaking capacity of most parties remains weak, and politics continue to be driven largely by leading personalities, with strong underlying ethnic and regional loyalties. The CDC in particular has struggled to maintain internal coherence since its defeat in the 2011 polls. In December 2012, President Johnson-Sirleaf appointed former CDC presidential candidate George Weah to lead the country's postconflict reconciliation process as a "peace ambassador," and in April 2013 she tapped Weah to chair the board of NOCAL after her son resigned from the post.

Ethnic and religious minority groups generally enjoy full political rights and electoral opportunities, though some minorities—especially the Mandingo and Fula peoples—continue to be stigmatized as outsiders. Candidates occasionally exploit these biases to rally their constituents.

C. Functioning of Government: 6 / 12

Corruption remained endemic in 2013, despite some continued progress in combating the problem. Liberia boasts a number of institutions devoted to fighting corruption—including the Liberia Anti-Corruption Commission (LACC), the General Auditing Commission, and the Public Procurement and Concessions Commission—but they lack the resources and capacity to function effectively.

Liberia was the first African state to comply with Extractive Industries Transparency Initiative (EITI) rules governing natural-resource extraction, and in 2013 it remained EITI compliant. Liberia was also the first West African country to pass a Freedom of Information Act. In July, the Office of the Independent Information Commissioner concluded the country's first freedom of information hearing, which resulted in an order instructing the LACC to disclose a number of asset-declaration forms requested by a Liberian nongovernmental organization. In October, the LACC published a report accusing the minister of defense and the police director, among other top officials, of obstructing efforts to verify their assets; while the outcome of the report remained to be seen at year's end, in 2012 Johnson-Sirleaf had suspended 46 officials, including her son Charles Sirleaf, for not disclosing their assets.

President Johnson-Sirleaf has been repeatedly accused of nepotism when filling lucrative bureaucratic posts within her administration. In September 2013, Robert Sirleaf resigned from his job as chairman of NOCAL, as well as his position as senior adviser to the president. The move came just days after the House of Representatives delayed a vote on a bill—drafted under Robert Sirleaf's supervision—that was intended to increase transparency and competition in the oil sector; critics complained that the bill had been drafted without any public comment or discussion. In addition to Charles Sirleaf, who was deputy governor of the central bank, a third son remained in place as head of the National Security Agency.

Corruption has been especially rife in connection with illegal narcotics trafficking and the natural resources sector. Twice in 2013, government officials allegedly impeded the arrests of heroin couriers, and criminal influence may extend to networks of higher-level government figures. Separately, a draft report of a government-commissioned audit found that just 2 of 68 contracts in the natural-resources sector signed since 2009 were in compliance with the country's laws. The government has exercised weak oversight of the alluvial gold sector, and there have been reports of illicit gold trafficking through Côte d'Ivoire and Guinea. Liberia's compliance with the Kimberley Process Certification Scheme in terms of resource exploration and extraction has been hampered by lack of government capacity to monitor diamond-mining activities regionally and in rural areas that are difficult to access. Illegal diamond trafficking is common between Liberia and Sierra Leone.

In July 2013, Transparency International ranked Liberia as one of the world's worst countries in terms of residents' perceptions of corruption. Ninety-seven percent of Liberians surveyed identified corruption in the public sector as a problem or a serious problem, and 85 percent viewed government anticorruption efforts as ineffective or very ineffective.

CIVIL LIBERTIES: 33 / 60 (-1)
D. Freedom of Expression and Belief: 10 / 16 (-1)

Liberia hosts a variety of newspapers, which publish mainly in the capital; numerous radio stations also operate across the country. The government does not restrict internet access, but poor infrastructure and high costs limit usage to a small fraction of the population. The 2010 Freedom of Information Act promotes unhindered access to public information and is considered a model for the region.

Nevertheless, libel laws pose a threat to media freedoms, with government officials, politicians, judges, and other powerful figures pursuing civil cases against critical journalists. In August 2013, a judge ordered the newspaper *FrontPage Africa* closed and its editor, Rodney Sieh, jailed after he failed to pay US$1.5 million in libel damages to former agriculture minister Chris Toe. The move provoked an international outcry from rights groups, including a letter to President Johnson-Sirleaf signed by Human Rights Watch (HRW), Amnesty International, and Global Witness. In November, Toe withdrew his libel action, Sieh was formally released, and the paper resumed publishing, but the incident renewed calls to reform the country's media legislation. Despite pledges to do so in recent years, Liberia again failed to abolish criminal defamation laws in 2013.

Religious freedom is affirmed in the constitution, and there is no official religion. However, Liberia is a de facto Christian state, and the Muslim minority reports discrimination.

The government does not restrict academic freedom, though educational quality and infrastructure remain grossly inadequate. In August 2013, a scandal erupted when none of the 25,000 students who took the University of Liberia's entrance exam passed. While the university subsequently admitted 1,800 of the students, the episode was a stark reminder of the poor quality of the country's schools.

E. Associational and Organizational Rights: 8 / 12

Freedoms of assembly and association are guaranteed and largely respected. Numerous civil society groups, including human rights organizations, operate in the country. The government has attempted to manage land disputes between local communities and large palm-oil concessions, with mixed results. In September 2013 the government dispatched police in response to local residents' attempts to block expanded cultivation by the company Equatorial Palm Oil. That month, 17 protesters were arrested during a peaceful march, fueling tensions. A high-level government delegation, including the acting vice president and two government ministers, visited to prevent the situation from deteriorating further.

The rights of workers to strike, organize, and bargain collectively are recognized, but labor laws remain in need of reform. Labor disputes often turn violent, particularly at the various rubber plantations throughout the country.

F. Rule of Law: 7 / 16

Despite constitutional provisions for an independent judiciary, judges are subject to executive influence and corruption. Case backlogs, prolonged pretrial detention, and poor security at correctional facilities continue to impede judicial effectiveness. Harmonization of formal and customary justice systems remains a challenge, and ritual killings, mob violence, and vigilantism persist. Many Liberians express a preference for these informal mechanisms of justice over the corrupt and understaffed courts.

Lack of discipline, absenteeism, and corruption continue to plague the police and armed forces. According to an August 2013 HRW report, the police are routinely accused of extortion, accepting bribes to release prisoners, and failing to investigate crimes if victims do not compensate them directly for their work. While the establishment of a Professional Standards Division has helped the police identify and, in some cases, address these abuses, they remain endemic. Prisons suffer from inadequate medical care, food, and sanitation, and conditions are often life-threatening.

The government lacks adequate legislation regulating weapons possession and trade, and it has been unable to effectively monitor arms trafficking, particularly in the border regions with Côte d'Ivoire, Sierra Leone, and Guinea. In some cases, the government has reportedly purchased weapons from Liberian mercenaries to remove them from circulation, but the chain of custody from that point forward has been opaque. In February 2013, a draft law to control domestic firearms was withdrawn from legislative consideration pending revisions; it had not been resubmitted by year's end.

The first half of 2011 featured an influx of some 180,000 combatants and refugees from political crises in Côte d'Ivoire, Guinea, and Sierra Leone. The effects of these crises continued to pose significant challenges in 2013, and observers said mercenary activity along Liberia's borders has provoked violence and obstructed efforts at refugee repatriation. Former fighters from Sierra Leone are reportedly engaged in illegal mining and trafficking of narcotics and weapons in the Gola Forest area. A series of cross-border raids into Côte d'Ivoire in March killed 10 people. In October, a Monrovia court suspended the trial of 18 men accused of involvement in earlier attacks across the Ivoirian border; the jury was disbanded pending an investigation into possible jury tampering, and a retrial was ordered.

Since its establishment in October 2010, the Independent National Human Rights Commission has made little progress in pursuing national reconciliation following the civil war and in implementing recommendations of the Truth and Reconciliation Commission (TRC), which was formed in 2005. Funding shortfalls, operational deficiencies, and a lack of political determination to break the cycle of impunity have hampered progress. Although recommended by the TRC, no war crimes tribunal has been established and no prosecutions pursued.

Former Liberian president Charles Taylor was apprehended in 2006, and his trial before a UN-backed special court for Sierra Leone opened in 2008 and concluded in 2011. In April 2012, he was convicted on 11 counts of war crimes and crimes against humanity for his role in Sierra Leone's civil war, and sentenced to 50 years in prison. His sentence was upheld on appeal in September 2013, and he began serving the term in a British prison facility the following month.

Under the penal code, "sodomy" is punishable with up to a year in prison. Although the law is rarely enforced, LGBT (lesbian, gay, bisexual, and transgender) people face social stigma and the threat of violence and harassment.

G. Personal Autonomy and Individual Rights: 8 / 16

Communal tensions over land access and ownership remain a potential threat to peace. Many of these conflicts originated in the civil war and the subsequent internal migration, displacement, and resettlement. Others are the result of opaque concession agreements granting foreign corporations access to lands for production of tropical timber, palm oil, and other products. A September 2012 estimate by Global Witness suggested that as much as one-quarter of the country's land mass had been granted to logging companies over the previous two years through licenses that allowed the companies to bypass environmental and social safeguards. President Johnson-Sirleaf placed a moratorium on issuing the logging licenses in January 2013, and in September the government announced that it would review at least 17 of them. Mechanisms for compensating local communities for the extraction of timber remain inadequate, raising the risk of future conflict.

Violence against women and children, particularly rape, is a pervasive problem. A specialized prosecution unit and a court with exclusive jurisdiction over sexual and gender-based violence are unable to effectively process the large number of cases brought before them.

Libya

Political Rights Rating: 4
Civil Liberties Rating: 5
Freedom Rating: 4.5
Freedom Status: Partly Free
Electoral Democracy: Yes

Population: 6,500,000
Capital: Tripoli

Ten-Year Ratings Timeline For Year Under Review (Political Rights, Civil Liberties, Status)

Year Under Review Rating	2004	2005	2006	2007	2008	2009	2010	2011	2012	2013
	7,7,NF	7,7,NF	7,7,NF	7,7,NF	7,7,NF	7,7,NF	7,7,NF	7,6,NF	4,5,PF	4,5,PF

INTRODUCTION

In 2013, Libya struggled, amid ongoing security challenges, to work toward a constitutional system following the 2011 overthrow of longtime dictator Mu'ammar al-Qadhafi. Procedures for electing a 60-member assembly tasked with drafting a new constitution were established in July by the General National Congress (GNC), and the country's electoral commission had begun accepting nominations for candidates by year's end.

Although the elected GNC and government continued to issue laws and decrees, their ability to enforce decisions was extremely limited. Meanwhile, growing citizen frustration, particularly with the country's multiple autonomous militias, led to regular protests and demonstrations, some of which ended in violence as participants confronted militias at their bases. In June in Benghazi, 32 people were killed when citizens mobilized to protest abuses by the Libya Shield 1 Brigade. In Tripoli in November, 43 people were killed as demonstrators demanded the withdrawal from the capital of regional militias from Zintan and Misrata. The government of Prime Minister Ali Zeidan promised investigations into the incidents, but there were no criminal prosecutions of the militias involved.

Among other signs of weak central authority and ongoing security threats, several foreign embassies were attacked, the prime minister was briefly kidnapped, and a vehicle carrying some $55 million belonging to the nation's central bank was robbed in Sirte. Regional militias, armed Islamist groups, international actors, criminal gangs, and smugglers all contributed to the insecurity. Harassment of women and attacks on vulnerable religious communities were serious concerns during the year. The southern border region, where illegal trafficking in arms, drugs, and people is common, has nominally been under martial law since 2012.

Political problems plagued the government, which sought to contend with the demands of both militias and civilian protesters. The independence of the GNC was challenged, notably during an incident in which militias surrounded government ministries in April and May to force the passage of a political exclusion law. The law has been criticized as too broad, potentially barring former Qadhafi officials from political life even if they had joined the opposition decades ago or defected during the 2011 revolt and contributed to the rebel victory.

In October, a regional group declared self-government in the oil-rich eastern region known as Cyrenaica, and the self-proclaimed authorities announced the creation of a separate state oil company and central bank in November. Militias advocating federalism in the region had shut down oil ports, contributing to the drop in Libya's oil production to as low as 10 percent of the previous capacity; oil production had also been upset by militia activity and peaceful demonstrations elsewhere in the country.

POLITICAL RIGHTS: 21 / 40 (-1)

A. Electoral Process: 9 / 12

The prime minister and cabinet are responsible to the 200-member GNC. The GNC, which replaced an unelected National Transitional Council, was elected in July 2012 after a series of delays prompted by continuing insecurity, the need to allow citizens more time to register, and the inability of the transitional government to investigate candidates and finalize preparations. The balloting represented Libya's first parliamentary elections since 1965, and more than 100 parties or lists registered to compete. The National Forces Alliance, a coalition headed by the relatively liberal politician Mahmoud Jibril, led the party-list portion of the voting with 39 of 80 seats, followed by the Muslim Brotherhood's Justice and Construction Party with 17. An array of smaller groups divided the remaining 24 party-list seats, and only independents ran for the 120 majoritarian seats. Election-related violence caused at least two deaths, but fears of extensive fighting and corruption proved unfounded, and the voting was regarded as generally free and fair.

While the GNC's initial choice for prime minister, Mustafa Abushagur, was unable to form a government, its second choice, Ali Zeidan, was named in October, and his cabinet was approved by the Congress. The GNC was tasked with appointing a body that would draft a new constitution, but in February 2013 it decided that the entity would be directly elected instead. It passed an electoral law to govern 2014 elections for the 60-member constituent assembly in July 2013. The High National Election Commission, established as a permanent body by the GNC in March, was responsible for vetting candidates, and nomination and voter-registration processes were under way at the end of 2013.

B. Political Pluralism and Participation: 9 / 16 (-1)

The 2011 uprising created more space for free political association and participation in Libya. Under the Qadhafi regime, political parties were illegal, and all political activity was strictly monitored. While only a few parties initially organized after al-Qadhafi's fall, the 2012 elections prompted a proliferation of over 100 parties or lists that spanned the political spectrum, from socialists to Islamists.

The May 2013 political exclusion law, passed under extreme pressure from militias, allows the barring of individuals from public life based on their past affiliations with the Qadhafi regime. An Integrity Commission was formed in July to carry out the legislation, but human rights groups were challenging its constitutionality at year's end.

Women held 33 seats in the GNC—candidate lists for the proportional-representation seats were required to alternate between men and women—and two seats in the cabinet in 2013. One of the seven national election commissioners was a woman. Six seats in the planned constituent assembly are reserved for women, and two each are reserved for three ethnic minorities—the Amazigh, the Tebu, and the Tuareg people. Moreover, the assembly's 60 seats will be divided equally among Libya's three historic provinces: Tripolitania, Cyrenaica, and Fezzan. Overseas populations will be allowed to vote. Some groups challenged the fairness of the rules, which give equal numbers of seats to the three ethnic minorities and the three regions despite their widely varying populations. In particular, Amazigh groups, who make up 10 percent of the country's population, objected to their allotment of only two seats. An Amazigh politician, Nouri Abusahmain, was elected as the new GNC president in June after his predecessor resigned due to the exclusion law.

Protests—including some by Amazigh groups that disrupted oil production in western Libya—were mounted during 2013 to push for the inclusion of cultural and linguistic rights of ethnic minorities in the new constitution.

C. Functioning of Government: 3 / 12

The nationwide authority of elected officials is limited in practice by autonomous regional militias and underdeveloped state institutions.

Corruption has long been pervasive in both the private sector and the government in Libya, which was ranked 172 out of 177 countries and territories surveyed in Transparency International's 2013 Corruption Perceptions Index. The fall of the Qadhafi regime raised some hopes that the level of graft would decline, but oil interests, foreign governments, smuggling groups, and armed militias often still wield undue influence, especially in the south, and opportunities for corruption abound in the absence of effective fiscal, judicial, and commercial institutions.

CIVIL LIBERTIES: 20 / 60 (-1)
D. Freedom of Expression: 8 / 16

The end of the Qadhafi regime, and of the civil war, brought some respite to Libya's long-repressed media sector. Citizen journalism has been on the rise, and more than 100 new print outlets have been established, representing a wide range of viewpoints. In June 2012,

Libya's Supreme Court struck down a law that would have restricted any speech deemed insulting to the country's people and institutions. However, media freedom advocacy groups reported an uptick in visa restrictions, filming bans, arbitrary detentions, and deportations of journalists in the months after the GNC elections in July 2012, especially in the name of security after a deadly September 2012 attack on the U.S. consulate in Benghazi. In 2013, journalists faced assaults, brief abductions, and raids on their offices, as well as criminal charges for defamation. News agency photographer Saleh Ayyad Hafyana was killed while covering the antimilitia protests in Tripoli in November.

Nearly all Libyans are Muslims, but Christians form a small minority. The Qadhafi regime closely monitored mosques for signs of religious extremism and Islamist political activity, and Muslims of various religious and political strains have been much freer to organize and debate their points of view since 2011. In some cases, however, this has led to verbal and armed clashes. Some Salafi Muslim groups, whose beliefs preclude the veneration of saints, have destroyed or vandalized Sufi Muslim shrines, and the government has lacked the will and capacity to halt such abuses. Violence against Christians by extremists and state repression of Christians suspected of proselytizing—a criminal offense—increased in 2013. Human rights organizations have called for the rights of religious minorities to be guaranteed in the forthcoming constitution.

Close state supervision of education has been lifted since al-Qadhafi's ouster, and his *Green Book* has been removed from school curriculums. However, laws have not been passed to guarantee academic freedom, and there were some reports of violence affecting school operations in 2013.

E. Associational and Organizational Rights: 5 / 12 (-1)

Freedom of assembly has increased dramatically since 2011. The GNC passed a freedom of assembly law in November 2012 that is generally compatible with international human rights principles. Although the ongoing presence of militia groups and the proliferation of firearms in the country deter peaceful assemblies and the public expression of dissenting views in certain areas, demonstrations by various groups were common during 2012 in the context of the GNC elections and the constitutional drafting process. In 2013, there were a number of protests associated with economic and cultural rights, as well as political interests. Chief among the myriad demands of citizens were calls for the state to disarm and disband militias and to establish a state security structure comprised of a regular army and police force. Some of these demonstrations were held in public spaces, while others marched to the headquarters of militias, where deadly violence ensued.

Although draft laws on freedom of association have yet to be adopted, domestic nongovernmental organizations have been allowed significantly more freedom to operate since the collapse of the Qadhafi regime, and they continued to expand in number and range of activities in 2013. However, political and civic activists faced the risk of violence and assassination. Human rights activist Abdelsalam Musmari, a vocal critic of intimidation by militias, was murdered by unidentified gunmen in Benghazi in July. Trade unions, previously outlawed, have made small strides since 2011, but they are in their organizational infancy and have received little official recognition.

F. Rule of Law: 1 / 16

The roles of the judiciary and Supreme Court remain unclear without a permanent constitution. The court system has begun to recuperate, with some functioning courts in city centers trying ordinary cases. However, investigations into a large number of cases involving torture and extrajudicial executions before and during the civil conflict, including the killing of Mu'ammar al-Qadhafi, have made little progress, and thousands of individuals remain in government or militia custody without any formal trial or sentencing. Among these detainees are high-profile suspects like Saif al-Islam al-Qadhafi, a son of Mu'ammar al-Qadhafi's, and former Qadhafi intelligence chief Abdullah al-Senoussi, who was extradited from Mauritania in September 2012. The Libyan government was still contesting the International Criminal Court's efforts to gain custody of and try Saif al-Islam at the end of 2013, but the court ruled in October that al-Senoussi could be tried in Libya. Both trials were still pending at year's end.

Abuses including arbitrary detention and torture, by both state and nonstate actors, continued to be reported in 2013. The year also featured an increase in assassinations, mostly targeting former members of the Qadhafi-era security forces in Benghazi and Derna, where Islamist militias are active. Human Rights Watch reported in August that more than 50 such killings had occurred since 2011. In the absence of a functioning police force and a capacity for witness protection, none of these murders have been fully investigated. The only suspect arrested by the end of 2013 escaped from custody.

In another sign of deficiencies in the rule of law, U.S. special forces entered Tripoli in October and seized Abu Anas al-Libi, who is suspected of involvement in the 1998 bombings of two U.S. embassies in East Africa. An American teacher was shot and killed near his home in Benghazi in December, reportedly in retaliation for al-Libi's capture.

Libyans from certain tribes and communities—often those perceived as pro-Qadhafi—have faced discrimination, violence, and displacement since the civil war. Migrant workers from sub-Saharan Africa have also been subject to discrimination and mistreatment, particularly at the hands of militia groups during and after the civil conflict.

G. Personal Autonomy and Individual Rights: 6 / 16

Freedom of movement is guaranteed by the interim constitution, but limitations have been imposed for individuals suspected of having ties with the previous regime. Government and militia checkpoints also restricted movement in 2013, particularly in the south, while poor security conditions more generally affected movement as well as access to work and education. There were reports of discrimination against the Tebu and Tuareg minorities in employment, housing, education, and other services.

Women enjoyed many of the same legal protections as men under the Qadhafi regime, but certain laws and social norms perpetuated discrimination, particularly in areas such as marriage, divorce, and inheritance. Extramarital sex is punishable with up to five years in prison, and this includes same-sex activity. The GNC has made some limited efforts to address gender inequality, but formal legal changes have yet to be made. There are reports that threats and harassment against women, especially against activists, are increasing.

Libya was rated a Tier 3 country in the U.S. State Department's 2013 *Trafficking in Persons Report*, which described widespread forced labor and sexual exploitation among trafficking victims from sub-Saharan Africa. The country lacks comprehensive laws criminalizing human trafficking, and the authorities have been either incapable of enforcing existing bans or complicit in trafficking activity.

Liechtenstein

Political Rights Rating: 1
Civil Liberties Rating: 1
Freedom Rating: 1.0
Freedom Status: Free
Electoral Democracy: Yes

Population: 37,027
Capital: Vaduz

Ten-Year Ratings Timeline For Year Under Review (Political Rights, Civil Liberties, Status)

Year Under Review	2004	2005	2006	2007	2008	2009	2010	2011	2012	2013
Rating	1,1,F	1,1,F	1,1,F	1,1,F	1,1,F	1,1,F	1,1,F	1,1,F	1,1,F	1,1,F

INTRODUCTION

Parliamentary elections in February 2013 saw a surge by a new grouping of independent candidates, in what was seen as a protest vote against austerity policies. The Progressive Citizens' Party (FBP) won the most seats and Adrian Hasler became prime minister.

In July, Liechtenstein's oldest bank agreed to a settlement with U.S. prosecutors to avoid criminal charges for facilitating tax evasion by U.S. clients. As part of the deal, Liechtensteinische Landesbank AG gave U.S. authorities information on more than 200 undeclared accounts.

POLITICAL RIGHTS: 39 / 40

A. Electoral Process: 12 / 12

Liechtenstein has the most politically powerful unelected monarch in Europe. The prince, as the hereditary head of state, appoints the prime minister on the recommendation of Parliament and possesses the power to veto legislation and dismiss the government. In a 2003 referendum, voters approved a constitutional amendment granting significantly more power to the monarch. The unicameral Parliament (Landtag) consists of 25 deputies chosen by proportional representation every four years. Voting is compulsory.

In 2004, Prince Hans-Adam II handed his constitutional powers to his son, Hereditary Prince Alois, though the elder prince retained his title as head of state. In a July 2012 referendum, 76 percent of voters rejected a proposal by prodemocracy advocates to prohibit the monarch from vetoing decisions made by the public in national referendums. Alois had threatened to abdicate if the proposal were approved.

In the February 2013 parliamentary elections, the FBP won 40 percent of the vote and 10 seats, while the Fatherland Union (VU) was second with 33.5 percent, for 8 seats. A new political grouping called the Independents (DU) took 15.3 percent, for 4 seats, capitalizing on public anger at the government's proposed austerity policies. The leftist Free List party took 11.1 percent, for 3 seats. The FBP's Adrian Hasler replaced the VU's Klaus Tschütscher as prime minister.

B. Political Pluralism and Participation: 15 / 16

Political parties can organize freely. The VU and the FBP, both conservative parties, have dominated politics over the last half-century; power last changed hands in 2013. However, after the DU's strong debut in the February 2013 elections, for the first time the parliament had four political groupings represented. There were no members of ethnic minorities represented.

C. Functioning of Government: 12 / 12

Liechtenstein's politics and society are largely free of corruption. Liechtenstein is a leading offshore tax haven and has traditionally maintained tight bank secrecy laws. However, in 2009, the principality agreed to comply with transparency and tax information–sharing standards as outlined by the Organisation for Economic Co-operation and Development (OECD). In July 2013, Liechtenstein's oldest and second-largest bank, Liechtensteinische Landesbank AG, reached a settlement with U.S. prosecutors, agreeing to pay $23.8 million to avoid criminal charges. The bank admitted that it had facilitated tax evasion by U.S. customers from 2001 to 2011, helping them conceal as much as $341 million. It turned over information on more than 200 undeclared accounts. Liechtenstein had amended its bank secrecy laws in 2012 to allow such data sharing.

The government of Nigeria in October 2013 accused Liechtenstein of using legal maneuvers to avoid returning €185 million ($243 million) allegedly stolen from the state by the late Nigerian dictator Sani Abacha. Liechtenstein's government said it was seeking to return the money but had to wait for the European Court of Human Rights to rule on a lawsuit brought by companies linked to Abacha's relatives. Nigeria first requested Liechtenstein's help with recouping the funds in 2000.

CIVIL LIBERTIES: 59 / 60
D. Freedom of Expression and Belief: 16 / 16

The constitution guarantees freedoms of expression and the press, though the law prohibits public insults directed against a race or ethnic group. Liechtenstein has one private television station, one privately held radio station, and two main newspapers that are roughly aligned with the major political parties; citizens have access to foreign broadcasting. Internet access is not restricted.

The constitution protects religious freedom, and the criminal code prohibits any form of discrimination against any religion or its adherents. However, the constitution also establishes the Roman Catholic Church as the national church. Catholic or Protestant religious education is mandatory in all primary schools, but exemptions are routinely granted. Islamic religious classes have been introduced in some primary schools since 2008. All religious groups are tax-exempt. The government respects academic freedom.

E. Associational and Organizational Rights: 12 / 12

Freedoms of assembly and association are protected, and the principality has one small trade union. A 2008 law provides civil servants with the right to strike. Domestic and international nongovernmental organizations are able to function freely.

F. Rule of Law: 15 / 16

The judiciary is independent and impartial despite the appointment of judges by the hereditary monarch. Due process is respected, and prison conditions meet international standards.

A third of the population is foreign born. Some native citizens have expressed concern over the growing number of immigrants from non-German-speaking countries, such as Turkey and Bosnia-Herzegovina. The government has responded by teaching recent immigrants the language and culture of Liechtenstein in formal integration programs. Foreigners have occasionally been the target of violence by right-wing groups. The laws provide for the granting of asylum or refugee status.

G. Personal Autonomy and Individual Rights: 16 / 16

A gender salary gap persists, with women earning on average 17.8 percent less than men for equal work in 2010. Following a 2005 reform, abortion is legal in the first 12 weeks of pregnancy, but only in cases where the mother's life is in danger or she was under 14 when she conceived. A law allowing same-sex registered partnerships took effect in 2011.

A February 2013 report by the European Commission against Racism and Intolerance cited "reports of discrimination in access to employment, as well as in remuneration," for immigrants.

Lithuania

Political Rights Rating: 1
Civil Liberties Rating: 1
Freedom Rating: 1
Freedom Status: Free
Electoral Democracy: Yes

Population: 2,956,000
Capital: Vilnius

Ten-Year Ratings Timeline For Year Under Review (Political Rights, Civil Liberties, Status)

Year Under Review	2004	2005	2006	2007	2008	2009	2010	2011	2012	2013
Rating	2,2,F	1,1,F	1,1,F	1,1,F	1,1,F	1,1,F	1,1,F	1,1,F	1,1,F	1,1,F

INTRODUCTION

In May 2013, the Lithuanian Parliament ratified the United Nations Convention on the Reduction of Statelessness and amended Lithuania's citizenship law, paving the way for the government to confer citizenship upon some of the country's 4,000 stateless residents.

In July, Labor Party founder Viktor Uspaskich and three other Labor Party officials were convicted in a fraud scheme. Uspaskich was sentenced to four years in prison and the others received lesser sentences; all four have filed appeals.

A report released in June by the country's state security department said Lithuania's dependence on Russian natural gas represented a threat to the country's energy security; in 2012, Lithuanian officials moved to sue Russia's state gas company, OAO Gazprom, for €1.4 billion ($1.9 billion) at the Stockholm Arbitration Tribunal, alleging that the firm had overcharged Lithuania for gas shipments. The case remained ongoing at year's end.

Lithuania, which joined the European Union (EU) in 2004, assumed the six-month, rotating EU presidency in July, becoming the first Baltic nation to hold the position. Soon after the presidency began, Russia took steps to discourage the import of Lithuanian goods in an apparent attempt to intimidate nations in the Eastern Partnership, a bloc of six former Soviet republics that had indicated a willingness to expand ties with the EU. Lithuania in November hosted a summit of the Eastern Partnership initiative, at which Moldovan and Georgian officials initialed partnership agreements with the EU. Russia in December lifted a ban on Lithuanian dairy products implemented earlier in the year.

In November, state intelligence agents interrogated journalists with the Baltic News Service (BNS) and confiscated several of the agency's computers in an attempt to compel the agency to reveal its sources. The order allowing the searches and questioning was later overturned.

POLITICAL RIGHTS: 37 / 40

A. Electoral Process: 12 / 12

Lithuania's 1992 constitution established a unicameral, 141-seat Parliament (Seimas), with 71 members elected in single-mandate constituencies and 70 chosen by proportional representation, all for four-year terms. The prime minister is named by the president, but is subject to confirmation by the parliament. The president is directly elected, and may serve up to two five-year terms. Recent presidential and parliamentary elections were deemed largely free and fair, though there were some reports of irregularities, including alleged bribery and forged ballots. Dalia Grybauskaitė, an independent candidate, was elected president in 2009 with nearly 70 percent of the vote, becoming the first woman to hold the post. She is expected to run for reelection in 2014, but had not formally announced her candidacy by the year's end.

In the 2012 parliamentary elections, voters, weary of austerity programs enacted by the Homeland Union–Lithuanian Christian Democrats (TS-LKD), dealt the governing coalition a major defeat. Following two rounds, the opposition Social Democratic Party of Lithuania (LSDP) finished first with 38 seats; the TS-LKD captured 33 seats; the Labor Party took 29 seats; the right-wing Order and Justice Party won 11 seats; and the Liberal Movement (LRLS) captured 10 seats. LSDP leader Algirdas Butkevičius became prime minister and assembled a four-party coalition comprising the LSDP, the Labor Party, Order and Justice, and the Lithuanian Poles' Electoral Action, which had won eight seats in the legislature.

B. Political Pluralism and Participation: 16 / 16

Lithuania's many political parties operate freely. While Lithuanian politics have been characterized by shifting coalitions, the LSDP and the TS-LKD—which formed in 2008 with the merger of the Homeland Union and the Lithuanian Christian Democrats—have dominated the political arena in recent years. Support for the Labor Party and the Order and Justice Party revolves around their charismatic patrons—respectively, the Russian-born Uspaskich and Rolandas Paksas, a former president who was impeached in 2004. Lithuania's Polish minority is represented by the Lithuanian Poles' Electoral Action. The Communist Party is banned.

In June 2013, Lithuania's state security department reported that Russian security services actively spy on Lithuanian institutions and have made efforts to influence government decision-making and inflame existing ethnic tensions in the country.

C. Functioning of Government: 9 / 12

Corruption remains a problem in Lithuania, though the country in recent years has attempted to prosecute a number of senior officials suspected of abusing their power. In July 2013, a court found four Labor Party officials, including Uspaskich, guilty of participating in a fraud scheme between 2004 and 2006 that benefited the Labor Party. Uspaskich, the party's founder and a member of Parliament, was sentenced to four years in prison; Vitalija Vonžutaitė, another Labor Party parliamentarian, received a three-year prison term; former Labor Party accountant Marina Liutkevičienė was sentenced to one year in prison; and Labor Party leader Vytautas Gapšys, who was also deputy parliament speaker, was ordered to pay a fine of about €10,000 ($14,000). All four filed appeals, but if the rulings against them are upheld, Uspaskich and Vonžutaitė will also be compelled to pay more than €870,000 ($1.2 million) in restitution to the state. In October, Gapšys stepped down as deputy parliament speaker ahead of a no-confidence vote that appeared likely to force him from the position; Parliament Speaker Vydas Gedvilas, also of Labor, stepped down as well. Gapšys also resigned as Labor Party head, and Loreta Graužinienė, a Labor Party MP, became the party's new leader as well as the new parliament speaker.

In April, a Vilnius court opened hearings concerning an apparent vote-buying scheme during the 2012 parliamentary elections that allegedly benefited the Labor Party. In November, it found four party members guilty of the scheme; two were ordered to pay a €7,500 ($10,200) fine, and the other two were ordered to perform 90 hours of community service and placed on a form of probation for one year. Meanwhile, in May, the Baltic Institute of Corporate Governance said Lithuania did not meet Organization for Economic Cooperation and Development (OECD) standards for operating public companies, citing inadequate anticorruption efforts and a tendency among politicians to consider political factors when making business decisions. Nevertheless, the OECD that same month mentioned Lithuania as a potential candidate to join the body.

Petty bribery remains a problem, though authorities have become increasingly resistant to such attempts in recent years. Despite these improvements, widespread belief remains that personal contacts inside the government are required to access ostensibly public services. Lithuania was ranked 43 out of 177 countries and territories surveyed in Transparency International's 2013 Corruption Perceptions Index.

CIVIL LIBERTIES: 53 / 60

D. Freedom of Expression and Belief: 16 / 16

The government generally respects freedoms of speech and the press. However, defamation is a criminal offense punishable by fines and jail terms of up to two years. Hate speech is a crime, as is the denial of war crimes and speech trivializing Nazi or Soviet crimes. In June 2013, a Vilnius court issued a €217 ($299) fine against a man who had displayed a portrait of Soviet leader Josef Stalin at a May ceremony commemorating the Soviet victory over Nazi Germany; the portrait was confiscated. The offender was found to have violated a measure barring the display of communist symbols at mass gatherings. In November, Lithuania's Special Investigation Service (SIS) took efforts to compel BNS, the largest news agency in the Baltics, to identify its sources. The pressure came after BNS, citing Lithuanian intelligence sources, had reported in October that Lithuanian intelligence agents had said Russian officials were planning to launch a misinformation campaign about Grybauskaitė. A subsequent judicial order prompted searches and interrogations of BNS journalists, and the confiscation of several computers. A court in December reversed the earlier order, following criticism of the searches from Grybauskaitė, BNS, and others.

A 2010 law bans the publication of material deemed harmful to minors, though no one has been prosecuted under it. Privately owned newspapers and independent broadcasters express a wide variety of views and criticize the government freely; however, the press suffers from inadequate standards for transparency of ownership. The government does not restrict internet access.

Freedom of religion is guaranteed by law and largely upheld in practice. However, nine so-called traditional religious communities, including the Roman Catholic Church, enjoy certain government benefits, including annual subsidies, which are not granted to other groups. Academic freedom is respected.

E. Associational and Organizational Rights: 11 / 12

Freedoms of assembly and association are generally observed. However, individuals and groups must obtain permission from authorities before staging protests larger than 15 people.

In May, authorities ruled that a member of the Lithuanian Poles' Electoral Action pay €145 ($199) for holding an unsanctioned demonstration; the fine was later canceled on appeal.

Nongovernmental organizations may register without facing serious obstacles, and human rights groups operate without restrictions. Workers may form and join trade unions, strike, and engage in collective bargaining, though there have been reports of employees being punished for attempting to organize.

F. Rule of Law: 13 / 16

The constitution guarantees judicial independence, which is largely respected in practice. Defendants generally enjoy due-process rights, including the presumption of innocence and freedom from arbitrary arrest and detention, but detained suspects are not always granted timely access to an attorney. Police abuse of detainees and lengthy pretrial detentions remain problems. Prisons suffer from overcrowding, and inmates have poor access to health care.

Discrimination against ethnic minorities, who comprise about 16 percent of the population, remains a problem, especially among the small Romany population. In recent years, Lithuania has moved to compensate the country's small Jewish community for property that was seized by the Nazi and Soviet regimes.

G. Personal Autonomy and Individual Rights: 13 / 16

Lithuanian residents may travel freely within the country and internationally, and residents generally enjoy economic freedom.

Marriage is defined in Lithuania's constitution as a union between a man and a woman, and members of LGBT community face discrimination. Vilnius officials in 2013 moved to ban Baltic Pride, an LGBT march, from taking place in the city center, but indicated that it could take place in a less central location. Baltic Pride's organizers successfully appealed the move, and the event took place peacefully in July. However, Vilnius mayor Artūras Zuokas later complained that the march amounted to socially divisive propaganda and asserted that Vilnius "needs no more of these festivals."

Men and women enjoy the same legal rights, though women earn about 12 percent less than men for every hour of work. However, that rate is comparatively better than the EU average, under which women earn about 16 percent less than men.

Domestic violence, including both spousal and child abuse, remains a serious problem. In March 2013, the European Court of Human Rights (ECHR) ruled that officials had failed to adequately investigate a woman's complaint of domestic abuse by her partner, and ordered that the government pay the woman €5,000 ($7,000) in damages. Lithuania continues to be a source, transit point, and destination for the trafficking of women and girls for the purpose of prostitution.

Luxembourg

Political Rights Rating: 1
Civil Liberties Rating: 1
Freedom Rating: 1.0
Freedom Status: Free
Electoral Democracy: Yes

Population: 543,000
Capital: Luxembourg

Ten-Year Ratings Timeline For Year Under Review (Political Rights, Civil Liberties, Status)

Year Under Review	2004	2005	2006	2007	2008	2009	2010	2011	2012	2013
Rating	1,1,F	1,1,F	1,1,F	1,1,F	1,1,F	1,1,F	1,1,F	1,1,F	1,1,F	1,1,F

INTRODUCTION

Prime Minister Jean-Claude Juncker submitted his resignation on July 11, 2013, after losing parliamentary support in the wake of a scandal over alleged misconduct by Luxembourg's intelligence service, including wiretapping and bribery. Prime minister since 1995, and from 2005 to January 2013 chairman of the Eurogroup—consisting of the finance ministers of the eurozone member nations—Juncker was the longest-serving European Union (EU) head of government when he resigned, and had had disproportionate influence in EU affairs.

In October general elections, Juncker's Christian Social People's Party (CSV) took 33.7 percent of the vote and lost three seats in parliament, its worst showing since 1999. However, it remained the largest party. In December, Xavier Bettel of the Democratic Party took over as prime minister, replacing Juncker, who had remained in office with his cabinet until then.

POLITICAL RIGHTS: 39 / 40 (-1)

A. Electoral Process: 12 / 12

Luxembourg's head of state is the unelected Grand Duke Henri, whose powers are largely ceremonial. The unicameral legislature, the Chamber of Deputies, consists of 60 members elected by proportional representation to five-year terms. The legislature chooses the prime minister. Voting is compulsory for Luxembourg's citizens. Foreigners constitute more than a third of the population.

In parliamentary elections on October 20, the CSV captured 23 seats, down from 26 in the 2009 election, while the Luxembourg Socialist Workers' Party (LSAP) and the Democratic Party (DP) each won 13 seats. The Greens took 6 seats, and smaller parties hold the remaining 5 seats. The elections were held seven months early as a result of the collapse of Juncker's government. On October 25, Grand Duke Henri asked DP leader Xavier Bettel, mayor of the city of Luxembourg, to form a government. Bettel was sworn in as prime minister December 4 as the head of a three-way coalition with the LSAP and the Greens joining his DP, excluding the CSV and ending Juncker's years in power.

B. Political Pluralism and Participation: 16 / 16

The political system is open to the establishment of new parties. There are three traditionally strong parties: the CSV, historically aligned with the Catholic Church; the LSAP, a formerly radical but now center-left party representing the working class; and the DP, which favors free-market economic policies. The CSV has governed since 1945, except for a brief hiatus in 1975–1979.

C. Functioning of Government: 11 / 12 (-1)

The government is largely free from corruption. However, Juncker resigned in response to the disclosure of abuses by the State Intelligence Service, including secret recordings of the conversations of politicians and taking of payments in return for access to local officials. A parliamentary review found that Juncker, to whom the intelligence service reported, had failed to control the service or report misconduct to lawmakers. He was forced to step down when the LSAP, the junior party in his coalition, withdrew its support for the government.

Luxembourg was ranked 11 out of 177 countries and territories surveyed in Transparency International's 2013 Corruption Perceptions Index. As one of the world's largest offshore financial centers, Luxembourg has been criticized for its bank secrecy rules. In April 2013, the government agreed to comply with the EU Savings Directive, changing its rules to allow the exchange of banking information with other EU governments as of 2015. In November, an Organization for Economic Co-operation and Development review found that Luxembourg was failing to meet international standards for tax transparency.

CIVIL LIBERTIES: 60 / 60
D. Freedom of Expression and Belief: 16 / 16

Freedom of expression is guaranteed by the constitution. A single conglomerate, RTL, dominates broadcast radio and television. Newspapers generally represent a broad range of opinion. Internet access is not restricted.

Although Roman Catholicism is the dominant religion, there is no state religion, and the state pays the salaries of clergy from a variety of Christian sects. Islamic clergy, however, are not supported. In October 2012, a government-commissioned report said that 95.6 percent of state funding for religious institutions went to the Catholic Church, and recommended a more equitable distribution for other faiths. School children must choose to study either the Roman Catholic religion or ethics; most choose the former. Academic freedom is respected.

E. Associational and Organizational Rights: 12 / 12

Freedoms of assembly and association are protected, and nongovernmental organizations operate freely. Luxembourgers may organize in trade unions, and approximately 40 percent of the workforce is unionized. The right to strike is constitutionally guaranteed.

F. Rule of Law: 16 / 16

The judiciary is independent, though judges are still appointed by the grand duke. Detainees are treated humanely in police stations and prisons.

Luxembourg's Muslim minority, mainly of Bosnian origin, faces no official hostility. A 2011 law increased penalties for hate speech. A July report by the European Asylum Support Office said Luxembourg rejected 98 percent of first-time asylum applications, the highest rejection rate in the EU. Luxembourg agreed to accept 60 Syrian asylum seekers in September 2013, although the government's plan to house them in an isolated former mental asylum drew criticism from an advocacy group for immigrant workers.

G. Personal Autonomy and Individual Rights: 16 / 16

Luxembourg protects private property rights, scoring 90.0 out of 100 on the Index of Economic Freedom.

While women comprise more than half of the labor force, they are underrepresented at the highest levels of government; 17 women currently serve in the 60-member parliament, and only four hold seats in the 15-member cabinet. While the law does not technically allow for abortion on demand, women can legally have abortions if in "distress." The Chamber of Deputies in November 2012 approved legislation that allowed abortions in a greater number of cases while maintaining current penalties for unapproved abortions. According to the 2013 U.S. State Department report on human trafficking, Luxembourg has not yet implemented comprehensive protections for victims of trafficking.

Same-sex couples have the right to registered partnerships. The new coalition agreement includes same-sex marriage and adoption rights for same-sex couples, both of which had previously been stalled in the parliament; no bill had been passed by year's end. In December, Bettel became the nation's first openly gay prime minister.

Macedonia

Political Rights Rating: 3
Civil Liberties Rating: 3
Freedom Rating: 3.0
Freedom Status: Partly Free
Electoral Democracy: Yes

Population: 2,066,000
Capital: Skopje

Ten-Year Ratings Timeline For Year Under Review (Political Rights, Civil Liberties, Status)

Year Under Review	2004	2005	2006	2007	2008	2009	2010	2011	2012	2013
Rating	3,3,PF	3,3,PF	3,3,PF	3,3,PF	3,3,PF	3,3,PF	3,3,PF	3,3,PF	3,3,PF	3,3,PF

INTRODUCTION

Macedonia began 2013 with a political crisis that had erupted in late December 2012, when the government of Prime Minister Nikola Gruevski unilaterally approved a 2013 budget after ejecting opposition lawmakers and journalists from the parliament chamber. In response, several opposition legislators quit the government, and the opposition began organizing antigovernment protests.

In January 2013, the crisis escalated when the opposition Social Democratic Union of Macedonia (SDSM) and its allies vowed to boycott local elections scheduled for March 24, saying Gruevski intended to rig the vote. The standoff continued until March 1, when, during European Union–brokered talks, Gruevski's governing Internal Macedonian Revolutionary Organization–Democratic Party for Macedonian National Unity (VMRO–DPMNE) and the SDSM-led opposition agreed to form a parliamentary commission to investigate the December incident. The conservative VMRO–DPMNE and its allies won the March elections, but initially refused to sign an August report by the parliamentary commission, which found that the December 2012 ejection of opposition legislators and journalists had been illegal. But the VMRO–DPMNE ultimately agreed to sign the report amid concerns that Macedonia's EU bid could be undermined if the crisis were to drag on.

On the first weekend of March, riots engulfed Skopje as ethnic Macedonians and ethnic Albanians clashed with each other and with police. On March 1, hundreds of ethnic Macedonians gathered to protest the recent appointment of Talat Xhaferi, a former Albanian separatist military leader, as defense minister. A day later, ethnic Albanians protested in response. At least 22 people were injured and 18 were arrested during the unrest.

In June, VMRO–DPMNE, following a rushed legislative process that omitted some usual legal processes and allowed little time for public debate, passed a controversial abortion law in a parliamentary session boycotted by all opposition lawmakers except one, who appeared to vote against it. The new law, adopted just two weeks after its proposal by the health ministry, required women seeking an abortion to file a request for one—a process requiring them to affirm that they had seen a gynecologist, had attended counseling, and had informed the "spouse" of their decision to have the procedure. The law additionally barred women from receiving more than one abortion per year.

POLITICAL RIGHTS: 26 / 40
A. Electoral Process: 8 / 12

Members of the unicameral, 123-seat Sobranie (Assembly) are elected to four-year terms by proportional representation. Parliament elects the prime minister. The president is elected to a five-year term through a direct popular vote, but the prime minister holds most executive power. Most postindependence elections have met international standards.

In 2009, university professor Gjorge Ivanov, running for the VMRO–DPMNE, won a presidential runoff against the SDSM's Ljubomir Frčkoski. In June 2011, Macedonia held early parliamentary elections, leading to a third consecutive victory for the VMRO–DPMNE-led coalition, which took 56 seats. An SDSM-led coalition followed with 42 seats; the ethnic Albanian Democratic Union for Integration (DUI) took 15 seats, the Democratic Party of Albanians captured 8, and the National Democratic Revival won 2. Gruevski secured a third term as prime minister. International observers called the polls competitive and transparent.

In the March 2013 local elections, 350 candidates competed for mayoral positions in 80 municipalities plus Skopje. The VMRO–DPMNE-led bloc won with 56 mayors, followed by the DUI with 14, and the SDSM with 4. In Skopje, incumbent Mayor Koce Trajanovski of the VMRO-DPMNE was reelected. The VMRO–DPMNE also won the most municipal council seats. Despite some irregularities, the polls were competitive and efficiently administered, according to an assessment by the Organization for Security and Cooperation in Europe (OSCE), whose monitors observed the elections.

Under the constitution and other legislation, citizens have the right to change their government peacefully. Suffrage is universal.

B. Political Pluralism and Participation: 11 / 16

Since Macedonian independence in 1991, power has alternated between center-left and center-right governments. The center-right VMRO–DPMNE has won every parliamentary election since 2006, ruling in coalition with several parties representing ethnic minorities. The left-leaning SDSM held power through much of the 1990s and early 2000s, and is the leading opposition party today.

Ethnic Albanians comprise 25 percent of the population. A political party representing Albanians has sat in each ruling coalition. In 2000 and 2001, Albanians mounted an armed insurgency, demanding better political representation. Unofficially, the insurgents also wanted control of smuggling routes in northwestern Macedonia. The August 2001 negotiations known as the Ohrid Accords prevented civil war, but ethnic violence between ethnic Macedonians and ethnic Albanians continues to erupt periodically.

In 2011, the Assembly added three seats for representatives of Macedonians living abroad. Certain types of legislation must pass by a majority of legislators from both main ethnic groups.

C. Functioning of Government: 7 / 12

Corruption is a serious problem. While relevant anticorruption legislation is in place and existing measures to clarify party funding sources and prevent conflicts of interest have been strengthened in recent years, implementation is weak. Graft and misconduct are widespread in public procurement. In July 2013, former Prime Minister Vlado Buckovski and four others were convicted for illegal procurement of tank parts in 2001. The judiciary lacks a track record of handling high-level corruption cases, and greater interagency cooperation is needed to identify problem areas in anticorruption efforts, according to the European Commission (EC). In a positive development, the Public Prosecutor's Office for Organized Crime and Corruption is now fully staffed, though its technical administrative capacity is subpar. Macedonia was ranked 67 out of 177 countries and territories surveyed in Transparency International's 2013 Corruption Perceptions Index.

CIVIL LIBERTIES: 38/60
D. Freedom of Expression and Belief: 11 / 16

The constitution provides for freedom of the press. However, the country's media face political pressure and harassment, resulting in self-censorship, and media outlets are divided along ethnic lines. In December 2010, Velija Ramkovski, the owner of the pro-opposition A1 Television channel, and more than a dozen associates were charged with crimes including tax evasion in a case widely regarded as politically motivated. During the investigation, A1 Television and three of Ramkovski's newspapers closed due to unpaid taxes. In March 2012, Ramkovski was convicted on numerous charges and sentenced to 13 years in prison. In June 2012, the Broadcasting Council shut down A2 Television, Ramkovski's last remaining media outlet, after it began broadcasting political content and hired journalists who had worked at A1 before its closure.

In November 2012, the government decriminalized libel under European standards, though steep new fines for libel were introduced, which journalists said would have a chilling effect. In 2013, the head of Macedonia's security services, Saso Mijalkov, sued the opposition-oriented weekly *Fokus* for libel over a report concerning the former Macedonian ambassador to the Czech Republic, Igor Ilievski. In a quotation published in the report, Ilievski appeared to accuse Mijalkov of masterminding his ouster to protect dubious business interests in the Czech Republic. The case was ongoing at year's end. In 2013, journalists also fought a new media law that would create a regulator empowered to revoke broadcasting licenses and impose sanctions to protect "citizens' interests," a vague term media watchdogs say could be abused to muzzle the press. In late December, parliament passed both the new media law and legislation on audio-visual services despite the objection of journalists and opposition legislators, who boycotted the vote. Throughout 2013, watchdogs including the OSCE criticized Macedonia for the incarceration of the journalist Tomislav Kezarovski, who was held in extended pretrial detention after being detained May 28 for allegedly revealing in print the identity of a protected witness in a murder case. In October, he was convicted and sentenced to four and a half years in prison. In early November, Kezarovski was released on house arrest awaiting appeal. Media coverage of the 2013 local elections was often partisan. Internet access is unrestricted.

The constitution guarantees freedom of religion. A long-standing dispute between the breakaway Macedonian Orthodox Church and the canonically recognized Serbian Orthodox Church remained unresolved in 2013. Hard-line Islamists reportedly control several mosques, with financing from Middle Eastern countries.

Though academic freedom is generally unrestricted, the education system is weak by European standards. Textbooks barely cover the postindependence period, primarily because ethnic Macedonians and ethnic Albanians interpret the 2001 conflict differently. In 2012, the European Association of History Educators urged history-education reform. Increasingly, schools are becoming ethnically segregated.

E. Associational and Organizational Rights: 8 / 12

Constitutional guarantees of freedoms of assembly and association are generally respected. In addition to the March riots, 2013 also saw peaceful protests over the political crisis, reproductive rights, and other issues. Nongovernmental organizations generally operate freely but are often polarized along political lines. Workers may organize and bargain collectively, though trade unions lack stable financing and skilled managers, and journalists have reportedly been fired over their union activities.

F. Rule of Law: 8 / 16

Improving judicial independence, impartiality, and efficiency remains a priority for Macedonia, though 2013 saw some relevant progress. From January 2013, all new first-instance judges must be graduates of the Academy for Judges and Prosecutors, a development meant to strengthen professionalism and independence. Courts continue to reduce the case backlog, and new software for judicial statistics was installed in courts and the Judicial Council in 2013 to help evaluate their performance, according to the EC. Prison conditions are generally unsatisfactory, with overcrowding and poor health care.

In June 2012, the parliament passed a lustration law aimed at removing former Yugoslav secret police collaborators from public office. The law, which the opposition SDSM had voted against, allows the names of informants to be published online. Critics said the law raises concerns about privacy.

In May 2013, the Macedonian Helsinki Committee for Human Rights released a study finding that crimes motivated by ethnic hatred and other discrimination are underreported because authorities have intentionally mislabeled them.

Roma, ethnic Albanians, and other vulnerable groups face discrimination. Minority groups say that the ongoing Skopje 2014 urban development plan ignores their heritage. Anti-LGBT sentiment is widespread, and in 2013 Human Rights Watch admonished authorities to thoroughly investigate a series of attacks against members of the LGBT community in June and July, including during Macedonia's first gay pride week, at which assailants attacked an LGBT-themed film screening in Skopje. A 2010 antidiscrimination law does not prohibit discrimination on the basis of sexual orientation.

G. Personal Autonomy and Individual Rights: 11 / 16

Travel is generally unrestricted. Membership in a party within the ruling coalition is often a precondition for employment in the public sector. While the government has streamlined procedures to launch a business, licensing fees can be prohibitively expensive. Official unemployment is 30 percent, but the actual figure is smaller given Macedonia's sizeable gray economy. While women in Macedonia enjoy the same legal rights as men, societal attitudes limit their participation in nontraditional roles, and women rarely participate in local politics. In Albanian Muslim areas, many women are subject to proxy voting by male relatives. Thirty-four women were elected to the 123-seat legislature in 2011. Despite the ongoing implementation of a strategy against domestic violence, it remains a serious problem, as does the trafficking of women for forced labor and prostitution.

Madagascar

Political Rights Rating: 5
Civil Liberties Rating: 4
Freedom Rating: 4.5
Freedom Status: Partly Free
Electoral Democracy: No

Population: 22,600,000
Capital: Antananarivo

Ratings Change: Madagascar's political rights rating improved from 6 to 5 due to the holding of competitive and peaceful presidential and parliamentary elections that were deemed free and fair by international and regional observers.

Ten-Year Ratings Timeline For Year Under Review (Political Rights, Civil Liberties, Status)

Year Under Review	2004	2005	2006	2007	2008	2009	2010	2011	2012	2013
Rating	3,3,PF	3,3,PF	4,3,PF	4,3,PF	4,3,PF	6,4,PF	6,4,PF	6,4,PF	6,4,PF	5,4,PF

INTRODUCTION

In October 2013, following numerous delays, Madagascar held a generally peaceful first-round presidential election that was deemed free and fair. The election marked a significant step toward resolving a protracted political crisis that began with a 2009 military coup and the installation of Andry Rajoelina as president. Rajoelina continued to lead a transitional government throughout 2013, and former president Marc Ravalomanana, who was ousted by Rajoelina, remained in exile. The Special Electoral Court rejected the candidacies of Rajoelina; Lalao Ravalomanana, Marc Ravalomanana's wife; and former president Didier Ratsiraka, who returned to Madagascar in April, ending an 11-year exile. A presidential runoff and legislative elections were held on December 20, though the official results had not yet been announced at year's end.

The 2009 coup and ensuing political crisis seriously damaged Madagascar's economy. Economic and security conditions remained strained in 2013, especially in the south. Following Rajoelina's takeover, the international community imposed severe sanctions on the country—but continued to provide humanitarian aid—and tourists and foreign businesses stayed away. In September, the African Union acknowledged the progress toward elections by lifting personal sanctions it had imposed on Rajoelina and his allies in 2010.

The World Bank estimated in early 2013 that 84 percent of Malagasies would be below the poverty line during the year, and as of September, 90 percent of the population lived on less than two dollars a day. Economic hardship was exacerbated by a cyclone that struck in February and a locust plague that threatened crops on nearly two-thirds of the island.

POLITICAL RIGHTS: 15 / 40 (+8)

A. Electoral Process: 6 / 12 (+5)

In early 2009, Ravalomanana handed power to the military following months of violent protests sparked by the closing of a television station owned by Rajoelina. The military quickly transferred power to Rajoelina, who suspended the elected bicameral parliament. Under an internationally mediated agreement in 2011, Rajoelina was recognized as interim president and appointed a transitional administration and parliament to serve until elections could be held.

In 2012, as part of the planned transition, a National Independent Electoral Commission was appointed to overhaul the inaccurate voter rolls and register voters for presidential and parliamentary elections. The elected president would serve up to two five-year terms, and the 151-seat National Assembly would serve five-year terms, with 64 seats filled through party-list voting in 32 multimember constituencies and 87 through majoritarian contests in single-member districts. Plans for the creation of an upper house, the Senate, were postponed indefinitely.

After further negotiations, the Southern African Development Community (SADC) endorsed a plan in December 2012 under which neither Rajoelina nor Ravalomanana would run in the presidential election. However, in April 2013, Lalao Ravalomanana filed papers to register her candidacy, prompting Rajoelina to renege and declare his own candidacy. The electoral commission approved both filings, as well as that of former president Ratsiraka, and delayed the vote until August 2013, prompting many international donors to suspend funding. In August, all three candidates were barred by the electoral court amid international pressure, and the first round of the presidential election was postponed again.

The presidential vote was finally held on October 25. Ravalomanana ally Jean Louis Robinson and Rajoelina ally Hery Rajaonarimampianina emerged as the leading candidates and faced off in a December 20 second round, which coincided with the National Assembly elections. The replacement of many regional governors with military officers in November raised concerns about possible rigging in the December balloting. Nevertheless, both the October and December elections were generally peaceful and deemed free and fair by the European Union and others. Both presidential candidates claimed victory, but official results were not released by year's end.

B. Political Pluralism and Participation: 8 / 16 (+3)

Prior to the 2009 coup, approximately 150 parties were registered in Madagascar. However, only a few had a national presence, and they tended to suffer from internal divisions, shifting alliances, and a lack of resources and clear ideology. After Rajoelina took power, opposition political activity was circumscribed through arbitrary bans on meetings and protests, as well as harassment, arrests, and killings of opposition supporters. In July 2013, police arrested presidential hopeful Laza Razafiarison, a former World Bank analyst, and seven others during an unauthorized campaign rally. However, political parties were generally able to operate with increased openness ahead of the October 2013 presidential election, and over 30 candidates took part. Political parties continued to openly hold rallies leading up to the December elections. Presidential rallies were controversially attended by Rajoelina and Lalao Ravalomanana in support of their respective candidates.

During Rajoelina's tenure, key political rivals were kept out of the country with the threat of arrest. Ravalomanana, who went into exile in South Africa after his ouster, was sentenced in absentia in 2010 to life in prison with hard labor for allegedly ordering the killing of at least 30 opposition protesters in February 2009. In 2012, a plane carrying the former president was prevented from landing in Madagascar. Also that year, despite pressure from SADC to pass an amnesty law that would allow for the unconditional return of all political exiles, the transitional parliament approved a law that excluded those who had committed "serious violations of human rights and fundamental freedoms," such as murder. This made Ravalomanana ineligible for the amnesty due to his 2010 conviction.

In February 2013, Ravalomanana lost his appeal of a South African court's order that he surrender his passport in connection with the 2009 massacre case. He remained in exile in South Africa at the end of 2013. Lalao Ravalomanana returned to Madagascar in March.

C. Functioning of Government: 1 / 12

Corruption worsened after the 2009 coup and remains a major problem, due in part to the transitional government's failure to enforce antigraft laws. In spite of a 2010 decree that prohibited the logging, transport, trading, and export of precious woods, the illegal trade continues. In 2011, the Extractive Industries Transparency Initiative (EITI) suspended

Madagascar on the grounds that the program could not be effectively implemented under the transitional government. Nevertheless, in 2012, Madagascar published its EITI report for 2010. The report showed that the government had doubled its income from natural resources to around $145 million, including a $100 million payment from China's Wuhan Iron & Steel Co. for exploratory iron-ore drilling. Illegally harvested rosewood and other precious timbers continued to be smuggled offshore in 2013. Madagascar was ranked 127 out of 177 countries and territories surveyed in Transparency International's 2013 Corruption Perceptions Index.

CIVIL LIBERTIES: 28 / 60

D. Freedom of Expression and Belief: 9 / 16

The constitution provides for freedoms of speech and of the press. However, Rajoelina has largely ignored these protections, and the independent outlets that have remained in operation are subject to government censorship, harassment, and intimidation. In 2012, Free FM, the last opposition radio station, shut down due to intimidation from the transitional government after having broadcast statements by the leaders of an army mutiny; it remained closed until December 2013, when it resumed broadcasting.

In late 2012, Free FM editors Lalatiana Rakotondrazafy and Fidel Razara Pierre were convicted and sentenced to three years in prison for allegedly organizing an illegal demonstration in May of that year, when thousands of people rallied in Antananarivo in support of the station. Despite the verdict, Rakotondrazafy and Pierre remained free pending an appeal during 2013, and they organized supporters of Free FM into a new political party that participated in the December parliamentary elections. Pierre stood as a candidate for the party.

The Malagasy people have traditionally enjoyed religious freedom, but the transitional authorities subjected a Protestant denomination associated with Ravalomanana to discrimination and harassment, and members of the Muslim community have reported some forms of discrimination. Academic freedom is generally respected.

E. Associational and Organizational Rights: 7 / 12

Freedom of assembly has been severely curtailed since the unrest in early 2009, and officials of the transitional government and the security forces routinely deny permission for demonstrations or forcibly repress gatherings. In July 2013, police advised protesters to avoid political demonstrations, alleging an opposition conspiracy to incite violence. In August, pro-Ravalomanana demonstrators took to the streets to protest the rejection of Lalao Ravalomanana's presidential candidacy by the Special Electoral Court.

Freedom of association is generally respected, and hundreds of nongovernmental organizations, including human rights groups, are active. Workers have the right to join unions, engage in collective bargaining, and strike. The transitional government has generally allowed strikes by public-sector unions to go forward. More than 80 percent of workers are engaged in agriculture, fishing, and forestry at a subsistence level.

F. Rule of Law: 5 / 16

The judiciary remains susceptible to corruption and executive influence. Its acquiescence in the face of Rajoelina's unconstitutional rise to power highlighted its weakness as an institution, and subsequent judicial decisions were tainted by frequent intimidation. Nevertheless, the Special Electoral Court demonstrated a degree of independence by barring Rajoelina, Lalao Ravalomanana, and Ratsiraka from participating in the 2013 elections. A lack of training, resources, and personnel hampers judicial effectiveness, and case backlogs are prodigious. More than half of the people held in the country's prisons are pretrial detainees, and prisoners suffer from harsh and sometimes life-threatening conditions. Customary-law courts in rural areas continue to lack due process guarantees and regularly issue summary and severe punishments.

The army and security forces have largely been beyond civilian control since the 2009 coup, and crime, violence, and insecurity have risen. Clashes in the south among villagers, security forces, and cattle thieves known as *dahalos*—who had come to be affiliated with criminal gangs—continued in 2013. Security operations to rein in the bandits have led to mass killings of civilians and indiscriminate burning of villages. In July 2013, at least 73 people were killed in clashes between cattle raiders and security forces. Separately, in March, a mob invaded a prison in search of suspects detained for the murder of a respected nun. Police fired into the crowd, killing two people.

A political cleavage has traditionally existed between the coastal *côtier* and the highland Merina peoples, of continental African and Southeast Asian origins, respectively. Due to past military conquest and long-standing political dominance, the status of the Merina tends to be higher than that of the côtier. Ethnicity, caste, and regional solidarity are often factors that lead to discrimination. LGBT (lesbian, gay, bisexual, and transgender) people also face discrimination from some segments of the state and society, and conditions reportedly grew worse after the 2009 coup.

G. Personal Autonomy and Individual Rights: 7 / 16

Despite government efforts and decentralized village patrols, free movement is hampered in the regions tormented by the well-armed dahalo groups. Dahalo raids have led to an uptick in domestic refugees, and security patrols cease operations after dark.

Malagasy women hold significantly more government and managerial positions than women in many continental African countries. However, they still face societal discrimination and enjoy fewer opportunities than men for higher education and employment. There have been reports of an increase in domestic violence since the coup, as personal conflicts arise over dwindling family resources. According to the U.S. State Department's 2013 *Trafficking in Persons Report*, weakened rule of law and a decline in economic development since the coup have led to an increase in the number of Malagasy women and children trafficked to the Middle East for forced labor and sex work. However, the report found that the transitional government made greater efforts to combat the problem than it had in previous years.

Malawi

Political Rights Rating: 3
Civil Liberties Rating: 4
Freedom Rating: 3.5
Freedom Status: Partly Free
Electoral Democracy: Yes

Population: 16,338,000
Capital: Lilongwe

Ten-Year Ratings Timeline For Year Under Review (Political Rights, Civil Liberties, Status)

Year Under Review	2004	2005	2006	2007	2008	2009	2010	2011	2012	2013
Rating	4,4,PF	4,4,PF	4,3,PF	4,4,PF	4,4,PF	3,4,PF	3,4,PF	3,4,PF	3,4,PF	3,4,PF

INTRODUCTION

In her first full year in office, President Joyce Banda of the People's Party (PP)—who succeeded President Bingu wa Mutharika following his sudden death in April

2012—struggled to maintain domestic support and implement reforms to revive Malawi's fragile economy. Upon taking office, Banda won praise from the international community for her initial efforts to restore respect for human rights and press freedom in the wake of Mutharika's increasingly repressive rule, and to implement economic reforms demanded by the International Monetary Fund (IMF) and other donors as a condition for restoring aid that had been cut off under Mutharika. These reforms included a 49 percent devaluation of the kwacha in May 2012. In return, the IMF in June 2012 agreed to restart a three-year, $157 million loan; other international donors also restored aid. Malawi—ranked 170 out of 187 countries and territories on the UN Development Programme's Human Development Index—relies on foreign donors for about 40 percent of its total budget.

The kwacha devaluation resulted in inflation, damaging Banda's domestic standing. By January 2013, popular outrage over the skyrocketing price of items such as maize, sugar, salt, and fuel led to protests and strikes by civil servants in several major cities. The strikes lasted until February, when Banda gave in to workers' demands for a substantial wage increase.

In March 2013, a commission of inquiry into the events surrounding Mutharika's death released a report finding that several high-ranking government officials had attempted to unconstitutionally transfer power to the president's brother, Peter Mutharika, rather than to Banda, the vice president, who had fallen out with the president and the then-ruling Democratic Progressive Party (DPP) in 2010. Soon after the commission released its report, 12 former officials of Mutharika's government were arrested and charged with treason. In June, the Malawi Electoral Commission (MEC) set a May 2014 date for the country's tripartite elections, in which long-delayed local elections would be held alongside presidential and parliamentary polls.

In October, a major corruption scandal known as Cashgate came to light, in which it was revealed that more than $250 million had been stolen from the government by mid-level officials and civil servants. This prompted international donors to suspend millions of dollars of crucial budget support, undermining Banda's efforts to revive the economy and potentially damaging her prospects in the 2014 election.

POLITICAL RIGHTS: 26 / 40
A. Electoral Process: 8 / 12

The president is directly elected for five-year terms and exercises considerable executive authority. The unicameral National Assembly is composed of 193 members elected by popular vote to serve five-year terms. In the 2009 presidential election, Mutharika defeated John Tembo, the head of the Malawi Congress Party (MCP), with approximately 66 percent of the vote. Mutharika's running mate, Banda, a grassroots women's rights activist, became Malawi's first female vice president. In concurrent parliamentary elections, Mutharika's DPP won 112 seats in the legislature; the MCP took 26, and the United Democratic Front (UDF) captured 17. According to international and domestic observers, the polls were the most free and competitive since the first multiparty elections in 1994. However, incumbents enjoyed a clear advantage due to the use of state resources during the campaign period and clear bias in the government-controlled media.

In late 2010, Mutharika unsuccessfully attempted to dismiss Banda as vice president. This sparked a crisis, as the vice president is an elected position that cannot be removed by the president. Banda refused to resign, and was supported by the courts. In December 2010, the DPP expelled Banda, who created her own party, the PP. Since Banda came to power, the PP has gained strength in the National Assembly, winning support from opposition defectors and holding about 80 seats as of June 2013. Some opposition members have called for section 65 of the constitution—which requires the speaker of the National Assembly to declare vacant the seat of any legislator who switched parties—to be applied, though no such action had been taken as of the end of the year.

While opposition groups had questioned the impartiality and legitimacy of the MEC in previous years, key observers concluded that it operated with sufficient transparency during the 2009 elections. In 2012, Banda, in consultation with several political parties, appointed 10 new MEC commissioners and a new chairperson. In June 2013, the MEC announced that all eligible voters would be required to re-register between July and January 2014.

B. Political Pluralism and Participation: 11 / 16

The main political parties are the PP, the DPP, the MCP, and the UDF. New political parties are allowed to register unhindered. There were reports of intimidation of the opposition when the DPP was in power under Mutharika, though this has reportedly lessened under the leadership of Banda and the PP. By August 2013, the four main parties had held their conventions and selected their 2014 presidential candidates: Banda for the PP, Peter Mutharika for the DPP, Atupele Muluzi—son of former president Bakili Muluzi—for the UDF, and Reverend Lazarus Chakwera of the MCP, which had ruled Malawi for nearly three decades after independence in 1963.

C. Functioning of Government: 7 / 12

Upon claiming the presidency, Banda made tackling corruption and waste a top priority. In October 2012, she announced that both she and Vice President Khumbo Kachali would take voluntary 30 percent pay cuts as part of a national austerity plan, and in September 2013, the Treasury announced that it would use the $15 million earned from selling the presidential jet—purchased by President Mutharika—to buy locally grown maize to feed Malawi's poor. Corruption remains endemic, however, with an estimated 30 percent of Malawi's annual budget lost to fraud.

Banda's administration was rocked by a corruption scandal sparked by the near-fatal shooting in September 2013 of Paul Mphwiyo, the budget director in the Finance Ministry who was reportedly conducting several corruption investigations. The shooting unearthed revelations of widespread government fraud and corruption, with some cases involving millions of kwacha in state funds discovered in the homes and cars junior officials and civil servants. As much as $250 million was believed to have gone missing since 2006. The fraud revelations led to a strike in early October by public health workers, who were protesting delays in the payment of their September salaries. Public hospitals also suffered from shortages of essential drugs and equipment. In late October, Kachali said the fraud was made possible by loopholes in the Integrated Finance Management Information System, a central payment system that the government began using in 2005.

The revelations caused public outrage and prompted calls for Banda and Finance Minister Ken Lipenga to resign. In response, Banda fired her entire cabinet on October 10, and announced the creation of a special unit to audit all government departments. Days later, she appointed a new cabinet, retaining 27 of the 32 members but replacing the Lipenga and Justice Minister Ralph Kasambara. Kasambara was later arrested in connection with Mphwiyo's shooting, and scores more were detained on fraud and corruption charges, although these were mainly lower-level officials. In November, the European Union, the United Kingdom, and Norway—members of a coalition called the Common Approach to Budgetary Support—withheld their portions of a $120 quarterly aid package to Malawi, due to a lack of confidence in the government's financial management system.

In November, the National Assembly passed a bill requiring high-level public officials to declare their assets and other financial interests (the constitution already requires the president and vice president to declare their assets to the speaker of the National Assembly when they are elected). However, Malawi lacked a Freedom of Information law, making it difficult for the public to obtain such information in practice.

Malawi was ranked 91 out of 177 countries and territories surveyed in the Transparency International (TI) 2013 Corruption Perceptions Index.

CIVIL LIBERTIES: 34 / 60
D. Freedom of Expression and Belief: 11 / 16

Freedom of the press is legally guaranteed, and although Mutharika cracked down on the media in 2011 and early 2012, the situation improved markedly under the Banda administration. The National Assembly in May 2012 repealed a Mutharika-era law granting the information minister power to ban publications deemed contrary to the public interest, and harassment and arrests of journalists declined after Banda took power. However, Banda in May 2013 refused calls from regional press freedom activists to become the third African head of state to endorse the Declaration of Table Mountain, which calls on African governments to abolish criminal defamation laws. (Libel is both a criminal and civil offense in Malawi.) Days earlier she had noted her displeasure with the press's criticism of her administration. There were incidents during the year in which government operatives harassed or assaulted journalists. In June, parliament's chief security officer was arrested for assaulting journalist Thoko Chikondi while she was photographing consumer rights advocate John Kapito in the parliament building. In August, a cabinet minister's bodyguards assaulted Zodiak Broadcasting Station journalist Raphael Mlozoa, after Mlozoa allegedly published false news about the minister.

In the past, the government-controlled Malawi Broadcasting Corporation and TV Malawi—historically the dominant outlets—displayed a significant bias in favor of the government. However, under Banda the MBC has made some progress in transforming into a true public broadcaster, giving air time to diverse viewpoints—including opposition figures—on its talk shows and news programs.

Religious and academic freedom are generally respected.

E. Associational and Organizational Rights: 7 / 12

The climate for civil society and opposition groups has improved notably under Banda, after being weakened under Mutharika. The right to organize labor unions and to strike is legally protected, with notice and mediation requirements for workers in essential services. Unions are active and collective bargaining is practiced, but workers face harassment and occasional violence during strikes. Since only a small percentage of the workforce is formally employed, union membership is low.

In January 2013, thousands of people peacefully demonstrated in major cities across Malawi to protest what they alleged were IMF-imposed economic reforms, after inflation topped 33 percent. Led by Kapito's lobby group Consumers Association of Malawi, they demanded a reversal of the kwacha devaluation, wage increases, and that Banda reduce her travel expenditures. In February, nearly all of the country's approximately 120,000 civil servants—including teachers and doctors—went on strike, demanding a 65 percent pay increase to address the rising cost of living. They were joined at one point by public school students, who marched on a private school run by the Joyce Banda Foundation. In February, Banda's government agreed to a 61 percent wage increase for the lowest-paid government workers. Labor relations remain fraught, however, as evidenced by the October health sector strike and repeated threats of labor action in other sectors through the end of the year.

F. Rule of Law: 9 / 16

Judicial independence is generally respected. However, the overburdened and inefficient court system lacks resources, personnel, and training. Banda appointed several new High Court judges in October 2012.

In early March 2013, a commission in inquiry—led by a respected former Supreme Court judge—released its report into the events surrounding Mutharika's death and attempts by his supporters to unconstitutionally take power. The report found that several high-ranking officials in the government had attempted to cover up the president's death until they could figure out a way to transfer power to Peter Mutharika rather than to Banda. However, the commander of the Malawian Defence Force, General Henry Odillo, refused to go along with the scheme, arguing that it was unconstitutional, and his support was key in Banda's eventual assumption of power.

Soon after the commission released its report, 12 officials of Mutharika's government—including Peter Mutharika and current Economic Planning Minister Goodall Gondwe—were arrested and charged with treason. (Gondwe resigned two days after his arrest.) The arrests sparked protests by DPP supporters in Lilongwe and Blantyre, and riot police fired tear gas to disperse the crowds. The alleged plotters were released on bail days after their arrest; soon after, the high court judge who granted their bail, Ivy Kamanga, received death threats, allegedly from high-ranking members of Banda's government. The treason trial was adjourned in early April, but resumed in November with nine of the defendants pleading not guilty.

Police brutality is reportedly common, as are arbitrary arrests and detentions. One of Banda's first actions was the replacement of the police inspector general, Peter Mukhito, with Loti Dzonzi, a noted human rights advocate who pledged to tackle corruption in the force. However, TI's 2013 Global Corruption Barometer, released in July, found that 95 percent of respondents believed that the police were corrupt or extremely corrupt. Prison conditions are dire, characterized by overcrowding and extremely poor health conditions; many inmates—some of whom are forced to wait up to three years to face trial—die from AIDS and other diseases. Abuse of younger inmates is commonplace.

Consensual sexual activity between same-sex couples is illegal and is punishable with up to 14 years in prison. Upon taking office, Banda had announced her intention to repeal these colonial-era laws, and in November 2012, then justice minister Kasambara said the laws would be suspended while their constitutionality was examined. While Kasambara soon backtracked on that statement and the laws remained in place as of the end of 2013, there was some evidence that the Banda government was giving increased support to LGBT (lesbian, gay, bisexual, and transgender) advocates.

G. Personal Autonomy and Individual Rights: 7 / 16

Property rights do not receive adequate protection, and starting a business can be a cumbersome process, with licensing costing more than 10 times the average annual income and taking more than 200 days. Business is also impeded by corruption in the various customs, tax, and procurement agencies.

Women recorded significant gains in the 2009 elections, winning 22 percent of the seats. Despite constitutional guarantees of equal protection, customary practices perpetuate discrimination against women in education, employment, business, and inheritance and property rights. Violence against women and children remains a serious concern, though in recent years there has been greater media attention on and criminal penalties for abuse and rape. Forced marriage, early marriage, and "wife inheritance," in which widows are passed on to a male relative, are still practiced in some areas. However, the Banda administration has made efforts to address these problems. In February 2013, the National Assembly passed the Gender Equality Bill, which brought the country's law into line with the 1979 Convention on the Elimination of All Forms of Discrimination against Women. In a March report to the United Nations, Gender Minister Anita Kalinde said the government had set up support centers across the country for victims of domestic violence, and that the number of reported cases of violence against women had increased significantly.

Trafficking in women and children, both locally and to locations abroad, is a problem. Penalties for the few successfully prosecuted traffickers have been criticized as too lenient, and the government's efforts to protect victims and prevent trafficking have been criticized by the U.S. State Department. A 2010 Child Care, Protection, and Justice Bill detailed the responsibilities of parents for raising and protecting their children and outlines the duties of local authorities to protect children from harmful, exploitative, or undesirable practices.

⬇ Malaysia

Political Rights Rating: 4
Civil Liberties Rating: 4
Freedom Rating: 4.0
Freedom Status: Partly Free
Electoral Democracy: No

Population: 29,794,000
Capital: Kuala Lumpur

Trend Arrow: Malaysia received a downward trend arrow due to electoral fraud and structural obstacles designed to block the opposition from winning power, a decision by an appellate court to forbid non-Muslims from using the term "Allah" to refer to God, and worsening hostility and prejudice faced by the LGBT community.

Ten-Year Ratings Timeline For Year Under Review (Political Rights, Civil Liberties, Status)

Year Under Review	2004	2005	2006	2007	2008	2009	2010	2011	2012	2013
Rating	4,4,PF	4,4,PF	4,4,PF	4,4,PF	4,4,PF	4,4,PF	4,4,PF	4,4,PF	4,4,PF	4,4,PF

INTRODUCTION

In 2013, the ruling Barisan Nasional (BN) coalition used a combination of economic rewards, and continued harassment of opposition leaders to ensure victory in the general elections on May 5. The BN won a minority of the popular vote, but took 60 percent of the seats in Parliament, and 10 out of 13 state governments.

The BN government has engaged in suppressing political opposition and dissent. In October, Parliament passed legislation that allows indefinite detention of suspects without trial. Critics argued that the provision was a bid to re-impose the most draconian elements of the Internal Security Act (ISA), which was repealed in 2012. Also in October, an appeals court ruled that non-Muslims cannot use the term "Allah" to refer to God which impacts freedom of speech and freedom of worship for all non-Muslims in Malaysia. In 2013 we also saw increasing attacks on Shiite practitioners, houses of Shiite adherents were raided, and the Youth wing of UMNO called on the government to amend the constitution's definition of Islam to specify Sunni Islam as the official religion. There was also increased government pressure on news media. The weekly publication *The Heat* was issued a "show cause" letter for an article on the prime minister and his wife's financial status. The publication was ordered to cease publishing on December 19. The LGBT community also faced increasing harassment from state and national government offices.

POLITICAL RIGHTS: 19 / 40 (-1)
A. Electoral Process: 6 / 12

The leader of the coalition that wins a plurality of seats in legislative elections becomes prime minister. Executive power is vested in the prime minister and cabinet. The paramount ruler, the titular head of state, is elected for five-year terms by fellow hereditary rulers in 9 of Malaysia's 13 states. Tuanku Abdul Halim Mu'adzam Shah was elected to the post in December 2011. The upper house of the bicameral Parliament consists of 44 appointed members and 26 members elected by the state legislatures, serving three-year terms. The lower house, with 222 seats, is popularly elected at least every five years.

The Election Commission (EC) is frequently accused of manipulating electoral rolls and gerrymandering districts to aid the ruling coalition, and the Registrar of Societies arbitrarily decides which parties can participate in politics. The first-past-the-post voting system also increases the power of the largest grouping. In April 2012, a government committee issued recommendations for electoral reforms, many of which had been called for by the Coalition for Free and Fair Elections (Bersih)—an alliance of civil society organizations working for electoral reforms, transparency in government, and an end to corruption. However, there was widespread skepticism that the existing EC could be trusted to implement the recommended changes. For example, one change implemented was the use of indelible ink to mark who had already voted; however, some voters and electoral watchdog groups charged that this ink was easily washed off.

The BN won the May 2013 parliamentary elections, capturing 133 seats in the lower house despite receiving only 47 percent of the overall popular vote. Among the three main opposition parties, the Democratic Action Party (DAP) took 38 seats, the People's Justice Party (PKR) took 30, and the Pan-Malaysian Islamic Party (PAS) won 21. The opposition and observers accused the BN of electoral fraud, citing irregularities like phantom voting and power outages that occurred in vote-tallying centers in a number of constituencies that the opposition parties hoped to win. There is also criticism of gerrymandering and other structural flaws in the electoral system which helps to ensure victory for the ruling coalition. To air grievances about the 2013 election, the Malaysian Electoral Roll Analysis Project (MERAP) published a report of the electoral irregularities, and in September a People's Tribunal was held to hear evidence in public from anyone who had a story to tell about electoral problems. Other heavy-handed tactics against opposition parties include the Registrar of Societies' (RoS) censure of the DAP for the conduct of their last two-party elections.

B. Political Pluralism and Participation: 7 / 16 (-1)

The BN coalition and its pre-1973 predecessor organization have governed Malaysia since independence. Most of its constituent parties have an ethnic or regional base, including the dominant United Malays National Organization (UMNO) and the United Traditional Bumiputera Party (PBB), whose stronghold is in Sarawak.

In addition to the skewed electoral framework, the three main opposition parties face obstacles such as unequal access to the media, restrictions on campaigning and freedom of assembly, and politicized prosecutions, all of which make it difficult for them to compete on equal terms with the BN. The effectiveness of these barriers in preventing a rotation of power was underscored by the 2013 election results.

PKR leader Anwar Ibrahim has been dogged by claims that he "sodomized" a young male aide in June 2008, a charge he said was a politically motivated fabrication. It followed a similar case against him in 2000. He was acquitted of the 2008 charges in January 2012, but a government appeal of the acquittal was pending at the end of 2013.

C. Functioning of Government: 6 / 12

Government favoritism and blurred distinctions between public and private enterprises create conditions conducive to corruption. Officials regularly move back and forth between the private and public sectors, fostering many opportunities for improper collusion and graft. Political parties are allowed to own or have financial holdings in corporate enterprises. Government and law enforcement bodies have suffered a series of corruption scandals in recent years. The Malaysian Anti-Corruption Commission (MACC) has itself come under scrutiny for its interrogation practices, as two suspects have died after falling from MACC office buildings since 2009. Inquests ruled one death a suicide and the other an accident. Malaysia was ranked 53 out of 177 countries surveyed in Transparency International's 2013 Corruption Perceptions Index. The Whistleblower Protection Act took effect in December 2010, but it did not significantly improve transparency. Corruption continues to be a significant problem. In 2013, new corruption allegations surfaced against former chief minister of Sarawak, now Governor, Abdul Taib Mahmud. The recent charges relate to a company linked to his son Mahmud Abdul Bekir that may have been used to as a front to receive RM6.6 million in commissions for a waste disposal project involving a state government joint venture with the German firm Trienekens GMBH. The charges were made by the rights group Global Witness.

CIVIL LIBERTIES: 28 / 60

D. Freedom of Expression and Belief: 8 / 16 (-1)

Freedom of expression is constitutionally guaranteed but restricted in practice. Parliament amended the 1984 Printing Presses and Publications Act (PPPA) in April 2012, retaining the home minister's authority to suspend or revoke publishing licenses but allowing judicial review of such decisions. The amendments also eliminated the requirement that publications and printers obtain annual operating permits. A 2012 amendment to the 1950 Evidence Act holds owners and editors of websites, providers of web-hosting services, and owners of computers or mobile devices used to publish content online accountable for information published on their sites or through their services. Malaysian press freedom advocates, bloggers, and opposition politicians staged a 24-hour internet blackout to protest the legislation. Critics of the amendment also charged that it would effectively shift the burden of proof to the accused.

Most private print outlets are controlled by parties or business groups allied with the BN. Privately owned television stations also have close ties to the BN and generally censor programming according to government guidelines. State outlets reflect government views. Books and films are directly censored or banned for profanity, violence, and political and religious material. Publications often face harassment from the government. In December of 2013, the Home Ministry temporarily suspended *The Heat* (a weekly news magazine) from publishing. This was in reaction to the magazine's publication of a front-page story on PM Najib and his wife's activities and spending of taxpayer money. The publication was first issued a "show cause" letter and then later told to cease publishing. The media outlet was suspended indefinitely. The internet has emerged as a primary outlet for free discussion and for exposing cases of political corruption. The government has responded in recent years by engaging in legal harassment of critical bloggers, charging them under defamation laws, the Official Secrets Act, and the Sedition Act, all of which can draw several years in prison. The Malaysian Communication and Multimedia Commission (MCMC), an agency responsible in part for regulating the internet, has been known to monitor online content and order outlets or bloggers to remove material it views as provocative or subversive. The government responds unevenly to cyber-blogging activity and sensational issues: sometimes allowing information to stay up, and sometimes censoring it.

While the BN government continues to articulate the need for a tolerant and inclusive form of Islam, religious freedom is restricted in Malaysia. Ethnic Malays are defined by the constitution as Muslims, and practicing a version of Islam other than Sunni Islam is prohibited. Muslim children and civil servants are required to receive religious education using government-approved curriculums and instructors. Proselytizing among Muslims by other religious groups is prohibited, and a 2007 ruling by the country's highest court effectively made it impossible for Muslims to have their conversions to other faiths recognized by the state; in very rare exceptions, non-Malays have been allowed to revert to their previous faiths after converting to Islam for marriage. Non-Muslims are not able to build houses of worship as easily as Muslims, and the state retains the right to demolish unregistered religious statues and houses of worship. Mainstream media outlets regularly attack the Shiite minority, with the newspaper *Utusan Malaysia* labeling Shiite beliefs as "deviant teachings" and "serious threats."

Discrimination against Shiites increased significantly in late 2013. Homes of Shiite adherents were raided, inflammatory sermons were given at Friday prayers denouncing Shiite believers and practices, and 16 people were arrested for supposedly spreading Shiite teachings, this reflects Malaysia's ban on the spreading of Shiite beliefs and practices. After the assassination of a religious affairs officer in November, UMNO amplified its effort to portray itself as a pious party by tabling a constitutional amendment that would identify Malaysia as a Sunni Muslim nation, and by calling for a government commission to protect Sunni Islam against "deviant" religious sects and the LGBT (lesbian, gay, bisexual, and transgender) community.

A court ruling in late 2009 overturned a government ban prohibiting non-Muslims from using the word Allah to refer to God, touching off a wave of January 2010 arson attacks and vandalism that struck Christian churches as well as some Muslim and Sikh places of worship. After much delay, an appeals court ruled in October 2013 that non-Muslims cannot use the word Allah to refer to God. The decision was seen as a devastating blow to both freedom of religion and freedom of private discussion, as Malay-speaking Christians had long used the word in their scriptures (in Malay-language Christian Bibles) and daily life but would now face potential criminal sanctions. As of the end of 2013 a final appeal was still pending.

The government restricts academic freedom; teachers or students espousing antigovernment views or engaging in political activity have long been subject to disciplinary action under the Universities and University Colleges Act (UUCA) of 1971. However, following a 2011 court finding that the constitution protected students' involvement in political campaigns, Parliament in April 2012 amended the UUCA to allow students to take part in political activities off campus. Students were especially targeted for participating in talks and meetings by opposition political parties, and in arrests following post-election rallies, known as the "Black 505" rallies demonstrating anger and opposition to the conduct and results of the May 2013 General Election.

Freedom of expression has also come under fire in 2013 when the director of a documentary on the Sri Lankan atrocities against the Tamil Tigers had a screening of her film shut down by the Censorship Board and some of the Malaysian organizers were taken into custody for questioning.

E. Associational and Organizational Rights: 6 / 12 (+1)

Freedoms of assembly and association are limited on the grounds of maintaining security and public order. The Peaceful Assembly Act, passed in late 2011, lifted a rule requiring police permits for nearly all public gatherings. However, other provisions were seen as a bid to restrict rather than safeguard freedom of assembly, including a prohibition on street protests and the levying of excessive fines for noncompliance with this rule. In addition, the law delineates 21 public places where assemblies cannot be held—including within 50 meters of houses of worship, schools, and hospitals—and prohibits persons under the age of 15 from attending any public assembly.

Demonstrations surrounding the 2013 elections attracted crowds up to 120,000 people. On May 22, at least 18 peaceful protesters and seven organizers were arrested and charged under the Peaceful Assembly Act. Some (including student leader Adam Adli) were also charged under the Sedition Act. Possible penalties could include various fines up to RM5,000 (approx. $1,800) and/or three years of jail time. Despite these threats and harassment of opposition leaders and civil society activists, repression of these activities was not as bad as in 2012. Thus, there seems to be somewhat more space to protest, this is particularly true on less political issues such as concerns over the environment. For example, protests were allowed to be carried out in Sarawak protesting the construction of the Baram Dam. Local residents and environmental organizations are upset about the possible environmental impact of the dam and the displacement of 20,000 indigenous people.

The Societies Act of 1996 defines a society as any association of seven or more people, excluding schools, businesses, and trade unions. Societies must be approved and registered by the government, which has refused or revoked registrations for political reasons. Numerous nongovernmental organizations operate in Malaysia, but some international human rights organizations are forbidden from forming Malaysian branches. Suaram, one of the leading human rights groups in the country, faced government harassment in 2012, including allegations of financial irregularities. This harassment continued in 2013 with staff members being investigated for their working to expose problems of corruption like the Scorpene case. Likewise, civil society groups and their leaders were detained and harassed for protesting the conduct and results of the 2013 election.

Most Malaysian workers—excluding migrant workers—can join trade unions, but the law contravenes international guidelines by restricting unions to representing workers in a single or similar trade. The director general of trade unions can refuse or withdraw registration arbitrarily, and the union recognition process can take from 18 to 36 months. Collective bargaining is limited. Unions in essential services must give advance notice of strikes; various other legal conditions effectively render strikes impossible. Amendments to the Employment Act further weakened workers' rights in 2011 by removing responsibility from employers and allowing greater use of subcontracting arrangements.

F. Rule of Law: 5 / 16

Judicial independence is compromised by extensive executive influence. Arbitrary or politically motivated verdicts are common, with the most prominent example being the convictions of opposition leader Anwar Ibrahim in 1999 and 2000 on charges of corruption and sodomy. The 2000 sodomy conviction was overturned in 2004, and Anwar was released from prison, but the corruption charge was upheld, delaying his return to elected office until 2008. A second charge of sodomy against him began that year, and although he won an acquittal in January 2012, the government's appeal of the verdict was pending at the end of 2013.

Malaysia's secular legal system is based on English common law. However, Muslims are subject to Sharia (Islamic law), the interpretation of which varies regionally, and the Constitution's Article 121 stipulates that all matters related to Islam should be dealt with in Sharia courts. This results in vastly different treatment of Muslims and non-Muslims regarding "moral" and family law issues.

The 1960 Internal Security Act (ISA) gave the police sweeping powers to hold any person acting "in a manner prejudicial to the security of Malaysia" for up to 60 days, extendable to two years without trial. The law was used to jail mainstream politicians, alleged Islamist militants, trade unionists, suspected communist activists, ordinary criminal suspects, and members of "deviant" Muslim sects, among others. Detainees have reported cases of torture while in custody; official documentation of these claims is rare. The ISA was replaced in June 2012 with the Security Offences (Special Measures) Act, which abolished preventive detention but left the definition of "security offences" so broad as to raise serious concerns about the intent of the measure. The new law allows police to detain anyone for up to 28 days without judicial review, and suspects may be held for 48 hours before being granted access to a lawyer. In October 2013 Parliament passed an amendment to the Prevention of Crime Act (PCA), a law ostensibly aimed at combating organized crime. The amendment allows a five-member board to order the detention of individuals listed by the Home Ministry for renewable two-year terms without trial or legal representation. The existing PCA had allowed detentions of 72 days. A New Year's Eve demonstration held December 31, 2013, to protest price increases on food, fuel, and tolls was organized by rights organizations such as Turun and was interpreted as anti-government, seditious, activity and organizers were facing arrest at year's end.

Although the constitution provides for equal treatment of all citizens, the government maintains an affirmative action program intended to boost the economic status of ethnic Malays and other indigenous people, known collectively as bumiputera. Bumiputera receive preferential treatment in areas including property ownership, higher education, civil service jobs, and business affairs, and bumiputera-owned companies receive the lion's share of large government contracts. In September 2013, the government announced a new "bumiputera economic empowerment" agenda, devoting close to 30 billion ringgits ($9.2 billion) in new funding to support for bumiputera-owned businesses.

LGBT people face discrimination and harassment. In 2012, Prime Minister Najib called the LGBT community an example of a "deviant culture" that threatens Malaysia. His remarks were consistent with those found in the country's mainstream media. Same-sex sexual relations are punishable by up to 20 years in prison under the penal code, and some states apply their own penalties to Muslims under Sharia statutes. In 2013, the government continued its increased attacks on LGBT individuals, the Ministries of Health and Education initiated "educational" campaigns warning parents, teachers, counselors, and young people to work to "prevent, overcome, and correct" symptoms of homosexuality in children. The Ministry of Information banned TV and radio shows depicting gay characters.

G. Personal Autonomy and Individual Rights: 9 / 16

Women are underrepresented in politics, the professions, and the civil service. Violence against women remains a serious problem. Muslim women are legally disadvantaged because their family grievances are heard in Sharia courts, where men are favored in matters such as inheritance and divorce; women's testimony is not given equal weight. Despite some progress in investigating and punishing sex-trafficking offenses, government efforts to combat trafficking are inadequate.

Foreign household workers are often subject to exploitation and abuse by employers. An estimated two million foreigners work in Malaysia illegally. If arrested and found guilty, they can be caned and detained indefinitely pending deportation. Questions are also being raised about indigenous rights in the planned displacement of possibly tens of thousands of people from the construction of the Baram Dam in Sarawak.

Maldives

Political Rights Rating: 4
Civil Liberties Rating: 4
Freedom Rating: 4.0
Freedom Status: Partly Free
Electoral Democracy: No

Population: 360,000
Capital: Malé

Ratings Change: The Maldives' political rights rating improved from 5 to 4 due to the largely free and fair presidential election held in November 2013, despite several delays and repeated interference by the Supreme Court.

Ten-Year Ratings Timeline For Year Under Review (Political Rights, Civil Liberties, Status)

Year Under Review	2004	2005	2006	2007	2008	2009	2010	2011	2012	2013
Rating	6,5,NF	6,5,NF	6,5,NF	6,5,NF	4,4,PF	3,4,PF	3,4,PF	3,4,PF	5,4,PF	4,4,PF

INTRODUCTION

A presidential election was held in Maldives in November 2013, following several aborted attempts; Abdullah Yameen of the Progressive Party of Maldives (PPM) ultimately prevailed. The polling, as well as the conduct of the Election Commission (EC), was deemed by both local and international observers to be free and fair, with high voter turnouts. However, repeated interference by the Supreme Court in the election weakened the overall democratic process.

The election followed the tumultuous events of 2012, in which President Mohamed Nasheed of the Maldivian Democratic Party (MDP) was forcibly removed from power after his administration's January 2012 arrest of judge Abdullah Mohamed. In 2013 Nasheed faced a politicized court case relating to the arrest, and briefly took refuge at the Indian embassy in Malé in February; in April, his trial was postponed until after the election and remained unresolved at year's end.

POLITICAL RIGHTS: 19 / 40 (+2)

A. Electoral Process: 7 / 12

Under Maldives' 2008 constitution, the president is directly elected for up to two five-year terms. The unicameral People's Majlis is composed of 77 seats, with members elected from individual districts to serve five-year terms.

Parliamentary elections held in May 2009 were largely transparent and competitive. Former president Maumoon Abdul Gayoom's Maldivian People's Party (DRP) won 28 of 77 seats, while the MDP captured 26.

A presidential election was held on September 7, 2013; turnout was almost 90 percent, and the process was deemed free and fair by both local and international monitors, including the independent EC. Former president Nasheed secured 45 percent of the vote, but failed to win enough votes to avoid a runoff. Abdullah Yameen, a half-brother of former president Gayoom and leader of the PPM, won 25 percent, while Gasim Ibrahim, a tycoon and resort owner, finished third with 24 percent. Sitting president Mohammed Waheed Hassan, who had replaced Nasheed the previous year, garnered only 5 percent.

Gasim challenged the results, and the Supreme Court issued rulings—based largely on a secret police report—nullifying the results and calling for a new first-round vote to be held by October 20. The court also designated the police to play a substantive role in handling the logistics for the election, and enumerated a list of 16 conditions for the election to take place; among them was a requirement that all candidates had to approve the voter lists prior to election day. The EC's attempt to hold a new election on October 19 was aborted when two of the three candidates—Gasim and Yameen—refused to sign the revised voter registry and the police refused to allow the election to move forward.

The election was finally held on November 9, with results broadly mirroring those of the September poll; Nasheed won nearly 47 percent of the votes, while Yameen received nearly 30 percent and Gasim again came third. In a runoff—which was delayed from November 10 to November 16 by the Supreme Court—Yameen pulled off a surprise win, aided by a last-minute endorsement from Gasim, taking 51 percent of the vote to Nasheed's 49 percent. Nasheed conceded, and Yameen was inaugurated as president on November 17.

B. Political Pluralism and Participation: 7 / 16 (+1)

Following several decades of rule by Abdul Maumoon Gayoom, Maldives' first multi-party presidential election was held in 2008, and the MDP's Mohamed Nasheed, a former political prisoner, triumphed over the incumbent. A number of political parties operate, and recent elections have been very competitive. The Political Parties Act, which restricts parties from registering and accessing official funds unless they have more than 10,000 members, was passed by the parliament in December 2012. The law was vetoed by President Waheed, but the parliament overrode the veto in March 2013 and the law took effect. As a result, 11 of Maldives' 16 parties were dissolved, including Waheed's Gaumee Itthihaad Party (GIP).

Former president Nasheed faced charges of abuse of power in 2013, which the MDP claimed were politically motivated. The high court issued a stay on proceeding to try the case in April 2013, pending investigation of the legality of a special court that had been established to adjudicate it, and the case remained unresolved at year's end. A number of other opposition lawmakers also faced being removed from their seats due to what the MDP alleged were politicized court cases; two were stripped of their seats by the Supreme Court in late October.

Political violence remained a concern in 2013, as the MDP faced some harassment surrounding attempted protests in support of Nasheed, although less than the previous year. The Supreme Court, the military, and the police repeatedly interfered in the electoral and democratic process in 2013.

C. Functioning of Government: 5 / 12 (+1)

The government functioned more regularly in 2013, allowing the election of a president from the political opposition. Nevertheless, political polarization and uncertainty, as well as corrupt behavior such as vote buying, limited elected officials' effectiveness in crafting policy or passing legislation. A law mandating access to government information is not implemented in practice.

The 2008 constitution and an independent auditor general have provided greater transparency in recent years, shedding light on pervasive corruption within all branches of government. An Anti-Corruption Commission (ACC), established in 2008, investigates cases of suspected corruption, but its work is hampered by inadequate manpower, and the vast majority of cases do not result in convictions. In 2013, the ACC requested that corruption charges be lodged against a former police commissioner; it also investigated the GIP regarding the issue of fraudulent party enrollments. In July, the ACC ruled out corruption regarding the lease of the Malé airport to the India-based company GMR Infrastructure; the government insists that the contract was illegal and will likely pursue the issue in court.

CIVIL LIBERTIES: 29 / 60

D. Freedom of Expression and Belief: 7 / 16

The constitution guarantees freedoms of expression and the press. However, journalists and media outlets faced attacks and harassment throughout 2013 as they attempted to cover the year's political turmoil, and news coverage has become more polarized since the February 2012 change in government. In March 2013, Ibrahim Waheed, the head of news at the pro-opposition Raajje TV, was attacked with an iron bar in Malé, and on October 7—the day the Supreme Court delayed the election—the station's offices were destroyed in an arson attack. The blocking of Christian websites by the Ministry of Islamic Affairs remains an issue. In July 2013, a political art show organized by Raaje TV was canceled after a government ministry refused access to the exhibition site.

Freedom of religion remains severely restricted. Islam is the state religion, and all citizens are required to be Muslims. Imams must use government-approved sermons. Non-Muslim foreigners are allowed to observe their religions only in private. In recent years, the rise of conservative strands of Islam has led to more rigid interpretations of behavior and dress, particularly for women, as well as an increase in rhetoric—and occasional physical attacks—against other religions as well as those who espouse more tolerant versions of Islam. There are no reported limitations on academic freedom, but many scholars self-censor.

E. Associational and Organizational Rights: 7 / 12

The constitution guarantees freedom of assembly, but a restrictive law passed in December 2012 limited the ability to protest outside of designated areas, required the media to have accreditation to cover protests, and defined "gatherings" as a group of more than one person. Preemptive detention is sometimes used to deter citizens from participating in protests. Police regularly used excessive force against peaceful protesters in 2013, including tear gas and pepper spray, and also beat and strip-searched unarmed civilians. In October, 65 MDP supporters were arrested following demonstrations protesting the delayed presidential vote.

Nongovernmental organizations (NGOs) struggle with funding and issues of long-term viability in a weak civil society environment, but a number of NGOs operate freely and comment on human rights and other sensitive issues. Harassment of NGOs increased in 2013, with threats and official investigations directed against Transparency Maldives and other groups that weighed in on sensitive political developments.

The constitution and the 2008 Employment Act allow workers to form trade unions and to strike, and a labor tribunal was established to enforce the act. Strikes do occur, although workers can sometimes face repercussions for industrial action. In February 2013, police broke up a strike by resort workers, arresting two. Nearly 30 others were dismissed from their positions with the resort.

F. Rule of Law: 7 / 16

The constitution provides for an independent judiciary, and a Judicial Services Commission (JSC) was established in 2009 to separate the judicial branch from the executive. However, a report released in early 2013 by a UN special rapporteur raised concerns regarding the transparency and politicization of the judiciary in general, and the JSC in particular. The role of the Supreme Court in repeatedly delaying the presidential election and nullifying the first round also raised concern.

Civil law is used in most cases, but it is subordinate to Sharia (Islamic law), which is applied in matters not covered by civil law and in cases involving divorce or adultery. As a result, the testimony of two women is equal to that of one man, and punishments such as internal exile and flogging continue to be carried out. Access to justice remains difficult for the substantial number of migrant workers in the country.

The constitution bans arbitrary arrest, torture, and prolonged detention without adequate judicial review. The abuse of individuals in custody remains a problem, although some cases are investigated by Maldives' Human Rights Commission (MHRC). Amid the political turmoil of 2012, protesters and political activists were arrested, detained, and tortured in custody, with MDP supporters in particular targeted for harsh treatment; there were fewer instances of these problems in 2013. An antitorture bill passed in December empowers the MHRC to combat the practice. The past several years have seen an increase in gang activity and violence, often linked to drugs and organized crime. More recently, political parties have used gangs to engage in political violence and attacks against opponents.

Religious minorities do not enjoy equal protection under the law. LGBT (lesbian, gay, bisexual, and transgender) individuals encounter societal intolerance; same-sex sexual conduct is prohibited by law and can draw penalties including house arrest, banishment, and lashes. Two men were charged with engaging in homosexual acts in August 2013.

G. Personal Autonomy and Individual Rights: 8 / 16

Freedom of movement both within and outside of Maldives is provided for by law and is generally allowed in practice. The close relationship between business owners and politicians led in 2013 to allegations that workers at some of the islands' tourist resorts had been fired due to their political sympathies or had been pressured to vote for a particular candidate in the presidential election. Property rights are generally weak, with most land owned by the government and then leased to private owners or developers.

Women are increasingly entering the civil service and receiving pay equal to that of men, though opportunities are sometimes limited by traditional norms, and women hold few senior government positions. Domestic violence against women is widespread, but a 2012 law criminalized several types of violence and provided protection for victims. International human rights groups have urged reform of severe legal punishments that primarily affect women, including the sentence of public flogging for extramarital sex. In a case that led to an international outcry, a 15-year-old rape victim was sentenced in February 2013 to 100 lashes and eight months of house arrest; the verdict was overturned by the high court in August. Efforts to address human trafficking have been sporadic and largely ineffective, and the exploitation of migrant workers, who comprise an estimated quarter of the country's population, is widespread.

Mali

Political Rights Rating: 5
Civil Liberties Rating: 4
Freedom Rating: 4.5
Freedom Status: Partly Free
Electoral Democracy: No

Population: 16,014,000
Capital: Bamako

Status Change: Mali's political rights rating improved from 7 to 5, its civil liberties rating improved from 5 to 4, and its status improved from Not Free to Partly Free due to the defeat of Islamist rebels, an improved security situation in the north, and successful presidential and legislative elections that significantly reduced the role of the military in politics.

Ten-Year Ratings Timeline For Year Under Review (Political Rights, Civil Liberties, Status)

Year Under Review	2004	2005	2006	2007	2008	2009	2010	2011	2012	2013
Rating	2,2,F	2,2,F	2,2,F	2,3,F	2,3,F	2,3,F	2,3,F	2,3,F	7,5,NF	5,4,PF

INTRODUCTION

Mali took steps toward returning to democracy in 2013, holding both presidential and parliamentary elections after a coup the previous year in which mutinous soldiers led by

Captain Amadou Sanogo overthrew the government due to its perceived inability to deal with the Tuareg rebellion in northern Mali. The coup had destabilized the country and allowed Tuareg separatists and Islamic militants to seize much of Mali's northern region.

In March 2012, mutinous soldiers led by Sanogo mounted a coup, removing democratically elected president Amadou Toumani Touré, suspending the constitution, and detaining government ministers. While some Malians welcomed the revolt, the international community condemned it, and the African Union (AU) and the Economic Community of West African States (ECOWAS) suspended Mali's membership. Sanogo handed power to interim president Dioncounda Traoré—the speaker of the National Assembly—in April, but the military maintained de facto authority over the civilian leadership until an elected president took office in September 2013.

Meanwhile, taking advantage of the turmoil in the capital, the Tuareg-led National Movement for the Liberation of the Azawad (MNLA) early in 2012 occupied the three main cities in Mali's north: Timbuktu, Kidal, and Gao; by April it had also taken the city of Douentza in central Mali. Over the course of the summer, Islamist militant groups that had cooperated with the MNLA— Al-Qaeda in the Islamic Maghreb (AQIM) and two splinter groups, Ansar Dine and the Movement for Unity and Jihad in West Africa (MUJAO)—turned on the Tuaregs and seized much of Mali's northern territory. By July, the MNLA was seeking a possible compromise with Mali's transitional government that included a level of autonomy short of full secession. Meanwhile, the Islamist groups in the north committed human rights abuses and destroyed religious monuments deemed un-Islamic.

In early January 2013, French forces began Operation Serval against Islamist groups in the north. The first strikes consisted of aerial bombardment, followed by a ground offensive by French and Malian forces. In total, 550 French soldiers were involved in the mission. France was later joined in the operation by the UN-authorized African-led International Support Mission to Mali (AFISMA), comprised of troops from mainly West and Central African countries. Between January and June 2013, the military government instituted a state of emergency, which gave the junta significant powers and severely limited freedom of assembly, by banning gathering of more than 50 people. The state of emergency was lifted in order to allow for elections campaigning.

By the end of January, the Islamist militants had been driven from Mali's northern cities; later in the year they turned to guerrilla tactics, including suicide bombings, raids, and landmines. In April 2013, the UN Multidimensional Integrated Stabilization Mission (MINUSMA), a peacekeeping force consisting of about 12,600 troops, began establishing itself on the ground; AFISMA formally transferred its authority to the UN force in July. As of December 2013, about 6,800 military personnel were deployed with a mandate to stabilize key centers in northern Mali, to help reestablish the authority of the Malian government, and to assist with the elections.

On June 18, 2013, the transitional government signed a peace agreement with MNLA rebels who were in control of Kidal that would allow the army to reenter the city. Fighting reoccurred in September and after a brief lull in October, fighting picked up again between MNLA supporters and the Malian army, as well as the MNLA supporters and Islamist groups.

With the Islamic militants being been driven underground and the Tuareg rebels agreeing to a fragile peace, Mali held presidential elections on July 28, with Ibrahim Boubacar Keïta emerging victorious. Legislative elections were in two rounds, on November 24 and December 15; Keïta's Rally for Mali (RPM) and its allies won an overwhelming majority.

POLITICAL RIGHTS: 17 / 40 (+12)

A. Electoral Process: 6 / 12 (+5)

According to the constitution—which had been suspended briefly in 2012 by the junta but was soon restored—the president, who appoints the prime minister, is elected by popular vote and can serve up to two five-year terms. Members of the 160-seat unicameral National Assembly serve five-year terms, with 13 seats reserved to represent Malians living abroad.

While the National Assembly was not dissolved following the coup, it was the interim government with Prime Minister Cheikh Modibo Diarra, appointed by interim President Dioncounda Traoré, that was in charge of preparing the parliamentary and presidential elections. The announcement was made in May 2013, with campaigning to start in early July. The military, however, remained ostensibly in charge until the new government of September 2013, and during the first half of the year it coordinated the military strategy with the French operation in the North.

The 2013 presidential elections were held over two rounds, on July 28 and August 11. Keïta, a former prime minister, won the presidency, taking about 40 percent of the vote and defeating Soumaïla Cissé—a former finance minister and leader of the Union for the Republic and Democracy (URD) party—who received about 20 percent. The elections were deemed generally free and fair by observers, and Cissé conceded shortly after the second round.

Security during the elections was overseen by French and AU forces; although there were several incidents of violence, the elections were generally peaceful. Turnout for the presidential elections was relatively high, at 49 percent. Keïta was sworn into office in September.

Legislative elections were held over two rounds, on November 24 and December 15. Keïta's RPM party won 66 seats; its allies won an additional 49 seats. The URD won 17 seats, and the Alliance for Democracy in Mali (ADEMA) party won 16. Turnout for parliamentary elections was lower than the presidential elections, at 38 percent. Foreign observers, including the EU mission and UN observers, declared both elections to have been conducted within the norm, despite high security.

A new electoral framework that was prepared for the cancelled elections prior to the 2012 coup as well as new biometric voter lists streamlined the elections process, although some criticism remained that such measures excluded the participation of those who did not receive their biometric voter ID cards on time.

B. Political Pluralism and Participation: 7 / 16 (+4)

The defeat of the Islamists in the north and the ousting of Sonogo's military junta led to circumstances in which political pluralism could return and all parties had equal chances of winning the presidential and legislative elections. The main parties in the 2013 elections were Rally for Mali (RPM), Union for the Republic and Democracy (URD), and Alliance for Democracy in Mali-Pan-African Party for Liberty, Solidarity and Justice (ADEMA).

No ethnic group dominates the government or security forces. Long-standing tensions between the more populous nonpastoralist ethnic groups and the Moor and Tuareg pastoralist groups have often fueled intermittent instability, leading up to the rebellion of 2012. Although the military government in the south and the Islamic militants in the north were ousted, Mali remains in a precarious position where insecurity limits full political rights.

C. Functioning of Government: 4 / 12 (+2)

Although Mali did not have an elected government through September 2013, the improving security situation has raised prospects of a functioning government moving forward.

A number of anticorruption initiatives had been launched under the administration of ousted president Touré, including the creation of a general auditor's office. However, while this office uncovered corruption in 2012, no legal proceedings have followed. However, corruption remained a problem in government, public procurement, and both public and private contracting. Seen by many as one of the main problems that led to the Islamist takeover in the North, fighting corruption is one of President Keita's main goals after winning elections, although several reports involve him in lavish expenses during his tenure as prime minister in 2000. Mali was ranked 127 out of 177 countries and territories surveyed in Transparency International's 2013 Corruption Perceptions Index.

CIVIL LIBERTIES: 27 / 60 (+8)

D. Freedom of Expression and Belief: 11 / 16 (+3)

Mali's media were considered among the freest in Africa before the 2012 rebellion and coup. Criminal libel laws had not been invoked by authorities since 2007, and there were no reports of harassment or intimidation of journalists in 2011. During 2012, however, an unprecedented number of journalists were illegally detained and tortured by the military and Islamist militants. Interviews with Touré and rebels were forbidden by the junta, and the national broadcaster was stormed by the military in April. The attacks on journalists decreased significantly in the second half of 2012. However, during 2013 Reporters Without Borders accused the Malian government of censoring reporters from reporting government abuses in the north and doing little to ensure their security. In November, two French journalists were kidnapped and murdered in the north. Mali is ranked 99th out of 179 countries in the 2013 Reporters Without Borders Press Freedom Index, a fall of 74 places since 2012.

Mali's population is predominantly Muslim, and the High Islamic Council has a significant influence over politics, especially by throwing their support for political candidates and parties. However, the state is secular, and minority religious rights are protected by law. In the north during 2012, Islamist militants imposed a crude form of Sharia (Islamic law) and destroyed Sufi Muslim shrines and other sacred sites that they deemed un-Islamic. Academic freedom was also suppressed in the rebel-held north. The situation improved in the second half of 2013, as the defeat of the Islamists allowed greater freedom of speech and belief, as well as increased academic freedom.

E. Associational and Organizational Rights: 6 / 12 (+2)

Freedoms of assembly and association were respected prior to the coup, and nongovernmental organizations (NGOs) operated actively without interference. The constitution guarantees workers the right to form unions and to strike, with some limitations regarding essential services and compulsory arbitration. Under the state of emergency that was in effect from January to July 2013, gatherings of more than 50 people were banned. However, with the overthrow of the rebels in the north and the restoration of an elected government in Bamako, people's freedom to protest, engage in civic advocacy, and assert labor rights has improved.

F. Rule of Law: 6 / 16 (+3)

The judiciary, whose members were appointed by the executive under the constitution, was not independent. Traditional authorities decided the majority of disputes in rural areas. The interim government made some improvements in 2012, including firing corrupt prosecutors. The situation also improved in 2013, relative to 2012, because coup leaders no longer controlled the judiciary after the elections, and Islamists in the North were no longer in control and committing extra-judicial executions. In a sign of relative independence from the military, the coup leader was arrested in November.

Detainees are not always charged within the 48-hour period set by law, and police brutality has been reported, though the courts have convicted some perpetrators. During 2012, however, people accused of crimes or perceived moral offenses were summarily punished and even executed in the north, while the junta regularly engaged in arbitrary arrests and detentions in the south.

In 2013, extrajudicial killings between Tuareg, Arab, and Malian army soldiers took place in northern Mali. There is also evidence that Tuareg and Arab populations in the north have been punished in an extrajudicial manner by Malian army troops. According to Human Rights Watch, there were at least 26 extrajudicial executions, 11 enforced disappearances, and over 50 cases of torture or mistreatment committed by the Malian army during the year. In November, a mass grave containing 21 soldiers was discovered near a military site in Kati, 30 km north of Bamako. These are the remains of mutinous soldiers who opposed General Sanogo and were summarily executed in 2012.

In November 2013, authorities arrested Sanogo, the leader of the 2012 coup. Sanogo was initially charged only with kidnapping, though prosecutors said they expected to add charges for the mass murder and torture of soldiers who opposed his coup.

G. Personal Autonomy and Individual Rights: 4 / 16

As a result of the intense fighting in 2012 and 2013, there was a significant uptick in Malian refugees fleeing into neighboring countries. As of the end of September, the UN Refugee Agency was attempting to address the needs of 152,856 Malian refugees in Algeria, Burkina Faso, Mauritania, and Niger. The estimated number of internally displaced persons inside Mali is about 254, 822 according to the Commission of Movements of Populations. According to the UN, over 1.3 million people in Mali are at risk of food insecurity as a result of climatic hazards and insecurity.

Women have been underrepresented in high political posts in Mali. The country's first female prime minister took office in 2011. Women won 14 seats, or about 9.5 percent, in the late 2013 legislative elections. Domestic violence against women is widespread, and cultural traditions hinder reform. Women faced heightened harassment, threats, and violence in the north in 2012 due to militants' enforcement of harsh restrictions on dress and behavior. The situation improved slightly in 2013 after the ouster of the militants.

Despite the creation of the National Coordinating Committee for the Fight Against Trafficking and Related Activities in 2011, adult trafficking has not been criminalized, and Mali remains a source, destination, and transit country for women and children trafficked for the purposes of sexual exploitation and forced labor. Prosecution of suspected traffickers is infrequent, with only two convictions in 2011. Traditional forms of slavery and debt bondage persist, particularly in the north, with thousands of people estimated to be living in conditions of servitude. The 2013 U.S. Trafficking in Persons' report placed Mali on its Tier 2 Watch List.

Malta

Political Rights Rating: 1
Civil Liberties Rating: 1
Freedom Rating: 1.0
Freedom Status: Free
Electoral Democracy: Yes

Population: 448,000
Capital: Valletta

Ten-Year Ratings Timeline For Year Under Review (Political Rights, Civil Liberties, Status)

Year Under Review	2004	2005	2006	2007	2008	2009	2010	2011	2012	2013
Rating	1,1,F	1,1,F	1,1,F	1,1,F	1,1,F	1,1,F	1,1,F	1,1,F	1,1,F	1,1,F

INTRODUCTION

After failing to pass a budget at the end of 2012, Prime Minister Lawrence Gonzi of the Nationalist Party (PN) met with President George Abela on January 7, 2013, to dissolve Parliament and call for early elections. Joseph Muscat and his Labor Party (PL) won the March elections. Gonzi stepped down as a member of Parliament on July 17.

Malta was also criticized for several incidents in 2013 involving immigrants, including a tanker carrying migrants that Malta refused to accept on its shores, and a violent fight in a migrant detention center.

POLITICAL RIGHTS: 39 / 40

A. Electoral Process: 12 / 12

The 69 members of Malta's unicameral legislature, the House of Representatives, are elected for five-year terms. Lawmakers elect the president, who also serves for five years. Former PL leader George Abela, who was very popular with voters from both parties, was sworn in as president in April 2009. The president names the prime minister, usually the leader of the majority party or coalition.

In elections on March 9, 2013, Joseph Muscat and his PL unseated the PN, which had been in power for 15 years. The PL won by over 35,000 votes, the largest gap since independence in 1964, giving it 39 seats against the PN's 26. The PN also gained an additional 4 seats to reflect the proportion of votes won.

In November 2013, the House of Representatives passed a bill lowering the voting age from 18 to 16 for local council elections.

B. Political Pluralism and Participation: 16 / 16

The ruling PL and opposition PN dominate national politics. The smaller Alternativa Demokratika party also competes but is not represented in Parliament.

C. Functioning of Government: 11 / 12

In January 2013, *MaltaToday* reported that a procurement committee member for the state oil company, Enemalta, received large sums of money from Trafigura, a Dutch commodities company, in return for contracts in 2004–2005. The investigation extended to the former Enemalta chairman and also involves alleged kickbacks from oil company Total. In a parallel case, Island Bunker Oils Ltd., an oil barge company that took over business from an Enemalta subsidiary, is under investigation for money laundering. Seven individuals were arraigned in February on corruption and fraud charges related to these cases.

A Whistleblower Act applicable in both the public and private sectors was passed by Parliament in July and went into effect in September 2013. The act establishes a whistleblowing officer in every ministry as well as an External Whistle Blowing Unit to investigate allegations.

A 2012 Eurobarometer survey showed that 51 percent of Maltese think that the most negative effect of private companies on society is corruption. In 2013, another Eurobarometer survey revealed that 83 percent of Maltese saw corruption as a major problem plaguing the country.

In June, the Criminal Code was amended to remove the statute of limitations on officials charged with corruption, and to allow for stricter penalties for those found guilty.

CIVIL LIBERTIES: 58 / 60
D. Freedom of Expression and Belief: 16 / 16

The constitution guarantees freedoms of speech and the press, though incitement to racial hatred is punishable by a jail term of six to eight months. Blasphemy is also illegal, and censorship remains an ongoing issue. There are several daily newspapers and weekly publications in Maltese and English, as well as radio and television stations. Residents also have access to Italian television broadcasts. In September 2012, Malta's first Freedom of Information Act went into effect but has since been criticized because of government red tape. The government does not restrict internet access.

Malta was plagued by libel suits in 2013. PL candidate Emmanuel Mallia, who later became minister of home affairs and national security, sought criminal proceedings against PN secretary-general Paul Borg Olivier in February after he was accused by the PN finance minister, Tonio Fenech, of involvement in the Enemalta fuel procurement scandal. In September, the Labor Party and newspaper *l-orizzont* were ordered to pay €5,000 ($6,600) to European Union (EU) Commissioner Tonio Borg for a 2007 advertisement that he claimed was slanderous.

The constitution establishes Roman Catholicism as the state religion, and the state grants subsidies only to Catholic schools. While the population is overwhelmingly Roman Catholic, small communities of Muslims, Jews, and Protestants are tolerated and respected. There is one Muslim private school. Academic freedom is respected.

E. Associational and Organizational Rights: 12 / 12

The constitution provides for freedoms of assembly and association, and the government generally respects these rights in practice. Nongovernmental organizations investigating human rights issues operate without state interference. The law recognizes the right to form and join trade unions as well as the right to strike. A compulsory yet seldom-used arbitration clause in the country's labor law allows the government to force a settlement on striking workers.

F. Rule of Law: 15 / 16

The judiciary is independent, and the rule of law prevails in civil and criminal matters. Prison conditions generally meet international standards, though the Council of Europe's Commission for Human Rights has criticized poor detention conditions for irregular migrants and asylum seekers. Migrant workers are reportedly often exploited and subjected to substandard working conditions.

Over the last decade, Malta has received an increasing number of immigrants, refugees, and asylum seekers, who subsequently settle in the country or proceed to other EU countries. Malta's treatment of migrants in detention and refusal to assist migrants trapped off its shores has been criticized. One such incident arose in August 2013 when Malta rejected a tanker carrying 102 immigrants from Africa. After it was stranded for three days, Italy accepted the migrants. In a separate case in July, the European Court of Human Rights (ECHR) ruled that it was illegal for Malta to return 45 immigrants to Libya.

Malta has also been criticized for poor conditions at holding centers for refugees and asylum seekers, which have led to rioting and even death. In July 2013, a fight broke out among 23 migrants held at the Safi detention center; 18 migrants were injured and 8 hospitalized.

Also in July, the ECHR ruled against Malta in a case involving a Somali migrant; she was held for 14 months in what were described as degrading conditions and suffered a miscarriage. Malta's commissioner for children also expressed concern over detention of children while families await the outcome of administrative procedures.

In December 2013, four former prison guards were sentenced to at least five years in prison for the 2008 beating of an escaped prisoner.

G. Personal Autonomy and Individual Rights: 15 / 16

The constitution prohibits discrimination based on gender. However, women are underrepresented in government, occupying only 10 seats in the parliament and 2 in the Cabinet of Ministers. A law legalizing divorce came into effect in October 2011. Violence against women remains a problem. Abortion is strictly prohibited in all cases. Malta is a source and destination country for human trafficking for the purposes of forced labor and sexual exploitation. A bill introduced in September to allow same-sex civil unions was not yet passed by year's end. In July, the Criminal Code was amended to allow for transgendered people to express their chosen gender identity on government-issued documents.

Marshall Islands

Political Rights Rating: 1
Civil Liberties Rating: 1
Freedom Rating: 1.0
Freedom Status: Free
Electoral Democracy: Yes

Population: 56,086
Capital: Majuro

Ten-Year Ratings Timeline For Year Under Review (Political Rights, Civil Liberties, Status)

Year Under Review	2004	2005	2006	2007	2008	2009	2010	2011	2012	2013
Rating	1,1,F	1,1,F	1,1,F	1,1,F	1,1,F	1,1,F	1,1,F	1,1,F	1,1,F	1,1,F

INTRODUCTION

In March 2013, the Republic of the Marshall Islands signed a new agreement with the United States to have U.S. Navy ships assist U.S. Coast Guard vessels and local officials to patrol the island nation's maritime exclusive economic zone.

The Marshall Islands maintains close relations with the United States under a Compact of Free Association, which allows U.S. military facilities to operate in the country in exchange for defense guarantees and development assistance. Citizens of the Marshall Islands can work, live, study, and obtain federal health care and social services in the United States; about one-third of the islands' citizens are in the United States. Compact funds pay for three quarters of the Marshall Islands' annual budget, and U.S. military facilities provide nearly 1,000 local jobs. The compact will run through 2023 with annual transfers of $57 million through 2013 and $62 million from 2014 to 2023.

The United States will have use of the Kwajalein missile-testing site until 2066. As the primary U.S. testing ground for long-range nuclear missiles, 67 atomic and nuclear bomb tests in the Bikini and Enewetak Atolls have left the former uninhabitable and the latter partly contaminated, and local populations worry about health and environmental hazards from testing activities. To compensate victims of the tests, the United States created a $150 million Nuclear Claims Fund, though critics say the fund is inadequate to fulfill the $2 billion in awards made to Marshall Islands residents by the Nuclear Claims Tribunal, which was established in 1988 as part of the first compact.

The Marshall Islands faces threats from climate change and rising sea levels. Additionally, a prolonged lack of rainfall has compelled the government to seek more international donations of emergency food, water, desalination machines, and spare parts to avert the spread of hunger and disease.

POLITICAL RIGHTS: 36 / 40

A. Electoral Process: 11 / 12

The Marshall Islands' unicameral parliament (Nitijela) has 33 members or senators, who are elected to four-year terms from 24 electoral districts that roughly correspond to each atoll. All citizens 18 years and older can vote. The senators then elect one of their own as president for a four-year term; the president holds most executive power. An advisory body, the Council of Chiefs (Iroij) has 12 traditional leaders who are consulted on customary law.

In the 2011 parliamentary elections, Aelon Kein Ad (AKA) took 20 seats. In January 2012, the parliament voted 21 to 11 for Christopher Loeak to replace Jurelang Zedkaia as the president.

B. Political Pluralism and Participation: 15 / 16

Citizens enjoy a high degree of political freedom. The AKA and the United Democratic Party are the two main parties. In 2011, Zedkaia left the AKA and formed Kein Eo Am to contest that year's elections. However, politicians typically run as independents and align with a party after they are elected.

C. Functioning of Government: 10 / 12

Corruption is a serious problem, and international donors have demanded improvements in accountability and transparency. In March 2013, the United States withheld $1 million in compact funds when the government could not answer for $3 million in spending, $2.5 million of which came out of compact funds.

In January 2013, the Marshall Islands' Public Service Commission stated that reform of the country's civil service was critically needed. An audit by the commission revealed numerous positions with no job descriptions, job titles that did not match actual work, and other problems.

CIVIL LIBERTIES: 55 / 60

D. Freedom of Expression and Belief: 16 / 16

The government generally respects freedoms of speech and the press. A privately owned newspaper, the *Marshall Islands Journal*, publishes articles in English and Marshallese. The government's *Marshall Islands Gazette* provides official news but avoids political coverage. Broadcast outlets include both government- and church-owned radio stations, and cable television offers a variety of international news and entertainment programs. Residents in some parts of the country can also access U.S. armed forces radio and television. Like many small island states, internet use is low; about 2 percent of residents have internet access, and only

25 percent have mobile phones. The lack of access is largely due to an outdated communication network and high costs.

Religious and academic freedoms are respected in practice. The quality of secondary education remains low, and four-year college education is rare. In April 2013, the United States announced that it would terminate funding that pays the salary of teachers who have no college education.

E. Associational and Organizational Rights: 11 / 12

Citizen groups, many of which are sponsored by or affiliated with church organizations and provide social services, operate freely. The government broadly interprets constitutional guarantees of freedoms of assembly and association to cover trade unions.

F. Rule of Law: 15 / 16

The constitution provides for an independent judiciary. In 2012, the Pacific Judicial Development Program gave the Marshall Islands the highest marks among 14 Pacific Island states for judicial transparency. Nearly all judges and attorneys are recruited from overseas. The government revived use of Traditional Rights Courts in 2010 to make advisory rulings to the High Court as a way to ease the backlog of land dispute cases. Limited resources in personnel and funding are the most fundamental problems, contributing to long waits. Police brutality is generally not a problem. Detention centers and prisons meet minimum international standards.

In January 2013, the mayor of Majuro banished a 25-year old man accused of repeatedly robbing local residents in the capital to an outer island for five years. The mayor indicated that this traditional punishment may be returning in order to help curb crime in the capital.

Tensions persist between the local population and Chinese migrants, who control much of the retail sector.

G. Personal Autonomy and Individual Rights: 13 / 16

Social and economic discrimination against women remain widespread despite a tradition of matrilineal inheritance in tribal rank and personal property. Hilda Heine was the only woman elected to the parliament in the 2011 general elections. Domestic violence against women and girls, while illegal, frequently goes unreported, and critics say the government has done little to stop it or to assist victims.

Same-sex relations were legalized in 2005 with the same age of consent (16 years) for both males and females, but there are no legal protections against discrimination based on sexual orientation or gender identity.

In July 2013, the U.S. Department of State named the country a sex trafficking destination and put it on its global watch list, citing a lack of effort to prevent trafficking. The Marshall Islands government claimed the report was baseless and excessive, noting that only a few incidents had occurred.

Mauritania

Political Rights Rating: 6
Civil Liberties Rating: 5
Freedom Rating: 5.5
Freedom Status: Not Free
Electoral Democracy: No

Population: 3,712,464
Capital: Nouakchott

Ten-Year Ratings Timeline For Year Under Review (Political Rights, Civil Liberties, Status)

Year Under Review	2004	2005	2006	2007	2008	2009	2010	2011	2012	2013
Rating	6,5,NF	5,4,PF	5,4,PF	4,4,PF	6,5,NF	6,5,NF	6,5,NF	6,5,NF	6,5,NF	6,5,NF

INTRODUCTION

On December 21, Mauritania held the second round of its parliamentary elections, which were boycotted by 10 opposition parties, including the main Rally of Democratic Forces (RFD). The ruling Union for the Republic (UPR) and its allies won the vast majority of the expanded national assembly, with UPR winning 74 of the 147 and its allies winning 34 seats. Opposition parties won 37 seats, with the largest number, 16, won by Tawassoul Islamist Party. The UPR similarly won 70 percent of the communes in the municipal elections.

While slavery has been abolished in Mauritania for decades and the government has previously rejected its existence, in 2013 it agreed to create an agency—named "The National Solidarity Agency for the Fight Against the Vestiges of Slavery, for Integration, and for the Fight Against Poverty"—in order to fight the practice. However, many anti-slavery activists remain skeptical of the agency and the government's will to fight slavery.

In May 2012, the Mauritanian army increased its presence along the border with Mali, which was fighting an Islamist rebellion, but the Mauritanian government ruled out direct intervention. The opposition alliance has criticized the government stance on Mali, as well as the death of Mauritanian citizens during the ongoing conflict. In early 2013, the RFD and other opposition parties demanded assurances that the Mauritanian army would not get involved in the conflict. By the end of 2013, Mauritania was host to about 70,000 Malian refugees who had fled the fighting.

In October 2013, Mauritania experienced unprecedented flooding that affected 5,600 people.

POLITICAL RIGHTS: 11 / 40

A. Electoral Process: 3 / 12

Under the 1991 constitution, the president is responsible for appointing and dismissing the prime minister and cabinet, and a 2006 amendment imposed a limit of two five-year presidential terms. The bicameral legislature consists of a newly expanded 147-seat National Assembly, elected by popular vote, and the 56-seat Senate, with 53 members elected by mayors and municipal councils and 3 members chosen by the chamber to represent Mauritanians living abroad. One-third of the Senate is elected on a rotating basis every two years. The last Senate elections were held after presidential elections in 2009, during which UPR held 38 seats and two of its allies had one seat each. An opposition parliamentary group comprised of RDF and UFP held 12 seats. As presidential, national assembly, and municipal elections were repeatedly postponed, no Senate elections have taken place. One-third of the Senate will be elected by the Municipal Councils elected in December 2013, but this had not occurred by the end of the year.

President Mohamed Ould Abdel Aziz came to power through a military coup on August 6, 2008. Upon removing the government, then-general Aziz and his allies announced that an 11-member junta, the High State Council (HSC), would run the country until new elections were held. While the international community strongly condemned the coup, the domestic reaction was mixed. A majority of lawmakers and mayors expressed support, while a coalition of four parties that supported the ousted president formed the National Front for the Defense of Democracy and refused to participate in the junta-led government.

In April 2009, Aziz announced that he would resign from the military in order to run for president. Despite initial resistance, opposition parties agreed to participate in the presidential vote. Under international pressure, the HSC handed power in June 2009 to a transitional government to supervise an election.

Aziz won the July 2009 election in the first round with 52.6 percent of the vote. Four opposition parties claimed that the results were predetermined, electoral lists had been tampered with, and fraudulent voters had used fake ballot papers and identity cards. However, the election was declared satisfactory by international observers. The opposition parties lodged a formal appeal with the Constitutional Council that was ultimately rejected, and the head of the electoral commission resigned over doubts about the election's conduct. While some opposition parties continued to protest the outcome, the Rally of Democratic Forces recognized Aziz's presidency in September 2010, citing the need for unity in the face of increased terrorist attacks by Islamist militants.

On August 3, 2013, Mauritania's communications minister, Mohamed Yahya Ould Hormah, announced that the country would hold National Assembly and municipal elections on October 12. The previous elections had been held in 2006, and had been postponed repeatedly. After the opposition threatened to boycott the elections, they were further postponed by six weeks in hopes of increasing party participation. However, talks between the opposition and the government failed by early October, and 10 out of the 11 parties within the Coordination of Democratic Opposition (COD) opposition coalition announced that they would boycott the elections, with only Tawassoul participating.

B. Political Pluralism and Participation: 3 / 16

Mauritania's party system is poorly developed, and clan and ethnic loyalties strongly influence the country's politics. While political parties are free to operate, the vast majority have boycotted the recent elections due to what they consider a system dominated by the president and his party, both of which have won with large majorities in the last elections. The military remains strongly influential and the shooting of President Abdel Aziz in 2012 brought the security apparatus in charge of civilian institutions for the duration of the President's treatment, drawing criticism from the opposition and complaints on the outsized role of the military in politics.

C. Functioning of Government: 5 / 12

Corruption is a serious problem, and political instability has prevented fiscal transparency. While several senior officials were charged with corruption in 2012—including a senior military official and the former minister of finance—these cases have either been dismissed or officials have been ordered to reimburse the government for the amount they supposedly embezzled, with no further legal ramifications. Mauritania was ranked 119 out of 177 countries and territories surveyed in Transparency International's 2013 Corruption Perceptions Index.

CIVIL LIBERTIES: 23 / 60

D. Freedom of Expression and Belief: 10 / 16

Despite constitutional guarantees for press freedom, some journalists practice self-censorship, and private newspapers face closure for publishing material considered offensive to Islam or threatening to the state. In 2011, the government ended a 51-year monopoly on broadcast media with a call for applications for licenses from private outlets. By the end of 2013, eight private television channels and 13 radio stations received licenses, in addition to foreign channels also being allowed to broadcast in the country. Defamation was decriminalized in 2011, though fines can still be levied. There were no reports of government restrictions on the internet.

Mauritania was declared an Islamic republic under the 1991 constitution, and proselytizing by non-Muslims is banned. Non-Muslims cannot be citizens, and those who convert from Islam lose their citizenship. In practice, however, non-Muslim communities have not been targeted for persecution. Academic freedom is respected.

E. Associational and Organizational Rights: 4 / 12

The 1991 constitution guarantees freedom of assembly, though organizers are required to obtain consent from the authorities for large gatherings. The environment for civil society groups and nongovernmental organizations (NGOs) in Mauritania has improved during the last few years, with fewer restrictions on their activities. However, antislavery activists continue to face harassment and arrest. In a protest in September, five activists from an unauthorized NGO were arrested and, according to the group, demonstrators were beaten while protesting against the government's failure to pursue criminal charges against an alleged slave master in Boutilimit. Similarly, a February protest by the February 25 Youth Movement was violently dispersed.

Workers have the legal right to unionize, but unions must be approved by the public prosecutor and encounter hostility from employers. Although only about a quarter of Mauritanians are formally employed, about 90 percent of workers in the industrial and commercial sectors are unionized. Nevertheless, workers are often wrongfully terminated, and organized workers are sometimes subject to pressure to withdraw their union membership or forego legal processes. The right to strike is limited by notice requirements and bans on certain forms of strike action. In June, Capital Drilling reportedly dismissed workers who had participated in a strike, allowing them to return only if they gave up union membership as well as their permanent contracts. Security forces used tear gas and batons against strikers in the cities of Zouerate and Nouadhibou in May.

F. Rule of Law: 4 / 16

The judicial system is heavily influenced by the government. Many judicial decisions are based on Sharia (Islamic law), especially in family and civil matters, which discriminates against women. Suspects are routinely held for long periods of pretrial detention, and security forces suspected of human rights abuses operate with impunity. Prison conditions are harsh. A June report by Amnesty International found that authorities tortured men, women, and children who were being held on both terrorism and other charges.

Members of Al-Qaeda in the Islamic Maghreb have carried out a number of attacks in Mauritania in recent years. A 2010 antiterrorism law removed previous restrictions on wiretaps and searches, allowed for individuals under 18 to be charged (which is illegal under Sharia), and granted immunity to terrorists that inform the authorities of a terrorism plot.

The country's three main ethnic groups are the politically and economically dominant White Moors of Arab and Berber descent; the black descendants of slaves, also known as Haratins or Black Moors; and black Africans, who are closer in ethnic heritage to the peoples of neighboring Senegal and Mali. Racial and ethnic discrimination persists in all spheres of political and economic life, with discrimination targeting almost exclusively black Africans.

Same-sex sexual activity is illegal in Mauritania, and punishable by death for men. Lesbian, gay, bisexual, and transgender individuals generally hide their sexual orientation.

G. Personal Autonomy and Individual Rights: 5 / 16

Despite a 1981 law banning slavery in Mauritania, an estimated half a million black Mauritanians are believed to live in conditions of servitude. According to the 2013 Global Slavery Index, Mauritania has the highest prevalence of slavery in the world. A 2007 law set penalties of 5 to 10 years in prison for all forms of slavery, but the law is hampered by a requirement that slaves themselves file a legal complaint before any prosecution can occur. In October, antislavery group the Initiative for the Resurgence of the Abolitionist Movement (IRA) alleged that judicial authorities convinced a plaintiff to drop a slavery complaint in exchange for a nominal sum. Those slave masters who are arrested are often released without charges. In September, the IRA reported that police refused to investigate a slavery complaint against a prominent family, and then protected the suspects in temporary custody while claiming that they had fled. Property disputes are frequent between slaves or former slaves and their masters, and human rights groups say that local authorities will favor the latter. The new antislavery agency established in 2013 will be tasked to deal with these issues.

Under a 2005 law, party lists for the National Assembly elections must include district-based quotas for female candidates, and 20 percent of all municipal council seats are reserved for women. Nevertheless, discrimination against women persists. Under Sharia, a woman's testimony is given only half the weight of a man's. Legal protections regarding property and pay equity are rarely respected in practice. Female genital mutilation (FGM) is illegal but widely practiced. Abortion is legal only when the life of the mother is in danger. The country is a source and destination for women, men, and children trafficked for the purposes of forced labor and sexual exploitation. In 2013 the U.S. Trafficking in Persons Report downgraded Mauritania to Tier 3 from the Tier 2 Watch List.

Mauritius

Political Rights Rating: 1
Civil Liberties Rating: 2
Freedom Rating: 1.5
Freedom Status: Free
Electoral Democracy: Yes

Population: 1,297,000
Capital: Port Louis

Ten-Year Ratings Timeline For Year Under Review (Political Rights, Civil Liberties, Status)

Year Under Review	2004	2005	2006	2007	2008	2009	2010	2011	2012	2013
Rating	1,1,F	1,1,F	1,2,F	1,2,F	1,2,F	1,2,F	1,2,F	1,2,F	1,2,F	1,2,F

INTRODUCTION

Prime Minister Navinchandra Ramgoolam's government faced opposition to the implementation of new biometric identity cards. The two main opposition parties, the Militant

Socialist Movement (MSM) and the Mauritian Militant Movement (MMM), highlighted privacy and security concerns, as well as soaring costs.

In April 2013 the Supreme Court rejected MSM leader Pravind Jugnauth's appeal to remove conflict of interest charges. The case, related to an inflated government bid on a hospital owned by Jugnauth's brother-in-law while Jugnauth was finance minister in 2010, remained pending at year's end.

POLITICAL RIGHTS: 38 / 40
A. Electoral Process: 12 / 12

The president, whose role is largely ceremonial, is elected by the unicameral National Assembly. Executive power resides with the prime minister, who is appointed by the president from the party or coalition with the most seats in the legislature. Of the National Assembly's 69 members, 62 are directly elected and 7 are appointed from among unsuccessful candidates who gained the largest numbers of votes. All members and the president serve five-year terms. Decentralized structures govern the country's small island dependencies. The largest of these, Rodrigues Island, has its own government and local councils, and two seats in the National Assembly.

In the 2010 legislative elections, Ramgoolam's Alliance of the Future—which included his Mauritian Labour Party (MLP), the MSM, and the Mauritian Social Democratic Party (PMSD)—captured 45 seats. Former prime minister Paul Bérenger's Alliance of the Heart—a coalition of the MMM, the National Union, and the Mauritian Social Democratic Movement—took 20. Three small parties hold the remaining 4 seats. Ramgoolam retained the premiership. In 2012, President Anerood Jugnauth resigned and the MSM formed a new coalition with the MMM, leaving the MLP and the PMSD with a 5-seat majority.

In 2012, the United Nations Human Rights Commission ruled that a law requiring potential candidates to declare their ethnic and religious status constitutes a human rights violation. While Prime Minister Ramgoolam said he supported electoral reforms, no changes were enacted by years' end.

B. Political Pluralism and Participation: 15 / 16

Political parties operate freely and the two highest political positions, the president and prime minister, have rotated between the three largest parties—the MLP, the MSM, and the MMM. All three parties champion democratic socialist doctrine. Smaller parties are often included in governing coalitions.

C. Functioning of Government: 11 / 12

The country's generally positive reputation for transparency and accountability has been damaged by the ongoing scandal surrounding the 2010 government purchase of a private hospital, as well as MSM allegations that the ruling MLP is using the Independent Commission Against Corruption (ICAC) as a political tool. In August 2013, the ICAC launched an investigation into corruption allegations against Minister of Higher Education Rajesh Jeetah involving conflicts of interest in the operation of a local university branch. Mauritius was ranked 52 out of 177 countries surveyed in Transparency International's 2013 Corruption Perceptions Index, and the country has been ranked first in the Ibrahim Index of African Governance since its inception in 2007.

CIVIL LIBERTIES: 52 / 60
D. Freedom of Expression and Belief: 15 / 16

The constitution guarantees freedom of expression. Several private daily and weekly publications criticize both the ruling and opposition parties, but the state-owned Mauritius

Broadcasting Corporation's radio and television services generally reflect government viewpoints. A small number of private radio stations compete with the state-run media. In 2012, the editor of the *Sunday Times*, Imran Hosany, was arrested and charged with outraging public and religious morality after publishing photographs of the dead body of a murdered tourist; in May 2013, Hosany was convicted and fined Rs 50,000 ($1,600). The internet is available and unrestricted by the government.

Religious and academic freedoms are respected.

E. Associational and Organizational Rights: 12 / 12

Freedoms of assembly and association are honored, though police have occasionally used excessive force in response to riots. There are more than 300 unions in Mauritius. However, tens of thousands of foreign workers employed in export processing zones suffer from poor living and working conditions, and their employers are reportedly hostile to unions. In September 2013, striking Bangladeshi textile workers demanding better working conditions clashed with riot police. Subsequently, the minister of labor issued a moratorium on visas for foreign construction workers.

F. Rule of Law: 13 / 16

The generally independent judiciary, headed by the Supreme Court, administers a legal system that combines French and British traditions and is considered transparent and nondiscriminatory. Mauritius has maintained the right of appeal to the Privy Council in London. Civil rights are largely respected, though individual cases of police brutality have been reported. Various ethnic cultures and traditions coexist peacefully, and constitutional prohibitions against discrimination are generally upheld. However, Mauritian Creoles—descendants of African slaves who comprise about a third of the population—are culturally and economically marginalized. Tensions between the Hindu majority and Muslim minority persist. In a 2011 report, the Truth and Justice Commission (TJC)—established to examine the country's history of slavery and indentured labor—recommended measures to encourage national reconciliation, such as promoting increased economic and political participation by non-Hindu Mauritians. Although in 2012 the chair of the ministerial committee of the TJC expressed disappointment that only 3 of the 19 measures recommended for immediate implementation had been adopted, the prime minister claimed that all 19 measures were being implemented as of September 2013.

G. Personal Autonomy and Individual Rights: 12 / 16

Women comprise about 36 percent of the labor force, but they receive less compensation than men for similar work. Women hold only 13 seats in the National Assembly and 2 cabinet posts. A 2012 gender quota law mandates that at least one-third of candidates in local elections be women, and women's representation at the local government level is 26 percent. However, Prime Minister Ramgoolam's plan to extend the quota to the national parliament for the 2015 elections has yet to be approved. Rape and domestic violence remain major concerns.

"Sodomy" is officially illegal, but the 2008 Equal Opportunities Act prohibits employment discrimination based on sexual orientation. Faced with a complaint to the Equal Opportunities Commission, in October 2013 the Ministry of Health removed a controversial measure requiring blood donors to report their sexual orientation. Attacks on the elderly are a growing problem: the Elderly Persons Protection Unit reported 544 cases of abuse from January to August 2013, up from 726 cases in 2012.

Mexico

Political Rights Rating: 3
Civil Liberties Rating: 3
Freedom Rating: 3.0
Freedom Status: Partly Free
Electoral Democracy: Yes

Population: 117,574,165
Capital: Mexico City

Ten-Year Ratings Timeline For Year Under Review (Political Rights, Civil Liberties, Status)

Year Under Review	2004	2005	2006	2007	2008	2009	2010	2011	2012	2013
Rating	2,2,F	2,2,F	2,3,F	2,3,F	2,3,F	2,3,F	3,3,PF	3,3,PF	3,3,PF	3,3,PF

INTRODUCTION

President Enrique Peña Nieto completed his first full year in power in 2013, having assumed office in December 2012. His Institutional Revolutionary Party (PRI) had previously ruled Mexico without interruption from 1929 to 2000, then lost two consecutive presidential races to the National Action Party (PAN) in 2000 and 2006. Contrary to the fears of many Mexicans, the PRI's return did not herald a rapid reversion to its old authoritarian mode of governance. Instead, the new administration offered a mix of reforms in some areas and continuity with the PAN government of former president Felipe Calderón in others. The three major parties—the ideologically amorphous PRI, the right-leaning PAN, and the left-wing Party of the Democratic Revolution (PRD)—maintained a tenuous alliance known as the Pact for Mexico for most of the year, allowing passage of a series of laws and constitutional amendments in areas including education, telecommunications, tax collection, political procedures and representation, and energy. The last of these opened the door to foreign and private investment in order to modernize Mexico's creaky energy sector, thereby altering a powerful symbol of Mexican nationalism and causing the PRD to withdraw from the Pact. However, the remaining parties have sufficient votes to continue with passage of both major reforms and the slew of secondary regulations necessary for their implementation.

Significantly less progress was made on Mexico's foremost governance challenge, establishing the rule of law. Although murder rates declined for a second straight year, the incidence of other serious crimes, including kidnapping and extortion, rose as increasingly fragmented crime syndicates diversified their operations beyond drug trafficking. In the state of Michoacán, frequent violence and crippling levels of extortion prompted residents in several municipalities to establish armed community self-defense groups. Despite the Peña Nieto administration's early rhetoric advocating demilitarization of the anticrime fight, several thousand troops were dispatched to Michoacán in May, and soldiers took over security duties in the port city of Lázaro Cárdenas in November following reports of large-scale smuggling by criminal groups. In a possible sign of progress, authorities captured the leaders of both the Gulf cartel and Zetas syndicates during the year, along with several dozen other important underworld figures.

Allegations of severe human rights violations continued to emerge from the security operations conducted by more than 45,000 soldiers in various parts of Mexico. In February, Human Rights Watch issued a report documenting 249 specific cases of disappearance, of which 149 were attributed to police and military units. Also that month, the government announced that it possessed a list containing the names of over 26,000 people registered as disappeared between 2007 and 2012. Officials subsequently claimed that the list would shrink substantially after further vetting, while rights groups criticized the methodology and demanded a more rigorous system of registering and tracking disappeared persons. Separately, a new Victims Law that entered into force in February established a set of rights for victims of state or criminal violence, including compensation.

POLITICAL RIGHTS: 28 / 40
A. Electoral Process: 9 / 12

The president is elected to a six-year term and cannot be reelected. The bicameral Congress consists of the 128-member Senate, elected for six years through a mix of direct voting and proportional representation, with at least two parties represented in each state's delegation, and the 500-member Chamber of Deputies, with 300 elected directly and 200 through proportional representation, all for three-year terms. As a result of the political reform approved in December, current members of Congress are barred from reelection; starting in 2018, elected senators will be allowed two six-year terms, and deputies up to four three-year terms. As a federal state, the elected governor and legislature in each of Mexico's 31 states have significant governing responsibility, including oversight of the bulk of Mexico's beleaguered police forces.

Peña Nieto won the July 2012 presidential election with 38 percent of the vote, followed by veteran PRD leader Andrés Manuel López Obrador with 32 percent. The PAN candidate trailed with 25 percent. López Obrador initially refused to accept the results, citing alleged infractions including widespread vote buying, manipulation of polls, overspending, and media bias, but the Federal Electoral Tribunal found insufficient evidence to invalidate the election. In concurrent congressional elections, the PRI emerged as the strongest force. Including allied parties, it garnered a narrow majority of 251 seats in the lower chamber. The PRD and its allies won 135, followed by the PAN with 114. No coalition gained a majority in the Senate, where the PRI–Green Party alliance held 61 seats, the PAN took 38, and the PRD won 22.

The Federal Electoral Institute (IFE), which supervises elections and enforces political party laws, has come to be viewed as a model for other countries. Following complaints about the fairness of the 2006 elections, an electoral reform was passed in 2007 to strictly regulate campaign financing and the content of political advertising. The 2012 elections were considered generally free and fair, but complaints persisted, particularly regarding vote buying and PRI collusion with the dominant broadcaster, Televisa, which helped spark a significant anti-PRI student movement. The 2013 political reform broadened the power of the national electoral authority to include supervision of state-level elections, while changing the agency's name to the National Electoral Institute (INE) and giving it the power to annul elections in which exceeding expenditure limits was deemed to have affected the outcome. Several current IFE members and outside analysts protested that several of the new provisions threatened to overwhelm INE's capacity as well as institutionalize electoral conflict.

At the state level, allegations of abuse of public resources to favor specific gubernatorial candidates have increased in recent years. Leaked audio recordings of PRI functionaries in Veracruz discussing ways of diverting social spending to purchase votes in July 2013 local elections raised political tensions at the national level in April. The July elections involved local races in 14 states as well as one gubernatorial race, won by a PAN-PRD candidate in Baja California.

B. Political Pluralism and Participation: 12 / 16

Mexico's multiparty system features few official restrictions on political organization and activity. Power has changed hands twice at the national level since 2000, and opposition parties are also competitive in many states. However, in states with lower levels of multiparty contestation, locally dominant political actors often govern in a highly opaque, caudillo-style manner that limits political activity and citizen participation and opens the door to corruption and the influence of organized crime. Politicians and municipal governments have faced growing pressure from criminal groups over the past five years. More than a dozen small-town mayors and candidates for office were killed between 2010 and 2013. In the run-up to local elections in 2013, several local functionaries and candidates, mostly from the PRD, were killed in Oaxaca, Guerrero, and Michoácan.

Female legislators make up over one-third of the Congress elected in 2012. Although indigenous Mexicans are not blocked from participating in the political process and provisions exist for the integration of traditional community customs with procedures prescribed by federal and state laws, indigenous groups remain underrepresented in formal political institutions.

C. Functioning of Government: 7 / 12

Organized crime and related violence have limited the effective governing authority of elected officials in some areas. In the most violence-plagued regions, provision of public services has become more difficult, and public-sector employees such as teachers are subject to extortion. In Michoacán in October 2013, gang attacks on gas stations and electrical installations left hundreds of thousands of residents without power.

Official corruption remains a serious problem. Billions of dollars in illegal drug money is believed to enter the country each year from the United States, and there is a perception that such funds affect politics, particularly on the state and local levels. Attempts to prosecute officials for alleged involvement in corrupt or criminal activity have often failed due to the weakness of the state's cases. Most punishment has focused on low- and mid-level officials, hundreds of whom have been dismissed or charged with links to drug traffickers. Some signs have emerged in recent years of more vigorous anti-graft efforts. A former governor of Tabasco, Andrés Granier, was arrested in August 2013 and charged with embezzling public funds. However, several army officers and other security personnel were released in 2013 after being arrested in 2012 on suspicion of accepting funds from drug traffickers. Mexico was ranked 106 out of 177 countries surveyed in Transparency International's 2013 Corruption Perceptions Index. A 2002 freedom of information law, despite some limitations, has been considered successful at strengthening transparency at the federal level, though implementation has slowed and many states lag far behind.

CIVIL LIBERTIES: 37 / 60
D. Freedom of Expression and Belief: 13 / 16

Legal and constitutional guarantees of free speech have been gradually improving, but the security environment for journalists has deteriorated markedly. Some major media outlets are no longer dependent on the government for advertising and subsidies, and the competitive press has taken the lead in denouncing official corruption, though serious investigative reporting is scarce, particularly at the local level. Broadcast media are dominated by a two-corporation duopoly that controls over 90 percent of the market, and the biggest, Televisa, has faced accusations of supporting specific politicians, usually from the PRI. Nonetheless, a constitutional amendment approved in 2013 establishes a new telecommunications agency and strengthens the Federal Economic Competition Commission, thereby potentially opening the spectrum to new competitors in television as well as cellular and internet service. Key secondary regulations were pending at year's end.

Since a sharp increase in violence in 2006, reporters probing police issues, drug trafficking, and official corruption have faced a high risk of physical harm. The National Human

Rights Commission (CNDH) reported 82 journalists killed between 2005 and 2012, making Mexico one of the world's most dangerous countries for media workers. At least three more journalists were killed during 2013, according to the Committee to Protect Journalists, though the motives were unconfirmed. Self-censorship has increased, and many newspapers in high-violence zones no longer publish stories involving in-depth reporting on organized crime. A 2012 constitutional amendment federalized crimes against journalists, and in May 2013 a federal special prosecutor gained authority to investigate such crimes, though press watchdog groups decried the office's slow initial pace.

The government does not restrict internet access, but criminals have extended their reach to citizens who attempt to report on crime via online outlets. Three individuals killed in Nuevo Laredo in 2011 were found with notes from the Zetas gang that tied their deaths to their online crime-reporting activities. A 2011 law passed in Veracruz to criminalize the "perturbation of public order" via social media was viewed as an attempt to intimidate Twitter users, though no prosecutions were reported in 2013.

Religious freedom is constitutionally protected and generally respected in practice. A constitutional amendment allowing increased public worship was promulgated in July 2013. Political battles over issues such as abortion and equal rights for LGBT (lesbian, gay, bisexual, and transgender) people have led to an increase in religious discourse in the public sphere in recent years. The government does not restrict academic freedom.

E. Associational and Organizational Rights: 8 / 12

Constitutional guarantees regarding free assembly and association are largely upheld, but political and civic expression is restricted in some regions. Civic observers criticized both protester vandalism and excessive force used by Mexico City police during demonstrations coinciding with Peña Nieto's presidential inauguration in December 2012. Protests carried out by teachers' unions led to violence and arrests in several states in 2013, as well as months of serious disruptions in Mexico City. Nongovernmental organizations, though highly active, sometimes face violent resistance, including threats and murders. The local chapter of press freedom group Article 19 received threats in April and October 2013. Three peasants' rights activists in Guerrero were found dead in June shortly after stating fears that they would be targeted by local police and government officials.

Trade unions' role as a pillar of the PRI has diminished significantly, but independent unions face government and management interference. Informal, nontransparent negotiations between employers and politically connected union leaders often result in "protection contracts" that govern employee rights but are never seen by workers. Several large unions, particularly the teachers' union, have long been considered opaque and overly antagonistic to necessary policy reforms. The day after the promulgation of an education reform in February 2013, longtime teachers' union leader Elba Esther Gordillo—widely perceived as extremely and visibly corrupt—was arrested and charged with embezzling over $150 million.

F. Rule of Law: 6 / 16

The justice system remains plagued by delays and unpredictability. A 2008 constitutional reform replaced the civil-inquisitorial trial system with an oral-adversarial one. The overhaul was widely expected to strengthen due process and increase efficiency and fairness, but human rights groups raised concerns about the vague definition of organized crime and weaker protections afforded to organized crime suspects. Implementation of the new system was expected to take eight years, and in 2013 civil society groups noted progress in some states but significant delays in many others. As of the end of 2013, approximately one-third of Mexican municipalities had implemented the reformed system.

Coordination on law enforcement between different branches of the federal government, as well as between federal authorities and the state and local police, has been problematic, and the Peña Nieto administration has pursued improved cooperation and streamlined chains of command. In crime-plagued zones, local police have been purged and temporarily replaced by federal troops. A 2009 law requires all members of the police to be vetted, but several states lagged behind on implementation in 2013, and analysts raised questions about the rigor of the procedures.

Lower courts and law enforcement in general are undermined by widespread bribery and incapacity. Most crimes go unreported because the underpaid police are viewed as either inept or in league with criminals. Moreover, only a small minority of crimes end in convictions even when investigations are opened. As of July 2013, sentences had been issued for less than 2 percent of the murders registered in 2012. Prisons are violent and overcrowded, and the CNDH had reported 108 deaths and 392 escapes as of mid-November 2013.

Presidential authority over the armed forces is extensive, but the military has historically operated beyond public scrutiny, and human rights advocates have warned that its strengthened counternarcotics role has not been accompanied by increased oversight of its conduct. Complaints of abuse including torture, forced disappearances, and extrajudicial executions have risen dramatically in recent years. Military personnel are generally tried in military courts, but in a series of cases starting in August 2012, the Supreme Court ruled that human rights violations against civilians must be tried in civilian courts. In 2013 rights groups criticized both the weakness and the pace of legislative reforms that would formally limit military courts' jurisdiction.

The number of deaths attributed to organized crime declined for a second straight year in 2013, after rising sharply each year between 2007 and 2011. Violence remained acute in many areas, however, including Acapulco and parts of Jalisco and Michoacán. The murders often featured extreme brutality designed to maximize the psychological impact on civilians, authorities, and rival groups. In addition, citizen perceptions of insecurity increased in line with rising rates of extortion, kidnapping, human trafficking, and other offenses.

The government has taken a number of steps in recent years to curb the violence and ease popular frustration, including consultations with civic leaders, the signing of a $1.5 billion counternarcotics aid agreement with the United States, the continued deployment of troops, the reformation of the federal police, and the decriminalization of possession of small quantities of drugs. The Peña Nieto administration has adopted a far less vocal, bellicose approach in its public discussions of the issue, but it has maintained many of the Calderón administration's basic strategies, particularly the use of the military. Starting in his 2012 campaign and continuing in 2013, Peña Nieto called for the formation of a hybrid military-police gendarmerie to help decrease the military role, but implementation was postponed to 2014 amid changing plans on the size, role, and composition of the force.

Mexican law bans discrimination based on categories including ethnic origin, gender, age, religion, and sexual orientation. Nevertheless, social and economic discrimination has marginalized much of Mexico's large indigenous population, with many groups relegated to extreme poverty in rural villages that lack essential services. Southern states with high indigenous concentrations suffer from particularly deficient services and limited political voice. The government has attempted to improve indigenous-language services in the justice system, an area of major concern. Indigenous groups have been harmed by the criminal violence in recent years, and in 2013 a series of indigenous communities in Guerrero formed community defense groups, several of which were legalized by the state government. In addition, disputes over land issues within indigenous groups at times becomes violent.

G. Personal Autonomy and Individual Rights: 10 / 16

In several states in recent years, criminals have impeded freedom of movement by blocking major roads. In 2013, the Knights Templar criminal group responded to the challenge from self-defense groups in several Michoacán municipalities by imposing a blockade on the communities in question. Rights groups frequently detail the persecution and criminal predation faced by migrants from Central America, many of whom move through Mexico to reach the United States. Mass graves containing hundreds of bodies found in Tamaulipas in 2011 included many migrants, and a wide range of abuses against migrants continued to be reported in 2013, despite some government initiatives to improve migrant rights protection undertaken by the Calderón and Peña Nieto administrations.

Sexual abuse and domestic violence against women are common. According to a 2012 study, 46 percent of women have suffered some form of violence, and perpetrators are rarely punished. Implementation of a 2007 law designed to protect women from such crimes remains halting, particularly at the state level, and impunity is the norm for the hundreds of women killed each year. Mexico is a major source, transit, and destination country for trafficking in persons, including women and children for sexual exploitation and forced labor. Abortion has been a contentious issue in recent years, with many states reacting to Mexico City's 2007 liberalization of abortion laws by strengthening their own criminal bans on the procedure.

Same-sex marriage is legal in Mexico City and the state of Quintana Roo, and marriages performed there are recognized nationwide. Same-sex civil unions are permitted in a number of other states.

Micronesia

Political Rights Rating: 1
Civil Liberties Rating: 1
Freedom Rating: 1.0
Freedom Status: Free
Electoral Democracy: Yes

Population: 106,841
Capital: Palikir

Ten-Year Ratings Timeline For Year Under Review (Political Rights, Civil Liberties, Status)

Year Under Review	2004	2005	2006	2007	2008	2009	2010	2011	2012	2013
Rating	1,1,F	1,1,F	1,1,F	1,1,F	1,1,F	1,1,F	1,1,F	1,1,F	1,1,F	1,1,F

INTRODUCTION

The Federated States of Micronesia (FSM) held parliamentary elections in March 2013 that were considered free and fair.

FSM has been embroiled in controversy over the government's attempts to build a 10,000-room casino, entertainment, hotel, golf, and convention complex to attract tourists and bolster the economy. The project is unpopular; many citizens have cited concerns about its size, consumption of water and other resources, and the social effects of the casino. A Chinese consortium was tapped to build the project, though the head of the company was one of several prominent Chinese businessmen to disappear unexpectedly amid an investigation into corruption allegations.

POLITICAL RIGHTS: 37 / 40

A. Electoral Process: 12 / 12

FSM's unicameral, 14-member Congress has one directly elected representative serving four-year terms from each of the four constituent states. The other 10 representatives are directly elected for two-year terms from single-member districts. Chuuk state, home to nearly half of the total population, holds the largest number of congressional seats, which has been a source of resentment among the three smaller states. The president and vice president are chosen by Congress from among the four state representatives to serve four-year terms. By informal agreement, the two posts are rotated among the representatives of the four states. Each state has its own constitution, elected legislature, and governor; the state governments have considerable power, particularly in budgetary matters. Traditional leaders and institutions exercise significant influence in society, especially at the village level.

In the March 2013 elections, voters selected representatives for the country's 10 elected congressional seats among 21 candidates. The elections were generally deemed free and fair. Both President Emanuel Mori and Vice President Alik L. Alik were reelected in 2011.

B. Political Pluralism and Participation: 15 / 16

There are no formal political parties, but there are no restrictions on their formation. Political loyalties are based mainly on geography, clan relations, and personality. All candidates ran as independents in the 2013 elections.

FSM relies heavily on economic and defense assistance from the United States for about a third of its revenue. This assistance, provided under a Compact of Free Association, also gives FSM citizens visa-free entry to the United States for education, work, and social services. In exchange, the United States maintains military bases in the islands. The current compact ends in 2023. China has also become an important donor to FSM, and Chinese aid has financed many local projects.

C. Functioning of Government: 10 / 12

Official corruption is a problem and a major source of public discontent. To meet U.S. demand for transparency and accountability in the use of compact funds, a new tracking system was adopted in 2009. In 2012, lawmakers passed legislation to improve the efficiency of the tax collection system and acceded to the UN Convention against Corruption. Nevertheless, a 2012 public auditor report found many fundamental weaknesses in the public payroll system, such as paychecks still going to employees who had been dismissed and overpayment for unauthorized work hours.

CIVIL LIBERTIES: 56 / 60

D. Freedom of Expression and Belief: 16 / 16

The news media operate freely. Print outlets include government-published newsletters and several small, privately owned weekly and monthly newspapers. Each state government runs its own radio station, and the Baptist church runs a fifth station. Television stations operate in three of the four states. Cable television is available in Pohnpei and Chuuk, and satellite television is increasingly common. Internet use is growing, but low income and small populations make it difficult for service providers to expand coverage.

Religious freedom is respected. There are no reports of restrictions on academic freedom, but lack of funds negatively affects the quality of and access to education.

E. Associational and Organizational Rights: 11 / 12

Freedom of assembly is respected, and citizens are free to organize civic groups. Several student and women's organizations are active. No labor unions exist, though there are no laws against their formation. No specific laws regulate work hours or set workplace health and safety standards. The right to strike and bargain collectively is not legally recognized.

F. Rule of Law: 15 / 16

The judiciary is independent, but lacks funds to improve functioning of the courts. The small national police force is responsible for local law enforcement, while the U.S. provides for national defense. There are no reports of abuses or inhumane treatment by police or prison officials.

G. Personal Autonomy and Individual Rights: 14 / 16

Women enjoy equal rights under the law, including those regarding property ownership and employment, though social and economic discrimination against women persists in a male-dominated culture. Although well represented in the lower and middle ranks of the state and federal governments, there are no women in Congress. A constitutional amendment passed in 2012 created four new congressional seats to be reserved for women, but it had not come into effect as of the 2013 elections. Domestic violence is a problem, and cases often go unreported because of family pressure or an expectation of inaction by the authorities. Offenders rarely face trial, and those found guilty usually receive light sentences.

Micronesia is a source country for women trafficked into prostitution. The Human Trafficking Act of 2012 made all trafficking activities in the FSM or by FSM nationals a criminal offense. Also in 2012, lawmakers approved FSM's accession to the Optional Protocol on the Sale of Children, Child Prostitution and Child Pornography under the UN Convention on the Rights of the Child and the Optional Protocol on the Involvement of Children in Armed Conflict.

Same-sex relations are legal but there are no legal protections against discrimination or hate crimes.

Moldova

Political Rights Rating: 3
Civil Liberties Rating: 3
Freedom Rating: 3.0
Freedom Status: Partly Free
Electoral Democracy: Yes

Population: 4,100,000
Capital: Chisinau

Note: The numerical ratings and status listed above do not reflect conditions in Transnistria, which is examined in a separate report.

Ten-Year Ratings Timeline For Year Under Review (Political Rights, Civil Liberties, Status)

Year Under Review	2004	2005	2006	2007	2008	2009	2010	2011	2012	2013
Rating	3,4,PF	3,4,PF	3,4,PF	3,4,PF	4,4,PF	3,4,PF	3,3,PF	3,3,PF	3,3,PF	3,3,PF

INTRODUCTION

The governing three-party coalition, known as the Alliance for European Integration (AIE), collapsed in early 2013 after a scandal over an illegal hunting excursion led to infighting among the alliance's principal leaders. In January, a civil society activist revealed that a businessman had been accidentally shot and killed during the illicit hunt, which took place in late 2012 in a national park and included senior judicial officials. Prosecutor General Valeriu Zubco, a member of the hunting party, was forced to resign after being accused of covering up the incident. He had been an appointee of the Democratic Party of Moldova (PDM), part of the AIE, and his ouster set off a series of escalating reprisals between the PDM and Prime Minister Vladimir Filat of the larger Liberal Democratic Party of Moldova (PLDM). Although a modified version of the old coalition formed a new government in May, the crisis revealed major weaknesses in Moldova's democratic institutions, including the politicization of law enforcement and judicial bodies and the manipulation of major laws for partisan ends.

The resolution of the political feud paved the way for Moldova to initial an Association Agreement with the European Union (EU) at a November summit, despite efforts by Moscow to derail the pact and compel the country to join a Russian-led customs union that also included Kazakhstan and Belarus. Among other measures, Russian officials banned imports of Moldovan wine in September, citing health and safety concerns. The EU responded in kind, lifting customs duties on Moldovan wine in December.

POLITICAL RIGHTS: 29 / 40
A. Electoral Process: 11 / 12

Voters elect the 101-seat unicameral Parliament by proportional representation for four-year terms. Parliament elects the president, who serves up to two four-year terms, with a three-fifths supermajority. The prime minister, who holds most executive power, must be approved by Parliament.

While some problems were reported, domestic and international observers hailed the 2010 parliamentary elections as a substantial improvement over the 2009 balloting, citing a more open and diverse media environment, impartial and transparent administration by the Central Election Commission, and a lack of restrictions on campaign activities. The opposition Communist Party of the Republic of Moldova (PCRM) took 42 seats, followed by the PLDM with 32, the PDM with 15, and the Liberal Party (PL) with 12. The latter three reconstituted their AIE coalition government. Several lawmakers then quit the PCRM, and with their support, the AIE was able to elect Nicolae Timofti as president in 2012, filling a post that had been vacant since 2009 due to partisan deadlock. The defections left the PCRM with only 34 seats in Parliament.

After the PLDM and PDM fell out over the 2013 hunting scandal, Prime Minister Filat lost a confidence vote in early March. In April, PL leader Mihai Ghimpu declared that he would not support Filat's bid to return as prime minister, but a splinter faction that included 7 of the PL's 12 lawmakers rejected his position. Further partisan wrangling ensued, and a new governing coalition was formed in late May, consisting of 31 PLDM deputies, the PDM's 15, and the 7 PL defectors, with support from several nonaligned lawmakers. Former foreign minister Iurie Leancă of the PLDM was confirmed as prime minister.

As part of a flurry of legislation passed during the negotiations between the PLDM and PDM in April, Parliament abruptly changed the electoral system so that 50 of its members would be chosen in single-mandate districts. The change was reversed in early May due to a new twist in the partisan battle, but a higher vote threshold for parties to enter Parliament—6 percent, up from 4 percent—was retained.

B. Political Pluralism and Participation: 12 / 16

The main political parties in Moldova are the leftist, Russophile PCRM, which governed from 2001 to 2009; the center-left PDM, reputedly controlled by powerful businessman Vladimir Plahotniuc; the reformist, center-right PLDM; and the conservative, pro-Romanian

PL. The PL splinter group moved to create a separate party, the Liberal Reformist Party, in August 2013. In a victory for the PCRM, the Constitutional Court struck down a 2012 ban on communist symbols in June 2013.

The Gagauz, a Turkic minority concentrated in the country's south, enjoy regional autonomy, but their leaders complain that their interests are not well represented at the national level. They and Moldova's various Slavic minorities tend to look to the PCRM, smaller leftist parties, and Russia for political support.

C. Functioning of Government: 6 / 12

Corruption remains a major problem in Moldova, and the country's leading politicians regularly trade accusations of graft and illegal business activities. The politicization of anticorruption mechanisms became especially apparent during the partisan feuding of early 2013. The National Anticorruption Center (CNA), led by a PDM nominee, launched cases against PLDM cabinet ministers and allied officials. The CNA was then shifted to the government's control under legislation passed in May, reversing an earlier reform that had placed it under Parliament. Separately, the agency failed to pursue allegations that embezzled funds linked to the high-profile Sergey Magnitsky case in Russia had been laundered through a Moldovan state-owned bank. Opposition parties and other observers criticized the government for holding a closed tender that in September 2013 awarded a 49-year management contract for Chisinau's airport to a Russian consortium. The deal was reportedly backed by the PDM. Moldova was ranked 102 out of 177 countries and territories surveyed in Transparency International's 2013 Corruption Perceptions Index.

CIVIL LIBERTIES: 35 / 60 (-1)
D. Freedom of Expression and Belief: 11 / 16

The public broadcaster has grown more impartial since 2009, and the entry of new private outlets has added to the diversity of national news coverage. However, several media outlets are perceived as party affiliates, including a number linked to the PDM's Plahotniuc. The media regulator's controversial 2012 closure of NIT, the only PCRM-aligned television station with national reach, was upheld on appeal in 2013. Several print outlets in both Romanian and Russian were closed or reduced production during the year due to financial difficulties. Reporters sometimes face physical abuse, threats of violence, or selective exclusion from events of public interest.

Although the constitution guarantees religious freedom, Moldovan law recognizes the "special significance and primary role" of the Orthodox Church. Despite some positive steps by the AIE government in recent years, the country's small religious minorities continue to encounter discrimination or hostility from local authorities, Orthodox clergy, and residents in some areas.

Moldovan officials do not restrict academic freedom, though opposition parties have accused the AIE of seeking to inject pro-Romanian ideology into school curriculums. The Gagauz community has complained of de facto exclusion from the mainstream higher education system, as most Gagauz are more fluent in Russian than Romanian, the language spoken by most Moldovans.

E. Associational and Organizational Rights: 8 / 12

The government generally upholds freedom of assembly. Opposition parties repeatedly mounted antigovernment protests in 2013. A gay pride march, protected by large numbers of police, was held in May, though it was relatively small and ended early due to the threat of clashes with counterprotesters. State relations with civil society groups have improved under the AIE, though some leading politicians have displayed wariness or hostility toward nongovernmental organizations (NGOs). Enforcement of union rights and labor standards is weak, with employers rarely punished for violations. Workers participating in illegal strikes face possible fines or prison time.

F. Rule of Law: 7 / 16 (-1)

Although the constitution provides for an independent judiciary, judicial and law enforcement officials have a reputation for politicization and corruption. Numerous cases of malfeasance and petty bribery among judges were reported during 2013, and an appellate judge was charged with firing the fatal shot in the illegal hunting scandal. The year's political crisis further exposed partisanship in judicial institutions, driven in part by agreements in which positions are parceled out among the ruling parties. PL and PDM nominees were appointed to fill vacancies on the Constitutional Court, which subsequently ruled in April that Filat could not return to the premiership due to suspected corruption in his cabinet. The decision drew criticism for its inversion of the presumption of innocence. In May, the president vetoed a law that would have allowed Parliament to dismiss Constitutional Court judges with a three-fifths vote. In addition, control over the prosecutor general's office became a bone of partisan contention, with the PDM ultimately securing the confirmation of its replacement for Zubco through a favorable Constitutional Court ruling.

Ill-treatment in police custody, excessive pretrial detention, and poor prison conditions are ongoing problems, despite some improvements in recent years. Abuse of military conscripts also remains a concern, with at least four accidental deaths or suicides among young soldiers reported during 2013.

Roma suffer serious discrimination in housing, education, and employment, and have been targets of police violence. LGBT (lesbian, gay, bisexual, and transgender) people are also subject to harassment. While the 2012 Law on Ensuring Equality's main article does not list sexual orientation among the banned grounds for discrimination, it is understood to be covered under a reference to "any other similar grounds." Moreover, sexual orientation—though not gender identity—is listed in a section on workplace discrimination. The law has been fiercely criticized by an alliance of opposition parties and Orthodox clergy. In June 2013, Parliament quietly passed legislation that imposed fines for the dissemination of information or acts meant to spread prostitution, pedophilia, pornography, or "any other relations than those related to marriage and family"—language that apparently targeted same-sex relationships. Under international pressure, the problematic phrase was removed in October. A 2012 municipal ban on "homosexual propaganda" in the city of Bălți was overturned by the courts in February 2013.

G. Personal Autonomy and Individual Rights: 9 / 16

Some 700,000 Moldovans work abroad, including an estimated 200,000 in Russia. In September 2013, Russia's migration service introduced new registration requirements that would deny reentry to those who fail to comply. The move was widely seen as part of Moscow's campaign to dissuade Moldova from pursuing EU integration. Meanwhile, the EU was expected to grant Moldovans visa-free travel privileges in 2014.

Women are underrepresented in public life; just 19 were elected to Parliament in 2010. Orders of protection for victims of domestic violence are inadequately enforced. Moldova is a significant source for women and girls trafficked abroad for forced prostitution. In mid-2013, the Constitutional Court overturned a 2012 law that imposed chemical castration on convicted pedophiles. The measure was designed to combat the problem of sex tourism by foreign pedophiles.

Monaco

Political Rights Rating: 2
Civil Liberties Rating: 1
Freedom Rating: 1.5
Freedom Status: Free
Electoral Democracy: Yes

Population: 37,172
Capital: Monaco

Ten-Year Ratings Timeline For Year Under Review (Political Rights, Civil Liberties, Status)

Year Under Review	2004	2005	2006	2007	2008	2009	2010	2011	2012	2013
Rating	2,1,F	2,1,F	2,1,F	2,1,F	2,1,F	2,1,F	2,1,F	2,1,F	2,1,F	2,1,F

INTRODUCTION

The Monegasque general election took place on February 10, 2013. Horizon Monaco won by a landslide, securing 20 of the 24 national seats. Union Monegasque won 3 seats, and a new political association, Renaissance, won 1 seat. On February 21, Laurent Nouvion of Horizon Monaco was elected president of the Conseil National.

POLITICAL RIGHTS: 31 / 40

A. Electoral Process: 10 / 12

Monaco is a principality governed as a constitutional monarchy. Only the prince, who serves as head of state, may initiate legislation and change the government, though all legislation and the budget require the approval of the Conseil National. Prince Albert II took the throne after his father's death in 2005. No constitutional provisions allow citizens to change the monarchical structure of government.

The 24 members of the unicameral Conseil National are elected for five-year terms; 16 are chosen through a majority electoral system and 8 by proportional representation. Horizon Monaco, the conservative former opposition, won the general election on February 10, 2013. The former ruling party, Union Monegasque, dropped from 21 seats to only 3, and Renaissance claimed the remaining seat. Laurent Nouvion of Horizon Monaco became president of the Conseil National, and Christophe Steiner became vice president. Voter turnout was approximately 75 percent.

The head of government, known as the minister of state, is traditionally appointed by the monarch from a candidate list of three French nationals submitted by the French government. The current minister of state, Michel Roger, has held the post since March 2010. The monarch also appoints five other ministers who comprise the cabinet.

B. Political Pluralism and Participation: 11 / 16

Monaco's political system is constructed of political associations, led by Horizon Monaco and Union Monegasque. Renaissance, the new association that first competed in the general election in 2013, was established by Monaco's largest hotel and casino company, SBM, along with trade union members.

Monaco's law on campaign finance was adopted in 2012 in response to the recommendations of GRECO. Changes included a €400,000 ($526,000) limit on campaign expenditures.

The constitution differentiates between the rights of Monegasque nationals and those of noncitizens. Only about 8,000 of the principality's residents are citizens, and they alone may elect the Conseil National. Citizens also benefit from free education, unemployment assistance, and the ability to hold elective office.

C. Functioning of Government: 10 / 12

Inadequate financial record keeping has traditionally made the country's level of corruption difficult to measure. However, in 2009 the principality started providing foreign tax authorities with information on accounts held by noncitizens, and by October of that year, the Organisation for Economic Co-operation and Development (OECD) removed Monaco from its list of uncooperative tax havens. Monaco took further steps toward improving financial transparency by signing tax information exchange agreements with 24 countries in 2009–2010, including with a number of OECD countries. The agreements ensure that Monaco will surrender relevant tax documents requested by the signatories.

In March 2013, senior official Jean-Sébastien Fiorucci was charged in a polling scandal in which the privacy of Monegasque citizens was said to have been compromised in 2012 when a French-based polling company sought information about people's opinions of candidates in the upcoming election. His trial was ongoing at the end of 2013.

In April 2013, Sherpa, a French nongovernmental organization against financial crimes, requested a preliminary inquiry into a BNP Paribas branch in Monaco that allegedly concealed a money laundering network between Monaco and several African countries, including Madagascar, Gabon, Senegal, and Burkina Faso.

CIVIL LIBERTIES: 57 / 60 (+1)

D. Freedom of Expression and Belief: 16 / 16 (+1)

The constitution provides for freedoms of speech and the press, although criticism of the ruling family is prohibited. There are no daily newspapers but there is an English-language monthly, *The Riviera Times*, as well as foreign and online newspapers that cover Monaco. Monaco Info is the only local TV channel. In May 2013, a news crossover went into effect in which *Riviera Times* editors host a weekly local news segment on Radio Monaco. In an effort to improve internet and telecommunications, two major providers, Monaco Telecom and Level 3 Communications, came to an agreement in June 2013 to connect Monaco to a global internet backbone.

The constitution guarantees freedom of worship, though Roman Catholicism is the state religion. There are no laws against proselytizing by formally registered religious organizations, but authorities strongly discourage proselytizing in public. Academic freedom is not restricted. The country's only institution of higher education, the private International University of Monaco, offers graduate and undergraduate programs in business administration, finance, and related fields. Monegasque students may attend French colleges and universities under various agreements between the two countries.

E. Associational and Organizational Rights: 12 / 12

The constitution provides for freedom of assembly, which is generally respected in practice. No restrictions are imposed on the formation of civic and human rights groups. Workers have the legal right to organize and bargain collectively, although they rarely do so. All workers except state employees have the right to strike, as did members of the Worker's Trade Union of Monaco in 2012. At the end of December 2012, the Union des Syndicats de Monaco (USM), which once had a monopoly on trade unions in Monaco, split to form the Fédération des syndicats de salariés de Monaco (F2SM) because of difference of opinion.

On December 30, employees of the Hotel de Paris began the longest strike in the country's history over wages during the hotel's renovations.

F. Rule of Law: 15 / 16

The legal rights to a fair public trial and an independent judiciary are generally respected. The justice system is based on the French legal code, and under the constitution, the prince delegates his judicial powers to the courts. The prince names five full members and two judicial assistants to the Supreme Court based on nominations by the Conseil National and other government bodies. Jail facilities generally meet international standards. After sentencing, criminal defendants are transferred to a French prison.

G. Personal Autonomy and Individual Rights: 14 / 16

Property rights are respected. Noncitizens holding a residence permit may purchase real estate and open businesses.

Women generally receive equal pay for equal work. There are five women in the Conseil National and two in the Crown Council. Abortion is legal only under special circumstances, including rape. Monaco does not recognize same-sex unions or marriages.

Mongolia

Political Rights Rating: 1
Civil Liberties Rating: 2
Freedom Rating: 1.5
Freedom Status: Free
Electoral Democracy: Yes

Population: 2,792,000
Capital: Ulaanbaatar

Ten-Year Ratings Timeline For Year Under Review (Political Rights, Civil Liberties, Status)

Year Under Review	2004	2005	2006	2007	2008	2009	2010	2011	2012	2013
Rating	2,2,F	2,2,F	2,2,F	2,2,F	2,2,F	2,2,F	2,2,F	2,2,F	1,2,F	1,2,F

INTRODUCTION

Incumbent president Ts. Elbegdorj won a second four-year term in the June 2013 presidential election, defeating two opponents in the first round of voting. In late July he pardoned his predecessor, N. Enkhbayar, who had been convicted on corruption charges in 2012. The country continued to experience economic growth based on its mineral wealth during 2013, even as corruption, the power of politicians associated with specific business interests, and the politicization of the media remained key challenges to freedom and democracy.

POLITICAL RIGHTS: 36 / 40
A. Electoral Process: 11 / 12

Under the 1992 constitution, the prime minister, who holds most executive power, is nominated by the party or coalition with the most seats in the 76-member parliament (the State Great Khural) and approved by the parliament with the agreement of the president. The president is head of state and of the armed forces, and can veto legislation, subject to a two-thirds parliamentary override. Candidates running for president are nominated by parties but may not be party members. Both the president and the parliament are directly elected for four-year terms.

Parliamentary balloting has varied from election to election between multimember and single-member districts. Currently, 48 of the parliament's 76 seats are awarded through majoritarian voting in single-member districts, while the remaining 28 are allocated through a proportional system according to parties' share of the national vote.

In the parliamentary elections held in June 2012, the Democratic Party (DP) won 33 seats, the Mongolian People's Party (MPP) 25, and the Justice Coalition—comprising the revived Mongolian People's Revolutionary Party (MPRP) and the Mongolian National Democratic Party (MNDP)—took 11, with the rest of the seats going to independents (3) and the Civil Will–Green Party (2). N. Altankhuyag of the DP became prime minister, leading a coalition cabinet that consisted of the DP, the Justice Coalition, and the Civil Will–Green Party. Ulaanbaatar city elections were held in conjunction with the parliamentary elections for the first time. The MPP leadership in the capital was replaced with a DP majority headed by democracy activist E. Bat-Uul.

In the June 2013 presidential election, the DP-backed Elbegdorj stood for a second term. The MPP nominated member of parliament B. Bat-Erdene, a former wrestler, while the MPRP nominated Health Minister N. Udval. The involvement of three candidates raised the possibility of a second-round runoff, but Elbegdorj was able to garner just over 50 percent of the votes, winning outright in the first round.

The General Election Commission in 2013 redeployed some of the innovations of the 2012 parliamentary elections, including electronic vote counting, a video feed from inside polling stations, and nonparty domestic observers. The commission also introduced new practices, such as the release of voting statistics by time of day and age group, and free mobile-telephone credits as a "reward" for voting. Following Mongolia's accession to the Organization for Security and Cooperation in Europe (OSCE) in late 2012, a large observation mission provided systematic monitoring of the election. Apart from administrative challenges with election officials at the local and national level, and some criticism of the politicization of the media, the mission confirmed previous smaller efforts and declared the election free and open.

B. Political Pluralism and Participation: 16 / 16

Mongolian democracy continues to be characterized by a vibrant multiparty landscape. The MPRP, which had ruled the country since the early 20th century, legalized opposition parties in 1990, and competitive elections have led to several peaceful transfers of power. In 2010, the MPRP rebranded itself as the MPP, but a faction led by former president Enkhbayar broke off the following year and formed a new MPRP.

While the top two parties command a large share of votes and dominate the parliament, smaller parties continue to be represented and remain viable. Political parties are largely built around patronage networks rather than political ideologies. Representatives of large business groups play an important role in funding and directing the large parties.

Voter participation in the 2013 presidential election rose slightly in the capital city, but declined further in the countryside, for a total of 66.5 percent.

C. Functioning of Government: 9 / 12

Corruption remains a serious problem in Mongolia and is viewed as pervasive. The Independent Authority Against Corruption (IAAC) has been actively investigating corruption allegations since 2007. In April 2012, the IAAC arrested former president and MPRP party leader Enkhbayar. He was convicted that August of relatively minor corruption and money-laundering charges, and sentenced to two and a half years in prison in November. Following his reelection in June 2013, Elbegdorj pardoned Enkhbayar. While anticorruption efforts have been stepped up, they have mostly targeted the political opposition.

Although the government operates with limited transparency, the first Citizens' Hall was established in Ulaanbaatar in 2009 to encourage civic participation in the legislative process. Citizens have the opportunity to provide feedback on draft laws and government services by attending such hearings or submitting their views. Citizens' Halls were given budgetary authority for the first time in 2013 through the dispersal of Local Development Funds. This measure is intended to foster local participation in politics as well as increase accountability regarding the spending of funds.

CIVIL LIBERTIES: 50 / 60
D. Freedom of Expression and Belief: 15 / 16

While the government generally respects press freedom, many journalists and independent publications practice a degree of self-censorship to avoid legal action under libel laws that place the burden of proof on the defendant. Journalists have been charged in defamation suits by members of parliament and businesspeople; in many cases, the charges were dropped.

There are hundreds of privately owned print and broadcast outlets, but the main source of news in the vast countryside is the state-owned Mongolian National Broadcaster. Some international media operations have moved into the Mongolian market. The government does not interfere with internet access.

Journalistic standards in Mongolia remain low. Media outlets tend to report rumors without confirmation. Political parties and their members have increasingly purchased media outlets, particularly television stations. This linkage between political interests and the press was criticized by the OSCE presidential election observation mission for blurring the lines between news and editorial content, and for not clearly identifying such politically connected ownership where it exists. However, most Mongolians are aware of the political positions of different media outlets.

Freedom of religion is guaranteed by the constitution. The fall of communism led to an influx of Christian missionaries to Mongolia and a revival of the country's traditional Buddhism and shamanism. Some Christian groups have reported registration obstacles and instances of harassment by local authorities. The Kazakh Muslim minority generally enjoys freedom of religion. Academic freedom is respected.

E. Associational and Organizational Rights: 11 / 12

Freedoms of assembly and association are observed in law and in practice. Numerous environmental, human rights, and social welfare groups operate without government restriction. Trade unions are independent and active, and the government has generally protected their rights in recent years. Collective bargaining is legal.

F. Rule of Law: 12 / 16

The judiciary is independent, but corruption among judges persists. The police force has been accused of making arbitrary arrests and traffic stops, holding detainees for long periods, and beating prisoners. Four senior police officers were tried for their roles in the death of rioters following the 2008 parliamentary elections. Prison deaths continue to be reported, as insufficient nutrition, heat, and medical care remain problems. President Elbegdorj issued a moratorium on the death penalty in January 2010.

Antidiscrimination laws do not address sexual orientation or gender identity, and LGBT (lesbian, gay, bisexual, and transgender) people reportedly face societal bias, cases of assault, and mistreatment by police.

G. Personal Autonomy and Individual Rights: 12 / 16

While women comprise 60 percent of all university students as well as 60 percent of all judges, they hold only 9 parliamentary seats despite a 20 percent quota on female candidates in the 2012 parliamentary elections and the candidacy of Udval in the 2013 presidential election. Spousal abuse is prohibited by law, but social and cultural norms continue to discourage victims from reporting such crimes, and the incidence—particularly in connection with alcohol abuse—remains high. Mongolia is a source, transit, and destination country for men, women, and children who are subjected to sex trafficking and forced labor. The government has continued efforts to eliminate trafficking, though funding for such programs has been inadequate.

Montenegro

Political Rights Rating: 3
Civil Liberties Rating: 2
Freedom Rating: 2.5
Freedom Status: Free
Electoral Democracy: Yes

Population: 623,000
Capital: Podgorica

Ten-Year Ratings Timeline For Year Under Review (Political Rights, Civil Liberties, Status)

Year Under Review	2004	2005	2006	2007	2008	2009	2010	2011	2012	2013
Rating	3,2,F	3,2,F	3,3,PF	3,3,PF	3,3,PF	3,2,F	3,2,F	3,2,F	3,2,F	3,2,F

Note: The ratings from 2004 and 2005 are for the State Union of Serbia and Montenegro.

INTRODUCTION

In early 2013, Montenegro's ruling Democratic Party of Socialists (DPS) came under fire after *Dan*, an independent media outlet known for criticism of the government, published leaked party meeting records that seemed to reveal underhanded political tactics. Among other allegations, the reports accused the DPS of trying to secure jobs for party loyalists and close a trade union led by a legislator from the opposition Democratic Front. After the state prosecutor declined to investigate the allegations in February, the opposition raised the possibility of boycotting the April presidential election, though they ultimately participated. Incumbent Filip Vujanović of the DPS defeated Democratic Front leader Miodrag Lekić. Prosecutors later in the year opened an investigation in connection with *Dan*'s reports. At year's end, no indictments had been filed.

In July, Montenegro's first gay pride event, in the coastal town of Budva, was disrupted by protesters, some of whom shouted "kill the gays" and threw rocks and other items at LGBT (lesbian, gay, bisexual, and transgender) activists. Some 20 people were detained, prompting authorities in the capital, Podgorica, to heighten security during its first gay pride event in October. Protesters nevertheless attempted to attack participants at that march, but police prevented them from doing so and made dozens of arrests.

Having officially opened membership talks with Montenegro in December 2012, the European Union (EU) in October 2013 expanded the negotiations to include issues related to the judiciary, media freedom, and security. Brussels also praised the Balkan nation's progress on key EU-backed reforms aimed at strengthening judicial independence, while calling for more transparency in public administration.

Montenegrin journalists faced increased pressure in 2013.

POLITICAL RIGHTS: 27 / 40

A. Electoral Process: 9 / 12

Members of the unicameral, 81-seat Skupština (Assembly) are elected for four-year terms. The president, directly elected for up to two five-year terms, nominates the prime minister, who requires legislative approval. International observers have deemed recent elections generally free and fair, despite some irregularities.

In July 2012, legislators voted to dissolve the parliament and call early elections so the government could begin the EU talks with a fresh mandate. A DPS-led coalition won snap polls held that October with a simple majority of 46 percent, or 39 seats. The Democratic Front took 20 seats, followed by the Socialist People's Party with 9, Positive Montenegro with 7, and the Bosniak Party with 3. The Croat Citizens' Initiative and two Albanian parties won 1 seat each. The DPS-led coalition took power with support from Albanian and Croatian minority parties, and DPS Chairman Milo Đukanović, who has served as Montenegro's prime minister or president for most of the last two decades, was elected to his seventh term as prime minister in December 2012.

On April 7, 2013, President Vujanović was reelected with 51.2 percent of the vote. The Democratic Front's Lekić followed with 48.8 percent. Opposition supporters protested the results, alleging fraud. However, the Organization for Security and Cooperation in Europe (OSCE), which monitored the election, said the poll had been professionally administered and competitive, and that "fundamental freedoms of expression, movement, and association were mostly respected" during the campaign.

B. Political Pluralism and Participation: 11 / 16

Numerous political parties compete for power, though the opposition is weak. The biggest opposition faction, the Democratic Front, comprises the reform-minded Movement for Changes and the New Serb Democracy. The current coalition government comprises the DPS, its ally the Social Democratic Party, and a handful of lawmakers from parties that represent Montenegro's ethnic minorities. The Roma ethnic minority is underrepresented in politics. Serbs, comprising 28.7 percent of the population, generally opposed the government's declaration of independence from Serbia in July 2006, but have adjusted to the new reality.

In September 2011, the parliament broke a four-year impasse to approve a landmark new election law that ensures the representation of minorities and improves technical voting issues. The law's passage had been delayed due to a controversy over the languages officially recognized in the country. In 2010, Montenegrin had become the official language of the state broadcaster, and a Montenegrin grammar text was introduced in schools. Critics countered that the government was promoting an artificial language derived from standard Serbian, and the opposition had vowed that it would not support the election law until the Serbian language was given equal status to Montenegrin in the education system. The law was passed after legislators agreed on a class to be taught in schools called "Montenegrin-Serbian, Bosnian, Croatian language and literature."

C. Functioning of Government: 7 / 12

Corruption remains a serious problem. Legislative frameworks to improve transparency in party financing and public procurement, among other anticorruption efforts, are in place, but implementation is mixed. Graft and misconduct remain widespread in key areas such as health care and public procurement, convictions in high-profile cases are low, and oversight of conflicts of interest is relatively weak, according to the European Commission's (EC) 2013 progress report; the report added that organized crime groups have significant influence in both the public and private sectors. Law enforcement does not take a proactive approach to corruption investigations, especially cases involving top officials. Regarding the corruption allegations against the ruling DPS that emerged in the media in early 2013, prosecutors eventually launched an investigation after initially dismissing the accusations; no indictments had been issued at year's end. Montenegro was ranked 67 out of 177 countries and territories surveyed in Transparency International's 2013 Corruption Perceptions Index.

CIVIL LIBERTIES: 45 / 60

D. Freedom of Expression and Belief: 13 / 16

A variety of independent media operate in Montenegro. While the government does not explicitly censor media outlets, journalists critical of Prime Minister Đukanović or the governing party have faced costly civil defamation suits. (Montenegro decriminalized libel in 2011.) In November 2013, Đukanović attended a so-called journalism conference in Podgorica that reportedly featured a display labeling outlets critical of the government as "enemy" media. Attacks against Montenegrin journalists are reported each year. In August, Reporters Without Borders criticized what it called an "oppressive climate for investigative journalism" after a bomb attack targeted the home of Tufik Softić, a reporter for a Montenegrin daily; he was not injured in the explosion. In December, an explosive device detonated outside the offices of the opposition daily *Vijesti*, though no one was injured.

The DPS-led government denies opposition media outlets advertising contracts from publicly owned entities, while directing significant funding toward the progovernment newspaper *Pobjeda*, which it continues to operate in evident violation of legislation prohibiting the state from founding print media outlets. The public broadcaster is being reformed but still lacks sustainable financing, according to the EC. Internet access is unrestricted.

The constitution guarantees freedom of religious belief. However, the canonically recognized Serbian Orthodox Church and a self-proclaimed Montenegrin Orthodox Church continue to clash over ownership of church properties and other issues.

Academic freedom is guaranteed by law, but political debates about the nature of Montenegrin identity and history have spilled over into the educational realm, as was the case when controversy over the Montenegrin language almost blocked the adoption of the 2011 election law.

E. Associational and Organizational Rights: 10 / 12

Citizens enjoy freedoms of association and assembly. After the violence at the July gay pride parade in Budva, authorities deployed 2,000 police officers to secure the Podgorica event, and some 60 counterdemonstrators were detained. Nongovernmental organizations generally operate without state interference, and civil society participates in state and local government, though the EC has urged closer cooperation. Most formally employed workers belong to unions, and the right to strike is generally protected. However, trade union members sometimes face discrimination, and dismissals of striking workers have been reported.

F. Rule of Law: 10 / 16

In 2013, the EC cited progress on judicial reform. In July, parliament passed constitutional amendments to improve judicial independence; these measures aim to curb political influence on judicial appointments by making the process more transparent and more focused on candidates' individual merit. However, the government has yet to institute a single nationwide recruitment system for judges and prosecutors based on transparent criteria, courts are subject to political influence, and the judicial and prosecutorial councils, while functional, are understaffed and underfunded, according to the EC. Legal proceedings are lengthy and often highly bureaucratic, particularly for proceedings involving business dealings. Prison conditions do not meet international standards for education or health care.

Ethnic Albanians, who comprise 5 percent of the population, maintain that they are underrepresented in the civil service, particularly in the police and judiciary. Roma, Ashkali,

Egyptians, members of the LGBT community, and other minority groups often face discrimination. As part of the Sarajevo Declaration Process, Montenegro continues to cooperate with Bosnia and Herzegovina, Croatia, and Serbia to reintegrate refugees from the conflicts in the former Yugoslavia in the 1990s.

G. Personal Autonomy and Individual Rights: 12 / 16

The state sector dominates much of Montenegro's economy, though the tourism industry has thrived in recent years, with significant foreign investment to develop Budva, Kotor, and other coastal towns. Official unemployment is 19 percent, but that figure is probably inflated, as many workers counted as officially unemployed work in Montenegro's sizeable gray economy. Since 2012, Montenegro has launched an electronic business registry, simplified licensing procedures, and taken other steps to improve the environment for starting a business. However, corruption continues to undermine the business climate.

Women in Montenegro are legally entitled to equal pay for equal work, but traditional patriarchal attitudes often limit their salary levels and educational opportunities. Women are underrepresented in government and business. New provisions requiring women to comprise 30 percent of candidate lists were implemented in the 2012 elections, but women hold only 14 seats in the 81-seat parliament. While domestic violence remains problematic, in January 2013 the government adopted the 2013–2017 Gender Equality Plan to address violence in the home and gender discrimination in the labor market. Trafficking in persons for the purposes of prostitution and forced labor remains a problem; the government has adopted an anti-trafficking strategy through 2018.

Morocco

Political Rights Rating: 5
Civil Liberties Rating: 4
Freedom Rating: 4.5
Freedom Status: Partly Free
Electoral Democracy: No

Population: 33,000,000
Capital: Rabat

Note: The numerical ratings and status listed above do not reflect conditions in Western Sahara, which is examined in a separate report.

Ratings Timeline (Political Rights, Civil Liberties, Status)

Year Under Review	2004	2005	2006	2007	2008	2009	2010	2011	2012	2013
Rating	5,4,PF	5,4,PF	5,4,PF	5,4,PF	5,4,PF	5,4,PF	5,4,PF	5,4,PF	5,4,PF	5,4,PF

INTRODUCTION

The struggling economy led to several demonstrations and riots including a September 22 protest in Rabat over the rising prices of fuel and foodstuffs. The demonstration consisted of a wide coalition of youth, labor, and Tamazight (Berber) protesters. The government fell in July when the centrist Istiqlal Party pulled out of the governing coalition over the government's handling of the economy. In October, a new government was formed when the National Rally of Independents (RNI) joined a new coalition.

In a particularly embarrassing moment for King Mohammed VI, a convicted child rapist was accidently released in July as part of broader amnesty of political prisoners. The mistaken release of Daniel Galván Viña, who had been convicted in 2011 of raping 11 children, appeared to be a combination of clerical error and diplomatic bungling with the Spanish foreign ministry. Although the pardon was revoked, widespread and violent protests took place in Casablanca and, especially, Rabat.

POLITICAL RIGHTS: 15 / 40 (-1)
A. Electoral Process: 5 / 12

Mohammed VI and his close advisors, often referred to as the *Makhzen*, hold political, social, and economic power in Morocco. The 2011 constitutional referendum was the last in a series of constitutional reforms the palace has engineered since the 1962 constitution. To be sure, the reform was significant. While it preserved the monarch's existing powers, it did nonetheless require him to choose the prime minister from the party that won the most seats in parliamentary elections, and consult the prime minister before dissolving Parliament. Other provisions included giving official status to Tamazight (Berbers), calling for gender equality, and emphasizing respect for human rights.

Even under the 2011 constitution, the monarch can dissolve Parliament, rule by decree, and dismiss or appoint cabinet members. He sets national and foreign policy, commands the armed forces and intelligence services, and presides over the judicial system. One of the king's constitutional titles is "commander of the faithful," giving his authority a claim to religious legitimacy. The king is also the majority stakeholder in a vast array of private and public sector firms; according to *Forbes*, Mohammed VI is worth $2.5 billion, making him one of the world's wealthiest people.

The lower house of Parliament, the Chamber of Representatives, has 395 directly elected members who serve for five-year terms. Sixty of these seats are reserved for women, and 30 for men under age 40. Members of the 270-seat upper house, the Chamber of Counselors, are chosen by an electoral college to serve nine-year terms. Under a rule that took effect in 2009, women are guaranteed 12 percent of the seats in local elections.

Parliamentary elections held in November 2011 resulted in a victory for the Justice and Development Party (PJD), with the Istiqlal placing second, followed by the National Rally of Independents, the Modernity and Authenticity Party, the socialist Social Union of Popular Forces (USFP), the Popular Movement, the Constitutional Union, the Party of Progress and Socialism (PPS) and ten small parties. Prime Minister Abdelilah Benkirane's PJD formed a coalition with the Istiqlal, the Popular Movement, and the PPS in January 2012. The government held office until July 2013, when the Istiqlal withdrew in protest of the PJD's handling of the economy. A new government took office in October, with the previously oppositional RNI joining the coalition.

B. Political Pluralism and Participation: 7 / 16

Morocco exhibits a multi-party system, a system developed by the current king's father, Hassan II. Multi-party politics ran contrary to the single-party rule evident in so many newly independent countries in the 1950s and 1960s. Although such pluralism is laudable, the result is that the parties are fragmented and generally unable to assert themselves. The PJD, which won the 2011 parliamentary vote, has long been a vocal opposition Islamist party, even as it remained respectful of the monarchy. The Islamist Justice and Charity Movement, by contrast, is illegal, though it is deftly tolerated by the authorities. Other Islamist groups are harassed by authorities and not permitted to participate in the political process. Parties emerge and disappear periodically, depending on reformation and fractures, as well as individual politicians' careerist maneuvers.

C. Functioning of Government: 3 / 12 (-1)

Elected officials of government are duly installed in government, although their power to shape policy is sharply constrained as the king and his advisers control most of the levers of power.

Despite the government's rhetoric on combating widespread corruption, it remains a problem, both in public life and in the business world. In the 2012 book, *Le Roi Prédateur,* journalists Catherine Graciet and Éric Laurent leveled sharp charges of corruption at the palace. Morocco was ranked 91 out of 177 countries and territories surveyed in Transparency International's 2013 Corruption Perceptions Index. In the November 2011 elections, the PJD ran on an anti-corruption platform, although it has found it challenging to root out graft. One of the deepest structural impediments is the king's own role in the economy; the king is the majority stakeholder in a vast array of private and public sector firms.

CIVIL LIBERTIES: 27 / 60
D. Freedom of Expression and Belief: 8 / 16

Although the independent press enjoys a significant degree of freedom when reporting on economic and social policies, the authorities use restrictive press laws and an array of financial and other, more subtle mechanisms to punish critical journalists, particularly those who focus on the king, his family, the status of the Western Sahara, or Islam. For example, the monarchy has instructed businesses not to buy ads in publications that have criticized the government.

Journalists have also been harassed, including Hamid Naïmi, who has investigated corruption and the marginalization of the Berber population in the northern Rif region, and Mohamed Sokrate, a blogger who has written sympathetically about the February 20 movement and advocates secularism.

The state dominates the broadcast media, but people have access to foreign satellite television channels. The authorities occasionally disrupt websites and internet platforms, while bloggers and other internet users are sometimes arrested for posting content that offends the monarchy. Youssef Jalili was convicted of defamation in January 2013 after reporting the misuse of public funds by a government official. Ali Anouzla, the founder and director of the Arabic edition of *Lakome*, was arrested in September after he posted a link to an article on the website of the Spanish newspaper *El Pais* which contained an Al Qaeda video. Anouzla had also broken the story on the release of the Spanish rapist Galvan. In October he was released, but the Arabic and French versions of *Lakome* remain blocked by authorities.

Nearly all Moroccans are Muslims. While the small Jewish community is permitted to practice its faith without government interference, Moroccan authorities are growing increasingly intolerant of social and religious diversity, as reflected in arrest campaigns against Shiites, Muslim converts to Christianity, and those opposed to a law enforcing the Ramadan fast.

While university campuses generally provide a space for open discussion, professors practice self-censorship when dealing with sensitive topics like Western Sahara, the monarchy, and Islam.

E. Associational and Organizational Rights: 6 / 12

Freedom of assembly is not always respected, though frequent demonstrations by unemployed graduates and unions are generally tolerated. Although such protests often occur without incident, activists say they are harassed outside of public events. As noted, the February 20 movement was deemed illegal by a Casablanca judge in July 2012.

Civil society and independent nongovernmental organizations are quite active, but the authorities monitor Islamist groups, arrest suspected extremists, and harass other groups that offend the government. Moroccan workers are permitted to form and join independent trade unions, and the 2004 labor law prevents employers from punishing workers who do so. However, the authorities have forcibly broken up labor actions that entail criticism of the government, and child laborers, especially girls working as domestic helpers, are denied basic rights.

F. Rule of Law: 6 / 16

The judiciary is not independent, and the courts are regularly used to punish opponents of the government. Arbitrary arrest and torture still occur, though they are less common than under Hassan. The security forces are given greater leeway with detainees advocating independence for Western Sahara, leading to frequent reports of abuse and lack of due process.

Police brutality and torture often goes uninvestigated. Ali Aarrass, who is serving a 12-year prison sentence after confessing to terrorism charges while allegedly being tortured, began a hunger strike in July that lasted nearly a month in protest to being ill-treated and not having been given a fair trial. His hunger strike ended on August 7 when Moroccan authorities assured lawyers and representatives from the Moroccan National Council for Human Rights he would receive due process. The government has also continued to accept payment from the EU to stop migrants at the northern border with Ceuta and Melilla, as well as to thwart passage across the Strait of Gibraltar and the passage to the Canary Islands. Human rights abuses are extensive against the transient population; according to a wide array of sources, the EU turns a blind eye to Moroccan human rights abuses.

G. Personal Autonomy and Individual Rights: 7 / 16

Many Moroccans have a mixed Tamazight (Berber) ancestry and the government has officially recognized Tamazight language and culture.

Women continue to face significant discrimination at the societal level. However, Moroccan authorities have a relatively progressive view on gender equality, which is recognized in the 2011 constitution. The 2004 family code has been lauded for granting women increased rights in the areas of marriage, divorce, and child custody, and various other laws aim to protect women's interests. But significant problems persist. Article 475 allows rapists to escape prosecution if they marry their victims. In March 2012, Amina Filali committed suicide by ingesting rat poison after being forced to marry her rapist. Subsequent protests led to a proposal in January 2013 to repeal Article 475. In addition, Article 486 treats rape as a matter of mere indecency, rather than violence. Additional efforts are being advocated for criminalizing marital rape. By December, progress was reported in both houses of parliament to amend Article 475—removing the ability to avoid prosecution by marrying the victim.

Finally, in October two 15-year-old boys and a 14-year-old girl were detained in Nador after posting a photo of one of the boys kissing the girl on Facebook. They were charged with public indecency under Article 484 of the penal code. A wave of solidarity spread, with people holding kiss-ins throughout the country and abroad. In November a court issued a reprimand.

Mozambique

Political Rights Rating: 4
Civil Liberties Rating: 3
Freedom Rating: 3.5
Freedom Status: Partly Free
Electoral Democracy: No

Population: 24,335,890
Capital: Maputo

Ten-Year Ratings Timeline For Year Under Review (Political Rights, Civil Liberties, Status)

Year Under Review	2004	2005	2006	2007	2008	2009	2010	2011	2012	2013
Rating	3,4,PF	3,4,PF	3,4,PF	3,3,PF	3,3,PF	4,3,PF	4,3,PF	4,3,PF	4,3,PF	4,3,PF

INTRODUCTION

At the start of 2013, the opposition Mozambique National Resistance (RENAMO)—a former rebel movement—was demanding stronger representation in the armed forces, revision of the electoral system, and a larger share of coal and natural gas income, after an ambush by the ruling Front for the Liberation of Mozambique (FRELIMO) on its leader in October 2012 prompted a cessation of the 1992 peace agreement. Negotiations failed early in the year. This led RENAMO and FRELIMO to several violent exchanges, beginning in April, when 1 RENAMO supporter and 4 members of the FIR (Rapid Response Force) were killed in Sofala province as RENAMO forces tried to free fellow supporters that had been jailed when the police invaded RENAMO's headquarters in Muxungue. Confrontations between the two sides continued in Sofala, resulting in dozens dead and many local people leaving the area. On October 21 the government took over RENAMO's base in Satunjira, Gorongosa. The fighting spread to other regions of Mozambique, reaching Nampula and Rapale. The government took over RENAMO's second base on October 28, and RENAMO conducted an increasing number of violent attacks in November and December against primarily military targets.

After 24 rounds of negotiations, no progress had been by the end of the year, as RENAMO demanded a revision of the 1992 Rome Peace Agreement that brought an end to the country's 1977–1992 civil war. Mozambicans faced a growing sense of lawlessness due to a significant spike in violent crimes—particularly kidnappings—in addition to the worsening political violence. Nevertheless, the heads of both FRELIMO and RENAMO declared that the country would return to peace in 2014.

November 2013 municipal elections were generally peaceful, and, although FRELIMO won the majority of municipalities, the opposition Democratic Movement of Mozambique (MDM) made major strides.

Despite the country's worst political and military crisis since 1992, Mozambique's GDP grew 7 percent in 2013. Extractive industries, financial services, transport, and communications drove the economy. Inflation was between 5 and 6 percent, 2 percent higher than in 2012 but still lower than the ceiling set by the Central Bank.

POLITICAL RIGHTS: 23 / 40

A. Electoral Process: 6 / 12

The president, who appoints the prime minister, is elected by popular vote for up to two five-year terms. Members of the 250-seat, unicameral Assembly of the Republic are also elected for five-year terms. The national government appoints the governors of the 10 provinces and Maputo. Despite the introduction of elected provincial assemblies and municipal governments, power remains highly centralized, particularly in the hands of the president. While international observers have deemed that the overall outcomes of Mozambique's national elections reflected the will of the people, general elections have repeatedly been riddled with problems.

Mozambique held presidential, legislative, and—for the first time—provincial elections in October 2009. Armando Guebuza was reelected with 75 percent of the vote. His opponents, Afonso Dhlakama of RENAMO and Daviz Simango of the newly formed MDM, received 16.4 percent and 8.6 percent, respectively. In the parliamentary contest, FRELIMO captured 191 of 250 seats, while RENAMO won 51, and the MDM took 8. FRELIMO also won absolute majorities in all 10 of the country's provincial assemblies. RENAMO and the MDM both alleged fraud, and international observer groups were highly critical of many pre-election processes. Observers also documented irregularities, though they concluded that the distortions were not significant enough to have impacted the overall results of the elections.

On July 29, 2013, RENAMO's leader announced that his party would not participate in the municipal elections set for November 20, and threatened to split the country into independent provinces because RENAMO was not adequately represented in the electoral bodies. Some analysts argued for postponing the elections in view of the growing military tension between RENAMO and FRELIMO, but a total of 18 parties ran. FRELIMO won the majority of the 53 municipalities in what were remarkably peaceful elections. MDM won several seats in a large number of municipal assemblies and control over three major cities: Beira (the second-largest city), Nampula (the third-largest city), and Quelimane.

National and provincial elections are set for October 15, 2014. RENAMO has declared that it will not participate if the electoral rules are not changed.

B. Political Pluralism and Participation: 10 / 16

Political parties are governed by a law that expressly prohibits them from identifying exclusively with any religious or ethnic group. FRELIMO, the political party that grew out of the former guerrilla group that had fought to win Mozambique's independence, is the only party to have held power nationally. Its unbroken incumbency has allowed it to acquire significant control over state institutions. In the lead-up to the 2009 elections, the government was heavily criticized for the electoral commission's disqualification of MDM candidates in 7 of the country's 11 parliamentary constituencies. Elements within FRELIMO are also believed to have instigated several violent attacks against opposition candidates and their supporters during the campaign. Meanwhile, popular support for RENAMO—which fought FRELIMO in the 16-year civil war—and its leader, Afonso Dhlakama, has dropped in recent years. MDM, which formed when certain RENAMO politicians had a break with the party, has quickly established itself as a viable political force.

C. Functioning of Government: 7 / 12

Corruption in government and business remains pervasive despite the passing of a new anticorruption law and the delegation of new powers to the Central Office for Combating Corruption in 2012. Observers note that anticorruption measures are not followed through, and those in charge of enforcing them—police and judicial bodies—are also often corrupt. Mozambique was ranked 119 out of 177 countries and territories surveyed in Transparency International's 2013 Corruption Perceptions Index. In the 2013 Revenue Watch Institute Natural Resources Management Index, Mozambique ranked 46 out of 58 countries. The country's poor performance was largely due to the government's failure to provide information on extractives, the confidential nature of contracts, and a lack of public oversight of the licensing process.

CIVIL LIBERTIES: 35 / 60 (-1)
D. Freedom of Expression and Belief: 12 / 16

Press freedom is legally protected and there are independent media outlets, but reporters are often pressured, threatened, and censored, in addition to practicing self-censorship. Mozambique has a government-run daily, *Noticias*, and the privately owned *Diario de Moçambique*. There is also a state news agency and a state radio and television broadcaster. Independent media include several weeklies and the daily *O País*, a number of radio stations, and news websites. However, the government persistently controls the media, both directly and through advertising and access to information. While there are no official government restrictions on internet use, opposition leaders have claimed that government intelligence services monitor online exchanges.

Religious freedom is well respected, and academic freedom is generally upheld. In August 2012 the government revised its 2011 ban on wearing a veil to school, allowing Muslim girls to do so during Ramadan. This change in policy followed intense pressure from throughout the Muslim community, which among other things threatened to vote against FRELIMO in the municipal and general elections.

E. Associational and Organizational Rights: 7 / 12

Associational and organizational rights are broadly guaranteed, but with substantial regulations. By law, the right to assemble is subject to notification and timing restrictions, and in practice it is also subject to governmental discretion. In March, Eduardo Mondlane University punished medical students who participated in a doctors' strike by forcing them to restart their residency.

While most campaign rallies in the lead-up to the 2013 municipal elections proceeded peacefully, a few were violently disrupted by rival party activists. On October 31, thousands in Maputo and other major Mozambican cities peacefully demonstrated against the threat of war, the increase in violent crime (for example the G-20 crime spree in Maputo), and the rapid rise in the number and violence of kidnappings. It was the largest-ever demonstration under FRELIMO rule.

Nongovernmental organizations (NGOs) operate openly but face bureaucratic hurdles in registering with the government, as required by law. Workers have the right to form and join unions and to strike.

F. Rule of Law: 7 / 16 (-1)

Following the establishment of the Superior Appeals Courts in late 2012, the National Assembly passed a new Penal Code in December 2013, the first new code in 120 years. Irrespective of these modernization efforts, judicial independence remains limited due to scarce resources, poor training, a backlog of cases, and corruption. In 2013, an external audit uncovered the misplacement of approximately $6 million from Mozambique's Administrative Court alone.

As of late 2013, only 25 percent of the estimated 15,000 prisoners in Mozambique had access to legal help, according to Samo Gonçalves, Mozambique's national director of prisons. As many as one-third of prisoners are in preventive detention, and the terms of around 25 percent of these have already expired. As a result, Mozambique's prisons are severely overcrowded. While the government is trying to address this issue, progress is sluggish. According to Amnesty International, in 2013 prisoners still had to take shifts sleeping and endure very poor sanitary conditions in several Mozambican prisons. Amnesty International has also reported numerous cases of arbitrary detention, expired prison terms, sexual abuse, beatings, and torture of prisoners. Several police precincts in Maputo, Moamba, and Nampula were repeatedly denounced for their ill treatment of detainees.

Amnesty International also condemned the use of excessive force by the police against the population. On March 19, Alfredo Tivane, a bus driver, was reportedly shot and killed by the police in Maputo after refusing to stop when asked.

Violence between FRELIMO and RENAMO and a rise in kidnappings have affected civilians. A RENAMO attack on a main road in April killed three people.

The law does not explicitly ban same-sex sexual activity, and in 2011 the minister of justice announced that it is not an offense in Mozambique. However, lesbian, gay, bisexual, and transgender (LGBT) individuals face discrimination, and the government does not recognize LAMBDA, the one NGO devoted to the rights of the LGBT community.

G. Personal Autonomy and Individual Rights: 9 / 16

Women comprise some 39 percent of the parliament. Mozambique has laws and national plans of action to reduce gender-based discrimination and violence against women, but the pace of change is slow. Children are particularly vulnerable due to a fragile national child protection system and persistent impunity. More than one in every two girls is married by the age of 18, and many are confronted with schoolteachers that offer passing grades in exchange for sexual favors.

Human trafficking has been on the rise, with Mozambicans and Asian immigrants taken to South Africa and sexually exploited. In November 2013, hours after an NGO organized a demonstration against human trafficking in a Mozambican border town, the police were alerted to a group of 22 children led by two men trying to cross illegally into South Africa.

Witch hunts continue to be a major problem in Mozambique, particularly in the south, where the elderly are murdered in high numbers after being accused of witchcraft.

Namibia

Political Rights Rating: 2
Civil Liberties Rating: 2
Freedom Rating: 2.0
Freedom Status: Free
Electoral Democracy: Yes

Population: 2,410,000
Capital: Windhoek

Ten-Year Ratings Timeline For Year Under Review (Political Rights, Civil Liberties, Status)

Year Under Review	2004	2005	2006	2007	2008	2009	2010	2011	2012	2013
Rating	2,3,F	2,2,F	2,2,F	2,2,F	2,2,F	2,2,F	2,2,F	2,2,F	2,2,F	2,2,F

INTRODUCTION

Infighting in Namibia's ruling South West Africa People's Organisation (SWAPO) party—which has governed the country since independence in 1990—continued in the wake of contentious party leadership elections in December 2012. Hage Geingob, the incumbent, won the crucial election for party vice president, positioning himself to be SWAPO's candidate for president in 2014. He defeated more radical rivals Jerry Ekandjo and Pendukeni Iivula-Ithana, both ministers in the current government. The SWAPO Youth League (SPYL) had supported Ekandjo, and in 2013, its members began openly criticizing Geingob. The intraparty rifts related to ideological differences such as the promotion of Black Economic Empowerment policies versus the Geingob faction's neoliberal economic policies.

Namibia experienced its worst drought in 30 years in 2013, with more than a third of the population facing food insecurity, according to the UN Children's Fund (UNICEF). Estimates made by the government—which declared a national emergency in May—showed that the 2013 harvest would yield 42 percent less than the previous year.

POLITICAL RIGHTS: 30 / 40

A. Electoral Process: 10 / 12

Namibia's bicameral legislature consists of the 26-seat National Council, whose members are appointed by regional councils for six-year terms, and the 72-seat National Assembly, whose members are popularly elected for five-year terms using party-list proportional representation. The president, who is directly elected for a five-year term (and eligible for a second term), appoints the prime minister and cabinet. Geingob was appointed prime minister after winning the SWAPO vice presidency.

President Hifikepunye Pohamba of SWAPO was reelected in November 2009 with 75 percent of the vote, while the candidate of the Rally for Democracy and Progress (RDP), an opposition party formed in 2007 mainly by SWAPO defectors, captured just 11 percent.

In concurrent parliamentary elections, SWAPO won 54 seats in the National Assembly, while the RDP took 8 seats; seven smaller parties won 1 or 2 seats each. The elections were praised as free and fair by domestic and international observers, although the latter raised some concerns about pro-SWAPO bias in the state-run Namibian Broadcasting Corporation (NBC), delays in the counting process, and organizational mishaps during the polling process. Nine opposition parties, led by the RDP, filed a legal challenge calling for the nullification of the parliamentary elections due to "gross irregularities"; the Supreme Court dismissed the case in October 2012.

B. Political Pluralism and Participation: 11 / 16

SWAPO has dominated the political landscape since Namibia gained independence in 1990. Significant opposition parties include the RDP, the Congress of Democrats, the Democratic Turnhalle Alliance, and the United Democratic Front. Since the RDP's formation in 2007 by SWAPO dissidents, its supporters have been subject to harassment and intimidation by SWAPO members, who occasionally disrupt RDP rallies. While these problems have subsided somewhat in recent years, the RDP experienced some difficulty in holding rallies before the 2009 elections.

Given SWAPO's previous electoral dominance, Geingob is expected to become Namibia's next president in November 2014 elections. From the minority Damara community, Geingob would become the first Namibian president who did not hail from the Oshiwambo-speaking majority.

C. Functioning of Government: 9 / 12

Although Pohamba has made anticorruption efforts a major theme of his presidency, official corruption remains a problem, and investigations of major cases proceed slowly. The Anti-Corruption Commission has considerable autonomy, reporting only to the National Assembly, though it lacks prosecutorial authority. In a survey by Afrobarometer released in April 2013 of 1,200 adult Namibians, 42 percent said the majority of police are corrupt, while 44 percent said most or all national government officials are corrupt. A major scandal surfaced in July 2010 over a scheme that cost the Government Institutions Pension Fund N$660 million (US$71.1 million) between 1994 and 2002. Following a forensic audit by the Office of the Auditor General, the Namibian police did not start an official investigation until January 2012. The complexity and magnitude of the case have led to delays in prosecutions, and the investigation was ongoing as of the end of 2013. Namibia was ranked 57 out of 177 countries and territories surveyed in Transparency International's 2013 Corruption Perceptions Index, and placed sixth out of 52 countries evaluated in the 2013 Ibrahim Index of African Governance.

CIVIL LIBERTIES: 46 / 60
D. Freedom of Expression and Belief: 14 / 16

The constitution guarantees free speech, and Namibia's media generally enjoy an open environment. However, government and party leaders at times issue harsh criticism and even threats against the independent press, usually in the wake of unflattering stories. In July 2013, former president Sam Nujoma sued the newly established independent weekly *Confidénte* for defamation for a May story alleging that Nujoma's herd of cattle was going to graze at a military base farm. Nujoma filed the suit even though *Confidénte* published a retraction and an apology on its front page. The case had not been resolved by the end of the year.

While many insist that the state-owned NBC is free to criticize the government, concerns have increased about excessive government influence over programming and personnel. Many private publications and websites are critical of the government. There is no access to information law in Namibia, despite prior government pledges to introduce the law and a strong civil society campaign backing it. The 2009 Communications Act raised concerns about privacy rights, as it allows the government to monitor telephone calls, e-mail, and internet usage without a warrant.

Freedom of religion is guaranteed and respected in practice. The government has in the past been accused of pressuring academics to withhold criticism of SWAPO, though there were no such reports in 2013.

E. Associational and Organizational Rights: 12 / 12

Freedoms of assembly and association are guaranteed by law and permitted in practice, except in situations of national emergency. Human rights groups generally operate without interference, but government ministers have threatened and harassed nongovernmental organizations (NGOs) and their leadership in the past. Activism in the LGBT (lesbian, gay, bisexual, and transgender) community has grown, with organizations such as Out-Right Namibia urging officials to reassess anti-sodomy laws.

Constitutionally guaranteed union rights are respected. However, essential public sector workers do not have the right to strike. Collective bargaining is not widely practiced outside the mining, construction, agriculture, and public service industries. The main umbrella union, the National Union of Namibian Workers, is affiliated with SWAPO and played a role in selecting the new party leaders.

F. Rule of Law: 11 / 16

The constitution provides for an independent judiciary, and the separation of powers is observed in practice. Access to justice, however, is obstructed by economic and geographic barriers, a shortage of public defenders, and delays caused by a lack of capacity in the court system, especially at lower levels. Traditional courts in rural areas have often ignored constitutional procedures. However, legislation to create greater uniformity in traditional court operations and better connect them to the formal judicial system was implemented in 2009. Allegations of police brutality persist. Conditions in prisons are improving, though overcrowding in certain facilities remains a problem.

Secessionist fighting in Namibia's Caprivi region between 1998 and 1999 led some 2,400 refugees to flee to neighboring Botswana. Treason trials for more than 100 alleged secessionists began in 2003. Ten defendants were found guilty in 2007 and sentenced to more than 30 years in prison; in July 2013, the Supreme Court ordered a retrial. However, the case against 65 defendants in the High Court had yet to be resolved as of the end of 2013.

Minority ethnic groups have claimed that the government favors the majority Ovambo—which also dominates SWAPO—in allocating funding and services. Attempts to ensure equal rights to the San indigenous group are progressing gradually. After a series of land invasions, in June 2013 the police inspector general ordered settlers without a certificate from the communal land board to vacate land traditionally occupied by the !Kung—a community of San—in Namibia's western Tsumkwe region. The order was issued after the UN Special Rapporteur on the Rights of Indigenous Peoples called for Namibia to boost efforts to protect the San from marginalization on their land.

A colonial-era law prohibits consensual sexual relations between men, but the law is generally not enforced. Members of the LGBT community report continued discrimination and persecution, including negative rhetoric by some public officials and discrimination in employment. A former Mr. Gay Namibia, Wendelinus Hamutenya, allegedly received death threats after he authored a list in early 2013 exposing affluent gay Namibians. His actions were condemned by Out-Right Namibia, which stated that public naming would not aid in productive discussion of LGBT issues. In May, an SPYL spokesperson made homophobic remarks at a press conference, denouncing homosexuality as un-African.

G. Personal Autonomy and Individual Rights: 9 / 16

The government respects constitutionally guaranteed rights to freedom of movement, foreign travel, emigration, and repatriation. The small white minority owns just under half of Namibia's arable land, and redistribution of property has been slow despite efforts to accelerate the process. In 2012, Pohamba warned that unequal land distribution could become a threat to political stability.

Women continue to face discrimination in customary law and other traditional societal practices. Widows and orphans have been stripped of their land, livestock, and other assets in rural areas. Lack of awareness of legal rights as well as informal practices have undermined the success of legal changes. Violence against women, including sexual violence, is reportedly widespread, and rights groups have criticized the government's failure to enforce the country's progressive domestic violence laws. In 2011, the government and a leading NGO launched a National Plan of Action on Gender-Based Violence, to run from 2012 to 2016; the plan included actions to address human trafficking, but sustainable progress has been lacking in government efforts to prosecute such crimes. In the 2009 elections, women won 19 seats in the National Assembly and 7 seats in the National Council.

Namibia's HIV infection rate, though high—an estimated 15 percent in 2013—is much lower than its southern African neighbors.

According to the U.S. State Department's 2013 Trafficking in Persons Report, Namibia serves as a source, transit, and destination country for human trafficking for forced labor and prostitution. Namibia was placed on the Tier 2 Watch List due to its failure to take legal action against offenders.

Nauru

Political Rights Rating: 1
Civil Liberties Rating: 1
Freedom Rating: 1.0
Freedom Status: Free
Electoral Democracy: Yes

Population: 10,560
Capital: Yaren

Ten-Year Ratings Timeline For Year Under Review (Political Rights, Civil Liberties, Status)

Year Under Review	2004	2005	2006	2007	2008	2009	2010	2011	2012	2013
Rating	1,1,F	1,1,F	1,1,F	1,1,F	1,1,F	1,1,F	1,1,F	1,1,F	1,1,F	1,1,F

INTRODUCTION

Nauru continued to struggle economically in 2013 as a result of the depletion of its phosphate supply. Mined for use as fertilizer, phosphate was the country's main source of revenue, but has since been exhausted; additionally, over-mining has left nearly 80 percent of the eight-square-mile island nation uninhabitable. As a result, Nauru relies heavily on foreign loans and international assistance; its survival is also threatened by climate change and rising sea levels.

In August 2013, Nauru signed a new agreement with Australia regarding the resettlement of refugees who had been seeking asylum in Australia; under the new deal, Nauru will receive about $27 million in a total aid package in exchange for giving refugees the option of resettling in Nauru once they are processed. The refugee detention center on Nauru has been criticized for harsh living conditions; much of the detention center was burned down in a February 2013 riot.

POLITICAL RIGHTS: 38 / 40
A. Electoral Process: 12 / 12

Nauru is an electoral democracy. The 19-member unicameral Parliament is popularly elected from 14 constituencies for three-year terms. Parliament chooses the president and vice president from among its members.

Intense political rivalries and the use of no-confidence votes have been a source of political instability. Several changes of government occurred between 2007 and 2011, the shortest lasting only days. Elected in 2011, President Sprent Dabwido made it a priority to introduce constitutional reforms that would increase political stability. Under the Electoral Act of 2012, Parliament was expanded by one seat to 19 to prevent legislative stalemate.

In May 2013, Parliament was dissolved after lack of a quorum forced adjournment of two consecutive sessions. In general elections held on June 8, voters chose 19 representatives out of 68 candidates. The new Parliament was the first to have 19 members; former education minister Baron Waqa, a lawmaker since 2003, was elected president, and Ludwig Scotty was named the new speaker of parliament.

B. Political Pluralism and Participation: 16 / 16

Although political parties are allowed, all candidates for public office are required to run as independents. Political parties include the Nauru First Party, the Democratic Party, and the Center Party. Alliances frequently shift.

C. Functioning of Government: 10 / 12

Corruption is a serious problem in Nauru. In 2011, President Marcus Stephen resigned amid allegations that he had accepted bribes from an Australian phosphate company.

CIVIL LIBERTIES: 54 / 60
D. Freedom of Expression and Belief: 15 / 16

The government does not restrict or censor the news media. There are several local weekly and monthly publications; foreign dailies, mostly in English, are widely available. The government publishes occasional bulletins, and the opposition publishes its own newsletters. Radio Nauru and Nauru TV, which are owned and operated by the government, broadcast content from Australia, New Zealand, and other international sources. There are no formal restrictions on internet usage.

The constitution provides for freedom of religion, which the government generally respects in practice. There have been no reports of government suppression of academic freedom.

E. Associational and Organizational Rights: 11 / 12

The government respects freedoms of assembly and association. There are several advocacy groups for women, as well as development-focused and religious organizations. There are no trade unions or labor protection laws, partly because there is little large-scale, private employment.

F. Rule of Law: 14 / 16 (-1)

The judiciary is independent, and defendants generally receive fair trials and representation. The Supreme Court is the highest authority on constitutional issues. Appeals in civil and criminal cases can be lodged with the high court of Australia. Traditional reconciliation mechanisms, rather than the formal legal process, are frequently used, typically by choice but sometimes under communal pressure. A civilian official controls the 100-person police force, and there have been few reported cases of abuse. Nauru has no armed forces; Australia provides defense assistance under an informal agreement.

In 2012, Nauru agreed to host refugees seeking asylum in Australia, and reopened a detention center that had previously been used to house asylum seekers. Detainees in Nauru's facilities have cited poor living conditions, with many engaging in violent protests and hunger strikes in attempts to pressure the Australian government into allowing them to settle there.

In February 2013, 80 percent of Nauru's detention center was burned down in a riot forcing detainees to live in tents and other temporary structures. By August, Nauru charged about 120 of the detainees with arson, property damage and rioting. Almost immediately, the asylum seekers and their advocates brought a counter suit, claiming unlawful detention in Nauru, but the court struck down their claims. Hearings were set for 2014.

In August, Nauru and Australia signed a new deal that would allow refugees to be resettled in Nauru after they are processed. The deal promised Nauru about $27 million in development assistance in addition to millions more to repair damage done to the detention center in the February riot.

G. Personal Autonomy and Individual Rights: 14 / 16

Societal pressures limit women's ability to exercise their legal rights. In 2013, Charmaine Scotty became the second woman to be elected to Nauru's parliament since the country became independent in 1968; she was also appointed Minister for Home Affairs,

Education, Youth, and Land Management. Sexual harassment is a crime, but spousal rape is not. Domestic violence is frequently associated with alcohol abuse. In 2011, Nauru pledged to decriminalize homosexuality—male homosexuality is punishable with 14 years of prison at hard labor—after a United Nations human rights audit. As of year's end, assault "with intent to have carnal knowledge of him or her against the order of nature" remains a criminal offense liable to 14 years of imprisonment with hard labor.

Nepal

Political Rights Rating: 4
Civil Liberties Rating: 4
Freedom Rating: 4.0
Freedom Status: Partly Free
Electoral Democracy: Yes

Population: 26,810,000
Capital: Kathmandu

Ten-Year Ratings Timeline For Year Under Review (Political Rights, Civil Liberties, Status)

Year Under Review	2004	2005	2006	2007	2008	2009	2010	2011	2012	2013
Rating	5,5,PF	6,5,PF	5,4,NF	5,4,NF	4,4,PF	4,4,PF	4,4,PF	4,4,PF	4,4,PF	4,4,PF

INTRODUCTION

After the Constituent Assembly (CA) elected in 2008 failed to adopt a permanent constitution despite multiple extensions of its original two-year mandate, Nepal finally held elections for a new CA in November 2013. International monitors deemed the voting generally free and fair, and two centrist parties—the Nepali Congress (NC) and the Communist Party of Nepal/United Marxist-Leninist (CPN-UML)—won a strong majority, sidelining the Communist Party of Nepal (Maoist), whose long-running insurgency had ended with a 2006 peace agreement. Negotiations on the formation of a new cabinet were ongoing at year's end. The Maoists' defeat suggested that previous elections that brought them to power may have been fraudulent. Parties hoping to restore Nepal's monarchy also did poorly in the November elections. Prior to the elections, the country had suffered from political paralysis and rising instability. Many observers in Nepal expect the renewed constitutional drafting process to take as long as three more years.

The human rights climate, meanwhile, continued to deteriorate in the run-up to the election. The National Human Rights Commission effectively disintegrated in September after the caretaker government in place before the elections allowed the terms of all of the commissioners to expire. It was reconstituted but it remained an extremely weak organization. This, along with a proposed amnesty law for perpetrators of violence during the civil war, which killed at least 17,000 people in the 1990s and early 2000s, made it highly unlikely that anyone would face justice for wartime abuses. In 2013, one case of a killing during the conflict was initiated at the behest of the rights commission before it was effectively disbanded.

China remained a major donor of military and nonmilitary aid to Nepal during 2013, and its influence was set to grow after the completion of a new road from the Chinese border through Mustang, one of the most remote parts of Nepal, expected in 2014 or 2015. Nongovernmental organizations (NGOs) working on Tibetan issues reported increasing harassment from Nepali security forces and repatriations of Tibetan refugees.

POLITICAL RIGHTS: 23 / 40 (+ 3)

A. Electoral Process: 8 / 12 (+ 3)

The Nepali state is operating under a 2007 interim constitution. In addition to its task of writing a permanent constitution, the CA serves as the interim legislature. Members are elected through a mixed system of first-past-the-post constituency races (240 seats), proportional representation (335 seats), and appointments by the cabinet (26 seats). Both the president and the prime minister are elected by a majority of the CA. The current president, Ram Baran Yadav of the NC, was elected in July 2008 and is expected to remain in office until a new constitution is in place.

The CA repeatedly extended its initial two-year mandate after May 2010, but by May 2012 it had still not passed a permanent constitution. It was forced to dissolve that month, leaving government in the hands of a caretaker administration until elections could be held.

The CA elections held in November 2013, after years of politicking between the major parties over how and when the vote should be conducted, were found by international monitors to be generally free and fair, despite violent incidents in the preelection period. The government deployed nearly 150,000 security personnel to keep order for the vote, but the campaign was still marred by multiple attacks on party supporters and campaign workers. Still, on voting day the vote was conducted relatively peacefully. Turnout reached record numbers for Nepal. Some Maoist leaders alleged that fraud had been committed during the election, a contention disputed by all international monitors of the election. The NC and CPN-UML dominated the results, with 196 and 175 seats, respectively. The Maoists placed a distant third with 80 seats, followed by over two dozen smaller parties and two independents with the remainder of the 575 elected seats. A new cabinet had yet to be formed at year's end, meaning the 26 appointed seats remained vacant.

B. Political Pluralism and Participation: 11 / 16

A diverse and competitive array of political parties operates in Nepal, though the system has featured considerable instability in recent years. Moreover, prior to the 2013 elections, the political environment suffered from growing extremism, including attacks by armed gangs linked to the main Maoist party on members of other parties, and on people who allegedly informed on the Maoists during the civil war. Gangs linked to the other leading parties were also accused of attacking supporters of the Maoists during 2013.

Unlike the 1990 constitution, the interim constitution has no limitation on parties formed along ethnic lines. Roughly a third of the seats in the CA are reserved for women through quotas in the party-list voting, and substantial allocations are also made for Madhesis, Dalits, and other minority groups.

C. Functioning of Government: 4 / 12

Nepal's governing process had essentially ceased to function by late 2013, and it remained to be seen whether the November elections would improve the situation. Prior to the elections, the caretaker government made little progress on critical tasks including drafting a permanent constitution, addressing the legacy of the civil war, and integrating former combatants into the national military.

Corruption is endemic in Nepali politics and government. While the Commission for the Investigation of Abuse of Authority is active, high-level officials are rarely prosecuted. Many lawmakers have been accused or convicted of corruption in the past. Graft is particularly prevalent in the judiciary, with frequent payoffs to judges for favorable rulings, and in the police force, which has been accused of extensive involvement in organized crime.

CIVIL LIBERTIES: 27 / 60
D. Freedom of Expression and Belief: 9 / 16

The interim constitution provides for press freedom and specifically prohibits censorship, although these rules can be suspended during an emergency. In practice, media workers frequently face physical attacks, death threats, and harassment by armed groups, security personnel, and political cadres, and the perpetrators typically go unpunished. Throughout 2013, supporters of political parties attacked journalists who wrote critical pieces about their organizations and leaders. There is a variety of independent radio and print outlets. Some have come to show a strong bias toward the Maoists, partly due to intimidation, but other outlets are critical of the party.

The interim constitution identifies Nepal as a secular state, signaling a break with the Hindu monarchy that was toppled as part of the resolution of the civil war in 2006 and formally abolished in 2008. Religious tolerance is broadly practiced, but proselytizing is prohibited, and members of some religious minorities occasionally report official harassment. Christian groups have considerable difficulty registering as religious organizations, leaving them unable to own land.

The government does not restrict academic freedom. However, Maoist strikes have repeatedly threatened the school system, and minorities, including Hindi- and Urdu-speaking Madhesi groups, have complained that Nepali is enforced as the language of education in government schools.

E. Associational and Organizational Rights: 6 / 12

Freedom of assembly is guaranteed under the interim constitution. While security forces have allowed large protests by Maoists and other political parties, Tibetan protests have been violently suppressed in recent years. In certain cases, authorities have detained Tibetan and Nepali monks and pressured them to sign pledges not to participate in future demonstrations.

NGOs played an active role in the movement to restore democracy in the mid-2000s, and restrictions on NGO activity imposed by the king toward the end of his rule have been lifted. However, groups working on Tibetan issues report increasing intimidation by security forces.

Labor laws provide for the freedom to bargain collectively, and unions generally operate without state interference. Workers in a broad range of "essential" industries cannot stage strikes, and 60 percent of a union's membership must vote in favor of a strike for it to be legal. Several unions linked to the Maoists have been accused of using violence to threaten employers and government officials to comply with union demands during bargaining processes. In the past two years, there has been a series of attacks by assailants supposedly linked to Maoist-backed unions on employers in the hotel and telecommunications industries.

F. Rule of Law: 5 / 16

The constitution provides for an independent judiciary, but most courts suffer from endemic corruption, and many Nepalese have only limited access to justice. Because of heavy case backlogs and a slow appeals process, suspects are frequently kept in pretrial detention for periods longer than any sentences they would face if tried and convicted.

Prison conditions are poor, with overcrowding and inadequate sanitation and medical care. The government has generally refused to conduct thorough investigations or take serious disciplinary measures against police officers accused of brutality or torture. A leading Nepali monitoring group, the Centre for Victims of Torture, found that 74 percent of respondents in a 2011 survey said they had been tortured while in custody.

Human rights groups have argued that no one has been punished for abuses during the decade-long civil war, in part because of the weakness of the judiciary and a prevailing climate of impunity. In 2013, the caretaker government essentially allowed the National Human Rights Commission to disband by failing to replace its members when their terms expired. Human rights organizations harshly criticized this development, which—combined with a proposed amnesty for anyone who committed abuses during the war—could mean that the legacy of the brutal conflict will go almost totally unexamined.

In the summer of 2013, a very small group of former Maoist fighters completed their training and were inducted into the national army, but this was only a fraction of the fighters originally expected to join the military.

A 2007 civil service law reserves 45 percent of posts for women, minorities, and Dalits, but their representation in state institutions remains inadequate, particularly at the highest levels of government. Members of the Hindu upper castes continue to dominate government and business, and low-caste Hindus, ethnic minorities, and Christians face discrimination in the civil service and courts. Despite constitutional protections and the 2012 Caste-Based Discrimination and Untouchability (Offense and Punishment) Act, which prohibits discrimination against Dalits and increases punishments for public officials found responsible for discrimination, Dalits continue to be subjected to exploitation, violence, and social exclusion.

Madhesis, plains-dwelling people with close connections to groups across the border in India, comprise 35 to 50 percent of Nepal's population, but they are underrepresented in politics, receive comparatively little economic support from the government, and—until an amendment to the citizenship law in 2006—had difficulty acquiring formal citizenship due to Nepali language requirements.

In 2007, the Supreme Court ordered the government to abolish all laws that discriminate against LGBT (lesbian, gay, bisexual, and transgender) people, and in 2008 it gave its consent to same-sex marriage. The government has yet to implement these rulings, though citizens can now obtain third-gender identity documents. LGBT people reportedly face harassment by the authorities and other citizens, particularly in rural areas.

In 2013, NGOs working on Tibetan issues warned that they were coming under mounting pressure from the Nepali government, on behalf of Beijing, to repatriate Tibetan refugees to China before they could register with UN officials in Kathmandu or transit to India. Nepali forces have also increasingly monitored the northern border, stopped Tibetan refugees, and sent them immediately back to China.

G. Personal Autonomy and Individual Rights: 7 / 16

Women rarely receive the same educational and employment opportunities as men, and domestic violence against women continues to be a major problem. The 2009 Domestic Violence Act provides for monetary compensation and psychological treatment for victims, but authorities generally do not prosecute domestic violence cases. The commission charged with providing reparations to women subjected to gender-based violence has also been severely criticized for failure to implement its mandate and politicized distribution of resources. Trafficking of young women from Nepal for prostitution in India is common. According to Human Rights Watch, kidnapping gangs have become rampant in recent years, abducting children to obtain small ransoms. Police rarely intervene in the kidnappings. Underage marriage of girls is widespread, particularly among lower-status groups.

Bonded labor is illegal but remains a problem. Similarly, the legal minimum age for employment is 14 years, but over two million children are believed to be engaged in various forms of labor, often under hazardous conditions.

Netherlands

Political Rights Rating: 1
Civil Liberties Rating: 1
Freedom Rating: 1.0
Freedom Status: Free
Electoral Democracy: Yes

Population: 16,798,000
Capital: Amsterdam

Ten-Year Ratings Timeline For Year Under Review (Political Rights, Civil Liberties, Status)

Year Under Review	2004	2005	2006	2007	2008	2009	2010	2011	2012	2013
Rating	1,1,F	1,1,F	1,1,F	1,1,F	1,1,F	1,1,F	1,1,F	1,1,F	1,1,F	1,1,F

INTRODUCTION

On January 28, 2013, three days before turning 75, Queen Beatrix announced that she would abdicate and clear the way for her son to become king. The coronation for King Willem-Alexander, age 45, was held on April 30.

Prime Minister Mark Rutte and his coalition government—which included his center-right People's Party for Freedom and Democracy (VVD) and the center-left Labor Party (PvdA)—had become increasingly unpopular due to austerity measures they put in place after taking office in late 2012 amid a continuing recession and rising unemployment. The right-wing Party for Freedom (PVV), known for its anti-immigration and anti–European Union views, had regained popularity since suffering a setback in the 2012 elections, and led in public opinion polls during 2013.

POLITICAL RIGHTS: 40 / 40

A. Electoral Process: 12 / 12

The Netherlands is governed under a parliamentary system. The monarchy is largely ceremonial; its residual political role of mediating coalition talks on government formation was eliminated in 2012. The leader of the majority party or coalition is usually appointed prime minister by the monarch. The monarch appoints the Council of Ministers (cabinet) and the governor of each province on the recommendation of the majority in parliament. The 150-member lower house of parliament, or Second Chamber, is elected every four years by proportional representation. The 75-member upper house, or First Chamber, is elected for four-year terms by the country's provincial councils, which in turn are directly elected every four years.

General elections were held in September 2012 after the government collapsed in April. Rutte led the VVD to first place, winning 41 seats, while the PvdA took 38 seats. The PVV, which campaigned in favor of leaving the EU and abandoning the euro, dropped to 15 seats.

Mayors are appointed from a list of candidates submitted by the municipal councils, which are directly elected every four years. Foreigners residing in the country for five years or more are eligible to vote in local elections. Aruba and the Netherlands Antilles have had voting rights in European Parliament elections since 2009.

B. Political Pluralism and Participation: 16 / 16

Political parties operate freely, and there are regular rotations of power in the country's multiparty system. Right-wing parties with anti-immigration and Euroskeptic platforms have enjoyed some popularity over the past decade, though they have remained out of government. The ruling coalition that stepped down in late 2012 relied on external support from the

PVV. In November 2013, Wilders and Marine Le Pen, leader of the far-right National Front in France, announced a new Euroskeptic alliance for the May 2014 European Parliament elections. Both parties were leading in the polls in their countries.

C. Functioning of Government: 12 / 12

The country has few problems with political corruption. The Netherlands was ranked 8 out of 177 countries and territories surveyed in Transparency International's 2013 Corruption Perceptions Index. In August 2013 the Organisation for Economic Co-operation and Development (OECD) issued a report warning that the Netherlands was failing to adequately enforce laws against bribery by Dutch individuals and companies doing business abroad. In March 2013, the parliament passed a new campaign financing law that took effect in May.

CIVIL LIBERTIES: 59 / 60
D. Freedom of Expression and Belief: 16 / 16

The news media are free and independent. The 1881 lèse majesté laws restricting defamation of the monarch are rarely enforced. The government does not restrict access to online media, though users and website operators can be punished for content deemed to incite discrimination. In April 2013, at the request of the Netherlands, Spanish police near Barcelona arrested Sven Olaf Kamphuis, a Dutch citizen accused of launching a massive cyberattack that had caused global internet disruptions in March. Kamphuis, whose companies CB3ROB and CyberBunker were known for hosting thousands of spam websites, was extradited to the Netherlands in May.

The constitution guarantees freedom of religion, and the Netherlands has long been known as a tolerant society. However, rising anti-immigrant sentiment in recent years has been accompanied by more open expression of anti-Islamic views. Members of the country's Muslim community have encountered increased hostility, including harassment and verbal abuse, as well as vandalism and arson attacks on mosques. Meanwhile, high-profile critics of Islam have faced the threat of violence. Politician Pim Fortuyn and filmmaker Theo van Gogh were assassinated in 2002 and 2004, respectively. In June 2011, PVV leader Geert Wilders was acquitted on charges of discrimination and inciting hatred of Muslims through his editorials and his film *Fitna*. The court ruled that Wilders' comments were part of public debate and were not a direct call for violence.

The government requires all imams and other spiritual leaders recruited from Muslim countries to take a one-year integration course before practicing in the Netherlands. In September 2011, the cabinet introduced a ban on clothing that covers the face, imposing a maximum fine of €380 ($460) for the first violation. However, the measure did not come to a vote in parliament and was shelved after the PVV-backed government fell in 2012. The VVD-PvdA coalition agreement of October 2012 also called for a ban on such clothing in public settings, including schools, hospitals, public transportation, and government buildings, and for withholding social security benefits from people who wore the garments.

Religious organizations that provide educational facilities can receive subsidies from the government. The government does not restrict academic freedom.

E. Associational and Organizational Rights: 12 / 12

Freedoms of assembly and association are respected in law and in practice. National and international human rights organizations operate freely without government intervention. Workers have the right to organize, bargain collectively, and strike.

F. Rule of Law: 15 / 16

The judiciary is independent, and the rule of law prevails in civil and criminal matters. The police are under civilian control, and prison conditions meet international standards. The population is generally treated equally under the law, although human rights groups have criticized the country's asylum policies for being unduly harsh and violating international standards. In December 2012, the government announced that it would propose legislation to criminalize living in the country without permission, with illegal residency punishable by fines and an entry ban of up to five years.

In January 2013, Russian citizen Aleksandr Dolmatov committed suicide in a Dutch detention center in Rotterdam, where he was being held while appealing the rejection of his application for political asylum. In April, a Dutch justice ministry report said Dolmatov should not have been held in detention.

In October 2013, the Council of Europe called on the Netherlands to stop evicting failed asylum seekers from refugee centers, warning that the government has an obligation to provide them with shelter, food, and clothing.

Also in 2013, a racial controversy erupted over the traditional figure of Zwarte Piet (Black Pete), a character central to the children's festivities of Sinterklaas, the December 5 Festival of St. Nicholas. In October it emerged that experts advising the UN Commission on Human Rights had sent a letter to the Dutch government in January, raising allegations that the character, typically portrayed by white performers wearing blackface, was a racist stereotype offensive to Dutch citizens of African descent. In November, the UN experts issued a statement urging the Dutch government to "facilitate an open debate in Dutch society" about the issue.

Dutch laws protect LGBT (lesbian, gay, bisexual, and transgender) people from discrimination and violence. The Netherlands was the first country in the world to legalize same-sex marriage, in 2001.

G. Personal Autonomy and Individual Rights: 16 / 16

Residents of the Netherlands generally enjoy freedom of movement and choice of residence, employment, and institution of higher education. Property rights are upheld by the country's impartial courts.

The government has vigorously enforced legal protections for women, including in employment and family law. In March 2013, the Supreme Court ruled that a "forced tongue kiss" should no longer be treated as rape, and instead should be classified as indecent assault, which carries a lesser sentence. The verdict narrowed a 1998 ruling by the court that any form of unwanted sexual penetration was rape.

The Netherlands is a destination and transit point for human trafficking, particularly in women and girls for sexual exploitation. A 2005 law expanded the legal definition of trafficking to include forced labor, and increased the maximum penalty for convicted offenders. Prostitution is legal and regulated in the Netherlands, though links between prostitution and organized crime have been reported.

New Zealand

Political Rights Rating: 1
Civil Liberties Rating: 1
Freedom Rating: 1
Freedom Status: Free
Electoral Democracy: Yes

Population: 4,450,000
Capital: Wellington

Ten-Year Ratings Timeline For Year Under Review (Political Rights, Civil Liberties, Status)

Year Under Review	2004	2005	2006	2007	2008	2009	2010	2011	2012	2013
Rating	1,1,F	1,1,F	1,1,F	1,1,F	1,1,F	1,1,F	1,1,F	1,1,F	1,1,F	1,1,F

INTRODUCTION

In April 2013, New Zealand became the 14th country, and the first in Asia, to legalize same-sex marriage with a 77 to 44 vote in parliament. The law took effect in late August.

In August, legislative amendments were passed that authorized the Government Communications Security Bureau—New Zealand's main intelligence agency—to collect data on residents and citizens. Surveillance was previously limited to those with no right of residency in New Zealand. Advocates of the change said it was needed to assist the police, military, and intelligence community in dealing with individuals like Kim Dotcom, a German national with residency in the country who had been charged with online piracy and money laundering. Opponents argued the law violates individual privacy and civil rights. Technology and communications firms also voiced their concerns.

New Zealand improved its ties with several countries in 2013; in February, it announced it would resume training police in Indonesia, and would provide $2 million in assistance to the country. A new defense pact with East Timor was signed in June. In July, however, the New Zealand government announced it would end its development assistance to Tonga due to safety concerns regarding a Chinese aircraft Tonga purchased for its domestic, inter-island air service. New Zealand also warned against traveling to Tonga; New Zealanders are the single largest group of tourists to Tonga.

POLITICAL RIGHTS: 39/ 40

A. Electoral Process: 12 /12

New Zealand is an electoral democracy and a member of the Commonwealth. A mixed-member electoral system combines voting in geographic districts with proportional representation balloting. The unicameral Parliament, or House of Representatives, has 121 members who are elected to three-year terms. The prime minister, the head of government, is the leader of the majority party or coalition and is appointed by the governor-general, the ceremonial head of state representing Queen Elizabeth II. Jerry Mateparae, a former military chief and head of the intelligence agency, has served as governor-general since 2011. He is the second Maori to hold this post.

In general elections held in 2011, the National Party was victorious, winning 59 parliamentary seats; the Labour Party won 34 seats, the Green Party won 14 seats, the New Zealand First Party won 8, and the Maori Party won 3. The National Party formed a ruling coalition with the New Zealand First Party and the United Future Party, and National Party leader John Key—who first became prime minister in 2008—was elected to another term.

In March 2013, the government announced a constitutional review; New Zealand has a so-called unwritten constitution, which consists of a collection of laws and statutes rather than a single document. An advisory panel was appointed to receive comments from the public and to formulate recommendations to the government; the panel delivered its findings to the government in December. Recommendations included combining all constitutional protections into a single document, as well as various measures that would enhance the governmental representation and decision-making powers of the indigenous Maori population. The panel also recommended increasing parliamentary terms and setting fixed election dates.

B. Political Pluralism and Participation: 15 / 16

The two main political parties are the center-left Labour Party and the center-right National Party. Smaller parties include the Maori Party, the New Zealand First Party, and the United Future Party. Seven of Parliament's constituency seats are reserved for the native Maori population. The Maori Party, the country's first ethnic party, was formed in 2004 to advance Maori rights and interests.

C. Functioning of Government: 12 / 12

New Zealand is one of the least corrupt countries in the world. It was ranked 1st out of 177 countries surveyed in Transparency International's 2013 Corruption Perceptions Index.

CIVIL LIBERTIES: 58 / 60
D. Freedom of Expression and Belief: 16 / 16

The media are free and competitive. Newspapers are published nationally and locally in English and in other languages for the growing immigrant population. Television outlets include the state-run Television New Zealand, three private channels, and a Maori-language public network. There is also a Maori-language radio station. The government does not control or censor Internet access, and competitive pricing promotes large-scale diffusion.

Freedom of religion is protected by law and respected in practice. Only religious organizations that collect donations need to register with the government. Though a secular state, businesses have been fined for opening on official holidays, including Christmas Day, Good Friday, and Easter Sunday. Exemptions are made for several categories of stores in response to demands from non-Christian populations. Academic freedom is enjoyed at all levels of instruction.

E. Associational and Organizational Rights: 12 /12

The government respects freedoms of assembly and association. Nongovernmental organizations are active throughout the country, and many receive considerable financial support from the government. Under the 2001 Employment Relations Act, workers can organize, strike, and bargain collectively, with the exception of uniformed personnel. There are numerous trade unions and many are affiliated with the Council of Trade Unions. Union membership overall is declining, estimated at no more than 20 percent of all workers.

F. Rule of Law: 15 / 16

The judiciary is independent, and defendants can appeal to the Privy Council in London. Prison conditions generally meet international standards. Allegations of discrimination against the Maori, who make up more than half of the prison population, persist. The police are learning to better deal with an increasingly racially and culturally diverse population and are looking to recruit more Maori and Pacific Islands to join the force.

Approximately 15 percent of the country's 4.4 million people identify themselves as Maori. Although no laws explicitly discriminate against the Maori and their living standards have generally improved, most Maori and Pacific Islanders continue to lag behind the

European-descended majority in social and economic status. The Maori population has become more assertive in its claims for land, resources, and compensation from the government.

In June 2013, the government concluded a historic agreement with the Tuhoe tribe to grant it greater control of the Te Urewea National Park, as well as $170 million for financial, commercial, and cultural redress. The Tuhoe had not signed the Treaty of Waitangi, the 1840 agreement that established British sovereignty in New Zealand in exchange for permanent land rights for the Maori; in 2009, the government agreed to pay $111 million in compensation—including both rent payments from state-owned forests and greenhouse gas emission credits—to eight tribes as a comprehensive settlement for grievances over land seizures and other breaches of the Treaty of Waitangi. Some observers worry that a new law proposed by parliament that would ban psychoactive substances would impact the legality of the traditional Maori drink kava, which is made from a root that contains natural sedatives. Several MPs have proposed changes to the law that would allow culturally significant substances like kava.

G. Personal Autonomy and Individual Rights: 15 / 16

Violence against women and children remains a problem, particularly among the Maori and Pacific Islander populations. One lawmaker claimed Pacific Island girls as young as 13 are engaged in prostitution. Some had run away from home; others see it as an attractive way to make money. Many governmental and nongovernmental programs work to prevent domestic violence and support victims, with special programs for the Maori community.

A 2007 law banning the spanking of children gave police the authority to determine whether a parent should be charged with abuse. A majority of voters rejected the law in a non-binding referendum in 2009, but the government has kept it in place.

Same-sex unions have been legal since 2005, giving same-sex couples many of the same rights as married couples. The legalization of same-sex marriage in 2013 allowed couples to jointly adopt children and allow their marriage to be recognized in other countries. Opinion polls indicated that two-thirds of the population favored the law, and Key and his coalition backed it.

Nicaragua

Political Rights Rating: 4
Civil Liberties Rating: 3
Freedom Rating: 3.5
Freedom Status: Partly Free
Electoral Democracy: No

Population: 6,000,000
Capital: Managua

Ratings Change: Nicaragua's political rights rating improved from 5 to 4 and its civil liberties rating improved from 4 to 3 due to the positive impact of consultations on proposed constitutional reforms, advances in the corruption and transparency environment, and gradual progress in women's rights and efforts to combat human trafficking.

Ten-Year Ratings Timeline For Year Under Review (Political Rights, Civil Liberties, Status)

Year Under Review	2004	2005	2006	2007	2008	2009	2010	2011	2012	2013
Rating	3,3,PF	3,3,PF	3,3,PF	3,3,PF	4,3,PF	4,4,PF	4,4,PF	5,4,PF	5,4,PF	4,3,PF

INTRODUCTION

During 2013, the Sandinista National Liberation Front (FSLN) continued to consolidate power following an overwhelming victory in the 2011 legislative and 2012 municipal elections that gave the party near-complete dominance over most of the country's institutions. Serious concerns remained about the politicization of institutions, particularly the Supreme Electoral Council (CSE), as well as political appointees with expired terms who had remained in their positions following a presidential decree.

The party's legislative dominance enabled it to pass important laws, including one granting a concession to a Chinese company for the development of an inter-oceanic canal. Disparate opposition groups formed an alliance, Unity for the Republic (UNIR), against President Daniel Ortega. At the end of the year, the FSLN was moving forward with a packet of constitutional changes, including the abolition of presidential term limits, that would further cement Ortega's power. Despite these controversies, popular support for Ortega remained among the highest for any leader in the hemisphere.

POLITICAL RIGHTS: 19 / 40 (+2)
A. Electoral Process: 6 / 12

The constitution provides for a directly elected president and a 92-member unicameral National Assembly. Two seats in the legislature are reserved for the previous president and the runner-up in the most recent presidential election. Both presidential and legislative elections are held every five years.

While the president is limited to two nonconsecutive terms under the constitution, the Supreme Court lifted the restriction in October 2009 in response to a petition by Ortega, who had been elected president in 2006 following an earlier period leading the country that had ended in 1990. In July 2009, Ortega publicly stated that the ban on consecutive presidential terms should be eliminated. The National Assembly opposed his initiative, and Ortega lacked the support to pass a constitutional amendment on the issue. Instead, he and more than 100 FLSN mayors filed a petition with the Constitutional Chamber of the Supreme Court claiming that the ban on consecutive terms violated their rights to participate in the political process. In October 2009, the Supreme Court found in favor of Ortega and the mayors, lifting the ban on consecutive terms. Although the ruling did not amend the constitution, the packet of constitutional reforms that passed a first reading in the National Assembly in December 2013 would eliminate term limits altogether.

In January 2010, Ortega decreed that appointed officials could remain in their posts until the National Assembly selected replacements, even if that occurred after the end of their terms. The decree affected 25 high-level posts, including the presidency and magistrates of the CSE, who had supported allowing Ortega to run for a second consecutive presidential term in 2011. The struggle over these appointments sent Nicaragua into a political crisis in 2010, as members of the National Assembly were unable to achieve the majority necessary to select replacements. In keeping with Ortega's decree, many officials remained in their posts after their terms expired in June, including the CSE president and members of the Supreme Court, which moved ahead with preparations for the 2011 elections.

Ortega's candidacy for another term was officially approved by the CSE in April 2011, effectively ending legal challenges to his candidacy. Fabio Gadea Mantilla's Nicaraguan Unity for Hope (UNE) coalition attempted to unite the opposition against Ortega, but former president Arnoldo Alemán refused to abandon his candidacy. Gadea's bloc, led by the Liberal Independent Party (PLI), included the Sandinista Renovation Movement as well as various liberal and conservative factions. Alemán was selected as the presidential candidate for the Conservative Party–Liberal Constitutionalist Party (PLC) alliance.

The CSE delayed issuing invitations to international observer teams until August 2011, significantly reducing the time available for observers to conduct their work. As with the 2008 municipal elections, several domestic observer groups with significant experience in electoral observation did not receive accreditation, though several international observer missions that were excluded in 2008—including the European Union, the Organization of American States, and the Carter Center—were invited to observe. There was some controversy over the rules for accompaniment issued by the CSE, which some observer teams feared would limit their capacity to effectively observe the electoral process.

Ortega won the presidential election in November 2011 with almost 63 percent of the vote, followed by Gadea with 31 percent and Alemán with almost 6 percent. In the legislative elections, the FSLN won 63 seats in the National Assembly, followed by the PLI with 27 and the PLC with 2. Though international observation teams noted irregularities and lamented a lack of transparency, there was no conclusive evidence of fraud. Observers did, however, report issues with the distribution of voting cards, the voter registry, difficulty accessing polling places, and concerns about the composition of electoral boards. Both Gadea and Alemán denounced the outcome and refused to recognize the results. Several protesters were killed and dozens of police officers were injured in postelection violence between supporters of the government and the opposition. In June 2012, the United States canceled its fiscal-transparency waiver—a policy in which U.S. aid to Nicaragua is contingent on financial and electoral transparency—over concerns about the 2011 elections, cutting approximately $3 million in aid.

In May 2012, the National Assembly approved numerous changes to the municipal electoral law, including adding the provision that mayors could run for reelection and instating a requirement that half of each party's candidates for mayor and council seats be women. The assembly also approved an increase in municipal council seats from 2,178 to 6,534.

The municipal elections were held in November 2012. The FSLN won 134 of 153 municipalities, the PLI took 13, the PLC captured 2, Yatama won 3, and the Nicaraguan Liberal Alliance took 1. The PLI and PLC challenged results in five municipalities, but the challenges were rejected by the CSE on procedural grounds. Opposition parties and observer groups noted irregularities in the electoral process, including outdated voter rosters, the presence of "phantom" parties and candidates, voters being turned away at the polls, and repeat voters. The abstention rate was also a matter of concern, though the figure was disputed by the CSE.

B. Political Pluralism and Participation: 7 / 16

In 1999, the PLC and FSLN agreed to a governing pact that guaranteed then president Alemán, who was accused of corruption throughout his presidency, a seat in both the Nicaraguan and the Central American parliaments, ensuring him immunity from prosecution. It also included reforms that lowered the vote threshold for winning an election without a runoff from 45 to 40 percent (or 35 percent if the winner had a lead of 5 percentage points). Using their combined bloc in the legislature, the two parties solidified their control over the Supreme Court and the electoral tribunal, among other institutions. During the subsequent years, the PLC experienced a sharp decline in support while support for the FSLN increased. An October 2013 Consulta Mitofsky poll showed that Ortega's approval rating was 66 percent.

The FSLN's majority in the National Assembly enabled it to pass laws without any support from opposition parties. In 2013 this included the controversial concession to a Chinese businessman for an inter-oceanic canal. In a potential further expansion of FSLN power, one of the proposed constitutional reforms would give Ortega's decrees the force of law.

In August 2013, opposition leaders in the National Assembly and several social movements formed UNIR as an anti-FSLN alliance. The group pledged to fight the "Ortega dictatorship" and to work together to promote popular participation and develop an agenda for the nation.

Minority groups, especially the indigenous inhabitants of Nicaragua's eastern and Caribbean regions, frequently complain that they are politically underrepresented and their grievances are largely ignored by the government and FSLN.

C. Functioning of Government: 6 / 12 (+2)

Nicaragua was ranked 127 out of 177 countries and territories surveyed in Transparency International's 2013 Corruption Perceptions Index. There have been incremental improvements in accountability over the past several years, though corruption and lack of transparency remain serious problems. Corruption charges against high-ranking government officials are still rare except in the most egregious of cases, and corruption cases against opposition figures are often criticized for being politically motivated. In 2003, Alemán was convicted of money laundering and sentenced to serve 20 years in prison. However, the former leader used his alliance with Ortega to secure his release from parole conditions in March 2007, as long as he did not leave the country. In May 2012, CSE alternate magistrate Julio César Osuna of the PLC was arrested on charges of money laundering, using his office to smuggle drugs, and selling false identification to drug traffickers. He was later stripped of his immunity by the National Assembly so that he could stand trial. Osuna pleaded guilty to racketeering and falsifying documents in exchange for a reduced sentence of 23 years in prison. CSE president Roberto Rivas insisted that Osuna had been working alone and that there was no wider scandal involving the CSE, though critics have suggested that is unlikely. In 2013 Rivas himself was implicated in a corruption scandal following allegations that he did not pay taxes on more than a dozen imported luxury vehicles.

The 2007 Law on Access to Public Information requires public entities and private companies doing business with the state to disclose certain information. However, it preserves the government's right to protect information related to state security. Concerns about the transparency of aid funds from the Venezuela-led Bolivarian Alliance for the Peoples of Our America organization, of which Nicaragua is a member, persisted in 2013. Concerns also remained about officials who retained their posts beyond their terms following the 2010 presidential decree. Although talks between the FSLN and PLI about replacements for those officials began in February 2013, more than 60 officials remained in their posts as of October 2013. One of the proposed constitutional reforms would enshrine into the charter the ability of such officials to remain in office until a replacement is approved.

The public consultation process leading up to the initial passage of the draft constitutional changes in 2013 represented a modest improvement on the government's previous practices, and the FSLN made some concessions in its proposals as a result, though a number of flaws in the process were noted by opposition and independent observers.

CIVIL LIBERTIES: 35 / 60 (+1)
D. Freedom of Expression and Belief: 12 / 16

The constitution calls for a free press but allows some censorship. Radio remains the main source of information. Before leaving office in 1990 after an earlier period in power, the FSLN privatized some radio stations and handed them to party loyalists. There are six television networks based in the capital, including a state-owned network, and many favor particular political factions. Three national newspapers cover the news from a variety of political viewpoints. The Communications and Citizenry Council, which oversees the government's press relations and is directed by First Lady Rosario Murillo, has been accused of limiting access to information and censoring the opposition. Access to the internet is unrestricted.

The press has faced increased political and judicial harassment since 2007, and the Ortega administration engages in systematic efforts to obstruct and discredit media critics.

Journalists have received death threats, and some have been killed in recent years, with a number of attacks attributed to FSLN sympathizers. Several reporters for the newspaper *El Nuevo Diario* have been subjected to threats. In 2013, reporter Ismael López Ocampo of the online news site Confidencial received threats after reporting on armed antigovernment groups, while Agence France-Presse photojournalist Hector Retamal was arrested and deported for alleged security and migration violations in May. In addition, members of the ruling elite have acquired stakes in media outlets and used their ownership influence to sideline independent journalists.

Religious and academic freedoms are generally respected.

E. Associational and Organizational Rights: 6 / 12

Freedoms of assembly and association are recognized by law, but their observance in practice has come under mounting pressure. While public demonstrations are generally allowed, opposition members have accused the police of partisan behavior and failing to protect demonstrators. In June 2013 a group of approximately 100 elderly people from the National Union of Older Adults (UNAM) who were advocating for the payment of partial pensions occupied the Social Security Institute's building in Managua for two days before being forcibly removed by the National Police. Protests continued outside the building in the ensuing days, and on June 22, some of the demonstrators were reportedly attacked by a group of FSLN supporters.

Although nongovernmental organizations are active and operate freely, they have faced harassment in recent years and have been weakened by the system of Citizens' Power Councils (CPCs) established by the Ortega administration in 2007. The CPCs, which operate from the neighborhood to the federal level, were formed to promote direct democracy and participation in the government's Zero Hunger food-production project. Critics argue that the bodies blur the lines between state and party institutions, and that CPCs are highly politicized.

The FSLN controls many of the country's labor unions, and the legal rights of non-FSLN unions are not fully guaranteed. Although the law recognizes the right to strike, unions must clear a number of hurdles, and approval from the Ministry of Labor is almost never granted. Employers sometimes form their own unions to avoid recognizing legitimate organizations. Employees have reportedly been dismissed for union activities, and citizens have no effective recourse when labor laws are violated by those in power.

F. Rule of Law: 7 / 16

The judiciary remains dominated by FSLN and PLC appointees, and the Supreme Court is a largely politicized body controlled by Sandinista judges. The court system also suffers from corruption, long delays, a large backlog of cases, and a severe shortage of public defenders. Access to justice is especially deficient in rural areas and on the Caribbean coast.

Despite long-term improvements, the security forces remain understaffed and poorly funded, and human rights abuses still occur. Forced confessions are also a problem, as are arbitrary arrests. Though Nicaragua has generally been spared the high rates of crime and gang violence that plague its neighbors to the north, the country—specifically the Caribbean coast—is an important transshipment point for South American drugs. The police have been active in combating trafficking and organized crime. Prison conditions are poor. One controversial amendment within the 2013 constitutional reform package would allow active-duty military officials to hold unelected office, potentially increasing the military's role in society.

The constitution and laws nominally recognize the rights of indigenous communities, but those rights have not been respected in practice. Approximately 5 percent of the population is indigenous and lives mostly in the Northern Atlantic Autonomous Region (RAAN) and the Southern Atlantic Autonomous Region (RAAS). In 2009, the Miskito Council of Elders in the RAAS announced the creation of a separatist movement demanding independence, citing government neglect and grievances related to the exploitation of natural resources. In 2012, the Nicaraguan constitution was translated into Miskito and Mayangna for the first time.

G. Personal Autonomy and Individual Rights: 10 / 16 (+1)

Property rights are protected on paper but can be tenuous in practice. Titles are often contested, and individuals with connections to the FSLN may enjoy an advantage during property disputes. The June 2013 canal deal prompted critics to worry that the highly favorable terms would lead to unfair land confiscations.

In 2013, Nicaragua was ranked 10th out of the 136 countries surveyed in the World Economic Forum's Global Gender Gap Report, indicating that its gender-based disparities are among the smallest in the world. However, violence against women and children, including sexual and domestic abuse, remains widespread and underreported; few cases are ever prosecuted. The murder rate for female victims increased significantly in recent years. In January 2012, the Comprehensive Law Against Violence Toward Women was passed by the National Assembly. The law, which went into effect in June 2012, addresses both physical and structural forms of violence, and recognizes violence against women as a matter of public health and safety. The law also sets forth sentencing guidelines for physical and psychological abuses against women, as well as the newly established crime of femicide. Opponents of the law challenged it before the Supreme Court, claiming that its prohibition of mediation between female victims and their abusers was unconstitutional. Religious officials claimed that the bill would lead to the disintegration of the family. In August 2013, the court ruled that the law was constitutional, but sent a proposal to the National Assembly that the law be amended to allow mediation. The National Assembly passed the reforms despite concerns from rights groups. Abortion is illegal and punishable by imprisonment, even when performed to save the mother's life or in cases of rape or incest. Scores of deaths stemming from the ban have been reported in recent years.

Same-sex marriage and civil unions remain barred in Nicaragua, and the country's LGBT (lesbian, gay, bisexual, and transgender) population is subject to intermittent threats and discriminatory treatment, such as the barring of a pride march on International LGBT Pride Day in Managua in June 2013.

Nicaragua is a source country for women and children trafficked for prostitution. In September 2010, the government passed a law that classifies human trafficking as a form of organized crime. In 2013, Nicaragua remained a Tier 1 country in the U.S. State Department's *Trafficking in Persons Report*, which stated that "Nicaraguan authorities significantly strengthened law enforcement efforts over the year, particularly through increased prosecutions and convictions, including forced labor." However, it also noted that efforts to combat human trafficking were much weaker in the RAAN and the RAAS. Child labor and other abuses in export-processing zones remain problems, though child labor occurs most often in the agricultural sector.

… Freedom in the World 2014

Niger

Political Rights Rating: 3
Civil Liberties Rating: 4
Freedom Rating: 3.5
Freedom Status: Partly Free
Electoral Democracy: Yes

Population: 16,900,000
Capital: Niamey

Ten-Year Ratings Timeline For Year Under Review (Political Rights, Civil Liberties, Status)

Year Under Review	2004	2005	2006	2007	2008	2009	2010	2011	2012	2013
Rating	3,3,PF	3,3,PF	3,3,PF	3,4,PF	3,4,PF	5,4,PF	5,4,PF	3,4,PF	3,4,PF	3,4,PF

INTRODUCTION

In August, President Mahamadou Issoufou of the Nigerien Party for Democracy and Socialism (PNDS) authorized a cabinet reshuffle to create what he called a government of national unity. The new cabinet was composed of 37 ministers—up from 26—and 10 members of the existing cabinet were dismissed. While the unity cabinet included members of opposition parties, the president's party retained key positions.

Issoufou characterized the reshuffle in part as a response to two terrorist attacks that had struck northern Niger on May 23, one at a military base in Agadez and another at a uranium mine in Arlit. More than 20 people were reported killed, in addition to several suicide bombers, and many more were wounded. The Movement for Unity and Jihad in West Africa—a militant group that had become more active since a conflict erupted in neighboring Mali in 2012—claimed responsibility. Algerian terrorist commander Mokhtar Belmokhtar also claimed a role in the attacks. Days later, on June 1, three guards were killed at a prison in the capital during what the government described as a botched escape attempt by four inmates held on terrorism charges.

In October, the government signed an agreement to cooperate with Nigeria against the Islamist militant groups Boko Haram and Al-Qaeda in the Islamic Maghreb (AQIM). Niger also authorized the U.S. government to establish bases for aerial surveillance in the region.

Already one of the world's poorest countries, Niger has been ravaged by extreme food shortages since a 2009 drought. The UN Office for the Coordination of Humanitarian Affairs announced that around 800,000 people would require food aid during 2013. Nevertheless, a study released in October by Save the Children found that the Nigerien government had targeted hunger and poor health care so effectively that it had made the greatest strides of any country in reducing child mortality.

POLITICAL RIGHTS: 26 / 40

A. Electoral Process: 9 / 12

A 2010 military coup that removed increasingly authoritarian president Mamadou Tandja led to the adoption of a new constitution that year. Drafted in broad consultation with civil society, the charter reinstated executive term limits, curbed executive power, and provided amnesty for the coup leaders. Under the constitution, the president is elected by popular vote for up to two five-year terms. Members of the 113-seat, unicameral National Assembly, who also serve five-year terms, are elected through party-list voting in eight multimember regional constituencies and eight single-member constituencies reserved for ethnic minorities.

Presidential, legislative, and municipal elections were held in January 2011 to replace the transitional government established by the junta and restore civilian rule. The junta forbade its members and representatives of the transitional government from running for office. The PNDS, headed by Issoufou, led the legislative voting with 37 seats. The pro-Tandja National Movement for a Developing Society (MNSD)—headed by former prime minister Seini Oumarou—placed second with 26 seats, while former prime minister Hama Amadou's Nigerien Democratic Movement for an African Federation took 25. Five smaller parties divided the remainder. In the first round of the presidential election, Issoufou and Oumarou emerged as the top two candidates; Issoufou then claimed victory with 58 percent of the vote in a March runoff election. Both the presidential and legislative elections were declared free and fair by international observers, despite minor irregularities. The PNDS and MNSD won the majority of positions across the country in local elections.

B. Political Pluralism and Participation: 10 / 16

After the 2010 military coup, Amadou returned from exile, three former legislators were released from jail, and there was a decrease in harassment of opposition politicians. Since assuming power in 2011, Issoufou has appointed former opponents and members of civil society to high positions in government to foster inclusivity, and the 2013 government reshuffle continued this pattern, though it left most key posts in the hands of Issoufou's allies.

The constitution reserves eight special constituency seats to ensure ethnic minorities' representation in the National Assembly. Such minorities, including the nomadic population, continue to have poor access to government services. Under a 2002 quota system, political parties must allocate 10 percent of their elected positions to women.

C. Functioning of Government: 7 / 12

Corruption is a serious problem in Niger, and observers have raised concerns regarding uranium-mining contracts. However, the 2010 constitution provides for greater transparency in government reporting of revenues from the extractive industries, and for the declaration of personal assets by government officials, including the president. In July 2011, the government created the High Authority to Combat Corruption, and it opened an anticorruption hotline that August. Key officials from the previous administration were indicted for fraud and corruption during 2011, and in July of that year, Issoufou was the target of a foiled assassination attempt thought to be motivated by his crackdowns on corruption in the military. In February 2013, authorities arrested some 20 doctors and other health workers on suspicion of embezzling funds from an international nongovernmental organization (NGO), which reportedly suspended its activities in Niger as a result of the alleged theft. Niger was ranked 106 out of 177 countries and territories surveyed in Transparency International's 2013 Corruption Perceptions Index.

CIVIL LIBERTIES: 30 / 60

D. Freedom of Expression and Belief: 11 / 16

In 2010, the transitional government made significant efforts to restore freedoms of speech and of the press. In June of that year, the National Assembly adopted a new press law that eliminated prison terms for media offenses and reduced the threat of libel cases that journalists had faced under Tandja. In November 2011, Issoufou became the first head of state to sign the Table Mountain Declaration, which calls on African governments to promote press freedom. The media are largely allowed to publish political facts and critiques without interference, but journalists still sometimes face police violence while covering protests and prosecutions for libel. In June 2013, an Al-Jazeera television crew was detained for two days, allegedly because its members had not obtained the proper permits. The crew had been filming a story on the living conditions of refugees from Nigeria's civil conflict. The government does not restrict internet use, though less than 2 percent of the population has access.

Freedom of religion is generally respected in this overwhelmingly Muslim country. In the aftermath of the 2010 coup, both Muslim and Christian leaders worked with the junta to restore peace and democracy. Academic freedom is guaranteed but not always observed in practice.

E. Associational and Organizational Rights: 8 / 12

Constitutional guarantees of freedoms of assembly and association are largely upheld. However, police sometimes used force to break up labor and other protests during 2013, in one case allegedly causing the death of a bystander. The government does not restrict the operations of NGOs, although a lack of security in the north prevents such groups from accessing or functioning in the region. While the constitution and other laws guarantee workers the right to join unions and bargain for wages, over 95 percent of the workforce is employed in subsistence agriculture and small trading.

F. Rule of Law: 5 / 16

The constitution provides for an independent judiciary, and courts have shown some autonomy in the past, though the judicial system has at times been subject to executive interference. The Ministry of Justice supervises public prosecutors, and the president has the power to appoint judges. Judicial corruption is fueled partly by low salaries and inadequate training. Prolonged pretrial detention is common, and police forces are underfunded and poorly trained. Prisons are characterized by overcrowding and poor health conditions.

Insecurity continues to plague many parts of the country, and several people have been kidnapped by groups such as AQIM. In October, four French citizens who had been abducted near Arlit and held by AQIM since 2010 were released.

The crisis in neighboring Mali led to an influx in 2012 of some 60,000 Malian refugees, of whom 47,000 remained in Niger in 2013, as well as 4,000 Nigerian refugees fleeing the situation in Northern Nigeria. This influx raised pressure on food supplies. Separately, in late October, the bodies of 92 migrants—predominantly women and children—who had died of thirst as they were attempting to cross illegally into Algeria were found close to Niger's border with that country. The government vowed to crack down on "criminal activities led by all types of trafficking networks," which it blamed for the deaths, and promised to close illegal migrant camps in the country's north. Just days after the discovery of the bodies, 127 migrants were stopped while attempting to cross via a similar route.

While two ethnic groups, Hausa and Djerma, still dominate many government and economic positions, minority groups are represented in these areas and their rights are protected by law. Same-sex sexual activity is not illegal in Niger, but same-sex rights are not recognized and there is no protection against discrimination based on sexual orientation. No NGOs work on LGBT (lesbian, gay, bisexual, and transgender) rights in Niger.

G. Personal Autonomy and Individual Rights: 6 / 16

The constitution guarantees freedom of movement and property rights and these are generally respected throughout the country, though bribery remains an issue for both.

Although the 2010 constitution prohibits gender discrimination, women suffer discrimination in practice. Family law gives women inferior status in property disputes, inheritance rights, and divorce. Sexual and domestic violence are reportedly widespread. Female genital mutilation was criminalized in 2003 and has declined, but it continues in a small percentage of the population.

While slavery was criminalized in 2003 and banned in the 2010 constitution, slavery remains a problem in Niger, with up to 43,000 individuals still in slavery. Niger remains a source, transit point, and destination for human trafficking. Despite a 2010 antitrafficking law and a five-year antitrafficking plan, investigation and prosecution efforts remained weak in 2013.

Nigeria

Political Rights Rating: 4
Civil Liberties Rating: 4
Freedom Rating: 4.0
Freedom Status: Partly Free
Electoral Democracy: No

Population: 173,615,000
Capital: Abuja

Ten-Year Ratings Timeline For Year Under Review (Political Rights, Civil Liberties, Status)

Year Under Review	2004	2005	2006	2007	2008	2009	2010	2011	2012	2013
Rating	4,4,PF	4,4,PF	4,4,PF	4,4,PF	4,4,PF	5,4,PF	4,4,PF	4,4,PF	4,4,PF	4,4,PF

INTRODUCTION

Human rights conditions continued to worsen in 2013, with increasing Islamic militancy in the north, a rising wave of kidnappings in the south, and ethnic and communal clashes in Kaduna and Plateau states. The situation in northeastern states continues to defy remedy, as the militant Islamist group Boko Haram (or "People Committed to the Propagation of the Prophet's Teachings and Jihad") increased its deadly attacks on civilians and government targets; Boko Haram was the second most deadly terrorist group in the world in 2013. Moreover, an October 15 report by Amnesty International revealed that security forces involved in the counterterrorist offensive against Boko Haram committed gross human rights violations, including extrajudicial killings, arbitrary mass arrests, illegal detentions, and torture against citizens living in the affected areas. According to the report, over 950 people died in military custody in the first six months of 2013. Meanwhile, in November, the International Criminal Court (ICC) classified the crisis involving Boko Haram and the Nigerian security forces as a non-international armed conflict. At year's end, the ICC also continued its investigations into whether Boko Haram has committed crimes against humanity.

Internal divisions rocked the ruling Peoples Democratic Party (PDP). A group of seven governors (known as the "G7") along with other high-ranking officials created a separate faction of the party that they have named the "New PDP." Meanwhile, both houses of the National Assembly (NASS) began deliberations on proposed amendments to the 1999 constitution that include, among other things, the guarantee of equal rights for minorities. In October, during Nigeria's 53rd independence celebrations, President Goodluck Jonathan announced the establishment of an advisory committee that will make recommendations on the convening of a national dialogue to address the main challenges to Nigeria's political and economic stability.

Nigeria's economy, the second largest in Africa, continues to grow by a rate of 6 percent per year. This growth is dominated by the production of oil, which accounts for 95 percent of export revenues and 80 percent of government revenue. However, unchecked government corruption has resulted in billions of dollars of lost public revenue over the last decade. A report by London-based think tank Chatham House revealed that for the first six months of 2013, over 100,000 barrels were stolen each day from oil facilities through elaborate networks involving Nigerian officials and international actors.

Nigeria has historically played an important role in regional security initiatives in West Africa. However, in July, the Nigerian military began withdrawing some of the more than

1,000 Nigerian troops from the Peace Support Operations in Mali (originally deployed in January) to support internal security operations directed at the insurgency in northern Nigeria. In October, Nigeria gained a nonpermanent seat on the United Nations Security Council.

POLITICAL RIGHTS: 20 / 40

A. Electoral Process: 6 / 12

According to the constitution, the president is elected by popular vote for no more than two four-year terms. Members of the bicameral National Assembly, consisting of the 109-seat Senate and the 360-seat House of Representatives, are elected for four-year terms. Although Nigeria's elections were marred by gross electoral irregularities and violence since the return of multiparty rule, the 2011 elections marked a significant departure from this trend. Following the passage of electoral reforms and the appointment of a new chairman of the electoral commission, domestic and international observers generally regarded the 2011 elections as free, fair, and credible, even in the wake of postelection violence that claimed the lives of 800 people and left 65,000 displaced.

Goodluck Jonathan of the PDP won the April 2011 presidential contest, defeating Muhammadu Buhari of the Congress for Progressive Change (CPC), with a margin of 59 percent to 32 percent. The vote seems to have exacerbated the ethnic and religious fault lines of the country, with Buhari winning mostly in the northern states and Jonathan gaining an overwhelming majority in the south. The CPC filed a petition to the Election Tribunal challenging the results of the presidential election, but in November 2011 the tribunal upheld the decision of the electoral commission declaring Jonathan as the winner. Meanwhile, PDP candidates won a reduced majority in legislative elections in April 2011. In the House of Representatives, the PDP claimed 202 of 360 seats, while the Action Congress of Nigeria (ACN) won 66, the CPC took 35, and the All Nigeria Peoples Party (ANPP) garnered 25. In the Senate, the PDP lost its two-thirds majority, winning 71 of 109 seats; the ACN took 18 seats, and the CPC and ANPP won 7 each. The PDP captured 18 of the 26 contested governorships.

B. Political Pluralism and Participation: 9 / 16

Nigeria's multiparty system provides opportunities for the participation of opposition parties in the political process. According to the Independent National Electoral Commission (INEC), 29 political parties are currently registered. The most recent are the All Progressives Congress (APC) and the Peoples Democratic Movement (PDM), which were both registered in July. Although the PDP continues to dominate both national and state elections, during the 2011 elections opposition parties made significant inroads, increasing representation in the NASS as well as the number of governorships relative to the 2007 elections. Furthermore, four prominent opposition parties—the ACN, the CPC, the ANPP, and a faction of the All Progressives Grand Alliance (APGA)—merged in February 2013 under the banner of the All Progressives Congress (APC), which INEC formally recognized in July. Meanwhile, in November, the APC increased in strength as members of the ruling PDP, including five state governors, defected from the party and joined the APC. Although the formation of the APC and the defection of members of the PDP have the potential of enhancing political pluralism in Nigeria, the ruling PDP has allegedly targeted and used government officials to disrupt the activities of these defectors, especially those with aspirations of contesting the 2015 presidential election.

C. Functioning of Government: 5 / 12

Corruption remains pervasive, and government efforts to improve transparency and reduce graft have been inadequate. During the year there were numerous high-profile corruption scandals. Following the 2012 "Oil Subsidy" scandal that revealed the misappropriation of $6.8 billion dollars of fuel subsidies, a September 2013 Chatham House report revealed that more than 5 percent of total oil output is stolen by a network of Nigerian politicians, military officers, oil industry authorities, and international actors. In addition, in October President Jonathan ordered an investigation into the purchase of two BMW 7 series armored cars valued at 255 million naira ($1.63 million) by the cash-strapped Nigerian Civil Aviation Authority under the approval of Minister of Aviation Stella Oduah. In October the Nigerian House of Representatives Committee on Aviation initiated an investigation into the scandal and in December found Minister Oduah culpable for breaching the 2013 Appropriations Act. The House further recommended that President Jonathan reconsider Oduah's appointment as minster.

Although Nigeria has established a robust legal and institutional framework to combat corruption, the government has not effectively prosecuted officials or eliminated the culture of impunity. For example, the Economic and Financial Crimes Commission (EFCC), Nigeria's main corruption agency, has successfully brought corruption charges against prominent politicians, such as former governor of Ogun state Otunba Gbenga Daniel in 2011 for allegedly misappropriating 58 billion naira ($372 million). However, the case is still before the courts. Since 2002, the anticorruption body has secured only four convictions, resulting in little or no jail time. The EFCC is hampered by political interference, an inefficient judiciary, and its own institutional weaknesses, and is subject to accusations that it targets those who have lost favor with the government.

Nigeria was ranked 144 out of 177 countries surveyed in the Transparency International (TI) 2013 Corruption Perceptions Index. In the 2013 Global Corruption Barometer, a public opinion survey by TI, 72 percent of Nigerian respondents believed that corruption had increased "a lot" since 2011. Corruption was perceived to be greatest among the Nigerian Police, political parties, and the parliament.

Despite the passage of the Freedom of Information Act in 2011, which guarantees the public the right to access public records, various nongovernmental organizations (NGOs), including the Media Rights Agenda, have criticized government agencies for routinely refusing to release information sought through the provisions of the law.

CIVIL LIBERTIES: 26 / 40
D. Freedom of Expression and Belief: 9 / 16

Freedoms of speech, expression, and the press are constitutionally guaranteed; however there is an increase in instances in which state and nonstate actors violate these rights. A recent report by the Committee to Protect Journalists (CPJ) documented 143 attacks on journalists in 2012. Of these cases, the government and security forces were associated with 79 percent, while Boko Haram were responsible for 16 percent.

The government frequently restricts press freedom by publicly criticizing, harassing, and arresting journalists, especially when they cover corruption scandals or separatist and communal violence. Moreover, Sharia statutes in 12 northern states impose severe penalties for alleged press offenses. In June, a reporter and a news editor from the *Leadership* newspaper were arrested and charged in an Abuja high court on counts of forgery for stories published on April 3 and 4 that revealed information about an alleged presidential directive. Earlier in the year, the National Film and Video Censors Board (NFCVB) banned "Fuelling Poverty," a 30-minute documentary by Ishaya Bako that details corruption in the oil industry and its impact on Nigeria's economic development. According to the NFCVB, the film is a threat to national security because of its potential to encourage public protests.

Journalists and media entities have also been the victims of attacks by nonstate actors, including Boko Haram. Moreover, cases of violence against journalists often go unsolved.

Nigeria ranks 11th in the world for deadly unpunished violence against the press. The most recent case was the January 2012 killing of Enenche Akogwu, a reporter and cameraman for Channels TV, who was shot dead while interviewing witnesses to terrorist attacks in Kano. No arrests had been made in the case as of the end of the year.

There were no reports of government restricting access to the internet or monitoring personal emails in 2013.

Religious freedom is constitutionally and legally protected and is generally respected by the government in practice. Nevertheless, in a few instances state and local governments have undermined religious freedom by placing limits on religious activities and endorsing a dominant religion. Nonstate actors have also attempted to limit religious freedom, especially in the north. For instance, Boko Haram has explicitly targeted Christians and their houses of worship, though Muslims still account for the majority of the group's victims. From January 2012 to August 2013, Boko Haram reportedly attacked approximately 50 churches, claiming the lives of 366 persons. Moreover, sectarian clashes between Muslims and Christians have continued in Kaduna and Plateau states, especially around the city of Jos, which have resulted in the deaths of hundreds and displacement of thousands more.

The federal government generally honors academic freedom. However, some state governments place restrictions on elementary and secondary curriculums by mandating religious instruction, and student admission and faculty hiring policies are subject to political interference.

Moreover, Boko Haram's targeted assault on western education has led to the destruction of numerous primary and secondary schools, the intimidation, injury and death of school children and teachers, and the forced closure of schools throughout the northeast. For instance, according to an Amnesty International report published in October 2013, over 50 schools were attacked in Borno state since the start of 2013.

E. Associational and Organizational Rights: 7 / 12

The rights to peaceful assembly and association are constitutionally guaranteed and generally respected. Nonetheless, federal and state governments have frequently banned public events that have the possibility of inciting political, ethnic, or religious tension. For example, in October, the Kaduna government banned all rallies and social gatherings in the state unless approved by the police. Kaduna-based NGOs criticized the ban as a violation of their constitutional rights of assembly. Additionally, NGOs operating in regions affected by the conflict between Boko Haram and the Nigerian security forces experienced difficulties in carrying out their work. Members of some organizations faced intimidation and physical harm for speaking out against Boko Haram, while members of NGOs also encountered challenges when investigating alleged human rights abuses of suspected Boko Haram suspects.

Under the constitution, workers have the right to form and join trade unions, engage in collective bargaining, and conduct legal strikes. At the same time, the government forbids strike action in a number of essential services, including public transportation and security. Following government abuse of NGOs during the fuel subsidy protests in 2012, the police prevented chapters of the Academic Staff Union of Universities from conducting public rallies to raise awareness about the ongoing labor dispute between them and the federal government in October 2013.

F. Rule of Law: 4 / 16

Judicial independence in Nigeria is constitutionally and legally enshrined. Although the judiciary has achieved some degree of independence and professionalism, political interference, corruption, and lack of funding, equipment, and training remain important challenges.

Certain departments, particularly the Court of Appeals, have frequently overturned decisions on election challenges or allegations of corruption against powerful elites, raising doubts about their independence.

Nigerian security forces commit abuses with near impunity, and corruption pervades their ranks. There were numerous allegations of extortion, bribe taking, and embezzlement within the Nigerian Police Force in 2013. However, corrupt officers act with impunity and are often supported by a chain of command that encourages and institutionalizes graft. Various domestic and international human rights groups have called for the government to take steps to stem human rights violations by security forces and the systemic corruption in the police force. For instance, Human Rights Watch (HRW) has called for the criminalization of torture, and the establishment of an independent commission to investigate and prosecute allegations of extortion, bribe taking, and embezzlement within the Nigerian Police Force. In January, the police introduced a new code of conduct to stem widespread human rights violations and promote discipline and professionalism among police officers. In May, Inspector General of Police Mohammed Abubakar claimed an 80 percent reduction in police corruption since the removal of police-manned roadblocks in 2012, but this figure has not been corroborated by other sources.

During 2013, Boko Haram continued to pose a serious threat to internal security in Nigeria. Under the leadership of Abubakar Shekau, the group has targeted police, military, government officials, and civilians, including Christians but also moderate Muslims mainly in northern Nigerian states. Both the scale and the geographic reach of Boko Haram attacks expanded in 2013. In September, the militant group killed 40 students during an attack on an agricultural college in Yobe state, while in July an attack on a boarding school claimed the lives to 29 students and one teacher. Boko Haram claimed responsibility for numerous other attacks throughout the year. In October, the UN Refugee Agency indicated that more than 10,000 Nigerians have crossed into Cameroon, Chad, and Niger, and 5,000 have been internally displaced because of the conflict.

The government's counterterrorism efforts, led by the Joint Task Force (JTF), have so far produced mixed results. In May, the federal government declared a state of emergency in the northeastern states of Borno, Yobe, and Adamawa, and the JTF's ground and air offensive has weakened the militant group's capacity and led to the capture or death of leading Boko Haram members. However, various international human rights groups have criticized the JTF for committing human rights abuses, including extrajudicial killings, in the course of their counterterrorism campaign. In an attempt to resolve the conflict, President Jonathan established a committee on Boko Haram in April that would pursue an amnesty and disarmament program for militants.

Violent crime in certain cities and regions remains a serious problem, and the trafficking of drugs and small arms is reportedly on the rise. Kidnapping and abductions continued unabated, especially in the Niger Delta and the southeastern states of Abia, Imo, and Anambara. Political figures, the wealthy, and foreigners were most frequently targeted. For instance, in September Anglican Archbishop Ignatius Kattey and his wife were kidnapped in Rivers state; they were released a few days after. In 2013, Nigeria recorded one of the highest rates of kidnappings in the world. Some states have introduced stringent anti-kidnapping laws that prescribe long prison sentences, and sometimes the death penalty, for those found guilty. Nevertheless, the conviction rate on kidnapping cases has been low because security personnel and local government officials are often involved in these networks.

Despite legal safeguards against ethnic discrimination in the Nigerian constitution, many ethnic minorities experienced discrimination by state governments and other societal groups in areas of employment, education and housing. For instance, in July the Lagos State

Government allegedly removed 70 persons of Igbo ethnicity from Lagos and forcibly relocated them to Anambra state, their perceived state of origin. According to many human rights activists, the forced relocation violated Nigerians' constitutionally enshrined right to reside in any part of the country, regardless of their state of origin.

The Nigerian government and society continue to discriminate against LGBT (lesbian, gay, bisexual, and transgender) people. Leading domestic and international human rights groups criticized the NASS for passing the Same Sex Marriage (Prohibition) Bill. The final version of the bill, which imposes sentences up to 14 years for engaging in same-sex relations and up to 10 years for any individual or group that supports or facilitates these relationships, was unanimously approved by the Senate in November, but has yet to be approved by the president at year's end. The new law complements existing state laws that make same-sex relationships illegal; in many southern states these relationships are punishable by up to 14 years in prison, while in northern states, Sharia statutes allow sentences up to the death penalty.

G. Personal Autonomy and Individual Rights: 6 / 16

Freedom of internal movement and foreign travel are legally guaranteed; however, security officials frequently restricted freedom of movement in areas affected by sectarian violence or terrorist attacks by imposing dusk-to-dawn curfews. This was especially the case in 2013 in many northern states, especially those under the state of emergency: Adamawa, Borno, and Yobe. Nigeria's largely unregulated property rights system continues to prevent citizen and private business from engaging in the efficient and legal purchase or sale of land and other types of property.

Nigerian women's educational opportunities have improved, and women hold several key governmental positions: 13 members of the current cabinet are women, while female candidates won 24 of 360 seats in the House of Representatives and 7 of 109 seats in the Senate. Moreover, women occupy key posts in the judiciary, including Justice Aloma Mukhtar, who was appointed in 2012 as the Chief Justice of Nigeria. However, throughout the country, women experience discrimination in employment and are often relegated to inferior positions. Discrimination against women is especially problematic in northern states governed by Sharia statutes, where women's rights have suffered particularly serious setbacks. In addition, women belonging to certain ethnic groups are often denied equal rights to inherit property throughout Nigeria. Women continue to be affected by domestic violence and rape, and the practices of female genital mutilation and child marriage are pervasive. Despite the existence of stiff laws against rape, domestic violence, female mutilation, and child marriages, there have been low rates of reporting and prosecution of these offenses.

Illegal human trafficking to, from, and within Nigeria for the purposes of forced labor and prostitution is reported to be on the rise. A recent report indicated that Nigerian authorities, through the National Agency for the Prohibition of Trafficking in Persons (NAPTIP), have become more successful in protecting human trafficking victims, prosecuting suspected traffickers, and dismantling human trafficking networks. For example, by the end of 2012, NAPTIP began 117 trafficking investigations, 25 of which led to convictions, with a majority of offenders punished with prison sentences. Forced labor is illegal but common, especially bonded labor and domestic servitude, and the government makes very little effort to combat the practice.

North Korea

Political Rights Rating: 7
Civil Liberties Rating: 7
Freedom Rating: 7.0
Freedom Status: Not Free
Electoral Democracy: No

Population: 24,720,000
Capital: Pyongyang

Ten-Year Ratings Timeline For Year Under Review (Political Rights, Civil Liberties, Status)

Year Under Review	2004	2005	2006	2007	2008	2009	2010	2011	2012	2013
Rating	7,7,NF	7,7,NF	7,7,NF	7,7,NF	7,7,NF	7,7,NF	7,7,NF	7,7,NF	7,7,NF	7,7,NF

INTRODUCTION

In January 2013, the UN Security Council voted unanimously to impose new sanctions on the Democratic People's Republic of Korea (DPRK, or North Korea) and to reiterate its commitment to enforce previous resolutions. The move followed the launch of a rocket into orbit by the DPRK the previous month. On February 12, North Korea conducted an underground nuclear weapons test, its third since 2006. The test fueled international protest and was followed by escalating threats by the DPRK, especially targeted at the U.S., South Korea, and Japan. In March, the Security Council unanimously adopted another resolution, the fifth since 2006, condemning North Korea's nuclear and ballistic missile program. The resolution imposed additional financial sanctions on North Korea, and called on states to step up inspections and interdictions of DPRK-affiliated shipments.

In April 2013, North Korea announced a new plan for the simultaneous development of its nuclear weapons and the economy (commonly referred to as the "byungjin line"). Satellite imagery throughout the year showed active construction at North Korea's two missile test sites, including possible new launch pads, improved roads, and more permanent instrumentation facilities, as well as additional tunneling activity at its nuclear test site. Major developments at the Yongbyon Nuclear Scientific Research Center were also noted. Various other instances of progress toward creating a nuclear weapon were seen during the year.

In June 2013, North Korea established the State Economic Development Committee (also referred to as Chosun Economic Development Committee), a "non-state" institution that was created for the purpose of developing special economic zones (SEZs). Plans include development of 14 SEZs, a considerable increase over the four that currently are under development. In July, the ruling Korean Workers' Party (KWP) created a centralized economy department with branches in each province.

These plans, however, exist outside the realm of the joint North-South Kaesong Industrial Complex (KIC). The KIC, which has in the past outlasted political disputes between the two Koreas, was shut down in April 2013 in response to high tensions on the peninsula. After six rounds of talks, an agreement was reached in August to reopen the complex, which included provisions to prevent unilateral actions to help avoid future shutdowns.

In July, a newly established Commission of Inquiry (COI), created by the UN Human Rights Council, began operations. The COI was tasked with investigating and evaluating North Korea's "systematic, widespread and grave violations of human rights." In September, COI chair Michael Kirby reported that the commission had found evidence of large-scale patterns that may constitute systematic and gross human rights violations. However, he also noted instances of "hope," including the DPRK's signing of the Convention on the Rights of Persons with Disabilities. The COI final report is scheduled to be issued in March 2014, including findings and recommendations for North Korea and the international community on how to improve the situation of human rights in the DPRK.

In December, North Korea publicly purged Kim Jong-un's uncle and vice-chairman of the National Defense Commission, Jang Song-thaek. During the December 8 KWP Central Committee Politburo meeting, Jang was arrested and removed from all posts and his arrest was broadcasted on KCTV. On December 13, the KCNA reported that Jang was tried for treason before a military tribunal on December 12 and was immediately executed.

POLITICAL RIGHTS: 0 / 40
A. Electoral Process: 0 / 12

Kim Jong-il led the DPRK following the 1994 death of his father, Kim Il-sung, to whom the office of president was permanently dedicated in a 1998 constitutional revision. Kim Jong-il's son, Kim Jong-un, became the country's new supreme leader after his father's death in December 2011. Kim Jong-un's titles include "first secretary" of the KWP, "first chairman" of the National Defence Commission (NDC), and "supreme commander" of the KPA. North Korea's parliament, the Supreme People's Assembly (SPA), is a rubber-stamp institution elected to five-year terms. All candidates for office, who run unopposed, are preselected by the ruling Korean Workers' Party (KWP) and two subordinate minor parties.

B. Political Pluralism and Participation: 0 / 16

North Korea functions as a single-party state under a totalitarian family dictatorship. The KWP, which was founded in 1926 and led by Kim Il-sung, is the only legally permitted party. Kim Jong-un currently serves as the "first secretary" of the KWP, with Kim Jong-il as the "eternal general secretary."

C. Functioning of Government: 0 / 12

Corruption is believed to be endemic at every level of the state and economy, and bribery is pervasive. North Korea was ranked 175 out of 177 countries and territories surveyed in Transparency International's 2013 Corruption Perceptions Index.

CIVIL LIBERTIES: 3 / 60
D. Freedom of Expression and Belief: 0 / 16

All domestic media outlets are run by the state. Televisions and radios are permanently fixed to state channels, and all publications are subject to strict supervision and censorship. In January 2012, the Associated Press opened a bureau office in Pyongyang. Since then, foreign media have been allowed limited access to key political events.

Internet access is restricted to a few thousand people, and foreign websites are blocked. The black market provides alternative information sources, including cellular telephones, pirated recordings of South Korean dramas, and radios capable of receiving foreign programs. Cellular phone service was launched in December 2008 by Koryolink, a joint venture between Egypt's Orascom and North Korea's Korea Post and Telecommunications Corporation. The network is limited to domestic use only, with foreign residents using a separate network. In May 2013, Koryolink reached two million subscriptions; however, the actual number of users may be notably less. Since January 2013, foreigners have been allowed to bring cell phones and smartphones into the country, enabling live social media feeds out of North Korea.

Although freedom of religion is guaranteed by the constitution, it does not exist in practice. State-sanctioned churches maintain a token presence in Pyongyang, and some North Koreans who live near the Chinese border are known to practice their faiths furtively.

However, intense state indoctrination and repression preclude free exercise of religion. Nearly all forms of private communication are monitored by a huge network of informers.

There is no academic freedom. All curriculum must be approved by the state, including domestically based foreigner-led educational opportunities. Although some North Koreans are permitted to study abroad—at both universities and short-term educational training programs—these opportunities are also subject to crackdowns. In October 2013, Pyongyang reportedly ordered its diplomats and state trading company officials to return their children to North Korea from educational institutions abroad out of concern that they could undermine the regime by spreading information or defecting.

E. Associational and Organizational Rights: 0 / 12

Freedom of assembly is not recognized, and there are no known associations or organizations other than those created by the state. Strikes, collective bargaining, and other organized-labor activities are illegal.

F. Rule of Law: 0 / 16

North Korea does not have an independent judiciary. The UN General Assembly has recognized and condemned severe DPRK human rights violations, including torture, public executions, extrajudicial and arbitrary detention, and forced labor; the absence of due process and the rule of law; and death sentences for political offenses. Updated South Korean reports estimate that there are 80,000–120,000 political prisoners held in detention camps in the country. This figure is lower than in past years due to the closing of two camps, the expansion of at least two other facilities, and the high mortality rates inside the camps. Inmates face brutal conditions, and collective or familial punishment for suspected dissent by an individual is a common practice.

In November 2012, U.S. citizen Kenneth Bae was arrested in North Korea and prosecuted for crimes against the state, including planning a religious coup and encouraging North Koreans to bring down the government. Bae was sentenced in April 2013 to 15 years of hard labor. While his mother has been allowed to visit him, the U.S. government has been unsuccessful in negotiating his release. In October 2013, 85-year-old Merrill Newman, another U.S. citizen, was detained while touring North Korea. Newman, who was removed from his plane just before its departure, released a videotaped confession in which he apologized for hostile acts committed against North Korea during the 1950–1953 Korean War. He was released and returned to the United States in December, and stated that his confession had been coerced.

The government operates a semihereditary system of social discrimination whereby all citizens are classified into 53 subgroups under overall security ratings—"core," "wavering," and "hostile"—based on their family's perceived loyalty to the regime. This rating determines virtually every facet of a person's life, including employment and educational opportunities, place of residence, access to medical facilities, and even access to stores.

G. Personal Autonomy and Individual Rights: 3 / 16

There is no freedom of movement, and forced internal resettlement is routine. Access to Pyongyang is tightly restricted; the availability of food, housing, and health care is somewhat better in the capital than in the rest of the country. Recently, this disparity has increased, with the capital featuring more luxuries for a growing middle class. Emigration is illegal, but many North Koreans have escaped via China or engaged in cross-border trade. Ignoring international objections, the Chinese government continues to return refugees and defectors to North Korea, where they are subject to torture, harsh imprisonment, or execution.

The economy remains both centrally planned and grossly mismanaged. Development is also hobbled by a lack of infrastructure, a scarcity of energy and raw materials, an inability to borrow on world markets or from multilateral banks because of sanctions, lingering foreign debt, and ideological isolationism. However, the growth of the black market has provided many North Koreans with a field of activity that is largely free from government control and continues to grow.

There have been widespread reports of trafficked women and girls among the tens of thousands of North Koreans who have recently crossed into China. UN bodies have noted the use of forced abortions and infanticide against pregnant women who are forcibly repatriated from China. Recent reports also suggest that prostitution of children continues unabated in North Korea and that the country's deteriorating economy has led to an increase in prostitution, which is now rampant in ordinary residential areas.

Norway

Political Rights Rating: 1
Civil Liberties Rating: 1
Freedom Rating: 1.0
Freedom Status: Free
Electoral Democracy: Yes

Population: 5,084,000
Capital: Oslo

Ten-Year Ratings Timeline For Year Under Review (Political Rights, Civil Liberties, Status)

Year Under Review	2004	2005	2006	2007	2008	2009	2010	2011	2012	2013
Rating	1,1,F	1,1,F	1,1,F	1,1,F	1,1,F	1,1,F	1,1,F	1,1,F	1,1,F	1,1,F

INTRODUCTION

Parliamentary elections in September 2013 resulted in a significant win for the Conservative Party, led by Erna Solberg, who ousted Jens Stoltenberg's red-green coalition. Initially enjoying huge personal popularity for his calm handling of the aftermath of the July 22, 2011, terrorist attacks in Norway, Stoltenberg was defeated in a campaign focused on domestic issues such as a badly functioning health care system and outdated infrastructure. His government also suffered from an August 2012 report by a government-appointed independent commission that found serious shortcomings in the police's response to the terrorist attacks. The Conservatives formed a coalition in October 2013 with the somewhat controversial right-wing Progress Party, whose restrictive immigration policy remains a divisive issue in Norway.

POLITICAL RIGHTS: 40 / 40
A. Electoral Process: 12 / 12

Norway's unicameral parliament, called the Storting, has 169 members who are directly elected for four-year terms through a system of proportional representation. The constitutional monarch, currently King Harald V, appoints the prime minister, who is the leader of the majority party or coalition in the Storting. While the monarch is officially the head of state and commander in chief of the armed forces, his duties are largely ceremonial.

The Conservative Party gained the most in the 2013 elections, winning 27 percent of the vote and 48 seats—an increase of 18 seats over previous elections. Although the Progress

Party lost 12 seats, its remaining 29 seats helped it to form a government with the Conservatives. The Labor Party remains the biggest party in parliament with 30 percent of the vote and 55 seats, but it lost 9 seats from the 2009 elections and joined the opposition for the first time in 8 years. The smaller center-right Christian Democratic and Center Parties, with 10 seats each, are expected to vote with the government on key issues, most notably immigration and social reforms.

B. Political Pluralism and Participation: 16 / 16

A range of political parties operates freely in the country. With some exceptions, political power in Norway has alternated between the Labor Party and Conservative-led coalitions. The Progress Party's critical stance on immigration has been widely debated in the media; how its transition from opposition to government party will affect its policy was not clear by year's end.

The indigenous Sami population, in addition to participating in the national political process, has its own parliament, or Sameting, which has worked to protect the group's language and cultural rights and influence the national government's decisions about Sami land and its resources. The Sameting is comprised of 39 representatives who are elected for four-year terms. The national government supports Sami-language instruction, broadcast programs, and subsidized newspapers in Sami regions. A deputy minister in the national government deals specifically with Sami issues.

C. Functioning of Government: 12 / 12

Norway remains one of the least corrupt countries in the world, ranked 5 out of 177 countries surveyed in Transparency International's 2013 Corruption Perceptions Index. However, isolated incidents of bribery and misconduct have occurred, and Norway's role in the international energy and mining industries has received particular scrutiny. In 2012 and throughout 2013, opposition parties strongly criticized Trade and Industry Minister Trond Giske for appointing friends and family to state bodies and state-owned firms; a parliamentary inquiry in 2013 found no overt wrongdoing.

CIVIL LIBERTIES: 60 / 60
D. Freedom of Expression and Belief: 16 / 16

Freedom of the press is constitutionally guaranteed and respected in practice. In an effort to promote political pluralism, the state subsidizes many newspapers, the majority of which are privately owned and openly partisan. The government does not impede internet access.

Freedom of religion is protected by the constitution and respected in practice. The monarch is the constitutional head of the Evangelical Lutheran Church of Norway, which counts 75.2 percent of Norwegians as members. Separation of state and church was achieved in 2012 with a constitutional amendment passed by Parliament, putting the Lutheran Church on par with all other denominations in Norway and absolving the requirement of half the cabinet to be members of the Lutheran Church. All religious groups must register with the state to receive financial support, which is determined by size of membership. Students must take a course on religion and ethics focusing on Christianity, though this is thought to violate international human rights conventions. Contrary to a recommendation from the government-appointed Faith and Ethics Policy Committee, Minister of Culture Hadia Tajik declared in parliament in January 2013 that hijabs will not be allowed in the Norwegian police force or judicial system. After a 2012 poll showed a rise in anti-Semitic attitudes, in 2013 anti-Semitic hate crimes were assigned their own category in police reports to facilitate tracking of new developments. Academic freedom is respected.

E. Associational and Organizational Rights: 12 / 12

The constitution guarantees freedoms of assembly and association. Norwegians are very active in nongovernmental organizations. Labor unions play an important role in consulting with the government on social and economic issues, and approximately 53 percent of the workforce is unionized, with 93 percent members of the four main unions. The right to strike is legally guaranteed, except for members of the military and senior civil servants, and is practiced without restrictions. All workers have the right to bargain collectively. There were no significant strikes in 2013.

F. Rule of Law: 16 / 16

The judiciary is independent, and the court system, headed by the Supreme Court, operates fairly at the local and national levels. The king appoints judges on the advice of the Ministry of Justice. The police are under civilian control, and human rights abuses by law enforcement authorities are rare. Prison conditions generally meet international standards and in many cases exceed them. Norway's recidivism rate of approximately 20 percent is the lowest in Scandinavia.

The 2011 terrorist attacks prompted hostility to Norway's multicultural agenda and its native Norwegian supporters. The attacks were perpetrated by Norwegian national and right-wing fundamentalist Anders Breivik, who killed 8 people in Oslo with a powerful bomb and then shot and killed 69 people attending a Labor Party summer youth camp on the island of Utøya. Prominent Norwegian right-wing extremist and heavy metal musician Kristian "Varg" Vikernes was arrested in July 2013 in France, where he will face charges of inciting racial hatred. Vikernes had informal connections to Breivik and had served a prison sentence for a 1994 murder in Oslo.

Immigration to Norway has increased fivefold since the 1970s, including recent asylum-seekers predominantly from Afghanistan, Syria, Sudan, and Eritrea. More than 10 percent of Norway's population was foreign-born in 2013, and by year's end approximately 11,983 people had applied for asylum in Norway, prompting the government to plan several new asylum centers. In 2012, Norwegian police raided a series of asylum centers and arranged forced repatriation of the more than 10,000 rejected asylum-seekers living illegally in Norway; no similar raids occurred in 2013. Immigration and asylum policies remain divisive in Norway.

G. Personal Autonomy and Individual Rights: 16 / 16

The Equality and Anti-Discrimination Ombud is responsible for all forms of discrimination and for enforcing the country's Gender Equality Act, the Anti-Discrimination Act, and other laws against discrimination. Although Norway is not a member of the European Union (EU), citizens within the European Economic Area (which includes all EU states plus Norway, Iceland, and Liechtenstein) do not need a residence permit to work in Norway.

The Gender Equality Act provides equal rights for men and women. A June 2013 law, taking effect in 2015, mandates gender-neutral conscription for the armed forces. This will make Norway the first NATO member to expand the draft to include women. In 2013, women won nearly 40 percent of seats in parliament. Norway is a destination country for human trafficking for the purposes of labor and sexual exploitation. In 2013 Save the Children called attention to 237 unaccompanied children missing from asylum centers over the last four years, citing fears of trafficking. However, according to the U.S. State Department's 2014 Trafficking in Persons Report, the country remains a leader in antitrafficking efforts.

In 2009 a gender-neutral marriage act was passed by Parliament, granting Norwegian same-sex couples identical rights as opposite-sex couples, including on adoption and assisted pregnancies. The Lutheran Church had at year's end failed to develop a liturgy for same-sex weddings, allowing priests to bless unions but not officiate them, reflecting the continued disagreement within the Church on the issue.

Oman

Political Rights Rating: 6
Civil Liberties Rating: 5
Freedom Rating: 5.5
Freedom Status: Not Free
Electoral Democracy: No

Population: 3,983,000
Capital: Muscat

Ten-Year Ratings Timeline For Year Under Review (Political Rights, Civil Liberties, Status)

Year Under Review	2004	2005	2006	2007	2008	2009	2010	2011	2012	2013
Rating	6,5,NF	6,5,NF	6,5,NF	6,5,NF	6,5,NF	6,5,NF	6,5,NF	6,5,NF	6,5,NF	6,5,NF

INTRODUCTION

The Omani government continued its suppression of dissent and free expression in 2013, arresting journalists, activists, and bloggers for making statements deemed unacceptable by the government. Few of the reforms promised by Sultan Qaboos bin Said al-Said following demonstrations in 2011 have been implemented, though most of the activists imprisoned for taking part in the 2011 and 2012 protests had been pardoned and released by July 2013.

POLITICAL RIGHTS: 9 / 40

A. Electoral Process: 2 / 12

Sultan Qaboos bin Said al-Said has ruled Oman since seizing power from his father, Sultan Said bin Taimur, in 1970. The 1996 basic law, promulgated by royal decree, created a bicameral parliament consisting of an appointed Council of State (Majlis al-Dawla) and a wholly elected Consultative Council. Citizens elect the 84-member Consultative Council for four-year terms, but the chamber has no legislative powers and can only recommend changes to new laws. The Consultative Council is part of a bicameral body known as the Council of Oman. The other chamber, the 59-member State Council, is appointed by the sultan, who has absolute power and issues laws by decree. The sultan serves as the country's prime minister; heads the ministries of defense, foreign affairs, and finance; and is the governor of Oman's central bank. In 2003, the sultan decreed universal suffrage for all Omanis over the age of 21. Parliamentary elections have been held twice since, once in 2007 and again in 2011, when Omanis elected 84 members of the new Majlis al-Shura from over 1,100 candidates. Oman held its first ever municipal elections in December 2012. Fifty percent of eligible voters participated, choosing between 1,475 candidates for seats on 192 local councils. Four women won seats in the elections.

B. Political Pluralism and Participation: 2 / 16

Political parties are not permitted, and no meaningful organized political opposition exists.

C. Functioning of Government: 2 / 12

Although corruption has not been perceived to be a serious problem, the issue was a factor in mobilizing protests in 2011 and 2012. Oman's legal code does not possess an effective or cohesive framework for prosecuting corruption, nor does not it include freedom of information provisions. However, after anti-corruption protests in 2011, Sultan Qaboos issued a royal decree mandating the State Financial and Administrative Audit Institution (SFAAI) to increase transparency and efficiency within government ministries, while reducing conflicts of interest. Government officials are required by law to declare their assets and sources of wealth. In August 2013, the SFAAI launched a smart phone application to go along with its social networking site to allow Omanis to report instances of abuse or corruption by government officials. Oman was ranked 61 out of 177 countries surveyed in Transparency International's 2013 Corruption Perceptions Index.

Discretionary Political Rights Question A: 3 / 4

Mechanisms exist for citizens to petition the government through local officials, and certain citizens are afforded limited opportunities to petition the sultan in direct meetings.

CIVIL LIBERTIES: 17 / 60
D. Freedom of Expression and Belief: 5 / 16

Freedom of expression is limited, and criticism of the sultan is prohibited. The 2004 Private Radio and Television Companies Law allows for the establishment of private broadcast media outlets. The government permits private print publications, but many of these accept government subsidies, practice self-censorship, or face punishment for crossing political "red lines." In September 2011, Youssef al-Haj and Ibrahim Ma'mari of the newspaper *Al-Zaman* were convicted of "insulting" the minister of justice and sentenced to five months in prison after reporting in May on allegations of corruption at the ministry. In January 2012, an appeals court upheld the convictions, but suspended their sentences. In August 2013, *The Week*, an English-language weekly newspaper was briefly suspended for publishing an article described as being sympathetic to Oman's gay community. The newspaper subsequently published an apology on its website for running the story; its editor-in-chief, Samir al-Zakwani, is being sued by the government for running the story.

Omanis have access to the internet through the national telecommunications company, and the government censors politically sensitive and pornographic content. The sultan issued a decree in 2008 expanding government oversight and regulation of electronic communications, including on personal blogs. In January 2013, eight Omanis received prison sentences ranging from 12 to 18 months for writings or blog posts that were considered slanderous to the sultan or in violation of cyber laws. Another eight citizens who received prison terms for similar charges had their prison sentences upheld in early 2013 by the Supreme Court. These detainees, however, were among more than 50 activists, writers, and bloggers pardoned by Sultan Qaboos. An additional 14 activists who were serving prison sentences for participating in the 2011 demonstrations in Sohar were pardoned and released on July 22. One of these activists, human-rights blogger Sultan Al-Sa'adi, was arrested again just one week later and charged with insulting the sultan on Twitter. Al-Sa'adi was released from prison on August 20 after being held for 22 days without access to legal representation.

Islam is the state religion. Non-Muslims have the right to worship, though they are banned from proselytizing. Non-Muslim religious organizations must register with the government. The Ministry of Awqaf (Religious Charitable Bequests) and Religious Affairs distributes standardized texts for mosque sermons and expects imams to stay within the outlines of these texts. The government restricts academic freedom by preventing the publication of material on politically sensitive topics.

E. Associational and Organizational Rights: 3 / 12

The right to peaceful assembly within limits is provided for by the basic law. However, all public gatherings require official permission, and the government has the authority to prevent organized public meetings without any appeal process.

After mass protests in 2011 calling for economic and political reforms, the sultan promised new jobs, an increase in social benefits, and measures to address government corruption. After the government was slow to implement the promised economic and political reforms, new protests erupted in 2012, leading to further crackdowns and arrests. By the end of 2012, more than 30 activists, writers, and bloggers had been arrested or detained, though most had been released by July 2013.

In August 2013, demonstrations were held in the town of Liwa to protest industrial pollution emanating from the Port of Sohar. Security forces used tear gas to disperse demonstrators. Among the protesters was Shura Council member Talib al-Mamari.

The basic law allows the formation of nongovernmental organizations, but civic life remains limited. The government has not permitted the establishment of independent human rights organizations and generally uses the registration and licensing process to block the formation of groups that are seen as a threat to stability.

Oman's 2003 labor law allows workers to select a committee to represent their interests but prevents them from organizing unions. Additional labor reforms enacted in 2006 brought a number of improvements, including protections for union activity, collective bargaining, and strikes. However, legal protections for Oman's 1.5 million migrant workers remain inadequate, and domestic servants are particularly vulnerable to abuse. In March 2013, several thousand migrant laborers working on an expansion project of the Muscat Airport went on strike to protest unsafe working conditions after a worker died on the job. The strike ended after one day when the contracting company agreed to improve safety conditions. In September, a four-day strike of over 9,000 foreign workers employed by an Omani construction company ended with the workers receiving higher base pay and improved working conditions. In October, teachers from several hundred schools throughout Oman went on strike demanding the creation of a teacher's union, increased pay and benefits, and improved working conditions. Most teachers went back to work despite their demands not being met.

F. Rule of Law: 4 / 16

The judiciary is not independent and remains subordinate to the sultan and the Ministry of Justice. Sharia (Islamic law) is the source of all legislation, and Sharia Court Departments within the civil court system are responsible for family-law matters, such as divorce and inheritance. In less populated areas, tribal laws and customs are frequently used to adjudicate disputes. The authorities do not regularly follow requirements to obtain court orders to hold suspects in pretrial detention. The penal code contains vague provisions for offenses against national security, and such charges are prosecuted before the State Security Court, which usually holds proceedings that are closed to the public. Prisons are not accessible to independent monitors, but former prisoners report overcrowding.

G. Personal Autonomy and Individual Rights: 5 / 16

The 1996 Basic Law banned discrimination on the basis of sex, religion, ethnicity, and social class. Omani law does not protect noncitizens from discrimination. Foreign workers risk deportation if they abandon their contracts without documentation releasing them from their previous employment agreement. Under these regulations, employers can effectively keep workers from switching jobs and hold them in conditions susceptible to exploitation.

Although the basic law prohibits discrimination on the basis of sex, women suffer from legal and social discrimination. Oman's personal status law, based on Sharia, favors the rights of men over those of women in marriage, divorce, inheritance, and child custody. According to official statistics, women constitute a very small percentage of the total labor force in Oman. Homosexual acts are illegal in Oman. Despite a 2008 antitrafficking law, Oman remains a destination and transit country for the trafficking of women and men.

⬆ Pakistan

Political Rights Rating: 4
Civil Liberties Rating: 5
Freedom Rating: 4.5
Freedom Status: Partly Free
Electoral Democracy: Yes

Population: 190,709,000
Capital: Islamabad

Trend Arrow: Pakistan received an upward trend arrow due to the successful transfer of power between two elected, civilian governments following voting that was deemed relatively free and fair.

Note: The numerical ratings and status listed above do not reflect conditions in Pakistani-controlled Kashmir, which is examined in a separate report.

Ten-Year Ratings Timeline For Year Under Review (Political Rights, Civil Liberties, Status)

Year Under Review	2004	2005	2006	2007	2008	2009	2010	2011	2012	2013
Rating	6,5,NF	6,5,NF	6,5,NF	6,5,NF	4,5,PF	4,5,PF	4,5,PF	4,5,PF	4,5,PF	4,5,PF

INTRODUCTION

In 2013, for the first time in Pakistan's history, a democratically elected government completed its full term and was replaced by another through constitutionally mandated procedures. Elections for the National Assembly (NA)—the lower house of Parliament—and the four provincial assembles took place on May 11. Although the elections featured intimidation and other flaws, they were relatively free, with vigorous competition and a high level of voter participation. The electoral process represented an improvement over previous balloting, having benefited from a number of reforms initiated after the 2008 elections. The outcome of the voting, which resulted in the formation of a national government by the Pakistan Muslim League–Nawaz (PML-N), formerly in opposition, was widely accepted. The new government took power on June 1.

During the year, three other vital state institutions experienced orderly leadership changes. A new president, Mamnoon Hussain, was elected on July 30 and assumed office on September 9, marking the first time an elected president completed his full term and was replaced by another. General Raheel Sharif succeeded two-term army chief General Ashfaq Pervez Kayani on November 29. Tassaduq Hussain Jillani became Pakistan's chief justice, replacing Iftikhar Muhammad Chaudhry on December 12.

Despite a visible strengthening of democratic processes, the country continued to suffer from multiple problems. In the month preceding the general elections, independent observers reported between 130 and 150 incidents of political violence resulting in more than 180 deaths. This intimidation, aimed at various parties and their supporters, skewed the playing field and affected turnout and participation in some areas. Broader violence involving terrorist, insurgent, and sectarian groups killed more than 3,000 people in 2013, with civilians accounting for most of the fatalities.

The new government, led by Prime Minister Nawaz Sharif, announced plans for peace negotiations with the Tehrik-i-Taliban Pakistan (TTP, or Pakistani Taliban) in October. However, the Islamist militant group's commander, Hakimullah Mehsud, was killed on November 1 in an apparent U.S. drone strike, casting doubt on the viability of such a dialogue. Drone strikes remained a source of resentment in many sections of the country. A reported drone attack on a religious seminary in Hangu District, Khyber Pakhtunkhwa (KPK), on November 21 prompted the KPK provincial government to organize a demonstration against the attack and block supply routes used by North Atlantic Treaty Organization (NATO) forces in Afghanistan. A perception persists that U.S. missile strikes encourage reprisal attacks by the TTP and other militants, fueling more unrest in the country.

Structural and societal impediments to freedom persisted, especially in relation to women, and non-Muslim minorities.

POLITICAL RIGHTS: 21 / 40 (+1)

A. Electoral Process: 7 / 12 (+1)

Pakistan consists of four provinces (Balochistan, KPK, Punjab, and Sindh) and two federal territories (the Federally Administered Tribal Areas, or FATA, and the Islamabad Capital Territory).

The Parliament (Majlis-i-Shoora) is bicameral, with a 342-member NA and a 104-member Senate. The latter is intended to provide equal representation to all units of the federation. The constitution envisages a parliamentary system of government headed by a prime minister, to be elected from the NA. An electoral college consisting of the Senate, the NA, and the provincial assemblies elects the president for up to two five-year terms.

Members of the NA are elected for five years. Of the 342 seats, 272 are filled through direct elections in single-member districts, 60 are reserved for women, and 10 are reserved for non-Muslim minorities. The reserved seats are filled through a proportional representation system with closed party lists. The seats for women are allocated in proportion to the number of general seats a party gains in each of the provinces. Parties fill the non-Muslim seats in proportion to the number of seats they win nationwide. The provincial assemblies employ a similar electoral system. The provincial assemblies elect senators for six-year terms, with half of the seats up for election every three years.

The 2013 general elections were held under an improved legal and regulatory framework. After the 2008 elections, three amendments to the constitution were introduced to establish a parliamentary procedure for appointing national and provincial caretaker governments and the leadership of the Election Commission of Pakistan (ECP). These improvements and extensive consultations that the ECP undertook with political parties and civil society in the months preceding the elections led to increased confidence in the neutrality of the relevant institutions.

The ECP also took a number of measures to streamline the election process, including an update of the voter rolls. About 37.2 million names were eliminated from the rolls, and approximately 36.7 million were added. The ECP introduced a service through which citizens could check their registration status, electoral district, and polling station location via mobile-telephone text messages.

Yet a number of weaknesses in the electoral process persisted. The candidacy requirements remained vague and subjective. Potential candidates were rejected on grounds including inadequate knowledge of Islamic teachings or a reputation for "bad" character. Procedural issues related to the counting of results and the lack of a proper dispute-resolution system also continued to undermine the system. The most serious problem was the lack of state capacity to guarantee law and order during the pre-election period. According to a report by the Islamabad-based Pak Institute for Peace Studies (PIPS), 298 people died and 885 were injured in election-related violence between January 1 and May 15.

Despite these concerns, prominent international and domestic election observers judged the elections favorably. 55 percent voter turnout was high in comparison with the last elections. There was active competition and campaigning by the parties and candidates. A number of parties that boycotted the 2008 elections contested in 2013. However, parties identified as secular—the Awami National Party (ANP) in KPK, and the PPP and the Muttahida Quami Movement (MQM) in Sindh—were subjected to intimidation by nonstate actors like the TTP, curtailing their capacity to campaign effectively.

Voters gave a clear mandate to the PML-N to replace the ruling Pakistan People's Party (PPP) at the federal level. The PML-N took 126 of the directly elected seats in the NA, followed by the PPP with 31 and Pakistan Tehreek-e-Insaf (PTI) with 28. Various smaller parties took less than 20 directly elected seats each. The PML-N formed a governing majority with the help of allied independents, and Nawaz Sharif became prime minister.

At the provincial level, the PML-N won in Punjab, the PPP formed a government in Sindh, and a coalition led by the National Party assumed power in Balochistan. In KPK, a PTI-led coalition took office.

B. Political Pluralism and Participation: 9 / 16

Pakistan has a thriving multiparty system. Notwithstanding election-related violence, parties actively campaigned across the country in 2013. Many rallies and processions came under attack, but the campaigning continued. The elections were also highly competitive. An average of 17 candidates contested each NA seat. These were the first elections in which parties could field candidates in the FATA. Party organization in the region was previously forbidden, meaning independents were elected based largely on tribal loyalty.

The success of the PTI, which had boycotted the last elections, demonstrated that the political system is open to the rise of new parties. Nonetheless, parties continue to be characterized by lack of internal democracy and transparency. Most party funds are generated through private, opaque means. Parties usually rely on charismatic leadership by individual personalities or political dynasties. Tribal and community loyalties play a powerful role in determining voters' choices.

Political participation is severely undermined by intimidation from nonstate actors, such as the TTP and associated Islamist militant groups. Baloch insurgents also carried out attacks, killing 14 people and injuring 78. The militant violence affected campaigning especially in KPK, Balochistan, the FATA, and Karachi, the capital of Sindh.

Clashes between political parties are also endemic. During the 2013 elections, according to PIPS, 97 such incidents took place, in which 128 leaders and workers of different political parties were killed. Karachi alone suffered 70 violent incidents of this kind.

Women remain underrepresented in all spheres of the electoral process. Only 44 percent of registered voters in the 2013 electoral rolls were women. According to the European Union observer mission, that translates into nearly 11 million unregistered women. Though the number of women candidates was nearly double the figure from 2008, it still was an abysmal 2.9 percent of the candidates for general seats. The ECP lacked female representation, and less than 2 percent of its staff members were women. Women were stopped from voting by local leaders in many constituencies in the FATA, KPK, and Punjab. Some polling stations for women reported zero turnout.

The participation of non-Muslims in the political system continues to be minimal. Few ran for the general seats in 2013, and only one was elected. Political parties nominate members to the seats reserved for non-Muslim minorities, leaving non-Muslim voters with little say in selecting the parliamentarians who supposedly represent them.

Ahmadis, members of a heterodox Muslim sect, continue to face political discrimination and are registered on a separate voter roll. Ahmadi representatives boycotted the 2013 elections.

C. Functioning of Government: 5 / 12

Three constitutional amendments adopted after the 2008 elections considerably reduced the powers of the indirectly elected president, in part by removing his authority to unilaterally dismiss elected governments. The changes restored the primacy of Parliament in Pakistan's political system. The election of a relatively unknown president in 2013 reflected the diminished stature of the office.

The role of the military in determining government policy also seems to have waned. General Kayani, who stepped down in November, was the longest-serving army chief in Pakistan's history to have never overturned a civilian government. By selecting a relative outsider to replace him, the new prime minister asserted his independence from the military command. In addition, Khawaja Muhammad Asif, once a fierce critic of the army, was appointed as defense minister. The new government's decision to put former military ruler Pervez Musharraf on trial for treason, despite strong sentiment in the army against the move, signaled an attempt to further affirm civilian control.

Notwithstanding these important changes, the military retains considerable autonomy and influence in matters of national security, foreign policy, and some elements of economic policy. The army remains the most powerful institution in the country.

Corruption, lack of accountability, and lack of transparency are pervasive problems at all levels of government, politics, and the military. Pakistan was ranked 127 of 177 countries assessed in Transparency International's 2013 Corruption Perceptions Index. The National Accountability Bureau has made little progress in tackling official graft, due largely to inadequate political will and institutional capacity. High-profile corruption cases against former president Asif Ali Zardari, reopened by the Supreme Court in 2012, are still under way. Procedural delays are a hallmark of such investigations.

CIVIL LIBERTIES: 21 / 60 (-1)
D. Freedom of Expression and Belief: 5 / 16

Pakistan has a vibrant media sector that presents a range of news and opinions. Over the last decade, its reach has extended to a large audience. There are about 90 television channels, 160 radio stations, and 200 daily newspapers. The English-language media primarily target the urban elite, while the Urdu media are read and viewed by the urban middle classes and rural population. The latter outlets are more conservative and sensationalist.

Despite this diverse media landscape, Pakistan is one of the world's most dangerous places for journalists. They are targeted by nonstate actors such as terrorists and criminals, as well as by political, military, and intelligence operatives. In 2013, reports of killings, threats, and kidnappings continued. According to International Federation of Journalists, 10 journalists were killed during the year. An investigative journalist with a leading weekly, the *Friday Times*, was abducted by Karachi police personnel on August 30, and although the incident was widely reported, no action was taken.

Media comes under censorship of both state and nonstate actors regularly. The constitution authorizes the government to curb speech on subjects pertaining to the armed forces, the judiciary, and religion. Blasphemy laws are occasionally used against the media.

During the elections, many media organizations and personalities received threats from the TTP and other militant organizations for failing to publish their unedited anti-election edicts. Media outlets in Karachi were especially affected. In Balochistan, most popular cable channels had to be taken off the air before the elections, due to pressure from the nonstate actors.

In October, the Shura-e-Mujahedeen, a TTP affiliate, reissued a year-old edict against several radio stations and popular political talk-show hosts, accusing them of promoting secular and Western values and spreading anti-Muslim propaganda. The state did not provide an adequate response or protection in these cases.

Online media has grown in reach and popularity in recent years. Pakistanis can use the internet to access foreign and independent news services. Political parties and organizations routinely disseminate their information online. However, access to the internet is subject to restrictions by the government. More than 200,000 websites are banned in the country because of their allegedly anti-Islamic, pornographic, or blasphemous content. Access is also restricted for security reasons. After an anti-Islamic video on YouTube sparked protests across the Muslim world in 2012, the site was blocked, and the blocking remained in place during 2013. In October, the popular online movie database IMDb was blocked without explanation for two days. Mobile telephony is sometimes restricted on security grounds during religious or national holidays.

Pakistan is an Islamic republic. Although the constitution provides for freedom of religion and the protection of minorities, violations by the government as well as nonstate actors are fairly common and rarely punished. 2013 was a particularly bad year for minorities. Bombings targeting Shiites and Christians occurred throughout the year. In January, explosions aimed at the Shiite Hazara minority killed roughly 150 people in Quetta and Swat. Lashkar-e-Jhangvi (LeJ), a Sunni Deobandi terrorist group, claimed responsibility for the Quetta blasts and a series of other attacks on the same community over the following months. In another high-profile incident, suicide attacks on a church in Peshawar killed 86 Christians in September.

Discriminatory legislation, particularly blasphemy laws, exacerbate religious extremism and vigilantism. In March 2013, a crowd burned down a Christian area in Lahore after a resident was accused of blasphemy.

Education is not free of political indoctrination. Pakistan's primary and secondary public schools as well as privately run religious seminaries use textbooks that promote prejudice and intolerance of religious minorities. In colleges and universities, the student wings of political parties and Islamist groups use intimidation to impose their beliefs, including Islamic codes of conduct. In the FATA and KPK, female access to education is under constant threat. In an egregious attack, fourteen female students of Sardar Bahadur Khan Women's University were killed and more than twenty injured in June, when LeJ blew up a bus in Quetta.

A 2013 decision by a Lahore school to teach its students a course on comparative religion came under criticism from both the provincial government and elements in civil society who suspected a conspiracy to convert students to other religions.

E. Associational and Organizational Rights: 6 / 12 (-1)

The constitution guarantees the rights to associate, demonstrate, and organize, but in practice the government often imposes arbitrary restrictions. Such official obstacles were less common during 2013, which featured many large demonstrations and gatherings, including during the election campaign. However, public assemblies were repeatedly targeted by nonstate militant groups during the year, killing hundreds of people.

The authorities generally allow nongovernmental organizations (NGOs) to function, including those that are highly critical of the government. Nevertheless, such groups face a number of challenges when working in violence-prone areas in the FATA, KPK, and Balochistan. Radical Islamist groups frequently threaten and attack NGOs devoted to female education and empowerment. A polio vaccination drive undertaken by international entities like the World Health Organization (WHO) and the UN Children's Fund (UNICEF) has been denounced by the TTP as a Western plot to sterilize Muslims. Over 30 polio workers have been murdered by them since mid-2012. Separately, several charitable and cultural organizations operating from Pakistan have links to Islamist militant groups.

The right of workers to organize and form trade unions is recognized in law. The constitution also grants unions the rights to collective bargaining and to strike. However, many groups are excluded from these protections: teachers, agricultural workers, those associated with the armed forces, state employees other than railway and postal workers, the security staff of airlines and energy companies, public-sector health workers, and workers in export-processing zones. These excluded groups make up approximately 60 percent of the country's workforce employed in the formal sector. The procedures that need to be followed for a strike to be legal are onerous. Nevertheless, strikes are organized regularly. Employers usually respond by harassing and firing workers for union activity. Nearly 70 percent of the workforce is employed in the informal sector and is not represented by unions.

F. Rule of Law: 4 / 16

Pakistan's judiciary consists of a Supreme Court, Provincial High Courts, and other lower courts that exercise civil and criminal jurisdiction. After the 18th and 19th constitutional amendments were adopted in 2010, a judicial commission and a parliamentary committee were established to oversee judicial appointments and reduce the chances of political interference.

Over the last decade, the higher judiciary has become comparatively free of the problems that are endemic in the broader justice system, including corruption, intimidation, a large backlog of cases, and political interference. Under Chief Justice Chaudhry, who retired in December 2013, the higher judiciary took on an activist role, which helped it assert its independence but also caused tensions with the political branches. By the end of the year, with a new democratic government and a new chief justice in place, the relationship between the branches appeared to have become less adversarial.

The 2009 National Judiciary Policy attempted to tackle inefficiency in the lower judiciary. Though its focus on speedy adjudication has reduced the courts' backlog, in many cases the policy has undermined the quality of justice by weakening due process safeguards, including through the use of special venues such as antiterrorism courts.

While the main court system operates on the basis of common law, parallel legal systems employ Sharia (Islamic law) and tribal law. A separate Federal Shariat Court is empowered to determine whether a provision of law goes against Islamic injunctions.

The FATA are governed by the president and federal administration under the Frontier Crimes Regulation (FCR), outside the jurisdiction of the Pakistan Supreme Court and Parliament. The FCR authorizes tribal leaders to administer justice according to Sharia and tribal custom, and despite amendments made to the regulation in 2011, it retains provisions that allow collective punishment of tribes for transgressions by individual members.

The existence of different legal systems results in unequal treatment. Moreover, many communities resort to informal, traditional forms of justice due to the inefficiency of the formal courts, leading to arbitrary and unjust decisions.

The police, the military, and the intelligence services continue to enjoy impunity for indiscriminate or excessive use of force. Extrajudicial killings, enforced disappearances, torture, and other abuses are common. Two ordinances issued in October 2013 expanded the power of law enforcement agencies to engage in detention without trial, electronic surveillance, searches and seizures, and the use of deadly force, ostensibly to combat terrorism and other serious crimes.

Enforced disappearances, particularly in Balochistan, remain a serious problem, highlighted during 2013 by a report from the UN Working Group on Enforced or Involuntary Disappearances, a separate report by the Human Rights Commission of Pakistan, and a 26-day march by families and friends of missing persons from Quetta to Karachi in October. Some victims were suspected of links to radical Islamist groups, and the abductions have also affected Balochi and Sindhi nationalists, journalists, researchers, and social workers.

A number of armed militants belonging to radical Sunni groups, with varying agendas, continued to attack foreign, government, and religious minority targets, as well as aid workers and human rights advocates, killing hundreds of civilians. There was no decline in the sectarian violence between the Sunni and Shiite groups.

Baloch activists continue to seek enhanced political autonomy, or outright independence, and more local control over Balochistan's natural resources. Armed Baloch militants carry out attacks on infrastructure, security forces, and non-Baloch teachers and educational institutions, while the army's counterinsurgency operations have led to increasing human rights violations and the displacement of civilians.

Ethnic violence in the city of Karachi is exacerbated by political rivalry between the traditionally dominant MQM, founded to represent refugees from India who came to Pakistan after 1947; the ANP, representing ethnic Pashtun migrants; and the PPP, which is allied with Baloch gangs. The criminal gangs that carry out much of the violence, regularly extort money from businesses in Karachi, Pakistan's economic hub.

According to the UN refugee agency, Pakistan hosts over 1.6 million registered Afghan refugees. A large number is unregistered. These populations are vulnerable to extortion, illegal detention, and harassment, and they are unable to work legally.

Pakistan has a number of religious, ethnic, and linguistic minorities and other marginalized groups. Multiple forms of discrimination are common. Non-Muslim religious minorities are especially exposed to violent attacks and legal persecution under blasphemy laws. The penal code makes it a criminal offense for Ahmadis to call themselves Muslims "directly or indirectly," to preach or propagate their faith, to outrage Muslims' religious feelings, or to refer to their places of worship as mosques.

Members of Pakistan's transgender and intersex community are authorized to register for official documents under a "third gender" classification recognized by the Supreme Court in 2009. In another ruling in 2011, the court granted them the right to vote, enabling them to participate in the 2013 elections.

Nonetheless, the LGBT (lesbian, gay, bisexual, and transgender) community continues to face societal and legal discrimination. The penal code prescribes prison terms for consensual sex "against the order of nature." Although prosecutions are rare, such laws deter LGBT from acknowledging their orientation or reporting abuses.

G. Personal Autonomy and Individual Rights: 6 / 16

There are few legal limitations on citizens' travel or their choice of residence, employment, or institution of higher learning. One exception affects Ahmadis, who are obliged to deny their faith to obtain a passport. Practical constraints on freedom of movement and related rights are common, ranging from insecurity and corruption to societal taboos. These are more pronounced in the case of women.

Pakistan's rampant corruption, weak regulatory environment, and ineffective legal system undermine property rights and economic freedom. The military controls a disproportionate share of the country's economy. Exploitative forms of labor remain common. Though bonded and child labor are outlawed, they are widespread in practice.

A number of reforms have been enacted in recent years to improve conditions for women. A 2010 law offered protections against workplace harassment, legislation passed in 2011 criminalized various forms of forced marriage, provided specific punishments for acid attacks, and addressed inheritance issues for women. In 2012, the National Commission on the Status of Women was made a permanent body tasked with monitoring implementation of relevant legislation and investigating violations.

The implementation of these laws has been weak, and violence against women continues unabated. In addition to acid attacks, domestic violence, rape, and so-called honor crimes, women face restrictions on voting and education, especially in KPK, the FATA, and Balochistan.

Palau

Political Rights Rating: 1
Civil Liberties Rating: 1
Freedom Rating: 1.0
Freedom Status: Free
Electoral Democracy: Yes

Population: 20,901
Capital: Melekeok

Ten-Year Ratings Timeline For Year Under Review (Political Rights, Civil Liberties, Status)

Year Under Review	2004	2005	2006	2007	2008	2009	2010	2011	2012	2013
Rating	1,1,F	1,1,F	1,1,F	1,1,F	1,1,F	1,1,F	1,1,F	1,1,F	1,1,F	1,1,F

INTRODUCTION

The legal status of gambling remained a controversial issue in Palau in 2013. In May, President Tommy Remengesau rejected a bill that would have legalized casinos, citing a 2011 referendum in which 75 percent of voters rejected legalizing the practice.

In March, Remengesau proposed banning commercial fishing and turning Palau's waters into a marine sanctuary to attract more tourists. A law passed in 2011 allowed for the exploitation of oil and gas resources in Palau's 200-nautical-mile exclusive economic zone.

POLITICAL RIGHTS: 37 / 40

A. Electoral Process: 12 / 12

Palau's bicameral National Congress or Olbiil Era Kelulau consists of the 9-member Senate and the 16-member House of Delegates. Legislators are elected to four-year terms by popular vote, as are the president and vice president. The president may serve only two consecutive terms. In 2012, Remengesau—who served as president from 2001 to 2009—defeated incumbent Johnson Toribiong with 58 percent of the vote. In concurrent parliamentary elections, all candidates ran as independents.

Palau is organized into 16 states, each of which is headed by a governor and has a seat in the House of Delegates. Every state is also allowed its own constitutional convention and to elect a legislature and head of state.

B. Political Pluralism and Participation: 15 / 16

There are no political parties, though no laws prevent their formation. The current system of loose political alliances that can quickly form and dismantle has had a destabilizing effect on governance.

A Compact of Free Association with the United States provides economic assistance in exchange for U.S. military access to the archipelago. In addition, citizens enjoy visa-free travel to the United States and can reside, study, and work there, as well as access to U.S. federal government programs. The compact runs through 2044. Palau's leaders have continued to lobby hard for the ratification of a 2010 financial agreement to increase total U.S. assistance, though the U.S. Congress has claimed its budget deficit is too large to justify further aid.

C. Functioning of Government: 10 / 12

Government corruption and abuse are problems, with several high-ranking public officials having faced charges in recent years. Anti-money laundering measures have been in place since 2007, but the general attorney's office lacks resources to implement them. In August 2013, the House of Delegates adopted a resolution asking the president to review all executive branch positions in order to avoid redundancy. Senate approval is needed for the resolution to take effect.

CIVIL LIBERTIES: 55 / 60
D. Freedom of Expression and Belief: 16 / 16

Freedoms of speech and the press are respected. There are several print publications, five privately owned radio stations, and one privately owned television station. Cable television rebroadcasts U.S. and other foreign programs. Internet access is limited by high cost and lack of connectivity outside the main islands.

Freedom of religion is respected. Although religious organizations are required to register with the government, applications have never been denied. There have been no reports of restrictions on academic freedom, and the government provides well-funded basic education for all. A December 2012 law requires Palauan language instruction in all primary and secondary schools chartered in Palau or receiving public funds.

E. Associational and Organizational Rights: 11 / 12

Freedoms of assembly and association are respected. Many nongovernmental groups represent youth, health, and women's issues. Workers can freely organize unions and bargain collectively. Union membership and activity are low, however, in an economy largely based on subsistence agriculture.

F. Rule of Law: 15 / 16

The judiciary is independent, and trials are generally fair. Palau had its first jury trial in 2012. In June 2013, Senator Hokkons Baules, who had been on probation for assault charges, was sentenced to 30 days in prison for attacking a patient at the Bureau of Behavioral Health with a chair; Baules was reportedly defending himself.

A 300-member police and first-response force maintains internal order. Palau has no military. There have been no reports of prisoner abuse, though overcrowding is a problem. The government announced in August 2013 it would build a new prison outside the capital after an escaped prisoner entered a hotel and robbed and injured a tourist.

In March 2013, Remengesau called on the United States to resettle six Uighur Chinese who had been transferred to Palau in 2009 from the U.S. detention camp in Guantanamo Bay, Cuba. The United States had paid Palau $600,000 to temporarily house the Uighurs; Palau says the funds have been exhausted.

Foreign workers account for about one-third of the population and 75 percent of the workforce. There have been reports of discrimination against and abuse of such workers, who cannot legally change employers once they arrive. In 2009, the government set the total number of foreign workers in the country at any time to 6,000.

In 2011, Palau pledged to end discrimination against gay men and lesbians following a UN audit of human rights. However, Palau continues to maintain laws that criminalize consensual sexual activity between same-sex adults.

G. Personal Autonomy and Individual Rights: 13 / 16

Palauans enjoy freedom of travel, choice of residence, employment and institution of higher learning. There are also no restrictions on property ownership or businesses for Palauans, but bureaucratic red-tape and official corruption are frequent complaints.

Women are highly regarded in this matrilineal society; land rights and familial descent are traced through women. Women are active in the economy and politics. The number of domestic violence and child abuse cases is small. Sexual harassment and rape, including spousal rape, are illegal.

Palau has been cited in multiple annual U.S. State Department Human Trafficking Reports as a destination country for forced prostitution (women) and labor (men and women). In 2012, police investigated several cases of forced labor and offered assistance and housing to victims, but law enforcement in general lacks training and resources to fight human trafficking.

Panama

Political Rights Rating: 2
Civil Liberties Rating: 2
Freedom Rating: 2.0
Freedom Status: Free
Electoral Democracy: Yes

Population: 3,850,000
Capital: Panama City

Ratings Change: Panama's political rights rating declined from 1 to 2 due to concerns that authorities were not investigating allegations of corruption against President Ricardo Martinelli and other officials, as well as verbal attacks against, and the withholding of information from, journalists who write about government corruption.

Ten-Year Ratings Timeline For Year Under Review (Political Rights, Civil Liberties, Status)

Year Under Review	2004	2005	2006	2007	2008	2009	2010	2011	2012	2013
Rating	1,2,F	1,2,F	1,2,F	1,2,F	1,2,F	1,2,F	1,2,F	1,2,F	1,2,F	2,2,F

INTRODUCTION

President Ricardo Martinelli's public approval rating remained high in 2013, even as he and his associates were implicated in numerous corruption scandals. Martinelli's administration continued to pressure journalists, particularly those who reported on the corruption allegations. Meanwhile, authorities displayed a reluctance to thoroughly investigate the charges against the president.

Nongovernmental organizations and others have expressed concern over the increasing militarization of the civilian security forces, following the successful demilitarization of the 1990s. Martinelli has continued to issue pardons for police officers accused of committing acts of violence against civilians, and has expressed firm support for a much-criticized law that keeps officers accused of crimes from being suspended or placed in pretrial detention.

POLITICAL RIGHTS: 35 / 40 (-1)

A. Electoral Process: 12 / 12

The president and deputies of the 71-seat unicameral National Assembly are elected by popular vote for five-year terms. Martinelli, of the center-right, business-oriented Democratic Change (CD) party, won the presidency in 2009 with 60 percent of the vote; he was backed by the Alliance for Change, a four-party coalition that included the CD, the Panameñista Party (PP), the Patriotic Union Party (PUP), and the Nationalist Republican Liberal Movement (MOLIRENA). Elections to the National Assembly were held concurrently, with the Alliance for Change winning 42 seats and the opposition One Country for All alliance, headed by the center-left Democratic Revolutionary Party (PRD), taking 27; the remaining seats went to independent candidates. The elections were considered free and fair by international observers.

The CD's alliance with the PP collapsed in August 2011 when Martinelli announced plans to hold a referendum on proposed electoral reforms, which included allowing consecutive terms in office for the president. However, the referendum was never held, and the current law—which prohibits a president seeking consecutive terms and mandates a two-term waiting period before running again—remains in place.

B. Political Pluralism and Participation: 15 / 16

High levels of electoral competition between political parties and voter participation characterize Panamanian politics. Turnover between government and opposition parties has been the norm since the return to democracy following the 1989 U.S. invasion that removed Manuel Noriega. The country's main political parties spent 2013 jockeying for position ahead of national elections set for May 2014.

On October 8, Panama's Electoral Tribunal prohibited a negative advertising campaign against the PRD's 2014 presidential candidate, Juan Carlos Navarro, ruling that it violated his dignity. The Supreme Court later overruled the Electoral Tribunal's decision, saying the tribunal had violated free speech; the Supreme Court's move drew complaints that it had acted outside of its jurisdiction, as the Electoral Tribunal is supposed to have final say over electoral matters. Additionally, the Supreme Court drew criticism for issuing a ruling by its president and two substitute judges at a time when the two judges assigned to the case were on vacation.

Indigenous groups continue to suffer political, economic, and social discrimination.

C. Functioning of Government: 8 / 12 (-1)

Corruption remains widespread, and electoral reforms have been criticized for failing to improve the transparency of campaign financing. In September 2012, Vice President Juan Carlos Varela of the PP accused officials associated with Martinelli of accepting bribes when signing a $250 million contract to buy helicopters and other equipment from Italy. Italian authorities are still investigating.

Martinelli, his son, and other government officials have also been implicated in the solicitation of bribes from Italian businessman Mauro Velocci and Valter Lavitola, an associate of former Italian prime minister Silvio Berlusconi, in exchange for contracts to build modular prisons and a new Metro system, and to expand the Panama Canal. Velocci in October 2013 confirmed the authenticity of audio recordings of a 2011 conversation—presented as evidence in Lavitola's Italian corruption trial—between himself, Lavitola, and Ricardo Martinelli Linares, President Martinelli's son, about bribery payments. The recordings were made by the Italian authorities and made public in October by leading Panamanian daily newspaper *La Prensa*; the paper's site was blocked for about eight hours after it published the recordings.

Former minister of government and current acting mayor of Panama City, Roxana Méndez, has also been implicated in the bribery scandal. Meanwhile, former PRD presidential candidate Balbina Herrera in October was sentenced to three years in prison, the maximum possible, after she was convicted of illegally disseminating e-mails that purported to show President Martinelli discussing bribes with Lavitola. Martinelli, however, pardoned Herrera days later, calling her an "idiot" who had not recovered from her loss in the 2009 presidential election. Panamanian prosecutors appear reluctant to investigate the bribery allegations.

Panama was ranked 102 out of 177 countries and territories surveyed in Transparency International's 2013 Corruption Perceptions Index.

CIVIL LIBERTIES: 47 / 60 (+1)
D. Freedom of Expression and Belief: 15 / 16

Panama's constitution protects freedom of speech and of the press, but these rights are not consistently upheld in practice. Libel is a criminal offense, though no one has been jailed for it since 2008. Independent or critical journalists and outlets face pressure from the government. In May 2013, Martinelli criticized a local reporter and businessman linked to *La Prensa* after the paper published stories accusing the president of improper ties with several hydroelectric dam contracts. In October, the government ordered its staff not to respond to questions posed by *La Prensa*.

In June, prosecutors issued orders compelling journalists working with the dailies *La Estrella* and *El Siglo* to reveal their sources, after the outlets had published articles raising concerns about government corruption. Prosecutors then attempted, without success, to search computers belonging to *La Estrella,* and separately issued an order allowing a search of *El Siglo*'s offices. The cases against the two papers remained unresolved at the end of 2013. Also in June, Frank LaRue, the UN special rapporteur on freedom of expression, and Catalina Botero, special rapporteur for freedom of expression for the Inter-American Commission on Human Rights, criticized Martinelli's government for illegally conducting surveillance of journalists, and for the detention of journalists. The country's media outlets are privately owned, with the exceptions of the state-owned television network and a network operated by the Roman Catholic Church; Martinelli himself has holdings in the print, radio, and television markets. Internet access is unrestricted.

Freedom of religion is respected, and academic freedom is generally honored. However, police in October arrested members of the Revolutionary Student Front (FER-29) who had participated in an anticorruption protest at the Instituto Nacional, a highly regarded public school. The police reportedly arrested 59 students, several of whom had not participated in protests, and later expelled 29 students without due process under orders from Education Minister Lucy Molinar. Days later, the government reportedly established rules allowing a permanent police presence in public schools.

E. Associational and Organizational Rights: 11 / 12 (+1)

Freedom of assembly is recognized, and nongovernmental organizations are free to operate. Violent clashes between government forces and protesters have taken place in recent years; however, no such incidents were reported in 2013. In 2012, three people were killed and six were injured when government forces clashed with protesters opposed to the sale of state-owned land in the duty-free zone in Colón; the protesters feared that the sale of the land would result in job losses. The government ultimately scrapped the plan. The National Medical Negotiating Committee (Comenenal), nursing unions, health technicians, and other health sector workers held nonviolent strikes in September and October to protest the government's move to recruit foreign doctors. Although only about 10 percent of the labor force is organized, unions are cohesive and powerful.

F. Rule of Law: 9 / 16

The judicial system remains overburdened, inefficient, politicized, and prone to corruption. Panama's Accusatory Penal System became operational in 2011 and is gradually being introduced throughout the country. The new system is intended to reduce congestion in the courts by resolving complaints more efficiently, while lower the number of people held in detention without conviction. The prison system is marked by violent disturbances in decrepit, overcrowded facilities. As of September 2013, the prison system was over capacity by more than 6,500 inmates.

The police and other security forces are poorly disciplined and corrupt. The government's militarization of the Panamanian Public Forces has prompted concern from human rights advocates. Many allegations of criminal activity committed by police officers go uninvestigated. Numerous officers accused of committing abuses against civilians have received presidential pardons. A 2010 law shields officers accused of crimes from pretrial detention and suspension from their positions. Human rights advocates have asked for the repeal of this law, but Martinelli asserted in November that he had no intention of scrapping it. Panama is experimenting with Community Police Units that are modeled on Brazil's Pacifying Police Units. The initial results have been promising.

One suspect has been arrested in connection with the September murder of Panamanian lawyer and PRD delegate Juan Ramon Messina. There are concerns that his shooting might have been politically motivated.

Panama's growing importance as a regional transport center makes it appealing to drug traffickers and money launderers. Intelligence sources claim that the Sinaloa Cartel, the Juarez Cartel, the Zetas, and the Beltran Leyva Organization, all of which are Mexico-based narcotics organizations, operate in Panama. Panamanian authorities over the summer discovered coca fields within the country, as well as laboratories at which coca leaves are processed to extract cocaine. However, drug seizures in Panama have now decreased over three consecutive years. Panama additionally struggles with criminal street gangs; the attorney general in August said there were 201 gangs operating in the country, and that more funding was needed to combat them.

Refugees from Colombia have faced difficulty obtaining work permits and other forms of legal recognition. The Martinelli administration had suggested measures to normalize the status of thousands of undocumented Colombians living in Panama without official refugee status, but minimal progress had been made on these measures. New immigration rules that took effect in 2008 tightened controls on foreigners, but other legislation grants recognized refugees who have lived in Panama for more than 10 years the right to apply for permanent residency.

Discrimination against darker-skinned Panamanians is widespread. The country's Asian, Middle Eastern, and indigenous populations are similarly singled out. While there are no laws prohibiting same-sex sexual relationships, members of the LGBT (lesbian, gay, bisexual, and transgender) face societal discrimination and harassment.

G. Personal Autonomy and Individual Rights: 12 / 16

The government generally respects freedom of internal movement and foreign travel. Indigenous communities enjoy a degree of autonomy and self-government, but some 90 percent of the indigenous population lives in poverty, 69 percent in extreme poverty as of 2012. Since 1993, indigenous groups have protested the encroachment of illegal settlers on their lands, and government delays in formal land demarcations. In July, the UN special rapporteur on the rights of indigenous peoples, James Anaya, called on the Panamanian government to work with indigenous authorities to protect indigenous lands and natural resources according to international standards.

Violence against women, including domestic violence, is widespread and common. In October, Martinelli signed a law to punish femicide—the act of killing a girl or woman— with up to 30 years in prison. Panama is a source, destination, and transit country for human trafficking. The government has worked with the International Labour Organization on information campaigns addressing the issue, and has created a special unit to investigate cases of trafficking for the purpose of prostitution. However, law enforcement is weak, the penal code does not prohibit trafficking for forced labor, and the government provides inadequate assistance to victims.

Papua New Guinea

Political Rights Rating: 3
Civil Liberties Rating: 3
Freedom Rating: 3
Freedom Status: Partly Free
Electoral Democracy: Yes

Population: 7,179,000
Capital: Port Moresby

Ratings Change: Papua New Guinea's political rights rating improved from 4 to 3 due to efforts by Prime Minister Peter O'Neill and his government to address widespread official abuse and corruption, enabling successful prosecutions of several former and current high-ranking officials.

Ten-Year Ratings Timeline For Year Under Review (Political Rights, Civil Liberties, Status)

Year Under Review	2004	2005	2006	2007	2008	2009	2010	2011	2012	2013
Rating	3,3,PF	3,3,PF	3,3,PF	3,3,PF	4,3,PF	4,3,PF	4,3,PF	4,3,PF	4,3,PF	3,3,PF

INTRODUCTION

In February 2013, the government of Papua New Guinea (PNG) government announced plans to substantially build up its military, increasing its troop levels from 1,900 to 10,000. It also announced it would receive $2 million in aid from China to purchase Chinese-made military equipment. Some former government officials have nevertheless expressed doubt that PNG would be able to afford or execute the troop buildup.

Natural-resource exploitation, including mining and logging, provides the bulk of government revenue, but the government has done little to improve infrastructure, education, health, and other indicators of development. High population growth is also a challenge for the country. Prime Minister Peter O'Neill has considered providing interest-free home loans to couples between the ages of 18 and 25 if they delay having children.

POLITICAL RIGHTS: 24 / 40 (+1)
A. Electoral Process: 9 / 12

Voters in PNG elect a unicameral, 109-member National Parliament to serve five-year terms. A limited preferential voting system allows voters to choose up to three preferred candidates on their ballots. The governor-general, who represents Britain's Queen Elizabeth as head of state, formally appoints the prime minister who leads the majority party or coalition in parliament.

In 2012, Peter O'Neill became prime minister when his People's National Congress (PNC) party was victorious in elections held in June and July; O'Neill was in a prolonged battle with former prime minister Michael Somare, who claimed he never legally left the post. The PNC won control of parliament in 2012 with 22 votes; while marred by violence, the elections were generally considered free and fair. O'Neill's government further consolidated its position in 2013, with many lawmakers joining its coalition; by May, the party and its allies held 46 seats in the parliament.

Shifting alliances and frequent use of no-confidence votes have undermined political stability and exacerbated fragmentation in politics. In February 2013, parliament approved O'Neill's proposal for a 30-month grace period in which no-confidence motions could not be held. Lawmakers also unanimously repealed three controversial laws passed during the political impasse between O'Neill and Somare that set an age ceiling for prime ministers and gave more power to the chief executive over the judiciary.

B. Political Pluralism and Participation: 10 / 16

There are numerous political parties but political loyalties are driven more by tribal, linguistic, geographic, and personal ties than party affiliation. Many candidates run as independents and align with parties after they are elected.

C. Functioning of Government: 5 / 12 (+1)

Prime Minister O'Neill has made fighting corruption a top priority and created an organization, Task Force Sweep (TFS), to investigate corruption in PNG. In August, TFS estimated that about $600 million intended for public development projects was lost to corruption in 2013. The organization also reported it had made 59 arrests, including Yori Yei, head of a United Nations agency office in PNG. Yei was accused of misappropriating funds intended for lobbying on PNG's behalf in the UN for his personal use. PNG's Auditor General's Office was also investigated in 2013 for numerous allegations of official abuse. Additionally, 23 members of parliament were investigated in 2014 for failing to comply with campaign finance laws. O'Neill has also proposed the creation of a formal Independent Commission Against Corruption, though parliament had not authorized it by the year's end.

In March, the government announced that China would help it create and implement a national electronic identification system intended to mitigate official abuse and prevent election fraud.

PNG was ranked 144 out of 177 countries surveyed in Transparency International's 2013 Corruption Perceptions Index.

CIVIL LIBERTIES: 36 / 60

D. Freedom of Expression and Belief: 12 / 16

Freedom of speech is generally respected, and the media provide independent coverage of controversial issues such as alleged police abuse, official corruption, and opposition views. However, the government and politicians have occasionally used media laws and libel and defamation lawsuits to limit critical reporting. Internet use is growing, but cost and lack of infrastructure limits its spread outside urban centers.

In July 2013, Anderson Agiru, governor of Hela Province put forth a proposal in parliament to determine whether non-Christian faiths should be banned. Church leaders immediately spoke out against it and there was little support in parliament. Nevertheless, rapid increase in the 5,000-member Muslim community in the predominantly Christian country in recent years has stirred anxiety among some locals.

Academic freedom is generally respected, but the government does not always tolerate criticism. In February 2013, the government ordered that English be used in PNG's schools, replacing the vernacular, also known as lingua franca.

E. Associational and Organizational Rights: 9 / 12

The constitution provides for freedoms of assembly and association, and the government generally observes these rights in practice. Marches and demonstrations require 14 days' notice and police approval. Many civil society groups provide social services and advocate for women's rights, the environment, and other causes. The government recognizes workers' rights to strike, organize, and engage in collective bargaining.

F. Rule of Law: 7 / 16

The judiciary is independent. The legal system is based on English common law. The Supreme Court is the final court of appeal and has jurisdiction on constitutional matters. Laypeople sit on village courts to adjudicate minor offenses under customary and statutory law. Suspects often suffer lengthy detentions and trial delays because of a shortage of trained judicial personnel.

Law enforcement officials have been accused of corruption, unlawful killings, extortion, rape, theft, the sale of firearms, and the use of excessive force in the arrest and interrogation of suspects. Weak governance and law enforcement have allegedly made PNG a base for organized Asian criminal groups. The correctional service is understaffed. Prison breaks are common. In March 2013, 49 escaped prisoners surrendered to authorities after telling the media about harsh prison conditions, including torture and a lack of medical care.

O'Neill's government has attempted to address the prison problems. In February 2013, it demoted 73 police officers for alleged brutality and other offenses, and arrested four correction officers in July for letting prisoners escape.

In May 2013, Australia agreed to provide additional military aid and police training to PNG for the operation of a detention center on Manus Island. The center had been opened in 2012 as part of a deal in which PNG would house refugees seeking asylum status in Australia in exchange for development assistance. In August, PNG signed an agreement to allow detainees to resettle within its borders in exchange for $463 million in development aid. In the weeks that followed, dozens of Iranians, who made up one-third of the detainees at the facility, opted for repatriation to Iran. By year's end, about 1,100 detainees were held in the detention center, the condition of which Amnesty International describes as unacceptable. The PNG government said it will begin processing their refugee claims in early 2014.

Opposition lawmakers have challenged the government's policy on refugees, and provincial governors and other local leaders cautioned hostile reactions from their communities. The government defended the detention policy on the grounds that asylum seekers had effectively consented to being held as a requirement for refugee status determination; it also defended the resettlement agreement, arguing that a new visa—not citizenship—would be offered to those opting to stay in PNG.

A referendum on the future of the Autonomous Bougainville Government (ABG) is scheduled between 2015 and 2020. The area was created following a multi-year, low-grade secessionist war in which landowners on Bougainville Island waged guerrilla attacks on a major Australian-owned copper mine, demanding compensation and profit-sharing. The 2005 treaty that ended the fighting stipulated that an independence referendum be held once

ABG disposed of its weapons and demonstrated self-reliance. Various reports in recent years, however, have found the island to be mired in poverty and corruption.

G. Personal Autonomy and Individual Rights: 8 / 16

Discrimination and violence against women and children are widespread. A 2013 UN survey found 61 percent of the PNG men surveyed reported to have raped someone at least once. Two other studies in 2013 claimed two-thirds of women in PNG are victims of physical or sexual assault and violence, and that nearly all cases went unreported and unpunished.

In May 2013, O'Neill publicly apologized for crimes against women and lawmakers increased penalties for such crimes. The new penalties included 50-year prison sentences with no possibility of parole for kidnapping, and the death penalty was reinstated for armed robbery, murder, and aggravated rape (including gang rape, rape of a child 10 years old and under, and rape involving a weapon). Parliament also repealed the Sorcery Act of 1971, which critics argued gave legitimacy to claims of sorcery and contributed to numerous deaths—particularly of women—each year. Nevertheless, police have been largely ineffective in controlling mob violence, tribal warfare, and other crimes.

In 2011, the government rejected a call by the United Nations to decriminalize homosexuality.

The U.S. State Department's 2013 Human Trafficking Report and rated PNG as a tier three country, in which both local and foreign victims are trafficked for sex work, child labor, and manual labor.

Paraguay

Political Rights Rating: 3
Civil Liberties Rating: 3
Freedom Rating: 3.5
Freedom Status: Partly Free
Electoral Democracy: Yes

Population: 6,797,859
Capital: Asunción

Ten-Year Ratings Timeline For Year Under Review (Political Rights, Civil Liberties, Status)

Year Under Review	2004	2005	2006	2007	2008	2009	2010	2011	2012	2013
Rating	3,3,PF	3,3,PF	3,3,PF	3,3,PF	3,3,PF	3,3,PF	3,3,PF	3,3,PF	3,3,PF	3,3,PF

INTRODUCTION

Horacio Cartes, a tobacco magnate and political newcomer, was elected president on April 21. Cartes's Colorado Party had governed Paraguay for 61 years before losing the presidency in 2008 to Fernando Lugo, who was controversially ousted in 2012. Cartes ran on a platform of change, promising increased investment in ailing public infrastructure as well as an end to official corruption and cronyism. The credibility of this pledge was complicated by the fact that President Cartes has himself been suspected of money laundering and involvement in Paraguay's growing drug trafficking network.

Upon taking office, the new Cartes government initiated a military and publicity offensive against the Paraguayan People's Army (EPP), a nationalist guerilla group that had renewed its activity in 2012. In response to the killing of five security guards in August 2013, allegedly by the EPP, the Senate one week later passed major reforms to the National Defense Law that give the president sweeping powers to deploy the military.

Increased drug trafficking and the growing presence of organized crime undermined public security. The high-profile murder of a well-known cattle farmer in May raised questions about the role of the EPP, possible complicity of the government, and the relative absence of effective state protection from criminal groups operating in Paraguay.

POLITICAL RIGHTS: 26 / 40 (-1)

A. Electoral Process: 10 / 12

The 1992 constitution provides for a president, a vice president, and a bicameral Congress consisting of a 45-member Senate and an 80-member Chamber of Deputies, all elected for five-year terms. The president is elected by a simple majority vote, and reelection is prohibited. Congress is elected by proportional representation. The constitution bans active-duty military from engaging in politics.

While the congressional vote impeaching Lugo in 2012 was technically constitutional, his swift ouster raised questions about the absence of due process. Presidential elections held in April 2013 brought the Colorado Party's Cartes to office with 46 percent of the vote, against 37 percent for his principal opponent, Efraín Alegre of the Partido Liberal Radical Auténtico (PLRA). In concurrent legislative elections, Colorado captured 19 Senate seats and 45 seats in the Chamber of Deputies, while the PLRA won 13 and 26 seats in the respective bodies. Several small parties also hold a handful of seats. The elections were marred by allegations of vote buying.

B. Political Pluralism and Participation: 12 / 16

The system is open to the rise of different political parties, although before President Lugo and the Alianza Patriótica por el Cambio (APC) came to power in 2008, the center-right Colorado Party had ruled Paraguay for over 60 years. The liberal PLRA is the other major political party. Smaller parties with congressional representation include the Patria Querida, the Unión Nacional de Ciudadanos Éticos, and the Partido Encuentro Nacional.

C. Functioning of Government: 4 / 12 (-1)

August reforms to the National Defense Law allow the president to deploy soldiers anywhere in the country at any time, with the sole requirement that the government inform Congress within 48 hours. While Congress can then vote to terminate the operation, human rights organizations and rural social movements condemned the law for diluting congressional oversight. The government argued the law would enable it to respond more effectively to the EPP.

Corruption is embedded in all levels of government. Corruption cases languish for years in the courts without resolution, and corruption often goes unpunished as judges favor the powerful and wealthy. Successive presidential administrations have pledged to increase overall transparency in government and reduce corruption, specifically in the judiciary, but progress has not been forthcoming. Paraguay was ranked 150 out of 177 countries and territories surveyed in Transparency International's 2013 Corruption Perceptions Index.

CIVIL LIBERTIES: 35 / 60

D. Freedom of Expression and Belief: 12 / 16 (+1)

The constitution provides for freedoms of expression and the press, but respect of these rights is significantly compromised in practice. Direct pressure by criminal groups and corrupt authorities lead journalists to censor themselves, especially in remote border areas, and threats against journalists are common. A local radio owner was murdered in February in a department bordering Brazil, and a journalist was shot to death in April in a city also near the border, presumably in connection with his reporting. Organized crime was suspected to be behind both assaults, although no one had been arrested by year's end. There are a number of private television and radio stations and independent newspapers, as well as two state-owned media outlets, *Radio Nacional* and *TV Pública*. Paraguay does not have a right to information law and continues to use defamation laws against the press. The government does not restrict internet use, nor does it censor its content.

The government generally respects freedom of religion. All religious groups are required to register with the Ministry of Education and Culture, but no controls are imposed on these groups, and many informal churches exist. The government does not restrict academic freedom.

E. Associational and Organizational Rights: 8 / 12

The constitution guarantees freedoms of association and assembly, and these rights are respected in practice. There are a number of trade unions, but they are weak and riddled with corruption. The labor code provides for the right to strike and prohibits retribution against strikers, though the government generally has failed to address or prevent employer retaliation. It is common for employers to illegally dismiss strikers and union leaders. According to the International Trade Union Confederation, nearly all collective agreements in the public sector are not recognized due to interference by the secretary for the civil service.

F. Rule of Law: 5 / 16 (-1)

The judiciary is nominally independent but is highly corrupt and subject to external influence. Corruption in the judiciary led to trial delays and extended pretrial detention in 2013. Courts are inefficient, and politicians routinely pressure judges and block investigations. The constitution permits detention without trial until the accused has completed the minimum sentence for the alleged crime. Illegal detention by police and torture during incarceration still occur, particularly in rural areas. Overcrowding, unsanitary conditions, and mistreatment of inmates are serious problems in the country's prisons.

Paraguay is the regional hub for money laundering, drug trafficking, and organized crime. After a six-year lull, the EPP—an armed leftist guerrilla group—renewed its campaign of kidnapping, extortion, and bombing attacks in 2012, continuing into 2013. EPP interests conflict with local farming, and the EPP was suspected in the May murder of a well-known cattle rancher and former mayor.

Another worrisome trend was Brazilian criminal organizations located in Paraguay with the aim of exerting greater control of the drug trade. The lack of security in border areas, particularly in the tri-border region adjacent to Brazil and Argentina, has allowed organized crime groups to engage in money laundering and the smuggling of weapons and narcotics. These gangs also took advantage of Paraguay's harsh geography. The "Red Command," a Brazilian drug-trafficking organization, reportedly exported one ton of cocaine monthly from Paraguay to Brazil in 2013. The EPP has also developed a closer connection with the drug trade.

The constitution provides Paraguay's estimated 108,000 indigenous people with the right to participate in the economic, social, and political life of the country. In practice, however, the indigenous population is unassimilated and neglected. Peasant organizations sometimes occupy land illegally, and landowners often respond with death threats and forced evictions by hired vigilante groups.

G. Personal Autonomy and Individual Rights: 10 / 16

Employment discrimination against women is pervasive. Sexual and domestic abuse of women continues to be a serious problem. Although the government generally prosecutes rape allegations and often obtains convictions, many rapes go unreported because victims fear their attackers or are concerned that the law will not respect their privacy. A 2013 U.S. Department of Labor report on Paraguay commended the Paraguayan government's advancements in combatting the worst forms of child labor, but lamented that children continue to work hazardous jobs in agriculture and domestic service. An estimated 450,000 minors work in Paraguay, according to a 2013 government report.

Same-sex sexual activity is legal, but Paraguay has a constitutional ban against recognition of same-sex relationships. President Cartes was criticized for remarks against human rights for the LGBT community during the election campaign.

Peru

Political Rights Rating: 2
Civil Liberties Rating: 3
Freedom Rating: 2.5
Freedom Status: Free
Electoral Democracy: Yes

Population: 30,475,140
Capital: Lima

Ten-Year Ratings Timeline For Year Under Review (Political Rights, Civil Liberties, Status)

Year Under Review	2004	2005	2006	2007	2008	2009	2010	2011	2012	2013
Rating	2,3,F	2,3,F	2,3,F	2,3,F	2,3,F	2,3,F	2,3,F	2,3,F	2,3,F	2,3,F

INTRODUCTION

President Ollanta Humala's approval rating declined during 2013 as his administration faced political turbulence, including multiple small crises that led to cabinet changes and added to a public perception of policy drift. Polling identified crime as the top source of discontent among Peruvian citizens, and the government's lack of effective action in preventing it—coupled with seemingly dismissive statements—contributed to the resignation of Prime Minister Juan Jiménez in October. Other prominent subjects of political debate included the possible 2016 presidential candidacy of the current first lady, an ongoing controversy over the medical and penal status of imprisoned former president Alberto Fujimori, and corruption investigations focused on the administrations of Humala's predecessors.

In March, Lima mayor Susana Villarán narrowly won a recall referendum led by allies of her predecessor, Luis Castañeda, whose administration Villarán had accused of corruption. Her opponents had pointed to her low poll numbers and accused her of mismanagement and ineffectiveness, but she secured 51 percent of the referendum vote.

In November a new scandal erupted when it was revealed that Óscar López Meneses, a close associate of Fujimori's notorious intelligence chief Vladimiro Montesinos, had been receiving 24-hour police protection. The police and the military engaged in mutual blame, and both Interior Minister Wilfredo Pedraza and presidential security adviser Adrián Villafuerte resigned. The subsequent discovery of a forged document with Humala's signature authorizing the protection brought additional attention to the shadowy links between disgraced former state operatives and their counterparts in active service.

Peru continued to face high levels of social conflict; while individual episodes are often sparked by environmental issues related to extractive industries, the conflicts also involve broader issues of class, inequality, and social marginalization, and are fueled by complex local politics. Nonetheless, protest-related violence declined considerably from 2012, as several of the most intractable disputes remained at a low simmer during the year.

POLITICAL RIGHTS: 30 / 40

A. Electoral Process: 10 / 12

The president and the 130-member, unicameral Congress are elected for five-year terms. Congressional balloting employs an open-list, region-based system of proportional representation, with a 5 percent vote hurdle for a party to enter the legislature.

The 2011 elections, while sharply polarized, were deemed generally free and fair by international observers. However, shortcomings included lack of enforcement of campaign finance norms and pressure on media outlets by powerful economic interests in support of losing presidential candidate Keiko Fujimori, daughter of the former president. With various candidates dividing the center, the leftist Humala and right-wing Fujimori were the top finishers in the April first round. In the runoff in June, Humala won by a margin of three points, 51.5 percent to 48.5 percent.

In the concurrent legislative elections, an alliance led by Humala's Peruvian Nationalist Party (PNP) captured 47 of the 130 seats, followed by Fujimori's Force 2011 grouping with 38 seats and former president Alejandro Toledo's Perú Posible with 21 seats. Two smaller parties, the Alliance for Major Change and the National Solidarity Alliance, secured 12 and 8 seats, respectively, and former president Alan García's Peruvian Aprista Party (APRA) captured just 4 seats. The new president's Peru Wins alliance forged a congressional majority with Perú Posible.

B. Political Pluralism and Participation: 13 / 16

Peruvian parties, while competitive, are both highly fragmented and extremely personalized. First Lady Nadine Heredia has denied any intention of succeeding her husband—which would be unconstitutional under current Peruvian law—but in late December 2013 she took over leadership of the PNP, fueling another round of speculation about her political aspirations.

Regional presidents have become important political actors over the last decade; former San Martín regional president César Villanueva was appointed prime minister in October 2013. Regional and local elections in October 2010 resulted in a moderately increased consolidation of regionally based political movements. The next round of regional elections will occur in October 2014. Despite political decentralization, the concerns of ethnic and cultural minorities, especially in remote mountain or jungle zones, remain inadequately addressed among parties with national scope, which contributes to regular episodes of acute social conflict in the provinces.

C. Functioning of Government: 7 / 12

Corruption is a serious problem. Checks on campaign financing are particularly weak at the local level, where drug traffickers' influence is perceived to have grown in recent years. Peruvians rated corruption as the most negative aspect of García's 2006–2011 presidency, and a congressional commission charged with investigating corruption among García administration officials neared completion of its work at the end of 2013, finding multiple areas of potential legal culpability for García and officials in his government. Perhaps the most prominent example was the alleged sale of presidential pardons, through which scores of convicted narcotics traffickers were released from prison. Meanwhile, a separate congressional commission continued to investigate former president Toledo regarding allegations of corrupt and fraudulent real estate transactions. Some government agencies have made progress on transparency, but much information related to defense and security policies remains secret under a 2012 law. Peru was ranked 83 out of 177 countries and territories surveyed in Transparency International's 2013 Corruption Perceptions Index.

CIVIL LIBERTIES: 41 / 60

D. Freedom of Expression and Belief: 15 / 16

The lively press is for the most part privately owned. Officials and private actors sometimes intimidate or even attack journalists in response to negative coverage. The local press watchdog Institute for Press and Society registered 60 attacks against journalists in 2013. Low pay leaves reporters susceptible to bribery, and media outlets remain dependent on advertising by large retailers. Defamation remains criminalized, and several journalists were convicted and given suspended sentences in 2013, with Áncash regional president César Álvarez proving especially aggressive in the use of legal cases to harass reporters. In August 2013, the El Comercio conglomerate, which already controlled a large swath of the newspaper market, purchased the EPENSA newspaper group, creating a company with a nearly 80 percent market share and sparking an intense debate over ownership concentration. The government does not limit access to the internet.

The constitution provides for freedom of religion, and the government generally respects this right in practice. However, the Roman Catholic Church receives preferential treatment from the state. The government does not restrict academic freedom.

E. Associational and Organizational Rights: 8 / 12

The constitution provides for the right to peaceful assembly, and the authorities uphold this right for the most part. However, the executive branch has issued several decrees in recent years that limit police and military responsibility in the event of injury or death during demonstrations. It has also frequently resorted to declarations of states of emergency and done little to prevent excessive use of force by security personnel when confronting protests. In June 2013 Congress passed a law that formally exempts security force members from responsibility for violence undertaken while "fulfilling their duties."

According to the government, 191 Peruvians died in episodes of social conflict during the García administration, including 38 police and soldiers; several thousand others faced charges for protest-related incidents. At least 24 more protesters were killed by government forces during the first 18 months of Humala's term, but deaths declined to nine in 2013. Analysts frequently observe that the government's approach to local grievances, which often involve environmental issues, typically eschews mediation and early intervention in favor of reactive repression by militarized police units and sometimes military forces. Over 50 community members involved in the 2009 Bagua protests, which left 10 protesters and 23 police officers dead and over 200 people injured, were facing trial in 2013, while very few members of the police or military have faced charges for protest-related incidents in recent years. As of year's end the Constitutional Tribunal (TC) had not yet ruled on the constitutionality of a 2010 law broadening military jurisdiction when the security forces are involved in civilian deaths.

Freedom of association is generally respected, but conservative politicians frequently allege that nongovernmental organizations (NGOs) hinder economic development. Antimining activists, including noted environmental leader Marco Arana, have been subjected to arbitrary arrest or faced questionable legal charges in recent years, while several NGOs have experienced various forms of intimidation.

Peruvian law recognizes the right of workers to organize and bargain collectively. Workers must notify the Ministry of Labor in advance of a strike, with the result that nearly all strikes are categorized as illegal in practice. Less than 10 percent of the formal-sector workforce is unionized. Parallel unionism and criminal infiltration of the construction sector in Lima have led to a series of disputes and murders.

F. Rule of Law: 8 / 16

The judiciary is widely distrusted and prone to corruption scandals. While the TC is relatively independent, its autonomy has undergone a mix of setbacks and advances in recent years. A 2008 Judicial Career Law improved the entry, promotion, and evaluation system for judges, and the judiciary's internal disciplinary body has been highly active. The terms of six of the TC's seven members had expired by the end of 2012, but the process of appointing new justices has been delayed on multiple occasions. In July 2013 Congress agreed to allocate the six TC seats, along with three Central Bank positions and a new ombudsman's office, along partisan lines. The TC appointments were particularly controversial, and thousands of Lima residents protested in response, causing the government to rescind all the appointments and initiate a new process that remained ongoing at year's end.

A majority of inmates are in pretrial detention, and the inmate population is far above the system's intended capacity. Since 2006, an adversarial justice system designed to improve the speed and fairness of judicial proceedings has slowly been implemented. Access to justice, particularly for poor Peruvians, remains problematic, and crime has risen. According to figures from the government's statistical agency, 41 percent of Peruvians reported being the victim of a crime in the first half of 2013. Although the government has formulated various reform plans, implementation has remained slow.

Ten years after the 2003 publication of Peru's Truth and Reconciliation Commission report on the internal conflict against Shining Path guerrillas, which took 69,000 lives in the 1980s and 1990s, rights watchers noted that although justice had been served in significant cases—above all the conviction of Alberto Fujimori for overseeing death-squad killings and two kidnappings—the military continues to place numerous obstacles in the path of investigators regarding past violations. The García government made almost no efforts to prioritize justice for cases of human rights abuses by state actors during the 1980s and 1990s, and the Humala administration has remained similarly passive. Lawyers for accused rights violators have focused in recent years on narrowing the legal definition of crimes against humanity, which under Peru's treaty obligations have no statute of limitations. To the dismay of rights groups, in September 2013 the TC ruled that the government's suppression of a 1986 prison riot, which killed 133 prisoners, could not be considered a crime against humanity. However, rights advocates hailed Humala's decision in June 2013 to deny Fujimori's request for a medical pardon.

Remnants of the Shining Path, which are involved in the drug trade, continue to clash with security forces in the Apurimac-Ene River Valley (VRAE) and Upper Huallaga zones. Coca eradication efforts and economic development programs in other regions have failed to reverse a trend toward increased coca production. However, deaths of security force members declined to three in 2013, from 20 the previous year, and in August the military killed two top Shining Path leaders in the VRAE zone. In 2012, the government sent Congress a bill that would criminalize the denial of terrorism; following complaints about the law's scope, the government submitted a narrower version, which remained under consideration throughout 2013.

G. Personal Autonomy and Individual Rights: 10 / 16

Discrimination against the indigenous population remains pervasive, particularly with regard to land use and property rights. Regulations to implement the 2011 Law of Prior Consultation were issued in April 2012, and the first formal process was completed in 2013. However, the process had yet to be tested in areas where the balance of resource extraction and environmental protection is highly contested, and rights groups worry that the government's need for mining revenue will continue to take precedence over indigenous people's environmental concerns. In October 2013 the Ministry of Culture presented a database of indigenous groups to whom the consultation mechanism would apply, but rights groups questioned both the database's methodology and the government's commitment to real engagement with indigenous groups.

In recent years, women have advanced into leadership roles in various companies and government agencies. Although legal protections have improved, domestic violence is epidemic, with over half of Peruvian women reporting instances of physical or emotional abuse. LGBT (lesbian, gay, bisexual, and transgender) people also face frequent discrimination in Peru. In 2013 a bill to prohibit discrimination on the basis of sexual orientation failed in Congress, and repeated attempts to introduce a bill legalizing same-sex civil unions have been unable to gain legislative traction.

Forced labor, including child labor, persists in the gold-mining region of the Amazon.

Philippines

Political Rights Rating: 3
Civil Liberties Rating: 3
Freedom Rating: 3.0
Freedom Status: Partly Free
Electoral Democracy: Yes

Population: 96,209,000
Capital: Manila

Ten-Year Ratings Timeline For Year Under Review (Political Rights, Civil Liberties, Status)

Year Under Review	2004	2005	2006	2007	2008	2009	2010	2011	2012	2013
Rating	2,3,F	3,3,PF	3,3,PF	4,3,PF	4,3,PF	4,3,PF	3,3,PF	3,3,PF	3,3,PF	3,3,PF

INTRODUCTION

Two sets of elections—congressional, provincial, and municipal polls in May and barangay (local district) council voting in October—took place in relatively peaceful conditions in 2013, though isolated incidents of election-related violence were reported. The congressional midterm elections gave President Benigno Aquino a rare majority in the Senate. The results also perpetuated the country's political dynasties, as former president Gloria Macapagal Arroyo, under hospital arrest for her alleged involvement in several graft scandals, retained her seat in the lower house, and former president Joseph Estrada, who was ousted for corruption in 2001, won the Manila mayoral race.

Corruption and state plunder, long-standing concerns in the Philippines, remained in the spotlight in 2013 as new instances of malfeasance were exposed. The state audit agency confirmed the organized abuse of Congress's Priority Development Assistance Funds (PDAF), which had originally been revealed by a local newspaper. Over 38 lawmakers and other officials were implicated for their alleged role for, among other things, creating bogus nongovernmental organizations (NGOs) to siphon off funds for fabricated development projects over several years, robbing the state of over $23 million. Investigation was ongoing at year's end. In November, the Supreme Court declared the fund unconstitutional and halted all usage of PDAF funds, including those remaining in the budget, as well as the president's discretionary "social" funds.

Negotiations continued between the Moro Islamic Liberation Front (MILF) and the government on a proposed peace deal that would lead to the disarming of the MILF and its entry into politics. Splinter elements of the rival Moro National Liberation Front (MNLF), which concluded a separate peace agreement with the government in 1996, argued that the terms of the MILF deal abrogated their own pact. The rogue militants declared independence in Zamboanga City and engaged in a 20-day confrontation with the Philippine army in September, resulting in over 200 deaths and the displacement of tens of thousands of people. The leader of the attack was at large at year's end. Separately, on December 8, the government and MILF signed an agreement over power sharing arrangements in a new self-governed region, Bangsamoro, in the region of Mindanao.

A long-running dispute with Malaysia over the region of Sabah in northern Borneo erupted into violence in February, when about 200 fighters loyal to a claimant to the Philippines' historical Sultanate of Sulu invaded the territory. The attack was not sanctioned by the Philippine government. The Malaysian army quelled the incursion, and both sides suffered causalities. The self-proclaimed sultan died in October of natural causes. Separately, the Philippines' relations with Taiwan suffered after the Philippine coast guard killed a Taiwanese fisherman in May.

On November 8, category 5 super-typhoon Haiyan ("Yolanda") hit the Philippines. One of the strongest hurricanes on record it resulted in over 6000 deaths, 14 million affected, 4 million displaced, and approximately $8.5 billion in damages.

POLITICAL RIGHTS: 26 / 40

A. Electoral Process: 9 / 12

Elections in the Philippines, while open and competitive, are typically marred by fraud, intimidation, and political violence, including assassinations by rival candidates, though conditions have improved in recent years. The country has a presidential system of government, with the directly elected president limited to a single six-year term. The national legislature, Congress, is bicameral. The 24 members of the Senate are elected on a nationwide ballot and serve six-year terms, with half of the seats up for election every three years. The 291 members of the House of Representatives serve three-year terms, with 233 elected in single-member constituencies and the remainder elected by party list. In April 2013, the Supreme Court ruled that the party-list system, traditionally meant to represent marginalized or underrepresented groups, could also be open to other groups, including national political parties, provided that they do not stand in the single-member constituency contests. Critics of the decision warned that it would allow the wealthy and powerful to gain more congressional seats at the expense of marginalized groups. Evidence suggests that a number of party-list groups gained seats in 2013 not from national sectoral votes as intended but by substantial support from single geographic regions. In October, the Philippines held village-level, "Barangay" elections, which were largely peaceful.

The Commission on Elections (Comelec) is appointed by the president, and with the president's permission it has the authority to unseat military, police, and government officials. Comelec was widely discredited by a 2005 audiotape scandal regarding cheating in the 2004 elections, but during the 2010 balloting and again in 2013, the commission was deemed to have improved its performance, due in part to the introduction in 2010 of optical-scan voting machines. Detainees were permitted to vote for the first time in 2010, and registration requirements for the approximately 900,000 overseas voters were eased in 2013. Another significant improvement dating to 2010 was the reduction in political violence, aided by restrictions on firearms for 30 days before elections and 15 days after. Appointments or promotions in government offices were also banned in the period surrounding elections. Election-related violence is typically tied to local rivalries and clan competition. In 2013, there were approximately 80 election-related deaths, a reduction from the 130 reported in

2010. Other persistent problems included media bias, which tended to favor wealthier candidates, and vote buying.

As the 2013 elections approached, people with election-day duties, including teachers who served as poll workers, raised concerns about their potential disenfranchisement. In 2010, approximately 300,000 polling-station workers were unable to vote. In response, in February Comelec passed new regulations on absentee voting, which enabled government workers, journalists, police officers, and military personnel who are assigned to work outside of their voting district or who must work on election day to vote for national offices in advance.

At the congressional level, a coalition led by Aquino's Liberal Party (LP) ultimately took 9 of the 12 contested Senate seats, giving the president's allies a total of 13 seats in the upper house (though his own party has only 4 seats). The remainder went to a coalition led by Estrada, United Nationalist Alliance (UNA). The LP also captured 110 seats in the lower house, followed by three allied parties with a combined 44 seats, giving the administration a clear majority in that chamber as well.

B. Political Pluralism and Participation: 10 / 16

Political parties typically have weak ideological identities. Their legislative coalitions are exceptionally fluid, and members of Congress often change party affiliation.

The persistence of political dynasties in politics and society is an ongoing concern. Distribution of power is strongly affected by kinship networks, as is the pattern of leadership. For example, Imelda Marcos, the wife of former authoritarian president Ferdinand Marcos, remains a member of Congress; her daughter is a governor, and her son is a senator. Former president Arroyo, herself the daughter of a president, also sits in Congress, while former president Estrada is now the mayor of Manila, and his son is a senator. Current president Aquino, the son of a former president, heads his own political dynasty. Each of these clans has a strong regional power base in the country, and draws on the support of other regional political families. The nature of election-related funding contributes to the concentration of power, with most candidates receiving support from a small number of donors. Almost half of the funds for the 2013 Senate campaigns came from under 4 percent (90) of the total donors.

The Roman Catholic Church in the Philippines has historically played a significant role in politics, especially related to issues such as corruption and family matters. In 2013, several dioceses publicly opposed the reelection of specific senators and House members who voted in support of the 2012 Responsible Parenthood and Reproductive Health Act (RH Law), which provided for free contraceptives at government health clinics. In the past, church leaders had merely described the attributes of a worthy candidate.

C. Functioning of Government: 7 / 12

President Aquino came to power in 2010 on a reform agenda and has made some progress on open and democratic governance. Since 2010, local governments have been required to post procurement and budget data on their websites, and beginning in 2012, the national government began participatory budgeting at various levels.

However, corruption and cronyism are rife in business and government. A few dozen leading families continue to hold an outsized share of land, corporate wealth, and political power. Local bosses often control their respective areas, limiting accountability and encouraging abuses of power.

High-level corruption also abounds, as indicated in the Commission on Audit's August 2013 report on PDAF abuses by members of Congress. All lawmakers receive annual budgets from the PDAF account, which they can direct to local development projects. While they had long been suspected of siphoning off funds, the scale and organized nature of the corruption was not previously known. Criminal cases against the 38 lawmakers and others implicated in the wake of the audit report were pending at year's end. In November, the Supreme Court found the PDAF to be unconstitutional, and halted the use of the funds as well as curbed the use of other funds such as the president's "special" fund. This is expected to change the power dynamic, giving the Executive greater control, as Congress members can no longer depend on special funds to secure support from their regions. Separately, in October, former president Arroyo was charged along with former cabinet officials and some 20 others for allegedly diverting funds from a discretionary presidential fund intended for victims of storms in 2009. Arroyo has been under hospital arrest since October 2012 based on charges related to the misuse of state lottery funds. She is implicated in several other corruption cases stemming from her tenure as president. Also in 2013, the Supreme Court blocked what was seen as a lenient plea bargain deal in a long-running case against former major general Carlos Garcia, who was accused along with his family of plundering nearly $7 million in state assets.

A culture of impunity, stemming in part from case backlogs in the judicial system, hampers the fight against corruption. The new ombudsman, installed in 2012, has focused on major cases with senior government officials and those involving large sums of money. However, cases take an average of six to seven years to be resolved in the Sandiganbayan anticorruption court. The country's official anticorruption agencies, the Office of the Ombudsman and the Presidential Anti-Graft Commission (PAGC), have mixed records. Many observers maintain that the former was compromised under the Arroyo administration, as convictions declined, while the PAGC lacks enforcement capabilities. The Philippines was ranked 94 out of 177 countries surveyed in Transparency International's 2013 Corruption Perceptions Index.

CIVIL LIBERTIES: 37 / 60
D. Freedom of Expression and Belief: 14 / 16

The constitution provides for freedoms of expression and the press. The private media are vibrant and outspoken, although content often consists more of innuendo and sensationalism than substantive investigative reporting. The country's many state-owned television and radio stations cover controversial topics and are willing to criticize the government, but they too lack strict journalistic ethics. While the censorship board has broad powers to edit or ban content, government censorship is generally not a serious problem in practice. The internet is widely available and uncensored.

Potential legal obstacles to press freedom include Executive Order 608, which established a National Security Clearance System to protect classified information, and the Human Security Act, which allows journalists to be wiretapped based on mere suspicion of involvement in terrorism. Libel is a criminal offense, and libel cases have been used frequently to quiet criticism of public officials. In September 2013, after a nine-year trial, Stella Estremera, the editor in chief of a local newspaper, was convicted along with her publisher of criminal libel for printing the name of a suspect who had already been mentioned in a publicly accessible police report. They were ordered to pay about $4,500 in fines and damages. Despite persistent lobbying by press freedom groups, Congress has yet to pass a draft Freedom of Information Act, which remained stalled in the lower house at the end of 2013. However, the controversial 2012 Cybercrime Prevention Act remains suspended pending a review of its constitutionality. In May 2013, the government said it would remove provisions that extended criminal libel rules to online content, though the law would still allow authorities to block websites and monitor traffic data without a court order, and would remove provisions that extended libel rules to those who copy or reprint libelous content (i.e., not the original author).

The Philippines remains one of the most dangerous places in the world for journalists to work, and impunity for crimes against them is the norm. The trial for alleged perpetrators of the 2009 Maguindanao massacre, in which 58 civilians—including 32 journalists—were killed to stop the registration of a local political candidate, continued in 2013. Although it was transferred to Manila to prevent local interference and has moved forward with unusual speed, the trial has featured a number of problems, including witness intimidation, flawed forensic investigations, and the fact that only 104 of the 196 suspects have been arraigned, and only 108 arrested. The Committee to Protect Journalists (CPJ) reported nine journalists killed in 2013, with a connection to the victims' reporting confirmed in three of the cases. Three journalists were killed in Mindanao in December alone. CPJ ranked the Philippines as the third-worst country in the world on its 2013 impunity index, with dozens of unresolved murder cases over the past decade.

Freedom of religion is guaranteed under the constitution and generally respected in practice. While church and state are separate, the Roman Catholic Church exerts political influence. The population is mostly Christian, with a Catholic majority. The Muslim minority is concentrated on the southern island of Mindanao and, according to the most recent census, represents about 5 percent of the total population. Perceptions of relative socioeconomic deprivation and political disenfranchisement, and resentment toward Christian settlement in traditionally Muslim areas, have played a central role in Muslim separatist movements. An obscure article of the penal code criminalizes acts that "offend religious feelings." The law was used for the first time in January 2013 to convict Carlos Celdran for protesting against the Catholic Church's opposition to the draft RH Law during a religious ceremony in 2010. While he faced a sentence of up to 13 months in jail, he remained free on bail pending appeal.

Academic freedom is generally respected in the Philippines. Professors and other teachers can lecture and publish freely.

E. Associational and Organizational Rights: 8 / 12

Citizen activism is robust, and demonstrations are common. However, permits are required for rallies, and antigovernment protests are often dispersed. The Philippines has many active human rights, social welfare, and other nongovernmental groups, as well as lawyers' and business associations. Various labor rights and farmers' organizations that are dedicated to ending extrajudicial killings and helping families of the disappeared face serious threats, and their offices are occasionally raided.

Trade unions are independent and may align with international groups. However, in order to register, a union must represent at least 20 percent of a given bargaining unit. Moreover, large firms are stepping up the use of contract workers, who are prohibited from joining unions. Only about 5 percent of the labor force is unionized. Collective bargaining is common, and strikes may be called, though unions must provide notice and obtain majority approval from their members. Violence against labor leaders remains a problem and has been part of the broader trend of extrajudicial killings over the last decade.

F. Rule of Law: 5 / 16

Judicial independence has traditionally been strong, particularly with respect to the Supreme Court. However, the efforts of the judiciary are stymied by inefficiency, low pay, intimidation, corruption, and high vacancy rates, which contribute to excessive delays and a backlog of more than 600,000 cases. In total, almost 24 percent of positions remain unfilled, according to the Supreme Court. The judiciary receives less than 1 percent of the national budget, and judges and lawyers often depend on local power holders for basic resources and salaries, leading to compromised verdicts. At least 12 judges have been killed since 1999, but there have been no convictions for the attacks.

Arbitrary detention, disappearances, kidnappings, and abuse of suspects continue to be reported. The police and military have been implicated in corruption, extortion, the torture of detainees, extrajudicial killings, and involvement in local rackets. In September 2013, a group of 13 police officers were charged with ambushing and murdering 13 people at a checkpoint in Atimonan in January as part of an illegal gambling turf war. In December, indigenous rights activist Rolen Langala was killed, allegedly by members of the local council for his work on land rights with regard to an oil palm plantation. The lack of effective witness protection has been a key obstacle to investigations against members of the security forces. Especially problematic is the fact that the Department of Justice oversees both the witness-protection program and the entity that serves as counsel to the military, leading to conflict of interest. Similarly, the Philippine National Police, tasked with investigating murders of journalists, falls under the jurisdiction of the military. Convictions for extrajudicial killings are extremely rare, and no military personnel were found guilty during Arroyo's presidency. At the end of 2012, Aquino signed a new law criminalizing enforced disappearances.

Firearms are common and poorly regulated, with estimates that 60 percent of guns are registered with fictitious data. In June the president signed a law that provides comprehensive rules for the possession, manufacture, and sale of guns and ammunition. In addition, a gun ban was in effect during both the national and Barangay elections in 2013, which is believed to have reduced the instance of electoral violence. Convictions for extrajudicial killings by non-state actors, often by so-called "death squads," are extremely rare. The Commission on Human Rights launched independent investigations into death squads in 2009 and noted that many witnesses and advocates fear for their safety if they testify, which impedes efforts to hold perpetrators accountable and to deter future cases. Kidnappings for ransom remains common in the south, perpetrated in large part by the militant group Abu Sayyaf. In May 2013, at least seven marines were killed trying to rescue six foreign and Filipino hostages from Abu Sayyaf. In March, an Australian who had been held for 15 months was released.

The Muslim separatist conflict has caused severe hardship for many of the 15 million inhabitants of Mindanao and nearby islands, and has resulted in more than 120,000 deaths since it erupted in 1972. Both government and rebel forces have committed summary killings and other human rights abuses. Several peace deals have fallen through as a result of the failure to effectively disarm, demobilize, and reintegrate former rebels. The MNLF and the government signed a peace deal in 1996, but the government has not implemented core provisions or has backpedaled on others. The MILF, which split from the MNLF in 1978, continued to fight after the 1996 deal. It reached a framework peace agreement with the government in October 2012, and has since been engaged in negotiations on a final deal. The agreement is perceived to supersede the original MNLF pact and would redistribute power in the south, creating a new autonomous entity, Bangsamoro, to replace the current Autonomous Region in Muslim Mindanao (ARMM). In response, Nur Misuari, the founder of the MNLF and former governor of the ARMM, led an MNLF splinter group that raised an independence flag in Zamboanga City on September 8, 2013. The group engaged in a violent standoff with the army that lasted for 20 days and resulted in over 200 deaths, the destruction of 10,000 homes, and the displacement of 60,000 people. Misuari and his fighters were charged with rebellion, but he remained at large at year's end. Meanwhile, the MILF negotiations continued with a signed agreement on December 8 on the power-sharing arrangement in Bangsamoro region. The various agreements provide the MILF with authority over the

Bangsomoro region by 2016, including control over the region's taxes (national taxes will still be controlled by Manila), 75 percent of mining revenues, and 50 percent of oil and gas revenues. It will be led by an elected assembly of 50 representatives who will elect a chief minister to run the regional government. The agreement also provides the right to Bangsamoro government to develop customary laws, including sharia courts. The MILF would decommission its military units and reform as a political group.

In the north, the government has been engaged in peace negotiations with the New People's Army (NPA), the militarized wing of the Communist Party. A possible peace deal made progress in 2011, but was stalled in 2012 and 2013, and deadly clashes between the NPA and the Philippine army resumed.

National law does not prohibit discrimination based on sexual orientation or gender identity, though some local protections are in place. LGBT (lesbian, gay, bisexual, and transgender) people reportedly face bias in employment, education, and other services. Indigenous rights are generally upheld, but indigenous activists regularly come into conflict over land disputes and local development projects. Rolen Langala (abovementioned) and Dexter Condez were both publicly murdered in 2013, allegedly related to land disputes. Cases against the perpetrators were still under investigation at year's end. The government's longstanding effort to end dispute over the Muslim southern region of Mindanao bore fruit this year with large advances in a final comprehensive peace agreement.

G. Personal Autonomy and Individual Rights: 10 / 16

Outside of conflict zones, citizens enjoy freedom of travel and choice of residence. Private business activity is subject to the support of local power brokers in a complex patronage system that extends through the country's social, political, and economic spheres.

Women have made many social and economic gains in recent years. The UN Development Programme notes that the Philippines is one of the few countries in Asia to have significantly closed the gender gap in the areas of health and education. Although more women than men now enter high schools and universities, women face some discrimination in private-sector employment, and those in Mindanao enjoy considerably fewer rights in practice. Divorce is illegal in the Philippines, though annulments are allowed under specified circumstances. A 2009 law known informally as the Magna Carta of Women included provisions calling for women to fill half of third-level government positions, requiring that each barangay has a "violence against women desk," and recognizing women's rights as human rights. Despite these measures, enforcement has been uneven. Violence against women continues to be a problem. Results from the National Statistics Office show that the number of cases of violence against women reported in 2012 was the highest since 1997, representing a 23 percent increase over the 2011 figure.

The landmark RH Law, signed in late 2012, provides state funding for contraceptives in public clinics, reproductive health care, and sex education in schools. Among other benefits, the law was expected to help reduce the growing transmission rate of HIV/AIDS. However, implementation was suspended in early 2013 pending a Supreme Court review of its constitutionality, and a ruling had yet to be issued at year's end.

The Philippines is a source country for human trafficking, which is a growing problem, though the president signed a stricter law on human trafficking in February 2013. The country's various insurgent groups have been accused of using child soldiers. In a bid to end economic exploitation of household workers, Aquino in January signed a Domestic Workers Act—under debate for 16 years—that entitles such workers to minimum wages, paid leave, and insurance, among other protections.

Poland

Political Rights Rating: 1
Civil Liberties Rating: 1
Freedom Rating: 1.0
Freedom Status: Free
Electoral Democracy: Yes

Population: 38,517,000
Capital: Warsaw

Ten-Year Ratings Timeline For Year Under Review (Political Rights, Civil Liberties, Status)

Year Under Review	2004	2005	2006	2007	2008	2009	2010	2011	2012	2013
Rating	1,1,F	1,1,F	1,1,F	1,1,F	1,1,F	1,1,F	1,1,F	1,1,F	1,1,F	1,1,F

INTRODUCTION

Although President Bronisław Komorowski remained Poland's most trusted politician in 2013, support for the ruling Civic Platform (PO) party, with which the president is affiliated, dwindled throughout the year, as did support for the government of second-term prime minister Donald Tusk. Supporters of Poland's two largest political parties—Tusk's center-right PO and former prime minister Jarosław Kaczyński's conservative Law and Justice (PiS) party—remained extremely polarized. In August, a conservative faction within the PO made an unsuccessful attempt to oust Tusk from his position as party leader. Amid growing public dissatisfaction with the ruling PO as well as the turmoil within it, PiS distanced itself somewhat from conspiracy theories associated with the death of President Lech Kaczyński and 95 other passengers in a 2010 plane crash. Instead, the opposition focused on PO's alleged mismanagement of the country's economy, which grew 1.6 percent in 2013 (compared with 1.9 percent in 2012).

Following public backlash against last year's pension reforms, which raised the minimum retirement age, the Tusk government appeared reluctant to initiate other long-awaited changes for most of 2013.

In September, the government announced plans to transfer a portion of private pension funds to the state, allowing the government to offset public debt. Critics of the resulting draft law equated it with the outright nationalization of private assets, a view backed in a legal opinion issued in late October by the State Treasury Solicitor's Office. The Polish central bank raised concern about the reforms' "legal risk" in remarks issued around the same time, but added that an overhaul of the pension system was needed. President Komorowski signed the new system into law on December 27 but announced simultaneously that he would refer the legality of the changes to the Constitutional Tribunal for review.

Poland continues to display the highest level of enthusiasm for European Union (EU) membership of all the Visegrad Group countries. (The Visegrad Group is comprised of the Czech Republic, Hungary, Poland and Slovakia, all of which have agreed to cooperate on various EU-backed reforms.) A 2013 poll showed that 78 percent of Polish respondents believe their country has benefited from EU accession, compared to 60 percent of Slovaks, 44 percent of Hungarians, and 43 percent of Czechs.

POLITICAL RIGHTS: 38 / 40
A. Electoral Process: 12 / 12

Voters elect the president for up to two five-year terms and members of the bicameral National Assembly for four-year terms. The president's appointment of the prime minister must be confirmed by the 460-seat Sejm, the National Assembly's lower house, which is elected by proportional representation. While the prime minister is responsible for most government policy, Poland's president also has influence, particularly over defense and foreign policy matters. The 100 Senate (upper house) members can delay and amend legislation but have few other powers.

Sejm speaker Bronisław Komorowski of PO became interim president following the deaths of President Lech Kaczyński of PiS and 95 other passengers in an April 2010 plane crash in Smolensk, Russia. Komorowski was then elected president in a poll held that June and July, winning 53 percent of the vote in the second round. Komorowski's presidency has seen increasing polarization between supporters of Jarosław Kaczyński's conservative PiS and Tusk's center-right PO.

In October 2011 elections to the lower house of parliament, the PO won 207 seats, followed by the PiS with 157. The liberal Palikot Movement captured 40 seats, the Polish People's Party (PSL) took 28, and the Democratic Left Alliance (SLD) won 27. A representative of the ethnic German minority held the remaining seat. In the Senate, the PO took 63 seats, the PiS won 31, the PSL received 2 seats, and the remainder went to independents. Prime Minister Tusk was reelected in October 2011, becoming the first head of government in postcommunist Poland to win a second consecutive term.

B. Political Pluralism and Participation: 16 / 16

Poland's political parties organize and operate freely. Following the collapse of Soviet hegemony in 1989, political power in Poland shifted in the 1990s between political parties rooted in the Solidarity movement and those with communist origins. The center-right PO party suffered several defections during 2013, including that of Jarosław Gowin, who had made an unsuccessful bid to replace Tusk as PO party leader in August. Gowin left PO altogether in September, after the government announced its controversial plan to offset public debt by transferring a portion of private pension funds to the state. Prime Minister Tusk had already removed Gowin from his position as minister of justice in April, apparently in response to Gowin's outspoken criticism of the party leadership's liberal stance on civil partnerships and in-vitro fertilization (IVF). In October, a referendum to remove Prime Minister Tusk's close ally, Warsaw mayor Hanna Gronkiewicz-Waltz, failed due to low voter turnout, but was nevertheless interpreted as an expression of growing dissatisfaction with the Tusk government.

Ethnic, religious, and other minority groups enjoy full political rights and electoral opportunities.

C. Functioning of Government: 10 / 12

Anticorruption laws are not always effectively implemented, and corruption within the government remains a notable problem, particularly in public procurement. In August, Polish prosecutors levied criminal charges against seven people, including three government officials, for allegedly accepting bribes in exchange for licenses for shale gas exploitation and exploration. Later in the year, a vote-buying scandal erupted when the Polish edition of *Newsweek* released recordings of two PO lawmakers apparently offering party officials employment at state-owned enterprises in return for supporting candidate Jacek Protasiewicz in a close, October 26 contest for the regional party leadership of Lower Silesia. The MPs allegedly involved have had their party membership rights suspended for three months while the matter is investigated. Poland was ranked 38 out of 177 countries and territories surveyed in Transparency International's 2013 Corruption Perceptions Index.

CIVIL LIBERTIES: 55 / 60

D. Freedom of Expression and Belief: 16 / 16

The constitution guarantees freedom of expression and forbids censorship. Libel remains a criminal offense, though a 2009 amendment to the criminal code eased possible penalties. In January 2013, an appeals court reduced the 2012 community service sentence and reversed the defamation charges levied against website creator Robert Frycz for satirizing President Komorowski online.

Article 18, section 1 of the Broadcasting Act prohibits programs or broadcasts that promote "actions contrary to law and Poland's *raison d'Etat* or propagate attitudes and beliefs contrary to the moral values and social interest." In July 2013, Poland's Supreme Court upheld a fine of 471,000 zloty (€108,500) against the television station TVN, which in 2008 broadcast guests on Kuba Wojewódzki's talk show placing miniature Polish flags in dog excrement—a reference to a controversial joke one of the guests, a well-known satirical cartoonist, had made two years earlier about street pollution. Supreme Court Judge Maciej Pacuda noted that freedom of expression is subject to limitations, pointing to laws that protect Poland's flag and national anthem.

Poland's print media are diverse and mostly privately owned. The dominant state-owned Polish Television and Polish Radio face growing competition from private domestic and foreign outlets. When the PO-controlled National Broadcasting Council (KRRiT) in 2012 refused a digital broadcasting license to TV Trwam, an ultraconservative TV station linked to PO's major political rival, PiS, PiS supporters protested, and the Constitutional Court later that year ruled to license TV Trwam through 2022. There are four spots available on the digital "multiplex" MUX-1, one of which is to go to Trwam when it is released by TVP before late April 2014.

A May 2012 court ruling found that the Central Anti-Corruption Bureau (CBA) had violated journalist Bogdan Wróblewski's privacy rights by monitoring his phone records between 2005 and 2007. Wróblewski was one of ten journalists considered critical of a previous, PiS-led coalition government whose phone records were monitored during that time. The CBA appealed the first-instance judgment in 2012, but the appeal was rejected in April 2013 and the agency was compelled to publish a formal apology to Wróblewski on the second page of three national newspapers.

The government does not restrict internet access.

The state respects freedom of religion. Religious groups are not required to register with the authorities but receive tax benefits if they do. In 2012, the 2011 acquittal of death-metal singer Adam Darski on charges of "offending religious feelings" was brought before the Supreme Court, which ruled that October that a person may be found guilty of blasphemy, a crime punishable by up to two years in prison, even if it was unintentional. In 2013, Darski's case was re-examined by a district court, and he was acquitted in June. Academic freedom in Poland is generally respected.

E. Associational and Organizational Rights: 12 / 12

Freedom of association is generally respected in law and in practice. Residents of Poland hold public demonstrations with some regularity. September 2013 saw some of the largest rallies in recent years as trade unions organized several days of marches against the government's recent changes in labor policy. The protesters also rejected the government's plan to offset public debt by transferring a portion of private pension funds to the state. Demonstrators additionally demanded higher wages, greater job security, health-care guarantees and retirement benefits, and a reversal of the 2012 decision to raise the retirement age to 67 for both men and women. A controversial amendment passed in October 2012 grants local authorities increased discretion to limit demonstrations in their districts, allegedly to maintain public order.

Nongovernmental organizations operate without government interference. Poland has a robust labor movement, though certain groups—including the self-employed and private contractors—may not join unions. Complicated legal procedures hinder workers' ability to strike, and labor leaders have complained of harassment by employers.

F. Rule of Law: 13 / 16

The judiciary is independent, but the courts are notorious for delays in adjudicating cases. Prosecutors' slow action on corruption investigations have prompted concerns that they are subject to political pressure. Pretrial detention periods can be lengthy, and prison conditions are poor by European standards.

Marcin Plichta, the founder of Amber Gold, an unregulated Polish lender and investment company that collapsed in August 2012, taking with it the holdings of nearly 11,000 investors, faces a sentence of up to 15 years if convicted of running a pyramid scheme. Plichta's wife, Katarzyna Plichta, is accused of being a co-conspirator and faces a possible 12-year sentence. An early 2013 investigative report by the Financial Supervision Authority (KNF) accused public institutions—including regional prosecutors in Gdańsk, where Amber Gold was based, the CBA, and the Office for Competition and Consumer Protection—of contributing to the Amber Gold debacle by ignoring KNF warnings over the course of several years. In June, Witold Niesiołowski was acquitted of disciplinary charges for alleged mishandling of Amber Gold when he was the regional prosecutor general for Gdańsk–Wrzeszcz.

Ethnic minorities generally enjoy generous legal rights and protections, including funding for bilingual education and publications. They also receive privileged representation in the parliament, as their political parties are not subject to the minimum vote threshold of 5 percent to achieve representation. Some groups, particularly the Roma, experience employment and housing discrimination, racially motivated insults, and, sometimes, physical attacks. Members of the LGBT (lesbian, gay, bisexual, transgender) community continue to face discrimination, though the first openly gay and transgender lawmakers entered the Sejm in November 2011.

G. Personal Autonomy and Individual Rights: 14 / 16

Citizens enjoy freedom of travel and choice of residence, employment, and institution of higher education. In global test score rankings of 15-year-olds published by the Organization for Economic Cooperation and Development in December 2013, Poland earned spots in the top 10 in reading (10) and science (9), and ranked highly in math (14).

Citizens have the right to own property and establish private businesses. Approximately two-thirds of GDP comes from the private sector.

Women hold senior positions in government and the private sector, including 24 percent of the seats in the Sejm. Poland's abortion laws are among the strictest in Europe. Women who undergo illegal abortions do not face criminal charges, but those who assist in the procedures—including medical staff—can face up to three years in prison. Domestic violence against women remains a serious concern, as does trafficking in women and girls for the purpose of prostitution.

Portugal

Political Rights Rating: 1
Civil Liberties Rating: 1
Freedom Rating: 1.0
Freedom Status: Free
Electoral Democracy: Yes

Population: 10,460,000
Capital: Lisbon

Ten-Year Ratings Timeline For Year Under Review (Political Rights, Civil Liberties, Status)

Year Under Review	2004	2005	2006	2007	2008	2009	2010	2011	2012	2013
Rating	1,1,F	1,1,F	1,1,F	1,1,F	1,1,F	1,1,F	1,1,F	1,1,F	1,1,F	1,1,F

INTRODUCTION

Portugal has been gripped by financial woes since the start of the European economic recession in the late 2000s. In 2012, after a year of protests and strikes against budget cuts and austerity measures, a challenge to the 2013 budget was filed with the Constitutional Court. In April 2013, the court ruled that four out of nine austerity measures were unconstitutional.

As unemployment rose as high as 18 percent and the government implemented pay cuts and tax hikes, protests and strikes continued throughout the year. A particularly large protest in October drew tens of thousands of people after the government unveiled its 2014 budget proposal, which included the harshest pay cuts and tax hikes the country has seen in nearly 40 years. In October, the European Union and International Monetary Fund approved steps taken by Portugal after a series of bailout reviews. The bailout was due to expire in mid-2014.

The Social Democratic Party (PPD/PSD) took a major hit in local elections in September 2013, as voters expressed frustration with government austerity measures and the country's continued grim financial situation. The Socialist Party (PS) won 36.7 percent of the vote while the PPD/PSD took just 18.9 percent. The PS now holds approximately 130 municipalities, compared to just 90 for the PPD/PSD.

POLITICAL RIGHTS: 39 / 40

A. Electoral Process: 12 / 12

The 230 members of the unicameral legislature, the Assembly of the Republic, are elected every four years using a system of proportional representation. The president can serve up to two five-year terms; while the position is largely ceremonial, the president can delay legislation through a veto, dissolve the assembly to trigger early elections, and declare war as the commander-in-chief of the armed forces. The legislature nominates the prime minister, who is then confirmed by the president. The constitution was amended in 1997 to allow Portuguese citizens living abroad to vote in presidential and legislative elections, as well as national referendums.

Early legislative elections were held in June 2011 after the PS government's fourth austerity budget proposal was rejected by all five opposition parties. The PPD/PSD rose to power with 108 seats and 40 percent of the vote, compared to the PS's 74 seats (29 percent). PPD/PSD leader Pedro Passos Coelho formed a coalition government with the Democratic Social Center/Popular Party (CDS/PP), which won 24 seats. The Unitarian Democratic Coalition (composed of the Portuguese Communist Party and the Greens) holds 16 seats and the progressive Left Bloc won 8.

Aníbal Cavaco Silva, a center-right candidate who had served as prime minister from 1985 to 1995, won the 2006 presidential election; he was reelected in January 2011.

B. Political Pluralism and Participation: 16 / 16

Political parties operate freely. The main political parties are the center-left PS, the center-right PPD/PSD, and the Christian-democratic CDS/PP. The 2011 elections saw a change of power from the PS to the PPD/PSD. The autonomous regions of Azores and Madeira—two island groups in the Atlantic—have their own political structures with legislative and executive powers.

C. Functioning of Government: 11 / 12

A 2009 police operation exposed companies engaged in illicitly obtaining industrial waste contracts. More than 30 people were charged with graft, money laundering, and influence peddling, including a number of officials linked to the PS. Their trials, which opened in 2011, continued throughout 2013, though no one had been prosecuted by the end of the year.

In June 2013, the Organisation for Economic Co-operation and Development (OECD) expressed concern over Portugal's reluctance to crack down on foreign bribary, particularly in regard to its relationship to its former colonies—Brazil, Angola, and Mozambique. Since joining an anti-bribery convention in 2001, Portugal had uncovered only 15 bribery allegations, none of which resulted in a prosecution. Furthermore, a Portuguese investigation into money laundering allegations involving Angola resulted in a media campaign against Portugal in an Angolan state-owned newspaper, including threats of economic retaliation.

In 2012, Transparency International released a report recommending that Portugal change its process for choosing a prosecutor general to allow for greater autonomy and less government influence. Portugal was ranked 33 out of 177 countries surveyed in Transparency International's 2013 Corruption Perceptions Index.

CIVIL LIBERTIES: 58 / 60

D. Freedom of Expression and Belief: 16 / 16

Freedom of the press is constitutionally guaranteed, and laws against insulting the government or armed forces are rarely enforced. In 2012, Portugal's national news agency, Lusa, went on strike for four days after it was announced that the government planned to cut its budget by more than 30 percent. However, in September 2013, government minister Miguel Poiares Maduro announced that funding for both Lusa and Rádio e Televisão de Portugal (RTP) would be maintained. Poorly funded public broadcasting channels already face serious competition from commercial television outlets. Internet access is not restricted.

In March 2013, the Committee to Protect Journalists expressed concern over Angola's increased influence over Portuguese media. In particular, powerful Angolans hold shares in the Newshold media group, which controls *Sol*—Portugal's third largest weekly—two major magazines, a tabloid, and a business paper. There have also been repercussions for journalists who critique Angola, creating an air of self-censorship. One RTP program was cancelled after an employee linked to the program accused the government of positively portraying the Angolan regime. The dire financial situation in Portugal is exacerbating the situation, as Angolan investments have become increasingly important to the Portuguese economy.

Although Portugal is overwhelmingly Roman Catholic, the constitution guarantees freedom of religion and forbids religious discrimination. The Religious Freedom Act provides benefits for religions that have been established in the country for at least 30 years (or recognized internationally for at least 60 years), including tax exemptions, legal recognition of marriage and other rites, and respect for traditional holidays. Academic freedom is respected.

E. Associational and Organizational Rights: 12 / 12

Freedoms of assembly and association are honored, and national and international nongovernmental organizations, including human rights groups, operate in the country without interference. Workers enjoy the right to organize, bargain collectively, and strike. However, a 2003 labor law mandated that workers assess a proposed strike's impact on citizens, and provide minimal services during such an event. Only 19 percent of the workforce is unionized. Thousands of people in 2013 participated in public protests and strikes amid high unemployment and other economic struggles. A strike paralyzed Lisbon and Porto in June 2013 when the General Confederation of the Portuguese Workers and the General Union of Workers shut down key public services, including transportation. The strike was only the fourth time in 25 years that these unions joined forces to mobilize their over 1 million members. On November 27, the government adopted a 2014 austerity budget despite massive protests the day before during which protestors stormed government buildings. On November 28, the head of Portugal's Public Safety Police after what was possibly the largest public safety protest in the country's history in Lisbon over potential cuts in the 2014 budget.

In August 2012 a new Labor Code went into effect including changes to the right of collective bargaining. However, in September 2013 a constitutional court ruled that 3 of the new provisions were unconstitutional.

F. Rule of Law: 15 / 16

The constitution provides for an independent judiciary, though staff shortages and inefficiency have contributed to a considerable backlog of pending trials. Human rights groups have expressed concern over unlawful police shootings and deaths in custody.

A 2012 investigation of Portugal's prisons and detention centers by the Council of Europe's Committee for the Prevention of Torture (CPT) found many cases of alleged ill-treatment of prisoners, including physical assaults, failure to give prisoners access to lawyers and inform them of their rights, poor conditions in detention cells, steadily increasing prison populations and overcrowding, lack of programmed activities to reduce extended confinement, long periods of solitary confinement, accommodation of juveniles with adults, and inadequate numbers of staff. A CPT follow-up visit in May 2013 found little improvement.

The constitution guarantees equal treatment under the law. The government has taken a number of steps to combat racism, including passing antidiscrimination laws and launching initiatives to promote the integration of immigrants and Roma. A 2007 immigration law facilitates family reunification and legalization for immigrants in specific circumstances. According to a 2008 study by the Observatory for Immigration, immigrants pay excessively high taxes, though little revenue is channeled to projects that benefit them directly. In September 2012, a new immigration law went into effect that more closely aligns with EU migration policy, including extending temporary visas and imposing higher penalties for employers who hire staff that are in the country illegally.

G. Personal Autonomy and Individual Rights: 15 / 16

Domestic violence against women and children remains a problem, and few domestic violence cases are prosecuted. Portugal is a destination and transit point for trafficked persons, particularly women from Eastern Europe and former Portuguese colonies in South America and Africa. Portugal legalized same-sex marriage in 2010.

Qatar

Political Rights Rating: 6
Civil Liberties Rating: 5
Freedom Rating: 5.5
Freedom Status: Not Free
Electoral Democracy: No

Population: 2,169,000
Capital: Doha

Ten-Year Ratings Timeline For Year Under Review (Political Rights, Civil Liberties, Status)

Year Under Review	2004	2005	2006	2007	2008	2009	2010	2011	2012	2013
Rating	6,5,NF	6,5,NF	6,5,NF	6,5,NF	6,5,NF	6,5,NF	6,5,NF	6,5,NF	6,5,NF	6,5,NF

INTRODUCTION

Qatar underwent a peaceful transition of power in June when Sheikh Hamad bin Khalifa al-Thani abdicated in favor of his 33-year-old son, Sheikh Tamim bin Hamad al-Thani. Maintaining an assertive foreign policy in the region, Qatar provided financial and material support to factions of the Syrian rebels attempting to remove Bashar al-Assad from power. Qatar also provided financial support to the Muslim Brotherhood–led government of Egypt until it was overthrown in June.

Large numbers of migrant workers have reportedly been subjected to slave-like conditions, which have received increased attention in the run-up to the 2022 football World Cup being held in Doha.

POLITICAL RIGHTS: 10 / 40
A. Electoral Process: 2 / 12

The head of state is the emir, whose family holds a monopoly on political power. The emir appoints the prime minister and cabinet, as well as an heir-apparent after consulting with the ruling family and other notables. In June 2013, Hamad abdicated, handing over power to his fourth-born son, 33-year-old Tamim bin Hamad bin Khalifa al-Thani. Sheikh Abdullah bin Nasser bin Khalifa al-Thani, the former head of state security, became prime minister as well as interior minister.

The constitution stipulates that 30 of the 45 seats of the parliament, the Advisory Council (Majlis Al-Shura), be filled through elections every four years; the emir appoints the other 15 members. However, elections for the Advisory Council have yet to take place, so all members are currently appointed. Elections scheduled to take place in 2013 were postponed due to the transfer of power to Tamim. The Advisory Council does not currently have the power to propose legislation, only to propose changes.

The country held its first elections in 1999 for a 29-member Central Municipal Council, a body designed to advise the minister on municipal affairs and agriculture. Its members serve four-year terms. In the most recent Municipal Council elections, held in May 2011, 4 of the 101 candidates were women; only one, who was running for reelection, won a seat. Voter turnout was 43 percent, with just 13,606 registered voters participating. In addition, Qataris voted in a 2003 referendum that overwhelmingly approved the country's first constitution, which came into force in 2005. The new constitution slightly broadened the scope of political participation without eliminating the ruling family's monopoly on power. Only a small percentage of the country's population is permitted to vote in those elections that do take place, or to hold office.

B. Political Pluralism and Participation: 2 / 16

The government does not permit the existence of political parties. The system is dominated by the ruling family.

C. Functioning of Government: 3 / 12

Critics continue to complain of a lack of transparency in government procurement, which favors personal connections. Official information is very tightly controlled. However, Qatar was ranked 28 out of 177 countries surveyed in Transparency International's 2013 Corruption Perceptions Index.

Discretionary Political Rights Question A: -3 / 0

Citizens can petition elected local government representatives with limited powers over municipal services; these representatives report to the appointed minister of municipal affairs and agriculture.

CIVIL LIBERTIES: 18 / 60
D. Freedom of Expression and Belief: 8 / 16

Although the constitution guarantees freedom of expression, both print and broadcast media content are influenced by leading families. The top five daily newspapers are privately owned, but their owners and boards include members of the ruling family. In 1996, Hamad permitted the creation of Al-Jazeera, which has achieved global reach. Although it is privately held, the government has reportedly paid for the channel's operating costs since its inception. As a result, Al-Jazeera generally does not cover Qatari politics. All journalists in Qatar practice a high degree of self-censorship and face possible jail sentences for slander. In October 2013, a 15-year prison sentence was upheld for poet Mohamed Ibn al-Dheeb al-Ajami, who was convicted in 2012 for insulting the emir through his poetry. Local news outlets were reportedly ordered by a Qatari court to refrain from covering the 2013 trial of two members of the royal family convicted for 19 deaths in a 2012 shopping mall fire.

In 2012, the Advisory Council approved a draft media law that would prevent journalists from being detained by authorities without a court order, and would allow them to protect their sources unless required to reveal them by a court. However, it also would impose fines of up to $275,000 for publishing or broadcasting material that criticizes the Qatari regime or its allies, insults the ruling family, or damages national interests. While state censorship is supposedly forbidden under the law, journalists would be required to obtain licenses and would be monitored by the Ministry of Arts, Heritage, and Culture. The draft law was still under consideration in 2013. In May, Qatar's government endorsed a new cyber law that would place greater restrictions on content posted on social media and news websites. Under the proposed law, any content spreading "false news" or undermining "general order" would be prohibited and the poster subject to arrest and prosecution. The law was still awaiting the emir's approval at year's end. Qataris currently have access to the internet, but the government censors content and blocks access to sites that are deemed pornographic or politically sensitive.

Islam is Qatar's official religion, though the constitution explicitly provides for freedom of worship. The Ministry of Islamic Affairs regulates clerical matters and the construction of mosques. Several churches have been built for Qatar's Christian community. The constitution guarantees freedom of opinion and academic research, but scholars often practice self-censorship on politically sensitive topics. Several foreign universities have established branches in Qatar under a program to strengthen Qatar's educational institutions.

E. Associational and Organizational Rights: 2 / 12

While the constitution grants freedoms of assembly and association, these rights are limited in practice. Protests are rare, with the government restricting the public's ability to organize demonstrations. However, in December 2012, the government permitted a 300-person demonstration calling for Arab leadership on climate change and for improved migrant worker rights. All nongovernmental organizations need state permission to operate, and the government closely monitors their activities. There are no independent human rights organizations, but a government-appointed National Human Rights Committee, which includes members of civil society and government ministries, investigates alleged abuses.

A 2005 labor law expanded some worker protections, but it restricts the right to form unions and to strike. The only trade union allowed to operate is the General Union of Workers of Qatar, which prohibits the membership of noncitizens or government-sector employees.

F. Rule of Law: 4 / 16

Despite constitutional guarantees, the judiciary is not independent in practice. The majority of Qatar's judges are foreign nationals who are appointed and removed by the emir. The judicial system consists of Sharia (Islamic law) courts, which have jurisdiction over a narrow range of issues including family law, and civil law courts, which have jurisdiction over criminal, commercial, and civil cases. Although the constitution protects individuals from arbitrary arrest and detention and bans torture, a 2002 law allows the suspension of these guarantees for the "protection of society." The law empowers the minister of the interior to detain a defendant for crimes related to national security on the recommendation of the director-general of public security.

In June 2013, two members of the ruling family—Sheikh Ali bin Jassim al-Thani and his wife, Iman al-Kuwari—along with three others were found guilty of negligence and faced prison sentences of up to six years in connection with a 2012 fire in a Doha shopping mall that killed 19 people, including 13 children in a daycare center they owned. The daycare center lacked proper safety features such as emergency exits.

The Penal Code punishes homosexual acts with imprisonment, and Sharia law, which applies only to Muslims, prohibits any sexual acts outside of marriage. Same-sex relationships must be hidden in public.

G. Personal Autonomy and Individual Rights: 4 / 16

The constitution treats women as full and equal persons, and discrimination based on gender is banned. The new emir appointed one female minister, for communication and information technology; she is the third-ever female minister. In 2006, Qatar implemented a codified family law, which regulates issues such as inheritance, child custody, marriage, and divorce. While this law offers more protections for women than they previously enjoyed, women continue to face disadvantages, including societal discrimination, and few effective legal mechanisms are available for them to contest incidents of bias.

Domestic violence is not criminalized and is prevalent. The Qatar Foundation for Child and Woman Protection (QFCWP) has noted a significant increase in cases of violence since 2004. The 2011–2016 National Development Strategy includes measures to better protect victims of abuse, including laws against domestic violence, increased legal protections for victims, and robust social support services. In July, the government reorganized a handful of social services organizations, including the QFPWC putting them under the purview of the Qatar Foundation for Social Work. The QFPWC operated a shelter for abused women and worked to coordinate with the public prosecutor's office to better facilitate charges against those suspected of domestic abuse. However, it is unclear if any domestic abuse charges were ever filed. Qatar is a destination for the trafficking of men and women, particularly for forced labor and prostitution.

While the constitution prohibits discrimination based on nationality, the government discriminates against noncitizens in the areas of education, housing, healthcare, and other services that are offered free of charge to citizens. Foreign nationals comprise 88 percent of the country's population and over 90 percent of the workforce, and most rights do not apply to noncitizen residents. Many foreign workers face economic abuses, including the withholding of salaries or contract manipulation, while others endure poor living conditions and excessive work hours. However, fear of job loss and deportation often prevents them from exercising their limited rights. Female domestic workers are particularly vulnerable to abuse and exploitation. In order to support infrastructure projects in preparation for the 2022 World Cup, Qatar is expected to import over 1.5 million migrant laborers. Human rights groups have documented unbearable working conditions, including withholding of wages, lack of food, water, and sanitation, and deaths.

Romania

Political Rights Rating: 2
Civil Liberties Rating: 2
Freedom Rating: 2.0
Freedom Status: Free
Electoral Democracy: Yes

Population: 21,269,000
Capital: Bucharest

Ten-Year Ratings Timeline For Year Under Review (Political Rights, Civil Liberties, Status)

Year Under Review	2004	2005	2006	2007	2008	2009	2010	2011	2012	2013
Rating	3,2,F	2,2,F	2,2,F	2,2,F	2,2,F	2,2,F	2,2,F	2,2,F	2,2,F	2,2,F

INTRODUCTION

Prime Minister Victor Ponta of the Social Democratic Party (PSD) continued his cohabitation with right-leaning president Traian Băsescu in 2013, though their relationship remained scarred by Ponta's attempt to have Băsescu removed in an impeachment referendum in July 2012.

The ruling Social Liberal Union (USL)—a coalition of the PSD, the National Liberal Party (PNL), and the small Conservative Party (PC)—in February announced the creation of a commission to draft amendments to the constitution, which were expected to be put to a referendum in late 2014. Planned revisions included a reduction of the president's powers, possible changes to the parliamentary electoral system, and a reorganization of the country's administrative divisions.

The government in 2013 struggled to implement economic plans such as the overhaul and privatization of indebted state-owned enterprises and a long-delayed mining project known as Roşia Montană. In late August, the government sent legislation to Parliament that would allow the controversial gold-mining project, led by a Canadian company, to move forward, setting off protests by environmentalists, academics, and local residents. By year's end the effort to activate Roşia Montană had suffered a series of defeats in Parliament.

POLITICAL RIGHTS: 35 / 40 (+3)
A. Electoral Process: 12 / 12 (+2)

The president is directly elected for up to two five-year terms and appoints the prime minister with the approval of Parliament. Members of the bicameral Parliament, consisting of the 176-seat Senate and 412-seat Chamber of Deputies, are elected for four-year terms. Elections since 1991 have been considered generally free and fair.

The presidential impeachment crisis of 2012 featured a number of legally dubious maneuvers by the USL government. Băsescu was temporarily suspended, and Senate president Crin Antonescu of the PNL served as acting president for several weeks. Băsescu resumed his post that August, after the Constitutional Court affirmed that the previous month's impeachment referendum had failed due to low turnout. The next presidential election is scheduled for November 2014; Băsescu is barred from running due to term limits.

In the December 2012 parliamentary elections, the USL took 273 of 412 seats in the lower house and 122 of 176 seats in the Senate. The opposition Democratic Liberal Party (PDL) and its Right Romania Alliance placed a distant second with 56 lower house seats and 24 Senate seats, followed by the People's Party–Dan Diaconescu with 47 and 21, the Democratic Union of Hungarians in Romania (UDMR) with 18 and 9, and various national minority representatives with a total of 18 seats in the lower house. The elections received a generally positive assessment from international observers, and enabled a return to normal political order in 2013.

B. Political Pluralism and Participation: 14 / 16

Romania's unfettered multiparty system features vigorous competition between rival blocs, and no single force has been able to dominate both the executive and legislative branches in recent years. However, some parties display little ideological consistency and tend to seek coalitions that will advance their leaders' personal or business interests. A splinter faction of the opposition PDL formed a new center-right party, the Popular Movement, in July 2013. Some PDL members and Băsescu had expressed frustration with Vasile Blaga's reelection as PDL leader at a party congress in March.

The constitution grants one lower house seat to each national minority whose representative party or organization fails to win any seats under the normal rules, and 18 such seats were allotted in 2012. The UDMR has long represented ethnic Hungarians, and in 2013 it lobbied for the creation of an autonomous region for the minority's Szekler subgroup. Political participation and representation of Roma are weak, though two Romany candidates with the USL and one representing a national minority party won seats in Parliament in 2012.

C. Functioning of Government: 9 / 12 (+1)

Romania, which joined the European Union (EU) in 2007, has struggled to meet the bloc's anticorruption requirements. In May 2013, a new National Anticorruption Directorate (DNA) chief was sworn in after a reported compromise on the post between Ponta and Băsescu. The director and two deputies were selected without an open application process.

Although political resistance and parliamentary immunity remained key obstacles in 2013, the year featured a number of new charges and successful convictions against high-ranking officials, including cabinet ministers and members of Parliament. Among several other cases, in July, Transport Minister Relu Fenechiu of the PNL was sentenced to five years in prison for illegally selling used electrical equipment as new to a state-owned enterprise through a firm he controlled. He was reportedly the first cabinet minister to be convicted of corruption while in office. He immediately lost his post, but remained a member of Parliament at year's end, pending an appeal. In September 2013, Senator Antonie Solomon was sentenced to three years in prison for taking a bribe from a businessman while mayor of Craiova. Also that month, PC founder and media mogul Dan Voiculescu was sentenced to five years in prison on fraud and corruption charges, having already resigned as a senator.

Economy Minister Varujan Vosganian of the PNL resigned in October due to accusations that he had harmed national interests by granting a special gas-pricing deal to an indebted chemical company, though the Senate rejected anticorruption officials' request to prosecute him. Also that month, Deputy Prime Minister Liviu Dragnea—the former PSD secretary general—and 74 local officials were charged with attempting to falsify the results of the 2012 impeachment referendum in a bid to ensure Băsescu's removal, but Dragnea denied the charges and refused to step down. Ponta accused Băsescu of manipulating the case against Dragnea, and the prosecutor who prepared it was reportedly removed from office.

Former prime minister Adrian Năstase, who was sentenced to two years in prison in January 2012 for misappropriating state funds for his 2004 presidential campaign, was released early for good behavior in March 2013.

In December 2013, the lower house passed a bill that would exempt many national and local elected officials, including the president and Parliament members, from most corruption charges in the criminal code. The measure was under review by the Constitutional Court at year's end. Romania was ranked 69 out of 177 countries and territories surveyed in Transparency International's 2013 Corruption Perceptions Index.

CIVIL LIBERTIES: 49 / 60
D. Freedom of Expression and Belief: 14 / 16

The constitution protects freedom of the press, and the media have been characterized by considerable pluralism. However, poor economic conditions have led some foreign media companies to sell their Romanian assets, leaving a larger share of important outlets in the hands of wealthy Romanian businessmen, who typically use them to advance their political and economic interests. Many outlets have also been forced to close, cut staff, or change to more entertainment-based formats. Financially hobbled public media remain dependent on the state budget and vulnerable to political influence. A Constitutional Court ruling in April 2013 created new ambiguity on defamation, raising the possibility that it could be treated as a criminal offense. In December the Chamber of Deputies passed a bill that would restore defamation to the criminal code, but the president promised to block it.

Religious freedom is generally respected, but the Romanian Orthodox Church remains dominant and politically powerful. Critics have described conflicts of interest whereby politicians with ties to construction firms ensure generous state funding for the building of new Orthodox churches, and clergymen then endorse the politicians during electoral campaigns. The government formally recognizes 18 religions, each of which is eligible for proportional state support, but the Orthodox Church accounts for about 85 percent of the population. Religious minorities report discrimination by some local officials and hostility from Orthodox priests.

The government does not restrict academic freedom, but the education system is weakened by widespread corruption.

E. Associational and Organizational Rights: 11 / 12

The constitution guarantees freedoms of assembly and association, and the government respects these rights in practice. Protests were held during 2013 on issues including shale gas exploration and the Roșia Montană gold-mining project. Thousands of ethnic Hungarians held demonstrations in October to call for a Szekler autonomous region.

Nongovernmental organizations operate freely and have increasing influence, though they suffer from funding shortages, often rely on foreign donors, and sometimes face hostility from politicians. Workers have the right to form unions and a limited right to strike, but in practice many employers work against unions, and enforcement of union and labor protections is weak. Employees at financially troubled state-owned companies mounted strikes and protests in 2013 over unpaid wages or cost-cutting plans as the firms prepared for privatization.

F. Rule of Law: 12 / 16

The country's courts continue to suffer from chronic problems such as corruption, political influence, staffing shortages, and inefficient resource allocation. In January 2013, Băsescu rejected the justice minister's nominees for chief prosecutor and DNA director, adhering to advisory opinions from the Superior Council of Magistrates. Ponta, temporarily acting as justice minister, subsequently nominated new candidates who took office in May. Critics noted that the appointments were made without an open application process as part of an apparent political compromise between the president and prime minister. Conditions in Romanian prisons remain poor, though overcrowding has eased in recent years.

Roma, members of the LGBT (lesbian, gay, bisexual, and transgender) community, people with disabilities, and HIV-positive children and adults face discrimination in education, employment, and other areas. Language in the draft constitution under consideration in 2013 would define marriage to exclude same-sex relationships.

G. Personal Autonomy and Individual Rights: 12 / 16

A large proportion of business activity in Romania takes place in the so-called gray economy and is exposed to criminal influences and practices. Despite tax cuts, tighter controls, and other improvements in recent years, nearly a quarter of working people in the country are unofficially employed, and tax evasion cost the state budget the equivalent of 13.8 percent of gross domestic product in 2012.

The constitution guarantees women equal rights, but gender discrimination is a problem. Less than 12 percent of the seats in Parliament are held by women. A 2012 legal amendment provided for restraining orders in domestic violence cases, which are rarely prosecuted. Trafficking of women and girls for forced prostitution remains a major concern, as does trafficking of children for forced begging.

⬇ Russia

Political Rights Rating: 6
Civil Liberties Rating: 5
Freedom Rating: 5.5
Freedom Status: Not Free
Electoral Democracy: No

Population: 143,500,000
Capital: Moscow

Trend Arrow: Russia received a downward trend arrow due to increased repression of two vulnerable minority groups in 2013: the LGBT community, through a law prohibiting "propaganda of nontraditional sexual relations," and migrant laborers, through arbitrary detentions targeting those from the Caucasus, Central Asia, and East Asia. Both efforts fed public hostility against these groups.

Ten-Year Ratings Timeline For Year Under Review (Political Rights, Civil Liberties, Status)

Year Under Review	2004	2005	2006	2007	2008	2009	2010	2011	2012	2013
Rating	6,5,NF	6,5,NF	6,5,NF	6,5,NF	6,5,NF	6,5,NF	6,5,NF	6,5,NF	6,5,NF	6,5,NF

INTRODUCTION

President Vladimir Putin devoted 2013 to strengthening his grip on power and eliminating any potential opposition. The government enforced a series of harsh laws passed the previous year in response to massive opposition protests in December 2011 and May 2012.

Among other restrictions, the laws increased controls on the internet, dramatically hiked fines for participating in unsanctioned street protests, expanded the definition of treason, and branded nongovernmental organizations (NGOs) that accepted foreign grants and engaged in vaguely defined "political activities" as "foreign agents." Although the authorities applied these measures with varying degrees of zeal, and even suffered some setbacks in the Constitutional Court, they repeatedly made it clear that they had the discretion to interpret the laws, and that members of civil society were always vulnerable.

In the face of this repression, opposition leader Aleksey Navalny demonstrated that it was possible to inspire an army of volunteers, raise money online for an opposition movement, and win more than a quarter of the votes in the Moscow mayoral election in September. Many civil society groups also demonstrated resilience by going about their business even as the government harassed and tried to marginalize them. However, Navalny and others operated under the threat of ongoing criminal cases or suspended prison sentences. Economist Sergey Guriyev was the most prominent figure to choose exile during the year rather than face such repercussions.

With the cooperation of the Russian Orthodox Church, the Kremlin also sought to bolster its popular support by scapegoating immigrants and minorities in Russian society. Putin signed laws in June and July that effectively outlawed LGBT (lesbian, gay, bisexual, and transgender) activism and expression and banned gay couples in foreign countries from adopting Russian children. The government's hostile stance encouraged a spate of homophobic attacks across the country. Meanwhile, police carried out a series of raids against irregular migrants, including after xenophobic rioting in October that came in response to the alleged murder of an ethnic Russian by an Azerbaijani. The riots reflected popular complaints that the police and other officials were corrupt and incompetent, and failed to protect the local population.

Late in the year, Putin issued a series of amnesties, releasing dissident businessman Mikhail Khodorkovsky, held for 10 years; two members of the antigovernment performance group Pussy Riot; 30 Greenpeace activists, who had been facing trial since September; four of the protesters arrested in the May 2012 Bolotnaya Square demonstrations; and thousands of lesser-known inmates. The amnesties seemed designed to boost Russia's worsening international image on the eve of the February 2014 Sochi Winter Olympics. However, of the 70 people that the human rights group Memorial identified as political prisoners in October, 33 remained in jail or under house arrest at the end of the year. Among these were Khodorkovsky's business partner, Platon Lebedev, and many of the Bolotnaya protesters. The upcoming Olympics put Russia's human rights record in the spotlight throughout the year, but the regime continued to harass a wide range of individuals who criticized abuses in the preparations for the games.

POLITICAL RIGHTS: 7 / 40

A. Electoral Process: 1 / 12

The 1993 constitution established a strong presidency with the power to dismiss and appoint, pending parliamentary confirmation, the prime minister. Putin served two four-year presidential terms from 2000 to 2008, and remained the de facto paramount leader while serving as prime minister until 2012, violating the spirit if not the letter of the constitution's two-term limit. The March 2012 presidential election was skewed in favor of Putin, who benefited from preferential media treatment, numerous abuses of incumbency, and procedural irregularities during the vote count, among other advantages. He won an official 63.6 percent of the vote against a field of weak, hand-chosen opponents, led by Communist Party leader Gennadiy Zyuganov with 17.2 percent. Under a 2008 constitutional amendment, Putin is set to serve a six-year term, and will be eligible for another in 2018.

The Federal Assembly consists of the 450-seat State Duma and an upper chamber, the 166-seat Federation Council. The 2008 constitutional amendment extended Duma terms from four to five years. The deeply flawed 2011 Duma elections were marked by a "convergence of the state and the governing party, limited political competition and a lack of fairness," according to the Organization for Security and Cooperation in Europe, but many voters used them to express a protest against the status quo. The ruling United Russia party captured just 238 seats, a significant drop from the 2007 elections. The Communist Party placed second with 92 seats, followed by A Just Russia with 64 and the Liberal Democratic Party of Russia with 56. Truly independent opposition parties were not allowed to run.

Since the 2007 elections, all Duma deputies have been elected on the basis of party-list proportional representation. Parties must gain at least 7 percent of the vote to enter the Duma. Furthermore, parties cannot form electoral coalitions. Russia frequently changes its electoral law, depending on the needs of the current incumbents, and there are ongoing discussions about returning to a system with 50 percent proportional representation and 50 percent single-member districts in the State Duma.

Half the members of the upper chamber are appointed by governors and half by regional legislatures, usually with strong federal input. Since 2011, only locally elected politicians have been eligible to serve in the Federation Council; the change was designed to benefit United Russia, as most local officeholders are party members.

A law signed in May 2012 restored gubernatorial elections, ending the system of presidential appointments dating to 2004. However, the new rules allowed federal and regional officials to screen the candidates for governor. United Russia won the eight gubernatorial elections held on September 8, 2013, the only day for regional elections during the year. In the vast majority of cases, various legal tools were used to prevent opposition candidates from running. United Russia also won more than 70 percent of the seats, on average, in the 16 regions that held legislative elections. In an exceptional case, anticorruption blogger Aleksey Navalny was allowed to participate in the Moscow mayoral election and was officially credited with 27.24 percent of the vote, a surprisingly large share given the essentially rigged nature of the contest. Since incumbent Sergey Sobyanin narrowly avoided a runoff with 51.37 percent, many opposition leaders assumed that the tally was falsified by at least 2 percentage points. Moreover, the campaign took place during the summer, when many residents were away, and Navalny had no access to the main television stations, which lavished praise on his opponent. Yevgeniy Roizman was the most prominent opposition figure to win a mayoral election, succeeding in Yekaterinburg, though the city manager there wields most executive powers. The only other opposition leader of a major city, Yaroslavl mayor Yevgeniy Urlashov, elected in April 2012, was arrested with four of his allies and charged with corruption in July 2013. Urlashov asserted that the arrest was politically motivated. He remained in jail at year's end.

In November 2013, Putin signed a law allowing regional legislatures to lower the number of deputies elected on the basis of proportional representation to 25 percent from the current 50 percent, and making it possible to remove proportional representation completely from the Moscow and St. Petersburg city councils. The move, backed by Sobyanin, will make it easier for progovernment candidates to gain a majority in the 2014 Moscow city council elections.

B. Political Pluralism and Participation: 3 / 16

Legislation enacted in April 2012 liberalized party registration rules, allowing the creation of hundreds of new parties. However, none posed a significant threat to the authorities, and many seemed designed to encourage division and confusion among the opposition. The

Opposition Coordinating Council, set up in October 2012 with the hope of unifying opposition strategy, ceased to exist one year later due to a lack of support from the various member groups.

It is exceedingly difficult for the opposition to win representation through the country's tightly controlled elections. However, Navalny was able to exploit the opportunities offered to him by the authorities in the Moscow mayoral election and organized an active campaign backed by 14,000 volunteers, demonstrating that there was significant opposition to the status quo in the capital.

Migration from the Caucasus (including Russia's North Caucasus republics) and Central Asia proved to be a major issue in Moscow's 2013 election. Official crackdowns on ethnic minorities before the voting sent a strong signal that the authorities endorsed widely held anti-immigrant attitudes and hoped to use this populist cause to win support.

C. Functioning of Government: 3 / 12

Corruption in the government and business world is pervasive, and a growing lack of accountability enables bureaucrats to act with impunity. The leadership frequently announces anticorruption campaigns, but their main purpose is to ensure elite loyalty and prevent the issue from mobilizing the opposition. In April 2013, Putin signed a decree forcing state officials to give up any assets they hold abroad, leaving them more vulnerable to disfavor from the Kremlin and less exposed to international human rights sanctions. A crackdown on the finances of the Skolkovo innovation center, a project supported by former president and current prime minister Dmitriy Medvedev, was interpreted as a move to discredit Medvedev and his comparatively liberal allies rather than a genuine attempt to root out procurement abuses. In December, Putin set up a new department in the presidential administration to fight corruption, but few observers expected it to produce real results. According to Transparency International, only 5 percent of the population thinks that the government's anticorruption efforts are effective.

There is little transparency and accountability in the day-to-day workings of the government. Decisions are adopted behind closed doors and announced to the population after the fact.

CIVIL LIBERTIES: 19 / 60 (-1)
D. Freedom of Expression and Belief: 6 / 16

Although the constitution provides for freedom of speech, vague laws on extremism grant the authorities great discretion to crack down on any speech, organization, or activity that lacks official support. The government controls, directly or through state-owned companies and friendly business magnates, all of the national television networks and many radio and print outlets, as well as most of the media advertising market. Only a small and shrinking number of radio stations and publications with limited reach offer a wide range of viewpoints. In December 2013, Putin abolished the state-owned news agency RIA Novosti, which had developed a reputation for objective reporting, and folded it into a new entity called Rossiya Segodnya (Russia Today), which would be run by pro-Kremlin television commentator Dmitriy Kiselyov and Margarita Simonyan, the head of RT, the Kremlin's propagandistic international television network. The Kremlin has also increased pressure on formerly outspoken outlets, such as the business newspaper *Kommersant*, which is now considered to be a progovernment publication.

More than 50 percent of Russian households have internet access, and penetration continues to increase. Discussion on the internet is largely unrestricted, but the government devotes extensive resources to manipulating online information and analysis. In November

2012, a broadly worded new law, ostensibly targeting information that is unsuitable for children, created a blacklist of internet outlets. The authorities currently block a wide range of sites that feature anti-Putin articles, Islamist materials, or information about suicide and drugs. In December 2013, Putin signed a similar law that allows the authorities to shut down—within 24 hours and without a court order—websites deemed to promote rioting or to contain extremist information. An antipiracy law adopted in July allows courts to put a temporary ban on websites that film copyright holders believe are distributing their products illegally without first confirming whether the claims are valid. While nominally aimed at protecting property rights, the bill opens the door to closures of websites without cause. Separately, a Moscow court ordered the closure of the online news agency Rosbalt in October on the grounds that its website included videos with obscene language. The agency's lawyers prepared an appeal, and the site continued to operate through the end of the year.

Freedom of religion is respected unevenly. A 1997 law on religion gives the state extensive control and makes it difficult for new or independent groups to operate. The Orthodox Church has a privileged position, working closely with the government on foreign and domestic policy priorities, and in 2009 the president authorized religious instruction in the public schools. Regional authorities continue to harass nontraditional groups, such as Jehovah's Witnesses and Mormons.

Academic freedom is generally respected, though the education system is marred by corruption and low salaries. Recent reforms have cut state spending, eliminated many faculty positions, and increased bureaucracy. In May 2013, the economist Sergey Guriyev, who served as rector of the New Economic School, went into exile to avoid harassment and possible arrest for a report that was critical of the cases against Khodorkovsky. Guriyev had coauthored the report at the request of then president Medvedev. In September, the Kremlin ordered a reform of the Russian Academy of Sciences that forced its research institutes to report to a new federal agency and essentially took control of their property. Russian intellectuals charged that the reforms gutted what had been a relatively independent organization.

E. Associational and Organizational Rights: 4 / 12

The government has consistently reduced the space for freedoms of assembly and association. Overwhelming police responses, the use of force, routine arrests, and harsh fines and prison sentences have discouraged unsanctioned protests, though pro-Kremlin groups are able to demonstrate freely. The authorities arrested 28 individuals for protesting Putin's inauguration on Moscow's Bolotnaya Square on May 6, 2012, and many continued to face criminal charges throughout 2013. The three sentenced by year's end received penalties including prison terms and, in the case of Mikhail Kosenko, indefinite psychiatric confinement. In late December, Putin amnestied four of the accused, but the rest continued to face charges. On December 31, police arrested opposition activist Sergey Mokhnatkin and charged him with attacking a police officer at a new demonstration. He had been arrested on the same charges in 2009, sentenced to 2.5 years in jail, declared a prisoner of conscience by Amnesty International, and then pardoned by President Medvedev in April 2012. When 30 members of Greenpeace, representing 18 different countries, protested Russian offshore oil production in the Arctic in September by trespassing at a drilling platform, border guards detained them on charges of piracy, later reduced to hooliganism. A court had granted them bail by late November, and Putin amnestied them in December, allowing them to leave Russia.

A law enacted in 2012 required all organizations receiving foreign funding and involved in vaguely defined "political activities" to register as "foreign agents" with the Justice Ministry. Noncompliance can be punished by steep fines and prison terms. Putin demanded that the authorities begin enforcing the law in February 2013, leading to hundreds of raids and inspections of NGO offices. However, the campaign seemed to ease by the summer. Overall, the authorities filed nine administrative cases against NGOs and an additional five administrative cases against NGO leaders for failing to register under the law, according to Human Rights Watch. Courts threw out the charges in nine of the cases. In one important case, the election-monitoring organization Golos was dissolved by the Justice Ministry in June, and its director fled the country. However, members reestablished the group the following month, set up a new website, and helped to monitor the Moscow mayoral election in September. Some regional branches continued to operate. Separately, the Kostroma Public Initiatives Support Center said at the end of October that it would have to shut down if it did not win a Constitutional Court appeal, which was still pending at the end of the year, as it could not afford a 300,000 ruble ($9,000) fine for failing to register as a foreign agent. The organization's mission was to convene roundtable discussions, some of which included foreigners.

While trade union rights are legally protected, they are limited in practice. Strikes and worker protests have occurred in prominent industries, such as automobile manufacturing, but antiunion discrimination and reprisals for strikes are not uncommon, and employers often ignore collective-bargaining rights. The largest labor federation works in close cooperation with the Kremlin, though independent unions are active in some industrial sectors and regions.

F. Rule of Law: 2 / 16 (-1)

The judiciary lacks independence from the executive branch, and career advancement is effectively tied to compliance with Kremlin preferences. In June 2013, Putin called for a merger of the commercial courts with the courts of general jurisdiction. Legislation to implement the change, including constitutional amendments, was still under consideration at year's end. The move was expected to harm the business community by reducing the independence of the commercial courts, which have ruled against the state more often than the rest of the judiciary. Seven high commercial court judges resigned to protest Putin's proposal.

In some cases, the courts have moderated or blocked harsh laws. The Constitutional Court overturned a law that banned people convicted of a crime from participating in politics for the rest of their lives in October, removed particularly onerous provisions of the law on demonstrations that imposed heavy fines on demonstrators and undue burdens on organizers in June, and found that citizens had the right to appeal the counting of votes in their specific precincts in April.

The criminal procedure code allows jury trials for serious cases, though they occur rarely in practice. While juries are more likely than judges to acquit defendants, such verdicts are frequently overturned by higher courts, which can order retrials until the desired outcome is achieved. Russian citizens often feel that domestic courts do not provide a fair hearing and have increasingly turned to the European Court of Human Rights. Critics charge that Russia has failed to address ongoing criminal justice problems, such as poor prison conditions and the widespread use of illegal detention and torture to extract confessions. Nadezhda Tolokonnikova, one of two members of the performance group Pussy Riot serving prison time for a 2012 anti-Putin protest action in an Orthodox cathedral, drew attention to the country's inhumane prison conditions in 2013 by going on hunger strike and publishing an open letter about her plight.

The justice system is used as a tool to harass the opposition, forcing activists to defend themselves against what are often blatantly trumped-up charges. Navalny, for example, was sentenced in July 2013 to five years in prison on widely ridiculed embezzlement charges, then released pending an appeal so that he could compete in the stage-managed Moscow mayoral election and lend it a sense of legitimacy. After the election, an appellate court suspended his prison sentence, allowing him to remain free but banning him from running for office again. A few days later, new but similar charges were filed against him, forcing him to go through the process again.

Parts of the country, especially the North Caucasus area, suffer from high levels of violence. Hundreds of officials, insurgents, and civilians die each year in bombings, gun battles, and assassinations. Suicide bombers struck three times in the city of Volgograd in late 2013, killing 40 people and demonstrating that the violence could spread to other parts of the country. In November, Putin signed a law that increased the number of crimes considered to be "terrorism" and required relatives of perpetrators to pay compensation for terrorist acts. Opponents argued that the law violated the presumption of innocence, marked a return to collective punishment, and would not deter terrorism.

Immigrants and ethnic minorities—particularly those who appear to be from the Caucasus or Central Asia—face governmental and societal discrimination and harassment. In a sign that the federal government is growing concerned about uncontrolled nationalism, Putin signed a law in October giving local authorities more responsibility for managing migration and interethnic relations, and providing for dismissal of municipal leaders who fail to suppress ethnic tensions.

The anti-LGBT law signed in June banned dissemination of information promoting "nontraditional sexual relationships," building on similar laws passed earlier in a number of municipalities. Putin claimed that the law did not outlaw homosexuality, but it triggered vigilante attacks on LGBT people. There have been at least three prosecutions under the law, and antigay activists have been emboldened to issue threatening statements. Moreover, the authorities have harassed LGBT support organizations under the auspices of the new law and the 2012 "foreign agent" law.

G. Personal Autonomy and Individual Rights: 7 / 16

The government places some restrictions on freedom of movement and residence. Adults must carry internal passports while traveling and to obtain many government services. Some regional authorities impose registration rules that limit the right of citizens to choose their place of residence, typically targeting ethnic minorities and migrants from the Caucasus and Central Asia.

State takeovers of key industries and large tax penalties imposed on select companies have illustrated the precarious nature of property rights in the country, especially when political interests are involved.

Women have particular difficulty achieving political power. They hold 13 percent of the Duma's seats (down from 14 percent in the previous term) and less than 5 percent of the seats in the Federation Council. Only two of 30 cabinet members are women. Domestic violence against women continues to be a serious problem, and police are often reluctant to intervene in what they regard as internal family matters. Economic hardships contribute to widespread trafficking of women abroad for prostitution.

# Rwanda

Political Rights Rating: 6
Civil Liberties Rating: 5
Freedom Rating: 5.5
Freedom Status: Not Free
Electoral Democracy: No
Population: 11,116,000
Capital: Kigali

Ratings Change: Rwanda's civil liberties rating improved from 6 to 5 due to increasing critical commentary on social media, as illustrated by the unhindered online debates regarding Paul Kagame's presidential tenure.

Ten-Year Ratings Timeline For Year Under Review (Political Rights, Civil Liberties, Status)

Year Under Review	2004	2005	2006	2007	2008	2009	2010	2011	2012	2013
Rating	6,5,NF	6,5,NF	6,5,NF	6,5,NF	6,5,NF	6,5,NF	6,5,NF	6,5,NF	6,6,NF	6,5,NF

INTRODUCTION

In parliamentary elections held in September 2013, the ruling coalition—led by the Rwandan Patriotic Front (RFP)—was victorious, winning over 76 percent of the vote and taking 40 out of 53 elected seats in the lower house. Independent election observer missions found the elections to be generally peaceful, free and fair, though the ballot counting process was reportedly not fully transparent in some polling stations. An absence of opposition party agents at most polling locations was also noted, which increased the election's susceptibility to manipulation, though no major abnormalities were observed.

A comprehensive access to information law was passed in March 2013 that was regarded as exemplary in its scope and for its effort to enhance government transparency and accountability. A new media law enacted the same month was similarly lauded for expanding the rights of journalists, but also contained some provisions that threatened to limit press freedom.

In July 2013, amendments to a vague 2008 law against "genocide ideology" were passed that reduced penalties and aimed to make the law more definitive and easier to interpret. In addition, there were indications of an improving climate for free expression in Rwanda, particularly on social media platforms, where citizens have become more vocal in discussing and debating political topics.

Meanwhile, the Rwandan government continued to target human rights organizations in 2013, and was accused of employing infiltration tactics to dismantle organizations from within. In August, for example, the Rwandan League for the Promotion and Defense of Human Rights (LIPRODHOR) saw its independent leadership illegally ousted and replaced with individuals believed to be favorable to the government. Similar strategies have been used against opposition political parties, and there are concerns that government crackdowns against critical voices may increase as the country prepares for the 2017 presidential elections.

Exiled opposition critics were increasingly threatened, attacked, forcibly disappeared, or even killed throughout the year, including Patrick Karegeya, the former head of Rwanda's external intelligence services, who was found dead in a Johannesburg hotel room on January 1, 2014.

POLITICAL RIGHTS: 9 / 40 (+1)

A. Electoral Process: 2 / 12

Ethnic strife in Rwanda culminated in a 1994 genocide in which the majority ethnic Hutus killed as many as 1 million minority Tutsis and moderate Hutus. The genocide occurred amid a guerilla war waged by the Tutsi-dominated RPF against the Hutu-dominated government that saw war crimes committed by both sides and caused millions of Rwandan refugees to flee the country.

Rwanda's 2003 constitution marked the end of a transition that began the nation's post-genocide political period. The constitution grants broad powers to the president, who can serve up to two seven-year terms and has the authority to appoint the prime minister and dissolve the bicameral Parliament. The 26-seat upper house, the Senate, consists of 12 members elected by regional councils, 8 appointed by the president, 4 chosen by a forum of political parties, and 2 elected representatives of universities, all serving eight-year terms. The 80-seat Chamber of Deputies, or lower house, includes 53 directly elected members, 24 women chosen by local councils, 2 from the National Youth Council, and 1 from the Federation of Associations of the Disabled; all serve five-year terms. Parliament generally lacks independence, merely endorsing government initiatives.

Parliamentary elections were held in September 2013. As anticipated, the RPF-led coalition won, taking over 76 percent of the vote and 40 out of 53 elected seats in the lower house. Independent election observer missions found the elections to be peaceful, free, and fair, though the African Union observer mission noted that the ballot counting process, while "generally transparent," was not fully transparent in some polling stations. The East African Community (EAC) observer mission noted an absence of party agents from the opposition at most polling stations, which increased the election's susceptibility to manipulation, though the mission did not observe any abnormalities.

The most recent presidential election, held in 2010, was regarded as administratively acceptable, despite presenting Rwandans with only a limited degree of choice. With no serious challengers on the ballot, President Paul Kagame won reelection with 93 percent of the vote. As the country gears up for the next presidential election in 2017, Kagame has been rumored to be seeking reelection to a third term, which would require a constitutional amendment to repeal term limits.

B. Political Pluralism and Participation: 2 / 16

The constitution officially permits political parties to exist, but only under strict controls, while the charter's emphasis on "national unity" effectively limits political pluralism. The RPF dominates the political arena, and parties closely identified with the 1994 genocide are banned, as are parties based on ethnicity or religion, though the RPF is still Tutsi-dominated. These restrictions have been used to ban other political parties that might pose a challenge to RPF rule.

In July 2013, Parliament passed amendments to the law governing political parties and politicians that further limited political pluralism by giving the Rwanda Governance Board the power to register political parties. It also banned foreign funding to political organizations.

Eleven political parties were registered in advance of the September parliamentary elections. The opposition Democratic Green Party (DGP) registered for the first time in August after a four-year effort, though it opted out of the September polls due to the limited timeframe it had left to campaign. Five of the remaining 10 parties were part of the RPF's ruling coalition.

In recent years, the government has been suspected of infiltrating opposition parties in an attempt to dismantle or divide them. In October 2013, DGP leader Frank Habineza alleged that there was a plot to replace him with someone more closely aligned with the RPF. A similar tactic against the opposition Social Party-Imberakuri was reported in 2010 when the party's president, Bernard Ntaganda, was ousted and replaced with a putatively more amenable leader. Ntaganda was subsequently arrested a few weeks prior to the 2010 presidential election; in 2011, he was tried and sentenced to four years in prison for threatening state security and fomenting "divisionism." The Supreme Court upheld these charges in April 2012.

In advance of the August 2010 presidential poll, the government prevented new political parties from registering and arrested the leaders of several other parties, effectively preventing them from fielding candidates. The most credible opposition candidate, Victoire Ingabire, the leader of the United Democratic Forces–Inkingi (FDU-Inkingi), was arrested on charges of denying the genocide and collaborating with a terrorist group. Kagame went on to win the election with an overwhelming majority. Ingabire was arrested again in October 2010 for allegedly engaging in terrorist activities and, after a year-long trial, was sentenced in October 2012 to eight years in prison. She launched an appeal against her conviction in April 2013.

Opposition critics residing outside of Rwanda have also been increasingly threatened, attacked, forcibly disappeared, or even killed. In August 2013, three former members of the Rwandan security forces living in exile went missing on separate occasions, including Kagame's former bodyguard Joel Mutabazi who had previously escaped a bungled abduction and survived an assassination attempt in July. He had been accused of having close ties with a prominent government critic living in South Africa. Pascal Manirakiza, another Rwandan asylum seeker in Uganda, was found unconscious a few days after his abduction at a cemetery near Kampala with serious injuries that indicated torture. The third abductee, Innocent Kalisa, remained missing as of December 2013. Meanwhile, on January 1, 2014, Patrick Karegeya, the former head of Rwanda's external intelligence services in exile known for his public criticisms of Kagame's government, was found dead in a hotel room in Johannesburg.

C. Functioning of Government: 5 / 12 (+1)

Government countermeasures have helped limit corruption, though graft remains a problem. In recent years, a number of senior government officials have been fired and faced prosecution for alleged corruption, embezzlement, and abuse of power. Government institutions focused on combating corruption include the Office of the Ombudsman, the auditor general, and the National Tender Board. Rwanda was ranked 49 out of 177 countries and territories surveyed in Transparency International's 2013 Corruption Perceptions Index. Rwanda is characterized as one of the least corrupt countries in Africa.

A comprehensive access to information law was passed in March 2013 that was praised for its scope and for its effort to enhance government transparency and accountability.

CIVIL Liberties: 17 / 40 (+1)
D. Freedom of Expression and Belief: 5 / 16 (+1)

The RPF has imposed both legal restrictions and informal controls on freedom of the press and expression. A vague 2008 law against "genocide ideology" prescribes heavy prison sentences and fines for an overly broad set of offenses. Amendments were passed in the lower house in July 2013 that aimed to make the law more definitive and easier to interpret; they also reduced prison sentences from 25 years to a maximum of 9, and required proof of criminal intent behind an offending act. A new media law was enacted in March 2013 that was lauded for expanding the rights of journalists and recognizing freedom for online communications. However, the new law also threatened to limit press freedom, including a provision that created a new government body with the power to set conditions for both local and foreign media outlets to operate in Rwanda.

The government has continually been accused of intimidating independent journalists. In February 2011, *Umurabyo* newspaper journalists Agnès Uwimana Nkusi and Saïdati

Mukakibibi were sentenced to 17 and 7 years in prison, respectively, for denying the genocide, inciting civil disobedience, and defaming public officials based on a 2009 article that criticized the president. Nkusi and Mukakibibi appealed their case in January 2012, and in April 2012, the Supreme Court reduced their sentences to four and three years, respectively. In November 2012, the editor of the Kinyarwandan-language paper *Umusingi*, Stanley Gatera, was found criminally liable for a controversial opinion piece published in June 2012. He was fined and sentenced to one year in prison for gender discrimination and inciting "divisionism"; an appellate court upheld the sentence in March 2013.

Rwanda's repressive media environment has led many journalists to flee the country and work in exile, though exiled opposition journalists and activists have also been subject to extralegal intimidation and violence. In November 2011, Charles Ingabire, editor of the Uganda-based online publication *Inyenyeri News* and an outspoken critic of the Kagame regime who fled Rwanda in 2007 due to threats, was shot dead in Uganda. His murder remained unsolved at the end of 2013. Meanwhile, there are increasing indications that e-mail and other private communications are being monitored. In August 2012, the lower house adopted amendments to the 2008 Law Relating to the Interception of Communications that expanded the surveillance and interception capabilities of security authorities.

Nevertheless, there is some indication that the ability of Rwandans to express themselves freely is increasing, particularly on social media platforms, where citizens have become more vocal in discussing and debating political topics such as Kagame's tenure. The government reportedly monitors online communications, and government censorship of online content has increased in recent years. In 2013, the weekly English-language newspaper, the *Chronicles*, was suspended, affecting both its print and online versions. The independent newspaper *Umuvugizi* frequently faced website blackouts since its 6-month suspension in 2010, and a few opposition sites continued to be blocked on some ISPs, including *Umusingi* and *Inyenyeri News,* which were both first blocked in 2011.

Religious freedom is generally respected, though relations between religious leaders and the government are sometimes tense, in part because of the involvement of clergy in the 1994 genocide. In July 2013, 11 members of a breakaway Catholic group were arrested for staging an allegedly illegal demonstration in front of the presidential residence. The group was urging the president to make political reforms.

Fear among teachers and students of being labeled "divisionist" restrains academic freedom. Following parliamentary commission reports on divisionism from 2004 and 2008, numerous students and teachers were expelled or dismissed without due process.

E. Associational and Organizational Rights: 2 / 12

Although the constitution codifies freedoms of assembly and association, these rights are limited in practice. Registration and reporting requirements for both domestic and foreign nongovernmental organizations (NGOs) are known to be excessively lengthy and onerous, and activities that the government defines as "divisive" are prohibited. Several organizations have been banned in recent years, leading others to refrain from criticizing the RPF, though civil society organizations that do not focus on sensitive subjects such as democracy and human rights are able to function without direct government interference. The government has been accused of employing infiltration tactics against human rights organizations similar to those used against opposition political parties. In August 2013, for example, the Rwandan League for the Promotion and Defense of Human Rights (LIPRODHOR) saw its independent leadership illegally ousted and replaced with individuals more favorable to the government.

The constitution provides for the rights to form trade unions, engage in collective bargaining, and strike. However, public workers are not allowed to unionize, and employees of the many "essential services" are not allowed to strike. The International Trade Union Confederation reported that although a 2009 labor code improved workers' rights, the government continues to pressure unions in indirect ways.

F. Rule of Law: 3 / 16

Recent improvements in the judicial system include an increased presence of defense lawyers at trials, improved training for court staff, and revisions to the legal code, but the judiciary has yet to secure full independence from the executive. In January 2013, Rwanda signed the Protocol to the African Charter on Human and Peoples' Rights, which allows individuals and NGOs to take cases before the African Court on Human and People's Rights based in Arusha, Tanzania.

The community-based *gacaca* courts officially completed their work in June 2012 after prosecuting hundreds of thousands of people accused of being involved in the genocide. The courts faced criticism from legal experts over their failure to address genocide-era crimes allegedly committed by the RPF, and because they routinely tried politically motivated cases. The national criminal court system, meanwhile, continued to try special cases of those accused of more serious crimes related to the genocide, including those transferred from the International Criminal Tribunal for Rwanda (ICTR). By the end of 2013, the ICTR had completed cases against 75 individuals, sentencing 46—of which 17 are being appealed—and acquitting 12. The ICTR aims to complete its work by the end of 2014. In February 2012, an international crimes chamber was created within Rwanda's High Court to prosecute extradited suspects.

Individual police officers sometimes use excessive force, and local officials periodically ignore due process protections. The construction of new prisons during the past decade has improved prison conditions, even as the gacaca trials increased the prison population. Nevertheless, alleged dissidents have been increasingly subject to unlawful imprisonment, torture, and ill-treatment in secret military detention centers.

Equal treatment for all citizens under the law is guaranteed, and legal protections against discrimination have increased in recent years. In practice, however, the Tutsi minority group is often accused of being given preferential treatment for high-ranking jobs and college scholarships under the pretext of an affirmative action program for "genocide survivors." A national identity card is required when Rwandans wish to move within the country, but these are issued regularly and no longer indicate ethnicity.

Same-sex conduct and sexual orientation is not criminalized in Rwanda, though social stigma still exists for sexual minorities.

G. Personal Autonomy and Individual Rights: 7 / 16

Rwanda was ranked 52 out of 185 countries on the World Bank's 2013 ease of doing business index, placing it third-best in sub-Saharan Africa. The country also ranked third-best in sub-Saharan Africa, and 66 out of 148 economies, in the World Economic Forum's Global Competitiveness Report 2013–2014, indicating the existence of relatively well-functioning institutions and a low level of direct government control over the economy.

There are no restrictions on property rights, freedom of travel, or choice of employment, residence, or institution of higher education, though Hutus often face unofficial discrimination when seeking public employment or government scholarships.

The 2003 constitution requires women to occupy at least 30 percent of the seats in each chamber of Parliament; women currently fill 10 of the 26 Senate seats and 51 of the 80 seats in the Chamber of Deputies. Legislation has strengthened women's rights to inherit land; however, de facto discrimination against women continues. Domestic violence is illegal but remains widespread.

⬇ Saint Kitts and Nevis

Political Rights Rating: 1
Civil Liberties Rating: 1
Freedom Rating: 1.0
Freedom Status: Free
Electoral Democracy: Yes

Population: 54,744
Capital: Basseterre

Trend Arrow: Saint Kitts and Nevis received a downward trend arrow due to the government's improper efforts to block consideration of a no-confidence motion that had been submitted by opposition legislators in December 2012.

Ten-Year Ratings Timeline For Year Under Review (Political Rights, Civil Liberties, Status)

Year Under Review	2004	2005	2006	2007	2008	2009	2010	2011	2012	2013
Rating	1,2,F	1,1,F	1,1,F	1,1,F	1,1,F	1,1,F	1,1,F	1,1,F	1,1,F	1,1,F

INTRODUCTION

Disharmony within the ruling Saint Kitts and Nevis Labour Party (SKNLP) erupted in early 2013 with the firing and resignation of two senators in Prime Minister Denzil Douglas's government. Among the numerous issues of contention were a bill that would increase the number of senators in the National Assembly, and a motion of no confidence submitted in December 2012 that Douglas refused to table for debate. The High Court ruled against the government in numerous cases throughout the year, including nullifying the appointment of a new attorney general and declaring the Senators Act unconstitutional.

General elections were held for the Nevis Island Assembly on January 22. The Concerned Citizens Movement (CCM) won a majority.

POLITICAL RIGHTS: 37 / 40 (-1)
A. Electoral Process: 12 / 12

The federal government consists of the prime minister, the cabinet, and the unicameral National Assembly. A governor-general represents Queen Elizabeth II as ceremonial head of state. Elected National Assembly representatives—8 from Saint Kitts and 3 from Nevis—serve five-year terms. In addition, the governor-general appoints 3 senators, plus the attorney general who is also a senator, under the advice of the prime minister and the leader of the opposition.

The January 2010 parliamentary elections were deemed generally free and fair. Denzil Douglas of the ruling SKNLP won a fourth term as prime minister. The SKNLP won 6 seats, and the opposition People's Action Movement (PAM) won 2 seats. For the Nevis seats, the pro-independence CCM and the Nevis Reformation Party (NRP) retained 2 and 1 seat, respectively.

The Nevis Island Assembly is composed of 5 elected and 3 appointed members. The local government provides its own services, with the exception of police and foreign relations. The constitution grants Nevis the option to secede. In March 2012, the High Court declared the 2011 election results for one of the assembly seats to be null and void, and the assembly was dissolved in November 2012 in preparation for new general elections, which were held on January 22. The CARICOM Election Observer Mission reported that the 2013 elections were peaceful and fair. The opposition CCM captured 3 of the 5 seats, defeating the NRP to become the majority party.

In preparation for the next general elections, constitutionally due in 2015, in July the National Assembly approved amendments to the election law designed to expedite ballot counting. The prime minister also announced plans that month to change the constituency boundaries, a move the opposition labeled as gerrymandering. On November 25, the High Court upheld an injunction filed by opposition legislators to prevent the governor-general from implementing the boundary changes. Although he approved a judicial review, the judge ruled that there was no evidence that the Constituency Boundaries Commission had acted improperly in the preparation of their report. The judicial review was pending at year's end.

B. Political Pluralism and Participation: 16 / 16

In general, people have the right to organize in different political parties and to form and operate new parties. The SKNLP and the PAM dominate politics. On June 17, former ministers Timothy Harris and Sam Condor launched the People's Labour Party, aligned with the opposition.

C. Functioning of Government: 9 / 12 (-1)

Increasing discord within the ruling SKNLP came to a head in early 2013 with the dismissal of Senior Minister Timothy Harris on January 25, and the resignation of Deputy Prime Minister Sam Condor on January 31. Harris was fired for publicly opposing a government-sponsored bill to increase the number of National Assembly senators to six, and for not stating how he would vote on the motion of no confidence. Condor resigned in response to "issues of good governance and constitutional integrity."

A few days later, Condor and the leader of the PAM opposition party filed an injunction in the High Court to prohibit newly appointed attorney general Jason Hamilton from continuing as a senator, and to block the Senators (Increase of Number) Act. Hamilton had been appointed on January 28, and was sworn in the next day, allowing him to cast the decisive vote to pass the Senators Act. On February 28, the High Court declared Hamilton's appointment null and void due to irregularities in procedures, and ruled the Senators Act unconstitutional. Hamilton was subsequently re-appointed under proper procedures.

In March, opposition legislators called for a debate on the no confidence motion, but the prime minister continued to avoid the issue. In November, the opposition requested the Organization of Eastern Caribbean States (OECS) Assembly to review the allegedly unconstitutional delays in debating the no confidence motion. The motion of no confidence had yet to be debated at year's end.

Saint Kitts and Nevis has generally implemented its anticorruption laws effectively. The government reiterated that freedom of information legislation was a priority in 2013, but a bill had yet to pass at year's end. The Integrity in Public Life Bill was passed in September, though government officials are not required to disclose financial assets. A Financial Intelligence Unit investigates financial crimes, but no independent body addresses allegations of governmental corruption. In November, the new premier of the Nevis Island Assembly accused the previous administration of misappropriating public funds; an investigation was ongoing at year's end.

CIVIL LIBERTIES: 53 / 60

D. Freedom of Expression and Belief: 15 / 16

Constitutional guarantees of freedom of expression are generally respected. On October 8, Prime Minister Douglas won EC$350,000 (US$130,000) in a defamation case initiated in 2011 against *The Democrat,* a newspaper aligned with the opposition PAM. The government owns the sole local television station, and the opposition faces some restrictions on access. In addition to both government and private radio stations, there is one privately owned daily newspaper, and political parties publish weekly newspapers. Internet access is not restricted.

Freedom of religion is constitutionally protected, and academic freedom is generally honored.

E. Associational and Organizational Rights: 12 / 12

The right to form civic organizations is generally respected, as is freedom of assembly. Workers may legally form unions. A union can engage in collective bargaining only if more than 50 percent of the company's employees are union members. The right to strike, while not specified by law, is generally respected in practice.

F. Rule of Law: 13 / 16 (+1)

The judiciary is largely independent, and legal provisions for a fair and speedy trial are generally observed. The highest court is the Eastern Caribbean Supreme Court, but under certain circumstances, there is a right of appeal to the Trinidad-based Caribbean Court of Justice. Additionally, an appeal may be made to the Privy Council in London. The islands' rule of law continues to be tested by the prevalence of drug-related crime and corruption. Law enforcement, particularly the Delta Squad, has been accused of using excessive force when conducting periodic raids. The national prison remains severely overcrowded.

Legal and social discrimination against the LGBT community persists; same-sex sexual conduct between men is criminalized with prison sentences of up to 10 years.

G. Personal Autonomy and Individual Rights: 13 / 16 (-1)

Eminent domain laws allow the government to seize private property and business, and the government does not always provide adequate and timely compensation.

While domestic violence is criminalized, violence against women remains a serious problem. Only one woman serves in the National Assembly. The government passed equal pay for equal work legislation in 2012.

Saint Lucia

Political Rights Rating: 1
Civil Liberties Rating: 1
Freedom Rating: 1.0
Freedom Status: Free
Electoral Democracy: Yes

Population: 170,311
Capital: Castries

Ten-Year Ratings Timeline For Year Under Review (Political Rights, Civil Liberties, Status)

Year Under Review	2004	2005	2006	2007	2008	2009	2010	2011	2012	2013
Rating	1,2,F	1,1,F	1,1,F	1,1,F	1,1,F	1,1,F	1,1,F	1,1,F	1,1,F	1,1,F

INTRODUCTION

Saint Lucia continued to suffer from slow economic growth (1.5 percent), a public debt at 78 percent of GDP, and an unemployment rate of 23.3 percent. The budget presented to Parliament in May reflected efforts to cut expenditures, but the opposition UWP protested the construction of a new government office in November during a time of economic hardship. Saint Lucia became a full member of the international cooperation organization Bolivarian Alliance for the Peoples of

Our America (ALBA) on July 30, which allows it to purchase Venezuelan petroleum products on concessionary terms. The leader of the United Workers Party (UWP) accused the prime minister of failing to consult the public or parliament about his intention to join ALBA. Criticism also mounted over an unlawful contract signed in 2000 between the prime minister and Jack Grynberg, the president of Texas-based RSM Production Company, that resulted in Grynberg filing an arbitration claim against the Saint Lucian government in November.

Members of the government employed threats and lawsuits to intimidate the media and restrict press freedom. Meanwhile, the United States responded to serious human rights violations by the Saint Lucia police by suspending all training and material assistance in August.

POLITICAL RIGHTS: 39 / 40

A. Electoral Process: 12 / 12

Under the 1979 constitution, the bicameral Parliament consists of the 17-member House of Assembly, elected for five years, and an appointed 11-member Senate. The prime minister is chosen by the majority party in the House of Assembly. The prime minister chooses 6 members of the Senate, the opposition leader selects 3, and 2 are chosen in consultation with civic and religious organizations. A governor general represents the British monarch as head of state. The island is divided into 11 quarters (districts), each with its own elected council and administrative services.

The Saint Lucia Labour Party (SLP) unseated the UWP in 2011 general elections with an 11-to-6 seat majority in the House of Assembly. Kenny Anthony, who served as SLP prime minister from 1997 to 2006, was sworn in for a third term.

In April 2013, the Constitutional Reform Commission presented a final report to Parliament, which will consider the recommendations in 2014. The governor-general also announced in April that legislative priorities for 2013–2014 would include proposed changes to the Elections Act in line with recommendations by the Electoral Commission.

B. Political Pluralism and Participation: 16 / 16

Political parties are free to organize, but the conservative UWP and the social-democratic SLP dominate politics. Five parties competed in the last general election, but no others gained representation. The Lucian People's Movement (LPM), launched before the 2011 elections, is especially active on the political scene.

C. Functioning of Government: 11 / 12

Saint Lucia has low levels of corruption and was ranked 22 out of 177 countries surveyed in Transparency International's 2013 Corruption Perceptions Index. Access to information is legally guaranteed, and government officials are required by law to present their financial assets annually to the Integrity Commission. However, there are cases of government corruption. An on-going legal battle continued in 2013 between Prime Minister Anthony and Jack Grynberg, the president of Texas-based RSM Production Company. Anthony signed a contract in 2000 granting RSM oil exploration rights to millions of acres of Saint Lucia's maritime territory, when legally only the governor general has authority to do so. In November 2013, Grynberg filed a corruption complaint against Saint Lucia with the U.S. Department of Justice under the Foreign Corrupt Practices Act; the case was ongoing at year's end.

CIVIL LIBERTIES: 53 / 60 (-1)

D. Freedom of Expression and Belief: 15 / 16 (-1)

The constitution guarantees freedom of speech, which is respected in practice. The media carry a wide spectrum of views and are largely independent. While there are no daily newspapers, numerous privately owned newspapers publish three issues per week. In 2013, the government took steps to merge the National Television Network (NTN) with the state-owned Radio St. Lucia to form the new National Broadcasting Network. Internet access is not restricted.

Libel offenses were removed from the criminal code in 2006. However, National Security Minister Philip Victor La Corbiniere initiated a wave of media intimidation in late September by announcing intended legal action against broadcast journalist Timothy Poleon and Radio Caribbean International (RCI) for criticizing his ministry. Two additional government officials announced in October that they would also sue Poleon for reading an article on his radio show from U.S.-based *Caribbean News Now* that allegedly contained defamatory words against them, although no names appeared in the article. On November 25, Poleon read an apology on air admitting his guilt. Leaders of both the UWP and LPM voiced solidarity with Poleon in what they labeled an attack on the media by the SLP administration.

The constitution guarantees freedom of religion, and that right is respected in practice. Academic freedom is generally honored as well.

E. Associational and Organizational Rights: 12 / 12

Constitutional guarantees regarding freedoms of assembly and association are largely upheld. Civic groups are well organized and politically active, as are labor unions, which represent the majority of wage earners. However, the Trade Union Federation faced lengthy governmental delays for a salary increase for public sector workers for the 2010–2013 period; negotiations only concluded in May 2013.

F. Rule of Law: 12 / 16

The judicial system is independent and includes a high court under the Eastern Caribbean Supreme Court (ECSC). A May 2013 ECSC ruling paves the way for Saint Lucia to adopt the Caribbean Court of Justice (CCJ) as its final court of appeal, replacing the Privy Council in London. In recent years, the record of Saint Lucia's police and judicial system has been blemished by incidents including the severe beatings of inmates by police and impunity in cases of police assault and unlawful killings. In August 2013, the U.S. government announced that it would no longer provide support to the Royal Saint Lucia Police Force (RSLPF) due to credible allegations of gross human rights violations related to 12 extrajudicial killings that took place in 2010 and 2011. The government responded by inviting CARICOM to investigate the killings and enlisting the Jamaican police to investigate the RSLPF. The government also passed legislation in November to create a new unit to address complaints against the police and to require search warrants before police may enter a property. Prison overcrowding remains a problem, with major backlogs in the judicial system leading to prolonged pretrial detentions.

Same-sex sexual relations are criminalized for both men and women, with punishments of up to 10 years in prison.

G. Personal Autonomy and Individual Rights: 14 / 16

Women are underrepresented in politics and other professions; there are currently five women serving in Parliament. Domestic violence is a serious concern and often goes unreported. Saint Lucia is considered a destination country for human trafficking for forced labor and prostitution; the government began prosecuting under the 2010 Counter-Trafficking Act in 2012.

Saint Vincent and the Grenadines

Political Rights Rating: 1
Civil Liberties Rating: 1
Freedom Rating: 1.0
Freedom Status: Free
Electoral Democracy: Yes

Population: 108,229
Capital: Kingstown

Ten-Year Ratings Timeline For Year Under Review (Political Rights, Civil Liberties, Status)

Year Under Review	2004	2005	2006	2007	2008	2009	2010	2011	2012	2013
Rating	2,1,F	2,1,F	2,1,F	2,1,F	2,1,F	2,1,F	1,1,F	1,1,F	1,1,F	1,1,F

INTRODUCTION

The government filed new charges against opposition senator Vynnette Frederick and arrested her for alleged false statements related to a complaint she lodged against Prime Minister Ralph Gonsalves following the 2010 general elections. Government officials also threatened and used libel lawsuits against the media and each other throughout the year. Meanwhile, the government passed important witness protection legislation.

The economy continued to show slow signs of recovery after the effects of torrential rains that wiped out the country's banana industry in 2011, destruction caused by Hurricane Tomas in 2010, and the global financial crisis. The annual percentage growth rate of GDP was 2.1 percent. However, the public debt remained over 70 percent of GDP, with close to one-third of all revenue servicing the debt.

POLITICAL RIGHTS: 36 / 40

A. Electoral Process: 11 / 12

A governor general represents the British monarch as head of state. The constitution provides for the election of 15 representatives to the unicameral House of Assembly. In addition, the governor general appoints 6 senators to the chamber: 4 selected on the advice of the prime minister and 2 on the advice of the opposition leader. All serve five-year terms. The prime minister is the leader of the majority party.

In the most recent general elections, in 2010, the incumbent social-democratic Unity Labour Party (ULP) won a slim majority of 8 of the 15 contested legislative seats, and Gonsalves retained his post as prime minister for a third term. Meanwhile, the conservative New Democratic Party (NDP) more than doubled its representation, taking 7 seats. Despite threats of legal challenges from NDP leaders, observers from the Caribbean Community, the Organization of American States, and the National Monitoring and Consultative Mechanism deemed the elections free and fair.

Prime Minister Gonsalves appointed three new senators to the cabinet in September 2013, including his son as minister of foreign affairs, foreign trade, and consumer affairs. Gonsalves's first cousin is also a minister.

Opposition senator Vynnette Frederick was accused of swearing falsely and lying under oath in relation to a private criminal complaint she had filed against the prime minister following the 2010 general elections. On February 15, police brought three charges against Frederick, in addition to three previous charges. All were dropped on July 11, but Frederick was arrested the same day on nine new but related charges. Her trial was pending at the end of the year.

Efforts to clean up the voters list, initiated by the supervisor of elections in early 2013, were ongoing at year's end.

B. Political Pluralism and Participation: 16 / 16

The political landscape is dominated by the NDP and the ULP, although the Green Party also contested the 2010 elections. The new Democratic Republican Party was formed in 2012, led by a former NDP senator.

C. Functioning of Government: 9 / 12

In recent years, there have been allegations of money laundering through Saint Vincent banks and drug-related corruption within the government and the police force. The government has taken some measures to prevent and prosecute such crimes, including the Amendment to the Proceeds of Crime and Money Laundering (Prevention) Act 2012. No independent body investigates government corruption, and the government has yet to pass legislation requiring government officials to disclose assets, incomes, and gifts. Saint Vincent and the Grenadines ranked 33 out of 177 countries and territories surveyed in the 2013 Corruption Perceptions Index.

CIVIL LIBERTIES: 53 / 60

D. Freedom of Expression and Belief: 15 / 16

The press is independent, and the constitution guarantees freedoms of speech and the press. While freedom of information legislation was enacted in 2003, it has yet to be fully implemented. There are several privately owned, independent weeklies and one daily newspaper. The national newspapers publish opinions critical of the government. The Saint Vincent and the Grenadines Broadcasting Corporation operates one television station, and satellite dishes and cable television are available. The main news radio station is partly government owned; radio talk shows are increasing. Internet access is not restricted.

Libel lawsuits continued in 2013. In one of numerous lawsuits against it, Nice Radio—which is considered to be aligned with the opposition NDP—paid the prime minister EC$206,000 (US$76,000) in February for a defamation judgment related to a statement radio host Eduardo Lynch had made close to a decade earlier questioning the financing of a trip Gonsalves had taken with his family. The same month, opposition leader Arnhim Eustace demanded an apology and compensation from the prime minister for alleged defamatory comments Gonsalves made on the radio on February 17, and in March, Gonsalves said he would open a second suit against Eustace for comments the latter had made during a town hall meeting in the United States. In August, the newspapers *The Vincentian* and *The News* issued apologies in response to separate threats of lawsuits by Gonsalves; in the *News* case, another newspaper considered to be aligned with the ULP had printed the same article yet was not asked to apologize.

Freedom of religion is constitutionally protected and respected in practice, and academic freedom is generally honored.

E. Associational and Organizational Rights: 12 / 12 (+1)

Freedoms of assembly and association are constitutionally protected, and nongovernmental organizations are free from government interference. Labor unions are active and permitted to strike and engage in collective bargaining.

F. Rule of Law: 12 / 16 (-1)

The government generally respects judicial independence. The highest court is the Eastern Caribbean Supreme Court, which includes a court of appeals and a high court. The country recognizes the original jurisdiction of the Caribbean Court of Justice, but the final court of appeal is still the Privy Council in London. There are often long judicial delays and a large backlog of cases caused by personnel shortages in the local judiciary. In December, parliament passed important witness protection legislation. Police occasionally use excessive force in arrest proceedings and in custody; in May, the police shot four people in ten days, including the shooting and killing of a man in police custody. Crowded prison conditions improved in 2012 after the long-awaited transfer of prisoners to a new correctional facility.

Same-sex sexual relations remain a criminal offense for both men and women, carrying sentences of up to 10 years in prison.

G. Personal Autonomy and Individual Rights: 14 / 16

Women are underrepresented in political decision-making positions, and hold only 3 of the 23 seats in parliament. Violence against women, particularly domestic violence, remains a problem. The Domestic Violence Summary Proceedings Act, which provides for protective orders, offers some tools that benefit victims.

The Prevention of Trafficking in Persons Act (2011) criminalizes forced labor and prostitution. On May 21, the government appointed a 12-member Reparations Committee to investigate genocide and forced deportation of the indigenous Garifuna and Callinago people, stealing of their land, and enslavement of African people in Saint Vincent and the Grenadines. In September, Prime Minister Gonsalves announced a CARICOM joint legal action against the United Kingdom, France, and the Netherlands for the legacy of the slave trade.

Samoa

Political Rights Rating: 2
Civil Liberties Rating: 2
Freedom Rating: 2.0
Freedom Status: Free
Electoral Democracy: Yes

Population: 190,000
Capital: Apia

Ten-Year Ratings Timeline For Year Under Review (Political Rights, Civil Liberties, Status)

Year Under Review	2004	2005	2006	2007	2008	2009	2010	2011	2012	2013
Rating	2,2,F	2,2,F	2,2,F	2,2,F	2,2,F	2,2,F	2,2,F	2,2,F	2,2,F	2,2,F

INTRODUCTION

In February, despite criticisms from gambling opponents, the Samoan government authorized licenses for the construction of two casinos in an effort to boost tourism. One of the licenses, granted to a Chinese firm, was canceled in August after the Chinese government arrested the owner of the company on corruption charges.

The new Crime Act went into effect in May. It increases penalties for many crimes and added others to the books, while dropping libel as a criminal offense.

POLITICAL RIGHTS: 32 / 40
A. Electoral Process: 9 / 12

Samoa is an electoral democracy. The 49-member legislature elects the head of state, who appoints the prime minister. Two legislative seats are reserved for at-large voters, mostly citizens of mixed or non-Samoan heritage who have no ties to the 47 village-based constituencies. All lawmakers serve five-year terms.

In the March 2011 parliamentary elections, the Human Rights Protection Party (HRPP) took 36 seats, while the Tautua Samoa Party (TSP) captured the remaining 13. The elections were generally regarded as fair and open, though the electoral court found four lawmakers from both parties guilty of bribing voters and stripped them of their seats. Special by-elections were held in July 2012 to fill the seats; the HRPP captured all four, boosting its majority to 40 seats. Prime Minister Tuilaepa Aiono Sailele Malielegaoi was elected to a third term.

B. Political Pluralism and Participation: 13 / 16

The centrist HRPP has dominated politics since Samoa gained independence in 1962. Prospective office holders seek endorsement by *matai*, traditional chiefs of extended families, as the latter are very influential in mobilizing their villagers to vote for their preferred candidates.

C. Functioning of Government: 10 / 12

Official corruption and abuse are a source of increasing public discontent. In June, the Samoan Customs Department launched an investigation into fraud within the agency that an opposition lawmakers say could have cost the government significant losses in revenue. The probe was ongoing at year's end.

CIVIL LIBERTIES: 49 / 60
D. Freedom of Expression and Belief: 14 / 16

Freedoms of speech and the press are generally respected. Several publicly and privately owned newspapers, radio, and television stations operate in Samoa. Moana TV, the first internet-based station in the South Pacific, was launched in 2012. Construction of a new broadband network to expand internet access is under way.

The Samoan media have made intermittent attempts over the past decade to create a self-regulating council to set standards for fairness, accuracy, and balance in news reporting, though little progress was made by the end of 2013. The Samoa Law Reform Commission recommended in its June 2012 report that the media industry be given two years to establish its own council. *Samoa Observer*, the leading newspaper, opposes such a body on the grounds that government supporters would dominate it.

The Newspaper and Printers Act of 1992 directs publishers and editors to reveal sources of information in cases of defamation claims by the prime minister, cabinet members, and heads of departments. As the 2013 crime law removes libel as a criminal offense, the attorney general said his office will review the 1992 law but made no promise to repeal it.

In May, the police department announced it was taking the prime minister's advice to end its weekly media briefs, replacing them with press releases and written responses. This policy change, made in the midst of investigations of several cases of police misconduct, spurred strong criticism from the media and the public. The following month, the prime minister reversed his position in the interest of more openness and transparency. In July, the government asserted that, under a 2012 law intended to bolster tourism, it has the power to prosecute anyone who makes false statements about Samoa that threaten to harm the country's tourism industry.

The government respects freedom of religion in practice, and relations among religious groups are generally amicable. There were no reports of restrictions on academic freedom in 2013.

E. Associational and Organizational Rights: 10 / 12

Freedoms of assembly and association are respected, and human rights groups operate freely. Workers, including civil servants, can strike and bargain collectively. Approximately 60 percent of adults work in subsistence agriculture, and about 20 percent of wage earners belong to trade unions.

F. Rule of Law: 13 / 16

The judiciary is independent and upholds the right to a fair trial. The Supreme Court is the highest court, with full jurisdiction over civil, criminal, and constitutional matters. The head of state, on the recommendation of the prime minister, appoints the chief justice. In August, the government adopted a new legal framework to help parties mediate disputes without going to court; it swore in 23 mediators to facilitate the process.

Prisons generally meet minimum international standards. In August, the police commissioner and several assistants were temporarily suspended in response to allegations of corruption and prisoner abuse.

A new crime law took effect on May 1. The law added new offenses, including computer-related crimes, human smuggling and trafficking, the distribution of sexual materials using mobile devices, and invasion of privacy. It also increased penalties for sex-related offenses, making sexual conduct with minors punishable by life in prison. In August, the government announced it would launch a National Human Rights Institution in the Ombudsman's Office to increase public awareness and public education on human rights.

Samoa has no military, and the small police force has little impact in the villages. Matai control local government and churches through the village *fono*, or legislature, which is open only to them. The fono settles most disputes. The councils vary considerably in their decision-making styles and in the number of matai involved. Light offenses are usually punished with fines; serious offenses result in banishment from the village. Individuals and entire families have been forced to leave villages for allegedly insulting a matai, embracing a different religion, or voting for political candidates not endorsed by the matai. Several controversial cases led the Supreme Court to rule in 2002 that village fono could not infringe on freedoms of religion, speech, assembly, or association.

In July 2013, eight defendants, including a lawmaker, were found guilty of blocking a road in Satapuala village the previous year; each was fined $635. The defendants had been protesting the government's claims over 8,000 acres of land near the airport, which they say were unlawfully taken from the village by colonial authorities and subsequently kept by the government without adequate compensation to the landowners.

Chinese presence in the local economy has grown rapidly in recent years, particularly in the fishing, retail, construction, and tourism industries. Business leaders have warned of rising social tensions because locals feel threatened and displaced by Chinese capital and migrants.

G. Personal Autonomy and Individual Rights: 12 / 16

Domestic violence against women and children is widespread. Spousal rape is not illegal, and social pressure and fear of reprisal inhibit reporting of domestic abuse. In addition to tougher penalties under the new crime law, the parliament passed the new Family Safety Act in February to protect victims of family violence and sexual abuse by giving more power to the police, public health officials, and educators to help affected families.

In June, the legislature unanimously passed a constitutional amendment to reserve at least five seats in parliament for women in the 2016 general election. If no women are elected in the polls, the five female candidates with the highest number of votes will claim these seats; the total number of lawmakers will be raised from 49 to 54.

In 2011, the government rejected a call by the United Nations to decriminalize homosexuality, arguing that it was contrary to Samoan culture and values.

San Marino

Political Rights Rating: 1
Civil Liberties Rating: 1
Freedom Rating: 1.0
Freedom Status: Free
Electoral Democracy: Yes

Population: 32,611
Capital: San Marino

Ten-Year Ratings Timeline For Year Under Review (Political Rights, Civil Liberties, Status)

Year Under Review	2004	2005	2006	2007	2008	2009	2010	2011	2012	2013
Rating	1,1,F	1,1,F	1,1,F	1,1,F	1,1,F	1,1,F	1,1,F	1,1,F	1,1,F	1,1,F

INTRODUCTION

In October, San Marino held a referendum to join the EU. Although a majority of voters were in favor, the referendum failed because the 22 percent of voters who turned out did not meet the required quorum of 32 percent.

In 2013, the trial began for seven individuals on corruption charges related to bribery at construction sites.

POLITICAL RIGHTS: 40 / 40

A. Electoral Process: 12 / 12

The 60 members of the Great and General Council, the unicameral legislature, are elected every five years. Executive power rests with the 10-member State Congress (cabinet), which is headed by two captains regent. As the joint heads of state, the captains regent are elected every six months by the Great and General Council from among its own members. Although there is no official prime minister, the secretary of state for foreign and political affairs is regarded as the head of government; Pasquale Valentini was elected to the post in December 2012. Under changes made to the electoral law in 2008 designed to increase accountability, government stability, and citizen participation, the winning coalition must hold 35 of the 60 parliamentary seats.

After the resignations of two members of parliament in July 2012, the captains regent dissolved the legislature in August, calling for early elections on November 11. The Sammarinese Christian Democratic Party (PDCS) captured 21 seats and formed a three-party coalition—San Marino Common Good—with the Party of Socialists and Democrats (PSD), which won 10 seats, and the Popular Alliance, which took 4 seats. Opposition groups include the Entente for the Country coalition with 12 seats, the Active Citizenship coalition with 9 seats, and the Civic Movement R.E.T.E. with 4 seats.

B. Political Pluralism and Participation: 16 / 16

The two main parties are the Christian-democratic PDCS and the social-democratic PSD. Due to the large number of small parties, the government is often run by changing coalitions of parties with similar platforms. In 2012, the PDCS and the Popular Alliance retained power, but the addition of the PSD marks a change of control.

C. Functioning of Government: 12 / 12

There is little government corruption in the country, though financial corruption has prompted the government to increase financial transparency. In 2010, San Marino became the 48th state to join the Council of Europe's Group of States against Corruption. In 2012, among those arrested for suspected criminal activity under a new antimafia commission established in 2011 was Livio Bacciocchi of the financial institution Fincapital, who was accused of money laundering and extortion. In April 2013, Bacciocchi was sentenced to five years and six months' imprisonment by a court in Bologna for the scandal, which came to be known as Vulcano2. Also in 2013, a trial began against Paolo Berardi and Davide Mularoni, two commissioners at San Marino's environmental hygiene agency, for illegally bribing building contractors. The case also implicated Bacciocchi and four others.

In January 2012, Marco Bianchini, the former head of the financial firm Karnak, was accused of extortion and corruption related to the Camorra, a Neapolitan mafia, in a scandal known as Criminal Minds; he was arrested after transferring €5 million ($6.5 million) into a Maltese bank. The case was investigated throughout 2013 but no one had been convicted by year's end.

In October, San Marino and Italy ratified a double-taxation agreement, a step toward Italy removing San Marino from its list of tax havens. The agreement will help San Marino crack down on Italian tax evaders.

CIVIL LIBERTIES: 60 / 60
D. Freedom of Expression and Belief: 16 / 16

Freedoms of speech and the press are guaranteed. There are several private daily newspapers; a state-run broadcast system for radio and television, RTV; and a private FM station, Radio Titano. The Sammarinese have access to all Italian print media and certain Italian broadcast stations. Access to the internet is unrestricted.

Religious discrimination is prohibited by law. There is no state religion, though Roman Catholicism is dominant. Academic freedom is respected.

E. Associational and Organizational Rights: 12 / 12

Freedom of assembly is respected, and civic organizations are active. Workers are free to strike, organize trade unions, and bargain collectively, unless they work in military occupations. Approximately half of the country's workforce is unionized.

F. Rule of Law: 16 / 16

The judiciary is independent. Lower court judges are required to be noncitizens—generally Italians—to ensure impartiality. The highest court is the Council of Twelve, a group of judges chosen for six-year terms from among the members of the Great and General Council. Civilian authorities maintain effective control over the police and security forces. With a very small prison population, San Marino considered improvements to its one prison in 2013 after a visit by the Council of Europe's Committee for the Prevention of Torture.

G. Personal Autonomy and Individual Rights: 16 / 16

A 2013 report by the European Commission against Racism and Intolerance noted that despite improvements since its 2008 report, several concerns remain about the status of foreigners in the country. San Marino has no formal asylum policy, although a decree adopted in 2010 introduced a "stay permit" in special cases of humanitarian need. A 2012 law loosened citizenship rules, including reducing the number of years' residency required for citizenship from 30 to 25; the European Convention on Nationality, which San Marino has not signed, recommends that such residence requirements not exceed 10 years. In 2012 San Marino withdrew a 16th-century law in order to give visa rights to foreign partners in same-sex relationships with Sammarinese citizens.

Women are given legal protections from violence and spousal abuse, and gender equality exists in the workplace and elsewhere. There are, however, slight differences in the way men and women can transmit citizenship to their children. Abortion is permitted only to save the life of the mother, though abortion laws in neighboring Italy are more liberal, and some women living in San Marino seek abortions there. Under a 2008 electoral law, no more than two-thirds of candidates from each party can be of the same gender. Ten women were elected to the Great and General Council in 2012, but none were elected to the 10-member State Congress.

São Tomé and Príncipe

Political Rights Rating: 2
Civil Liberties Rating: 2
Freedom Rating: 2.0
Freedom Status: Free
Electoral Democracy: Yes

Population: 188,132
Capital: São Tomé

Ten-Year Ratings Timeline For Year Under Review (Political Rights, Civil Liberties, Status)

Year Under Review	2004	2005	2006	2007	2008	2009	2010	2011	2012	2013
Rating	2,2,F	2,2,F	2,2,F	2,2,F	2,2,F	2,2,F	2,2,F	2,2,F	2,2,F	2,2,F

INTRODUCTION

The year was marked by the continued slow-down of São Tomé and Príncipe's economy, as well as brewing tensions between the government coalition and the Independent Democratic Action party (ADI), which boycotted certain parliamentary activities for the first half of the year. In addition to exchanging corruption accusations, the ADI and the ruling Movement for the Liberation of São Tomé and Príncipe-Social Democratic Party (MLSTP-PSD) disagreed on items including the appointment of an attorney general.

POLITICAL RIGHTS: 34 / 40

A. Electoral Process: 11 / 12

São Tomé and Príncipe's president is elected for up to two five-year terms. Members of the unicameral, 55-seat National Assembly are elected by popular vote to four-year terms. In the August 2010 parliamentary elections, which were considered free and fair, the ADI captured 26 seats, followed by the MLSTP-PSD with 21 seats, and the Democratic Convergence Party (PCD) with 7; the Force for Change Democratic Movement captured only 1 seat. ADI leader Patrice Trovoada was appointed prime minister.

Former strongman Manuel Pinto da Costa, who ruled São Tomé and Príncipe for the first 15 years after independence, won the August 2011 presidential election as an independent candidate. He defeated the incumbent ADI party's Evaristo Carvalho in a runoff election with 52.9 percent of the vote. Foreign observers deemed the highly contested elections credible and fair.

Following a no-confidence vote that brought down the ADI government in November 2012, MLSTP-PSD leader Gabriel Costa assumed office as the new prime minister on December 10. Meanwhile, ADI's members boycotted parliament from November 2012 until February 15, when the now MLSTP-PSD-controlled National Assembly voted to cut the salaries of absent members. The ADI continued to boycott parliamentary commissions until early July, at which point the National Assembly ordered the cancellation of car privileges for nonparticipating members. On July 18, after returning to full participation, ADI submitted a request for a no-confidence vote, accusing the MLSTP-PSD government of corruption, human rights' violations, and endangering the health of São Tomeans. The president of the National Assembly refused the request on the grounds that it did not fulfill procedural requirements.

In May, President Pinto da Costa postponed municipal and regional elections, originally scheduled for July, until 2014. Consultations on revisions to a draft electoral law were ongoing at year's end.

B. Political Pluralism and Participation: 14 / 16

The multiparty system features vigorous competition between the ADI, the MLSTP-PSD, the PCD, and other parties. Though political parties are free to operate there is evidence that some of the opposition leaders have been victim of political persecution.

As indicated by the president, São Tomeans are losing trust in political parties as they are appear to be more concerned with their own interests than those of the country. As a result, São Tomeans are increasingly turning to civil society organizations.

Although immigrants represent a very small share of the population in São Tomé, they have yet to be allowed to participate in elections and vote.

C. Functioning of Government: 9 / 12

Following the approval of a new anticorruption law and the establishment of the Public Integrity Center in 2012, the new prime minister warned in January that money laundering and narco-trafficking were on the rise. In August, following pressure from international donors, the National Assembly approved a new law to prevent and fight money laundering. In April, to promote transparency, the government submitted to the Supreme Court a list of all assets controlled by its cabinet members.

A slew of alleged corrupt deals came to the fore in 2013. In March, the government declared that €572,000 ($753,000) was missing from a state fund financed through the sale of rice donated by Japan. In May, the ADI accused the minister of agriculture and fisheries of establishing a private company within the Fisheries Department and cozying up to a private Spanish company. The ADI also accused the Ministry of Commerce of illicitly buying 3,000 tons of tainted rice from Cameroon. In June, the PCD accused former prime minister Trovoada of money laundering, including €624,600 ($821,800) sent under suspicious circumstances to Gabon. This exchange of corruption allegations contributed to political instability. São Tomé and Príncipe was ranked 72 out of 177 countries surveyed in Transparency International's 2013 Corruption Perceptions Index.

CIVIL LIBERTIES: 47 / 60
D. Freedom of Expression and Belief: 15 / 16

Freedom of expression is guaranteed and respected. While the state controls a local press agency and the only radio and television stations, no law forbids independent broadcasting. Opposition parties receive free airtime, and newsletters and pamphlets criticizing the government circulate freely. Residents also have access to foreign broadcasts. Internet access is not restricted, though a lack of infrastructure limits penetration.

Freedom of religion is respected within this predominantly Roman Catholic country. The government does not restrict academic freedom. However, although the government has identified education as a top priority, limited funds and poor training undermine the quality of teaching.

E. Associational and Organizational Rights: 10 / 12

Freedoms of assembly and association are respected, and citizens have the constitutional right to demonstrate with two days' advance notice to the government. The tainted rice case caused public demonstrations, which led to the government's July decision to recall the rice.

In May 2013 the Federation of NGOs in São Tomé and Príncipe that represents approximately 100 NGOs inaugurated its new headquarters. NGOs are free to operate though their capacity to intervene is limited as most have very limited funding. Workers' rights to organize, strike, and bargain collectively are guaranteed and respected. In October the teachers' union called for a strike that disrupted schooling for 80,000 students. The prime minister headed the negotiations with the union, which called off the strike after signing an agreement with the government addressing several of the teachers' demands.

F. Rule of Law: 12 / 16

The constitution provides for an independent judiciary, though it is susceptible to political influence and is understaffed and inadequately funded. The country's one prison is overcrowded, and inmates suffer from inadequate food and medical care. In January, Elsa Pinto was appointed as the new attorney general by presidential decree. As Pinto is prominent in the MLSTP-PSD party, the Bar Association and others argued that her political ties jeopardized the office's independence. Just two weeks after her appointment, Pinto was dismissed. She was replaced by Frederique Samba. On July 30, after an audit of the courts' finances and rumors of poor management, the head judge of the Supreme Court, José Bandeira, dissolved the courts' Board of Administration and nominated a new board that he presides over. Critics called it an abuse of power, arguing that only the National Assembly may perform this type of structural change.

Although the 2012 penal code removed restrictions, same-sex relationships are generally hidden due to discrimination. São Tomé was among the countries that signed a UN joint declaration to decriminalize homosexuality in 2011.

G. Personal Autonomy and Individual Rights: 10 / 16

While São Tomeans are free to travel and seek employment, they have limited access to secondary and higher education.

São Tomé and Príncipe is one of the smallest economies in Africa and extremely dependent on international aid (85 percent of its budget is financed by donors). Economic activity is growing but it is still challenging to establish private businesses in view of red tape and corruption. Access to economic opportunities is also uneven, with São Tomé and Príncipe exhibiting one of the highest Gini coefficients in sub-Saharan Africa (50.8).

There are currently 10 women in the National Assembly. The constitution provides equal rights for men and women, but women encounter discrimination in all sectors of society. Domestic violence is common and rarely prosecuted.

Saudi Arabia

Political Rights Rating: 7
Civil Liberties Rating: 7
Freedom Rating: 7.0
Freedom Status: Not Free
Electoral Democracy: No

Population: 30,054,000
Capital: Riyadh

Ten-Year Ratings Timeline For Year Under Review (Political Rights, Civil Liberties, Status)

Year Under Review	2004	2005	2006	2007	2008	2009	2010	2011	2012	2013
Rating	7,7,NF	7,6,NF	7,6,NF	7,6,NF	7,6,NF	7,6,NF	7,6,NF	7,7,NF	7,7,NF	7,7,NF

INTRODUCTION

The kingdom's rulers worked to suppress reform activism throughout 2013. Saudi courts in March sentenced two founding members of the Saudi Civil and Political Rights Association (ACPRA) to lengthy prison terms for calling for political reform and championing human rights, and disbanded their organization. Another member of the ACPRA was sentenced in June to eight years in prison for "slandering the king," among other charges. Those sentences were part of a much broader campaign against political dissidents and activists in various fields. In one case, two women's rights activists were each sentenced to 10 months in jail in June for "supporting a wife without her husband's knowledge, thereby undermining the marriage," after aiding an apparently abused woman.

Authorities also continued to target members of the country's minority Shiite Muslim community, mostly in the country's Eastern Province. Shiites began protesting against discrimination and calling for greater political rights in 2011, and during 2013 security forces killed at least one person and arrested dozens of others for related activity, including several who were accused of spying for Iran in March. In June, seven Shiites were sentenced to between 5 and 10 years in prison for supporting protests on Facebook. A Shiite woman was sentenced in April to eight lashes for sending a text message that included information on Shiite religious services.

Despite formidable obstacles, women continued to press for greater social and political rights during the year, including through an ongoing campaign to lift the ban on women driving. While the movement has broad societal support, members of the country's consultative assembly, the Majlis al-Shura, have refused to back the effort.

POLITICAL RIGHTS: 3 / 40

A. Electoral Process: 0 / 12

The 1992 Basic Law declares that the Koran and the Sunna (the guidance set by the deeds and sayings of the prophet Muhammad) are the country's constitution. The cabinet, which is appointed by the king, passes legislation that becomes law once ratified by royal decree. The king also appoints a 150-member Majlis al-Shura (Consultative Council) every four years, though it serves only in an advisory capacity. Limited elections for advisory councils at the municipal level were introduced in 2005, and the second round of elections was held in 2011. Half of the seats on the 285 councils were open to nonpartisan voting by adult male citizens, while the remainder was filled through appointment by the king. The next municipal council elections are scheduled for 2015.

B. Political Pluralism and Participation: 0 / 16

Political parties are forbidden, and organized political opposition exists only outside the country. Political dissent is criminalized.

Activists who challenge the country's record on political inclusion or call for constitutional changes are treated harshly. Several high-profile activists were convicted in 2013 for advocating reform, including ACPRA cofounders Muhammad Qahtani and Abdullah al-Hamed, who were sentenced in March to 10- and 11-year prison terms, respectively, for their work. As part of the sentencing, the court disbanded the ACPRA and seized its assets. In June, another ACPRA founding member, Abd al-Kareem al-Khoder, was sentenced to eight years in prison for calling for the creation of a constitutional monarchy. In August, authorities released a fourth founding member of the group, Muhammad al-Bajadi, who had been arrested in 2011 and sentenced in 2012 to four years in prison. However, he was quickly rearrested and apparently remained behind bars at year's end.

Women are generally excluded from political affairs. However, in January 2013 a royal decree established that women would receive at least 20 percent of the seats on the Consultative Council. Thirty women were duly appointed the following month. A 2011 decree gave women the right to vote and seek seats in the 2015 municipal council elections.

C. Functioning of Government: 1 / 12

Corruption remains a significant problem. After widespread floods killed more than 120 people in November 2009, King Abdullah bin Abdul Aziz al-Saud in May 2010 ordered the prosecution of over 40 officials in the city of Jeddah on charges of corruption and mismanagement related to improper construction and engineering practices. A second round of floods in January 2011 killed over 10 people and displaced several thousand, sparking small protests that alleged ongoing corruption. In May 2012, a government official and a local businessman were fined and sentenced to five years in prison on charges of corruption related to the 2009 floods. Several other cases remained pending in 2013. A 2011 royal decree established an anticorruption commission to monitor government departments, though administrative obstacles have hindered the commission's success. Individuals who accuse officials of corruption can face defamation charges and other repercussions.

Although the Saudi government generates massive revenue from the sale of oil, which it redistributes to social welfare programs and as patronage, little is known about the government's accounting or the various direct ways that the state's wealth becomes a source of private privilege for the royal family and its clients.

Discretionary Political Rights Question A: 2 / 4

In addition to the advisory councils, the monarchy has a tradition of consulting with select members of Saudi society, but the process is not equally open to all citizens. From the king to local governors, royal family officials periodically host meetings for citizens to air grievances and seek access to money or power. These meetings are irregular, and while they afford some citizens rare opportunities to meet with the powerful, the outcomes reinforce the personalized nature of authority.

CIVIL LIBERTIES: 7 / 40

D. Freedom of Expression and Belief: 3 / 16

The government tightly controls domestic media content and dominates regional print and satellite-television coverage, with members of the royal family owning major stakes in news outlets in multiple countries. Government officials have banned journalists and editors who publish articles deemed offensive to the religious establishment or the ruling authorities.

A 2011 royal decree amended the country's press law to criminalize any criticism of the country's grand mufti, the Council of Senior Religious Scholars, or government officials; violations can result in fines and forced closure.

The regime has taken steps to limit the influence of new media, blocking access to over 400,000 websites that are considered immoral or politically sensitive. A 2011 law requires all blogs and websites, or anyone posting news or commentary online, to have a license from the Ministry of Information or face fines and possible closure of the website.

Many writers and activists have been incarcerated for using the internet to express their views. Prominent author and intellectual Turki al-Hamad was released in June 2013 after six months of detention without charge, having been arrested after criticizing Islamists on the social-media site Twitter. Human rights activist Mikhlif al-Shammari was sentenced to five years in prison in June, based in part on the authorities' claim that he had uploaded a video to YouTube that appeared to document abuse against women. Raef Badawi, who was arrested in 2012 for comments about religion that he made on his website and on television, was sentenced to seven years in prison and 600 lashes in July. In October, officials released writer Hamza Kashgari, who had been was arrested in Malaysia in 2012 and extradited back to Saudi Arabia to face charges of apostasy, which carries a mandatory death sentence. He had used Twitter to express views on Islam and the prophet Muhammad that are criminalized in the kingdom. In October Waleed al-Bukhair was sentenced to three months in prison for criticizing abuses in the judicial and criminal systems.

Islam is the official religion, and all Saudis are required by law to be Muslims. The government prohibits the public practice of any religion other than Islam and restricts the religious practices of the Shiite and Sufi Muslim minority sects. Although the government recognizes the right of non-Muslims to worship in private, it does not always respect this right in practice. The building of Shiite mosques is banned.

Academic freedom is restricted, and informers monitor classrooms for compliance with curriculum rules, such as a ban on teaching secular philosophy and religions other than Islam. Despite changes to textbooks in recent years, intolerance in the classroom remains an important problem, as some teachers continue to espouse discriminatory and hateful views of non-Muslims and Muslim minority sects.

E. Associational and Organizational Rights: 0 / 12

Freedoms of assembly and association are not upheld. The government frequently detains political activists who stage demonstrations or engage in other civic advocacy. While there have been no large-scale protests in the kingdom, smaller demonstrations have become more common. Regular protests by relatives of political prisoners took place outside the Ministry of the Interior in Riyadh and in the town of Burayda throughout 2013. Authorities arrested hundreds of protesters, mostly women, typically releasing them after several hours or days of detention. Small demonstrations also occurred in predominantly Shiite villages in Eastern Province, where protesters periodically took to the streets to demand political reform and express support for antigovernment protests in neighboring Bahrain.

Saudi Arabia has no associations law and has historically approved licenses only for charitable organizations. In May 2013, the authorities rejected an application for the registration of the Adala Center, an independent human rights society based in Eastern Province. There are no laws protecting the rights to form independent labor unions, bargain collectively, or engage in strikes. Workers who engage in union activity are subject to dismissal or imprisonment. The Ministry of Labor reported in 2013 that it is in the process of enacting regulations that will allow for some form of workers' organization for business that have more than 100 employees.

F. Rule of Law: 2 / 16

The judiciary, which must coordinate its decisions with the executive branch, is not independent. A Special Higher Commission of judicial experts was formed in 2008 to write laws that would serve as the foundation for verdicts in the court system, which is grounded in Sharia (Islamic law). While Saudi courts have historically relied on the Hanbali school of Islamic jurisprudence, the commission incorporates all four Sunni Muslim legal schools in drafting new laws.

The penal code bans torture, but allegations of torture by police and prison officials are common, and access to prisoners by independent human rights and legal organizations is strictly limited. In 2011, the authorities issued a draft of a sweeping new antiterrorism law that would include significant prison sentences for criticizing the government or questioning the integrity of the king or crown prince. It had not been adopted by the end of 2013, though elements of the measure, including the penalization of criticism of the royal family, appeared to have been implemented.

Substantial prejudice against ethnic, religious, and national minorities prevails. Shiites, who represent 10 to 15 percent of the population, are underrepresented in major government positions and have also faced physical assaults. As a result, Shiite activists and demonstration organizers became more confrontational in 2012. Authorities responded harshly, issuing a most-wanted list of activists and violently dispersing protests. Security forces continued their crackdown in 2013, arresting 16 people in March for allegedly participating in an Iranian spy ring. In June, a 19-year-old Shiite man was killed by stray gunfire from police who were pursuing another suspect. Also that month, seven Shiites were sentenced to between five and ten years in prison for posting their support for protests on Facebook.

G. Personal Autonomy an Individual Rights: 2 / 16

Freedom of movement is restricted in some cases. The government punishes activists and critics by limiting their ability to travel outside the country, and reform advocates are routinely stripped of their passports. Journalist and activist Iman al-Qahtani was banned from traveling abroad in July 2013 as a result of her writing on human rights issues.

While a great deal of business activity is connected to members of the government, the ruling family, or other elite families, officials have given assurances that special industrial and commercial zones will be free from royal family interference.

Women are not treated as equal members of society, and many laws discriminate against them. They are not permitted to drive cars or travel within or outside of the country without a male relative. According to interpretations of Sharia in Saudi Arabia, daughters generally receive half the inheritance awarded to their brothers, and the testimony of one man is equal to that of two women. Moreover, Saudi women seeking access to the courts must be represented by a male. The religious police enforce a strict policy of gender segregation and often harass women, using physical punishment to ensure that they meet conservative standards of dress in public. All sexual activity outside marriage, including homosexual acts, is criminalized, and the death penalty can be applied in certain circumstances.

Education and economic rights for Saudi women have improved somewhat in recent years, with more than half of the country's university students now female, though they do not enjoy equal access to classes and facilities. Women gained the right to hold commercial licenses in 2004. In 2008, the Saudi Human Rights Commission established a women's branch to investigate cases of human rights violations against women and children, but it has not consistently carried out serious investigations or brought cases against violators.

In August 2013, the government enacted a law that defines and criminalizes domestic abuse, prescribing fines and up to a year in prison for perpetrators. However, according to an analysis by Human Rights Watch, the law lacks clarity on enforcement mechanisms. In July, prominent women's rights activists Wajeha al-Huwaider and Fawzia al-Oyouni were sentenced to 10 months in prison and banned from traveling abroad for two years for a 2011 attempt to assist a woman who was apparently being domestically abused.

Saudi women continued to agitate and press for the right to drive in 2013. About 60 women reported driving on October 26 as part of a coordinated protest; several participants uploaded videos of themselves driving onto YouTube.

A 2005 labor law that extended various protections and benefits to previously unregulated categories of workers also banned child labor and established a 75 percent quota for Saudi citizens in each company's workforce. However, the more than six million foreign workers in the country have virtually no legal protections. Many are lured to the kingdom under false pretenses and forced to endure dangerous working and living conditions. Female migrants employed in Saudi homes report regular physical, sexual, and emotional abuse. In 2013, Saudi Arabia launched a campaign to deport expatriate workers who had allegedly overstayed their visas or were no longer employed by their original hosts. The roughly one million people affected included some 300,000 Yemenis and over 100,000 Ethiopians. Efforts to crackdown on workers who had overstayed their visas led to labor unrest and rare riots between foreign laborers and authorities in November. Over 100 people were injured. Tens of thousands of expatriates, including those assaulted by authorities, were deported in the fall.

Senegal

Political Rights Rating: 2
Civil Liberties Rating: 2
Freedom Rating: 2.0
Freedom Status: Free
Electoral Democracy: Yes

Population: 13,497,000
Capital: Dakar

Ratings Change: Senegal's civil liberties rating improved from 3 to 2 due to improvements in the media environment and for freedom of assembly since President Macky Sall took office in 2012.

Ten-Year Ratings Timeline For Year Under Review (Political Rights, Civil Liberties, Status)

Year Under Review	2004	2005	2006	2007	2008	2009	2010	2011	2012	2013
Rating	6,5,NF	6,5,NF	6,5,NF	6,5,NF	4,5,PF	4,5,PF	4,5,PF	4,5,PF	4,5,PF	4,5,PF

INTRODUCTION

After reactivating the Court of Repossession of Illegally Acquired Assets (CREI) and establishing the National Anti-Corruption Commission (OFNAC) in 2012, President Macky Sall intensified his fight against corruption in 2013. Several members of the former ruling party were under investigation. Karim Wade, a former government minister and the son of former president Abdoulaye Wade, was arrested in April on charges of the corrupt acquisition of up to $1.4 billion while in office. The CREI re-indicted Karim Wade and prolonged his detention in October, which his lawyers and some human rights advocates claimed was not allowed under the legal code. Sall has also targeted corruption in his own administration, including by responding to a drug-trafficking scandal within the police. He publicly declared his assets in 2012 as required by the constitution and has worked both informally and through legislation to encourage similar behavior among other public officials.

Senegal received widespread praise in July for setting up the Extraordinary African Chambers that the government had authorized in 2012 to try former Chadian dictator Hissene Habré for offenses committed in Chad under his regime, and for indicting Habré for torture, war crimes, and crimes against humanity. However, Senegal's judiciary remains dependent on the executive branch in practice, with no new reforms implemented in 2013.

In June, Sall drew criticism from human rights advocates for publicly expressing his opposition to the decriminalization of homosexuality, a position he shared with large segments of Senegalese society.

POLITICAL RIGHTS: 33 / 40 (+1)

A. Electoral Process: 11 / 12

Members of Senegal's 150-seat National Assembly are elected to five-year terms; the president serves seven-year terms with a two-term limit. A 100-member upper house that had been created in 2007 was abolished in 2012. The president appoints the prime minister; Sall in September 2013 fired Prime Minister Abdoul Mbaye and appointed Justice Minister Aminata Touré to the post.

The National Autonomous Electoral Commission (CENA) is the domestic monitor of elections. It is nominally independent, but its members are appointed by the president on the advice of other public figures, and it is financially dependent on the government, which funds its monitoring and oversight operations. The Interior Ministry organizes the elections.

In January 2012, ahead of the February presidential election, Wade's candidacy for a third term was validated the Constitutional Council, whose members he had appointed. Wade had previously failed to secure passage of a constitutional amendment allowing him to run for a third term and lowering the threshold for victory in the first round of a presidential election from 50 percent to 25 percent. Nevertheless, the council upheld his argument that his first term had not counted toward the two-term limit, which was imposed the year after he first took office.

The presidential campaign period featured significant violence and intimidation, but the election ultimately resulted in a peaceful transfer of power. After placing second in the first round, Sall—a former member of Wade's Senegalese Democratic Party (PDS) who had previously served as his prime minister and campaign director, and as the president of the National Assembly—garnered support from other opposition parties in the March runoff. He took 66 percent of the vote, and Wade quickly conceded defeat.

In the July 2012 parliamentary elections, Sall's United in Hope coalition, which included his Alliance for the Republic party, captured 119 of the 150 seats, followed by the PDS with 12. About a dozen parties divided the remainder.

Both the presidential and National Assembly elections were declared free and fair by international observers.

B. Political Pluralism and Participation: 13 / 16

There is a significant opposition vote, and there are viable opportunities for the opposition to win presidential, legislative, and local offices. Opposition figures are active in politics, and there are over 200 registered political parties, which operate freely. The March 2012 presidential election marked the second victory by an opposition candidate in 12 years.

The opposition still faces certain disadvantages when competing with incumbents, namely major inequalities in financial resources. There is no public financing of political parties in Senegal, and international funding of parties is illegal. The ruling party can deploy a vast set of state resources to attract and maintain support, whereas opposition party leaders must often rely on personal wealth.

C. Functioning of Government: 9 / 12 (+1)

Corruption has long been a serious problem in Senegal and provoked growing public outrage during Wade's second term. Upon his election in 2012, Sall began a public works audit to investigate corruption under the Wade administration. In 2013, Sall intensified his efforts to reduce corruption and improve governance in Senegal. He used the CREI and the OFNAC to monitor current officials and pursue corruption charges against members of the previous government.

Sall has been praised for his crackdown on corruption and is supported in these efforts by the World Bank, but the selection of cases is not always viewed as objective. Recent investigations have focused on allegations of corruption by PDS politicians close to Wade, although Sall himself was Wade's close associate until 2008. In April 2013, Karim Wade was arrested, and the CREI investigated charges that he had embezzled up to $1.4 billion while in office. By the end of 2013, he had been re-indicted and was still in detention, despite criticism of the re-indictment by his lawyers and some human rights advocates. Several other PDS officials prominent during Abdoulaye Wade's last years in office were under investigation.

Although PDS officials denounce investigations into their colleagues as political revenge, Sall has fought corruption within his own administration as well. In July 2013, the director general of the police, Abdoulaye Niang, was accused of complicity in drug trafficking in his former position as director of the Central Office for the Repression of Drug Trafficking (OCRTIS). Both he and his accuser, current OCRTIS director Cheikhna Cheikh Sadibou Keïta, were temporarily relieved of their duties as the investigation continued. The Directorate for the Inspection of Security Services (DISS) presented the results of its investigation to Sall, and the council of ministers discussed the case at the end of July; the DISS report cleared Niang and implicated Keita. By the end of 2013, the public prosecutor had issued a ruling that echoed the findings of the DISS. Separately, in April, the Division of Criminal Investigation (DIC) promptly pursued a complaint filed by then prime minister Mbaye about trafficking in false passports within the Ministry of Foreign Affairs.

Sall publicly declared his assets in 2012 as required by the constitution. He invited government ministers and National Assembly members to do so as well, sparking public debate. In July 2013, the council of ministers began discussing a legislative text that would require asset declarations by a wide range of public officeholders. Senegal was ranked 77 out of 177 countries and territories surveyed in Transparency International's 2013 Corruption Perceptions Index.

Private resource-extraction companies provide local development funds to the government, but there is little transparency regarding who manages the funds or how the money is spent.

CIVIL LIBERTIES: 46 / 60 (+3)

D. Freedom of Expression and Belief: 15 / 16 (+1)

The constitution guarantees freedom of speech, and freedom of expression overall appears to be less restricted under Sall than during the end of Wade's presidency. The country has a number of free and independent media outlets in addition to state-controlled or affiliated radio stations, newspapers, and one state television channel. Several privately owned newspapers have existed for decades and are widely read. Access to the internet is not restricted. Independent journalists regularly critique the government, and libel, blasphemy, and security laws are generally not used to silence them.

However, criminal defamation laws are still in place, and a notable exception to the general improvement in freedom of the press was the August 2013 sentencing of the editor of the private newspaper *Le Quotidien* and an intern reporter to one month in jail for defamation in an article about the former foreign minister. The defendants were also ordered to pay fines of $2,000 each and, along with the paper's publisher, a total of $20,500 in damages. An appeal was filed, and the paper remained in operation at year's end. Earlier, in April, the DIC questioned several PDS members about possible "offenses to the chief executive" after they told the media that Sall had laundered money and included gay politicians in the government. Bara Gaye, youth leader of the PDS, was detained in May for offense against the head of state after a speech at a regional PDS meeting. At the end of 2013, he was still awaiting a trial verdict in prison.

There is no state religion, and freedom of worship is constitutionally protected and respected in practice. Muslims make up about 94 percent of the population. The country's Sufi Muslim brotherhoods are influential, including in the political arena. Academic freedom is legally guaranteed and generally respected.

E. Associational and Organizational Rights: 11 / 12 (+1)

Freedom of assembly is constitutionally guaranteed and respected in practice. The Interior Ministry must approve opposition leaders' requests to lead protests and demonstrations, and it sometimes dictates the hours and locations at which such activities can occur. It is also standard practice for the administration to deploy security forces to monitor demonstrations. PDS supporters in 2013 protested Karim Wade's incarceration, among other complaints about Sall's government, and were not harassed by the police. The authorities' tolerance of such demonstrations represented an improvement over the repression of protests and violence against participants that occurred under the previous administration during 2011 and early 2012.

Freedom of association is legally guaranteed, and the Sall administration did not impede nongovernmental organizations (NGOs) from operating in 2013. NGO and political party leaders must register their organizations at the Interior Ministry. Although workers' rights to organize, bargain collectively, and strike are legally protected for all except security employees, the labor code requires the approval of the Interior Ministry for the initial formation of a trade union.

F. Rule of Law: 10 / 16

The law guarantees fair public trials and defendants' rights. The judiciary is formally independent, but inadequate pay and lack of tenure expose judges to external influences and prevent the courts from providing a proper check on the other branches of government. The president controls appointments to the Constitutional Council. Sall has promised to shift power away from the executive, but has not yet implemented reforms. Geographic, educational, bureaucratic, and financial hurdles hinder public access to the courts.

Senegalese prisons are overcrowded, an issue the minister of justice spoke out against in October 2013. The Dakar-based NGO Tostan cites poor living conditions, inadequate sanitation, and limited access to medical care as problems faced by prisoners in the country.

Sall agreed in mid-2012 to try Hissene Habré, the former Chadian dictator, for crimes committed under his regime in Chad in the 1980s. Habré had long resided in Senegal. In February 2013, the government set up the Extraordinary African Chambers, and by July it had indicted Habré for crimes against humanity, torture, and war crimes.

The low-level separatist conflict in Senegal's southern Casamance region continues, but did not lead to further large-scale displacement of the population in 2013.

Individuals of lower castes in Senegalese society are still sometimes subject to discrimination. Consensual same-sex activity is a criminal offense, and most of the population opposes its decriminalization. Sall expressed his unwillingness to change the law in a widely publicized joint press conference with U.S. president Barack Obama during a June 2013 visit by Obama to Senegal. Members of the LGBT (lesbian, gay, bisexual, and transgender) community face societal discrimination, physical attacks, and police harassment.

G. Personal Autonomy and Individual Rights: 10 / 16 (+1)

Citizens generally enjoy freedom of travel and residence. The civil code facilitates the ownership of private property, but the enforcement of land registration and tenure is not consistent in rural areas. The government provides compensation when it expropriates land.

Women are not able to obtain credit as easily as men, early marriage remains an issue, and women who marry foreigners forgo Senegalese citizenship for their children. Some elements of Islamic and local customary law, particularly regarding inheritance and marital relations, discriminate against women. Rape, female genital cutting, and domestic abuse persist, and reports of violence against women more generally are on the rise. At a September 2013 workshop on combating gender-based violence, Prime Minister Aminata Touré and Justice Minister Sidiki Kaba both spoke about procedures and reforms undertaken by the government that they said would aid victims. First implemented in the July 2012 National Assembly elections, a 2010 gender parity law has resulted in women holding 64 seats in the 150-seat legislature, but there is not parity in the selection of assembly vice presidents and committee chairs.

The U.S. State Department's 2013 *Trafficking in Persons Report* cites estimates that over 50,000 children attending *daaras* (Koranic schools) are required to beg in the streets, and states that other forms of forced labor and sex trafficking are also current concerns. Child labor is a problem in the gold mines of eastern Senegal.

Serbia

Political Rights Rating: 2
Civil Liberties Rating: 2
Freedom Rating: 2.0
Freedom Status: Free
Electoral Democracy: Yes

Population: 7,136,000
Capital: Belgrade

Ten-Year Ratings Timeline For Year Under Review (Political Rights, Civil Liberties, Status)

Year Under Review	2004	2005	2006	2007	2008	2009	2010	2011	2012	2013
Rating	6,5,NF	6,5,NF	6,5,NF	6,5,NF	4,5,PF	4,5,PF	4,5,PF	4,5,PF	4,5,PF	4,5,PF

Note: The ratings through 2005 are for the State Union of Serbia and Montenegro. Kosovo is examined in a separate report.

INTRODUCTION

In late June, just over a year after Serbia had won European Union (EU) candidacy status, the EU agreed to begin membership talks with the country by January 2014. At a

December meeting in Brussels, EU foreign ministers scheduled the opening conference for January 21. The political milestone came primarily as a result of significant progress in an EU-led "dialogue" designed to improve relations between Serbia and Kosovo, which had unilaterally declared independence from Serbia in 2008.

After many setbacks in the dialogue, launched in 2011, Serbian prime minister Ivica Dačić and his Kosovo counterpart, Hashim Thaçi, reached a landmark agreement in Brussels in April 2013. Under the complex deal, Belgrade effectively agreed to recognize the Kosovo government's authority in Kosovo's ethnic Serb enclaves. In exchange, Priština agreed to grant the Kosovo Serb community, which comprises about 9 percent of Kosovo's population, increased autonomy. The agreement aimed to weaken parallel health, education, and other state structures that Belgrade has long funded in a largely Serb enclave located to the north of the Ibar River in Kosovo. Dačić and Thaçi also agreed that their respective countries would not block the other's EU bid, though Belgrade continues to maintain that it will never recognize Kosovo's independence. The dialogue continued throughout 2013, as Serbian and Kosovo leaders worked to implement the April agreement's technical provisions.

Also in April, Serbian president Tomislav Nikolić, a former ultranationalist, made further headway on improving neighborly relations by apologizing for Serbia's role in the 1995 Srebrenica massacre of some 8,000 Bosnian Muslim men and boys by Bosnian Serb forces, the worst atrocity committed on European soil since World War II. However, Nikolić refused to acknowledge that the killings constituted an act of genocide, even though it had been recognized as such by both the International Criminal Tribunal for the former Yugoslavia (ICTY) in The Hague and the International Court of Justice, the United Nations' primary judicial body.

In September, Serbian authorities canceled a Belgrade gay pride parade for the third straight year, citing lingering security concerns following violent counterdemonstrations at the 2010 event. In October, the government announced that it would implement a package of public-sector wage cuts, tax hikes, and other emergency measures designed to shore up an economy facing recession and double-digit unemployment rates. Without these austerity measures, Finance Minister Lazar Krstić warned, Serbia would go bankrupt within two years. Furthermore, Deputy Prime Minister Aleksandar Vučić in December indicated that Serbia planned to open negotiations with the International Monetary Fund (IMF) on a new aid package in early 2014.

POLITICAL RIGHTS: 30 / 40

A. Electoral Process: 9 / 12

The National Assembly is a unicameral, 250-seat legislature, with deputies elected to four-year terms according to party lists. The prime minister is elected by the assembly. The president, a largely ceremonial post, is elected for up to two five-year terms. International monitors have deemed recent elections largely free and fair.

In April 2011, the Constitutional Court clarified and extended its 2010 decision to prohibit a practice whereby politicians elected on a party ticket had to file a letter of resignation with the party before taking office. This had allowed party leaders to replace elected officials who proved disloyal. The court declared the system unconstitutional and invalidated any postelection reallocation of parliamentary seats.

In May 2012, Nikolić's opposition Serbian Progressive Party (SNS)—which had emerged as a moderate offshoot of the ultranationalist Serbian Radical Party in 2008—and its allies led parliamentary elections with 73 seats. The ruling bloc headed by the Democratic Party (DS) took 67 seats, followed by the Socialist Party of Serbia (SPS) with a surprisingly strong 44 seats. Later that month, Nikolić upset incumbent and DS leader Boris Tadić in a presidential runoff with 51.2 percent of the vote. In July, the SNS formed a coalition with the SPS, whose strong performance in the elections had made it the kingmaker in any future government; Dačić, the SPS president and a onetime spokesman for former authoritarian leader Slobodan Milošević, became prime minister. The DS went into opposition, and Tadić effectively assumed blame for its electoral loss by giving up the party leadership that November.

B. Political Pluralism and Participation: 14 / 16

Under Serbia's multiparty system, the leading factions compete for influence, and a single party has rarely dominated the legislative and executive branches simultaneously since Milošević's ouster amid massive demonstrations in 2000. An exception came after elections in 2007 and early 2008, when the DS controlled the presidency, the premiership, and a working parliamentary majority. Despite concerns that Serbia would take a more nationalist tack given the results of the 2012 elections, the country remained on the path to EU integration.

Of Serbia's 91 registered political parties, 53 represent minorities. Parties representing pensioners, veterans, and ethnic groups such as Bosniaks and Roma sit in the current government coalition. Nevertheless, ethnic minorities have a relatively muted voice in Serbian politics in practice.

C. Functioning of Government: 7 / 12

Corruption remains a serious concern, but the European Commission (EC) noted some improvements in its 2013 progress report. In 2013, Belgrade adopted a new anticorruption strategy and action plan to last through 2018; meanwhile, several notable high-profile corruption cases were prosecuted. During the year, criminal charges were filed against two former ministers, and a former high-level judicial official was convicted of abuse of office and sentenced to six and a half years in prison. However, implementation of anticorruption legislation is relatively weak, law enforcement agencies need to take a more proactive approach, and the judiciary has yet to establish a track record of convictions in corruption cases, according to the EC. Serbia was ranked 72 out of 177 countries and territories surveyed in Transparency International's 2013 Corruption Perceptions Index.

CIVIL LIBERTIES: 48 / 60

D. Freedom of Expression and Belief: 15 / 16

The press is generally free, although most media outlets are thought to be aligned with specific political parties. In May 2011, public broadcaster RTS apologized for its role in supporting authoritarian governments during the 1990s, but advocacy groups noted that RTS remains subject to strong government influence. Funds for media advertising are controlled by a few economic and political actors, creating incentives for self-censorship. Media ownership is not fully transparent. Journalists face threats and even attacks, which also lead to self-censorship. The government in 2013 made no progress on implementation of its 2011 media strategy, the EC has noted. In a positive development, the government decriminalized defamation in December 2012; authorities had previously claimed that decriminalization was not a condition for EU membership. Internet access is unrestricted.

The constitution guarantees freedom of religion, which is generally respected in practice. Acts of religiously motivated discrimination continued to decline in 2013, but remain a concern. Critics say the 2006 Law on Churches and Religious Communities privileges seven "traditional" religious communities by giving them tax-exempt status, while forcing other groups to go through cumbersome and inconsistent registration procedures. However, in 2012, the Constitutional Court ruled that the law was constitutional and not discriminatory. Relations between factions within the Muslim community in the largely Bosniak region of

Sandžak—and between one of the factions and the Serbian government—have deteriorated in recent years, but did not worsen in 2013. There were no reports of government restrictions on academic freedom in 2013. In Sandžak, a Bosnian-language school curriculum was introduced in 2013.

E. Associational and Organizational Rights: 10 / 12

Citizens enjoy freedoms of assembly and association, though a 2009 law bans meetings of fascist organizations and the use of neo-Nazi symbols. In recent years, the LGBT (lesbian, gay, bisexual, and transgender) community's right to assembly has been restricted. In September 2013, authorities in the capital banned a scheduled gay pride parade due to security concerns. The 2010 parade was attacked by several thousand counterdemonstrators, and Belgrade has banned the event three years running despite the objection of rights groups. Nevertheless, hundreds of gay activists defied the 2013 ban and marched in Belgrade on September 28.

Radical right-wing organizations and violent "sports fans" remain a serious concern. Foreign and domestic NGOs generally operate freely. Workers may join unions, engage in collective bargaining, and strike, but the International Confederation of Trade Unions has reported that organizing efforts and strikes are substantially restricted in practice.

F. Rule of Law: 10 / 16

In July 2012, the Constitutional Court abrogated a controversial reappointment procedure in effect during 2009 and 2010 that cost hundreds of judges and prosecutors their jobs, and the officials who had appealed their "nonreappointment" were reinstated. To reintegrate these judges and prosecutors, the government announced plans in October 2012 to roughly double the court network in 2013, in what was also described as an effort to improve citizens' access to justice following a 2010 judicial overhaul that merged the country's 138 municipal courts into just 34 basic courts. The parliament in November 2013 then approved legislation by which the court network would be expanded to 66 basic courts in January 2014. In addition, Serbia would no longer administer courts in northern Kosovo, according to the legislation, which is part of the government's 2013–2018 judicial reform strategy to improve independence, competency, and efficiency. The strategy also calls for strengthening the High Judicial and State Prosecutorial Councils.

Despite these positive steps, the judiciary is vulnerable to political influence, especially regarding appointments, and efficiency remains problematic, with the case backlog standing at over 3 million at the end of 2012. Prisons generally meet international standards, though overcrowding is an issue, and health care facilities are often inadequate. A national amnesty of 3,600 prisoners in 2012 had an immediate impact on overcrowding, the EC said.

Ethnic minorities are underrepresented in government. The country's main minority groups are the Bosniaks (Muslim Slavs), concentrated in the Sandžak region; and the Hungarian community, concentrated in Vojvodina. Serbia is also home to Roma, Albanian, Croat, Montenegrin, and other communities. In June 2013, the parliament adopted its 2013–2018 antidiscrimination strategy to address widespread prejudice and mistreatment of ethnic and other minorities, including the LGBT community. In January 2013, a court in northern Serbia fined a man for using an antigay epithet against a colleague—the country's first verdict on discrimination based on sexual orientation. To address widespread discrimination against the Roma, the government in June 2013 adopted measures to improve the socioeconomic status of the group. Also during the year, the government began implementation of a law enabling the roughly 6,500 people in Serbia without a birth certificate, most of them Roma, to obtain documentation, but the reforms have yet to be fully implemented.

G. Personal Autonomy and Individual Rights: 13 / 16

The state sector remains a large portion of Serbia's economy, as does the gray economy. Since 2009, Serbia has struggled with recession and stagnation. Unemployment hovers around 25 percent, and youth unemployment is of particular concern. In December 2013, the government said Serbia would in early 2014 begin talks on a new financial aid package from the IMF to shore up the economy. The IMF had suspended an earlier deal in 2012 after Serbian leaders failed to adhere to previously agreed debt and deficit targets.

Women comprise 33 percent of the parliament. According to electoral regulations, women must account for at least 30 percent of a party's candidate list. Although women are legally entitled to equal pay for equal work, traditional attitudes often limit their economic role. A 2009 law on gender equality provides a range of protections in employment, health, education, and politics. Domestic violence is a serious problem. Serbia is a source, transit, and destination country for the trafficking of men, women, and children for forced labor and prostitution.

Seychelles

Political Rights Rating: 3
Civil Liberties Rating: 3
Freedom Rating: 3.0
Freedom Status: Partly Free
Electoral Democracy: Yes

Population: 93,388
Capital: Victoria

Ten-Year Ratings Timeline For Year Under Review (Political Rights, Civil Liberties, Status)

Year Under Review	2004	2005	2006	2007	2008	2009	2010	2011	2012	2013
Rating	3,3,PF	3,3,PF	3,3,PF	3,3,PF	3,3,PF	3,3,PF	3,3,PF	3,3,PF	3,3,PF	3,3,PF

INTRODUCTION

During the year, the Seychelles government signed a bilateral trade agreement with the European Union (EU) and took steps to strengthen bilateral economic relations with China, including the signing of a mutual visa waiver agreement. Corruption and extensive drug trafficking continue to plague the archipelago.

In 2011, the country modified its law to allow pirates captured anywhere in the world to be prosecuted in the Seychelles. In February 2013, the EU transferred nine Somali pirates to the Seychelles for prosecution. In October 2013, 11 Somali pirates arrested in 2012 by the Dutch navy were convicted by the Seychelles Supreme Court and sentenced to between 18 months and 16 years' imprisonment. Somali pirates make up approximately 20 percent of the Seychelles' prison population.

POLITICAL RIGHTS: 25 / 40
A. Electoral Process: 8 / 12

The president and the unicameral National Assembly are elected by universal adult suffrage for five-year terms. The head of government is the president, who appoints the cabinet. President James Michel, running for the People's Party (Parti Lepep, or PL), won a third term in May 2011 with 55 percent of the vote. The opposition Seychelles National Party (SNP) boycotted parliamentary elections held later that year, citing alleged misconduct by the PL in the presidential vote and Michel's failure to implement electoral reforms. Of the National Assembly's 32 members, 25 are directly elected and 7 are allocated on a proportional basis to parties gaining at least 10 percent of the vote. The PL holds all the elected seats and 6 of 7 allocated seats. The ninth seat is held by the Popular Democratic Movement, formed by a dissident SNP member who disagreed with its decision to boycott. Despite the boycott, both the 2011 presidential and parliamentary elections were generally regarded as having met basic international norms.

The Forum for Electoral Reform, made up of representatives from every registered political party, was established by the Electoral Commission (EC) following the 2011 parliamentary elections to review existing electoral registration. In 2013, the Forum completed these reviews and made recommendations to the EC. The proposed reforms were subsequently published by EC.

B. Political Pluralism and Participation: 10 / 16

The ruling PL—formerly the Seychelles People's Progressive Front (SPPF)—remains the dominant party, having held continuous power since 1977. The leftist SPPF was the only legal party until a 1992 constitutional amendment legalized opposition parties. A proposal to increase the number of signatures needed to form a political party—currently just 100—was pending at year's end. The centralist opposition SNP has claimed that its sympathizers face job discrimination in the public sector and police harassment. The conservative Democratic Party has endured reduced support in recent elections.

C. Functioning of Government: 7 / 12

Concerns over government corruption have focused on a lack of transparency in the privatization and allocation of government-owned land. A December 2011 report released by the auditor-general revealed nearly two decades of dysfunction in government finances, including unprofessional book-keeping, illegal procedures, and embezzlement. President Michel launched an investigation that was pending at year's end. The Seychelles was ranked 47 out of 177 countries surveyed in Transparency International's 2013 Corruption Perceptions Index.

CIVIL LIBERTIES: 42 / 60

D. Freedom of Expression and Belief: 11 / 16

The government controls much of the nation's print and broadcast media, including the daily *Seychelles Nation* newspaper. Strict libel laws are sometimes used to harass journalists, leading to self-censorship. The first domestic commercial radio station, Pure FM, began broadcasting in August. The government can restrict the broadcast of material considered to be objectionable. The board of directors of the officially nonpartisan Seychelles Broadcasting Corporation includes several non-PL members, though coverage is biased in favor of the ruling party. There have been reports that the state monitors e-mail, chat rooms, and blogs, and opposition activists claim that the government blocks access to opposition party websites.

Religious freedom is constitutionally guaranteed and respected in practice. Churches in this predominantly Roman Catholic country have been strong voices for human rights and democratization, and they generally function without government interference. Academic freedom is also respected, though PL loyalists are reportedly favored in high-level academic appointments.

E. Associational and Organizational Rights: 9 / 12

The constitution protects freedoms of assembly and association. While public demonstrations are generally tolerated, the government has occasionally impeded opposition gatherings. In 2012, the Electoral Commission submitted a proposal to President Michel outlining a new Public Order Act to modernize outdated statutes accompanying constitutional guarantees for freedoms of speech and assembly. Passage of the law, which would allow political parties to hold public meetings upon giving five days' notice to the police commissioner instead of requiring permission, was still pending at the end of 2013.

Human rights groups and other nongovernmental organizations operate in the country. Workers have the right to strike, though strikes are illegal until all arbitration procedures have been exhausted. Collective bargaining is rare.

F. Rule of Law: 11 / 16

Judges generally decide cases fairly, but face interference in cases involving major economic or political interests. The majority of the members of the judiciary are naturalized citizens or foreign nationals from other Commonwealth countries, and the impartiality of the non-Seychellois magistrates can be compromised because they are subject to contract renewal. Security forces have at times been accused of using excessive force, including torture and arbitrary detention. Prolonged pretrial detention and overcrowding in prisons are common. Pretrial detainees account for approximately a quarter of the prison population, in large part due to inefficiencies in the judicial process.

The country's political and economic life is dominated by people of European and South Asian origin. Islanders of Creole extraction face discrimination, and prejudice against foreign workers has also been reported.

Sexual relations between men are illegal. However, a 2006 amendment to the Employment Act prohibits discrimination based on sexual orientation, and the Seychelles pledged in 2011 that it would decriminalize homosexuality.

G. Personal Autonomy and Individual Rights: 11 / 16

The government does not restrict domestic travel but may deny passports for unspecified reasons of "national interest."

The Seychelles boasts one of the world's highest percentages of women in parliament: 14 women were elected in 2011 with no quota system. Gender discrimination in employment is illegal, but most women are engaged in subsistence agriculture. Inheritance laws do not discriminate against women. Despite a 2008 National Strategy on Domestic Violence, rape and domestic violence remain widespread.

Sierra Leone

Political Rights Rating: 3
Civil Liberties Rating: 3
Freedom Rating: 3.0
Freedom Status: Partly Free
Electoral Democracy: Yes

Population: 6,200,000
Capital: Freetown

Ratings Change: Sierra Leone's political rights rating declined from 2 to 3 and its status declined from Free to Partly Free due to high-profile corruption allegations against bankers, police officers, and government officials as well as long-standing accounting irregularities that led to the country's suspension from the Extractive Industries Transparency Initiative.

Ten-Year Ratings Timeline For Year Under Review (Political Rights, Civil Liberties, Status)

Year Under Review	2004	2005	2006	2007	2008	2009	2010	2011	2012	2013
Rating	4,3,PF	4,3,PF	4,3,PF	3,3,PF	3,3,PF	3,3,PF	3,3,PF	3,3,PF	2,3,F	3,3,PF

INTRODUCTION

Corruption remained rampant in all sectors of Sierra Leone's government and economy in 2013, and the year witnessed several high-profile suspensions or indictments of bankers, police officers, and government officials. In February, Sierra Leone was suspended from the Extractive Industries Transparency Initiative (EITI) for its failure to resolve accounting irregularities. The suspension provoked an increase in regulatory activity by the government, though the results of those initiatives remain to be seen. The administration of President Ernest Bai Koroma continues to harass journalists and suppress freedom of the press. In October, two journalists from a prominent local newspaper were arrested for an article that insulted the president, provoking an international outcry.

At the same time, Sierra Leone continued to take steps toward open and accountable government in 2013. Since 2012's presidential and parliamentary elections—widely considered a landmark for peace in the country—the government has launched a constitutional review, passed a long-awaited freedom of information law, and, partly in response to its suspension from the EITI, expanded efforts to regulate the lucrative natural resources industries.

POLITICAL RIGHTS: 29 / 40 (-1)

A. Electoral Process: 10 / 12

Of the unicameral Parliament's 124 members, 112 are chosen by popular vote, and 12 seats are reserved for indirectly elected paramount chiefs. Parliamentary and presidential elections are held every five years, and presidents may seek a second term. After a 1991–2002 civil war, Sierra Leone has progressed toward increasing fairness and transparency in its electoral process. In 2012, Koroma, of the All People's Congress (APC) party, was reelected with 59 percent of the vote; the candidate of the opposition Sierra Leone People's Party (SLPP), former military ruler Julius Maada Bio, secured 37 percent. In concurrent parliamentary elections, the APC increased its majority from 59 to 69 seats, and the SLPP held on to its 43 seats. The SLPP refused to accept the results and filed a petition later in November alleging numerous irregularities, including the absence of voter registers in some parts of the APC-dominated north, and the intimidation of SLPP partisans by the police. In December, however, Koroma and Bio issued a joint statement recognizing the APC's victory, and reversing the SLPP's earlier threat of a government boycott. International observers determined that both the presidential and parliamentary elections were free and fair, and they were widely considered a milestone for the consolidation of peace in the country.

The country implemented its first biometric voting registration system in advance of the 2012 polls, and the Political Parties Registration Commission, created in 2002, trained and deployed monitors throughout the country and publicized violations of electoral laws committed by both the APC and SLPP.

B. Political Pluralism and Participation: 12 / 16

The APC and the SLPP are the main political parties. Other parties include the People's Movement for Democratic Change, the National Democratic Alliance, and the United Democratic Movement. Both the All Political Parties Women's Association and the All Political Parties Youth Association, which became operational in 2011, play important roles in promoting peaceful electoral campaigning, dialogue, and participation.

In accordance with recommendations made by the country's Truth and Reconciliation Commission, the government launched a formal and long-delayed constitutional review in July 2013. While it remains to be seen whether the review will increase political pluralism or improve functioning of government, it will at the very least provide a catalyst to convene representatives from the 10 registered political parties for discussions.

Sierra Leone has been praised by the UN and other organizations for its culture of tolerance across ethnic and religious divides. Inter-religious marriage is common, many Sierra Leoneans practice Christianity and Islam simultaneously, and ethnic and religious minorities typically enjoy full political rights and electoral opportunities.

C. Functioning of Government: 7 / 12 (-1)

Corruption remains a serious problem. In its 2013 Global Corruption Barometer, Transparency International found that Sierra Leone had the highest incidence of reported bribery among the countries it surveyed sub-Saharan Africa. While the government disputed these findings, complaints of corruption are pervasive in nearly every sector of the country's economy. Koroma has encouraged and supported the work of the Anti-Corruption Commission, which has established a secretariat to oversee implementation of the National Anti-Corruption Strategy and is active in investigating and prosecuting corrupt officials, but the scope of the problem is daunting. In January, the government said it had suspended 10 senior Ministry of Health and Sanitation officials over allegations of corruption and misuse of funds. In July, the commission indicted four police officers on charges of bribery, following complaints from drivers. Also in July, dozens of bankers and tax officials—including the managing director of Sierra Leone's largest commercial bank—were charged with fraud; as part of the investigation, a travel ban was imposed on all of the country's banking and tax workers.

In February, Sierra Leone was suspended from the EITI for its failure to account for royalty and tax irregularities in its contracts with international mining companies. In response, the country's government has worked toward better regulation of the historically opaque and corruption-prone sector, including through the efforts of a new regulatory organization, the National Minerals Agency, but progress has been slow. In October 2013, the parliament passed the long-anticipated Right to Access Information Act, winning praise from a variety of domestic and international rights groups.

CIVIL LIBERTIES: 38 / 60 (-2)
D. Freedom of Expression and Belief: 12 / 16 (-1)

Freedoms of speech and the press are constitutionally guaranteed, but sometimes violated in practice. In June 2010, the Sierra Leone Broadcasting Corporation (SLBC) was officially launched as the independent national broadcaster. The APC and the SLPP relinquished control of their radio stations in 2010, allowing for incorporation into the SLBC. Numerous independent newspapers circulate freely, and there are dozens of public and private radio and television outlets. The government does not restrict internet access, though the medium is not widely used.

However, the government continued to use the country's antiquated libel and sedition laws to target journalists, delivering especially severe punishments in 2013. In October, two journalists with the *Independent Observer* newspaper were arrested over a piece in which Koroma was compared to a rat. They were charged with 26 counts, including "conspiracy to commit acts with seditious intent," under the draconian and antiquated Public Order Act of 1965. The journalists spent 19 days in jail before being released on bail; their trial is ongoing. Also in October, the country's media commission suspended the newspaper *Watchman* for a month for reporting that the radical Islamist group Al-Shabaab was planning to attack a government building in Freetown.

Freedom of religion is protected by the constitution and respected in practice. In its 2012 International Religious Freedom Report, the U.S. State Department recorded no reports of abuse or discrimination on the basis of religion, and in July 2013 the UN Special Rapporteur on freedom of religion or belief praised the country for establishing an atmosphere of religious tolerance and pluralism. Academic freedom is similarly upheld.

E. Associational and Organizational Rights: 7 / 12 (-1)

While freedoms of assembly and association are constitutionally guaranteed and generally observed in practice, this year witnessed several high profile incidents of police brutality against peaceful protestors, especially in the natural resource sectors. In October, the police used tear gas to disperse protestors from the Sierra Leone Dock Workers' Union, and in December the police opened fire on local residents protesting the development of a palm oil plantation in the southern province of Pujehun. Nongovernmental organizations (NGOs) and civic groups operate freely, though a 2008 law requires NGOs to submit annual activity reports and renew their registration every two years. While workers have the right to join independent trade unions, serious violations of core labor standards occur regularly.

F. Rule of Law: 9 / 16

The judiciary has demonstrated a degree of independence, and a number of trials have been free and fair. However, corruption, poor salaries, police unprofessionalism, prison overcrowding, and a lack of resources threaten to impede judicial effectiveness. Drug trafficking and other crimes continue to pose a threat to the rule of law and the stability of the wider Mano River region.

The Special Court for Sierra Leone, a hybrid international and domestic war crimes tribunal, has been working since 2004 to convict those responsible for large-scale human rights abuses during the civil war. The trial of former Liberian president Charles Taylor, accused of fostering the insurgency that roiled the conflict, concluded in March 2011, and in April 2012, he was convicted on 11 counts of war crimes and crimes against humanity. His 50-year prison sentence was upheld in September 2013, and in October he was transferred to the United Kingdom to serve his term.

While Sierra Leone's laws increasingly recognize the rights of minority groups, women and members of the LGBT community continue to face discrimination and violence. In May, a gay rights activist was severely beaten after a story about his personal life appeared in the Exclusive newspaper, and in September the Deputy Minister of Education was fired after being accused of raping a 24-year-old university student. Reports of sexual and gender-based violence rarely result in conviction, and the Sierra Leonean police unit responsible for investigating and prosecuting SGBV remains underfunded and understaffed.

G. Personal Autonomy and Individual Rights: 10 / 16

Sierra Leone has become increasingly attractive to international investors since the end of the civil crisis in 2002, but the country still struggles to effectively regulate these investors, especially in the lucrative natural resource sector, where reports of economic exploitation are common. Furthermore, while most citizens enjoy freedom of travel and choice of residence, large-scale natural resource extraction projects have resulted in forced displacements and serious disruptions to local subsistence economies.

Laws passed in 2007 prohibit domestic violence, grant women the right to inherit property, and outlaw forced marriage. Despite these laws and constitutionally guaranteed equality, gender discrimination remains widespread, and female genital mutilation and child marriages are common. In its 2013 *State of the World's Mothers* report, Save the Children ranked Sierra Leone the third-worst country in the world for mothers and children based on health, educational, economic, and political indicators. Rape is reportedly widespread and not generally viewed as a crime, despite the 2012 passage of the Sexual Offenses Act, which increased penalties for rape to 15 years in prison. In September, women's rights groups criticized various media outlets for improper reporting of a high-profile rape case; critics said the publication by some outlets of the name and an identifiable photograph of the alleged victim violated the Sexual Offenses Act.

In 2011, the government and the UN Integrated Peacebuilding Office in Sierra Leone drafted a gender equality bill recommended by the Truth and Reconciliation Commission. If passed, the law would reserve a minimum of 30 percent of parliamentary seats and one ward per local council for women. The bill continues to await passage.

Singapore

Political Rights Rating: 4
Civil Liberties Rating: 4
Freedom Rating: 4.0
Freedom Status: Partly Free
Electoral Democracy: No

Population: 5,444,000
Capital: Singapore

Ten-Year Ratings Timeline For Year Under Review (Political Rights, Civil Liberties, Status)

Year Under Review	2004	2005	2006	2007	2008	2009	2010	2011	2012	2013
Rating	5,4,PF	5,4,PF	5,4,PF	5,4,PF	5,4,PF	5,4,PF	5,4,PF	4,4,PF	4,4,PF	4,4,PF

INTRODUCTION

There were several signs in 2013 that the ruling party's monopoly on power was weakening. The opposition Workers' Party increased its presence in Parliament by winning a January by-election, and citizens mounted a number of demonstrations—some of them unusually large—on issues including government plans on immigration, new internet regulations, and gay rights. Separately, in a rare case of unrest, hundreds of migrant workers briefly rioted and clashed with police in early December after an Indian worker was struck and killed by a bus. The incident has also raised debate online by Singaporeans on the issues of overcrowding and increasing numbers of migrant workers in the country. It also highlighted ongoing ethnic tensions within Singapore, rising income inequality, the country's heavy reliance on foreign labor, and the working conditions of migrants.

POLITICAL RIGHTS: 19 / 40
A. Electoral Process: 4 / 12

The president, whose role is largely ceremonial, is elected by popular vote for six-year terms, and a special committee is empowered to vet candidates. The prime minister and cabinet are appointed by the president. Of the unicameral legislature's 87 elected members, who serve five-year terms, 12 are elected from single-member constituencies, while 75 are elected in Group Representation Constituencies (GRCs), a mechanism intended to foster ethnic minority representation. The top-polling party in each GRC wins all of its four to six seats, so the system has historically bolstered the majority of the dominant People's Action Party (PAP). Up to nine Parliament members can be appointed from among leading opposition parties to ensure a minimum of opposition representation, only three of these seats needed to be awarded in the latest elections. Up to nine additional, nonpartisan members can be appointed by the president. The GRC system is now being questioned as the best way to ensure minority representation. Maruah, a human rights NGO, has proposed replacing the GRC with a reversion to single member constituencies nationwide, combined with a requirement that all parties contesting multiple constituencies maintain a minimum share of minority candidates.

Elections are free from irregularities and vote rigging, but the PAP dominates the political process. The country lacks an independent election authority. The May 2011 parliamentary elections featured a more vigorous and coordinated campaign effort by the opposition, which put forward candidates for 82 of the 87 directly elected seats, the highest number since independence. The opposition Workers' Party took an unprecedented six directly elected seats, including a five-seat GRC, demonstrating that the PAP's advantage in the GRC system could be challenged. The Workers' Party also received two seats under the system guaranteeing the opposition a representation of at least nine seats. Another party, the Singapore People's Party (SPP), was awarded the remaining seat allocated to the opposition. The PAP took 81 seats, even though it had secured only 60 percent of the overall vote.

The first contested presidential election since 1993 was held in August 2011, with all candidates running as independents in keeping with the constitution. Former deputy prime minister Tony Tan, the PAP-backed candidate, won with 35.2 percent of the vote, narrowly defeating three opponents. The results confirmed the growing strength of the opposition, and the increased willingness of the electorate to vote against the ruling party.

In a May 2012 by-election for the Hougang single-member constituency, Png Eng Huat of the Workers' Party defeated the PAP candidate, 62 percent to 38 percent, retaining the seat for the opposition. In a January 2013 by-election, Workers' Party candidate Lee Li Lian defeated the PAP nominee to win the party's seventh elected seat, reducing the PAP to 80.

B. Political Pluralism and Participation: 8 / 16

Although the opposition has been gaining ground in recent years, its campaigns and activities have historically been hamstrung by a ban on political films and television programs, the threat of libel suits, strict regulations on political associations, and the PAP's influence on the media and the courts.

The PAP has governed without interruption since the British colony of Singapore obtained home rule in 1959, entered the Malaysian Federation in 1963, and gained full independence in 1965. Moreover, the country has had only three prime ministers. Lee Kuan Yew, the first of the three, governed for more than three decades, transforming the port city into a regional financial center and exporter of high-technology goods, but restricting individual freedoms and political competition. Lee transferred the premiership to Goh Chok Tong in 1990 but stayed on as "senior minister." Lee's son, Lee Hsien Loong, became prime minister in 2004, and the elder Lee assumed the title of "minister mentor." After the 2011 elections, Lee Kuan Yew resigned from that position, ending over half a century in government.

C. Functioning of Government: 7 / 12

Singapore has traditionally been lauded for its lack of corruption, though issues of transparency remain a concern. The country was ranked 5 out of 177 countries and territories surveyed in Transparency International's 2013 Corruption Perceptions Index. However, there is increasing concern over the deeply entrenched position of the country's political elites.

CIVIL LIBERTIES: 32 / 60 (-1)

D. Freedom of Expression and Belief: 9 / 16 (-1)

The government maintains that racial sensitivities and the threat of Islamist terrorism justify draconian restrictions on freedoms of speech, but such rules have been used to silence criticism of the authorities. Singapore's media remain tightly constrained. All domestic newspapers, radio stations, and television channels are owned by companies linked to the government. Although editorials and news coverage generally support state policies, newspapers occasionally publish critical pieces. Mainstream media offered more balanced coverage of the opposition ahead of the 2011 elections. Self-censorship is common among journalists. The Sedition Act, in effect since the colonial period, outlaws seditious speech, the distribution of seditious materials, and acts with "seditious tendency." Popular videos, music, and books that reference sex, violence, or drugs are also subject to censorship. Foreign broadcasters and periodicals can be restricted for engaging in domestic politics, and all foreign publications must appoint legal representatives and provide significant financial deposits.

The internet is widely accessible, but authorities monitor online material and block some content through directives to licensed service providers. Singaporeans' increased use of social-networking websites has sparked interest in social activism and opposition parties, contributing to opposition electoral gains. The enforcement of internet restrictions was eased in the run-up to the 2011 voting, allowing broader online discussion of political issues.

In May 2013, the Media Development Authority issued new regulations requiring news websites to apply for individual licenses that will be subject to annual renewal. The sites will also be obliged to post a financial bond with the regulator, and respond to government takedown orders within 24 hours. The new rules drew strong objections from bloggers and civil liberties activists, who organized a "free my internet" protest event. Bloggers increasingly risk being charged with defamation, the *Straits Times* changed editorship, and in December, the independent Breakfast Network news website decided to shut down after the government imposed burdensome registration requirements and required them to show that they received no foreign funding. Another regulation banned major websites in Singapore from "advocating homosexuality or lesbianism." These are examples of increasing control over print and internet information.

The constitution guarantees freedom of religion as long as its practice does not violate any other regulations, and most groups worship freely. However, religious actions perceived as threats to racial or religious harmony are not tolerated, and unconventional groups like the Jehovah's Witnesses and the Unification Church are banned. All religious groups are required to register with the government under the 1966 Societies Act. Adherents of the Falun Gong spiritual movement have been arrested and prosecuted on vandalism charges in recent years for displaying posters in a public park that detail the persecution of fellow practitioners in China. The government in 2013 faced renewed calls to allow Muslim women to wear headscarves ("tudong" in Malay) in all workplaces, including public-sector fields like nursing.

All public universities and political research institutions have direct government links that enable at least some influence. Academics engage in political debate, but their publications rarely deviate from the government line on matters related to Singapore. Scholars who do address issues related to Singaporean politics have been denied tenure in recent years.

E. Associational and Organizational Rights: 4 / 12

Public assemblies must be approved by police. A 2009 law eliminated a previous threshold requiring permits for public assemblies of five or more people, meaning political events involving just one person could require official approval. Permits are not needed for indoor gatherings as long as the topic of discussion does not relate to race or religion. In the 2011 campaign period, opposition parties held rallies without significant interference. Protests mounted during 2013 included one in February in which participants voiced opposition to a government plan to increase the population and workforce through further large-scale immigration, which had already put pressure on the country's infrastructure, job market, and cost of living. The rally drew some 4,000 people, reportedly making it the largest political protest since independence.

The Societies Act restricts freedom of association by requiring most organizations of more than 10 people to register with the government, and the government enjoys full discretion to register or dissolve such groups. Only registered parties and associations may engage in organized political activity, and political speeches are tightly regulated. Singaporeans for Democracy, a civil society organization active in promoting greater political and civil rights, dissolved in August 2012, asserting that government rules and regulations had made their activities increasingly impossible.

Unions are granted fairly broad rights under the Trade Unions Act, though restrictions include a ban on government employees joining unions. Union members are prohibited from voting on collective agreements negotiated by union representatives and employers. Strikes must be approved by a majority of a union's members, as opposed to the internationally accepted standard of at least 50 percent of the members who vote. In practice, many restrictions are not applied. Nearly all unions are affiliated with the National Trade Union Congress, which is openly allied with the PAP. Workers in "essential services" are required to give 14 days' notice to an employer before striking. In November 2012, Singapore saw its first strike in more than two decades when 171 migrant Chinese public bus drivers went on strike to protest wage discrimination. The action was regarded as illegal because public transportation is considered an essential service, and the strikers had not provided 14 days' notice. Three of the strikers were dismissed from their jobs, 29 were deported, and one was sentenced to six weeks in prison.

F. Rule of Law: 7 / 16

The government's overwhelming success in court cases raises questions about judicial independence, particularly because lawsuits against opposition politicians and parties often drive them into bankruptcy. It is unclear whether the government pressures judges or simply appoints those who share its conservative philosophy. Defendants in criminal cases enjoy most due process rights. Prisons generally meet international standards.

The Internal Security Act (ISA) and Criminal Law Act (CLA) allow warrantless searches and arrests to preserve national security, order, and the public interest. Government agencies, including the Internal Security Department, conduct surveillance using extensive networks and sophisticated methods to monitor telephone and other private conversations. The ISA, previously aimed at communist threats, is now used against suspected Islamist terrorists. Suspects can be detained without charge or trial for an unlimited number of two-year periods. A 1989 constitutional amendment prohibits judicial review of the substantive grounds for detention under the ISA and of the constitutionality of the law itself. The CLA is mainly used to detain organized crime suspects; it allows preventive detention for an extendable one-year period.

The Misuse of Drugs Act empowers authorities to commit suspected drug users, without trial, to rehabilitation centers for up to three years. The death penalty applies to drug trafficking as well as murder, but reforms that took effect in 2013 grant judges the discretion to impose lighter sentences under some circumstances. The penal code mandates caning, in addition to imprisonment, for about 30 offenses, though the punishment is applied inconsistently.

There is no legal racial discrimination, though ethnic Malays reportedly face discrimination in both private- and public-sector employment. The LGBT (lesbian, gay, bisexual, and transgender) community in Singapore faces significant legal obstacles. Section 377A of the penal code criminalizes consensual sex between adult men, which is punishable by up to two years in prison. The law is not actively enforced, however, and a number of court challenges seeking to overturn it were pending at the end of 2013. Over time, there have been more attempts to promote tolerance and acceptance of LGBT Singaporeans. In June 2013, Singapore Democratic Party treasurer Vincent Wijaysingha came out as gay and attended the "Pink Dot" gay pride event that month, which drew about 20,000 people, the largest crowd to date. Wijeysingha later resigned from the party to pursue LGBT activism.

G. Personal Autonomy and Individual Rights: 12 / 16

Citizens enjoy freedom of movement, though the government occasionally enforces its policy of ethnic balance in public housing, in which most Singaporeans live. Opposition politicians have been denied the right to travel.

Women enjoy the same legal rights as men on most issues, and many are well-educated professionals. There are no explicit constitutional guarantees of equal rights for women, and no laws that mandate nondiscrimination in hiring practices on the basis of gender. Few women hold top positions in government and the private sector. Twenty women won seats in the 2011 parliamentary elections.

Singapore's 180,000 household workers are excluded from the Employment Act and regularly exploited. A 2006 standard contract for foreign household workers addresses food deprivation and entitles replaced workers to seek other employment in Singapore, but it fails to provide other basic protections, such as vacation days. A new law that took effect in January 2013 requires that all new contracts grant household workers one day off per week. However, the law allows employers to offer compensation in place of the day off if the worker agrees.

Slovakia

Political Rights Rating: 1
Civil Liberties Rating: 1
Freedom Rating: 1.0
Freedom Status: Free
Electoral Democracy: Yes

Population: 5,414,000
Capital: Bratislava

Ten-Year Ratings Timeline For Year Under Review (Political Rights, Civil Liberties, Status)

Year Under Review	2004	2005	2006	2007	2008	2009	2010	2011	2012	2013
Rating	1,1,F	1,1,F	1,1,F	1,1,F	1,1,F	1,1,F	1,1,F	1,1,F	1,1,F	1,1,F

INTRODUCTION

The first year and a half of Prime Minister Robert Fico's second, nonconsecutive term in office was characterized by significant polarization and discord between his ruling center-left Direction–Social Democracy (Smer-SD) party—which controls a comfortable majority in the parliament—and the center-right opposition parties. Having refused to appoint the prosecutor general who was lawfully elected by the previous parliament in 2011, President Ivan Gašparovič called for new elections to the post in 2013, resulting in the swift confirmation of a new, government-backed candidate by July. Opposition lawmakers, who accused Gašparovič of intentionally breaching the constitution to promote Smer-SD's interests, had launched the first-ever impeachment attempt against a Slovakian president in January, but the motion was voted down by the parliament in March.

Also in March, the parliament adopted controversial public-procurement legislation that was initially introduced by the interior minister in 2012. The law allows major contracts to be awarded without an open, competitive tender process.

Police in June carried out a violent raid on a Romany settlement, prompting international concern, but a flawed government investigation into the events found that police had not acted inappropriately.

POLITICAL RIGHTS: 37 / 40
A. Electoral Process: 12 / 12

Voters elect the president for up to two five-year terms. Members of the 150-seat, unicameral National Council are elected for four-year terms through nationwide proportional representation. Parties must obtain at least 5 percent of the vote to win seats. The prime minister is appointed by the president but must have majority support in the parliament to govern. The presidency is mostly ceremonial, though the president has the power to name judges to the Constitutional Court and veto legislation. In 2009, Gašparovič, a Smer-SD ally, became the first Slovakian president to win reelection.

Early elections in March 2012 resulted in a landslide victory for Fico's Smer-SD, which won 83 seats. The two main parties in the outgoing center-right government, the Christian Democratic Movement (KDH) and the Slovak Democratic and Christian Union–Democratic Party (SDKÚ–DS), fared poorly after being implicated in two major corruption scandals. They captured 16 and 11 seats, respectively. Most-Hid (Bridge), which advocates better cooperation between the country's ethnic Hungarian minority and ethnic Slovak majority, took 13 seats, and the Freedom and Solidarity (SaS) party won 11 seats. A new party composed of former SaS members, the Ordinary People and Independent Personalities (OLaNO), secured 16 seats by appealing to citizens who were disillusioned with the government.

The elections were deemed free and fair by international monitors, though the Organization for Security and Cooperation in Europe (OSCE) expressed concern about a lack of oversight and transparency in campaign financing.

The government in August 2013 agreed on laws that would unify voting procedures across the country and set campaign spending limits and finance regulations, as well as prescribe fines for violating election rules. The changes under discussion would also limit when parties are allowed to campaign, and included a moratorium on campaigning during the two days that precede each election. The unified rules also contained measures designed to cut election costs by introducing electronic communication between the election committee and subcommittees, and by placing a cap of eight members on district election committees. Opposition members argued that the new rules would be selectively applied to the advantage of ruling parties. They demanded amendments to the proposed legislation, eventually resulting in the postponement of its adoption until 2014.

B. Political Pluralism and Participation: 15 / 16

Slovakia is home to a competitive, multiparty political system. Since the country joined the European Union (EU) in 2004, power has shifted between coalitions of center-left and center-right parties. The left-leaning Smer-SD, then in opposition, won the 2012 parliamentary elections by a margin large enough to form Slovakia's first single-party government.

Relations between Smer-SD and the opposition center-right parties remained confrontational throughout 2013, with the opposition accusing Smer-SD of using its majority to rush through legislation or block other factions' proposals.

Slovakia's first-ever Romany representative, Peter Pollak, was elected to the legislature in March 2012 and later became the government's top policy coordinator for the Roma, known as the plenipotentiary for Romany communities.

C. Functioning of Government: 10 / 12

Corruption remains a problem, most notably in public procurement and the health sector. According to Transparency International (TI), many state-owned companies still do not publish even basic information, such as annual reports. Controversial revisions to Slovakia's public-procurement rules, originally proposed by Interior Minister Robert Kaliňák in September 2012, were extensively modified and then adopted by the parliament in late March 2013, with most entering into force in July. The changes introduced an electronic marketplace designed to increase competition and transparency in procurements, but included a variety of exemptions that would allow ministries and offices to award substantial contracts without a tender process. A new, nine-member council was established to serve as an appeal body for the Public Procurement Office (ÚVO), in order to speed up appeal proceedings and unify ÚVO decision-making. The council is headed by the chair and vice-chair of ÚVO. Municipalities and nongovernmental organizations (NGOs) will nominate candidates to serve as the remaining seven members, who are formally appointed by the cabinet.

Investigators probing alleged misconduct by politicians implicated in the "Gorilla file"—a document, leaked in late 2011, concerning the Slovak intelligence service's wiretapping of a flat where politicians allegedly met with prominent businessmen to discuss corrupt dealings—had yet to secure enough evidence to press charges against any specific individual at the end of 2013. One thread of the investigation, related to the privatization of the M. R. Štefánik airport in Bratislava, was declared closed in October 2013.

In late May, Smer-SD deputies on the parliamentary committee responsible for military affairs, despite objections from opposition politicians, voted not to investigate an allegedly suspicious transfer of assets from two military intelligence agencies (now merged as Military Intelligence, or VS) under the Fico government of 2006–2010. The accusations were based on a classified report allegedly shared with the daily newspaper *SME* by an anonymous source. The still-classified case was immediately handed over to the public prosecutor's office and police. *SME* reported on another leaked file on June 12, this time pointing to misuse of power by former Military Defense Intelligence (VOS) head and incumbent VS deputy director Róbert Tibenský between 2004 and 2008. The government dismissed the accusations. Two weeks later, state prosecutors charged former Military Intelligence Service (VSS) officer Katarína Svrčeková and former VSS head Roman Mikulec—who had launched the original investigation into the suspected embezzlement of agency assets—with leaking classified information.

In 2012, Slovakia's parliament voted unanimously to lift the immunity of its deputies from criminal prosecution; only judges remain immune from prosecution. Slovakia was ranked 61 out of 177 countries and territories surveyed in TI's 2013 Corruption Perceptions Index.

In 2013 the government prepared an amendment that would have limited of the scope of freedom of information legislation. Although pushback from civil society prompted the Ministry of Justice to drop the disputed provisions, a new draft amendment to the freedom of information act was under way at year's end.

CIVIL LIBERTIES: 54 / 60 (-1)

D. Freedom of Expression and Belief: 16 / 16

Freedom of speech and of the press is protected by the constitution, but media outlets sometimes face political interference. Journalists continue to encounter verbal attacks and libel suits by public officials, though these have occurred less frequently in recent years. The OSCE in 2013 expressed concern about two defamation suits filed against media outlets by members of the judiciary: In the ongoing "Bonanno" case, filed in February 2013, past and current members of the judiciary sought a total of €940,000 ($1.23 million) from a publication that reported on a 2010 social gathering at which the plaintiffs appeared to make light of a recent mass murder. In the second case in March, a court ordered *SME* to publish an apology to Special Court judge Michal Truban on its front page for three consecutive days, after Truban sued the outlet for reporting that he had received an illegal gift in the form of free hunting privileges on a trip in 2012.

The government respects religious freedom in this largely Roman Catholic country. Registered religious organizations are eligible for tax exemptions and government subsidies. However, religious groups must have at least 20,000 members to register, effectively preventing the small Muslim community and other groups from claiming government benefits. Academic freedom is respected.

E. Associational and Organizational Rights: 12 / 12

Authorities uphold freedom of assembly and association. NGOs generally operate without government interference. Labor unions are active, and organized workers freely exercise their right to strike. A new labor code with guarantees related to overtime and severance pay, as well as rules on hiring temporary workers, took effect in 2013.

F. Rule of Law: 12 / 16 (-1)

The constitution provides for an independent judiciary. Despite some reforms pushed through by the previous, center-right government of Prime Minister Iveta Radičová in 2011, the court system continues to suffer from corruption, intimidation of judges, and a significant backlog of cases. As a result, public trust in the judicial system is low. In July 2013, two students launched a website, Otvorené Súdy (Open Courts), with the aim of increasing the transparency of the judicial system by making information on judges and rulings more easily accessible.

The circumstances surrounding the appointment of a new prosecutor general in 2013 raised fresh concerns about political influence on the judicial system. In mid-2011, the parliament had selected Jozef Čentéš, a candidate backed by the center-right parties, to fill the position, but the left-leaning President Gašparovič had refused to confirm the appointment. He cited concerns about Čentéš's moral character and the procedures surrounding his election, despite an October 2011 Constitutional Court ruling that the election process had been legitimate. In March 2013, the Smer-SD parliamentary majority elected in 2012 voted down the opposition's proposal to impeach Gašparovič for allegedly breaching the constitution by stalling on the appointment without concrete justification. The issue of Čentéš's election remained mired in the Constitutional Court for several more months as both Gašparovič and Čentéš filed petitions challenging the impartiality of the judges. An amendment to the Law on the Constitutional Court was adopted in an accelerated legislative procedure in April, permitting the assignment of cases to judges who had previously been disqualified for lack of impartiality.

Čentéš was not permitted to run in the new elections held on June 17. The vote was boycotted by the opposition, while Smer-SD deputies all voted for their party's proposed candidate, Jaromír Čižnár, the regional prosecutor of Bratislava and Fico's former university classmate. Gašparovič appointed Čižnár in July, before the Constitutional Court could issue a final ruling on Čentéš's case. The court then canceled a hearing on Čentéš's case that was planned for October after Gašparovič again accused the judges assigned to deal with Čentéš's complaint of bias.

In late October 2013, the Constitutional Court assessed several disciplinary motions filed against Supreme Court president Štefan Harabin by Lucia Žitňanská, the justice minister under the Radičová government. On October 29, the court upheld its earlier decision to penalize Harabin by reducing his salary for obstructing a 2010 audit of the Supreme Court by the Finance Ministry. However, the next day it rejected three separate motions against him that had been outstanding. Among other charges, Žitňanská had accused Harabin of manipulating the assignment of judges to cases in his court, a process that is supposed to be random.

Prison conditions meet most international standards, but overcrowding remains a concern. NGOs and members of the Romany community report that Romany suspects are often mistreated by police during arrest and while in custody.

The rights of national minorities and ethnic groups are constitutionally guaranteed. Minority groups in Slovakia—including the country's sizable Hungarian and Romany populations—have the right to develop their own culture, the right to information and education in their mother tongue, and the right to use their language in official communication.

Nevertheless, minority groups—most notably the Roma—experience widespread discrimination, including forced evictions and segregation of Romany children in schools. In late February 2013, Fico made a controversial public address in which he suggested that Slovakia had been established for Slovaks, not for minorities. The prime minister later said his words had been taken out of context. On June 19, dozens of police officers raided a Romany settlement known as Budulovska, allegedly in search of seven convicted or suspected criminals. Violence erupted during the search, and several residents were injured. Although none of the raid's targets were found, police detained 15 others. Members of the community who were involved in the incident were not interviewed during a subsequent investigation by the Interior Ministry. Instead, the final report, which cleared the police of any wrongdoing, included testimony from non-Romany residents of a nearby town who complained of the Romany community's "inappropriate" behavior and "arrogance." A number of Slovak cities have built walls to isolate Romany neighborhoods since 2008.

Members of the LGBT (lesbian, gay, bisexual, and transgender) community continue to report discrimination. However, Bratislava's fourth annual gay pride parade took place in September 2013 without serious incident.

G. Personal Autonomy and Individual Rights: 14 / 16

Although women enjoy the same legal rights as men, they continue to be underrepresented in senior-level government and business positions. Domestic violence is punishable by imprisonment but remains widespread. Slovakia is a source, transit, and destination for the trafficking of men, women, and children for forced labor and prostitution.

Slovenia

Political Rights Rating: 1
Civil Liberties Rating: 1
Freedom Rating: 1.0
Freedom Status: Free
Electoral Democracy: Yes

Population: 2,060,000
Capital: Ljubljana

Ten-Year Ratings Timeline For Year Under Review (Political Rights, Civil Liberties, Status)

Year Under Review	2004	2005	2006	2007	2008	2009	2010	2011	2012	2013
Rating	1,1,F	1,1,F	1,1,F	1,1,F	1,1,F	1,1,F	1,1,F	1,1,F	1,1,F	1,1,F

INTRODUCTION

In February 2013, parliament voted to dissolve the government of prime minister and Slovenian Democratic Party (SDS) leader Janez Janša, whose coalition had been teetering amid public protests over government corruption and unpopular austerity measures introduced in 2012 to combat a dual economic and banking crisis. In March, parliament approved a new left-leaning government led by Alenka Bratušek, Slovenia's first woman prime minister and head of the Positive Slovenia party. Janša was subsequently convicted of taking bribes in a year that saw several high-profile corruption cases.

Also in March, Slovenia and Croatia reached a deal to end a 20-year dispute over a Slovenian bank, Ljubljanska Banka, which had received savings from Yugoslav citizens in the 1970s. When a Slovenian bank acquired its assets in 1994, thousands of non-Slovene customers lost their deposits, prompting several government-supported lawsuits in Croatia. After years of requests from Slovenia, Croatia suspended the suits in March 2013, and the countries agreed to seek a final ruling on the issue from the Bank for International Settlements.

Throughout 2013, fears persisted that Slovenia would need a bailout from the European Union (EU) and International Monetary Fund (IMF) to shore up an ailing economy struggling with recession and some €8 billion in bad bank loans. In late October, the IMF urged Slovenia to immediately recapitalize its banks. In December, the Finance Ministry announced plans to inject €3 billion into the country's three largest banks in a move welcomed by the EU.

POLITICAL RIGHTS: 38 / 40
A. Electoral Process: 12 / 12

An EU member since 2004, Slovenia has a bicameral Parliament. Members of the 90-seat National Assembly, which chooses the prime minister, are elected to four-year terms. Members of the 40-seat National Council, a largely advisory body representing professional groups and local interests, are elected to five-year terms. The president is directly elected for up to two five-year terms.

In early elections held in December 2011, the center-left Positive Slovenia, then led by Ljubljana Mayor Zoran Janković, won with 28 seats, upsetting the center-right SDS, which took 26 seats, followed by the Social Democrats (SD) with 10. However, Janković failed to secure a parliamentary majority to form a government or become prime minister. In January 2012, Parliament elected Janša prime minister and, a month later, approved a new SDS-led coalition government; Positive Slovenia went into opposition. Janša's government lost a no-confidence vote in February, and a new center-left coalition headed by Bratušek, who had been elected Positive Slovenia's leader in January, took power.

In a presidential runoff in December 2012, SD head and former Prime Minister Borut Pahor defeated incumbent Danilo Türk, a law professor and former diplomat, with 67.4 percent of the vote to Türk's 32.6 percent.

B. Political Pluralism and Participation: 15 / 16

After 1990, center-left governments administered Slovenia for more than a decade, with Janez Drnovšek's Liberal Democracy of Slovenia (LDS) dominating the political stage. Drnovšek served as prime minister almost continuously from 1992 to 2002, when he was elected president. In the 2004 parliamentary elections, Janša's SDS finally unseated the LDS-led government, and he became prime minister. The LDS has since lost most of its support and failed to win enough votes in the 2011 election to enter parliament. Meanwhile, Positive Slovenia has gained significant support in recent years.

In the National Assembly, one seat each is reserved for Slovenia's Hungarian and Italian minorities. Roma are automatically given seats on 20 municipal councils. In the 2010 municipal elections, Ghanian-born doctor Peter Bossman was elected mayor of Piran, making him the first black mayor of an Eastern European city.

C. Functioning of Government: 11 / 12

While less extensive than in some other Central European countries, corruption remains a problem in Slovenia, usually taking the form of conflicts of interest and contracting links between government officials and private businesses. Only 5,000 of Slovenia's 80,000 public servants are subject to financial disclosure laws, according to the U.S. State Department. In January 2013, Slovenia's anticorruption commission accused Janša and Janković of failing to declare assets. Following his ouster as prime minister in February, Janša in June 2013 was sentenced to almost two years in prison for taking bribes in an arms deal in 2006, during his first term as prime minister. Just weeks later, Igor Bavčar, who served as interior minister in Slovenia's first democratically elected government, was sentenced to seven years in prison for a complex stock trading scheme that cost the Istrabenz conglomerate €24.3 million in 2007, when Bavčar was the firm's chairman. Slovenia was ranked 43 out of 177 countries and territories surveyed in Transparency International's 2013 Corruption Perceptions Index.

CIVIL LIBERTIES: 53 / 60

D. Freedom of Expression and Belief: 14 / 16

Freedoms of speech and the press are constitutionally guaranteed, though defamation remains a criminal offense, journalists can be legally compelled to reveal their sources, and hate speech is outlawed. The government maintains stakes in a number of media outlets. Janša's government in 2012 dismissed four members of public broadcaster Radio Televizija Slovenija's supervisory board before the expiration of their terms, prompting criticism from Reporters Without Borders; the four had been appointed by the previous government. Internet access is unrestricted.

The constitution guarantees freedom of religion and contains provisions that prohibit incitement to religious intolerance or discrimination. Approximately 58 percent of Slovenians identify themselves as Roman Catholics. In June 2010, the Constitutional Court annulled certain provisions of the 2007 Religious Freedoms Law, including requirements for legal registration of religious communities and the payment of social security contributions to priests working in prisons and hospitals. Though societal discrimination against the small Muslim community has been problematic in the past, interfaith relations were generally civil during the year. After a 44-year struggle to build a mosque in Ljubljana, construction began in 2013, with Prime Minister Bratušek helping to lay the foundation stone during a groundbreaking ceremony in September. There were no reports of government restrictions on academic freedom during the year.

E. Associational and Organizational Rights: 12 / 12

The government respects freedoms of assembly and association. Numerous nongovernmental organizations operate freely and play a role in policymaking. Workers may establish and join trade unions, strike, and bargain collectively. The Association of Free Trade Unions of Slovenia has some 300,000 members and controls the four trade union seats in the National Council. On January 23, 100,000 public-sector employees held a strike over wage cuts, following months of antiausterity demonstrations.

F. Rule of Law: 14 / 16

The constitution provides for an independent judiciary, and the government respects judicial freedom. Introduced in 2005, the Lukenda Project has helped the judiciary steadily reduce case backlogs and was partially extended through 2014. Prison conditions meet international standards, though overcrowding has been reported.

A two-decade border dispute with Croatia—which concerns the delineation of the countries' maritime border in the Bay of Piran, and parts of their common territorial border—remains a key foreign policy issue in Slovenia. In 2009, former prime minister Pahor and his Croatian counterpart at the time, Jadranka Kosor, agreed that Slovenia would lift its veto of Croatia's EU accession and allow an international arbitration panel to settle the dispute. Following parliamentary approval in both states and a successful 2010 referendum in Slovenia, the Arbitral Tribunal held its first meeting in April 2012. No decision was reached by year's end.

The so-called "erasure" of citizens of the former Yugoslavia remains an issue. More than 25,000 non-Slovene citizens, mostly from other constituent republics within the former Yugoslavia who had remained in Slovenia after independence, were removed from official records after they failed to apply for citizenship or permanent residency during a brief window of opportunity in 1992. In 2009, Pahor's government began enforcing a 2003 Constitutional Court ruling intended to provide retroactive permanent residency status to those who had been "erased." In March 2010, Parliament adopted legislation to reinstate the legal status of those "erased" in 1992, but implementation has been problematic. In 2012, the European Court of Human Rights (ECHR) ruled that the "erasures" had been grave human rights violations and ordered Slovenia to pay six applicants compensation of €20,000 each. Subsequently, an additional 648 suits were filed with the ECHR, and the Slovenian government gave the "erased" until July 24, 2013, to request compensation. Roma face widespread poverty and societal marginalization.

G. Personal Autonomy and Individual Rights: 13 / 16

Of the post-communist countries that joined the EU in 2004, Slovenia enjoyed arguably the fastest and most stable economic transition, even meeting the bloc's strict euro adoption criteria to join the currency union by 2007. However, the post-2008 global slowdown sent Slovenia into recession and, despite rebounding in 2010, its economy contracted in 2012 and 2013. Unemployment is 12 percent. Much of the economy remains state controlled.

Women hold the same legal rights as men, but they are underrepresented in political life and face discrimination in the workplace. There are 31 women in the National Assembly and 3 in the National Council. Domestic violence remains a concern. Prostitution has been decriminalized in Slovenia. Slovenia is a transit point and destination for women and girls trafficked for the purpose of prostitution.

Although discrimination based on sexual orientation is technically illegal, in practice members of the lesbian, gay, bisexual, and transgender community face discrimination and even occasional attack.

Solomon Islands

Political Rights Rating: 4
Civil Liberties Rating: 3
Freedom Rating: 3.5
Freedom Status: Partly Free
Electoral Democracy: No

Population: 581,000
Capital: Honiara

Ten-Year Ratings Timeline For Year Under Review (Political Rights, Civil Liberties, Status)

Year Under Review	2004	2005	2006	2007	2008	2009	2010	2011	2012	2013
Rating	3,3,PF	3,3,PF	4,3,PF	4,3,PF	4,3,PF	4,3,PF	4,3,PF	4,3,PF	4,3,PF	4,3,PF

INTRODUCTION

In summer 2013, the military component of the Australian-led Regional Assistance Mission to the Solomon Islands (RAMSI)—which has kept peace between the country's two dominant ethnic groups, the Gwale and Malaitans, since 2000—withdrew. The police component—a 150-member force from Australia, New Zealand, and other Pacific Island countries—will remain through 2017 to train and support the local police.

POLITICAL RIGHTS: 22 / 40

A. Electoral Process: 6 / 12

Elections in the Solomon Islands have been plagued with problems from flawed voter rolls and allegations of bribery to fraudulent ballots, stealing of ballot boxes, and voter intimidation and violence.

Members of the 50-seat, unicameral National Parliament are elected for four-year terms. A parliamentary majority elects the prime minister. Gordon Darcy Lilo was elected prime minister in 2011 after his predecessor Danny Philip resigned amid allegations of corruption. A governor-general, appointed on the advice of Parliament for a five-year term, represents the British monarch as head of state. The governor-general appoints the cabinet on the advice of the prime minister. To prepare for general elections in 2014, the Electoral Office will establish a new voter registry using biometrics and 700 registration centers across the country. By year's end, biometric registration had begun.

B. Political Pluralism and Participation: 10 / 16

Though there are multiple political parties, alliances are driven more by personal ties and clan identities. The last general election was in 2010.

In October, the government withdrew the Political Party Integrity Bill, citing lack of support. The bill has been in existence since 2010. The goal is to curb the frequent changing of party affiliations by lawmakers, which has a destabilizing effect on government. Opponents questioned constitutionality of the bill, which calls for a commission to regulate political parties, including their registration, constitutions, and rules.

C. Functioning of Government: 6 / 12

Public offices are widely seen as opportunities for personal enrichment. Many lawmakers and officials have faced charges of official abuse and corruption and even former prime ministers have been convicted.

The Leadership Code Commission, which investigates allegations of misconduct against lawmakers, resumed its work in March 2013. The commission had been unable to perform its duties because Prime Minister Lilo—who is among the politicians being investigated—had not appointed replacements for two members whose terms ended in 2012. In June, the commission reported that 36 lawmakers, including 26 cabinet members, have yet to declare their personal finances.

In March 2013, the government pushed through the Constituency Development Fund bill. The government says the new law will increase transparency and accountability in the use of constituency development funds, monies that lawmakers can spend at their discretion on roads, services, and assistance among others to improve livelihood for their constituent communities. Critics say the new law puts more money in lawmakers' hands—effectively creating a slush fund—without clear measures to monitor how funds are managed and spent, and that little time was given to public consultation.

Lawmakers have been criticized for giving themselves pay raises and other benefits despite the economic hardship suffered by the population. In April 2013, public controversy compelled the government to withdraw a bill that would provide former prime ministers and their surviving spouses with generous monthly pension payments (80 percent of current pay for sitting prime ministers) and other benefits including free housing and utilities, free health care, and a service staff.

CIVIL LIBERTIES: 43 / 60
D. Freedom of Expression and Belief: 14 / 16

Freedoms of expression and of the press are generally respected, but politicians and elites sometimes use legal and extralegal means to intimidate journalists. The print media include a privately owned daily, a weekly, and two monthly publications. The government operates the only radio station. There is no local television station, but foreign broadcasts can be received via satellite. Internet use is growing, but access is limited by lack of infrastructure and high costs.

Freedom of religion is generally respected, as is academic freedom. In April 2013, the country's first university, the Solomon Islands National University, opened in Honiara.

E. Associational and Organizational Rights: 9 / 12

The constitution guarantees freedom of assembly, and the government generally recognizes this right in practice. Organizers of demonstrations must obtain permits, which are typically granted. Civil society groups operate without interference. Workers are free to organize, and strikes are permitted. The teachers' union went on strike three times in 2013 to demand pay increases and other benefits. In July, the High Court ordered the teachers to return to work but also required the government to provide them with back pay.

F. Rule of Law: 8 / 16

Threats against judges and prosecutors have weakened the independence and rigor of the judicial system. Judges and prosecutors have also been implicated in scandals relating to corruption and abuse of power. A lack of resources limits the government's ability to provide legal counsel and timely trials. Victims in rural areas have even less access to the formal justice system. The ombudsman's office has far-reaching powers to investigate complaints of official abuse and unfair treatment, but generally lacks funds to do so. Poor training, abuse of power, and factional and ethnic rivalries are common in the police force. Prison escapes are not uncommon.

The country went several months without a police commissioner in 2013 after the government failed to renew commissioner John Michael Lansley's contract in May; a new commissioner was finally appointed in September.

A Truth and Reconciliation Commission, modeled after South Africa's, was launched in 2009 to investigate crimes and address impunity connected to ethnic violence between 1998 and 2003. The commission submitted a report to Prime Minister Lilo in February 2012, though he has yet to send it to parliament for approval and release to the public, claiming that more time is needed for review. There have been widespread calls for the report's release. In April 2013, commission member Terry Brown posted a copy of the report on the internet, a move Lilo claimed was illegal.

G. Personal Autonomy and Individual Rights: 12 / 16

The Chinese economic presence in the Solomon Islands continues to grow, fostering public resentment; many have urged the government to enforce laws that reserve certain jobs for native islanders.

Discrimination limits the economic and political roles of women. Rape and other forms of abuse against women and girls are widespread. While rape is illegal, no laws prohibit domestic violence and marital rape. A 2012 World Bank study ranked the country worst in the world for violence against women. The country is also a source and destination for men and women trafficked for forced prostitution and labor. The government rejected a call by the United Nations to decriminalize homosexuality in 2011, saying it is against traditional values.

Somaliland

Political Rights Rating: 4
Civil Liberties Rating: 5
Freedom Rating: 4.5
Freedom Status: Partly Free

Population: 3,500,000
Capital: Hargeisa

Ten-Year Ratings Timeline For Year Under Review (Political Rights, Civil Liberties, Status)

Year Under Review Rating	2004	2005	2006	2007	2008	2009	2010	2011	2012	2013
	--	--	4,4,PF	4,4,PF	5,4,PF	5,5,PF	4,5,PF	4,5,PF	4,5,PF	4,5,PF

INTRODUCTION

The government of Somaliland, which had declared independence from Somalia in 1991, showed mixed signals regarding its commitment to political and civil rights in 2013. The administration continued its heavy-handed response to political criticism. Though arrests of journalists were less frequent than last year, the Somaliland government appeared to focus its energies those it considered key threats. In July, Kalsan TV, a London-based private television station, was banned indefinitely by Somaliland authorities who said the station lacked a license. Officials of the television station attributed the ban to the network's airing of a political debate that the government had not wanted broadcast.

In June, President Ahmed Mohamed Mohamoud Silanyo announced a major reshuffle and expansion of his administration, increasing the size of his cabinet from 33 to 45. The president dismissed five ministers and two deputies, named new officials, and established two new ministries. Opposition groups criticized the move, suggesting it would strain government resources for little benefit and was at odds with Silanyo's 2010 election promise to consolidate government.

Fears mounted that UK-based bank Barclays PLC would be successful in its efforts to close more than 250 Somali money-transfer operators, including Dahabshiil Holdings Ltd., the largest money-transfer operation in Somaliland and Somalia, due to concerns over money laundering. The bank's attempts to pull out were put on hold in November when Dahabshiil won an injunction delaying the closeout until the completion of a full trial, which was scheduled for 2014.

In October, the police in Hargeisa, the capital, conducted a sweep of 53 suspects accused of causing insecurity and violence. Similar security operations had led to the arrest of 270 others, according to Brigadier General Abdilahi Iman Fadal.

POLITICAL RIGHTS: 21 / 40
A. Electoral Process: 5 / 12

According to Somaliland's constitution, the president is directly elected for a maximum of two five-year terms and appoints the cabinet. The presidential election of 2010, originally scheduled for 2008, resulted in a smooth transfer of power from the United People's Democratic Party (UDUB) to the main opposition party, the Peace, Unity, and Development Party (Kulmiye). Silanyo, the leader of Kulmiye, captured almost 50 percent of the vote, comfortably ahead of the incumbent, Dahir Riyale Kahin, who received 33 percent. International monitors identified some irregularities, but declared the vote free and fair.

Somaliland has a well-developed electoral framework. Members of the 82-seat lower house of parliament, the House of Representatives, are directly elected for five-year terms, while members of the 82-seat upper house, or Guurti, are clan elders indirectly elected for six-year terms. In 2013, the terms of the lower and upper houses were extended for a second time, until 2015 and 2016, respectively. The terms were first extended in 2010 on the grounds that Somaliland could not organize another election so soon after the presidential poll. On November 28, 2012, the region held municipal elections for local councils, the first such elections in a decade. The United Nations alleged that elections did not take place in certain areas of the disputed eastern Sanaag, Sool, and Buhodle areas; those reports were unconfirmed by the Somaliland government. Overall, the elections were deemed free and fair by a coalition of civil society observers, though large protests followed a recount in Hargeisa's city council elections and the elections prompted Silanyo to call for a new voter roll before the upcoming parliamentary elections.

B. Political Pluralism and Participation: 10 / 16

Although parties defined by region or clan are technically prohibited, party and clan affiliations often coincide. A constitutional restriction allows for a maximum of three officially recognized political parties. The region's Registration and Approval Committee (RAC) reviewed the 18 parties and associations in existence to determine which could contest the November 2012 local elections. From the seven parties that contested those elections the three parties that received the most votes would be officially sanctioned and therefore would be the only parties able to stand in elections for the coming decade. The three that emerged on top in November 2012 were: Wadani, the Justice and Welfare Party (UCID), and the ruling Kulmiye party. Wadani is the newest of these parties; it was formed by breakaway members of UCID in October 2011 and later added members of the Horyaal and Nasiye political groups in September 2012 to solidify its position in the lead-up to the local council elections. In July 2013, Wadani and UCID agreed to align their strategies and form a coalition against Silanyo's Kulmiye party.

C. Functioning of Government: 6 / 12

Corruption in Somaliland was a serious problem under the government of President Riyale, but there have been signs of improvement under Silanyo. In March 2012, three top officials charged with mismanaging food aid were fired. A bill to strengthen the five-member Good Governance and Anti-Corruption Commission, an informal body established in 2010, passed parliament in the fall of 2012. In April 2013, the president followed through on his rhetorical commitments to the fight corruption by firing both the head and the second in command of the Hargeisa Power Agency on corruption-related charges. In July, Hassan Omer Horri was named the new Director General of the Good Governance and Anti-Corruption Commission.

CIVIL LIBERTIES: 25 / 60
D. Freedom of Expression and Belief: 7 / 16

While freedoms of expression and the press are guaranteed by the constitution, these rights are limited in practice. Journalists continued to face government interference and harassment in 2013. In April, the offices of *Hubaal*, an independent daily newspaper, were attacked and shots were fired at the paper's manager, and there were allegations that the assailants were police. In June, acting attorney general Aden Ahmed Mouse suspended *Hubaal* without explanation. The next month, a Somaliland court charged the newspaper's editor and its manager, Hassan Hussein Abdullahi and Mohamed Ahmed Jama, with defamation, reporting false news, and wrongly accusing Ethiopian consulate workers of smuggling alcohol into Somaliland. The suspension was lifted in August and both Abdullahi and Jama were granted presidential pardons. Citizens demonstrated in Hargeisa after one of the police officers accused of attacking the newspaper in April was released without charge in early December. Four journalists who covered the story for other news outlets were arrested and detained for seven days following the protest. *Hubaal* was again shut down after a police raid against its headquarters in December and remained closed through the year's end. Journalist Jama Jiir was released on appeal several months after his arrest on charges of insulting the state related to a February *Gufaan Times* article he had written criticizing the ruling party for what he called slow movement on anticorruption measures and unfair distribution of resources.

Islam is the state religion, and nearly all Somaliland residents are Sunni Muslims. While the Somaliland constitution allows for freedom of belief, it prohibits conversion from Islam and proselytizing by members of other faiths. It also requires that candidates for the presidency, vice presidency, and House of Representatives be Muslim. Academic freedom is less restricted than in neighboring Somalia. The territory has at least 10 universities and colleges of higher learning, though none are adequately resourced.

E. Associational and Organizational Rights: 5 / 12

Freedoms of assembly and association are constitutionally guaranteed, though the government has taken a heavy-handed stance on critical demonstrations. In 2012, the government banned political demonstrations after the May arrests of three opposition leaders in Hargeisa who were protesting the decision to disqualify their groups from participating in local elections. In September 2013, witnesses alleged that police fired live ammunition at protesters chanting antigovernment slogans and burning tires in Erigavo in the disputed Sanaag region; the protesters were demonstrating against the Somaliland government's ban on the official Somali currency in the region. At least 10 people were wounded, according to witnesses. After the violence, the government imposed a curfew in the region.

International and local nongovernmental organizations operate without serious interference. The constitution does not specifically mention the right to strike, though it does permit collective bargaining. The right to belong to a union is generally respected.

F. Rule of Law: 7 / 16

The judiciary is underfunded and lacks independence, and the Supreme Court is largely ineffective. Somaliland has approximately 100 judges, most of whom do not have formal legal training. Somaliland's constitution allows for three legal systems, based respectively on Sharia (Islamic law), civil law, and customary law. Upon taking office, Silanyo pledged to strengthen the independence of the judiciary and release all prisoners who had not been charged with a crime, apart from those accused of terrorism or theft. Somaliland's police and security forces, while more professional than those in Somalia, have at times used excessive force. In October, discussions began for the drafting of an Administration Procedure Act, which would outline the separation of powers and clarify roles within the Somaliland government.

Societal fault lines are largely clan-based. Larger, wealthier clans have more political clout than the less prominent groups, and clan elders often intervene to settle conflicts. There has been increased discrimination against foreigners.

G. Personal Autonomy and Individual Rights: 6 / 16

In 2013, the Somaliland government placed new emphasis on tightening legal strictures around human trafficking, specifically related to youth emigration for employment. According to the Somaliland National Youth Organisation, about 50 Somaliland youth are smuggled out of the region every month. According to the Somaliland Youth Ambition Development Group, in May, a group of 325 young people were smuggled out of Somaliland, bound for Libya; of the group that left Somaliland, almost half wound up imprisoned in Libya or Tunisia, 15 died en route—killed either by smugglers or by harsh conditions—and over 30 remain unaccounted for. In an effort to curb illegal migration, Silanyo created a committee to prevent migration and promote job creation in June. In October, Somaliland police arrested a man they said was a top regional official in a major international human trafficking network led by Yasin Mahi Ma'alin, a Swedish citizen of Somali origin.

While society in Somaliland is patriarchal, women have made modest advances in public life. The idea of a quota for political representation of women has been frequently discussed, but never adopted, and Kulmiye in 2010 expressed support for a 25 percent quota across all political institutions. In 2013, Silanyo appointed two new female ministers, bringing the total number of women in his cabinet to four. However, the only female member of the Guurti, Fadumo Jama Eleye, resigned in March, citing the challenge of creating sufficient change as the only woman in the upper house. Baar Saeed, a member of the House of Representatives, is now the region's sole female legislator.

The government showed a renewed commitment to combatting rape after an increase in cases in 2013, with a heavy-handed approach to arrests and prosecutions. In August, the government handed 5- and 10-year prison sentences to 21 individuals for the gang rape of two women in Hargeisa. According to a human rights worker, in the two weeks prior to the sentencing, six additional gang-rape cases were seen in the city. Female genital mutilation, while illegal, is practiced on the vast majority of women.

South Africa

Political Rights Rating: 2
Civil Liberties Rating: 2
Freedom Rating: 2.0
Freedom Status: Free
Electoral Democracy: Yes

Population: 52,982,000
Capital: Tshwane/Pretoria

Ten-Year Ratings Timeline For Year Under Review (Political Rights, Civil Liberties, Status)

Year Under Review	2004	2005	2006	2007	2008	2009	2010	2011	2012	2013
Rating	1,2,F	1,2,F	2,2,F	2,2,F	2,2,F	2,2,F	2,2,F	2,2,F	2,2,F	2,2,F

INTRODUCTION

The year 2013 in South Africa was marked by the continued decline of prosecutorial independence; high-profile corruption scandals; strikes by, and rivalries among, the country's powerful trade unions; ongoing service-delivery protests; and the emergence of new opposition parties. The year was capped by the passing of the country's iconic first black president, Nelson Mandela, in December, highlighting South Africa's ongoing transition from single-party dominance by Mandela's Africa National Congress (ANC) to a more competitive electoral landscape. The ANC has dominated every election since the end of the apartheid system of white minority rule in 1994.

Ahead of national elections scheduled for May 2014, the year saw the emergence of a number of new opposition parties. In February, Mamphele Ramphele—a well-known anti-apartheid activist, former university chancellor, and businesswoman—formed the centrist Agang party. Meanwhile, former ANC Youth League (ANCYL) leader Julius Malema, who had been expelled from the ANC in 2012, launched the radical Economic Freedom Fighters (EFF) party in July. In December, the National Union of Metalworkers South Africa (NUMSA)—the country's largest trade union and an affiliate of the ANC-allied labor federation Congress of South African Trade Unions (COSATU)—resolved to withhold its usual electoral support from the ANC in 2014 and explore forming a new labor party.

A sometimes violent rivalry between the ANC-affiliated National Union of Mineworkers (NUM) and the more militant Association of Mineworkers and Construction Union (AMCU) in the mining sector continued in 2013, resulting in nearly a dozen deaths and helping drive a number of strikes. The labor unrest exacerbated the nation's flagging economy and high unemployment rate, which was stood at approximately 25 percent nationally and around 36 percent for youth.

President Jacob Zuma became embroiled in another corruption scandal in 2013 surrounding R200 million ($20.9 million) of state spending on renovations to his homestead in Nkandla, KwaZulu-Natal.

POLITICAL RIGHTS: 33 / 40 (-1)

A. Electoral Process: 12 / 12

Elections for the 400-seat National Assembly, the lower house of the bicameral Parliament, are determined by party-list proportional representation. The 90 members of the upper chamber, the National Council of Provinces (NCOP), are selected by the provincial legislatures. The National Assembly elects the president to serve concurrently with its five-year term, and presidents can serve a maximum of two terms. The Independent Electoral Commission (IEC) is largely independent and voter registration ahead of 2014 elections proceeded well in 2013, although allegations of corruption in awarding construction tenders for new headquarters has slightly weakened perceptions of the institution's integrity.

The ANC—which has won every election since the end of apartheid in 1994—claimed another sweeping victory in the April 2009 elections, although with a smaller majority than in the previous elections. The ANC took 65.9 percent of the national vote, 264 seats in the 400-seat National Assembly, and clear majorities in eight of nine provinces. The Democratic Alliance (DA) remained the largest opposition party, winning 67 National Assembly seats and outright control of Western Cape Province. The smaller opposition Congress of the People (COPE) party—launched in 2008 by disaffected ANC members—won 30 seats, and the traditionally Zulu-nationalist Inkatha Freedom Party (IFP), led by Mangosuthu Buthelezi, took 18. Zuma was easily elected state president by the National Assembly the following month, winning 277 of the 400 votes.

B. Political Pluralism and Participation: 13 / 16 (-1)

The ANC, which is part of a tripartite governing alliance with COSATU and the South African Communist Party, dominates the political landscape. The DA is the leading opposition party. Factionalism within the ANC and COSATU, as well as tensions between the alliance partners, has been a hallmark of South African politics in recent years. Political violence and allegations of vote buying marked ANC nomination contests ahead of the party's December 2012 national conference, especially in North West, Limpopo, Mpumalanga, and KwaZulu-Natal provinces. The run-up to the conference showcased the most recent of many leadership battles within the ANC, pitting Zuma against backers of Deputy President Kgalema Motlanthe. Zuma ultimately defeated Motlanthe decisively. Prominent ANC figure and business tycoon Cyril Ramaphosa, a former labor leader, was elected deputy president of the party, replacing Motlanthe, who remained deputy president of the republic.

The emergence of new and more assertive opposition parties evoked government restrictions on some political events and rallies in 2013, a trend that will likely continue before the 2014 elections. A number of events sponsored by Malema's EFF were blocked or delayed by authorities on technical grounds. Some also saw scuffles between supporters of the EFF, the ANCYL, or the ANC-affiliated South African Students Congress (SASCO). Meanwhile, parts of Rustenberg have become "no-go" areas for ANC politicians and affiliated unions, as a result of the violence against striking workers at Marikana in 2012. The ANCYL also occasionally used vandalism to protest the DA government in the Western Cape and some of the party's political events in Gauteng and the Eastern Cape.

C. Functioning of Government: 8 / 12

Several agencies are tasked with combating corruption, but enforcement is inadequate. Public servants regularly fail to declare their business interests as required by law, and the ANC has been criticized for charging fees to business leaders for access to top government officials. The tender process for public contracts is often politically driven and opaque. The delivery of government services is undermined by maladministration, although a newly formed procurement office and more training for public servants may improve the situation. According to the auditor general's report for the 2012–2013 fiscal year (April 1–March 31), "wasteful" expenditure increased by 43 percent over 2011–2012 to about R2.1 billion ($220 million), while "irregular expenditure" hit R26.4 billion ($2.76 billion), with health, education, and public works departments among the worst offenders. South Africa was ranked 72 out of 177 countries and territories surveyed in Transparency International's 2013 Corruption Perceptions Index.

Zuma, who was charged with corruption three times between 2005 and 2009 in connection with the "arms deal" scandal, continued to face scrutiny in 2013. Although the National

Prosecuting Authority (NPA) has repeatedly declined to prosecute Zuma for corruption related to the arms deal, in August, a North Gauteng High Court granted a request by the DA to make public the so-called spy tapes—secret recordings of the NPA's justifications for dropping fraud and corruption charges against Zuma in 2009. Zuma appealed the decision in October. Former acting NPA head Nomgcobo Jiba previously had obstructed the tapes' release.

In late November, leaks from Public Protector Thuli Madonsela's provisional report concluded that Zuma had derived "substantial" personal benefit from the upgrades to Nkandla, ostensibly for security, and may have misled Parliament in this regard. By contrast, a December report by an inter-ministerial task team—led by security ministers close to Zuma—concluded that while there was substantial misallocation of spending, Zuma bore no responsibility. The inter-ministerial report was met by wide skepticism by most civil society and independent media entities. Madonsela's final report is due in early 2014.

CIVIL LIBERTIES: 48 / 60 (+1)
D. Freedom of Expression and Belief: 15 / 16

Freedoms of expression and the press are protected in the constitution and generally respected in practice, though press freedom has deteriorated in recent years. Most South Africans receive the news via radio outlets, a majority of which are controlled by the South African Broadcasting Corporation (SABC). The SABC also dominates the television market, but two commercial stations are expanding their reach. Private newspapers and magazines are often very critical of powerful figures and institutions and remain a critical check on the government. However, political allies of the government own a growing share of independent media. In December 2013, *Cape Times* editor Alide Danois was fired after the newspaper—which is part of Independent News & Media South Africa, recently acquired by the politically connected Sekunjalo Investments—ran an article about an allegedly irregular government tender awarded to the Sekunjalo consortium to manage the country's fishery vessels. Internet access is unrestricted and growing rapidly, though many South Africans cannot afford the service fee.

The government is highly sensitive to media criticism and has increasingly encroached on the editorial independence of the SABC. Some government critics have been barred from SABC programs, and a number of documentaries and specials produced by the broadcaster have been canceled due to political considerations. In December 2013, SABC executives reportedly ordered staff not to broadcast footage of Zuma being booed at a high-profile memorial service for Mandela, or subsequent calls for his resignation by senior leaders of NUMSA. The government has also recently enacted or proposed several potentially restrictive laws, although there has been significant pushback from civil society and judicial authorities. In 2012, the Constitutional Court (CC) found sections of the 2009 Film and Publications Amendment Act that require prepublication classification of material dealing with "sexual conduct" to be unconstitutional, and two bans on films by the government's Film and Publications Board for encouraging child pornography have been overturned by the courts. In part because of substantial opposition from civil society and opposition parties, Zuma has yet to sign into the law a revised, less onerous version of the controversial Protection of State Information Bill, which would allow state agencies to classify a wide range of information as in the "national interest" and thus subject to significant restrictions on publication. The revised law removed a clause criminalizing the disclosure of information about state security, but still does not allow a "public interest" defense for violations.

Freedom of religion and academic freedom are constitutionally guaranteed and actively protected by the government.

E. Associational and Organizational Rights: 12 / 12 (+1)

Freedoms of association and peaceful assembly are guaranteed by the constitution. South Africa hosts a vibrant civil society. Nongovernmental organizations (NGOs) can register and operate freely, and lawmakers regularly accept input from NGOs on pending legislation. Freedom of assembly is generally respected, and South Africa has a vibrant protest culture; demonstrators must notify police ahead of time but are rarely prohibited from gathering. In recent years, however, a growing number of community protests over public-service delivery have turned violent and been forcibly dispersed by police. According to the University of Johannesburg, there were 287 service delivery protests in 2013, down from 470 in 2012.

South Africans are generally free to form, join, and participate in independent trade unions, and the country's labor laws offer unionized workers a litany of protections; contract workers and those in the informal sector enjoy fewer safeguards. Growing union rivalries, especially in mining, have led to an increase in violent tactics to win and retain members, as well attacks on rivals. COSATU, the nation's largest trade union federation, claims about two million members. Strike activity is very common, and unionized workers often secure above-inflation wage increases. Violent and "wildcat strikes" (strikes not sanctioned by labor law) are increasing. The year 2013 saw several clashes between members of the NUM and the AMCU, leading to at least 6 deaths.

Nonetheless, the year's labor unrest was less deadly than in 2012; in August of that year, police killed 34 striking mineworkers during a violent confrontation in Marikana near Rustenberg, marking the worst incident of state violence in the post-apartheid era. The Farlam Commission, a government-sponsored inquiry into the violence at Marikana, was ongoing at year's end; significant evidence of excessive lethal force by police was presented during the year. After a court battle, in October the South Guateng High Court ruled that the state, through Legal Aid South Africa, was compelled to fund legal representation for strikers and their families.

F. Rule of Law: 10 / 16

Judicial independence is guaranteed by the constitution, and the courts—particularly the CC and the Supreme Court of Appeal—operate with substantial autonomy. Nevertheless, judicial and prosecutorial independence has come under pressure in recent years amid the Zuma corruption cases, prompting several instances of judicial and political misconduct. In a positive step, Parliament in 2012 approved a 17th amendment to the constitution, making the CC the apex court, the Supreme Court of Appeal a general appellate court, and the CC chief justice—not the justice minister—South Africa's chief judicial authority. CC judges are appointed by the Judicial Services Commission, based on both merit and government efforts to racially transform the judiciary. In November 2013, the National Assembly passed the controversial Legal Practice Bill, which allows the state to regulate the previously self-regulating legal profession with a 22-member council (3 members of which are appointed by the Justice Minister) in order to facilitate racial transformation. If, as expected, it is passed by the NCOP and signed by Zuma, the law will likely be challenged as unconstitutional.

Prosecutorial independence continued to suffer under the Zuma administration. Although judicial authorities continued to push back on infringements, the senior-most ANC leaders generally retained impunity from punishment for a range of alleged offenses. In August 2013, Zuma appointed a new head of the NPA, Mxolisi Sandile Oliver Nxasana; the office had remained vacant since 2011 and has seen a string overtly political hirings and firings. Also, Vasantrai Soni was appointed the new head of the NPA's Special Investigation Unit. In September, a North Gauteng High Court overturned former NPA official Lawrence

Mrwebi's February 2012 decision to drop corruption charges against suspended police spy boss Richard Mdluli, as well as a separate decision to drop murder, kidnapping, and assault charges against Mdluli.

Judicial staff and resource shortages undermine defendants' procedural rights, including the rights to a timely trial and state-funded legal counsel. There were about 50,000 pretrial detainees in South African prisons in 2013, comprising about 31 percent of the prison population. They wait an average of three months before trial, and some beyond the legal maximum of two years. Lower courts have proven more susceptible to corruption than the higher panels, and there have been reports of physical intimidation of judges and magistrates.

Despite constitutional prohibitions and some government countermeasures, there are many reports of police torture and excessive force during arrest, interrogation, and detention. Prisons often feature overcrowding, inadequate health care, and abuse of inmates by staff or other prisoners; both HIV/AIDS and tuberculosis are problems. The Judicial Inspectorate for Correctional Services (JICS) investigates prisoners' complaints but has limited resources and capacity. According to a JICS report released in October 2013, inmate complaints about assaults by other inmates increased by 55 percent and by guards by 73 percent in April 2012–March 2013, and prison rapes increased by 40 percent. The government paid out R1.3 billion ($161 million) to compensate prisoners and families for assaults and rape in 2012, but prevention programs are almost nonexistent.

South Africa has one of the highest rates of violent crime in the world. After declining in recent years, murder, attempted murder, armed robbery, sexual offenses, home robberies, and carjackings all increased from April 2012–March 2013, according to a report by the South African Police Service (SAPS). The Zuma administration has given the police more latitude to use force against criminals. Mostly due to police incapacity, vigilantism is a problem.

The constitution prohibits discrimination based on a range of categories, including race, sexual orientation, and culture. State bodies such as the South African Human Rights Commission and the Office of the Public Protector are empowered to investigate and prosecute cases of discrimination. Affirmative-action legislation has benefited previously disadvantaged groups (defined as "Africans," "Coloureds," "Asians," and, as of 2008, "Chinese") in public and private employment as well as in education. Racial imbalances in the workforce persist, and a majority of the country's business assets remain white-owned. The government's Black Economic Empowerment program aims to increase the black stake in the economy, mostly by establishing race-based ownership thresholds for government tenders and licenses.

The number of foreign nationals in South Africa is uncertain, with estimates ranging from two to seven million, including between one and three million Zimbabweans. South Africa receives the highest number of asylum applications in the world—overwhelmingly from other African countries. However, it accepts only about 15 percent, and closed three of seven refugee reception offices in 2012. The 2011 Immigration Amendment Act reduced the period asylum seekers have to make a formal application at refugee reception centers after entering the country, from 14 days to 5 days; also that year, the government resumed deportations of Zimbabwean migrants. Conditions at migrant detention centers are poor, and deportees are subject to physical and sexual abuse by police and immigration officers. Increased immigration, particularly from Zimbabwe, Mozambique, and Somalia, has spurred xenophobic violence by police and vigilantes. Sporadic attacks continued in 2013, often tied to wider service-delivery protests in which immigrants were scapegoated.

Separately, the nomadic Khoikhoi and Khomani San peoples, indigenous to South Africa, suffer from social and legal discrimination.

South Africa has one of the world's most liberal legal environments for LGBT (lesbian, gay, bisexual, and transgender) people. Discrimination on the basis of sexual orientation is prohibited in the constitution; a 2002 Constitutional Court ruling held that same-sex couples should have the same adoption rights as married couples; and the 2006 Civil Unions Act legalized same-sex marriage. Nevertheless, societal bias remains strong. LGBT people are routinely subject to physical attacks, including an increase in instances of so-called corrective rape, in which lesbians are raped by men who claim this can change the victim's sexual orientation.

G. Personal Autonomy and Individual Rights: 11 / 16

The state generally protects citizens from arbitrary deprivation of property. However, some 80 percent of farmland is owned by white South Africans, who make up 9 percent of the population. As a result, thousands of black and colored farmworkers suffer from insecure tenure rights; illegal squatting on white-owned farms is a serious problem, as are attacks on white owners. The government has vowed to transfer 30 percent of land to black owners by 2014; however, only about 6 percent of land has been transferred since 1994. A 2013 government land audit revealed the state owns between 14 and 21 percent of the country's land. In 2013, the government replaced its "willing buyer, willing seller" approach to land reform with a more aggressive "just and equitable" approach, echoing language in the constitution, and proposed a number of bills to this effect, although all are in preliminary stages.

Equal rights for women are guaranteed by the constitution and promoted by the Commission on Gender Equality. While the constitution allows the option and practice of customary law, it does not allow such law to supersede women's rights as citizens. Nevertheless, women suffer de facto discrimination with regard to marriage (including forced marriage), divorce, inheritance, and property rights, particularly in rural areas. A draft Traditional Courts Bill would strengthen the legal authority of traditional leaders, sparking concerns among civic groups about women's rights. The bill was rejected by 5 of 9 provincial legislatures but had not yet been withdrawn from consideration as of the end of 2013.

Despite a robust legal framework criminalizing domestic violence and domestic rape, both are extremely grave problems. South Africa has one of the world's highest rates of sexual abuse: 127 per 100,000, according to the 2013 SAPS report. Under-reporting is prevalent; a separate police report estimated that only 1 in 36 rapes is reported. Women are also subject to sexual harassment and wage discrimination in the workplace, and are not well represented in top management positions. Women are better represented in government, holding some 41 percent of the seats in the National Assembly and leading five of nine provincial governments. The main opposition DA party is led by Helen Zille, the premier of Western Cape Province.

South Korea

Political Rights Rating: 2
Civil Liberties Rating: 2
Freedom Rating: 2.0
Freedom Status: Free
Electoral Democracy: Yes

Population: 50,220,000
Capital: Seoul

Ratings Change: South Korea's political rights rating declined from 1 to 2 due to high-profile scandals involving corruption and abuse of authority, including alleged meddling in political affairs by the National Intelligence Service.

Ten-Year Ratings Timeline For Year Under Review (Political Rights, Civil Liberties, Status)

Year Under Review	2004	2005	2006	2007	2008	2009	2010	2011	2012	2013
Rating	1,2,F	1,2,F	1,2,F	1,2,F	1,2,F	1,2,F	1,2,F	1,2,F	1,2,F	2,2,F

INTRODUCTION

In February 2013, Park Geun-hye was inaugurated as South Korea's first female president. Park is the daughter of former president Park Chung-hee, who assumed office in 1963 after a military coup. She also served as first lady under her father after the assassination of her mother in 1974. While she has acknowledged the human rights abuses perpetrated under her father's rule, she is still criticized for his legacy. Her inauguration came soon after North Korea's third nuclear weapons test, forcing her to demonstrate early on how she would implement her "trustpolitik" approach to North Korea. This approach, combining deterrence and trust building between the two Koreas, was tested repeatedly throughout the year.

After nearly a year of investigations, state prosecutors announced in November that agents from the National Intelligence Service (NIS), the country's spy agency, had posted more than 1.2 million "tweets" the previous year in a clandestine online campaign to try to help Park win the 2012 presidential election. The tweets praised Park and ridiculed opposition rivals. Prosecutors did not say what impact the campaign had on the election results; Park won by only 1 million votes. The opposition Democratic Party held a series of rallies demanding an apology from Park and calling for the dismissal of Justice Minister Hwang Kyo-ahn, a political appointee of Park's, for lack of impartiality, though he remained in office at year's end.

In March, South Korea, China, and Japan began the first round of negotiations for a trilateral free-trade agreement. The same month, the annual joint U.S.–Republic of Korea training exercises included a flyover of U.S. B-52 bombers to reaffirm the U.S. "nuclear umbrella" over South Korea. North Korea responded by threatening to abandon the armistice agreement and cut the hotline to the South. At the end of the month, tensions had risen to dangerous levels. North Korea declared a "state of war" against the South and threatened nuclear attack against the United States. The United States responded by bolstering defense forces in the region.

In April, North Korea denied entry by South Koreans to the Kaesong Industrial Complex (KIC), and recalled all 53,000 North Korean workers. The KIC is an inter-Korean economic cooperation project that has historically continued to function regardless of the political climate on the peninsula. South Korean staff stayed on for a short period, but were all withdrawn by early May. Several rounds of talks took place starting in July, when political tensions began to thaw, and operations at the KIC were resumed in September.

In December, the Korean Railway Workers' Union (KRWU) led thousands of workers on a strike against the possible privatization of the Korea Railroad Corporation (KORAIL). Tensions between strike leaders and the government escalated to the point of mass arrests, but a political agreement led most strikers to return to work by year's end.

POLITICAL RIGHTS: 35 / 40 (-1)
A. Electoral Process: 11 / 12

The 1988 constitution vests executive power in a directly elected president, who is limited to a single five-year term. Of the unicameral National Assembly's 300 members, 246 are elected in single-member districts and 54 are chosen through proportional representation, all for four-year terms.

In the April 2012 National Assembly elections, the ruling conservative Saenuri Party won 152 seats, while the liberal Democratic United Party—later renamed the Democratic Party—took 127 seats. The United Progressive Party captured 13 seats, the Liberty Forward Party took 5, and independent candidates won 3. In that December's presidential election, Park of the Saenuri Party defeated DUP candidate and former human rights lawyer Moon Jae-in, 52 percent to 48 percent.

In April 2013, two new voting systems came into effect. One was early voting, intended to expand electoral participation, which was launched in by-elections that month. Voters were able to show up at a polling station during the early voting period and cast their ballots without applying in advance. The other was a new integrated voter register, which allowed voters to cast their ballots simply by showing their identification cards at any polling station across the country, regardless of their home district.

B. Political Pluralism and Participation: 14 / 16 (-1)

Political pluralism is robust, with multiple parties competing for power. Although party structures and coalitions are relatively fluid, the two dominant parties during 2013 were the ruling Saenuri and the opposition Democratic Party.

In order to restrict the power of the ruling party, under the 2012 National Assembly Advancement Act, a three-fifths majority is required to bring closely contested bills from standing committees to the plenum for a floor vote.

Given that Park won the 2012 presidential election by a narrow margin, investigations into the NIS-led online campaign have led some observers to question whether such activity harmed the country's electoral process. Charges have been filed against Won Sei-hoon, former NIS chief; Lee Jong-myung, former third deputy director of the NIS; Min Byung-joon, director of psychological intelligence; and six other officials. Kim Yong-pan, former chief of the Seoul Metropolitan Police, was also indicted in June for obstruction of the police investigation.

C. Functioning of Government: 10 / 12

Despite anticorruption efforts by the government, bribery, influence peddling, and extortion persist in politics, business, and everyday life. In July 2013, Won Sei-hoon, the former NIS director, was arrested on bribery charges. He was charged with accepting cash, gold, and other gifts totaling 150 million won ($135,000) from the head of a construction company since 2009 in exchange for helping the company win construction projects.

In another case, investigations begun in May revealed that substandard parts and fabricated testing certificates had been supplied to nuclear power plants, which led to the shutdown of two reactors. The investigation also resulted in criminal charges against close to 100 high-ranking officials linked to the nuclear power industry. These included the former vice minister of knowledge economy Park Young-joon, who was indicted in September for receiving 60 million won ($54,000) in bribes from a local contractor to help Hankook Jungsoo Industries win a contract from the Korea Electric Power Corporation (KEPCO) under a deal to build a nuclear power plant in the United Arab Emirates. Park had already been jailed for a separate corruption charge. Also indicted was Kim Jong-shin, former president of the state-run Korea Hydro and Nuclear Power, for receiving 130 million won ($117,000) for steering business to Hankook Jungsoo Industries.

In March, an investigation began into several influential figures, including Vice Justice Minister Kim Hak-ui, in relation to allegations that they received sex services from women hired by a local construction contractor who sought business favors in 2009. Although he resigned from his post, Kim was cleared of charges in November for lack of evidence.

The Park administration has launched a series of reforms of key government agencies including the National Tax Service, the Board of Audit and Inspection, and the Supreme Prosecutors' Office to help address pervasive corruption. In April, the administration eliminated the Central Investigation Division (CID) of the Supreme Prosecutors' Office, which reportedly had a long record of corruption problems and whose neutrality had been doubted. In September, the ruling and opposition parties agreed to reestablish the National Integrity Commission to facilitate full-scale anticorruption efforts. However, the National Assembly's special committee on judicial reform has failed to reach an agreement on several key issues, including the establishment of a special investigator's office. South Korea was ranked 46 out of 177 countries and territories surveyed in Transparency International's 2013 Corruption Perceptions Index.

CIVIL LIBERTIES: 50 / 60

D. Freedom of Expression and Belief: 14 / 16

The news media are generally free and competitive. Newspapers are privately owned and report aggressively on government policies and alleged official and corporate wrongdoing. However, although media censorship is illegal, official censorship, particularly of online content, increased during Lee Myung-bak's 2008–2013 presidency. Under the National Security Law, enacted in 1948 to prevent espionage and other threats from the North, listening to North Korean radio is illegal, as is posting pro-North messages online; authorities have deleted tens of thousands of web posts deemed to be pro-North. The Office of the UN High Commissioner for Human Rights and Amnesty International have called for the law to be scaled back or repealed, insisting that its broadly written provisions are being abused to silence political opposition. The government has also attempted to influence reporting by media outlets and has interfered with the management of major broadcast media.

The constitution provides for freedom of religion. Academic freedom is unrestricted, though the National Security Law limits statements supporting the North Korean regime or communism.

The government generally respects citizens' right to privacy. A wiretap law sets the conditions under which the government may monitor telephone calls, mail, and e-mail.

E. Associational and Organizational Rights: 11 / 12

South Korea respects freedoms of assembly and association, which are protected under the constitution. However, several other legal provisions conflict with these principles, creating tension between the police and protesters over the application of the law. For instance, Article 3 of the Law on Assembly and Demonstration prohibits activities that might cause social unrest. Police must be notified of all demonstrations. Local nongovernmental organizations (NGOs) have alleged that police who mistreat demonstrators have not been penalized equally with protesters under this law.

Under the Act on Electric Source Development, Korea Electric Power Company (KEPCO) can expropriate land for electric installation. KEPCO and residents of Miryang in South Gyeongsang Province have been in conflict for the past eight years over the construction of high-voltage transmission towers. When KEPCO resumed construction at five sites in the area in October, a few hundred protesters, mostly in their 70s and 80s, demonstrated. Clashes ensued with 2,000 riot police stationed at the five sites, causing at least three injuries.

Human rights groups, social welfare organizations, and other NGOs are active and generally operate freely. The country's independent labor unions advocate workers' interests, organizing high-profile strikes and demonstrations that sometimes lead to arrests. However, labor unions in general have diminished in strength and popularity, as is the global trend, especially as the employment of temporary workers increases. In October, the government revoked the legal status of the Korean Teachers' and Education Workers' Union (KTU), after the union refused to revise a provision regarding union membership (the administration offered KTU one month to change its bylaws). KTU allows retired and dismissed workers to keep union membership, which is an internationally accepted practice.

For 22 days in December, railway workers went on strike to protest the government's plans to create a subsidiary company (Suseo KTX Corporation) under the state-run KORAIL to operate the Suseo High Speed Railway—a step the workers said could lead to privatization. Tensions between railway workers and the government escalated quickly, as KORAIL fired thousands of striking unionists and filed complaints against strike leaders, and the government declared the strike illegal. On December 22, 600 police officers raided the headquarters of the Korea Confederation of Trade Unions (KCTU) to arrest nine KRWU leaders, but ended up arresting 136 KCTU officials and members who resisted the police. This led to a general strike rally in Seoul organized by the KCTU, where tens of thousands gathered to speak out against the government. The KORAIL strike ended on December 30, as Saenuri and Democratic lawmakers held talks and agreed to form a subcommittee on railway development to address the issues raised by the strike.

F. Rule of Law: 13 / 16

South Korea's judiciary is generally considered to be independent. Judges render verdicts in all cases; while there is no trial by jury, there has been an advisory jury system since 2008, and judges generally respect juries' decisions. Although South Korea's prisons lack certain amenities, such as hot water in the winter, there have been few reports of beatings or intimidation by guards. In March 2013, an activist with the Catholic Human Rights Commission filed a constitutional appeal arguing that the overcrowding of jails was a violation of human dignity.

The country's few ethnic minorities face legal and societal discrimination. Residents who are not ethnic Koreans have extreme difficulties obtaining citizenship, which is based on parentage rather than place of birth. Lack of citizenship bars them from the civil service and limits job opportunities at some major corporations. Same-sex intercourse is legal, but same-sex marriage is not. Such relationships are gaining acceptance but still largely hidden. A celebrity couple symbolically held a wedding in October to challenge public views on same-sex marriage. In March, the Seoul Western District Court ruled that transgender individuals can legally change their gender without having reassignment surgery, as an earlier decision had required.

Comprehensive antidiscrimination legislation was proposed in February 2013 that would prohibit discrimination based on religion, political ideology, or sexual orientation. Facing fierce opposition from conservatives, it was withdrawn in April. This marked the third attempt since 2007 to introduce an antidiscrimination act in the National Assembly.

G. Personal Autonomy and Individual Rights: 12 / 16

Travel both within South Korea and abroad is unrestricted, except for travel to North Korea, which requires government approval.

Although South Korean women enjoy legal equality and a 2005 Supreme Court ruling granted married women equal rights with respect to inheritance, women face social and employment discrimination in practice. Women continued to be underrepresented in government following the December 2012 elections, holding just 15.7 percent of National Assembly seats. The Park administration's emphasis on fighting sex crimes and protecting victims' rights led to revisions of the sex-crime laws in June and bolstering of police sex-crime units. Some features of the new laws include a redefinition of potential victims of sex crimes to include men, a lifting of the statute of limitations for several types of cases, and harsher punishments for offenders. In addition, people accused of sex offenses can now be investigated and prosecuted without a direct complaint from the victim; third-party reports can be accepted as grounds to start an official investigation.

South Sudan

Political Rights Rating: 6
Civil Liberties Rating: 6
Freedom Rating: 6.0
Freedom Status: Not Free
Electoral Democracy: No

Population: 9,782,000
Capital: Juba

Ratings Change: South Sudan's civil liberties rating declined from 5 to 6 due to increased armed conflict and mass killings along ethnic lines, triggered by intolerance for dissent within the ruling party and politically motivated arrests in December.

Ten-Year Ratings Timeline For Year Under Review (Political Rights, Civil Liberties, Status)

Year Under Review	2004	2005	2006	2007	2008	2009	2010	2011	2012	2013
Rating	--	--	--	--	--	--	--	6,5,NF	6,5,NF	6,6,NF

INTRODUCTION

Less than three years after achieving independence, South Sudan was in danger of unraveling at the end of 2013 following an outbreak of political violence that quickly assumed ethnic dimensions. The year was characterized by runaway corruption, political discord, stalled progress on constitutional reform, and widespread abuses by the country's security forces. It was capped in December by factional fighting within the army that turned into a full-scale rebellion against the government of President Salva Kiir. According to the United Nations, more than 1,000 people were killed and approximately 180,000 displaced in just two weeks of fighting as the year drew to a close. The violence showed no sign of subsiding by December 31, despite calls for a cease-fire. Fighting affected half of South Sudan's 10 states and government forces had lost control of two state capitals, including the strategically important town of Bentiu, the center of oil production in the country.

The backdrop to the violence was a political split within the ruling party, the Sudan Peoples' Liberation Movement (SPLM), aggravated by long-standing rivalry between President Salva Kiir and his deputy, Riek Machar. Kiir fired Machar as vice president in July, along with his entire cabinet. Kiir justified the move as a good-governance measure, appointing a new, slimmed-down cabinet a week later. Machar announced his intention to oppose the president in the next elections, scheduled for 2015. However, when an armed confrontation broke out within the presidential guard on December 15 between members of the Dinka and Nuer, South Sudan's two largest ethnic groups, the president accused Machar of trying to launch a coup. Machar denied the allegations, but as the fighting spread and degenerated into communal violence, he placed himself at the head of the revolt and declared that his rival was an illegitimate president whose "dictatorial tendencies" made him unfit for office. Kiir ordered the arrest of Machar and several other senior SPLM leaders. While Machar evaded capture, 12 of his allies were detained. They included nine former government ministers, a former state governor, the suspended secretary general of the party, and the former head of mission to the United States.

Meanwhile, relations with Sudan continued to be volatile throughout 2013. Summits between Kiir and his Sudanese counterpart, President Omar al-Bashir, in April, September, and October, saw both leaders vowing to cooperate on trade and resolve other disputes. South Sudan was cast an economic lifeline in April when an agreement between the countries allowed oil exports to resume through Sudan's oil pipeline.

POLITICAL RIGHTS: 8 / 40 (-3)
A. Electoral Process: 4 / 12

Kiir was elected president of the semiautonomous region of Southern Sudan with an overwhelming majority in 2010, five years after taking over as head of the region's dominant party, the SPLM, following the death of longtime leader John Garang. Upon the country's independence in July 2011, Kiir became president of the new nation of South Sudan. A revised version of Southern Sudan's 2005 interim constitution, adopted at independence, gives sweeping powers to the executive. The president cannot be impeached and has the authority to fire state governors and dissolve the parliament and state assemblies. Kiir made use of his wide powers in 2013, dismissing his entire cabinet and the vice president. He also fired two state governors, appointing interim governors in their place and missing constitutional deadlines to elect permanent replacements.

A permanent constitution is due to be passed by 2015. A 55-member National Constitutional Review Commission, established in 2012, was charged with writing a draft text by early 2013, but its work has been hamstrung by administrative delays and lack of an operational budget; the draft had yet to be produced by the end of the year. Some opposition politicians boycotted the constitutional consultation process, claiming it was insufficiently inclusive and dominated by members of the SPLM.

South Sudan's bicameral National Legislature was reconfigured after independence. The SPLM holds 90 percent of the 332 seats in the lower house, the National Legislative Assembly (NLA). In addition to members of the old, pre-independence Southern legislature—who were elected in 2010—the chamber includes 96 former members of Sudan's National Assembly and 66 additional members appointed by the president. The upper chamber, the Council of States, includes 20 former members of Sudan's Council of States, plus 30 members appointed by Kiir. The SPLM dominates the new 21-member cabinet appointed in September. South Sudan has a decentralized system, with significant powers devolved to the 10 state assemblies. Nine of the 10 state governors are members of the SPLM.

The government has begun preparations for the country's first national elections, scheduled for 2015. In 2012, it passed an elections act and established a National Elections Commission. But the head of the commission said in September 2013 that the government had failed to provide adequate funding for the process and warned that the electoral timetable might slip as a result; the head of the National Bureau of Statistics the previous day said there was not enough money to conduct a census, which was constitutionally required in advance of the elections.

B. Political Pluralism and Participation: 2 / 16 (-3)

Opposition parties have no chance of winning real political power; five opposition parties are represented in the NLA, but they lack both the resources to operate effectively and the experience to formulate policy and set party platforms The SPLM is intolerant of opposition. It has repeatedly accused the largest opposition party, the SPLM–Democratic Change (DC), of supporting armed groups and threatened to rescind its party registration. However, in an apparent change of heart, a presidential "pardon" was issued to the leader of the SPLM-DC, Lam Akol, in October, although he had never been charged with an offense.

The SPLM is also deeply intolerant of internal dissent. The December 2013 crisis was preceded by Kiir's decision to marginalize a significant portion of South Sudan's political leadership, his refusal to convene a meeting of the SPLM's executive body to discuss complaints about his governing style, and his failure to promote internal party democracy. Kiir has been accused of allowing his decisions to be led by a group of close advisers, described by his opponents as "regional and ethnic lobbies and close business associates." Accusations persist that members of the country's largest ethnic group, the Dinka, dominate the SPLM's leadership and the security services to the detriment of other groups, such as the Nuer.

South Sudan's military, the Sudan Peoples' Liberation Army (SPLA), continues to exercise strong influence over political affairs.

C. Functioning of Government: 2 / 12

Endemic corruption is undermining public confidence in the state. In an open letter to mark two years of independence in July, a group of U.S. activists and academics known for their strong support of South Sudan lamented that the country had become "synonymous with corruption." Government appointments are typically handed to SPLM loyalists or potential rivals with little regard for merit, and corrupt officials take advantage of inadequate budget monitoring to divert public funds. So-called ghost workers are used to artificially inflate the public payroll, allowing corrupt officials to steal the surplus. In August, the interior minister said an ongoing investigation had so far been unable to confirm the identities of half the members of South Sudan's police force, supposed to total 52,000. In September, Kiir accused the SPLA of rampant corruption, asking why it lacked the most basic equipment despite its significant budget.

In June, two senior cabinet ministers were suspended pending an investigation into the theft of $8 million of public money. In September, the head of South Sudan's Anti-Corruption Commission said the funds had been recovered and recommended that the two men face charges. However, there were no signs of progress in a separate investigation into 75 current and former officials accused of stealing a total of $4 billion. Kiir made the allegations in June 2012, demanding the immediate return of the money. But he refused to name the suspects and no one has yet been prosecuted.

CIVIL LIBERTIES: 16 / 60 (-4)

D. Freedom of Expression and Belief: 7 / 16 (-1)

Private media in South Sudan has proliferated, with more than three dozen FM radio stations, more than half a dozen newspapers, and several online news sites. The sole national television channel is government-owned. There is one private satellite television channel, Ebony TV. In the summer of 2013, parliament passed bills governing public broadcasting in South Sudan, setting up a media oversight authority, and guaranteeing the public right of access to information. All three bills were awaiting presidential approval at the end of the year. The media authority bill has been criticized by some for establishing statutory regulation of the press, empowering the president to appoint members to the regulator's board and remove board members through a majority vote by parliament. Oliver Modi Philip, chair of the Union of Journalists of Southern Sudan, welcomed the legislation but warned that it would only confer all of its benefits if fully implemented.

Meanwhile, journalists going about their work encountered increasing hostility from public officials and security forces. Members of the National Security Service (NSS) harassed and unlawfully detained members of the media for critical coverage of the government. Journalists were warned not to report on a press conference held by Machar in December in which he called for political reform and criticized the president. After violence broke out on December 15, the authorities detained a Reuters correspondent and a freelance photojournalist for two nights without charge for their reporting on a media briefing by Kiir. In other incidents during the year, seven journalists were held in January when they tried to cover violent demonstrations in the city of Wau. Security officials harassed and sometimes unlawfully detained members of the media for critical coverage of the government. In May, top editors from the *Juba Monitor* newspaper were arrested in connection with a story that accused a senior government official of involvement in a murder, and one of them was detained for three days, reportedly without access to a lawyer. In July, a Catholic radio station had its license suspended after it reported on the suspicious death of a prisoner. In early January, the government claimed to have made arrests in connection with the murder of an online journalist and critic of the government, Diing Chan Awuol, who was shot dead on his doorstep in 2012. However, it released no further details and there were no outward signs that the investigation was making progress. In May, the United States expressed alarm about worsening press freedom conditions in South Sudan.

Religious freedom is guaranteed by the interim constitution and generally respected in practice. The church is the strongest nongovernmental organization (NGO) in South Sudan and plays an important role in mediating state-society relations. There are no restrictions on academic freedom, although basic access to education is limited outside state capitals. The university system was seriously disrupted in 2012 by austerity measures and ethnic violence, which forced the closure of the country's main institution of higher learning, Juba University, for three months. The December 2013 violence also disrupted the education system.

Public discussion of political issues is muted for fear of harassment from the authorities. The government uses the NSS to track and intimidate perceived critics.

E. Associational and Organizational Rights: 3 / 12 (-1)

Freedoms of assembly and association are enshrined in the interim charter, and authorities typically uphold them in practice. South Sudan is highly dependent on assistance from foreign NGOs, which largely operate freely in the country. However, the government has hindered the approval of visas for some nationalities and obstructed the work of international organizations it considers unhelpful. A UN human rights official was expelled in 2012 in response to a report accusing the SPLA of committing abuses in Jonglei state. The country's widespread instability has also interfered with the work of international organizations. Members and staff of the UN Mission in South Sudan (UNMISS) have come under attack from armed groups. In the most serious incident, in April, 12 people traveling in a UNMISS convoy were killed by unidentified attackers in Jonglei. When violence broke out in Jonglei in December, armed youth attacked a UN compound in Akobo, killing two UN peacekeepers and approximately 20 Dinka civilians who had been seeking shelter.

Domestic civil society organizations, including unions, remain nascent. A Workers' Trade Union Federation, formed in 2010, has 65,000 members. Legislation to codify labor rights has stalled in the National Assembly.

F. Rule of Law: 1 / 16 (-2)

The interim constitution provides for an independent judiciary. The president's Supreme Court appointments must be confirmed by a two-thirds majority in the NLA. The court system is under huge strain. In 2011, the chief justice said that the courts had the capacity to handle 100,000 cases a year, but faced four times that number. There are allegations that the courts have been used by the government to harass opponents of Kiir. The president was accused of using the alleged December 15 coup as a pretext to detain prominent political rivals. Twelve senior SPLM current and former officials were arrested on suspicion of involvement in an attempted coup. Only one had been released by the end of the year, despite protests by the international community.

There is a culture of impunity within the security forces, with serious abuses carried out against civilians, reportedly with the full knowledge or on the orders of some senior commanders. The South Sudan National Police Service (SSNPS) is ill-equipped, unprofessional, and overwhelmed by the country's security challenges. There were numerous reports of arbitrary arrest, police brutality, and bribe-taking. Factions of the SSNPS were believed to be responsible for a spate of violent crime and robberies in Juba in 2012. In 2011, UN inspectors uncovered evidence of brutality and rape at the main police training academy; at least two recruits died of their injuries, and no one has been prosecuted. The National Security Service (NSS), an unregulated agency reporting directly to the president, has been responsible for arbitrary arrests and abuses.

While there have been modest improvements to the penal system, prison facilities are poor, with unsanitary conditions and insufficient food for inmates. Children and the mentally ill are routinely detained with adult prisoners. According to Human Rights Watch, one-third of detainees are on remand. Inefficiencies in the justice system have led to indefinite detention.

The army routinely performs policing functions, and the SPLA has committed serious human rights violations while carrying out such duties and in its other capacities. These include the murder, rape, and torture of civilians and the looting and destruction of property during the ongoing counter-insurgency campaign in Jonglei. Much of the violence has targeted the Murle ethnic group; Human Rights Watch documented almost 100 unlawful killings of Murle civilians and security officials by the security forces between December 2012 and July 2013 in one county alone. Little has been done to investigate abuses by the army, although in a positive step, the army announced in August that it had arrested a brigadier general whose soldiers were accused of serious violence against civilians.

While members of some armed insurgent groups—including the South Sudan Liberation Army (SSLA)—reached a deal with the government and handed over their weapons in April, other groups, particularly one led by David Yau Yau, continued to wreak havoc in Jonglei. In an attack widely attributed to Yau Yau's rebels, more than 70 people were killed in October when gunmen attacked villages, burned property, and stole cattle. Yau Yau denied that his rebels had been involved in the attack. In their response to the insurgency in Jonglei, South Sudanese security forces were accused of attacking civilians and destroying property on a large scale, and raping women with impunity.

The state authorities are unable to protect vulnerable populations from violence and are themselves responsible for some of the most serious abuses. The United Nations logged 269 separate incidents of armed violence across the country from January–September 2013. The worst-affected area remained Jonglei state, where ethnic clashes had caused almost two thousand deaths since independence and the displacement of more than 100,000 people, even before the violence of December 2013.

Foreign workers in South Sudan have complained of harassment and discrimination. In August, foreign motorcycle-taxi operators were banned from working in the country, a decision that forced an estimated 1,000 Ugandans to leave South Sudan.

Since 2005, more than two million refugees and internally displaced people have moved back to the South. The government encouraged their return but has largely failed to provide them with even the most basic assistance.

Same-sex sexual conduct is not explicitly illegal in South Sudan, but "carnal intercourse against the order of nature" is punishable by up to 10 years in prison. LGBT (lesbian, gay, bisexual, and transgender) individuals face widespread discrimination and stigma.

G. Personal Autonomy and Individual Rights: 5 / 16

Land use and ownership are frequent causes of conflict in South Sudan, and returning refugees have exacerbated the problem. Unclear or nonexistent laws have been exploited by SPLM officials and overseas investors to uproot people from their land.

The interim constitution guarantees the rights of women to equal pay and property ownership. Nonetheless, women are routinely exposed to discriminatory practices and domestic abuse. Women hold a quarter of the posts in the NLA, fulfilling a constitutional gender quota. The prevalence of child marriage contributes to low levels of educational attainment among girls. Official figures suggest that almost half of girls aged 15–19 are married and, according to a March 2013 Human Rights Watch report, the government is failing to adequately address the problem. The SPLA continues to use child soldiers, despite a pledge to end the practice.

Spain

Political Rights Rating: 1
Civil Liberties Rating: 1
Freedom Rating: 1.0
Freedom Status: Free
Electoral Democracy: Yes

Population: 46,600,000
Capital: Madrid

Ten-Year Ratings Timeline For Year Under Review (Political Rights, Civil Liberties, Status)

Year Under Review	2004	2005	2006	2007	2008	2009	2010	2011	2012	2013
Rating	1,1,F	1,1,F	1,1,F	1,1,F	1,1,F	1,1,F	1,1,F	1,1,F	1,1,F	1,1,F

INTRODUCTION

Following a decade-long housing and construction boom, the global financial crisis that started in 2008 revealed the troubled state of the Spanish financial sector. In June 2012, Spain began the process of obtaining a €41 billion ($55.6 billion) bailout of its banking sector, initiating a deep reform. The continuation of stringent austerity measures imposed in response to the financial crisis, an unemployment rate that remained above 25 percent for all of 2013—with youth unemployment at 54.3 percent at the end of the year—and a wave of foreclosures and evictions have resulted in social discontent across large sectors of Spanish society. Spain's economy returned to growth in the second half of 2013 after nine consecutive quarters of decline, and was projected to grow slightly in 2014.

In 2013, several notorious corruption investigations in Spain, implicating politicians at all levels, resulted in mounting public anger toward the country's political and economic elite, the destabilization of the Spanish government, and, according to some analysts, threats to investor confidence in the country. Public anger was also directed at ongoing cuts to education spending coupled with a controversial education reform passed by parliament in November. A law approved by the government in December that made abortions illegal except in the case of rape or when a pregnancy poses a serious mental or physical risk to the woman drew condemnation from women's rights groups and opposition politicians; the law was considered likely to be approved by parliament.

A referendum on the independence of Catalonia, planned for 2014 by the regional Catalan president but deemed illegal by the Spanish government, further strained relations between the regional and central governments. Diplomatic tensions between Spain and the UK mounted over the British colony of Gibraltar, but critics accused the Spanish government of using this as a smoke screen to divert attention from domestic issues.

POLITICAL RIGHTS: 39 / 40

A. Electoral Process: 12 / 12

The Congress of Deputies, the lower house of Spain's bicameral parliament, has 350 members elected in multimember constituencies, except for the North African enclaves of Ceuta and Melilla, which are each assigned one single-member constituency. The Senate has 264 members, with 208 elected directly and 56 chosen by regional legislatures. Members of both the Senate and Congress serve four-year terms. Following legislative elections, the monarch selects the prime minister—usually the leader of the majority party or coalition. The parliament must then elect the candidate. The country's 50 provinces are divided into 17 autonomous regions; with powerful regional parliaments, Spain is one of the most decentralized countries in Europe. National and regional elections are considered free and fair. Spain is a member of the European Union.

In early general elections held in November 2011, the right-wing Popular Party (PP) trounced the center-left Socialist Party (PSOE), capturing 186 out of 350 seats in the lower house, while the PSOE took only 111 seats, its worst showing in 30 years. PP leader Mariano Rajoy replaced the PSOE's José Luis Rodríguez Zapatero as prime minister.

B. Political Pluralism and Participation: 16 / 16

People have the right to organize political parties and other competitive groups of their choice. For example, the Bildu party in the Basque region, which was formed after the political wing of the militant Basque separatist group Euskadi Ta Askatasuna (ETA), or Basque Fatherland and Freedom, was permanently banned in 2002, won seats in regional elections in 2012. The opposition has realistic opportunities to gain power, but due to the electoral law, only two major parties, the PP and the PSOE, have a genuine chance. Other parties such as the left-wing Izquierda Unida or the liberal Unión Progreso y Democracia have seen increasing gains in elections. However, some regional electoral reforms make it more difficult for these parties to win seats. An independence movement in the region of Catalonia has gained steam, and Catalan President Artur Mas continues to press ahead with plans to hold a referendum on Catalan independence in November 2014; the Spanish government says it will block the referendum, which it claims violates the Spanish constitution.

C. Functioning of Government: 11 / 12

There was a string of developments in high-profile corruption investigations in 2013, most notoriously connected to the so-called Bárcenas case, involving the ruling PP. The case concerned allegations that a slush fund—allegedly administered by a former party treasurer, Luis Bárcenas—had been used for many years to make illegal cash payments to party leaders, including to Rajoy, possibly in exchange for favorable treatment of the construction companies that allegedly made the illegal donations. Rajoy and other party leaders denied receiving payments. Bárcenas is in jail awaiting trial. Another ongoing case has implicated the son-in-law of King Juan Carlos I, Iñaki Urdangarín, who is accused of misappropriating millions of euros in his role as chairman of a charitable organization. Urdangarín's wife, Princess Cristina, was also under investigation. High-profile corruption scandals have also rocked the Catalonian and Andalusian regional governments. All these events contributed to Spain's slump to rank 40 out of 177 countries and territories in Transparency International's 2013 Corruption Perceptions Index.

CIVIL LIBERTIES: 57 / 60
D. Freedom of Expression and Belief: 15 / 16 (-1)

Spain has a free and active press, with more than 100 newspapers (many of them regional) covering a wide range of perspectives and actively investigating high-level corruption. However, due to the economic crisis, Spanish media have suffered from ownership consolidation: very few media groups control most TV and radio stations, and most newspapers and magazines are also in the hands of a few. Media organizations had suffered over the course of the economic crisis, and according to a study released in December 2013 by the Madrid Press Association, more than 4,400 journalists lost their jobs in 2013 as 73 media organizations closed. In August 2012, the state-owned broadcaster, RTVE, removed several journalists who strongly criticized the ruling PP. Excessive political intervention into the creation of new TV and radio stations is considered an obstacle to freedom of the press, especially at the regional and local levels.

Freedom of religion is guaranteed through constitutional and legal protection. Roman Catholicism is the dominant religion and enjoys privileges that other religions do not, such as financing through the tax system. The role of Catholicism in political decision-making is evident in the proposed law restricting abortions and in elements of the education reform law passed in 2013 that increase the role of religion in the classroom. Jews, Muslims, and Protestants have official status through bilateral agreements with the state, while other groups, including Jehovah's Witnesses and Mormons, have no such agreements.

The government does not restrict academic freedom. However, large protests by educators and students in October demonstrated discontent with ongoing austerity-driven cuts to education funding that critics say will disadvantage lower-income students, particularly with respect to paying for university. There was also public dissatisfaction with a reform to the education system passed in November that gave greater weight to exam scores and prioritized the Spanish language over regional languages in schools, among other measures.

E. Associational and Organizational Rights: 12 / 12

The constitution provides for freedom of assembly, and the government respects this right in practice. Large anti-austerity protests and strikes took place across the country throughout 2013. A draft bill approved by the government late in 2013 that set fines of up to €30,000 ($40,000) for several protest-related offenses was criticized by civil liberties groups as an affront to freedom of assembly. The bill was expected to pass in the PP-dominated parliament. Domestic and international nongovernmental organizations operate without government restrictions. With the exception of members of the military, workers are free to strike, organize, and join unions of their choice.

F. Rule of Law: 15 / 16 (+1)

The Constitution provides for an independent judiciary. However, some important members of judicial institutions such as the Constitutional Court and the General Public

Prosecutor are elected by politicians. Experts believe a new reform approved by the government in June weakens judicial independence by removing the power of judges to nominate members of the General Council of the Judiciary and reducing the number of permanent positions on that body. The European Court of Human Rights in Strasbourg stopped several foreclosures in Spain during 2013 that were the result of onerous mortgage terms. In October, the same court struck down the "Parot doctrine," a Spanish sentencing practice that was used to keep some prisoners (mostly ETA terrorism detainees) incarcerated for most of the 30-year maximum allowed by law; the court ruling applied only to the particular sentence challenged in the case, but it was expected to have wider ramifications as the court found that the Parot doctrine violated the European Convention on Human Rights. An austerity measure adopted in 2012 denies public health coverage to illegal immigrants.

G. Personal Autonomy and Individual Rights: 15 / 16

A lack of access to credit has created obstacles to private business activity, especially for small and medium-sized firms. Women enjoy legal protections against rape, domestic abuse, and sexual harassment in the workplace. Violence against women, particularly within the home, remains a serious problem, with up to 50 women killed in 2013. The proposed abortion law was criticized by the opposition and abortion rights groups for rolling back women's rights. Same-sex marriages are legal, and same-sex couples may adopt children. Trafficking in men, women, and children for the purposes of sexual exploitation and forced labor remains a problem.

⬇ Sri Lanka

Political Rights Rating: 5
Civil Liberties Rating: 4
Freedom Rating: 4.5
Freedom Status: Partly Free
Electoral Democracy: No

Population: 20,501,000
Capital: Colombo

Trend Arrow: Sri Lanka received a downward trend arrow due to intensified attacks by hardline Buddhist groups against the Christian and Muslim minorities, including their properties and places of worship, often with official sanction.

Ten-Year Ratings Timeline For Year Under Review (Political Rights, Civil Liberties, Status)

Year Under Review	2004	2005	2006	2007	2008	2009	2010	2011	2012	2013
Rating	3,3,PF	3,3,PF	4,4,PF	4,4,PF	4,4,PF	4,4,PF	5,4,PF	5,4,PF	5,4,PF	5,4,PF

INTRODUCTION

The government, led by President Mahinda Rajapaksa of the United People's Freedom Alliance (UPFA), tightened its grip on power in 2013 by intimidating critical voices in the media and civil society and by weakening judicial independence through the confirmation of Parliament's impeachment of the chief justice of the Supreme Court in January.

Authorities continued to reject credible allegations of war crimes committed in the final phase of the military's campaign against the Liberation Tigers of Tamil Eelam (LTTE, or Tamil Tigers) rebel group in 2009. Implementation of recommendations made in late 2011 by the Lessons Learnt and Reconciliation Commission (LLRC), a government-backed investigative body, was uneven in 2013. Among other steps, the LLRC had called on the administration to gradually remove security forces from civilian affairs, establish a more distanced relationship between the police and institutions managing the armed forces, implement a policy of trilingualism, devolve power to local government institutions, and commence investigations into the myriad abductions, disappearances, and harassment of journalists that have taken place in recent years.

In light of the government's continued failure to address such problems, the UN Human Rights Council in March adopted a second resolution criticizing Sri Lanka's rights record and encouraging the government to allow an independent investigation into alleged war crimes. Following a visit to the country in August, UN High Commissioner for Human Rights Navi Pillay noted little progress on issues of accountability.

In September, elections for the Northern Provincial Council were held for the first time in decades. Despite complaints of intimidation and subterfuge by the military in the run-up to the vote, the Tamil National Alliance (TNA)—the main party representing the interests of the island's ethnic Tamil population—won 30 of the council's 38 seats. Meanwhile, the ruling UPFA won comfortably in the other two provinces that held elections. Despite the long-delayed voting in Northern Province, most executive power there remained in the hands of a quasi-military administration headed by an appointed governor.

A number of global heads of state refused to attend the Commonwealth Heads of Government meeting in Colombo in November, and Sri Lanka's human rights record and conduct during the end of the war overshadowed media coverage of the event itself. Media attention also focused on official attempts to stifle local protest and dissent during the meeting.

POLITICAL RIGHTS: 16 / 40

A. Electoral Process: 6 / 12

The 1978 constitution vested strong executive powers in the president, who is directly elected for six-year terms and can dissolve Parliament. The prime minister heads the leading party in Parliament but has limited authority. The 225-member unicameral legislature is elected for six-year terms through a mixed proportional representation system.

In the January 2010 presidential election, called almost two years ahead of schedule, Rajapaksa won a second term with nearly 58 percent of the vote. His main opponent, former head of the armed forces Sarath Fonseka, received around 40 percent. In parliamentary elections held later that year, the ruling UPFA secured 144 of 225 seats, but fell short of a two-thirds majority. The opposition United National Party (UNP) won 60 seats, while the Democratic National Alliance (DNA) coalition, led by the People's Liberation Front (JVP), won 7, and the TNA took 14.

In both the presidential and parliamentary elections, monitoring groups such as the independent Center for Monitoring Election Violence alleged inappropriate use of state resources—particularly transport, infrastructure, police services, and the media—to benefit the ruling coalition, in violation of orders issued by election officials. More than 1,000 incidents of violence, including at least four deaths, were reported prior to the presidential election, and in Northern and Eastern Provinces, inadequate provisions for transport and registration of displaced persons contributed to a low turnout. The parliamentary elections were less beleaguered by violence; nevertheless, irregularities led to the nullification or suspension of results in several districts. The provincial elections held in 2013 were also reportedly affected by violence and intimidation, primarily perpetrated by the military and progovernment forces; violence was particularly widespread in the Northern Province.

B. Political Pluralism and Participation: 6 / 16

A range of political parties—some of which explicitly represent the interests of ethnic and religious minority groups—are able to operate freely and contest elections. However, in recent years opposition parties' chances of gaining power have been steadily reduced by the ruling coalition's abuse of state resources during election periods. The ruling coalition has also weakened the opposition through strategies such as co-opting opposition members of Parliament to encourage defections.

Harassment of opposition politicians continues to occur. Shortly after he placed second in the 2010 presidential contest, Fonseka was arrested on charges of plotting a coup and subsequently sentenced to a 30-month prison term for engaging in politics while still an active military officer and not adhering to procurement rules. He was released in May 2012, but forbidden from holding office for seven years. In the north and east, members of Tamil political parties that do not support the government are particularly prone to threats. In 2013, during the run-up to the Northern Province elections, TNA candidates and their staff faced attacks and harassment by the military and progovernment supporters.

C. Functioning of Government: 4 / 12

Some observers charge that Rajapaksa's centralized, authoritarian style of rule has led to a lack of transparent, inclusive policy formulation. The Centre for Policy Alternatives (CPA) and others have noted the concentration of power in the hands of the Rajapaksa family. The president himself holds multiple ministerial portfolios—including defense, finance, and law and order—and his brothers serve in other key posts: Gotabaya is defense secretary, Basil is minister for economic development, and Chamal is speaker of Parliament. A growing number of other relatives, including the president's son Namal, also hold important political or diplomatic positions. The president and his family consequently control approximately 70 percent of the national budget. In January, Parliament passed the controversial Divi Neguma Bill, which would combine all local and provincial development agencies under the central minister for economic development, effectively transferring an additional fund of 80 billion rupees ($620 million) to Basil Rajapaksa without oversight provisions.

The 18th Amendment to the constitution, passed in 2010, gave a government-dominated parliamentary council the authority to advise the president regarding appointments to independent commissions that oversee the police, the judiciary, human rights, and civil servants. A politically neutral constitutional council had previously made the nominations. The new amendment also removed the two-term limit on presidents. Separately, the government has repeatedly stalled the passage of freedom of information legislation.

Official corruption remains a significant concern. The current legal and administrative framework is inadequate for promoting integrity and punishing corrupt behavior, and enforcement of existing safeguards has been weak. The Commission to Investigate Allegations of Bribery or Corruption (CIABOC) has insufficient resources and personnel to deal with a heightened level of complaints; local activists charge that the commission has failed to investigate some cases brought to its attention, though it typically receives several thousand claims each year, of which dozens are investigated. A March 2012 parliamentary report also alleged widespread corruption in 229 public enterprises, leading to the removal of a number of chairmen. Sri Lanka was ranked 91 out of 177 countries and territories surveyed in Transparency International's 2013 Corruption Perceptions Index.

CIVIL LIBERTIES: 26 / 60 (-1)
D. Freedom of Expression and Belief: 7 / 16 (-1)

Although freedom of expression is guaranteed in the constitution, a number of laws and regulations restrict this right, including the Official Secrets Act, antiterrorism regulations, and laws on defamation and contempt of court. State-run media outlets have fallen under government influence, while official rhetoric toward critical journalists and outlets has grown increasingly hostile, often equating any form of criticism with treason and threatening physical violence.

Journalists throughout Sri Lanka, particularly those who cover human rights or military issues, encounter considerable levels of intimidation, which has led to increased self-censorship over the past several years. A number of journalists received death threats in 2013, and others were assaulted. In February, journalist Faraz Shauketaly of the *Sunday Leader* survived an assassination attempt by unknown assailants, while Mandana Ismail Abeywickrema, an editor at the same paper, fled the country in September after receiving threats. Tamil-language outlets such as the *Uthayan* newspaper, based in Jaffna, also face regular attacks and harassment. Past attacks on journalists and media outlets, such as the murder of Lasantha Wickrematunga in 2009 and the disappearance of Prageeth Eknaligoda in 2010, have not been adequately investigated, leading to a climate of complete impunity.

Web-based media, particularly Tamil-language news sites and other independent outlets, are occasionally subject to government-authorized blocks. State authorities reportedly conduct surveillance on the personal communications of individuals known to be critical of the government.

The constitution gives special status to Buddhism, and religious minorities face discrimination and occasional violence. Tensions between the Buddhist majority and the Christian minority—particularly evangelical Christian groups, which are accused of forced conversions—sporadically flare into attacks on churches and individuals by Buddhist extremists. Muslims have also faced harassment, and Buddhist militant groups such as the Bodu Bala Sena stepped up hostile rhetoric and attacks during 2013. In August, a mosque in Colombo was forced to close after being attacked by a Buddhist mob. Also that month, the CPA raised concerns about a proposed defamation of religions bill that would establish a government regulatory board to monitor the publication of materials on Buddhism; the initiative had not been passed by year's end. In recent years, the minority Ahmadiyya Muslim sect has faced increased threats and attacks from Sunni Muslims who accuse Ahmadis of being apostates. Work permits for foreign clergy are limited to one year, with the possibility of extension.

Academic freedom is generally respected. However, some commentators report increasing politicization on university campuses, lack of tolerance for antigovernment views, and a rise in self-censorship by professors and students. Academics who study Tamil issues have reported official harassment following their participation in conferences overseas, according to the Federation of University Teachers' Associations (FUTA). Other FUTA members have faced threats due to their activism and critiques of growing political interference in the education sector. In 2011, authorities introduced mandatory "leadership training" for all university undergraduates, conducted by the army at military camps. The curriculum allegedly promotes Sinhalese nationalist viewpoints and discourages respect for ethnic diversity and political dissent. Several student leaders arrested in Jaffna in late 2012 were released in early 2013 after being kept in detention centers for several months; a larger number have faced questioning from authorities and attempts to restrict their ability to organize peaceful demonstrations and events.

E. Associational and Organizational Rights: 6 / 12

Although demonstrations regularly take place, authorities sometimes restrict freedom of assembly. In October, the government announced a ban on rallies in Colombo during the Commonwealth heads of government summit in November. Security forces broke up those that did occur. Police occasionally use excessive force to disperse protesters. In August, three protesters were killed and several dozen were injured when security forces opened fire on a demonstration demanding access to clean drinking water in the town of Weliweriya.

The army has imposed more widespread restrictions on assembly, particularly for planned memorial events concerning the end of the war, in the north and east. In March, authorities prevented 11 busloads of northerners from traveling to Colombo to present a petition to UN representatives regarding their disappeared or detained relatives, according to Amnesty International.

Nongovernmental organizations (NGOs) experience some official harassment and curbs on their activities, and since 2010 the Defence Ministry has controlled the registration of both local and foreign NGOs. Human rights and peace-seeking groups—particularly those willing to document abuses of human rights or accountability and to discuss them at international forums, such as the CPA, the National Peace Council, and the local branch of Transparency International—face surveillance, smear campaigns, threats to their staff, and criminal investigations into their funding and activities. In August 2013, human rights activists and others who met with Navi Pillay, the visiting UN high commissioner for human rights, were later harassed and threatened by the military. Many NGOs had difficulty acquiring work permits in the northern and eastern areas of the country. However, the United Nations and other humanitarian organizations were generally given adequate access to the former conflict zones.

Most of Sri Lanka's 1,500 trade unions are independent and legally allowed to engage in collective bargaining, but this right is poorly upheld in practice. Except for civil servants, most workers can hold strikes, though the 1989 Essential Services Act allows the president to declare a strike in any industry illegal. While more than 70 percent of the mainly Tamil workers on tea plantations are unionized, employers routinely violate their rights. Harassment of labor activists and official intolerance of union activities, particularly in export processing zones, are regularly reported. In May 2013, the government threatened to fire public-sector workers who took part in a nationwide strike to protest rising prices.

F. Rule of Law: 5 / 16

Judicial independence was significantly weakened in late 2012 when Parliament successfully impeached the chief justice of the Supreme Court, Shirani Bandaranayake, after the court issued an important ruling that was unfavorable to the government. The Supreme Court found in early 2013 that the impeachment proceedings were unconstitutional, but the president nevertheless ratified the parliamentary vote, and Bandaranayake was replaced with a government ally, Mohan Peiris, in mid-January. The International Commission of Jurists condemned the impeachment for violating due process and the fundamentals of a fair trial, and the local bar association also protested the move. Other judges have faced physical attacks, intimidation, and political interference. Concerns about broader politicization of the judiciary have grown in recent years; judicial independence had already been eroded by the 18th Amendment, which granted advisory powers to a parliamentary council and greater responsibility for judicial appointments to the president. Corruption remains common in the lower courts, and those willing to pay bribes have better access to the legal system. Lawyers who specialize in human rights issues and who have campaigned to protect judicial independence, such as J. C. Weliamuna, faced death threats in early 2013.

The security forces have engaged in a number of abusive practices, including arbitrary arrest, extrajudicial execution, forced disappearance, custodial rape, torture, and prolonged detention without trial, all of which disproportionately affect Tamils. A February Human Rights Watch report detailed the use of rape and other forms of sexual violence against Tamil men and women held in custody on suspicion of links to the LTTE. Abuse is facilitated by the Prevention of Terrorism Act (PTA), under which suspects can be detained for up to 18 months without trial, as well as 2006 antiterrorism regulations. These laws have been used to detain a variety of perceived enemies of the government, including political opponents, critical journalists, members of civil society, and Tamil civilians suspected of supporting the LTTE. Several thousand remained in detention without charge at the end of 2013, according to human rights groups.

Separately, of the roughly 11,000 Tiger cadres who surrendered in the war's final stages, around 230 remained in military-run "rehabilitation" programs during 2013, after several hundred more were released in 2012. Human rights groups have claimed that insufficient registration policies in the postwar camps for internally displaced persons (IDPs) contributed to widespread disappearances and removals without accountability, and the status of hundreds of Tamils who disappeared during the war's closing offensives remains unclear.

Impunity in cases of abuse remains the norm; most past human rights abuses are not aggressively investigated or prosecuted, and victims and witnesses are inadequately protected. In October, the Supreme Court dismissed a case in which the parents of a deceased Tamil prisoner alleged that he had been illegally killed in detention. The National Human Rights Commission (NHRC) is empowered to investigate abuses, but it has traditionally suffered from insufficient authority and resources, and its independence was weakened by the adoption of the 18th Amendment in 2010.

Tamils maintain that they face systematic discrimination in areas including government employment, university education, and access to justice. Legislation that replaced English with Sinhala as the official language in 1956 continues to disadvantage Tamils and other non–Sinhala speakers. Tensions between the three major ethnic groups (Sinhalese, Tamils, and Muslims) occasionally lead to violence, and the government generally does not take adequate measures to prevent or contain it.

Members of the LGBT (lesbian, gay, bisexual, and transgender) community face social discrimination and some instances of official harassment. Sex "against the order of nature" is a criminal offense, though cases are rarely prosecuted.

G. Personal Autonomy and Individual Rights: 8 / 16

Freedom of access to educational institutions is affected by rampant corruption, with parents forced to pay bribes for admission, materials, and unofficial projects. The problem continued in 2013 despite a presidential directive to stop such practices, according to Transparency International.

Freedom of movement is restricted by the use of security checkpoints, particularly in the north of the country. Government appropriation of land in the north and east, as part of economic development projects or "high security zones," has prevented local people from returning to their property, and observers have expressed concerns that the land will be allotted to southerners or on politically motivated grounds. Seizures of land in the north and east by the military remained a problem in 2013, contributing to tensions between local Tamils and the predominantly Sinhalese security forces. According to humanitarian groups, around 90,000 people remained internally displaced in 2013, the vast majority of whom were residing with host families. Muslims forcibly ejected from the north by the LTTE in the early 1990s told the LLRC in 2010 that many were unable to return to their homes, as their land was still being occupied by Tamils. In general, there have been few official attempts to help this group of returnees. Other former residents of the conflict area live as refugees in India.

Since the end of the war, the military has exercised control over most aspects of daily life in the north and east (about 10–15 percent of the country), including local government in some districts. The military has also expanded its economic activities in the north and east, running shops and growing agricultural produce for sale in the south, while local businesspeople are pushed out of the market. Throughout the country, the military's role in a variety of economic sectors—from tourism to agriculture and infrastructure projects—has expanded significantly, providing jobs and revenue for a force that has tripled in size under the current president.

Women are underrepresented in politics and the civil service. Female employees in the private sector face some sexual harassment and discrimination in salary and promotion opportunities. Rape and domestic violence remain serious problems, with hundreds of complaints reported annually; existing laws are weakly enforced. Violence against women increased along with the general fighting in the civil conflict, and has also affected female prisoners and interned IDPs. The entrenchment of the army in the north and east has increased the risk of harassment and sexual abuse for female civilians in those areas, many of whom are widows. Although women have equal rights under civil and criminal law, matters related to the family—including marriage, divorce, child custody, and inheritance—are adjudicated under the customary law of each ethnic or religious group, and the application of these laws sometimes results in discrimination against women.

The government remains committed to ensuring that children have access to free education and health care, and it has also taken steps to prosecute those suspected of sex crimes against children. However, child rape is a serious problem. Although the government has increased penalties for employing minors, and complaints involving child labor have risen significantly, thousands of children continue to be employed as household servants, and many face abuse.

Sudan

Political Rights Rating: 7
Civil Liberties Rating: 7
Freedom Rating: 7.0
Freedom Status: Not Free
Electoral Democracy: No

Population: 34,200,000
Capital: Khartoum

Ten-Year Ratings Timeline For Year Under Review (Political Rights, Civil Liberties, Status)

Year Under Review	2004	2005	2006	2007	2008	2009	2010	2011	2012	2013
Rating	7,7,NF	7,7,NF	7,7,NF	7,7,NF	7,7,NF	7,7,NF	7,7,NF	7,7,NF	7,7,NF	7,7,NF

INTRODUCTION

The government of President Omar al-Bashir faced the most sustained challenge to its 24-year-long rule in 2013 when a decision in September to end fuel subsidies triggered spontaneous street protests and riots in several cities, including the capital, Khartoum. The regime quelled the disturbances violently, using live ammunition and detaining hundreds of protesters. Human rights monitoring groups put the number of dead at more than 200, while Sudan's Interior Ministry said it had arrested 700 "criminals."

Meanwhile, armed groups continued their push to topple the regime by force. Operating under the banner of the Sudan Revolutionary Front (SRF), the groups staged one of their biggest offensives to date in April, launching attacks on several areas of Northern and Southern Kordofan states. The SRF also formalized links with Sudan's political parties, signing what the groups called a New Dawn Charter for democratic change in January with the National Consensus Forces (NCF), a coalition of the main opposition parties and some civil society groups.

The conflicts in the Darfur region and Southern Kordofan and Blue Nile states continued in 2013. Ten years after the war in Darfur entered its deadliest phase, the year saw a surge in fighting that led to the displacement of an additional 400,000 people, according to estimates by the United Nations. Khartoum continued to obstruct the efforts of humanitarian agencies to assist civilians affected by the conflicts. In September, the United Nations reported that government restrictions on movement as well as intertribal fighting in Eastern Darfur state were delaying efforts to reach 150,000 newly displaced people. In Southern Kordofan and Blue Nile, well over one million people were believed to be displaced or otherwise severely affected by the fighting. The bleak situation facing civilians was compounded by severe food shortages. Indiscriminate aerial bombing was a feature of the Southern Kordofan and Blue Nile conflicts.

Relations with South Sudan remained volatile in 2013. Joint cooperation on oil production restarted in April, when South Sudan resumed using Sudan's pipelines in exchange for the payment of transit fees. But Khartoum made repeated threats to stop exports in protest of what it said was South Sudan's ongoing support of armed rebels in Sudan. Meetings between al-Bashir and his South Sudanese counterpart, Salva Kiir, in April, September, and October helped ease tensions. The two leaders agreed to open their shared border to trade and to stop interfering in each other's conflicts. But no solution was found for the contested border area of Abyei, whose status is due to be decided by a long-delayed referendum. Frustrated by the impasse, residents of Abyei conducted an unofficial referendum in October that was criticized by the governments in both Khartoum and Juba.

POLITICAL RIGHTS: 2 / 40

A. Electoral Process: 2 / 12

Sudan is governed according to a 2005 interim constitution. The document is being redrafted following the independence of South Sudan in July 2011, though the process has stalled. Members of the opposition and civil society have so far been excluded from consultations over the constitution-writing process and claim that proposed revisions would lead to a more repressive system of governance.

Although the first multiparty elections in 24 years were held in 2010, they were plagued by irregularities and failed to meet international standards, according to monitors from the United States, the European Union, and Sudan itself. Members of the lower house of the bicameral legislature, the 450-seat National Assembly, were elected using a mixed majoritarian and party-list system. State legislatures chose the 50 members of the upper house, the Council of States. All lawmakers serve five-year terms. As a result of South Sudan's secession in 2011, the two chambers were reduced to 354 and 32 seats, respectively. Under the interim constitution, the president may serve a maximum of two five-year terms.

In the 2010 elections, the Sudan People's Liberation Movement (SPLM)—the dominant party in the South—and other leading opposition parties boycotted the national presidential and some legislative elections, citing unfair campaign conditions. Al-Bashir's long-ruling National Congress Party (NCP) manipulated the census used to compile the electoral roll, overstating the population in areas of core support and undercounting opposition strongholds. Although 72 political parties nominated candidates for the elections, many of them were not allowed to campaign freely and rarely received official permission to hold public events. The voting period was plagued by irregularities, with reports of inaccurate voter rolls, ballot stuffing, and cash handouts to NCP voters.

As a result of the boycott, al-Bashir won the presidency convincingly, capturing 68 percent of the vote. The NCP won 323 seats in the National Assembly, 91 percent of the state assembly seats in the North, and 32 seats in the Council of States.

B. Political Pluralism and Participation: 3 / 16

The NCP's dominance of the political system in Sudan was reinforced by the independence of South Sudan, which signaled the end of a power-sharing government with the SPLM and the withdrawal of the South's representatives from parliament. The Khartoum government also launched a crackdown on other political parties. The SPLM-North (SPLM-N), an offshoot of the southern liberation movement, was banned from operating in 2011, following the outbreak of fighting in Blue Nile. Senior members of opposition parties, including the Popular Congress Party, Umma, and the Sudanese Communist Party (SCP), were detained for short periods without charge during student-led protests in June 2012. This pattern was repeated when protests broke out once more in September 2013. Amnesty International catalogued the arrest of at least 17 members of the SCP and noted reports of the arrest of 15 members of the Sudanese Congress Party. Additionally, several opposition leaders associated with the New Dawn Charter had been arrested in January and held until April, when al-Bashir announced that all political prisoners would be released.

The influence of the military clique within the NCP has subverted the political system to such an extent that analysts believe a "soft coup" may have taken place in 2011, with senior generals taking over responsibility for key government decisions.

C. Functioning of Government: 1 / 12

Sudan is considered one of the world's most corrupt countries. Power and resources are concentrated in and around Khartoum, while outlying states are neglected and impoverished. Members of the NCP, particularly those from favored ethnic groups, tightly control the national economy and use the wealth they have amassed in banking and business to buy political support. The International Crisis Group estimates that the party's top leadership owns more than 164 companies, which get the pick of the government's contracts. While the authorities have appealed for public help in exposing corruption, a whistleblower who provided information about graft in the police force was himself convicted of charges including ruining the reputation of the police, and was sentenced to four years in prison in August 2013.

Discretionary Political Rights Question B: -4 / 0

The government stands accused of attempting to change the ethnic distribution of the country through its response to an insurgency led by marginalized Muslim but non-Arab ethnic groups in Darfur. In 2004, government-supported Arab militias known as *janjaweed* began torching villages, massacring the inhabitants, and raping women and girls. The military also bombed settlements from the air. More than two million civilians were displaced. The scale of the violence led to accusations of genocide by international human rights groups and the United States. In 2009, the International Criminal Court (ICC) issued an arrest warrant for al-Bashir on charges of war crimes and crimes against humanity in Darfur; a charge of genocide was added in 2010. Accusations of ethnically targeted violence have also been leveled against the government for its handling of the war in Southern Kordofan, beginning in 2011, in which Sudan's military launched aerial bombardments and indiscriminate shelling of civilian areas thought to be strongholds of support for the SPLM-N.

CIVIL LIBERTIES: 5 / 60

D. Freedom of Expression and Belief: 3 / 16

The 2005 interim constitution recognizes freedom of the press, but the media face significant obstacles in practice. The 2009 Press and Publication Act allows a government-appointed Press Council to prevent publication or broadcast of material it deems unsuitable, temporarily shut down newspapers, and impose heavy fines for violations of media regulations. Members of the National Intelligence and Security Services (NISS) routinely raid printing facilities to confiscate editions of newspapers considered to be in violation of the act. By waiting until editions are printed, the authorities impose crippling financial losses on media houses. Media workers whose reports meet with official disapproval or who cover sensitive topics risk arrest. According to the Committee to Protect Journalists, an online journalist with *Al-Taghyeer* was arrested at a funeral in September 2013 and detained for eight days before being released. Foreign reporters were not immune to violence and threats. A British correspondent for Bloomberg reported being arrested and beaten up by police officers while covering an opposition party meeting in June, and said he had fled the country after his ordeal.

The pressure on the media intensified during and after the September protests. Journalists were ordered to describe the protesters as "vandals" and "saboteurs." The biggest-circulation newspaper in Sudan, *Al-Intibaha*, was closed in September for refusing to follow the government line and only resumed publication more than a month later after its chairman—the president's uncle—stood down. At least three other newspapers were ordered to suspend publication for several days. Foreign media organizations including Al-Arabiya and Sky News had their Khartoum offices closed and their licenses temporarily suspended after they were accused by the authorities of trying to foment an Arab Spring–style uprising. During the height of the protests, the government shut down the internet altogether. At other points in the year, it prevented access to specific websites, including the opposition news site *Hurriyat* and the forum Sudanese Online.

Religious freedom, though guaranteed by the 2005 interim constitution, is not upheld in practice. Approximately 97 percent of Sudan's population is Muslim, nearly all of whom are Sunni. The authorities showed increased intolerance of Christians in late 2012 and 2013, destroying or shuttering several churches in the Khartoum area, closing church-affiliated nongovernmental organizations (NGOs), ordering expatriate Christian workers out of the country, and detaining a number of Evangelical Christians. These included Salwa Fahmi Suleiman Gireis, a Sudanese Christian and NGO worker who was arrested in February 2013 in Khartoum and held for seven weeks before being released without charge.

The law prohibits apostasy, blasphemy, and conversion to any religion apart from Islam. The government uses religious laws to persecute political opponents. In 2011, 129 Darfuris were charged with apostasy, which carries a maximum sentence of death, although they were released after agreeing to follow the government's interpretation of Islam. In December 2012, two Coptic Orthodox priests and three other Christians were held on suspicion of apostasy for converting a Muslim woman to their faith. They were later released. During the fighting in Southern Kordofan in 2012, government forces shelled churches, claiming that rebels used them as safe houses. The U.S. Commission on International Religious Freedom in its 2013 report recommended that the U.S. State Department renew its designation of Sudan as a country of particular concern.

Respect for academic freedom is limited. The government administers public universities, monitors appointments, and sets the curriculum. Authorities do not directly control private universities, but self-censorship among instructors is common. Student associations are closely monitored for signs of antigovernment activities. Authorities responded harshly to protests connected to universities in 2011 and 2012, with security services in 2012 burning dormitories at Omburman University, attacking female students protesting against increased fees at Khartoum University, and raiding campuses across the country, rounding up hundreds of students. Universities were again targeted during the 2013 demonstrations. In September, police fired tear gas into the campus of Ahfad University for Women during protests against the regime. Darfuri students were targeted for arrest on multiple occasions during sporadic university protests throughout the first half of the year.

Sudan's security and intelligence service, the NISS, seeks to intimidate citizens who engage in private discussions on issues of a political nature. In May, two members of a doctors committee in El Geneina in Darfur were summoned by NISS agents and beaten after they held discussions with government officials over a pay dispute. The NISS accused them of inciting strike action. Members of a student group at Red Sea University were detained overnight after plans to hold a press conference on a controversial dam project were discovered in June.

E. Associational and Organizational Rights: 1 / 12

Freedom of assembly and association are provided for by the interim constitution and by law. Free assembly was violently curtailed when a series of mostly peaceful street protests against the government's decision to end fuel subsidies broke out in September. Security forces turned live ammunition on demonstrators in Khartoum, Wad Madani, and other towns. The African Centre for Justice and Peace Studies, which monitors human rights in Sudan, confirmed the deaths of 170 protesters killed by gunfire during the protests. At least 15 of the dead were children. In one incident, security forces opened fire on mourners as they left a funeral for a young pharmacist killed during protests the day before.

The operating environment for NGOs is difficult. All NGOs must register with a government body, the Humanitarian Assistance Commission (HAC). The HAC regularly places restrictions or bans on the operations of NGOs and the movements of their workers, particularly in conflict-affected areas such as Darfur, Southern Kordofan, and Blue Nile.

Trade union rights are minimal, and there are no independent unions. The Sudan Workers' Trade Unions Federation has been co-opted by the government. All strikes must be approved by the government.

F. Rule of Law: 0 / 16

The judiciary is not independent. Lower courts provide some due process safeguards, but the higher courts are subject to political control, and special security and military courts do not apply accepted legal standards. Sudanese criminal law is based on Sharia (Islamic law) and allows punishments such as flogging and cross-amputation (removal of the right hand and left foot). In February 2013, Human Rights Watch cited credible reports that government doctors had carried out a sentence of cross-amputation that month on a convicted armed robber in Khartoum.

In April, al-Bashir announced the release of all political prisoners. Those who were set free in the following weeks included senior military officers accused of a coup plot against the government in late 2012 and political leaders associated with the New Dawn Charter. But a wave of fresh arrests took place in the wake of the September street protests. According to the African Centre for Justice and Peace Studies, at least 800 people were detained, including some who were arrested as they sought medical treatment. Many of those arrested were held under the 2010 National Security Act, which gives the NISS sweeping authority to seize property, conduct surveillance, search premises, and detain suspects for up to four and a half months without judicial review. The police and security forces routinely exceed these broad powers, carrying out arbitrary arrests and holding people at secret locations without access to lawyers or their relatives. Human rights groups accuse the NISS of systematically detaining and torturing opponents of the government, including Darfuri activists, journalists, and members of youth movements such as Girifna and Sudan Change Now.

The Sudanese government continues to wage war and inflict political terror on marginalized groups in Darfur, Southern Kordofan, and Blue Nile. This has included indiscriminate bombing of civilians, murder, forced displacement of communities, the burning of villages, and the use of rape as a weapon of war. In addition, the authorities have impeded the efforts of NGOs to reach conflict-affected communities with emergency humanitarian supplies, leading to accusations that the government is engaged in "starvation warfare." Following the major SRF military offensive in April, national security agents in Khartoum arbitrarily rounded up more than 25 Darfuri civilians, as well as Nuba civilians from Southern Kordofan, in what Human Rights Watch described as an act of retaliation. Some were still being held incommunicado two months later.

At least 55 members of the joint UN–African Union peacekeeping force in Darfur have been killed since 2007. They included seven members of a patrol who were shot dead in a firefight following an ambush by unidentified assailants in Southern Darfur in July 2013 and three Senegalese members of a police unit killed in Western Darfur by unknown assailants in October. Separately, shells fired at a UN base in Southern Kordofan had killed an Ethiopian peacekeeper in June in an incident blamed on rebels.

The approximately one million Southerners who remained in the North following South Sudan's independence face serious discrimination. Under a political agreement reached by Khartoum and Juba in 2012, Southerners living in Sudan were guaranteed rights of residency and movement as well as the right to engage in economic activity and acquire property. However, the agreement, which has yet to be fully implemented, does not address the question of citizenship, putting some people at risk of being reclassified as "foreigners" even if they have lived in Sudan their entire lives.

More than 125,000 refugees from neighboring Chad and Eritrea live in Sudan. In October, the office of the UN High Commissioner for Refugees announced that Sudan would grant work permits to 30,000 mostly Eritrean refugees in the east of the country.

G. Personal Autonomy and Individual Rights: 1 / 16

Unresolved disputes over portions of the new international boundary between Sudan and South Sudan have curtailed freedom of movement and trade across the border and caused serious hardship to pastoralist groups whose migratory routes have been interrupted.

Female politicians and activists play a role in public life in Sudan, and women are guaranteed a quarter of the seats in the National Assembly. In daily life, however, women face extensive discrimination. Islamic law denies women equitable rights in marriage, inheritance, and divorce. Two women convicted of adultery in separate cases in 2012 were sentenced to death by stoning, although the death penalty was eventually dropped in both cases. Police use provisions of Sudan's Criminal Act outlawing "indecent and immoral acts" to prohibit women from wearing clothing of which they disapprove. In March, 150 women were arrested in one day in Southern Darfur because some of them were wearing what the authorities described as tight clothes, and some were not wearing socks. They were all convicted of public order violations and fined. Female genital mutilation is widely practiced. There are no laws specifically prohibiting domestic violence, spousal rape, or sexual harassment.

The U.S. State Department in its 2013 Trafficking in Persons Report named Sudan as a source, transit, and destination country for persons trafficked for forced labor and sexual exploitation. The Sudanese military and Darfur rebel groups continue to use child soldiers.

Suriname

Political Rights Rating: 2
Civil Liberties Rating: 2
Freedom Rating: 2.0
Freedom Status: Free
Electoral Democracy: Yes

Population: 558,460
Capital: Paramaribo

Ten-Year Ratings Timeline For Year Under Review (Political Rights, Civil Liberties, Status)

Year Under Review	2004	2005	2006	2007	2008	2009	2010	2011	2012	2013
Rating	1,2,F	2,2,F	2,2,F	2,2,F	2,2,F	2,2,F	2,2,F	2,2,F	2,2,F	2,2,F

INTRODUCTION

In 2013, the government failed to establish a constitutional court, which is required to review the constitutionality of the revised amnesty law. In April 2012, the government had extended the 1992 amnesty law to apply to the period during which current president Desiré Bouterse and 24 others allegedly murdered 15 political opponents in December 1982. Bouterse led a military regime from 1980 to 1987.

The president's son, Dino Bouterse, a senior official in Suriname's counterterrorism unit, was arrested in Panama in August and extradited to the United States to face drug-trafficking and weapons charges. Additional charges of aiding a terrorist organization and supplying fake Surinamese passports were brought against him in November. He pleaded not guilty to all charges.

Suriname's economy continued to grow in 2013. The country took steps toward South American integration in July when it became an associate member of Mercosur, the South American trade bloc. In December, Suriname became a full member of the Caribbean Development Bank, which will facilitate the country's access to subsidized loans.

POLITICAL RIGHTS: 33 / 40

A. Electoral Process: 12 / 12

The 1987 constitution provides for a unicameral, 51-seat National Assembly, elected by proportional representation for five-year terms. The body elects the president to a five-year term with a two-thirds majority. If it is unable to do so, a United People's Assembly—consisting of lawmakers from the national, regional, and local levels—convenes to choose the president by a simple majority. A Council of State made up of the president and representatives of major societal groupings—including labor unions, business, the military, and the legislature—has veto power over legislation deemed to violate the constitution.

In 2010 legislative elections, Desiré Bouterse's Mega Combination coalition—comprising the National Democratic Party (NDP) and a number of smaller parties—captured 23 seats, while the New Front for Democracy and Development (NF) took 14 seats. A-Combination took 7 seats, the People's Alliance won 6, and the Party for Democracy and Development in Unity gained 1 seat. Bouterse was elected president with 71 percent of the parliamentary vote, defeating NF candidate Chandrikapersad Santokhi.

In June 2013, Bouterse dismissed two cabinet members from his own party, the minister of public works and the minister of land management and forestry, without providing an official explanation. He replaced the minister of education in July, claiming to want to depoliticize and increase efficiency in the ministry. In October, the president dismissed his finance minister as part of an effort to undertake a thorough review of the country's finances. This was the 10th minister to be dismissed from Bouterse's cabinet since he took office in 2010.

B. Political Pluralism and Participation: 13 / 16

Suriname's political parties largely reflect the cleavages in the country's ethnically diverse society and often form coalitions in order to gain power. The major coalitions are the NF, an alliance of the National Party of Suriname and several smaller parties; the People's Alliance; the Mega Combination; and the A-Combination, which has strong support among Maroon communities (descendants of former slaves). Suriname's Amerindians and Maroons were historically marginalized from the political process until 2005, when a coalition of Maroon political parties gained 5 seats in parliament. However, women continue to be sidelined from the political process, holding just 12 percent of parliamentary seats and one of the 17 cabinet positions.

C. Functioning of Government: 8 / 12

The Ministry of Justice and Police is in charge of combating corruption, but the country has no dedicated anticorruption legislation. Suriname has been plagued by corruption cases in recent years, and organized crime and drug networks continue to hamper governance and undermine the judicial system. While legislation is in place to combat money laundering, it is weakly implemented. Suriname was ranked 94 out of 177 countries and territories surveyed in Transparency International's 2013 Corruption Perceptions Index. The country lacks freedom of information legislation.

In August, Dino Bouterse, who held a senior position in Suriname's counterterrorism unit, was arrested in Panama and sent to the United States to face drug-trafficking charges and a weapons offense, to which he pleaded not guilty. In November, U.S. prosecutors further charged the younger Bouterse with attempting to support a terrorist organization, based on his alleged agreement to receive $2 million in exchange for allowing sources of the U.S. Drug Enforcement Agency, posing as members of the Lebanese group Hezbollah, to establish a base in Suriname in order to carry out attacks on the United States. Bouterse denied all charges, including charges that he supplied false Surinamese passports, and his lawyers accused the United States of fabricating evidence against their client. The case was ongoing at year's end.

CIVIL LIBERTIES: 44 / 60
D. Freedom of Expression and Belief: 15 / 16

The constitution provides for freedoms of expression and the press, and the government generally respects these rights in practice. However, defamation and libel remain criminal offenses, with punishments ranging from fines to up to seven years in prison for publicly expressing enmity, hatred, or contempt toward the government. Dismissed government minister Ramon Abrahams sued Jaap Hoogendam, publisher of the monthly magazine *Parbode*, in October 2013, seeking 1 million Surinamese dollars (US$300,000) in damages and a retraction for an article that accused him of corruption while in office. Hoogendam refused to give up the identity of his sources; the trial was ongoing at year's end. Some media outlets engage in occasional self-censorship, and there is a lack of investigative journalism. There are three privately owned daily newspapers and close to 30 radio stations, which compete with the government-owned radio and television broadcasting systems, resulting in a generally pluralistic range of viewpoints. However, not all private media have equal access to government advertising or press conferences. The government does not restrict internet access.

The authorities generally respect freedom of religion, which is protected by law and the constitution, and do not infringe on academic freedom.

E. Associational and Organizational Rights: 11 / 12

The constitution provides for freedoms of assembly and association, and the government respects these rights in practice. Workers can join independent trade unions, though civil servants have no legal right to strike. Collective bargaining is legal and conducted fairly widely. The labor movement is active in politics.

F. Rule of Law: 8 / 16

The legal system of Suriname is based on the Dutch Civil System. The judiciary is susceptible to political influence and suffers from a significant shortage of judges and a large backlog of cases. Suriname is a signatory to the 2001 agreement establishing the Caribbean Court of Justice (CCJ) as the final venue of appeal for member states of the Caribbean Community, but has yet to ratify the CCJ as its own final court of appeal. Police abuse detainees, particularly during arrests. Suriname is a major transit point for cocaine en route to Africa, Europe, and the United States, which has contributed to a rising tide of narcotics-related money laundering and organized crime. Temporary detention centers are overcrowded and in poor condition.

A judicial investigation was launched in 2000 into the December 1982 abduction and murder of 15 political opponents of the Bouterse military regime. The victims—who included labor union leaders, attorneys, military officers, professors, businessmen, and journalists—were allegedly killed by Bouterse and members of the armed forces. While Bouterse continued to deny direct involvement in the murders, he accepted "political responsibility" and offered a public apology in 2007. The long-awaited trial of Bouterse and 24 other suspects began in November 2007. In April 2012, a month before the trial's expected conclusion, the National Assembly controversially voted 28 to 12 to extend the country's 1992 amnesty law for crimes committed in defense of the state to include the period during which the murders were committed. Immunity was therefore granted to Bouterse and the 24 other suspects.

Questions on the constitutionality of the new amnesty law and whether a trial against the defendants could proceed led to the trial's adjournment in May 2012. The Prosecutor's Office subsequently stated that the amnesty law's constitutionality must be reviewed in a constitutional court, which would need to be formed by the government. While a military court denied a request to dismiss the case in February 2013, it appeared unlikely that the trial would proceed as long as interested parties remain in power.

International travel has occasionally proven difficult for Bouterse due to a Europol arrest warrant that was issued after his conviction in absentia for drug trafficking in the Netherlands in 1999. However, he remains protected from arrest in Suriname because the country lacks an extradition treaty with the Netherlands and he is head of state.

Discrimination based on race or ethnicity is prohibited by law. However, the government does not recognize or offer any special protections for indigenous groups. Indigenous Amerindians and Maroons, who live primarily in the country's interior, are significantly disadvantaged in the areas of socioeconomic development and infrastructure, employment, education, and access to government services, and they have limited opportunities to participate in the decision-making processes that affect their lands, traditions, and natural resources. Collective land rights are not acknowledged, and these populations continue to face problems due to illegal logging and mining on their land.

Same-sex intercourse is legal, but LGBT (lesbian, gay, bisexual, and transgender) individuals face some discrimination.

G. Personal Autonomy and Individual Rights: 10 / 16

Constitutional guarantees of gender equality are not adequately enforced. Domestic violence remains a serious problem. While the law provides for women's equal access to education and employment, women do not receive the same wages as men for performing the same work. Suriname serves as a source, destination, and transit country for the trafficking of men, women, and children for the purposes of forced labor and prostitution.

Swaziland

Political Rights Rating: 7
Civil Liberties Rating: 5
Freedom Rating: 6.0
Freedom Status: Not Free
Electoral Democracy: No

Population: 1,238,364
Capital: Mbabane

Ten-Year Ratings Timeline For Year Under Review (Political Rights, Civil Liberties, Status)

Year Under Review	2004	2005	2006	2007	2008	2009	2010	2011	2012	2013
Rating	7,5,NF	7,5,NF	7,5,NF	7,5,NF	7,5,NF	7,5,NF	7,5,NF	7,5,NF	7,5,NF	7,5,NF

INTRODUCTION

Although parliamentary elections in September were peaceful and saw significant turnover among members (at least 46 of the 55 elected members are new, with 6 former ministers losing seats), the polls were neither free nor fair, according to international observers. In one positive development, long-time prodemocracy advocate and trade unionist Jan Sithole—now leader of the Swaziland Democratic Party (SWADEPA) political association—was elected.

Before the elections, King Mswati III had raised hopes of reform by announcing that Swaziland's political system would now be called "monarchical democracy," under which the people would provide advice to the king before he made decisions. However, he later clarified to the international press that it was no more than a name change.

The country remains mired in a deep financial crisis brought on by a sharp drop in revenue from a regional customs union, maladministration of public funds, and lavish spending by the royal family. The crisis has led to massive cuts in public services, including pensions, education, and health care since 2010. Swaziland has the world's highest rate of HIV infection: 26 percent of Swazis between 15 and 49 are living with the disease. The financial crisis has led to shortages in antiretroviral drugs, as well as in HIV testing.

POLITICAL RIGHTS: 1 / 40

A. Electoral Process: 0 / 12

King Mswati III is an absolute monarch. The 2005 constitution removed the king's ability to rule by decree, but reaffirmed his ultimate authority over the cabinet, legislature, and judiciary. Members of the bicameral Parliament, all of whom serve five-year terms, cannot initiate legislation. Of the House of Assembly's 65 members, 55 are elected by popular vote within the tinkhundla system, in which local chiefs vet all candidates; the king appoints the other 10 members. The king also appoints 20 members of the 30-seat Senate, with the remainder selected by the House of Assembly. Traditional chiefs govern designated localities and typically report directly to the king.

Parliament passed a series of election reform bills in the weeks leading up to the 2013 elections. Some provisions were considered to be restrictive or politically motivated. An important development was the establishment of the Elections and Boundaries Commission, although its creation after the start of the election process limited its impact in 2013.

B. Political Pluralism and Participation: 1 / 16

According to the constitution, election to public office is based on individual merit rather than political parties. This, in effect, makes political parties illegal. Instead, political associations have organized, the two largest being the banned People's United Democratic Movement (PUDEMO) and the Ngwane National Liberatory Congress (NNLC). Both PUDEMO and the NNLC boycotted the 2013 elections. The political associations SWADEPA and Sive Siyinqaba participated.

In June, police searched the offices of certain members of Parliament who had led a motion of no confidence against the government in October 2012. Authorities said the search was to gather information on alleged embezzlement charges.

C. Functioning of Government: 0 / 12

Corruption is a major problem, and government corruption was widely blamed for contributing to Swaziland's financial crisis. Corruption and nepotism are frequent in areas such as contracts, government appointments, and school admissions. In 2012, legislators voted to revoke their own 10 percent pay cuts. There is no oversight of the king's budget. Swaziland was ranked 82 out of 177 countries and territories surveyed in Transparency International's 2013 Corruption Perceptions Index.

CIVIL LIBERTIES: 19 / 60 (-1)

D. Freedom of Expression and Belief: 8 / 16

Constitutional rights to free expression are severely restricted in practice and can be suspended by the king. Publishing criticism of the ruling family is banned. Self-censorship is widespread, as journalists are routinely threatened and attacked by the authorities and are subject to very high libel penalties. However, South African media are available, and both the private, royal-owned *Swazi Observer* and the independent *Times of Swaziland* occasionally criticize the government. In March, two senior editors at the *Swazi Observer* were reinstated after an eight-month suspension for reporting too negatively on the king. In April, an editor and the publishers of the independent monthly the *Nation* were found guilty of contempt of court and ordered to pay a 200,000-emalangeni ($20,000) fine or serve two years in jail for articles from 2009 and 2010 that criticized Chief Justice Michael Ramodibedi; the ruling is still being appealed. The government reportedly has monitored internet communication. About a quarter of the population had access to the internet in 2013.

Freedom of religion is not explicitly protected under the constitution, but is mostly respected in practice, although security forces have been accused of intimidating church leaders deemed sympathetic to the prodemocracy movement. Academic freedom is limited by prohibitions against criticizing the monarchy, as well as restrictions on political gatherings.

E. Associational and Organizational Rights: 2 / 12 (-1)

The government restricts freedoms of assembly and association, and permission to hold political gatherings is frequently denied. Demonstrators routinely face violence and arrests by police. The government has sweeping powers under the 2008 Suppression of Terrorism Act to declare any organization a "terrorist group," a practice that has been abused by authorities. In 2012, the government secured an Industrial Court order prohibiting antigovernment marches, and PUDEMO leader Mario Masuku was placed under house arrest to prevent him from attending a rally in support of striking teachers. Police harassment and surveillance of civil society organizations has increased in recent years, as have forced searches of homes and offices, torture in interrogations, and the use of roadblocks to prevent demonstrations.

Swaziland has active labor unions, some of whom have called for democratic reforms. Workers in most areas of the economy, with the exception of essential services such as police and health care, can join unions; however, government pressure and crackdowns on strikes have limited union operations. After approving the registration of the new Trade Union Congress of Swaziland (TUCOSWA)—a merger between the Swaziland Federation of Trade Unions, the Swaziland Federation of Labour, and the Swaziland National Association of Teachers—in January 2012, the government deregistered it the following April, days after the new union voiced support for an election boycott. The union has continued to function without official government recognition, but faces harassment. On May 1, 2013, police raided its offices and placed five members under house arrest, disrupting May Day celebrations.

F. Rule of Law: 5 / 16

The dual judicial system includes courts based on Roman-Dutch law and traditional courts using customary law. The judiciary is independent in most civil cases, though the king has ultimate judicial powers, and the royal family and government often refuse to respect rulings with which they disagree. However, the Swazi High Court has made a number of notable antigovernment rulings in recent years. In 2011, Judge Thomas Masuku—head of the Judicial Services Commission—was suspended for allegedly insulting the king in a ruling. In 2013, Lawyers for Human Rights Swaziland filed a complaint with the Gambia-based African Commission on Human and Peoples' Rights calling for his reinstatement.

Incidents of police torture, beatings, and suspicious deaths in custody continued in 2013. Security forces generally operate with impunity. Prisons are overcrowded, and inmates are subject to rape, beatings, and torture.

Discrimination against whites and people of mixed race is common, including difficulty in obtaining official documents. People with albinism are at risk of murder for ritual purposes. Discrimination against members of the LGBT (lesbian, gay, bisexual, and transgender) community is widespread, and many people hide their sexual orientation.

G. Personal Autonomy and Individual Rights: 4 / 16

The constitution grants women equal rights and legal status as adults, but these rights remain restricted in practice. While both the legal code and customary law provide some protection against gender-based violence, it is common and often tolerated with impunity. There are only four female members of the House of Assembly, down from nine in 2008. The Commonwealth Observer Mission reported two cases of traditional authorities telling people not to vote for certain female candidates in 2013, one of whom wore pants and the other a widow. The former took her case to court and won.

Sweden

Political Rights Rating: 1
Civil Liberties Rating: 1
Freedom Rating: 1.0
Freedom Status: Free
Electoral Democracy: Yes

Population: 9,592,000
Capital: Stockholm

Ten-Year Ratings Timeline For Year Under Review (Political Rights, Civil Liberties, Status)

Year Under Review	2004	2005	2006	2007	2008	2009	2010	2011	2012	2013
Rating	1,1,F	1,1,F	1,1,F	1,1,F	1,1,F	1,1,F	1,1,F	1,1,F	1,1,F	1,1,F

INTRODUCTION

Six nights of riots in May 2013 spread from Stockholm suburbs to several Swedish cities. The riots were initially seen as a response to a police shooting in which a mentally ill man of immigrant descent was killed after violently resisting arrest. However, the riots, concentrated in areas with large immigrant populations, came to be understood as an indication of larger social problems concerning marginalization of immigrants. They prompted a searing national debate on the future of the Swedish welfare model and economic inequality. Material damage was widespread, with more than 100 vehicles and several buildings torched and 30 police officers reported injured. There were no further riots in 2013.

In September 2013, the *Dagens Nyheter* newspaper exposed a registry of Roma residing in Sweden, kept by the Skåne County police and comprising well over 4,000 names, including those of children. Maintaining such a registry violates several Swedish laws as well as the European Convention on Human Rights.

POLITICAL RIGHTS: 40 / 40

A. Electoral Process: 12 / 12

Sweden has a unicameral parliament, the Riksdag, whose 349 members are elected every four years by proportional representation. A party must receive at least 4 percent of the vote nationwide or 12 percent in one of the 29 electoral districts to win representation. The prime minister is appointed by the speaker of the Riksdag and confirmed by the body as a whole. King Carl XVI Gustaf, crowned in 1973, is the ceremonial head of state.

In the September 2010 parliamentary elections, eight political parties won representation in the Riksdag. Fredrik Reinfeldt secured a second term as prime minister after his center-right Moderate Party took 107 seats. It formed a minority government with the Center Party (23 seats), the Liberal People's Party (24 seats), and the Christian Democrats (19 seats). The Social Democratic Party (SDP), also known as the Workers' Party, was the largest single faction with 112 seats, but remained in opposition. Two other opposition groups, the Green Party and the Left Party, took 25 and 19, respectively. The controversial far-right Sweden Democrats (SD) entered the parliament for the first time with 20 seats, though the other seven parties vowed not to rely on the SD for significant votes, leaving it politically isolated. Peaceful protests were mounted against the SD and against racism in the period surrounding the elections. Nevertheless, during 2012 and 2013 the party moved toward broader public acceptance, with slightly but steadily rising poll numbers.

B. Political Pluralism and Participation: 16 / 16

The SDP ruled for most of the last century with the support of the Left Party and, in later decades, the Green Party, all of which are in opposition since the 2010 elections.

The country's principal religious, ethnic, and immigrant groups are represented in the parliament.

Since 1993, the indigenous Sami community has elected its own parliament, which has significant powers over community education and culture and serves as an advisory body to the government. In April 2011, the Supreme Court issued a landmark ruling in the so-called Nordmaling case, granting Sami reindeer herders common-law rights to disputed lands; the case had been ongoing for 14 years.

C. Functioning of Government: 12 / 12

Corruption rates are generally low in Sweden, which was ranked 3 out of 177 countries and territories surveyed in Transparency International's 2013 Corruption Perceptions Index. The country has one of the most robust freedom of information statutes in the world. However, the Organisation for Economic Co-operation and Development published a critical report in June 2012, admonishing Sweden for insufficient enforcement of its foreign bribery laws.

CIVIL LIBERTIES: 59 / 60 (-1)

D. Freedom of Expression and Belief: 16 / 16

Freedom of speech is guaranteed by law. However, hate-speech laws prohibit threats or expressions of contempt based on race, color, national or ethnic origin, religious belief, or sexual orientation.

Sweden's media are independent. Most newspapers and periodicals are privately owned, and the government subsidizes daily newspapers regardless of their political affiliation. Public broadcasters air weekly radio and television programs in several immigrant languages. The ethnic minority press is entitled to the same subsidies as the Swedish-language press. Under the 2009 Intellectual Property Rights Enforcement Directive (IPRED), internet-service providers must reveal information about users who are found to be engaged in illegal file-sharing. A ruling in 2012 by the European Court of Justice determined that IPRED followed European legislation on privacy and data protection. In 2012, Sweden adopted a data retention law after a six-year delay due to privacy concerns. The law, which puts Sweden in compliance with EU directives, requires telecommunications carriers to store data, including records on telephone calls and internet traffic, for three years.

The 2008 Signals Intelligence Act gives the National Defense Radio Establishment the authority to monitor communications without a court order. Only the military and government can request surveillance, and those who have been monitored must be notified. In 2013, *Dagens Nyheter* revealed that the National Defense Radio Establishment has exploited a loophole in the law to gather extensive personal telephone and internet records, the use of which remained unclear.

Religious freedom is constitutionally guaranteed. Although the population is 66 percent Lutheran, all churches, as well as synagogues and mosques, receive some state financial support. The Lutheran church was denationalized in 2000. Academic freedom is ensured for all.

E. Associational and Organizational Rights: 12 / 12

Freedoms of assembly and association are respected in law and practice. The rights to strike and organize in labor unions are guaranteed. Trade union federations, which represent about 80 percent of the workforce, are strong and well organized. The labor code was amended in 2010 after the European Court of Justice ruled that employees at the Swedish branches of foreign companies are subject to their home country's collective agreements, not those of Swedish unions. A nationwide bus strike in June 2013 over salary concerns and outsourcing was resolved after a nine-day walkout.

F. Rule of Law: 15 / 16 (-1)

The judiciary is independent. Swedish courts have jurisdiction to try suspects for genocide committed abroad. In 2011, Sweden sought the extradition of Julian Assange, founder of the antisecrecy group WikiLeaks, from the United Kingdom so that he could be questioned regarding rape and sexual assault allegations stemming from two incidents in Stockholm in 2010. In June 2012, Assange sought refuge in the Ecuadorean embassy in London, where he was granted asylum; he remained there at year's end.

A 2013 survey by the EU Agency for Fundamental Rights found that Swedish Jews were more than twice as likely as Jews in other European countries to hide their religious affiliation, prompting concern. Malmö's longtime mayor, Ilmar Reepalu, resigned in February 2013 under a cloud of controversy over comments that were considered anti-Semitic. While official nationwide statistics on hate crimes with anti-Semitic motives had not yet been released by year's end, and previously showed only modest fluctuation, regional data indicated a significant increase in anti-Semitic discrimination and harassment in the southern part of Sweden. A new unit for hate crimes was formed by the Malmö police. At the national level, a permanent hate-crime police unit had been established in 2009, and an Equality Ombudsman position was created in 2008 to oversee efforts to prevent discrimination on the basis of gender, ethnicity, disability, and sexual orientation.

Following intense media scrutiny of the Skåne police's unlawful Roma registry in 2013, the politically appointed Commission on Security and Integrity Protection launched an investigation, which found significant problems regarding a lack of transparency on the list's purpose and usage, but no proof that citizens were on the registry primarily because of their ethnicity. Minister of Justice Beatrice Ask publicly apologized, and the Skåne police department filed a complaint against itself, requesting an internal investigation led by a prosecutor that was still ongoing at year's end.

The government announced in October 2013 that it would grant permanent residency as well as family reunification to all Syrian refugees—making Sweden the only country in Europe to do so. While Sweden's liberal refugee policy continues to enjoy broad support, a geographically unequal distribution of refugees, coupled with a shortage of housing and jobs in the affected municipalities, has caused both public and political frustration at the local level. On the national level, the Swedish Democrats were seen as the main beneficiaries of the emerging debate on immigration.

G. Personal Autonomy and Individual Rights: 16 / 16

Sweden is a global leader in gender equality. Approximately 45 percent of Riksdag members are women. Of the 24 government ministers, 13 are women. About 72 percent of women work outside the home, earning the equivalent of 94 percent of men's wages, when differences in age, sector, and experience are taken into account. Same-sex couples are legally allowed to adopt, and the country granted lesbian couples the same rights to artificial insemination and in vitro fertilization as heterosexual couples in 2005. Same-sex marriage was legalized when the parliament adopted gender-neutral legislation on marriage in 2009, the same year the Lutheran Church voted to allow same-sex ceremonies.

The country is a destination and transit point for women and children trafficked for the purpose of sexual exploitation. The 2004 Aliens Act helped to provide more assistance to trafficking victims, and a special ambassador has been appointed to aid in combating human trafficking.

Switzerland

Political Rights Rating: 1
Civil Liberties Rating: 1
Freedom Rating: 1.0
Freedom Status: Free
Electoral Democracy: Yes

Population: 8,078,000
Capital: Bern

Ten-Year Ratings Timeline For Year Under Review (Political Rights, Civil Liberties, Status)

Year Under Review	2004	2005	2006	2007	2008	2009	2010	2011	2012	2013
Rating	1,1,F	1,1,F	1,1,F	1,1,F	1,1,F	1,1,F	1,1,F	1,1,F	1,1,F	1,1,F

INTRODUCTION

Amid rising tensions over immigration, Swiss voters approved stricter asylum laws in a June referendum. Authorities in one town reacted to the opening of a new federal housing center for asylum seekers by banning them from local public facilities, including a swimming pool. The southern canton of Ticino became the nation's first to ban face-covering veils in public places.

The Swiss banking industry continued to face pressure from an international crackdown on tax evasion. The oldest Swiss bank pleaded guilty to conspiracy in January and announced that it would close. In August, the government struck an agreement with the United States allowing Swiss banks that were not already under investigation to avoid prosecution if they disclose involvement in tax evasion by U.S. customers and pay fines.

POLITICAL RIGHTS: 39 / 40
A. Electoral Process: 12 / 12

The constitution provides for a Federal Assembly with two directly elected chambers: the 46-member Council of States (in which each canton has two members and each half-canton has one) and the 200-member National Council. All lawmakers serve four-year terms. The Federal Council (cabinet) is a seven-person executive council, with each member elected by the Federal Assembly. The presidency is largely ceremonial and rotates annually among the Federal Council's members.

The federal elections held in October 2011 saw a modest strengthening of the political center in Switzerland. The right-wing Swiss People's Party (SVP) while still the leading party, lost seats in the National Council for the first time since 1975, retaining 54 seats—8 fewer than it won in 2007. The Social Democratic Party (SPS) won 46 seats, the Free Democratic Party (FDP) took 30 seats, and the Christian Democratic People's Party (CVP) garnered 28 seats. Seven smaller parties are also represented. In a June 2013 referendum, voters rejected a proposal backed by the SVP to hold direct elections for Federal Council members.

B. Political Pluralism and Participation: 15 / 16

Political parties are free to operate, but the system is extremely stable, with a coalition of the same four parties (or their precursors) governing since 1959. By common agreement, since 2008 the Federal Council has been comprised of two members each from the SVP, the SPS, and the FDP, and one member from CVP.

Restrictive citizenship laws and procedures tend to exclude many immigrants and their family members in successive generations from political participation.

C. Functioning of Government: 12 / 12

The Swiss political system is characterized by decentralization. The 26 cantons have significant control over economic and social policy, with the federal government's powers largely limited to foreign affairs and some economic matters. Referendums, which are used extensively, are mandatory for any amendments to the federal constitution, the joining of international organizations, or major changes to federal laws.

The government is free from pervasive corruption. Switzerland was ranked 7 out of 177 countries and territories surveyed in Transparency International's 2013 Corruption Perceptions Index.

As the world's largest offshore financial center, however, the country has been criticized for failing to comply with recommended international norms on preventing tax evasion, money laundering, and terrorist financing. In June 2013, the National Council rejected a bill that would have allowed banks to disclose information about their U.S. customers in order to avoid indictment by the U.S., which was pursuing banks that allegedly helped U.S. customers conceal assets and evade taxes. In August, the Swiss and U.S. governments reached an agreement to allow approximately 100 Swiss banks to avoid prosecution for aiding tax evasion by admitting wrongdoing, turning over customer information, and paying a fine equal to at least 20 percent of the hidden deposits. However, the agreement excluded banks already under investigation, which includes most of the nation's largest banks. Wegelin & Co., the oldest Swiss bank, pleaded guilty in January to conspiracy to help approximately 100 U.S. customers evade at least $1.2 billion in taxes; the bank paid nearly $58 million in fines and said it would close.

In October 2013, Switzerland signed an Organisation for Economic Cooperation and Development convention against tax evasion, in which nations pledge to share information for tax enforcement. However, ratification requires both parliamentary approval and a referendum, which had not taken place by year's end.

CIVIL LIBERTIES: 57 / 60
D. Freedom of Expression and Belief: 15 / 16

Freedom of speech is guaranteed by the constitution. Switzerland has a free media environment, although the state-owned Swiss Broadcasting Corporation dominates the broadcast market. Consolidation of newspaper ownership in large media conglomerates has forced the closure of some small and local newspapers. The law penalizes public incitement to racial hatred or discrimination as well as denial of crimes against humanity. There is no government restriction on access to the internet.

Freedom of religion is guaranteed by the constitution, and most cantons support one or more churches. The country is roughly split between Roman Catholics and Protestants, though some 400,000 Muslims form the largest non-Christian minority, at about 5 percent of the population. Voters in a November 2009 referendum approved a ban on the future construction of minarets on mosques. In September 2012, the Swiss parliament rejected a proposal to ban face-covering veils for Muslim women in public spaces. However, in 2013 voters in the Italian-speaking southern canton of Ticino became the first to approve such a ban. About 65 percent of voters backed the ban in a referendum.

Most public schools provide religious education, depending on the predominant creed in the canton. Religion classes are mandatory in some schools, although waivers are regularly granted upon request. The government respects academic freedom.

E. Associational and Organizational Rights: 12 / 12

Freedoms of assembly and association are provided by the constitution. The right to collective bargaining is respected, and approximately 25 percent of the workforce is unionized.

In March 2013, about 20,000 civil servants demonstrated in Bern against austerity measures by the canton including pay freezes and reduced spending on education and health care.

F. Rule of Law: 15 / 16

The judiciary is independent, and the rule of law prevails in civil and criminal matters. Most judicial decisions are made at the cantonal level, except for the federal Supreme Court, which reviews cantonal court decisions when they pertain to federal law. Some incidents of police discrimination and excessive use of force have been documented. In November 2013, representatives of minority youth groups raised allegations of police discrimination, including repeated stops and intrusive searches. Prison and detention center conditions generally meet international standards, and the Swiss government permits visits by independent human rights observers.

Increasing anxiety about the growing foreign-born population has led to the passage of stricter asylum laws. According to the government, 21,465 people applied for asylum in Switzerland in 2013, down 25 percent from 2012. In a June referendum, about 80 percent of voters approved a proposal to tighten asylum laws. Under the new rules, asylum seekers may no longer apply from abroad, and military desertion is not valid grounds for asylum; desertion has been the reason most commonly cited by Eritreans, the largest contingent of asylum seekers in Switzerland. In August, human rights groups denounced the town of Bremgarten for banning asylum seekers from using a swimming pool and other public facilities; at the beginning of the month about 150 asylum seekers had been housed by federal authorities in a former military barracks in the town.

The rights of cultural, religious, and linguistic minorities are legally protected, though minorities—especially those of African and Central European descent, as well as Roma—face increasing societal discrimination. In August, black American talk show host Oprah Winfrey sparked a controversy over Swiss racial attitudes by alleging that a shop assistant in Zurich had refused her request to see a $38,000 handbag, telling the billionaire Winfrey that the item was too expensive for her.

G. Personal Autonomy and Individual Rights: 15 / 16

In a November referendum, voters rejected a proposal to limit executives' salaries to 12 times those of the lowest-paid employees at their companies.

Women were only granted universal suffrage at the federal level in 1971, and the half-canton of Appenzell Innerrhoden denied women the right to vote until 1990. There are 62 women in the 200-member National Council and 9 in the Council of States. The constitution guarantees men and women equal pay for equal work, but pay differentials remain. Switzerland was ranked 9 out of 136 countries surveyed in the World Economic Forum's 2013 Gender Gap Report, which analyzes equality in the division of resources and opportunities between men and women.

In a 2005 referendum, voters approved same-sex civil unions. Recognized since 2007, these unions grant many of the legal rights of marriage, with the exception of adoption. In December 2012, the National Council passed a bill allowing members of same-sex unions to adopt the children of their partners but not other children. That narrowed the original measure passed by the Council of States, which would have allowed all couples unrestricted adoption rights regardless of marital status or sexual orientation.

Syria

Political Rights Rating: 7
Civil Liberties Rating: 7
Freedom Rating: 7.0
Freedom Status: Not Free
Electoral Democracy: No

Population: 21,900,000
Capital: Damascus

Trend Arrow: Syria received a downward trend arrow due to the worsening conditions for civilians, the increased targeting of churches for destruction and kidnapping of clergy, the implementation of harsh Sharia-inspired restrictions in some areas, and unchecked violence against women, including the use of rape as a weapon of war.

Ten-Year Ratings Timeline For Year Under Review (Political Rights, Civil Liberties, Status)

Year Under Review	2004	2005	2006	2007	2008	2009	2010	2011	2012	2013
Rating	7,7,NF	7,7,NF	7,6,NF	7,6,NF	7,6,NF	7,6,NF	7,6,NF	7,7,NF	7,7,NF	7,7,NF

INTRODUCTION

The civil war that started in the wake of a peaceful 2011 uprising continued unabated in 2013. By year's end it had produced more than 2 million refugees, 5 million internally displaced persons, and nearly 130,000 fatalities, according to the British-based Syrian Observatory for Human Rights.

While the demise of the Syrian regime had been predicted by many observers, it survived and even made some gains in the fighting during the year. President Bashar al-Assad raised the possibility that he would run for reelection in 2014, and he was increasingly supported by minority groups in Syria as they grew alarmed by the rise of radical Islamism in the country.

The moderate armed opposition in Syria was mainly represented by the Free Syrian Army (FSA), a loose alliance of units founded by those who had participated in the nonviolent uprising in 2011 as well as defecting army officers and soldiers. The radical Islamist opposition was splintered among many groups. The National Coalition of Syrian Revolutionary and Opposition Forces (SOC), the latest political structure formed by the opposition in exile to support the uprising, remained ineffective in 2013.

The regime and the opposition drew varying levels of assistance from allies in the international community. On the regime's side were Russia, Iran, and the Lebanese Shiite group Hezbollah, which actively participated in the fighting in key areas. The opposition was supported by regional states including Saudi Arabia, Qatar, the United Arab Emirates, and Turkey, in addition to France, Britain, and the United States, though the latter countries avoided providing meaningful or direct shipments of arms due to concerns that they would fall into the hands of radical Islamists. The U.S. government threatened to conduct a punitive missile strike on the Assad regime following its use of chemical weapons against civilians in August, but the proposal faltered amid a lack of congressional support and a British parliamentary vote against participation. Russia helped broker a deal under which al-Assad began handing over his forces' chemical weapons to international experts, though the regime's overall military campaign was not affected by the agreement, and the aborted U.S. attack reportedly demoralized moderate opposition forces.

POLITICAL RIGHTS: -2 / 40 (-1)
A. Electoral Process: 0 / 12

Al-Assad took power after the death of his father, longtime president Hafez al-Assad, in 2000 and secured a second seven-year term in 2007 with 97.6 percent of the vote in a tightly controlled referendum. Constitutional revisions adopted in 2012 provided for future presidential elections, replacing the presidential referendum system, in which the sole candidate was nominated by the ruling Baath Party. However, among other restrictions, candidates would need support from at least 35 lawmakers to qualify. During a media interview in October 2013, al-Assad said he was considering a run for reelection in 2014, despite a two-term limit introduced in the 2012 constitution.

Members of the 250-seat, unicameral People's Council serve four-year terms and hold little independent legislative power. Almost all power rests in the executive branch. The last legislative elections were held in May 2012 amid open warfare and an opposition boycott. The Baath Party and allied factions took 168 seats, progovernment independents secured 77, and a nominal opposition group won 5.

The rebel-held parts of the country continued to lack an effective or unified governing structure in 2013, but the SOC, formed in 2012, was regarded as the international face of the moderate opposition. Made up of delegates from opposition groups in exile, it has been recognized as the legitimate representative of the Syrian people by the Arab League, the United States, and many European countries, formally taking Syria's seat in the Arab League in March 2013. The SOC elected Moaz al-Khatib as its first president, but he resigned in April 2013. George Sabra served as interim president until Ahmad al-Jarba was elected in July. Ghassan Hitto, who was elected as the coalition's first prime minister in March, stepped down in July, citing his inability to form a government. Ahmed Tumeh was named to succeed him in September and formed a cabinet two months later. Nevertheless, the SOC's links to local leaders inside Syria remained tenuous.

While provisional local councils in many rebel-held areas have held rudimentary elections, the proceedings are undermined by ongoing government shelling and other insecurity, minimal turnout, and competing sources of authority, such as jihadist groups. Local council elections were held in Deir Ezzour in February 2013 and for the Aleppo governorate in March, though the latter voting was conducted across the Turkish border by delegates from municipal committees.

B. Political Pluralism and Participation: 0 / 16

In the formal political system, parties based on religious, tribal, or regional affiliation are banned. Until a 2011 decree allowed the formation of new parties, the only legal factions were the Baath Party and its several small coalition partners. Independent candidates are heavily vetted and closely allied with the regime. A 2012 constitutional referendum relaxed rules regarding the participation of non-Baathist parties, but the armed conflict and ongoing state restrictions have continued to limit political activity in practice.

Political activity in rebel-held areas, while more diverse, is also minimal. Local councils are typically sponsored or appointed by prominent families and armed groups, and their work is dominated by pressing humanitarian needs and basic service delivery.

Nationwide, the political views of various segments of the population are largely overridden by whatever armed group controls a given area. Territory is held by a multitude of armed factions, ranging from the government's forces and allies on the one hand, to moderate, Islamist, radical jihadist, and autonomous Kurdish units on the other. The size, strength, and affiliations of these factions were all in flux during 2013, making any assessment highly provisional.

The government and its security forces are dominated by the extended Assad family. Maher al-Assad, Bashar's brother, commands the Fourth Armored Division, an elite military unit tasked with protecting the regime, and his cousins head units responsible for presidential security and security in the capital. While the ruling family and its inner circle belong to the Alawite minority, the outer circle of the Baath Party and state apparatus is composed of Sunni allies, including Prime Minister Wael Nader al-Halqi and Deputy Prime Ministers Walid Muallem and Fahd Jassem al-Freij. In April 2013, al-Halqi survived an assassination attempt in Damascus. Al-Assad also has allies among the Sunni religious elite; one such cleric, Sheikh Ramadan al-Bouti, was killed in a bomb attack in March. The regime is reportedly assisted by Iranian forces and Shiite militias from Syria and across the region.

The Supreme Military Command (SMC), formed in late 2012, represents the moderate armed opposition in its dealings with the international community. Its chief of staff is Salim Idriss, a former general who defected from the Syrian army. The FSA leadership is incorporated into the SMC to the extent that the two names can be used interchangeably. The FSA consists of roughly 30 armed groups, including some of the more moderate or nationalist Sunni Islamist factions fighting in Syria. The group receives financial and political support and limited arms supplies from Arab and Western states.

The Sunni Islamist groups fighting in Syria include both those with a national focus and global jihadists. Among the more nationally oriented Islamist groups are the Syrian Islamic Liberation Front, founded in September 2012, and the Syrian Islamic Front (SIF), established in December 2012. While such groups tend to support the creation of an Islamic state in Syria based on Sharia (Islamic law), they generally do not call for the creation of a transnational Islamic caliphate. SIF leaders are not incorporated into the SMC structure, and the group receives funding from wealthy private donors in the Gulf.

There are two groups affiliated with Al-Qaeda in Syria: Jabhat al-Nusra (JN) and the Islamic State in Iraq and Greater Syria (ISIS). JN, which was designated as a terrorist organization by the United States in December 2012, aims to establish an Islamic caliphate based in Greater Syria, and its members include fighters from around the world. JN sometimes collaborates with other antigovernment groups in Syria on an ad hoc basis, reportedly including the FSA, but both JN and ISIS have also fought with opposition forces.

Kurdish militias have operated autonomously in northeastern Syria, reportedly clashing with Islamist factions and cooperating with other groups and allegedly with the regime in some instances.

C. Functioning of Government: 0 / 12 (-1)

Even before the armed conflict, Syrian government institutions lacked public accountability and were plagued by corruption. Those who question their policies and actions are often imprisoned or otherwise censored or punished. Members of the ruling family and their inner circle are said to own and control a major portion of the Syrian economy. The president's own fortune has been estimated at $550 million to $1.5 billion, while his cousin Rami Makhlouf is said to be worth $5 billion. Makhlouf was designated as profiting from public corruption by the U.S. Treasury Department in 2008. Syria was ranked 168 out of 177 on Transparency International's 2013 Corruption Perceptions Index.

Faced with serious financial and economic constraints as a result of the war, the government made some efforts to impose internal discipline in 2013. It approved a draft anticorruption law in August, and from June to August close to 100 civil servants were dismissed over charges of corruption. The head of the terrorism court was appointed in August to lead the anticorruption agency, known as the Central Commission for Monitoring and Inspection. Despite such moves, there is little or no transparency regarding the use of aid from allied states and other forms of assistance.

Corruption is also present in rebel-held areas, albeit on a smaller scale. Some rebel commanders, including from the FSA, have been accused of looting or seizing goods and selling them in Turkey. In addition, local administrators and activists complain that little of the international aid reportedly given to opposition representatives abroad seems to reach them, raising suspicions of graft.

Discretionary Political Rights Question B: -2 / 0

The armed conflict has grown increasingly sectarian over time, with Sunni civilians bearing the brunt of government attacks, some Islamist factions persecuting minorities and secularists, and civilians of all confessions seeking safety among their respective groups. The result has been significant and ongoing changes in the demographics of the country.

CIVIL LIBERTIES: 3 / 60 (-3)

D. Freedom of Expression and Belief: 1 / 16 (-1)

Freedom of expression is heavily restricted in Syria. Most domestic news outlets are either state controlled or aligned with rebel factions, and access to information is made difficult by both the opposition and regime forces. At least 28 journalists were killed in 2013, the majority of whom were Syrian. In addition, foreign, Syrian, and other Arab journalists were abducted during the year. According to the Committee to Protect Journalists, by early October at least 14 journalists were missing. Reporters Without Borders noted that month that 37 foreign journalists had disappeared since the beginning of the uprising, more than 60 Syrian journalists had been kidnapped or arrested by rebels, and more than 200 had been arrested by the regime. However, some kidnapped journalists have been returned to their families.

Because professional journalists do not have access to many areas, citizens have stepped in to fill the void of information. They have used social media, especially Facebook and YouTube, to upload reports and videos of human rights violations by both the regime and rebels. Government interrogators now reportedly ask detainees for access to Facebook or Skype accounts rather than the names of collaborators. The regime has stopped trying to block Facebook and uses it for surveillance, monitoring the pages of opponents and dissidents. Meanwhile, the progovernment Syrian Electronic Army has mounted a series of cyberattacks on opposition supporters, activists, and news outlets, including major foreign media.

While the constitution mandates that the president be a Muslim, there is no state religion in Syria, and historically freedom of worship has been respected to a greater extent than most other rights. However, the government tightly monitors mosques and controls the appointment of Muslim religious leaders. The war has increased sectarian hostility and polarization in both government and rebel-held areas, particularly as jihadist elements gained prominence. Two Orthodox bishops were kidnapped in Aleppo in March 2013, and churches were torched in cities such as Raqqa and smaller towns such as Tal Abyad. Alawite civilians have been killed by radical Islamists: at least 67 were massacred in progovernment villages in the Latakia governorate in August 2013.

Academic freedom is heavily restricted. University professors in government-held areas have been dismissed or imprisoned for expressing dissent, and some have been killed in response to their outspoken support for regime opponents. Education in general has been greatly disrupted by the civil war, with school facilities regularly attacked or commandeered by combatants.

E. Associational and Organizational Rights: 0 / 12

Freedom of assembly is harshly restricted. Any opposition protests in government-held areas are met with gunfire, mass arrests, and torture. Some rebel factions have also been severely intolerant of civilian demonstrations. Foreign journalists in Damascus reported an incident in May 2013 in which rebel fighters opened fire on a small progovernment demonstration.

The regime generally denies registration to nongovernmental organizations with reformist or human rights missions, and regularly conducts raids and searches to detain civic and political activists. An umbrella group of grassroots activists known as the Local Coordination Committees (LCC) emerged at the time of the 2011 uprising, organizing and monitoring the activities of the peaceful protest movement and documenting human rights abuses. However, LCC figures and other activists have faced violence and intimidation by armed groups. Human rights attorney Razan Zaitouneh, an LCC cofounder, was abducted along with three others near Damascus in December 2013.

Professional syndicates in state-held areas are controlled by the Baath Party, and all labor unions must belong to the General Federation of Trade Unions, a nominally independent grouping that the government uses to control union activity. The economic and political pressures of the war have made normal labor relations virtually impossible across the country.

F. Rule of Law: 0 / 16

Government interference in the civil judiciary is forbidden by the constitution, but all judges and prosecutors must belong to the Baath Party and are beholden to the political leadership in practice. Military officers can try civilians, both in conventional military courts and in field courts. While civilians may appeal military court decisions to the military chamber of the Court of Cassation, military judges are not independent or impartial, as they are subordinate to the military command. The Supreme State Security Court (SSSC), which heard national security cases and featured sweeping restrictions on due process, was disbanded in 2011, but there have been no notable improvements in the rights of defendants.

Human rights violations have increased during the armed conflict, reaching the level of war crimes and crimes against humanity, according to the Office of the UN High Commissioner for Human Rights. While abuses have been committed by all sides, the bulk of violations have been attributed to the Assad regime.

Government forces in 2013 engaged in the indiscriminate killing of civilians using air strikes, artillery bombardments, and chemical weapons, most notably a chemical attack near Damascus in August that killed hundreds of people and injured thousands. There is also evidence of mass executions by progovernment forces, including operations in the towns of Al-Bayda and Baniyas in May that killed nearly 250 people.

Government forces are responsible for the arrest and torture of tens of thousands of people since the start of the uprising in 2011. Human Rights Watch in 2012 identified 27 facilities where people have been subjected to more than 20 types of torture, including beatings, torture with electricity or battery acid, rape, and mock execution. Most victims are men between 18 and 35 years of age, but women, the elderly, and children are also detained and tortured. Rape is being used as an instrument of war, and while most reported victims are women, men and boys have also been raped. Human rights groups report that the overwhelming majority of documented sexual assaults in Syria are perpetrated by government forces and their allies.

Rebel and jihadist forces have been accused of committing summary executions; indiscriminate killings of civilians, particularly of Alawites and other minorities; and high-profile incidents of torture and mutilation of captured combatants. Some Islamist rebels and jihadists have also set up so-called Sharia courts in their areas, imposing crude punishments, including execution, for perceived religious offenses by civilians.

The Kurdish minority has historically faced discrimination and severe restrictions on cultural and linguistic expression. As many as 300,000 Syrian Kurds were long denied citizenship, passports, identity cards, and birth certificates, preventing them from owning land, obtaining government employment, and voting. While the government pledged in 2011 to extend citizenship rights to this population, conditions for Kurds remained harsh, and Kurdish militias have taken up arms to defend their areas amid the civil war.

G. Personal Autonomy and Individual Rights: 2 / 16 (-2)

The proliferation of military and rebel checkpoints, heavy combat, and general insecurity have severely restricted freedom of movement and shipments of vital supplies since 2011, affecting resident civilians, the internally displaced, and those attempting to flee abroad. The Assad regime has systematically blockaded regions controlled by rebels, with especially tight cordons surrounding districts under military siege or assault. Such tactics have led to widespread malnutrition and disease, including an outbreak of polio, which had previously been eradicated in Syria. Rebel and jihadist forces have also intermittently blocked shipments of aid and medicine for civilians.

Syria was ranked 133 out of 136 countries in the World Economic Forum's Gender Gap Report. In addition to sexual violence associated with the armed conflict, domestic abuse is endemic. Rates of early marriage are reportedly high, with displaced and refugee families in particular marrying off young daughters as a perceived safeguard against rape, a means of covering up such crimes, or a response to economic pressure. Forced prostitution and human trafficking are also serious problems among these populations.

Women faced legal and other forms of discrimination even before the uprising. While Syria was one of the first Arab countries to grant female suffrage, women have been underrepresented in Syrian politics and government. They hold just 12 percent of the seats in the legislature, though some have been appointed to senior positions, including one of the two vice presidential posts. A husband may request that the Interior Ministry block his wife from traveling abroad, and women, unlike men, are generally barred from taking their children out of the country without proof of the spouse's permission. Perpetrators of killings classified as "honor crimes" are punished with reduced sentences ranging from five to seven years in prison. Personal status law for Muslims is governed by Sharia and is discriminatory in marriage, divorce, and inheritance matters. Church law governs personal status issues for Christians, in some cases barring divorce. According to the penal code, "unnatural sexual intercourse" is punishable with up to three years in prison.

Taiwan

Political Rights Rating: 1
Civil Liberties Rating: 2
Freedom Rating: 1.5
Freedom Status: Free
Electoral Democracy: Yes

Population: 23,361,000
Capital: Taipei

Ten-Year Ratings Timeline For Year Under Review (Political Rights, Civil Liberties, Status)

Year Under Review	2004	2005	2006	2007	2008	2009	2010	2011	2012	2013
Rating	2,1,F	1,1,F	2,1,F	2,1,F	2,1,F	1,2,F	1,2,F	1,2,F	1,2,F	1,2,F

INTRODUCTION

The administration of incumbent president Ma Ying-jeou, who was reelected in Taiwan's fifth direct presidential election in 2012, continued pursuing closer ties with China during 2013. Having signed the bilateral Economic Cooperation Framework Agreement (ECFA) trade pact in 2010, the two governments agreed on another deal in June 2013 that would open up their service sectors. The agreement was under legislative review at year's end.

In one of a series of high-profile corruption cases, a former cabinet secretary general was acquitted of bribery charges in April, though he was sentenced to over seven years in prison for lesser offenses. Former president Lee Teng-hui, who was indicted in 2011 for alleged embezzlement and money laundering, was found not guilty in November.

Concerns about abuses at the Special Investigation Division of the Supreme Prosecutor's Office, which is administered by the Ministry of Justice, mounted during the year. Prosecutor General Huang Shih-ming was indicted in October for allegedly leaking wiretap information to President Ma without authorization.

Two deals initiated by private media owners in 2012 that had triggered nationwide concern over reduced news diversity both fell through in 2013. After a lengthy review, the National Communications Commission (NCC) in February rejected a media conglomerate's bid to purchase the country's second-largest cable provider. The second deal, a buyout of the Taiwan assets of Hong Kong's Next Media Group, collapsed in March, after the consortium of buyers reportedly withdrew to avoid potential antitrust scrutiny.

In August, the death of an army conscript triggered a mass protest featuring significant youth participation. Several other large-scale demonstrations held during 2013 were organized by civil society groups instead of political parties, with a growing focus on nonpartisan issues.

POLITICAL RIGHTS: 36 / 40

A. Electoral Process: 11 / 12

The president is directly elected for up to two four-year terms, appoints the prime minister, and can dissolve the national legislature (Legislative Yuan), which consists of 113 members serving four-year terms. The Executive Yuan, or cabinet, is made up of ministers appointed by the president on the recommendation of the prime minister. The three other branches of the government are the judiciary (Judicial Yuan), a watchdog body (Control Yuan), and a branch responsible for civil-service examinations (Examination Yuan). Direct elections for both the president, since 1996, and for the legislature, since 1991, have been considered generally free.

President Ma, the candidate of the ruling nationalist Kuomintang (KMT) party, won a second term in the January 2012 presidential election. The KMT also retained its majority in concurrent legislative elections, taking 64 seats. The proindependence Democratic Progressive Party (DPP) remained the largest opposition faction with 40 seats, and the remainder went to independents and smaller parties.

B. Political Pluralism and Participation: 15 / 16

Taiwan's multiparty system features vigorous competition between the two main parties, the KMT and the DPP. Opposition parties are able to function without interference. The KMT has dominated both the executive and legislative branches since 2008. Although the KMT holds a clear advantage in campaign funding from the business sector, which in general favors the Ma administration's China-friendly policy, the opposition parties have been able to compete freely during major elections, including the presidential and legislative balloting in January 2012.

C. Functioning of Government: 10 / 16

Though significantly less pervasive than in the past, corruption remains a problem in Taiwan. Instances of vote buying occur at the local level during elections. Politics and big business are closely intertwined, leading to malfeasance in government procurement. In April 2013, former Executive Yuan secretary general and KMT lawmaker Lin Yi-shih was acquitted of the core corruption charges issued against him in October 2012. He had faced a life sentence for allegedly demanding NT$63 million (US$2.1 million) in bribes from a businessman seeking a contract, but the Taipei District Court instead sentenced him to seven years and four months in prison for unexplained wealth and extortion.

After former president Chen Shui-bian was given an additional 10-year prison term in December 2012 for taking bribes during his presidency, the Ministry of Justice announced in June that Chen, who was already serving a sentence of 18 and a half years on other corruption charges, would serve a total of 20 years—the maximum sentence for such crimes according to Taiwan's criminal code. Another former president, Lee Teng-hui, was acquitted in November in an embezzlement and money-laundering case; his former aide, Liu Tai-ying, was convicted and sentenced to two years and eight months in prison in the same case. Both Lee and Liu had been indicted in 2011 for diverting secret diplomatic funds to launch a private research organization.

Taiwan was ranked 36 out of 177 countries and territories surveyed in Transparency International's 2013 Corruption Perceptions Index.

CIVIL LIBERTIES: 52 / 60
D. Freedom of Expression and Belief: 14 / 16

Taiwan's media reflect a diversity of views and report aggressively on government policies and corruption allegations, though many outlets display strong party affiliation in their reporting. After two and a half years of disputes over the leadership of the Public Television Service (PTS), a new board of directors was formed in June 2013, and a former chief of the now defunct Government Information Office was elected as the chairman.

Growing media ownership by conglomerates with business interests in China has raised public concerns about self-censorship on topics considered sensitive by Beijing. The NCC in February rejected a bid by Want Want Broadband, a subsidiary of the Want Want Group conglomerate, to purchase the country's second-largest cable provider. The regulator had granted conditional approval for the proposed merger in 2012, requiring Want Want owner Tsai Eng-meng and his associates to avoid any involvement in the management of a news channel controlled by the company, and to establish guidelines to ensure the editorial independence of another television network, among other stipulations. Want Want attempted to meet the requirements by placing the majority of the news channel's shares in a trust with a Taiwanese bank in December 2012, but the NCC concluded that such an arrangement left the controlling relations unchanged. Critics had warned that the bid would enable Tsai, who is known for his pro-Beijing stance, to monopolize Taiwan's media landscape.

In March, the proposed buyout of the Taiwan assets of Next Media Group fell through after raising similar concerns. The consortium of buyers, most of whom had large business operations in China, reportedly withdrew to avoid potential antitrust scrutiny. The print assets of Next Media Group, including the popular *Apple Daily* newspaper, which is known for its nonpartisan and investigative reporting, continued to operate under original owner Jimmy Lai of Hong Kong. In April, Next TV was sold to the chairman of ERA Communications, Taiwan's largest distributor of news channels. That sale was approved by the NCC in November.

Taiwanese of all faiths can worship freely. Religious organizations that choose to register with the government receive tax-exempt status.

Educators in Taiwan can generally write and lecture without interference. In September 2013, a court ruled in favor of a university professor who was sued by a Taiwanese petrochemical conglomerate for defamation in April 2012, after he published a report alleging that one of its factories was emitting a carcinogen.

E. Associational and Organizational Rights: 11 / 12

Freedom of assembly is generally respected in Taiwan, and several large-scale demonstrations during 2013 featured increased youth participation compared with previous years. In August, more than 110,000 protesters turned out for a rally demanding military reforms after a 24-year-old army conscript died of internal bleeding and organ failure while being punished for minor misconduct. The defense minister resigned that month.

Taiwan's Assembly and Parade Law enables police to prosecute protesters who fail to obtain a permit or follow orders to disperse. In July, a professor was detained at a rally against forced house demolitions in the village of Dapu in northern Taiwan. He was charged with offense against public safety in September, having attempting to enter a restricted area for the presidential motorcade while shouting antigovernment slogans.

All civic organizations must register with the government, though registration is freely granted. Nongovernment organizations (NGOs) typically operate without harassment.

Trade unions are independent, and most workers enjoy freedom of association. However, military personnel and government employees (with the exception of teachers) are barred from joining unions and bargaining collectively.

F. Rule of Law: 14 / 16

Taiwan's judiciary is independent, and trials are generally fair. However, scandals at the Ministry of Justice and its Special Investigation Division (SID) have raised concerns about political interference and illegality among prosecutors. The SID is administered by the Ministry of Justice and tasked with investigating high-profile cases. In October, Prosecutor General Huang Shih-ming, who leads the division, was indicted for allegedly disclosing wiretapped conversations to President Ma. Huang reportedly briefed the president in August and September on ongoing investigations, and suggested that Wang Jin-pyng, speaker of the Legislative Yuan, had lobbied Justice Minister Tseng Yung-fu to interfere with a commercial lawsuit involving a DPP lawmaker. Tseng resigned in September after being accused of pressuring prosecutors not to appeal the lawmaker's acquittal. The KMT attempted to revoke Wang's party membership, but he retained his position after winning a court ruling that month. The case against Huang was pending at year's end. The scandal prompted calls to abolish the SID.

Separately, after 18 years of litigation, the Supreme Court in August 2013 handed down guilty verdicts against two former prosecutors for leaking information to a gambling-arcade tycoon, who was jailed in 1997 for running a network of illegal video-gambling parlors. One prosecutor was sentenced to eight years and four months in prison, and the other was sentenced to one year.

Police largely respect the ban on arbitrary detention, and attorneys are allowed to monitor interrogations to prevent torture. Despite international criticism, Taiwan executed six inmates in 2013, while 50 people were awaiting execution after exhausting all appeals. Family members of inmates are typically not informed about scheduled dates of executions. Police corruption remains a problem in parts of Taiwan. Most instances involve officers being paid to provide information to venues that are targeted for raids. In July, six officers were indicted for taking bribes from the operator of an illegal gambling ring in Taipei through a number of journalists who acted as middlemen.

The constitution provides for the equality of all citizens, though the island's indigenous people continue to face social and economic discrimination. Disputes over their reserve lands continued as efforts to pass the Indigenous Autonomy Act stalled in 2013. LGBT (lesbian, gay, bisexual, and transgender) people are protected by law. Same-sex marriage is not permitted.

Taiwanese law does not allow for asylum or refugee status, and a 2010 bill that would address the problem was under legislative review at year's end.

G. Personal Autonomy and Individual Rights: 13 / 16

A program launched in 2011 by the government allowed Chinese tourists from 26 cities to travel to Taiwan without supervision. The daily quota was increased to 3,000 from 500 in 2013.

The constitution guarantees women equal rights, though Taiwanese women continue to face discrimination in employment and compensation. After 2012 elections, women held 30 percent of the seats in the legislature. Women from China and Southeast Asian countries are often at risk for sex trafficking and forced labor, but the government has stepped up efforts to tackle such issues in recent years.

According to official statistics, there were at least 469,000 foreign workers in Taiwan in 2013. Cases of abuse and exploitation are not unusual.

Tajikistan

Political Rights Ratings: 6
Civil Liberties Ratings: 6
Freedom Rating: 6.0
Freedom Status: Not Free
Electoral Democracy: No

Population: 8,100,000
Capital: Dushanbe

Ten-Year Ratings Timeline For Year Under Review (Political Rights, Civil Liberties, Status)

Year Under Review	2004	2005	2006	2007	2008	2009	2010	2011	2012	2013
Rating	6,5,NF	6,5,NF	6,5,NF	6,5,NF	6,5,NF	6,5,NF	6,5,NF	6,5,NF	6,6,NF	6,6,NF

INTRODUCTION

President Emomali Rahmon was reelected in November 2013 with 83.6 percent of the vote against a field of candidates that included his own supporters; the Organization for Security and Co-operation in Europe (OSCE) determined that the government had not offered voters a meaningful choice. Opposition parties—including the only legal Islamic party in Central Asia, the Islamic Renaissance Party of Tajikistan (IRPT)—had united to support the candidacy of a human rights lawyer, Oinihol Bobonazaroa. Bobonazarova's candidacy, however, was disqualified by the Central Electoral Commission, which ruled that the signatures of migrant laborers, who make up nearly 45 percent of Tajikistan's electorate, could not be used to meet the extremely high threshold for the nomination petition.

Throughout 2013, the government continued to take steps to arbitrarily limit free speech, access to information, the right to civic organization, and took especially harsh measures against former elites who attempted to join the political opposition.

POLITICAL RIGHTS: 8 / 40
A. Electoral Process: 2 / 12

Tajikistan's 1994 constitution provides for a strong, directly elected president who enjoys broad authority to appoint and dismiss officials. In the Assembly of Representatives (lower chamber), 63 members are elected by popular vote to serve five-year terms. In the

33-seat National Assembly (upper chamber), 25 members are chosen by local assemblies, and eight are appointed by the president, all for five-year terms.

Shortly after independence from the USSR in 1991, long-simmering tensions between regional elites, combined with various anticommunist and Islamist movements, ignited a five-year civil war from 1992 to 1997. Emomali Rakhmonov, a senior member of the Communist Party, was installed as president in September 1992 by party hardliners in the midst of the conflict; he was elected to office in 1994 and has never left the position. (Rakhmonov changed his surname to "Rhamon" in 2007 to make it sound less Russian.)

Following a December 1996 ceasefire, Rakhmonov signed a formal peace agreement in 1997 with the United Tajik Opposition (UTO), led by Said Abdullo Nuri. A coalition of secular and Islamist groups, the UTO emerged as the main force fighting against Rakhmonov's government; both sides committed to a reintegration process to be overseen by a politically balanced National Reconciliation Commission. A September 1999 referendum that permitted the formation of religion-based political parties paved the way for the legal operation of the Islamist opposition, including the IRPT. Rakhmonov's People's Democratic Party (PDP) has consistently dominated legislative elections and important provisions of the 1997 peace accord were never unimplemented.

The ruling PDP won 55 of 63 lower house seats in February 2010 parliamentary elections for the current legislature; elections failed to meet basic democratic standards according to OSCE monitors.

In November, Rahmon was reelected to a fourth term in office with 83.6 percent of the vote; OSCE observers noted the election "lacked a real choice" and failed to meet international standards. Six candidates were on the ballot, but several of them supported President Rahmon, and opposition candidates were disqualified on technicalities. The incumbent administration took advantage of its nearly absolute control over media coverage, the extremely high threshold for signatures required to participate, and the exclusion of migrant workers—who make up a significant part of the country's population and up to 45 percent of its electorate—from the nomination process to cement its dominance over the electoral process.

B. Political Pluralism and Participation: 4 / 16

Opposition parties were promised 30 percent of senior government posts as part of the 1997 peace accords, but this quota was never met. The Islamic and secular opposition are frequently persecuted and have become increasingly alienated from the political process. Several legal opposition parties, including the IRPT, united behind consensus candidate Oinihol Bobonazaroa in the presidential election; she was disqualified when the Electoral Commission rejected signatures of migrant workers from her petition to participate. Police reportedly harassed and arrested activists attempting to collect signatures on her behalf.

In May, businessman Zayd Saidov was arrested on charges of rape, statutory rape, theft, extortion, and polygamy shortly after announcing the formation of a new political party; in August, family members who protested his arrest were themselves jailed for "undermining public order." Throughout the year, members of the IRPT were beaten, harassed, and imprisoned, and one member in Isfara was hospitalized after he "fell" from a third floor window during a police interrogation.

C. Functioning of Government: 2 / 12

Corruption is pervasive. Patronage networks and regional affiliations are central to political life, with officials from the president's native Kulyob region dominant in government. At least two of Rahmon's children hold senior government posts, and various family members reportedly maintain extensive business interests in the country.

In January 2013, Tajikistani businessman and opposition leader Umarali Quvatov released a series of alleged phone records between himself and members of the presidential family that revealed the government's deep nepotism and corruption. Quvatov had been apprehended in late 2012 in Dubai and was held until September 2013, at which time Dubai denied an extradition request from Tajikistan.

Major irregularities at the National Bank of Tajikistan and the country's largest industrial company, TALCO Aluminum, have been documented. Tajikistan was ranked 154 out of 177 countries and territories surveyed in Transparency International's 2013 Corruption Perceptions Index.

CIVIL LIBERTIES: 16 / 60

D. Freedom of Expression and Belief: 5 / 16

Despite constitutional guarantees of freedom of speech and the press, independent journalists face harassment and intimidation, and the penal code criminalizes defamation. Crippling libel judgments have been common, particularly against newspapers that are critical of the government. Though Tajikistan decriminalized libel in 2012, reclassifying it as a civil offense, the act of publicly insulting the president remains punishable by a jail term of up to five years and charges against critical journalists are not limited to libel or insult.

In March 2013, Salimboy Shamsiddinov, a journalist critical of the government and a leader of the Uzbek minority in Khatlon province, disappeared after publicly encouraging Uzbeks to support an opposition candidate in the presidential election. In July, officials claimed he was found dead in Uzbekistan. In October, journalist Mahmadyusuf Ismoilov was sentenced to 11 years in prison on bribery charges after publishing an article in March that criticized local authorities.

The government controls most printing presses, newsprint supplies, and broadcasting facilities, and most television stations are state-owned or only nominally independent. The government blocks some critical websites and online news outlets, and increased these obstructions in the run-up to the 2013 presidential election.

The government has imposed a number of restrictions on religious freedom. A 2009 law restricts religious activities to state-approved houses of prayer. Authorities limit the number of mosques allowed in the country's towns, and in recent years have undertaken a campaign to shutter those that are not properly registered. Throughout 2013, Tajikistan continued to prosecute dozens of citizens for alleged membership in extremist religious organizations, and stepped up pressure against the IRPT.

Tajikistan's limited religious education institutions have failed to integrate most of the 1,500 students who were pressured to return from religious schools abroad in 2010, and some have faced prosecution. In 2011, unprecedented new legislation on "parental responsibility" that came into force banned minors from attending regular religious services in mosques, and banned private religious education. Many religious leaders criticized the law or quietly refused to obey it. Wearing of the *hijab* (headscarf) in schools and higher educational institutions has been banned since 2005.

E. Associational and Organizational Rights: 4 / 12

The government limits freedoms of assembly and association. Local government approval is required to hold public demonstrations, and officials reportedly refuse to grant permission in many cases.

Nongovernmental organizations (NGOs) must register with the Ministry of Justice, making them vulnerable to shutdown for minor technicalities. In January 2013, Khujend city officials banned the NGO Civil Society after 11 years of operations on charges that the address on their registration form was incorrect; a regional court upheld the closure in April. Citizens have the legal right to form and join trade unions and to bargain collectively, but unions are largely subservient to the authorities.

F. Rule of Law: 3 / 16

The judiciary lacks independence. Many judges are poorly trained and inexperienced, and bribery is reportedly widespread. Police frequently make arbitrary arrests and beat detainees to extract confessions. Overcrowding and disease contribute to often life-threatening conditions in prisons. Tajikistan is a major conduit for the smuggling of narcotics from Afghanistan to Russia and Europe, which has led to an increase in drug addiction within Tajikistan.

G. Personal Autonomy and Individual Rights: 4 / 16

Sexual harassment, discrimination, and violence against women, including spousal abuse, are reportedly common, but cases are rarely investigated. Reports indicate that women sometimes face societal pressure to wear headscarves, even though official policy discourages the practice. Despite some government efforts to address human trafficking, Tajikistan remains a source and transit country for persons trafficked for prostitution. Child labor, particularly on cotton farms, also remains a problem.

⬇ Tanzania

Political Rights: 3
Civil Liberties: 3
Freedom Rating: .0
Freedom Status: Partly Free
Electoral Democracy: Yes

Population: 49,100,000
Capital: Dar-es-Salaam

Trend Arrow: Tanzania received a downward trend arrow due to an increase in acts of extrajudicial violence by security forces, mob and vigilante violence, and violence against vulnerable groups including women, albinos, members of the LGBT community, and those at high risk of contracting HIV.

Ten-Year Ratings Timeline For Year Under Review (Political Rights, Civil Liberties, Status)

Year Under Review	2004	2005	2006	2007	2008	2009	2010	2011	2012	2013
Rating	4,3,PF	4,3,PF	4,3,PF	4,3,PF	4,3,PF	4,3,PF	3,3,PF	3,3,PF	3,3,PF	3,3,PF

INTRODUCTION

The year 2013 saw a general increase in acts of extrajudicial violence committed by security forces, mob and vigilante violence, and political violence. There was also an increase in violence against women, albinos, and people at risk of contracting HIV. Press freedom deteriorated due to the shutdown of key news outlets and an increase in attacks on journalists. Corruption continued to plague political and civilian life, with a number of new large-scale scandals exposed. New concerns also arose regarding a land rights dispute with the Maasai community and the revelation of the large-scale use of child labor in Tanzanian gold mining.

A draft constitution that proposed relatively revolutionary ideas was introduced in June, but the law that prompted the constitutional review was altered in September, making it likely the changes would not be implemented.

POLITICAL RIGHTS: 29 / 40 (+1)
A. Electoral Process: 9 / 12

The president is elected by direct popular vote for a maximum of two five-year terms. A unicameral National Assembly (the Bunge), which currently has 357 members serving five-year terms, holds legislative power. Of these, 239 are directly elected in single-member constituencies, 102 are women chosen by political parties according to their representation, 10 are presidential appointees, 5 are members of the Zanzibar legislature, and the last is reserved for the attorney general. Zanzibar elects its own president and legislature, and maintains largely autonomous jurisdiction over the archipelago's internal affairs.

Despite some notable irregularities, the October 2010 elections were judged to be the most competitive and legitimate in Tanzania's history. While the ruling Chama Cha Mapinduzi (CCM) party retained its dominant position, winning 186 seats, the opposition gained its largest representation in Tanzania's history. The Civic United Front (CUF) took 24 seats and Chama Cha Demokrasia na Maendeleo (CHADEMA) won 23. President Jakaya Kikwete of the CCM—first elected in 2005—was reelected with 61 percent of the vote, compared with 26 percent for CHADEMA's Wilibrod Slaa.

The National Electoral Commission and Zanzibar Electoral Commission maintain the electoral framework. Both are appointed by the president, and remain suspect institutions lacking in capacity and impartiality. In addition, the executive maintains the ability to appoint regional and district commissioners, who are influential during the election process. There was a significant decline in voter turnout during the 2010 elections, despite higher registration rates.

In 2013 the Tanzanian Constitutional Review Commission produced two draft constitutions (one in June and one in December). The most recent draft suggested a three-tiered federal state, fewer cabinet members, independent candidature, limits on executive appointment, and an explicit Bill of Rights. However, on September 6, the Constitution Review Act of 2011 was amended under protest from opposition parties to ensure that the Constituent Assembly, which debates the draft constitutions and ultimately approves the final version, would consist of legislators and presidential appointees. This potentially limited debate on the draft constitution, especially over controversial issues such as the future government structure. As of December 2013, the constituent assembly had not yet been convened.

The government began to make plans in 2013 to implement a biometric voter list that would address past issues with voter registration. By-elections for council seats in four wards in the Arusha region were held on July 14 and were generally peaceful, despite some reported issues with registration.

B. Political Pluralism and Participation: 12 / 16

Tanzanians have the right to organize into political parties. Coalitions are prohibited, as is independent candidature. There are opportunities for opposition parties to increase their support, although they still face significant hurdles. Opposition parties are not denied registration or the right to organize, yet continue to report harassment. On June 15, 2013, four people were killed and dozens injured in a grenade attack at a CHADEMA rally in Arusha. Later that month, Tanzanian police banned a CUF demonstration in Dar es Salaam and apparently tortured six party members in Mtwara. In July, the registrar of political parties threatened to de-register CHADEMA.

There is a growing opposition vote and comparatively stable opposition parties. Despite the proliferation of opposition parties, the same five have consistently won parliamentary seats—the CUF, CHADEMA, National Convention for Construction and Reform–Mageuzi, Tanzania Labor Party, and United Democratic Party. The constitution also permits political parties to form "shadow governments" while in opposition.

People's choices are hindered by threats from military forces and the use of material inducements by the ruling party. During the 2010 elections, security forces issued a threatening statement largely perceived as a warning to opposition parties. Local CCM representatives are widely reported to use small bribes to influence voting.

Cultural, ethnic, religious, and other minority groups have full political rights, but parties formed on explicitly religious, ethnic, or religious bases are prohibited.

C. Functioning of Government: 8 / 12 (+1)

The government is not free from pervasive corruption, despite the presence of the Prevention and Combating Corruption Bureau (PCCB). Corruption is pervasive in all aspects of political and commercial life, but especially in the energy and natural resources sectors. Tanzania was ranked 111 out of 177 countries and territories surveyed in Transparency International's 2013 Corruption Perceptions Index. In 2013, a large-scale corruption scandal was revealed involving the Commodity Import Support project; the PCCB was scheduled to investigate 23 public institutions for corruption practices (without resolves as of December 2013). The PCCB also introduced a record 823 cases into court.

The government remains sporadically responsive to citizen input between elections and citizens have access to public information, although they are not necessarily influential. The parliament of Tanzania publishes legislation, committee reports, budgets, and Q&A sessions. Most recently, the Tanzania Constitutional Forum (TCF), a civil society organization, helped coordinate opposition to the amended Constitution Review Act and pressured Kikwete to veto the bill, but unsuccessfully.

CIVIL LIBERTIES: 35 / 40 (-3)
D. Freedom of Expression and Belief: 10 / 16 (-1)

Although the constitution provides for freedom of speech, it does not specifically guarantee freedom of the press. Independent media on mainland Tanzania have come under increasing pressure. Current laws allow authorities broad discretion to restrict media on the basis of national security or public interest. Difficult registration processes hinder print and electronic media. The Committee to Protect Journalists recorded 22 attacks or threats against members of the press in 2013; among the most notable incidents was the severe beating of *New Habari* reporter Absalom Kibanda in March. Members of the press report frequent intimidation, leading to self-censorship and a dearth of reporting on important issues like protests in the town of Mtwara in May and June. The ban on the newspaper *MwanaHalisi*—imposed in July 2012—continued, and in September the newspapers *Mwananchi* and *Mtanzania* were shut down for 14 and 90 days, respectively. Press freedom in Zanzibar is even more constrained. The Zanzibari government owns the only daily newspaper, and private media other than radio is nearly non-existent. Internet access, while limited to urban areas, is growing. The authorities monitor websites that are critical of the government.

Freedom of religion is generally respected. Relations between the various faiths are largely peaceful, though there have been periodic instances of violence. In May 2013, a Catholic church in Arusha was bombed, killing 3 people and injuring 60.

Tensions between Muslims and Christians on Zanzibar continued in 2013. The Zanzibar government appoints a *mufti*, a professional jurist who interprets Islamic law, to oversee Muslim organizations. Some Muslims have criticized this practice, arguing that it represents excessive government interference. In February, Father Evarist Mushi was shot at the entrance of his church in Zanzibar, and just two days later, Zanzibar's Evangelical Church of Siloam was set on fire. In three separate incidents between June and September, acid was thrown at Catholic priests in Zanzibar.

There are few government restrictions on academic freedom. People are generally able to engage in private discussions, yet the ruling party CCM maintains a system of party-affiliated cells in urban and rural areas, which theoretically are responsible for every 10 households. This provides the ruling party with an effective tool of public monitoring that is used to stifle freedom of expression.

E. Associational and Organizational Rights: 7 / 12

The constitution guarantees freedoms of assembly, but the government can limit this right since all assemblies require police approval and critical political demonstrations are at times actively discouraged. A CUF demonstration was banned in June 2013, and a joint opposition rally was banned in September.

There is freedom for nongovernmental organizations (NGOs), and there are over 4,000 registered. While current law gives the government the right to de-register an NGO, there is little interference in NGO activity. Many, such as the Legal and Human Rights Centre (LHRC) and Research and Education for Democracy in Tanzania, publish reports that are critical of the government.

Trade unions are ostensibly independent of the government and are coordinated by the umbrella Trade Union Congress of Tanzania and Zanzibar Trade Union Congress. The Tanzania Federation of Cooperatives represents most of Tanzania's agricultural sector. Essential public services workers are barred from striking, and other workers are restricted by complex notification and mediation requirements. Strikes are infrequent on both the mainland and Zanzibar. In late August the Tanzanian-Zambian Railway Authority went on strike for two weeks.

F. Rule of Law: 9 / 16 (-2)

Tanzania's judiciary remains under political influence, and suffers from underfunding and corruption. All judges are political appointees, and the judiciary does not have an independent budget. There is therefore pressure from the executive regarding what cases the judiciary considers.

Rule of law does not always prevail in civil and criminal matters. Despite improvements, arrests and pretrial detention rules are often ignored. Prisons suffer from harsh conditions, including overcrowding and safety and health concerns. Security forces reportedly routinely abused, threatened, and mistreated civilians throughout 2013 with limited accountability. According to the LHRC, in the first half of 2013 at least 22 people were killed due to excessive force by security forces. Moreover, security forces were repeatedly unable to enforce rule of law; 597 deaths were reported due to mob violence, and 303 people accused of witchcraft people were killed.

Important segments of the population are not given equal treatment under the law or adequate protection from violence. Tanzania's albino population faced continued discrimination and violence in 2013. Consensual same-sex sexual relations are illegal and punishable by lengthy prison terms, and members of the LGBT (lesbian, gay, bisexual, and transgender) community face discrimination and police abuse. In 2013 Human Rights Watch reported an increase in the number of abuses committed by authorities against Tanzania's LGBT community, as well as against people at risk of contracting HIV. The report also uncovered a rise in cases of medical professionals refusing to treat or verbally abusing sex workers, LGBT people, and drug users.

Over 250,000 refugees from conflicts in neighboring countries reside in Tanzania. The 2002 Prevention of Terrorism Act has been criticized by NGOs and gives the police and immigration officials sweeping powers to arrest suspected illegal immigrants. In 2013, there was an increased crackdown on illegal immigration, including the deportation of nearly

4,000 people and several reported police abuses. Moreover, there has been increasing pressure to rapidly repatriate Rwandan refugees due to disputes with the Rwandan government over Tanzania's involvement in the Democratic Republic of Congo.

G. Personal Autonomy and Individual Rights: 9 / 16

Citizens generally enjoy freedom of travel, residence, employment, and education. However the prevalence of petty corruption can inhibit these freedoms.

Tanzanians have the right to establish private businesses, but often are required to pay petty bribes during the process. All land remains state-owned, and can only be leased to private entities. In 2013 nearly 70,000 Maasai living in the Loliondo region were threatened with eviction in order to create a new hunting ground licensed to the United Arab Emirates–owned OBC Corporation. In September 2013, after a strong public reaction, the plan was tabled.

Women's rights are constitutionally guaranteed but not uniformly protected. Traditional and Islamic customs frequently discriminate against women in family law, especially in rural areas and Zanzibar. Rape and domestic violence are reportedly common but rarely prosecuted. In 2013 there was a reported increase in gender-based violence, including an increase in female genital mutilation. The minimum female age for marriage is 15, but can be lower if customary law prevails. Trafficking of women and children from rural areas is also a growing concern.

Equality of economic opportunity is limited and there is continued economic exploitation. Poverty, especially in rural areas, impacts approximately 33 percent of the population. Most recently a 2013 Human Rights Watch report exposed the prevalent use of child labor in hazardous Tanzanian gold mines.

Thailand

Political Rights Rating: 4
Civil Liberties Rating: 4
Freedom Rating: 4.0
Freedom Status: Partly Free
Electoral Democracy: Yes

Population: 66,185,000
Capital: Bangkok

Ten-Year Ratings Timeline For Year Under Review (Political Rights, Civil Liberties, Status)

Year Under Review	2004	2005	2006	2007	2008	2009	2010	2011	2012	2013
Rating	2,3,F	3,3,PF	7,4,NF	6,4,PF	5,4,PF	5,4,PF	5,4,PF	4,4,PF	4,4,PF	4,4,PF

INTRODUCTION

Thailand remained divided in 2013 between the elected populist government of Prime Minister Yingluck Shinawatra and her Puea Thai Party (PTP)—with its so-called "red shirt" supporters—and antigovernment "yellow shirt" forces that included the opposition Democratic Party (DP), the pressure group People's Democratic Reform Council (PDRC), and a traditional political establishment encompassing the military, the senior bureaucracy, and royalists.

While much of 2013 was relatively peaceful until more street protests and violence erupted in November and December, the government's popularity fell as the year progressed, and it faced mounting obstacles on multiple fronts. In June Yingluck shuffled the cabinet after the government's attempt to cut rice subsidies drew protests from farmers. The subsidy program had been criticized for causing the government a loss of approximately $4 billion in a single year, but it was considered a boon to rice farmers from the central region, one of one of PTP's main constituencies.

The PTP-led parliament in September passed key amendments to the 2007 constitution that would make the partly appointed Senate wholly elected, a move that was denounced by opponents as a power grab. In November, the lower house of parliament passed a PTP-backed bill that would have provided blanket amnesty to military personnel, politicians, protesters, and even thugs who played active roles during Thailand's political crises of 2004–2010. The bill was widely seen as an attempt to allow Yingluck's brother, former prime minister Thaksin Shinawatra, to return to Thailand; he had gone into self-imposed exile after being deposed in a 2006 military coup, and faced a two-year jail term for corruption if he were to return. Still, many red shirts joined a public outcry against the proposed amnesty, as it applied amnesty to their opponents as well.

The amnesty bill was defeated in the Senate on November 11, but the controversy reinvigorated antigovernment protests. As pressure on Yingluck escalated, the Constitutional Court on November 20 struck down the constitutional amendment that would have made the Senate a wholly elected body on the grounds that the amendment undermined Thailand's checks and balances; the amendment had been passed by both houses of parliament. Clashes between red-shirt and yellow-shirt protesters escalated on November 30 and led to several deaths, and DP members resigned from the parliament on December 8. The next day, the prime minister announced the parliament's dissolution and called elections for February 2014. Antigovernment protesters opposed any new voting, calling instead for an appointed assembly to oversee reforms that would weaken electoral democracy.

At year's end, DP leader Abhisit Vejjajiva was facing murder charges related to a 2010 crackdown on protests while he was prime minister. Prosecutors in October had dropped similar charges against Thaksin for his alleged role in fomenting the 2010 unrest. The year concluded with ongoing protests, mounting violence, and continued political impasse.

POLITICAL RIGHTS: 22 / 40

A. Electoral Process: 8 / 12

Thailand's 2007 constitution was drafted by a military-controlled council after the 2006 military coup that ousted Thaksin and dissolved his Thai Rak Thai (TRT) party. The new charter, approved in an August 2007 referendum, provided amnesty for the 2006 coup leaders, and in a clear response to the premiership of Thaksin, it limited prime ministers to two four-year terms and set a lower threshold for launching no-confidence motions.

The elected prime minister and the bicameral parliament, comprising elected and appointed members, determine the policies of the government. Whereas the old Senate was fully elected, the Senate created by the 2007 constitution consists of 77 elected members and 73 appointed by a committee of judges and members of independent government bodies. Senators, who serve six-year terms, cannot belong to political parties. For the 500-seat lower chamber, the House of Representatives, the new constitution altered the system of proportional representation to curtail the voting power of the northern and northeastern provinces, where support for Thaksin remains strong.

Thaksin supporters, regrouped as the People's Power Party (PPP), won the first postcoup elections in December 2007, but the resulting government fell a year later when the Constitutional Court disbanded the PPP for alleged electoral fraud. A new government was formed by Abhisit and the opposition DP. After extensive red-shirt protests and government crackdowns in 2009 and 2010, elections were called for July 2011. The voting was considered relatively free and fair, yielding a strong victory for pro-Thaksin forces, this time reconstituted as the PTP. The party took 265 of 500 seats in the lower house, followed by the DP with 159; small parties divided the remainder. Although the influential military weighed in against the PTP prior to the vote, it was unable to decisively affect the outcome. The Asian Network for Free Elections, a leading monitoring organization, reported that representatives of several political parties tried to influence voters' choices inside polling stations, and that vote buying had increased compared with previous parliamentary polls.

B. Political Pluralism and Participation: 9 / 16

The two main political factions in Thailand's multiparty system are the DP—which is today associated with the traditional establishment —and the TRT and its successors (PPP and PTP), which first took office under Thaksin following the 2001 elections and has won every election since.

The power of the courts to dissolve political parties has played a central role in politics since 2006. The judiciary dissolved the TRT that year and the PPP in 2008. It also banned many senior members of the TRT and PPP from politics for five-year periods. In 2013, the DP and PAD filed several petitions asking the Constitutional Court to rule on whether various PTP proposals threatened to overthrow the constitutional order, but the court declined to issue rulings that would disband the ruling party.

The military and the monarchy have played significant roles in party politics. Thailand's approximately 18 military coups since 1932 have fostered a political culture that has tolerated such intervention by powerful unelected groups. Until the attempted passage of the amnesty bill in late 2013, Yingluck had sought to work with the military and the palace, avoiding highly contentious issues and confrontational stances regarding antigovernment protests. In September, Yingluck authorized a military reshuffle that, despite the military's stated goal of reducing top-level positions, increased the number of senior figures, including the addition of 215 new generals. Observers saw the move as another indicator of rapprochement between the military and the prime minister's office.

The Shinawatra family's domination of the populist political faction was reinforced with the victory of Yaowapa Wongsawat—the sister of Thaksin and Yingluck—in an April by-election for a lower house seat in Chiang Mai. She was among the senior party figures who had been banned from politics for five years upon the dissolution of the TRT. Concentration of power among prominent families is common on both sides of the political divide. Some 42 percent of the lawmakers elected in 2011 replaced family members.

C. Functioning of Government: 5 / 12

Corruption is widespread at all levels of Thai society. Both the DP and PTP include numerous lawmakers who have faced persistent corruption allegations. Thailand was ranked 102 out of 177 countries and territories surveyed in Transparency International's 2013 Corruption Perceptions Index. Former deputy interior minister Pracha Maleenont was sentenced in absentia in September 2013 to 12 years in prison for his role in the graft-laden purchase of fireboats and trucks. In April, the anticorruption agency cleared Yingluck of irregularities in her mandatory disclosure of assets.

The controversial amnesty bill considered by the parliament in November would have forced the cessation of over 25,000 corruption cases, including those ready for indictment, according to the anticorruption commission.

CIVIL LIBERTIES: 32 / 60 (+1)

D. Freedom of Expression and Belief: 10 / 16 (+1)

The government and military control licensing and transmission for Thailand's six main television stations and all 525 radio frequencies. Community radio stations are generally unlicensed. Print publications are for the most part privately owned and are subject to fewer restrictions than the broadcast media. Most print outlets take a clearly partisan political position.

The 2007 constitution restored freedom of expression guarantees that were eliminated by the 2006 coup, though the use of laws to quash criticism is growing. Defamation is a criminal offense in Thailand if the slander results in loss of reputation or hatred, and defamation charges are often used by politicians to silence opponents, critics, and activists. In August 2013, the Court of Appeal overturned the slander conviction of Jatuporn Prompan, a former PTP member of parliament and leading red-shirt activist. Jatuporn was originally convicted in 2009 for sitting improperly in the presence of the king.

The 2007 Computer Crimes Act assigns significant prison terms for the publication of false information deemed to endanger the public or national security, and permits the government to review the individual data of web users for the preceding 90 days. In August, a posting on Facebook citing rumors of a military coup resulted in police questioning of four individuals, including an editor of a public television channel. A senior police official announced to the media that anyone who "likes" the post on Facebook would face charges. In December, the Thai Navy filed criminal defamation and computer crime charges against two journalists, one Thai and one Australian, for an article they wrote alleging the trafficking of Muslim Rohingya asylum seekers by Thai Navy personnel. The case was pending at year's end.

The government in 2013 continued the practice of blocking websites for allegedly insulting the monarchy, and continued to observe webmasters and internet users. The authorities did ease restrictions on some red-shirt websites and community radio stations, but DP supporters have criticized the government for its unsympathetic approach to media and artists associated with their side of the political divide.

Aggressive enforcement of Thailand's lèse-majesté laws since the 2006 coup has created widespread anxiety and stifled freedom of expression not just online but also in print and broadcast media and even at public events, such as film festivals. Due to the secrecy surrounding most lèse-majesté cases, it is unclear how many went to trial in 2013, though the annual figure is believed to be in the hundreds, and has increased steadily since the 2006 coup. It is estimated the number of lèse-majesté cases rose from 33 in 2005 to 478 in 2010. The charges have been used to target activists, scholars, students, journalists, foreign authors, and politicians. Defendants can face decades in prison for multiple counts, and any leniency tends to come only through pressure by the media and activists.

Among other high-profile cases during the year, Somyot Prueksakasemsuk, a labor activist and former editor of a pro-Thaksin paper, was sentenced in January to 11 years in prison for publishing articles deemed to be lèse-majesté. Individuals and the media cannot report on the offending content in such cases, as they would risk being prosecuted as well. Some lèse-majesté convicts are pardoned by the king, as was red-shirt activist Surachai Danwattananusorn in October. He had been sentenced in 2012 to 12 and a half years in prison for speeches made in 2009–2011. Those accused of lèse-majesté usually spend the length of their trial in detention without bail.

Some harassment and violence against journalists continued in 2013, mostly in restive areas affected by the insurgency in the south. In October, five journalists were injured by a roadside bomb in the region.

The constitution explicitly prohibits discrimination based on religious belief. However, while there is no official state religion, the constitution requires the monarch to be a Buddhist, and speech considered insulting to Buddhism is prohibited by law. The conflict in the south, which pits ethnic Malay Muslims against ethnic Thai Buddhists, continues to undermine citizens' ability to practice their religions: Buddhist monks report that they are unable to travel freely through southern communities to receive alms, and many Buddhist schoolteachers have been attacked by insurgents as part of escalating violence against civilian targets since the failure of peace negotiations with the government. Nevertheless, religious freedom in the majority of the country is generally respected, religious organizations operate freely, and there is no systemic or institutional discrimination based on religion.

Academic freedom is respected, though subject also to lèse-majesté laws.

E. Associational and Organizational Rights: 6 / 12

The 2007 constitution guarantees freedom of assembly, though the government may invoke the Internal Security Act (ISA)—in which the armed forces assist the police to maintain order—or declare a state of emergency to curtail major demonstrations. The ISA was invoked several times in parts of Bangkok in 2013 for protests related to the amnesty bill, as well as to curb potential unrest stemming from an unfavorable November decision by the International Court of Justice regarding a border dispute with Cambodia. It also remained in place in the restive south. Political parties and organizations campaigned and met freely during the year, engaging in regular pro- or antigovernment demonstrations. Protesters' interactions with security forces were less violent for much of 2013 compared with the 2008–2010 period, but protests became increasing aggressive in November and December, including the storming and occupation of the Finance Ministry.

Thailand has a vibrant civil society sector, with groups representing farmers, laborers, women, students, environmentalists, and human rights interests. However, attacks on civil society leaders have been reported, and even in cases where perpetrators are prosecuted, there is a perception of impunity for the ultimate sponsors of the violence.

Thai trade unions are independent, and more than 50 percent of state-enterprise workers belong to unions, though less than 2 percent of the total workforce is unionized. Antiunion discrimination in the private sector is common, and legal protections for union members are weak and poorly enforced. Violent protests by rubber farmers demanding subsidies amid declining global prices led to the death of at least one protester in October and injuries among police officers. Rubber is grown mostly in the southern regions, where the opposition DP is strong, whereas heavily subsidized rice is grown in the central regions, where PTP is strong, prompting accusations of political bias.

In October, the government signed a memorandum of understanding with labor groups that was expected to pave the way to increased rights for workers, including migrant workers, state employees, and members of the military and police. In 2012, new rules increased the rights of household workers, mandating paid sick leave and days off, and raising the minimum working age to 15. Household workers had not been included in laws setting general labor protections.

F. Rule of Law: 6 / 16

The 2007 constitution restored judicial independence after the 2006 coup and reestablished an independent Constitutional Court. A separate military court adjudicates criminal and civil cases involving members of the military, as well as cases brought under martial law. Sharia (Islamic law) courts hear certain types of cases pertaining to Muslims. A new court specifically for tourists opened in 2013.

The Thai courts have played a decisive role in determining the outcome of political disputes, generating complaints of judicial activism and political bias. Since the coup, courts have voided an election won by Thaksin's party; disbanded two parties linked to him (TRT and PPP); disqualified about 200 of his allies from assuming office; sentenced Thaksin to jail in absentia; and seized 46 billion baht ($1.6 billion) of his wealth. However, the Constitutional Court during 2013 rejected multiple petitions by PD and PAD affiliates concerning the PTP's proposed constitutional amendments that could have led to the ruling party's dissolution.

As the debate over the proposed amnesty bill ramped up in September, an independent government body released a report on the 2010 killings in Bangkok during antigovernment protests, warning that unresolved issues surrounding the violence could lead to a resumption of the conflict. The report blamed the deaths of over 90 people—including protesters, security personnel, journalists, and others—on the military as well as nonmilitary instigators it called the "black shirts." The report also urged opposing factions to decrease their use of lèse-majesté laws and noted that the monarchy should be above political conflict.

A combination of martial law and emergency rule remains in effect in the four southernmost provinces, where Malay Muslims form a majority and a separatist insurgency has been ongoing—with varying intensity and multiple rebel groups—since the 1940s. The government has been divided on how to deal with the rebellion. Peace negotiations assisted by Malaysia made headway in February 2013, when the government signed an agreement to begin the first formal peace negotiations with a southern group, the dominant National Revolutionary Front (BRN). However, the negotiations broke down and violence escalated later in the year, with almost daily attacks, including ambushes and bombings. The BRN announced its withdrawal from the talks in August, and the negotiations were suspended indefinitely in mid-November. There are concerns that the BRN does not have control over insurgents in some regions of the south.

Counterinsurgency operations have involved the indiscriminate detention of thousands of suspected insurgents and sympathizers, and there are long-standing and credible reports of torture and other human rights violations, including extrajudicial killings, by security forces. To date there have been no successful criminal prosecutions of security personnel for these transgressions. Separatist fighters and armed criminal groups regularly attack government workers, police, teachers, religious figures, and civilians.

In Thailand's north, so-called hill tribes are not fully integrated into society. Many continue to struggle without formal citizenship, which renders them ineligible to vote, own land, attend state schools, or receive protection under labor laws. A 2008 amendment to the Nationality Act was supposed to facilitate citizenship registration, but in practice a lack of documentation made this difficult.

Thailand is known for its tolerance of the LGBT (lesbian, gay, bisexual, and transgender) community, though same-sex couples do not have the same rights as opposite-sex couples, and social tolerance is higher among tourists and expatriates than nationals. Since 2005, gay people have been able to serve openly in the military. A proposed bill to recognize same-sex civil partnerships with most of the benefits of marriage was pending at the end of 2013.

Thailand has not ratified UN conventions on refugees, and the authorities have forcibly repatriated some Burmese and Laotian refugees.

G. Personal Autonomy and Individual Rights: 10 / 16

Except in areas in which the ISA, martial law, or emergency rule have been imposed, citizens have freedom of travel and choice of residence. Citizens also enjoy freedom of employment and higher education. The rights to property and to establish businesses are protected by law, though in practice business activity is affected by some bureaucratic delays, and at times by the influence of security forces and organized crime in certain areas.

While women have the same legal rights as men, they remain subject to economic discrimination in practice, and are vulnerable to domestic abuse, rape, and sex trafficking. Sex tourism has been a key part of the economy in some urban and resort areas. A 2007 law criminalized spousal rape. Yingluck Shinawatra is the country's first female prime minister.

Exploitation and trafficking of migrant workers from Burma, Cambodia, and Laos are serious and ongoing problems, as are child and sweatshop labor. Labor shortages in Thailand have led to the trafficking of migrants, especially from Burma, into the fishing industry. A March 2013 report by the Environmental Justice Foundation pointed to restrictive labor laws, expensive immigration processes, and government indifference as reasons for the expansion of migrant smuggling networks. Thai military and immigration officers were accused in 2013 of trafficking Rohingya refugees from western Burma.

Togo

Political Rights Rating: 4
Civil Liberties Rating: 4
Freedom Rating: 4.0
Freedom Status: Partly Free
Electoral Democracy: No

Population: 6,168,497
Capital: Lomé

Ratings Change: Togo's political rights rating improved from 5 to 4 due to successful elections for the national legislature, which suffered from alleged irregularities but were generally deemed fair by international observers and did not feature serious violence.

Ten-Year Ratings Timeline For Year Under Review (Political Rights, Civil Liberties, Status)

Year Under Review	2004	2005	2006	2007	2008	2009	2010	2011	2012	2013
Rating	6,5,NF	6,5,NF	6,5,NF	5,5,NF	5,5,PF	5,4,PF	5,4,PF	5,4,PF	5,4,PF	4,4,PF

INTRODUCTION

Legislative elections intended for October 2012 were finally held in July 2013 after being postponed due to disagreement over electoral reforms. Talks between opposing political parties were facilitated by Nicodème Barrigah-Bénissan, former president of Togo's Truth, Justice and Reconciliation Commission (TJRC), and U.S. ambassador to Togo Robert Whitehead.

The electoral proceedings were largely conducted peacefully and considered to be credible and transparent by international observers. However, the results were contested by the opposition, as recent redistricting meant that President Faure Gnassingbé's allies in the Union for the Republic (UNIR) party won fewer votes but significantly more seats (62 of the total 91). In addition to zone borders favoring UNIR candidates, many observers attributed opposition losses to divisions between the various opposition parties.

Given Togo's recent history of electoral violence and human rights violations, the peaceful nationwide legislative election was cautiously applauded. Nonetheless, the controversy around electoral reforms was only temporarily fixed rather than resolved. Outstanding issues include the composition of the electoral commission, the distribution of electoral seats among electoral zones, access to state media for civil society and the political opposition, the number of election rounds, and presidential term limits.

Deadly market fires in January in Lomé and Kara were a controversial issue throughout the year, as 39 members of the opposition were arrested in connection with the fires. Some of the most high profile detainees were released on bail after a month, and ten others were released in May. The others remained in prison at year's end, one of whom died in prison due to poor medical care. Amnesty International and a number of European governments condemned the arrests were condemned, and the investigation into the cause of the fires has produced no publicly available results by the end of the year. Representatives of the opposition Save Togo Collective (CST), including failed former presidential candidate Jean-Pierre Fabre, accused the police of staging the fire as an excuse to crack down on opposition activities.

POLITICAL RIGHTS: 18 / 40 (+2)

A. Electoral Process: 5 / 12 (+1)

The president is elected to a five-year term and appoints the prime minister. In March 2010, Gnassingbé won reelection with more than 60 percent of the vote amid numerous irregularities, including vote buying and partisanship within the electoral commission. However, the problems were not considered serious enough to have influenced the outcome of the vote. The unicameral National Assembly is elected to five-year terms, but the previous elections were held in 2007. Progress was seen in 2013 when legislative elections were finally held. The election itself was considered to be credible and transparent by international observers, though the opposition protested the results in the streets and with the Constitutional Court. UNIR won 62 of the total 91 seats, as well as 23 of the country's 28 electoral zones, including some opposition strongholds. The CST won 19 seats, the Rainbow Alliance won 6 seats, the Union of Forces for Change (UFC) won 3, and an independent candidate won 1 seat.

Notwithstanding the negotiations that enabled the legislative elections to take place, a number of controversial electoral reforms—including electoral district allocations and presidential term limits—remain unresolved. In protest, newly elected opposition members boycotted the vote for the president of the National Assembly, which UNIR member Dama Dramani won by a large margin.

B. Political Pluralism and Participation: 8 / 16

Although opposition parties are free to operate, the structure of the electoral system, including districting as well as the single round of elections, help ensure that Gnassingbé and his party remain in power. Gnassingbé's family has ruled the country for nearly 50 years, and the likelihood that the opposition will gain power remains slim. The 2013 electoral process weakened the opposition's electoral clout due in part to divisions within the opposition, as well as district allocations dramatically favoring UNIR.

C. Functioning of Government: 5 / 12 (+1)

The new National Assembly was freely elected and has influence over policy, but corruption remains a serious problem. The anticorruption commission was reformed under the current president so its members would be appointed by the National Assembly rather than the president, but it has been slow to make progress and appears to still be aligned with President Eyadéma and UNIR. Togo was ranked 123 out of 177 countries and territories surveyed in Transparency International's 2013 Corruption Perceptions Index.

CIVIL LIBERTIES: 29 / 60 (+2)

D. Freedom of Expression and Belief: 9 / 16 (+1)

Freedom of the press is guaranteed by law, though often disregarded in practice. Impunity for crimes against journalists and frequent defamation suits encourage self-censorship, but 2013 saw a reduction in the number of attacks against journalists and the availability of diverse and critical voices in the media has been increasing. Most notable among the improvements in 2013 was when when the Constitutional Court rejected a proposed amendment to the 2009 Press Law that would have given the state broadcasting council, the High Authority of Broadcasting and Communications (HAAC), the power to shut down media outlets without a court order. The decision followed peaceful protests against the proposed amendment in which three journalists were reportedly injured by security forces. However, the HAAC can still impose severe penalties—including the suspension of publications or broadcasts and the confiscation of press cards—if journalists are found to have made "serious errors" or are "endangering national security," and is known for cracking down on opposition voices. During the year, the HAAC shut down the private station, Legende FM, for a month starting midway through election day in 2013, and closed it completely in August. Legende had previously been targeted by the HAAC for inciting ethnic hatred; while the station's director believed they were being reprimanded for coverage of antigovernment protests, other observers believe the accusations of ethnically fractious content were warranted.

During the 2013 election, official media outlets, which have the largest reach of any media outlet in the country, remained inaccessible for opposition candidates. Nonetheless, the number of attacks on journalists reported was particularly low for an election year in Togo; most took place during coverage of opposition demonstrations or during the journalists' demonstration against the proposed amendment to the Press Law.

Private print and broadcast outlets have low capacity, are often politicized, and journalists are often easily corruptible due to low pay. Access to the internet is generally unrestricted, but few people use the medium due to high costs.

Religious freedom is constitutionally protected and generally respected. Islam and Christianity are recognized as official religions, and other religious groups must register as associations. In September 2012, the Pew Forum on Religion and Public Life ranked Togo among the highest in the world in a study on global religious tolerance. While political discussion is prohibited on religious radio and television outlets, citizens are increasingly able to speak openly. Government security forces are believed to maintain a presence on university campuses and have cracked down on student protests in the past, though no such overt repression took place in 2013.

E. Associational and Organizational Rights: 6 / 12

Freedom of assembly is sometimes restricted. A 2011 law requires that demonstrations receive prior authorization and only be held during certain times of the day. After the arrest of opposition supporters in connection with the market fires, opposition-led protests in May calling for their release ended with police using tear gas. At the end of that month, the government temporarily banned protests led by either the CST or the Rainbow Alliance. These parties then led street demonstrations beginning in August protesting the July election results and accusing the Constitutional Court, which confirmed the results, of corruption. The closing of Legende FM provoked angry protests from the opposition, who fought with security forces and briefly took two police officers hostage until Nicodème Barrigah-Bénisson intervened.

Freedom of association is largely respected, and human rights organizations generally operate without government interference. Togo's constitution guarantees the right to form and join labor unions. In April, a spontaneous student protest in the northern Togolese city of Dapaong erupted in support of a teacher's strike. Local authorities violently dispersed protesters, and two students were killed, including a 12-year-old boy.

F. Rule of Law: 7 / 16 (+1)

The judicial system lacks resources and is heavily influenced by the presidency, though the Constitutional Court demonstrated some independence when it declared the amendment to the media law, which was favored by the president, unconstitutional. Lengthy pretrial detention is a serious problem. Prisons suffer from overcrowding and inadequate food and medical care. The government moved to reduce prison overcrowding in 2012 by releasing hundreds of prisoners on parole. A year later, persistently poor prison conditions came into the national spotlight with the death of Etienne Kodjo Yakanou, one of the opposition activists arrested in connection with the market fires. While the official statement was that he died of malaria, the opposition accused the prison authorities of withholding medical care. Months after his death, another of the detainees in relation to the market fires, Abass Kaboua, was released for health reasons. The International Federation for Human Rights also made accusations of torture and mistreatment of detainees.

The TJRC—which was tasked with investigating the political violence and human rights violations that occurred in Togo between 1958 and 2005, particularly during the 2005 election—recommended in April 2012 financial and medical compensation for victims, the abolition of the death penalty, the implementation of mechanisms for the prevention of torture, constitutional reform ensuring the separation of powers, a return to a two-term limit for the presidency, and improved oversight of the police and the military. According to the 2013 Afrobarometer survey, nearly half of Togolese respondents believe that the government will enact none or very few of the TJRC recommendations.

Ethnic tensions have historically divided the country between the north and south along political, ethnic, and religious lines. Discrimination among the country's 40 ethnic groups occurs though was not widely reported in 2013. Same-sex sexual activity is punishable by fines and up to three years in prison.

G. Personal Autonomy and Individual Rights: 7 / 16

While the majority of Togo's economy comprises of agriculture employing more than 60 percent of the population, it is increasingly seen as a western-friendly investment environment and has made moves to privatize a number of industries including telecommunications and the banking sector. Starting a business in Togo also improved slightly in 2013 as the government lifted some of the bureaucratic restrictions and reduced of some of the fees associated with the process.

In May, Gnassingbé submitted a law to the National Assembly guaranteeing equal representation of women in the legislature, and a 2013 amendment to the Electoral Code now requires that women have equal representation on the lists of electoral candidates submitted by political parties. The Law on Political Party and Electoral Campaign Funding, passed after the legislative election this year, also requires that public campaign funding be distributed to political parties in proportion to the number of women elected from each party in this year's election. In the 2010 presidential election, Togo saw its first female presidential candidate, and of the 91 seats in the National Assembly, 16 are currently held by women, up from just 6 previously. Despite constitutional guarantees of equality, women's opportunities for education and employment are limited. Customary law discriminates against women in divorce and inheritance, giving them the legal rights of minors, and children can only inherit citizenship from their father. Spousal abuse is widespread, and spousal rape is not a crime. Child trafficking for the purpose of slavery remains a serious problem, and prosecutions under a 2005 child-trafficking law are rare.

# Tonga

Political Rights Rating: 2
Civil Liberties Rating: 2
Freedom Rating: 2.0
Freedom Status: Free
Electoral Democracy: Yes

Population: 103,000
Capital: Nuku'alofa

Ratings Change: Tonga's political rights rating improved from 3 to 2 due to the orderly implementation of constitutional procedures in response to the prime minister's incapacitation by illness, and the opposition's increasing ability to hold politically dominant nobles accountable to the electorate.

Ten-Year Ratings Timeline For Year Under Review (Political Rights, Civil Liberties, Status)

Year Under Review	2004	2005	2006	2007	2008	2009	2010	2011	2012	2013
Rating	5,3,PF	5,3,PF	5,3,PF	5,3,PF	5,3,PF	5,3,PF	3,3,PF	3,3PF	3,2,F	2,2,F

INTRODUCTION

Prime Minister Lord Tu'ivakanō suffered a mild stroke in September while in New York for the UN General Assembly Plenary Session. King Tupou VI and the deputy prime minister were also overseas at the time, and lawmakers subsequently discovered that existing laws were not clear on who was to become acting prime minister in such a situation. Affairs in Tonga continued for several weeks without a resident head of state or head of government. On October 1, lawmakers named Lord Ma'afu, the most senior cabinet minister, the "minister in charge," which allowed him to represent the government in parliament but not to change policy. On October 15, Lord Tu'ivakanō resumed the prime ministership.

In September, the defense services were renamed "His Majesty's Armed Forces." Opposition lawmakers complained that the change was inconsistent with recent democratic reforms.

Also in September, the parliament passed the Family Protection bill and the king issued final approval of the measure in November, with full implementation expected in 2014. The legislation was first introduced in 2011, and includes provisions to safeguard victims of domestic violence. A crisis center for victims opened in November.

POLITICAL RIGHTS: 31 / 40 (+2)
A. Electoral Process: 11 / 12

The unicameral Legislative Assembly has 26 members, including 17 popularly elected representatives and 9 nobles elected by their peers; all members serve four-year terms. The Legislative Assembly elects the prime minister. The king appoints the chief justice, judges of the court of appeal, and the attorney general on the advice of the Privy Council, whose members the king also selects.

In 2010, Tonga held parliamentary elections under a new system by which a majority of seats were filled through universal suffrage for the first time. Candidates from the prodemocracy Democratic Party of the Friendly Islands won 12 of the 17 popularly elected seats, and independents took 5 seats. That December, the new parliament chose Lord Tu'ivakanō as prime minister.

In March 2012, King Tupou V died at the age of 63 while receiving medical treatment in Hong Kong. His brother, Prince Tupouto'a Lavaka, assumed the throne, taking the title King Tupou VI. For two weeks in early October 2013, Lord Ma'afu, the most senior cabinet minister, served as "minister in charge" to represent the government in parliament after the prime minister had a stroke. Lord Tuʻivakanō returned to his post as prime minister on October 15.

Lord Tuʻihaʻateiho resigned as acting speaker of the parliament in August 2013, to the dismay of many lawmakers. He said only that he felt "incompetent for the position." However, the resignation came in the wake of a criminal charge against him for illegal possession of a firearm. Justice Minister Clive Edwards protested that the acting speaker was innocent until proved guilty and should remain in his post, which he did, after posting bail. In November, Lord Tuʻihaʻateiho pleaded not guilty to the firearms possession charge. Proceedings were expected to continue in 2014.

B. Political Pluralism and Participation: 14 / 16

The monarchy, hereditary nobles, and a few prominent nonnobles dominate politics and the economy. While popularly elected representatives hold a greater number of seats in the parliament than nobles do, nobles nevertheless have great influence over Tongan politics, and frequently draw public ire with their actions.

There are no restrictions against forming political parties. Unlike Tonga's 33 titleholders, who select their own representatives, commoners run for offie under the banner of political parties or as independents. Ethnic, gender, and other minorities do not have reserved seats in the parliament.

C. Functioning of Government: 6 / 12 (+2)

Lawmakers duly followed constitutional guidelines by electing Lord Maʻafu as "minister-in-charge" to assume leadership after the prime minister became incapacitated due to illness in September. This allowed the affairs of government to continue to function smoothly until the return of Lord Tuʻivakanō as prime minister.

Corruption is widespread, with royals, nobles, and their top associates allegedly using state assets for personal benefit. The Anti-Corruption Commission, established in 2007, lacks power and resources to operate. In January 2013, a parliamentary report alleged that former prime minister Lord Feleti Sevele had mishandled a Chinese loan.

The election of commoners to the parliament in 2010 marked a fundamental change for democracy in Tonga. However, solidarity among the nobles and their success in courting support from the five independent lawmakers allow considerable influence in selecting the prime minister, law making, and other affairs of state. In 2012, the government introduced a freedom of information policy to promote greater openness and accountability, but its potential impact on official abuse and corruption is still unproven.

CIVIL LIBERTIES: 44 / 60
D. Freedom of Expression and Belief: 13 / 16

The constitution guarantees freedom of the press. Criticisms of the government appear regularly in all newspapers, including those wholly or partly owned by the state, but the government and individual leaders nevertheless have a history of suppressing the media. In June 2013, *Keleʻa*, a local newspaper, as well as its editor, its publisher, and the author of a letter to the editor the paper had printed, were collectively fined $138,000 in a civil defamation case brought by the prime minister and six cabinet ministers. The letter to the editor alleged that the courts allowed impunity for certain individuals, and criticized what it called improper government spending. *Keleʻa* has appealed the fine. In September, the publisher and the editor of *Keleʻa* were held in contempt of court in connection with their decision to print an editorial criticizing the earlier ruling against the newspaper, and were each ordered to pay a fine of $1,385 or serve one month in prison. *Kele'a* issued an apology to the court for the editorial following the ruling.

A new high-speed internet cable network went into operation in August 2013. Despite high costs and poor infrastructure, internet use is growing rapidly.

Freedom of religion is generally respected, but the government requires all religious references on broadcast media to conform to mainstream Christian beliefs.

There are no government restrictions on academic freedom. To conduct research in Tonga, scholars must provide details of proposed research and receive a permit from the prime minister's office. In 2012, Tongan was made the only language taught at early levels, with English added at higher grades. The rules exempt children whose native language is not Tongan.

E. Associational and Organizational Rights: 8 / 12

Freedoms of assembly and association are upheld. There has been a gradual decline in actions by the government and powerful elites to limit the creation or activities of nongovernmental organizations, including those that engage in work of a political nature. The 1963 Trade Union Act gives workers the right to form unions and to strike, but regulations for union formation were never promulgated. A number of professional associations exist, including ones for teachers, nurses, seafarers, and public servants. They do not have official powers to bargain collectively.

F. Rule of Law: 11 / 16

The judiciary is generally independent, though a shortage of judges has created serious case backlogs. Traditional village elders frequently adjudicate local disputes. Nobles have increasingly faced scrutiny in society and the courts. Prisons are basic, and are only lightly guarded, as violent crimes are rare.

In February 2013, Tongan police commissioner Grant O'Fee announced that he had found that Tongan police officers had forged letters to immigration authorities in New Zealand that declared falsely that certain individuals who had been convicted of crimes had no police record, allowing those people to improperly secure New Zealand visas. Several senior police officers were implicated in the scheme, which Tongan authorities are investigating. An Australian investigation also found that a number of Tongans with criminal records had been improperly granted Australian visas, after their criminal records were effectively wiped through similar means.

Six people, five of whom were members of the Tongan police force, were implicated in the 2012 death of a New Zealand police officer who had died of head injuries while in the custody of Tongan police. Three of the police officers implicated were released from custody in April 2013, with authorities citing a lack of evidence against them. The other three suspects face manslaughter charges; the cases against them were ongoing at year's end.

G. Personal Autonomy and Individual Rights: 12 / 16

The economy depends heavily on foreign aid and remittances from Tongans abroad. China's outreach to islands in the Pacific has allowed Tonga access to millions of dollars in Chinese investment and aid, including a $60-million loan for which China has agreed to indefinitely defer payment. The gift of a Chinese-made MA60 aircraft sparked a row with New Zealand when Tonga added it to its commercial fleet. New Zealand—the source of a significant number of tourists to Tonga—alleged that the aircraft is unsafe; in July 2013 it advised against travel to Tonga and suspended $8 million in tourism aid to the kingdom.

Women enjoy equal access to education and hold several senior government jobs. However, no woman was elected in 2010. Domestic violence is common. Tonga has signed but not ratified the UN Convention for the Elimination of Discrimination Against Women. Women cannot own land. A January 2013 UN report on human rights in Tonga found shortcomings in gender equality and women's rights, and urged Tongan authorities to permit women to become landowners. The king gave his assent to the Family Protection Act on November 5, after the parliament approved it in September, and the new law will come into force in mid-2014. Under the new measure, police can grant on-the-spot protection orders for up to seven days, and counselors will be available to assist victims of domestic violence and the courts that hear their cases. In November, the Women and Children's Crisis Center began providing access to free counseling, medical care, and the police in a single place. Colonial-era antisodomy laws remain on the books, but there is little evidence of government persecution or discrimination on the basis of gender or sexual preference. Conservative Christian values coexist with a traditional tolerance for more fluid notions of gender and sexuality.

Trinidad and Tobago

Political Rights Ratings: 2
Civil Liberties Rating: 2
Freedom Rating: 2.0
Freedom Status: Free
Electoral Democracy: Yes

Population: 1,300,000
Capital: Port-of-Spain

Ten-Year Ratings Timeline For Year Under Review (Political Rights, Civil Liberties, Status)

Year Under Review	2004	2005	2006	2007	2008	2009	2010	2011	2012	2013
Rating	3,3,PF	3,2,PF	2,2,F	2,2,F	2,2,F	2,2,F	2,2,F	2,2,F	2,2,F	2,2,F

INTRODUCTION

In 2013, a rise in the murder rate coincided with an increase in gang activity in Port-of-Spain, Trinidad's capital. Official corruption remains an issue, especially within the law enforcement community. After disappointing growth in 2012, Trinidad and Tobago experienced modest economic growth in 2013.

POLITICAL RIGHTS: 33 / 40

A. Electoral Process: 11 / 12

Tobago is a ward of Trinidad. The president is elected to a five-year term by a majority of the combined houses of Parliament, though executive authority rests with the prime minister. Parliament consists of the 41-member House of Representatives and the 31-member Senate; members of both houses are elected to five-year terms. The president appoints 16 senators on the advice of the prime minister, 6 on the advice of the opposition, and 9 at his or her own discretion.

Faced with a no-confidence vote, Prime Minister Patrick Manning of the People's National Movement (PNM) dissolved Parliament in April 2010 and called for elections in May. Kamla Persad-Bissessar's People's Partnership (PP) coalition—comprising the United National Congress (UNC), the Congress of the People, and the Tobago Organization of the People—won 29 of 41 seats, while the PNM took only 12. The PP's victory ended nearly 40 years of PNM rule.

B. Political Pluralism and Participation: 13 / 16

Political parties are technically multiethnic, though the PNM is favored by Afro-Trinidadians, while the UNC is affiliated with Indo-Trinidadians. The PP coalition was multiethnic.

The multiethnic population consists of Afro-Trinidadians, Indo-Trinidadians, and those of mixed race. The Indo-Trinidadian community continues to edge toward numerical, and thus political, advantage. Racial disparities persist, with Indo-Trinidadians comprising a disproportionate percentage of the country's upper class.

C. Functioning of Government: 9 / 12

The country suffers high-level corruption. Trinidad's Integrity Commission, established in 2000, has the power to investigate public officials' financial and ethical performance. Following the resignations of several commission members in 2009 due to suspicions of their ineligibility to serve, including because of allegations of malfeasance, a new Integrity Commission was appointed in 2010. In April 2013, Minister of National Security Jack Warner resigned in response to a report that he was involved in financial misbehavior while he served on the regional football association CONCACAF.

Drug-related corruption extends to the business community, and a significant amount of money is believed to be laundered through front companies. The 2000 Proceeds of Crime Act imposes severe penalties for money laundering and requires that major financial transactions be strictly monitored. Trinidad and Tobago was ranked 83 out of 177 countries surveyed in Transparency International's 2013 Corruption Perceptions Index.

CIVIL LIBERTIES: 48 / 60
D. Freedom of Expression and Belief: 15 / 16

Freedom of speech is constitutionally guaranteed. Press outlets are privately owned and vigorously pluralistic. There are four daily newspapers and several weeklies, as well as private and public broadcast media outlets. Internet access is unrestricted. The constitution guarantees freedom of religion, and the government honors this provision in practice. Academic freedom is generally observed.

E. Associational and Organizational Rights: 11 / 12

Freedoms of association and assembly are respected. Civil society is relatively robust, with a range of interest groups engaged in the political process. Labor unions are well organized and politically active, though union membership has declined in recent years. Strikes are legal and occur frequently.

F. Rule of Law: 9 / 16

The judicial branch is independent, though subject to some political pressure and corruption. Rising crime rates have produced a severe backlog in the court system. Corruption in the police force, which is often drug-related, is endemic, and inefficiencies result in the dismissal of some criminal cases. Despite the efforts of human rights groups, Trinidad and Tobago is the only country in the region that imposes a mandatory death sentence for murder. Most prisons are severely overcrowded.

Most abuses by the authorities go unpunished. An October 2011 Amnesty International report criticized the use of excessive force by police and noted that such violence was seldom investigated. Reports of police brutality still persist in 2013.

The government has struggled in recent years to address violent crime. Many Trinidadians of East Indian descent, who are disproportionately targeted for abduction, blame the increase in violence and kidnapping on government and police corruption. According to government statistics, 407 murders and 116 kidnappings occurred in 2013, showing an increase in the murder rate over 2012, but a decline in kidnappings. In addition to the increase in the number of murders, the kind of killings in Trinidad are becoming more brutal (e.g., beheadings), indicating an uptick in gang activity according to an October 2013 report by the Council on Hemispheric Affairs.

G. Personal Autonomy and Individual Rights: 13 / 16

Women hold 12 seats in the House of Representatives and 7 seats in the Senate. Domestic violence remains a significant concern. A draft National Gender and Development Policy, which will provide a framework for promoting gender equality, was submitted to the Cabinet in 2012 for approval. Human rights groups have criticized the government's unwillingness to address the discrimination and violence against LGBT (lesbian, gay, bisexual, and transgender) persons in Trinidad and Tobago. A proposed change to legislation that would extend death benefits of civil servants to include same-sex domestic partners was rejected in 2013.

Tunisia

Political Rights Rating: 3
Civil Liberties Rating: 3
Freedom Rating: 3.0
Freedom Status: Partly Free
Electoral Democracy: Yes

Population: 10,900,000
Capital: Tunis

Ratings Change: Tunisia's civil liberties rating improved from 4 to 3 due to gains in academic freedom, the establishment of new labor unions, and the lifting of travel restrictions.

Ten-Year Ratings Timeline For Year Under Review (Political Rights, Civil Liberties, Status)

Year Under Review	2004	2005	2006	2007	2008	2009	2010	2011	2012	2013
Rating	6,5,NF	6,5,NF	6,5,NF	7,5,NF	7,5,NF	7,5,NF	7,5,NF	3,4,PF	3,4,PF	3,3,PF

INTRODUCTION

Progress on the drafting of a constitution and the passage of an election law were hampered for much of 2013 by a political standoff between the governing coalition, led by the Islamist party Ennahda, and secular opposition parties. The February assassination of leftist opposition politician Chokri Belaid by suspected Islamist militants prompted opposition parties to accuse Ennahda of complicity or excessive tolerance of extremist groups. Prime Minister Hamadi Jebali resigned and was replaced by another Ennahda figure, former interior minister Ali Laarayedh. The new cabinet led a crackdown on violent ultraconservative Salafi Muslim groups, but political tensions escalated in July, when a second secular opposition leader, Mohamed Brahmi, was assassinated.

After many weeks of opposition protests and deadlock in the Constituent Assembly, Ennahda agreed in October to hand power to a politically neutral caretaker government that would be tasked with overseeing elections in 2014. Further negotiations over who would lead the caretaker administration ended in December, when the parties settled on Industry Minister Mehdi Jomaa. However, the agreement was not fully implemented by year's end. The Ennahda government remained in place pending the selection of a caretaker cabinet, work on the final draft of the constitution was still in progress, an election law had yet to be enacted, and an election commission had yet to be nominated.

POLITICAL RIGHTS: 27 / 40 (+1)
A. Electoral Process: 9 / 12

Tunisia was governed in 2013 by a 217-seat Constituent Assembly tasked with drafting a new constitution. It was elected in October 2011, nine months after longtime authoritarian president Zine el-Abidine Ben Ali fled the country amid a wave of antigovernment protests. Parties from across the ideological spectrum participated. The voting was observed by international monitoring groups, and was widely touted as the first free and fair elections in Tunisia's history. While there were isolated reports of irregularities and one documented violation of campaign finance rules, the transitional authorities acted quickly on those problems, in some instances invalidating seats that were gained unfairly. However, the electoral framework gave rural districts a disproportionately high number of seats. Turnout was 52 percent, a substantially higher rate than in previous Tunisian elections.

Ennahda, the formerly outlawed Islamist party, won a plurality of the vote and 89 of the 217 seats. Two left-leaning parties, the Congress for the Republic (CPR) and Ettakatol, joined Ennahda in a governing coalition after winning 29 and 20 seats, respectively. A variety of other parties and independents also won seats. The new assembly chose Ennahda's Hamadi Jebali as prime minster, Ettakatol's Mustafa Ben Jaafar as speaker, and the CPR's Moncef Marzouki to serve in the largely ceremonial presidency.

In the absence of local elections and in a process that lacks transparency, the transitional government has appointed many local and regional officials. This has led in some cases to the spontaneous emergence of rival provisional councils, forcing the Ennahda government to review some of its appointees in a process that was ongoing at the end of 2013.

In December 2012 the Constituent Assembly passed legislation on the creation of an election commission, the Independent High Authority for Elections (ISIE). The body's nine members were to be selected by a two-thirds vote in the assembly, raising concerns that it could be biased toward Ennahda, the largest party. Due to legal challenges and ongoing political negotiations, the formation of the ISIE remained incomplete at the end of 2013.

B. Political Pluralism and Participation: 12 / 16

More than 100 legal political parties exist, including a right-wing Salafi party. As of 2013, members of old ruling party, the Constitutional Democratic Rally (RCD), who served in the government under Ben Ali were disqualified from participating in politics.

The Tunisian military has historically been marginalized by the political leadership. In the 2011 revolution, the military remained politically neutral, though it performed nonmilitary security functions to protect the population during the transition. For example, it provided security at polling stations during the Constituent Assembly elections.

The transitional government and both domestic and international nongovernmental organizations (NGOs) have worked to increase the political participation of marginalized groups, including disabled Tunisians, and ensure their inclusion in future elections.

C. Functioning of Government: 6 / 12 (+1)

The removal of Ben Ali and his close relatives and associates, who had used their positions to create private monopolies in several sectors, represented an important first step in combating corruption and conflicts of interest. While an anticorruption commission was established in the wake of Ben Ali's departure, the state's willingness to prosecute corruption cases remains questionable. More than 100 cases have been sent to the judiciary, but it has initiated prosecutions only in rare instances. A strong legal framework and systematic practices aimed at curbing corruption had yet to take shape at the end of 2013. A majority of citizens say that corruption has increased in the last two years, with political parties and the police perceived as the most corrupt institutions, and tax services and permits as the most common areas for bribery. Tunisia was ranked 77 of 177 countries and territories assessed in Transparency International's 2013 Corruption Perceptions Index.

In 2011, Tunisia enacted a new information law that instructed public institutions to make internal documents available to the public. In July 2013, an online tool called Marsoum41 was created to enable citizens to directly request public documents. Later in the year, the government introduced draft amendments that would strengthen the 2011 law and create an independent commission to monitor compliance, but these plans were not complete at the end of 2013.

The political elite's negotiations and compromises during the year, particularly the government's agreement to step down in favor of a caretaker administration, were widely hailed as a positive sign of democratic accountability and responsiveness to public pressure.

CIVIL LIBERTIES: 36 / 60 (+3)
D. Freedom of Expression and Belief: 11 / 16 (+1)

The Ben Ali regime used an array of legal, penal, and economic measures to silence dissenting voices in the media, and the transitional government in 2011 almost immediately proclaimed freedom of information and expression as a foundational principle for the country. However, the media continued to face a number of obstacles during 2013. The government frequently used the legal system to punish independent reporting, with several journalists either arrested or convicted on defamation and other charges. Several other criminal cases, some resulting in imprisonment, were brought against internet users for content they posted online. Some lawmakers in May proposed creating a commission to monitor journalists who insult Constituent Assembly members. In September, the president indicated that journalists were not above the law, but that infringements should be dealt with through civil rather than criminal proceedings.

Members of a new media regulator, the High Independent Authority of Audiovisual Communication (HAICA), were finally agreed upon in May 2013, but the government by that time had already appointed directors of state-owned media outlets, who in turn continued to name subordinates without consulting the regulator, raising objections from journalists who expressed concern about politicization. Journalists, opposition supporters, and civil society groups held a one-day strike to protest such appointments in September.

Muslims form the dominant religious group in Tunisia, but the small populations of Jews and Christians have generally been free to practice their faiths. While the draft constitution identifies Islam as the state religion and requires the president to be a Muslim, Ennhada has not sought a constitutional provision identifying Sharia (Islamic law) as a source of legislation. Other language in the draft would protect freedom of belief and conscience.

After Ben Ali's ouster, ultraconservative and Salafi Muslims, like all religious groups, had more freedom to openly discuss the role that religion should play in the public sphere and to express their beliefs without state interference. However, this resulted in periodic violent clashes with their political and ideological opponents, attacks on purveyors of alcohol or allegedly blasphemous art, and public threats by Salafis against state institutions. At least four Sufi Muslim shrines, which Salafi Muslims consider un-Islamic, were destroyed, and several others were forced to close. Extremists in 2013 continued to attack citizens and businesses participating in activities they viewed as religiously offensive, at times without intervention by police, prompting accusations that the government was too lenient toward radical groups.

Authorities limited academic discussion of sensitive topics under the Ben Ali regime, and its removal created a more open environment for students and faculties. Academic freedom continued to improve in practice in 2013, and an article of the draft constitution called for protection of academic freedom and state support of scientific research.

E. Associational and Organizational Rights: 9 / 12 (+1)

Some human rights groups questioned the government's commitment to freedom of assembly in 2013. Although demonstrations on political, social, and economic issues took place throughout the year, many featured violent clashes with police, who were criticized for using excessive force. Temporary curfews were imposed in some cases.

NGOs were legally prohibited from pursuing political objectives and activities under the Ben Ali regime. However, many new groups began operating after the revolution. A number of conferences were held by NGOs across the country during 2013, and advocacy groups have mounted protests on issues such as women's rights, the role of religion in the state, and the needs of nomadic Berber communities. No formal registration process has been instated for these organizations, and their existence is not protected by a legal framework.

New labor organizations were established in 2011, including the Tunisian Labor Union (UTT) and the General Confederation of Tunisian Workers (CGTT). In 2013, these organizations, along with the oldest labor union in Tunisia, the General Union of Tunisian Workers (UGTT), grew more active in pursuing their demands for substantial governmental labor reform, better wages, and improved workplace conditions. The Constituent Assembly gave these issues little attention, leading the UGTT to both call for strikes and support protests against the authorities.

F. Rule of Law: 6 / 16

Under Ben Ali, the judicial system was carefully managed by the executive branch, which controlled the appointment and assignment of judges through the Supreme Council of Magistrates. Trials of suspected Islamists, human rights activists, and journalists were typically condemned as grossly unfair and politically biased by domestic and international observers. Politicized imprisonment and similar abuses have declined significantly since 2011, but concerns about the misuse of the legal system against journalists and others persisted in 2013.

In April the Constituent Assembly passed legislation replacing the old executive-controlled Supreme Council of Magistrates with an independent temporary body tasked with overseeing the judiciary, including its appointments, promotions, assignments, and disciplinary procedures, until a permanent structure is established by the new constitution. The final bill reflected changes demanded in February by the Union of Tunisian Judges, which argued that the original draft exposed the judiciary to interference from the executive and legislative branches by allowing nonjurists to sit on the temporary board.

Security issues, particularly threats from radical Salafi Muslim groups, were a major concern for the coalition government during 2013, and security forces stepped up patrols of the southern border regions, where Islamist militant groups have been active. Police cracked down on riots by supporters of the extremist group Ansar al-Sharia. The Ennahda government made progress in investigating the year's two political assassinations, and by the end of the year authorities had identified several suspects.

The draft constitution under consideration in 2013 referred to state protections for persons with special needs, prohibiting all forms of discrimination and providing aid to integrate them into society. The draft also guaranteed the right to culture for all citizens and called for the state to create a culture of diversity. LGBT (lesbian, gay, bisexual, and transgender) people continue to face discrimination in law and society. Article 230 of the penal code prescribes up to three years in prison for "sodomy."

Tunisia is a signatory to the 1951 UN convention on refugees and its 1967 protocol, and the government reportedly remains committed to developing an asylum law. In June 2013, the country's Shousha transit camp was closed after more than 3,000 refugees and asylum seekers, most of them from the Horn of Africa, were accepted for resettlement in third countries.

G. Personal Autonomy and Individual Rights: 10 / 16 (+1)

Freedom of movement has improved substantially since 2011, and international travel is unrestricted, though police checkpoints have increased in the southern border area. The draft constitution under discussion in 2013 guaranteed freedom of movement within Tunisia, as well as freedom to leave the country. Women do not require the permission of a male relative to travel.

Tunisia has long been praised for relatively progressive social policies, especially in the areas of family law and women's rights. The 1956 Personal Status Code giving women equality with men has remained in force. It grants women equal rights in divorce, and children born to Tunisian mothers and foreign fathers are automatically granted citizenship. The country legalized medical abortion in 1973. There are currently 58 women in the Constituent Assembly, representing the largest proportion of female representatives in the Arab world. Party lists for the 2011 elections were required to alternate between male and female candidates. In 2012, women's rights advocates criticized language in the draft constitution that referred to "complementarity" rather than equality between the sexes. Government officials backtracked on the change after the public outcry. Areas of ongoing concern for women's rights include discrimination in society as well as unequal inheritance laws for men and women.

⬇ Turkey

Political Rights Rating: 3
Civil Liberties Rating: 4
Freedom Rating: 3.5
Freedom Status: Partly Free
Electoral Democracy: Yes

Population: 76,100,000
Capital: Ankara

Trend Arrow: Turkey received a downward trend arrow due to the harsh government crackdown on protesters in Istanbul and other cities and increased political pressure on private companies to conform with the ruling party's agenda.

Ten-Year Ratings Timeline For Year Under Review (Political Rights, Civil Liberties, Status)

Year Under Review	2004	2005	2006	2007	2008	2009	2010	2011	2012	2013
Rating	3,3,PF	3,3,PF	3,3,PF	3,3,PF	3,3,PF	3,3,PF	3,3,PF	3,3,PF	3,4,PF	3,4,PF

INTRODUCTION

In January 2013, the government began new talks with Abdullah Öcalan, the jailed leader of the separatist Kurdistan Workers' Party (PKK) militant group, in an attempt to end a conflict that had claimed over 40,000 lives since the 1980s. In March, Öcalan called a cease-fire and announced that the PKK would withdraw its fighters from Turkish territory into northern Iraq. This cease-fire remained in effect throughout the year. However, in September, the PKK announced that it was suspending the withdrawal because of insufficient efforts by the government to carry out legal reforms that would help resolve the Kurdish question.

Meanwhile, in May, protests broke out in Istanbul over government-backed development plans that would supplant the city's Gezi Park. While the dispute was initially framed as an environmental issue, protests spread to other cities and assumed a broader antigovernment character, directed against what the protesters saw as creeping authoritarianism on the part of Prime Minister Recep Tayyip Erdoğan and his Justice and Development Party (AKP), in power since 2002. For two weeks in June, tens of thousands of protesters occupied Taksim Square in the heart of Istanbul, and over 2.5 million Turks were estimated to have participated in protests nationwide. After a tense standoff, police forcibly cleared Taksim Square and other protest sites. Across Turkey by mid-July, five protesters had been killed, over 8,000 had been injured, and nearly 5,000 had been detained by police. The government's response was condemned by Turkish and international observers. Government officials subsequently blamed the protests on external forces including the foreign media and the Jewish diaspora, and police raided residences and offices to arrest additional suspects accused of having instigated or assisted the demonstrations.

In September, the AKP unveiled a long-awaited democratization package, which touched on, among other issues, Kurdish-language education in private schools, possible changes to the electoral system, freedom to wear the Islamic headscarf, and greater protections for freedom of expression. Implementation of most of the proposals remained to be seen at year's end, and critics charged that the reforms were both insincere and insufficient, particularly in light of their failure to repeal sweeping antiterrorism laws or introduce protections for the Alevi minority.

In December, police raided dozens of homes and offices in a bribery and money-laundering investigation that targeted prominent businesspeople and family members of cabinet ministers. Erdoğan ordered a purge of the police officials responsible and claimed that the investigation was a politically motivated move by elements of a "parallel state" engaged in an international plot to undermine Turkey. Three cabinet ministers resigned, with one suggesting that Erdoğan himself should resign. The crisis remained unresolved at year's end.

POLITICAL RIGHTS: 28 / 40

A. Electoral Process: 11 / 12

In Turkey's semipresidential system, the prime minister is head of government and currently holds most executive authority, while the president is head of state and has powers including a legislative veto and authority to appoint judges and prosecutors. In 2007, the AKP's Abdullah Gül was elected by the parliament to a single seven-year term as president. Beginning in 2014, the president will be elected by popular vote for a once-renewable, five-year term. A full delineation of the directly elected president's powers has yet to be enacted.

The unicameral parliament, the Grand National Assembly, is elected every four years using a proportional-representation system. The June 2011 parliamentary elections were widely judged to have been free and fair, although 12 candidates from the largely Kurdish Peace and Democracy Party (BDP) were barred from running. The 2011 elections were notable for featuring the first legal campaigning in Kurdish. The AKP ultimately won nearly 50 percent of the vote and 326 of 550 seats. The opposition Republican People's Party (CHP) and Nationalist Action Party (MHP) took 135 and 53 seats, respectively, and independents, mostly from the BDP, won the remaining 36 seats.

A party must win at least 10 percent of the nationwide vote to secure parliamentary representation, while independents must win 10 percent of the vote in their provinces. This is the highest electoral threshold in Europe. In 2011, the BDP ran candidates as independents to get around the party requirement. The government proposed changes to this system in its September 2013 democratization package, including lowering the threshold to 5 percent or adopting a system of single-member districts. The proposals would be subject to public and parliamentary debate.

B. Political Pluralism and Participation: 10 / 16

Turkey has a competitive multiparty system, but at present parties can still be disbanded for endorsing policies that are not in agreement with constitutional parameters. The rule has frequently been applied to Islamist and pro-Kurdish parties. An effort to repeal this measure in 2010 narrowly failed. No effort has been made to ban the BDP, but many of the party's officials have been arrested as part of a law enforcement campaign against the Union of Communities of Kurdistan (KCK), which the government describes as the PKK's urban arm. In July 2013, 13 Kurdish politicians, including local BDP leaders, were given more than six years in prison for belonging to an illegal organization. Separately, three members of parliament from the CHP were convicted in August in the Ergenekon trial, a sprawling case against an alleged conspiracy to create disorder and overthrow the AKP government, which has Islamist roots. The case formally closed that month with convictions of over 250 individuals, including military officers, state bureaucrats, and journalists. Both the KCK and Ergenekon cases have been criticized for alleged politicization and due process violations.

In September, the government proposed lowering the threshold for state funding for political parties from 7 percent of the vote to 3 percent, which would benefit smaller parties such as the BDP.

The military has historically been a dominant force in politics, forcing out an elected government most recently in 1997. Over the past decade, AKP-led reforms have increased control and oversight of the military by elected civilian officials, but problems persist in areas such as supervision of defense expenditures. The verdicts delivered in the Ergenekon case in August 2013 included a life sentence for the former military chief of staff, İlker Başbuğ.

C. Functioning of Government: 7 / 12

Corruption remains a major problem in Turkey. Reports in October 2013 noted weaknesses related to transparency, with government ministries refusing to hand over information to the Court of Accounts and pressuring the court to alter its reports on corruption. There is also concern over the awarding of government contracts, as major projects have allegedly benefited AKP party officials and the armed forces. The high-level corruption investigation that emerged in December, causing three cabinet ministers to resign, also led several AKP lawmakers to leave the party in protest. Many reports described the case as a manifestation of a rift between the AKP and the Hizmet movement, inspired by the Islamic scholar Fethullah Gülen, who had previously backed the government and whose supporters are well represented in the police and judiciary.

CIVIL LIBERTIES: 32 / 60 (-1)

D. Freedom of Expression and Belief: 9 / 16

Freedom of expression is guaranteed in the constitution but restricted by law and in practice. In November 2013, PEN International reported that 73 writers and intellectuals were being held in Turkish jails, up from 60 in 2012. The Committee to Protect Journalists reported that 40 journalists were incarcerated in Turkey as of December 2013, more than in any other country. Most of those behind bars were Kurdish and charged under antiterrorism laws in KCK-related cases. In one round of arrests during 2013, 11 journalists were held in January for allegedly belonging to a terrorist organization. In August, over 20 journalists were convicted as part of the Ergenekon trial.

The government has imposed gag orders on coverage of certain events, including the Gezi Park protests. In June, television stations that aired independent coverage of the protests were fined by the government for inciting violence. Nearly all media organizations are owned by giant holding companies with ties to political parties or business interests in other industries, contributing to self-censorship. Dozens of journalists were fired or forced to resign in the aftermath of the Gezi protests, apparently in retaliation for their sympathetic coverage of the demonstrators. Erdoğan labeled social-media platforms such as Twitter, which was instrumental in the protests, as a "menace to society," and some Twitter users were detained for their online activity. While the government began investigating Twitter, bans on social media did not materialize. News outlets have met with state pressure for critical coverage of other issues as well. In December, the daily *Taraf* faced prosecution for leaking information about government surveillance and profiling of individuals tied to religious movements and organizations.

The constitution protects freedom of religion. In the past, the state's official secularism led to restrictions on expressions of religious belief, but since 2010 women have been allowed to wear the Islamic headscarf at universities, and in keeping with an element of the September 2013 democratization package, restrictions were similarly loosened for teachers and other public employees outside the police, military, and judiciary. Female lawmakers from the AKP consequently began wearing headscarves in the parliament in October. Critics have expressed concern about the AKP government's alleged religious agenda—exemplified in a May statement by an AKP official calling for the "annihilation of atheists"—as well as laws that prohibit expression of critical views of religion. In April, Fazıl Say, a renowned Turkish pianist, was convicted under Article 216 of the penal code for insulting religion in comments he made on Twitter, receiving a suspended jail sentence. In May, Sevan Nişanyan, an ethnic Armenian journalist, was sentenced to over a year in prison under the same article for comments he made on a blog.

Three non-Muslim religious groups—Jews, Orthodox Christians, and Armenian Christians—are officially recognized. However, disputes over property, prohibitions on training of clergy, and interference in the internal governance of religious organizations remain concerns. The Alevis, a non-Sunni Muslim group, lack protected status. Historically, they have been targets of violence and discrimination, and their houses of worship—known as cemevis—do not receive state support, as mosques do. The government has made overtures to the Alevi community, but Alevi issues were pointedly not included in the 2013 democratization package. In September, construction began in Ankara on a joint mosque-cemevi complex, which was seen by some as a positive step but also generated some protests and controversy.

Academic freedom is limited by self-censorship and legal or political pressure regarding sensitive topics such as the Kurds, the definition of World War I–era massacres of Armenians as genocide, and the legacy of Mustafa Kemal Atatürk, founder of the Turkish Republic. Scholars linked to the Kurdish issue have been jailed in the anti-KCK campaign. Separately, six scholars, including the former head of the Higher Education Council, were sentenced to jail terms in August 2013 as part of the Ergenekon case. The government has allegedly favored the appointment of more religiously oriented staff at universities and interfered in issues such as the teaching of evolution.

E. Associational and Organizational Rights: 6 / 12 (-1)

Freedoms of association and assembly are protected in the constitution, and Turkey has an active civil society. However, the police have forcibly broken up public gatherings, with the government justifying its actions by citing the need to maintain order and alleging the presence of violent hooligans and radical groups among the protesters. The crackdown on the Gezi protests, labeled a "brutal denial of the right to peaceful assembly" by Amnesty International, received the most scrutiny during 2013, but earlier protests over the demolition of a historic theater in April and May Day demonstrations in Istanbul both featured violence between police and protesters. In August, ahead of the Ergenekon verdicts, police raided the offices of a secularist association, political party, and television station, detaining 20 people for inciting demonstrations. In September, the police forcibly dispersed student protesters at Middle East Technical University in Ankara who had mobilized against plans to build a highway through their campus.

Laws to protect labor unions are in place, and there are four national union confederations. Many trade unions participated in the Gezi protests and other demonstrations in 2013. However, union activity remains limited in practice. Regulations for the recognition of legal strikes are onerous, and penalties for participating in illegal strikes are severe. Union officials were arrested on antiterrorism charges on multiple occasions in 2012, and in February 2013, 169 members of the Confederation of Public Service Workers (KESK) were rounded up in an anti-KCK operation.

F. Rule of Law: 8 / 16 (+1)

The constitution stipulates an independent judiciary, and in June 2012 the parliament passed a long-awaited measure to establish an ombudsman. In practice, however, the government can influence judges through appointments, promotions, and financing. Critics of the government are concerned about pressure put on judges, particularly in cases involving alleged coup plots and journalists. Defense lawyers in KCK cases have themselves been placed under investigation. In September 2013, the Turkish Economic and Social Science Foundation issued a report that criticized flaws in the judicial system, including lengthy detention periods and poor prison conditions. The government has enacted laws and introduced training to prevent torture, but reports of mistreatment continue. During the Gezi protests, the media and human rights groups documented harsh beatings, threats of and actual sexual assault by police, and widespread use of unofficial detention. In September, over 30 police chiefs and riot police were put under investigation for such abuses.

Constitutional amendments in 2010 limited the jurisdiction of military courts to military personnel and removed provisions that prevented the prosecution of leaders of the 1980 military coup, who subsequently went on trial in April 2012. In September 2013, a trial began against 103 defendants, mostly from the military, who were charged with illegal actions linked to the 1997 "soft coup" that removed an elected Islamist government. Many observers have expressed concern that the various trials against military, secularist, and nationalist defendants, including Ergenekon, are politically motivated and rest on flimsy or doctored evidence.

The latest cease-fire between the PKK and the government has improved the security situation in the country. Many past restrictions on the Kurdish language have been lifted, and as a result of the September 2013 democratization package, Kurdish-language education in private schools is now allowed, Kurdish names have been restored to several villages and provinces, a committee has been formed to investigate hate crimes, and a mandatory pledge by schoolchildren that affirms their Turkishness and was viewed as offensive by many Kurds is no longer conducted. Critics of the package argued that these changes, even if fully implemented, remained inadequate. The reforms did not address demands for more autonomy for local governments or the release of the estimated 2,000 to 3,000 people detained under antiterrorism laws in the anti-KCK campaign.

Despite the improved security associated with the PKK cease-fire, the situation along the Syrian border remained tense in 2013. By year's end, Turkey was hosting over 600,000 refugees from Syria's civil war, including Syrian opposition and rebel leaders. In May, car bombs killed over 40 people in the Turkish city of Reyhanli, and the attack was blamed on agents of the Syrian government, prompting some residents to attack Syrian nationals and cars with Syrian license plates.

Homosexual activity is not prohibited, and there was a gay pride parade in Istanbul in June 2013, but LGBT (lesbian, gay, bisexual, and transgender) people are subject to widespread discrimination, police harassment, and occasional violence. In August, the government rejected a proposal to add constitutional protections for LGBT people, and in September, a court issued a ban on an online gay dating platform.

G. Personal Autonomy and Individual Rights: 9 / 16 (-1)

Property rights are generally respected in Turkey, with notable exceptions. Non-Muslim religious communities that lack a corporate legal identity have difficulty owning property or regaining property previously seized by the state. Since 2002, the government has returned $2.5 billion worth of property to Greeks, Jews, and Armenians. In many cases, this was the result of rulings against Turkey by the European Court of Human Rights (ECHR), where a sizable percentage of cases have involved property claims, including 23 of 117 judgments against Turkey in 2012. In September 2013, the ECHR issued additional judgments against Turkey on the property of two Armenian foundations and denial of inheritance to Greek nationals.

The property rights of business owners who displease the government have increasingly come under pressure. In the aftermath of the Gezi protests, companies that were perceived to have supported the demonstrators—including Koç Holding, the country's largest conglomerate—reportedly faced intrusive government inspections, tax audits, and denial of government contracts. Erdoğan had denounced Koç Holding after one of its Istanbul hotels gave shelter to protesters fleeing police tear gas. In November 2013, the government proposed closing private test-preparation centers, many of which are operated under the aegis of the Hizmet movement. This action generated opposition across the political spectrum, both on personal freedom grounds and for restricting private economic activity.

The constitution grants women full equality before the law, but the World Economic Forum ranked Turkey 120 out of 136 countries surveyed in its 2013 Global Gender Gap Index. Only about a third of working-age women participate in the labor force, the lowest rate in Europe. Women hold just 79 seats (14 percent) in the parliament, though this is an increase from 48 after the 2007 elections. Reports of domestic abuse have increased in recent years, and so-called honor crimes continue to occur. A March 2012 report found that 42 percent of Turkish women have been subjected to physical or sexual violence. In August 2012, the Ministry of Family and Social Policies announced its 2012–2015 Action Plan to Combat Violence Against Women, but critics argue that the government has not done enough, focusing more on family integrity than women's rights.

Erdoğan has equated abortion with murder, and while he has backed away from plans to ban the procedure, the government passed measures in February 2013 that would limit access to abortion services. In June, women's groups took part in the Gezi protests and highlighted several issues, including lack of accountability for domestic violence, restrictions on state family-planning services, and the AKP's sexist rhetoric, which has included statements that men and women are not equal and a suggestion that women should have at least three children. In November, Erdoğan caused a major stir by suggesting that government action was necessary to prevent male and female university students from sharing private housing. This aggravated concerns about state imposition of religious values on private life.

Turkmenistan

Political Rights Rating: 7
Civil Liberties Rating: 7
Freedom Rating: 7.0
Freedom Status: Not Free
Electoral Democracy: No

Population: 5,240,000
Capital: Ashgabat

Ten-Year Ratings Timeline For Year Under Review (Political Rights, Civil Liberties, Status)

Year Under Review	2004	2005	2006	2007	2008	2009	2010	2011	2012	2013
Rating	7,7,NF	7,7,NF	7,7,NF	7,7,NF	7,7,NF	7,7,NF	7,7,NF	7,7,NF	7,7,NF	7,7,NF

INTRODUCTION

The government hailed the December 2013 parliamentary elections as the first under a new "multiparty" system, but all participating factions were loyal to President Gurbanguly Berdymukhammedov, and international observers considered the balloting no more free or fair than in the past. In a June by-election, for the first time in its history since independence, a seat in the Mejlis, or parliament, had gone to a member of a party other than the ruling Democratic Party of Turkmenistan (DPT).

A new media law passed with much fanfare in January banned press monopolies and divested the president of his majority stakes in all major newspapers. However, it simply transferred control of the papers to the cabinet of ministers, of which Berdymukhammedov is the head, and other government offices under the president's direct control. The law also banned censorship, but the government nevertheless continues to severely restrict independent media.

POLITICAL RIGHTS: 1 / 40

A. Electoral Process: 0 / 12

None of Turkmenistan's elections since independence in 1991 have been free or fair. The election commission has no meaningful independence from the executive branch. President Berdymukhammedov has maintained all the means and patterns of repression established by his predecessor, Saparmurat Niyazov, whose authoritarian rule lasted from 1985 to 2006. Niyazov's death was followed by the rapid and seemingly well-orchestrated ascent of Berdymukhammedov, then the deputy prime minister, to the position of acting president, in a process that appeared to circumvent constitutional norms. Berdymukhammedov was formally elected to his first five-year presidential term in 2007. Since then, he has gradually removed high-ranking Niyazov loyalists and taken steps to replace Niyazov as the subject of the state's cult of personality.

Under a new constitution approved in 2008, the Mejlis became the sole legislative body and the number of seats expanded from 50 to 125, with members elected to five-year terms from individual districts. The new charter also gave citizens the right to form political parties; a new law outlining the processes necessary for a party's formation was then approved by the Mejlis in 2012. A single deputy from the new Party of Industrialists and Entrepreneurs was seated in the Mejlis following a June 2013 by-election, marking the first time a member of a party other than the ruling DPT had been elected to the legislature. In the December 2013 elections, the DPT took 47 seats, followed by the Federation of Trade Unions with 33, the Women's Union with 16, the Party of Industrialists and Entrepreneurs with 14, and a youth organization and other "citizen groups" with 8 and 7, respectively. Despite this new appearance of pluralism, the Mejlis remained under the president's absolute control.

Turkmenistan's last presidential election was held in February 2012. While Berdymukhammedov had promised that the polls would include opposition candidates and adhere to international norms, all seven of his challengers were minor figures associated with the DPT. Berdymukhammedov was reelected to a second five-year term with 97 percent of the vote and 96 percent turnout, according to the election commission.

B. Political Pluralism and Participation: 1 / 16

The DPT, formerly the Soviet-era Communist Party of Turkmenistan, was the only party permitted to operate legally and field candidates for elections until 2013. The 2012 law on political parties specified the legal basis for any citizen to form an independent party, and barred parties formed on professional, regional, or religious lines, among other restrictions. Shortly after the law was passed, Berdymukhammedov announced plans to form two new political parties—the Agrarian Party and the Party of Entrepreneurs and Industrialists. His announcement violated two sections of the new law, by proposing profession-based parties and tasking a government official with their creation. Both parties were openly organized by sitting members of the DPT; only the latter ultimately registered and participated in the 2013 elections. Aside from the DPT and the Party of Entrepreneurs and Industrialists, the entities that won seats were unions and civic groups, all affiliated with the state.

C. Functioning of Government: 0 / 12

Corruption is widespread. Many individuals holding public office are widely understood to have bribed their way into their positions. The government's lack of transparency affects nearly all spheres of the economy and public services. According to a 2013 article published by the exile-based Turkmen Initiative for Human Rights in cooperation with Global Witness and the Eurasian Transition Group, bribes are needed to accomplish ordinary tasks like placing a student in a university or obtaining medical care. Moreover, decisions to award large-scale contracts to foreign companies are ultimately made by the president without any effective legal controls or oversight, and bribes are a key part of the process.

Allocation of state profits from hydrocarbon exports remains opaque. A 2011 amendment to the 2008 Law on Hydrocarbon Resources expanded the president's near-total control over the hydrocarbon sector and the revenue it produces; additional amendments in 2012 allowed the state agency for hydrocarbon resources to establish companies, buy a direct stake in foreign companies, and open branches abroad. According to a 2011 report by Crude Accountability, an environmental group that works in the Caspian Sea region, only 20 percent of revenues from the sale of state-owned hydrocarbons are transferred to the state budget; the rest is controlled by the hydrocarbon agency, which is directly subordinate to the president.

Turkmenistan was ranked 168 out of 177 countries and territories surveyed in Transparency International's 2013 Corruption Perceptions Index.

CIVIL LIBERTIES: 6 / 60

D. Freedom of Expression and Belief: 2 / 16

Freedom of the press is severely restricted by the government, which controls nearly all broadcast and print media. Turkmenistan's main internet service provider, run by the government, blocks undesirable websites and monitors users' activity. The authorities remained hostile to news reporting in 2013, and sought to suppress any independent sources of information. Although the new media law passed in January banned press monopolies and censorship, the government continues to severely restrict independent media. The very few independent reporters that still operate in Turkmenistan risk detention by the authorities; rights groups suspect that imprisoned journalists are subject to torture.

The government restricts freedom of religion. Practicing an unregistered religion remains illegal, with violators subject to fines. In 2010, an Islamic cleric reportedly died in prison under unclear circumstances.

The government places significant restrictions on academic freedom. Since 2009, students bound for university study abroad have routinely been denied exit visas.

E. Associational and Organizational Rights: 0 / 12

The constitution guarantees freedoms of peaceful assembly and association, but in practice, these rights are severely restricted. Sporadic protests, usually focused on social issues, have taken place in recent years. A 2003 law on nongovernmental organizations (NGOs) deprived all such groups of their registration; the few groups that were subsequently reregistered are tightly controlled. Turkmenistan is still home to a few dedicated activists, but there is virtually no organized civil society sector. The government-controlled Association of Trade Unions of Turkmenistan is the only central trade union permitted. Workers are barred by law from bargaining collectively or staging strikes.

F. Rule of Law: 1 / 16

The judicial system is subservient to the president, who appoints and removes judges without legislative review. The authorities frequently deny rights of due process, including public trials and access to defense attorneys. According to a 2013 report by Amnesty International, methods of torture used by security forces against criminal suspects include "electric shocks, asphyxiation, rape, forcibly administering psychotropic drugs, deprivation of food and drink, and exposure to extreme cold." Prisons suffer from overcrowding, and prisoners are poorly fed and denied access to adequate medical care. The U.S. Department of State characterizes prison conditions as "unsanitary, overcrowded, harsh, and life threatening."

The government has released a number of political prisoners since Niyazov's death, but many others remain behind bars. Nothing is known about the condition of jailed former foreign ministers Boris Shikhmuradov and Batyr Berdyev, and some 28 others. Rights activists Annakurban Amanklychev and Sapardurdy Khajiev, convicted on dubious espionage charges in 2006, were finally freed at the end of their scheduled terms in February 2013. Unanswered questions still surround the 2006 death in custody of Radio Free Europe/Radio Liberty correspondent Ogulsapar Muradova, who was convicted in the same trial.

Employment and educational opportunities for ethnic minorities are limited by the government's promotion of Turkmen national identity. The law does not protect LGBT (lesbian, gay, bisexual, and transgender) people from discrimination, and traditional social taboos make even discussion of LGBT issues difficult. Sexual activity between men is illegal in Turkmenistan and punishable with up to two years in prison and an additional term of up to five years in a labor camp.

G. Personal Autonomy and Individual Rights: 3 / 16

Freedom of movement is restricted, with a reported blacklist preventing some individuals from leaving the country. A few activists who hold dual citizenship and continue to reside in Turkmenistan are able to travel abroad using their Russian passports. In June 2013, the government approved the issuance of Turkmen travel documents for tens of thousands of Turkmen-Russian dual citizens who had spent years with no clear legal status after the Turkmen parliament in 2003 approved a measure revoking a dual-citizenship pact with Russia.

A Soviet-style command economy and widespread corruption diminish equality of opportunity. The constitution establishes the right to private property, but the deeply flawed judiciary provides little protection to businesses and individuals. Arbitrary evictions and confiscation of property are common practices.

Traditional social and religious norms, inadequate education, and poor economic conditions limit professional opportunities for women, and NGO reports suggest that domestic violence is common.

Tuvalu

Political Rights Rating: 1
Civil Liberties Rating: 1
Freedom Rating: 1.0
Freedom Status: Free
Electoral Democracy: Yes

Population: 10,000
Capital: Funafuti

Ten-Year Ratings Timeline For Year Under Review (Political Rights, Civil Liberties, Status)

Year Under Review	2004	2005	2006	2007	2008	2009	2010	2011	2012	2013
Rating	1,1,F	1,1,F	1,1,F	1,1,F	1,1,F	1,1,F	1,1,F	1,1,F	1,1,F	1,1,F

INTRODUCTION

For several months, Prime Minister Willy Telavi used legal and political maneuvering to forestall opposition attempts to remove him from office through a no-confidence vote. After the sudden death of Finance Minister Lotoaloa Metia in December 2012, Telavi repeatedly delayed the by-election to elect Metia's replacement. Once the High Court ruled the by-election be held, Teavi refused to convene parliament leading to Governor General Iakoba Italei's order to reconvene the parliament. On August 3, the opposition, now holding a majority in the 15-member parliament after the Metia by-election, ousted Telavi and elected Enele Sopoaga prime minister.

Tuvalu faces a serious threat from global climate change and rising sea levels. Additionally, scarce rainfall has resulted in a dangerously low fresh water supply and declarations of state of emergency. In August, a climate change adaptation agreement with the United Nations Development Program was signed to bring in economic assistance to protect local fisheries and to fund disaster management.

POLITICAL RIGHTS: 37 / 40
A. Electoral Process: 12 /12

Britain's Queen Elizabeth II is the head of state and is represented by a governor general, who must be a citizen of Tuvalu. The prime minister, chosen by Parliament, leads the government. The unicameral, 15-member Parliament is elected to four-year terms. A six-person council administers each of the country's nine atolls. Council members are chosen by universal suffrage for four-year terms. In the October 2010 general elections, 26 candidates—all independents—competed. Within two months, a no-confidence vote ousted Prime Minister Maatia Toafa and parliament replaced him with Willy Telavi. Telavi held on to power till August 2013 when the opposition ousted him with a no-confidence vote and chose Enele Sopoaga to replace him.

B. Political Pluralism and Participation: 15 / 16

There are no formal political parties, though there are no laws against their formation. Political allegiances revolve around geography, tribal loyalties, and personalities. Intense personal and political rivalries frequently prompt new alliances and no-confidence votes to change governments.

C. Functioning of Government: 10 / 12

Tuvalu is one of the few places in the Pacific Islands where corruption is less severe, though international donors have called for improvements in governance. About 10 percent of its annual budget comes from an overseas investment fund set up by Britain, Australia, and South Korea in 1987 to provide development assistance. Sales of fishing licenses, lease of its internet suffix (.tv), and remittances from Tuvalu workers overseas also supplement the state budget.

CIVIL LIBERTIES: 57 / 60
D. Freedom of Expression and Belief: 16 /16

The constitution provides for freedoms of speech and the press, and the government generally respects these rights in practice. The semi-public Tuvalu Media Corporation (TMC) operates the country's sole radio and television stations, as well as the biweekly newspaper *Tuvalu Echoes* and the government newsletter *Sikuelo o Tuvalu*. Human rights groups have criticized the TMC for its limited coverage of politics and human rights issues, but there have been no allegations of censorship or imbalances in reporting. Many residents use satellite dishes to access foreign programming. Internet use is largely limited to the capital because of cost and connectivity challenges, but authorities do not restrict access.

Religious freedom is upheld in this overwhelmingly Christian country, where religion is a major part of life. Academic freedom is generally respected.

E. Associational and Organizational Rights: 12 / 12

The constitution provides for freedoms of association and assembly, and the government upholds these rights in practice. Nongovernmental organizations provide a variety of health, education, and other services.

Workers have the right to strike, organize unions, and choose their own representatives for collective bargaining. With two-thirds of the population engaged in subsistence farming and fishing, Tuvalu has only one registered trade union with about 600 members who work on foreign merchant vessels. Public sector employees—fewer than 1,000—are members of professional associations that do not have union status.

F. Rule of Law: 15 / 16

The judiciary is independent and provides fair trials. Tuvalu has a two-tier judicial system. The higher courts include the Privy Council in London, the Court of Appeal, and the High Court. The lower courts consist of senior and resident magistrates, the island courts, and the land courts. The chief justice, who is also the chief justice of Tonga, visits twice a year to preside over the High Court. A civilian-controlled constabulary force maintains internal order. There are no reports of abuse in the prison system. Jails meet minimum standards, but limited capacity can mean long waits in the legal system and restricted access to proper counsel.

Sexual relationships between men are illegal and punishable by up to 15 years in prison. To date, no one has been charged or imprisoned.

G. Personal Autonomy and Individual Rights: 14 / 16

Traditional customs and social norms condone discrimination against women and limit their role in society. Women enjoy equal access to education, but they are underrepresented in positions of leadership in business and government. There are currently no women in Parliament. No law specifically addresses sexual harassment. There have been few reports of violence against women. Rape is illegal, but spousal rape is not included in the definition.

Uganda

Political Rights Rating: 6↓
Civil Liberties Rating: 4
Freedom Rating: 5.0
Freedom Status: Partly Free
Electoral Democracy: No

Population: 36,890,500
Capital: Kampala

Ratings Change: Uganda's political rights rating declined from 5 to 6 due to the continued, repeated harassment and arrest of prominent opposition leaders, the passage of the Public Order Management Bill to further restrict opposition and civil society activity, and new evidence of the limited space for alternative voices within the ruling National Resistance Movement.

Ten-Year Ratings Timeline For Year Under Review (Political Rights, Civil Liberties, Status)

Year Under Review	2004	2005	2006	2007	2008	2009	2010	2011	2012	2013
Rating	5,4,PF	5,4,PF	5,4,PF	5,4,PF	5,4,PF	5,4,PF	5,4,PF	5,4,PF	5,4,PF	6,4,PF

INTRODUCTION

In 2013, President Yoweri Museveni governed in an increasingly repressive manner, attempting to muzzle the political opposition, civil society, independent media, and dissidents within his long-ruling National Resistance Movement (NRM). Nevertheless, these groups generally remained resilient, continuing to challenge Museveni's government on sensitive issues including corruption, transparency in the oil sector, and the condition of the economy.

In May, a major controversy erupted when the widely read, independent *Daily Monitor* newspaper published a letter written by highly influential Gen. David Sejusa warning of an alleged plot to assassinate senior officials who opposed a plan for Museveni's son, Brig. Muhoozi Kainerugaba, to succeed him as president. The police questioned *Daily Monitor* editors and reporters in an effort to obtain the source of the letter, and eventually raided the *Daily Monitor* and the tabloid *Red Pepper*, which had also reported on the letter. The raid led to the temporary closure of the papers and of two radio stations that shared a building with the *Daily Monitor*, prompting street protests by local press freedom groups and condemnation from local and international advocacy groups.

Throughout the year, there were numerous confrontations between authorities and opposition figures, including former Forum for Democratic Change (FDC) presidential candidate Kizza Besigye and embattled Kampala mayor Erias Lukwago. Both were arrested numerous times and police used force to disperse organized opposition rallies as well as spontaneous gatherings that erupted when Besigye managed to elude his near-constant police minders.

In August, the National Assembly passed the Public Order Management Bill, which significantly expanded the government's power to restrict freedom of assembly and expression by imposing broad new limitations on "public meetings." In December, the assembly passed the Anti-Homosexuality Bill, which imposed harsher penalties for same-sex sexual relations as well as the "promotion" of homosexuality. Both bills were condemned by international human rights groups as a violation of international standards.

POLITICAL RIGHTS: 11 / 40 (-1)
A. Electoral Process: 3 / 12

Uganda's single-chamber National Assembly and the powerful president are elected for five-year terms. Of the legislature's 386 members, 238 are directly elected and 137 are indirectly elected from special interest groups including women, the military, youth, the disabled, and trade unions. Eleven ex-officio seats are held by cabinet ministers, who are not elected and do not have voting rights. In 2005, voters approved a package of constitutional amendments in which a ban on political parties was lifted in exchange for an end to presidential term limits.

Museveni, a former rebel leader who took power in 1986, won the February 2011 presidential election with 68 percent of the vote. Besigye, who had been cleared of treason, terrorism, murder, and firearms charges in 2010, placed second with 26 percent. In concurrent parliamentary elections, the NRM took 263 of 375 elected seats, followed by the FDC with 34. According to observers from the European Union (EU) and the Commonwealth, the elections were undermined by flawed administration, extensive state media bias, and government spending on behalf of the ruling party. Museveni and his party exploited the advantages of incumbency; observers criticized the passage of a $256 million supplementary budget shortly before the election, with much of the funds going to the president's office.

Despite questions over the independence of the electoral commission, Museveni renewed the panel and its chairman for a second seven-year term in 2009.

B. Political Pluralism and Participation: 5 / 16 (-1)

The NRM is the dominant party, and the FDC is the main opposition party. There are significant concerns about the ability of the opposition to compete with the ruling NRM. The opposition is hindered by harassment of its leaders; restrictive party registration requirements, voter, and candidate eligibility rules; the use of government resources to support NRM candidates; a lack of access to state media coverage; and paramilitary groups—such as the Kiboko Squad and the Black Mambas—that intimidate voters and government opponents. The passage of the Public Order Management Bill further infringed on the opposition's ability to freely hold rallies and meet with constituents.

As in previous years, Besigye, the former FDC leader who was now led the banned For God and My Country (4GC) political pressure group—as well as Lukwago and other top opposition figures were subject to frequent arrest and harassment in 2013. Besigye's home was under near-constant surveillance and his movements closely tracked by the police, making it extremely difficult for him to lead rallies or even move freely among the public. In July, police carried out a "preventive arrest" of Besigye as he was leaving his home, on the grounds that he was planning illegal rallies, after 4GC announced upcoming economic demonstrations. The group launched another round of such protests in November; those protests were dispersed and Besigye was again arrested and charged with belonging to an unlawful society.

In late November, Lukwago, after months of conflict with the Kampala Capital City Authority (KCCA)—which had already taken over many of city mayor's powers under 2010 legislation—was impeached on the grounds of incompetence and abuse of office, in the wake of a report by a government-appointed tribunal into his conduct as mayor. On the day of the impeachment, nearly 20 journalists were prevented from covering the proceedings, in Kampala's City Hall. Lukwago's lawyer was roughed up by the police; and protests against the impeachment were reportedly dispersed violently. Three days after the impeachment, a High Court judge issued a ruling staying the implementation of the report that had led to Lukwago's impeachment. As of the end of 2013, a court was still considering whether the KCCA's impeachment of Lukwago was legal.

NRM legislators have recently attempted to assert some independence from Museveni by censuring high-level executive officials, seeking greater transparency in Uganda's growing oil sector, and exercising oversight to influence a number of government actions and policies. However, in April 2013 the NRM expelled four legislators for "indiscipline"; according to NRM leaders, the four had committed offenses including participating in a group that challenged the party's oil policy and voicing criticism of Museveni. The legislators challenged their expulsion in the Supreme Court, which began hearing the case in September and had not reached a decision by year's end.

The military, controlled by Museveni, exerts a powerful role behind the scenes. The May controversy over the letter by Sejusa—the coordinator of intelligence services—made public the extent of military involvement in the government. The publication of the letter, to the director general of the Internal Security Organisation, prompted Sejusa to flee to the United Kingdom; he continued to denounce Museveni's regime from exile. In June, Kainerugaba denied that there was a plan for him to succeed his father, but indicated that he might have his own political ambitions. Sejusa, who was one of the 10 military members of parliament, was dismissed from that role in November after being absent without permission for a lengthy period of time.

In July, Museveni swore in Gen. Aronda Nyakairima as internal affairs minister despite ambiguity surrounding the constitutionality of appointing active military personnel to the cabinet. The constitution bars armed forces members from seeking political office. The inspector general of police, Gen. Kale Kayihura, is also a member of the military.

C. Functioning of Government: 3 / 12

Although Uganda has a variety of laws and institutions tasked with combating corruption, enforcement is weak in practice. In July 2013, the Constitutional Court suspended one of these institutions—the Anti-Corruption Court—a specialized branch within the High Court, after a lawyer filed a petition challenging its composition. The Constitutional Court ruled in late December that its members were indeed legally appointed, and it was set to reopen in early 2014. In late 2012, the EU and several European nations had frozen aid to Uganda in response to a report by the auditor general's office revealing that $13 million in donor money had been embezzled by Prime Minister Amama Mbabazi's office. In January 2013, Uganda paid back $5.4 million to Ireland; it has reportedly repaid other European donors as well. However, instead of taking concrete action on promises of reform in the wake of this scandal, the government in 2013 stepped up its harassment of anticorruption activists. An October 2013 report by Human Rights Watch and Yale Law School's Allard K. Lowenstein International Human Rights Clinic found that despite the recent high-profile scandals and investigations, as well as the laws and institutions that exist to combat corruption, no top government official had ever been imprisoned for corruption in Uganda.

Uganda was ranked 140 out of 177 countries and territories surveyed in Transparency International's 2013 Corruption Perceptions Index. Uganda was also rated last in the agency's 2013 East African Bribery Index.

In December 2012, the National Assembly passed the Petroleum Bill, which gave wide-ranging powers over the sector to the energy minister and was criticized by the opposition and international monitoring groups such as Global Witness for the lack of parliamentary or independent oversight of the energy minister's decisions.

CIVIL LIBERTIES: 26 / 40 (-2)

D. Freedom of Expression and Belief: 10 / 16 (-1)

The constitution provides for freedom of expression and of the press; however, these rights are often undermined by provisions in the penal code, including laws on criminal libel and treason, as well as by extralegal actions by the government. The media sector has flourished in the last decade, with nearly 200 private radio stations and dozens of television stations and print outlets. Independent journalists are often critical of the government, but in recent years they have faced substantial, escalating government restrictions and intimidation, which encourage self-censorship. Continuing a pattern from previous years, throughout 2013 journalists were regularly prevented from covering opposition-related events or were attacked while doing so, summoned for questioning about content they had produced, or verbally threatened by officials. In covering these events, police often assumed journalists to be opposition supporters rather than neutral observers.

Numerous press freedom violations were recorded during the confrontation between the authorities and the *Daily Monitor* in May. The authorities initially sought to obtain the source of Sejusa's letter by summoning the authors of the story and a *Daily Monitor* editor to police headquarters. After the *Monitor* employees refused to turn over the information, the police on May 20 carried out a court order to search the *Daily Monitor*'s offices as well as the offices of *Red Pepper*, leading to the closure of both papers. Police also shut down two of the *Daily Monitor*'s sister radio stations, KFM and Dembe FM. The court order was revoked two days later; however, the police continued their search for the letter and the outlets remained closed. The search continued despite reports that the police had obtained a copy of the letter from another source, leading to allegations that the shutdown was being used as a tactic to intimidate the *Daily Monitor*. When journalists and media freedom groups staged a march and sit-in outside the *Daily Monitor* offices to protest the shutdown, police responded with force, injuring several protesters and arresting three. The impasse was eventually resolved at the end of May after a meeting between the heads of the Nation Media Group (NMG), which owned the *Daily Monitor*, and Museveni and other top government officials; however, the NMG apparently agreed to certain conditions that could compromise the editorial integrity of the *Daily Monitor*.

In December, parliament passed the Anti-Pornography Bill—also known as the "Miniskirt Bill" for its provisions to ban short skirts and other clothing deemed sexually explicit. The legislation defines pornography in broad terms and sets up a nine-member Pornography Control Committee with wide-ranging powers to determine what amounts to pornographic material. The committee is also mandated to develop software that would allow internet service providers to monitor websites for pornography. Critics and free expression advocates expressed concern that media outlets and websites could easily violate the law due to its sweeping and opaque provisions.

There is no state religion, and freedom of worship is constitutionally protected and respected in practice. Academic freedom is also generally respected.

E. Associational and Organizational Rights: 4 / 12

Freedom of assembly is officially recognized but is restricted in practice. Since leading a "walk to work" campaign of marches against corruption and the rising cost of living in 2011, Besigye has been arrested numerous times, as have other opposition leaders, and their freedom of movement and expression has been severely curtailed. In August 2013, the National Assembly passed the Public Order Management Bill, which severely restricts freedom of assembly. Among the most repressive provisions of the bill, groups are required to register with the local police in writing three days before any gathering to discuss political issues, either in public or in private. The police have broad authority to deny approval for such meetings if they are not deemed to be in the "public interest," or if another event is planned at the same time. Certain sites, such as the areas around the parliament and court buildings, are off-limits. The bill also authorizes the use of force to disperse assemblies deemed unlawful; makes no provision for the protection of media members covering the assemblies; and allows for organizers to be held liable for any criminal conduct by third parties.

Freedom of association is guaranteed in the constitution and the law but is often restricted; nevertheless, civil society in Uganda remains vibrant. Several nongovernmental organizations (NGOs) address politically sensitive issues, but their existence and activities are vulnerable to legal restrictions, including the manipulation of burdensome registration requirements under the 2006 NGO Registration Amendment Act. In 2013, the National NGO Board, which regulates NGOs under the act, announced that the more than 10,000 NGOs in Uganda would be required to "update their files" via a form on the Ministry of Internal Affairs website (which was reportedly difficult to access), starting September 1 and ending November 29. The board stated that any group failing to do so within the required period was subject to deregistration. However, amid strong objections for the NGO community, the board dropped this requirement in October.

In 2013, the government continued to harass civil society groups that advocate for sensitive issues, such as combating corruption, transparency in the oil sector, and LGBT (lesbian, gay, bisexual, and transgender) rights. On at least three occasions during 2013, police arrested activists who were part of the Black Monday coalition of anticorruption civil society groups. Meanwhile, other NGOs that focus on issues such as service delivery are largely allowed to operate freely.

Workers' rights to organize, bargain collectively, and strike are recognized by law, except for those providing essential government services, but legal protections often go unenforced. Many private firms refuse to recognize unions, and strikers are sometimes arrested.

F. Rule of Law: 5 / 16 (-1)

Executive influence undermines judicial independence. In July, Museveni reappointed 70-year-old Benjamin Odoki as chief justice of the Supreme Court, despite that fact that Odoki was past the age of mandatory retirement; the reappointment was being challenged in Constitutional Court.

Prolonged pretrial detention, inadequate resources, and poor judicial administration impede the fair exercise of justice. The country has also faced criticism over the military's repeated interference with court processes. The prison system is reportedly operating at nearly three times its intended capacity, with pretrial detainees constituting more than half of the prison population. Rape, vigilante justice, and torture and abuse of suspects and detainees by security forces remain problems. The Joint Anti-Terrorism Task Force, established under the 2002 Anti-Terrorism Act, has committed many of the worst rights abuses. It reportedly has stepped up its efforts in the wake of bombings in Kampala in 2010 by the Somali Islamist group Al-Shabaab, illegally detaining and abusing terrorism suspects as well as expanding the scope of the law to crack down on the political opposition. The Kampala attack was in retaliation for Uganda's leading role in the African Union (AU) peacekeeping mission in Somalia. Security was stepped up after Al-Shabaab's deadly September 2013 terrorist attack on the Westgate shopping mall in neighboring Kenya.

Northern Uganda continues to struggle to recover economically from 20 years of attacks by the cult-like rebel group the Lord's Resistance Army (LRA), with residents of the region voicing allegations of neglect by the central government and corruption related to donor funds earmarked for the north. The LRA has not staged attacks in Uganda itself since 2005, but Uganda had a leading role in an international effort to eliminate the group from neighboring countries.

Uganda's society and government is overtly prejudiced against gays and lesbians, creating a climate of fear and insecurity for members of the LGBT community. In December 2013, the National Assembly passed the Anti-Homosexuality Bill, which had been surrounded by international controversy since it was first introduced in 2009. If signed by Museveni in 2014, the bill would toughen penalties for same-sex relations in a number of areas, including mandating a 14-year prison sentence for a first conviction of same-sex sexual behavior, with a lifetime sentence for repeat offenders or those convicted of "aggravated homosexuality." It would punish individuals for the "promotion" of homosexuality and for not reporting violations within 24 hours, potentially threatening health workers and advocates for LGBT rights. It would also endanger freedom of expression by imposing penalties on speech seen as sympathetic to the LGBT community. Even before the bill's passage, societal and legal harassment of the LGBT community continued unabated. In mid-November 2013, prominent activist Samuel Ganafa was arrested on charges of infecting another man, Disan Twesiga, with HIV. Ganafa alleged that police searched his home without a warrant and that he was involuntarily tested for HIV. Also in November, Briton Bernard Randall went on trial for trafficking obscene publications after a newspaper published photos of him having sex with his partner, Albert Cheptoyek; the photos had been obtained from a video on a laptop that was stolen from Randall's home. Randall, 65, faced a two-year sentence. Cheptoyek was charged with the more serious offense of engaging in "acts of gross indecency," which carried up to a seven-year prison term. Their cases had yet to be decided as of the end of 2013.

G. Personal Autonomy and Individual Rights: 7 / 16

Travel is largely unrestricted; however, the government has occasionally enforced travel restrictions for security purposes, particularly in the north. Bribery is common practice in many facets of life, such as interacting with traffic police and in gaining admittance to some institutions of higher education. Licenses are required for starting a business, construction permits, and to register property, and the multistage processes involve numerous public officials who are in a position to extract bribes.

Although Articles 2(2) and 21(2) of the constitution prohibit discrimination on the basis of gender and acknowledge the equal rights of women, gender discrimination remains pronounced, particularly in rural areas. Women hold nearly 35 percent of the National Assembly seats, and one-third of local council seats are reserved for women. The law gives women the right to inherit land, but discriminatory customs often trump legal provisions in practice. A proposed Marriage and Divorce Bill, which would have required asset-sharing in cases of divorce and explicitly made marital rape illegal, was debated at length in parliament but did not pass by year's end. Rape and domestic violence are widespread and underreported, and offenders are often not prosecuted. Cultural practices such as female genital mutilation persist. Sexual abuse of minors is a significant problem. Ritual sacrifice of abducted children has reportedly increased in recent years, with wealthier individuals paying for the killings to secure good fortune. Uganda continues to be a source and destination country for men, women, and children trafficked for the purposes of forced labor and prostitution.

↓ Ukraine

Political Rights Rating: 4
Civil Liberties Rating: 3
Freedom Rating: 3.5
Freedom Status: Partly Free
Electoral Democracy: Yes

Population: 45,500,000
Capital: Kyiv

Trend Arrow: Ukraine received a downward trend arrow due to violence against journalists and media manipulation associated with the controversy over President Viktor Yanukovych's decision to forego a European Union agreement and accept a financial assistance package from Russia—a decision made without public consultation and against the wishes of a large portion of the Ukrainian people.

Ten-Year Ratings Timeline For Year Under Review (Political Rights, Civil Liberties, Status)

Year Under Review	2004	2005	2006	2007	2008	2009	2010	2011	2012	2013
Rating	4,3,PF	3,2,F	3,2,F	3,2,F	3,2,F	3,2,F	3,3,PF	4,3,PF	4,3,PF	4,3,PF

INTRODUCTION

Domestic political life for much of 2013 revolved around President Viktor Yanukovych's unrelenting efforts to tilt the playing field in his favor in advance of the March 2015 presidential election. The unpopular president worked to eliminate potential opponents from the race, stack the electoral commission, strengthen his control of the judiciary, and exert greater influence over the media. Although the country's business magnates, or "oligarchs," often had separate interests from Yanukovych's, they were careful not to assert them forcefully and risk costly repercussions.

As the growth of its unreformed economy ground to a halt, Ukraine came under increasing pressure to choose an orientation toward Russia or the European Union. Yanukovych made it clear during the year that he intended to initial an Association Agreement with the EU at a November 28–29 summit in Vilnius, but with only days left before the gathering, on November 21, he abruptly decided not to proceed with the deal.

Yanukovych apparently chose to forego the EU agreement because he calculated that it would be the best way to preserve his political power. Moving closer to the EU would have forced long-delayed political, economic, and legal reforms on Ukraine. While such reforms could stimulate economic growth in the long term, they would impose short-term difficulties that might have undermined Yanukovych's ability to win reelection. Most importantly, the EU demanded that Yanukovych release former prime minister Yuliya Tymoshenko, potentially his most formidable political rival, from jail. Ukraine's pliant courts had sentenced her to seven years in prison in 2011 on the grounds that she had abused her power while in office by signing a deal that allowed Russia to charge more for natural gas than the judge deemed fair. The case was widely seen as politically motivated, and in May 2013 the prosecutor general filed murder charges against Tymoshenko to further undermine her standing. Yanukovych reportedly feared releasing her with a full pardon, which would allow her to resume an active political role and endanger his reelection bid in 2015. As the Vilnius summit drew closer, Yanukovych was urged to release Tymoshenko for medical treatment in Germany without giving her a pardon, effectively sending her into exile. However, no such decision was made, and she remained in prison at year's end.

Another crucial factor behind Yanukovych's failure to conclude the EU pact was increasing pressure from Russia, against the backdrop of a fiscal crisis that put Ukraine on the verge of defaulting on its foreign debts. During the latter part of the year, Yanukovych met with Russian president Vladimir Putin several times for secret negotiations, and after he backed away from the EU agreement, Putin on December 17 pledged to lend Ukraine $15 billion (in $3 billion installments and for just two years) and cut natural gas prices by a third (though the price is reviewed every three months). Moreover, unlike the EU, Putin raised no objections to Yanukovych's authoritarian bent or Tymoshenko's imprisonment, and demanded no economic reforms. Neither leader explained what Ukraine would provide in return for the Kremlin's assistance. An Association Agreement between the EU and Ukraine would have been a major defeat for Putin, who counted on Ukraine becoming a key member of a Russian-sponsored Customs Union. But despite his apparent tilt toward Russia, Yanukovych continued to claim that he wanted to work with the EU.

Immediately after Yanukovych announced that he would not sign the EU agreement, supporters of closer ties with Europe began to occupy Kyiv's Maidan Nezalezhnosti (Independence Square) and several nearby buildings, including city hall, remaining in place through the end of the year. Smaller protests were mounted in cities across the country. The Kyiv protests included a permanent encampment of several thousand people, with crowds swelling to hundreds of thousands on evenings and weekends for political speeches and concerts. A police attempt to clear the square on November 30, accompanied by savage beatings, drew many more protesters to the city center. In addition, unidentified assailants targeted activists and journalists in many regions. The leaders of Ukraine's main opposition parties sought to ensure that the protests remained peaceful, particularly watching for so-called *titushki*, young thugs hired by the authorities to carry out assaults. Meanwhile, some observers raised questions about the role and democratic credentials of the radical nationalist party Svoboda, which was crucial in organizing the protests.

Following the police violence, the main demands of the protesters were the resignation of Yanukovych and the holding of early presidential and parliamentary elections, but the government appeared unlikely to comply, and the crisis remained unresolved at year's end.

POLITICAL RIGHTS: 20 / 40 (-1)
A. Electoral Process: 8 / 12

The president is elected to a maximum of two five-year terms. In the 2010 presidential election, which met most international standards, Yanukovych defeated Tymoshenko in the second round of voting, 49 percent to 46 percent. He quickly reversed many of the changes adopted in the wake of the 2004 Orange Revolution, securing Constitutional Court rulings that enabled him to oust Tymoshenko as prime minister and replace her with a loyalist, and to annul the 2004 constitutional compromise that had reduced the power of the presidency. Under the restored 1996 constitution, the president issues decrees; exercises power over the courts, the military, and law enforcement agencies; appoints the prime minister with the parliament's approval and removes the prime minister at will; appoints and fires all other ministers without the parliament's approval; and appoints regional governors without consulting the prime minister. The parliament can dismiss the entire cabinet, but not individual ministers. The expansion of presidential power raised serious questions about whether the next presidential election in March 2015 would be free and fair.

Citizens elect delegates to the Verkhovna Rada (Supreme Council), the 450-seat unicameral parliament, for four-year terms. The 2004 constitutional amendments, which were annulled in 2010, had extended this term to five years. Under the ruling Party of Regions, the parliament has largely become a rubber-stamp body. According to a new electoral law adopted in December 2011, Ukraine returned to a system in which half of the members are elected by proportional representation and half in single-member districts; blocs of parties are not allowed to participate. In the 2012 parliamentary elections, the Party of Regions retained a plurality with 185 seats, followed by Tymoshenko's Fatherland with 101, professional boxer Vitaliy Klychko's Ukrainian Democratic Alliance for Reform (UDAR) with 40, the radical nationalist Svoboda party with 37, and the Communist Party with 32. Independents won 43 seats, and four small parties divided the remainder. As expected, and in sharp contrast with the other major parties, the Party of Regions won most of its seats in the revived single-member districts, giving it enough seats overall to forge working parliamentary majorities with the Communist Party and independents. Five seats remained unfilled because ballot tampering made it impossible to determine the winner, though the opposition claimed that they had won the seats. Legislation inspired by the EU and adopted in September 2013 cleared the way to hold fresh elections in those districts. Amid widespread allegations of misconduct, the elections held on December 15 produced victory for the opposition in only one seat, with the rest effectively going to the Party of Regions.

In May 2013, the Constitutional Court approved the postponement of Kyiv's mayoral and city council elections to October 2015, well after the March 2015 presidential election. It was clear that a fair vote would remove Yanukovych's ally, acting mayor Galyna Hereha, from city hall. The last elected mayor had resigned in mid-2012. The head of the city administration holds the real power in Kyiv, and this post was occupied by Oleksandr Popov until mid-December 2013, when Yanukovych replaced him in response to the failed November 30 effort to clear protesters from the central square by force. The acting city administrator at year's end was Popov's first deputy, Anatoliy Holubchenko.

In July Yanukovych appointed Mykhailo Okhendovsky as the head of the Central Electoral Commission, ensuring that the body was led by an ally ahead of the presidential election. He also appointed another member, Oleksandr Kopylenko, to the commission, provoking objections from the opposition, which argued that he had ignored his legal obligation to consult the parliament first.

B. Political Pluralism and Participation: 8 / 16 (-1)

Political parties are typically little more than vehicles for their leaders and financial backers, and they generally lack coherent ideologies or policy platforms.

Yanukovych has sought to eliminate potential 2015 presidential challengers by keeping Tymoshenko in jail and signing legislation in November 2013 that was designed to prevent Klychko from running because he has residency status in Germany. Klychko had formally announced his candidacy for the office in October and protested the adoption of the legislation. In another blow against Tymoshenko's party, police raided its offices on December 9 and confiscated its computer servers.

Both the Kremlin and Yanukovych's inner circle of relatives and associates, known as the "Family," exercise undue influence over the country's political affairs. During the countdown to the EU summit in November 2013, Russia, which accounted for 26 percent of Ukrainian commodities exports and 39 percent of services exports in 2012, put heavy pressure on Ukraine to dissuade it from going through with the Association Agreement. The Russian government imposed significant trade restrictions on Ukrainian exports to Russia and charged Ukraine a higher price for natural gas than that paid by European customers. Putin aide Sergey Glazyev warned in October that signing the Association Agreement would be "suicidal" for Ukraine. After Yanukovych rejected the EU deal, without public consultation, Russia responded with loans and reduced gas prices. The opaque change of course effectively served the short-term personal interests of Yanukovych and his allies while forestalling reform and potentially harming long-term national interests.

C. Functioning of Government: 4 / 12

Corruption, one of the country's most serious problems, continues to worsen. Business magnates benefit financially from their close association with top politicians. A *Forbes* study has shown that businessmen affiliated with the Party of Regions win a considerable portion of state tenders. Yanukovych has become the de facto owner of a huge estate outside of Kyiv, raising suspicions of illicit wealth, and his two sons have amassed both power and immense personal fortunes. The corruption of the administration, and the precedent set by its politicized pursuit of charges against Tymoshenko and former members of her government, have increased Yanukovych's incentives to remain in power indefinitely. Small and medium-sized businesses continue to suffer at the hands of corrupt bureaucrats, tax collectors, and corporate raiders.

CIVIL LIBERTIES: 35 / 60 (-1)
D. Freedom of Expression and Belief: 9 / 16 (-1)

The constitution guarantees freedoms of speech and expression. Libel is not a criminal offense. However, conditions for the media have worsened since Yanukovych's election in 2010. The media do not provide the population with unbiased information, as business magnates with varying political interests own and influence many outlets, and the state exercises politicized control over a nationwide television network and television stations at the regional level. Some 69 percent of Ukrainians get their news from television, and the medium now features fewer alternative points of view, open discussions, and expert opinions than in previous years.

Pressure on independent media increased dramatically during 2013. TVi, one of the last independent television channels with national reach, went through a change of ownership in May, and 30 of its top journalists left as a result. In June, 27-year-old Serhiy Kurchenko, apparently a stand-in for the president's inner circle, took over Ukrainian Media Holding, which controls dozens of newspapers, other periodicals, and websites. Editor Vladimir Fedorin and other leading journalists with *Forbes Ukraine*, which was part of the group, left after the sale, stating that the magazine had lost its independence. Kurchenko also gained control of *Korrespondent*, a prominent opposition publication whose key journalists similarly quit. *Ukrayinska Pravda*, the country's most influential news site, came under a different from of pressure attributed to the president's allies, with the establishment of look-alike websites and publications meant to tarnish its image.

Other television channels remain in the hands of oligarchs who compete with the president's "Family" for influence, including oil baron Ihor Kolomoysky and Viktor Pinchuk. In February 2013, the largest television network in Ukraine, Inter, was bought by the head of the presidential administration, Serhiy Levochkin, but observers said its coverage remained relatively balanced. Levochkin is closely allied with gas oligarch Dmitro Firtash, but not part of the Yanukovych "Family." He opposed the use of force against the protesters in late 2013 and resigned from his government post. While state television ignored the protests, the oligarch-controlled channels provided comparatively objective coverage as their owners apparently sought to hedge their bets and balance between Yanukovych and the opposition. Newly created independent internet news sites, such as Hromadske TV, broadcast many of the protest-related events in real time.

Despite this limited degree of pluralism, self-censorship is rampant at the oligarch-owned media outlets, as the businessmen must be careful not to directly antagonize the authorities and thereby endanger their assets. Topics like corruption and especially the president's lavish residence at Mezhyhirya are considered off limits.

Journalists continue to face the threat of violence in the course of their work, with a total of 101 acts of physical violence against Ukrainian journalists documented in 2013. Assailants badly beat journalist and opposition activist Tetyana Chornovol on December 25. She claimed that Yanukovych had ordered the attack because she was investigating the construction of a new mansion even grander than Mezhyhirya. Yanukovych denied ordering the beating. A group of thugs beat reporters Olha Snitsarchuk and Vladyslav Sodel in Kyiv in May during an opposition rally. Police at the scene failed to intervene. Oleh Bogdanov, a journalist who covers abuses by traffic police and other authorities, was severely beaten in Donetsk in July. In January, a court sentenced the Interior Ministry's former surveillance department chief, General Oleksey Pukach, to life in prison for killing journalist Heorhiy Gongadze in 2000. The Organization for Security and Cooperation in Europe called for further investigations to identify those who had ordered the killing.

The constitution and the 1991 Law on Freedom of Conscience and Religion define religious rights in Ukraine, and these are generally well respected. However, among other problems, Yanukovych publicly associates himself with one of the country's competing branches of the Orthodox Church (that associated with the Moscow patriarchate), and there have been some signs of anti-Semitism in political campaigns in recent years.

Academic freedom has come under pressure since Yanukovych took power. Education Minister Dmytro Tabachnyk has curtailed many programs designed to promote Ukrainian language and culture, and in 2010 he began a process aimed at bringing Ukrainian textbooks into line with those in Russia. Ministry budget cuts have focused heavily on schools with liberal reputations and universities in Kyiv and western Ukraine, while universities in the eastern Donetsk region have gained more funding.

E. Associational and Organizational Rights: 8 / 12

The constitution guarantees the right to peaceful assembly but requires organizers to give the authorities advance notice of any demonstrations. Before the EU-related protests began in November 2013, a growing number of court rulings had prohibited peaceful assembly, and the administration sought to pressure protest leaders. However, the government lost control of the situation when thousands of protesters began camping in downtown Kyiv after the rejection of the EU agreement. A brutal police effort to remove the protesters on November 30 failed and brought more people into Independence Square. After a second attempt to clear the square collapsed on December 11, the authorities effectively ceded the downtown area to the protesters through the end of the year.

Beyond the late 2013 protests, social, political, cultural, and economic movements of different sizes and with various agendas have remained active despite serious obstacles. Leaders of the civic activist group Femen have complained of intimidation and repeated physical assaults. Trade unions function in the country, but strikes and worker protests are infrequent. Factory owners are still able to pressure their workers to vote according to the owners' preferences.

F. Rule of Law: 7 / 16

The judiciary is subject to intense political pressure and largely carries out the will of the executive branch, as the imprisonment of Tymoshenko demonstrated in 2011. In April 2013, Yanukovych pardoned former interior minister Yuriy Lutsenko, who had been sentenced to four years in prison in 2012 and was the subject, along with Tymoshenko, of an international campaign accusing Ukraine of selective justice. The president also pardoned former environment minister Heorhiy Filipchuk, another jailed Tymoshenko ally.

In July 2013 Yanukovych appointed Vyacheslav Ovcharenko, a judge from his hometown of Yenakiyeve, to be chairman of the Constitutional Court. He had served on the court since 2006, and would henceforth be in a position to approve potential legal changes designed to keep Yanukovych in power, such as holding presidential elections in one round or holding a referendum on constitutional amendments. Observers questioned Ovcharenko's qualifications and alleged that he may have had a hand in removing criminal records describing Yanukovych's youthful convictions.

In other politically fraught judicial developments, the High Administrative Court in February 2013 canceled the elections of two independent members of parliament who had already been confirmed by the Central Electoral Commission but refused to work with the Party of Regions. In March, the court stripped Serhiy Vlasenko, Tymoshenko's unpaid legal defender, of his seat in parliament for allegedly engaging in commercial activity beyond his official duties. An obscure Party of Regions deputy later lost his seat as well in a possible bid to cover the political motives of Vlasenko's removal.

An extensive reform of the legal system linked to the planned conclusion of the EU Association Agreement would have improved judicial independence and prison conditions. However, the president's decision not to proceed meant that the reforms were not enacted, leaving the courts, prosecutors, and law enforcement agencies under the effective control of the executive.

Reports of police torture have grown in recent years. Townspeople in Vradiyivka in the southern Mykolayiv region stormed the local police station after officers were accused in the brutal beating and rape of a 29-year-old woman, Iryna Krashkova, in June 2013. The incident reportedly followed years of police abuses and impunity in the region. Four defendants, including three police officers, were ultimately sentenced to prison in November. Separately, the number of raids by tax police and the security service against opposition-aligned businesses has increased. Since 2010, Ukrainian authorities have misused psychiatric treatment to intimidate civil society activists.

Crimean Tatars, many of whom returned to Ukraine after being exiled en masse in 1944, continue to suffer discrimination at the hands of local authorities and communities in Crimea in terms of access to land ownership, employment, social services, and educational opportunities in their native language. Their representative organizations, such as the Mejlis, have not won official recognition. The country's Romany population also suffers from discrimination. However, the national government has generally interceded to protect the rights of most ethnic and religious minorities, including the Tatar community.

G. Personal Autonomy and Individual Rights: 11 / 16

Gender discrimination is prohibited under the constitution, but government officials demonstrate little interest or understanding of the problem. Human rights groups have complained that employers openly discriminate on the basis of gender, physical appearance, and age. The trafficking of women abroad for the purpose of prostitution remains a major problem.

LGBT (lesbian, gay, bisexual, and transgender) people continue to face discrimination and hostility in Ukraine. The country's first LGBT rally took place in May 2013, proceeding peacefully with police protection despite counterdemonstrators and an initial court ban.

United Arab Emirates

Political Rights Rating: 6
Civil Liberties Rating: 6
Freedom Rating: 6.0
Freedom Status: Not Free
Electoral Democracy: No

Population: 9,300,000
Capital: Abu Dhabi

Ten-Year Ratings Timeline For Year Under Review (Political Rights, Civil Liberties, Status)

Year Under Review	2004	2005	2006	2007	2008	2009	2010	2011	2012	2013
Rating	6,6,NF	6,6,NF	6,5,NF	6,5,NF	6,5,NF	6,5,NF	6,5NF	6,6,NF	6,6,NF	6,6NF

INTRODUCTION

In 2013, the ongoing suppression by the government of the United Arab Emirates (UAE) culminated in the trial of 94 activists, students, academics, journalists, lawyers, and judges accused of being members of the Islamic group Al-Islah. The widely criticized trial resulted in 69 defendants being convicted and receiving sentences ranging from 7 to 15 years in prison. The UAE also supported a crackdown on Islamists in Egypt by joining Saudi Arabia in pledging $8 billion in economic aid after the Egyptian military overthrew the democratically elected Muslim Brotherhood government.

POLITICAL RIGHTS: 8 / 40

A. Electoral Process: 1 / 12

In the United Arab Emirates, all decisions about political leadership rest with the dynastic rulers of the seven emirates, who form the Federal Supreme Council, the highest executive and legislative body in the country. These seven leaders select a president and vice president, and the president appoints a prime minister and cabinet. The emirate of Abu Dhabi, the major oil producer in the UAE, has controlled the federation's presidency since its inception.

In 2006, Sheikh Mohammed bin Rashid al-Maktoum succeeded his late brother as ruler of the emirate of Dubai and prime minister of the UAE. The first-ever elections for 20 of the 40-seat, largely advisory Federal National Council (FNC) were held that year, with participation limited to a small electoral college appointed by the emirates' seven rulers. The UAE government appointed the remaining 20 members in February 2007.

The 40-member FNC serves only as an advisory body, reviewing proposed laws and questioning federal government ministers. Half of the FNC's members were elected for the first time in 2006 by a 6,689-member electoral college chosen by the seven rulers. The other half of the council is directly appointed by the government for two-year terms. In September 2011, the UAE held elections to the FNC after having expanded the electoral college to just over 129,000 members; however, only about 36,000 voters participated.

B. Political Pluralism and Participation: 2 / 16

Political parties are banned in the UAE. The allocation of positions in the government is determined largely by tribal loyalties and economic power. In December 2011, authorities cited security concerns in their decision to revoke the citizenship of seven men affiliated with the Islamist group the Association for Reform and Guidance, or *Al-Islah*; the seven men had signed a petition earlier in the year calling for legislative reform and free elections. Since 2011, the UAE has aggressively cracked down on suspected members of Al-Islah—a group formed in the UAE in 1974 to peacefully advocate for democratic reform—accusing them of being foreign agents of the Muslim Brotherhood intent on violently overthrowing the government. The crackdown culminated in 69 alleged members of the group being convicted and sentenced to prison terms ranging from 7 to 15 years.

C. Functioning of Government: 2 / 12

The UAE is considered one of the least corrupt countries in the Middle East. It was ranked 69 out of 177 countries surveyed in Transparency International's 2013 Corruption Perceptions Index. In April 2009, ABC News publicized a video filmed in 2004 that showed Issa bin Zayed al-Nahyan, the brother of President Khalifa bin Zayed bin Sultan Al Nahyan, torturing an Afghan grain dealer, and the Justice Department subsequently launched an investigation into the actions depicted in the video. In January 2010, a court acquitted al-Nahyan of charges of torture and rape stemming from the publication of the video; al-Nahyan's lawyer said the court had agreed with the defense's somewhat implausible argument that al-Nahyan had been drugged and therefore committed the crime unknowingly.

Discretionary Political Rights Question A: 3 / 0

Citizens have limited opportunities to express their interests through traditional consultative sessions.

CIVIL LIBERTIES: 13 / 60 (-1)
D. Freedom of Expression and Belief: 4 / 16

Although the UAE's constitution provides for some freedom of expression, the government restricts this right in practice. UAE Federal Law No. 15 of 1980 for Printed Matter and Publications regulates all aspects of the media and is considered one of the most restrictive press laws in the Arab world. The law prohibits criticism of the government, allies, and religion, and also bans pornography. Consequently, journalists commonly practice self-censorship, and the leading media outlets frequently publish government statements without criticism or comment. The UAE has three media free zones (MFZ)—areas in which foreign media outlets produce print and broadcast material intended for foreign audiences—located in Dubai, Abu Dhabi, and Ras al-Khaimah. Although these areas are subject to UAE media laws, the press operates with relative freedom.

In 2013, local media showed bias in favor of the government in the trial of the 94 alleged members of Al-Islah. International media was banned from the courtroom during the proceedings. Journalist Khalifah Rabia was arrested in July for reporting allegations on his Twitter feed that members of the so-called UAE 94 were tortured by security officials. Shortly after his arrest, 24.ae, a television network affiliated with the government, accused Rabia of having terrorist ties. In July, the UAE's Telecommunications Regulator attempted to censor the U.S.-based Arabic news website Watan.com by threatening legal action against its Germany-based internet hosting service. Furthermore, the web site's creator, Nezam Mahdawi, has reportedly been subject to threats and intimidation by UAE authorities over Watan's coverage of the UAE 94 trial.

In 2012, the UAE passed a cyber law giving authorities more latitude to crack down on activists using the internet or social media to criticize the government or to organize demonstrations. The law allows for the imprisonment of anyone who publishes material to the internet in which they insult the state, organize antigovernment protests, or publicize information deemed a threat to national security. Offenders can also be fined as much as $272,000. During the UAE 94 trial, family members of the defendants who posted trial updates on Twitter were arrested and charged under the cyber law. Abdullah al-Hadidi, the son of one of the defendants, was arrested and sentenced to 10 months in prison for posting "false news" on Twitter. Several other family members of the defendants, along with activists, were arrested under the cyber law for tweeting about the trial. Waleed al-Shehhi was also convicted of tweeting trial updates under the cyber law and was sentenced to 2 years in prison and fined 200,000 Euros.

The constitution provides for freedom of religion. Islam is the official religion, and the majority of citizens are Sunni Muslims. The minority Shiite Muslim sect and non-Muslims are free to worship without interference. The government controls content in nearly all Sunni mosques. Academic freedom is limited, with the Ministry of Education censoring textbooks and curriculums in both public and private schools. Several Western universities have opened satellite campuses in the UAE, although faculties take care to not criticize the UAE government or its policies out of fear of losing funding. In 2012, several academics critical of UAE government policies were dismissed from their positions and either arrested or expelled from the country. The RAND Corporation, a U.S.-based research institute, was forced to close its Abu Dhabi office in December 2012.

E. Associational and Organizational Rights: 2 / 12

The government places restrictions on freedoms of assembly and association. Public meetings require government permits. NGOs must register with the Ministry of Labor and Social Affairs, and registered NGOs receive subsidies from the government. After members of two prominent teachers' and lawyers' associations publicly pledged support for democratic reforms in the UAE, authorities in April 2011 dissolved their elected boards of directors and replaced them with pro-regime sympathizers. In March 2011, over 130 intellectuals and activists signed a petition calling for political reforms, including the expansion of legislative powers for the FNC. Five of the country's most outspoken reform advocates were subsequently arrested and convicted of insulting the country's leaders, though they were pardoned by the president in November 2011. Seven signatories had their citizenship stripped in late 2011, leaving them stateless and without legal documentation. In March 2012, the UAE forced the closures of the offices of two NGOs: the National Democratic Institute in Dubai and Konrad-Adenauer-Stiftung in Abu Dhabi.

In July 2012, two prominent human rights lawyers, Mohamed al-Roken and Mohamed al-Mansoori, were arrested along with other activists under suspicion of "committing crimes that harm state security." They stood trial in 2013 along with 92 other activists, lawyers, judges, students, and journalists charged with being members of Al-Islah. Al-Mansoori and al-Roken were among the 69 defendants convicted, and each received a 10-year prison sentence. In June, a combination of 30 Egyptians and Emiratis were arrested and charged with setting up an illegal branch of the Muslim Brotherhood. Their trial was still pending at year's end.

The UAE's mostly foreign workers do not have the right to organize, bargain collectively, or strike. Expatriate workers can be banned from working in the UAE if they try to leave their employer prior to at least two years of service. Workers occasionally protest against unpaid wages and poor working and living conditions, but such demonstrations are frequently broken up. In May 2013, thousands of laborers working for the Emirati construction company Arabtec went on strike in Dubai, calling for an increase in wages and demanding back pay for overtime. The strikes ended after five days. Hundreds of the striking laborers were deported and there were reports of a violent police crackdown in the worker camps.

F. Rule of Law: 3 / 16 (-1)

The judiciary is not independent, with court rulings subject to review by the political leadership. The legal system is divided into Sharia (Islamic law) courts, which address family and criminal matters, and secular courts, which cover civil law. Sharia courts sometimes impose flogging sentences for drug use, prostitution, and adultery. As part of its crackdown on dissent, the UAE arrested former judge Khamis Saeed al-Zyoudi in September 2012. In October 2012, the UAE arrested Mohammed Saeed Ziab Abdouly, president of the penal circuit in the Appellate Court of Abu Dhabi. Al-Zyoudi was acquitted in the UAE 94 trial, while Abdouly received a 10-year prison sentence. The trial of the UAE 94 was widely regarded as unfair and in violation of international standards. The International Commission of Jurists issued a report in October that called the trial "manifestly unfair" and criticized the proceedings for various irregularities, including not giving the defendants expedient or adequate access to legal counsel during interrogations, holding the defendants at length in unofficial detention centers, holding some defendants in solitary confinement for over 200 days, and not adequately investigating allegations of torture.

While the federal Interior Ministry oversees police forces in the country, each emirate's force enjoys considerable autonomy. Arbitrary arrests and detention have been reported, particularly of foreign residents. Prisons in the larger emirates are overcrowded. At least two foreign nationals were detained by security forces in 2013. In February, in a separate case from the UAE 94 trial, Qatari doctor Mahmood al-Jaidah was arrested and detained without charge for seven months until he was ultimately charged with being a supporter of Al-Islah in November. Salah Yafai, a member of the Bahraini branch of Al-Islah, was arrested at the Dubai airport in April and was held in an unknown location before being released in June.

G. Personal Autonomy and Individual Rights: 4 / 16

Discrimination against noncitizens and foreign workers, who comprise more than 80 percent of the UAE's population, is common. Stateless residents, known as *bidoon*, are unable to secure regular employment and face systemic discrimination. While the Interior Ministry has established methods for stateless persons to apply for citizenship, the government uses unclear criteria in approving or rejecting such requests. Under UAE's *kafala* system, a migrant worker's legal status is tied to an employer's sponsorship; foreign workers are often exploited and subjected to harsh working conditions, physical abuse, and the withholding of passports with little to no access to legal recourse.

The constitution does not address gender equality. Muslim women are forbidden to marry non-Muslims and receive smaller inheritances than men. Women are underrepresented in government, though they have received government appointments at various levels in recent years, including to the cabinet, and there are several women in the FNC.

In March 2013, a Norwegian woman who was raped while on a business trip in Dubai was arrested and charged with having extramarital sex, consuming alcohol, and perjury, and sentenced to 16 months in prison. An international outcry led to her charges being dismissed. The charges against her attacker, who received a lesser 13-month sentence for having extramarital sex and consuming alcohol, were also dismissed. Despite a 2006 antitrafficking law and the opening of new shelters for female victims, the government has failed to adequately address human trafficking.

United Kingdom

Political Rights: 1
Civil Liberties: 1
Freedom Rating: 1
Status: Free
Electoral Democracy: Yes

Population: 64,100,000
Capital: London

Ten-Year Ratings Timeline For Year Under Review (Political Rights, Civil Liberties, Status)

Year Under Review	2004	2005	2006	2007	2008	2009	2010	2011	2012	2013
Rating	1,1,F	1,1,F	1,1,F	1,1,F	1,1,F	1,1,F	1,1,F	1,1,F	1,1,F	1,1,F

INTRODUCTION

The scale and oversight of British intelligence agencies sparked debate in 2013 after the revelation that the Government Communications Headquarters (GCHQ) had been complicit in a mass surveillance program perpetrated by the U.S. National Security Agency (NSA).

Press freedom in the United Kingdom also came under scrutiny with the unveiling of new regulations on the media as well as the alleged harassment by authorities of the journalists who published the surveillance leaks.

The Labour Party took a sharp turn to the left in 2013, while the right wing of Prime Minister David Cameron's Conservative Party grew increasingly impatient with some of his policies. The populist United Kingdom Independence Party (UKIP) made considerable gains in local elections in May. Cameron's failure to secure enough votes to authorize British intervention in Syria in August was seen as a weakness by many of his critics.

The British economy experienced a robust recovery in 2013 after a contraction the previous year, growing at its fastest pace in three years, at 1.8 percent in the first three quarters. The recovery gave a boost to Conservatives, though the manufacturing sector trailed the service sector.

POLITICAL RIGHTS: 40 / 40

A. Electoral Process: 12 / 12

Each of the members of the House of Commons, the dominant lower chamber of the bicameral Parliament, is elected in a single-member district. Parliamentary elections must be held at least every five years. Executive power rests with the prime minister and cabinet, who must have the support of the Commons.

The House of Lords, Parliament's upper chamber, can delay legislation initiated in the Commons. If it defeats a measure passed by the Commons, the Commons must reconsider, but it can ultimately overrule the Lords. The Lords' membership, currently around 800, consists mostly of "life peers" nominated by successive governments. There are also 92 hereditary peers (nobles) and 26 bishops and archbishops of the Church of England. The monarch, currently Queen Elizabeth II, plays a largely ceremonial role as head of state.

The struggle between unionists and Irish nationalists over governance in Northern Ireland largely ended with a 1998 peace agreement, which established the Northern Ireland Assembly. However, the assembly was suspended a number of times before further peace talks, and the formal disarmament of the Irish Republican Army (IRA)—an outlawed Irish nationalist militant group—paved the way for fresh assembly elections in 2007. Those elections resulted in the formation of a power-sharing local government between Sinn Féin and the Democratic Unionist Party (DUP). A March 2011 referendum increased the Welsh

Assembly's autonomy, giving it authority to make laws in 20 subject areas without consulting Parliament. Sinn Féin and the DUP consolidated their control in the May 2011 elections for the Northern Irish legislature, while the ruling Scottish National Party (SNP) made major gains in Scotland's election held the same day.

In the May 2010 Parliamentary elections, the Conservatives led with 306 seats. Labour placed second with 258, the Liberal Democrats took 57, and smaller parties divided the remainder. Conservative leader David Cameron, lacking a majority, formed a rare coalition government with the Liberal Democrats. Local elections in May 2013 resulted in considerable gains for the populist UKIP, which came third in the average share of votes.

Despite clashes on certain issues, the coalition government persevered throughout 2013. In January, Prime Minister Cameron announced that he would renegotiate Britain's membership with the European Union (EU) and hold a referendum on leaving it if Conservatives won the next elections. A bill guaranteeing a referendum by the end of 2017 passed in July with the unanimous support of MPs in the House of Commons; Labour and the Liberal Democrats boycotted the vote. Business lobby groups and investors were disturbed by the news of a possible British exit. Cameron lost an important vote on intervention in Syria in August, becoming the first prime minister in British history to be prevented by Parliament from going to war.

B. Political Pluralism and Participation: 16 / 16

The Conservative Party recovered in popular opinion polls during 2013 after seeing their popularity lag the previous year; the Liberal Democrats and their leader Nick Clegg continued to lose voters' support. Labour Party leader Ed Miliband took a sharp turn to the left at his party's conference in September, promising to increase the minimum wage and freeze energy prices if his party wins the 2015 elections.

Other parties include the Welsh nationalist Plaid Cymru and the SNP. In Northern Ireland, the main Catholic and republican parties are Sinn Féin and the Social Democratic and Labour Party, while the leading Protestant and unionist parties are the Ulster Unionist Party and the DUP. Parties that have never won seats in Parliament, such as the UKIP and BNP, fare better in races for the European Parliament, which feature proportional-representation voting.

After much debate between Westminster and the Scottish Parliament over the terms of a referendum on Scotland's independence from the United Kingdom, a compromise was reached in 2012 between Cameron and Scottish first minister Alex Salmond. The agreement scheduled a vote for the fall of 2014, with a single yes-or-no question on independence. Polls conducted in 2013 predicted varying results for the referendum, though most have indicated it would fail.

C. Functioning of Government: 12 / 12

Corruption is not pervasive in Britain, but high-profile scandals have damaged political reputations under both Labour and Conservative governments. The Bribery Act, which is considered one of the most sweeping anti-bribery legislation in the world, came into force in July 2011. Editors involved in a scandal with the *News of the World* paper were accused of repeatedly bribing public officials and the police.

A 2013 World Bank study concluded that the United Kingdom's freedom of information laws are "reasonably successful"; the government has proposed reforms that would limit freedom of information requests, which have been criticized by civil liberties groups and the press. The UK placed 14 of 177 countries on Transparency International's 2013 Corruption Perceptions Index.

CIVIL LIBERTIES: 57 / 60

D. Freedom of Expression and Belief: 15 / 16

Press freedom is legally protected, and the media are lively and competitive. Daily newspapers span the political spectrum, though the economic downturn and rising internet use have driven some smaller papers out of business. On rare occasions, the courts have imposed so-called superinjunctions, which forbid the media from reporting certain information or even the existence of the injunction itself.

The state-owned British Broadcasting Corporation (BBC) is editorially independent and faces significant private competition. A series of scandals have plagued the broadcaster in recent years, however, as several BBC employees were convicted of sexual and verbal abuse, and senior managers were accused of receiving inordinately high severance payouts.

In October 2013, Rebekah Brooks, the former head of the tabloid *News of the World*, and seven of the paper's journalists stood trial for allegedly hacking into the telephone messages of hundreds of public figures and crime victims. The scandal led to the closing of the paper, which was owned by media mogul Rupert Murdoch's News Corporation. The trial is expected to last until Easter 2014.

The scandal led to the creation of a new regulatory system in October 2013 to prevent future press transgressions. The new regulations—which were adopted via an arcane legislative procedure, the royal charter, to avoid accusations of state regulation—will make it easier to file complaints about press intrusion and establish fines of up to £1 million ($1.6 million) for offenders. The regulations have been staunchly opposed by the British media, as well as numerous press freedom organizations, which argue that they could be used to stifle press freedom. The new rules could be amended by a two-thirds majority in both houses of Parliament and the unanimous agreement of the recognition panel approving the regulator.

British authorities allegedly harassed the *Guardian* and its journalists after the paper published the leaks linking the GCHQ to the NSA's surveillance program. In July, two security agents threatened journalists in the *Guardian*'s offices and compelled them to destroy computer hard drives, and in August, the partner of investigative journalist Glenn Greenwald, who first reported on the program, was detained and questioned at Heathrow Airport for the maximum nine hours allowed under British law.

England's libel laws—which had been regarded as claimant-friendly—were significantly overhauled in April 2013 with the Defamation Act. The law introduced a "public interest" defense, set more stringent requirements for claimants, and made it more difficult for foreigners to file a complaint.

The government does not restrict internet access. A draft communications data bill announced in 2012 would require internet and phone companies to keep metadata up to a year, allowing public authorities to see details about the identities, locations, and duration of online communications, mobile phone calls, and voice calls placed over the internet. However, the so-called snoopers' charter was shelved after criticism by privacy rights organizations and the Liberal Democrats announcement in April 2013 that they were not supporting the bill.

Although the Church of England and the Church of Scotland have official status, freedom of religion is protected in law and practice. Nevertheless, minority groups, particularly Muslims, report discrimination, harassment, and occasional assaults. A 2006 law banned incitement to religious hatred, with a maximum penalty of seven years in prison. In May 2013, Islamic extremists killed a British soldier in Woolwich. Two people were arrested after the attack for making incendiary comments on social media, and a third was charged with malicious communications.

Academic freedom is respected.

E. Associational and Organizational Rights: 12 / 12

Freedoms of assembly and association are respected in law and in practice. There are certain laws and practices, however, which the United Nations Special Rapporteur on the rights to freedom of peaceful assembly and of association deemed unnecessarily harsh during his January 2013 visit. Such practices include the criminal charge of "aggravated trespass" used occasionally against protesters, and the use of "kettling"—a policing tactic when protesters are contained in a limited area by a cordon of policemen. The former tactic was used in June against 21 climate activists protesting at a power station.

Violence in Northern Ireland has abated in recent years. Nevertheless, protests were held throughout 2013 as a reaction to the Belfast City Council's vote limiting the time the Union Flag is flown at city hall. Demonstrations in January and February descended into violent rioting, and by April police had arrested more than 200 people in connection with the protests.

Civic and nongovernmental organizations may operate freely. Groups labeled as terrorist organizations are banned under UK law. A bill being considered by the House of Lords was heavily criticized for limiting the amount of money charities could spend during election years, with opponents asserting that the bill's ambiguous language could lead to self-censorship and hinder the work of smaller charities.

Workers have the right to organize trade unions, which have traditionally played a central role in the Labour Party.

F. Rule of Law: 15 / 16

A new Supreme Court began functioning in 2009, replacing an appellate body within the House of Lords. A Justice and Security Act adopted in April 2013 allows civil courts to hear secret evidence in private in cases related to national security. Critics charged that the act violates fair trial rights, denying defendants the right to counter evidence against them in closed material proceedings and allowing ministers, rather than judges, to decide which evidence would be withheld or presented in court.

The police maintain high professional standards, and prisons generally adhere to international guidelines. In October 2013, the Supreme Court denied two prisoners the right to vote despite a European Court of Human Rights ruling that the UK should abolish its blanket ban on prisoners' votes. The Supreme Court, however, stopped short of ruling the ban lawful.

In 2013 the government banned undercover agents from having sexual relations with their targets; several agents had been criticized in recent years for improper conduct.

The leaks of the GHCQ's surveillance programs revealed that the agency was wiretapping millions of phone calls and more than 200 fiberoptic cables. Critics argued that the legal rationale behind the spying was outdated, particularly the Regulation of Investigatory Powers Act, which allows the interception of broad categories of communications if one end of the communication is non-domestic.

Britain's strict antiterrorism laws have undergone several changes in recent years. In January 2011, the detention of terrorism suspects without charge was limited to 14 days. Britain's "control order" regime—including the use of forcible relocation of terrorism suspects and restrictions on their internet usage—was replaced in January 2012 with new Terrorism Prevention and Investigation Measures (TPIMs). The 2013 report of the Independent Reviewer of Terrorism Legislation stated that, despite several problems, TPIMs provided a "broadly acceptable response." The detention of David Miranda, the partner of *Guardian* investigative journalist Glenn Greenwald, was seen by many as an abuse of the Terrorism Act.

The government has been accused of "outsourcing" torture by extraditing terrorism suspects to their home countries, where they could be abused in custody, but has consistently denied complicity in illegal rendition and torture. The United Nations Committee against Torture published a scathing report in May 2013 criticizing the government for delaying public inquiries into allegations of torture and rendition, creating loopholes in legislation that shield British officials from prosecution in case of torture, and deporting Sri Lankan asylum seekers who were allegedly tortured afterward. The committee also expressed concerns about the secret court procedures introduced by the Justice and Security Act.

Britain's large numbers of immigrants and their locally born offspring receive equal treatment under the law, but their living standards are lower than the national average, and they complain of having come under unwarranted suspicion amid the recent terrorist attacks and plots. An immigration report released in November 2012 found that the UK has a large backlog of asylum cases, with some 147,000 asylum seekers who made a claim before March 2007 having waited an average of seven years for a decision. The Home Affairs Committee found in 2013 that in some instances asylum seekers who were lesbian, gay, bisexual, or transgender (LGBT) had to "prove" their sexual orientation to the UK Border Agency.

The Conservative Party pledged to reduce the number of immigrants significantly by 2015. A new Immigration Bill being considered by Parliament at the end of 2013 would require landlords to check the immigration status of their tenants and banks to perform background checks before opening an account; it would also clamp down on "sham" marriages and compel temporary migrants, such as students, to pay £200 ($320) annually to the National Health Service (NHS). The bill was criticized for increasing the risk of homelessness and discrimination.

In a pilot project that was part of conservatives' plans to reduce immigration, vans were placed around in London with a sign reading "go home or face arrest." The project was canceled amid criticism from the Liberal Democrats. The Islamic community has been threatened by protests and occasional violence by the far-right English Defence League (EDL).

A 2010 equality act consolidated previous antidiscrimination laws for age, disability, race, religion, sex, and sexual orientation.

G. Personal Autonomy and Individual Rights: 15 / 16

While women receive equal treatment under the law, they remain underrepresented in top positions in politics and business. Women won 143 seats in the House of Commons in the 2010 elections. A report released in May 2013 revealed that women were affected disproportionately by the government's austerity measures. Abortion is legal in Great Britain but heavily restricted in Northern Ireland, where it is allowed only to protect the life or the long-term health of the mother.

Despite considerable opposition in his own party, Prime Minister David Cameron managed to push a same-sex marriage bill through Parliament, which became law in July 2013, making the UK the ninth country in Europe to legalize the practice. The law allowed religious organizations to refuse to conduct same-sex marriages.

United States of America

Political Rights Rating: 1
Civil Liberties Rating: 1
Freedom Rating: 1.0
Freedom Status: Free
Electoral Democracy: Yes

Population: 316,158,000
Capital: Washington, D.C.

Note: The numerical ratings and status listed above do not reflect conditions in Puerto Rico, which is examined in a separate report.

Ten-Year Ratings Timeline For Year Under Review (Political Rights, Civil Liberties, Status)

Year Under Review Rating	2004	2005	2006	2007	2008	2009	2010	2011	2012	2013
	1,1,F	1,1,F	1,1,F	1,1,F	1,1,F	1,1,F	1,1,F	1,1,F	1,1,F	1,1,F

INTRODUCTION

For the second consecutive year, a polarized political environment seriously weakened the ability of the United States to adopt new policies through the normal legislative process. Indeed, legislative gridlock precluded the adoption of a federal budget for much of the year and triggered a previously mandated "sequestration," or automatic reductions in federal spending across broad categories. In October, continued failure to reach a spending accord resulted in a partial shutdown of the federal government that lasted for about two weeks. The opposition Republican Party, which holds a majority in the House of Representatives, refused to pass essential spending bills unless they included provisions that defunded the 2010 Affordable Care Act, a federal health insurance measure championed by President Barack Obama that was set for implementation in 2014. Republican leaders eventually agreed to drop the demand and pass legislation that funded the government through January 2014 and extended federal borrowing power through February.

Compounding the perception of the federal government as ineffectual was a major technical failure on the Affordable Care Act's website, which temporarily prevented uninsured individuals from signing up for insurance coverage as required under the law.

The Obama administration also faced an international furor over revelations that the National Security Agency (NSA), a Defense Department division responsible for electronic surveillance, had been amassing a huge database of information on telephone calls, e-mail messages, mobile phone exchanges, and other forms of communication. The existence of the NSA programs was made public through voluminous leaks provided by Edward Snowden, a contract worker for the agency who fled the United States and settled, at least temporarily, in Russia to avoid prosecution by U.S. authorities. While much of the data collection focused on individuals outside the United States and was meant to serve either traditional espionage or counterterrorism purposes, information on communications within the United States was also amassed.

The NSA controversy was the latest chapter in an ongoing series of debates over America's counterterrorism tactics that stretched back to the 2000–2008 administration of President George W. Bush. While many of the more contentious policies were eliminated during the latter part of the Bush administration or Obama's first term, Obama failed in his efforts to close the military detention facility for terrorism suspects in Guantanamo Bay, Cuba. During 2013, Obama again attempted to persuade Congress to ease the transfer or release of Guantanamo detainees, but was thwarted by resistance from the Republican Party. Obama himself was criticized for his administration's failure to fully exercise its existing authority and release more detainees to their home or third countries.

In August, Army private Chelsea Manning (then known as Bradley Manning) was sentenced to 35 years in prison for providing hundreds of thousands of classified documents to the antisecrecy organization WikiLeaks. The leaks were published over the course of 2010, exposing internal diplomatic and military communications on the wars in Iraq and Afghanistan, among other topics. Manning, who had been held under military detention conditions that were widely criticized, would be eligible for parole in roughly seven years.

POLITICAL RIGHTS: 37 / 40

A. Electoral Process: 11 / 12

The United States is a presidential republic, with the president serving as both head of state and head of government. Cabinet secretaries and other key officials are nominated by the president and confirmed by the Senate, the upper house of the bicameral Congress. Presidential elections are decided by an Electoral College, meaning it is possible for a candidate to win the presidency while losing the national popular vote, as happened most recently in 2000. Electoral College votes are apportioned to each state based on the size of its congressional representation. In most cases, all of the electors in a particular state cast their ballots for the candidate who won the statewide popular vote, regardless of the margin. Two states, Maine and Nebraska, have chosen to divide their electoral votes between the candidates based on their popular-vote performance in each congressional district, and other states are now considering similar systems. The president may serve up to two four-year terms. In the 2012 election, incumbent Barack Obama of the Democratic Party won the Electoral College tally by 332 to 206 and the popular vote by 51 to 47 percent, defeating his Republican Party challenger, Mitt Romney.

The Senate consists of 100 members—two from each of the 50 states—serving six-year terms, with one-third coming up for election every two years. The lower chamber, the House of Representatives, consists of 435 members serving two-year terms. All national legislators are elected directly by voters in the districts or states they represent. In the 2012 congressional elections, Democrats strengthened their hold on the Senate, with 53 seats plus two independents who generally vote with the party, versus 45 for the Republicans. In the House, Republicans retained control with 234 seats, versus 201 for the Democrats. Republicans also held the majority of state governorships and legislatures.

A great deal of government responsibility rests with the 50 states. Most criminal cases are dealt with at the state level, as are education, family matters, gun ownership policies, and many land-use decisions. States also have the power to raise revenues through taxation. In some states, citizens have a wide-ranging ability to influence legislation through referendums. Such direct-democracy mechanisms, often initiated by signature campaigns, have been hailed by some as a reflection of the openness of the U.S. system. However, they have also been criticized on the grounds that they can lead to incoherent governance, undermine representative democracy, and weaken the party system. Recent referendums in various states have resulted in the legalization of same-sex marriage, legalization of recreational use of marijuana, and approval of certain forms of gambling.

Election campaigns are long and expensive. The two main parties and the constituency and interest groups that support them have used an array of methods to circumvent legal restrictions on campaign spending, and the Supreme Court on several occasions has struck down such restrictions, finding that they violated free speech rights. The cost of the 2012 presidential race alone reached at least $5.8 billion, with billions more spent on elections for Congress and state and local offices. In general, candidates with a financial advantage are more likely to prevail, though a number of Senate races were won by candidates who trailed in fund-raising.

B. Political Pluralism and Participation: 16 / 16

The intensely competitive U.S. political environment is dominated by two major parties, the right-leaning Republicans and the left-leaning Democrats. The country's "first past the post" or majoritarian electoral system discourages the emergence of additional parties, as do a number of specific legal and other hurdles. However, on occasion, independent or third-party candidates have significantly influenced politics at the presidential and state levels, and a number of newer parties, such as the Green Party or groups aligned with organized labor, have modestly affected politics in certain municipalities in recent years.

While the majoritarian system has discouraged the establishment of parties based on race, ethnicity, or religion, religious groups and minorities have been able to gain political influence through participation in the two main parties. A number of laws have been enacted to ensure the political rights of minorities. However, new laws in a number of states require voters to present driver's licenses, birth certificates, or other forms of identification before casting ballots. Sponsors claim that the intent is to combat voter fraud, but critics contend that such fraud is a minor problem at most, and accuse Republicans of adopting the laws to suppress voting by demographic groups that tend to support Democrats, particularly low-income blacks. While the courts have struck down some voter identification laws, others have been given approval by the judiciary. In the 2012 presidential election, participation rates for minority voters were relatively high, especially for black Americans, who voted in higher percentages than did whites.

C. Functioning of Government: 10 / 12

American society has a tradition of intolerance toward corrupt acts by government officials, corporate executives, or labor leaders. In the wake of the 2008–2009 financial crisis, the Justice Department and some state governments launched several high-profile prosecutions directed at various forms of misconduct in banking and financial institutions. Several of the more prominent cases have resulted in multibillion-dollar settlements. Cases of corruption involving administration officials, members of Congress, and others in the federal government have been relatively rare or small in scale in recent years. The most serious instances of political corruption have instead been uncovered among state-level officials. In New York State, a number of state legislators and municipal officials have been convicted on charges of bribery, theft, and other forms of graft. The media are aggressive in reporting on cases of corporate and official corruption; newspapers often publish investigative articles that delve into questions of private or public malfeasance. However, there are concerns that financial difficulties in the newspaper industry have reduced the press's willingness to devote resources to investigative journalism. Moreover, the expanding influence of interest groups and lobbyists on the legislative and policymaking processes, combined with their crucial role in campaign fund-raising, has given rise to public perceptions of enhanced corruption in Washington. A controversy erupted during 2013 when it was revealed that the Internal Revenue Service had applied special scrutiny to applications for tax-exempt status submitted by nonprofit organizations with a conservative political profile. It later emerged that the agency had given similar scrutiny to some liberal groups, and charges appeared unlikely at year's end.

The United States has a history of open and transparent government. It was the first country to adopt a freedom of information law. In an action widely praised by scholars and civil libertarians, Obama in 2009 ordered that millions of government documents from the Cold War era be declassified, and instructed federal agencies to adopt a cooperative attitude toward public information requests. A substantial number of auditing and investigative agencies function independently of political influence. Such bodies are often spurred to action by the investigative work of journalists. Federal agencies regularly place information relevant to their mandates on websites to broaden public access.

However, the Obama administration has encountered criticism in recent years for engendering an atmosphere of secrecy, especially in relations with the press. In addition to prosecutors' efforts to compel journalists to reveal the sources of leaked national security information, the administration has been accused of implementing an aggressive policy to discourage government officials from having contact with the media. A report issued by the Committee to Protect Journalists in October 2013 criticized the administration's "Insider Threat Program," under which federal employees are obliged to monitor the behavior of colleagues to prevent unauthorized leaks. Some have also criticized the administration for its efforts to arrest Edward Snowden and for the military's prosecution of Chelsea Manning. Nevertheless, both cases are controversial, and many observers have argued that the government's actions are justified on national security grounds.

CIVIL LIBERTIES: 55 / 60 (-1)
D. Freedom of Expression and Belief: 15 / 16 (-1)

The United States has a free, diverse, and constitutionally protected press. While newspapers have been in economic decline for the past decade, the media environment retains a high degree of pluralism. News websites now constitute a major source of political news, along with cable television networks and talk-radio programs. News coverage has also grown more polarized, with particular outlets and their star commentators providing a consistently right- or left-leaning perspective.

In May 2013, the Justice Department revealed that three months earlier it had secretly subpoenaed and seized records for 20 Associated Press (AP) telephone lines for a two-month period in 2012. The subpoena was part of an investigation into an AP story about American covert operations in Yemen. It was also revealed that the Justice Department had secretly subpoenaed and seized the e-mail and telephone records of James Rosen, a Fox News correspondent, in connection with an investigation into Stephen Jin-Woo Kim, a former State Department contractor accused of illegally disclosing classified information.

The AP and Fox News cases provoked a firestorm of criticism from the media, civil libertarians, and members of Congress. Subsequently, Obama and Attorney General Eric Holder held meetings with media representatives, issued statements expressing the administration's commitment to journalistic freedom, and indicated a more favorable attitude toward a national shield law. While such shield laws, which protect journalists' sources and materials from government scrutiny, have been adopted in 39 states, a similar measure at the federal level has yet to win congressional approval. Furthermore, after a policy review prompted by the AP and Fox News revelations, the Justice Department issued new guidelines that significantly narrowed conditions under which the government could gain access to records of journalists' communications with sources.

The United States has a long tradition of religious freedom. The constitution protects the free exercise of religion while barring any official endorsement of a religious faith, and there are no direct government subsidies to houses of worship. The debate over the role of religion in public life is ongoing, however, and religious groups often mobilize to influence political discussions on the diverse issues in which they take an interest.

The academic sphere features a healthy level of intellectual freedom. Nevertheless, universities have faced problems related to their establishment of overseas branches in such authoritarian settings as China, Singapore, and Dubai. Critics have charged such universities with agreeing to a form of academic self-censorship by avoiding discussion of sensitive issues at their foreign campuses, and agreeing to tamp down student political activism. U.S.

universities have also been accused of caving in to pressure from activist groups that object to speakers who have been invited to campus events. Speakers have regularly been disinvited or decided to withdraw from speaking engagements after protests were launched.

Americans generally enjoy open and free private discussion, including on the internet. However, civil libertarians in 2013 pointed to the potential effect of NSA data collection on the rights of U.S. citizens, and free speech organizations asserted that the surveillance revelations—combined with the year's scandals over the seizure of journalists' records—were causing some to practice self-censorship.

E. Associational and Organizational Rights: 11 / 12

In general, officials respect the right to public assembly. Demonstrations against government policies are frequently held in Washington, New York, and other major cities. In response to acts of violence committed in the course of some past demonstrations, local authorities often place restrictions on the location or duration of large protests directed at meetings of international institutions, political party conventions, or targets in the financial sector.

The United States gives wide freedom to trade associations, nongovernmental organizations, minority rights advocates, and issue-oriented pressure groups to organize and pursue their civic or policy agendas.

Federal law guarantees trade unions the right to organize and engage in collective bargaining. The right to strike is also guaranteed. Over the years, however, the strength of organized labor has declined, so that less than 7 percent of the private-sector workforce is currently represented by unions. While public-sector unions have higher rates of membership, they have come under pressure from officials concerned about the cost of compensation and pensions to states and municipalities. The country's labor code and decisions by the National Labor Relations Board (NLRB) during Republican presidencies have been regarded as impediments to organizing efforts. Union organizing is also hampered by strong resistance from private employers. In 2012, Michigan became the 24th state to adopt "right to work" legislation, which makes union organizing more difficult. Organized labor's political clout at the national level has diminished along with its membership, but unions provided significant support to Obama and other Democratic candidates during the 2012 election campaign.

F. Rule of Law: 14 / 16

Judicial independence is respected. Although the courts have occasionally been accused of intervening in areas that are best left to the political branches, most observers regard the judiciary as a linchpin of the American democratic system. In recent years, much attention has been paid to the ideological composition of the Supreme Court, which has issued a number of major decisions by a one-vote margin and is currently seen as having a conservative majority. In 2013, however, a pair of Supreme Court rulings removed important obstacles to same-sex marriage. Concern has also been raised about a trend toward the politicization of judicial elections in some states.

While the United States has a strong rule-of-law tradition, the criminal justice system's treatment of minority groups has long been a problem. Black and Latino inmates account for a disproportionately large percentage of the prison population. Civil liberties organizations and other groups have also advanced a broader critique of the justice system, arguing that there are too many Americans in prison, that prison sentences are often excessive, that too many prisoners are relegated to solitary confinement or other maximum-security arrangements, and that too many people are incarcerated for minor drug offenses. Although the incarceration rate has declined somewhat in recent years, the United States still has the highest proportion of citizens in prisons or jails in the world. Additional calls for prison reform have focused on the incidence of violence and rape behind bars.

The United States has the highest rate of legal executions in the democratic world, though the number has declined from a peak in the late 1990s. There were 39 executions in the United States in 2013. The death penalty has been formally abolished by 18 states, most recently Maryland in May 2013; in another 13 states where it remains on the books, executions have not been carried out for the past five years or more. Of particular importance in this trend has been the exoneration of some death-row inmates based on new DNA testing, as well as legal challenges to the constitutionality of the prevailing methods of lethal injection. The Supreme Court has ruled out the death penalty in cases where the perpetrator is a juvenile or mentally disabled, among other restrictions. In 2012, the court further decided that juvenile offenders could not be sentenced to life imprisonment without the possibility of parole.

The United States is one of the world's most racially and ethnically diverse societies. In recent years, residents and citizens of Latin American ancestry have replaced black Americans as the largest minority group, and the majority held by the non-Latino white population has declined. An array of policies and programs are designed to protect the rights of minorities, including laws to prevent workplace discrimination, affirmative-action plans for university admissions, quotas to guarantee representation in the internal affairs of some political parties, and policies to ensure that minorities are not treated unfairly in the distribution of government assistance. The black population, however, continues to lag in overall economic standing, educational attainment, and other social indicators. Affirmative action in employment and university admissions remains a contentious issue. The Supreme Court has given approval to the use of race or ethnicity as a factor in university admissions under certain narrow conditions. However, affirmative action has been banned, in whole or in part, through referendums in five states.

The United States has generally maintained liberal immigration policies in recent decades. Most observers believe that the country has struck a balance that both encourages assimilation and permits new legal immigrants to maintain their religious and cultural customs. Many Americans remain troubled by the large number of illegal immigrants in the country, and the government has responded by strengthening border security and stepping up efforts to deport illegal immigrants, especially those found guilty of criminal offenses. Some states have enacted laws to restrict various economic and civil rights of undocumented immigrants, though the federal courts have struck down key sections of these laws, partly because of their potential side effects on the rights of U.S. citizens. At the same time, some states have actually adopted policies that discourage local law enforcement officials from identifying or reporting illegal immigrants, except in cases of serious crimes. Although the Obama administration and most Democrats support proposed plans that would offer many current illegal immigrants a path to resident status and eventual citizenship, such immigration reform has been opposed by most Republican elected officials. The Obama administration has recently refocused its enforcement policies to target criminals and other high-priority categories of migrants while sparing groups like those who entered the country illegally as children.

G. Personal Autonomy and Individual Rights: 15 / 16

Citizens of the United States enjoy a high level of personal autonomy. The right to own property is protected by law and is jealously guarded as part of the American way of life. Business entrepreneurship is encouraged as a matter of government policy.

Women have made important strides toward equality over the past several decades. They now constitute a majority of the American workforce and are well represented in professions like law, medicine, and journalism. Although the average compensation for female workers is roughly 80 percent of that for male workers, women with recent university degrees have effectively attained parity with men. Nonetheless, many female-headed families continue to live in conditions of chronic poverty. In recent years there has been a renewed effort in some states to restrict women's access to abortion. In the past, most such measures were ultimately struck down by the Supreme Court, but the new laws are being tailored to push the boundaries of prior court decisions, and some have survived initial judicial scrutiny, adding to state-by-state variation in access.

Federal antidiscrimination legislation does not include LGBT (lesbian, gay, bisexual, and transgender) people as a protected class, though most states have enacted such protections. Many states have passed laws or constitutional amendments explicitly banning same-sex marriage, but an increasing number have granted gay couples varying degrees of family rights, and by the end of 2013 same-sex marriage was legal in Washington, D.C., and 15 states, including such populous states as California, New York, and Illinois. A pair of Supreme Court rulings in June paved the way for same-sex marriage in California and struck down a federal law that had barred federal agencies from recognizing the marriages of same-sex couples and conferring related benefits.

The United States prides itself as a society that offers wide access to economic and social advancement and favors government policies that enhance equality of opportunity. Recently, however, studies have shown a widening inequality in wealth and a narrowing of access to upward mobility, trends that have been accentuated in the years since the 2008–2009 financial crisis. Obama has cited the reduction of inequality as a major objective of his administration. The government has proposed an increase in the federal minimum wage, and a number of states and municipalities have proposed substantial rises in their own minimum wage levels. At the same time, Americans seem resistant to increases in tax rates, and Democratic Party leaders have generally failed to win passage of tax measures that call for wealthier citizens to contribute more. Among the world's prosperous, stable democracies, the United States is unique in having a large underclass of poor people who have at best a marginal role in economic life.

Uruguay

Political Rights Rating: 1
Civil Liberties Rating: 1
Freedom Rating: 1.0
Electoral Status: Free
Electoral Democracy: Yes

Population: 3,400,000
Capital: Montevideo

Ten-Year Ratings Timeline For Year Under Review (Political Rights, Civil Liberties, Status)

Year Under Review	2004	2005	2006	2007	2008	2009	2010	2011	2012	2013
Rating	1,1,F	1,1,F	1,1,F	1,1,F	1,1,F	1,1,F	1,1,F	1,1,F	1,1,F	1,1,F

INTRODUCTION

After over a year of public deliberation, the parliament in December 2013 passed legislation that made it legal to consume marijuana, grow cannabis plants at home, and purchase the drug from licensed pharmacies. While polls revealed that the majority of Uruguayans were still against drug legalization in 2013, opposition to the bill waned toward the end of the year as supporters argued effectively that prohibition fostered organized crime and carried greater health risks.

Uruguay still boasts some of the lowest crime rates and strongest state institutions in the region. However, it has experienced a rise in crime and insecurity in recent years due primarily to drug trafficking and small-scale gang activity. The change in the country's drug laws attempted to address and reverse this trend.

In May 2013, Uruguayan courts for the first time convicted a serving general for human rights violations committed during the country's dictatorship. General Miguel Dalmao, who was a 23-year-old lieutenant when the crime was committed in 1974, was sentenced to 28 years in prison for the torture and murder of a communist professor.

POLITICAL RIGHTS: 40 / 40 (+1)
A. Electoral Process: 12 / 12

The 1967 constitution established a bicameral General Assembly consisting of the 99-member Chamber of Representatives and the 30-member Senate, with all members directly elected for five-year terms. The president is directly elected for a single five-year term.

In general elections held in October 2009, the Broad Front (FA) coalition won 50 seats in the lower house, the Nationalist Party (PN) won 30, the Colorado Party 17, and the Independent Party (PI) 2. In the Senate, the FA won 16 seats, the PN took 9, and the Colorado Party won 5. The FA's Jose Mujica was elected president. The next general elections will be held in October 2014.

B. Political Pluralism and Participation: 16 / 16

Uruguay is home to an open and competitive multiparty system. The major political parties and groupings are the Colorado Party, the PI, the PN (also known as the Blanco Party), and the ruling FA coalition. The FA includes the Movement of Popular Participation, the New Space Party, the Socialist Party, and the Uruguayan Assembly, among other factions.

C. Functioning of Government: 12 / 12 (+1)

Corruption levels in Uruguay are low by regional standards, and by 2013 government institutions had established a fairly strong track record of accountability to the electorate. The country's Transparency Law criminalizes a broad range of potential abuses of power by officeholders, including the laundering of funds related to public corruption cases. Uruguay was ranked 19 out of 177 countries and territories surveyed in Transparency International's 2013 Corruption Perceptions Index, making it one of the best performers in Latin America.

CIVIL LIBERTIES: 58 / 60
D. Freedom of Expression and Belief: 16 / 16

Constitutional guarantees regarding free expression are respected, and violations of press freedom are rare. The press is privately owned, and the broadcast sector includes both commercial and public outlets. There are numerous daily newspapers, many of which are associated with political parties. A 2009 law eliminated criminal penalties for the defamation of public officials. President Mujica sent a draft broadcast media law to the parliament in May 2013; the bill includes provisions restricting broadcast oligopolies, safeguards against censorship, more transparent licensing procedures, and a requirement that at least 60 percent of the programming on each channel be produced or coproduced in Uruguay. If passed, the bill would be a step toward increased pluralism and transparency in the press. The government does not place restrictions on internet usage.

Freedom of religion is broadly respected. The government does not restrict academic freedom.

E. Associational and Organizational Rights: 12 / 12

Rights to freedom of assembly and association are provided for by law, and the government generally observes these in practice. A widespread array of community organizations are active in civic life. Numerous women's rights groups focus on problems such as violence against women and societal discrimination. Workers exercise their right to join unions, bargain collectively, and hold strikes. Unions are well organized and politically powerful.

F. Rule of Law: 15 / 16

The judiciary is relatively independent, but the court system remains severely backlogged. Pretrial detainees often spend more time in jail than they would if convicted of the offense in question and sentenced to the maximum prison term. Overcrowded prisons, poor conditions, and violence among inmates remain serious problems. The prison system held an estimated 10,000 inmates in 2013, 120 percent of intended capacity. Medical care for prisoners is substandard, and many rely on visitors for food.

Uruguay's efforts to bring to justice those responsible for human rights violations committed under the military regime that ended in 1985 have been inconsistent and at times contradictory. A 1986 amnesty law gave the executive branch, rather than the judiciary, final say over which cases could be tried. A majority of Uruguayans supported the amnesty and voted to maintain it in two separate referendums in 1989 and 2009. However, court rulings have historically reinterpreted the law to allow for higher-level officers to be tried. Going against popular opinion, in November 2011, Mujica signed a law nullifying the amnesty, opening the door for additional convictions. However, in April 2013 the Supreme Court ruled that the 2011 law was unconstitutionally retroactive.

Uruguay has historically been one of the most peaceful countries in the region. However, homicides increased by 45 percent in 2012, compared with 2011, making it Uruguay's most violent year on record. Gun ownership rates are unusually high in Uruguay, and more than half of the weapons in the country are illegal. Officials have attributed the rise in crime to warring drug gangs, with Uruguay becoming an increasingly important transit point for narcotics. The Mujica administration's response included an increased police presence in the capital and the bill to legalize and regulate the production and distribution of marijuana. The president signed the legislation in late December 2013. Meanwhile, the "Seven Zones Plan," which began implementation in 2013, expanded social programs and law-enforcement measures in the poorest districts of Montevideo. A bill that was still awaiting approval at the end of 2013 would tighten controls on the possession of shotguns and handguns.

The small Afro-Uruguayan minority, comprising an estimated 4 percent of the population, continues to face economic and social inequalities and is underrepresented in the government.

G. Personal Autonomy and Individual Rights: 15 / 16

Women enjoy equal rights under the law but face traditional discriminatory attitudes and practices, including salaries averaging approximately two-thirds those of men. Violence against women remains a problem. Women hold only 12 percent of the seats in the Chamber of Representatives and 13 percent of the Senate. However, under a 2009 quota law, women must comprise one-third of a party's candidate list beginning in 2014. Women make up approximately 25 percent Uruguay's armed forces, compared to an average of 4 percent in Latin American countries.

The parliament approved same-sex civil unions in 2007, legalized abortion for any reason during the first trimester in 2012, and voted overwhelmingly to legalize gay marriage in April 2013.

Lawmakers approved ratification of the Domestic Workers Convention in April 2012, making Uruguay the first country worldwide to do so. The convention, which mandates domestic workers' core labor rights, came into effect in September 2013.

Uzbekistan

Political Rights Rating: 7
Civil Liberties Rating: 7
Freedom Rating: 7.0
Freedom Status: Not Free
Electoral Democracy: No

Population: 30,215,000
Capital: Tashkent

Ten-Year Ratings Timeline For Year Under Review (Political Rights, Civil Liberties, Status)

Year Under Review	2004	2005	2006	2007	2008	2009	2010	2011	2012	2013
Rating	7,6,NF	7,7,NF	7,7,NF	7,7,NF	7,7,NF	7,7,NF	7,7,NF	7,7,NF	7,7,NF	7,7,NF

INTRODUCTION

As in previous years, Uzbekistan's government suppressed all political opposition in 2013. The few remaining civic activists and critical journalists in the country faced physical violence, prosecution, hefty fines, and arbitrary detention. In June, noting three consecutive years without significant improvements, the U.S. State Department downgraded Uzbekistan to Tier 3 in its annual *Trafficking in Persons Report*, finding that "Uzbekistan remains one of only a handful of governments around the world that subjects its citizens to forced labor through implementation of state policy."

In response, Uzbekistan met one of the report's recommendations and for the first time allowed representatives from the International Labor Organization to monitor the annual cotton harvest. However, minors who were forced to participate in the harvest wrote on social media that they were instructed to lie to the monitors. Although significant steps have been taken toward eliminating forced child labor, reports by multiple international monitors confirmed that people 15 years of age and older were still systematically forced to work in the fields to meet government quotas.

POLITICAL RIGHTS: 0 / 40

A. Electoral Process: 0 / 12

After Uzbekistan gained independence from the Soviet Union through a December 1991 referendum, Islam Karimov, the incumbent Communist Party leader, was elected president amid fraud claims by rivals. His first term was extended by means of a 1995 referendum, and he was reelected in 2000, with no genuine opposition candidate allowed to participate.

The constitution barred Karimov from running for reelection after his second legal term in office ended in January 2007. Nevertheless, despite the lack of any formal ruling on this legal obstacle, he won a new term in December 2007 with an official 88 percent of the vote. The legislature quietly altered the constitution in 2011 to reduce future presidential terms to five years, from seven. In 2013 the 75-year-old Karimov gave no indication that he intended to step down from power.

Uzbekistan has a bicameral parliament. The lower house has 150 seats, with 135 members directly elected in single-member constituencies and 15 representing the newly formed Ecological Movement of Uzbekistan, which holds separate indirect elections. The 100-member upper house, or Senate, has 84 members elected by regional councils and 16 appointed by the president. All members of the parliament serve five-year terms. The last parliamentary elections in 2009 offered voters no meaningful choice, as all participating parties supported the government.

B. Political Pluralism and Participation: 0 / 16

Only four political parties, all progovernment, are currently registered, and no genuine opposition parties operate legally. The legal parties indulge in mild criticism of one another and occasionally of government ministers below the president. Unregistered opposition groups function primarily in exile, and domestic supporters or family members of exiled opposition figures are frequently persecuted.

In June 2013, 71-year-old Hasan Choriyev—the infirm father of Bahodyr Choriyev, leader of the U.S.-based Birdamlik (Solidarity) political action group—was taken by police from his home in rural Qashqdaryo province and, after almost two weeks of detention, charged with rape. According to Birdamlik and human rights investigators, on the morning of the alleged rape, Choriyev had been in the prosecutor's office. He had previously reported receiving threats from an official related to his son's political activity. In August, Hasan Choriyev was sentenced to five and a half years in prison in a closed trial. Activists and Choriyev family members noted that the arrest took place almost immediately after Bahodyr Choriyev said in an interview that he would run for president in Uzbekistan's 2015 election.

Also in August, a member of the unregistered opposition Erk (Freedom) Party, Fakhriddin Tillayev, and his wife were beaten by a mob after an incident in which, according to Tillayev, a woman appeared at their door nude and began screaming that Tillayev was raping her.

C. Functioning of Government: 0 / 12

There are no free elections in Uzbekistan, and the legislature does not meaningfully debate new laws or regulations; instead, it serves as a rubber stamp for the executive branch. Police, security services, and judges interpret the laws as they choose or according to political dictates, leaving little recourse to appeal.

Corruption is pervasive. Uzbekistan was ranked 168 out of 177 countries and territories surveyed in Transparency International's 2013 Corruption Perceptions Index. Graft and bribery among low and mid-level officials are part of everyday life and are sometimes even transparent. However, international investigations that were launched in 2012, after the local affiliate of Swedish telecommunications giant Teliasonera was shut down by the state, appeared to reveal corruption within Karimov's family in unprecedented detail. In January 2013, new documents released as part of a Swedish criminal investigation showed that Teliasonera had sought to negotiate directly with the president's daughter, Gulnara Karimova. The company was under investigation for allegedly paying more than $300 million in bribes to an offshore shell company controlled by associates of the president's family.

In February, the chief executive of Teliasonera was forced resign after an external review showed serious failures of due diligence. Swedish criminal proceedings were ongoing at year's end. In May, documents leaked to the Swedish media appeared to show that Karimova had aggressively dictated the terms of the contract and threatened the company with obstruction from multiple government ministries if Teliasonera did not agree to payments. Related money-laundering investigations in Switzerland and Sweden continued throughout the year, with hundreds of millions of dollars frozen in accounts connected to the case.

CIVIL LIBERTIES: 4 / 60

D. Freedom of Expression and Belief: 1 / 16

Despite constitutional guarantees, freedoms of speech and the press are severely restricted. The state controls major media outlets and related facilities, and state-run television has aired "documentaries" that smear perceived opponents of the government. Although official censorship was abolished in 2002, it has continued through semiofficial mechanisms that strongly encourage self-censorship. Foreign reporters are generally excluded from the country.

State restrictions on free expression continued during 2013. Even recording artists must obtain special licenses from a government authority to perform in public, and in June a number of them found that their licenses had been revoked on the grounds of "meaningless" content that was deemed insufficiently patriotic and edifying according to Uzbek national values. In July the Tashkent-based online outlet Uzmetornom was temporarily shut down after a military prosecutor threatened the site's owner for covering a deadly clash on the Uzbek-Kyrgyz border. In September, journalist Sergey Naumov, well regarded for his reporting on forced labor in the cotton harvest, disappeared from his home city of Urgench for several days. Friends and relatives later learned that he had been arrested, charged with sexual assault, and sentenced to 12 days in prison without a lawyer present.

The government systematically blocks websites with content that is critical of the regime. Mainstream news, information, and social-media sites based outside the country are sometimes blocked as well. Authorities maintain and frequently update a list of banned proxy sites that allow users to access blocked content anonymously.

The government permits the existence of approved Muslim, Jewish, and Christian denominations, but treats unregistered religious activity as a criminal offense. The state exercises strict control over Islamic worship, including the content of sermons. Suspected members of banned Muslim organizations and their relatives have been subjected to arrest, interrogation, and torture. Arrested believers are frequently accused of founding previously unknown religious organizations, a charge that carries high penalties. In most cases, little evidence that such organizations exist is presented at the closed trials. In February 2013, a group of 11 Namangani men were sentenced to terms of up to 12 years in prison for participating in a group allegedly called "Jihadism," and in July some 20 others were sentenced to lengthy terms for membership in another new group called "Hizb-ut Nusrat," though no evidence of the existence of either organization was available for independent analysis.

Members of other religions are regularly arrested and fined as well. Throughout the year, Christian groups faced increasingly harsh fines following raids of churches and private homes in which religious literature, including Bibles, was seized. In August, a group of nine Baptists in Qarshi was fined more than $21,000 for possessing religious texts and holding private services.

The government reportedly limits academic freedom. Bribes are commonly required to gain entrance to exclusive universities and obtain good grades. Open and free private discussion is limited by the *mahalla* committees, traditional neighborhood organizations that the government has turned into an official system for public surveillance and control.

E. Associational and Organizational Rights: 0 / 12

Despite constitutional provisions for freedom of assembly, authorities severely restrict this right in practice, breaking up virtually all unsanctioned gatherings and detaining participants. In January 2013, Valeriy Nazarov, a Birdamlik activist who had planned to travel to Tashkent for a protest event, was reported missing for a month. He reappeared after fellow Birdamlik activists drew media attention to his case. According to his friends, he arrived home drugged and disoriented. Birdamlik members suspected that he had been held in the Urganch Psychiatric Hospital.

In July, a group of family members and activists from the Uzbekistan Human Rights Alliance and Birdamlik attempted a picket in front of the Qashadaryo regional prosecutor's office to protest the charges against Hasan Choriyev. They reported being attacked and severely beaten by a group of women who robbed them and ripped their clothes; after the violence, police, who had done nothing to intervene, arrested the demonstrators. The group was subsequently fined more than $15,000 in total for holding an "illegal demonstration."

Freedom of association is tightly constrained, and unregistered nongovernmental organizations face extreme difficulties and harassment. After a major episode of unrest in the city of Andijon in 2005, the government shut down virtually all foreign-funded organizations in Uzbekistan; Human Rights Watch, the last international monitoring group with a presence in the country, was forced to close its office in 2011. Throughout 2013, human rights activists continued to face harassment, prosecution, travel restrictions, and violence. In August, 75-year-old activist Turaboy Juraboyev was sentenced to five years in prison for extortion and fraud; independent media connected his arrest to his investigation of the murder of a local man involved in a business deal with Jizzakh-area government officials.

In September, Bobomorod Rizzakov, the Bukharan regional head of Ezgulik, the only registered human rights organization permitted to operate in Uzbekistan, was sentenced to four years in prison on human trafficking charges after he criticized local government officials for corruption.

The Council of the Federation of Trade Unions is dependent on the state, and no genuinely independent union structures exist. Organized strikes are extremely rare.

F. Rule of Law: 0 / 16

The judiciary is subservient to the president, who appoints all judges and can remove them at any time. The creation in 2008 of a Lawyers' Chamber with compulsory membership increased state control over the legal profession. Law enforcement authorities routinely justify the arrest of suspected Islamic extremists or political opponents by planting contraband or filing dubious charges of financial wrongdoing. In April 2013, the government released Mamadali Mahmudov, who had spent 14 years in a labor camp and had three more years added to his sentence days before his surprise release. At least 12 other high-profile political prisoners remain incarcerated indefinitely despite international pressure.

Prisons suffer from severe overcrowding and shortages of food and medicine. As with detained suspects, prison inmates—particularly those sentenced for their religious beliefs—are often subjected to abuse or torture.

Although racial and ethnic discrimination is prohibited by law, the belief that senior positions in government and business are reserved for ethnic Uzbeks is widespread. Moreover, the government appears to be systematically closing schools for the Tajik-speaking minority.

Sex between men is illegal in Uzbekistan and punishable with up to three years in prison. The law does not protect LGBT (lesbian, gay, bisexual, and transgender) people from discrimination, and traditional social taboos make even discussion of LGBT issues difficult.

G. Personal Autonomy and Individual Rights: 3 / 16

Permission is required to move to a new city, and bribes are commonly paid to obtain the necessary documents. Restrictions on foreign travel include the use of exit visas, which are often issued selectively. Despite such controls, millions of Uzbeks seek employment abroad, particularly in Russia and Kazakhstan.

Widespread corruption and the government's tight control over the economy limit equality of opportunity.

Women's educational and professional prospects are limited by cultural and religious norms and ongoing economic difficulties. Victims of domestic violence are discouraged from pressing charges against perpetrators, who rarely face prosecution. The trafficking of women abroad for prostitution remains a serious problem. A 2009 law imposed tougher penalties for child labor, and in August 2012 Uzbekistan's prime minister pledged to end the practice completely. However, while reports indicated that forced labor for children under 15 were less pervasive than in the past, multiple organizations confirmed the ongoing use of forced labor—especially of college and university students—during the cotton harvest in 2013. Anecdotal reports show that parents are required to sign a contract agreeing to compulsory unpaid cotton labor by their children before they can be admitted to vocational college at age 15. In at least one region, mothers were denied social welfare payments with the explanation that this was the price for excusing their minor children from labor in the cotton fields.

Vanuatu

Political Rights Ratings: 2
Civil Liberties Ratings: 2
Freedom Rating: 2.0
Freedom Status: Free
Electoral Democracy: Yes

Population: 300,000
Capital: Port Vila

Ten-Year Ratings Timeline For Year Under Review (Political Rights, Civil Liberties, Status)

Year Under Review	2004	2005	2006	2007	2008	2009	2010	2011	2012	2013
Rating	2,2,F	2,2,F	2,2,F	2,2,F	2,2,F	2,2,F	2,2,F	2,2,F	2,2,F	2,2,F

INTRODUCTION

In March 2013, Prime Minister Sato Kilman resigned before a parliamentary no-confidence vote. Subsequently, parliament selected Moana Carcasses Kalosil, leader of the Green Party and finance minister in the Kilman coalition government, to fill the top post. Kalosil quickly introduced a 68-point plan of action to reform the government during his first 100 days in office. Many of his proposed changes threaten entrenched interests.

The government devised a legal scheme to exploit the desire of mainland Chinese to acquire residency in Hong Kong. In order for Chinese citizens to participate in Hong Kong's Capital Investment Entrant Scheme and gain permanent residency in Hong Kong, they must first have resident status in a country other than China. If approved, paying a $3,000 application fee and registering a business in Vanuatu would grant applicants permanent resident status in Vanuatu without having to live there. By February 2013, Vanuatu had earned $4.3 million from granting 1,400 Chinese persons permanent residency status (and none relocated to Vanuatu).

POLITICAL RIGHTS: 32 / 40

A. Electoral Process: 9 / 12

The constitution provides for parliamentary elections every four years. The prime minister, who appoints his own cabinet, is chosen by the 52-seat unicameral Parliament from among its members. Members of Parliament and the heads of the six provincial governments form an electoral college to select the largely ceremonial president for a five-year term. The National Council of Chiefs works in parallel with Parliament, exercising authority mainly over language and cultural matters.

B. Political Pluralism and Participation: 15 / 16

Many political parties are active, but politicians frequently switch affiliations. Politics is also driven by linguistic and tribal identity. The major parties include the Vanua'aku Party (VP), the Union of Moderate Parties (UMP), the People's Progressive Party (PPP), and the National United Party (NUP). In June 2013, a former VP member launched the People's National Party (PNP). No-confidence votes have forced several changes of government in recent years. In July, a no-confidence motion was lodged against Kalosil based on allegations of bribery in the 2012 general elections. The motion was rejected on the grounds that several of the 28 signatures in the petition were forged.

C. Functioning of Government: 8 / 12

Corruption is a serious problem, and official abuse is serious and widespread. Politicians also regularly use allegations of corruption to discredit adversaries. Local critics and international donors have long censured the practice of politicians granting passports for personal gain. There are concerns, too, with lack of transparency and accountability in the new permanent residency program. In December 2013, a Ministry of Justice inquiry implicated several past political appointees and diplomats in the selling of passports between 2002 and 2008.

CIVIL LIBERTIES: 47 / 60
D. Freedom of Expression and Belief: 15 / 16

The government generally respects freedoms of speech and the press, though elected officials have been accused of threatening journalists for critical reporting. In May 2013, police used anti-terrorism and sedition laws to arrest a journalist, Gratien Tiona, after he posted on Facebook that he hoped the aircraft carrying the Council of Ministers to Port Vila would crash. The next day, the public prosecutor ordered the charges dropped and Tiona was released. The number of internet users is growing, but access is limited by high cost and lack of infrastructure.

The government generally respects freedom of religion in this predominantly Christian country. There were no reports of restrictions on academic freedom.

E. Associational and Organizational Rights: 11 / 12

The law provides for freedoms of assembly and association, and the government typically upholds these rights. Public demonstrations are permitted by law and generally allowed in practice. Civil society groups are active on a variety of issues.

Workers can bargain collectively and strike. Five independent trade unions are organized under the umbrella Vanuatu Council of Trade Unions.

F. Rule of Law: 10 / 16

The judiciary is largely independent, but a lack of resources hinders the hiring and retention of qualified judges and prosecutors. Tribal chiefs often adjudicate local disputes, but their punishments are sometimes deemed excessive. Long pretrial detentions are common, and prisons fail to meet minimum international standards. Harsh treatment of prisoners and police brutality provoke frequent prison riots and breakouts.

There are no laws targeting LGBT persons nor were there reports of violence against them in 2013.

G. Personal Autonomy and Individual Rights: 11 / 16

Discrimination against women is widespread. No laws prohibit spousal rape, domestic abuse, or sexual harassment, which women's groups claim are common and increasing. Most cases go unreported due to victims' fear of reprisal or family pressure, and the police and courts rarely intervene or impose strong penalties. In June 2013, the Council of Ministers agreed to a proposal to reserve 30 percent of parliament seats for women.

At year's end, parliament amended the constitution to allow dual citizenship. This change and other schemes have primarily attracted primarily mainland Chinese applicants and investors. The rapid expansion of Chinese-owned businesses has fueled resentment among native Vanuatu residents. To appease them, the government in December 2013 added seven occupations to the list of reserved jobs open only to those native to Vanuatu.

⬇ Venezuela

Political Rights Rating: 5
Civil Liberties Rating: 5
Freedom Rating: 5.0
Freedom Status: Partly Free
Electoral Democracy: No

Population: 29,700,000
Capital: Caracas

Trend Arrow: Venezuela received a downward trend arrow due to an increase in the selective enforcement of laws and regulations against the opposition in order to minimize its role as a check on government power.

Ten-Year Ratings Timeline For Year Under Review (Political Rights, Civil Liberties, Status)

Year Under Review	2004	2005	2006	2007	2008	2009	2010	2011	2012	2013
Rating	3,4,PF	4,4,PF	4,4,PF	4,4,PF	4,4,PF	5,4,PF	5,5,PF	5,5,PF	5,5,PF	5,5,PF

INTRODUCTION

President Hugo Chávez died of cancer in March 2013 after 14 years in power that left Venezuela sharply divided. To his supporters, Chávez's social initiatives and stirring rhetoric offered millions of formerly marginalized citizens unprecedented voice, political power, and concrete living improvements. To his detractors, his authoritarian tactics led to the replacement of liberal democracy with a quasi-socialist, personality-based state in which the lack of any institutional checks on executive power caused increasing economic, social, and political dysfunction, as well as frequent abuses of Venezuelans' political rights and civil liberties.

An election to replace Chávez, who had just been reelected in 2012, took place in April. His vice president and anointed successor, Nicolás Maduro, narrowly defeated opposition leader Henrique Capriles amid opposition claims of irregularities. Protests in the election's immediate aftermath left nine people dead and hundreds injured, with each side claiming that the other's supporters were responsible for, or misrepresenting the extent of, the violence. Maduro's victory was eventually confirmed by the Chavista-dominated electoral commission and courts.

Although early analyses had suggested that Maduro might prove more pragmatic than Chávez, he and his allies repeatedly used polarizing rhetoric—including scores of accusations that the opposition was conspiring with the United States and other foreign actors to sabotage the economy and stage a coup—and took actions aimed at weakening the opposition. A brawl in the National Assembly in late April left several opposition members injured, with most observers identifying Chavista legislators as the instigators. In May, opposition deputy Richard Mardo was stripped of his seat following money-laundering allegations that the opposition denounced as absurd.

Government policy following the election focused on attempts to stabilize the economy, which suffered from fiscal and monetary stresses—especially a mismanaged exchange-rate regime—that generated widespread shortages of consumer goods and the hemisphere's highest inflation rate. Other domestic policy initiatives included the deployment of the military to contain one of the world's highest crime rates and an anticorruption campaign that resulted in the arrest of several mid-level Chavista figures but no high-ranking officials.

As December local elections approached, Maduro declared that "speculators" were charging illegally high prices, leading to a series of arrests. He also sent the National Guard to occupy electronics stores and enforce lower prices, setting off a buying frenzy. In November, the National Assembly ousted another opposition member, María Mercedes Aranguren, over corruption charges, giving the government the three-fifths majority needed to pass a bill providing Maduro with decree power on economic issues.

The December local elections resulted in a decisive victory for Chavismo, with government-backed candidates taking nearly 55 percent of the vote and over 75 percent of the mayoralties.

Relations with the United States, which is one of the primary customers for Venezuelan oil but has lacked an ambassador in Caracas since 2010, fluctuated during the year. Washington was slower than Latin American states to recognize Maduro's presidential victory, but there were some early signs of détente, most prominently a handshake between Foreign Minister Elías Jaua and Secretary of State John Kerry in June. Relations subsequently deteriorated, however, and in late September Maduro ordered the expulsion of three U.S. embassy officials for allegedly scheming with the opposition to sabotage the Venezuelan economy. More broadly, the ongoing bilateral friction was attributable to Venezuela's long-standing aspirations to regional leadership as well as its history of rhetorical support for and economic cooperation with Cuba, Iran, Syria, and other authoritarian states. Venezuela formally withdrew from the American Convention on Human Rights in September 2013, a year after announcing plans for the move in response to a series of decisions against it at the Inter-American Court of Human Rights.

POLITICAL RIGHTS: 14 / 40 (-1)

A. Electoral Process: 5 / 12

While the act of voting is relatively free and the count is generally considered fair, the political playing field favors government-backed candidates, and the separation of powers is virtually nonexistent.

The president serves six-year terms, and both he and other elected officials are, since 2009, not subject to term limits. Ahead of the April 2013 election, two controversial rulings by the Supreme Tribunal of Justice (TSJ) favored Maduro: One allowed him to take over the presidency from the late Chávez despite a plausible constitutional argument that National Assembly head Diosdado Cabello was the legal successor, while the other allowed Maduro to remain in the presidency rather than temporarily step down during the campaign period. Maduro won the election by a razor-thin margin, 50.6 percent to 49.1 percent, following a brief, lackluster campaign that nonetheless produced turnout of nearly 80 percent.

The opposition denounced the results, accusing the government of multiple violations, including election-day abuses and the rampant misuse of state resources during the campaign. The opposition specifically complained that its witnesses were ejected from multiple voting centers, and that the Chavista-dominated National Electoral Commission (CNE) failed to protect against ballot fraud. Maduro was officially declared the winner by the CNE, but the opposition refused to accept the outcome's legitimacy and pursued several avenues of redress, including requests for a detailed cross-check of votes, signatures, and fingerprints by the CNE and the annulment of a significant portion of the results by the similarly progovernment TSJ. Neither forum accepted the opposition's arguments. The CNE's limited audit revealed few discrepancies, while the TSJ rejected the opposition's cases in August, thereby concluding the electoral process.

The unicameral, 165-seat National Assembly is popularly elected for five-year terms. In the run-up to the 2010 legislative elections, the ruling Unified Socialist Party of Venezuela (PSUV) benefited from significant exposure on state-run media and pressure on public employees and neighborhood groups. The opposition, grouped together as the Democratic Unity Roundtable (MUD), took more than 47 percent of the vote, the PSUV captured 48 percent, and the opposition-leaning Fatherland for All (PPT) party obtained over 3 percent. Due to electoral rules revised in 2009, however, PSUV candidates secured 98 of the 165 seats, MUD candidates took 65, and the PPT won the remaining two. The ruling party's legislative majority has acted as a reliable rubber stamp for the executive, and Chávez's control of the 2006–2010 assembly allowed him to curb the already tenuous independence of institutions including the judiciary, the intelligence services, and the Citizen Power branch of government, which was created by the 1999 constitution to fight corruption and protect citizens' rights. The 2011–2015 assembly features a much larger opposition presence, but it has been unable to check government power. The legislature has voted to hand the president wide-ranging decree powers several times in recent years.

The opposition's attempt to use the December 2013 local elections as a referendum on the Maduro administration backfired when Chavista candidates won 5.7 million votes, to 4.6 million for opposition-backed candidates. Although the opposition won the mayoral races in most of Venezuela's largest cities, Chavista candidates won nearly 260 of the 335 races in total. The central government has stripped opposition-led municipalities of responsibilities and resources in recent years, leaving those officials with a reduced governance role.

In all recent elections, the CNE has failed to limit the use of state resources by the PSUV. The promotion of social and infrastructure projects often blurs the line between PSUV candidates' official roles and their electoral campaigns. Public employees are subjected to heavy pressure to support the government, and state vehicles are frequently used to transport supporters to rallies and voting sites.

Ballot secrecy has long been a source of controversy. After a failed 2004 presidential recall referendum, tens of thousands of people who had signed petitions in favor of the effort found that they could not get government jobs or contracts, or qualify for public assistance programs; they had apparently been placed on a blacklist of Chávez's alleged political opponents.

B. Political Pluralism and Participation: 7 / 16 (-1)

The merger of government-aligned parties into the PSUV that began in 2007 is largely complete, though several groups retain nominal independence. PSUV leaders are generally selected by the president, rather than through internal elections, a pattern that continued during the selection of candidates for the 2013 local elections.

In 2009, opposition parties established the MUD, which selected unity candidates—in part via primaries—for the 2010 parliamentary and 2012 presidential elections. Opposition leadership in some states and localities has been blunted in recent years by laws allowing the national government to cut budgets and strip important functions from subnational administrations. Primaries for some of the opposition's 2013 local election candidates were held in early 2012, while other candidates were chosen by consensus.

Rather than stimulating pluralistic policymaking, the opposition's sizable presence in the National Assembly has resulted in a new forum for polarized and occasionally violent partisan confrontation. Two opposition members were stripped of their seats in 2013 despite a lack of formal charges against them. The government's majority ensures that the opposition is denied any meaningful opportunity to play a role in proposing and debating legislation and monitoring government operations.

C. Functioning of Government: 2 / 12

The government plays a major role in the economy and has created regulatory restrictions that increase opportunities for corruption, particularly via the selective disbursement of scarce U.S. dollars at the greatly distorted official exchange rate. Several large development funds are controlled by the executive branch without independent oversight. The largest, the National Development Fund (FONDEN), has received over $100 billion since 2005 and provides half of Venezuela's public investment, with no legislative examination of its many large-scale, unproductive allocations. The government's strong reliance on oil revenue to pay for services and distribute welfare benefits increases the probability that falling oil income will affect political stability.

Anticorruption efforts have been a low government priority, and the lack of state transparency makes citizen investigation and exposure of corruption difficult. The creation in September 2013 of a new body, the Strategic Center for Security and Protection of the Homeland (CESPPA), threatened to produce further restrictions on transparency, given the extensive classification and censorship powers included in the agency's mandate. Maduro's announcement of an anticorruption campaign in May was followed by several arrests in June and July, including of managers in several state-owned enterprises. Corruption scandals continued to emerge, however, including the revelation of tens of millions of dollars in fraud at the Sports Ministry in October. Venezuela was ranked 160 out of 177 countries surveyed in Transparency International's 2013 Corruption Perceptions Index.

CIVIL LIBERTIES: 24 / 60
D. Freedom of Expression and Belief: 8 / 16 (-1)

Although the constitution provides for freedom of the press, the media climate is permeated by intimidation, sometimes including physical attacks, and strong antimedia rhetoric by the government is common. The 2004 Law on Social Responsibility of Radio and Television gives the government the authority to control radio and television content. Opposition-oriented outlets make up a large portion of the print media, but their share of the broadcast media has declined in recent years, in part due to closures by regulators and other forms of official pressure, such as selective exchange-rate controls. Coverage of election campaigns by state media has been overwhelmingly biased in favor of the government; private outlets have also exhibited bias, though to a somewhat lesser degree.

Local press watchdog Public Space registered 219 press violations during the year, including a large number of arbitrary detentions and acts of aggression against reporters covering social problems such as prison riots and food lines. Two U.S. journalists were among those detained in 2013. One, *Miami Herald* correspondent Jim Wyss, was held by the military for several days in November while investigating cross-border smuggling into Colombia. Shortages of newsprint forced several papers to suspend publication. The sale of the markedly pro-opposition television station Globovisión to new owners was announced in March. While the new management took initial steps to assuage opposition fears that the station would join the progovernment media, by late May several prominent opposition and independent voices had left the channel and complained about a lack of editorial independence.

The government does not restrict internet access, but in 2007 it nationalized the dominant telephone company, CANTV, giving the authorities a potential tool to hinder access. During the 2013 election CANTV shut down broadband access for approximately 30 minutes, ostensibly to assist a government investigation of hacking attempts against officials' Twitter microblog accounts. A law passed during the December 2010 lame-duck legislative session extended the 2004 broadcasting law's restrictions to the internet. In recent years, dozens of prominent opposition activists and journalists have found that their Twitter accounts had been hacked and used to disseminate antiopposition messages.

Constitutional guarantees of religious freedom are generally respected, though government tensions with the Roman Catholic Church remain high. Government relations with the small Jewish community have also been strained at times.

Academic freedom came under mounting pressure during Chávez's tenure, and a school curriculum developed by his government emphasizes socialist concepts. A 2008 Organic Education Law included ambiguities that could lead to restrictions on private education and increased control by the government and communal councils. In universities, elections for student associations and administration positions have become more politicized, and rival groups of students have clashed repeatedly over both academic and political matters.

Freedom of private discussion suffered during 2013 due to a series of releases of illegally recorded conversations of prominent Venezuelans—including hard-line Chavista television host Mario Silva and opposition leader María Corina Machado—as well as increased fear regarding the economic repercussions, such as loss of employment, resulting from criticism of the government.

E. Associational and Organizational Rights: 4 / 12

Freedom of peaceful assembly is guaranteed in the constitution. However, the right to protest has become a sensitive topic in recent years, and rights groups have criticized legal amendments that make it easier to charge protesters with serious crimes. Workers, particularly employees of state-owned enterprises, are the most frequent demonstrators, followed by citizens protesting poor delivery of public services and high crime rates. Although most protests are permitted and occur without incident, Maduro barred the opposition from holding a march in downtown Caracas a few days after the April 2013 election.

Nongovernmental organizations (NGOs) are also frequent antagonists of the government, which has sought to undermine the legitimacy of human rights and other civil society groups by questioning their international ties. In December 2010, the lame-duck parliament passed the Law on Political Sovereignty and National Self-Determination, which threatens sanctions against any "political organization" that receives foreign funding or hosts foreign visitors who criticize the government. Dozens of civil society activists have been physically attacked in recent years, and other forms of harassment are common, including bureaucratic hurdles to registration. In October 2013 the National Assembly created a commission charged with investigating NGOs that were allegedly receiving foreign financing with the intent of plotting to undermine the government.

Workers are legally entitled to form unions, bargain collectively, and strike, with some restrictions on public-sector workers' ability to strike. Control of unions has shifted from traditional opposition-allied labor leaders to new workers' organizations that are often aligned with the government. The growing competition has contributed to a substantial increase in labor violence as well as confusion during industrywide collective bargaining. Labor strife has also risen due to the addition of thousands of employees of nationalized companies to the state payroll, and the government's failure to implement new collective-bargaining agreements. In 2013 rights groups accused the government of firing opposition sympathizers from jobs in state-owned enterprises following the April election.

F. Rule of Law: 4 / 16

Politicization of the judicial branch increased dramatically under Chávez, and high courts generally do not rule against the government. Conviction rates remain low, the public defender system is underfunded, and nearly half of all judges and prosecutors lack tenure, undermining their autonomy. The National Assembly has the authority to remove and appoint judges to the TSJ, which controls the rest of the judiciary. In December 2010 the outgoing legislature appointed nine new TSJ judges who are generally viewed as friendly to the government. In April 2012 a fired and exiled TSJ judge, Eladio Aponte, accused administration officials of instructing judges on how to rule in sensitive cases. Judge María Lourdes Afiuni was released from house arrest in June 2013, though her trial on corruption charges was ongoing at year's end. She was arrested in 2009 after angering the government by ordering the release of a prominent banker who had been held without conviction for more than the maximum of two years.

Venezuela's murder rate is among the world's highest. The nongovernmental Venezuelan Violence Observatory cited at least 24,700 murders in 2013, a figure that represents a rate of approximately 79 homicides per 100,000 citizens. The government claimed a figure of 39 murders per 100,000, but offered no further details. The police and military have been prone to corruption, widespread arbitrary detention and torture of suspects, and extrajudicial killings. In 2009, the justice minister admitted that police were involved in up to 20 percent of crimes; few officers are convicted, partly due to a shortage of prosecutors. Several anticrime initiatives formulated during Chávez's second term received praise from policy analysts and rights groups, but a continued rise in violence prompted Maduro to deploy National Guard forces to the streets in May 2013, leading the same observers to decry the trend toward militarization. Prison conditions in Venezuela remain among the worst in the Americas. The NGO Venezuelan Prison Observatory reported 289 violent deaths within prison walls in the first six months of 2013, including at least 61 during a massive riot in January at a prison in Barquisimeto.

Following a short-lived military coup in 2002, Chávez began to purge the military of unsympathetic officers, politicize those who remained, and heighten military participation in the delivery of public services. Military officials, many of them in active service, occupy top positions in several government ministries, and the armed forces perform routine government duties, blurring the lines between civilian and military functions. Foreign officials assert that the military has adopted a permissive attitude toward drug trafficking, as evidenced by the confiscation of over one ton of cocaine on an Air France flight arriving in Paris from Caracas in September 2013. Eight members of the National Guard, which is tasked with airport security, were arrested. In recent years, the division of responsibility between the military and civilian militias has become less clear, and informal progovernment groups have carried out attacks on press outlets and, occasionally, individual journalists and opposition supporters.

The formal and constitutional rights of indigenous people, who make up about 2 percent of the population, improved under Chávez, though such rights are seldom enforced by local authorities. The constitution reserves three seats in the National Assembly for indigenous people. Indigenous communities trying to defend their land rights are subject to abuses, particularly along the Colombian border. In March 2013, indigenous leader Sabino Romero, who had sought greater land rights for the Yukpa indigenous group, was killed in Zulia State. Afro-Venezuelans also remain marginalized and underrepresented among the country's political and economic elite. Although discrimination based on sexual orientation is barred, LGBT (lesbian, gay, bisexual, and transgender) Venezuelans face de facto discrimination similar to the situation in much of Latin America, and are occasionally subjected to violence.

G. Personal Autonomy and Individual Rights: 8 / 16 (+1)

Property rights are affected by the government's penchant for price controls and nationalizations. While the pace of nationalizations has declined from previous years—due in part to the state's dominant position in many strategic industries—the government continues to threaten to nationalize businesses deemed to lack commitment to revolutionary goals. Accusations of mismanagement, underinvestment, corruption, and politicized hiring practices within state-owned enterprises and utilities are common, with several large blackouts in 2013 illustrating the problem. The incidence of consumer-goods shortages rose sharply in 2013. The opposition pointed to the perverse effects of price controls and other economic policies, while the government blamed speculators and capitalist conspirators, culminating in the November forced price cuts, arrests, and the enabling law that gave Maduro decree power on economic issues.

Women are guaranteed progressive rights in the 1999 constitution, as well as benefits under a major 2007 law. However, despite some improvements on implementation of these pledges, domestic violence and rape remain common and are rarely punished in practice. Trafficking of women remains inadequately addressed by the authorities. Women are poorly represented in government, with just 17 percent of the seats in the National Assembly, but they hold a number of important offices in the executive branch.

Vietnam

Political Rights Ratings: 7
Civil Liberties Ratings: 5
Freedom Rating: 6.0
Freedom Status: Not Free
Electoral Democracy: No

Population: 89,700,000
Capital: Hanoi

Ten-Year Ratings Timeline For Year Under Review (Political Rights, Civil Liberties, Status)

Year Under Review Rating	2004	2005	2006	2007	2008	2009	2010	2011	2012	2013
	7,6,NF	7,5,NF	7,5,NF	7,5,NF	7,5,NF	7,5,NF	7,5,NF	7,5,NF	7,5,NF	7,5,NF

INTRODUCTION

In 2013, Vietnam continued its intense crackdown on free expression online, in print, and in the public. The state convicted more than twice as many dissidents for activities like "conducting propaganda against the state" in 2013 than it did in 2012. In September, the state introduced a new law, Decree 72, that restricted all websites and social media from publishing anything that "provides information that is against Vietnam," an incredibly broad provision that could essentially permit the government to arrest any Internet user in the country.

The repression did not stop the public from venting its anger—through social media and other forums—at perceptions of nepotism and vast corruption within the Communist Party of Vietnam (CPV), and at the slowing economy. Party leaders, including President Truong Tan Sang, acknowledged this anger and criticized some of the government's actions, but did not enact meaningful reforms to stop corruption or promote political pluralism.

Despite the overall worsening climate for civil liberties and political freedoms, the CPV decided in November to lift its ban on gay marriage. Though it did not officially legalize same-sex marriage, Vietnam is the first country in Asia to allow same-sex unions.

The country also enhanced its strategic ties with influential democracies in 2013, including Japan and the United States, which hosted Vietnam's president for a White House visit and launched a "comprehensive partnership" with Vietnam. Vietnam also joined the negotiations for a major regional free trade deal, the Trans-Pacific Partnership.

POLITICAL RIGHTS: 3 / 40 (+1)

A. Electoral Process: 0 / 12

The CPV, Vietnam's the sole legal political party, controls politics and the government, and its Central Committee is the top decision-making body. The National Assembly, whose 500 members are elected to five-year terms, generally follows CPV dictates. The president, elected by the National Assembly for a five-year term, appoints the prime minister, who is confirmed by the legislature.

Tightly controlled elections for the one-party National Assembly were held in May 2011, with the CPV taking 454 seats, officially vetted nonparty members securing 42 seats, and self-nominated candidates garnering the remaining 4. In July 2011, the legislature approved Nguyễn Tấn Dũng, the prime minister since 2006, for another term, and elected Trương Tấn Sang as the state president.

B. Political Pluralism and Participation: 1 / 16

The CPV is the only legally allowed party in Vietnam. The Vietnam Fatherland Front, essentially an arm of the CPV, vets all candidates for the National Assembly. Membership in the Party is now primarily seen as a means to business and societal connections.

Although splits within different factions of the party have become more noticeable to outsiders and some educated Vietnamese, they are not openly aired, and websites or other media in Vietnam that discuss these splits are shut down and prosecuted. Many urban Vietnamese participate in political debate by using remote servers and social media to criticize nepotism and mismanagement by party leaders.

C. Functioning of Government: 2 / 12 (+1)

Vietnam's government has become increasingly saddled by corruption, splits, and an inability to manage the country's problems. Although the CPV has since the late 1980s overseen a long period of economic expansion, growth has slowed in the past four years, and the government has failed to address serious problems, including a widening wealth gap and vast debts within state-owned enterprises. Splits within the CPV have become slightly more open, and the government has failed to seriously address corruption within the party or nepotism in the Party and state companies.

Although senior CPV and government officials have acknowledged growing public discontent, they have not responded with comprehensive reforms. Government decisions are still made with little transparency. A plan announced in spring 2013 to make state companies more transparent was not put into practice.

CIVIL LIBERTIES: 17 / 60

D. Freedom of Expression and Belief: 4 / 16

The government tightly controls the media, silencing critics through the courts and other means of harassment. A 1999 law requires journalists to pay damages to groups or individuals found to have been harmed by press articles, even if the reports are accurate. A

2006 decree imposes fines on journalists for denying revolutionary achievements, spreading "harmful" information, or exhibiting "reactionary ideology." Foreign media representatives legally cannot travel outside Hanoi without government approval, though they often do in practice. The CPV or other state entities control all broadcast media. Although satellite television is officially restricted to senior officials, international hotels, and foreign businesses, many homes and businesses have satellite dishes. All print media outlets are owned by or are under the effective control of the CPV, government organs, or the army.

The government restricts internet use through legal and technical means. A 2003 law bans the receipt and distribution of antigovernment e-mail messages, websites considered "reactionary" are blocked, and owners of domestic websites must submit their content for official approval. Internet cafés must register the personal information of and record the sites visited by users. Internet-service providers face fines and closure for violating censorship rules.

In 2013, the government increased its repression of print and online journalists, jailing more than twice as many writers and bloggers in 2013 as it did the previous year. In June, the government arrested Pham Viet Dao, perhaps the best-known blogger in Vietnam, and charged him with "abusing democratic freedoms." In September, the state introduced Decree 72, which restricted all websites and social media from publishing anything that "provides information that is against Vietnam," an incredibly broad provision. The law also bans anyone using social media from writing about anything but "personal information," and requires foreign Internet companies, like Google and Yahoo!, to maintain servers inside Vietnam, making it easier for Hanoi to censor any information that appears on their sites.

Religious freedom also remains restricted, having declined somewhat after a series of improvements in the mid-2000s. All religious groups and most individual clergy members must join a party-controlled supervisory body and obtain permission for most activities. The Roman Catholic Church can now select its own bishops and priests, but they must be approved by the government. Catholic leaders continued to be arrested around the country in 2013, and in September, Vietnamese authorities forcibly broke up a protest by Catholics in a town south of Hanoi, injuring at least 40 people.

Academic freedom is limited. University professors must refrain from criticizing government policies and adhere to party views when teaching or writing on political topics. Although citizens enjoy more freedom in private discussions than in the past, the authorities continue to punish open criticism of the state.

E. Associational and Organizational Rights: 1 / 12

Freedoms of association and assembly are tightly restricted. Organizations must apply for official permission to obtain legal status and are closely regulated and monitored by the government. A small but active community of nongovernmental groups promotes environmental conservation, land rights, women's development, and public health. Land rights activists are frequently arrested; in April 2013, a court sentenced a group of fish farmers who fought back against land eviction to two to five years in jail. Occasional protests have erupted in major cities against China in the past two years, but these demonstrations are encouraged by the Vietnamese government and closely monitored. Human rights organizations and other private groups with rights-oriented agendas are banned. In early 2013, Vietnam allowed a representative of Amnesty International to visit the country for the first time in decades for a "dialogue," but that discussion has thus far produced no tangible results.

The Vietnam General Conference of Labor (VGCL), closely tied to the CPV, is the only legal labor federation. All trade unions are required to join the VGCL. However, in recent years the government has permitted hundreds of independent "labor associations" without formal union status to represent workers at individual firms and in some service industries. Farmer and worker protests against local government abuses, including land confiscations and unfair or harsh working conditions, have become more common. The central leadership often responds by pressuring local governments and businesses to comply with tax laws, environmental regulations, and wage agreements. Enforcement of labor laws covering child labor, workplace safety, and other issues remains poor.

F. Rule of Law: 4 / 16

Vietnam's judiciary is subservient to the CPV, which controls courts at all levels. Defendants have a constitutional right to counsel, but lawyers are scarce, and many are reluctant to take on human rights and other sensitive cases for fear of harassment and retribution—including arrest—by the state. Defense attorneys cannot call or question witnesses and are rarely permitted to request leniency for their clients. Police can hold individuals in administrative detention for up to two years on suspicion of threatening national security. The police are known to abuse suspects and prisoners, and prison conditions are poor. Many political prisoners remain behind bars, and political detainees are often held incommunicado. After an 18-month hiatus to re-examine the death penalty, Vietnam resumed using capital punishment in August 2013.

G. Personal Autonomy and Individual Rights: 8 / 16

Ethnic minorities, who often adhere to minority religions, face discrimination in mainstream society, and some local officials restrict their access to schooling and jobs. Minorities generally have little input on development projects that affect their livelihoods and communities.

Despite the overall worsening of the climate for political rights and civil liberties in Vietnam, over the past two years the government has allowed increasingly open displays of Lesbian, Gay, Bisexual, and Transgender (LGBT) rights. LGBT supporters held pride days in 2012 and 2013 in Vietnam, and the country's state media aired a gay-themed sitcom. In November 2013, the government passed a law removing its ban on gay marriages, though it stopped short of recognizing same-sex unions.

Women hold 122 seats in the National Assembly. Women generally have equal access to education and are treated similarly in the legal system as men. Although economic opportunities have grown for women, they continue to face discrimination in wages and promotion. Many women are victims of domestic violence, and thousands each year are trafficked internally and externally and forced into prostitution.

Yemen

Political Rights Rating: 6
Civil Liberties Rating: 6
Freedom Ratings: 6.0
Freedom Status: Not Free
Electoral Democracy: No

Population: 25,200,000
Capital: Sanaa

Ten-Year Ratings Timeline For Year Under Review (Political Rights, Civil Liberties, Status)

Year Under Review	2004	2005	2006	2007	2008	2009	2010	2011	2012	2013
Rating	5,5,PF	5,5,PF	5,5,PF	5,5,PF	5,5,PF	6,5,PF	6,5,NF	6,6,NF	6,6,NF	6,6,NF

INTRODUCTION

Yemen continued to face political uncertainty in 2013. After replacing long-time president Ali Abdullah Saleh in 2012, President Abu Rabu Mansur Hadi struggled to address a series of national challenges. The secessionist movement in southern Yemen staged protests throughout the year against corruption and lack of political inclusion. Security forces responded violently to protests several times during the year, including in February when authorities killed at least 9 people in response to demonstrations in Aden. Hadi took steps to limit the lingering influence of Saleh and his family in June when he sacked several of the former president's family members from prominent positions in the military and reassigned them to diplomatic posts abroad.

The country's National Dialogue Conference (NDC), a months-long initiative including over 500 delegates aiming to resolve issues such as corruption and Yemen's political future launched in March. Originally scheduled to conclude in September and to put forward a new constitution for a national referendum in October, the NDC was extended and the referendum delayed through the end of the year due to ongoing tensions with the South.

Low level clashes in the North between the Ansar Allah, a Houthi rebel movement, and their Salafi and Al-Islah Sunni opponents spilled into Sanaa with the spread of demonstrations and random violence there. Security killed 10 Houthi protestors in June.

Al-Qaeda in the Arabian Peninsula (AQAP) carried out regular attacks during the year. Insecurity in the south and Yemeni and American concerns about terrorism led the United States to continue its controversial policy of using to unmanned aerial drones to strike at targets in the country.

POLITICAL RIGHTS: 10 / 40 (+1)

A. Electoral Process: 3 / 12

Elections have been marred by flaws including vote buying, the partisanship of public officials and the military, and exploitation of state control over key media platforms. The original six-year mandate of the current parliament expired in 2009, and elections were postponed again amid the turmoil of 2011. The political system has long been dominated by former president Saleh's General People's Congress (GPC) party, and there are few limits on the authority of the executive branch. The president is elected for seven-year terms, and appoints the 111 members of the largely advisory upper house of parliament, the Majlis al-Shura (Consultative Council). The 301 members of the lower house, the House of Representatives, are elected to serve six-year terms. Provincial councils and governors are also elected.

B. Political Pluralism and Participation: 4 / 16

Yemen's relatively well-developed and experienced opposition parties have historically been able to wring some concessions from the government. The 2011 ouster of President

Saleh was accomplished through a sustained campaign of protests motivated primarily by grievances over imbalances of power and levels of corruption, but also over lack of access to decision-making and political participation by regular citizens. Under sustained pressure from the United States, the United Nations, and the Gulf Cooperation Council, Saleh signed a Saudi-brokered agreement in November 2011 that transferred his powers to Yemen's vice president, Abdu Rabu Mansur Hadi, in exchange for immunity from prosecution for his role in the violent crackdown during the 2011 demonstrations. In 2012, Yemeni voters selected Hadi, who ran unopposed, as the country's new president.

As part of the transitional agreement, the Yemeni government and the opposition launched the country's NDC in March. The NDC, while boycotted by some in the opposition, was attended by 565 delegates, including members of the Southern separatist movement as well as rebels from the north. The Dialogue was not free of controversy, as some Yemenis were displeased with which delegates were selected to participate. The NDC was meant to move forward a new constitution that would be put up for a national referendum in October. The referendum was delayed due to tensions between Sanaa and the South. In December, several political parties agreed that giving limited autonomy to the South based vaguely on the notion of federalism would help break through stalled dialogue talks. It remained unclear at the end of the year what political force the agreement would have.

C. Functioning of Government: 3 / 12 (+1)

Corruption is endemic. Despite recent efforts by the government to fight graft, Yemen lacks most legal safeguards against conflicts of interest. Auditing and investigative bodies are not sufficiently independent of executive authorities. Yemen was ranked 167 out of 177 countries surveyed in Transparency International's 2013 Corruption Perceptions Index.

Since coming to power, Hadi has struggled to consolidate his political authority. Yemen's political stability has been adversely affected by meddling by Saleh and his supporters within the military. Hadi took steps to address Saleh's lingering influence within the military in 2012 by restructuring the army and dismissing military leaders closely related to Saleh, including his son, brother, and one of his nephews. Hadi took additional measures in 2013, assigning Saleh's son Ahmed Ali Saleh as the country's ambassador to the UAE and sending Saleh's nephew Ammar Muhammad Abdullah Saleh to Ethiopia, where he took up a diplomatic post as military attaché.

CIVIL LIBERTIES: 16 / 60
D. Freedom of Expression and Belief: 6 / 16

The government does not respect freedoms of expression and the press. Article 103 of the Press and Publications Law bans direct personal criticism of the head of state and publication of material that "might spread a spirit of dissent and division among the people" or that "leads to the spread of ideas contrary to the principles of the Yemeni Revolution, [is] prejudicial to national unity or [distorts] the image of the Yemeni, Arab, or Islamic heritage." The government controls most terrestrial television and radio; however, seven privately-owned radio stations launched between 2012 and the end of 2013. Although they have diminished in scale as the 2011 protest movement receded, attacks on journalists have continued. In February Wagdi al-Shabi, who previously worked for the Yemeni daily *Al-Ayyam*, was killed by unknown assailants wearing military uniforms in his home in Aden. In April an explosive device was found in the offices of Shabab TV in Sanaaand disarmed before it could detonate. Mansoor Noor, a correspondent for the *September 26* newspaper, was shot in Aden and had to have his leg amputated. Also in April two Al Jazeera journalists were attacked by members of the Southern secessionist movement.

Abdulelah Haider Shaye, who had reported on American responsibility for military strikes that killed civilians and was arrested and convicted in 2011 of allegedly having ties to Al-Qaeda, was transferred from prison to house arrest in July, where he will spend the remaining two years of his sentence despite having been pardoned by former-president Saleh shortly after his conviction. His continued imprisonment is the result of pressure from the U.S. government.

Access to the internet is not widespread, and the authorities block websites they deem offensive. Although the ban on most news website has been lifted, some websites and forums where political debate takes place are blocked due to security concerns.

The constitution states that Islam is the official religion and declares Sharia (Islamic law) to be the source of all legislation. Yemen has few non-Muslim religious minorities, and their rights are generally respected in practice. The government has imposed some restrictions on religious activity in the context of the rebellion in the northern province of Saada. Mosques' hours of operation have been limited in the area, and imams suspected of extremism have been removed. Strong politicization of campus life, including tensions between supporters of the ruling GPC and the opposition al-Islah party, infringes on academic freedom at universities.

E. Associational and Organizational Rights: 3 / 12

Yemenis have historically enjoyed some freedom of assembly, with periodic restrictions and sometimes deadly interventions by the government. Over the past four years, southern Yemenis have mounted growing protests to challenge the government's alleged corruption and abuse of power, the marginalization of southerners in the political system, and the government's inability to address pressing social and economic concerns. The protest movement has in the past called for secession by the south, although several of the movement's leaders agreed to participate in the NDC.

Freedom of association is constitutionally guaranteed. Several thousand nongovernmental organizations work in the country, although their ability to operate is restricted in practice. The law acknowledges the right of workers to form and join trade unions, but some critics claim that the government and ruling party elements have increased efforts to control the affairs of these organizations. Virtually all unions belong to a single labor federation, and the government is empowered to veto collective bargaining agreements.

F. Rule of Law: 2 / 16

The judiciary is nominally independent, but it is susceptible to interference from the executive branch. Authorities have a poor record on enforcing judicial rulings, particularly those issued against prominent tribal or political leaders. Lacking an effective court system, citizens often resort to tribal forms of justice or direct appeals to executive authorities. Arbitrary detention is partly the result of inadequate training for law enforcement officers and a lack of political will on the part of senior government officials to eliminate the problem. Security forces affiliated with the Political Security Office (PSO) and the Ministry of the Interior torture and abuse detainees, and PSO prisons are not closely monitored. As part of the November 2011 agreement for him to step down from power, Ali Abdullah Saleh was granted immunity from prosecution for his role in the country's deadly crackdown in 2011.

Tensions between Zaidis, Yemen's largest Shiite community, and Sunnis escalated and spread in 2013. Ongoing unrest between Ansar Allah, a Houthi rebel movement and the state in the North continued in 2013. Clashes between Houthis an Sunni Salafis in the north killed more than 250 people in November and December. Tensions also spread to Sanaa where the two communities waged low level violence against one another, including random attacks, struggles to control mosques, and staging competing demonstrations. State authorities responded harshly against Zaidi protests, killed 10 in one demonstration in June.

Same-sex sexual activity is illegal and punishable by death. In 2013 there were credible reports of AQAP killing men for allegedly being gay. Due to the severe threat against them, few LGBT Yemenis reveal their sexuality or gender identity.

Yemen's penal code allows lenient sentences for those convicted of "honor crimes"—assaults or killings of women by family members for alleged immoral behavior. Although the law prohibits female genital mutilation, it is still prevalent.

G. Personal Autonomy and Individual Rights: 5 / 16

Yemen is relatively ethnically and racially homogeneous. However, the Akhdam, a small minority group, live in poverty and face social discrimination. Thousands of refugees seeking relief from war and poverty in the Horn of Africa are smuggled annually into Yemen, where they are routinely subjected to theft, abuse, and even murder. Up to 200,000 Yemenis working in Saudi Arabia either faced or were forcibly deported from the oil-rich kingdom in 2013. Yemen's economy has struggled over the last year, with inflation rising from 5.5 percent in November 2012 to over 14 percent in September.

Women continue to face discrimination in several aspects of life. A woman must obtain permission from her husband or father to receive a passport and travel abroad, cannot confer citizenship on a foreign-born spouse, and can transfer Yemeni citizenship to their children only in special circumstances. Women are vastly underrepresented in elected office; there is just one woman in the lower house of parliament. School enrollment and educational attainment rates for girls fall far behind those for boys.

⬇ Zambia

Political Rights Rating: 3
Civil Liberties Rating: 4
Freedom Rating: 3.5
Freedom Status: Partly Free
Electoral Democracy: Yes

Population: 14,200,000
Capital: Lusaka

Trend Arrow: Zambia received a downward trend arrow due to the ruling party's ongoing repression and harassment of the political opposition, including through the increased use of the Public Order Act, hindering its ability to operate in general and to campaign in by-elections.

Ten-Year Ratings Timeline For Year Under Review (Political Rights, Civil Liberties, Status)

Year Under Review	2004	2005	2006	2007	2008	2009	2010	2011	2012	2013
Rating	4,4,PF	4,4,PF	3,4,PF	3,4,PF	3,3,PF	3,4,PF	3,4,PF	3,4,PF	3,4,PF	3,4,PF

INTRODUCTION

In 2013, President Michael Sata and his Patriotic Front (PF) party achieved some progress on economic reforms but generally failed to fulfill other promises—such as promulgating a new constitution, media-sector reforms, and rooting out corruption—that they made ahead of the 2011 elections, in which they ousted the long-governing Movement for Multiparty Democracy (MMD). Instead, Sata and the PF governed in an increasingly autocratic manner, using repressive laws and policies as well as extralegal intimidation against the opposition, media, and civil society.

As part of what many alleged was a concerted effort to undermine the MMD and another opposition faction, the United Party for National Development (UPND), the PF government prevented numerous political gatherings throughout the year by invoking the colonial-era Public Order Act and filing multiple legal cases against UPND leader Hakainde Hichilema and MMD leader Nevers Mumba. In addition, more than 35 by-elections were held during 2012 and 2013 due to successful PF court challenges regarding seats it had lost in the 2011 polls, as well as a PF strategy of enticing opposition legislators to change sides with offers of government posts. (A party switch automatically triggers a by-election.) With the opposition further weakened by internal discord in the MMD, the PF has been able to win several new seats and gain an outright majority in the National Assembly.

The year's increased harassment of opposition and independent media outlets included the blocking of the critical *Zambian Watchdog* and *Zambia Reports* websites and the arrest of journalists allegedly associated with the *Zambian Watchdog*.

In April 2012, a draft of a long-promised new constitution was unveiled, containing several encouraging provisions, such as a requirement that presidential candidates gain more than 50 percent of the vote to win, a strengthened bill of rights, and greater independence for the electoral commission. However, critics have asserted that the draft awards too much power to the president. The final version was scheduled for submission by late 2012, but the process was plagued by delays and a lack of clarity in the way consultations with the public were conducted, and civil society groups criticized the lack of a timeline for a promised national referendum. The draft was eventually finalized in late October 2013. In early November, the technical committee in charge of drafting the charter refused an order from the Justice Ministry that it print only 10 copies, to be given to the president and his close aides. The committee claimed that its terms of reference required it to provide the final draft to both the president and the public at the same time. The committee ultimately handed over the final draft to Sata on December 31, sparking concern from civil society that the government could alter provisions it did not like.

POLITICAL RIGHTS: 25 / 40 (-3)
A. Electoral Process: 8 / 12 (-1)

The president and the unicameral National Assembly are elected to serve concurrent five-year terms. The National Assembly includes 150 elected members, as well as 8 members appointed by the president. In the September 2011 presidential election, Sata defeated incumbent Rupiah Banda of the MMD, 43 percent to 36 percent. In concurrent parliamentary elections, the PF won a plurality, taking 61 seats, followed by the MMD with 55 and the UPND with 29. Although the elections were characterized by fierce campaigning, the misuse of state resources by the MMD, and isolated rioting, the voting was deemed free and credible by international observers.

The numerous by-elections in 2012 and 2013 altered the balance of power in the National Assembly, and analysts have warned that the PF's maneuvers to increase its parliamentary representation could jeopardize Zambia's democratic credentials. As of the end of 2013, the PF held 68 elected seats (plus the 8 appointed by the president), while the MMD's count had dropped to 42 and the UPND's had moved to 30. Several of the by-election campaigns have been characterized by violence between party cadres on all sides, as well as blatant misuse of state resources and the media by the PF to win votes and discredit the opposition. In one notable episode in late February 2013, the by-election in Livingstone was postponed for two weeks after PF official Harrison Chanda was killed during the last days of campaigning. Several members of the UPND were charged with Chanda's murder, and Hichilema was charged with inciting violence. It was later found that Chanda had been killed by another PF member. The PF candidate won the by-election.

B. Political Pluralism and Participation: 10 / 16 (-2)

The major political parties are the PF, the MMD, and the UPND. Since its 2011 election loss, the MMD has been weakened considerably due to infighting and the PF's effort to coopt its members. Throughout 2013, the PF-led government harassed and intimidated the MMD, the UPND, and smaller opposition parties. It utilized the colonial-era Public Order Act to prevent the opposition from holding meetings and rallies. According to reports, the authorities employed the act to arrest both Hichilema and Mumba during meetings with their constituents, and—citing previous violence by opposition supporters—told the party leaders that they needed permission for all rallies or meetings. In May 2013, police prevented the small opposition National Restoration Party from conducting an indoor strategy workshop. Party president Elias Chipimo Jr. was arrested and charged with unlawful assembly.

Mumba and Hichilema were subjected to other forms of legal harassment during the year, facing arrest numerous times on charges such as abuse of office and defamation. Opposition supporters were at times physically attacked by PF cadres, including an assault on Hichilema and his staff in September near Kasama. Opposition leaders and supporters have also been responsible for inflammatory statements and violence.

C. Functioning of Government: 7 / 12

Corruption is believed to be widespread. The Sata government has taken some steps to fight graft, but many of its prosecutions have allegedly been politically motivated. In 2012, the National Assembly reinserted the key "abuse of office" clause of the Anti-Corruption Act, which had been removed by the MMD-dominated legislature in 2010. The clause allows for the prosecution of public officials for violations such as abuse of authority or misuse of public funds. Meanwhile, Sata's administration launched corruption investigations against several former MMD ministers and officials. In March 2013, the National Assembly voted to lift former president Banda's immunity from prosecution; he was subsequently arrested, and his passport was confiscated temporarily. Among other charges, he was accused of abuse of power in connection with a $2.5 million oil deal with a Nigerian company from which he allegedly benefitted during his 2008–2011 presidency. Banda denied the charges, and suggested that the case was retribution by the director of public prosecutions, Mutembo Nchito, for a case against Nchito and another close Sata ally, *Post* newspaper owner Fred M'membe, that had begun while Banda was president. In that case, Nchito and M'membe were ordered in 2012 to repay at least $2.5 million to the Development Bank of Zambia, having borrowed it in an effort to finance Zambian Airways, which collapsed in 2009. In response, Sata had suspended the judges who issued the ruling. In December 2013, the Supreme Court sent the case back to the High Court for a retrial, citing irregularities in the first trial. Meanwhile, the case against Banda was ongoing at year's end.

Sata's government has made repeated promises to pass an access to information law, but had not taken action on an existing draft by the end of 2013. Zambia was ranked 83 out of 177 countries and territories surveyed in Transparency International's 2013 Corruption Perceptions Index.

CIVIL LIBERTIES: 34 / 60
D. Freedom of Expression and Belief: 11 / 16

Freedoms of speech and the press are constitutionally guaranteed, but the government often restricted these rights in practice in 2013. Although Sata had pledged to free the public media—consisting of the Zambia National Broadcasting Corporation (ZNBC) and the widely circulated *Zambia Daily Mail* and *Times of Zambia*—from government control, these outlets have generally continued to report along progovernment lines, and journalists practice self-censorship. The other main daily is the private but pro-PF *Post*; as a result of the PF's move into government in 2011, all the major print and broadcast outlets now favor the ruling party. The ZNBC dominates the broadcast media, although several private stations have the capacity to reach large portions of the population. Only about 13 percent of the population had internet access, according to 2012 figures.

The government has the authority to appoint the management boards of ZNBC and the Independent Broadcasting Authority (IBA), which regulates and grants licenses to broadcasters. In October 2013, IBA board chairman Emmanuel Mwamba, the information and broadcasting permanent secretary, extended nationwide broadcasting licenses to several local radio stations. However, later that month Sata ordered Mwamba to revoke the nationwide licenses issued to privately owned Radio Phoenix and Q-FM because they had aired statements by opposition politicians; the two stations were allowed to keep their licenses to broadcast in Lusaka. Sata said only the ZNBC and religious stations should be allowed to have nationwide licenses. Mwamba was fired soon thereafter.

The government stepped up legal harassment and intimidation of independent journalists in 2013. It targeted in particular the highly critical *Zambian Watchdog*, which is hosted outside Zambia, employs anonymous reporters, and often uses inflammatory language against the authorities. In late June, the site was blocked by certain internet service providers in Zambia. Eventually, it became completely inaccessible via web browsers inside Zambia and, for some periods, outside the country as well, although its content could be accessed on mobile phones, using circumvention tools, and via Facebook and Twitter. Another critical website, *Zambia Reports*, was also blocked at times. In early July, the government raided the homes of two journalists whom they accused of writing for the *Zambian Watchdog*—Clayson Hamasaka and Thomas Zyambo—and searched for seditious material and drugs. The police confiscated their computers and other equipment, and the two journalists were detained without charge for over 24 hours. Zyambo was ultimately charged with sedition in connection with documents about Sata that were found in his home. Hamasaka was charged with possession of pornography. Another journalist allegedly associated with the *Zambian Watchdog*, Wilson Pondamali, was arrested in mid-July and faced several charges, including malicious damage to property and attempted escape from lawful custody. He was held for two weeks before being granted bail. Separately, Richard Sakala, the owner of the *Daily Nation*, one of the few remaining independent print outlets, appeared in court with two others in December to face the charge of publishing false news. None of the cases had been resolved at year's end.

Constitutionally protected religious freedom is respected in practice. The government does not restrict academic freedom.

E. Associational and Organizational Rights: 7 / 12

Freedom of assembly is guaranteed under the constitution but is not consistently respected by the government. Under the Public Order Act, police must receive a week's notice before all demonstrations. While the law does not require permits, the police in 2013 frequently broke up "illegal" rallies and demonstrations led by opposition groups because the organizers lacked permits. The police can choose where and when rallies are held, as well as who can address them. In October, the High Court dismissed a petition in which the independent Law Association of Zambia (LAZ) asked the court to review the constitutionality of the Public Order Act. The LAZ argued that the act infringed on freedoms of expression, assembly, and association, and discriminated against the opposition.

Freedom of association is guaranteed by law but not always respected in practice. Nongovernmental organizations (NGOs) are required to register and to reregister every five years under the 2009 NGO Act, which was signed into law by Banda but not implemented until 2013. The implementation of the law by the PF government was considered a setback for free association in Zambia; the PF in its 2011 campaign had vowed to review the act, which established a government-appointed board to provide guidelines and regulate NGO activity, and grants the government broad discretion to deny reregistration. Every group was initially required to reregister by November 11 or face a ban, but in December the deadline was extended to February 2014.

The law provides for the right to join unions, strike, and bargain collectively. Historically, Zambia's trade unions were among Africa's strongest, but the leading bodies, including the Zambia Congress of Trade Unions, have faced marginalization under PF rule. While labor activism continues, government tolerance for worker action varies widely. In October 2013, the government demanded that the South African–owned retailer Shoprite reinstate striking workers and pay them higher wages. Conversely, a major strike by public-sector nurses and midwives over wages and working conditions in November was met with a harsh government reaction, and resulted in the dismissal of over 200 workers.

F. Rule of Law: 8 / 16

While judicial independence is guaranteed by law, the government does not respect it in practice. Upon taking office, Sata replaced most top judges and judicial officials, alleging that the system was corrupt and needed reform. In a disturbing trend, Sata has set up tribunals to probe alleged misconduct by judges (including the judges who ruled against Sata's allies in the Zambian Airways case), in violation of constitutional provisions on judicial independence. In June 2012, Sata installed his ally and cousin, Lombe Chibesakunda, as acting chief justice of the Supreme Court after forcing out her predecessor. In October 2013, the LAZ mounted protests against and legal challenges to her appointment, which had never been ratified by the National Assembly because she was past the constitutionally mandated retirement age of 65. She has been accused of making biased decisions in favor of the ruling party, including in cases involving PF challenges to opposition victories in the 2011 parliamentary elections.

Zambia's courts lack qualified personnel and resources, and significant trial delays are common. Pretrial detainees are sometimes held for years under harsh conditions, and many of the accused lack access to legal aid owing to limited resources. In rural areas, customary courts of variable quality and consistency—whose decisions often conflict with the constitution and national law—decide many civil matters.

Allegations of police corruption and brutality are widespread, and security forces have generally operated with impunity. There are reports of forced labor, abuse of inmates by authorities, and deplorable health conditions in the country's prisons.

Western Province, a traditionally poor and marginalized region, has repeatedly demanded to secede from Zambia, and successive administrations have had a contentious relationship with its people, the Lozi. This has continued under the PF. In 2012, separatists in the region declared independence after Sata reneged on a campaign promise to honor the 1964 Barotseland Agreement, which gave the area limited local self-governance and provided for future discussions of greater autonomy or independence. In August 2013, the authorities arrested more than 45 people after a separatist leader, Afumba Mombotwa, was declared its administrator general. The detainees were among 64 Barotseland activists detained on charges of treason; they were released in late November.

Consensual sexual activity between members of the same sex is illegal and punishable by prison sentences of up to 15 years, and members of the LGBT (lesbian, gay, bisexual, and transgender) community faced increased public harassment and legal prosecution in 2013. In April, prominent LGBT rights activist Paul Kasonkomona was arrested after calling for same-sex relations to be decriminalized on a live show on privately owned Muvi TV. The management of Muvi TV refused police requests to halt the interview. The trial of Kasonkomona, who was charged with "soliciting for immoral purposes," was ongoing as of the end of 2013. In May, two men, Philip Mubiana and James Mwape, were arrested for engaging in homosexual acts. They pleaded not guilty in a court in the town of Kapiri Mposhi. As of the end of 2013, their trial was ongoing, and they were refused bail. In a surprising development, First Lady Christine Kaseba-Sata, a respected doctor of obstetrics and gynecology, said in early November that no one should be discriminated against based on their sexual orientation.

Persons living with disabilities and with HIV/AIDS routinely face discrimination in society and employment.

G. Personal Autonomy and Individual Rights: 8 / 16

The government generally respects the constitutionally protected rights of free internal movement and foreign travel. However, internal movement is often hindered by petty corruption, such as police demands for bribes at roadblocks, for which perpetrators are rarely prosecuted.

Societal discrimination remains a serious obstacle to women's rights. Women won just 17 of the 150 elected seats in the National Assembly in the September 2011 polls. Women are denied full economic participation, and rural, poor women often require male consent to obtain credit. Discrimination against women is especially prevalent in customary courts, where they are considered subordinate with respect to property, inheritance, and marriage. Rape, while illegal and punishable with up to life in prison with hard labor, is widespread, and the law is not adequately enforced. Spousal rape is not considered a crime. Domestic abuse is common, and traditional norms inhibit many women from reporting assaults.

There is significant labor exploitation in some sectors of the economy. In particular, labor abuses in Chinese-operated copper mines, including unsafe working conditions and resistance to unionization, have been reported. A February 2013 report by Human Rights Watch found that these violations have largely continued despite pledges by Sata to make workers' rights a priority. However, the report also noted that the government's 2013 budget nearly doubled the allocation to the Mines Safety Department, showing some commitment to improving conditions.

The use of children between the ages of 7 and 14 in the most dangerous forms of labor, such as agriculture and mining, is a problem in Zambia. According to the U.S. State Department's 2013 *Trafficking in Persons Report*, the most prevalent forms of exploitation in Zambia were internal trafficking of women and children for domestic servitude and forced labor in agriculture, mining, textile work, and construction.

Zimbabwe

Political Rights Rating: 5
Civil Liberties Rating: 6
Freedom Rating: 5.5
Freedom Status: Not Free
Electoral Democracy: No

Population: 13,038,000
Capital: Harare

Ratings Change: Zimbabwe's political rights rating improved from 6 to 5 due to a decline in harassment and violence against political parties and opposition supporters during the 2013 elections.

Ten-Year Ratings Timeline For Year Under Review (Political Rights, Civil Liberties, Status)

Year Under Review	2004	2005	2006	2007	2008	2009	2010	2011	2012	2013
Rating	7,6,NF	7,6,NF	7,6,NF	7,6,NF	7,6,NF	6,6,NF	6,6,NF	6,6,NF	6,6,NF	5,6,NF

INTRODUCTION

A new constitution passed with approximately 95 percent in favor in a March referendum that saw a record turnout, and was approved by parliament and signed by President Robert Mugabe in May. The new charter paved the way for elections that would the end of the Government of National Unity (GNU, or the "inclusive government") between Mugabe's Zimbabwe African National Union–Patriotic Front (ZANU-PF) and two factions of the Movement for Democratic Change (MDC). The GNU—in which Mugabe served as president and MDC-T leader Morgan Tsvangirai served as prime minister—had been formed in late 2008 to bring to an end an outbreak of severe political violence, mostly targeting MDC supporters, that had followed a contested first-round 2008 presidential vote.

Exploiting their influence over the judiciary, Mugabe and ZANU-PF secured a presidential and parliamentary election date of July 31 despite a deeply flawed voter roll, an underresourced and biased electoral commission, and incomplete media and security sector reforms called for in the new constitution. According to the Zimbabwe Electoral Coalition (ZEC), Mugabe won the presidential vote with 61 percent of the vote, with 34 percent going to Tsvangirai. Meanwhile, ZANU-PF took 197 of the 270 seats in the House of Assembly. While voting day was largely peaceful, the run-up saw crackdowns on civil society and some independent media. Pro-ZANU-PF security forces and militias were deployed to intimidate voters in swing provinces such as Masvingo and Manicaland and to "encourage" turnout in provincial strongholds like Mashonaland and Midlands. Observers from the African Union (AU) and the Southern African Development Community (SADC) endorsed the results as reflective of the people's will, but also cited some irregularities. Tsvangirai and the MDC-T accused ZANU-PF of vote rigging but abandoned a legal challenge of the results in August. Mugabe was sworn in on August 22, and the new parliament was sworn in on September 17.

In September, the European Union (EU) lifted sanctions on the state-owned diamond mining firm Zimbabwe Mining Development Corporation, despite allegations by both domestic and international nongovernmental organizations (NGOs) that the company's resources may have been used to fund parts of ZANU-PF's election campaign. The following month the EU allowed exports of diamonds from mines in the Marange fields, echoing a 2011 decision by the Kimberley Process—an international mechanism designed to prevent the use of diamonds to fund armed conflicts—to lift a suspension of Zimbabwean diamond exports from a number of mines in Marange due to improvements in labor conditions and transparency. Nonetheless, it is clear that some of the mines are controlled by security forces or powerful generals closely tied to the ruling party, and a November 2012 report by Partnership Africa Canada alleged that at least $2 billion in diamonds had been stolen from Marange by military and government officials. Although the EU removed many other sanctions on Zimbabwean individuals and businesses after the constitutional referendum, it retained a small number. The United States retained targeted sanctions, including travel restrictions and asset freezes on Mugabe and other senior ZANU-PF figures, as well as restrictions on the Zimbabwe Mining Development Corporation—which owned the Marange fields—and other firms.

POLITICAL RIGHTS: 12 / 40 (+1)
A. Electoral Process: 3 / 12

The March 2013 constitutional referendum was deemed credible by a range of domestic and outside observers, although the vote was preceded by a widespread crackdown on prodemocracy civil society. The new constitution included a Declaration of Rights (including a range of basic political and civil rights), limited the president to two five-year terms, eliminated the post of prime minister, removed the presidential power to veto legislation and dismiss parliament, devolved some powers to provinces and retained Zimbabwe's bicameral legislature, but failed to introduce reforms to the heavily politicized security sector. The term limit was not retroactive, however, giving Mugabe—who has been the country's president since its independence in 1980—the chance to serve two more terms. It also empowered the president's party, and not parliament, to select a presidential successor in the case of a death in office, a critical provision given that Mugabe turned 89 in early 2013.

The 210 members of the lower House of Assembly are elected by proportional representation (which must include 60 women until the 2023 election), while the 80-member Senate includes 6 members elected from each of the 10 provinces and 20 appointments, including 18 traditional leaders and 2 members representing the disabled.

Although less violent than the 2008 elections, the July 2013 presidential and parliamentary elections were marred by serious irregularities, especially an outdated and incomplete voter roll riddled with hundreds of thousands of "ghost voters." According to the ZEC, over 300,000 voters were rejected at the polls over registration issues, and the Zimbabwe Election Support Network (ZESN)—a domestic observer group—claims that up to 1 million voters were omitted from the roll and/or turned away at the polls. The Electoral Amendment Act in September 2012 had reconstituted the ZEC with new, more independent commissioners, but the president and much of the staff remained partisan, and two of the new commissioners resigned after the July vote, casting doubt on the integrity of the ZEC and its handling of the 2013 election. According to a number of independent political analysts, electoral irregularities ultimately had a greater impact on parliamentary results than on the presidential election, although both were affected. Voting by Zimbabwe's substantial expatriate community was not allowed.

B. Political Pluralism and Participation: 6 / 16 (+1)

State-sponsored political violence against the political opposition is a serious and chronic problem, although violence was much less severe in 2013 than in previous election years, especially in the post-election period. In general, MDC politicians, activists, and supporters were still subject to harassment, assault, and occasional arbitrary detention by security forces, militias, and supporters of ZANU-PF. Some attacks were also perpetrated by affiliates of the MDC. According to the Zimbabwe Human Rights NGO Forum, between July and September 2013, 66 percent of political violence cases targeted MDC-T supporters, the victims of 31 percent of cases had unknown party affiliations, 2 percent targeted other MDC formations, and 1 percent targeted ZANU-PF supporters.

In a June report, Human Rights Watch accused the army of deploying troops to threaten, and in some cases attack, potential MDC supporters or government critics; it also alleged that the army exploited channels such as food-aid distribution and education projects to campaign for ZANU-PF in communities across the country. Traditional leaders—especially in more rural provinces like Mashonaland Central, Mashonaland West, Mashonaland East, Manicaland, and the Midlands provinces—were often "encouraged" to ensure their villages voted for ZANU-PF under the threat of collective retribution. In December 2012, 24 of 29 MDC members who had been detained for 19 months on charges of murdering a Harare policeman were released on bail, and 21 were acquitted of the charge in September 2013.

The new constitution failed to introduce greater civilian control over or require the professionalization of the highly partisan security forces. As such, both the Joint Operations Command, composed of the heads of the security services, and the Central Intelligence Organization (CIO) remain closely tied presidency and free of any concrete or enforceable regulation by the legislature or bureaucracy. The JOC continues to play a central role in government decision-making.

C. Functioning of Government: 3 / 12

Historically, Zimbabwe had a much more professional and less corrupt civil service than most other countries in sub-Saharan Africa. Since 2000, however, corruption has become endemic, including at the highest levels of government. The collapse in public-service delivery and the politicization of food and agricultural aid has made the problem ubiquitous at the local level. In November 2013, Comptroller and Auditor General Mildred Chiri reported widespread abuse of state resources across a range of government ministries in 2011, including hundreds of thousands of dollars of unaccounted-for expenditures by both the presidency and the office of then prime minister Tsvangirai. The Zimbabwe Revenue Authority in October 2013 said the country lost about $2 billion to corruption in 2012. The Zimbabwe Anti-Corruption Commission was enshrined in the new constitution, although its enforcement powers remain unclear. Zimbabwe was ranked 157 out of 177 countries and territories surveyed in Transparency International's 2013 Corruption Perceptions Index.

CIVIL LIBERTIES: 16 / 60 (+2)
D. Freedom of Expression and Belief: 6 / 16

Freedom of the press is restricted. Although the new constitution's Declaration of Rights protects freedom of the media and of expression, the country's draconian legal framework—including the Access to Information and Protection of Privacy Act, the Official Secrets Act, the Public Order and Security Act (POSA), and the Criminal Law (Codification and Reform) Act—has yet to be reformed. In general, these laws restrict who may work as a journalist, require journalists to register with the state, severely limit what they may publish, and mandate harsh penalties, including long prison sentences, for violators. In May, Dumisani Muleya, the editor of the weekly *Zimbabwe Independent*, and the paper's chief reporter, Owen Gagare, were arrested, detained for seven hours, and charged under the Criminal Law (Codification and Reform) Act (CLCRA) after the newspaper reported that Tsvangirai had met secretly with officials from the security forces. Journalists covering both ZANU-PF and MDC were occasionally threatened and beaten during the election campaign (including at least four in the month of June, according to the Committee to Protect Journalists), while a number of journalists from independent media were briefly detained during campaign rallies and on election day for various public safety offenses, restricting coverage. Freedom of expression received a significant boost in October when the Constitutional Court ruled that CLCRA provisions which criminalize undermining the authority of the president and publishing falsehoods detrimental to the state are unconstitutional and cannot be used to prosecute offenders.

The government continues to dominate the broadcast sector via the state-controlled Zimbabwe Broadcasting Corporation (ZBC) and the NewZiana news agency. Access to international news via satellite television is prohibitively expensive for most Zimbabweans. Ahead of the March constitutional referendum, police announced a ban on the possession of "specially designed radios," apparently targeted at hand-cranked and solar-powered radios distributed by NGOs and used to access expatriate radio stations like Radio Voice of The People, Studio 7, and Short Wave Radio Africa. Devices were confiscated during a number of raids, including a March raid on the offices of Radio Dialogue in Bulawayo. Election-day coverage was biased in favor of ZANU-PF. According to the Media Monitoring Project of Zimbabwe, 90 percent of the coverage of MDC across new outlets that day was negative. The Broadcasting Authority of Zimbabwe (BAZ) issued two new radio licenses in 2012, one for Star FM and the other for ZiFM Stereo, both of which are affiliated with ZANU-PF. In October 2013, BAZ invited applications for private radio licenses in 25 new areas; some media advocacy groups claim the government intends to again award licenses only to pro-ZANU-PF outlets to try to crowd out competition from the generally antigovernment shortwave broadcasters. The government had yet to license a single private television broadcaster by year's end. Internet access and use (especially from mobile devices) has expanded rapidly in recent years. Internet content is rarely blocked or filtered, though various ruling party officials publicly expressed a desire and intent to do so as access expands.

While freedom of religion has generally been respected in Zimbabwe, church attendance has become increasingly politicized. In the 2000s, some religious groups and individual pastors faced harassment and arrest. The mainstream Anglican Church was one of the churches most affected by political struggles, culminating in a November 2012 Supreme Court ruling that returned control of Anglican Church properties to Bishop Chad Gandiya of Harare. The ruling ended a six-year campaign by excommunicated pro-Mugabe bishop Nolbert Kunonga to seize the sites. Religious communities were somewhat less affected by political struggles in 2013.

While academics rank among the regime's most vociferous critics, academic freedom is somewhat limited. Mugabe serves as the chancellor of all eight state run-universities, and the ZANU-PF-controlled Ministry of Higher Education supervises education policy at the universities. In 2013, the Progressive Teachers Union of Zimbabwe accused ZANU-PF supporters of intimidating teachers in rural areas to pledge their support to the party and claimed that teachers from the rival, ZANU-PF–linked Zimbabwe Teacher's Association were complicit in political indoctrination. Education aid has often been based on parents' political loyalties. Security forces and ZANU-PF thugs harass dissident university students, who have been arrested or expelled for protesting against government policy.

E. Associational and Organizational Rights: 3 / 12

Freedom of assembly is limited. The 2002 POSA requires police permission for public meetings and demonstrations and allows police to impose arbitrary curfews and forbids criticism of the president. The nongovernmental sector is active and professional, but NGOs are regularly subject to legal restrictions under POSA, the Criminal Law (Codification and Reform) Act, and the Private Voluntary Organisations Act. This legislation is often implemented in a partisan manner. In addition to legal harassment, NGOs, human rights lawyers, and civil society workers face extralegal harassment and arbitrary arrest by security services.

The lead-up to the March referendum saw significant crackdowns on civil society organizations, including raids on over a dozen of Zimbabwe's most prominent NGOs in which files and equipment were confiscated and leaders arrested. In January, Saviour Kasukuwere, then minster for youth and indigenization, declared that all youth organizations must be registered with the government's Zimbabwe Youth Council or be banned; that same month, over 40 members of the National Youths for Democracy Trust were arrested in Bulawayo during a voter registration campaign. Following the referendum, four employees from the prime minister's office and a lawyer for two of them, prominent human rights attorney Beatrice Mtetwa, were detained during a raid, held for a week, and charged with a variety of offenses. Mtetwa was acquitted in November of "defeating or obstructing the course of justice."

The Labor Relations Act allows the government to veto collective-bargaining agreements that it deems harmful to the economy. Strikes are allowed except in "essential" industries. Because the Zimbabwe Congress of Trade Unions (ZCTU) has led resistance to Mugabe's rule, it has become a particular target for repression. In recent years, Gertrude Hambira, secretary general of the General Agriculture and Plantation Workers' Union, has also been subject to focused harassment by the authorities. The ZCTU vocally rejected the 2013 elections results, citing pre-election violence and intimidation and flawed voter rolls.

F. Rule of Law: 2 / 16 (+1)

Pressure from the executive branch has substantially eroded judicial independence. The Constitutional Court's May 2013 ruling that elections had to be held by July 31 was largely considered to be a product of political interference by Mugabe and ZANU-PF, which favored an earlier election date. The Constitutional Court also ruled the elections were free and fair in the face of evidence to the contrary. Although the new constitution creates an independent prosecutorial authority and includes a range of criminal rights, the accused are often denied access to counsel and a fair, timely trial, and the government has repeatedly refused to enforce court orders. It has also replaced senior judges or pressured them to resign by stating that it could not guarantee their security; judges have been subject to extensive physical harassment. Vacancies for scores of magistrate posts have caused a backlog of tens of thousands of cases.

The GNU and the new constitution failed to introduce greater civilian control over or require the professionalization of the highly partisan security forces. Both the Joint Operations Command—which is composed of the heads of the security services and plays a central role in government decision-making—and the Central Intelligence Organization remain closely tied to the presidency and free of any concrete or enforceable regulation by the legislature or bureaucracy.

Security forces abuse citizens with impunity, often ignoring basic rights regarding detention, searches, and seizures. The government has taken no clear action to halt the incidence of torture and mistreatment of suspects in custody. Formed in 2009 as part of the agreement that created the GNU, the Joint Monitoring and Implementation Committee helped expose abuses of power by security forces, but the body had almost no enforcement powers and was formally disbanded after the swearing in of the new government in September 2013.

Lengthy pretrial detention remains a problem, and despite some improvements in recent years, prison conditions remain harsh and sometimes life-threatening. Zimbabwe's 72 prison facilities house more than 17,500 prisoners, and overcrowding, poor sanitation, and food shortages have contributed to HIV and tuberculosis infections and other illnesses among inmates.

The Declaration of Rights contained in the new constitution is considered an improvement because it guarantees equal treatment of citizens under the law. The new constitution gives those arrested the rights to contact relatives and advisors; visitors; to be informed of their rights; and released after 48 hours unless court ordered to remain detained, although these rights are rarely respected in practice.

G. Personal Autonomy and Individual Rights: 5 / 16 (+1)

The state has extensive control over travel and residence. The government has seized the passports of its domestic opponents, and foreign critics are routinely expelled or denied entry. High passport fees inhibit legal travel. At the same time, badly underfunded immigration and border authorities lack the capacity to effectively enforce travel restrictions. In a positive development, the new constitution gives citizenship rights back to Zimbabwean nationals born to foreign parents; these nationals were stripped of automatic citizenship by an amendment to the Citizenship Act in 2001. Aside from a brief period surrounding the election, travel within the country is freer of roadblocks by security forces, and foreign travelers are subject to less harassment upon leaving and entering the country.

Property rights are not respected. Operation Murambatsvina in 2005 entailed the eviction of hundreds of thousands of city dwellers and the destruction of thousands of residential and commercial structures, many of which had been approved by the government. Despite a government resettlement program called Operation Garikai, by 2013 the majority of victims still lacked adequate housing and had no means of redressing the destruction of their property. Most victims have moved into existing, overcrowded urban housing stock or remained in rural areas. In rural areas, the nationalization of land has left both commercial farmers and smallholders with limited security of tenure, and the lack of title to land means that they have little collateral to use for bank loans.

The 2007 Indigenization and Economic Empowerment Act, which stipulates that 51 percent of shares in all companies operating in Zimbabwe must be owned by black Zimbabweans, came into effect in 2010. Although details concerning the implementation and enforcement of the law remained murky, by 2012 nearly every foreign-owned mining company had submitted an indigenization plan to the government and most had been approved by year end 2013. After the election, the government indicated it would press ahead with the indigenization of banks and foreign owned shops, although the policy was not implemented by year's end. Fewer than 400 white-owned farms remain out of the 4,500 that existed when land invasions started in 2000, and any avenues of legal recourse for expropriated farmers have been closed.

Women enjoy extensive legal protections, but societal discrimination and domestic violence persist. Women serve as ministers in national and local governments and the 2013 constitution mandates that for the two parliamentary elections following its adoption, at least 60 of the 270 House of Assembly seats be allocated to women. The World Health Organization has reported that Zimbabwean women's "healthy life expectancy" of 34 years is the world's shortest, largely due to the country's HIV prevalence rate, which remains one of the highest in the world. Sexual abuse is widespread, and past election periods have seen rape used as a political weapon. Female members of the opposition often face particular brutality at the hands of security forces. The prevalence of customary laws in rural areas undermines women's civil rights and access to education. About one-third of Zimbabwean girls do not attend primary school and two-thirds do not attend secondary school due to poverty, abuse, and discriminatory cultural practices.

Sex between men is a criminal offense and can be punished with a fine and up to a year in prison. Mugabe has been vocal in his opposition to homosexuality and LBGT groups have been subject to regular harassment by security forces.

Abkhazia

Political Rights Rating: 4
Civil Liberties Rating: 5
Freedom Rating: 4.5
Freedom Status: Partly Free

Population: 242,800

Ten-Year Ratings Timeline For Year Under Review (Political Rights, Civil Liberties, Status)

Year Under Review	2004	2005	2006	2007	2008	2009	2010	2011	2012	2013
Rating	6,5,NF	5,5,PF	5,5,PF	5,5,PF	5,5,PF	5,5,PF	5,5,PF	5,5,PF	4,5,PF	4,5,PF

INTRODUCTION

In May 2013, the authorities in Sukhumi suspended issuance of Abkhaz passports to residents of the predominantly ethnic Georgian district of Gali, yielding to fierce opposition criticism that warned of Abkhazia's "Georgianization." In June, the former ruling party United Abkhazia moved to the opposition, citing disappointment with President Aleksandr Ankvab's policies and government spending.

Moscow continued to exert significant military and financial control over Abkhazia, providing hundreds of millions of dollars in infrastructure and budgetary support to the territory. Despite security concerns in the lead-up to the 2014 Winter Olympics in Sochi, which borders Abkhazia, no significant disruptions had been reported by year's end.

At the end of 2013, only Russia, Venezuela, Nicaragua, and the Pacific Island states of Nauru and Tuvalu recognized Abkhazia's independence from Georgia.

POLITICAL RIGHTS: 18 / 40
A. Electoral Process: 7 / 12

Abkhazia's 1999 constitution established a presidential system, in which the president and vice president are elected for five-year terms. The parliament, or People's Assembly, consists of 35 members elected for five-year terms from single-seat constituencies. Under the constitution, only ethnic Abkhaz can be elected to the presidency. The more than 200,000 ethnic Georgians who fled the region during the 1992–1993 war—in which Abkhazia secured de facto independence—cannot vote in Abkhazia's elections. None of Abkhazia's elections have been recognized internationally.

In May 2011, Abkhaz president Sergey Bagapsh died unexpectedly after surgery, resulting in a snap August presidential election between Vice President Aleksandr Ankvab, Prime Minister Sergey Shamba, and former defense minister Raul Khadjimba. Amid 70 percent turnout, Ankvab won with 55 percent of the vote, followed by Shamba with 21 percent and Khadjimba with 19.5 percent. The election was considered genuinely competitive. Moscow did not publicly endorse a candidate, but all three promised to maintain strong ties with Russia.

The 2012 parliamentary elections marked a significant shift toward independents, who captured 28 of the 35 seats, compared with 4 for opposition parties and only 3 for the ruling United Abkhazia party. Six of the nine incumbents seeking reelection were defeated, including the outgoing speaker of parliament. Amid a low 44 percent turnout, only 13 candidates won majorities in the first round, requiring runoff votes for the remaining 22 seats.

B. Political Pluralism and Participation: 7 / 16

Abkhazia's opposition has grown stronger in recent years. In June 2013, United Abkhazia announced that it was moving into the opposition, citing "growing disappointment" with the policies of Ankvab's government and concerns about high unemployment and ineffective use of funds from Russia. Khajimba, the opposition leader who orchestrated the move, had also spearheaded protests in Sukhumi in February after the government announced an increase in electricity and bread prices. In response to the relatively large protests, Ankvab agreed to raise prices by a fraction of the original amount.

Following a protracted public debate, the authorities suspended issuance of Abkhaz passports to Gali Georgians in May. The passports carry significant legal benefits, entitling residents to vote, own property, run a business, and obtain Russian citizenship and pensions. The Georgian government elected in 2012 adopted a softer policy toward Abkhazia, no longer discouraging Gali Georgians from seeking Abkhaz passports, and about 25,000 of them had received the documents. The Abkhaz opposition consequently argued that Ankvab's government was allowing the "Georgianization" of Abkhazia. Meanwhile, Abkhaz authorities have reportedly seized Georgian passports from Gali residents in some cases.

C. Functioning of Government: 4 / 12

The ability of elected authorities in Abkhazia to set and implement policies is limited in practice by the influence of Moscow, which continues to exert significant military and economic control over the territory. This is a source of concern among both the Abkhaz leadership and the local population, who complain that a lack of international recognition has led to a growing dependence on Russia and an inability to diversify the economy.

Moscow has spent at least $465 million since 2008 to build or rehabilitate military infrastructure in Abkhazia, including the largest military airfield in the South Caucasus and a strategic naval base close to Tbilisi. According to Russian officials, roughly 5,000 Russian military and other security personnel are currently stationed in Abkhazia.

Moscow also provides direct budgetary support amounting to roughly a fifth of Abkhazia's state budget, additional funds for aid projects and civilian infrastructure, and some $70 million annually in pension payments, as most Abkhaz residents hold Russian passports.

Corruption is believed to be extensive, and government officials are not required to provide declarations of income. In 2013, Russia's Audit Chamber reported that only half of the aid funds allocated for 2010–2012 had been spent, citing poor planning and oversight as well as noncompetitive contracting practices. In 2011 the Audit Chamber had accused the Abkhaz leadership of misappropriating $12 million in aid funds.

CIVIL LIBERTIES: 22 / 60

D. Freedom of Expression and Belief: 8 / 16

Local broadcast media are largely controlled by the government, which operates the Abkhaz State Television and Radio Company (AGTRK). In 2011, the authorities granted permission to Abaza, the sole independent television station, to expand its broadcast range and cover the entire territory. All the major Russian television stations also broadcast into Abkhazia. Facing persistent opposition complaints of progovernment bias at AGTRK, Ankvab in October 2011 fired its director, who had held his post for 15 years and was seen as an impediment to reform.

The print media are considered more influential, consisting of several weekly newspapers. The government publication *Respublika Abkhazii* competes with two main independent papers, *Chegemskaya Pravda* and *Novaya Gazeta*, which are openly critical of government policies.

Internet access has increased since 2008, with over a quarter of the population believed to be online. Some legal restrictions apply to both traditional and online media, including criminal libel statutes.

Religious freedom in Abkhazia is affected by the political situation. In 2011, the Abkhaz Orthodox Church split into two factions; while both officially support autocephaly, or independence, for the Abkhaz church, the newer faction accused the established leadership of acquiescing to de facto control by the Russian Orthodox Church. Outside Abkhazia, the territory is still formally considered to be in the Georgian Orthodox Church's jurisdiction. Debate over the church's status continued in 2013, with a poll showing that the majority of Abkhaz support the newer faction.

Abkhazia's Muslims, who make up about 30 percent of the population, are allowed to practice freely, though a series of murders and assassination attempts have targeted local religious leaders in recent years. Jehovah's Witnesses continue to practice openly, but they were banned by a 1995 decree and have recently reported increased pressure from local authorities. In March 2012, a Witness prayer building was attacked with a grenade, causing property damage but no deaths.

The Abkhaz constitution offers some protection for education in minority languages. Armenian-language schools generally operate without interference, but Gali's schools are officially allowed to offer instruction only in Russian or Abkhaz. While Georgian is often used in these schools in practice, enforcement by the authorities has reportedly been on the rise. Some ethnic Georgian students regularly travel to Georgian-controlled territory to attend classes. Ethnic Georgian residents without Abkhaz passports are restricted from attending Sukhumi State University.

E. Associational and Organizational Rights: 5 / 12

Freedom of assembly is somewhat limited, but the opposition and civil society groups mounted regular protests in 2013. Although most nongovernmental organizations (NGOs) rely on funding from outside the territory, the NGO sector exerts significant influence on government policies.

F. Rule of Law: 4 / 16

The judicial code is based on Russia's, and the criminal justice system suffers from chronic problems including limited defendant access to qualified legal counsel, violations of due process, and lengthy pretrial detentions. Local NGOs have petitioned for significant judicial reform.

Gali's ethnic Georgian residents continue to suffer from widespread poverty and undefined legal status within Abkhazia, though the security situation in Gali is reported to have improved considerably following an increase in violence over the previous two years, during which eight Abkhaz officials and one Russian soldier were killed, according to Abkhaz sources. In September 2013, a Russian consulate official was shot dead in Sukhumi by an unknown attacker. The new Georgian government has reportedly disbanded covert Georgian paramilitary units stationed in Gali.

G. Personal Autonomy and Individual Rights: 5 / 16

Travel and choice of residence are limited by the ongoing separatist dispute. Most ethnic Georgians who fled Abkhazia during the early 1990s live in Tbilisi and western Georgia. As many as 47,000 former Gali residents have returned to Abkhazia since 1994, with an additional 5,000 who commute between Abkhazia and Georgia. The process of obtaining travel permits remains expensive and burdensome, and travel has become more difficult since Russian border guards closed the administrative line between Abkhazia and Georgia and took control of the sole official crossing point in 2012.

About 90 percent of Abkhazia's residents hold Russian passports, as Abkhaz travel documents are not internationally recognized. However, since the 2008 war, ethnic Abkhaz have had greater difficulty receiving visas to travel abroad, including to the United States and European Union countries.

Equality of opportunity and normal business activities are limited by corruption, criminal organizations, and economic reliance on Russia, which accounts for nearly all foreign investment.

Under a law preventing foreigners from buying Abkhaz property, ethnic Russians have been barred from acquiring residences in the territory, and some have reported that their homes have been confiscated.

A strong NGO sector has contributed to women's involvement in business and civil society. However, Abkhaz women complain of being underrepresented in government positions, holding only one of the 35 legislative seats.

Gaza Strip

Political Rights Rating: 7 ↓
Civil Liberties Rating: 6
Freedom Rating: 6.5
Freedom Status: Not Free
Population: 1,816,000

Ratings Change: The Gaza Strip's political rights rating declined from 6 to 7 due to the continued failure to hold new elections since the term of the 2006 Palestinian legislature expired in 2010.

Note: Whereas past editions of *Freedom in the World* featured one report for Israeli-occupied portions of the West Bank and Gaza Strip and another for Palestinian-administered portions, the latest four editions divide the territories based on geography, with one report for the West Bank and another for the Gaza Strip. As in previous years, Israel is examined in a separate report.

Ten-Year Ratings Timeline For Year Under Review (Political Rights, Civil Liberties, Status)

Year Under Review	2004	2005	2006	2007	2008	2009	2010	2011	2012	2013
Rating	--	--	--	--	--	--	6,6,NF	6,6,NF	6,6,NF	7,6,NF

INTRODUCTION

In 2013, residents of the Gaza Strip worked to recover from large-scale strikes by the Israel Defense Forces (IDF) in November 2012, an operation dubbed "Pillar of Defense" by Israel, that led to a boost in support for Hamas among Palestinians across both Gaza and the West Bank. Rocket fire toward Israel continued, but very sporadically. Restrictions on press freedom and other civil liberties persisted throughout 2013.

Negotiations aimed at repairing the six-year-old rift between the Hamas regime in Gaza and the Fatah-led Palestinian Authority (PA) in the West Bank made little tangible progress during 2013, and no date for long-overdue elections was set. However, Hamas continued to support diplomatic plans for the Fatah-led Palestine Liberation Organization (PLO) to assert

Palestinian statehood within UN institutions. In November 2012 the PLO had won recognition for Palestine as a nonmember observer state at the UN General Assembly.

POLITICAL RIGHTS: 5 / 40 (-4)

A. Electoral Process: 2 / 12 (-3)

Residents of Gaza were never granted citizenship by either Egypt or Israel, and are mostly citizens of the PA. The current Hamas-controlled government in the territory claims to be the legitimate leadership of the PA. However, the authority—a quasi-sovereign entity created by the 1993 Oslo Accords—is effectively fractured, and the Hamas government implements PA law selectively.

The PA president is elected to four-year terms, and international observers judged the 2005 presidential election to be generally free and fair. However, PA president Mahmoud Abbas lost control over Gaza after the 2007 Fatah-Hamas schism, and Prime Minister Ismail Haniya of Hamas continues to lead the government in Gaza despite being formally dismissed by Abbas. Other Hamas ministers remained in their posts in Gaza after almost all Fatah-affiliated officials were expelled or fled to the West Bank. When Abbas's elected term expired in 2009, Hamas argued that the PA Basic Law empowered the head of the Palestinian Legislative Council (PLC)—Aziz Dweik of Hamas—to serve as acting president.

The unicameral, 132-seat PLC serves four-year terms. Voting in Gaza during the 2006 PLC elections was deemed largely fair by international observers. Hamas won 74 seats, while Fatah took 45. The subsequent Hamas-Fatah rift, combined with Israel's detention of many (especially Hamas-affiliated) lawmakers, has prevented the PLC from meeting since 2007, and its term expired in 2010. No elections have been held since 2006.

B. Political Pluralism and Participation: 2 / 16

Since the 2007 schism, Gaza has effectively functioned as a one-party state, with Fatah largely suppressed and smaller factions tolerated to varying degrees. There is little to no public display of opposition party activities, and little in the way of party organizing. In May 2011, Hamas and Fatah agreed to form a national unity government that would organize presidential and parliamentary elections and increase security coordination, but negotiations on implementing the pact soon stalled. In January 2013, ahead of a new round of talks in Cairo, Hamas authorities allowed a mass rally by Fatah supporters in Gaza for the first time in several years. By the end of 2013, however, no unity government had been formed, and elections were still not planned.

C. Functioning of Government: 1 / 12 (-1)

The expiration of the presidential and parliamentary terms in 2009 and 2010 has left Gaza's government with no electoral mandate, and its continued failure to set new election dates in 2013 further undermined its legitimacy. The ability of local authorities to make and implement policy is limited in practice by Israeli and Egyptian border controls, Israeli military actions, and the fact that the Palestinian political collective is split between Gaza and the West Bank.

Humanitarian organizations and donor countries allege that Hamas exerts almost total control over the distribution of funds and goods in Gaza, and allocates resources according to political criteria with little or no transparency, creating ample opportunity for corruption.

CIVIL LIBERTIES: 10 / 60

D. Freedom of Expression and Belief: 4 / 16

The media are not free in Gaza. In 2008, Hamas replaced the PA Ministry of Information with a government Media Office and banned all journalists not accredited by it; authorities also closed down all media outlets not affiliated with Hamas. According to the Palestinian Center for Development and Media Freedoms (MADA), the 2011 political reconciliation deal promised to end Hamas's ban on the import of three West Bank newspapers—*Al-Ayyam*, *Al-Quds*, and *Al-Hayat al-Jadida*—that are generally associated with Fatah, but the ban had not yet been lifted in 2013. Blogging and other online media activity have reportedly increased in recent years.

During Operation Pillar of Defense in November 2012, the Israeli air force reportedly attacked media offices in Gaza, injuring several journalists, and killed two news photographers in a car marked as a press vehicle. MADA noted that Palestinian broadcasting frequencies were seized by the IDF to urge Palestinian residents not to cooperate with Hamas during the fighting. The Israeli operation accounted for most of the press freedom violations documented in 2012, but the onus shifted to Hamas authorities in Gaza in 2013. According to MADA, Palestinian actors were responsible for all 50 of the violations in the territory during the year, compared with 37 out of 100 in 2012. The incidents included arrests, detentions, and threats, often targeting journalists who expressed opinions about political affairs in Egypt, where President Mohamed Morsi, seen as a Hamas ally, was deposed in a July 2013 coup.

Freedom of religion is restricted in Gaza. The PA Basic Law declares Islam to be the official religion of Palestine and states "respect and sanctity of all other heavenly religions (Judaism and Christianity) shall be maintained." Hamas authorities have enforced orthodox Sunni Islamic practices and conservative dress, and have regularly harassed worshippers at mosques not affiliated with Hamas. Christians, who make up less than 1 percent of the population, have also suffered routine harassment, though violent attacks have reportedly declined in recent years. There is one Christian member of the PLC based in Gaza.

Hamas has taken over the formal education system, aside from schools run by the United Nations. A teachers' strike in 2009 led to the replacement of many strikers with new, Hamas-allied teachers. Hamas security officials have confiscated copies of "immoral" novels from (mostly university) bookstores, according to Human Rights Watch (HRW). The Egyptian and Israeli blockade has restricted access to school supplies. While university students are ostensibly allowed to leave Gaza, they must be escorted by foreign diplomats or contractors. In practice, Gazans are now mostly absent from West Bank universities.

E. Associational and Organizational Rights: 3 / 12

Since 2008, Hamas has significantly restricted freedoms of assembly and association, with security forces violently dispersing unapproved public gatherings of Fatah and other groups. A rare, 500-person demonstration took place in September 2012 in the Bureij refugee camp, with protesters calling for the overthrow of Hamas following the death of a three-year-old boy in a fire during a power failure. The demonstration was quickly dispersed by Hamas forces.

There is a broad range of Palestinian nongovernmental organizations (NGOs) and civic groups, and Hamas itself operates a large social-services network. However, following a 2009 conflict between Hamas and Israel (dubbed "Operation Cast Lead" by Israel), Hamas restricted the activities of aid organizations that would not submit to its regulations, and many civic associations have been shut down for political reasons since the 2007 PA split. In July 2011, Hamas began enforcing its 2010 demand to audit the accounts of some 80 international NGOs in Gaza.

Independent labor unions in Gaza continue to function, and PA workers have staged strikes against Hamas-led management. However, the Fatah-aligned Palestinian General Federation of Trade Unions, the largest union body in the territories, has seen its operations greatly curtailed. Its main Gaza offices were taken over by Hamas militants in 2007, and the building was severely damaged in a December 2008 Israeli air raid.

F. Rule of Law: 0 / 16

Laws governing Palestinians in the Gaza Strip derive from Ottoman, British Mandate, Jordanian, Egyptian, PA, and Islamic (Sharia) law, as well as Israeli military orders. The judicial system is not independent, and Palestinian judges lack proper training and experience. In 2007, Abbas ordered judges to boycott judicial bodies in Gaza, and Hamas began appointing new prosecutors and judges in 2008. Hamas security forces and militants continued to carry out arbitrary arrests and detentions during 2013, and torture of detainees and criminal suspects continued to be reported. The Palestinian human rights ombudsman agency, the Independent Commission for Human Rights, is banned from Hamas detention centers and Gaza's central prison.

According to B'Tselem, a total of 9 Palestinians in Gaza were killed by the IDF during 2013, down from 246 in 2012, the year of Operation Pillar of Defense. B'Tselem notes Israel's continued use of "targeted killings" of alleged terrorist leaders, whereby, between Israel's withdrawal from the territory in 2005 and May 2013, 155 Palestinians (including 68 bystanders, 34 of whom were minors) were killed by the IDF.

Hamas executed 3 Palestinians in Gaza during 2013. In 2012, in addition to 6 executed by hanging, several people who had been convicted of collaboration with Israel were taken from prisons and shot in the street during Operation Pillar of Defense. HRW has reported that some of those sentenced to death in Gaza were convicted based on evidence gathered during torture, or were minors at the time of the alleged offense.

Rocket fire from the Gaza Strip into Israel continued sporadically throughout 2013, but declined markedly from more than 2,000 rockets launched in 2012 to fewer than 50 in 2013.

G. Personal Autonomy and Individual Rights: 3 / 16

Freedom of movement is severely restricted. Although Egypt had opened the Rafah border crossing to women, children, and men over 40 in mid-2011, soon after the July 2013 overthrow of President Morsi, the Egyptian authorities closed the Rafah crossing (in August), and it remained closed by year's end. Between 40,000 and 50,000 Gaza Palestinians lack identity cards, severely limiting their ability to travel in and out of Gaza. Human rights groups such as B'Tselem have urged Israel, as the state controlling the Palestinian Population Registry, to rectify the problem. The regular clashes between Israeli forces and Gaza-based militants greatly restrict freedom of movement within the Gaza Strip, as does the presence of unexploded ordnance.

Freedom of residence has been limited by the violent conflicts in and around Gaza. The conflict with Israel that ended in January 2009 was fought to a large extent in civilian neighborhoods, leading to the damage or destruction of some 50,000 homes. The November 2012 conflict resulted in the displacement of 3,000 Palestinians and the destruction of or severe damage to 450 homes, according to the United Nations.

Under Hamas, personal status law is derived almost entirely from Sharia, which puts women at a stark disadvantage in matters of marriage, divorce, inheritance, and domestic abuse. Rape, domestic violence, and so-called "honor killings" are common, and these crimes often go unpunished. The government has barred women from wearing trousers in public and declared that all women must wear hijab in public buildings, though these and other such controls on women's behavior have been enforced less frequently in recent years. However, in March 2013 Hamas banned women from participating in an annual marathon organized by UN Relief and Works Agency, leading the agency to cancel the race. In April,

Hamas introduced a law requiring children aged nine and up to be educated in sex-segregated classrooms.

The blockade of Gaza's land borders and coastline has greatly reduced economic opportunity in the territory, though these conditions improved slightly in 2011 and 2012, before worsening again in 2013. A dense network of tunnels beneath Gaza's border with Egypt facilitates much economic activity but is also used to transport weapons. The tunnels are routinely bombed by Israel, and after the July 2013 coup in Egypt, Egyptian authorities made a serious attempt to shut down the tunnels. Israel had begun easing the entry of construction materials and other previously restricted commercial goods in 2012, but the ban on building supplies was reimposed in October 2013, after Israeli security forces discovered a tunnel leading from Gaza into Israel. Also during 2013, the IDF restricted the coastal waters open to Gazan fishermen from 6 to 3 nautical miles from shore in March, then expanded the limit back to 6 nautical miles in May. According to the Palestinian Centre for Human Rights, there were multiple incidents during the year in which Israeli forces fired on Palestinian fishing boats operating within the 6-mile limit.

Hong Kong

Political Rights Rating: 5
Civil Liberties Rating: 2
Freedom Rating: 3.5
Freedom Status: Partly Free

Population: 7,205,000

Ten-Year Ratings Timeline For Year Under Review (Political Rights, Civil Liberties, Status)

Year Under Review	2004	2005	2006	2007	2008	2009	2010	2011	2012	2013
Rating	5,2,PF	5,2,PF	5,2,PF	5,2,PF	5,2,PF	5,2,PF	5,2,PF	5,2,PF	5,2,PF	5,2,PF

INTRODUCTION

Hong Kong chief executive Leung Chun-ying, who was elected in March 2012 by a committee dominated by pro-Beijing elites, faced growing public discontent in 2013 over his close ties to the Chinese central government and the slow progress of political reforms under his leadership. Leung survived an impeachment attempt initiated by prodemocracy members of the territory's Legislative Council (Legco), which is also dominated by pro-Beijing interests.

Official discussion on reforms that would allow universal suffrage for future chief executive and Legco elections stalled in 2013. In September, the director of Beijing's Liaison Office in Hong Kong publicly rejected the open nomination of candidates for the next chief executive election in 2017—the clearest indication yet that the central government would not permit major electoral reforms.

The Independent Commission Against Corruption (ICAC) continued to investigate several high-profile graft scandals from 2012. Two property tycoons, along with a senior official who allegedly received bribes from them, were scheduled to face trial in May 2014. In September 2013, an independent review found that a former ICAC commissioner had breached rules on personal travel and entertainment expenses during his tenure. The agency was widely criticized for failing to enforce its own employee guidelines.

In October, the Hong Kong government issued free-to-air television licenses to two companies, ending a long-standing duopoly. However, critics noted that both new licensees are controlled by billionaire tycoons with close ties to the central government, and that a third applicant was rejected without explanation. Meanwhile, the number of physical attacks on journalists increased during the year, adding to concerns about a broader decline in freedom of expression.

POLITICAL RIGHTS: 16 / 40

A. Electoral Process: 3 / 12

Hong Kong's Basic Law calls for the election of a chief executive and a unicameral Legislative Council (Legco). Under electoral reforms adopted in 2010, the chief executive, who serves a five-year term, is chosen by a 1,200-member election committee: some 200,000 "functional constituency" voters—representatives of various elite business and social sectors, many with close ties to Beijing—elect 900 of the committee's members, and the remaining 300 consist of Legco members, Hong Kong delegates to China's National People's Congress (NPC), religious representatives, and members of the Chinese People's Political Consultative Conference (CPPCC), an advisory body to the NPC. Candidates for chief executive must be nominated by at least 150 members of the election committee.

The 2010 amendments to the Basic Law added 10 seats to the Legco, giving it a total of 70 seats after the 2012 elections. While 30 members are still elected by the functional constituency voters, 35—up from 30—are chosen through direct elections in five geographical constituencies. Hong Kong's 18 district councils nominate candidates for the remaining 5 Legco seats from among themselves, and the nominees then face a full popular vote. All 70 members serve four-year terms. The Basic Law restricts the Legco's lawmaking powers, prohibiting legislators from introducing bills that would affect Hong Kong's public spending, governmental operations, or political structure.

In March 2012, the election committee chose Leung Chun-ying, a member of the CPPCC, as the new chief executive. He won 689 of the 1,050 valid votes cast following an usually competitive race against two other candidates—Henry Tang, a high-ranking Hong Kong civil servant who took 285 votes, and Democratic Party leader Albert Ho, who secured 76. Tang was initially Beijing's preferred candidate, but after his popularity fell due to a series of scandals, the central government switched its backing to Leung. Officials from China's Liaison Office reportedly lobbied members of the election committee to vote for Leung and pressured media outlets to remove critical coverage of him ahead of the balloting. Leung took office in July 2012.

During the Legco elections in September 2012, pro-Beijing parties won 43 seats, though only 17 of those were directly elected. Prodemocracy parties took 27 seats, which enabled them to retain a veto on constitutional changes.

B. Political Pluralism and Participation: 7 / 16

Over a dozen factions in Hong Kong's multiparty system are currently represented in the Legco. The main parties in the prodemocracy camp are the Civic Party, the Democratic Party, and the Labor Party. The largest pro-Beijing party is the Democratic Alliance for the Betterment and Progress of Hong Kong. The Chinese Communist Party (CCP) is not formally registered in Hong Kong but exercises considerable influence, both officially and through indirect economic and other pressure.

Hong Kong residents' political choices are limited by the semidemocratic electoral system, which ensures the dominance of pro-Beijing interests. While the Basic Law states that universal suffrage is the "ultimate aim," only incremental changes have been permitted to date. The NPC ruled in 2007 that it might allow universal suffrage for the 2017 chief executive election and the 2020 Legco election, but official discussion on such a move stalled in

2013. In September, Liaison Office director Zhang Xiaoming rejected a proposal to allow the registration of candidates who receive the endorsement of at least 2 percent of the electorate. Meanwhile, Chief Executive Leung expressed opposition to interference by foreign governments after Hugo Swire, minister of state at Britain's Foreign Office, published an article expressing support for universal suffrage in the territory.

C. Functioning of Government: 6 / 12

Hong Kong is generally regarded as having low rates of corruption, though business interests exercise a strong influence in the government. The ICAC continued to prosecute public officials and corporate executives linked to high-profile cases throughout the year. However, graft complaints reported in the first 10 months of 2013 were down 35 percent compared with the same period of the previous year, leading critics to argue that the drop showed a lack of confidence in the ICAC. The commission was widely criticized in September after an independent review found that former ICAC chief Timothy Tong had breached spending rules on 42 occasions during his 2007–2012 tenure. Meanwhile, pretrial proceedings continued for billionaire property developers Thomas and Raymond Kwok, who were accused of bribing Rafael Hui, a former second-rank executive official who was also facing trial for his part in the alleged arrangement. Prodemocracy Legco members tried unsuccessfully to impeach Leung as chief executive in January 2013, claiming that he had been dishonest about illegal construction on his property. Hong Kong was ranked 15 out of 177 countries and territories surveyed in Transparency International's 2013 Corruption Perceptions Index.

CIVIL LIBERTIES: 51 / 60

D. Freedom of Expression and Belief: 14 / 16

Under Article 27 of the Basic Law, Hong Kong residents enjoy freedoms of speech, press, and publication. Residents have access to dozens of daily newspapers, international radio broadcasts, and satellite television. Foreign media operate without interference. However, the government continued to impose controls on access to information in 2013. The administration held fewer press conferences, and several official visits to Beijing were unannounced, including a trip by Leung in October. The territory's Code on Access to Information, which lacks a centralized system for retrieving government data, remained unchanged despite calls for amendment. In February, Leung sent a legal letter to a local newspaper, seeking the retraction of an article that he believed was defamatory. The newspaper denied the accusation and said Leung had set a bad precedent for freedom of speech in Hong Kong. In October, the ICAC dropped its controversial attempt to obtain a magazine's internal records on an interview with a former supporter of Leung. In the interview, published in January in *iSun Affairs*, former CPPCC Standing Committee member Lew Mon-hung alleged that Leung had lied about his handling of illegal construction on his property and considered democratic politicians his "enemies."

Direct and indirect efforts by Beijing to interfere in news reporting in Hong Kong persisted in 2013. Several media owners are current or former members of the NPC and CPPCC, and many have significant business interests in mainland China. The Hong Kong government in October issued free-to-air television licenses to PCCW and i-Cable Communications, ending the nearly 40-year duopoly of Television Broadcasts Limited (TVB) and Asia Television Limited (ATV). However, officials failed to explain why they rejected the application of a third company that was seen as more independent; both PCCW and i-Cable are controlled by pro-CCP tycoons. Separately, in September Louie King-bun, a former executive editor of the pro-Beijing newspaper *Ta Kung Pao*, took the executive director position at ATV, whose former employees have alleged increasing self-censorship and political interference.

Though violence against journalists has historically been rare in Hong Kong, a series of attacks occurred in 2013, including beatings, assaults during protests, and an incident in which unidentified men threatened newspaper distribution workers and destroyed 26,000 copies of the critical *Apple Daily*.

Religious freedom is generally respected in Hong Kong. Adherents of the Falun Gong spiritual movement, which is persecuted in mainland China, are free to practice in public. However, they are frequently confronted by members of the Hong Kong Youth Care Association (HKYCA), which has ties to the CCP. In July 2013, a teacher was filmed berating police for allegedly favoring HKYCA in their handling of a standoff between protesters from the two groups, leading to a smear campaign against the teacher and a broader debate over civil liberties in the territory.

University professors can write and lecture freely, and political debate on campuses is lively. Although a pro-Beijing curriculum for Hong Kong schools was shelved in 2012, controversy over national education continued in 2013. In July, copies of a booklet about the Basic Law that contained CCP-style nationalistic rhetoric were reportedly distributed in local primary schools.

E. Associational and Organizational Rights: 9 / 12

The Basic Law guarantees freedoms of assembly and association, and police permits for demonstrations are rarely denied. Several large protests against the Chinese government took place during 2013. The annual June 4 vigil to commemorate the 1989 Tiananmen Square massacre drew 150,000 people, including activists who came from mainland China, where such events are banned. In October, more than 100,000 protesters attended a rally to demand an explanation from the government after it rejected the third applicant for a free-to-air television broadcasting license. Other major demonstrations were held during the year to demand Leung's resignation.

Hong Kong authorities have demonstrated reduced respect for freedom of assembly in recent years, and activists have complained that police are not punished for arresting protesters whose cases are subsequently dropped or dismissed. In an alleged case of selective enforcement, a resident was investigated by a serious crime squad and charged with criminal damage in April for writing graffiti that cursed Chinese president Xi Jinping.

Hong Kong hosts a vibrant and largely unfettered nongovernmental organization sector, and trade unions are independent. However, there is limited legal protection for basic labor rights. Collective-bargaining rights are not recognized, protections against antiunion discrimination are weak, and there are few regulations on working hours.

F. Rule of Law: 15 / 16

The judiciary is independent, and the trial process is generally fair. The NPC reserves the right to make final interpretations of the Basic Law, effectively limiting the power of Hong Kong's Court of Final Appeal. In November 2013, after that court's former chief justice said the NPC should not use its authority to overrule the Hong Kong judiciary, a former NPC deputy warned that no one should question the Beijing body's power to interpret the Basic Law.

Police are forbidden by law to employ torture and other forms of abuse. They generally respect this ban in practice, and complaints of abuse are investigated. Arbitrary arrest and detention are illegal; suspects must be charged within 48 hours of their arrest. Prison conditions generally meet international standards.

Citizens are treated equally under the law, though Hong Kong's 300,000 foreign household workers remain vulnerable to abuse and poor housing accommodation. Since foreign workers face deportation if dismissed, many are reluctant to bring complaints against employers. In 2013, the Court of Final Appeal upheld the 2012 reversal of a lower court ruling that would have allowed foreign household workers, like other foreigners in Hong Kong, to apply for permanent residency after seven years of uninterrupted stay. South Asians also routinely complain of discrimination. In early 2013, a young South Asian construction worker accused the police of racial bias after he was detained for a year on suspicion of robbery in a case that was finally dropped due to lack of evidence. Antidiscrimination laws do not specifically protect LGBT (lesbian, gay, bisexual, and transgender) people.

G. Personal Autonomy and Individual Rights: 13 / 16

Hong Kong maintains its own immigration system, but the authorities periodically deny entry to political activists and Falun Gong practitioners, particularly at sensitive times, raising suspicions that the government enforces a Beijing-imposed political blacklist. In 2013, the immigration department stopped processing a work visa application for Chang Ping, an outspoken journalist from the mainland, after he reportedly waited two years whereas an official response usually takes no more than four weeks.

Many mainland women have given birth in Hong Kong with the aim of accessing its advanced welfare system or skirting China's one-child policy, spurring public resentment in the territory. A regulation that bans mainland women without Hong Kong spouses from giving birth in the territory came into effect in January. In April, a woman from Guangdong Province who gave birth in Hong Kong through a sham marriage with a local resident was sentenced to one year in prison.

Women in Hong Kong are protected by law from discrimination and abuse, and they are entitled to equal access to schooling and to property in divorce settlement. However, they continue to face de facto inequality in employment opportunities, salary, inheritance, and welfare. Only 11 of the 70 Legco members are women, and all of the judges on the Court of Final Appeal are men. Despite government efforts, Hong Kong remains a destination and transit point for human trafficking linked to sexual exploitation and forced labor.

Indian Kashmir

Political Rights Rating: 4
Civil Liberties Rating: 4
Freedom Rating: 4.0
Freedom Status: Partly Free

Population: 12,541,300

Ten-Year Ratings Timeline For Year Under Review (Political Rights, Civil Liberties, Status)

Year Under Review	2004	2005	2006	2007	2008	2009	2010	2011	2012	2013
Rating	5,5,PF	5,5,PF	5,4,PF	5,4,PF	4,4,PF	4,5,PF	4,4,PF	4,4,PF	4,4,PF	4,5,PF

INTRODUCTION

Negotiations between India and Pakistan over the divided region of Jammu and Kashmir were threatened in 2013 as each side accused the other of gunfire and incursions across the Line of Control. These incidents increased around a September meeting between the two countries' prime ministers in New York. In October, Indian military officials said they had challenged up to 40 armed militants entering from Pakistan, though the details remained unclear. Exchanges of fire across the de facto border that month wounded at least 10 civilians in Indian-held regions and displaced dozens more. Nevertheless, a 2003 cease-fire remained in place, and the peace talks tentatively continued. Hundreds of people attended a political rally for peace in the summer capital, Srinagar, in November.

Pakistani-backed Islamist militants and proindependence groups continued to orchestrate attacks against Indian rule during the year. Militant assaults on police and army bases in March and September killed more than a dozen people. However, the level of violence has declined over the past decade. New Delhi withdrew 15,000 troops from the southern Jammu region in 2009 after the number of militancy-related fatalities decreased for seven consecutive years. Despite this improvement, the unpopular Armed Forces Special Powers Act (AFSPA) has remained in effect. Extended to the territory in 1990 after an armed insurgency gained momentum in 1989, the AFSPA allows the army to make arrests and conduct searches without a warrant, and to use deadly force with virtual impunity. Though Chief Minister Omar Abdullah supports partially revoking the act, his efforts bore no fruit in 2013.

Relations between the Indian government and moderate Kashmiri independence movements, though significantly improved in the past decade, remained brittle during the year. Three people were killed in February when civilians defied curfews to protest the execution of a militant convicted of involvement in a 2001 attack on the Indian Parliament. The execution, which many locals believed was the result of an unfair trial, and the mysterious death of a Kashmiri student who led a related protest in Hyderabad three weeks later, continued to fuel unrest. Though security forces responded better than they had in 2010, when weeks of clashes with protesters left more than 100 civilians dead, they were accused of fatally shooting another protester in March, and two more in June, prompting further demonstrations. In September, security forces in southern Shopian district killed four supposed militants. Police subsequently identified three of them as local civilians, and hundreds of people protested, resulting in a fifth death after security forces fired on protesters throwing stones. The state government launched a judicial investigation.

Communal violence was also reported during 2013, as local tensions were exacerbated by activists promoting the Hindu nationalist Bharatiya Janata Party ahead of national elections scheduled for 2014. Dozens of houses were burned and at least two people killed during riots between Muslim and Hindu populations of Kishtwar in August. Local authorities imposed curfews in several towns.

POLITICAL RIGHTS: 20 / 40
A. Electoral Process: 8 / 12

Jammu and Kashmir received substantial autonomy under Article 370 of India's constitution and a 1952 accord, but India annulled such guarantees in 1957 and formally annexed the portion of Jammu and Kashmir under its control. It is largely governed like other Indian states, with an elected bicameral legislature and a chief minister entrusted with executive power. An appointed governor serves as symbolic head of state. Members of the 87-seat lower house, or legislative assembly, are directly elected, while the 36-seat upper house has a combination of members elected by the assembly and nominated by the governor.

India has never held a referendum allowing Kashmiri self-determination as called for in a 1948 UN resolution. The state's residents can change the local administration through elections, which are supposed to be held at least once every six years. The Election Commission of India monitors the polls, but historically they have been marred by violence, coercion, and ballot tampering. Militants have enforced boycotts called for by separatist political parties, threatened election officials and candidates, and killed political activists and civilians during balloting.

In the most recent state elections, held in November and December 2008, turnout was higher than expected, exceeding 60 percent on most polling dates, as voters largely ignored separatist groups' calls for a boycott. While early voting dates were generally peaceful, some violence affected later polling—particularly in early December—when antielection protesters clashed with security forces. The elections were considered mostly free and fair, however, with significantly reduced levels of voter intimidation, harassment, and violence compared with previous elections. The pro-India National Conference (NC) party won a plurality of 28 seats, followed by the People's Democratic Party (PDP) with 21 seats and the Congress party with 17. The NC allied itself with Congress to form a governing coalition. The next elections are scheduled for 2014.

Panchayat (local council) elections were held across Kashmir in 2011 for the first time since 2001, and were described as the first truly open panchayat elections since 1978. Although separatist groups urged citizens to boycott the polls, turnout was reported at about 80 percent. Unfortunately, more than 700 panchayat leaders resigned in 2012, facing death threats after several were assassinated. Municipal elections originally slated for 2011 have been repeatedly delayed.

B. Political Pluralism and Participation: 8 / 16

The state is governed under a multiparty system, but normal party politics and electoral activities are often disrupted by militant violence, intimidation, and boycotts. The NC won state elections in 1987 that were undermined by arrests of members of a new, Muslim-based opposition coalition, leading to widespread unrest. Although opposition parties joined together to form the All Parties Hurriyat Conference (APHC) in 1993, they boycotted the 1996 state elections, and the NC was able to form a government. The APHC also declined to participate in the 2002 elections, which were particularly violent, but the NC nevertheless lost more than half of its assembly seats, allowing the Congress party and the PDP to form a coalition government. That coalition collapsed in June 2008, when the PDP withdrew its support amid a high-profile dispute over land set aside for a Hindu pilgrimage site, leading to that year's elections. Women and minority religious groups are underrepresented in government, though the PDP is headed by a woman, Mehbooba Mufti.

C. Functioning of Government: 4 / 12

Corruption remains widespread, though the government has taken some steps to combat it. The 2011 Jammu and Kashmir State Vigilance Commission Act established an anticorruption commission with the power to investigate alleged offenses under the state's 2006 Prevention of Corruption Act. Its first commissioners were appointed in 2013.

CIVIL LIBERTIES: 29 / 60

D. Freedom of Expression and Belief: 9 / 16

India's 1971 Newspapers (Incitement to Offences) Act, which is in effect only in Jammu and Kashmir, gives district magistrates the authority to censor publications in certain circumstances, though it is rarely invoked. During the February 2013 unrest over the executed militant, authorities temporarily shut down mobile internet service to discourage protests, and blocked journalists from visiting Kishtwar during the communal riots in August. Protest-related violence in 2010 had led some newspapers to suspend circulation, and curfews inhibited journalists from covering important stories, though conditions have since improved. Foreign journalists are generally able to travel freely, meet with separatist leaders, and file reports on a range of issues, including government abuses.

As in the rest of India, print media are thriving in Kashmir, and online media have proliferated, providing new platforms for public discussion. By the end of 2012 there were over 1,100 registered publications in Jammu and Kashmir, compared with 30 in 1989. At times, the Public Safety Act (PSA), which allowed detention without charge or trial before it was partially amended in 2012, has been used to arrest journalists, and the government has withheld official advertising from disfavored media outlets. Journalists also face threats from militant groups.

Freedom of worship and academic freedom are generally respected by the authorities. Since 2003, the state government has permitted separatist groups to organize a procession marking the prophet Muhammad's birthday. However, militants at times attack Hindu and Sikh temples.

E. Associational and Organizational Rights: 6 / 12

Freedoms of assembly and association are often restricted. Although local and national civil rights groups are permitted to operate, they sometimes encounter harassment by security forces. The separatist APHC is allowed to function, but its leaders are frequently subjected to short-term preventive detention, and its requests for permits for public gatherings are often denied. Protection of labor union rights in Kashmir is generally poor and has resulted in prolonged strikes by both public- and informal-sector workers.

F. Rule of Law: 6 / 16

The courts in Kashmir, already backlogged by thousands of pending cases, are further hampered by intermittent lawyers' strikes. These were particularly severe in 2011, mounted in part to protest the 10-month PSA detention of Kashmir High Court Bar Association president Mian Abdul Qayoom for speaking out against Indian rule and fomenting protests, and separately to force the High Court to stay a cabinet decision transferring the power to register land and property from judicial officers to the revenue department. The Bar Association implemented several short-term strikes in 2013 to protest against alleged human rights violations.

The government and security forces frequently disregard court orders. Broadly written legislation such as the AFSPA and the Disturbed Areas Act allow security forces to search homes and arrest suspects without a warrant, shoot suspects on sight, and destroy buildings believed to house militants or arms. Under the AFSPA, prosecutions of security personnel cannot proceed without the approval of the central government, which is rarely granted. In April 2012, the PSA was amended after a particularly critical 2011 report by Amnesty International (AI); changes included the prohibition of the detention of minors and new rules that are expected to reduce the amount of time prisoners are held before trial. However, a follow-up report from AI indicated some continuing problems, including "revolving door" detentions in which detainees reaching the maximum detention threshold are released and quickly rearrested. Chief Minister Omar Abdullah has supported revoking the AFSPA in six districts where militant activity is rare, but says the army opposes the move.

Indian security personnel based in Kashmir carry out arbitrary arrests and detentions, torture, forced disappearances, and custodial killings of suspected militants and their alleged civilian sympathizers. Meanwhile, militant groups based in Pakistan continue to kill pro-India politicians, public employees, suspected informers, members of rival factions, soldiers, and civilians. The militants also engage in kidnapping, extortion, and other forms of intimidation. Terrorist-related violence reached the lowest point in more than 20 years in 2012, according to the South Asian Terrorist Portal, but increased again slightly in 2013. A total of 181 civilians, security personnel, and militants were killed, up from 117 the previous year.

A pattern of violence targeting Pandits, or Kashmiri Hindus, dates to 1990 and has forced several hundred thousand Hindus to flee their homes in region over the years. Many continue to reside in refugee camps near Jammu. Other religious and ethnic minorities such as Sikhs and Gujjars have also been targeted.

G. Personal Autonomy and Individual Rights: 8 / 16

Freedom of movement and property rights are hampered by transient factors such as police curfews, checkpoints, and military activity, as well as by long-term obstacles and displacement related to the standoff with Pakistan.

As in other parts of India, women face some societal discrimination as well as domestic violence and other forms of abuse. Female civilians continue to be subjected to harassment, intimidation, and violent attacks, including rape and murder, at the hands of both the security forces and militant groups.

Nagorno-Karabakh

Political Rights Rating: 5
Civil Liberties Rating: 5
Freedom Rating: 5.0
Freedom Status: Partly Free

Population: 146,600

Ten-Year Ratings Timeline For Year Under Review (Political Rights, Civil Liberties, Status)

Year Under Review	2004	2005	2006	2007	2008	2009	2010	2011	2012	2013
Rating	5,5,PF	5,5,PF	5,5,PF	5,5,PF	5,5,PF	5,5,PF	6,5,NF	6,5,NF	5,5,PF	5,5,PF

INTRODUCTION

While there was no major escalation of violence along the cease-fire line in 2013, international observers expressed concern about the possibility of renewed fighting between Karabakh and Azerbaijani forces.

Peace talks on a final status for Nagorno-Karabakh remained at a standstill during the year, after highly anticipated Russian-brokered negotiations between the presidents of Armenia and Azerbaijan in 2011 ended in deadlock. Baku's rapid military buildup, with a defense budget that reached $3.7 billion in 2013, further escalated tensions. The Azerbaijani government has openly threatened to consider a military solution to the conflict.

Regional relations were also strained during the year by renewed discussion of plans to reopen Stepanakert's airport, which was closed during the separatist conflict in 1991 but appeared to be ready for normal operations by 2013. The revival of the facility had been delayed in 2012 amid threats from Baku.

In October, two students from Nagorno-Karabakh were sentenced to 10 and 11 years in prison, respectively, on counts of high treason and espionage after being charged with passing state secrets via the internet to a foreign intelligence agent living in Istanbul.

POLITICAL RIGHTS: 12 / 40
A. Electoral Process: 4 / 12

Nagorno-Karabakh has enjoyed de facto independence from Azerbaijan since 1994 and retains close political, economic, and military ties with Armenia. All Karabakh elections are considered invalid by the international community, which does not recognize the territory's independence.

The president is directly elected for up to two five-year terms and appoints the prime minister. Of the unicameral National Assembly's 33 members, 17 are elected by party list and 16 from single-mandate districts, all for five-year terms.

Several 2009 amendments to the election code reduced the vote threshold for representation from 10 percent to 6 percent and changed the proportion of party-list and single-mandate constituency seats. The previous legislature had been composed of 22 party-list and 11 single-mandate seats.

President Bako Saakian, the incumbent since 2007, was reelected in July 2012 with 66.7 percent of the vote. His main opponent, former deputy defense minister Vitaly Balasanian, received 32.5 percent. The two main candidates had nearly identical foreign-policy goals—achieving international recognition of Nagorno-Karabakh's independence—though Balasanian also called for social justice and accused the government of allowing corruption and fiscal mismanagement. Balasanian claimed that administrative resources were misused to aid Saakian during the campaign.

The presidential contest was considered an improvement over the 2010 parliamentary elections, in which no genuine opposition candidates participated. Administrative resources were used to support the progovernment candidates, and the election commission was uniformly composed of progovernment officials. The balloting was swept by the three parties of the ruling coalition. Azat Hayrenik (Free Fatherland), the party of Prime Minister Ara Harutiunian, won 14 of the 33 seats, followed by the Democratic Party of Artsakh (AZhK) with 10 and the Armenian Revolutionary Federation–Dashnaktsutiun party with 6. The remaining seats were captured by Hayrenik loyalists with no formal party affiliation. Parliament speaker Ashot Ghulian was reelected to his post.

B. Political Pluralism and Participation: 5 / 16

The three main political parties are Azat Hayrenik, the AZhK, and the Armenian Revolutionary Federation–Dashnaktsutiun, all of which currently support the government. Given the territory's uncertain status, dissent—including political opposition—is generally regarded as a sign of disloyalty and a security risk. As a consequence, opposition groups have either disappeared or been brought into the government over the past several years. Balasanian, the defeated challenger in the 2012 presidential election, announced in August of that year that he was forming a new opposition group.

C. Functioning of Government: 3 / 12

The ability of Karabakh officials to set and implement government policies is limited in practice by security threats along the cease-fire line, warnings from Baku, and the dominant role played by the Armenian government.

Nagorno-Karabakh continues to suffer from significant corruption, particularly in the construction industry, as well as favoritism in filling civil service positions.

CIVIL LIBERTIES: 19 / 60
D. Freedom of Expression and Belief: 6 / 16

The territory officially remains under martial law, which imposes restrictions on civil liberties, including media censorship. However, the authorities maintain that these provisions have not been enforced since 1995, a year after the cease-fire was signed.

The government controls many of Nagorno-Karabakh's media outlets, and the public television station has no local competition. Most journalists practice self-censorship, particularly on subjects related to the peace process. The popular independent newspaper *Demo* and Karabakh-Open.com, the territory's only independent news website, were both closed by their publishers in 2008. The internet penetration rate is low but expanding. During the 2012 presidential election, the opposition campaigned heavily via social media.

In March 2013, an Armenian-sponsored radio station began broadcasting in Talysh, an Iranian language, from Nagorno-Karabakh into southeastern Azerbaijan, home to the country's minority Talysh population. Iran denied involvement with the broadcasts, which some Azerbaijani officials called a "provocation" meant to promote anti-Azerbaijani sentiments. The station broadcasts three hours a day in both Talysh and Azeri.

Most residents belong to the Armenian Apostolic Church, and the religious freedom of other groups is limited. A 2009 law banned religious activity by unregistered groups and proselytism by minority faiths, and made it more difficult for minority groups to register. Although at least three were subsequently registered, a Protestant group and the Jehovah's Witnesses were reportedly denied registration. Unregistered groups have been fined for their religious activities, and conscientious objectors have been jailed for refusing to serve in the Karabakh army.

E. Associational and Organizational Rights: 3 / 12

Freedom of assembly is formally restricted under martial law provisions. Freedom of association is also limited, but trade unions are allowed to organize. The handful of nongovernmental organizations (NGOs) that are active in the territory are virtually all progovernment, and they suffer from lack of funding and competition from government-organized groups.

F. Rule of Law: 5 / 12

The judiciary is not independent in practice, and the courts are influenced by the executive branch as well as by powerful political, economic, and criminal groups.

In March 2013, two students from Nagorno-Karabakh were arrested on counts of high treason and espionage after allegedly passing state secrets via the internet to a foreign intelligence agent living in Istanbul. Both admitted to sharing sensitive information but claimed that they did not know the recipient was an intelligence officer. In July, the two men, both in their early twenties, were found guilty and sentenced to 10 and 11 years in prison, respectively. The verdict was appealed in August, with the defendants' attorney submitting a complaint listing almost 20 violations committed by the prosecution during the trial. In October, a higher court ruled to dismiss the appeal, upholding the original sentences, and Karabakh's Supreme Court followed suit in December.

A 2011 amnesty law released or commuted the sentences of up to 20 percent of the prison population. The law applied to inmates who had fought in the 1991–1994 war or had family killed in the conflict. The amnesty also stipulated the closure of at least 60 percent of pending criminal cases and the release of suspects from pretrial detention.

The security of the population is affected by regular incidents of violence along the cease-fire line. Hundreds or thousands of cease-fire violations are reported each month, and soldiers on both sides are killed or injured each year. A spike in violence in June 2012 resulted in the death of a dozen soldiers on both sides.

G. Personal Autonomy and Individual Rights: 5 / 16

The majority of Azeris who fled the territory during the separatist conflict continue to live in poor conditions in Azerbaijan, despite Baku's increased efforts to provide new housing in recent years. Land-mine explosions and other dangers in the conflict zone cause deaths and injuries each year and limit freedom of movement. According to the International Committee of the Red Cross, at least 50,000 antipersonnel mines were laid during the war. In many cases, records of minefield locations were lost or never created.

The continued control of major economic activity by powerful elites limits opportunities for most residents, though the government has instituted a number of economic rehabilitation projects in recent years.

Men and women have equal legal status, though women are underrepresented in government and the private sector. Women are not subject to military conscription. The government administers a "birth-encouragement program" with the goal of repopulating the territory. Couples receive several hundred dollars when they marry and additional money for the birth of each child.

Northern Cyprus

Political Rights Rating: 2
Civil Liberties Rating: 2
Freedom Rating: 2.0
Freedom Status: Free

Population: 286,257

Ten-Year Ratings Timeline For Year Under Review (Political Rights, Civil Liberties, Status)

Year Under Review	2004	2005	2006	2007	2008	2009	2010	2011	2012	2013
Rating	2,2,F	2,2,F	2,2,F	2,2,F	2,2,F	2,2,F	2,2,F	2,2,F	2,2,F	2,2,F

Note: See also the country report for Cyprus.

INTRODUCTION

In February 2013, Greek Cypriots elected to the presidency Nicos Anastasiades, who supports a plan initially suggested in 2003 by then–UN Secretary General Kofi Annan to reunite the island of Cyprus by creating a single federation comprised of the Republic of Cyprus (Cyprus) and the Turkish Republic of Northern Cyprus (TRNC), which is recognized only by Turkey. Anastasiades met with TRNC President Derviş Eroğlu in May, but reunification negotiations made no headway, in part because Cyprus was preoccupied with serious economic difficulties. Turkish Cypriots often suggest that any settlement must recognize "realities on the island," and both Eroğlu and the Turkish government have suggested that a two-state solution may eventually become necessary. Cyprus and the TRNC have also been involved in disputes over rights to explore for oil and gas in the eastern Mediterranean.

The TRNC, which is generally dependent upon the Turkish government for both security and economic support, experienced its own economic problems in 2013. These problems were generated in part by cuts in Turkish financial assistance, as well as by the economic troubles in the Republic of Cyprus. In response, the TRNC government, led by the nationalist National Unity Party (UBP), enacted austerity measures, which were unpopular and seen as having been imposed by Turkey. The government lost a vote of confidence in May, prompting new parliamentary elections in late July. A coalition government, headed by Özkan Yorgancıoğlu of the center-left and prounification Republican Turkish Party (CTP), took office in September. The main priority of the government is economic revival, although it is also committed to solving the Cyprus dispute through the creation of a federation.

POLITICAL RIGHTS: 32 / 40
A. Electoral Process: 11 / 12

Elections have been generally free and fair. The president is elected by popular vote to a five-year term, while members of the Assembly are elected to five-year terms through party-list voting. A party must win 5 percent of the vote in order to be seated in the legislature.

While the prime minister is the head of the government, the president is the head of state, with the primary responsibility of representing the TRNC internationally.

Parliamentary elections were held in July, after the government of Prime Minister İrsen Küçük of the UBP lost a confidence vote. Five parties ran a list of candidates for the 50-seat Assembly, and four parties won seats. The CTP, which previously had been the main opposition party, won the most seats, taking 21. It formed a coalition with the Democratic Party (DP), which won 12 seats. Eroğlu of the UBP, who was elected in 2010 to a five-year term, remains president.

Minority Greek and Maronite residents of the TRNC are legally citizens of the Republic of Cyprus, and are thus not eligible to vote in TRNC elections.

B. Political Pluralism and Participation: 12 / 16

Turkish Cypriots are free to organize political parties, and elections are competitive. However, there is a widespread perception that Turkish officials wield most political power in the TRNC; elected TRNC governments have limited room to adopt policies over any objections from Ankara. In 2013, Turkish influence was seen mainly in the economic arena, with Ankara forcing the TRNC to adhere to an economic protocol that demanded austerity measures and privatization, and threatening to cut off funds if such measures were not implemented. Some reports also suggested that Turkey interfered in intraparty politics of the UBP, and later tried unsuccessfully to influence the formation of the new coalition government.

C. Functioning of Government: 9 / 12

Many observers suggest that the effective functioning of the TRNC government is hampered by interference from Turkey. Corruption among TRNC politicians is also a concern. The eight members of the Assembly who defected from the UBP in May and forced early elections accused Prime Minister Küçük of excessive tolerance of bribes, nepotism, and corruption. Serdar Denktaş, leader of the DP, complained in August of a lack of transparency in the €650-million ($873.5-million) privatization of the TRNC's Ercan international airport. The new coalition government announced a variety of measures in September designed to combat corruption, including the end of parliamentary immunity and of temporary civil service jobs.

CIVIL LIBERTIES: 47 / 60 (+1)
D. Freedom of Expression and Belief: 14 / 16 (+1)

Freedom of the press is guaranteed by law, and some media outlets are openly critical of the government. However, in recent years some journalists who espouse antigovernment positions were physically attacked, apparently by members of nationalist groups, though there were no such incidents in 2013. Some journalists and editors in the TRNC have reportedly been summoned to the Turkish embassy and urged to tone down criticism of Ankara. In June, Channel T was sued by two DP Assembly members for airing an interview that suggested they had engaged in bribery.

A 1975 agreement with Republic of Cyprus authorities provides for freedom of worship, and the TRNC is a secular state. However, according to an April 2013 report from the U.S. Commission on International Religious Freedom, religious activities of non-Muslims are subject to some regulations, and there are still disputes over the condition of Christian churches and access to religious sites. In January the United Nations Development Programme reached an agreement with TRNC authorities to restore the monastery of Apostolos Andreas. Academic freedom is generally respected, and there is open private discussion.

E. Associational and Organizational Rights: 9 / 12

Freedoms of assembly and association are generally upheld, though police have been criticized for disrupting protests and allegedly using excessive force. Nongovernmental organizations generally operate without restrictions. Workers may form independent unions, bargain collectively, and strike. Large protests and periodic strikes took place over government austerity measures in 2011 and 2012, but these were less pronounced in 2013. In June, some demonstrations in the TRNC expressed sympathy with the Gezi Park protesters in Turkey. Police briefly clashed with the demonstrators, but there were no injuries.

F. Rule of Law: 12 / 16

The judiciary is independent, and trials generally meet international standards of fairness. Turkish Cypriot police, who are under the control of the Turkish military, sometimes fail to respect due process rights, and there have been allegations of abuse of detainees. Lawyers' associations and journalists have actively worked to remedy irregularities in the justice system.

G. Personal Autonomy and Individual Rights: 12 / 16

All European Union citizens, including Greek Cypriots, can now travel to the north by presenting identity cards and no longer require passports or visas. Most governments do not recognize TRNC travel documents, so thousands of Turkish Cypriots have obtained Republic of Cyprus passports since this option became available in 2004. However, in 2008, Turkey began forbidding Turkish Cypriots from leaving the TRNC through Turkey without TRNC passports. The only direct flights from the TRNC are to Turkey.

There is a right to private property. The TRNC formed a property commission in 2006 to resolve claims by Greek Cypriots who owned property in the north before the island's division. The European Court of Human Rights (ECHR) recognized the commission in 2010 as an "accessible and effective" mechanism. As of September 2013, over 5,000 applications have been lodged with the commission, some 400 of which have been resolved.

A few hundred Greek Cypriots and Maronites continue to live in the TRNC. They reside primarily in their ancestral villages and face difficulties at border checkpoints, as well as alleged surveillance by TRNC authorities. There is some tension between native Turkish Cypriots and recent immigrants from Turkey, who, according to the 2011 census, make up 36 percent of the TRNC's population.

According to Articles 171 and 173 of the criminal code, male homosexuality is punishable with jail time, although this law is rarely enforced. In July 2012, a case was filed with the ECHR against Turkey—deemed responsible for administering the TRNC—in an attempt to force the TRNC to decriminalize homosexuality. In April 2013 the TRNC government suggested it would change the law. However, as of the end of 2013, this had yet to occur.

Women have equal legal rights with men, but face discrimination. Women are underrepresented in politics, and no woman was named to the new government's cabinet in August. This elicited protests from women's organizations; subsequently, Sibel Siber, who had previously served as interim prime minister, was elected speaker of the Assembly. In 2011, the government adopted the Council of Europe's Convention on Violence Against Women, but surveys suggest domestic violence is a major problem. The TRNC is a destination for trafficking in women for the purpose of prostitution, and local officials have done little to address this problem. Abortion is legal, but married women must receive permission from their husbands.

… Freedom in the World 2014

Pakistani Kashmir

Political Rights Rating: 6
Civil Liberties Rating: 5
Freedom Rating: 5.5
Freedom Status: Not Free

Population: 5,595,000

Ten-Year Ratings Timeline For Year Under Review (Political Rights, Civil Liberties, Status)

Year Under Review	2004	2005	2006	2007	2008	2009	2010	2011	2012	2013
Rating	7,5,NF	7,5,NF	7,5,NF	7,5,NF	6,5,NF	6,5,NF	6,5,NF	6,5,NF	6,5,NF	6,5,NF

INTRODUCTION

The Pakistani-controlled territories of Azad Jammu and Kashmir (AJK) and Gilgit-Baltistan (GB) continued to suffer from political and sectarian tensions in 2013. A prominent proindependence activist in AJK was assassinated in May, and supporters blamed the Pakistani government for the crime.

Separately, a series of attacks on Shiite Muslim communities in Pakistan during the year killed a number of GB residents, leading to protests in GB itself, and deadly sectarian clashes struck the territory in December. In June, Islamist extremists killed a group of foreign tourists preparing to climb a mountain in GB.

AJK women living near the frontier with Indian-controlled Kashmir mounted protests against militant activity that had triggered cross-border shelling. Other protests during the year focused on issues including teacher salaries, power outages, and demands for royalties from hydroelectric projects in the region.

POLITICAL RIGHTS: 8 / 40

A. Electoral Process: 3 / 12

Pakistan seized control of both AJK and GB following the partition of British India in 1947. The former enjoys nominal self-government, while Pakistan assumed direct administration of the latter. Pakistan never formally incorporated either territory, leaving them neither sovereign nor a province of Pakistan. Instead the relationship has been determined by various provisional arrangements pending a final settlement of the dispute with India. Article 1 of the constitution of Pakistan, which defines the territories of the country, obliquely refers to these areas as "such States and territories as are or may be included in Pakistan, whether by accession or otherwise."

Pakistan has governed AJK through different acts promulgated in 1960, 1964, 1968, and 1970. Under the 1970 act, AJK was given a rudimentary constitution with a presidential system. In 1974 the elected AJK legislature enacted a new interim constitution approved by the government of Pakistan, this time with a parliamentary system. A president, elected by the Legislative Assembly, serves as head of state, while the prime minister is the chief executive. There is also an AJK Council based in Pakistan's capital, Islamabad. It consists of both Kashmiri and Pakistani officials and holds a number of key executive, legislative, and judicial powers, such as the authority to appoint superior judges and the chief election commissioner. The constitution can theoretically be amended by a majority of the total membership of the Legislative Assembly and the Council in a joint sitting.

Of the AJK Legislative Assembly's 49 seats, 41 are filled through direct elections: 29 with constituencies based in the territory and 12 representing Kashmiri "refugees" throughout Pakistan. Another eight are reserved seats: five for women and one each for representatives of overseas Kashmiris, technocrats, and religious leaders. The system disproportionately favors nonresident refugees over AJK residents, and the nonresident elections are more vulnerable to manipulation by the federal authorities; the party in office at the federal level invariably wins these seats. In the 2011 legislative elections, the Azad Kashmir Peoples' Party (AKPP)—affiliated with Pakistan's then ruling Pakistan People's Party (PPP)—won 20 of the 41 seats, followed by the Pakistan Muslim League–Nawaz (PML-N) with nine seats and the Muslim Conference (MC) party with five. AKPP leader Chaudhry Abdul Majid became prime minister, and Sardar Muhammad Yaqoob Khan was installed as president. The elections were marred by allegations of rigging and vote buying, as well as some violence and harassment, with at least three election-related killings reported.

GB was until recently governed under the Frontier Crimes Regulation (FCR) of 1901 and the Legal Framework Order of 1994. They were replaced in 2009 by the Gilgit-Baltistan Empowerment and Self-Governance Order (GBESGO), which can only be amended by the Pakistani government. The political structure under the GBESGO includes the 33-member GB Legislative Assembly (GBLA), as well as the 15-member Gilgit-Baltistan Council (GBC), headed by the Pakistani prime minister and vice-chaired by a federally appointed governor. The GBC consists of six members of the GBLA and nine Pakistani Parliament members appointed by the governor. The GBLA in turn is composed of 24 directly elected members, six seats reserved for women, and three seats reserved for technocrats; the reserved seats are filled through a vote by the elected members. It has the authority to choose the chief minister and introduce legislation on 61 subjects. Ultimate authority rests with the governor, who has significant power over judicial appointments and whose decisions cannot be overruled by the GBLA. Many fiscal powers remain with the GBC rather than the elected assembly. A majority of high-level positions in the local administration are reserved under the GBESGO for Pakistani bureaucrats.

In November 2009 elections for the GBLA, the PPP won 12 of the 24 directly elected seats; 10 of the remainder were divided among four other parties and four independents, and voting for two seats was postponed. Syed Mehdi Shah, head of the PPP's Gilgit-Baltistan chapter, became chief minister. Following the death of Governor Shama Khalid from cancer in September 2010, Pir Karam Ali Shah, a member of the GBLA, was appointed as governor in January 2011.

No proindependence candidates won seats in the 2009 GBLA elections. Local nationalist leaders accused the authorities of preventing their parties from holding public gatherings, and a number of nationalist leaders and candidates were arrested during the campaign period. Although violence erupted between supporters of rival candidates, the elections themselves were largely peaceful. Independent observer missions characterized the elections as competitive, despite flaws including an inaccurate voter list, allegations of rigging and interference, and misuse of state resources to benefit the PPP.

B. Political Pluralism and Participation: 4 / 16

The interim constitution of AJK bans political parties that do not endorse the territory's eventual accession to Pakistan, and government employees must declare loyalty to the cause of accession. Similar rules prevail in GB, meaning nationalist leaders and parties are denied access to the political process and public employment. Those who oppose Pakistani rule are also subject to surveillance, harassment, and sometimes imprisonment.

Historically, it has been the norm for the party in office at the federal level to form the local governments in AJK and GB. If there were a change at the federal level, a transition would be effected in the local assemblies through cross voting and party switching. This has been a source of considerable political corruption. However, in 2013, after a PML-N government replaced the PPP in Pakistan, the new federal ruling party stopped the local units from undertaking a full-fledged political coup. Nevertheless, the federal government continues to exercise control over the AJK and GB political processes. PML-N candidates won by-elections that were held to fill empty seats in the local assemblies.

C. Functioning of Government: 3 / 16

The federal authorities have direct control over matters including defense and foreign affairs, and indirect control over many other areas of governance through the AJK Council and GBC. The areas of responsibility left to the local authorities are consequently limited. Even on those issues, effective authority is exercised by senior civil servants appointed by the federal government, such as the chief secretary, finance secretary, inspector general of police, accountant general, development commissioner, and health secretary.

Accountability and transparency are hampered by the two territories' lack of representation in the federal government. Because Pakistan maintains that their final status cannot be decided until a UN-sponsored plebiscite is held for the whole disputed region, the two units are left in constitutional limbo and do not enjoy the same rights as other provinces. They do not have seats in the Pakistan Parliament or in constitutional bodies established for consultation and coordination between the federal government and the provinces, such as the Council of Common Interests, the National Economic Council, and the National Finance Commission. AJK and GB do not have representation in Indus River System Authority and do not receive a share in the profits from hydroelectric projects located in their territory.

AJK receives a large amount of financial aid from Islamabad, but successive administrations have been tainted by corruption and incompetence. Aid agencies have also been accused of misusing funds.

Discretionary Political Rights Question B: -2 / 0

The pre-1947 princely state of Jammu and Kashmir barred outsiders from seeking permanent residence or naturalization. In the 1970s, this rule was abolished in GB, opening it up to immigration from different parts of Pakistan. The Sunni Muslim share of the population has since increased significantly. State agencies are suspected of deliberately engineering a demographic change in the sparsely populated Shiite-majority region. Under the 2009 GBESGO, the settlers were given formal citizenship rights in GB. The pre-1947 restrictions on acquiring citizenship are still in place in AJK.

CIVIL LIBERTIES: 21 / 60
D. Freedom of Expression and Belief: 6 / 16

AJK and GB are subject to laws that curb freedom of expression, particularly related to the political status of the region. Media houses need permission from the AJK Council and the federal Ministry of Kashmir Affairs and Gilgit-Baltistan to operate. Though a wide range of media are present and active, censorship of political content, both direct and indirect, is common. Self-censorship is also prevalent as a means of avoiding state harassment. A number of local dailies have faced bans. In GB there have been reports of journalists being fired if they refuse to toe the government line. The government is known to withdraw advertisements, which are a source of revenue for media houses, from outlets seen as too critical. In May 2013, the Skardu Press Club in GB was closed by the district administration, prompting protests by members of the group. Journalists have been targeted by nonstate actors as well. However, after the 2005 earthquake in the region, the media became somewhat more open, with a focus on local news and humanitarian emergencies and efforts. AJK and GB have access to the internet, with the same restrictions as in Pakistan. Usage is largely limited to urban areas.

Pakistan is an Islamic republic and has numerous restrictions on religious freedoms, including blasphemy laws, that are also enforced in AJK and GB. In recent years, sectarian violence predominantly targeting the Shiite community has increased. Sectarian tensions are sharper in GB, a Shiite-majority region. A series of large-scale attacks on Shiite communities throughout Pakistan in 2013 killed some residents of GB, leading to protests and strikes in the region. Sectarian clashes in December left three people dead and several others injured. A 2012 code of conduct enacted by the GBLA aimed to curb sectarian violence by banning prayer leaders from issuing edicts against other sects, but it has not been effectively enforced.

Educational opportunities in the region are limited. Academics are not free of political indoctrination. Any expression of views contradicting the official line on the region's status can invite censure and even legal action. Student union activity has long been under state surveillance for signs of nationalist political views. Local languages and scripts are not taught in government schools. In many areas of GB, there are no schools for girls. Government teachers are paid very low wages. AJK benefits from higher overall literacy rates and better education facilities than those in GB.

E. Associational and Organizational Rights: 5 / 16

There are restrictions on freedom of assembly and association. The AJK interim constitution bans activities that are prejudicial to AJK's accession to Pakistan. Nationalist groups are subject to persecution. Sardar Arif Shahid, a Kashmiri nationalist leader and chair of the All Parties National Alliance (APNA), was shot and killed by unidentified assailants in May 2013. His supporters alleged that it was a targeted killing by the state. Shahid had been prohibited from traveling abroad since 2009. The police had also registered a case against him for publishing a magazine that allegedly contained anti-Pakistan material.

Custodial torture and intimidation of independence supporters and other activists have been reported. In GB, a nascent free Balwaristan movement, seeking independence for GB and neighboring areas under Chinese control, has been crushed ruthlessly.

However, despite the restrictions, demonstrations and protests on various topics remain common, especially in AJK. The harsh curbs on assembly are limited mostly to issues that concern the region's status vis-à-vis Pakistan.

Humanitarian nongovernmental organizations (NGOs) operate freely. The Aga Khan Foundation sponsors several development projects in GB. After the 2005 earthquake, a large number of organizations from across the world were granted access to AJK. However, NGOs working on political or human rights face intense government scrutiny and, in some cases, harassment.

AJK is subject to labor laws similar to those in Pakistan, though with fewer protections for workers. Unions and professional organizations are frequently barred. Labor laws and activities are at a very nascent stage of development in GB. In 2013 there were frequent demonstrations by teachers and nurses demanding better working conditions and salaries.

F. Rule of Law: 4 / 16

AJK has a multi-tiered, dual judicial system with a Supreme Court, High Courts, and district courts. Islamic judges handle criminal cases involving Sharia (Islamic law), while regular judges deal with other criminal and civil cases. The president of AJK, in consultation with the AJK Council, appoints the chief justice of the Supreme Court. Other judges of the superior courts are appointed by the AJK president on the advice of the council, after consultation with the chief justice. Under the constitution the president is bound by the advice of the prime minister. The judicial appointments are therefore easily susceptible to manipulation by the executive in AJK and by federal institutions through the AJK Council. This has led to a politicized judiciary. Charges of nepotism, favoritism, and corruption are common, as are delays in judicial proceedings, due in part to unfilled vacancies in the courts.

GB has a Supreme Appellate Court and a GB Chief Court. The chief judge and judges of the Supreme Appellate Court are appointed on a contractual basis by the prime minister of Pakistan in his capacity as chairman of the GBC, on the recommendation of the governor. Though the 2009 GBESGO is silent about the role of the Ministry of Kashmir Affairs and Gilgit-Baltistan, all appointments to the top judiciary have been routed through the ministry in practice. The process of appointments is consequently lengthy and gives disproportionate influence to the federal government. There have been instances in which the ministry has not honored the recommendations of the local government in a timely manner, leading to delays and dysfunction in the courts. Some areas in GB have parallel or informal judicial systems, including those operated by religious authorities.

The federal government, army, and intelligence agencies have a considerable presence in AJK and GB, and surveillance of political activities is the norm. Arbitrary arrests, torture, and deaths in custody at the hands of security forces have been reported.

Extremist groups devoted largely to attacks on Indian-administered Jammu and Kashmir operate from the region and have links with similar factions based in Pakistan and Afghanistan. Internecine tension between pro-Pakistan and nationalist Kashmiri militant groups is common. In 2013, in a widely reported campaign, women in the Neelum Valley came together to demand an end to militant activity in the area, as it was leading to renewed firing between Indian and Pakistani troops across the Line of Control (LoC), endangering local residents.

The militant groups have been able to expand their influence in both AJK and GB. The Tehrik-e-Taliban Pakistan (TTP) and its affiliates have frequently targeted the Shiite population. In June 2013, the TTP killed a group of 10 foreign mountaineers and their Pakistani guide in the Nanga Parbat base camp. In another attack in August, the militants killed security officials who were investigating the crime. TTP claimed that the attack on foreigners was in retaliation for the killing of their leader, Waliur Rehman, in a U.S. drone strike in Pakistan's tribal areas. A number of foreign climbing expeditions were canceled as a result.

G. Personal Autonomy and Individual Rights: 6 / 16

The citizens of AJK and GB have Pakistani national identity cards and passports. They are internationally recognized as Pakistani nationals. However, there are reports of passports being denied or not renewed for citizens suspected of questioning Pakistani control over the region. Pakistan has been reluctant to offer citizenship to migrants displaced from Indian-administered Jammu and Kashmir. Many of these refugees have been subjected to abuse and arbitrary arrest for demanding their rights.

The pre-1947 state subject law, which bars outsiders from seeking permanent residency and is still in effect in AJK, allows only legal residents to own property. Procedures for establishing private enterprises are onerous.

The status of women varies between AJK and GB. Instances of violence against women and honor killings are rarer in the former. At least 12 honor crimes in GB were reported in the media in 2013. Though the law prohibits discrimination on the basis of sex, treatment is unequal in practice. While women are legally permitted to marry without the consent of their family, they frequently face societal censure if they do so. Many women are victims of forced marriages. Inheritance laws are skewed heavily against women, who in most cases receive far less than their rightful share. In remote areas of GB there have been instances in which Islamist militants target women who work outside the home.

AJK and GB are economically dependent on federal assistance. The Pakistani government exercises full control over decisions on how the natural resources of the region are used. GB is rich in minerals, and AJK has abundant water. Four large hydropower projects that supply electricity to the rest of Pakistan have been undertaken in AJK. Nevertheless, the region faces persistent electricity cuts. In 2013, this led to recurrent protests in AJK. In May, more than 50 people were injured when protesters clashed with police. Residents have been demanding royalty payments as well as an uninterrupted power supply. The hydropower projects have displaced a number of people who are still awaiting their resettlement compensation packages.

Pakistan has signed agreements with China for investment in mineral exploration and infrastructure development in GB. Local residents resent the Chinese presence, as the workers are seen to be taking away jobs and revenue from the exploitation of the region's resources. There have been instances of attacks on Chinese nationals.

Puerto Rico

Political Rights Rating: 1
Civil Liberties Rating: 2
Freedom Rating: 1.5
Freedom Status: Free

Population: 3,640,272

Ten-Year Ratings Timeline For Year Under Review (Political Rights, Civil Liberties, Status)

Year Under Review	2004	2005	2006	2007	2008	2009	2010	2011	2012	2013
Rating	1,2,F	1,2,F	1,1,F	1,1,F	1,1,F	1,1,F	1,1,F	1,1,F	1,2,F	1,2,F

INTRODUCTION

Just as for others in the region, 2013 has been a serious test for the viability of the economy of Puerto Rico, a U.S. commonwealth. In August, government officials reported that income from sales-and-use taxes, which are mainly contributed by consumers, dropped to $553 million in fiscal year 2013 from $797 million five years earlier. According to data from Puerto Rico's Government Development Bank, the island's economy shrank by 5.4 percent in August as compared to a year earlier.

POLITICAL RIGHTS: 37 / 40
A. Electoral Process: 12 / 12

As a U.S. commonwealth, Puerto Rico exercises approximately the same control over its internal affairs as do the 50 states. The commonwealth constitution, modeled after that of the United States, provides for a governor elected for four-year terms and a bicameral legislature. The 27-member Senate and the 51-member House of Representatives are also elected for four-year terms. Puerto Ricans are U.S. citizens guaranteed all civil liberties granted in the United States, though they cannot vote in U.S. presidential elections. A single delegate represents Puerto Rico in the U.S. Congress and is allowed to vote on floor amendments to legislation, but not on the final passage of bills. Pedro Pierluisi of the opposition New Progressive Party (PNP) was reelected to this post in 2012 by a narrow margin. In the November 6, 2012, gubernatorial election, Senator Alejandro García Padilla of the Popular Democratic Party (PPD) received 47.7 percent of the vote, narrowly defeating incumbent governor Luis Fortuño of the PNP, who captured 47.1 percent. Four other candidates received less than 3 percent each. In legislative elections held the same day, the PPD won 18 Senate seats to the PNP's 8; the Puerto Rican Independence Party won 1 seat. Three smaller parties won no seats. In the Puerto Rico House of Representatives, the PPD won 28 seats and the PNP won the remaining 23.

A two-part, nonbinding referendum on Puerto Rico's territorial status was held the same day as the elections. The first question, asking whether voters wanted Puerto Rico to maintain its current territorial status, was supported by only 46 percent of the voters. A second question asked voters to choose whether they preferred statehood, independence, or a sovereign free associated state; the statehood option was selected by 61 percent of voters. However, with more than 470,000 voters choosing not to answer the question, in effect only 45 percent supported statehood. Governor García Padilla subsequently made it clear that he does not support statehood.

B. Political Pluralism and Participation: 15 / 16

Power has alternated between the pro-commonwealth Popular Democratic Party (PPD) and the pro-statehood New Progressive Party (PNP) for several decades. Puerto Ricans have consistently been nearly equally divided between support for commonwealth status and full U.S. statehood, while a third option of independence enjoys little popular support.

C. Functioning of Government: 10 / 12

Corruption is common in Puerto Rican politics. A number of leading political figures have been indicted in recent years on various corruption charges. The commonwealth was ranked 33 out of 177 countries and territories surveyed in Transparency International's 2013 Corruption Perceptions Index.

CIVIL LIBERTIES: 52 / 60
D. Freedom of Expression and Belief: 16 / 16

Puerto Rico's tradition of varied and vigorous news media has been challenged by a decline in newspapers that has stemmed from the ongoing economic crisis and other factors. While internet access in Puerto Rico is slower and more expensive than in the mainland United States, first amendment rights on the internet are not restricted. Freedom of religion is guaranteed in this largely Roman Catholic territory. A substantial number of Evangelical churches have also been established on the island in recent years. Academic freedom is guaranteed.

E. Associational and Organizational Rights: 10 / 12

Freedom of assembly is protected by law, and Puerto Ricans frequently protest local or federal government policies. Civil society is robust, with numerous nongovernmental organizations representing special interests. The government respects trade union rights, and unions are generally free to organize and strike.

F. Rule of Law: 12 / 16

The legal system is based on U.S. law, and the island's Supreme Court heads an independent judiciary. However, concerns about politicization at the Supreme Court emerged in 2010, when the four justices approved a congressional resolution expanding the court from seven to nine members—ostensibly to deal with a heavy caseload—over the objections of a three-justice minority.

Crime is a serious problem in Puerto Rico. The center of the narcotics trade has shifted from San Juan to smaller communities, leaving housing projects in some towns under virtual siege by drug gangs. During 2013, 883 homicides were recorded, 12.1 percent fewer than in 2012. Puerto Rico, like surrounding Caribbean countries, remains a main trafficking route for international drug cartels. In October, a sting operation in the island by the Federal Bureau of Investigation (FBI) dismantled one of the most powerful drug gangs to operate in the Caribbean in the last 20 years.

In September 2011, a U.S. Justice Department report accused the Puerto Rico Police of "profound" and "longstanding" patterns of civil rights violations and other illegal practices that have left it in a state of "institutional dysfunction." According to the report, police frequently attack nonviolent protesters and journalists in a manner that compromises their constitutionally protected rights to freedom of speech and assembly. The report also accused police of unwarranted searches and seizures, among other things. The police superintendent at the time and the Puerto Rico Justice Department claimed the report was untrustworthy and lacked objectivity. A June 2012 American Civil Liberties Union (ACLU) report on Puerto Rico's police force further corroborated the Justice Department findings, charging that the Puerto Rico Police "use of excessive or lethal force is routine, and civil and human rights violations are rampant." The ACLU report cited targeting of poor, African-descent Puerto Ricans and Dominican immigrants.

In July 2013, the U.S. Justice Department announced a lawsuit against the Puerto Rico Police for sustained racial and sexual discrimination against one of its female police officers. Earlier in the month both sides had signed a major civil rights agreement to reform the pattern of police misconduct.

Increasing numbers of homicides include hate violence against members of the LGBT (lesbian, gay, bisexual, and transgender) community; in 2010 and 2011, 18 LGBT people were murdered on the island. In May 2013, the government signed a bill prohibiting employment discrimination based on gender or sexual orientation.

G. Personal Autonomy and Individual Rights: 14 / 16

Puerto Ricans enjoy freedom of travel and choice of residence. There are no limitations on rights to enter institutions of higher education or choose one's place of employment. While organized crime is a problem in Puerto Rico, rights to own property or operate a private business are generally not inhibited. The government is the largest employer on the island.

Although women enjoy equal rights under the law, the 2011 U.S. Justice Department report cited evidence that police officers failed to investigate incidents of sexual assault and domestic violence, including spousal abuse by fellow officers.

Somalia

Capital: Mogadishu
Political Rights Rating: 7
Civil Liberties Rating: 7
Freedom Rating: 7.0
Freedom Status: Not Free
Electoral Democracy: No

Population: 10,383,000

Note: The numerical ratings and status listed above do not reflect conditions in Somaliland, which is examined in a separate report.

Ten-Year Ratings Timeline For Year Under Review (Political Rights, Civil Liberties, Status)

Year Under Review	2004	2005	2006	2007	2008	2009	2010	2011	2012	2013
Rating	6,7,NF	6,7,NF	7,7,NF	7,7,NF	7,7,NF	7,7,NF	7,7,NF	7,7,NF	7,7,NF	7,7,NF

INTRODUCTION

In early December, Prime Minister Abdi Farah Shirdon, who had been in power for just over a year, lost a no-confidence vote, reportedly after he refused to approve President

Hassan Sheikh Mohamud's cabinet picks ahead of a planned reshuffle. Mohamud soon afterward tapped Abdiweli Sheikh Ahmed, an economist, to serve as Somalia's new prime minister, and the parliament approved the appointment in late December. A new cabinet had yet to be installed at year's end. A constitutional referendum set for 2015 requires an electoral framework that has not yet been established.

The active African Union (AU) force in Somalia, as well as Kenyan forces, in 2011 and 2012 successfully pushed the Shabaab, an extremist group that once controlled most of southern Somalia, out of its major strongholds in Mogadishu and Kismayo—a development that effectively cut off the group's financial lifelines. However, security challenges remain pervasive, with the Shabaab retaining an active presence in the south-central region of the country. International actors, including the United States, have assisted in targeting the Shabaab's leaders in Somalia.

While pirates continue to use Somalia as a launchpad for attacks, the number of attacks has declined dramatically. According to the European Union Naval Force–Somalia, there were only 7 attacks by pirates in the Gulf of Aden in 2013, down from 35 in 2012 and 176 in 2011. The last successful hijacking in the region occurred in May 2012. In October 2013, pirate ringleader Mohamed Abdi Hassan, who was thought to be responsible for dozens of hijackings since 2008, was captured at an airport in Brussels, Belgium.

Questions remain regarding the status of the many federated regions of Somalia that have operated with relative autonomy since General Siad Barre's regime collapsed in 1991, giving way to more than two decades without a permanent federal government. Since then, the northwestern region of Somaliland has functioned with relative stability as a self-declared independent state, though it has not received international recognition. In 1998, the northeastern region of Puntland declared temporary autonomy until the establishment of a permanent federal government in Somalia. However, calls for full independence have been on the rise and the Puntland government has yet to formally accept the new Somali government. Further, Puntland has suspended relations with the new Somali federal government until a federal constitution is adopted. A new Puntland legislature was appointed by clan elders in December, after plans for direct elections were scrapped due to security concerns and a lack of necessary infrastructure.

POLITICAL RIGHTS: 0 / 40

A. Electoral Process: 0 / 12

Prior to the swearing-in of President Mohamud and the House of the People, the lower house of the Federal Parliament, in 2012, the state had largely ceased to exist in most respects, and had no governing authority with the ability to protect political rights and civil liberties. The new government is working to create permanent institutions, but has little capacity to govern beyond Mogadishu.

Mohamud was elected to a four-year term by Somalia's provisional legislature in September 2012, from a field of 22 candidates. The 275 members of the House of the People serve four-year terms and were selected by traditional Somali elders. After being vetted for links with militant groups as well as for basic literacy, were sworn in in August 2012. A number of the elders involved in the selection process were chosen by the previous transitional government, which had been deeply unpopular domestically and had faced corruption allegations. Additionally, the U.S. embassy in Somalia ahead of the new legislature's swearing-in had cited "multiple credible reports of intimidation and corruption" during the process by which the new lawmakers were selected. The Upper House, which would have 54 members, had yet to be formed.

In December, Prime Minister Shirdon lost a no-confidence vote amid disagreements with Mohamud, who then tapped Abdiweli Sheikh Ahmed as his replacement.

The region of Puntland has a 66-member legislature nominated by clan elders to five-year terms. Plans for direct elections in May were scrapped amid security concerns and a lack of necessary infrastructure. A new legislature was then approved in December 2013. Puntland's president is elected by the legislature, and may serve up to two five-year terms. A presidential election is set for January 2014; President Abdirahman Mohamed Farole plans to run for a second term. Relations between authorities in Puntland and federal authorities in Mogadishu have been tense. In August, Farole suspended cooperation with the new Somali government until a federal constitution is adopted and national consultations held.

Jubaland, a semiautonomous region in the country's south, held a presidential election in May, drawing complaints from Mogadishu. Some 500 tribal elders in Jubaland elected Sheikh Ahmed Mohamed Islam as the region's first president, though Somali President Mohamud called the vote illegitimate. Jubaland authorities dispute allegations from Mogadishu of secessionist activity, and maintain that the regional administration is permitted under Somalia's federal constitution. In August, the Somali federal government signed an agreement officially recognizing the Jubaland administration, and in November held a reconciliation conference with Jubaland officials in Mogadishu.

B. Political Pluralism and Participation: 0 / 16

While the creation of several political parties has been announced in recent years, the political process is largely driven by clan loyalty. Nevertheless, the new Somali parliament is highly regarded. Since taking power in mid-2012, federal leaders have outlined an ambitious agenda and have begun hearings to tackle the country's most critical challenges.

Somali citizens have little power to exert influence over the system, either as individuals or through civil society. Citizens rarely have relationships with or access to their local members of parliament. There are few accountability mechanisms for government officials; however, to the extent that these mechanisms exist, they largely come from the international community.

C. Functioning of Government: 0 / 12

Corruption in Somalia is rampant. A July report by the UN Monitoring Group on Somalia and Eritrea indicated that 80 percent of withdrawals from Somalia's central bank were made for private purposes. The report further stated that an average of 33 percent of customs and port fees deposited to the bank monthly are unaccounted for. The UN linked the irregularities to Central Bank Governor Abdusalam Omer, who was replaced in September. In October, however, Omer's successor, Yussur Abrar, resigned, citing pressure from fellow government officials to make illegal withdrawals from foreign banks. Corruption is also pervasive in Puntland, where the authorities have been complicit in piracy. Somalia ranked 175 out of 177 countries and territories surveyed in Transparency International's 2013 Corruption Perceptions Index.

CIVIL LIBERTIES: 2 / 40
D. Freedom of Expression and Belief: 1 / 16

While the new constitution calls for freedom of speech and the press, the new government has taken a heavy-handed approach toward the media. For example, in January, journalist Abdiaziz Abdinuur was arrested for conducting an unpublished interview with a woman allegedly raped by government soldiers. After being held without charge for 19 days, Abdinuur was assigned a one-year prison sentence for "offending state institutions" and "false reporting." He was released in March after the Supreme Court threw out the case, citing insufficient evidence. In October, federal authorities raided the Mogadishu offices of the Shabelle Media Network, beating several journalists and shutting down two radio stations. In November, Mohamed Bashir, a Radio Shabelle reporter, and Abdiimalik Yusuf, the head of the Shabelle Media Network, were detained in connection with an interview of an alleged rape victim; her alleged attackers reportedly were two journalists with a government-run radio station, and one had filed a defamation suit in response to the interview. The two Shabelle workers were tried in December; Bashir received a six-month prison sentence and Yusuf, one year. Both were also given the option to pay a fine, which they chose to do in order to avoid prison. However, the alleged rape victim was handed a six-month suspended sentence.

Meanwhile, in July, the federal cabinet passed a draft media law that includes a proclamation of media freedom and initiatives to encourage media transparency. However, it also permits censorship by the Information Ministry, requires broadcasters to seek permission to air foreign media, and prohibits the dissemination of material "harming the country, the people or the religion." The law had not been adopted at year's end.

In Puntland, authorities in March banned broadcasters from airing programs that were produced outside the region, specifically noting two Kenya-based stations and one Somaliland-based station, all of which receive significant funding from European nations. Horseed FM, a Puntland-based independent broadcaster, was suspended by Puntland authorities in October 2012 and remains off the air. In September, Puntland officials indefinitely suspended the private television station Universal TV, reportedly because it did not offer a live broadcast of a speech delivered in Brussels by Puntland's president. In December, however, Puntland's government adopted a media law that won some praise from local journalists.

Somalia remains one of the most dangerous countries in the world for journalists. According to the Committee to Protect Journalists, 52 journalists have been killed since 1992, including 4 in 2013 and 12 in 2012. In March, Radio Abudwaq reporter Rahmo Abdulkadir was fatally shot in Mogadishu by two gunmen after leaving an internet café with a friend. The following month, Radio Mogadishu journalist Mohamed Ibrahim Raage was murdered by two unidentified gunmen near his home in the capital. In July, Liban Abdullahi Farah, a Puntland-based journalist, was shot and killed in that region, and in October, Mohamed Mohamud of Universal TV was shot and killed in Mogadishu. The federal government at the beginning of 2013 established a task force to address violence against journalists, but it has not taken any meaningful action.

Radio is the primary news medium in Somalia. Internet and mobile telephone services are widely available in large cities, though poverty and illiteracy limit access to these resources.

Nearly all Somalis are Sunni Muslims, but there is a very small Christian community. Both Somalia's new constitution and Puntland's charter recognize Islam as the official religion, though the constitution does include religious freedom clauses. The Shabaab has imposed crude versions of Islamic law in areas under its control, banning music, films, and certain clothing, and in one area has prohibited men and women from walking together or talking in public. Anyone accused of apostasy risks execution by the Shabaab, which has also denied religious freedom to moderate Muslims and has caused deep offense among many Somalis by destroying the graves of Sufi saints. The education system is severely degraded due to the breakdown of the state.

E. Associational and Organizational Rights: 0 / 12

Freedom of assembly has not been respected amid ongoing instability and violence in Somalia. Many nongovernmental organizations (NGOs) and UN agencies operating in the country have reduced or suspended their activities in recent years. In October 2012, the

Shabaab banned Islamic Relief, one of the few remaining aid organizations, claiming that the group was "covertly extending the operations of banned organizations." According to the Aid Worker Security Database, a total of 15 aid workers were killed in 2013, which included nine domestic and six international aid workers.

Freedom of assembly was also seriously stifled in Puntland in 2013. Demonstrations against Farole's government were met with a heavy security response and live ammunition fired toward protesters, leaving at least one person wounded.

Existing labor laws are not adequately enforced. With the exception of a journalists' association, unions in the country are not active.

F. Rule of Law: 0 / 16

There is a weak judicial system functioning at the national level. The new constitution outlines a judicial framework that includes the creation of a Constitutional Court, Federal Government courts, and Federal Member State courts, though these institutions have yet to be established. The harshest codes are enforced in areas under the control of the Shabaab, where people convicted of theft or other minor crimes are flogged or have their limbs amputated, usually in public.

The Shabaab is based in Somalia, and controls large swaths of the south-central region. In one notable attack that the group claimed responsibility for, a suicide bomber in October killed 13 people and injured another 10 in Beledweyne. Its most notable act in 2013 was the September attack on Westgate shopping mall in Nairobi, the Kenyan capital, in which 67 people were killed. Four suspects in that strike, reportedly ethnic Somalis, have since been arrested in Kenya.

Various foreign military forces occasionally carry out operations against the group on Somali territory. In late October, Ibrahim Ali, a key Shabaab explosives specialist, was killed in a U.S. air attack in the Somali town of Jilib. Days before, the Kenyan military had successfully targeted a Shabaab training base in Somalia's Dinsoor region, killing an estimated 300 fighters, according to Kenyan military officials. Additionally, U.S. Navy SEALs (Sea, Air, Land Forces) in early October embarked on an unsuccessful raid in Baraawe in a reported attempt to capture a Shabaab commander known as Ikrima. However, the commandoes reportedly retreated without capturing him after encountering a high number of civilians.

The Somali government has had limited success in prosecuting suspected Shabaab members. A federal military court in October convicted four individuals suspected of belonging to the Shabaab in connection with various acts of terrorism, including a bombing at a military base in Mogadishu. However, the Shabaab is believed to have undercover agents operating within the Somali government. In late October, a former custodial corps chief who had been convicted in absentia of having ties to the Shabaab was apprehended.

Most Somalis share the same ethnicity, but clan divisions have long fueled violence in the country. The larger, more powerful clans continue to dominate political life and are able to use their strength to harass weaker clans.

Same-sex sexual activity is punishable by up to three years in prison. LGBT (lesbian, gay, bisexual, and transgender) individuals are not protected by antidiscrimination statutes and are subject to broad social stigma and hostility. They face harsh punishments in areas controlled by the Shabaab.

G. Personal Autonomy and Individual Rights: 1 / 16

The autonomy and individual rights of Somali citizens are severely restricted in practice, primarily because the absence of functional democratic institutions over a period of many years has given way to a lawless environment. Residents must also contend with abuses committed by warlords, clan leaders, and the Shabaab in the absence of government control in several areas of the country—which, among many other violations, have reportedly included the recruitment of child soldiers.

Somalia's economy is largely informal. Agricultural activity accounts for about 40 percent of gross domestic product, though telecommunications and businesses handling the administration of remittance payments also account for some economic activity. More than 40 percent of Somali residents rely on remittances, which total an estimated $1 billion annually. There had been serious concerns in Somalia in 2013 about a plan by British banking giant Barclays PLC to close an account held by the Dubai-based money-transfer operator Dahabshiil Holdings Ltd.; such a move would block many Somalis from collecting remittance payments. However, Dahabshiil obtained an injunction against the planned move by Barclays, and its operations in Somalia, which lacks a formal banking system, remained undisturbed at the year's end.

Women in Somalia face considerable discrimination. Although outlawed under the new constitution, female genital mutilation is still practiced in some form on nearly all Somali girls. Sexual violence is rampant due to lawlessness and impunity for perpetrators, and rape victims are often stigmatized. The new constitution outlines the expectation that women be included in all branches of government and includes a nondiscrimination clause that specifically mentions women. Of the 275 seats in Somalia's new parliament, women hold 38, or 14 percent, falling short of the country's new 30-percent quota.

South Ossetia

Political Rights Rating: 7
Civil Liberties Rating: 6
Freedom Rating: 6.5
Freedom Status: Not Free

Population: 70,000

Ten-Year Ratings Timeline For Year Under Review (Political Rights, Civil Liberties, Status)

Year Under Review Rating	2004	2005	2006	2007	2008	2009	2010	2011	2012	2013
	--	--	--	--	7,6,NF	7,6,NF	7,6,NF	7,6,NF	7,6,NF	7,6,NF

INTRODUCTION

In May 2013, Russian border guards began installing wire fencing to separate Georgia and South Ossetia, shifting the de facto boundary in the affected area by about 300 meters into Georgian territory and hampering previously unimpeded movement between villages on both sides. Following significant international criticism of this "borderization" and its contravention of Moscow's commitments under a cease-fire agreement that ended the 2008 conflict with Georgia, the Russian guards suspended the fence installation by mid-September, though there was no official comment from Moscow about whether the suspension was temporary.

After a protracted and chaotic election process in 2011–2012, new South Ossetian president Leonid Tibilov oversaw a period of relative political stability in 2013. At the same time, he greatly increased the territory's ties to Moscow, signing a series of agreements with Russia during the year. The Russian government now exerts almost complete control over the territory and funds the entirety of the South Ossetian government's budget.

At the end of 2013, only Russia, Venezuela, Nicaragua, and the Pacific Island states of Nauru and Tuvalu recognized South Ossetia's independence from Georgia.

POLITICAL RIGHTS: -3 / 40
A. Electoral Process: 0 / 12

Under the South Ossetian constitution, the president and the 33-seat parliament are elected for five-year terms. Elections held by the separatist government are not monitored by independent observers or recognized by the international community, and most ethnic Georgians have either declined or been unable to participate in the elections since separatist forces first seized territory in the early 1990s and expanded their control in the 2008 conflict.

In 2009, South Ossetia held parliamentary elections that resulted in a legislature dominated by supporters of Eduard Kokoity, the president since 2001, amid accusations that he had shut out and threatened opposition parties.

In June 2011, however, the parliament rejected efforts by Kokoity supporters to lift term limits and allow him to participate in the presidential election set for November. Eleven candidates ultimately ran in the first round on November 13, including several Kokoity loyalists; six other candidates were forced or pressured to withdraw. Opposition candidate Alla Dzhioyeva, a former education minister who opposed Russian annexation, and Moscow-backed candidate Anatoliy Bibilov, South Ossetia's emergency situations minister, each won about 25 percent of the vote and advanced to the November 27 runoff. Results showed Dzhioyeva as the second-round winner with nearly 57 percent, but amid questionable claims of electoral violations, the Supreme Court declared the election invalid and ordered a new vote for March 2012.

The ruling triggered protests by Dzhioyeva's supporters that continued until mid-December 2011, when Russia brokered a compromise under which Dzhioyeva would accept the court's ruling if Kokoity stepped down immediately and the parliament fired the prosecutor general and the Supreme Court chairman. Kokoity stepped down, and Prime Minister Vadim Brovtsev became acting president. However, the parliament rejected the other conditions, prompting Dzhioyeva to announce that she would go ahead with her inauguration on February 10, 2012. On February 9, about 200 security personnel raided her headquarters and attempted to detain her. She was hospitalized after the confrontation, with some reports saying she was struck with a rifle and the authorities maintaining that she fainted due to high blood pressure.

Four new candidates, all favorable to Russia, ran in the repeat election on March 25, 2012. Dzhioyeva was barred from running, and neither her nor Kokoity's camp succeeded in fielding a candidate. Leonid Tibilov, who had led South Ossetia's Committee for State Security (KGB) in the 1990s, received 42 percent of the vote, followed by human rights ombudsman David Sanakoyev with about 25 percent. Tibilov won the April 8 runoff with 54 percent and was sworn in as president on April 19.

B. Political Pluralism and Participation: 0 / 16

In keeping with his campaign pledge of national unity, Tibilov brought members of the approved opposition into his government, including Sanakoyev as foreign minister and Dzhioyeva as deputy prime minister. During the 2011 election period, the leading opposition candidates had been prevented from registering, due in part to a 10-year residency requirement that was added to the constitution earlier in the year. Other opposition candidates were beaten or jailed, and one senior member of a disqualified candidate's party was murdered in North Ossetia.

Tibilov has ushered in a period of apparent political liberalization. Since his inauguration, several new political parties have been registered, including Sanakoyev's Nauag Iryston (New Ossetia). However, Tibilov has significantly increased ties with Russia, and officials endorsed by Moscow have held key government positions in recent years, many appointed directly by Russia or from Russia's North Ossetia republic.

In September 2013, Russian president Vladimir Putin appointed Vladislav Surkov, the reputed architect of Russia's nominally pluralistic but tightly managed party system, as his presidential aide responsible for social and economic issues in South Ossetia and Abkhazia.

C. Functioning of Government: 0 / 12

Russia exerted almost complete control over South Ossetia in 2013, and Tibilov has spoken repeatedly of formally uniting the territory with Russia's North Ossetia republic or joining the Russian Federation directly.

In February, Russian officials reportedly discussed integrating South Ossetia into its tax and revenue system, after Russia set up a treasury on the territory. In May, South Ossetia signed a memorandum with Russia's North Caucasus republic of Kabardino-Balkariya to increase cooperation on standards and practices between their respective parliaments. In June, South Ossetia signed an interparliamentary cooperation agreement with Russia to harmonize Ossetian laws with Russian legislation and to provide assistance in implementing international agreements. And in July, South Ossetia signed a memorandum of cooperation on antiterrorism with Moscow to enhance security and the protection of state borders. In 2011, South Ossetia's parliament had signed a 49-year agreement allowing Russia to build and operate a new military base in the territory; roughly 4,000 Russian troops are stationed in South Ossetia.

Having pledged to root out his predecessor's allegedly rampant corruption and increase stability, Tibilov initiated an investigation of Kokoity's suspected embezzlement and replaced a number of reputedly corrupt officials in 2012. He also left some officials in their posts, including Bibilov. By August 2013, South Ossetia's new prosecutor general, Merab Chigoyev, had opened some 70 criminal investigations, some aimed at former government officials, and Interpol was asked to issue international arrest warrants for nine people, including three former South Ossetian cabinet ministers.

Kokoity's alleged embezzlement of Russian funds earmarked for postwar reconstruction was a major issue in the 2011–2012 elections. A Russian report released in December 2009 found that only a fraction of the money had been used for its intended purposes, and Tskhinvali residents mounted several protests over the issue in 2010. After the Russian Audit Chamber conducted an investigation on embezzlement, subsidies for 2013 were reduced to 4.25 billion rubles ($134 million), compared with 6.4 billion in 2011 and 5.5 billion in 2012, though Moscow later lauded Tibilov for spending funds "efficiently" since he took power, and promised to increase both budgetary subsidies and money earmarked for infrastructure projects during the year.

Discretionary Political Rights Question B: -3 / 0

During the 2008 war, Ossetian forces seized or razed property in previously Georgian-controlled villages, and large numbers of ethnic Georgians fled the fighting. Authorities in South Ossetia have since barred ethnic Georgians from returning to the territory unless they renounce their Georgian citizenship and accept Russian passports.

CIVIL LIBERTIES: 8 / 60

D. Freedom of Expression: 4 / 16

South Ossetia's local electronic and print media are almost entirely controlled by the authorities, and private broadcasts are prohibited. Foreign media, including broadcasts from Russia and Georgia, are accessible. During the 2011–2012 election period, independent or opposition-oriented journalists in the territory faced various forms of intimidation, including trumped-up criminal charges.

Freedom of religion has sometimes been adversely affected by the political and military situation. While the majority of the population is Orthodox Christian, there is a sizeable Muslim community, many members of which migrated from the North Caucasus. The educational system reflects government views, and many South Ossetians receive higher education in Russia.

E. Associational and Organizational Rights: 0 / 12

While antigovernment protests were extremely rare before the 2008 war, opposition groups mounted demonstrations following the flawed 2009 elections, and Tskhinvali residents protested repeatedly over the slow postwar reconstruction process and related government corruption. In the run-up to the presidential election in 2011, one human rights activist was beaten and another threatened after leading such demonstrations. Dzhioyeva's supporters held weeks of peaceful protests after the annulment of the first presidential election, which Kokoity called unauthorized and threatened with violence.

Though some nongovernmental organizations (NGOs) operate in the territory, in practice they are largely controlled by the state and funded by Russia. Activists operate under the close scrutiny of the authorities and are subject to intimidation. In August 2013, South Ossetia's parliament amended the territory's NGO laws, requiring the groups to provide information to the government about the source of their funding.

F. Rule of Law: 1 / 16

South Ossetia's justice system has been manipulated to punish perceived opponents of the separatist leadership, while government allies allegedly violate the law with relative impunity. Russian prosecutors have attempted to curb malfeasance by local officials, but the Russian court system itself remains deeply flawed.

Physical abuse and poor conditions are reportedly common in South Ossetian prisons and detention centers. Arbitrary arrests of ethnic Georgians have been reported.

G. Personal Autonomy and Individual Rights: 3 / 16

Freedom of movement in and out of the territory is restricted in various ways. In May 2013, Russian troops began installing wire fencing along the administrative border, dividing Georgian-controlled areas from South Ossetia and effectively halting previously unimpeded movement between local villages on both sides. They had erected 27 kilometers of fencing through 15 villages by September, pushing 300 meters into Georgian territory. The United States, the North Atlantic Treaty Organization (NATO), and the European Union Monitoring Mission (EUMM) called on Russia to halt construction and adhere to its commitments under the August 2008 cease-fire agreement. By mid-September, Russian forces had halted the installation.

South Ossetian authorities detained dozens of people for crossing the administrative border during 2013. The detainees were typically released after paying fines. Russian authorities have prevented ethnic Ossetians from entering Georgia, but travel to Russia is unimpeded. In September, the Ossetian authorities toughened restrictions on vehicles and limited the amount of cargo passing through checkpoints along the border. Meanwhile, the Georgian government elected in late 2012 has eased the previous government's policy of detaining and intimidating Ossetian residents travelling to Georgia.

Tibet

Population: 3,000,000 [Note: This figure from China's 2010 census covers only the Tibet Autonomous Region. Areas of eastern Tibet that were incorporated into neighboring Chinese provinces are also assessed in the report below.]
Political Rights Rating: 7
Civil Liberties Rating: 7
Freedom Rating: 7.0
Freedom Status: Not Free

Ten-Year Ratings Timeline For Year Under Review (Political Rights, Civil Liberties, Status)

Year Under Review	2004	2005	2006	2007	2008	2009	2010	2011	2012	2013
Rating	7,7,NF	7,7,NF	7,7,NF	7,7,NF	7,7,NF	7,7,NF	7,7,NF	7,7,NF	7,7,NF	7,7,NF

INTRODUCTION

The security clampdown established after an uprising in 2008 was sustained during 2013 and increasingly extended to Tibetan areas outside the Tibet Autonomous Region (TAR). Over the course of the year, a total of 26 Tibetans set themselves on fire to protest Chinese Communist Party (CCP) rule. The authorities responded with communications blackouts, "patriotic education" campaigns, travel restrictions, and intrusive new controls on monasteries. Despite the repressive atmosphere, many Tibetans expressed solidarity with the self-immolators, protested discriminatory language policies, and quietly maintained contact with the exile community.

Intermittent talks between the government and representatives of the Dalai Lama, last held in 2010, did not resume during 2013, marking the longest period without negotiations since 2002. Meanwhile, Beijing continued to press foreign leaders to refrain from meeting with the Dalai Lama and to endorse the official Chinese position on Tibet.

While the region had been periodically accessible to tourists and journalists under special conditions since 2008, travel restrictions on Tibetans and foreigners attempting to enter the TAR intensified in 2012, and access remained extremely limited in 2013. The U.S. ambassador to China was allowed to visit the TAR in June, the first such visit by an American official in over two years.

POLITICAL RIGHTS: -2 / 40
A. Electoral Process: 0 / 12

The Chinese government rules Tibet through administration of the TAR and 12 Tibetan autonomous prefectures or counties in the nearby provinces of Sichuan, Qinghai, Gansu, and Yunnan. Under the Chinese constitution, autonomous areas have the right to formulate their own regulations and implement national legislation in accordance with local conditions. In practice, decision-making power is concentrated in the hands of senior, ethnic Chinese CCP officials. In August 2011, Zhang Qingli was replaced as TAR party secretary by Chen Quanguo. The few ethnic Tibetans who occupy senior positions serve mostly as figureheads and echo official doctrine on Tibet. Padma Thrinley (known as Pema Choling in the Chinese press) was replaced by Losang Gyaltsen as chairman of the TAR government in January 2013; both men are Tibetans.

B. Political Pluralism and Participation: 0 / 16

All political activity outside the CCP is illegal and harshly punished, as is any evidence of loyalty to or communication with the Tibetan government in exile in Dharamsala, India.

The exile government includes an elected parliament serving five-year terms, a Supreme Justice Commission that adjudicates civil disputes, and—since 2001—a directly elected prime minister, also serving five-year terms. The unelected Dalai Lama, who served as head of state, renounced his political role in March 2011. Lobsang Sangay was elected prime minister the following month, replacing a two-term incumbent and becoming the exile government's top political official.

C. Functioning of Government: 1 / 12

Corruption is believed to be extensive in Tibet, as in the rest of China. Nevertheless, little information was available during the year on the scale of the problem or official measures to combat it.

Discretionary Political Rights Question B: -3 / 0

The Chinese government's economic development programs in Tibet have strongly encouraged ethnic Chinese migration to the region, disproportionately benefited ethnic Chinese residents, and exacerbated the marginalization of ethnic Tibetans, who have also been displaced by mass resettlement campaigns. Intrusive and discriminatory government policies on education and religious institutions have added to Tibetan fears of cultural assimilation.

CIVIL LIBERTIES: 3 / 60
D. Freedom of Expression: 0 / 16

Chinese authorities tightly restrict all media in Tibet. Such measures intensified in 2013 as the authorities sought to suppress information about self-immolations and related security crackdowns. International broadcasts are jammed and communications devices periodically confiscated. The online restrictions and monitoring in place across China are enforced even more stringently in the TAR. In July 2012, Human Rights Watch reported new media controls and invigorated state propaganda efforts, particularly in the TAR. These included distribution of satellite receivers fixed to government channels and a pilot project for broadcasting official messages via loudspeakers in 40 villages. A number of Tibetans who transmitted information abroad suffered repercussions including long prison sentences. Some internet and mobile-telephone users have been arrested solely for accessing banned information. On several occasions in 2013, the authorities cut off the internet and mobile-phone text-messaging near the sites of self-immolations in Sichuan and Gansu Provinces. According to overseas Tibetan groups, scores of writers, intellectuals, and musicians have been arrested since 2008, with some sentenced to lengthy prison terms. Among other such detentions during 2013, Chinese officials in October arrested three writers who provided information to outside observers, on the grounds that they carried out "political activities aimed at destroying social stability and dividing the Chinese homeland."

Authorities continued to restrict access to the TAR for foreign journalists, human rights researchers, and even tourists in 2013. They were denied entry surrounding politically sensitive dates, such as the anniversary of the 2008 protests. During other periods, they were required to travel in groups and obtain official permission to visit the TAR, but even then, last-minute travel bans were sometimes imposed. Foreign journalists were consistently prevented from entering Tibetan areas of Sichuan and other provinces, though no permission is technically required for travel there. Residents who assist foreign journalists are reportedly harassed. In May 2013, a French television station aired a documentary that was filmed undercover by a reporter visiting the TAR on a tourist visa. Chinese officials subsequently harassed and threatened the journalist and his station. The Foreign Correspondents' Club of China condemned Beijing's aggressive attempts to prevent reporting on the region.

The authorities regularly suppress religious activities, particularly those seen as forms of dissent or advocacy of Tibetan independence. Possession of Dalai Lama–related materials can lead to official harassment and punishment, though many Tibetans secretly possess such items. CCP members, government employees, and their family members are not allowed to practice Buddhism, at least within the TAR. The Religious Affairs Bureaus (RABs) control who can study in monasteries and nunneries. Officials allow only men and women over age 18 to become monks and nuns, and they are required to sign a declaration rejecting Tibetan independence, expressing loyalty to the government, and denouncing the Dalai Lama. In January 2012, the CCP announced that new committees of government officials were being set up within monasteries to manage their daily operations and enforce party indoctrination campaigns. Under the previous arrangement, managing committees comprised monks and nuns who had been deemed politically reliable. That system was reportedly retained in Tibetan regions outside the TAR, but with a government official appointed as deputy director. In addition, police posts are increasingly common even in smaller monasteries. In June 2013, exile groups and activists decried the demolition of historic sections of Lhasa adjacent to UNESCO World Heritage sites of religious significance, reportedly as part of a plan to construct a large shopping mall and other commercial or tourist facilities.

Ideological education campaigns that had been conducted sporadically since 1996 began to escalate in 2005, intensified again after 2008, and expanded further in 2013, reaching most monasteries and nunneries in the region. Such campaigns typically force participants to recognize the CCP claim that China "liberated" Tibet and to denounce the Dalai Lama. Some monks and nuns have reportedly left their institutions to avoid the sessions. The effort has also been extended to the lay population in recent years, with students, civil servants, and farmers required to participate in discussions, singing sessions, and propaganda film screenings. In a program initiated in 2011, tens of thousands of CCP cadres have been sent to villages across the TAR to scrutinize residents' views and enforce the government's message.

University professors cannot lecture on certain topics, and many must attend political indoctrination sessions. The government restricts course materials to prevent the circulation of unofficial versions of Tibetan history.

E. Freedom of Association: 0 / 12

Freedoms of assembly and association are severely restricted in practice. Independent trade unions and human rights groups are illegal, and even nonviolent protests are often harshly punished. Nongovernmental organizations (NGOs) focused on development and public health operate under highly restrictive agreements. Despite the risks, Tibetans continue to seek avenues for expressing dissatisfaction with government policies. Most self-immolation protesters in 2012 and 2013 were lay Tibetans, including farmers facing eviction from their land, whereas in 2011 the majority were monks and nuns. Authorities responded to the immolations with information blackouts, a heightened security presence, and increased surveillance. Since late 2012, officials have employed collective punishment tactics, canceling public benefits for the households of self-immolators and ending state-funded projects in their villages. Notices offered rewards of up to 200,000 yuan ($31,500) for information on alleged organizers.

In addition to the self-immolations, Tibetans staged periodic demonstrations or vigils to protest CCP rule or express solidarity with the immolators. Authorities sometimes responded violently. In October, security forces repeatedly opened fire on Tibetan demonstrators in Driru, in the TAR, wounding scores, reportedly killing at least 4, and detaining hundreds more. The Tibetans were protesting government orders to fly the Chinese flag from their homes.

F. Rule of Law: 0 / 16

The judicial system in Tibet remains abysmal, and torture is reportedly widespread. The Tibetan Center for Human Rights and Democracy reported an increase in arrests and detentions of Tibetans in 2013, the majority of which occurred during peaceful protests. Defendants lack access to meaningful legal representation. Trials are closed if state security is invoked, and sometimes even when no political crime is listed. Chinese lawyers who offer to defend Tibetan suspects have been harassed or disbarred. Security forces routinely engage in arbitrary detention, and detainees' families are often left uninformed as to their whereabouts or well-being.

In December 2012 the central authorities unveiled guidelines indicating that engaging in self-immolations and organizing, assisting, or gathering crowds related to such acts should be considered criminal offenses, including intentional homicide in some cases. In 2013 the government implemented the new policy by arresting relatives and friends of self-immolators and handing down lengthy prison sentences. In August, a man received a death sentence after his wife self-immolated; he was accused of murdering her, reportedly after refusing to blame her death on domestic problems.

G. Personal Autonomy: 3 / 16

Heightened restrictions on freedom of movement—including the use of troop deployments, roadblocks, and passport restrictions—were employed during 2012 and continued in 2013, particularly in areas where self-immolations took place. Increased security efforts kept the number of Tibetans who successfully crossed the border into Nepal at less than 200 in 2013, continuing a trend of annual declines from over 2,000 in 2007. Some Tibetan students who were accepted by foreign schools were denied passports, preventing them from studying abroad.

Tibetans receive preferential treatment in university admission examinations, but this is often not enough to secure entrance. The dominant role of the Chinese language in education and employment limits opportunities for many Tibetans. Private employers favor ethnic Chinese for many jobs, and Tibetans reportedly find it more difficult to obtain permits and loans to open businesses.

Since 2003, the authorities have intensified efforts to resettle rural Tibetans—either by force or with inducements—in permanent-housing areas with little economic infrastructure. According to Human Rights Watch, over 2 million TAR residents have been resettled since 2006, while more than 300,000 nomadic herders in Qinghai Province have been relocated and "sedentarized." Many have reportedly tried to return to their previous lands, risking conflict with officials.

China's restrictive family-planning policies are more leniently enforced for Tibetans and other ethnic minorities. As a result, the TAR is one of the few areas of China without a skewed sex ratio. Officials limit urban Tibetans to two children and encourage rural Tibetans to stop at three.

Transnistria

Political Rights Rating: 6
Civil Liberties Rating: 6
Freedom Rating: 6.0
Freedom Status: Not Free

Population: 505,153

Ten-Year Ratings Timeline For Year Under Review (Political Rights, Civil Liberties, Status)

Year Under Review	2004	2005	2006	2007	2008	2009	2010	2011	2012	2013
Rating	6,6,NF	6,6,NF	6,6,NF	6,6,NF	6,6,NF	6,6,NF	6,6,NF	6,6,NF	6,6,NF	6,6,NF

INTRODUCTION

International negotiations on the status of Transnistria—also known as the Pridnestrovskaya Moldavskaya Respublika (PMR)—continued during 2013 under the so-called 5+2 format, with the Organization for Security and Cooperation in Europe (OSCE), Russia, and Ukraine attempting to mediate between Moldova and the separatist PMR, and the United States and the European Union (EU) joining as observers. The talks focused on minor issues related to freedom of movement across the de facto border separating Transnistria from the rest of Moldova, and generally failed to address the overarching political questions.

In May 2013, the PMR parliament rejected a proposal by President Yevgeniy Shevchuk to relocate the legislature from Tiraspol to Bender, a separatist-controlled city on the right bank of the Dniester River where the Moldovan government has also maintained some presence. However, the PMR government issued a decree in June that included Bender and other contested areas within its "state border." Some observers speculated that these and other provocative actions by separatist authorities formed part of Russia's campaign to dissuade Moldova from moving closer to the EU at a summit scheduled for November. Moldovan representatives nevertheless initialed an EU Association Agreement as planned.

POLITICAL RIGHTS: 10 / 40

A. Electoral Process: 3 / 12

Residents of Transnistria cannot choose their leaders democratically, and they are unable to participate freely in Moldovan elections. While the PMR maintains its own legislative, executive, and judicial branches of government, no country recognizes its independence. Both the president and the 43-seat, unicameral Supreme Council are elected to five-year terms. In 2011, the legislature approved constitutional amendments that created a relatively weak post of prime minister and set a two-term limit on the presidency.

The Obnovleniye (Renewal) party maintained its majority in December 2010 legislative elections, winning 25 of 43 seats. Party leader Anatoliy Kaminsky was reelected as speaker. While the December 2011 presidential election, like all voting for PMR institutions, was not recognized internationally, it featured increased competition and a somewhat broader choice for voters compared with previous polls. Founding PMR president Igor Smirnov, whom Moscow had urged not to seek a fifth term, was eliminated in the first round, taking 24 percent of the vote in a field of six. Shevchuk, a former parliament speaker, led with 39 percent, followed by Kaminsky, who had Russia's endorsement, with 26 percent. Shevchuk went on to win the runoff against Kaminsky, securing 74 percent of the vote. Kaminsky resigned as parliament speaker and head of Obnovleniye in June 2012. He was replaced in both posts by his deputy, Mikhail Burla.

In June 2013, Tatyana Turanskaya was appointed as the PMR's acting prime minister, and lawmakers approved her permanent appointment to the post in July. Shevchuk had promoted her multiple times since 2012; previously she had worked at a local tax inspectorate.

B. Political Pluralism and Participation: 5 / 16

Shevchuk, who had fallen out with Smirnov in 2009 and was expelled from Obnovleniye in July 2011, formed the Vozrozhdeniye (Revival) movement to back his presidential bid. Although he was committed to maintaining strong ties with Russia, he pledged to tackle corruption and laid out plans to reduce barriers to travel and trade with Moldova.

Obnovleniye, which remains the majority party in the legislature, is associated with Transnistria's monopolistic business conglomerate, Sheriff Enterprises, and maintains a close relationship with the ruling party in Russia. All of the PMR's political establishment, including nominal opposition parties, supports the separatist system and Russia's role as patron.

Moscow's strong political influence in Transnistria is undergirded by the presence of roughly 1,000 Russian troops, who are ostensibly stationed in the territory to guard Soviet-era ammunition depots and uphold a 1992 cease-fire between the PMR and the Moldovan government. During 2013, Russia pressed Moldova and Ukraine to allow it to bring in new military supplies and reopen a defunct military airport in Tiraspol.

Native Romanian speakers are poorly represented in government. While the authorities do not allow voting in Moldovan elections to take place in PMR-controlled territory, residents with Russian citizenship had access to two dozen polling stations for Russia's tightly controlled presidential election in 2012. Shevchuk strongly endorsed the candidacy of Vladimir Putin.

C. Functioning of Government: 2 / 12

Corruption and organized crime are serious problems in Transnistria. The authorities are entrenched in the territory's economic activities, which rely in large part on smuggling schemes. In 2012, the deputy director of Moldova's Information and Security Service (SIS) alleged that criminal groups used the PMR's banking system to launder proceeds from trafficking in persons, drugs, and arms. PMR officials strongly denied the claims. The EU assists Ukraine and Moldova in efforts to maintain customs controls along their internationally recognized border. Russia has a major stake in the Transnistrian economy and backs the PMR through loans, direct subsidies, and natural gas supplies. Transnistria has not paid the state-owned Russian energy giant Gazprom for gas imports since 2007, building up a debt of about $4 billion. Individuals associated with the Smirnov administration have been accused of embezzling Russian aid and Transnistrian public assets.

CIVIL LIBERTIES: 14 / 60 (-1)
D. Freedom of Expression and Belief: 5 / 16 (-1)

The media environment is restrictive. Nearly all media are state owned or controlled and refrain from criticizing the authorities. A government decision in October 2013 offered bonuses to journalists at state-run outlets for coverage of official activities. The few independent print outlets have small circulations. Critical reporting draws harassment by the government, which also uses tactics such as bureaucratic obstruction and the withholding of information to inhibit independent media. Sheriff Enterprises dominates the private broadcasting, cable television, and internet service markets. Opposition groups reported in mid-2013 that a series of 10 websites with antigovernment content had been blocked without explanation beginning in late 2012. They included news portals and opposition party sites.

Religious freedom is limited. Orthodox Christianity is the dominant faith, and authorities have denied registration to several smaller religious groups. Unregistered groups face harassment by police and Orthodox opponents. There are no legal exemptions from military service for conscientious objectors, leading to criminal punishment of Jehovah's Witnesses and others.

Several schools that provide instruction in Romanian using the Latin alphabet, which is associated with support for unity with Moldova, face harassment by PMR officials and are forced to use substandard facilities. A 2012 ruling by the European Court of Human Rights found Russia liable for the PMR's restrictions on Romanian-language education, ordering Moscow to pay about $1.4 million in damages to a group of Transnistria residents who had sued in 2004 and 2006.

E. Associational and Organizational Rights: 2 / 12

The authorities severely restrict freedom of assembly and rarely issue required permits for public protests. In July 2013, opposition politicians and free speech advocates were allowed to hold a small protest against the recent website blocking, but its impact was limited by other events, such as a military band concert, that were scheduled for the same time and location.

Freedom of association is similarly circumscribed. All nongovernmental activities must be coordinated with local authorities, and groups that do not comply face harassment, including surveillance and visits by security officials. The region's trade unions are holdovers from the Soviet era, and the United Council of Labor Collectives works closely with the government.

F. Rule of Law: 2 / 16

The judiciary is subservient to the executive and generally implements the will of the authorities. Defendants do not receive fair trials, and the legal framework falls short of international standards. Politically motivated arrests and detentions are common. Human rights groups have received credible accounts of torture in custody, and prison conditions are considered harsh and unsanitary. A UN report issued in February 2013 found excessive use of pretrial detention, lengthy sentences for minor crimes, and an "alarming" health situation in prisons, including multiple cases of drug-resistant tuberculosis. There is no separate juvenile justice system, and addicts face forced medical treatment. Suspicious deaths of military conscripts occur periodically amid reports of routine mistreatment.

Despite constitutional guarantees of equality, authorities discriminate against the Romanian-speaking plurality. Ethnic Russians and ethnic Ukrainians together account for some 60 percent of the population. LGBT (lesbian, gay, bisexual, and transgender) people are also reportedly subject to discrimination.

G. Personal Autonomy and Individual Rights: 5 / 16

Travelers are frequently detained and questioned by the PMR authorities. In the 5+2 negotiations during 2013, Moldovan representatives said they were considering lifting travel restrictions on Transnistrian residents who held passports issued by Russia or Ukraine. The majority of residents hold Russian, Ukrainian, or other countries' passports, though many are believed to have multiple citizenship. Transnistrian negotiators are also seeking acceptance of PMR-issued vehicle licenses, shipping permits, and university diplomas.

The 2013 UN report found that many residents have lost their rights to housing or agricultural land following flawed privatizations of factories and collective farms.

Women are typically underrepresented in positions of authority, making up less than 10 percent of the legislature, though Shevchuk's government includes several high-ranking women. Domestic violence against women is a widespread problem, and police sometimes refuse to take complaints from victims. Transnistria is a significant source and transit point for trafficking in women for the purpose of prostitution.

West Bank

Political Rights Rating: 6
Civil Liberties Rating: 5
Freedom Rating: 5.5
Freedom Status: Not Free

Population: 2,731,000

Note: Whereas past editions of *Freedom in the World* featured one report for Israeli-occupied portions of the West Bank and Gaza Strip and another for Palestinian-administered portions, the latest four editions divide the territories based on geography, with one report for the West Bank and another for the Gaza Strip. As in previous years, Israel is examined in a separate report.

Ten-Year Ratings Timeline For Year Under Review (Political Rights, Civil Liberties, Status)

Year Under Review	2004	2005	2006	2007	2008	2009	2010	2011	2012	2013
Rating	--	--	--	--	--	--	6,5,NF	6,5,NF	6,5,NF	6,5,NF

INTRODUCTION

In 2013, the Palestinian Authority (PA) in the West Bank continued to operate without an electoral mandate or a functioning legislature, despite the administration's ongoing state-building efforts. Negotiations aimed at repairing the six-year-old rift between the Hamas regime in Gaza and the Fatah-led PA in the West Bank made little tangible progress during the year, and no date for long-overdue elections was set. However, Hamas continued to support diplomatic plans for the Fatah-led Palestine Liberation Organization (PLO) to assert Palestinian statehood within UN institutions. In November 2012 the PLO had won recognition for Palestine as a nonmember observer state at the UN General Assembly. U.S.-mediated peace talks between the PA and Israel were ongoing at the end of 2013.

Israel doubled new West Bank settlement construction in 2013. Meanwhile, attacks by Jewish settlers on Palestinian individuals and property continued.

POLITICAL RIGHTS: 7 / 40 (+1)

A. Electoral Process: 2 / 12

Most Palestinian residents of the West Bank are citizens of the PA, a quasi-sovereign entity created by the 1993 Oslo Accords. Jewish settlers in the West Bank are Israeli citizens.

The PA president is elected to four-year terms. The prime minister is nominated by the president and requires the support of the unicameral, 132-seat Palestinian Legislative Council (PLC), which also serves four-year terms. Voting in the West Bank during the 2005 presidential and 2006 PLC elections was deemed largely free and fair by international observers. Fatah's Mahmoud Abbas won the presidency with 62 percent of the vote, but Hamas led the PLC balloting with 74 seats, leaving Fatah with 45. The two factions formed a unity government headed by Prime Minister Ismail Haniya of Hamas.

After the violent bifurcation of the PA in 2007, Abbas appointed a new cabinet in the West Bank—with Salam Fayyad as prime minister—that lacked the PLC's approval. In 2008, PA security forces arrested hundreds of Hamas members and supporters. The rift, combined with Israel's detention of many Palestinian lawmakers, prevented the PLC from functioning, and its term expired in 2010.

The PLO indefinitely extended Abbas's presidential term after his electoral mandate expired in 2009. Moreover, Abbas issued a law permitting the Fatah-affiliated minister of local government to dissolve municipal councils, leading to the replacement of nearly all

Hamas-affiliated municipal officials in the West Bank with Fatah loyalists. Elections were held for over 90 municipalities in October 2012 amid some accusations of unfairness, with Hamas and Islamic Jihad boycotting the voting. Only half of eligible Palestinians registered to participate, and only 54 percent of those registered actually voted. Fatah won 40 percent of the seats at stake, and others were taken by independents, many of whom were former Fatah members.

In June 2013, Abbas appointed Rami Hamdallah to replace Fayyad as prime minister.

B. Political Pluralism and Participation: 5 / 16

The PA and Israeli forces in the West Bank have largely suppressed Hamas since 2007. However, a number of smaller Palestinian parties continue to operate in the West Bank, including through membership in the PLO. A May 2011 Hamas-Fatah agreement envisioned a unity government that would organize presidential and parliamentary elections, but no such government had been formed by the end of 2013, nor had a timetable for elections been set.

After Israel annexed East Jerusalem in 1967, Arab residents were issued Israeli identity cards and given the option of obtaining Israeli citizenship. However, most have rejected this option. They can vote in municipal and PA elections, but are subject to restrictions imposed by the Israeli municipality. In the 2006 PLC elections, Israel barred Hamas from campaigning in the city. By law, Israel strips Arabs of their Jerusalem residency if they remain outside Jerusalem for more than three months.

C. Functioning of Government: 2 / 12

The 2007 schism left the West Bank PA with a cabinet that lacked the support of the legislature, and the expiration of the presidential and parliamentary terms in 2009 and 2010 further undermined the government's legitimacy. The PA's ability to implement policy decisions is limited in practice by direct Israeli control over much of the West Bank.

Abbas has overseen some improvements on corruption, and Fayyad was credited with significantly reducing corruption at the higher levels of the PA. Nevertheless, a 2013 report by the Coalition for Accountability and Integrity (AMAN) detailed endemic corruption, especially graft, and partly attributed the lack of transparency and poor functioning of government to the split between Hamas in Gaza and Fatah in the West Bank.

Discretionary Political Rights Question B: -2 / 0 (+1)

Plans to build Jewish settlements in a crucial area east of Jerusalem known as E1, first announced in 2012, were halted by the Israeli government in late 2013. The PA and international observers had warned that such construction could scuttle peace talks and prevent the formation of a viable Palestinian state. Peace negotiations were ongoing at year's end. Nevertheless, settlement building elsewhere in the West Bank continued, effectively doubling from the previous year, with 2,534 new housing units begun in 2013.

According to the human rights group B'Tselem, the Israel Defense Forces (IDF) demolished 175 Palestinian housing units in the West Bank (not including East Jerusalem) in 2013 due to lack of building permits, leaving 528 people homeless, including 270 minors. In East Jerusalem, the number of home demolitions was 72, and 301 people were left homeless, including 176 minors.

CIVIL LIBERTIES: 24 / 60
D. Freedom of Expression and Belief: 8 / 16

The media are not free in the West Bank. Under a 1995 PA press law, journalists may be fined and jailed, and newspapers closed, for publishing "secret information" on PA security forces or news that might harm national unity or incite violence. Several small media outlets are routinely pressured to provide favorable coverage of the PA and Fatah. Journalists who criticize the PA or Fatah face arbitrary arrests, threats, and physical abuse. Since 2007, both the PA and Israeli forces have shut down most Hamas-affiliated broadcast outlets in the West Bank.

According to a report by the Palestinian Center for Development and Media Freedoms (MADA), there were a total of 179 media freedom violations—ranging from physical violence to detentions, threats, and equipment confiscations—in the West Bank in 2013, a slight decrease from the previous year. Of those violations, 151 were allegedly committed by Israeli forces. International press freedom groups regularly criticize Israel for blocking journalists' access to conflict zones, harming and sometimes killing reporters during armed clashes, and harassing Palestinian journalists. Israel insists that reporters risk getting caught in crossfire but are not targeted deliberately.

The PA Basic Law declares Islam to be the official religion of Palestine and states that "respect and sanctity of all other heavenly religions (Judaism and Christianity) shall be maintained." Blasphemy against Islam is a criminal offense. Synagogues are occasionally attacked by Palestinian militants. Some Palestinian Christians have experienced intimidation and harassment by radical Islamist groups and PA officials.

Israel generally recognizes freedom of religion in the West Bank, though recent years have featured a spike in mosque vandalism and other attacks by radical Israeli settlers. Citing the potential for violence, Israel occasionally restricts Muslim men under age 50 from praying at the Temple Mount/Haram al-Sharif compound in Jerusalem.

The PA has authority over all levels of Palestinian education. Israeli military closures, curfews, and the security barrier restrict access to academic institutions, particularly those located between Israel and the barrier. Schools have sometimes been damaged during military actions, and student travel between the West Bank and the Gaza Strip has been limited. Israel accuses the PA of teaching incitement in schools, though a February 2013 report by the Council of Religious Institutions of the Holy Land—funded by a U.S. State Department grant—found that "dehumanizing and demonizing characterizations of the other as seen in textbooks elsewhere and of concern to the general public are rare in both Israeli and Palestinian books."

Israeli academic institutions in the West Bank are increasingly subject to international and domestic boycotts. Primary and secondary education in West Bank settlements is administered by Israel, though religious schools have significant discretion over curriculum. According to the Association for Civil Rights in Israel (ACRI), East Jerusalem's schools are badly underfunded compared with schools in West Jerusalem.

E. Associational and Organizational Rights: 6 / 12

The PA requires permits for demonstrations, and those against PA policies are generally dispersed. However, in December 2012 the authorities allowed the first Hamas rally in several years. Israel's Military Order 101 requires an IDF permit for all "political" demonstrations of more than 10 people, though demonstrations are routinely broken up with force, which occasionally results in fatalities. In 2013, Israeli forces continued to restrict and disperse frequent and sometimes violent demonstrations in opposition to the security barrier, declaring some protest areas to be closed military zones. They regularly used rubber-coated bullets, stun grenades, and tear gas to break up demonstrations. According to B'Tselem, Israeli security forces killed 27 Palestinians in the West Bank in 2013, compared with 8 in 2012. B'Tselem also reported that in June 2013 IDF soldiers were filmed beating a reporter and a photojournalist from a Palestinian television station during a demonstration. The journalists were detained for two days.

A broad range of Palestinian NGOs operate in the West Bank, and their activities are generally unrestricted. Since 2007, however, many Hamas-affiliated civic associations have been shut down for political reasons. Researchers, lawyers, and activists are sometimes beaten by the PA security services, according to Human Rights Watch.

Workers may establish and join unions without government authorization. Palestinian workers seeking to strike must submit to arbitration by the PA Labor Ministry. There are no laws in the PA-ruled areas to protect the rights of striking workers. Palestinian workers in Jerusalem are subject to Israeli labor law.

F. Rule of Law: 5 / 16

The PA judicial system is partly independent. West Bank laws derive from Ottoman, British Mandate, Jordanian, Israeli, and PA legislation, as well as Israeli military orders. The High Judicial Council oversees most legal proceedings. Israel's Supreme Court hears petitions from non-Israeli residents of the West Bank regarding home demolitions, land confiscations, road closures, and IDF tactics. Decisions in favor of Palestinian petitioners, while rare, have increased in recent years.

Though most applications have been rejected, the Israeli Supreme Court has repeatedly ordered changes to the route of the West Bank security barrier after hearing petitions from NGOs and Palestinians; for example, a section of the barrier near Bil'in was moved in June 2011, four years after the relevant ruling. In April 2013 the Supreme Court accepted a conditional access compromise (involving an underground passageway) between the Israeli state and the Hajajleh family, whose home is being cut off from the village of Al-Walajah by the barrier.

The PA also has a military court system that lacks almost all due process, including the right to appeal sentences, and can impose the death penalty. No executions have been carried out since Abbas took power in 2005, however. These courts handle cases on a range of security offenses, collaborating with Israel, and drug trafficking. There are reportedly hundreds of administrative detainees in Palestinian jails. Human rights groups regularly document torture complaints, but security officers rarely face punishment for such abuses. The Independent Commission for Human Rights (ICHR), the Palestinian human rights ombudsman, received 145 torture complaints from the West Bank in 2013, down slightly from 160 in 2012.

Palestinians accused of security offenses by Israel are tried in Israeli military courts, which grant some due process protections but limit rights to counsel, bail, and appeal. According to B'Tselem, as of the end of December 2013 there were 4,387 Palestinian security detainees and prisoners from the West Bank being held in Israeli prisons. Under terms set during Israeli-Palestinian peace negotiations, Palestinian prisoners were released in three batches of 26 in August, October, and December.

A temporary order in effect since 2006 permits the detention of suspects accused of security offenses for 96 hours without judicial oversight, compared with 24 hours for other detainees. Most convictions in Israeli military courts are based on confessions, sometimes obtained through coercion. Israel outlawed the use of torture to extract security information in 2000, but milder forms of coercion are permissible when the prisoner is believed to have vital information about impending terrorist attacks. Human rights groups criticize the Israeli interrogation methods, which include binding detainees to a chair in painful positions, slapping, kicking, and threatening violence against detainees and their relatives.

According to Defence for Children International (DCI) Palestine, there were 154 Palestinian children being held in Israeli jails as of December 2013, including 14 youths aged 12 to 15. Most were serving sentences of less than a year for throwing stones at Israeli forces in the West Bank, handed down by a special court for minors; acquittals on such charges are very rare. A 2012 report from DCI found that of 311 testimonies gathered from minors detained between 2008 and 2012, 90 percent reported being blindfolded, 95 percent had their hands tied, 75 percent experienced physical violence, and 60 percent were arrested between midnight and 5 a.m. East Jerusalem Palestinian minors are tried in Israeli civil juvenile courts.

Militant Jewish settlers escalated attacks on Palestinian individuals and property in 2013 as part of their "price tag" campaign, so named to imply retribution for Israeli policies aimed at limiting settlement—though the attacks increasingly lack any specific triggering action by Israeli authorities. A report by the human rights watchdog group Yesh Din revealed that of 211 incidents of vandalism to Palestinian fruit trees from 2005 to June 2013, only four led to indictments, while 183 cases were closed in what the group termed "investigative failure." Settlers also occasionally face violence from Palestinians. In 2013, according to B'Tselem, two Israeli civilians were killed by Palestinians in the West Bank.

Israeli soldiers accused of harassing or assaulting Palestinian civilians are subject to Israeli military law. Soldiers convicted of abuses typically receive relatively light sentences. Citing B'Tselem figures, an August 2013 report by Yesh Din showed that some 5,000 Palestinians had been killed by Israeli forces in the occupied territories since September 2000. Of 179 criminal investigations opened against soldiers for the deaths of Palestinians from 2003 to 2013, only 16 led to indictments.

G. Personal Autonomy and Individual Rights: 5 / 16

The easing of checkpoints and roadblocks and the wider deployment of PA security forces has improved freedom of movement in the West Bank in recent years. B'Tselem cites OCHA's count of 256 "flying checkpoints" as of December 2013, down from the previous year, and notes that as of February 2013 there were 98 fixed checkpoints, including 40 representing the last point before entry into Israel. These obstacles stunt trade and restrict Palestinian access to jobs, hospitals, and schools.

Israel's West Bank security barrier, which was declared illegal by the International Court of Justice in 2004, has meant that 150 Palestinian communities need special permits to access their land. It was 62 percent complete by mid-2013. Some 11,000 Palestinians currently live in the zone between the barrier and the pre-1967 border, or Green Line.

All West Bank residents must have identification cards to obtain entry permits to Israel and East Jerusalem. While most roads are open to both Israelis and Palestinians, 65 kilometers are open only to Israelis.

Palestinian women are underrepresented in most professions and encounter discrimination in employment, though they have full access to universities and to many professions. Palestinian laws and societal norms, derived in part from Sharia (Islamic law), put women at a disadvantage in matters of marriage, divorce, and inheritance. For Christians, such personal status issues are governed by ecclesiastical courts. Rape, domestic abuse, and so-called "honor killings" are not uncommon. These murders often go unpunished.

Western Sahara

Political Rights Rating: 7
Civil Liberties Rating: 7
Freedom Rating: 7.0
Freedom Status: Not Free

Population: 554,800

Ten-Year Ratings Timeline For Year Under Review (Political Rights, Civil Liberties, Status)

Year Under Review	2004	2005	2006	2007	2008	2009	2010	2011	2012	2013
Rating	7,6,NF	7,6,NF	7,6,NF	7,6,NF	7,6,NF	7,6,NF	7,6,NF	7,7,NF	7,7,NF	7,7,NF

INTRODUCTION

Twenty-two years after a UN-brokered cease-fire between Morocco and the pro-independence Polisario Front—a nationalist liberation movement comprised of members of the Sahrawi ethnic group—a promised referendum on independence for Western Sahara has yet to be held. The year 2013 marked Morocco's second of its two-year position on the UN Security Council, allowing authorities in the Moroccan capital of Rabat to deepen control over Western Sahara. Morocco considers it to be its "Southern Province," but the Polisario has declared a Sahrawi Arab Democratic Republic (SADR). Longstanding support for Morocco from France and the United States—based on geopolitical calculations—continues to give Rabat the upper hand. The support of French president François Holland is especially crucial, particularly in the context of France's January 2013 intervention in nearby Mali. The Sahara and the Sahel have been framed as zones of insecurity and a theater in the global war on terror; Rabat points to evidence that Al Qaeda in the Islamic Maghreb (AQIM) is reaching into Western Sahara and calls for support from its western allies in fighting extremism.

The power of Morocco's status on the Security Council was particularly evident in April, when the United States sought to expand the mandate of the UN Mission for the Referendum in Western Sahara (MINURSO) to include a human rights monitoring effort. The move was angrily blocked by Rabat as an "attack on the national sovereignty of Morocco." France backed Morocco's position, and the mission was ultimately renewed without the human rights clause. In response to the U.S. initiative, Morocco in April 2013 canceled its annual participation in "African Lion," a joint military exercise with the U.S. African Command (AFRICOM) and the North Atlantic Treaty Organization (NATO). Relations were eventually smoothed over, and the exercises were planned for 2014.

In 2009, UN Secretary General Ban Ki-moon named Christopher Ross to be the UN Special Envoy for Western Sahara. In 2012, Rabat had called for his dismissal because it perceived Ross to be biased, but the secretary general rejected the calls. In 2013, Ross continued his shuttle diplomacy, traveling to the region in October.

POLITICAL RIGHTS: -2 / 40

A. Electoral Process: 0 / 12

There are no free elections within Western Sahara. As the occupying power, Morocco, which controls about 85 percent of the territory, holds authority over municipal elections and excludes candidates who support independence, and works to retain the territory as a vital component of the kingdom. Some members of the Moroccan Parliament represent districts in Western Sahara.

The Polisario government-in-exile in Tindouf, Algeria, is formed from a General Popular Congress, which is made up of delegates from refugee camps in Polisario-controlled areas of Western Sahara and in Algeria.

B. Political Pluralism and Participation: 0 / 16

Within the territory—and in Morocco—the Moroccan monarchy continues to react toward Sahrawi activism with harsh repression and an unwillingness to compromise. The Polisario remains fragmented between hardline elements demanding full independence, with other wings more willing to accept a degree of autonomy from Rabat.

C. Functioning of Government: 0 / 12

Corruption among Moroccan authorities in Western Sahara and within the Polisario as well is rampant and goes uninvestigated. Although the territory possesses extensive natural resources, including phosphate, iron ore deposits, hydrocarbon reserves, and fisheries, the local population remains largely impoverished.

Discretionary Political Rights Question B: -2 / 0

Morocco has tried to bolster its claim to Western Sahara over the years by working to alter its demographics. Moroccan authorities offer financial incentives for Moroccans to move to Western Sahara, and for Sahrawis to move to Morocco.

CIVIL LIBERTIES: 7 / 60
D. Freedom of Expression and Belief: 3 / 16

Freedom of expression within Moroccan-controlled areas of Western Sahara is sharply curtailed. Moroccan authorities detain or expel Sahrawi, Moroccan, and foreign reporters who seek to cover sensitive issues relating to Western Sahara from both Morocco and from Western Sahara; additionally, Moroccan law bars the media and individuals from challenging Morocco's sovereignty over Western Sahara, leading to self-censorship. Freedom of expression within the Polisario is also constrained, and there have been reports of restrictions by Polisario (and Algerian) authorities in refugee camps in Tindouf. Access to the internet and independent satellite broadcasts are largely unavailable in the territory due to economic constraints.

Nearly all Sahrawis are Sunni Muslims, as are most Moroccans, and Moroccan authorities generally do not interfere with their freedom of worship. There are no major universities or institutions of higher learning in Western Sahara.

E. Associational and Organizational Rights: 0 / 12

Freedom of assembly is severely restricted, and Sahrawis are not permitted to form independent nongovernmental organizations. As in previous years, activists supporting independence and their suspected foreign sympathizers were subject to harassment.

After the UN vote in late April to extend MINURSO's mandate, protests among Sahrawis angry about the lack of a human rights mandate within the mission took place across the territory. In Laayoune, it was reported that six detainees arrested at a pro-independence rally in May, including a minor, were tortured in detention in order to extract confessions. One, 17-year-old El Hussein Bah, was rearrested after he reported to Amnesty International that he had been tortured. In September, demonstrations took place to protest the killing of Rashid al-Mamoun Shin, a young protester who was shot by Moroccan police at a Sahrawi rally held earlier that month in Assa, Morocco. Demonstrations over his death also took place in September outside the Moroccan embassy in Paris.

The third anniversary of the November 2010 Gdeim Izik clashes—in which Moroccan forces had violently dispersed the Gdeim Izik protest camp's Sahrawi residents—saw Moroccan forces clash with Sahrawi demonstrators. In February 2013, a Moroccan military court sentenced two dozen people detained during the 2010 clashes and accused of killing members of the Moroccan security forces. Eight of the detainees were jailed for life, 4 received 30-year sentences, 8 received 25-year sentences, and 2 received 20-year sentences. The 2 remaining detainees were given two-year sentences and released for time served, while another person was convicted in absentia and sentenced to life.

Sahrawis are technically subject to Moroccan labor laws in Moroccan-controlled areas, but there is little organized labor activity in the territory.

F. Rule of Law: 0 / 16

The government of Morocco asserts judicial and penal administration within the Western Sahara. In the Western Sahara territory that Morocco does not fully control—principally the eastern part of the territory—and the refugee camps in Algeria, the Polisario is ostensibly the governing power. The Polisario's General Popular Congress is responsible for administration of the refugee camps.

Activists and dissidents have in the past disappeared after being detained by Moroccan authorities, although there were no reported cases in in 2013. Torture has been reported in Moroccan-run detention facilities. In April, Amnesty International called for the Moroccan authorities to examine claims by Sahrawi activist Mohamed Dihani that he had been tortured while in detention. Dihani in 2011 had received a 10-year sentence in connection with terrorism charges but was appealing the case; Amnesty also called on Moroccan authorities to exclude from court proceedings any previous confessions from Dihani extracted through torture.

In September, a team of forensic experts from the University of the Basque Country in Spain said its members, while working in Western Sahara, had identified the remains of eight Sahrawi people and had confirmed that the people died after being shot by Moroccan forces in 1976, corroborating scenes the deceased's relatives claimed to have witnessed. None of the eight people had been mentioned in the 2004 Equity and Reconciliation (IER) Commission—the body that investigated human rights abuses under former Moroccan King Hassan II. Morocco's Advisory Council on Human Rights mentioned four of the deceased in a later report, but that investigation found that the four had been arrested and died later while in detention. The forensic team said remains belonging to possibly hundreds of other Sahrawi victims were likely still unexamined in shallow graves in the territory.

G. Personal Autonomy and Individual Rights: 4 / 16

Morocco and the Polisario Front both restrict free movement in potential conflict areas. The SADR government routinely signs contracts with firms for the exploration of oil and gas, but these contracts cannot be formally implemented given the territory's status, and no credible free market exists. For its part, Morocco signs contracts as well and grants access to Western Sahara's abundant territorial waters to foreign fishing fleets.

The National Union of Sahrawi Women was created in 1974 and is especially present in Tindouf. It also has representation and influence in Western Sahara, although its scope is difficult to gauge. According to journalistic accounts, women in Sahrawi society are understood to enjoy relatively strong civil liberties. They are certainly prominent in activist circles. Some attribute this to the liberal interpretation of Islam in Sahrawi society, as well as the nomadic roots of the culture. Others ascribe it to the ordeal of living in refugee camps or under occupation. LGBT (lesbian, gay, bisexual, and transgender individuals) face high levels of discrimination, similar to the situation in Morocco.

Freedom in the World 2014
Survey Methodology

INTRODUCTION

Freedom in the World is an annual global report on political rights and civil liberties, composed of numerical ratings and descriptive texts for each country and a select group of related and disputed territories. The 2014 edition covers developments in 195 countries and 14 territories from January 1, 2013, through December 31, 2013.

The report's methodology is derived in large measure from the Universal Declaration of Human Rights, adopted by the UN General Assembly in 1948. *Freedom in the World* is based on the premise that these standards apply to all countries and territories, irrespective of geographical location, ethnic or religious composition, or level of economic development. *Freedom in the World* operates from the assumption that freedom for all peoples is best achieved in liberal democratic societies.

Freedom in the World assesses the real-world rights and freedoms enjoyed by individuals, rather than governments or government performance per se. Political rights and civil liberties can be affected by both state and nonstate actors, including insurgents and other armed groups.

Freedom House does not equate legal guarantees of rights with the on-the-ground fulfillment of those rights. While both laws and actual practices are factored into the ratings decisions, greater emphasis is placed on implementation.

Countries and territories with small populations are not penalized for lacking pluralism in the political system or civil society if these limitations are determined to be a function of size and not overt restrictions by the government or other powerful actors.

Territories are selected for inclusion in *Freedom in the World* based on their political significance and size. Freedom House divides territories into two categories: related territories and disputed territories. Related territories are in some relation of dependency to a sovereign state, and the relationship is not currently in serious legal or political dispute. Disputed territories are areas within internationally recognized sovereign states whose status is in serious political or violent dispute, and whose conditions differ substantially from those of the relevant sovereign states. They are often outside of central government control and characterized by intense, longtime, and widespread insurgency or independence movements that enjoy popular support. Freedom House typically takes no position on territorial or separatist disputes as such, focusing instead on the level of political rights and civil liberties in a given geographical area.

HISTORY OF *FREEDOM IN THE WORLD*

Freedom House's first year-end reviews of freedom began in the 1950s as the *Balance Sheet of Freedom*. This modest report provided assessments of political trends and their implications for individual freedom. In 1972, Freedom House launched a new, more comprehensive annual study called *The Comparative Study of Freedom*. Raymond Gastil, a Harvard-trained specialist in regional studies from the University of Washington in Seattle, developed the methodology, which assigned political rights and civil liberties ratings to 151 countries and 45 territories and categorized them as Free, Partly Free, or Not Free. The findings appeared each year in Freedom House's *Freedom at Issue* bimonthly journal (later titled *Freedom Review*). *Freedom in the World* first appeared in book form in 1978 and included short narratives for each country and territory rated in the study, as well as a series of essays by leading scholars on related issues. *Freedom in the World* continued to be produced by Gastil until 1989, when a larger team of in-house analysts was established. In the mid-1990s, the expansion of the country and territory narratives demanded the hiring of outside analysts—a group of regional experts from the academic, media, and human rights communities—and the project has continued to grow in size and scope in the years since.

CHANGES TO *FREEDOM IN THE WORLD* 2014

The methodology is reviewed periodically, and a number of modest changes have been made over the years to adapt to evolving ideas about political rights and civil liberties. However, the time-series data are not revised retroactively, and any changes to the methodology are introduced incrementally in order to ensure the comparability of the ratings from year to year.

This year, the following changes were made to the narrative report format:

- The Overview section, which had included an Executive Summary paragraph and a chronological review of historical events, now focuses on major political and other developments during the current edition's coverage period.
- The Political Rights and Civil Liberties section has been divided into 7 subsections that correspond to the 7 methodological subcategories (see below) used by the analysts to score their countries. The subcategory scores, and the resulting aggregate scores for political rights and civil liberties, are now listed at the beginning of each subsection, drawing a clearer connection between the scores and the descriptive text.

A few minor changes to the subquestions used by the analysts to score their countries were also made, including more specific references to LGBT rights.

RESEARCH AND RATINGS REVIEW PROCESS

Freedom in the World is produced each year by a team of in-house and external analysts and expert advisers from the academic, think tank, and human rights communities. The 2014 edition involved more than 60 analysts and nearly 30 advisers. The analysts, who prepare the draft reports and scores, use a broad range of sources, including news articles, academic analyses, reports from nongovernmental organizations, and individual professional contacts. The analysts score countries based on the conditions and events within their borders during the coverage period. The analysts' proposed scores are discussed and defended at annual review meetings, organized by region and attended by Freedom House staff and a panel of the expert advisers. The final scores represent the consensus of the analysts, advisers, and staff, and are intended to be comparable from year to year and across countries and regions. The advisers also provide a detailed review of and commentary on a number of key country and territory reports. Although an element of subjectivity is unavoidable in such an enterprise, the ratings process emphasizes methodological consistency, intellectual rigor, and balanced and unbiased judgments.

RATINGS PROCESS

Freedom in the World uses a three-tiered rating system, consisting of **scores**, **ratings**, and **status**. The complete list of the questions used in the scoring process, and the tables for converting scores to ratings and ratings to status, appear at the end of this essay.

Scores – A country or territory is awarded 0 to 4 points for each of 10 political rights indicators and 15 civil liberties indicators, which take the form of questions; a score of 0 represents the smallest degree of freedom and 4 the greatest degree of freedom. The political rights questions are grouped into three subcategories: Electoral Process (3 questions), Political Pluralism and Participation (4), and Functioning of Government (3). The civil liberties questions are grouped into four subcategories: Freedom of Expression and Belief (4 questions), Associational and Organizational Rights (3), Rule of Law (4), and Personal Autonomy and Individual Rights (4). The political rights section also contains two additional discretionary questions. For additional discretionary question A, a score of 1 to 4 may be added, as applicable, while for discretionary question B, a score of 1 to 4 may be subtracted, as applicable (the worse the situation, the more points may be subtracted). The highest score that can be awarded to the political rights checklist is 40 (or a total score of 4 for each of the 10 questions). The highest score that can be awarded to the civil liberties checklist is 60 (or a total score of 4 for each of the 15 questions). The scores from the previous edition are used as a benchmark for the current year under review. A score is typically changed only if there has been a real-world development during the year that warrants a decline or improvement (e.g., a crackdown on the media, the country's first free and fair elections), though gradual changes in conditions, in the absence of a signal event, are occasionally registered in the scores.

Political Rights and Civil Liberties Ratings – A country or territory is assigned two ratings (7 to 1)—one for political rights and one for civil liberties—based on its total scores for the political rights and civil liberties questions. Each rating of 1 through 7, with 1 representing the greatest degree of freedom and 7 the smallest degree of freedom, corresponds to a specific range of total scores (see tables 1 and 2).

Free, Partly Free, Not Free Status – The average of a country's or territory's political rights and civil liberties ratings is called the Freedom Rating, and it is this figure that determines the status of Free (1.0 to 2.5), Partly Free (3.0 to 5.0), or Not Free (5.5 to 7.0) (see table 3).

Trend Arrows – A country or territory may be assigned an upward or downward trend arrow to highlight developments of particular significance or concern. A trend arrow must be linked to a specific score change and can be assigned only when the score change is not large enough to trigger a broader ratings change. Most score changes do not warrant trend arrows; whether a country or territory should receive a trend arrow is left to the discretion of the analyst, in consultation with the expert advisers and Freedom House staff.

Electoral Democracy – *Freedom in the World* assigns the designation "electoral democracy" to countries that have met certain minimum standards for political rights; territories are not included in the list of electoral democracies. According to the methodology, an electoral democracy designation requires a score of 7 or better in the Electoral Process subcategory and an overall political rights score of 20 or better. Freedom House's term "electoral democracy" differs from "liberal democracy" in that the latter also implies the presence of a substantial array of civil liberties. In *Freedom in the World*, all Free countries can be considered both electoral and liberal democracies, while some Partly Free countries qualify as electoral, but not liberal, democracies.

RATINGS AND STATUS CHARACTERISTICS
POLITICAL RIGHTS

1 – Countries and territories with a rating of 1 enjoy a wide range of political rights, including free and fair elections. Candidates who are elected actually rule, political parties are competitive, the opposition plays an important role and enjoys real power, and the interests of minority groups are well represented in politics and government.

2 – Countries and territories with a rating of 2 have slightly weaker political rights than those with a rating of 1 because of such factors as political corruption, limits on the functioning of political parties and opposition groups, and foreign or military influence on politics.

3, 4, 5 – Countries and territories with a rating of 3, 4, or 5 either moderately protect almost all political rights or strongly protect some political rights while neglecting others. The same factors that undermine freedom in countries with a rating of 2 may also weaken political rights in those with a rating of 3, 4, or 5, but to a greater extent at each successive rating.

6 – Countries and territories with a rating of 6 have very restricted political rights. They are ruled by one-party or military dictatorships, religious hierarchies, or autocrats. They may allow a few political rights, such as some representation or autonomy for minority groups, and a few are traditional monarchies that tolerate political discussion and accept public petitions.

7 – Countries and territories with a rating of 7 have few or no political rights because of severe government oppression, sometimes in combination with civil war. They may also lack an authoritative and functioning central government and suffer from extreme violence or rule by regional warlords.

CIVIL LIBERTIES

1 – Countries and territories with a rating of 1 enjoy a wide range of civil liberties, including freedoms of expression, assembly, association, education, and religion. They have an established and generally fair legal system that ensures the rule of law (including an independent judiciary), allow free economic activity, and tend to strive for equality of opportunity for everyone, including women and minority groups.

2 – Countries and territories with a rating of 2 have slightly weaker civil liberties than those with a rating of 1 because of such factors as limits on media independence, restrictions on trade union activities, and discrimination against minority groups and women.

3, 4, 5 – Countries and territories with a rating of 3, 4, or 5 either moderately protect almost all civil liberties or strongly protect some civil liberties while neglecting others. The same factors that undermine freedom in countries with a rating of 2 may also weaken civil liberties in those with a rating of 3, 4, or 5, but to a greater extent at each successive rating.

6 – Countries and territories with a rating of 6 have very restricted civil liberties. They strongly limit the rights of expression and association and frequently hold political prisoners. They may allow a few civil liberties, such as some religious and social freedoms, some highly restricted private business activity, and some open and free private discussion.

7 – Countries and territories with a rating of 7 have few or no civil liberties. They allow virtually no freedom of expression or association, do not protect the rights of detainees and prisoners, and often control or dominate most economic activity.

The gap between a country's or territory's political rights and civil liberties ratings is rarely more than two points. Politically oppressive states typically do not allow a well-developed civil society, for example, and it is difficult, if not impossible, to maintain political freedoms in the absence of civil liberties like press freedom and the rule of law.

Because the designations of Free, Partly Free, and Not Free each cover a broad third of the available scores, countries or territories within any one category, especially those at either end of the range, can have quite different human rights situations. For example, those at the lowest end of the Free category (2 in political rights and 3 in civil liberties, or 3 in political rights and 2 in civil liberties) differ from those at the upper end of the Free group (1 for both political rights and civil liberties). Also, a designation of Free does not mean that a country or territory enjoys perfect freedom or lacks serious problems, only that it enjoys comparatively more freedom than those rated Partly Free or Not Free (and some others rated Free).

FREEDOM IN THE WORLD 2014
CHECKLIST QUESTIONS

The bulleted subquestions are intended to provide guidance to the analysts regarding what issues are meant to be considered in scoring each checklist question. The analysts do not need to consider every subquestion during the scoring process, as the relevance of each varies from one place to another.

POLITICAL RIGHTS (0–40 POINTS)

A. **ELECTORAL PROCESS (0–12 points)**
   1. **Is the head of government or other chief national authority elected through free and fair elections?**
      - Did established and reputable national and/or international election monitoring organizations judge the most recent elections for head of government to be free and fair? (*Note*: Heads of government chosen through various electoral frameworks, including direct elections for president, indirect elections for prime minister by parliament, and the electoral college system for electing presidents, are covered under this and the following sub-questions. In cases of indirect elections for the head of government, the elections for the legislature that chose the head of government, as well as the selection process of the head of government himself, should be taken into consideration.)
      - Have there been undue, politically motivated delays in holding the most recent election for head of government?
      - Is the registration of voters and candidates conducted in an accurate, timely, transparent, and nondiscriminatory manner?
      - Can candidates make speeches, hold public meetings, and enjoy media access throughout the campaign free of intimidation?

- Does voting take place by secret ballot or by equivalent free voting procedure?
- Are voters able to vote for the candidate or party of their choice without undue pressure or intimidation?
- Is the vote count transparent, and is it reported honestly with the official results made public? Can election monitors from independent groups and representing parties/candidates watch the counting of votes to ensure their honesty?
- Is each person's vote given equivalent weight to those of other voters in order to ensure equal representation?
- Has a democratically elected head of government who was chosen in the most recent election subsequently been overthrown in a violent coup? (*Note*: Although a peaceful, "velvet coup" may ultimately lead to a positive outcome—particularly if it replaces a head of government who was not freely and fairly elected—the new leader has not been freely and fairly elected and cannot be treated as such.)
- In cases where elections for regional, provincial, or state governors and/or other subnational officials differ significantly in conduct from national elections, does the conduct of the subnational elections reflect an opening toward improved political rights in the country, or, alternatively, a worsening of political rights?

2. **Are the national legislative representatives elected through free and fair elections?**
    - Did established and reputable domestic and/or international election monitoring organizations judge the most recent national legislative elections to be free and fair?
    - Have there been undue, politically motivated delays in holding the most recent national legislative election?
    - Is the registration of voters and candidates conducted in an accurate, timely, transparent, and nondiscriminatory manner?
    - Can candidates make speeches, hold public meetings, and enjoy media access throughout the campaign free of intimidation?
    - Does voting take place by secret ballot or by equivalent free voting procedure?
    - Are voters able to vote for the candidate or party of their choice without undue pressure or intimidation?
    - Is the vote count transparent, and is it reported honestly with the official results made public? Can election monitors from independent groups and representing parties/candidates watch the counting of votes to ensure their honesty?
    - Is each person's vote given equivalent weight to those of other voters in order to ensure equal representation?
    - Have the representatives of a democratically elected national legislature who were chosen in the most recent election subsequently been overthrown in a violent coup? (*Note*: Although a peaceful, "velvet coup" may ultimately lead to a positive outcome—particularly if it replaces a national legislature whose representatives were not freely and fairly elected—members of the new legislature have not been freely and fairly elected and cannot be treated as such.)
    - In cases where elections for subnational councils/parliaments differ significantly in conduct from national elections, does the conduct of the subnational elections reflect an opening toward improved political rights in the country, or, alternatively, a worsening of political rights?

3. **Are the electoral laws and framework fair?**
    - Is there a clear, detailed, and fair legislative framework for conducting elections? (*Note*: Changes to electoral laws should not be made immediately

preceding an election if the ability of voters, candidates, or parties to fulfill their roles in the election is infringed.)
- Are election commissions or other election authorities independent and free from government or other pressure and interference?
- Is the composition of election commissions fair and balanced?
- Do election commissions or other election authorities conduct their work in an effective and competent manner?
- Do adult citizens enjoy universal and equal suffrage? (*Note*: Suffrage can be suspended or withdrawn for reasons of legal incapacity, such as mental incapacity or conviction of a serious criminal offense.)
- Is the drawing of election districts conducted in a fair and nonpartisan manner, as opposed to gerrymandering for personal or partisan advantage?
- Has the selection of a system for choosing legislative representatives (such as proportional versus majoritarian) been manipulated to advance certain political interests or to influence the electoral results?

B. **POLITICAL PLURALISM AND PARTICIPATION (0–16 points)**
  1. **Do the people have the right to organize in different political parties or other competitive political groupings of their choice, and is the system open to the rise and fall of these competing parties or groupings?**
     - Do political parties encounter undue legal or practical obstacles in their efforts to be formed and to operate, including onerous registration requirements, excessively large membership requirements, etc.?
     - Do parties face discriminatory or onerous restrictions in holding meetings, rallies, or other peaceful activities?
     - Are party members or leaders intimidated, harassed, arrested, imprisoned, or subjected to violent attacks as a result of their peaceful political activities?
  2. **Is there a significant opposition vote and a realistic opportunity for the opposition to increase its support or gain power through elections?**
     - Are various legal/administrative restrictions selectively applied to opposition parties to prevent them from increasing their support base or successfully competing in elections?
     - Are there legitimate opposition forces in positions of authority, such as in the national legislature or in subnational governments?
     - Are opposition party members or leaders intimidated, harassed, arrested, imprisoned, or subjected to violent attacks as a result of their peaceful political activities?
  3. **Are the people's political choices free from domination by the military, foreign powers, totalitarian parties, religious hierarchies, economic oligarchies, or any other powerful group?**
     - Do such groups offer bribes to voters and/or political figures in order to influence their political choices?
     - Do such groups intimidate, harass, or attack voters and/or political figures in order to influence their political choices?
     - Does the military control or enjoy a preponderant influence over government policy and activities, including in countries that nominally are under civilian control?
     - Do foreign governments control or enjoy a preponderant influence over government policy and activities by means including the presence of foreign military troops, the use of significant economic threats or sanctions, etc.?

4. **Do cultural, ethnic, religious, or other minority groups have full political rights and electoral opportunities?**
   - Do political parties of various ideological persuasions address issues of specific concern to minority groups?
   - Does the government inhibit the participation of minority groups in national or subnational political life through laws and/or practical obstacles?
   - Are political parties based on ethnicity, culture, or religion that espouse peaceful, democratic values legally permitted and de facto allowed to operate?

C. **FUNCTIONING OF GOVERNMENT (0–12 points)**

1. **Do the freely elected head of government and national legislative representatives determine the policies of the government?**
   - Are the candidates who were elected freely and fairly duly installed in office?
   - Do other appointed or non–freely elected state actors interfere with or prevent freely elected representatives from adopting and implementing legislation and making meaningful policy decisions?
   - Do nonstate actors, including criminal gangs, the military, and foreign governments, interfere with or prevent elected representatives from adopting and implementing legislation and making meaningful policy decisions?

2. **Is the government free from pervasive corruption?**
   - Has the government implemented effective anticorruption laws or programs to prevent, detect, and punish corruption among public officials, including conflict of interest?
   - Is the government free from excessive bureaucratic regulations, registration requirements, or other controls that increase opportunities for corruption?
   - Are there independent and effective auditing and investigative bodies that function without impediment or political pressure or influence?
   - Are allegations of corruption by government officials thoroughly investigated and prosecuted without prejudice, particularly against political opponents?
   - Are allegations of corruption given wide and extensive airing in the media?
   - Do whistleblowers, anticorruption activists, investigators, and journalists enjoy legal protections that make them feel secure about reporting cases of bribery and corruption?
   - What was the latest Transparency International Corruption Perceptions Index score for this country?

3. **Is the government accountable to the electorate between elections, and does it operate with openness and transparency?**
   - Are civil society groups, interest groups, journalists, and other citizens able to comment on and influence pending policies or legislation?
   - Do citizens have the legal right and practical ability to obtain information about government operations and the means to petition government agencies for it?
   - Is the budget-making process subject to meaningful legislative review and public scrutiny?
   - Does the government publish detailed accounting expenditures in a timely fashion?
   - Does the state ensure transparency and effective competition in the awarding of government contracts?
   - Are the asset declarations of government officials open to public and media scrutiny and verification?

ADDITIONAL DISCRETIONARY POLITICAL RIGHTS QUESTIONS

A. **For traditional monarchies that have no parties or electoral process, does the system provide for genuine, meaningful consultation with the people, encourage public discussion of policy choices, and allow the right to petition the ruler? (0–4 points)**
   - Is there a non-elected legislature that advises the monarch on policy issues?
   - Are there formal mechanisms for individuals or civic groups to speak with or petition the monarch?
   - Does the monarch take petitions from the public under serious consideration?

B. **Is the government or occupying power deliberately changing the ethnic composition of a country or territory so as to destroy a culture or tip the political balance in favor of another group? (-4–0 points)**
   - Is the government providing economic or other incentives to certain people in order to change the ethnic composition of a region or regions?
   - Is the government forcibly moving people in or out of certain areas in order to change the ethnic composition of those regions?
   - Is the government arresting, imprisoning, or killing members of certain ethnic groups in order change the ethnic composition of a region or regions?

CIVIL LIBERTIES (0–60 POINTS)

D. **FREEDOM OF EXPRESSION AND BELIEF (0–16 points)**
   1. Are there free and independent media and other forms of cultural expression? (*Note:* In cases where the media are state controlled but offer pluralistic points of view, the survey gives the system credit.)
      - Are print, broadcast, and/or internet-based media directly or indirectly censored?
      - Is self-censorship among journalists common, especially when reporting on politically sensitive issues, including corruption or the activities of senior officials?
      - Are libel, blasphemy, or security laws used to punish journalists who scrutinize government officials and policies or other powerful entities through either onerous fines or imprisonment?
      - Is it a crime to insult the honor and dignity of the president and/or other government officials? How broad is the range of such prohibitions, and how vigorously are they enforced?
      - If media outlets are dependent on the government for their financial survival, does the government withhold funding in order to propagandize, primarily provide official points of view, and/or limit access by opposition parties and civic critics? Do powerful private actors engage in similar practices?
      - Does the government attempt to influence media content and access through means including politically motivated awarding of broadcast frequencies and newspaper registrations, unfair control and influence over printing facilities and distribution networks, selective distribution of advertising, onerous registration requirements, prohibitive tariffs, and bribery?
      - Are journalists threatened, arrested, imprisoned, beaten, or killed by government or nongovernmental actors for their legitimate journalistic activities, and if such cases occur, are they investigated and prosecuted fairly and expeditiously?
      - Are works of literature, art, music, or other forms of cultural expression censored or banned for political purposes?

2. **Are religious institutions and communities free to practice their faith and express themselves in public and private?**
    - Are registration requirements employed to impede the free functioning of religious institutions?
    - Are members of religious groups, including minority faiths and movements, harassed, fined, arrested, or beaten by the authorities for engaging in their religious practices?
    - Are religious practice and expression impeded by violence or harassment from nonstate actors?
    - Does the government appoint or otherwise influence the appointment of religious leaders?
    - Does the government control the production and distribution of religious books and other materials and the content of sermons?
    - Is the construction of religious buildings banned or restricted?
    - Does the government place undue restrictions on religious education? Does the government require religious education?
    - Are individuals free to eschew religious beliefs and practices in general?
3. **Is there academic freedom, and is the educational system free of extensive political indoctrination?**
    - Are teachers and professors free to pursue academic activities of a political and quasi-political nature without fear of physical violence or intimidation by state or nonstate actors?
    - Does the government pressure, strongly influence, or control the content of school curriculums for political purposes?
    - Are student associations that address issues of a political nature allowed to function freely?
    - Does the government, including through school administration or other officials, pressure students and/or teachers to support certain political figures or agendas, including pressuring them to attend political rallies or vote for certain candidates? Conversely, does the government, including through school administration or other officials, discourage or forbid students and/or teachers from supporting certain candidates and parties?
4. **Is there open and free private discussion?**
    - Are people able to engage in private discussions, particularly of a political nature (in places including restaurants, public transportation, and their homes) without fear of harassment or detention by the authorities or powerful nonstate actors?
    - Do users of personal online communications—including private e-mail, text messages, or personal blogs with a limited following—face legal penalties, harassment, or violence from the government or powerful nonstate actors in retaliation for critical remarks?
    - Does the government employ people or groups to engage in public surveillance and to report alleged antigovernment conversations to the authorities?

E. **ASSOCIATIONAL AND ORGANIZATIONAL RIGHTS (0–12 points)**
1. **Is there freedom of assembly, demonstration, and open public discussion?**
    - Are peaceful protests, particularly those of a political nature, banned or severely restricted?
    - Are the legal requirements to obtain permission to hold peaceful demonstrations particularly cumbersome and time consuming?
    - Are participants of peaceful demonstrations intimidated, arrested, or assaulted?

- Are peaceful protestors detained by police in order to prevent them from engaging in such actions?

2. **Is there freedom for nongovernmental organizations?** (*Note*: This includes civic organizations, interest groups, foundations, etc.)
    - Are registration and other legal requirements for nongovernmental organizations particularly onerous and intended to prevent them from functioning freely?
    - Are laws related to the financing of nongovernmental organizations unduly complicated and cumbersome?
    - Are donors and funders of nongovernmental organizations free of government pressure?
    - Are members of nongovernmental organizations intimidated, arrested, imprisoned, or assaulted because of their work?

3. **Are there free trade unions and peasant organizations or equivalents, and is there effective collective bargaining? Are there free professional and other private organizations?**
    - Are trade unions allowed to be established and to operate free from government interference?
    - Are workers pressured by the government or employers to join or not to join certain trade unions, and do they face harassment, violence, or dismissal from their jobs if they do?
    - Are workers permitted to engage in strikes, and do members of unions face reprisals for engaging in peaceful strikes? (*Note*: This question may not apply to workers in essential government services or public safety jobs.)
    - Are unions able to bargain collectively with employers and able to negotiate collective bargaining agreements that are honored in practice?
    - For states with very small populations or primarily agriculturally based economies that do not necessarily support the formation of trade unions, does the government allow for the establishment of peasant organizations or their equivalents? Is there legislation expressively forbidding the formation of trade unions?
    - Are professional organizations, including business associations, allowed to operate freely and without government interference?

F. **RULE OF LAW (0–16 points)**
  1. **Is there an independent judiciary?**
     - Is the judiciary subject to interference from the executive branch of government or from other political, economic, or religious influences?
     - Are judges appointed and dismissed in a fair and unbiased manner?
     - Do judges rule fairly and impartially, or do they commonly render verdicts that favor the government or particular interests, whether in return for bribes or other reasons?
     - Do executive, legislative, and other governmental authorities comply with judicial decisions, and are these decisions effectively enforced?
     - Do powerful private concerns comply with judicial decisions, and are decisions that run counter to the interests of powerful actors effectively enforced?
  2. **Does the rule of law prevail in civil and criminal matters? Are police under direct civilian control?**
     - Are defendants' rights, including the presumption of innocence until proven guilty, protected?
     - Are detainees provided access to independent, competent legal counsel?
     - Are defendants given a fair, public, and timely hearing by a competent, independent, and impartial tribunal?

- Are prosecutors independent of political control and influence?
- Are prosecutors independent of powerful private interests, whether legal or illegal?
- Is there effective and democratic civilian state control of law enforcement officials through the judicial, legislative, and executive branches?
- Are law enforcement officials free from the influence of nonstate actors, including organized crime, powerful commercial interests, or other groups?

3. **Is there protection from political terror, unjustified imprisonment, exile, or torture, whether by groups that support or oppose the system? Is there freedom from war and insurgencies?**
    - Do law enforcement officials make arbitrary arrests and detentions without warrants or fabricate or plant evidence on suspects?
    - Do law enforcement officials beat detainees during arrest and interrogation or use excessive force or torture to extract confessions?
    - Are conditions in pretrial facilities and prisons humane and respectful of the human dignity of inmates?
    - Do citizens have the means of effective petition and redress when their rights are violated by state authorities?
    - Is violent crime either against specific groups or within the general population widespread?
    - Is the population subjected to physical harm, forced removal, or other acts of violence or terror due to civil conflict or war?

4. **Do laws, policies, and practices guarantee equal treatment of various segments of the population?**
    - Are members of various distinct groups—including ethnic and religious minorities, LGBT people, and the disabled—able to exercise effectively their human rights with full equality before the law?
    - Is violence against such groups widespread, and if so, are perpetrators brought to justice?
    - Do members of such groups face legal and/or de facto discrimination in areas including employment, education, and housing because of their identification with a particular group?
    - Do women enjoy full equality in law and in practice as compared to men?
    - Do noncitizens—including migrant workers and noncitizen immigrants—enjoy basic internationally recognized human rights, including the right not to be subjected to torture or other forms of ill treatment, the right to due process of law, and the rights of freedom of association, expression, and religion?
    - Do the country's laws provide for the granting of asylum or refugee status in accordance with the 1951 UN Convention Relating to the Status of Refugees, its 1967 Protocol, and other regional treaties regarding refugees? Has the government established a system for providing protection to refugees, including against *refoulement* (the return of persons to a country where there is reason to believe they fear persecution)?

G. **PERSONAL AUTONOMY AND INDIVIDUAL RIGHTS (0–16 points)**
1. **Do citizens enjoy freedom of travel or choice of residence, employment, or institution of higher education?**
    - Are there restrictions on foreign travel, including the use of an exit visa system, which may be issued selectively?

- Is permission required from the authorities or nonstate actors to move within the country?
- Do state or nonstate actors determine or otherwise influence a person's type and place of employment?
- Are bribes or other inducements needed to obtain the necessary documents to travel, change one's place of residence or employment, enter institutions of higher education, or advance in school?

2. **Do citizens have the right to own property and establish private businesses? Is private business activity unduly influenced by government officials, the security forces, political parties/organizations, or organized crime?**
   - Are people legally allowed to purchase and sell land and other property, and can they do so in practice without undue interference from the government or non-state actors?
   - Does the government provide adequate and timely compensation to people whose property is expropriated under eminent domain laws?
   - Are people legally allowed to establish and operate private businesses with a reasonable minimum of registration, licensing, and other requirements?
   - Are bribes or other inducements needed to obtain the necessary legal documents to operate private businesses?
   - Do private/nonstate actors, including criminal groups, seriously impede private business activities through such measures as extortion?

3. **Are there personal social freedoms, including gender equality, choice of marriage partners, and size of family?**
   - Is violence against women, including wife-beating and rape, widespread, and are perpetrators brought to justice?
   - Is the trafficking of women and/or children abroad for prostitution widespread, and is the government taking adequate efforts to address the problem?
   - Do women face de jure and de facto discrimination in economic and social matters, including property and inheritance rights, divorce proceedings, and child custody matters?
   - Does the government directly or indirectly control choice of marriage partners and other personal relationships through means such as requiring large payments to marry certain individuals (e.g., foreign citizens), not enforcing laws against child marriage or dowry payments, restricting same-sex relationships, or criminalizing extramarital sex?
   - Does the government determine the number of children that a couple may have?
   - Does the government engage in state-sponsored religious/cultural/ethnic indoctrination and related restrictions on personal freedoms?
   - Do private institutions, including religious groups, unduly infringe on the rights of individuals, including choice of marriage partner, dress, gender expression, etc.?

4. **Is there equality of opportunity and the absence of economic exploitation?**
   - Does the government exert tight control over the economy, including through state ownership and the setting of prices and production quotas?
   - Do the economic benefits from large state industries, including the energy sector, benefit the general population or only a privileged few?
   - Do private interests exert undue influence on the economy through monopolistic practices, cartels, or illegal blacklists, boycotts, or discrimination?

- Is entrance to institutions of higher education or the ability to obtain employment limited by widespread nepotism and the payment of bribes?
- Are certain groups, including ethnic or religious minorities, less able to enjoy certain economic benefits than others? For example, are certain groups restricted from holding particular jobs, whether in the public or the private sector, because of de jure or de facto discrimination?
- Do state or private employers exploit their workers through activities including unfairly withholding wages and permitting or forcing employees to work under unacceptably dangerous conditions, as well as through adult slave labor and child labor?

KEY TO SCORES, PR AND CL RATINGS, STATUS

Table 1

Political Rights (PR)

Total Scores	PR Rating
36–40	1
30–35	2
24–29	3
18–23	4
12–17	5
6–11	6
0–5*	7

Table 2

Civil Liberties (CL)

Total Scores	CL Rating
53–60	1
44–52	2
35–43	3
26–34	4
17–25	5
8–16	6
0–7	7

Table 3

Combined Average of the PR and CL Ratings (Freedom Rating)	Freedom Status
1.0 to 2.5	Free
3.0 to 5.0	Partly Free
5.5 to 7.0	Not Free

* It is possible for a country's or territory's total political rights score to be less than zero (between -1 and -4) if it receives mostly or all zeros for each of the 10 political rights questions *and* it receives a sufficiently negative score for political rights discretionary question B. In such a case, it would still receive a final political rights rating of 7.

Tables and Ratings

Independent Countries

Country	Freedom Status	PR	CL	Trend Arrow
Afghanistan	Not Free	6	6	↓
Albania*	Partly Free	3	3	
Algeria	Not Free	6	5	
Andorra*	Free	1	1	
Angola	Not Free	6	5	
Antigua and Barbuda*	Free	2	2	
Argentina*	Free	2	2	
Armenia	Partly Free	5	4	
Australia*	Free	1	1	
Austria*	Free	1	1	
Azerbaijan	Not Free	6	6 ▼	
Bahamas*	Free	1	1	
Bahrain	Not Free	6	6	↓
Bangladesh*	Partly Free	3	4	↓
Barbados*	Free	1	1	
Belarus	Not Free	7	6	
Belgium*	Free	1	1	
Belize*	Free	1	2	↓
Benin*	Free	2	2	↓
Bhutan*	Partly Free	3 ▲	4 ▲	
Bolivia*	Partly Free	3	3	
Bosnia and Herzegovina*	Partly Free	3	3	
Botswana*	Free	3	2	
Brazil*	Free	2	2	
Brunei	Not Free	6	5	
Bulgaria*	Free	2	2	
Burkina Faso	Partly Free	5	3	
Burma	Not Free	6	5	
Burundi	Partly Free	5	5	
Cambodia	Not Free	6	5	
Cameroon	Not Free	6	6	
Canada*	Free	1	1	

Country	Freedom Status	PR	CL	Trend Arrow
Cape Verde*	Free	1	1	
Central African Republic	Not Free ▼	7 ▼	7 ▼	
Chad	Not Free	7	6	
Chile*	Free	1	1	
China	Not Free	7	6	
Colombia*	Partly Free	3	4	
Comoros*	Partly Free	3	4	
Congo (Brazzaville)	Not Free	6	5	
Congo (Kinshasa)	Not Free	6	6	
Costa Rica*	Free	1	1	
Côte d'Ivoire	Partly Free	5	4 ▲	
Croatia*	Free	1	2	
Cuba	Not Free	7	6	↑
Cyprus*	Free	1	1	
Czech Republic*	Free	1	1	
Denmark*	Free	1	1	
Djibouti	Not Free	6	5	
Dominica*	Free	1	1	
Dominican Republic*	Free	2	3 ▼	
East Timor*	Partly Free	3	4	
Ecuador*	Partly Free	3	3	
Egypt	Not Free ▼	6 ▼	5	
El Salvador*	Free	2	3	
Equatorial Guinea	Not Free	7	7	
Eritrea	Not Free	7	7	
Estonia*	Free	1	1	
Ethiopia	Not Free	6	6	
Fiji	Partly Free	6	4	
Finland*	Free	1	1	
France*	Free	1	1	
Gabon	Not Free	6	5	
The Gambia	Not Free	6	6	↓
Georgia*	Partly Free	3	3	
Germany*	Free	1	1	
Ghana*	Free	1	2	
Greece*	Free	2	2	
Grenada*	Free	1	2	
Guatemala*	Partly Free	3	4	

Tables and Ratings 849

Country	Freedom Status	PR	CL	Trend Arrow
Guinea	Partly Free	5	5	
Guinea-Bissau	Not Free	6	5	
Guyana*	Free	2	3	
Haiti	Partly Free	4	5	
Honduras*	Partly Free	4	4	
Hungary*	Free	1	2	
Iceland*	Free	1	1	
India*	Free	2	3	
Indonesia*	Partly Free ▼	2	4 ▼	
Iran	Not Free	6	6	
Iraq	Not Free	5 ▲	6	
Ireland*	Free	1	1	
Israel*	Free	1	2	
Italy*	Free	1 ▲	1	
Jamaica*	Free	2	3	
Japan*	Free	1	1 ▲	
Jordan	Not Free	6	5	
Kazakhstan	Not Free	6	5	↓
Kenya*	Partly Free	4	4	
Kiribati*	Free	1	1	
Kosovo	Partly Free	5	4	
Kuwait	Partly Free	5	5	
Kyrgyzstan	Partly Free	5	5	
Laos	Not Free	7	6	
Latvia*	Free	2	2	
Lebanon	Partly Free	5	4	↓
Lesotho*	Free	2	3	
Liberia*	Partly Free	3	4	
Libya*	Partly Free	4	5	
Liechtenstein*	Free	1	1	
Lithuania*	Free	1	1	
Luxembourg*	Free	1	1	
Macedonia*	Partly Free	3	3	
Madagascar	Partly Free	5 ▲	4	
Malawi*	Partly Free	3	4	
Malaysia	Partly Free	4	4	↓
Maldives	Partly Free	4 ▲	4	
Mali	Partly Free ▲	5 ▲	4 ▲	

Country	Freedom Status	PR	CL	Trend Arrow
Malta*	Free	1	1	
Marshall Islands*	Free	1	1	
Mauritania	Not Free	6	5	
Mauritius*	Free	1	2	
Mexico*	Partly Free	3	3	
Micronesia*	Free	1	1	
Moldova*	Partly Free	3	3	
Monaco*	Free	2	1	
Mongolia*	Free	1	2	
Montenegro*	Free	3	2	
Morocco	Partly Free	5	4	
Mozambique	Partly Free	4	3	
Namibia*	Free	2	2	
Nauru*	Free	1	1	
Nepal*	Partly Free	4	4	
Netherlands*	Free	1	1	
New Zealand*	Free	1	1	
Nicaragua	Partly Free	4 ▲	3 ▲	
Niger*	Partly Free	3	4	
Nigeria	Partly Free	4	4	
North Korea	Not Free	7	7	
Norway*	Free	1	1	
Oman	Not Free	6	5	
Pakistan*	Partly Free	4	5	↑
Palau*	Free	1	1	
Panama*	Free	2 ▼	2	
Papua New Guinea*	Partly Free	3 ▲	3	
Paraguay*	Partly Free	3	3	
Peru*	Free	2	3	
Philippines*	Partly Free	3	3	
Poland*	Free	1	1	
Portugal*	Free	1	1	
Qatar	Not Free	6	5	
Romania*	Free	2	2	
Russia	Not Free	6	5	↓
Rwanda	Not Free	6	5 ▲	
Saint Kitts and Nevis*	Free	1	1	↓
Saint Lucia*	Free	1	1	

Country	Freedom Status	PR	CL	Trend Arrow
Saint Vincent and Grenadines*	Free	1	1	
Samoa*	Free	2	2	
San Marino*	Free	1	1	
São Tomé and Príncipe*	Free	2	2	
Saudi Arabia	Not Free	7	7	
Senegal*	Free	2	2 ▲	
Serbia*	Free	2	2	
Seychelles*	Partly Free	3	3	
Sierra Leone*	Partly Free ▼	3 ▼	3	
Singapore	Partly Free	4	4	
Slovakia*	Free	1	1	
Slovenia*	Free	1	1	
Solomon Islands	Partly Free	4	3	
Somalia	Not Free	7	7	
South Africa*	Free	2	2	
South Korea*	Free	2 ▼	2	
South Sudan	Not Free	6	6 ▼	
Spain*	Free	1	1	
Sri Lanka	Partly Free	5	4	↓
Sudan	Not Free	7	7	
Suriname*	Free	2	2	
Swaziland	Not Free	7	5	
Sweden*	Free	1	1	
Switzerland*	Free	1	1	
Syria	Not Free	7	7	↓
Taiwan*	Free	1	2	
Tajikistan	Not Free	6	6	
Tanzania*	Partly Free	3	3	↓
Thailand*	Partly Free	4	4	
Togo	Partly Free	4 ▲	4	
Tonga*	Free	2 ▲	2	
Trinidad and Tobago*	Free	2	2	
Tunisia*	Partly Free	3	3 ▲	
Turkey*	Partly Free	3	4	↓
Turkmenistan	Not Free	7	7	
Tuvalu*	Free	1	1	
Uganda	Partly Free	6 ▼	4	
Ukraine*	Partly Free	4	3	↓

Country	Freedom Status	PR	CL	Trend Arrow
United Arab Emirates	Not Free	6	6	
United Kingdom*	Free	1	1	
United States*	Free	1	1	
Uruguay*	Free	1	1	
Uzbekistan	Not Free	7	7	
Vanuatu*	Free	2	2	
Venezuela	Partly Free	5	5	↓
Vietnam	Not Free	7	5	
Yemen	Not Free	6	6	
Zambia*	Partly Free	3	4	↓
Zimbabwe	Not Free	5 ▲	6	

PR and CL stand for political rights and civil liberties, respectively; 1 represents the most free and 7 the least free rating.

▲ ▼ up or down indicates an improvement or decline in ratings or status since the last survey.

↑ ↓ up or down indicates a trend of positive or negative changes that took place but were not sufficient to result in a change in political rights or civil liberties ratings.

* indicates a country's status as an electoral democracy.

NOTE: The ratings reflect global events from January 1, 2013, through December 31, 2013.

Related Territories

Territory	Freedom Status	PR	CL	Trend Arrow
Hong Kong	Partly Free	5	2	
Puerto Rico	Free	1	2	

Disputed Territories

Territory	Freedom Status	PR	CL	Trend Arrow
Abkhazia	Partly Free	4	5	
Gaza Strip	Not Free	7 ▼	6	
Indian Kashmir	Partly Free	4	4	
Nagorno-Karabakh	Partly Free	5	5	
Northern Cyprus	Free	2	2	
Pakistani Kashmir	Not Free	6	5	
Somaliland	Partly Free	4	5	
South Ossetia	Not Free	7	6	
Tibet	Not Free	7	7	
Transnistria	Not Free	6	6	
West Bank	Not Free	6	5	
Western Sahara	Not Free	7	7	

PR and CL stand for political rights and civil liberties, respectively; 1 represents the most free and 7 the least free rating.

▲ ▼ up or down indicates an improvement or decline in ratings or status since the last survey.

↑ ↓ up or down indicates a trend of positive or negative changes that took place but were not sufficient to result in a change in political rights or civil liberties ratings.

NOTE: The ratings reflect global events from January 1, 2013, through December 31, 2013.

Combined Average Ratings – Independent Countries

FREE

1.0
Andorra
Australia
Austria
Bahamas
Barbados
Belgium
Canada
Cape Verde
Chile
Costa Rica
Cyprus
Czech Republic
Denmark
Dominica
Estonia
Finland
France
Germany
Iceland
Ireland
Italy
Japan
Kiribati
Liechtenstein
Lithuania
Luxembourg
Malta
Marshall Islands
Micronesia
Nauru
Netherlands
New Zealand
Norway
Palau
Poland
Portugal
Saint Kitts and Nevis
Saint Lucia
Saint Vincent and the Grenadines
San Marino
Slovakia
Slovenia
Spain
Sweden
Switzerland
Tuvalu
United Kingdom
United States
Uruguay

1.5
Belize
Croatia
Ghana
Grenada
Hungary
Israel
Mauritius
Monaco
Mongolia
Taiwan

2.0
Antigua and Barbuda
Argentina
Benin
Brazil
Bulgaria
Greece
Latvia
Namibia
Panama
Romania
Samoa
São Tomé and Príncipe
Senegal
Serbia
South Africa
South Korea
Suriname
Tonga
Trinidad and Tobago
Vanuatu

2.5
Botswana
Dominican Republic
El Salvador
Guyana
India
Jamaica
Lesotho
Montenegro
Peru

PARTLY FREE

3.0
Albania
Bolivia
Bosnia and Herzegovina
Ecuador
Georgia
Indonesia
Macedonia
Mexico
Moldova
Papua New Guinea
Paraguay
Philippines
Seychelles
Sierra Leone
Tanzania
Tunisia

3.5
Bangladesh
Bhutan
Colombia
Comoros
East Timor
Guatemala
Liberia
Malawi
Mozambique
Nicaragua
Niger
Solomon Islands
Turkey
Ukraine
Zambia

4.0
Burkina Faso
Honduras
Kenya
Malaysia
Maldives
Nepal
Nigeria
Singapore
Thailand
Togo

4.5
Armenia
Côte d'Ivoire
Haiti
Kosovo
Lebanon
Libya
Madagascar
Mali
Morocco
Pakistan
Sri Lanka

5.0
Burundi
Fiji
Guinea
Kuwait
Kyrgyzstan
Uganda
Venezuela

NOT FREE

5.5
Algeria
Angola
Brunei
Burma
Cambodia
Congo (Brazzaville)
Djibouti
Egypt
Gabon
Guinea-Bissau
Iraq
Kazakhstan
Mauritania
Oman
Qatar
Russia
Rwanda
Zimbabwe

6.0
Afghanistan
Azerbaijan
Bahrain
Cameroon
Congo (Kinshasa)
Ethiopia
The Gambia
Iran
South Sudan
Swaziland
Tajikistan
United Arab Emirates
Vietnam
Yemen

6.5
Belarus
Chad
China
Cuba
Laos

7.0
Central African Republic
Equatorial Guinea
Eritrea
North Korea
Saudi Arabia
Somalia
Sudan
Syria
Turkmenistan
Uzbekistan

Combined Average Ratings – Related Territories

FREE	PARTLY FREE
1.5	3.5
Puerto Rico	Hong Kong

Combined Average Ratings – Disputed Territories

FREE

2.0
Northern Cyprus

PARTLY FREE

4.0
Indian Kashmir

4.5
Abkhazia
Somaliland

5.0
Nagorno-Karabakh

NOT FREE

5.5
Pakistani Kashmir
West Bank

6.0
Transnistria

6.5
Gaza Strip
South Ossetia

7.0
Tibet
Western Sahara

Electoral Democracies (122)

Albania	Hungary
Andorra	Iceland
Antigua and Barbuda	India
Argentina	Indonesia
Australia	Ireland
Austria	Israel
Bahamas	Italy
Bangladesh	Jamaica
Barbados	Japan
Belgium	Kenya
Belize	Kiribati
Benin	Latvia
Bhutan	Lesotho
Bolivia	Liberia
Bosnia-Herzegovina	Libya
Botswana	Liechtenstein
Brazil	Lithuania
Bulgaria	Luxembourg
Canada	Macedonia
Cape Verde	Malawi
Chile	Malta
Colombia	Marshall Islands
Comoros	Mauritius
Costa Rica	Mexico
Croatia	Micronesia
Cyprus	Moldova
Czech Republic	Monaco
Denmark	Mongolia
Dominica	Montenegro
Dominican Republic	Namibia
East Timor	Nauru
Ecuador	Nepal
El Salvador	Netherlands
Estonia	New Zealand
Finland	Niger
France	Norway
Georgia	Pakistan
Germany	Palau
Ghana	Panama
Greece	Papua New Guinea
Grenada	Paraguay
Guatemala	Peru
Guyana	Philippines
Honduras	Poland

Portugal	Suriname
Romania	Sweden
St. Kitts and Nevis	Switzerland
St. Lucia	Taiwan
St. Vincent and the Grenadines	Tanzania
Samoa	Thailand
San Marino	Tonga
São Tomé and Príncipe	Trinidad and Tobago
Senegal	Tunisia
Serbia	Turkey
Seychelles	Tuvalu
Sierra Leone	Ukraine
Slovakia	United Kingdom
Slovenia	United States
South Africa	Uruguay
South Korea	Vanuatu
Spain	Zambia

The Survey Team

AUTHORS

Michael E. Allison is an associate professor of political science at the University of Scranton in Pennsylvania. He received his master's degree and PhD in political science from Florida State University. His teaching and research interests include the comparative study of civil war and civil war resolution, particularly as it relates to the transformation of armed opposition groups into political parties in Latin America. His work has appeared in *Latin American Politics and Society*, *Conflict Management and Peace Science*, and *Studies in Comparative International Development*. He also blogs at *Central American Politics*. He served as an Americas analyst for *Freedom in the World*.

Lindsay J. Benstead is an assistant professor of political science in the Mark O. Hatfield School of Government at Portland State University. Her research focuses on electoral politics, public opinion, women and politics, and survey methodology in the Middle East and North Africa. She has coconducted surveys in Morocco, Algeria, Tunisia, Libya, and Jordan. Her work has appeared in the *International Journal of Public Opinion Research*, *Politics & Religion*, *Democratization*, and *Foreign Affairs*. She holds a PhD in public policy and political science and an MAE in applied economics from the University of Michigan in Ann Arbor. She served as a Middle East and North Africa analyst for *Freedom in the World*.

Robert Blair is a PhD candidate in political science at Yale University and a research fellow at AidData. Beginning in the fall of 2015 he will be an assistant professor of political science and international studies at Brown University. His research addresses the dynamics of state consolidation after civil war, with a regional focus on West Africa. He has worked in various capacities for the Political Instability Task Force, the Small Arms Survey, and the UN Office of Rule of Law and Security Institutions, among others. He served as a sub-Saharan Africa analyst for *Freedom in the World*.

S. Adam Cardais is a contributing editor at *Transitions Online*, a Prague-based internet magazine covering politics, economics, and society in postcommunist Europe and the former Soviet Union. He received a master's degree in European studies, with a focus on postconflict peacebuilding in the former Yugoslavia, from New York University. He served as a Central and Eastern Europe analyst for *Freedom in the World*.

Katherine Blue Carroll is an assistant professor and the director of the program in public policy studies at Vanderbilt University. She received her master's degree and PhD in politics from the University of Virginia. Her teaching and research interests include the comparative politics of the Middle East, political violence, and the U.S. military. Her work has appeared in *Middle East Policy* and the *Middle East Journal*. She served as a Middle East and North Africa analyst for *Freedom in the World*.

Fotini Christia is an associate professor of political science at the Massachusetts Institute of Technology. Her research interests center on conflict and cooperation in the Muslim world. She has done extensive ethnographic, survey, and experimental research on the effects of development aid in postconflict, multiethnic societies, with a focus on Afghanistan and Bosnia and Herzegovina. She is the author of *Alliance Formation in Civil Wars*, which received the 2013 Gregory M. Luebbert Award for Best Book in Comparative Politics, the Lepgold Prize for Best Book in International Relations, and the Distinguished Book Award of the Ethnicity, Nationalism, and Migration Section of the International Studies Association. Her research has also been published in *Science* and the *American Political Science Review*, among other journals, and she has written opinion pieces for *Foreign Affairs*, the *New York Times*, the *Washington Post*, and the *Boston Globe*. She received a PhD in public policy from Harvard University. She served as an Asia-Pacific analyst for *Freedom in the World*.

Sarah Cook is a senior research analyst for East Asia at Freedom House. She manages the team that produces the *China Media Bulletin*, a biweekly news digest of press freedom developments related to China. She previously served as assistant editor on three editions of Freedom House's *Freedom on the Net* index, which assesses internet and digital media freedom around the world. She coedited the English version of Chinese attorney Gao Zhisheng's memoir, *A China More Just*, and was a delegate to the UN Human Rights Commission for an organization working on religious freedom in China. She received a master's degree in politics and a master of laws degree in public international law from the School of Oriental and African Studies in London, where she was a Marshall Scholar. She served as an Asia-Pacific analyst for *Freedom in the World*.

Britta H. Crandall is an adjunct professor at Davidson College in North Carolina. She is the author of *Hemispheric Giants: The Misunderstood History of U.S.-Brazilian Relations*. Previously, she was associate director for Latin American sovereign risk analysis at Bank One and worked as a Latin American program examiner for the U.S. Office of Management and Budget. She received a PhD from the Johns Hopkins University School of Advanced International Studies. She served as an Americas analyst for *Freedom in the World*.

Zselyke Csaky is a research analyst for *Nations in Transit*, Freedom House's annual survey of democratic governance from Central Europe to Eurasia. She also writes reports for *Freedom of the Press*. Prior to joining Freedom House, she worked for the Hungarian and U.S. offices of Amnesty International. She holds master's degrees in international relations and European studies and in human rights from Central European University. She served as a Europe analyst for *Freedom in the World*.

Julian Dierkes is an associate professor and the Keidanren Chair in Japanese Research at the University of British Columbia's Institute of Asian Research, where he coordinates the Program on Inner Asia. His research has focused on history education and supplementary education in Japan, as well as contemporary Mongolia. He is the editor of *Change in Democratic Mongolia: Social Relations, Health, Mobile Pastoralism, and Mining*. He received a PhD in sociology from Princeton University. He served as an Asia-Pacific analyst for *Freedom in the World*.

Jake Dizard is a PhD candidate in political science at the University of Texas at Austin. He was previously the managing editor of *Countries at the Crossroads*, Freedom House's annual survey of democratic governance. His area of focus is Latin America, with a specific emphasis on the Andean region and Mexico. He received a master's degree from the Johns Hopkins University School of Advanced International Studies. He served as an Americas analyst for *Freedom in the World*.

Richard Downie is deputy director and a fellow of the Africa Program at the Center for Strategic and International Studies. Previously, he was a journalist for the British Broadcasting Corporation (BBC). He received a master's degree in international public policy from the Johns Hopkins University School of Advanced International Studies. He served as a sub-Saharan Africa analyst for *Freedom in the World*.

Jennifer Dunham is the project manager for *Freedom in the World* and *Freedom of the Press* at Freedom House, and writes country reports on Southern and East Africa for both publications. She holds a bachelor's degree in history-sociology from Columbia University and a master's degree in international relations from New York University. She served as a sub-Saharan Africa analyst for *Freedom in the World*.

Madeline Earp is the Asia research analyst for *Freedom on the Net*. She works with regional analysts to produce internet freedom assessments of 15 countries in South, Southeast, and East Asia. She was previously the senior Asia program researcher at the Committee to Protect Journalists in New York. Earp holds an MA in East Asian Studies from Harvard University and a BA from Cambridge University. She served as an Asia-Pacific analyst for *Freedom in the World*.

Amy Freedman is a professor and the department chair of political science and international studies at Long Island University, C. W. Post Campus. Her research touches on various questions relating to democratization and political economy in Southeast Asia. Her most recent book is *The Internationalization of Internal Conflicts* (Routledge, 2013), and she is a coeditor of the journal *Asian Security*. She received a master's degree and PhD in political science from New York University. She served as an Asia-Pacific analyst for *Freedom in the World*.

T. R. Goldman is a freelance journalist in Washington, DC, and writes for a variety of national publications. He is a former reporter and editor at Reuters and Agence France-Presse. He received a master's degree in international public policy from the Johns Hopkins University School of Advanced International Studies. He served as a sub-Saharan Africa analyst for *Freedom in the World*.

Eva Hoier Greene is a former research assistant at Freedom House. Previously, she covered nuclear disarmament and other issues at the Permanent Mission of Denmark to the United Nations. She received a bachelor's degree in international development in Denmark. She served as a Western Europe analyst for *Freedom in the World*.

Holger Henke is assistant provost at York College, City University of New York, and a political scientist with a variety of research interests in international relations. He has authored and edited six books, including *Constructing Vernacular Culture in the Trans-Caribbean*, and has published numerous articles in journals such as *Cultural Critique* and *Latin American Perspectives*. He is the editor of *Wadabagei: A Journal of the Caribbean and its Diasporas*. He received a master's degree in political science from the Geschwister-Scholl-Institute of Political Science at the Ludwig Maximilians University of Munich and a PhD in government from the University of the West Indies at Mona, Jamaica. He served as an Americas analyst for *Freedom in the World*.

Ted Henken is an associate professor and chair of the Department of Sociology and Anthropology at Baruch College, City University of New York. He holds a joint appointment in Baruch's Black and Latino Studies Department. He is a past president of the Association for the Study of the Cuban Economy. He is the coauthor with Archibald Ritter of *Entrepreneurial Cuba: The Changing Policy Landscape* (October 2014), coeditor with Miriam Celaya and Dimas Castellanos of *Cuba in Focus* (2013), and author of *Cuba: A Global Studies Handbook* (2008). He has published articles about Cuba in the journals *Nueva Sociedad*, *Cuban Studies*, *Latino Studies*, and *Latin American Research Review*, as well as in the *New York Times* and the blog of the Committee to Protect Journalists. He also writes about contemporary Cuba on his blog, *El Yuma*. He received a PhD in Latin American studies from Tulane University in 2002. He served as an Americas analyst for *Freedom in the World*.

Franklin Hess is the coordinator of the Modern Greek Program at Indiana University, a senior lecturer at the Institute for European Studies, and codirector of a working group on the sovereign debt crisis. His scholarly work examines Greek popular culture, exploring the economic, geopolitical, and geocultural contexts of its production. His other research interests include immigration and the cinematic representation of violence. He served as the secretary of the Modern Greek Studies Association from 2007 to 2009. He received a PhD in American studies from the University of Iowa, focusing on the influence of American television programming on Greek culture. He served as a Western Europe analyst for *Freedom in the World*.

Rola el-Husseini holds a PhD from the École des Hautes Études en Sciences Sociales in Paris and is currently a research assistant professor at the City University of New York Graduate Center. She has previously held positions at Texas A&M University and Yale University. Her first book, *Pax Syriana: Elite Politics in Postwar Lebanon*, was published in 2012. She served as a Middle East and North Africa analyst for *Freedom in the World*.

Morgan Huston is a former member of the research team at Freedom House, where she also contributed to the *Freedom of the Press* publication. She received a master's degree in international human rights from the Josef Korbel School of International Studies at the University of Denver. She served as a sub-Saharan Africa analyst for *Freedom in the World*.

Toby Craig Jones is an associate professor of history and the director of the Center for Middle Eastern Studies at Rutgers University, New Brunswick. From 2012 to 2014 he served as codirector of the Rutgers Center for Historical Analysis. Previously, he was the Persian Gulf analyst at the International Crisis Group. He is the author of *Desert Kingdom: How Oil and Water Forged Modern Saudi Arabia* and is currently writing a book entitled *America's Oil Wars*. He is an editor of *Middle East Report* and has published widely, including in the *International Journal of Middle East Studies*, the *New York Times*, and *Foreign Affairs*. He received a PhD from Stanford University. He served as a Middle East and North Africa analyst for *Freedom in the World*.

Karin Deutsch Karlekar is the project director of *Freedom of the Press*, Freedom House's annual survey of global media freedom. A specialist on media freedom trends and measurement indicators, she also developed the methodology for and edited the pilot edition of *Freedom on the Net*, Freedom House's assessment of internet and digital media freedom. She has written South Asia reports for several Freedom House publications, and has been on research and advocacy missions to Afghanistan, Nigeria, Pakistan, Sri Lanka, South Africa, Uganda, Zambia, and Zimbabwe. She previously worked as a consultant for Human Rights Watch and as an editor at the Economist Intelligence Unit. She received a PhD in Indian history from Cambridge University. She served as an Asia-Pacific analyst for *Freedom in the World*.

Catherine Kelly is a postdoctoral fellow at Washington University in St. Louis in the Department of International and Area Studies. She received her PhD from Harvard University (2014). Based on over 16 months of research in Senegal, her dissertation is about the sources and consequences of party proliferation in Africa. Her research and teaching address African politics, political party development, elections, democratization, and Islam in politics. A former Fulbright Scholar and Title VI Foreign Language and Area Studies fellow, her work has appeared in the *Journal of Democracy* and *Electoral Studies*, and on the blogs of the Council on Foreign Relations and the Social Science Research Council. She served as a sub-Saharan Africa analyst for *Freedom in the World*.

Nicholas Kerr is an assistant professor of comparative politics in the Department of Political Science at the University of Alabama. His research interests include African politics, electoral institutions, electoral integrity, and public opinion. His current research project explores the factors that influence the design of electoral commissions in Africa, and probes how the design and performance of these institutions influence electoral integrity. He recently published an article in *Electoral Studies* that examines citizens' evaluation of electoral integrity in Nigeria. He served as a sub-Saharan Africa analyst for *Freedom in the World*.

Sylvana Habdank-Kołaczkowska is the project director of *Nations in Transit*, Freedom House's annual report on democratic governance from Central Europe to Eurasia. She also writes reports on Central Europe for *Freedom of the Press*. Previously, she was the managing editor of the *Journal of Cold War Studies*, a peer-reviewed quarterly. She received a master's degree in Eastern European and Eurasian studies from Harvard University. She served as a Central and Eastern Europe analyst for *Freedom in the World*.

Paul Kubicek is a professor of political science and director of the International Studies Program at Oakland University. He is the author of numerous works on postcommunist and Turkish politics, which have appeared in journals including *Comparative Politics*, *Democratization*, and *Political Science Quarterly*. He is currently coeditor of *Turkish Studies* and is working on a book-length project examining the role of Islam in Muslim-majority democracies. He has taught in Ukraine, Turkey, and Austria, and was a Fulbright Scholar in Slovenia. He received a PhD in political science from the University of Michigan. He served as a Western Europe analyst for *Freedom in the World*.

Joshua Kurlantzick is a senior fellow for Southeast Asia at the Council on Foreign Relations. Previously, he was a scholar at the Carnegie Endowment for International Peace, where he focused on Southeast Asian politics and economics and China's relations with Southeast Asia. He is a longtime journalist whose articles have appeared in *Time*, the *New Republic*, the *Atlantic Monthly*, *Foreign Affairs*, and the *New Yorker*, among others. He is the author of the recently released book *Democracy in Retreat: The Revolt of the Middle Class and the Worldwide Decline of Representative Government*. He received a bachelor's degree in political science from Haverford College. He served as an Asia-Pacific analyst for *Freedom in the World*.

Astrid Larson is the language center administrative director for the French Institute Alliance Française. She has served as an analyst for Western Europe, sub-Saharan Africa, and the South Pacific for Freedom House's *Freedom of the Press* report. She received a master's degree in international media and culture from the New School University. She served as a Western Europe analyst for *Freedom in the World*.

Beatrice Lindstrom is a human rights attorney with the Institute for Justice & Democracy in Haiti (IJDH), focusing on rule of law and access to justice. Prior to joining IJDH, she worked with the Bureau des Avocats Internationaux in Port-au-Prince, Haiti, where her activities included election monitoring, human rights reporting, and managing grassroots participation in the UN Universal Periodic Review. She received a juris doctor degree from New York University School of Law, where she was a Root Tilden Kern scholar. She served as an Americas analyst for *Freedom in the World*.

Joshua Lustig is editor of *Current History*, an international affairs journal based in Philadelphia. Previously, he was a senior editor at *Facts On File World News Digest*, covering Western Europe. He received a bachelor's degree in English literature from Columbia University. He served as a Western Europe analyst for *Freedom in the World*.

Katherin Machalek is institutional development officer and project manager for capacity-building projects in Russia and Ukraine for the Geneva-based Human Rights Information and Documentation Systems (HURIDOCS), helping civil society organizations in Eurasia improve their use of information and communication technologies and digital advocacy. She received a master's degree in political science from the University of North Carolina, Chapel Hill. She served as a Eurasia analyst for *Freedom in the World*.

Eleanor Marchant is a PhD student at the Annenberg School for Communications at the University of Pennsylvania, specializing in political communications and new technology in Africa. She is also a research associate at the Center for Global Communication Studies, where she advises on African and transnational media research projects. Previously, she worked at the Programme in Comparative Media Law and Policy at Oxford University, the Media Development Investment Fund, and the Media Institute in Nairobi. She also served as assistant editor for Freedom House's *Freedom of the Press* report. She received a master's degree in international relations from New York University. She served as a sub-Saharan Africa analyst for *Freedom in the World*.

Susana Moreira is an extractive-industries specialist at the World Bank. She received a PhD from the Johns Hopkins University School of Advanced International Studies, focusing on Chinese national oil companies' investment strategies in Latin America and sub-Saharan Africa. She is involved in several other research projects, including the African Crisis Management in Comparative Perspective project, sponsored by the U.S. military's Africa Command. She served as a sub-Saharan Africa analyst for *Freedom in the World*.

Yonatan L. Morse is a visiting assistant professor of government and the associate director of the Democracy and Governance Program at Georgetown University. He has researched and authored publications on democratization, electoral authoritarianism, and African political parties. He received his PhD in government from Georgetown University. He served as a sub-Saharan Africa analyst for *Freedom in the World*.

Maura Moynihan is a journalist and researcher who has worked for many years with Tibetan refugees in India and Nepal. Her works of fiction include *Yoga Hotel* and *Kaliyuga*. She is a contributor to the *Asian Age* newspaper. She served as an Asia-Pacific analyst for *Freedom in the World*.

Bret Nelson is a research analyst for *Freedom in the World* and *Freedom of the Press* at Freedom House. He received master's degrees in political science from Fordham University and in Middle East studies from the City University of New York Graduate Center. He served as a Middle East and North Africa analyst for *Freedom in the World*.

Alysson Akiko Oakley is a PhD candidate at the Johns Hopkins University School of Advanced International Studies (SAIS) and an adjunct professor at Georgetown University. Previously, she served as a senior adviser at the International Republican Institute and a program director at the U.S.-Indonesia Society. She has lived in Indonesia, with frequent postings to East Timor, for over 10 years. She received a master's degree in international economics and Southeast Asian studies from SAIS and a bachelor's degree in international relations from Brown University. She served as an Asia-Pacific analyst for *Freedom in the World*.

Robert Orttung is assistant director of the Institute for European, Russian, and Eurasian Studies at George Washington University's Elliott School of International Affairs, president of the Resource Security Institute, and a visiting scholar at the Center for Security Studies at the Swiss Federal Institute of Technology (ETH) in Zurich. He is managing editor of *Demokratizatsiya: The Journal of Post-Soviet Democratization* and a coeditor of the *Russian Analytical Digest* and the *Caucasus Analytical Digest*. He received a PhD in political science from the University of California, Los Angeles. He served as a Eurasia analyst for *Freedom in the World*.

Shannon O'Toole is an MA candidate in international relations at Central European University. Previously, she worked as an editor and writer at *Facts On File World News Digest*, where she covered Eastern Europe, Russia, and the Balkans. She holds a bachelor's degree in history and anthropology from the University of Missouri, Columbia. She served as a Central and Eastern Europe analyst for *Freedom in the World*.

Amy Padilla is a research assistant at the Johns Hopkins University School of Advanced International Studies, where she received her master's degree in international economics and Southeast Asia studies. Previously, she worked with the Center for Strategic and International Studies and the Liberty Institute of New Delhi, expanding their Empowering India initiative to improve transparency in Indian elections. She is a former staff member of Freedom House and has worked on its Southeast Asia, exchanges, and advocacy programs. Prior to joining Freedom House, she was a fellow with Kiva Microfunds in Cambodia. She served as a Southeast Asia analyst for *Freedom in the World*.

Alessandra Pinna is a program associate for the Global Emergency Assistance Program at Freedom House. Previously, she worked as a researcher and teaching assistant at Roma Tre University. She received her PhD in political science and democracy studies from the Istituto Italiano di Scienze Umane (Florence). She participated in several research programs, both in Italy and abroad, and has published articles and book chapters on democratization and democracy promotion. Her most recent publications are *The International Dimension of Democratization* (2014) and *U.S. Democracy Promotion in Serbia and Croatia* (2013). She served as a Western Europe analyst for *Freedom in the World*.

Arch Puddington is vice president for research at Freedom House and coeditor of *Freedom in the World*. He has written widely on American foreign policy, race relations, organized labor, and the history of the Cold War. He is the author of *Broadcasting Freedom: The Cold War Triumph of Radio Free Europe and Radio Liberty* and *Lane Kirkland: Champion of American Labor*. He received a bachelor's degree in English literature from the University of Missouri, Columbia. He served as an Americas analyst for *Freedom in the World*.

Ellora Puri is on the faculty of the Department of Political Science, University of Jammu, India. She received her degrees from University of Michigan, Ann Arbor, and Jawaharlal Nehru University, New Delhi. Her research interests include South Asian politics, political violence, and gender. She has been associated with a variety of policy groups and think tanks working on human rights and peace and conflict studies in South Asia. She served as a South Asia analyst for *Freedom in the World*.

Mark Y. Rosenberg is a senior Africa analyst at Eurasia Group, focusing on the Southern Africa region. Previously, he worked as a researcher at Freedom House and assistant editor of *Freedom in the World*. His opinion articles have appeared in the *New York Times*, the *Jerusalem Post*, and *Business Day* (South Africa), and his research has been cited by publications including the *Economist* and the *Financial Times*. He received a master's degree and a PhD in political science from the University of California, Berkeley, where he was a National Science Foundation Graduate Fellow. He served as a sub-Saharan Africa analyst for *Freedom in the World*.

Tyler Roylance is a staff editor at Freedom House and is involved in a number of its publications. Previously, he worked as a senior editor for *Facts On File World News Digest*. He received a master's degree in history from New York University. He served as a Central and Eastern Europe and Eurasia analyst for *Freedom in the World*.

Sergio Rozalén coordinates media and communication for the International Network for Economic, Social and Cultural Rights, a collaborative initiative of over 200 groups and 50 individual advocates from around the world working to secure economic and social justice through human rights. As a journalist, he worked for more than five years in the press department of the European Commission in Spain. He has developed media strategies for numerous nongovernmental organizations and foundations via a public relations agency he founded in Spain. He holds a BA in journalism and an MA in marketing. He served as a Western Europe analyst for *Freedom in the World*.

Adrian Shahbaz is a research analyst for *Freedom on the Net* at Freedom House, where he covers the European Union and the Middle East and North Africa. Previously, he was a political affairs analyst and researcher at the United Nations, the European Parliament, and the Organization for Security and Cooperation in Europe. He received a master's degree in international relations from the London School of Economics and Political Science. He served as a Middle East and North Africa analyst for *Freedom in the World*.

Yvonne Shen was a founding editor of the *China Media Bulletin*, Freedom House's biweekly news digest of press freedom developments related to China. Previously, she was a research fellow at the Taiwan Foundation for Democracy in Taipei, and received a master's degree from New York University's Wagner School of Public Service. She served as an Asia-Pacific analyst for *Freedom in the World*.

Mira Sucharov is an associate professor of political science at Carleton University in Ottawa, Canada. She is the author of *The International Self: Psychoanalysis and the Search for Israeli-Palestinian Peace*, and has published articles in *International Studies Perspectives*, the *Journal of International Relations and Development*, the *International Journal*, and the *Journal of Political Science Education*. She blogs at *Haaretz* and the *Jewish Daily Forward*. She received a master's degree in political science from the University of Toronto and a PhD in government from Georgetown University. She served as a Middle East and North Africa analyst for *Freedom in the World*.

Farha Tahir is a program officer at the National Democratic Institute focusing on governance issues in Africa. She also provides economic analysis for Pragnya Group. She previously served as project manager at the International Interfaith Peace Corps (IIPC), overseeing the Dakar Vaccination Summit, an effort with the government of Senegal to identify the challenges associated with vaccinating resistant and hard-to-reach Muslim communities throughout Africa. She also worked as a program coordinator and research associate at the Center for Strategic and International Studies, where she provided research regarding U.S. strategic priorities on the continent. She received bachelor's and master's degrees from the University of Wisconsin, Madison. She served as a sub-Saharan Africa analyst for *Freedom in the World*.

Leigh Tomppert is a human rights policy specialist in the Leadership and Governance Section of the United Nations Entity for Gender Equality and the Empowerment of Women. She previously coedited Freedom House's *Women's Rights in the Middle East and North Africa* publication. She received master's degrees in comparative and cross-cultural research methods from the University of Sussex and in the social sciences from the University of Chicago. She served as an Americas analyst for *Freedom in the World*.

Silvana Toska is a PhD candidate in political science at Cornell University, focusing on the causes and spread of revolutions. She received master's degrees in African studies from Oxford University, where she wrote on the effects of foreign aid on ethnic conflict, and in Arab studies from Georgetown University. She served as a sub-Saharan Africa analyst for *Freedom in the World*.

Jenny Town is the assistant director of the U.S.-Korea Institute at Johns Hopkins University's School of Advanced International Studies. Previously, she worked for the Human Rights in North Korea Project at Freedom House. She received a master's degree from Columbia University's School of International and Public Affairs, with a concentration in human rights. She served as an Asia-Pacific analyst for *Freedom in the World*.

Mai Truong is a program officer and Africa research analyst for *Freedom on the Net*, Freedom House's annual assessment of internet and digital media freedom. Prior to joining Freedom House, she worked on projects related to international development, food security, and women's rights issues in sub-Saharan Africa. She received a master's degree in international relations from Yale University's Jackson Institute for Global Affairs. She served as a sub-Saharan Africa analyst for *Freedom in the World*.

Noah Tucker has worked both in the nonprofit sector and as a researcher on Central Asian religion, human rights, security, and conflict. He served as a U.S. embassy policy specialist for Kyrgyzstan in 2011 and returned to Central Asia for fieldwork most recently in the summer of 2012. He received a master's degree from Harvard University's Davis Center for Russian and Eurasian Studies. He served as a Eurasia analyst for *Freedom in the World*.

Vanessa Tucker is vice president for analysis at Freedom House. Previously, she was the project director of *Countries at the Crossroads*, Freedom House's annual survey of democratic governance. Prior to joining Freedom House, she worked at the Harvard University Kennedy School's Women and Public Policy Program, at the Kennedy School's Program on Intrastate Conflict, and with the Carter Center's Democracy Program. She received a master's degree in international relations from Yale University. She served as a Middle East and North Africa analyst for *Freedom in the World*.

Daria Vaisman is a New York–based writer and producer. Her first book, a narrative nonfiction account of U.S. foreign policy in the former Soviet Union, will be published in 2014. She is also codirector of a documentary film on diplomatic recognition and sovereignty, currently in production. Previously, she was an analyst at Transparency International and deputy director of the Eurasia Foundation in Tbilisi, Georgia, and a journalist covering the Caucasus and Central Asia. She received a master's degree from Columbia University's School of International and Public Affairs and is a PhD candidate in criminal justice at the City University of New York Graduate Center. She served as a Eurasia analyst for *Freedom in the World*.

Christine Wade is an associate professor of political science and international studies at Washington College, where she is also the curator of the Louis L. Goldstein Program in Public Affairs. She has authored and coauthored numerous publications on Central American politics. She received a PhD in political science from Boston University. She served as an Americas analyst for *Freedom in the World*.

Greg White is a professor of government at Smith College. He is the author of *Climate Change and Migration: Borders and Security in a Warming World* and the forthcoming coedited volume *North Africa: From Status Quo to (R)Evolution*. He is also the recipient of a Mellon Foundation New Directions Fellowship, as well as Fulbright-IIE and Fulbright-Hays scholarships to Tunisia and Morocco, respectively. He received a PhD from the University of Wisconsin, Madison. He served as a Middle East and North Africa analyst for *Freedom in the World*.

Anny Wong is an adjunct political scientist with the RAND Corporation and a research fellow with the John G. Tower Center for Political Studies at Southern Methodist University in Dallas, Texas. She also serves on the board of the Japan-America Society of Dallas–Fort Worth and provides analyses on politics and economics in East and Southeast Asia for senior business executives. Her research covers science and technology policy, international development, military manpower, and U.S. relations with states in the Asia-Pacific region. She received a PhD in political science from the University of Hawaii, Manoa. She served as an Asia-Pacific analyst for *Freedom in the World*.

Min Zin is a regular contributor to *Foreign Policy*'s *Transitions* blog. He also serves as a Burma country analyst for several research foundations. His writings appear in *Foreign Policy*, the *New York Times*, the *Irrawaddy*, the *Bangkok Post*, *Far Eastern Economic Review*, the *Wall Street Journal*, and other publications. He is a PhD candidate in political science at the University of California, Berkeley. He served as an Asia-Pacific analyst for *Freedom in the World*.

ACADEMIC ADVISERS

Eva Bellin is Myra and Robert Kraft Professor of Arab Politics in the Department of Politics and the Crown Center for Middle East Studies at Brandeis University.

Julio F. Carrión is an associate professor and founding director of the Center for Global and Area Studies at the University of Delaware.

Kathleen Collins is an associate professor in the Department of Political Science at the University of Minnesota in Minneapolis.

Tulia Falleti is the Class of 1965 Term associate professor of political science and senior fellow of the Leonard Davis Institute for Health Economics at the University of Pennsylvania.

Robert Lane Greene is a Berlin-based correspondent for the *Economist*, and a former adjunct assistant professor of global affairs at New York University.

Steven Heydemann is vice president of Applied Research on Conflict and director of Syria programs at the U.S. Institute of Peace, and previously served as director of the Center for Democracy and Civil Society at Georgetown University.

Melissa Labonte is an associate professor of political science at Fordham University.

Thomas R. Lansner is a visiting professor at the Sciences Po Paris School of International Affairs.

Adrienne LeBas is an assistant professor of government at American University's School of Public Affairs.

Peter Lewis is an associate professor and director of the African Studies Program at Johns Hopkins University's School of Advanced International Studies.

Adam Luedtke is an assistant professor of political science at City University of New York–Queensborough Community College.

Ellen Lust is a professor of political science at Yale University and founding director of the Program on Governance and Local Development.

Peter Mandaville is a professor of government and politics and director of the Ali Vural Ak Center for Islamic Studies at George Mason University.

Rajan Menon is the Anne and Bernard Spitzer Professor of Political Science, Department of Political Science, City College of New York/City University of New York.

John S. Micgiel is president and executive director of the Kosciuszko Foundation and visiting professor at the University of Warsaw's Eastern Studies Center.

Carl Minzner is a professor at Fordham Law School.

Alexander J. Motyl is a professor of political science at Rutgers University, Newark.

Philip Oldenburg is a research scholar at Columbia University's South Asia Institute.

Tsveta Petrova is a fellow at the Harriman Institute, Columbia University.

J. Mark Ruhl is the Glenn and Mary Todd Professor of Political Science at Dickinson College.

Martin Schain is a professor of politics at New York University.

Samer S. Shehata is an associate professor and Middle East Studies Program coordinator at the University of Oklahoma.

Scott Taylor is an associate professor at the School of Foreign Service and director of the African Studies Program at Georgetown University.

Joseph Tulchin is a visiting scholar at the David Rockefeller Center for Latin American Studies at Harvard University and a senior scholar at the Woodrow Wilson International Center for Scholars.

Bridget Welsh a senior research associate at the Center for East Asia Democratic Studies, National Taiwan University.

Susanna Wing is an associate professor at Haverford College.

PRODUCTION

Ida Walker, Proofreader

Selected Sources for *Freedom in the World 2014*

PUBLICATIONS/BROADCASTS/BLOGS

Publications/Broadcasts/Blogs
38 North [North Korea], www.38north.org
ABC Color [Paraguay], www.abc.com.py
Africa Confidential, www.africa-confidential.com
Africa Daily, www.africadaily.com
Africa Energy Intelligence, www.africaintelligence.com
AFRICAHOME dotcom, www.africahome.com
Africa News, www.africanews.com
AfricaOnline.com, www.africaonline.com
African Elections Database, http://africanelections.tripod.com
Afrol News, www.afrol.com
Aftenposten [Norway], www.aftenposten.no
Agence France-Presse (AFP), www.afp.com
Al-Arab al-Yawm [Jordan]: www.alarabalyawm.net
Al-Arabiya, www.alarabiya.net
Al-Ahram, www.ahram.org.eg
Al-Akhbar [Beirut], www.al-akhbar.com
Al-Dustour [Egypt], www.addustour.com
Al-Hayat, www.alhayat.com
Al-Jazeera, http://english.aljazeera.net
allAfrica.com, www.allafrica.com
Al-Masry al-Youm [Egypt], www.almasryalyoum.com
Al-Ray Al-'am [Kuwait], www.alraialaam.com
Al-Raya [Qatar], www.raya.com
Al-Quds al-Arabi, www.alquds.co.uk
Al-Thawra [Yemen], www.althawra.gov.ye
Al-Watan [Qatar], www.al-watan.com
American Broadcasting Corporation News (ABC), www.abcnews.go.com
The Analyst [Liberia], www.analystliberia.com
Andorra Times, www.andorratimes.com
An-Nahar [Lebanon], www.annahar.com
Annual Review of Population Law (Harvard Law School), annualreview.law.harvard.edu
Arab Advisors Group, www.arabadvisors.com
Arabianbusiness.com, www.arabianbusiness.com
Arabic Network for Human Rights Information (ANHRI), www.anhri.net
Arab Media, http://arab-media.blogspot.com
Arab News [Saudi Arabia], www.arabnews.com
Asharq Alawsat, www.asharqalawsat.com
Asia Sentinel, www.asiasentinel.com
Asia Times, www.atimes.com
Asia-Pacific Journal, www.japanfocus.org
As-Safir [Lebanon], www.assafir.com
Associated Press (AP), www.ap.org
The Atlantic Monthly, www.theatlantic.com
Austrian Times, www.austriantimes.at
Australia Broadcasting Corporation News Online, www.abc.net.au/news
The Australian, www.theaustralian.news.com.au
Awareness Times [Sierra Leone], www.news.sl
Bahrain Post, www.bahrainpost.com
Balkan Insight, www.balkaninsight.com
The Baltic Times, www.baltictimes.com
Bangkok Post, www.bangkokpost.co.th
Boston Globe, www.boston.com
British Broadcasting Corporation (BBC), www.bbc.co.uk
BruDirect.com [Brunei], www.brudirect.com
Budapest Times, www.budapesttimes.hu
Business Day [South Africa], www.bday.co.za
Cabinda.net, www.cabinda.net
Cable News Network (CNN), www.cnn.com
Cameroon Tribune, www.cameroon-tribune.cm
Caribbean & Central America Report (Intelligence Research Ltd.)
CBS News, www.cbsnews.com
Central Asia-Caucasus Analyst (Johns Hopkins University), www.cacianalyst.org
Central News Agency [Taiwan], http://focustaiwan.tw
China Post, www.chinapost.com.tw
Chosun Ilbo [South Korea], http://english.chosun.com
Christian Science Monitor, www.csmonitor.com
CIA World Factbook, www.cia.gov/cia/publications/factbook
Civil Georgia, www.civil.ge
Congo Siasa, http://congosiasa.blogspot.co.uk
Contemporary Pacific, http://pidp.eastwestcenter.org/pireport/tcp.htm
Copenhagen Post [Denmark], www.cphpost.dk
Corriere della Sera [Italy], www.corriere.it
Czech News Agency, www.ceskenoviny.cz/news

Selected Sources 871

Daily Excelsior [India-Kashmir], www.dailyexcelsior.com
Daily Star [Lebanon], www.dailystar.com.lb
Danas [Serbia], www.danas.rs/danasrs/naslovna.1.html
Dani [Bosnia-Herzegovina], www.bhdani.com
Dawn [Pakistan], www.dawn.com
Der Spiegel [Germany], www.spiegel.de
Der Standard [Austria], www.derstandard.at
Die Zeit [Germany], www.zeit.de
Deutsche Presse-Agentur [Germany], www.dpa.de
Deutsche Welle [Germany], www.dwelle.de
East Africa Standard [Kenya], www.eastandard.net
The Economist, www.economist.com
Economist Intelligence Unit, www.eiu.com
Ekho Moskvy [Russia], http://echo.msk.ru
Election Watch, www.electionwatch.org
El Mercurio [Chile], www.elmercurio.cl
El Nuevo Herald [United States], www.miami.com/mld/elnuevo
El Pais [Uruguay], www.elpais.com.uy
El Tiempo [Colombia], www.eltiempo.com
El Universal [Venezuela], www.eluniversal.com.ve
Epoch Times, www.theepochtimes.com
Eurasia Review, www.eurasiareview.com
Federal Bureau of Investigation Hate Crime Statistics, www.fbi.gov/ucr/2003/03semimaps.pdf
Federated States of Micronesia Congress press releases www.fsmcongress.fm
Federated States of Micronesia Information Services www.fsmpio.fm
Fijilive, www.fijilive.com
Fiji Times Online, www.fijitimes.com
Fiji Village, www.FijiVillage.com
Financial Times, www.ft.com
Folha de Sao Paulo, www.folha.com.br
Foreign Affairs, www.foreignaffairs.org
Foreign Policy, www.foreignpolicy.com
France 24, www.france24.com
Frankfurter Allgemeine Zeitung [Germany], www.faz.net
Friday Times [Pakistan], www.thefridaytimes.com
FrontPageAfrica [Liberia], www.frontpageafrica.com
Gazeta.ru [Russia], www.gazeta.ru
Global Insight, www.globalinsight.com
Global News Wire, www.lexis-nexis.com
Grupo consultor de la sociedad civil cubana [Cuba] http://grupoconsultorcuba.wordpress.com
The Guardian [Nigeria], www.ngrguardiannews.com
The Guardian [United Kingdom], www.guardian.co.uk

Gulf Daily News [Bahrain], www.gulf-daily-news.com
Gulf News Online [United Arab Emirates], www.gulf-news.com
Gulf Times [Qatar], www.gulf-times.com
Haaretz [Israel], www.haaretz.com
Hankyoreh Shinmun [South Korea], http://english.hani.co.kr/kisa
Harakah Daily [Malaysia], http://bm.harakahdaily.net
Harper's Magazine, www.harpers.org
Haveeru Daily [Maldives], www.haveeru.com.mv
Hindustan Times [India], www.hindustantimes.com
Hurriyet [Turkey], www.hurriyetdailynews.com
Iceland Review, www.icelandreview.com
The Independent [United Kingdom], www.independent.co.uk
Index on Censorship, www.indexoncensorship.org
India Today, www.india-today.com
Indian Express, www.indian-express.com
Insight Namibia Magazine, www.insight.com.na
Integrated Regional Information Networks (IRIN), www.irinnews.org
Inter Press Service, www.ips.org
Interfax News Agency, www.interfax-news.com
International Herald Tribune, www.iht.com
IRIN news, www.irinnews.org
Irish Independent, www.unison.ie/irish_independent
Irish Times, www.ireland.com
Islands Business Magazine, www.islandsbusiness.com
Izvestia, www.izvestia.ru
Jakarta Post, www.thejakartapost.com
Jamaica Gleaner, www.jamaica-gleaner.com
Jeune Afrique [France], www.jeuneafrique.com
Joongang Ilbo [South Korea], http://joongangdaily.joins.com/?cloc=home|top|jdaily
Jordan Times, www.jordantimes.com
Journal of Democracy, www.journalofdemocracy.org
Jyllands-Posten [Denmark], www.jp.dk
Kaselehlie Press [Micronesia], www.bild-art.de/kpress
Kashmir Times [India-Kashmir], www.kashmirtimes.com
Kedaulatan Rakyat [Indonesia], www.kedaulatan-rakyat.com
Khaleej Times [United Arab Emirates], www.khaleejtimes.com
Kommersant [Russia], www.kommersant.ru
Kompas [Indonesia], www.kompas.com
Korea Central News Agency [North Korea], www.kcna.co.jp/index-e.htm
Korea Economic Daily [South Korea], http://english.hankyung.com

Korea Times [South Korea], http://times.hankooki.com
Kuensel [Bhutan], www.kuenselonline.com
Kurier [Austria], www.kurier.at
L'Informazione di San Marino, www.libertas.sm/News_informazione/news_frameset.htm
La Nación [Argentina], www.lanacion.com.ar
La Repubblica [Italy], www.repubblica.it
La Tercera [Chile], www.tercera.cl
Latin American Regional Reports, www.latinnews.com
Latin American Weekly Reports, www.latinnews.com
Le Faso [Burkina Faso], www.lefaso.net
Le Figaro [France], www.lefigaro.fr
Le Messager [Cameroon], www.lemessager.net
Le Monde [France], www.lemonde.fr
Le Quotidien [Senegal], www.lequotidien.sn
Le Temps [Switzerland], www.letemps.ch
Le Togolais [Togo], www.letogolais.com
The Local [Sweden], www.thelocal.se
L'Orient-Le Jour [Lebanon], www.lorientlejour.com
Los Angeles Times, www.latimes.com
Mail & Guardian [South Africa], www.mg.co.za
Malaysiakini [Malaysia], www.malaysiakini.com
Manila Times, www.manilatimes.net
Marianas Business Journal, www.mbjguam.net
Marianas Variety [Micronesia], www.mvariety.com
Marlborough Express [New Zealand], www.stuff.co.nz/marlborough-express
Matangi Tonga Magazine, www.matangitonga.to
The Messenger [Georgia], www.messenger.com.ge
Miami Herald, www.miami.com/mld/miamiherald
Middle East Desk, www.middleeastdesk.org
Middle East Online, www.middle-east-online.com
Middle East Report, www.merip.org
Minivan News [Maldives], www.minivannews.com
Mirianas Variety [Micronesia], www.mvariety.com
Misr Digital, http://misrdigital.blogspirit.com
Mongolia Focus, http://blogs.ubc.ca/mongolia
The Mongolist, www.themongolist.com
Mother Jones, www.motherjones.com
Moscow Times, www.themoscowtimes.com
Munhwa Ilbo [South Korea], www.munhwa.com
Nacional [Croatia], www.nacional.hr
The Namibian, www.namibian.com.na
The Nation, www.thenation.org
The Nation [Thailand], www.nationmultimedia.com
The National [Papua New Guinea], www.thenational.com.pg
The National [UAE], www.thenational.ae
National Business Review [New Zealand], www.nbr.co.nz
National Public Radio (NPR), www.npr.org
National Review, www.nationalreview.com
Neue Zurcher Zeitung [Switzerland], www.nzz.ch
New Dawn [Liberia], www.thenewdawnliberia.com
New Mandala, http://asiapacific.anu.edu.au/newmandala
New York Times, www.nytimes.com
New Yorker, www.newyorker.com
New Zealand Herald, www.nzherald.co.nz
New Zealand government press releases, www.beehive.govt.nz
Nezavisimaya Gazeta [Russia], www.ng.ru
NIN [Serbia], www.nin.co.rs
NiuFM News [New Zealand], www.niufm.com
North Korea Economy Watch, www.nkeconwatch.com
Nyasa Times [Malawi], www.nyasatimes.com
The Observer [Liberia], www.liberianobserver.com
O Estado de Sao Paulo, www.estado.com.br
O Globo [Brazil], www.oglobo.globo.com
OFFnews [Argentina], www.offnews.info
Oman Arabic Daily, www.omandaily.com
Outlook [India], www.outlookindia.com
Pacific Business News, http://pacific.bizjournals.com/pacific
Pacific Daily News, www.guampdn.com
Pacific Islands Report, http://pidp.eastwestcenter.org/pireport
Pacific Magazine, www.pacificmagazine.net
Pacific Scoop [New Zealand], http://pacific.scoop.co.nz
Página/12 [Argentina], www.pagina12.com.ar
PANAPRESS, www.panapress.com
Papua New Guinea Post-Courier, www.postcourier.com.pg
Philippine Daily Inquirer, www.inquirer.net
Phnom Penh Post, www.phnompenhpost.com
Planet Tonga, www.planet-tonga.com
Politics.hu [Hungary], www.politics.hu
Politika [Serbia], www.politika.rs
Prague Post, www.praguepost.com
Radio and Television Hong Kong, www.rthk.org.hk
Radio Australia, www.abc.net.au/ra
Radio France Internationale, www.rfi.fr
Radio Free Europe-Radio Liberty, www.rferl.org
Radio Okapi [Congo-Kinshasa], www.radioOkapi.net
Radio New Zealand International, www.rnzi.com
Republika [Indonesia], www.republika.co.id
Reuters, www.reuters.com
Ritzau [Denmark], www.ritzau.dk
Rodong Sinmun [North Korea], www.rodong.rep.kp
Royal African Society's African Arguments, http://africanarguments.org
Sahel Blog, http://sahelblog.wordpress.com

Saipan Tribune, www.saipantribune.com
Samoa News, www.samoanews.com
Samoa Observer, www.samoaobserver.ws
San Marino Notizie, www.sanmarinonotizie.com
Semana [Colombia], www.semana.com
Slobodna Bosna [Bosnia-Herzegovina], www.slobodna-bosna.ba
Slovak Spectator, www.slovakspectator.sk
SME [Slovakia], www.sme.sk
Sofia Echo, www.sofiaecho.com
Solomon Islands Broadcasting Corporation, www.sibconline.com.sb
Solomon Star, www.solomonstarnews.com
Somaliland Times, www.somalilandtimes.net
South Asia Tribune [Pakistan], www.satribune.com
South China Morning Post [Hong Kong], www.scmp.com
The Statesman [India], www.thestatesman.net
Straits Times [Singapore], www.straitstimes.asia1.com.sg
Sub-Saharan Informer, www.ssinformer.com
Suddeutsche Zeitung [Germany], www.sueddeutsche.de
Sud Quotidien [Senegal], www.sudonline.sn
Tageblatt [Luxembourg], www.tageblatt.lu
Taipei Times, www.taipeitimes.com
Talamua [Samoa], www.talamua.com
Tamilnet.com, www.tamilnet.com
Tax-News.com, www.tax-news.com
Téla Nón Diário de São Tomé e Príncipe, www.telanon.info
The Telegraph [United Kingdom], www.telegraph.co.uk
Tempo [Indonesia], www.tempointeraktif.com
Texas in Africa, texasinafrica.blogspot.co.uk
This Day [Nigeria], www.thisdayonline.com
Tico Times [Costa Rica], www.ticotimes.net
Time, www.time.com
Times of Central Asia, www.times.kg
Today's Zaman [Turkey], www.todayszaman.com
TomPaine.com, www.TomPaine.com
Tongan Broadcasting Commission, http://tonga-broadcasting.com
Transcaucasus: A Chronology, www.anca.org/resource_center/transcaucasus.php
Trinidad Express, www.trinidadexpress.com
Tuvalu News, www.tuvalu-news.tv
Union Patriótica de Cuba (UNPACU), www.unpacu.org/acerca-de/sobre-unpacu
University World News, www.universityworldnews.com
U.S. News and World Report, www.usnews.com
U.S. State Department Country Reports on Human Rights Practices, www.state.gov/g/drl/rls/hrrpt
U.S. State Department Country Reports on Human Trafficking Reports, www.state.gov/g/tip
U.S. State Department International Religious Freedom Reports, www.state.gov/g/drl/irf
The Vanguard [Nigeria], www.vanguardngr.com
Vedomosti [Russia], www.vedomosti.ru
Voice of America, www.voa.gov
Waikato Times [New Zealand], www.stuff.co.nz/waikato-times
Walfadjri [Senegal], www.walf-groupe.com
Wall Street Journal, www.wsj.com
Washington Post, www.washingtonpost.com
Washington Times, www.washingtontimes.com
Weekly Standard, www.weeklystandard.com
West African Democracy Radio, http://wadr.org
World News, www.wn.com
Xinhua News, www.xinhuanet.com
Yap State Government press release, www.yapstategov.org
Yedioth Ahronoth [Israel], www.ynetnews.com
Yemen Times, www.yementimes.com
Yokwe Online [Marshall Islands], www.yokwe.net
Yonhap News Agency [South Korea], www.yonhapnews.co.kr
Zambia Reports, http://zambiareports.com
Zawya, www.Zawya.com

ORGANIZATIONS

ActionAid Australia, www.actionaid.org.au
Afghan Independent Human Rights Commission, www.aihrc.org.af
African Elections Project [Liberia], www.africanelections.org/liberia
African Health Observatory (WHO), www.aho.afro.who.int
Afrobarometer, www.afrobarometer.org
Alternative ASEAN Network on Burma, www.altsean.org
American Bar Association Rule of Law Initiative, www.abanet.org/rol
American Civil Liberties Union, www.aclu.org
Amnesty International, www.amnesty.org
Anti-Slavery International, www.antislavery.org
Asan Institute for Policy Studies, www.asaninst.org/eng
Asia Foundation, http://asiafoundation.org
Asian Center for Human Rights [India], www.achrweb.org
Asian Human Rights Commission [Hong Kong], www.ahrchk.net
Asian Philanthropy Forum, www.asianphilanthropyforum.org

Assistance Association for Political Prisoners [Burma], www.aappb.org
Australian Department of Education, Employment and Workplace Relations, www.deewr.gov.au/Pages/default.aspx
Balkan Human Rights Web, www.greekhelsinki.gr
Belarusian Institute for Strategic Studies, www.belinstitute.eu
Brookings Institution, www.brookings.edu
B'Tselem–The Israeli Information Center for Human Rights in the Occupied Territories, www.btselem.org
Cabindese Government in Exile, www.cabinda.org
Cairo Institute for Human Rights, www.cihrs.org
Cambridge International Reference on Current Affairs, www.circaworld.com
Canadian Department of Foreign Affairs and International Trade, www.dfait-maeci.gc.ca
Carnegie Endowment for International Peace, www.carnegieendowment.org
Carter Center, www.cartercenter.org
Center for Strategic and International Studies, www.csis.org
Centre for International Governance, www.cigionline.org
Centre for Policy Alternatives [Sri Lanka], www.cpalanka.org
Centre for the Study of Violence and Reconciliation, www.csvr.org.za
Chad/Cameroon Development Project, www.essochad.com
Charter '97 [Belarus], www.charter97.org
Chatham House [United Kingdom], www.chathamhouse.org
Child Rights Information Network, www.crin.org/resources/infodetail.asp?ID=22188
Committee for Human Rights in North Korea, www.hrnk.org
Committee for the Prevention of Torture, www.cpt.coe.int
Committee to Protect Journalists, www.cpj.org
Coordinating Ministry of Economic Affairs [Indonesia], www.ekon.go.id
Council of Europe, www.coe.int
Council on Foreign Relations, www.cfr.org/index.html
Danish Institute for Human Rights, www.humanrights.dk
Danish Ministry of Foreign Affairs, the Global Advice Network, www.business-anti-corruption.com
Ditshwanelo – Botswana Centre for Human Rights, www.ditshwanelo.org.bw
Earth Institute Advisory Group for Sao Tome and Principe, www.earthinstitute.columbia.edu
East Asia Institute, www.eai.or.kr/english
Electoral Institute of Southern Africa, www.eisa.org.za
Eurasia Group, www.eurasiagroup.net
European Bank for Reconstruction and Development, www.ebrd.org
European Roma Rights Center, www.errc.org
European Union, www.europa.eu
European Union Agency for Fundamental Rights, http://fra.europa.eu
Executive Mansion of Liberia, www.emansion.gov.lr
Extractive Industries Transparency Initiative, www.eiti.org
Federal Chancellery of Austria, www.bka.gv.at
Forum 18, www.forum18.org
Forum for Human Dignity [Sri Lanka], www.fhd.8m.net
Forum of Federations/Forum des Federations, www.forumfed.org
Friends of Niger, www.friendsofniger.org
Global Integrity, www.globalintegrity.org
Global Policy Forum, www.globalpolicy.org
Global Rights, www.globalrights.org
Global Witness, www.globalwitness.org
Globe International [Mongolia], www.globeinter.org.mn/old/en/index.php
Government of Botswana Website, www.gov.bw
Government of Mauritania Website, www.mauritania.mr
Government of Sierra Leone State House, www.statehouse.gov.sl
Heritage Foundation, www.heritage.org
Hong Kong Human Rights Monitor, www.hkhrm.org.hk
Human Rights Commission of Pakistan, www.hrcp-web.org
Human Rights First, www.humanrightsfirst.org
Human Rights Watch, www.hrw.org
Hyundai Research Institute, www.hri.co.kr
Indonesian Institute of Sciences, www.lipi.go.id
Indonesian Survey Institute, www.lsi.or.id
INFORM (Sri Lanka Information Monitor)
Institute for Democracy in Eastern Europe, www.idee.org
Institute for Far Eastern Studies, www.isn.ethz.ch/Digital-Library/Organizations/Detail//?id=48861
Institute for War and Peace Reporting, www.iwpr.net
Inter-American Dialogue, www.thedialogue.org
Inter-American Press Association, www.sipiapa.com
Internal Displacement Monitoring Center, www.internal-displacement.org
International Alert, www.international-alert.org
International Bar Association, www.ibanet.org
International Campaign for Tibet, www.savetibet.org

International Centre for Ethnic Studies, www.icescolombo.org
International Centre for Not-for-Profit Law: NGO Law Monitor, www.icnl.org
International Commission of Jurists, www.icj.org
International Crisis Group, www.crisisgroup.org
International Federation of Journalists, www.ifj.org
International Foundation for Electoral Systems, www.ifes.org
International Freedom of Expression Exchange, www.ifex.org
International Helsinki Federation for Human Rights, www.ihf-hr.org
International Institute for Democracy and Electoral Assistance, www.idea.int
International Labour Organization, www.ilo.org
International Legal Assistance Consortium, www.ilacinternational.org
International Lesbian and Gay Association, www.ilga.org
International Monetary Fund, www.imf.org
International Network for Higher Education in Africa, www.bc.edu/bc_org/avp/soe/cihe/inhea
International Organization for Migration, www.iom.int
International Press Institute, www.freemedia.at
International Republican Institute, www.iri.org
International Society For Fair Elections And Democracy [Georgia], www.isfed.ge
Jamestown Foundation, www.jamestown.org
Kashmir Study Group, www.kashmirstudygroup.net
Korea Development Institute, www.kdi.re.kr
Korea Institute for National Unification, www.kinu.or.kr
Legislature of Liberia, http://legislature.gov.lr
Macedonian Information Agency, www.mia.mk
MADA—Palestinian Center for Development and Media Freedoms, www.madacenter.org/index.php?lang=1
Malta Data, www.maltadata.com
Media Institute of Southern Africa, www.misa.org
Media Rights Agenda [Nigeria], www.mediarightsagenda.org
Migrant Assistance Programme Thailand, www.mapfoundationcm.org/eng
Millennium Challenge Corporation, www.mcc.gov
National Anti-Corruption Network [Burkina Faso], www.renlac.org
National Bureau of Asian Research, www.nbr.org
National Committee on North Korea, www.ncnk.org
National Democratic Institute for International Affairs, www.ndi.org
National Elections Commission of Liberia, www.necliberia.org
National Elections Commission of Sierra Leone, www.nec-sierraleone.org
National Endowment for Democracy, www.ned.org
National Human Rights Commission [India], www.nhrc.nic.in
National Human Rights Commission of Korea, www.humanrights.go.kr
National Peace Council of Sri Lanka, www.peace-srilanka.org
National Society for Human Rights [Namibia], www.nshr.org.na
Nicaragua Network, www.nicanet.org
Observatory for the Protection of Human Rights Defenders, www.omct.org
Odhikar [Bangladesh], www.odhikar.org
Office of the High Representative in Bosnia and Herzegovina, www.ohr.int
Open Government Partnership, www.opengovpartnership.org
Open Society Institute, www.soros.org
Organization for Economic Cooperation and Development, www.oecd.org
Organization for Security and Cooperation in Europe, www.osce.org
Oxford Analytica, www.oxan.com
Pacific Islands Forum Secretariat, www.forumsec.org
People's Forum for Human Rights [Bhutan]
Population Reference Bureau, www.prb.org
Portal for Parliamentary Development, www.agora-parl.org
Publish What You Pay Campaign, www.publishwhatyoupay.org
Refugees International, www.refugeesinternational.org
Reliefweb, http://reliefweb.int
Reporters Sans Frontières, www.rsf.org
Samsung Economic Research Institute, www.seriworld.org
Save the Children, www.savethechildren.org
Shan Women's Action Network, www.shanwomen.org
Sierra Leone Legal Information Institute, www.sierralii.org
South African Human Rights Commission, www.sahrc.org.za
South African Press Association, www.sapa.org.za
South Asia Terrorism Portal [India], www.satp.org
South East Europe Media Organisation, http://seemo.org
State House of Sierra Leone, www.statehouse.gov.sl
Sweden.se, www.sweden.se
Syria Comment, www.joshualandis.com
Tibet Information Network, www.tibetinfo.net

Transitions Online, www.tol.cz
Transparency International, www.transparency.org
Truth and Reconciliation Commission of Liberia, www.trcofliberia.org
Turkish Ministry of Foreign Affairs, www.mfa.gov.tr
United Nations Development Program, www.undp.org
United Nations High Commissioner for Refugees, www.unhcr.org
United Nations High Commissioner on Human Rights, www.unhchr.ch
United Nations Integrated Peacebuilding Office in Sierra Leone (UNIPSIL), http://unipsil.unmissions.org
United Nations Interim Mission in Kosovo, www.unmikonline.org
United Nations Mission in Liberia (UNMIL), www.unmil.org
United Nations Office for the Coordination of Humanitarian Affairs (OCHA), http://unocha.org
United Nations Population Division, www.un.org/esa/population
United Nations Security Council, www.un.org
United States Agency for International Development, www.usaid.org
United States Department of the Interior, www.doi.gov/oia/index.cfm
United States Department of State, www.state.gov
University Teachers for Human Rights-Jaffna, www.uthr.org
U.S.–Korea Institute at SAIS, www.uskoreainstitute.org
Washington Office on Latin America, www.wola.org
World Bank, www.worldbank.org
World Press Freedom Committee, www.wpfc.org

FREEDOM HOUSE BOARD OF TRUSTEES

Kenneth I. Juster, *Chairman*
Thomas A. Dine, *Vice Chair*
Ruth Wedgwood, *Vice Chair*
David Nastro, *Treasurer*
John Norton Moore, *Secretary, Governance and Ethics Officer*
Bette Bao Lord, *Chairman Emeritus*

Carol C. Adelman, Kenneth Adelman, Zeinab Al-Suwaij, Goli Ameri, Stephen E. Biegun, David E. Birnbaum, Ellen Blackler, Dennis C. Blair, James H. Carter, Lee Cullum, Charles Davidson, Kim G. Davis, Paula J. Dobriansky, Eileen C. Donahoe, James C. Duff, Alan P. Dye, Alison B. Fortier, Susan Ginsburg, Rebecca G. Haile, D. Jeffrey Hirschberg, Kathryn Dickey Karol, Jim Kolbe, Jay Mazur, Theodore N. Mirvis, Alberto Mora, Joshua Muravchik, Andrew Nathan, Diana Villiers Negroponte, Douglas E. Schoen, Faryar Shirzad, Scott Siff, William H. Taft IV, Wendell Willkie II, Jennifer L. Windsor

David J. Kramer, *President*

Freedom House supports global freedom through comprehensive analysis, dedicated advocacy, and concrete assistance for democratic activists around the world.

Founded in 1941, Freedom House has long been a vigorous proponent of the right of all individuals to be free. Eleanor Roosevelt and Wendell Willkie served as Freedom House's first honorary co-chairpersons.

Kenneth I. Juster
Chair
Freedom House Board of Trustees

David J. Kramer
President

Arch Puddington
Vice President for Research

www.freedomhouse.org

Support the right of every individual to be free.
Donate now.

WITHDRAWN